CW01335233

THE OXFORD HANDBOOK OF
WORLD WAR II

THE OXFORD HANDBOOK OF

WORLD WAR II

Edited by

G. KURT PIEHLER

and

JONATHAN A. GRANT

OXFORD
UNIVERSITY PRESS

OXFORD
UNIVERSITY PRESS

Oxford University Press is a department of the University of Oxford. It furthers
the University's objective of excellence in research, scholarship, and education
by publishing worldwide. Oxford is a registered trade mark of Oxford University
Press in the UK and certain other countries.

Published in the United States of America by Oxford University Press
198 Madison Avenue, New York, NY 10016, United States of America.

© Oxford University Press 2023

All rights reserved. No part of this publication may be reproduced, stored in
a retrieval system, or transmitted, in any form or by any means, without the
prior permission in writing of Oxford University Press, or as expressly permitted
by law, by license, or under terms agreed with the appropriate reproduction
rights organization. Inquiries concerning reproduction outside the scope of the
above should be sent to the Rights Department, Oxford University Press, at the
address above.

You must not circulate this work in any other form
and you must impose this same condition on any acquirer.

Library of Congress Cataloging-in-Publication Data
Names: Piehler, G. Kurt, author. | Grant, Jonathan A., 1963– author.
Title: The Oxford handbook of World War II / G. Kurt Piehler and Jonathan A. Grant.
Description: New York, NY : Oxford University Press, [2023] |
Includes bibliographical references and index.
Identifiers: LCCN 2022032447 (print) | LCCN 2022032448 (ebook) |
ISBN 9780199341795 (hardback) | ISBN 9780197676578 (epub) |
ISBN 9780199352425
Subjects: LCSH: World War, 1939–1945.
Classification: LCC D743 .P516 2022 (print) | LCC D743 (ebook) |
DDC 940.54—dc23/eng/20220920
LC record available at https://lccn.loc.gov/2022032447
LC ebook record available at https://lccn.loc.gov/2022032448

DOI: 10.1093/oxfordhb/9780199341795.001.0001

Printed by Sheridan Books, Inc., United States of America

To the memory of Judy Barrett Litoff
1944–2022

Contents

Maps	xi
Acknowledgments	xxi
Contributors	xxiii

Introduction: Freed from the Shadows of the Cold War:
A Global War Reconsidered   1
    G. KURT PIEHLER AND JONATHAN A. GRANT

1. The Collapse of the Versailles System   15
    MICHAEL H. CRESWELL

2. Ideological Origins of World War II   38
    VLADIMIR TISMANEANU AND BOGDAN C. IACOB

3. Ethiopia and the Spanish Civil War before and during World War II   56
    PETER GARRETSON AND STEPHEN MCVEIGH

4. The Sino–Japanese War   73
    GAO BEI

5. Forging Alliances: The Axis   94
    RICKY W. LAW

6. German Victories, 1939–1940   116
    EUGENIA C. KIESLING

7. The Battle of Britain: Britain and the British Empire Alone   138
    ANDREW STEWART

8. The Battle of the Atlantic, 1939–1945   154
    MARC MILNER

9. The Axis Invasion of the Soviet Union, 1941–1943   173
    JONATHAN A. GRANT

10.	The Middle East during World War II HAKAN GÜNGÖR AND PETER GARRETSON	190
11.	Pearl Harbor and Japan Ascendant SIDNEY PASH	202
12.	The United Nations and the Grand Alliance DAVID B. WOOLNER	219
13.	The Air War: Germany and Italy M. HOUSTON JOHNSON V	237
14.	North Africa and Italy DOUGLAS PORCH	256
15.	Eastern Europe in World War II DEBORAH S. CORNELIUS AND JONATHAN A. GRANT	274
16.	The Eastern Front, 1943–1945 DAVID R. STONE	287
17.	From D-Day to the Elbe PETER MANSOOR	304
18.	The Land War in Asia: China, Burma, and India ALAN JEFFREYS	327
19.	The Pacific War KYLE P. BRACKEN	342
20.	The Air War and Conflict Termination in the Pacific CONRAD C. CRANE	357
21.	Home Fronts at War JUDY BARRETT LITOFF	375
22.	Neutral Powers in a Global War NEVILLE WYLIE	392
23.	Western Religious Leaders, Communities, and Organizations before and during World War II VICTORIA J. BARNETT	414
24.	Science and Technology RONALD E. DOEL AND KRISTINE C. HARPER	431

25. The Environmental Impact 448
    CHARLES CLOSMANN

26. Medicine and Disability 466
    JOHN M. KINDER

27. The Holocaust 482
    JAN-RUTH MILLS

28. The Humanitarian Impulse 497
    HILLARY SEBENY

29. Rendering Justice 515
    MICHAEL S. BRYANT AND JAMES BURNHAM SEDGWICK

30. Cultural Responses to Total War, 1930s–1945 539
    ANNIKA A. CULVER

31. Postwar Settlements and Internationalism 562
    REGINA GRAMER AND YUTAKA SASAKI

32. Reintegrating Veterans and Demobilizing Populations 580
    R. M. DOUGLAS

33. The Memory and Commemoration of War 600
    BRIAN M. PUACA AND SHIZUE OSA

Index 617

Maps

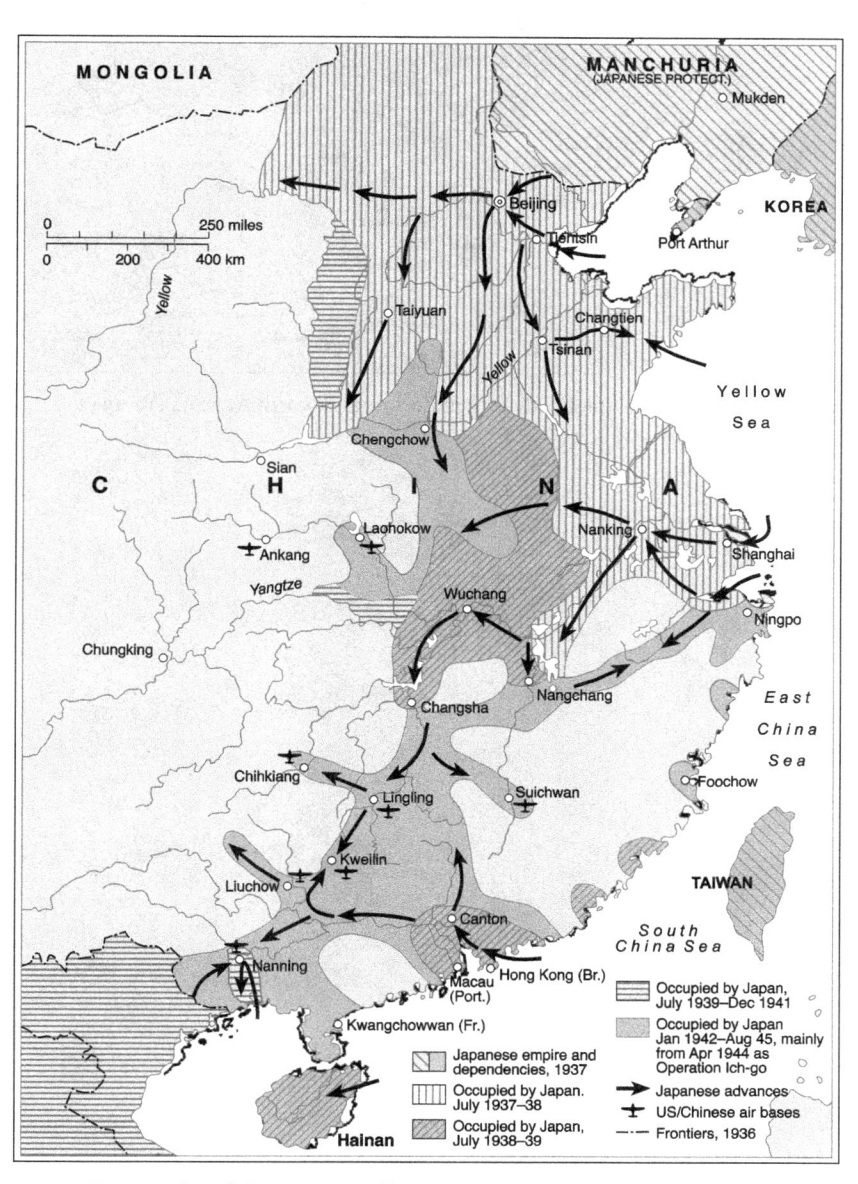

MAP 1 Japanese Land Campaign in China, 1937–1945

MAP 2 The Axis Territorial Advance in Europe and North Africa, 1939–1942

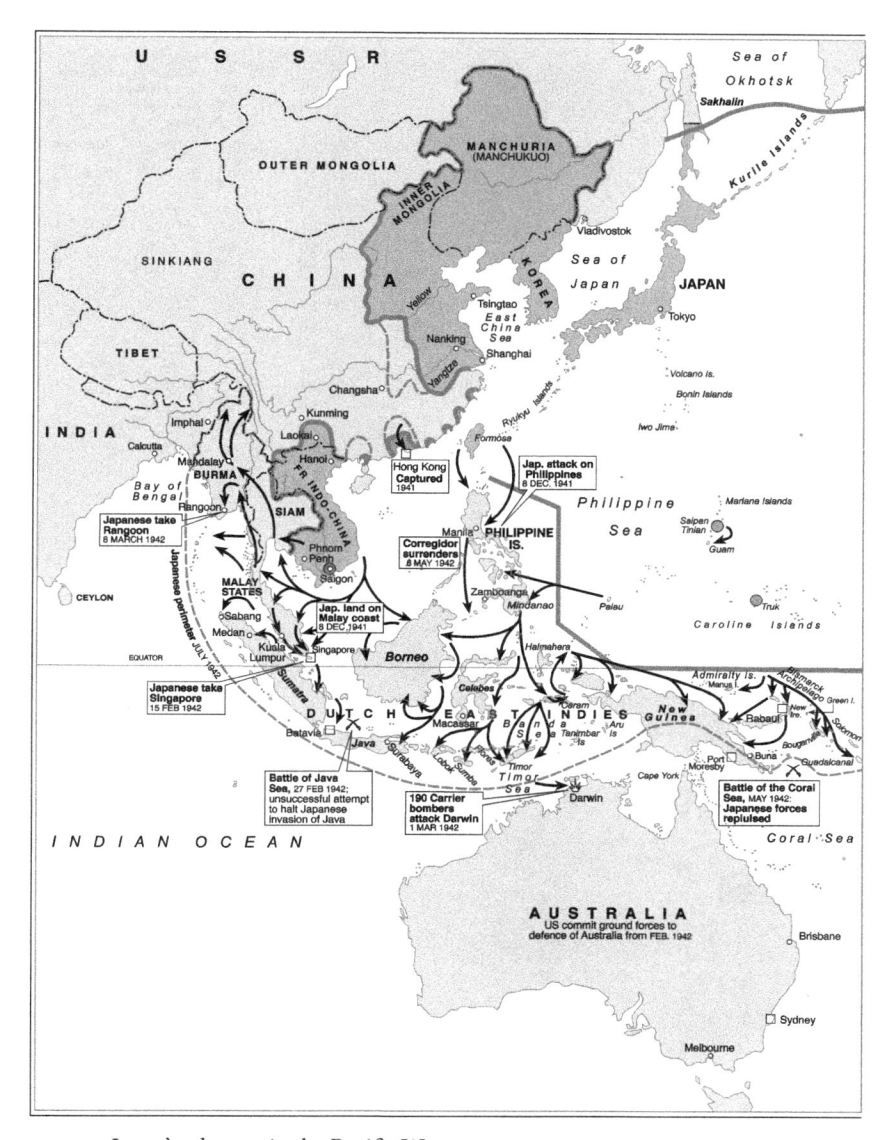

MAP 3 Japan's advance in the Pacific War, 1941–42

xiv MAPS

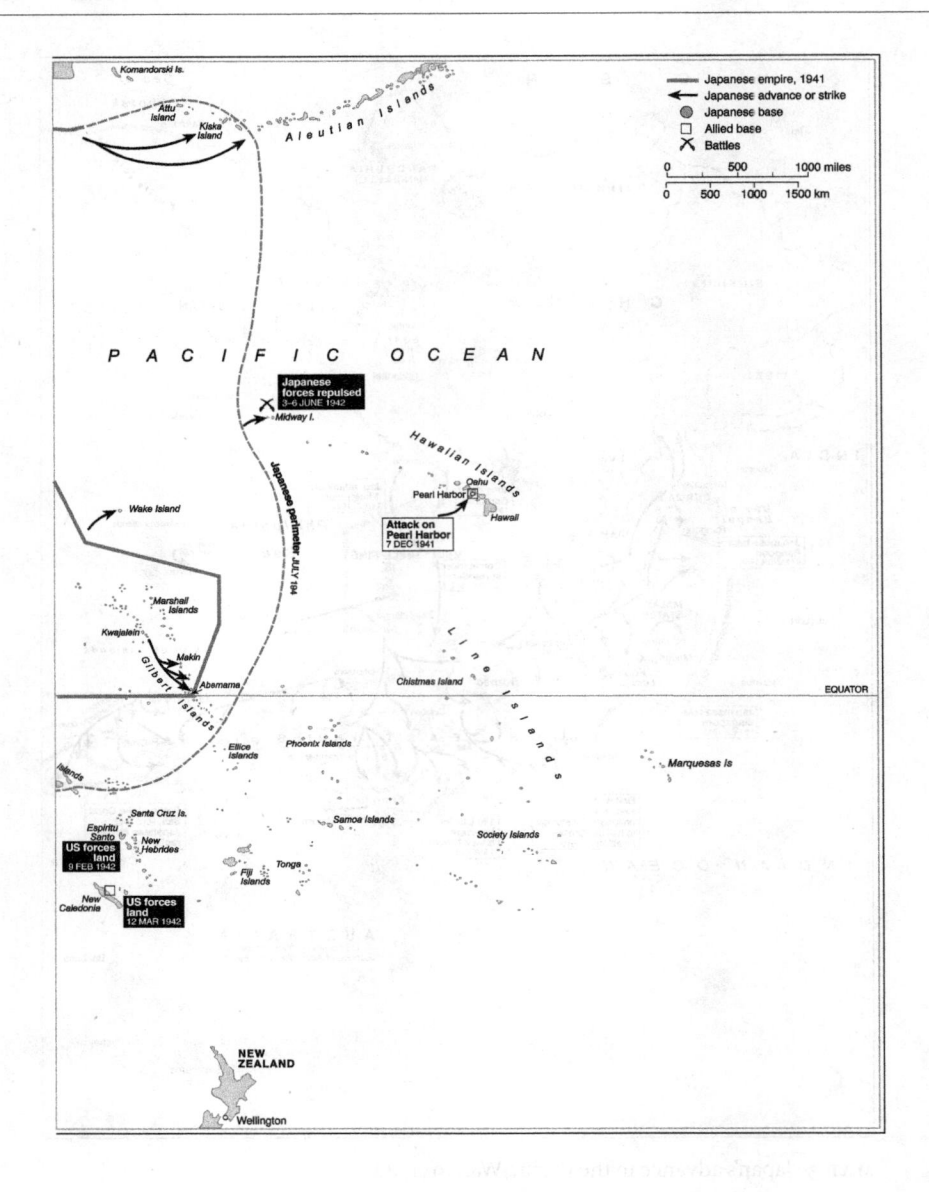

MAP 4 Major Concentration Camps/Death Camps Europe

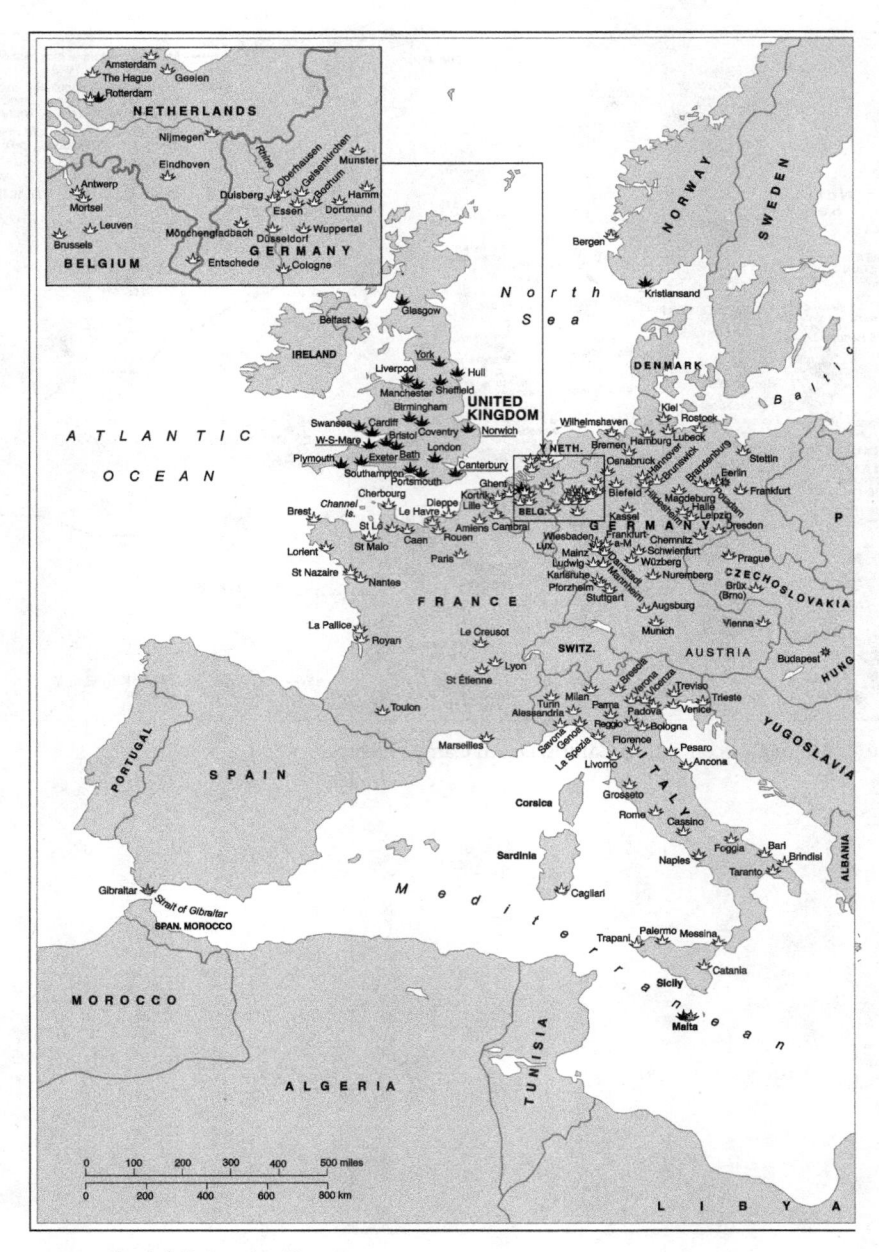

MAP 5 Aerial Campaign Europe

MAPS xvii

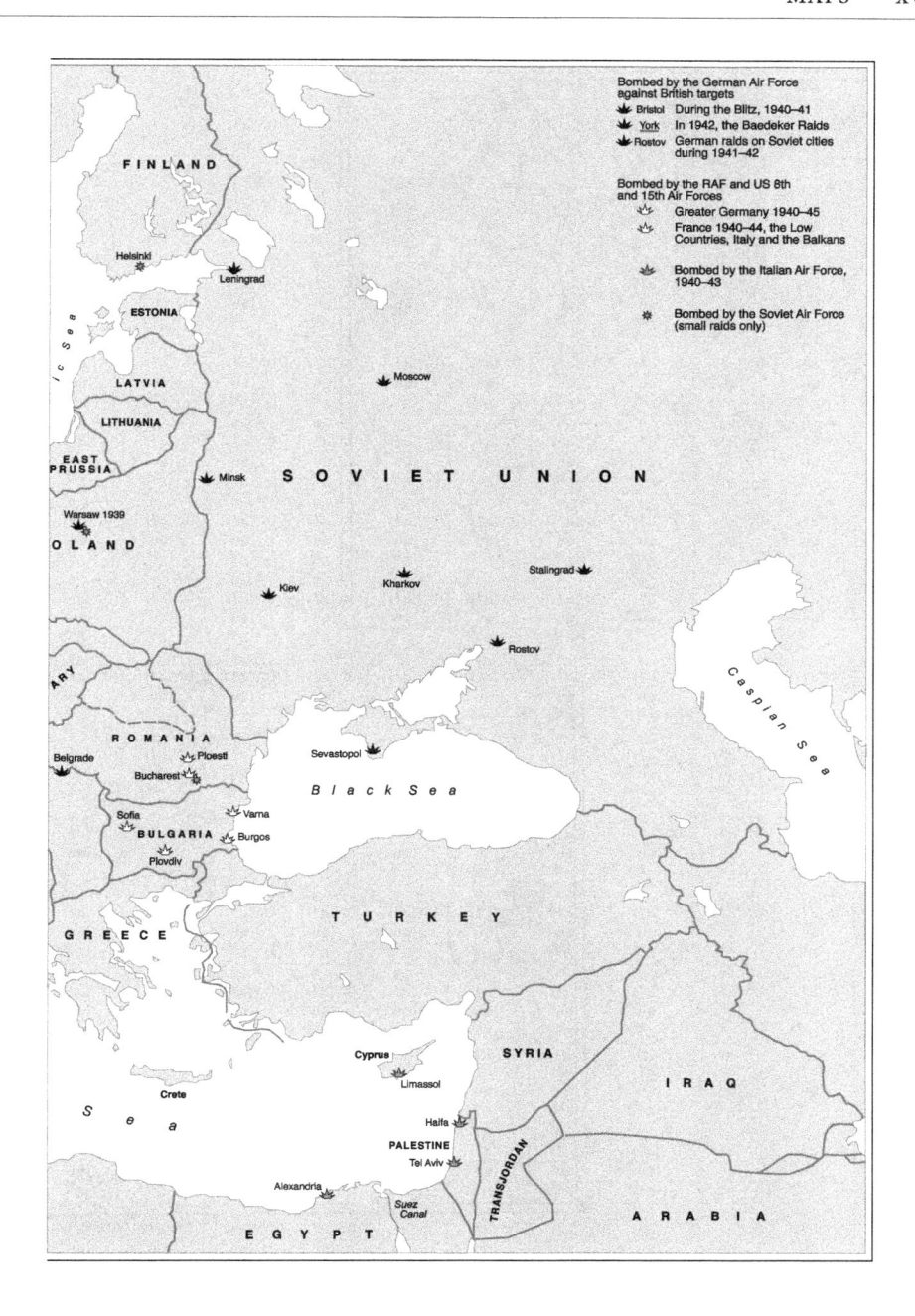

xviii   MAPS

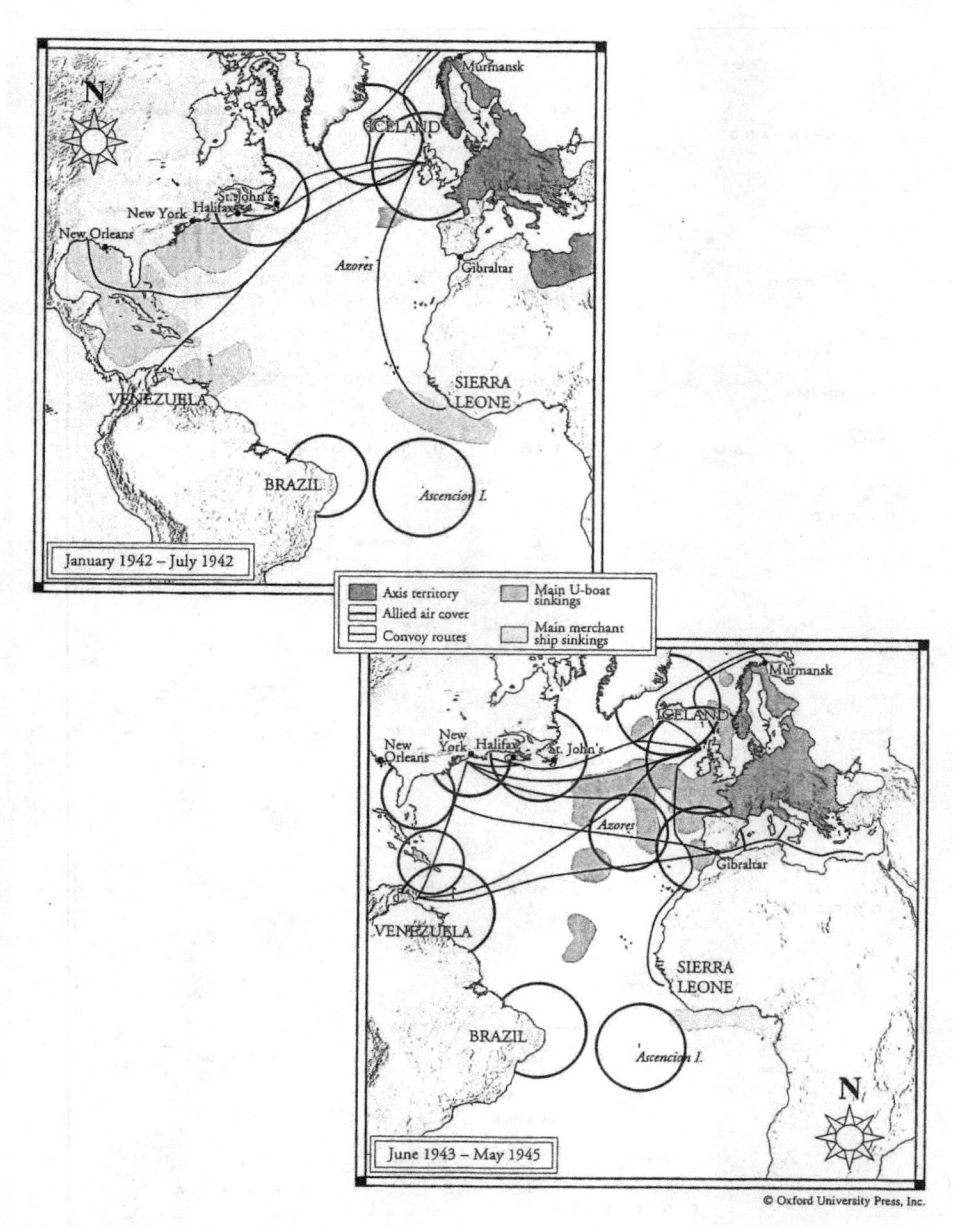

MAP 6 Battle of the Atlantic

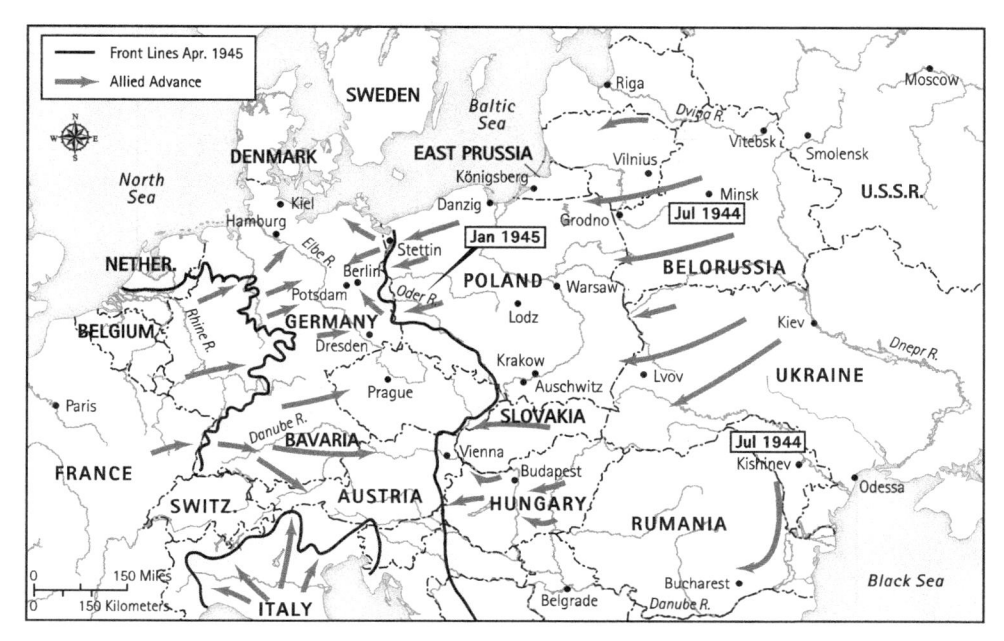

MAP 7 Defeat of Germany, 1945

John Ferris and Evan Mawdsley (eds.), *The Cambridge History of the Second World War*, Vol. 1 (Cambridge: Cambridge University Press, 2015), p. 414.

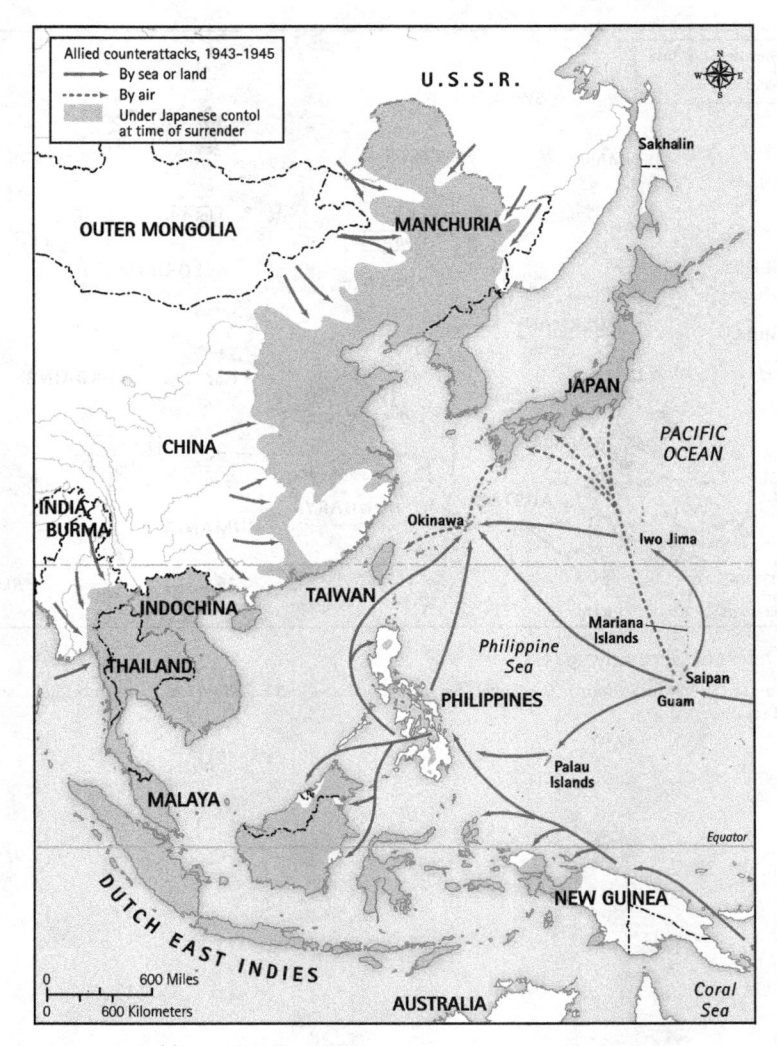

MAP 8 World War II in Eastern Asia, 1943–45.

Rhodes Murphy, A History of Asia, Fifth edition (Pearson Longman: New York, 2006). p. 376

Acknowledgments

We want to express our appreciation to Nancy Toff, who conceived the need for a comprehensive and concise handbook focusing on the global history of World War II. Nancy dedicated considerable time to this project and offered editorial suggestions for every chapter in the volume. Soon after the project was commissioned, Nancy graciously provided space at the headquarters of Oxford in Manhattan for a one-day writers', conference held in conjunction with an annual meeting of the American Historical Association. Jordan Bolan, former senior undergraduate assistant at the Institute on World War II and the Human Experience at Florida State University, helped with myriad logistical details that brought together many of the authors of this volume.

Gabriella Maduro, Angela Stevens, Mallory Malman, and Megan Quinn served at various points as editorial assistants on this project and offered invaluable assistance. Angela, Gabriella and Megan worked on this project while completing an internship in Florida State's outstanding Editing, Writing Media program. Anne Marsh, former administrator for the Institute on World War II, spot checked citations and bibliographies in this volume for accuracy. At Oxford, we appreciate Shunmugapriyan, A. Usharani, and Zara Cannon-Mohammed for shepherding this project through production and Jessie Coffey for copyediting the manuscript.

This project took several years to complete and we are indebted to patience of our families, especially our respective spouses, Susan G. Contente, and Lynn Wray-Grant.

Editors of reference works are indebted to the individual contributors who participated in this project. Sadly as this work went into production, one contributor, Judy Barrett Litoff suddenly passed away. We wish to dedicate this volume in memory of Judy whose scholarship did much to preserve the American women's voices, especially their correspondence from the World War II generation. Judy was an outstanding teacher and supportive colleague, may her memory be a blessing.

Contributors

Victoria J. Barnett is the Director (retired), Programs on Ethics, Religion and the Holocaust, U.S. Holocaust Memorial Museum. She is author of *For the Soul of the People: Protestant Protest under Hitler* and *Bystanders: Conscience and Complicity during the Holocaust*.

Michael S. Bryant is a Professor of History and Legal Studies at Bryant University in Smithfield, Rhode Island, and an adjunct professor of law at Creighton University Law School in Omaha, Nebraska. He is the author of four books: *Confronting the "Good Death": Nazi Euthanasia on Trial, 1945–53*; *Eyewitness to Genocide: The Operation Reinhard Death Camp Trials 1955–66*; *A World History of War Crimes: From Antiquity to the Present*; *Nazi Crimes and Their Punishment: A Short History with Documents*. He has also co-authored two additional books: a casebook, *Comparative Law: Global Legal Traditions* and an edited volume (with John and Susan Michalczyk), Hitler's *Mein Kampf* and the *Holocaust*.

Kyle P. Bracken earned his doctorate from Florida State University, studying World War Two and the twentieth century United States. He is a historian at the Defense Prisoner of War/Missing in Action Accounting Agency in Honolulu, Hawai'i.

Charles Closmann is an associate professor of History at the University of North Florida in Jacksonville. His research focuses on the history of environmental policies at military bases in the U.S. South, and on issues of environmental justice in the late-twentieth century. *War and the Environment: Military Destruction in the Modern Age*.

Deborah S. Cornelius is a professor of Eastern European history. She received her PhD from Rutgers University in 1994 and is the author numerous articles and of several books, including: *In Search of the Nation* and *Hungary in World War II: Caught in the Cauldron*.

Conrad C. Crane is currently Senior Research Historian at the Strategic Studies Institute of the US Army War College. He is the author of *American Airpower Strategy in World War II: Bombs, Cities, Civilians, and Oil, American Airpower Strategy in Korea, 1950–1953*, and *Cassandra in Oz: Counterinsurgency and Future War*.

Michael H. Creswell is an associate professor of history at Florida State University, an executive editor at *History: Reviews of New Books*, and the author of *A Question of Balance: How France and the United States Created Cold War Europe*.

Annika A. Culver is associate professor of East Asian History at Florida State University and a scholar in the U.S.–Japan Network for the Future whose research and teaching has featured themes related to war and society, wartime cultural production, and propaganda from transnational perspectives. She is the author of *Democratizing Luxury: Name Brands, Advertising, and Consumption in Modern Japan*, *Japan's Empire of Birds: Aristocrats, Anglo-Americans, and Transwar Ornithology*, *Glorify the Empire: Japanese Avant-Garde Propaganda in Manchukuo*, winner of the Southeast Conference of the Association for Asian Studies (SECAAS) 2015 Book Prize, and co-editor of *Manchukuo Perspectives: Transnational Approaches to Literary Production*, with Norman Smith.

Ronald E. Doel is an associate professor of history at Florida State University.

R. M. Douglas is the Russell Colgate Distinguished University Professor of History at Colgate University in Hamilton, New York. He is currently working on a study of conflict-related sexual violence during the Second World War.

Gao Bei is associate professor of International Studies at the University of North Carolina Wilmington. She holds a PhD in history and is the author of *Shanghai Sanctuary: Chinese and Japanese Policy toward European Jewish Refugees during World War II*.

Peter Garretson taught Middle Eastern and African History at Florida State University for over thirty years, as well as administering its International Programs and a Middle East Center, before retiring as an Emeritus Professor. His major areas of interest and research are Modern Ethiopian, Sudanese and Kurdish history, and he has published several books and numerous articles on the first two countries. He is author of *Victorian Gentleman & Ethiopian Nationalist: the Life and Times of Hakim Warqenah, Dr. Charles Martin*.

Regina Gramer is a clinical associate professor in Liberal Studies at New York University and the Managing Editor of *The Interdependent*: Journal of Undergraduate Research in Global Studies. She has published various essays and reviews on topics related to World War II and the Cold War.

Jonathan A. Grant is a professor of Modern Russian History in the Department of History at Florida State University in Tallahassee. His most recent book, *Between Depression and Disarmament: The International Armaments Business, 1919-1939* examines the armaments business in Eastern Europe from 1919 to 1939.

Hakan Güngör is assistant professor of History at Ordu University, Turkey. He specializes in World War II history of Turkey and the Middle East. He is the author of *Turkish–American Relations in World War II: Survival of Turkish Neutrality* and *Jewish Immigration from the Balkans to Palestine in World War II* and numerous articles.

Kristine C. Harper is a professor of History and Philosophy of Earth Sciences at the University of Copenhagen. Her research focuses on the history of the atmospheric, oceanographic, and hydrographic sciences in the twentieth century.

Bogdan C. Iacob is a researcher at the "Nicolae Iorga" Institute of History (Bucharest) of the Romanian Academy. He co-authored the monograph *1989. A Global History of Eastern Europe*.

Alan Jeffreys is Head of Equipment and Uniform at the National Army Museum, London and a visiting research fellow at the University of Greenwich. He is the author of *Approach to Battle: Training the Indian Army during the Second World War*, *London at War 1939–1945: A Nation's Capital Survives*, and editor of *The Indian Army in the First World War: New Perspectives*.

M. Houston Johnson V serves as Professor of History and Head of the Department of History at the Virginia Military Institute, where his teaching focuses on the twentieth-century United States. His research examines the development of commercial aviation in the United States, aviation infrastructure development, and World War II. He is author of *Taking Off: The Foundations of American Commercial Aviation, 1918-1938*.

Eugenia C. Kiesling teaches military and ancient history at the United States Military Academy at West Point.

John M. Kinder is Director of American Studies and Associate Professor of History at Oklahoma State University. He is the author of *Paying with Their Bodies: American War and the Problem of the Disabled Veteran* and co-editor with Jason Higgins of *Service Denied: Marginalized Veterans in Modern American History*.

Ricky W. Law is associate professor of History at Carnegie Mellon University. His research focuses on German, Japanese, and transnational histories. He is the author of *Transnational Nazism: Ideology and Culture in German–Japanese Relations, 1919–1936*.

Judy Barrett Litoff was a professor of History at Bryant University in Smithfield, Rhode Island and is the author of fourteen hardcover books (and eight paperback editions) and more than one hundred articles, book chapters, and reviews in American women's history. Over the last two decades, her research made a significant contribution to the history of American women and the Second World War.

Peter Mansoor is the General Raymond E. Mason Jr. Chair of Military History at The Ohio State University. He is the author of a monograph on the combat performance of U.S. Army infantry divisions in Europe during World War II, *The GI Offensive in Europe: The Triumph of American Infantry Divisions, 1941–1945*, which was awarded the Society for Military History distinguished book award and the Army Historical Society distinguished book award.

Stephen McVeigh is associate professor in War and Society and Director of Learning and Teaching for the College of Arts and Humanities at Swansea University. Dr. McVeigh is the series editor of *War, Culture and Society*, a research monograph series published by Bloomsbury Academic. He is also a member of the editorial board of the *Journal of War and Culture Studies*.

Jan-Ruth Mills earned her PhD from Florida State University in 2021. She was awarded a Fulbright Research Fellowship in 2018–2019, and her research focuses on Austria and the Holocaust.

Marc Milner is professor Emeritus at the University of New Brunswick and is best known for his many books and articles on the Battle of the Atlantic. He worked on the official histories of the RCAF and RCN in the Second World War before teaching military history at University of New Brunswick and serving as Director of its Gregg Centre for the Study of War and Society until his retirement in 2019. His recent work has focused on the Normandy campaign, including *Stopping the Panzers* which won the Brigadier General James Collins Prize for the best book of 2014–15 awarded by the US Commission on Military History.

Sidney Pash is professor of History at Fayetteville State University and a former Fulbright Scholar at the University of Tokyo. His is the author of *The Currents of War: A New History of American–Japanese Relation* and, with G. Kurt Piehler, the co-editor of *The United States and the Second World War: New Perspectives on War, Diplomacy, and the Home Front*.

G. Kurt Piehler is Director of the Institute on World War II and the Human Experience at Florida State University. He is author of *A Religious History of the American GI in World War II* and *Remembering War the American Way*. As founding director of the Rutgers Oral History Archives (1994–1998), he conducted over two hundred interviews with World War II veterans.

Douglas Porch is Distinguished Professor Emeritus at the Naval Postgraduate School. He is the author of several books on French and military history, including the two-volume *France at War 1939–1945*.

Brian M. Puaca is professor of History at Christopher Newport University in Virginia where he teaches courses on the history of modern Germany, World War II, and postwar Europe. His monograph, *Learning Democracy: Education Reform in West Germany, 1945–1965*, received the 2011 New Scholar's Book Award from the American Educational Research Association (Division F). He has published several articles and book chapters on school reform, history instruction, democratization, and German memory.

Yutaka Sasaki is a professor of American Political/Diplomatic History at Kyoto University of Foreign Studies, Kyoto, Japan. He has published various articles on U.S.–East Asian relations in the twentieth century. His latest essay is "SSRC's Committee on Comparative Politics and the Struggle to Construct a General Theory of Political Modernization Using the Japanese Model: Scholarly Endeavors of Robert

E. Ward" in Hiroo Nakajima, ed., *International Society in the Early Twentieth Century Pacific: Imperial Rivalries, International Organizations, and Experts.*

Hillary Sebeny earned her doctorate writing a dissertation on US activity in Antarctica. She currently works as a historian in support of the Defense POW/MIA Accounting Agency, focusing on World War II air losses and war graves in the Pacific Theater.

James Burnham Sedgwick is an associate professor of history at Acadia University in Wolfville, Nova Scotia. His work explores global histories of catastrophe and response, memory and mass violence, empire and atrocity, with a particular focus on the Asia-Pacific region.

Shizue Osa is professor in Japan Studies at the Graduate School of Intercultural Studies Kobe University, specializing in Japanese modern history. He is the author of *The Occupation Period: Occupied Territory and Memories of the War* and co-editor of *Japanese History from a Gender Perspective* (Otuki-syoten).

Andrew Stewart is a military historian and Visiting Professor at King's College London where he studied for his doctorate. Having taught for nearly twenty years at the Defence Academy of the United Kingdom, he has recently held professorships at the Australian National University and the Zayed Military University in Abu Dhabi. He is currently working on an expanded version of the wartime diaries of General Sir Edmund Ironside.

David R. Stone is the William E. Odom Professor of Russian Studies in the Strategy and Policy Department of the U.S. Naval War College in Newport, Rhode Island. He is the author of several works on Russian military history including *The Soviet Union at War, 1941–1945* and *The Russian Army in the Great War: The Eastern Front, 1914–1917.*

Vladimir Tismaneanu is professor of Politics at the University of Maryland (College Park) and Global Fellow, Woodrow Wilson International Center for Scholars. In 2996 he chaired the Presidential Commission for the Analysis of the Communist Dictatorship in Romania. He is the author of numerous books, including *Stalinism for All Seasons: A Political History of Romanian Communism. Fantasies of Salvation: Democracy, Nationalism, and Myth in Post-Communist Europe, The Devil in History: Communism, Fascism, and Some Lessons of the Twentieth Century*, and, co-authored with Kate Langdon, *Putin's Totalitarian Democracy: Ideology, Myth, and Violence in the Twenty-First Century.*

David B. Woolner is Senior Fellow and Resident Historian of the Roosevelt Institute, Professor of History at Marist College, and Senior Fellow of the Center for Civic Engagement at Bard College. He is the author of *The Last 100 Days: FDR at War and at Peace*, and is editor/co-editor of five books, including *Progressivism in America: Past Present and Future, FDR's World: War, Peace and Legacies*, and *FDR the Vatican, and the Roman Catholic Church in America.*

Neville Wylie is professor of International History and Deputy Principal at the University of Stirling, UK. He has written extensively on the Second World War, including *Barbed Wire Diplomacy. Britain, Germany and the Politics of Prisoners of War 1939–1945*, *Britain, Switzerland and the Second World War* and was the editor of *European Neutrals and Non-Belligerents during the Second World War*.

INTRODUCTION

*Freed from the Shadows of the Cold War:
A Global War Reconsidered*

G. KURT PIEHLER AND JONATHAN A. GRANT

BIAS is inevitable in the writing of history even when scholars strive for objectivity. The divide between Communist and Capitalist worlds during the Cold War fostered a bipolar view of World War II. In the case of the West, it led to scholarship and public discourse minimizing the vital role the Soviet Union played in achieving military victory against Nazi Germany. In the Soviet bloc, most notably in East Germany, the victory against fascism was commemorated as the valiant resistance of Communists against fascist tyranny. Although Nazi war crimes were remembered, the racialized nature of the Holocaust was largely forgotten. In Asia, the Cold War spurred reconciliation between the United States and Japan, limiting American interest in prosecuting perpetrators of war crimes. Paradoxically, Maoist China did relatively little to promote a memory of World War II; instead, it triumphed the long struggle against the Kuomintang and final victory in 1949.[1]

The end of the East–West ideological division in Europe led to the final peace settlement that saw the victorious Allied powers—the Soviet Union, the United States, Great Britain, and France—relinquish their occupation rights over Germany, which permitted the reunification of the country. German reunification contributed to a renewed interest in questions of collaboration, resistance, and the ideological divides engendered by World War II. During the Cold War era, there was an effort to make a distinction between the evil nature of the Nazi regime, and the average German as misguided, even a victim of the war. In a number of countries, most notably France, a growing amnesia emerged regarding the extent of collaboration under the Vichy regime and instead it emphasized commemorating the heroism of the resistance, especially by President Charles De Gaulle and his supporters.[2] In Europe, the fall of the Berlin Wall combined with the coming of age of a generation that had no living memory of the war energized scholarly inquiry, promoting renewed interest in asking difficult questions of complicity and collaboration, especially with regard to the Holocaust.

The end of the Cold War in Asia served to rekindle public discussion of Japan's actions as a colonial occupier. Women in several Asian countries, most notably South Korea, sought compensation and an official apology from the government of Japan for being coerced into prostitution as "comfort women" by Japanese troops. The emergence of China into a quasi-capitalist nation that no longer embraced the Maoist vision of solidarity with the fraternity of communist and socialist regimes ironically served to foster renewed tensions between Japan and China over the legacy of World War II. The Chinese government invested in new history textbooks, monuments, and museums that stressed Japanese war crimes. This effort to promote a memory of World War II led to a remarkable rehabilitation by the Chinese Government and scholars regarding the role Chiang Kai-Shek and the Kuomintang played in opposing Japanese aggression.

There is a vast scholarly and popular literature on World War II, especially focused on the land war in Western Europe. A growing body of work has documented the origins of the Final Solution by the Nazi regime, as well as the global response to the Holocaust. Other topics, however, have not received significant analysis. Relatively little attention has been paid to the broader humanitarian issues that surrounded World War II, such as the Bengal famine in India, the treatment of prisoners of war, and the role of non-governmental organizations in ameliorating suffering. Despite the strategic importance of the Middle East during the war, scholarship on this conflict is scant, especially for Iran, Iraq, and Turkey, where World War II served to reshape the region, fostering greater nationalism and bolstering this region.

To study World War II is to grapple with a conflict that left no nation or territory of the world untouched. Only a handful of nations, most significantly Ireland, Portugal, Spain, Sweden, Switzerland, and Vatican City, were able to remain officially neutral throughout the entire war. But even these nations had their sovereignty limited and they played important roles in providing belligerents with necessary goods or serving as centers of espionage. A number of countries had their neutrality compromised over the course of war. Some, such as the Netherlands and Norway, that had been neutral in World War I faced an unprovoked German invasion. Even Argentina, which strived to remain neutral for ideological reasons, and Turkey, which resisted entry into the conflict for strategic reasons, declared war against Germany in the closing months of the conflict.

This conflict witnessed the unprecedented mobilization of whole societies politically, economic, socially, and culturally to engage in war. The battle of production, as Richard Overy argues in *Why the Allies Won*, was one that the Grand Alliance decisively won. Great Britain, the Soviet Union, and the United States produced staggering amounts of aircraft, artillery pieces, and naval vessels. Even in 1940, and under direct aerial attack by the *Luftwaffe*, British aircraft production exceeded that of Germany.

Adolf Hitler began rearmament soon after coming to power and gained a significant head start over his adversaries, but historians debate whether he waged his war too early. In terms of armaments, Germany lagged behind after the outbreak of the war. German production peaked in 1944. Despite these gains, the Nazi regime could not compete with those of the Allied powers, despite drawing on the extensive resources and labor of the territories it conquered. Strategically, Germany, Japan, and Italy lacked the resources to sustain what ultimately became a war of attrition.[3]

The war witnessed a scale of state-sanctioned violence that staggers the imagination with over one hundred million casualties. World War II saw an almost complete collapse of boundaries that sought to avoid the unnecessary loss of civilian life. Even Allied nations were willing to accept the death of civilians in pursuing victory. Anglo-American use of strategic bombing killed not only enemy civilians, but also scores of citizens living under enemy occupation. Historians and philosophers have hotly debated both the effectiveness and morality of the Allied campaign. There is a greater consensus regarding the actions of the Axis Powers. In the case of Nazi Germany, the regime planned and implemented a policy of genocide aimed at the destruction of European Jewry and other groups deemed racially inferior. Japan never developed a policy to implement genocide against the peoples they conquered, but they suppressed resistance brutally, especially in China. Moreover, both the Nazis and the Japanese engaged in medical experimentation on enemy civilians.

The Interwar Interlude

It is generally accepted that World War II began on September 1, 1939, with the invasion of Poland representing the failure of the victors of World War I to create an enduring international order at the Paris Peace Conference of 1919. The Treaty of Versailles and associated treaties imposed on Germany, Austria, and Hungary have been considered by most scholars as a victor's peace that sowed the seed of another world war. Germany endured significant limitations on its sovereignty with regard to defense, was required to pay reparations to compensate the victorious powers, and endured significant territorial losses, including the entire overseas empire. This punitive peace, accepted by the Weimar Republic led by the Social Democrats that came to power after the abdication of Kaiser Wilhelm II, earned almost uniform condemnation from all sectors of German society.[4]

The world order created by the Treaty of Versailles was heavily influenced by the ideals of President Woodrow Wilson. National self-determination based on ethnic identity espoused by Wilson in the Fourteen Points led to the dismemberment of the Austro-Hungarian Empire and the formation of a series of ethnically based nations in eastern Europe. Wilson wanted the newly formed League of Nations to counter the threat posed by aggressor nations through collective security.

Peace rested on a slender reed, even in the 1920s. Despite proposing the creation of the League, the United States never joined the organization nor offered security guarantees to France against a resurgent Germany. Moreover, the United States insisted that former allies repay their war debts and maintained large custom barriers stifling the world economy. The Soviet Union had not been a party to the Treaty of Versailles and was initially excluded from the League of Nations. Eventually, all major Western powers, even the United States, recognized this Communist regime, and the Soviet Union became a member of the League. Ideologically, the Soviet Union remained committed under Vladimir Lenin and his successor, Joseph Stalin, to challenge the liberal world order. As an outlier regime, the Soviet Union found common ground, both with Weimar Germany and later Nazi Germany. Under Joseph Stalin the Communist movement vacillated over how to respond to rise of the Nazi party. Was fascism simply another manifestation of the historical development of capitalism? Or did this movement pose such a threat that Communists should join with socialists and liberals in fighting fascism?

Fascism gained significant traction during the interwar years and first emerged as a political force in Italy. Benito Mussolini's rise to power resulted from a combination of ruthlessness and his ability to tap into public disenchantment with Italy's meager gains from the Paris Peace conference. Despite being a major force in world politics during the interwar years, there existed significant national variations of fascism in different countries. For instance, the cult of personality that surrounded Mussolini palled compared to the emergence of Adolf Hitler as the Führer when the Nazis seized power in 1933. In the case of Japan, no single leader had the same stature of either Hitler or Mussolini. The ideological common thread that all fascist regimes embraced centered on ultranationalism and a belief that war remained a positive good.

The Versailles system provided a measure of stability for a brief period. In the 1920s there existed promising signs that Germany could be politically and economically reintegrated into the international order. The United States revitalized the German economy through the Dawes Plan by providing this country access to private capital. Germany not only joined the League of Nations, but also signed the Treaty of Locarno with France, Great Britain, Italy, and Belgium. This treaty appeared to augur a new era of harmony between former adversaries and appeared to settle the boundaries of Western Europe permanently.

Power politics must be layered on top of the question of ideology. Germany and the Soviet Union as outlier regimes in the Versailles system signed the Treaty of Rapollo in 1922, which established diplomatic ties between them. In a secret clause, German officers were permitted to train in the Soviet Union while Germany provided the Soviet regime military technology. The two principal defenders of the Versailles system, Great Britain and France, turned inward. The British faced the burdens of imperial defense and sought to forge a trading block with its empire. France devoted enormous resources to a defensive network, the Maginot Line, and was riven by intense political and economic divisions internally.

The Great Depression toppled everything. Massive unemployment and economic contraction provided the Nazi Party the perfect opportunity to challenge the mainstream parties of the right and left. In the case of the Western democracies, the Great Depression fostered a desire to turn inward politically. Ideologically, the Soviet Union gained enormous traction during the 1930s by trumpeting its success in spurring industrialization and maintaining full employment. For Japan, the Great Depression empowered militarists and undermined civilian control over the questions of war and peace.

Without consulting senior military or civilian leaders in Tokyo, the Kwantung Army stationed in Manchuria provoked a war with China. The Manchurian Incident in 1931 represented the first failure of collective security. Neither the League of Nations nor the United States took any significant actions, aside from diplomatic protest to halt Japanese aggression. The annexation of Manchuria did not lead to full-scale war in part because of the internal discord within China.

The Tripartite Pact, signed on September 27, 1940, between Germany, Italy, and Japan was not inevitable. Ricky Law observes in his examination of Axis diplomacy there existed considerable tension between Italy and Germany in the early 1930s, over the status of southern Tyrol and the sovereignty of Austria. Initially, Germany had a close economic and military alliance with China, not Japan. German military advisors played a crucial role in training Chiang Kai-Shek armies in the late 1920s and 1930s. The shift to Japan only came in the late 1930s when aid to China ceased and there was a concerted effort to cultivate stronger relations with Japan that ultimately culminated in their joining the Axis alliance.[5]

The fragile strategic position of Great Britain and France influenced how these two powers viewed relations with Italy and responded to the Spanish Civil War. Until June 1940, both nations courted Mussolini as a potential ally and sought to forestall a German–Italian military alliance. Great Britain and France supported only limited sanctions by the League of Nations in response to Mussolini's invasion of Ethiopia and they failed to aid the Spanish Republican regime. The Western democracies' fears regarding Communism shaped their policies toward the Spanish Civil War. Deep suspicion, especially on the part of the French and British government regarding the Soviet Union hindered efforts to create an effective popular front that united liberals, socialists, and communists.

Confrontation between Chinese and Japanese forces on the Marco Polo Bridge in July 1937 led to the outbreak of a full scale, but undeclared war, between China and Japan. Initially, this conflict remained regional with the Western powers offering little diplomatic or military support to the regime of Chiang Kai-Shek. Militarily, Chiang Kai-Shek forces fought bravely, especially in the defense of Shanghai, but in the end the Nationalists were driven from the coastal cities and forced to move their capital to the Chungking. Despite the military reverses, the war promoted Chinese nationalism, especially in urban areas. It also pressured both the Chiang Kai-Shek and Communist forces under Mao Tse-Tung to come to a truce, forestalling their final conformation until Japan's defeat.

In considering the course of events that led to the outbreak of World War II in Europe—the German occupation of the Rhineland, the Anschluss with Austria, the Munich Pact, the annexation of Czechoslovakia, and the invasion of Poland—scholars have generally accepted the verdict rendered in the Nuremberg War Crimes Tribunal—the Nazis had a deliberate plan to wage aggressive war. In contrast to the historiography of World War I, there is no significant historiographical literature that seeks to rehabilitate the Nazi regime or shift blame to other parties.

The controversy surrounding the coming of World War II is often asked: Why did the West not do more to meet the threat posed by fascism to the world order? In sharp contrast, the debate over what caused World War I has been hotly contested one. At the Paris Peace conference, the victors inserted a war guilt clause and declared Germany entirely responsible for causing the conflict. The war guilt clause not only fostered substantial debate during the interwar years, but it also sparked a major revisionist movement among historians. As a result, there is a vast and complicated historiography that has sought to understand the underlying and immediate causes for World War I.

Two events in the summer of 1939 altered the course of World War II. In a short, undeclared war on the Mongolian–Soviet border, the Soviet Army prevailed against Japanese forces at the Battle of Nomonhan. Ideologically, Japanese militarists viewed communism as a grave threat and many contemplated waging war toward the North. This stunning loss provoked renewed debate in Tokyo over strategy.[6] Ultimately, the Japanese Government opted to turn to the South and eventually go to war attacking European and American colonial possessions in the Pacific.

The other pivotal event that stunned the world was the signing of the Non-Aggression Pact between the Soviet Union and Germany, announced in August 1939. Both regimes managed to subsume ideological considerations for an agreement that allowed the Soviet Union several territorial concessions, including a free hand in the Baltics and Eastern Poland, along with access to German technology. In turn, Hitler gained reassurance that he could wage war against Poland and turn West without worry of Soviet intervention, and he also gained access to considerable amounts of raw materials. For several decades, Soviet apologists have seen the pact as tactical move by Stalin to strengthen his defenses.[7] Other scholars have portrayed Stalin and the Soviet leadership as quite enthusiastic partners with the Nazi regime. For instance, the Soviets scrupulously fulfilled its trade obligations with Germany.[8] Under the treaty's secret protocols, Stalin entered the war against Poland and incorporated a portion of the country into the Soviet Union.

Axis Success and the Road to Allied Victory

One of the essential questions asked by both Allied and Axis leaders was how to win the war or avoid losing it. The Allied triumph did not end the debate, with many historians in the West minimizing the strategy and military effectiveness of the American, British, and Soviet armed forces. A generation of scholars maintain that Germany had been defeated by superior numbers, especially on the Russian front, and possessed better soldiers. This view has become hotly contested, especially after the Cold War ended and there has been a major reappraisal of combat effectiveness of Soviet and Western Allied armies. But debate continues regarding the wisdom of the North African and Italian campaigns that delayed the opening of a major front until June 6, 1944, at Normandy, France.

The story of World War II began with a stunning German "Blitzkrieg" invasion and conquest of Poland in a matter of weeks. France and Great Britain declared war on Germany in support of Poland but rendered no effective assistance to Poland. From October until April 1940, a Phoney War prevailed, with neither side taking significant military actions. This lull ended in April 1940 with the German invasion of Denmark and Norway, followed on May 10, 1940, by a simultaneous attack on Belgium, the Netherlands, and France. Although the Dutch and Belgian governments retreated into exile in Great Britain, France surrendered to the Nazi regime in June 1940. The French armistice with Germany meant that Britain and its empire fought alone until Nazi Germany invaded the Soviet Union in 1941.

After France's defeat in June 1940, British propaganda stressed how this island nation fought alone and hailed the valor of Royal Air Force in meeting the onslaught of *Luftwaffe* in the strategically significantly Battle of Britain in the summer and fall 1940. Britain drew heavily upon the resources of the Empire and Commonwealth throughout the war, but especially during the pivotal year following the fall of France. British survival rested not just in prevailing over the skies of their island nation, but also grappling with the submarine threat posed by the German navy. Even after the United States entered the war, British and Canadian navies bore the brunt of fighting in the Battle of the Atlantic.

The German invasion of the Soviet Union on June 22, 1941, proved decisive in shifting the strategic balance in Europe. By turning east and abrogating the Soviet–German Non-Aggression Pact, Adolf Hitler confronted an enemy with vast manpower resources. For the rest of the war, the bulk of the German army would fight on the Eastern Front. For Great Britain, the invasion of the Soviet Union made any invasion of the British Isles unlikely and British Prime Minister Winston Churchill offered moral support and limited aid to the Soviet Union, further overstretching British resources that could have been sent to the Far East to meet the growing threat from Japan.

Many of the popular and even scholarly works during the Cold War gave the Soviet effort short shrift. After V-E Day, American intelligence operatives conducted extensive interviews with defeated German generals and accepted their claims that their forces were overwhelmed by superior numbers and hindered by a deranged leader.[9] In point of fact, the Soviet Union, while facing grave defeats in the opening months of the war, managed to not only stabilize the front by December 1941, but also launched a major counter-offensive. Initiative rested with Germany until 1943 and only after the hard-fought victories at Stalingrad and Kursk did strategic balance shift in favor of the Soviet Union. If the Soviet Union armies had not halted Germany's advance, especially on the Southern Front, the British position in the Middle East would have proven untenable.

The decision by Japan to attack Pearl Harbor on December 7, 1941, brought the United States into the war. It also turned what had been a regional conflict in China into another theater of global conflict. Honoring the Axis Pact with Japan, Adolf Hitler declared war on the United States three days later. The Japanese attack and Germany's declaration of war ended the bitter debate within the United States over American involvement and the majority of non-interventionists lined up in support of the war.

The forging of the Grand Alliance took a torturous path. After signing the Non-Aggression Pact with Germany, the Soviet Union earned the ire of the Western Powers by waging war against Finland in the winter of 1939–1940 and annexing the Baltic States. The United States proved willing to provide military aid to Great Britain after the fall of France, but only after it became clear that this country and empire were on the verge of economic collapse. Even though support for aid to Britain and the Soviet Union grew among Americans, most of the public opposed joining the fight. After some debate within the Roosevelt Administration regarding the ability of Stalin's army to survive the Nazi onslaught, it extended aid to the Soviet Union.

Even before the United States entered the war, President Franklin D. Roosevelt joined with Winston Churchill in issuing the Atlantic Charter, which offered a vision for the postwar world built around democratic values stressing the territorial integrity of nations. Churchill and Roosevelt clashed throughout the war over the future of colonialism. The British prime minster remained determined to maintain the British Empire while the American president envisioned the European colonial empires falling away.

The alliance of the United Nations proclaimed in January 1942 that it affirmed the unity of all the signatories in their struggle against the Axis Powers. The coalition was broad. As a result of American diplomacy, a number of Latin American nations joined the United Nations. The United Nations would be dominated by the United States, Great Britain, and the Soviet Union. Cooperation between Britain and the United States would be close, even leading to the formation of Combined Chiefs of Staff and the appointment of unified Allied Commanders for the different theaters. Relations with the Western Allies and the Soviet Union were more limited, although the United States provided massive amounts of material assistance and the British and Canadian navies took significant losses trying to keep the sea-lanes to Murmansk open.

Even after the United States joined the fight, the bulk of Japan's army remained deployed in China. Japan launched a successful offensive that drove Britain out of Burma, cutting off all ground transportation to this country. Broadening the war failed to break the stalemate in China. Even though the Nationalist government suffered perilous losses, it managed to continue the struggle. Although the amount of supplies was small, the United States Army Air Force launched a major airlift operation to ferry supplies from India to China. Until the retaking of Burma by British, Indian, and American forces and the construction of the Ledo Road, this perilous air route remained the principal line of communication for the Chinese government with the outside world.

Japan, like Great Britain, was a major maritime power and island nation that depended heavily on imported food, petroleum, and other raw materials to maintain its economy. In fact, the decision of Japan to pursue war against the United States, Britain, and the Netherlands stemmed from a need for petroleum and other resources necessary to sustain its economy and imperial ambitions. In the opening months of the war, Japan inflicted a series of devastating defeats on the American and British navies. Naval dominance, combined with air superiority, allowed Japan to conquer the Dutch East Indies, Malaysia, the Philippines, and several smaller colonial possessions of the Western powers in the Pacific in a matter of months. Although the Australian and American troops proved able to hold Japanese forces in New Guinea, Australians rightly feared a possible invasion in 1942.

The United States dominated the naval war against the Pacific and the key to victory by Allies rested heavily on gaining control of the Pacific Ocean. The Battle of Midway in June 1942 ranks among El Alamein and Stalingrad as one of the crucial turning points of the war. Midway is remarkable on several counts, beginning with the slim resources the United States possessed at the time. With most of the battleships of the Pacific fleet out of action as a result of Pearl Harbor, the defense of the island of Midway rested heavily on only three aircraft carriers. By breaking the Japanese naval code, American forces ignored the Japanese attack in the Aleutians in favor of the strategically important Midway. An element of good fortune turned the battle decisively in favor of the U.S., despite the naval superiority of the Japanese fleet going into battle. At a crucial moment, American aviators managed to strike the Japanese aircraft carriers with their decks filled with aircraft in the midst of refueling and rearming.

Midway reflected the overreach of the Japanese Imperial Navy that also abandoned efforts to seize Ceylon (Sri Lanka). The American landing on Guadalcanal in August 1942, initially unopposed by Japanese forces, began the long Allied offensive against Japan. Although the hold on Guadalcanal proved initially tenuous as the U.S. Navy struggled to maintain control of the sea-lanes around the island, the island would be secured by early 1943.

Germany, unlike Japan, was a land power and by 1941 the British navy had sunk or bottled up in port most of the German surface fleet. At several points in the war, most notably in late 1941 and 1942, German submarines afflicted grievous losses on Allied shipping. Still, Germany never seriously challenged British and later Allied dominance of the Atlantic in the way Japan did in the Pacific in 1941 and the first half of 1942. The route to victory in the Pacific War required the U.S. Navy to engage in several epic battles that eventually destroyed the Japanese navy as an effective fighting force.

Both the Japanese and German air forces earned the condemnation of world public opinion for attacking cities and killing civilians. During the Battle of Britain, the German air force initially targeted airfields and other military installations, but they switched to attacking London and other British cities in the later part of the campaign. While the German Air Force did engage in strategic bombing, it primarily remained a force that provided tactical support for ground forces. By contrast, both the American and British air forces focused their resources on conducting sustained strategic bombing campaigns that sought to deal a decisive blow to the enemy. Historians have fiercely debated the military effectiveness and morality of the air campaign, especially the area bombing undertaken by the British and the use of the atomic bomb against Japan.

The older view of the military conflict against Nazi Germany emphasized that the Soviet Union's road to victory from 1943 to 1945 depended on Russian hordes overwhelming the more skilled, but smaller, German army. The revisionist reassessment of the reasons for Soviet victory, drawing on scholarship that has tapped Russian sources, shows that the Soviet military leadership grew increasingly adept on the operational level while also managing to gain technological superiority over the Germans. Fuel shortages, diversions of aircraft to the defense of the fatherland, and battle losses meant that the German army became increasingly de-mechanized in the final two years of the war.

In considering the military and diplomatic course of the war, greater scholarly interest shines a light on the impact of the war on Eastern Europe, the Balkans, and the Mediterranean theaters. In the case of war against Japan, the pivotal role of the Burma campaign in restoring lines of communication with China, the multiethnic composition of the Allied war effort, and the vital role the Indian army played in this campaign now offer a more comprehensive picture.

Legacies of War

Some nations, most notably in the Americas, remained largely sheltered from direct enemy attack. Both the United States and Canada underwent an economic mobilization that altered gender roles for the duration of the conflict. Civilians in most countries were not safe from the ravages of enemy attack. For societies under Nazi occupation, populations suffered a grim fate, especially Jews, the Roma, and others that were placed in concentration camps and later killed in an extensive network of death camps. Other non-combatants faced the quandary of how to respond to enemy occupation. Some segments of society, especially business elites, actively collaborated, even participating in the implementation of the Final Solution. A distinct minority in most countries engaged in covert, even armed, resistance against Nazi occupation. Most fell into a more nebulous category that neither embraced their conquerors nor fought them.

Most scholarship examining religion and World War II has understandably centered on the Holocaust, especially the relationship of the Vatican with the Italian and German states. There is a more complex story to be told about the role of religion with both Axis and Allied regimes seeking to mobilize religious institutions and ideals. In the case of Japan, the government fostered state-sponsored Shintoism to bolster support for the war among soldiers and the broader society. Even in Germany, where the Nazis had an antagonistic relationship with Protestant and Catholic churches in the 1930s, both churches still embraced the war effort in September 1939. A small minority of religious dissenters at times challenged the policies of governments, even in Germany. For instance, Roman Catholic Bishop Von Galen publicly preached against Hitler's euthanasia program to the extent that the regime was required to place a veil of secrecy over it. In Great Britain and the United States, a small segment of the religious community was one of the few groups to publicly question the Army Air Force bombing doctrine that resulted in high levels of civilian deaths.

The relationship between culture and politics remained complex for most societies under war. All regimes at war, even Allied nations, imposed some form of censorship of the press and often restricted the rights of artists and intellectuals. The Soviet Union and Germany imposed rigid restrictions on artists and other intellectuals, with both regimes promoting realism as a superior aesthetic. In contrast, both Italy and Japan offered greater range for artistic expression. For instance, Japanese avant-garde artists acquired patronage from the Japanese state and in turn supported the imperial enterprise in Manchuria.

All the major powers, but most notably Germany, Great Britain, and the United States, devoted significant resources to scientific and technological research that had a far-reaching impact on the war and during postwar era. Modern computers, radar, ballistic missiles, and jet aircrafts were among the most important technological advances that emerged from the war, but there were countless others. Moreover, the war changed the relationship between science and the state. Government funds displaced private individuals and corporations as the largest source of patronage for science. The role of medicine in this conflict is far less researched. Physicians and nurses were healers, but they also remained crucial cogs in waging war. The ability of the U.S. Army and Marines to effectively cope with malaria through the use of DDT played a pivotal role in a number of Pacific theater battles, especially at Guadalcanal. The vast number of disabled veterans and civilians continues to be one of the lasting legacies of the war and all societies struggled with providing care for them.

The evolution of the United Nations into an international organization remains one of the most enduring legacies of the war. In a series of war-time conferences, Great Britain, the Soviet Union, and the United States enshrined great power dominance over the organization's Security Council, which was established to preserve peace and maintain collective security. This body granted the permanent five members of the council (the original Big Three, along with France and China) the right to veto any resolution, ensuring the organization could only act decisively with support of the great powers. In a bow to Wilsonian internationalism, the United Nations Organization offered each member nation one vote in the less powerful General Assembly. The ability of the United Nations to enforce collective security waxed and waned, especially during the Cold War. Nonetheless, the United Nations has proven more durable and effective on matters of peace and security than the League of Nations that it replaced. In contrast to its predecessor, virtually every nation in the world has joined the organization.

Equally significant legacies of the war are the International Momentary Fund (IMF), the International Bank for Reconstruction and Development (World Bank), and the General Agreement on Trade and Tariffs (GATT) established by the Bretton Wood Agreements. While the Bretton Wood financial system, which was based on a fixed exchange rate pegged to the United States dollar, collapsed in the early 1970s, the IMF and the World Trade Organization (WTO) (the organization that replaced the General Agreement on Trade and Tariffs) have provided stability to the global economy and played a critical part in several financials crises. In the 1970s and 1980s, the IMF played a crucial role as the lender of last resort to nations cut off from international credit markets. Support for free trade and stable currency exchange remained strong among elites in the postwar era in the West and, after the collapse of the Soviet bloc, globalization seemed unstoppable. It may be no coincidence that with the passing of the World War II generation, support for free trade and support of multilateral institutions has faltered.

The crimes of Germany and Japan were countless and the understanding of them has shifted both in historiography and popular memory. Perhaps the most significant is the explosion of scholarship on the Holocaust that began in the 1970s. Two generations of scholars have offered new insights into the causes and frightening outcomes of these crimes against humanity. Less well understood, especially in Western historiography, is the extent and nature of Japanese war crimes.

The Allied response to the Holocaust has produced a heated debate over the failures of the West's response to the Holocaust into a wider consideration of humanitarianism in an age of global war. The response to the Holocaust must also be seen in the context of the failure of British authorities to prevent over three million deaths in Bengal from famine. At the same time, the wartime Allies established an international humanitarian organization, the United Nations Relief and Rehabilitation Administration (UNRRA), that provided crucial aid to civilian populations of war-torn Europe and Asia.

An enduring precedent established as a result of World War II would be the creation of international courts to try war criminals for the first time. A rich and varied historiography and memoir literature has documented the International Military Tribunal at Nuremberg and the Israeli trial of Adolf Eichmann. More recent scholarship has sought to broaden the focus to examine efforts by individual nations to render justice and to examine the trials organized by the occupying powers in Germany. The Tokyo trials have received scant attention and the view that they simply demonstrated victors' justice has prevailed for several decades.[10] This view has been challenged persuasively by a new wave of scholarship arguing that while the quest for justice was incomplete, these courts accomplished a great deal. In the case of the Tokyo War Crimes trial, the court was decisively international in character and included representatives from fifteen nations as judges, including India and the Philippines. The court also established new precedents regarding crimes against humanity involving sexual violence waged against women.

Victory over Nazi Germany and Imperial Japan led to some ambiguous legacies. In redrawing the map of Europe, the borders of Germany and Poland were fundamentally reordered with the Soviet Union gaining at the expense of Poland. In turn, the Polish border was moved westward, and East Prussia disappeared. The German city of Danzig, a free city under the control of the League of Nations during the interwar years, became the Polish city of Gdansk. Czechs took revenge against the ethnic Germans by murdering scores and expelling others from the Sudeten region. In Asia, the collapse of Japan led to the mass expulsion of Japanese colonizers from China, Korea, and other parts of Asia.

The war devastated the Soviet Union and the nation even experienced famine in the immediate postwar period. But the Soviet military power crushed opposition movements in Eastern Europe and this region became part of the Eastern Bloc until the collapse of the Soviet Union in the early 1990s. Although the Baltic states annexed by the Soviet Union gained independence, the reordered borders remained extant.

The war hastened the decline of European empires, beginning with the ideological impact of the Atlantic Charter that bolstered the cause of anti-colonial movement. The growing independence movement in India during the interwar years led to a growing consensus among British leaders, fiercely opposed by Winston Churchill, for granting independence. Churchill's electoral defeat in 1945 empowered the Labour Government of Prime Minister Clement Attlee to grant independence in 1947. The onset of the Cold War complicated decolonization, but ultimately only delayed it. For instance, the United States eventually supported French efforts to retain Indochina, but it only delayed their inevitable defeat in 1954.

Historians are not the only group in society to engage in the history of World War II. Considering how different societies remember and commemorate this conflict suggests the lingering trauma experienced by many nations engulfed in this conflict. For the United States, the war has increasingly been termed the "good war" whereas in the Soviet Union, now Russia, it has been deemed the Great Patriotic War. In Japan, there exists a fundamental debate over how to name the conflict. Time has not dimmed all memories of suffering among the dwindling band of survivors of wartime atrocities nor the wider societies. Moreover, there are significant unsettled legacies from the war, most notably the lack of a peace treaty between Japan and Russia and the continued division of the Korean Peninsula.

Despite the outpouring of scholarship on World War II, there is much we still need to learn. The social history of combatants who fought in the air and on the high seas warrants further study. We have a vast literature on the D-Day landing on June 6, 1944, but far less on the major landings that preceded it in North Africa, Sicily, and Italy. Humanitarianism in response to what many consider a total war warrants further investigations, especially with regard to the treatment of prisoners of war. Above all, there is a need to try in writing the history of war to transcend a narrow, national parochialism to see the global dimensions.

Notes

1. Zheng Wang, *Never Forget National Humiliation: Historical Memory in Chinese Politics and Foreign Relations* (New York: Columbia University Press, 2012); Akiko Takenaka, *History, Memory, and Japan's Unending Postwar* (Honolulu: University of Hawaii Press, 2015).
2. Henry Rousso, *The Vichy Syndrome: History and Memory in France Since 1944* (Cambridge: Harvard University Press, 1991).
3. Richard Overy, *Why the Allies Won* (New York: W. W. Norton, 1995).
4. John Maynard Keynes, *Economic Consequences of the Peace* (New York, 1920); Norman A. Graebner and Edward M. Bennett, *The Versailles Treaty and Its Legacy: The Failure of the Wilsonian Vision* (Cambridge: Cambridge University Press, 2011).
5. Ricky Law, *Transnational Nazism: Ideology and Culture in German–Japanese Relations, 1919–1939* (New York: Cambridge University Press, 2019).
6. Stuart Goldman, *Nomonhan, 1939: The Red Army's Victory That Shaped World War II* (Annapolis, MD: Naval Institute Press, 2012).
7. Geoffrey Roberts, *The Soviet Union and the Origins of the Second World War: Russo–German Relations and the Road to War, 1933–1941* (New York: St. Martin's Press, 1995); Caroline Kennedy-Pipe, *Russia and the World 1917–1991* (New York: Oxford University Press, 1998).

8. Roger Morehouse, *The Devils' Alliance: Hitler's Pact with Stalin, 1939–1941* (New York: Basic Books, 2014).
9. Max Hasting, *Armageddon: The Battle for Germany, 1944–1945* (New York: Vintage, 2005); Erich von Manstein, *Lost Victories*, trans. Anthony G. Powell (Chicago: H. Regnery, 1958).
10. Richard H. Minear, *Victor's Justice: The Tokyo War Crimes Trial* (Princeton, NJ: Princeton University Press, 1971).

CHAPTER 1

THE COLLAPSE OF THE VERSAILLES SYSTEM

MICHAEL H. CRESWELL

THE outbreak of World War I generated high expectations among the belligerents. Many people in each of the warring nations firmly believed that the conflict would be short and that their side would triumph. But as the trench lines hardened and the human and material costs of the war mounted, optimism was replaced by pessimism and disillusionment. The victors therefore sought to devise a plan to ensure that never again would such a deadly and destructive war be fought. At the Paris Peace Conference in 1919, the victors tried to create a system that would reflect the catchphrase made popular during the conflict, that the war would be "the war to end war."[1]

The postwar system the victors cobbled together at Paris contained several elements. The settlement included the creation of the League of Nations, protection for minorities, the establishment of mandates to oversee the colonies of the defeated powers, supervised population exchanges, as well as the resolution of other important matters. Five separate treaties were concluded at the Paris Peace Conference, one for each of the defeated powers; but the centerpiece of the system was the settlement the Allies imposed upon defeated Germany. The Treaty of Versailles limited the size of Germany's armed forces, compelled the country to cede territory in both its east and west, stripped it of its colonies, forced it to accept moral responsibility for the war (as spelled out in Article 231 of the treaty), and saddled it with substantial financial reparations. These and other elements of the treaty were the foundation stones of the Versailles System—a system designed to prevent Germany from committing future aggression and starting another world war.

Yet, like the optimism that reigned at the outset of the conflict, the confidence that greeted the new system would soon dissipate. By the 1920s, Germany was finding ways to avoid paying reparations. The Ruhr Crisis of 1923 marked a turning point. The crisis occurred when Germany defaulted on part of its reparations to France, whereupon France and Belgium invaded the Ruhr region to force collection by commandeering goods from German mines and factories and shipping them home. But German workers refused to cooperate, going so far as to sabotage Ruhr mines and factories. France was now convinced that the Versailles System was unenforceable, something future events would confirm. In the early 1930s, Germany continued violating the terms of the Versailles Treaty, and those charged with defending the system proved either unable or unwilling to enforce it. By the late 1930s, the Versailles System was in tatters. Then, on September 1, 1939, Germany invaded Poland and World War II began, ending only after tens of millions of people had perished.

We are left with several questions, but two of them stand out. Why, given the safeguards established at the Paris conference, was catastrophe not averted? What did the Allied powers overlook or misunderstand? In fact, there was no isolated decision, hasty move, or simple oversight that caused the system to fail and end in a second global cataclysm. Many factors were involved and, taken together, they opened the door to World War II.

The Defeat of Germany and the German Revolution

The failure of the Versailles System is rooted in the conditions under which Germany lost the war. After years of slogging it out on the battlefield, Germany decided in 1918 to make one final push for victory. Russia's defeat and the signing of the Treaty of Brest-Litovsk (March 3, 1918) ended the war in the east and gave Germany a relatively free hand for operations in the west. Although Germany still had to occupy Ukraine, as well as try to keep its main ally, the Austro-Hungarian Empire, from collapsing, the German military command, dominated by General Erich Ludendorff, undertook a major offensive in France, hoping to defeat the Western powers before American troops could arrive in sufficient numbers to turn the tide against Berlin.

At the outset of the 1918 campaign Germany appeared to be in a strategically sound position. Russia had exited the conflict and American troops had yet to cross the Atlantic in substantial numbers. Although some political moderates urged Berlin to seek a diplomatic end to the war, the military and most civilian leaders were convinced that if the Reich struck swiftly, it could achieve an outright victory before large numbers of American forces arrived in France. The military leaders probably knew that taking this decision was a huge gamble because Germany would run out of trained reserves by summer. Unless the gamble of a western offensive paid off, Germany would likely suffer defeat.

Between March 21 and July 15, 1918, the German Army undertook five offensives in the west. By midsummer, German forces had again reached the Marne River, where they had been stopped in September 1914. But the Marne was as far as they got. On July 18, French and American troops launched a counterattack, forcing Ludendorff to abandon further offensive action.[2] With hundreds of thousands of American troops arriving in

France, the Allies were now forcing the Germans back. By mid-August, after the British victory at Amiens (which Ludendorff called the "black day of the German Army"), it was beginning to look like a rout.[3]

In late September, the Allies launched four coordinated attacks on the western front. Germany's high command and many political officials in Berlin realized that the country could not halt the Allied advance and that it would face either invasion by the Allies or a Bolshevik-style revolution, or both. In addition, Germany received another strategic setback when Bulgaria, a member of the Central Powers, signed an armistice on September 29. Bulgaria was strategically important because it was a land bridge linking Germany and Austria-Hungary with the Ottoman Empire, another German ally. Sofia's exit from the war also opened Austria-Hungary to the prospect of an Allied invasion. On the same day Bulgaria surrendered, Ludendorff and Field Marshal Paul von Hindenburg, who technically was Ludendorff's superior, demanded that Germany seek an immediate armistice from President Woodrow Wilson. In an effort to obtain favorable peace terms and to foist responsibility for the impending defeat onto the parliamentary politicians, they would come to advocate the formation of a government based on wider popular support.[4]

On October 3, Prince Max of Baden was appointed chancellor of Germany. Prince Max was a prominent moderate and critic of Germany's prosecution of the war. The next day the prince sent a note to Wilson asking for an armistice and peace based on the president's Fourteen Points. Unveiled in a January 8, 1918 speech on war aims Wilson delivered to a joint session of the U.S. Congress, the Fourteen Points called for self-determination, freedom of the seas, and other high-minded principles. This new world order was intended to replace the previous one, which was based purely on power considerations.[5] Angered when, on October 14, Wilson demanded more from Germany in return for an armistice, Ludendorff reversed course and recommended renewing the fighting. But by October 23, Prince Max's Cabinet had agreed to Wilson's terms. Infuriated by the supreme command's about face, the Kaiser accepted Ludendorff's resignation on October 26.[6] Ludendorff was succeeded by General Wilhelm Groener, who had expressed mildly democratic sympathies. Germany's leadership had finally recognized that securing a favorable peace required wholesale political change.

Indeed, with the end near, Germany's government sought to adopt a new public face to avoid harsh treatment at the hands of the Allies and to forestall revolution at home. On October 28, Prince Max pushed through a series of measures that reformed the constitution and transformed Germany into a constitutional monarchy. On November 4, the Germans accepted the Allies' military terms for an armistice. Revolution then swept through Germany in early November. These were not simply antiwar uprisings. The Kiel mutiny of November 3, which saw sailors of the German High Seas Fleet revolt in concert with industrial workers, triggered other revolutions in the country, first in the Rhineland and north Germany, and then the spectacular revolutions in Munich on November 7 and Berlin on November 9, which toppled the Bavarian (Wittelsbach) and Prusso-German (Hohenzollern) dynasties. The revolutions were political and left-wing in nature, not simply antiwar. The High Command informed the ineffectual Kaiser

Wilhelm II that he had lost the support of his soldiers, and he then fled from headquarters to exile in Holland on November 10. Wilhelm formally abdicated the throne on November 28. With the political Right and Center in disarray, the socialists filled the vacuum. On November 9, 1918, the Social Democratic Party declared Germany a parliamentary republic, and the country signed an armistice two days later.[7]

The new regime, the Weimar Republic, was handicapped by deep political division from the start. While the military high command had told Germany's political leadership that defeat was inevitable, the German public was left in the dark. This failure to publicly disclose the country's true military situation, in part, gave rise to the stab-in-the-back theory. The Weimar Republic was forced to shoulder the blame for a defeat that most German people were unprepared for, as heavy censorship and deceptive reports by the military had prevented bad news from the front from reaching them.[8] The demand for an armistice was so unexpected that it caused many Germans to look for a scapegoat. The search for villains gave rise to the "stab in the back" myth—the belief that leftists, Jews, and war profiteers had conspired to cause Germany to lose the war. The Weimar Republic was unable to dispel or overcome this deeply held belief, which left it politically vulnerable throughout its relatively brief existence.

Following the 1918 revolution in Germany that brought the socialist Left into power, Kurt Eisner, a leader of the radical Independent Social Democratic Party, counseled the new revolutionary government to fully admit Germany's war guilt to secure better terms in the upcoming Paris negotiations. To this end, Eisner and others promoted the opening of the German archives to place the blame for starting the war on the previous government of the Kaiser. The journalist and Marxist theoretician Karl Kautsky then began to assemble a collection of relevant documents from government offices.[9]

Kautsky's efforts spurred considerable opposition from Germany's military leadership and from the Foreign Office. To put the best possible face on its prewar conduct, officials from these two institutions launched a public relations campaign that attempted to justify Germany's policies and strategies to an international audience. They doubled their efforts when the Foreign Office learned that the war guilt question would form the legal basis for the Entente's peace terms. To rebut any such accusations, Foreign Office officials began assembling diplomatic documents to make the case that Germany alone should not be blamed for the war. They argued instead that the other powers, especially France and Russia, should be blamed because the latter had mobilized first and together with Britain had encircled Germany before the war. Germany's primary goal was to obtain a more moderate peace based on Wilson's Fourteen Points. The Germans also hoped to gain access to badly needed American credits.[10]

The Paris Peace Conference

The victors of the Great War descended on Paris in January 1919 full of confidence. The British diplomat Sir Harold Nicolson, then a junior member of his country's delegation to the conference, recalled how the conferees saw their task: "We were preparing not Peace only, but Eternal Peace."[11] Representing the victors were the Big Four: British Prime Minister David Lloyd George, French Premier Georges Clemenceau, Italian Premier Vittorio Orlando, and President Woodrow Wilson.

Wilson's arrival in Europe was greeted with great fanfare by the public. His Fourteen Points and his visionary rhetoric had led many Europeans to see him as a savior from the New World, returning to redeem the Old. They believed that through Wilson some lasting good could emerge from the long and terrible war. But Wilson's idealistic notions raised popular expectations too high.

These notions began to unravel when it became clear that reality differed from expectations. Perhaps most importantly, the Big Four made decisions at Paris that violated the principle of self-determination. The newly created Czechoslovakia, for example, was stitched together from the remnants of the Austro-Hungarian Empire plus a small amount of territory from Germany. The new state contained Czechs, Slovaks, Hungarians, and ethnic Germans. The latter group did not fare as well economically or politically in the new Czechoslovakia as it had in Austria-Hungary, a fact that the Austrian-born Adolf Hitler would later exploit.

France had much it wanted to accomplish at Paris, and French Prime Minister Clemenceau played a critical role. Given how France had suffered at the hands of its German neighbor, many observers expected Paris to seek a punitive peace. But while Clemenceau did not completely renounce France's ambition to annex or otherwise control the left bank of the Rhine, his main goal in Paris was to maintain France's alliance with Britain and the United States.[12] Moreover, Clemenceau entertained suggestions from certain conservative circles (large banks and major industrial firms) in France to seek some sort of accommodation with Germany. Indeed, Clemenceau pursued a "three-tiered" strategy at the peace conference.[13] Although known as "the Tiger," Clemenceau was in fact politically subtler than historians have usually given him credit for.[14]

Lloyd George also greatly influenced the establishment of the Versailles System. Although one of the main treaty makers at the peace conference, he sought short-term tactical advantage for Britain instead of pursuing long-term objectives that might have led to a durable peace. Indeed, Britain took a harder line on reparations at Paris than did France, as Lloyd George was inclined to make Germany pay a high price for the war. While he had campaigned in 1918 for a harsh peace, he could easily have adopted a more moderate stance with few domestic repercussions.[15]

Poland posed a unique set of challenges to the establishment of a durable postwar settlement. Between 1772 and 1795, the Polish–Lithuanian Commonwealth experienced three partitions carried out by the great powers of the day, with the final partition ending its national existence. The Allies of 1919 decided to recreate the country from territory ceded by Austria, Germany, and Russia. To give the Poles access to the sea, the Allies created the Danzig Corridor, which left East Prussia separated from the rest of Germany, a decision that would have momentous repercussions. Indeed, Hitler later pressured Poland to return some of this territory to Germany.

The Versailles Treaty diminished Germany's territory by fourteen percent and its population by 6.5 million people. Although most of the 6.5 million were not Germans, some were and, together with the Austrian Germans now living in Czechoslovakia, constituted a large German minority living in non-German lands.[16] These compromises violated some of Wilson's Fourteen Points, and they would become rallying cries for those Germans who wanted to overturn the Versailles System. One facet of the stab-in-the-back myth is that some on the German Right believed Wilson had tempted the German Left with promises of a soft peace, only to then impose an extremely harsh one.[17] Almost all Germans mistakenly expected a peace based on the Fourteen Points. The Nazis later exploited these dashed expectations to the fullest.[18]

Another challenge to the Versailles System was the fate of the Rhineland. According to the armistice agreement of November 11, 1918,[19] American, Belgian, British, and French forces were to occupy the Rhineland. The zone on the western bank of the Rhine would be demilitarized. German troops were banned from all territory west of the Rhine and within fifty kilometers east of the Rhine. The amount of territory to be occupied by the Allies was twelve thousand square miles. These strictures were among the strongest guarantees of French security the Allies imposed on Germany.[20]

However, the Rhineland strategy failed to work as envisioned because it lacked strategic coherence and was followed inconsistently. Debate over the Rhineland had flared at Paris, primarily between France on one side and Britain and the United States on the other. The three reached a compromise agreement in April 1919. France received American and British assurances against future German attack, as well as Allied occupation of the left bank and strategic bridgeheads on the right bank for at least five years in the north and fifteen years in the south. Moreover, the left bank and a fifty-kilometer strip on the right bank would be permanently demilitarized. Demilitarizing the Rhineland was also a way to avoid calls for it to be an independent state linked to France and the Benelux countries through collective security, as Marshal Foch and others had advocated.[21]

Despite the agreement, differences between London, Paris, and Washington over policy, tactics, and strategy continued. On December 26, 1922, the Reparations Commission, which had been created by the Treaty of Versailles and charged with setting a final reparations figure,[22] declared Germany in default on its reparation payments. France first imposed sanctions. Then on January 11, 1923, French and Belgian forces occupied the Ruhr District, which prompted Germany to stop reparation payments and deliveries in kind. Britain chose not to support France's strategy; such support would have allowed French military forces to operate in the British zone, which would have harmed Anglo-German relations.[23]

Britain was left in the difficult position of either disobeying the Inter-Allied Rhineland High Commission (IARHC), which oversaw the occupation of the Rhineland,[24] or being seen as favoring the French over the Germans. The IARHC was the highest representative of the four occupying powers—Belgium, Britain, France, and the United States. This body wielded great legal power. It could enact legally binding decrees concerning occupation military forces, and it could declare martial law. The IARHC also operated through majority rule. In the case of a tie, the French representative, president by law, would cast the tiebreaker vote. Following the departure of the American delegate from the IARHC, the British high commissioner saw his influence decline.[25]

Britain's unwillingness to support France risked increasing tensions with the French. Britain wanted to prevent France from growing too powerful, and it also wanted to ensure that Germany would be able to buy British goods. Although the crisis passed, it revealed early on that the Treaty of Versailles, as crafted, was simply unenforceable. This was also a major underlying condition of appeasement: if you cannot enforce a treaty, modify it.[26]

While tensions mounted between Britain and France, some of the Allies' hard feelings toward Germany began to subside. As noted previously, Germany attempted to rebut the charges leveled against it in Paris. But while its campaign to deflect blame provided no relief at the Peace Conference, it achieved some success in the near and medium term.[27] Over time, many foreign observers softened their stance toward Germany, which in the Versailles Treaty had been held responsible for starting the war. Rather than singling out Germany, which had rid itself of those responsible (i.e., the Hohenzollern dynasty and those in government and the military who had wanted war), many foreigners began to blame the alliance system that existed before the war for touching off the conflict. Others saw the war as an accident—a conflict that no one had wanted.

Economic issues presented another challenge, as the problem of war debts and reparations would confound policymakers. The two issues were intertwined and sparked considerable debate on both sides of the Atlantic over how to respond. The international economic system was thriving during the 1920s, as production was increasing in almost every Western country (although European economies lagged behind the United States). However, this prosperity ended with the onset of the Great Depression, which began with the financial panic of October 1929. The Depression fueled the rise of economic nationalism and caused some countries to blame others for their own economic distress. Weimar Germany argued that it was overburdened by huge reparation payments that undermined the German economy, while Britain and France argued in vain for the United States to moderate its demand for full repayment of the debts they had incurred during the war.

But despite Germany's complaints, the economic terms of the Versailles Treaty were relatively moderate. Even so, for many years scholars were overwhelmingly united in their condemnation of the peace settlement. Many of them castigated France for seeking to punish Germany by adopting a vengeful strategy at the Peace Conference and beyond. That consensus has largely crumbled. Few scholars today adopt the traditional view.

Ultimately, the cardinal mistake the Allies committed was failing to develop a sound war termination strategy in 1918. The goal of war is to make a better peace, but military victory alone is insufficient to ensure a better peace. Military victories must be sealed by political agreements that all sides accept. The Treaty of Versailles contributed to postwar instability because Britain and France were too exhausted to enforce the peace, and the United States chose to limit its political and military involvement in the international system. Balancing the relationship among national security objectives, military objectives, and war termination from 1917[28] to 1919 posed a daunting strategic challenge to the victors. The Allied leadership arrived at Paris with different policy goals.[29] As a result, successful war termination proved elusive.

THE DEPRESSION YEARS

During the years 1919–1933, Germany worked strenuously to halt reparations payments. So successful was Germany that it actually received payments from the United States. But while Germany succeeded in obtaining a short-term benefit for itself, it also did much harm to the international monetary system, primarily by contributing to the abandonment of the gold standard in 1931, which was followed by the adoption of an autarchic, or go-it-alone, strategy in many countries.[30]

Germany was not alone in being asked to pay up. To prosecute the war, many of the Allied governments had borrowed a considerable amount of money from the United States. But during the 1920s, Americans united around one issue: collecting the $10 billion debt that the Allies owed to the United States. Although the Allies had argued at the Paris Peace Conference that their efforts came in support of a common cause, and that therefore debts should be forgiven or reduced, Wilson rejected this line of argument, knowing that it would be a political nonstarter at home. He was correct in his assessment, as much of that debt was owed to private banks over which Wilson and the other presidents in the 1920s had little influence. Wilson also welcomed the Europeans' indebtedness to the United States, as it would enable him to shape the peace along his lines.

Postwar U.S. tariff policy posed another problem, as it stifled international economic cooperation. After the Republicans' victory in the 1920 election, Congress raised tariffs to help American farmers in the face of a recovering European agricultural sector, as well as to help American manufacturers who had enjoyed a boom during the war but who were now experiencing a downturn. The Emergency Tariff Act of 1921 and the Fordney-McCumber Tariff Act of 1922 made it increasingly difficult for European companies to sell their goods in the United States, something that they needed to do if their governments were to repay the debts owed to the U.S. government and banks. The Congress also passed legislation that prevented the executive branch from unilaterally deferring or canceling debts.[31]

In addition to raising tariffs and striving to ensure that foreign debts were repaid, by the fall of 1925 the Commerce and State Departments became concerned about lending abroad. But, despite the risk, Wall Street remained very willing to provide loans to Germany.[32] The issue began to boil in 1931–1933 when the Europeans either halted payment on their debts or refused to pay interest on them.[33] In response, Congress passed the Johnson Debt Default Act of 1934, which forbade lending to countries that were in default on previous loans made to them by the United States. Senator Hiram Johnson, an isolationist Republican from California, spoke for many Americans when he complained that international bankers were "driving us deeper and deeper in the European maelstrom."[34]

The continued economic woes of American farmers prompted calls for greater protection. Herbert Hoover, running as the Republican candidate for president in 1928, promised help to farmers. Meanwhile, calls for protection also came from other sectors of society, including manufacturers. The stock market crash of 1929, which began on October 24, strengthened protectionist sentiment. These calls resulted in the Tariff Act of 1930, also known as the Smoot-Hawley tariff, which excluded European exports from U.S. markets. Smoot-Hawley's tariff increases burdened the economies of countries already struggling from the Great Depression and the costs of post-World War I reconstruction.

In 1931, with the Great Depression in full force, President Hoover, who blamed the Depression in part on the failures of the Paris Peace Conference, suspended reparations repayments and inter-Allied war debts.[35] The onset and duration of the Great Depression meant that unresolved problems created by the Great War further undermined trust and commitment, which in turn prevented the international coordination of monetary policy. The fragility of postwar political institutions, the continuing dilemma of how to deal with war debts and reparations, and the lingering specter of the early 1920s inflation were the primary causes that prevented coordination. The war had caused great economic, material, and political damage to Europe, and the continent was slow to recover.[36] The bleak economic landscape provided fertile soil for the rise and growth of extremist ideologies.

Poverty often gives rise to disillusionment and opens the door to political demagogues who attempt to show solidarity with the downtrodden, identify scapegoats who supposedly caused the economic misery, and promise actions that will lead to the return of good times. Adolf Hitler, Benito Mussolini, and Josef Stalin were three such men who gained control of their respective countries by employing some variant of this formula. All three adopted autarky to some degree to help their nations get through the Great Depression. The strategy of economic self-sufficiency led countries to engage in beggar-thy-neighbor strategies in which one country attempted to solve its own economic problems in ways that harmed the economies of its neighbors. Such strategies normally involve erecting trade barriers to lower the price of exports and thus drive up the price of imports, while at the same time preserving employment at home. These three authoritarian regimes—Hitler's Germany, Mussolini's Italy, and Stalin's Soviet Union—seemed to weather the Great Depression better than other countries, which earned them a significant degree of international respect.

DISARMAMENT INITIATIVES

Efforts to promote disarmament produced another failure during the interwar years. Many politicians and much of the public believed that the arms race that occurred before 1914 paved the way for the catastrophe that followed. Revulsion at the Great War, a desire to reduce the profits made by arms manufacturers, and the desire of some states—particularly Italy and Japan—to prevent Britain and the United States from pulling too ahead of them, all led to several disarmament initiatives during the interwar period. One area of concern was naval power, in which the United States took a particular interest. The country feared that its aspirations for naval supremacy might end, as Britain and Japan sought to build technologically advanced fleets. Charles Evans Hughes, the U.S. secretary of state under presidents Warren G. Harding and Calvin Coolidge, recognized the importance of military power in support of diplomacy. Rather than seek unilateral naval reductions, or engage in an expensive arms race, the United States sought to achieve balanced reductions though international agreement. The most important of these efforts were the Washington Naval Conference (November 12, 1921 to February 6, 1922), the Geneva Naval Conference (June 20, 1927 to August 4, 1927), and the London Naval Treaty (April 22, 1930).[37]

One early setback occurred with the failure of the Washington Conference, which was intended to regulate naval ships among the great naval powers and to craft security agreements for the Pacific region. However, it did result in the drafting and signing of several major and minor agreements. Signed by Britain, France, Japan, and the United States on December 13, 1921, the Four-Power Pact was intended to create a framework that would help them avoid clashing over their interests in the Pacific. Deep-seated differences between the powers were papered over, making the agreement toothless. It also annulled the 1902 Anglo-Japanese Alliance, which had maintained the balance of power in Asia.[38]

The Five-Power Naval Limitation Treaty resulted from a U.S. proposal to scrap almost two million tons of warships. Signed by Britain, France, Italy, Japan, and the United States on February 6, 1922, the ratio of capital ships between the countries was set at five each for Britain and the United States, three for Japan, and 1.67 each for France and Italy. However, while the agreement limited the total tonnage of each navy's warships, it left some classes of ships unrestricted. This loophole led to a new race to build cruisers after 1922, prompting the signatories to return to the negotiating table in 1927 and 1930 to amend the treaty. The Naval Limitation Treaty remained in force until the mid-1930s, when Japan insisted on equality with the United States and Britain regarding the size and number of its capital ships. When the other signatories rejected this demand, Japan notified them that it intended to terminate the treaty, which then expired at the end of 1936.

Another reason for the collapse of the Versailles System was that two of its main pillars, Britain and France, were economically, militarily, and politically hamstrung during the interwar period. Britain did not begin rearming until 1934, and France was mired in political turmoil that hindered its military effectiveness. Anglo-French weakness opened the way for Berlin's growing ambitions.

Obstacles to British rearmament were evident by 1935. The Conservative Party had pledged to undertake a series of social welfare initiatives and to build public housing. Reneging on this pledge and focusing instead on rearmament could have triggered a serious public backlash. Britain was simply unable to meet its domestic challenges and simultaneously guard its empire, take part in the League of Nations, and confront the territorial ambitions of Germany, Italy, and Japan.

France also faced problems during this period that prevented it from opposing the military and territorial ambitions of Germany and Italy. One problem was the severe polarization of France's domestic politics. This division worked against any full-scale French mobilization of resources for defense. The political Right in France was willing to align itself with the Nazis in Germany, and the Left with the communist Soviet Union. The Socialists opposed greater military spending, pledged to fight only under the auspices of the League of Nations, and demanded economic sanctions on its former ally, Italy, when the latter country invaded Ethiopia in 1935. This stance tended to drive Italy into the arms of Germany.

The Popular Front, a left-leaning coalition of parties primarily intended to combat fascism, was formed in 1934. It stressed national defense above all. Even the French communists pledged to set aside their traditional demands for things like the redistribution of wealth to focus on the Nazi threat. The Popular Front went on to win the 1936 legislative elections.[39] This victory gave the premiership to Léon Blum, a prominent socialist.

The Spanish Civil War brought all these issues facing France to a head, as symbolized by the political violence that occurred in the late 1930s and the defeat of Blum in 1937. The Popular Front chose not to offer material aid to the Republicans in Spain out of fear of sparking a crisis in France itself. The Fascists won the Spanish Civil War and thus deprived Britain and France of a potential ally in any conflict against Germany and Italy. Ultimately, France lacked both sufficient military power and the political unity needed to prevent a further collapse of the Versailles System.

France had begun thinking about a potential second world conflict soon after the Great War.[40] Marshal Ferdinand Foch, who served as supreme allied commander during World War I, rued the Treaty of Versailles: "This is not a peace. It is an armistice for twenty years."[41] France was militarily unprepared in 1939. The main problem was that France had no powerful eastern ally, as Russia had been in 1914 (this is why France supported the Little Entente, an alliance between Czechoslovakia, Romania, and Yugoslavia). It was also surrounded (again, unlike 1914) by regimes in Spain and Italy that were sympathetic to Germany. And although by the 1930s France had repaired some of the problems that had weakened its army during the 1920s,[42] its military budget was limited by the economic conditions of the time. These problems prevented France from playing a stronger role in Europe during the interwar period.

France was also hampered because relations with Britain were at times less than cordial.[43] In fact, there was mutual distrust. For example, Paris failed to share its military plans with London. Despite the importance of Belgium in any war against Germany, the British knew little about the plan devised by the chief of the French General Staff, General Maurice Gamelin, for the Franco–Belgian theater of operations. Britain also contributed to the problem of poor communication between it and France. Even in the months leading up to the outbreak of war, Britain provided only enough intelligence to prevent any damage to relations with France. Britain mistrusted France, who it thought might leak secret information.[44] Anglo–French mutual mistrust and lack of comprehension were thus partly responsible for the fall of the Versailles System.

An Ineffective League of Nations

One of the main factors in the fall of the Versailles System was its failure to stop international aggression. The weakness of the League of Nations was largely to blame. During its existence, the League compiled a dismal record of preventing war and punishing aggressors. It did nothing to punish Italy's aggression against Ethiopia in 1935, Germany's remilitarization of the Rhineland in 1936, Berlin's cooperation with Rome against the Spanish Republic (1936–1938), Japan's invasion of China in 1937, or the Soviet Union's attack on Finland in 1939. Given such abject failure, no international system designed to prevent war could survive.

The League suffered from several flaws. For reasons of self-interest, no nation wanted to take the lead militarily in repelling an aggressor because this would potentially involve devoting significant human and material resources over an extended period against a powerful enemy that might not be a direct threat. In addition, attempting to generate public support for intervention against an aggressor was a very hard sell in the 1930s. Such considerations led to buck-passing, as some nations tried to make others do the hard work.[45] Ultimately, these flaws made the League a weak reed incapable of propping up the Versailles System.

Further contributing to the weakness of the League was the fact that the United States did not take part. Despite his great rhetorical gifts, Woodrow Wilson's postwar speaking tour in support of the League failed to generate sufficient public and Congressional support for joining it. Domestic politics created political alignments that made it impossible for Wilson to gain Senate approval for the Versailles Treaty.[46] Indeed, isolationist sentiment was rapidly rising in the United States. The country's refusal to ratify the Treaty of Versailles led Britain to renege on an Anglo–American security guarantee to France.[47]

Germany Takes a Turn for the Worse

After ridding itself of the many of the people responsible for starting the war, Germany seemed to have turned a page in the 1920s. Its most successful statesman during this period was Gustav Stresemann. After serving as chancellor briefly in 1923, he was Germany's foreign minister from 1923 to 1929. Stresemann's successes included negotiating the Locarno Treaties, for which he shared the Nobel Peace Prize in 1926. In October and November of 1925, Germany reached agreement with the Western powers on several issues. Germany agreed to accept its new western border, submit disputes concerning its eastern border with Poland to arbitration, and join the League of Nations. For their part, Britain and France agreed that Germany need not be bound by League of Nations' sanctions against Russia; they also agreed to evacuate Cologne. Part of the agreement recognized the postwar border between France and Germany, and it was guaranteed by Italy and the United States.[48]

But despite Stresemann's success, the Locarno agreement generated parliamentary anger in Germany. The treaty had failed to achieve the rescission of Article 231, the hated war guilt clause.[49] Stresemann also failed to elicit a statement from Britain and France that the lessening of international tension and German adherence to the Treaty of Versailles would shorten the period of Allied occupation. Stresemann shared some of the blame for this, as he had earlier raised expectations that the Allies would evacuate the entire Rhineland zone and not just certain areas.[50] Many Germans were angry simply because he had cooperated with France.

The anger and disappointment in Germany surrounding Locarno caused political repercussions. The Deutschnationale Volkspartei (DNVP), a conservative nationalist party formed in the wake of Germany's defeat in the Great War, voted against ratification of the Locarno Treaty. The DNVP rejected Stresemann's conciliatory foreign policy approach and instead sought confrontation. The DNVP suffered electoral losses in 1928, however, losing many votes to the National Socialist Party. Germany's shift even further to the right would in time have powerful repercussions.

Unfortunately for Germany, Stresemann died of a stroke on October 3, 1929. He would be the last constructive leader Germany would have until after World War II. In the summer of 1931, the German government decided the time had come to abandon the Young Plan. Signed in 1929, it reduced Germany's reparations payments and lifted foreign controls on the country's economy. Now Berlin renounced definitively all reparations payments.[51]

All German parties regarded the Versailles Treaty as humiliating and intolerable. Any party that promised to get rid of it was bound to find support. Once in power, though, the National Socialists quickly made good on their promise to eliminate the Versailles System, and they gained enormous popular support when they repudiated the treaty. Although initially reluctant to do so, President Paul von Hindenburg asked the leader of the National Socialist Party, Adolf Hitler, to form a government in January 1933. In this way the Nazi era in Germany began. After Hindenburg's death in August 1934, Hitler combined the offices of president and chancellor. He now wielded unprecedented power, as he was both head of state and head of government. Still, Hitler remained somewhat vague about his future plans.

The Asia Factor

The Versailles System was not immune to happenings outside of Europe, as even events in Asia would play a role in its downfall. One important development in Asia occurred when Japan abandoned diplomacy and turned to militarism. Forced out of parts of Asia (half of Russia was still in Asia) by its devastating loss in the Russo-Japanese War (1904–1905), Russia became embroiled in the pre-World War I great power competition in Europe, leaving Asia vulnerable to Japan's ambition to dominate the region militarily to create a self-sufficient Japanese empire.[52]

Japan was also more economically powerful than it had been before the Great War. Its production of steel doubled, its exports increased, and it became a creditor as opposed to a debtor nation. Japan also benefitted from World War I as German influence in the Far East was eliminated. Finally, the European powers were focused on their own regional concerns, thereby giving Japan more or less a free hand in Asia. Japan took advantage of this newly permissive environment by engineering the Mukden Incident as a pretext for the invasion of northeast China, also known as Manchuria.[53]

However, Japan's aggression against China would produce important consequences. One consequence is that it created a border dispute with the Soviet Union. To defeat Japan's threat to its interests, the Soviet Union signed a neutrality pact with Germany in August 1939. The Molotov–Ribbentrop Pact ensured the Soviet Union peace (temporarily) on its European border, thus enabling it to confront Japan's threat in the Far East. Germany, for its part, had solved the dilemma that it had faced since the lapsing of the Reinsurance Treaty in 1890; that is, a possible two-front war against France and Russia.[54]

Appeasement

One of Hitler's many grievances was the fate of German-speaking citizens in the Sudetenland region of the new state of Czechoslovakia. When the Sudetenland was part of the multiethnic Austro-Hungarian Empire, ethnic Germans were the unquestioned rulers. But once it became part of Czechoslovakia, the Sudeten Germans fared less well economically and socially.

With tension growing between Germany and Czechoslovakia and the odds mounting that Europe might again find itself at war, a last-ditch effort to avoid disaster took place at Munich in September 1938. There, Britain's prime minister, Neville Chamberlain, and France's premier, Édouard Daladier, met with Hitler and Mussolini. Chamberlain sought to master the situation and avoid having events spiral out of control as they had back in the fateful summer in 1914. Though Daladier believed that Hitler sought to dominate Europe, he nonetheless followed Chamberlain's lead and acquiesced in the Munich Agreement. Signed on September 30, 1938, the agreement permitted Germany to annex the Sudetenland, thereby transforming Sudeten Germans into citizens of Hitler's Greater German Reich. In return, Hitler pledged to respect the sovereignty of what remained of Czechoslovakia. Chamberlain returned home from Munich and waved his copy of the agreement in front of a crowd of cheering admirers, proclaiming that it represented "peace for our time."

While most Englishmen and women supported Chamberlain at the time, Conservative MP Winston Churchill condemned the Munich Agreement. On October 5, 1938, Churchill stood before the House of Commons and sharply criticized Chamberlain's strategy: "This is only the beginning of the reckoning. This is only the first sip, the first foretaste of a bitter cup which will be proffered to us year by year unless, by a supreme recovery of moral health and martial vigour, we arise again and take our stand for freedom, as in the olden time."[55]

Churchill has been lauded for seeing the danger facing Britain, while Chamberlain has been pilloried for cravenly giving in to a dictator. The strategy Chamberlain pursued, appeasement, has since become a political epithet on both sides of the Atlantic. However, this traditional view has been challenged by the release of official archives and new interpretive approaches.

Over the years, three schools of thought about the strategy of appeasement have taken shape. The first is the traditionalist approach, which sees appeasement as a reflection of the strategically incompetent decisions made by British leaders such as Chamberlain. The second is the revisionist approach, which views appeasement as strategically sound because Britain was economically and militarily unprepared for conflict with Germany. The third is the counter-revisionist approach, which asserts that Chamberlain obdurately chose appeasement despite warnings and despite viable alternative strategies. According to the counter-revisionists, his myopic insistence on appeasement reveals that Chamberlain's strategies were wrong and appeasement was a pervasive and a personal failure. Recent scholarship is shifting the pendulum away from previously established revisionist work and in the direction of counter-revisionism.[56]

Hitler soon tore up the Munich Agreement and grabbed all of Czechoslovakia in March 1939. Humiliated, Chamberlain told the House of Commons that, "in the event of any action which clearly threatened Polish independence, and which the Polish Government accordingly considered it vital to resist with their national forces, His Majesty's Government would feel themselves bound at once to lend the Polish Government all support in their power." He added that "the French Government have authorised me to make it plain that they stand in the same position in this matter as do His Majesty's Government." In other words, Britain and France would declare war.[57] Chamberlain had finally drawn a line in the sand. Yet, this threat was simply too little, too late. Based on British and French actions since 1919, Hitler had no reason to believe the British prime minister was doing anything other than bluffing.

Conclusion

When World War II began on September 1, 1939, the Versailles System had long since collapsed.[58] No one event or decision produced this outcome. Rather, the Paris Peace

Conference failed to secure long-term peace because there was a fundamental mismatch between the victors' policy, tactics, and strategy.[59] The first mistake the Allies committed was failing to develop a sound war termination strategy in 1918. Because the Allies had not decisively defeated Germany, many Germans believed that they had lost the war not on the battlefield but through treachery on the home front. As Carl von Clausewitz had stated, the end of one conflict can plant the seeds for future wars.[60] The failure to secure proper war termination is a common pitfall of coalition warfare. While the Allies had a common interest in victory, they differed over the meaning of victory and the shape and character of the peace that would follow.[61]

Another problem was that France's military leadership had little confidence in what the political leadership had decided at the time. Marshal Ferdinand Foch believed that the Treaty of Versailles was too lenient. In fact, he boycotted the signing ceremony and declared the peace no more than a twenty-year armistice.[62] Cynicism appeared elsewhere as well. The U.S. military leadership thought that Britain and France fought not to save democracy, but to prop up their failing empires.[63] The U.S. Navy even developed war plans in case of conflict with Britain.[64]

The Versailles System also faltered because the winning coalition disintegrated, thereby preventing it from maintaining a durable peace. Russia left the war in early 1918, and thereafter adopted an antagonistic stance toward Britain, France, and the United States. Britain seemed more focused on defending its empire in the 1920s than promoting security in Europe. Moreover, financial constraints perhaps led British military planners to be less sympathetic to France's security concerns.[65] For its part, Italy succumbed to domestic political turmoil, which led to the rise of a fascist government that eventually ended up on a collision course with the country's former partners. Finally, the United States limited its international responsibilities to the financial arena, neglecting the role that military might play in securing peace. There was a lack of close cooperation in every area between Britain, France, and the United States. Anglo–American relations went through peaks and valleys during the 1920s.[66] And American military planners viewed Britain in a less than positive light because they believed London had fought the war for empire and not democracy.[67]

Ultimately, the Versailles System was poorly designed and weakly enforced. Its collapse was simply a matter of time. During the interwar period, many sensed another war approaching and attempted to prepare for what they saw as the inevitable. However, their attempts to prepare for it failed to stave off the collapse of the Versailles System.

Acknowledgments

I thank Max Paul Friedman, William G. Gray, Jon Harrison, Michael S. Neiberg, Nicholas E. Sarantakes, Marc Trachtenberg, Janice M. Traflet, and David Valladares for their valuable comments on earlier drafts of this chapter.

Notes

1. The victors confronted other topics as well, including the fate of colonial empires. See Erez Manela, *The Wilsonian Moment: Self-Determination and the International Origins of Anticolonial Nationalism* (New York: Oxford University Press, 2009); Chad Williams, "W. E. B. Du Bois, World War I, and the Question of Failure," *Black Perspectives* (February 19, 2018), https://www.aaihs.org/w-e-b-du-bois-world-war-i-and-the-question-of-failure/; Chad Williams, "World War I in the Historical Imagination of W. E. B. Du Bois," *Modern American History* 1, no. 1 (March 2018): 3–22.
2. David Stevenson, "1918 Revisited," *Journal of Strategic Studies* 28, no. 1 (2005): 113; Robert A. Doughty, *Pyrrhic Victory: French Strategy and Operations in the Great War* (Cambridge, MA: The Belknap Press of Harvard University Press, 2005), 470–473.
3. Martin Samuels, "Shock and Friction as Explanations for Disaster at the Battle of Amiens, 8 August 1918," *War & Society* 35, no. 4 (2016): 275–297.
4. Stevenson, "1918 Revisited," 114–115.
5. For the text of the Fourteen Points, see http://avalon.law.yale.edu/20th_century/wilson14.asp.
6. Stevenson, "1918 Revisited," 120, 128.
7. Thomas Weber, *Becoming Hitler: The Making of a Nazi* (New York: Basic Books, 2017); Robert Gerwarth, *The Vanquished: Why the First World War Failed to End* (New York: Farrar, Straus and Giroux, 2016).
8. See Klaus Schwabe, "World War I and the Rise of Hitler," *Diplomatic History* 38, no. 4 (2014): 864–865.
9. Schwabe, "World War I and the Rise of Hitler," 869–870; Holger H. Herwig, "Clio Deceived: Patriotic Self-Censorship in Germany after the Great War," *International Security* 12, no. 2 (Fall 1987): 9.
10. Herwig, "Clio Deceived," 5–7, 9–11, 13.
11. Harold Nicolson, *Peacemaking 1919: Being Reminiscences of the Paris Peace Conference* (London: Grosset & Dunlap, 1933), 32.
12. David Stevenson, "French War Aims and Peace Planning," in *The Treaty of Versailles: A Reassessment After 75 Years*, ed. Manfred F. Boemeke, Gerald D. Feldman, and Elisabeth Gläser (New York: Cambridge University Press, 1998), 97; Georges-Henri Soutou, "French Peacemakers and their Home Front," in *The Treaty of Versailles: A Reassessment After 75 Years*, ed. Manfred F. Boemeke, Gerald D. Feldman, and Elisabeth Gläser (New York: Cambridge University Press, 1998), 170–172; Stephen A. Schuker, "The Rhineland Question: West European Security at the Paris Peace Conference of 1919," in *The Treaty of Versailles: A Reassessment After 75 Years*, ed. Manfred F. Boemeke, Gerald D. Feldman, and Elisabeth Gläser (New York: Cambridge University Press, 1998), 282.
13. Soutou, "French Peacemakers and their Home Front," in *The Treaty of Versailles*, 168–181.
14. Peter Jackson, "A Tran-Atlantic Condominium of Democratic Power: The Grand Design for a Post-war Order in French Policy at the Paris Peace Conference," *Journal of Military and Strategic Studies* 16, no. 2 (2015): 179–207.
15. Antony Lentin, "A Comment," in *The Treaty of Versailles: A Reassessment After 75 Years*, ed. Manfred F. Boemeke, Gerald D. Feldman, and Elisabeth Gläser (New York: Cambridge University Press, 1998), 222, 225–227.
16. Schwabe, "World War I and the Rise of Hitler," 864.

17. Schwabe, "World War I and the Rise of Hitler," 867.
18. Roger Moorhouse, "'The Sore That Would Never Heal": The Genesis of the Polish Corridor," *Diplomacy & Statecraft* 16, no. 3 (2005): 603–613.
19. "Terms of the Armistice Agreement of November 11, 1918," https://www.census.gov/history/pdf/armistice11-11-1918.pdf
20. Walter A. McDougall, *France's Rhineland Diplomacy, 1914–1924: The Last Bid for a Balance of Power in Europe* (Princeton: Princeton University Press, 1978); Alan Sharp, *The Versailles Settlement: Peacemaking in Paris, 1919* (New York: St. Martin's Press, 1991), 17.
21. Elspeth O'Riordan, "The British Zone of Occupation in the Rhineland," *Diplomacy & Statecraft* 16, no. 3 (2005): 441.
22. The Versailles Treaty: Part VIII, Article 232, June 28, 1919, http://avalon.law.yale.edu/imt/partviii.asp.
23. D. G. Williamson, "Great Britain and the Ruhr Crisis, 1923–1924," *British Journal of International Studies* 3, no. 1 (April 1977), 74.
24. The Versailles Treaty: Part XIV, Section One, Articles 428–431, June 28, 1919, http://avalon.law.yale.edu/imt/partxiv.asp.
25. Stanislas Jeanneson, "French Policy in the Rhineland," *Diplomacy and Statecraft* 16, no. 3 (2005): 476.
26. O'Riordan, "The British Zone of Occupation in the Rhineland," 448–449, 452.
27. Herwig, "Clio Deceived," 6–7.
28. David Stevenson, "The Failure of Peace by Negotiation 1917," *The Historical Journal* 34, no. 1 (1991): 65–86.
29. Stevenson, "1918 Revisited," 109, 121.
30. Stephen A. Schuker, "American Reparations to Germany, 1919–1933," in *Die Nachwirkungen der Inflation auf die deutsche Geschichte 1924–1933*, ed. Gerald D. Feldman et al. (Munich: Oldenbourg, 1985), 336.
31. Melvyn Leffler, "The Origins of Republican War Debt Policy, 1921–1923: A Case Study in the Applicability of the Open Door Interpretation," *Journal of American History* 59, no. 3 (December 1972): 592, 595.
32. Schuker, "American Reparations to Germany, 1919–1933," 344; Barry Eichengreen and Richard Portes, "The Interwar Debt Crisis and Its Aftermath," *The World Bank Research Observer* 5, no. 1 (January 1990), 73.
33. Franklin D. Roosevelt, "Message to Congress on the Payment of War Debts to the United States, June 1, 1934," *The Public Papers and Addresses of Franklin D. Roosevelt*, Vol. 3: *The Advance of Recovery and Reform, 1934* (New York: Random House, 1938), 275–283.
34. Quote from Mira Wilkins, *The History of Foreign Investment in the United States, 1914–1945* (Cambridge: Harvard University Press, 2004), 354.
35. Adam Tooze, *The Deluge: The Great War, America and the Remaking of the Global Order, 1916–1931* (New York: Viking, 2015), 496.
36. Nikolaus Wolf, "Europe's Great Depression: Coordination Failure After the First World War," *Oxford Review of Economic Policy* 26, no. 3 (October 1, 2010): 340.
37. Joseph Maiolo, *Cry Havoc: How the Arms Race Drove the World to War, 1931–1941* (New York: Basic Books, 2010), 123.
38. Maiolo, *Cry Havoc*, 123; Sadao Asada, "The Revolt against the Washington Treaty: The Imperial Japanese Navy and Naval Limitation, 1921–1927," *Naval War College Review* 46, no. 3 (Summer 1993): 82–97.
39. Schuker, "France and the Remilitarization of the Rhineland," 316–317.

40. Eugenia C. Kiesling, *Arming Against Hitler: France and the Limits of Military Planning* (Lawrence: University Press of Kansas, 1996), 1.
41. Williamson Murray and Jim Lacey, *The Making of Peace: Rulers, States, and the Aftermath of War* (New York: Cambridge University Press, 2009), 209.
42. Alexander and Philpott, "The Entente Cordiale and the Next War: Anglo-French Views on Future Military Cooperation, 1928–1939," *Intelligence and National Security* 13 (1998): 63.
43. Hines H. Hall III, "British Air Defense and Anglo–French Relations, 1921–1924," *Journal of Strategic Studies* 4, no. 3 (1981): 271–284; John Ferris, "The Theory of a 'French Air Menace': Anglo-French Relations and the British Home Defence Air Force Programmes of 1921–25," *Journal of Strategic Studies* 10, no. 1 (1987): 62–83; Arthur Turner, "Anglo–French Financial Relations in the 1920s," *European History Quarterly* 26, no. 1 (1996): 31–55; Andrew Barros, "Disarmament as a Weapon: Anglo–French Relations and the Problems of Enforcing German Disarmament, 1919–28," *Journal of Strategic Studies* 29, no. 2 (2006): 301–321.
44. Alexander and Philpott, "The Entente Cordiale and the Next War," 63–64, 72.
45. Mark L. Haas, "Ideology and Alliances: British and French External Balancing Decisions in the 1930s," *Security Studies* 12, no. 4 (2003): 34–79; Norrin M. Ripsman and Jack S. Levy, "The Preventive War that Never Happened: Britain, France, and the Rise of Germany in the 1930s," *Security Studies* 16, no. 1 (2007): 32–67; B. J. C. McKercher, "National Security and Imperial Defence: British Grand Strategy and Appeasement, 1930–1939," *Diplomacy & Statecraft* 19, no. 3 (2008): 391–442; Martin Thomas, "Appeasement in the Late Third Republic," *Diplomacy & Statecraft* 19, no. 3 (2008): 566–607.
46. Jack Snyder, "Dueling Security Stories: Wilson and Lodge Talk Strategy," *Security Studies* 24, no. 1 (2015): 196–197.
47. McDougall, *France's Rhineland Diplomacy*.
48. Jon Jacobson, *Locarno Diplomacy Germany and the West, 1925–1929* (Princeton, NJ: Princeton University Press, 1972), 64–65.
49. Schwabe, "World War I and the Rise of Hitler," 874.
50. Jacobson, *Locarno Diplomacy*, 65–66.
51. Schuker, "American Reparations to Germany, 1919–1933," 348–349.
52. Michael A. Barnhart, *Japan Prepares for Total War: The Search for Economic Security, 1919–1941* (Ithaca, NY: Cornell University Press, 1988).
53. Rana Mitter, *Forgotten Ally: China's World War II, 1937–1945* (New York: Houghton Mifflin Harcourt, 2013).
54. Stuart Goldman, *Nomonhan, 1939: The Red Army's Victory That Shaped World War II* (Annapolis, MD: Naval Institute Press, 2013).
55. Hansard, House of Commons 5th series Vol. 5th October 1938 c 360-371 (361), https://api.parliament.uk/historic-hansard/commons/1938/oct/05/policy-of-his-majestys-government#column_360.
56. Tim Bouverie, *Appeasement: Chamberlain, Hitler, Churchill, and the Road to War* (Emeryville, CA: Tim Duggan Books, 2019); P. E. Caquet, *The Bell of Treason: The 1938 Munich Agreement in Czechoslovakia* (New York: Other Press, 2019); Adrian Phillips, *Appeasement Round Three: Fighting Churchill, Appeasing Hitler: Neville Chamberlain, Sir Horace Wilson & Britain's Plight of Appeasement: 1937–1939* (New York: Pegasus Books, 2019).
57. "Statement by the Prime Minister in the House of Commons on March 31, 1939," http://avalon.law.yale.edu/wwii/blbk17.asp. A formal alliance was concluded between Britain

and Poland on August 25, 1939. See Agreement of Mutual Assistance between the United Kingdom and Poland, London, August 25, 1939, http://avalon.law.yale.edu/wwii/blb k19.asp.
58. Keith Neilson, *Britain, Soviet Russia and the Collapse of the Versailles Order* (New York: Cambridge University Press, 2006).
59. Schuker, "The Rhineland Question," 276.
60. Carl von Clausewitz, *On War*, trans. and ed. Michael Howard and Peter Paret (Princeton, NJ: Princeton University Press, 1976), 80.
61. Stevenson, "1918 Revisited," 121–122.
62. Quoted in Williamson Murray, "Versailles: The Peace Without a Chance," in *The Making of Peace: Rulers, States, and the Aftermath of War*, ed. Williamson Murray and Jim Lacey (New York: Cambridge University Press, 2009), 209.
63. Stoler, *Allies and Adversaries: The Joint Chiefs of Staff, the Grand Alliance, and U.S. Strategy in World War II* (Chapel Hill: University of North Carolina Press, 2003), ch. 2–6.
64. Christopher M. Bell, "Thinking the Unthinkable: British and American Naval Strategies for an Anglo-American War, 1918–1931," *The International History Review* 19, no. 4 (November 1997), 789–808.
65. Alexander and Philpott, "The Entente Cordiale and the Next War," 54.
66. Robert Self, *Britain, America and the War Debt Controversy: The Economic Diplomacy of an Unspecial Relationship, 1917–45* (London: Routledge, 2006), 4–5.
67. Stoler, *Allies and Adversaries*, 8.

Bibliography

Alexander, Martin S., and William J. Philpott. "The Entente Cordiale and the Next War: Anglo-French Views on Future Military Cooperation, 1928–1939." *Intelligence and National Security* 13 (1998): 1: 53–84.

Asada, Sadao. "The Revolt against the Washington Treaty: The Imperial Japanese Navy and Naval Limitation, 1921–1927." *Naval War College Review* 46, no. 3 (Summer 1993): 82–97.

Barnhart, Michael A. *Japan Prepares for Total War: The Search for Economic Security, 1919–194.* Ithaca, NY: Cornell University Press, 1988.

Barros, Andrew. "Disarmament as a Weapon: Anglo-French Relations and the Problems of Enforcing German Disarmament, 1919–28." *Journal of Strategic Studies* 29, no. 2 (2006): 301–321.

Bell, Christopher M. "Thinking the Unthinkable: British and American Naval Strategies for an Anglo-American War, 1918–1931." *The International History Review* 19, no. 4 (November 1997): 789–808.

Bouverie, Tim. *Appeasement: Chamberlain, Hitler, Churchill, and the Road to War*. Emeryville, CA: Tim Duggan Books, 2019.

Browning, Christopher. *The Origins of the Final Solution: The Evolution of Nazi Jewish Policy, September 1939–March 1942*. Lincoln: University of Nebraska Press, 2004.

Caquet, P. E. *The Bell of Treason: The 1938 Munich Agreement in Czechoslovakia*. New York: Other Press, 2019.

Clausewitz, Carl von. *On War*. Translated and edited by Michael Howard and Peter Paret. Princeton, NJ: Princeton University Press, 1976.

Cooper, Jr., John Milton. *The Warrior and the Priest: Woodrow Wilson and Theodore Roosevelt.* Cambridge, MA: Belknap Press of Harvard University Press, 1985.

Doughty, Robert A. *Pyrrhic Victory: French Strategy and Operations in the Great War.* Cambridge, MA: The Belknap Press of Harvard University Press, 2005.

Eichengreen, Barry, and Richard Portes. "The Interwar Debt Crisis and Its Aftermath." *The World Bank Research Observer* 5, no. 1 (January 1990): 69–94.

Ferris, John. "The Theory of a 'French Air Menace': Anglo–French Relations and the British Home Defence Air Force Programmes of 1921–25." *Journal of Strategic Studies* 10, no. 1 (1987): 62–83.

Gerwarth, Robert. *The Vanquished: Why the First World War Failed to End.* New York: Farrar, Straus and Giroux, 2016.

Goldman, Stuart. *Nomonhan, 1939: The Red Army's Victory That Shaped World War II.* Annapolis, MD: Naval Institute Press, 2013.

Haas, Mark L. "Ideology and Alliances: British and French External Balancing Decisions in the 1930s." *Security Studies* 12, no. 4 (2003): 34–79.

Herwig, Holger H. "Clio Deceived: Patriotic Self-Censorship in Germany after the Great War." *International Security* 12, no. 2 (Fall 1987): 5–44.

Hall, III, Hines H. "British Air Defense and Anglo-French Relations, 1921–1924." *Journal of Strategic Studies* 4, no. 3 (1981): 271–284.

Jackson, Peter. "A Tran-Atlantic Condominium of Democratic Power: The Grand Design for a Post-war Order in French Policy at the Paris Peace Conference." *Journal of Military and Strategic Studies* 16, no. 2 (2015): 179–207.

Jacobson, Jon. *Locarno Diplomacy Germany and the West, 1925–1929.* Princeton, NJ: Princeton University Press, 1972.

Jeanneson, Stanislas. "French Policy in the Rhineland." *Diplomacy and Statecraft* 16, no. 3 (2005): 475–486.

Kiesling, Eugenia C. *Arming Against Hitler: France and the Limits of Military Planning.* Lawrence: University Press of Kansas, 1996.

Leffler, Melvyn. "The Origins of Republican War Debt Policy, 1921–1923: A Case Study in the Applicability of the Open Door Interpretation." *Journal of American History* 59, no. 3 (December 1972): 585–601.

Lentin, Antony. "A Comment." In *The Treaty of Versailles: A Reassessment After 75 Years*, edited by Manfred F. Boemeke, Gerald D. Feldman, and Elisabeth Gläser. New York: Cambridge University Press, 1998, 221.

McDougall, Walter A. *France's Rhineland Diplomacy, 1914–1924: The Last Bid for a Balance of Power in Europe.* Princeton, NJ: Princeton University Press, 1978.

McKercher, B. J. C. "National Security and Imperial Defence: British Grand Strategy and Appeasement, 1930–1939." *Diplomacy & Statecraft* 19, no. 3 (2008): 391–442.

Maiolo, Joseph. *Cry Havoc: How the Arms Race Drove the World to War, 1931–1941.* New York: Basic Books, 2010.

Manela, Erez. *The Wilsonian Moment: Self-Determination and the International Origins of Anticolonial Nationalism.* New York: Oxford University Press, 2009.

Mitter, Rana. *Forgotten Ally: China's World War II, 1937–1945.* New York: Houghton Mifflin Harcourt, 2013.

Moorhouse, Roger. "'The Sore That Would Never Heal': The Genesis of the Polish Corridor." *Diplomacy & Statecraft* 16, no. 3 (2005): 603–613.

Murray, Williamson. "Versailles: The Peace Without a Chance." In *The Making of Peace: Rulers, States, and the Aftermath of War*, edited by Williamson Murray and Jim Lacey. New York: Cambridge University Press, 2009, 208–239.

Murray, Williamson, and Jim Lacey. *The Making of Peace: Rulers, States, and the Aftermath of War*. New York: Cambridge University Press, 2009.

Neilson, Keith. *Britain, Soviet Russia and the Collapse of the Versailles Order*. New York: Cambridge University Press, 2006.

Nicolson, Harold. *Peacemaking 1919: Being Reminiscences of the Paris Peace Conference*. London: Grosset & Dunlap, 1933.

O'Riordan, Elspeth. "The British Zone of Occupation in the Rhineland." *Diplomacy & Statecraft* 16, no. 3 (2005): 439–454.

Pedersen, Susan. *The Guardians: The League of Nations and the Crisis of Empire*. New York: Oxford University Press, 2015.

Phillips, Adrian. *Appeasement Round Three: Fighting Churchill, Appeasing Hitler: Neville Chamberlain, Sir Horace Wilson & Britain's Plight of Appeasement: 1937–1939*. New York: Pegasus Books, 2019.

Ripsman, Norrin M., and Jack S. Levy. "The Preventive War that Never Happened: Britain, France, and the Rise of Germany in the 1930s." *Security Studies* 16, no. 1 (2007): 32–67.

Roosevelt, Franklin D. "Message to Congress on the Payment of War Debts to the United States, June 1, 1934." *The Public Papers and Addresses of Franklin D. Roosevelt*. Vol. 3: *The Advance of Recovery and Reform, 1934*, edited by Samuel I. Rosenman. New York: Random House, 1938, 275–282.

Roosevelt, Franklin D. "Inaugural Address, March 4, 1933." *The Public Papers and Addresses of Franklin D. Roosevelt*. Vol. 2: *The Year of Crisis, Public Papers of the Presidents of the United States, Franklin D. Roosevelt, 1933*, edited by Samuel I. Rosenman. New York: Random House, 1938, 11–16.

Samuels, Martin. "Shock and Friction as Explanations for Disaster at the Battle of Amiens, 8 August 1918." *War & Society* 35, no. 4 (2016): 275–297.

Self, Robert. *Britain, America and the War Debt Controversy: The Economic Diplomacy of an Unspecial Relationship, 1917–45*. London: Routledge, 2006.

Schuker, Stephen A. "The Rhineland Question: West European Security at the Paris Peace Conference of 1919." In *The Treaty of Versailles: A Reassessment After 75 Years*, edited by Manfred F. Boemeke, Gerald D. Feldman, Elisabeth Gläser. New York: Cambridge University Press, 1998, 275–312.

Schuker, Stephen A. "American Reparations to Germany, 1919–1933." In *Die Nachwirkungen der Inflation auf die deutsche Geschichte 1924–1933*, edited by Gerald D. Feldman et al. Munich: Oldenbourg, 1985, 445–493.

Schwabe, Klaus. "World War I and the Rise of Hitler." *Diplomatic History* 38, no. 4 (2014): 864–879.

Sharp, Alan. *The Versailles Settlement: Peacemaking in Paris, 1919*. New York: St. Martin's Press, 1991.

Snyder, Jack. "Dueling Security Stories: Wilson and Lodge Talk Strategy." *Security Studies* 24, no. 1 (2015): 171–197.

Soutou, Georges-Henri. "French Peacemakers and their Home Front." In *The Treaty of Versailles: A Reassessment After 75 Years*, edited by Manfred F. Boemeke, Gerald D. Feldman, and Elisabeth Gläser. New York: Cambridge University Press, 1998, 170–172.

Stevenson, David. "1918 Revisited." *Journal of Strategic Studies* 28, no. 1 (2005): 107–139.

Stevenson, David. (1998) "French War Aims and Peace Planning." In *The Treaty of Versailles: A Reassessment After 75 Years*, edited by Manfred F. Boemeke, Gerald D. Feldman, and Elisabeth Gläser. New York: Cambridge University Press, 1998, 87–109.

Stevenson, David. "The Failure of Peace by Negotiation 1917." *The Historical Journal* 34, no.1 (1991): 65–86.

Stoler, Mark A. *Allies and Adversaries: The Joint Chiefs of Staff, the Grand Alliance, and U.S. Strategy in World War II*. Chapel Hill: University of North Carolina Press, 2003.

Thomas, Martin. "Appeasement in the Late Third Republic." *Diplomacy & Statecraft* 19, no. 3 (2008): 566–607.

Tooze, Adam. *The Deluge: The Great War, America and the Remaking of the Global Order, 1916–1931*. New York: Viking, 2015.

Turner, Arthur. "Anglo-French Financial Relations in the 1920s." *European History Quarterly* 26, no. 1 (1996): 31–55.

Weber, Thomas. *Becoming Hitler: The Making of a Nazi*. New York: Basic Books, 2017.

Williams, Chad. "W. E. B. Du Bois, World War I, and the Question of Failure." *Black Perspectives*, February 19, 2018. https://www.aaihs.org/w-e-b-du-bois-world-war-i-and-the-question-of-failure/.

Williams, Chad. "World War I in the Historical Imagination of W. E. B. Du Bois." *Modern American History* 1, no. 1 (March 2018): 3–22.

Williamson, D. G. "Great Britain and the Ruhr Crisis, 1923–1924." *British Journal of International Studies* 3, no. 1 (April 1977): 70–91.

Wilkins, Mira. *The History of Foreign Investment in the United States, 1914–1945*. Cambridge: Harvard University Press, 2004.

Wilson, Woodrow. "Fourteen Points." January 8, 1918. http://avalon.law.yale.edu/20th_century/wilson14.asp.

Wolf, Nikolaus. "Europe's Great Depression: Coordination Failure After the First World War." *Oxford Review of Economic Policy* 26, no. 3 (October 1, 2010): 339–369.

"Terms of the Armistice Agreement of November 11, 1918." https://www.loc.gov/law/help/us-treaties/bevans/m-ust000002-0009.pdf.

The Versailles Treaty. Part VIII, Article 232. June 28, 1919. http://avalon.law.yale.edu/imt/partviii.asp.

The Versailles Treaty. Part XIV, Section One, Articles 428–431. June 28, 1919. http://avalon.law.yale.edu/imt/partxiv.asp.

Hansard, House of Commons 5th series Vol. 5th October 1938 c 360-371 (361).

HC Deb 05 October 1938 vol 339 cc337-454. https://api.parliament.uk/historic-hansard/commons/1938/oct/05/policy-of-his-majestys-government

"Statement by the Prime Minister in the House of Commons on March 31, 1939." HC Deb 25 March 1920 vol 127 cc613-4, https://api.parliament.uk/historic-hansard/commons/1920/mar/25/statement-by-prime-minister.

The British War Blue Book. "Statement by the Prime Minister in the House of Commons on March 31, 1939." New York: Farrar & Rinehart, 1939, 48.

The British War Blue Book. "Agreement of Mutual Assistance between the United Kingdom and Poland, August 25, 1939." New York: Farrar & Rinehart, 1939, 49–52.

CHAPTER 2

IDEOLOGICAL ORIGINS OF WORLD WAR II

VLADIMIR TISMANEANU AND BOGDAN C. IACOB

No century witnessed and documented so much atrocious suffering, organized hatred, and devastating violence as the twentieth. At the center of the destruction lay World War II. This chapter discusses the ideological origins of World War II by exploring the role played by the most influential revolutionary movements of the past century, Communism and Fascism, in fueling the tumult and tribulations of the interwar period. This intensely polarized universe was the setting for what would be the most ruinous war in recent history.

Understanding the nature of World War II and its specificities, such as barbarization, Holocaust, exterminism, and ethnic cleansing, is impossible if we do not acknowledge the impulse from the revolutionary right and left party movements to reshape the human condition in the name of presumably inexorable historical laws. The particular outlook of World War II was circumscribed by a clash of modernities. The interwar years witnessed the formulation and, by late 1930s, the rise of visions of development, collective identities, and geopolitics that were alternative to and competing with bourgeois modernity.

On the one hand, there was the showdown among democracy, Fascism, and Communism that triggered civil, ethnic, and social strife. On the other hand, there was the conflict among colonialisms, as Britain and France desperately sought to keep the world order unchanged under the pressure from a resurgent, post-1933 Germany, Mussolini's dreams of Mediterranean empire, and Japan's anti-Western push for imperial hegemony and racial superiority across East Asia.

With all this in mind, one can better understand the sense of historical mission, of divine calling intrinsic to images of the upcoming war among the most important revisionist powers—Germany, Italy, Japan, and the Soviet Union. In Hitler's world view, National Socialism was not just another political movement; it actually incarnated the "will to create mankind anew."[1] The Nazi dictator, the main culprit of the cataclysm that shattered the world between 1939 and 1945, wrote in *The Secret Book*, his sequel to *Mein Kampf*, unpublished in his lifetime, that "If... politics is history in the making and history itself is the presentation of the struggle of men and nations for self-preservation and continuance, then politics is in truth the execution of a nation's struggle for existence."[2]

In similar fashion, Benito Mussolini proclaimed in 1922, the year of his March on Rome, that the time for myth had come: "Everything is to be done. Only the myth can give the strength and energy to a people about to hammer out its own destiny."[3] Along the same lines, at the opposite corner of the world in Japan, the military and conservative elite had fully embraced the idea of their country's divine mission (especially in China) and their will for racially founded hegemony throughout East Asia.[4] Last but not least, in the aftermath of 1917 and the failure of a Europe-wide revolution (1919–1923), Lenin (and later Stalin) espoused the metaphor of "an oasis of Soviet power in the middle of the raging imperialist sea."[5] It was premised on an overwhelming and axiomatic expectancy for a new world war. In fact, the idea of the inevitability of an "international civil war" was at the core of the Bolshevik Weltanschauung of global revolution.[6]

Setting the Stage—War and Revolution

Born out of the cataclysmic barbarism and unprecedented violence of World War I, Fascism and Communism proclaimed the advent of the millennium in this world. In reestablishing and recreating social order, these states proved to be both repressive and paternalistic. Society was structured according to categories such as class, race, nationality, and gender, each with specific consequences on the inclusion–exclusion axis. The Soviet Union and Germany were realigned demographically, geographically, and biologically according to imagined projects of the perfect citizenry. They created blueprints for radical movements and politicians across the world that challenged domestic establishments and the international order.

After 1918, the socialist Left and the nationalist Right increasingly began to conceive of politics in terms of the future tense.[7] The new radicalisms became intoxicated with the ideological rationale for totalist projects to engineer reality.[8] But the sense of crisis and the fear of social upheaval were augmented by a momentous corollary to the Great War—the Bolshevik revolution of 1917. Among the far Left, this event, to use Stalin's words, seemed to have "inflicted a mortal wound on world capitalism from which the latter will never recover." In the West and in the Central and Southeastern European states that were the result of the Versailles treaties, the new Bolshevik power triggered widespread fear of further revolutionary contamination. This state of things encouraged either radical nationalisms or state policies geared toward the fixed idea of removing the threat of 1917.[9]

What appeared to give credence to such views was the overlap between Lenin's attempts to export revolution to Poland, Hungary, or Germany in the early 1920s and the formation of an international communist movement under the umbrella of the Comintern. The Red Army's drive toward Warsaw coincided with the Second Congress of the Comintern. If the founding gathering of this organization had been rather underwhelming, its follow-up brought together about two hundred delegates from more than thirty countries. In the Comintern, Lenin had the organization to dictate the rhythm and tone of the much-anticipated insurrection(s) against capitalism and imperialism.

From the beginning, the Comintern, with the imposition of the twenty-one conditions of adherence of individual parties, was part and parcel of the Soviet state. The October revolution (as both an event and a founding myth of a global illusion) combined with the consolidation of the Comintern and the conspicuous presence of communist parties in the post-1918–1921 period gave Communism, and particularly the Soviet Union, a world dimension and ambition. This was a crucial ingredient in the ideological alchemy behind the onset of World War II.

We see our approach within Dan Diner's overview of the twentieth century as a universal civil war based on the profound antagonism between Communism and its opponents.[10] As an offspring of nineteenth-century antibourgeois, often antimodern, ideologies of resentment, Fascism did not need Bolshevism to emerge and mature. The cult of race, the blending of pseudoscientism (social Darwinism) with the neo-pagan worship of blood and soil, and the resentful rejection of liberal values predated Leninism.

It is hard to deny, though, that the triumph of Bolshevism and the intensity and scope of the Red Terror, together with the traumatic effects of World War I mobilized the Fascist offensive against the universalistic traditions of the Enlightenment. Fascism itself was a radical experiment aiming to change participatory democracy and the meaning of the modern nation-state by transforming ultra-nationalism into a secular religion. It exalted the supremacy of the national community over individualism by means of social control and engineering.[11] Ultimately, Nazism's crusade against democracy and Communism was essentially targeting the perceived decadence of both.

Fascism and Communism, as revolutionary party movements, execrated and denounced liberalism, democracy, and parliamentarianism as degradations of true politics, and claimed to transcend all divisions through the establishment of perfect communities (defined as classless or racially unified). Fundamentally atheistic, Communism and Fascism organized their political objectives in discourses of alleged emancipation. They operated as political religions seeking to deliver the individual from the impositions of traditional morality and legality.

To employ Italian political thinker Emilio Gentile's terminology, they were forms of the sacralization of politics. They rejected coexistence with other political ideologies and movements, denied the autonomy of the individual in relation with the collective, and decreed the mandatory compliance to their commandments and participation in their political cult. They sanctified violence as a legitimate means against their foes as well as an instrument of regeneration.[12] Fascism and Communism entered together into the theater of history,[13] dominating most of the interwar period and World War II. They continuously augmented their destructive impact on parliamentary democracy to the point of fundamental rupture and global cataclysm.

Where does Japan stand in a narrative centered on the clash among democracy, Communism, and Fascism? The country had its coming onto the scene of great powers after the victory in the war with tsarist Russia (1904–1905). At the same time, its society and political system had experienced shattering changes during the Meiji modernization. The ideologues of the new order deified Japan itself to provide the doctrinal cement for their new worldview.[14] These transformations created the premises for the escalating extolment of collectivism and ethnic millennialism at home and for aggrandizing imperialist expectations among Japan's ruling elites.

The end of World War I and the Versailles Treaty had a radicalizing effect on Japan as well, but of a different sort than the one it had on Germany and Italy. It confirmed that in East Asia there was no room for its expansion because of the Western powers. For nationalist politicians and intellectuals, Japan could not expect support for its imperial designs from the international community. It would would have to rely instead on state power and its people's vitality.[15] By the 1930s, this option would be imbued with a double-edged racism: against "the White peril" and against the other nations in what became the Greater Asia Co-Prosperity Sphere.[16]

In East Asia, along with Communism and less Fascism (which was, like in Europe, an object of emulation), the Japanese essentially anti-Western vision of empire had near revolutionary consequences. It weakened an already difficult to defend British empire (and a moribund French one), thus further making London wary about engagement in Europe. It also emboldened national liberation movements. The best example is the simultaneous heightening of para-fascist nationalism and the gradual ascendency of Communism in China.[17]

Moreover, the rise of self-determination after the Great War could not be limited to Europe. The ideal had a long-term subversive impact on European empires as the calls for self-government or independence among colonial peoples grew louder during the interwar years.[18] Political movements, particularly in Asia but also in Africa, challenged liberal imperialism in their respective metropoles, at the League of Nations (established in 1920),[19] or through institutions such as the League Against Imperialism, which vacillated between Communism and various forms of nationalism.[20] This budding insurgency from the provinces of empires reached its apex after World War II, as the conflagration had a dissolutive effect on colonial rule first in Asia, then in Africa.

WHAT WAS NEW?

In the context of the Great Depression and of the social, economic, institutional, and cultural wreckage it left behind, Communism and Fascism presented themselves as creative forms of revolutionary nihilism—extremely utilitarian and contemptuous of universal rights. They challenged the uneasy balance between tradition and innovation created during the 1920s that relied on the concert of powers (with British and French colonial empires at its center), the ideal of collective security, the League of Nations, disarmament, and on the gold standard as global management of capital.[21] Instead, Communism and Fascism envisioned societies as communities of "bearers of beliefs," and every aspect of their private life and behavior was expected to conform to these beliefs. Upon coming into power and implementing their vision of the perfect society comprising new men and women, the two political movements established dictatorships of purity in which people were compensated or disciplined according to politically defined criteria of virtue.[22] They set the stage for the 1930s, which was a decade of ideological crusades that seemed to confirm the demise of the bourgeois democracy.

Most telling for the extreme contestation of the status-quo was Hitler's vision of National Socialism as creative destruction generated by the imperative of reestablishing the chosen community on the right track of history. In July 1934, Hitler stated that, "when a deathly check is violently imposed upon the natural development of a people, an act of violence may serve to release the artificially interrupted flow of evolution to allow it once again the freedom of natural development."[23] As a zenith of surging extremisms, National Socialism preconditioned reconstruction by unleashing revolutionary destruction—also a cardinal principle to the Bolshevik project centered on bringing about social Utopia at home and abroad.

Hitler and Mussolini were not mere representatives of local nationalist traditions. Both fascist leaders internalized a lineage of ethnocentrisms, but they put their own stamp on it. In Mussolini's case, the most pervasive myth he had in common with pre-war political establishments was the pursuit of national *grandezza*.[24] In his ideological vision, the latter morphed into the narrative of a third Rome that could satisfy nationalist frustrations at home, justify the regime's imperial dreams, and consolidate the purported sacred mission of Fascism.[25] But Mussolini and his followers were driven by something much more radical than turn-of-the-century dreams of national greatness. For him, fascism was "a religious conception of life, in which man is seen in his immanent relationship with a superior law, with an objective will, which transcends any individual and raises him to the status of an initiated member of a spiritual society."[26] Mussolini saw Fascism as the foundation of a new civilization.

Similarly, the success of National Socialism relied on its ability to turn long-cherished myths to its own purposes. It claimed to embody an idealized and transcendent Volk that symbolized the desired unity of a racially defined nation.[27] Hitler successfully convinced large sections of the German population (including some portions of the

Left's working-class electorate) that he had found the right combination between social and national consciousness. A mixture of revolutionary anti-capitalism and ultra-nationalist German racism led to Hitler's chiliastic dreams of Aryan supremacy.

At a speech in the Berlin Sports Palace on February 10, 1933, Hitler formulated with religious fervor his "predestined mission" to resurrect the German nation:

> For I cannot divest of my faith in my people, cannot dissociate myself from the conviction that this nation will one day rise again, cannot divorce myself from my love for this, my people, and I cherish the firm conviction that the hour will come at last in which the millions who despise us today will stand by us and with us will hail the new, hard-won and painfully acquired German Reich we have created together, the new German kingdom of greatness and power and glory and justice. Amen.[28]

A comparable ideological frenzy was also at the core of Communism. Such a sense of mission was apparent at the Congress of Victors (the Seventeenth Congress of the Communist Party of the Soviet Union) in January–February 1934, as the Soviet regime entered the second five-year plan and finalized the Cultural Revolution, after Stalin had murdered, starved, and deported millions of kulaks in Ukraine and forcibly resettled several ethnic groups, and as he consolidated his position as the undisputed leader of the Bolshevik party. At such a "glorious moment," almost two-and-a-half years before the beginning of the Great Terror, Politburo member Lazar Kaganovich praised Stalin as the creator "of the greatest revolution that human history has ever known."[29]

Such proclamations grew louder outside of the USSR, too. The Great Depression, the rise of fascism, and the Five-Year Plan ushered in a new age of worldwide fascination with the Soviet experiment.[30] Mussolini's ascent to power, the coming of the Third Reich, the Italian invasion of Ethiopia, the Spanish Civil War, and Nazi Germany's attack on the Soviet Union in 1941 generated transnational waves of anti-fascist solidarity that nurtured global left-wing mobilizations. This phenomenon further destabilized the Eurocentric status-quo preparing the ground for decolonization after 1945.[31]

On the path to permanent transformation, both Communism and Fascism engineered the extinction of the individual by inventing equally binding criteria of faith, loyalty, and status crystallized into a master political myth. Despite the presence of party or leader despotism, each of the two radical movements were regimes of continuous revolution.[32] They were founded upon programs of total societal mobilization intended to achieve a radical transformation of the body politic.

The first step in the revolutions promoted by Communism and Fascism (German and Italian) was the takeover of power, which was fundamentally exclusionary in relation to all other political formations or adversaries. For Lenin, once imposed via the Bolshevik insurrection, the "dictatorship of the proletariat" was irreversible and unrestrained by any law. In March 1933, Hitler, too, announced, "The government will embark upon a systematic campaign to restore the nation's moral and material health. The whole educational system, theater, film, literature, the press, and broadcasting— all these will be used as means to this end."[33] Indeed, during the trial of the army officers imprisoned for their involvement with National Socialism in Leipzig in 1930, Hitler had declared that he aimed at a "legal revolution." Once in power, National Socialism would "mold the state into the shape we hold suitable."[34]

Such an approach was disturbingly reminiscent of the Bolshevik precedent. Lenin believed that any wavering in taking power was a criminal act. Lenin's party, the Bolsheviks, neither forged nor led the revolution from below, but they alone understood its direction and flourished in its aftermath.[35] Just like the Nazis and Italian Fascists, Bolsheviks knew that they wanted to rule because they believed in a perceived historical, transformative, and redemptive mission.

In Japan, the first decade of the postwar order enhanced the influence of the military in the state and within society, although it increasingly became more divided. To make matters worse, there was a significant difference between how the Army and the Navy envisaged Japanese imperial expansion. The former had its eyes fixed on the mainland (Manchuria and Korea), which implied that the Soviet Union became the inevitable foe. The latter turned its gaze to the Pacific, targeting the United States and Britain as the future cardinal antagonists. Furthermore, just as in Europe, the post-Versailles period brought about a proliferation of nationalist leagues and, by 1936, there were more than 750 active groups.[36]

As military radicalism deepened and multiple strands of nationalisms engulfed Japan, local officials called for "autonomous diplomacy" that departed in two ways from the country's policies before and in the first years after the war. First, it meant liberating Japanese imperial interests in Asia from their embedding in relations with the West. Second, such autonomy effectively green-lit the ambitions of Japan's colonial armies in East and Southeast Asia.[37] Armed with this new doctrine, Japan embarked on a unilateral expansionist path that played its part in the subversion of efforts to stabilize the postwar order. This particular form of isolationism spelled doom to the possibility for a liberal democratic alternative in the country.

The Leap into the Abyss

Fascism and Communism presented themselves as voicing the protest of those who had lost out in the aftermath of the Great War. If, during the stabilization of the 1920s, such politics of resentment seemed marginal and innocuous, the Great Depression and the chronic weakness of the international system radically altered the horizon of expectations of both revolutionaries (Left or Right) and of their rapidly swelling constituencies.

After the failed insurrection in Germany in October 1923, communist parties across Europe acquired a paradoxical status of revolutionary parties in a non-revolutionary environment. Their Bolshevization and subsequent Stalinization[38] represented the umbilical cord that tied them to policies and dynamics within the Soviet Union. Between the fifth and the sixth congresses of the Comintern, the imperatives and the defense of the Soviet state became synonymous with the idea of revolution at home and abroad.

Until the mid-1930s, the USSR's vacillation between the foreign strategies of revolution and diplomacy further increased the disruptive potential of communist movements across Europe. The Comintern's sectarianism reached its climax during the "third period" (1928 to 1934), when its leadership claimed that there was no difference between fascists and left-wing socialists, and that the communists were the only representatives of the proletariat.[39] In this context social democrats were labeled "social fascists."

Stalin's control over the Comintern and the USSR's sacred status in the international communist movement came at a price. Between 1929 and 1933, the Moscow-appointed German Communist Party (KPD) leadership stubbornly refused to depart from the Comintern-imposed "general line," turning a blind eye to the profound political and ideological upheaval that was under way in the Weimar Republic. In November 1932 the communists had joined a big strike led by the Nazis against the Berlin transport board.

The KPD had adopted the slogan "First Hitler, them our turn!"[40] This mindset was also reflected in April 1934 when the newspaper *Rundschau* proclaimed that "the momentary calm after the victory of Fascism is only a passing phenomenon. The rise of the revolutionary tide in Germany will inevitably continue. The resistance of the masses against Fascism will inevitably increase. The open dictatorship of Fascism destroys all democratic illusions, frees the masses from the influence of the Social-democratic Party and thus accelerates the speed of Germany's march towards the proletarian revolution."[41] Stalin himself, at the 1934 Congress of the Communist Party of the Soviet Union, despite doomsday predictions of an imminent war, pointed out that even though the USSR was far from enthusiastic about the fascist regime in Germany, Fascism in Italy had not prevented the development of bilateral relations with that country.

Nevertheless, after 1933, an ideological abyss had opened across Europe. Hitler's fascist revolution encouraged other right-wing extremisms and authoritarianisms in Europe and beyond, accentuating the transnational impact of Fascism on the world. In countries as diverse as France, Romania, Austria, Holland, Brazil, and Argentina, various local fascist movements mushroomed.[42] To make matters worse, Hitler's success also validated various antisemitic narratives, which became state policies by the end of the decade in many European states. After 1941, as Hitler invaded the Soviet Union, the continental wave of antisemitism stoked in the previous years would be a central factor in various countries' collaboration in the Nazis' implementation of the Holocaust.

A chasm triggered by radicalism had occurred in Japan as well. The economic crisis deeply affected the country: famine and rice riots ravaged the society. As in Europe, these circumstances fostered politics of violence and nationalist extremism. In 1936, a group of young officers attempted a coup that aimed to eliminate more liberal military and civil authorities. What set Japan apart from Europe was the fact that these radicalisms did not coalesce into one ideological party. Only in 1940, the movements that shaped up during 1930s were brought together in a para-fascist organization, the Imperial Rule Assistance Association, which was created by prime minister Fumimaro Konoe. He was the same politician who, in 1937 during a previous stint as head of government, adopted the vision of the world extolled by the military.

The new realities in Japan reflected in the governmental policies advanced during the 1930s. They resembled in spirit the measures taken by Hitler or Mussolini to draw the support of their populations upon coming into power. But the overarching element in the ideological radicalization of the Japanese society and establishment was the celebration of *kokutai*. This concept encapsulated the idea of a mystical unity of the Japanese people founded upon the mythical origins of the nation, all under the benevolent authority of a divine emperor.[43]

For the extremists in the Japanese military and political establishment, *kokutai* meant the life-world of the nation in support of which no means were too extreme nor sacrifice too great if deemed necessary for its survival.[44] The pervasiveness of this form of *völkisch* political thought, combined with radicalism among politicians and the military, created an environment in which totalizing mobilization came simultaneously from above and from below.[45] It generated forms of state rule increasingly similar with the radical movements that ascended to power (or attempted to) in European states.

Returning to Europe, Hitler's success in Germany with its grievous consequences were finally tackled by the Soviet leadership and the Comintern. The policies of "popular front" and "struggle for peace" were adopted at the organization's seventh congress in 1935. The standard bearer of the new line was Bulgarian communist, Georgi Dimitrov, the general secretary, nominated by Stalin after he became an anti-fascist icon during the Leipzig trail, when he was falsely accused of involvement in the Reichstag Fire.[46]

Dimitrov's famous definition of fascism formulated in August 1934, as a follow-up to the popular front line, symbolizes the contradictions of the new turn. According to him, Fascism was "the open terrorist dictatorship of the most reactionary, most chauvinist and most imperialist elements of finance capital."[47] To fight against it, communists had to ally with democratic and progressive political forces; popular fronts sprung up in France, Spain, and Chile to counter the fascization of these countries. The ultimate goal, however, remained the communist seizure of power, as Dimitrov underlined: "We state frankly to the masses: Final salvation this government [of the Popular Front] cannot bring . . . Consequently it is necessary to prepare for the socialist revolution! Soviet power and only soviet power can bring such salvation!"[48]

Across Europe, and increasingly throughout the world, contemporaries took for granted the fact that the zeitgeist of the period was determined by the polarization between Communism and Fascism. The outbreak of the Spanish Civil War in 1936 only seemed to confirm such views. However, rather than a conflict between Communism and Fascism, as credited by the Italian, German, and Soviet intervention, the Spanish conflict revealed the quicksand progressively engulfing the idea of non-totalitarian democracy. Although an extreme case, Spain signaled the ascendency of ideological radicalisms at the expense of centrist, democratic politics.[49]

In the second half of 1930s, Hitler consolidated his rule at home and became ever bolder in his revisionist designs (seconded closely by Italy's and Japan's own struggle for empire). By 1938, he had completed his political revolution, breaking away from the conservatives that assisted his takeover of power. The changing nature of the dictatorship was revealed by the creation, in peace time, of the general headquarters (OKW)—a symbol of the centrality and paramount role of the Führer, an institution foreboding war.

Hitler also provided for "a climate of permission" within the party apparatus and state institutions to expand and accelerate plans for racial hygiene and economic imperialism.[50] In this context, governmental disorder became an inescapable facet of the Nazi polity's cumulative radicalization. The Nazi state was transformed into a complex of overlapping and competing agencies that depended on the will of the Führer.[51]

Around the same time, Stalin began the second phase of his own consolidation of the Soviet dictatorship in the aftermath of the Congress of Victors (1934). From the mid-1930s onward, the communist leadership (in the Soviet Union and of the Comintern) seemed to witness the fulfillment of its own catastrophist visions of capitalist modernity. The USSR appeared besieged and vulnerable to a war on two, if not three, fronts (if Japan is taken into account). The situation created an all-powerful paranoia in the Kremlin and the Comintern. From 1936 until 1938, Stalin used show-trials to eliminate all his former contesters, while also engineering murderous mobilization from below among regional leaderships and the rank-and-file. The Great Terror along with the social and national operations (which reignited de-kulakization and massive campaigns of ethnic cleansing against "enemy" nationalities) appeared to Stalin and his henchmen a form of preparation for war.[52]

The terror campaigns actually worsened the USSR's position, bargaining power, and influence in relation with the West. Despite its calls for collective security, its extolling of the popular front, its intervention in Spain, and its use of the banner of anti-fascism in the struggle for international support, the Soviet Union pursued domestic policies that brought the country into an ever more hermetic autarchy.[53] Nevertheless, Stalin, in contrast with Hitler, for most of his rule, was successful in finding a synthesis between government and ideology, system-building and ideological expansion. His politics of mobilization, however destructive for the Soviet population, did not obliterate the formal mechanisms of state administration.[54]

If we look outside of Europe, in Japan the toxic mix between ultra-nationalism and totalizing state control facilitated cumulative radicalization at home and abroad similar to the situation in Germany and the Soviet Union. The Manchurian incident in 1931 is an ideal example in this sense. The army representatives who engineered the attack against China proclaimed their determination to export the revolution in Japan: "When we return to the homeland this time we shall carry out a coup d'état and do away with the party political system of government. Then we shall establish a nation of National Socialism with the Emperor as the center."[55] Their vision of revolution via imperial expansion was founded on the reconceptualization of the Japanese nation's paramount role in a future world order.

The Japanese intelligentsia extolled a new regionalism that was premised on the ideas of liberation from the West and subordination of East Asian peoples. It was the expression of *kodo* (the Imperial Way) that putatively enabled all nations and races to find their place in the world. Japan was at the center of this realignment: the pure Yamato race would rule over other nations, assigned subservient and dependent roles.[56] The shock of postwar mass politics combined with the polyarchy of nationalism and imperialism pushed Japan into an accelerated scramble for empire ever more soaked in exterminist practices and mindsets.

Less in the case of Mussolini's Italy and in a different way for imperial Japan, the end of the 1930s witnessed the entrenchment of "states of terror"[57] with Hitler's Germany and Stalin's Soviet Union as pinnacles of such specific state-forms. At its core, the new world conflagration was about the rise and fall of three empires—Germany, Japan, Italy—and about the Soviet state's achievement of a central role in the contemporary political universe.[58]

In their most accomplished state-forms, Fascism and Communism appeared to have successfully constructed two radical, revolutionary civilizations that rivaled, and even overshadowed, the project of bourgeois modernity. Stalin's etatization of social Utopia was founded on a secular eschatology (Marxism-Leninism), a radical vision of the world (capitalist encirclement and the touchstone theory of proletarian internationalism spelled out by Stalin in the 1920s), and ultimately, an alternative idea of modernity (based upon anti-capitalism and state managed collectivism) self-identified as infallibly righteous.[59]

The characterization of Stalinism as civilization comes very close to the assessment made by Anthony Stevens, a Jungian analyst, of National Socialism. According to Stevens, Nazism had its Messiah (Hitler), its Holy Book (*Mein Kampf*), its cross (the Swastika), its religious processions (the Nuremberg Rally), its ritual (the Beer Hall Putsch Remembrance Parade), its anointed elite (the SS), its hymns (the "Horst Wessel Lied"), excommunication for heretics (the concentration camps), its devils (the Jews), its millennial promise (the Thousand Year Reich), and its Promised Land (the East).[60]

On the brink of war, Germany and the Soviet Union represented two totalizing dictatorships. Their legitimacy was based upon a synthesis between coercion and consent. In this sense, these extreme, ideological polities were embodied by the masses, who gave them life and direction.[61] Both party movements pretended to purify humanity of agents of corruption, decadence, and dissolution and to restore a presumably lost unity of humanity (excluding, of course, those regarded as subhuman, social, and racial enemies).

Hitler saw the war with the Soviet Union and Western democracies as a crusade meant to totally destroy the ideologically dehumanized enemy. Robert Gellately quotes the recollections of one of Hitler's secretaries: "We will win this war, because we fight for an idea, and not for Jewish capitalism, which drives the soldiers of our enemies. Only Russia is dangerous, because Russia fights with the same fanaticism as we do for its worldview. But the good will be the victor, there is nothing else for it."[62] Nazi ideology merged antisemitism with biological determinism to the extent that genocide itself represented purification and "a ritual act of sacrifice performed to redeem history from chaos and decadence."[63] In the case of the Soviet Union, after the war on the peasants, the Stalinist repressive machine, especially during the Great Terror, attacked all social strata.

The above remarks bring us to a crucial dilemma that haunts any attempt at understanding the ideological origins of World War II: the difficulty of fathoming how so many people approved of and sustained extreme violence as normal and justifiable practice.[64] Here is where the understanding of Fascism and Communism's revolutionary passion becomes vital. It is this spirit of radical transformation and renewal that mobilized the masses who pushed forward both movements throughout their existence.[65]

Fascism and Communism assigned to the state its own morality, granting only to it the right to define the meaning and ultimate aim of human existence. The premises for waging war were founded on a moral inversion that made "the state's crimes explicable not as crimes but as necessary precautions to prevent greater injustice."[66] Both Fascism and Communism decided they had found the key to happiness, virtue, and infallibility, and they were prepared to kill in applying it to specific societies.

In late 1930s, the domestic build-up in Germany and the Soviet Union had two main consequences tremendously relevant for the onset of World War II. Hitler accelerated the creation of a Nazi New World Order, which was rooted in the unification of all Germans and the fulfillment of their alleged need for *Lebensraum* (living space). His vision drew from the colonial experience of other European empires: occupied peoples and allied nations existed only to serve the interests of Greater Germany.[67] By 1939, many on the right were convinced they were contemporaries with the collapse of interwar liberalism. German military successes reinforced the conviction in the apparent viability and righteousness of collaboration.

In his turn, Stalin reverted to the idea of a war of attrition between capitalist states, pursuing his own form of appeasement toward Hitler, parallel to the one adopted by Britain and France. Western efforts for peace on the Continent were subverted by their inescapable ambiguity. France and Britain were hostile to fascist ambition, but they were no friend to communism either.[68] They had reached a European settlement with Hitler in Munich (September 1938), while ignoring the Soviet Union. Their subsequent efforts to construct an anti-Nazi alliance with Stalin had scant chance of success, if any at all, especially if we keep in mind that the latter had begun his own courting of Hitler.

Was the Non-Aggression Pact between the Soviet Union and Nazi Germany (August 1939) a forgone conclusion? Taking into account the creation in 1936 of the Anti-Comintern Pact, Hitler's obsession with the inevitable showdown with Bolshevism, and the West's last-ditch efforts to woo the Soviets, the answer is negative. But the Pact was not entirely surprising either. From 1922 until 1941, only five years saw a total absence of co-operation between the USSR and Germany. Even during these five years of Nazi hostility, Soviet diplomats maintained the hope of finding some common ground with the new regime in Berlin.[69]

At first glance, the Non-Aggression Pact offered great advantages for both dictators: Hitler was now convinced he could localize conflict in East-Central Europe and had avoided the danger of a war on two fronts; Stalin made sure he kept the USSR out of a war that now seemed inevitable to him (as it did throughout the interwar years), while also pursuing his own revolutionary imperialism in East-Central Europe and Finland. This logic was further confirmed when the Soviet Union signed a similar non-aggression pact with Japan in 1941. At a deeper level, though, the Pact made war more likely, if not unavoidable. It epitomized the pinnacle of ideological extremism's constant and accelerated offensive against parliamentary democracy. It signaled the demise of the post-Great War international order.

The position adopted by Stalin in 1939 resembled the Comintern's political line in Germany at the beginning of 1930s. In September, he told Dimitrov that, "it is not a bad thing if Germany is the means of shaking up the position of the richest capitalist countries (England in particular). Hitler is, unwittingly and without wanting it himself, upsetting and undermining the foundations of the capitalist system." It was a return to the principle of "first Hitler, then our turn." Dimitrov would conform to his master's views, publishing at the beginning of November an article in which he lambasted the "myth" of the anti-fascist nature of the war, which was attributed to the social democrats.[70] From 1928 until 1939, the circle was complete. Neither Hitler nor Stalin had a master plan for destroying the postwar order. Nevertheless, their revisionisms, deeply imbedded in radical ideological Weltanschauungs, made direct contact with one another in central Poland[71] as the world had been plunged into another world war.

Conclusion

In 1919, Marshal Foch, the Allied Generalissimo during World War I, gave a grim prophecy concerning the Treaty of Versailles: "This is not peace. It is an armistice for twenty years."[72] However, World War II was far from inevitable or preordained by the problems of the post-1918 order. The onset of the new world conflagration was not sudden. At the level of international politics, it was the result of a gradual but systematic dismantling of the achievements from the stabilization period of the 1920s.

At the level of ideology, war and its upward scale of barbarism until 1945 were the outcome of the tremendous challenge that right-wing and left-wing extremisms posed to post-1914 democratic societies and parliamentary systems. Fascism and Communism were equally antibourgeois doctrines, and their visions of the future were rooted in the idea of the inescapable decadence of the Western democracies. They were born in a Europe that seemed to have entered a new era in which politics had to be radically redefined toward the glorious dawn of new left or right civilizations.

Fascism (in its Italian and German avatars) and Communism, along with Japanese nationalism, challenged not only domestic establishments, but also the very idea of a postwar world order with the British empire at its center, seconded closely by the French empire and a reluctant United States. During 1920s, Britain's vision of liberal imperialism, combined with France's shaky and only apparent hegemony in Europe and with America's deepening political isolationism, did not amount to a solid foundation for either Europe or the world.

In the 1930s, the post-Versailles establishment increasingly clashed, domestically and at the international level, with the alternative modernities that found state-forms in

Italy, Germany, and the Soviet Union. Japan, with its belief in national supremacy and its calls for Asia to belong to the Asians, basically turned the entire world on its axis.[73] This quadruple ideological challenge at home and abroad generated an explosive situation rooted in projected certainties of liberal democratic demise.

As radical movements took over states in the second half of the 1930s and founded regimes of violence, persecution, exclusion, and extermination, ideology took hold by belief and osmosis. True believers indulged in their millenialist fantasies by state means. The vacillating majority of the populations under their grip allowed themselves to be engulfed.[74] In either case, ideology became the territory in which individuals would fall back once the fog of war took hold of Europe and the rest of the world. Just as war had been a catalyst for revolution and radicalisms between 1914 and 1918, from 1939, and especially since 1941 until 1945, war stoked by ideology, with the Holocaust at its center, made the limits of the conceivable ever wider with multiple cycles of previously unthinkable destruction and extermination.

Before 1939, there was a high level of entanglement among the ideologies and states discussed in this chapter (Fascism, Communism, nationalisms—Germany, Italy, the Soviet Union, and Japan). The war proved an ideal opportunity for the unprecedented expansion of interwar visions of radical transformation. With France's collapse, Germany's invasion of the Soviet Union, and Japan's Pearl Harbor attack, World War II truly entered its global phase. Once this stage was reached, achieving the right form of modernity became literally a matter of life or death.[75] Such novel alignment of the globe would be, until 1989–1991, the lasting legacy of the second world conflagration in the twentieth century and of its ideological origins. Europe, the initial breeding ground, remained center stage only as the most symbolic theater of conflict between the victorious superpowers: the United States and the USSR.

Notes

1. Roger Griffin, *A Fascist Century* (New York: Palgrave Macmillan, 2008), 42.
2. P. M. H. Bell, *The Origins of the Second World War in Europe* (New York: Routledge, 2013), 91.
3. Richard Overy, with Andrew Wheatcroft, *The Road to War* (London: Penguin, 1999), 172.
4. Louise Young, *Japan's Total Empire: Manchuria and the Culture of Wartime Imperialism* (Los Angeles: University of California Press, 1999).
5. Overy, with Wheatcroft, *The Road*, 211.
6. Silvio Pons, *The Global Revolution: A History of International Communism 1917–1991* (Oxford: Oxford University Press, 2014), 96–97.
7. Peter Fritzsche, *German into Nazis* (Cambridge: Harvard University Press, 2003), 81.
8. Roger Griffin, *Modernism and Fascism: The Sense of Beginning under Mussolini and Hitler* (London: Palgrave Macmillian, 2007), 9–10.
9. Overy, with Wheatcroft, *The Road*, 353.
10. Dan Diner, *Cataclysms: A History of the Twentieth Century from Europe's Edge* (Madison: University of Wisconsin Press, 2008), 4.

11. Griffin, *A Fascist Century*, 32.
12. Emilio Gentile and Robert Mallett, "The Sacralisation of Politics: Definitions, Interpretations and Reflections on the Question of Secular Religion and Totalitarianism," *Totalitarian Movements and Political Religions* 1, no. 1 (2000): 18–9.
13. François Furet, *The Passing of an Illusion: The Idea of Communism in the Twentieth Century* (Chicago: University of Chicago Press, 1999), 23.
14. M. G. Sheftall, "An Ideological Genealogy of Imperial Era Japanese Militarism," in *The Origins of the Second World War: An International Perspective*, ed. Frank Mcdonough (London: Continuum, 2011), 59.
15. Overy, with Wheatcroft, *The Road*, 268.
16. David Earhart, *Certain Victory: Images of World War II in the Japanese Media* (London: M.E. Sharpe, 2008), 215–307.
17. Rana Mitter, *China's War with Japan, 1937–1945: The Struggle for Survival* (New York: Penguin Books, 2013).
18. Erez Manela, *The Wilsonian Moment: Self-Determination and the Origins of Anticolonial Nationalism* (Oxford: Oxford University Press, 2007).
19. Susan Pedersen, *The Guardians: The League of Nations and the Crisis of Empire* (Oxford: Oxford University Press, 2015).
20. Daniel Brückenhaus, *Policing Transnational Protest: Liberal Imperialism and the Surveillance of Anticolonialists in Europe, 1905–1945* (Oxford: Oxford University Press, 2017).
21. Zara Steiner, *The Lights that Failed: European International History 1919–1933* (Oxford: Oxford University Press, 2005).
22. David Priestland, *Stalinism and the Politics of Mobilization: Ideas, Power, and Terror in Interwar Russia* (Oxford: Oxford University Press, 2007), 39.
23. Richard Evans, *The Coming of the Third Reich* (London: Penguin Books, 2003), 460.
24. Alan Cassels, "Mussolini and the Myth of Rome," in *The Origins of the Second World War Reconsidered. A.J.P. Taylor and the Historians*, 2nd ed., ed. Gordon Martel (New York: Routledge, 1999), 58.
25. Aristotle Kallis, *The Third Rome 1922–1943: The Making of the Fascist Capital* (New York: Palgrave MacMillan, 2014), 15; Simonetta Falasca-Zamponi, *Fascist Spectacle: The Aesthetics of Power in Mussolini's Italy* (Los Angeles: University of California Press, 1997), 90–99.
26. Emilio Gentile, *The Sacralization of Politics in Fascist Italy* (Cambridge: Harvard University Press, 1996), 59.
27. George Mosse, *The Crisis of German Ideology: Intellectual Origins of the Third Reich* (New York: Schocken Books, 1981), vi, 51.
28. Evans, *The Coming*, 324.
29. Timothy Snyder, *Bloodlands: Europe between Hitler and Stalin* (New York: Basic Books, 2010), 65.
30. Michael David-Fox, *Showcasing the Great Experiment: Cultural Diplomacy and Western Visitors to the Soviet Union, 1921–1941* (Oxford: Oxford University Press, 2011); Silvio Pons and Stephen Smith, eds., *The Cambridge History of Communism*, Vol. 1: *World Revolution and Socialism in One Country 1917–1941* (Cambridge: Cambridge University Press, 2017).
31. Kasper Braskén, Nigel Copsey, and David Featherstone, eds., *Anti-fascism in a Global Perspective: Transnational Networks, Exile Communities, and Radical Internationalism* (New York: Routledge, 2021).

32. Michael Mann, "Contradictions of Continuous Revolution," in *Stalinism and Nazism: Dictatorships in Comparison*, ed. Ian Kershaw and Moshe Lewin, (Cambridge: Cambridge University Press, 1997), 136.
33. Evans, *The Coming*, 397.
34. Evans, *The Coming*, 455.
35. Stephen F. Cohen, *Bukharin and the Bolshevik Revolution: A Political Biography, 1888-1938* (New York: Oxford University Press, 1973), 46.
36. Overy, with Wheatcroft, *The Road*, 271-272.
37. Louise Young, "Japan at War: History-writing on the Crisis of the 1930s," in *The Origins*, ed. Martel, 155.
38. Norman LaPorte, Kevin Morgan, and Matthew Worley, eds., *Bolshevism, Stalinism and the Comintern Perspectives on Stalinization, 1917-53* (New York: Palgrave MacMillan, 2008).
39. Franz Borkenau, *The Communist International* (London: Faber and Faber, 1938), 335.
40. Norman LaPorte, "Presenting a Crisis as an Opportunity: The KPD and the Third Period, 1929-1933," in *In Search of Revolution: International Communist Parties in the Third Period*, ed. Matthew Worley (London: I. B. Tauris, 2004), 41.
41. Borkenau, *The Communist*, 376-377.
42. Arnd Bauerkèamper and Grzegorz Rossolinski, eds., *Fascism without Borders: Transnational Connections and Cooperation between Movements and Regimes in Europe From 1918 to 1945* (New York: Berghahn Books, 2017).
43. Sheftall, "An Ideological," 60.
44. Julia Thomas, *Reconfiguring Modernity: Concepts of Nature and Japanese Political Ideology* (Los Angeles: University of California Press, 2001).
45. Young, "Japan at War," 163.
46. Ivo Banac, ed., *The Diary of Georgi Dimitrov 1933-1949*, trans. Jane T. Hedges, Timothy D. Sergay, and Irina Faion (New Haven: Yale University Press, 2012).
47. David Beetham, *Marxists in the Face of Fascism* (Manchester: Manchester University Press, 1983), 22.
48. Stanley Payne, *Civil War in Europe, 1905-1949* (Cambridge: Cambridge University Press, 2011), 113. Also see Kevin McDermott and John Agnew, *The Comintern: A History of International Communism from Lenin to Stalin* (London: MacMillan, 1996), 130-132, 155-159.
49. Stanley Payne, *The Spanish Civil War, the Soviet Union, and Communism* (London: Yale University Press, 2004).
50. Richard Overy, "Misjudging Hitler: A. J. P. Taylor and the Third Reich," in *The Origins*, ed. Martel, 101-103.
51. Ian Kershaw, *Hitler 1936-45: Nemesis* (New York: W.W. Norton, 2000), 321.
52. Amir Weiner, *Making Sense of the War: The Second World War and the Fate of the Bolshevik Revolution* (Princeton: Princeton University Press, 2002), 17.
53. Katerina Clark, *Moscow the Fourth Rome: Stalinism, Cosmopolitism, and the Evolution of Soviet Culture, 1931-1941* (Cambridge: Harvard University Press, 2011), 145.
54. Yoram Gorlizki and Hans Mommsen, "The Political (Dis)Orders of Stalinism and National Socialism," in *Beyond Totalitarianism: Stalinism and Nazism Compared*, ed. Michael Geyer and Sheila Fitzpatrick (Cambridge: Cambridge University Press, 2009), 41-86.
55. Overy, with Wheatcroft, *The Road*, 275.
56. Overy, with Wheatcroft, *The Road*, 280.

57. Richard Overy, *The Dictators: Hitler's Germany and Stalin's Russia* (London: Penguin Books, 2005), 176.
58. David Reynolds, "World War II and Modern Meanings," *Diplomatic History* 25, no. 3 (2001): 457–471; Amir Wiener, "In the Long Shadow of War: The Second World War and the Soviet and Post-Soviet World," *Diplomatic History* 25, no. 3 (2001): 443–456.
59. Stephen Kotkin, *The Magnetic Mountain: Stalinism as Civilization* (Berkeley: University of California Press, 1995), 225–237; Astrid Hedin, "Stalinism as a Civilization: New Perspectives on Communist Regimes," *Political Studies Review* 2, no. 2 (2004): 166–184.
60. Griffin, *Modernism and Fascism*, 274.
61. Felix Patrikeeff, "Stalinism, Totalitarian Society and the Politics of 'Perfect Control,'" *Totalitarian Movements and Political Religions* 4, no. 1 (2003): 40.
62. Robert Gellately, *Lenin, Stalin, and Hitler: The Age of Social Catastrophe* (New York: Alfred Knopf, 2007), 310.
63. Griffin, *Modernism and Fascism*, 332–333. Also, Enzo Traverso, *The Origins of Nazi Violence* (London: New Press, 2003), 136, 144; Omer Bartov, *Mirrors of Destruction: War, Genocide, and Modern Identity* (Oxford: Oxford University Press, 2000), 111.
64. Ian Kershaw and Moshe Lewin, "Introduction: The Regimes and their Dictators: Perspectives of Comparison," in *Stalinism and Nazism*, 25.
65. Griffin, *Modernism and Fascism*, 4.
66. Overy, *The Dictators*, 303–306.
67. Mark Mazower, *Hitler's Empire: How the Nazis Ruled Europe* (London: Penguin Books, 2008), 7.
68. Overy, with Wheatcroft, *The Road*, 246.
69. Overy, with Wheatcroft, *The Road*, 245.
70. Pons, *Global Revolution*, 93–94.
71. Overy, with Wheatcroft, *The Road*, 211.
72. Zara Steiner, *The Triumph of the Dark: European International History 1933–1939* (Oxford: Oxford University Press, 2011), 1037.
73. Overy, with Wheatcroft, *The Road*, 280.
74. Diner, *Cataclysms*, 179.
75. Odd Westad, "The Cold War and the International History of the Twentieth Century," in *Cambridge History of the Cold War*, Vol. I: *Origins*, ed. Melvyn Leffler and Odd Westad (Cambridge: Cambridge University Press, 2010), 13.

Bibliography

Diner, Dan. *Cataclysms: A History of the Twentieth Century from Europe's Edge*. Madison: University of Wisconsin Press, 2008.

Evans, Richard. *The Coming of the Third Reich*. London: Penguin Books, 2003.

Gentile, Emilio. *The Sacralization of Politics in Fascist Italy*. Cambridge: Harvard University Press, 1996.

Geyer, Michael, and Sheila Fitzpatrick, eds. *Beyond Totalitarianism: Stalinism and Nazism Compared*. Cambridge: Cambridge University Press, 2009.

Griffin, Roger. *Modernism and Fascism: The Sense of Beginning under Mussolini and Hitler*. London: Palgrave Macmillan, 2007.

LaPorte, Norman, Kevin Morgan, and Matthew Worley, eds. *Bolshevism, Stalinism and the Comintern Perspectives on Stalinization, 1917–53*. New York: Palgrave MacMillan, 2008.

Overy, Richard, with Andrew Wheatcroft. *The Road to War*. London: Penguin, 1999.

Pons, Silvio. *The Global Revolution: A History of International Communism 1917–1991*. Oxford: Oxford University Press, 2014.

Pons, Silvio, and Stephen Smith, eds. *The Cambridge History of Communism*. Vol. 1: *World Revolution and Socialism in One Country 1917–1941*. Cambridge: Cambridge University Press, 2017.

Reynolds, David. "World War II and Modern Meanings." *Diplomatic History* 25, no. 3 (2001): 457–471.

Snyder, Timothy. *Bloodlands: Europe between Hitler and Stalin*. New York: Basic Books, 2010.

Steiner, Zara. *The Lights that Failed: European International History 1919–1933*. Oxford: Oxford University Press, 2005.

Steiner, Zara. *The Triumph of the Dark: European International History 1933–1939*. Oxford: Oxford University Press, 2011.

Thomas, Julia. *Reconfiguring Modernity: Concepts of Nature and Japanese Political Ideology*. Los Angeles: University of California Press, 2001.

Tismaneanu, Vladimir. *The Devil in History: Communism, Fascism, and Some Lessons of the Twentieth Century*. Berkeley: University of California Press, 2012.

Young, Louise. *Japan's Total Empire: Manchuria and the Culture of Wartime Imperialism*. Los Angeles: University of California Press, 1999.

CHAPTER 3

ETHIOPIA AND THE SPANISH CIVIL WAR BEFORE AND DURING WORLD WAR II

PETER GARRETSON AND Stephen McVEIGH

When discussing the "small European wars of the 1930s," historians have generally emphasized those in Ethiopia and Spain, and their significance to World War II. They have focused on four major issues: the maneuverings of the Great Powers during those small wars, their impact on global diplomacy, their military significance, and the issue of collective security. Parallel to these four international issues have been two important internal developments within Ethiopia—Ethiopian resistance to the Italian invasion and the impact on Ethiopia of weapons of mass destruction.

The Ethiopian victory at Adwa in 1896 was a major turning point in Italo–Ethiopian relations. Italy had been bent on making Ethiopia its colony through military means, but after defeat, it turned largely to economic penetration as its strategy. The 1906 Tripartite Treaty between Britain, France, and Italy recognized economic spheres of influence for each of the powers, carving up Ethiopia for a potential future power grab. The French demanded the least (its colony of Djibouti and influence over its railway to the capital of Addis Ababa) and thus, for several decades, remained Ethiopia's closest international ally. Italy focused on the hinterlands in Ethiopia of Eritrea and Somalia, while Britain looked enviously at western Ethiopia and especially the watershed of the Blue Nile and Lake Tana, the key to the dominant need for water in Egypt and the Sudan. After Mussolini's seizure of power in 1922, Italy became more and more militaristic and nationalistic, and it was only a matter of time before this fascist state would turn again toward a military solution in Ethiopia, seeking revenge for the humiliation of Adwa. However, the 1920s saw continued "rapprochement," first in 1924 when the emperor was welcomed in Rome while visiting Europe, and then a peak in good relations was reached by the 1928 Treaty of Friendship between the two countries. Only the 1930s began to reveal Italy's true intentions, when there was a substantial increase in the military budgets of the Italian colonies bordering Ethiopia. The governor of Eritrea in 1932 drew up a detailed program for a probable war with Ethiopia. Increasingly, Italy followed two policies in Ethiopia: subversion and diplomacy.[1] The groundwork was set, and Italy was now only looking for an excuse to colonize Ethiopia; this was its major aim during the peace negotiations after World War I.

While these policies were barely noticed, taking place in far off Africa, events in Europe were moving apace to Ethiopia's detriment. The rise of Germany under Hitler quickly became the major concern of France and Britain, who both desperately wanted to keep Mussolini from forging an alliance with his fellow fascist. Ethiopia became an expendable pawn in these machinations. Although Haile Selassie understood international affairs better than any previous Ethiopian emperor, he still seriously misjudged the international diplomatic field in the mid-1930s. Because of increasing fears of Germany, France, who had supported an independent Ethiopia against Italy and Britain, now changed its policy in the Horn of Africa. Wanting to please Mussolini, it withdrew opposition to Italian expansion in Ethiopia for compensation elsewhere. Great Britain would soon follow suit, seeing its priorities in Europe as far greater than any in Northeast Africa.

Once it was clear to Mussolini that there would be no significant opposition from France to an invasion of Ethiopia, he launched a massive push on war preparations in both Italian colonies (Eritrea and Somalia) and in Italy. General Emilio De Bono led the effort, first as Minister of Colonies and then as High Commissioner of Eritrea. Italy expanded a great deal of infrastructure and constructed major port facilities, roadways, airports, and hospitals. All that remained by mid-1935 was a *casus belli*. This was provided by the so-called Wal Wal Incident.

The Italian military in Italian Somaliland had been slowly advancing into the Ethiopian province of Ogaden in the early 1930s, fortifying the major oases, including one of the most important at Wal Wal. Wal Wal was vital in supporting the people and livestock of this very dry province and it was an important watering hole and stop-off point for cattle and camels being exported from the Northeast through British Somaliland to the port of Aden.

By the terms of the 1928 Friendship Treaty between Ethiopia and Italy, Wal Wal was well beyond the agreed boundary and, as such, a clear encroachment into Ethiopian territory. On November 22, 1934, a one-thousand-strong Ethiopian militia and its commanders formally requested that the Somali Dubats stationed in the fort withdraw from Ethiopian territory. The Somali officer commanding the garrison refused the request but proceeded to inform the Italian commander of a garrison at Warder, some twenty kilometers away, of these events. The following day, confronted by arriving Italian troops, a protest was made by the Anglo–Ethiopian Territory Commission, which was engaged in surveying the border between British Somaliland and Ethiopia. The British contingent of the survey group protested. However, the Commission, which had an escort of Ethiopian territorial troops, preferred to withdraw rather than embarrass Italy, a situation to be avoided because Britain was keen to maintain Italian friendship against a strengthening Germany. Although the British members of the Commission withdrew, the Ethiopian troops did not. They set up camp in Wal Wal, in provocatively close proximity to the Italian contingent. Tensions simmered and, in early December 1934, violence erupted.

According to the Italian account, the Ethiopians opened fire on the Somali troops with rifles and machine guns. Perhaps unsurprisingly, the Ethiopians claimed the Italians had attacked them, reporting that the Italian forces were supported by two tanks and three aircraft. Regardless, between the December 5 and December 7, 107 Ethiopians and fifty Italians and Somalis were killed in skirmishes. Irrespective of how Mussolini would come to paint the incident at Wal Wal, it was not the cause of the Italian invasion and, in fact, the incident was "settled" by a League of Nations report on September 4, 1935, which attributed blame to neither side. It did, however, provide Mussolini with "evidence" of aggressive acts on the part of Ethiopia and it became a ready justification for a major military buildup in the bordering Italian territories of Eritrea and Somaliland. By May, the Italian government claimed a position as the "civilised nation" confronted by "barbaric" Ethiopia. By October, Mussolini had ordered his forces to prepare for the total conquest of Ethiopia.

On October 3, 1935, two large armies crossed into Ethiopian territory, one from Eritrea and the other from Italian Somaliland. The size of the Italian force made it apparent that preparations had been in process for some time. Half-a-million men and several million tons of equipment had been transported from Italy to form the basis of the invasion. The nature of the war waged by Italy was vividly modern in its application of industrialized warfare and new strategies. The Ethiopian forces were, by comparison, extremely poorly equipped with many soldiers using spears or long curved swords. Most of the rifles that were available dated from the end of the nineteenth century. Furthermore, Ethiopia did not have the means to acquire better weaponry because the international community refused to make available the resources with which to purchase them and because of sanctions imposed on them. The Italian troops, by contrast, were equipped with modern rifles and machine guns, and had motorized columns which were able to move rapidly toward the heart of Ethiopia. The ground offensive was supported by aircraft. With such obvious inequalities in terms of equipment and training, Italy was able to defeat the Ethiopian forces in almost every battle. In May 1936, Italian forces captured the capital, Addis Ababa. King Victor Emmanuel was named Emperor of Ethiopia in place of Haile Selassie. The country was united with Eritrea and Italian Somaliland, and the new country was renamed Italian East Africa.

WEAPONS OF MASS DESTRUCTION AND ETHIOPIAN RESISTANCE

Chemical weapons of mass destruction played a key role in the invasion and following "pacification." Both Italy and Spain used weapons of mass destruction between World War I and World War II, Spain in Spanish Morocco and Italy in Libya and Ethiopia.[2]

Their use in Morocco and Libya were on a very small scale, but Italy's use of bombs, "casket" or barrel bombs, and spraying from airplanes was the greatest use of weapons of mass destruction between World War I and Saddam Hussein's use of them against the Kurds in the mid-1980s. Needless to say, these uses were against African peoples who would be unable to retaliate. These two regimes felt they could use chemical weapons against Black Africans with impunity, but not against Europeans. Furthermore, Emperor Haile Selassie in his autobiography distinguished three stages in the use of Italy's chemical weapons of mass destruction. First, at the beginning of the invasion, Italian airplanes dropped "tear-gas bombs upon my armies"; they didn't do much damage as the soldiers knew to scatter until the wind blew the gas away. During the second stage, however, they "began to drop yperite gas, Casks containing yperite" (barrel bombs). These caused more harm but were soon recognized for what they were, and they killed and injured only a few. However, the third stage, was different: airplanes, specially equipped, sprayed "a fine rain bringing death . . . over vast tracts of country." Mussolini "made this the principal means of warfare."[3] No distinction was made between combatants and civilians.[4] As Haile Selassie described it, "There has not been seen a previous example of a government that has set out to extinguish methodically and by means of cruelty, the entire stock of another people . . . to exterminate innocent human being by powerful and toxic poison gas."[5]

Ethiopian resistance to the Italians and their invasion of Ethiopia went through three stages.[6] The first stage began after the Italian occupation of the capital of Addis Ababa in May 1936 and continued until February 1937, the second stage occurred from February 1937 to June 1940, and the final stage lasted from 1940 to the defeat of Italy in 1941.

After Addis Ababa had fallen in May 1936, Italy had conquered less than one-half of Ethiopia, and throughout the Occupation (1936–1941) it only really controlled the major cities. In this initial period, the upper nobility led widespread resistance. The Italians moved swiftly to co-opt or eliminate this elite and they were largely successful. The climax to this effort came with the "Graziani massacre" of February 1937, which started with the attempted, but unsuccessful, assassination of the Italian Viceroy of Ethiopia, General Rodolfo Graziani. He and his staff overreacted and slaughtered ten thousand Ethiopians, many of them part of the small, educated elite, mostly in the capital. This generated a horrified national reaction against Italian occupation and the beginning of the second phase of resistance led by the lower nobility. This resistance was national, occurring in virtually every province of Ethiopia, but it was strongest in the center and northern provinces of Ethiopia. Guerrilla movements sprang up throughout Ethiopia, often fighting more among themselves than against the Italians, but also tying down some 250,000 troops to contain the conflict. This included both Italians and their colonial troops, as well as militias from Eritrea and Somalia. These guerrillas, known in Ethiopia as "arbegna," were precursors of the National Liberation Army movements of the Cold War years. The third and final stage of resistance came after the Italian declaration of war against the Allies in June 1940. Ethiopians fighting against the Italian forces created a greater degree of unity in the resistance than had existed before, and they played a major role in the final defeat of Italy and the liberation of Ethiopia.

The Ethiopian Crisis and the End of Collective Security

The Italian invasion of Ethiopia proved a key development in the continuum of European conflict which would culminate in World War II as it involved two members of the League of Nations. Haile Selassie had protested the Italian aggression and the incursion into Ethiopian territory at Wal Wal to the League of Nations on December 6, 1934. On December 8, however, claiming Wal Wal was within Italian territory, Mussolini demanded an apology from Ethiopia and on December 11 made additional demands for financial and strategic compensation. Haile Selassie placed his faith in the League of Nations and, in particular, in Britain and France, two of the League's most influential and powerful members, to support his call for arbitration, a remedy specifically provided for in the 1928 treaty. Ethiopia, the last independent African nation, had become a member of the League in 1923, and pursued the line of negotiation and arbitration in the face of Italian hostility and refusal throughout. In this regard, the League did not live up to the terms of its Covenant. The Ethiopian emperor invoked elements of the League's Articles pertaining to the stated commitment to respect and preserve territorial integrity from external aggression and the principles of collective security. However, the League's response was weak and far removed from the level of consideration and protection described by the Covenant.

A number of factors account for the League's weak response. The rise of Germany exerted an immense influence over the handling of the crisis in Ethiopia. Britain and France were beholden to the notion that Italy was an important bulwark against German ambitions, especially in Austria, and so they were reluctant to do anything that might jeopardize Italian relations. The political and diplomatic activity that followed Haile Selassie's protest to the League was directed at averting hostilities but primarily in a manner that favored Italy, the aggressor in this case. Efforts by British and French politicians to defuse the conflict were made outside of the auspices of the League. The British and French entered into a number of diplomatic engagements, all with the aim of maintaining Italian support but which ultimately served to create the space for Italy to prepare for the invasion largely unimpeded. The meetings that were triggered by the Ethiopian crisis then had very little to do with the Ethiopian people or the nation's right to independence and everything to do with restricting German resurgence. One of the earliest negotiations formally signed between France and Italy, on January 7, 1935, permitted Italy a free hand in Ethiopia. Pierre Laval, French Foreign Minister, hoped that such consideration would guarantee Italian support against any future German aggression, while Mussolini had established the space he required to pursue his military buildup.

In June 1935, Mussolini's determination to attack Ethiopia was further reinforced as a consequence of the Anglo-German Naval Agreement. The British were moved to attempt to limit German expansion and the treaty was intended to act as a preliminary arms limitation measure. The treaty was highly controversial and divisive. The French contended that the British had no legal right to release Germany from adhering to the naval clauses of the Versailles treaty. Inevitably, the pact fostered a political rift between Britain and France. Mussolini was also outraged that Britain had acted alone and his reaction was dramatic. To this point, his invasion plans had been somewhat restrained so as not to antagonize his allies; however, the betrayal he felt in the wake of the naval accord removed any lingering impediments to the invasion. Italy invaded Ethiopia in October 1935.

In November 1935, in response to Haile Selassie's protest to the League about Mussolini's invasion, the League condemned Italian actions and instructed members to impose sanctions upon Italy immediately. This was a weak response and it compounded the sense that the League had no teeth. There was little urgency to the imposition of sanctions; it took six weeks for sanctions to be organized. Still more damagingly, the impact of the sanctions would be limited. The restrictions did not include vital war resources, most especially oil. Restricting items such as gold and textiles had only a negligible impact and were, for the most part, an inconvenience that could be borne by Italy. A limit upon the supply of oil would have severely restricted the Italian war machine. The excuse for excluding oil from the sanctions was the argument that Italy could acquire oil from the United States, a non-League country and so not bound by the sanctions. Britain and France remained at pains not to provoke Mussolini, continuing to believe Italy to be an important ally and they were prepared to go to some lengths to retain Italian friendship in the face of the ever-resurgent Germany. Britain was also concerned not to upset the situation in the Mediterranean, the site of two large naval bases at Gibraltar and Malta. Whether Britain and France overestimated Italian naval capabilities is open to debate, but their anxiety was great enough to keep the Suez Canal open. If the canal had been closed, Italy would have had great difficulty supplying its forces in the region as the conflict played out. It is also the case that self-interest of a more general variety informed British and French thinking. This was simply a faraway war in a comparatively unimportant region and, consequently, not worth the commitment of resources or the potential of stirring up international antagonisms.

The urge, then, was to bring about an end to conflict without provoking Mussolini. A meeting between the British foreign secretary, Samuel Hoare, and the French prime minister, Pierre Laval, in December 1935 was so aimed at ending the war this way. Their plan was to give two large areas of Ethiopia to Italy, with the land in between, the so-called "corridor of camels," allocated to Ethiopia. The south of the country would be made available to Italian economic interests. In return for the land, Italy would stop the war. Mussolini was prepared to accept the plan, but it was derailed by popular opinion once the details went public in Britain. Generating an enormous outcry, the British public saw the plan as a betrayal of the Ethiopian people. In response, Hoare resigned, the plan was dropped, and Mussolini continued his invasion.

In June 1936, Haile Selassie travelled to Geneva to personally request assistance from the League of Nations, to, in his words, "claim that justice which is due to my people and the assistance promised to it eight months ago, by fifty-two nations who asserted that an act of aggression had been committed in violation of international treaties."[7] He was the first head of state to address the League in person and his speech to Council was heartfelt, rational, and, in some ways, prophetic. The core of his address was a demand that the League live up to its responsibilities and protect Ethiopia's rights as a member:

> I assert that the issue before the Assembly today is a much wider one. It is not merely a question of the settlement in the matter of Italian aggression. It is a question of collective security; of the very existence of the League [of Nations]; of the trust placed by States in international treaties; of the value of promises made to small States that their integrity and their independence shall be respected and assured. It is a choice between the principle of the equality of States and the imposition upon small Powers of the bonds of vassalage. In a word, it is international morality that is at stake. Have treaty signatures a value only in so far as the signatory Powers have a personal, direct and immediate interest involved?[8]

Referring to the words of the League at the onset of the invasion, he lamented the lack of action:

> The Ethiopian Government never expected other Governments to shed their soldiers' blood to defend the Covenant when their own immediately personal interests were not at stake. Ethiopian warriors asked only for means to defend themselves. On many occasions I asked for financial assistance for the purchase of arms. That assistance was constantly denied me. What, then, in practice, is the meaning of Article 16 of the Covenant and of collective security?[9]

Haile Selassie saw in the League's response to the invasion a portent of things to come:

> Is that the guidance that the League of Nations and each of the States Members are entitled to expect from the great Powers when they assert their right and their duty to guide the action of the League? Placed by the aggressor face to face with the accomplished fact, are States going to set up the terrible precedent of bowing before force?[10]

The Italian victory answered his question, a question that would resonate in the coming years.

The loss of Ethiopian independence was not the most significant and damaging aspect of the British and French attempts to end the conflict. There were wider consequences and precedents established. The unanimity of the League was irrevocably damaged because its key members were willing to act outside of its remit to service their own agendas. Further, the plans, accommodations, and agreements indicated the preparedness of two major European powers, significant and influential members of the League of Nations, to negotiate with the aggressor in an international conflict rather than speak with and for the weaker, embattled nation. The actions of the international powers and the inaction of the League marked a significant turning point. The League had already looked weak in relation to its position on the Japanese invasion of Manchuria but there were, perhaps, acceptable excuses in that case: "the test had come in a part of the world remote from the vital, immediate interests of the most important members of the League."[11] Its involvement with Ethiopia, however, was a disaster. It was made clear that there were real inequalities in the status of members. Given its failure on every level, perhaps the most impactful consequence of the League's handling of the conflict was that the sanctions attempted by the League upon Italy to bring her into line in fact turned her away from international cooperation and toward Nazi Germany. This pairing, which had its beginnings in the Second Italo–Ethiopian War, would develop on the battlefields, military and ideological, of the Spanish Civil War.

THE SPANISH CIVIL WAR, 1936–1939

The civil war in Spain was waged with a ferocity and brutality of immense scale. Half-a-million Spaniards died during the war and its legacies continue to be felt in Spain to the present day. The significance of this civil war, however, far exceeds Spain's borders. The international participants in the Ethiopian crisis were all centrally engaged with the Spanish Civil War. The war's origins are a complex combination of longstanding issues related to poverty and social inequalities, and the more immediate political antagonisms generated between the forces of conservatism and modernization as Spain developed in the early twentieth century. The origins of the war have very little to do with issues external to Spain except insofar as the urge to modernity in the wake of World War I catalyzed many long-standing issues. However, approaching the war with a view to exploring its international implications, the Spanish Civil War emerges very clearly as an ideological war, the landscape of which evinces something of the ideological conflict of World War II. Although it is important to consider the war as it was fought by the Republican and Nationalist armies, it is fair to say that the outcome of the Spanish Civil War was decided, to paraphrase Francisco Romero Salvado, in the chancelleries of Europe rather than the battlefields of Spain. From this perspective, the decisions taken by the European powers in relation to Spain, or, more precisely, the actions undertaken by some states and the inaction of others, are revealed as important steps on the path to World War II.

Viewed from an internal perspective, the Spanish Civil War was the culmination of a long and sustained political and social disquiet predicated upon the polarization of the rich and poor in Spain. The forces of Spanish conservatism were ranged in three major groups. Millions of Spanish citizens subsisted as landless, rural peasants or urban laborers, at the mercy of the powerful and wealthy *latifundistas*, owners of immense agricultural estates or factory-owning industrialists. This wealthy, moneyed class represented a powerful bloc of conservative elites. The repression of the poor was facilitated by the Catholic church, an important force of control in much of Spanish society. The church had responsibilities for education, although rather than empowering the individual or encouraging any freedom of thought or expression, the church taught the peasants to accept their lot now and that their reward would come in the next life. The church in this way was a vital instrument of repression and it worked in tandem with landowners and factory owners to maintain the status quo. Such concern with resisting change was also central to the third group in conservative Spain–the army. The army came to consider the defense of the status quo against any kind of regional, social, or economic modernization or development to be at the core of its mission at the beginning of the twentieth century. After the defeat in the Spanish–American War of 1898, wherein Spain lost the last vestiges of its once substantial empire and the army lost its external function, a situation which Spanish officers blamed on civilian politicians, the army had increasingly looked inwards for a purpose. The army became the guardian of traditional Spanish values and any threat to their conception of *la patria*, the Spanish fatherland, would be treated as a foreign threat.

In this context, the election of a left-leaning reformist government in April 1931 with a clear agenda to modernize Spain was provocative. The Spanish left was not a coherent grouping, but was rather a fractious mosaic of different positions and prone to conflict among themselves. The Second Republic was composed mainly of Republicans and Socialists, but the left also included Anarchist groups, trade unions, Marxists, and the Spanish Communists, as well as Basque and Catalan separatist groups, with their influence changing over time. From the morrow of the election, conservative forces began to organize resistance to this left-wing challenge to their dominance. The reforms planned by the administration of the Second Republic, were ambitious, indeed overly so given the powerful interests opposing them, as well as the Spanish left's inexperience in government. The moneyed classes, the clergy, and the military class looked on anxiously as the new Republican government began to define agrarian reform measures and undertake the redistribution of land as it sought to modify the relationship between the Church and the Spanish state in terms of education, as well as its financial arrangements, and as it initiated a reform of the military which targeted the officer class. Their anxiety about these challenges to their longstanding hegemony undergirded an attempt to engage in the political arena, which resulted in the formation of a coalition of conservative groups in the form of the Confederación Española de Derechas Autónomas (CEDA), which resulted in the election of a rightist government in November 1933. Before the proclamation of the Second Republic in 1931, there had been no political party of the right, and the Spanish right was a patchwork groups including fascists, monarchists, and Catholic conservatives. Unlike the left, though, they were more effectively able to work together primarily because they shared the desire to prevent change in Spain. The CEDA administration immediately moved to roll back what little reform had been undertaken. Such overt resistance to reform mobilized another coalition of the left in the form a Popular Front which narrowly defeated CEDA and came to power in the elections of February 1936. The right subsequently moved away from engaging political means to resolve their concerns in favor of more direct action and the plotting of a military coup.

The coup, in the form of a Generals' rebellion, came on July 18, 1936. The expectation among the officers at the center of the uprising was of a speedy victory and the swift takeover of the whole of Spain. Such confidence was soon dispelled, however, as Spanish workers took up arms and repelled the coup in key locations, including Madrid and Barcelona. It was in this moment that the nature of the struggle for Spain transitioned from military *pronunciamento* (proclamation) to civil war, which contributed much to the military and diplomatic patterning in Europe in the late 1930s. The broad historical consensus that the Spanish Civil War was won and lost in the corridors of the European powers obscures the actual fighting of the war between the two Spanish armies.

The consequence of the rebellion was that the Republic, while retaining control of the war ministry, lost a significant number of professional officers. Republican military forces were made of militias with little training. Indeed, the revolutionary chaos which ensued in the aftermath of the coup meant that the Republic only began to exert some control in October 1936. The Nationalist force, on the other hand, was led by well-trained men with field experience, largely gained from fighting in Morocco. But Republican problems were not simply related to military experience and training. The ideological divisions on the left played out in the military organization of Republic forces and prevented the unity of purpose which was necessary to face the skilled soldiers of the Nationalists.

The main conflict was between the Anarchist concept of a revolutionary army and the Communist preference for a more traditional adherence to military organization and discipline. The Nationalist armies had no such problems given the rebellion was first and foremost a military rebellion which aimed to impose a military order rather than a political one. Leadership was another telling difference between the forces. While Nationalists might not have been ideologically united, Franco established himself quickly as a leader and the figurehead of the nationalist cause behind whom all groups could support. Republican command had some capable figures but none that provided the kind of authority and stability that Franco was able to project. This issue of leadership and competency impact on the nature of the military encounters. Republican forces were able to devise bold and imaginative plans, like the diversionary offensive on the Aragon front in June 1937 or the Battle of Teruel in the winter of 1937–1938, an attempt to deflect Franco's focus on Madrid. However, in all cases, the lack of trained soldiers and appropriate materiel meant any Republican gains were short-lived and they were pushed back. The Nationalists' resistance and counter-offensives, combined with their use of aircraft and artillery, made even the smallest advance extremely costly for Republican forces. The outcome at Teruel made clear that an outright military victory over the Nationalist forces was unlikely. A sustained military resistance was the best the Republic could hope for to create the space for the diplomatic effort to compel the Western powers to intervene.

Both sides attempted to engage support from the international community. Despite the complexity of the origins of the war, both broadcast their aims in vividly simplistic and sensational terms. The Republicans cast themselves as heroically fighting fascism to defend democracy. For the Nationalists, they exclaimed that they were engaged in a holy crusade, resisting the Bolsheviks, who were bent on nothing less than the destruction of the Catholic Church. Consequently, many outside Spain began to consider the war as consequential for the whole world. The ways in which the outside world did or did not take part reveals the relationship between the Spanish Civil War and World War II.

International Interventions and Non-Intervention

All the international actors shared one common feature: each nation's policy in Spain was driven by concerns and ambitions that had nothing to do with Spain at all. In this sense, the engagement of other nations followed broadly the political patterns that framed the Ethiopian crisis. The actions of the British and French were intended to avoid antagonizing Germany and so avoid a general war. Italy took the opportunity to establish a new ally and further its leader's ambitions to become a great European power. Germany used the conflict to test international resolve in its quest for greater dominance in Europe as Hitler pursued German rearmament and resurgence. Italy and Germany were very directly involved in the civil war. Since 1936, Mussolini had moved closer to Hitler. Annoyed with the League and the sanctions it imposed on Italy in response to the invasion of Ethiopia, Mussolini had looked to create a new alliance. In October 1936, the two leaders agreed to work together on matters of common interest. Mussolini called this arrangement the Rome–Berlin Axis. British, French, and American involvement was, in tangible terms, non-existent as they adhered to a policy of non-intervention in the conflict. However, their refusal to intervene on behalf of the democratically elected Republic was, as well as a violation of international norms, in reality an intervention in support of Franco's Nationalists.

The Republican government in Madrid expected assistance from the European democracies and looked to France for support in the first instance, as both countries were governed by a left-leaning Popular Front administration. Upon the first approach, the French Prime Minister, Léon Blum, was prepared to aid the Republic. He initially agreed to send aircraft and artillery to reinforce the Republic. However, the British, led by Prime Minister Stanley Baldwin and Foreign Secretary Anthony Eden, applied pressure to dissuade such intervention. This pressure stemmed from a number of connected anxieties about the possible implications of the Spanish Civil War. For one thing, British politicians were uncomfortable with the notion that, given the Republics' reforming agenda was predicated upon concepts of redistribution and collectivization, they may find themselves supporting a revolutionary or even Bolshevist government. Connectedly, they were also concerned about the future of British economic interests in Spain under this leftist administration. And, once more, they were responding in fear that any intervention could escalate into another general European war.

The British government made clear to the French that should they aid the Spanish Republic, and should that aid lead to hostilities with Germany, Britain would not join the fighting in their support. This, in combination with concerns voiced by members of his own cabinet, changed Blum's mind. He now took the lead, with Baldwin's support, in calling for all European nations to remain aloof from the war in Spain. Out of this emerged the disgraceful, cowardly, and damaging policy of non-intervention. Non-intervention was the diplomatic initiative proposed by the British and French governments which they hoped would prevent both a proxy war in Spain and its escalation into a pan-European conflict. On August 3, 1936, the French presented their plan. The Non-Intervention Agreement was accepted in principle immediately by Britain. By the end of August, Britain, France, Italy, Germany, Portugal, and the USSR had signed up to the agreement, which renounced the traffic of all war material. The Non-Intervention Committee met for the first time in London on September 9, 1936. The committee's function was to uphold the terms of the agreement and to oversee the prohibition of men and materiel reaching the warring parties in Spain. Eventually, twenty-seven countries signed into the agreement.

The stated function of the committee may have been to prevent the supply of men and materiel to the antagonists in the civil war. The reality was, however, different. The committee was little more than diplomatic theater. The European nations who joined the committee agreed not to supply arms to either the Republicans or the Nationalists. However, it was an open secret that not all signatories were complying with these terms. Those sitting at the committee table had knowledge of the support given by the Germans and Italians to Franco's Nationalists. This did not prevent Britain and France from adhering rigidly to the concept of non-intervention anyway. Even when Italian submarines attacked British ships heading for Republican ports, Britain turned a blind eye. In this way, non-intervention, which was intended to guarantee neutrality, was in actual fact an endorsement of Franco and the Nationalist cause and did the most to doom the Republic to defeat. As Paul Preston says, by adhering to this policy of non-intervention, the Western powers "passed a death sentence on the Spanish Republic."[12]

From the very beginning of the war, both the Nationalists and the Republicans recognized the vital need for external support. Without the military aid received by the Nationalists from Germany and Italy in July 1936, the coup would have failed before it began. Aircraft supplied by the fascist powers were crucial in the early moments of the rebellion, essential for the transportation of Franco's troops from North Africa to mainland Spain. The transport of the Army of Africa represents the first airlift in military history. Hitler observed the pivotal role played by the aircraft sent by Germany and Italy, saying that, "Franco ought to erect a monument to the glory of the Junkers 52. It is this aircraft that the Spanish revolution has to thank for its victory."[13]

Between 1936 and 1938, the Axis powers delivered substantial amounts of military materiel, aircraft, weapons, ammunition, and troops and advisors into the Nationalist Zone. Italy provided seventy-three thousand troops, 759 aircraft, 157 tanks, eighteen hundred big guns, and 320 million rounds of ammunition. Germany sent some sixteen thousand troops, six hundred aircraft and half-a-billion marks worth of war materials. Perhaps the most infamous German contribution to the Nationalist efforts was the Condor Legion of the *Luftwaffe*. A portent of the conflagration to come between 1939 and 1945 can be seen in the devastation wrought upon the small town of Guernica in

Northern Spain on April 26, 1937. The bombing of the culturally important Basque town was sustained for over three hours. German bombers, supported by German and Italian fighter aircraft, dropped one hundred thousand pounds of explosive and incendiary ordinance on the town. Whilst the Nationalists and the Germans would later claim they were attacking strategically legitimate sites, it is clear that civilians were deliberately targeted in the operation. For many observers and commentators, this attack was an experiment. It was a test of aerial warfare and strategy, often cited as the origin of the tactic of bombing civilian populations in an attempt to demoralize the enemy. However, Guernica was not the first instance of this tactic, as Mussolini had deployed bombers in the war in Ethiopia. Also, twenty days before the attack on Guernica, the Condor Legion had bombed the town of Durango, a town without any military value, resulting in the death of some 250 civilians. Nevertheless, it was the destruction of Guernica which captured the world's attention. Guernica was one of the first sites ever to be destroyed by a bombing attack carried out without regard for those traditionally considered non-combatants.

The Republicans had greater difficulty securing international support and aid, an outrage given its legitimacy as a national government. The French, British, and Americans had persuaded themselves of the necessity of non-intervention and its fallacious neutrality. Consequently, the majority of the aid supplied to the Republic came from the Soviet Union. Soviet aid consisted of around one thousand aircraft, nine hundred tanks, fifteen hundred guns, and large supplies of ammunition. In addition, there were about one thousand troops, most of whom acted as advisors and technicians. However, this aid came at an enormous cost. The Soviets expected the Republic to pay for these military supplies in gold. On the outbreak of the war, Spain had the world's fourth-largest reserves of gold. During the war, approximately $500 million, or two-thirds of Spain's gold reserves, were shipped to the Soviet Union.

Perhaps most evocative, when considering international involvement in the Spanish Civil War, are the volunteers recruited by the communist parties of foreign countries who travelled to Spain to fight in the International Brigades. Forty thousand young volunteers fought in the Brigades and more than one-third were killed in action. This contribution vividly illustrates the international implications of the war. The men who volunteered were fighting in defense of the Republic and their testimony reveals that their participation was underpinned by class loyalties and by the fear that their own nations might be similarly embattled if a stand was not taken against the Nationalists in Spain. In this way, their involvement was motivated by defending the Spanish Republic and supporting with their blood the global struggle against the spread of fascism.

This awareness that the civil war and its implications had resonance beyond Spain's borders is in many ways the conflict's most impactful contribution to the coming of World War II. The conflict in Spain affected the way in which many Europeans considered war and its role in the contemporary world. The idea abroad in the 1920s and early 1930s, that war was a thing of the past, and that World War I had been the war to end all wars, emphatically shifted during the civil war. Many, even those who considered themselves pacifist, realizing what was at stake, came to believe that the only viable response was to take up arms against the threat posed by fascism. The ideological battle at the core of the Spanish Civil War, the clash between fascism and democracy, how that was broadcast to the world, and the demand it made to take a stand confirmed, in the final analysis, the principle that war was once again necessary.

Ethiopia, Spain, and World War II

Ethiopia and Spain not only set the stage that led to World War II, but they played interesting roles in the war itself. Ethiopia contributed greatly to the action on the East African Front with widespread resistance to the Italians, where Allied forces engaged in a series of battles with Axis troops, primarily Italian, between June 1940 and November 1941. This led directly to the liberation of Ethiopia from Italian occupation in 1941. Thus, Ethiopia was the first country in World War II to be freed from Axis occupation. The Spanish contribution is perhaps less straightforward.

Once the war began, Spain remained aloof from Europe. The cost of three years of devastating civil conflict had left Spain in no condition to enter into another war. Spanish society was divided, and the economy was in ruins. The Nationalist victory in April 1939 had guaranteed General Franco's accession to the Head of State, in the form of a dictatorship, and a primary focus for Franco during the early phase of World War II was the consolidation of his position. This task he pursued with characteristic ruthlessness and violence.

At the start of the war, Franco did have a natural inclination to support the other fascist dictatorships. This inclination ran along ideological lines but was also an acknowledgement of his indebtedness to Germany and Italy for the aid he had received and its enormous contribution to the Nationalist victory. However, he managed his relationships with Italy and Germany very carefully.

Much of Franco's, and consequently Spain's, behaviour during World War II has been obscured by certain myths that emerged after 1945. By the war's end, it was clear that any association Franco had had with the Axis was a potentially serious diplomatic problem. To address this, myths about the nature and success of Franco's deliberate neutrality were circulated. In this myth, the facts of the relationship between Franco, Hitler, and Mussolini were rewritten, or at least obscured. In the revised version of events, Franco had singlehandedly resisted Hitler to guarantee Spanish neutrality. The fact is that, while Franco did not declare war, Spain was hardly neutral, especially in the early part of the war. United Nations investigations conducted in the aftermath of World War II found evidence that Spain had allowed German aircraft engaged in attacks on Allied shipping to operate from Spanish airfields. Spanish ports were covertly used to refuel and repair German naval vessels. More generally, the state-controlled media in Spain persistently broadcast pro-Axis propaganda. Spain's neutrality was not a consequence of ideological differences with Germany.

The reasons why Spain remained neutral, despite such intimations of support, are to be found elsewhere. The implications of timing for Spain's neutral stance are important. In the early stages of World War II, it was assumed to be an inevitability by the Axis and Franco alike that Spain would enter into the war on the side of fascism. The roadblock to Spanish entry came in the terms Franco stipulated, terms which were focused on expanding the Spanish empire. At the meeting between Hitler and Franco at Hendaye on October 23, 1940, Franco stated his demand for North Africa, which Hitler dismissed because he did not wish to alienate either Vichy, France or Mussolini, both of which had claims on the territory. It is likely that had Hitler accepted the demand, Franco would have joined the Axis. By the time Hitler was ready to welcome Spanish intervention and so accede to Franco's imperial terms, Franco's attention had shifted. He was now more concerned with facilitating the flow of American aid into Spain and this necessitated the maintenance of Spanish neutrality. It was this then—the combination of economic and military weakness—that explains Spanish neutrality, rather than Franco's diplomatic will. It is also worth observing that, even if Franco was tempted, early on, to join Hitler, his experience as a soldier and officer meant he was fully cognizant of his country's shortcomings as a military force. Other circumstances help explain Franco's reticence.

The German failure to defeat Britain in the summer of 1940 was a significant concern for Franco. The Italian setbacks against the British in East Africa in the autumn of that year served to further increase his wariness of joining Hitler's war against the Allies. The German invasion of Russia did reinvigorate Franco's inclination toward the Axis, in large part because of the ideological echoes with his own civil war: the authoritarian right fighting the revolutionary left. Franco sent twenty thousand Spanish volunteers in the guise of the Blue Division to fight with the Germans on the Eastern Front. The instructions under which they were sent, though, give another clear illustration of Franco's carefulness. The volunteers who traveled did so in the understanding that they would only fight against the Bolsheviks and not engage the Western allies or the populations of any Western occupied countries. In this way, Franco was able to lend support to Germany as a measure of repayment for the assistance he had received while still maintaining the necessary peace with the Allies. Mussolini's downfall in July 1943 compelled Franco to move much more publicly toward neutrality and definitively away from the Axis. Once it looked certain that Germany would lose the war, Franco quickly moved to expunge all overt elements of fascism from his regime.

After 1945, it was made illegal to make any comparison between Franco's leadership and Hitler's Germany or Mussolini's Italy. Franco's ruling party was renamed from the *Falange* to the *Movemiento Nacionale*, to remove the fascist connotations of the former, and the fascist salute was outlawed. In such reconfigurations it becomes apparent that Franco wanted to legitimize his regime by distancing it and himself from the taint of the Axis. The success of this exercise can be best illustrated by Franco's longevity. He would remain the Spanish head of state until his death on November 20, 1975.

The wars in Ethiopia and Spain are complex insofar as they represent both the culmination of longstanding issues and the direct consequences of contemporary political, cultural, and social forces. Although both wars were limited and contained, their implications were significant and rippled out into the wider sweep of European history as it headed toward war. Only in this context of comparison to the conflagration that would consume Europe in September 1939 can these immensely significant and resonant conflicts be categorized as small wars.

Notes

1. Bahru Zewde, *A History of Modern Ethiopia 1855–1991* (Oxford: James Currey, 2001), 152.
2. There are many references to the use of weapons of mass destruction in Morocco, Libya, and Ethiopia. The best single documented one is Sebastian Balfour, *Deadly Embrace: Morocco and the Road to the Spanish Civil War* (New York: Oxford University Press, 2002), chapter 5, and especially p. 128.
3. Emperor Haile Sellassie I, *The Autobiography of Emperor Haile Sellassie I: 'My Life and Ethiopia's Progress' 1892–1937* (Oxford University Press, 1976), 201.
4. Asfa-Wossan Asserate, *King of Kings: The Triumph and Tragedy of Emperor Haile Selassie I of Ethiopia* (London: Haus Publishing, 2015), 119.
5. Sellassie I, *The Autobiography of Emperor Haile Sellassie I*, 300.
6. See Zewde, *A History of Modern Ethiopa*, 167, 171.
7. This and the following quotes are in Haile Selassie's speech from Joel Larus, ed., *From Collective to Preventative Diplomacy: Readings in International Organization and the Maintenance of Peace* (New York: Wiley 1965), 136–143.
8. Ibid.
9. Ibid.
10. Ibid.
11. George Scott, *The Rise and Fall of the League of Nations* (London: Hutchinson, 1973), 239–240.
12. Paul Preston, *A Concise History of the Spanish Civil War* (London: Fontana Press, 1996), 115.
13. Hugh Thomas, *The Spanish Civil War* (London: Penguin, 2003), 357.

Bibliography

Alpert, Michael. *The Republican Army in the Spanish Civil War, 1936–1939*. Cambridge: Cambridge University Press, 2013.

Asserate, Asfa-Wossan. *King of Kings: The Triumph and Tragedy of Emperor Haile Selassie I of Ethiopia*. London: Haus Publishing, 2015.

Baer, George W. "Sanctions and Security: The League of Nations and the Italo-Ethiopian War, 1935–1936." *International Organization* 27, no. 2 (Spring 1973): 165–179.

Balfour, Sebastian. *Deadly Embrace: Morocco and the Road to the Spanish Civil War*. Oxford: Oxford University Press, 2002.

Barker, A. J. *The Civilizing Mission: A History of the Italo-Ethiopian War of 1935–1936*. New York: Dial Press, 1968.

Baxell, Richard. "Myths of the International Brigades." *Bulletin of Spanish Studies* 90, no. 1–2 (January–February 2014): 11–25.

Brenan, Gerald. *The Spanish Labyrinth: An Account of the Social and Political Background of the Spanish Civil War* (1943). Repr. Cambridge: Cambridge University Press, 2014.

Burns, Emile. *Abyssinia and Italy*. London: Victor Gollancz, 1935.
Coffey, Thomas M. *Lion by the Tail: The Story of the Italian-Ethiopian War*. New York: Viking Press, 1974.
Esdaile, Charles J. *The Spanish Civil War: A Military History*. New York: Routledge, 2019.
Garratt, Geoffrey T. *Mussolini's Roman Empire*. London: Penguin, 1938.
Graham, Helen. *War and its Shadow: Spain's Civil War in Europe's Long Twentieth Century*. Eastbourne: Sussex Academic Press, 2012.
Hurcombe, Martin. *France and the Spanish Civil War: Cultural Representations of the War Next Door, 1936-1945*. Surrey: Ashgate, 2011.
Iadarola, Antoinette. "Ethiopia's Admission into the League of Nations: An Assessment of Motives." *The International Journal of African Historical Studies* 8, no. 4 (1975): 601–622.
Keene, Judith. *Fighting for Franco: International Volunteers in Nationalist Spain During the Spanish Civil War, 1936-1939*. London: Hambledon Continuum, 2007.
Larus, Joel, ed., *From Collective to Preventative Diplomacy: Readings in International Organization and the Maintenance of Peace*. New York: Wiley, 1965.
Kowalsky, Daniel. "Operation X: Soviet Russia and the Spanish Civil War." *Bulletin of Spanish Studies* XCI, no. 1–2 (January–February 2014): 159–179.
Matthews, James. *Reluctant Warriors: Republican Popular Army and Nationalist Army Conscripts in the Spanish Civil War, 1936–1939*. Oxford: Oxford University Press, 2012.
McDonaugh, Frank. *The Origins of the Second World War: An International Perspective*. London: Continuum, 2011.
Nicolle, David. *The Italian Invasion of Abyssinia, 1935–36*. London: Osprey, 1997.
Pike, David Wingeate. "The View from Next Door: The French Third Republic." *Bulletin of Spanish Studies* XCI, no. 1–2 (January–February 2014): 227–239.
Preston, Paul. *A Concise History of the Spanish Civil War*. London: Fontana Press, 1996.
Preston, Paul. *Franco: A Biography*. London: Fontana Press, 1995.
Preston, Paul. *The Spanish Holocaust: Inquisition and Extermination in Twentieth Century Spain*. London: HarperPress, 2012.
Sbacchi, Alberto. *Ethiopia under Mussolini: Fascism and the Colonial Experience*. London: Zed Books, 1985.
Scott, George. *The Rise and Fall of the League of Nations*. London: Hutchinson, 1973.
Sellassie I, Haile. *The Autobiography of Emperor Haile Sellassie I: 'My Life and Ethiopia's Progress' 1892-1937*. Oxford: Oxford University Press, 1976.
Stone, Glyn Arthur. "Neville Chamberlain and the Spanish Civil War, 1936–9." *The International History Review* 35, no. 2 (2013): 377–395.
Thomas, Hugh. *The Spanish Civil War*. London: Penguin, 2003.
Tierney, Dominic. *FDR and the Spanish Civil War: Neutrality and Commitment in the Struggle that Divided America*. Durham, NC: Duke University Press, 2007.
Waley, Daniel. *British Public Opinion and the Abyssinian War 1935-36*. London: Maurice Temple Smith, 1975.
Zewde, Bahru. *A History of Modern Ethiopia 1855-1991*. Oxford: James Currey, 2001.

CHAPTER 4

THE SINO–JAPANESE WAR

GAO BEI

On the evening of September 18, 1931, an explosion on a small section of the South Manchurian Railway track outside the city of Mukden triggered one of the most important regional, and later international, conflicts of the twentieth century. The damaged portion of the track was only three feet in length, but the Kwantung army's leaders claimed that Chinese soldiers were responsible for the explosion, and they retaliated immediately. The Kwantung army had been stationed in Manchuria since 1906, following the end of the Russo–Japanese War, to defend Japan's Kwantung Leased Territory and to protect the railway system there. The day after the explosion the Japanese Consul General in Mukden, Hayashi Hisajiro, received a report from officials of the South Manchurian Railway Company. The company, which had been established by the Japanese government in 1906 to manage the railway system in Manchuria, was sending workers to repair the railway tracks, and the officials informed the consul general that the military was standing by near the scene. Nevertheless, Hayashi wrote in a telegram to Foreign Minister Shidehara Kijūrō that, "it appears to me that this incident was indeed planned by the [Kwantung] army."[1] Japanese forces attacked and captured Mukden on the morning of September 19, and over the next three days the Kwantung army took the other four major cities in Manchuria.

The Manchurian/Mukden Incident set the stage for Japan's subsequent invasion of China. The initial indifference of the Western powers and the Soviet Union, and their later appeasement of Tokyo, encouraged Japan's military expansion into China. The Sino–Japanese conflict steadily intensified and escalated into a full-scale war after the Marco Polo Bridge Incident of 1937. After the hostilities in China became deadlocked, Japan marched into Southeast Asia in the summer of 1940 in pursuit of natural resources that would permit it to continue the war and crush the Chinese resistance. But Japan's southward thrust increased tensions with the Western powers and made confrontation and war with the United States inevitable. Japan's December 1941 attack on Pearl Harbor cemented an alliance between China and Western democracies that guaranteed Japan's military destruction. Nevertheless, Pearl Harbor and the Pacific War could have been prevented had the great powers acted decisively after Mukden. Their diplomacy, which was tantamount to the appeasement of Tokyo, amounted to a Munich moment in East Asia.

In his 1987 work *The Origins of the Second War in Asia and the Pacific*, Akira Iriye raised a critical question: "Why did the Western powers, which stood by while Japanese forces overran Manchuria in 1931, end up by coming to China's assistance ten years later even at the risk of war with Japan?"[2] This question suggests that the Western powers were uninvolved in the Sino–Japanese confrontation before late 1941. In fact, the world's great powers became engaged in the East Asian conflict, in one manner or another, soon after the Manchurian Incident. Their complex diplomacies with Germany, the Soviet Union, and the United States were at the heart of the two combatants' strategic calculations and directly and indirectly shaped the course of the war between China and Japan. At the same time, the great powers assisted and, from time to time, sacrificed the interests of the belligerents as they pursued their own strategic interests in East Asia. Nevertheless, China and Japan proved that they were not simply pawns of the more powerful nations. The two countries articulated their own national, regional, and international priorities, and they attempted to harness the political influence and military strength of powerful patrons in support of their war efforts. Their national, regional, and international agendas connected countries across the globe to the Sino–Japanese War. Therefore, even before the attack on Pearl Harbor, the Sino–Japanese War had already been thoroughly internationalized. It was fought as a world war and began in Manchuria in 1931.

The Manchurian Incident was, in fact, plotted and executed under the leadership of Kwantung army staff officers, Colonel Itagaki Seishirō and his subordinate, Lt. Colonel Ishiwara Kanji. Previously, in the summer of 1928, Kwantung army officers also assassinated the Manchurian warlord Zhang Zuolin, even though the Tokyo government professed its willingness to cooperate and negotiate with him. Army leaders in Japan always considered the Soviet Union a potential enemy and many believed that it was vital to control Manchuria as they prepared for a possible conflict with the Russians. In addition, the Great Depression of 1929 had caused the Japanese economy to deteriorate badly. Controlling Manchuria, which was rich in natural resources and uncultivated land, became even more important for Japan, and for the army in particular, who wished to establish a self-contained economy there, and if possible, help supply the homeland. As Ishiwara Kanji later contended to the League of Nations' Commission of Inquiry following the Manchurian Incident, "If we are unable to utilize the resources of Manchuria and Mongolia, it will be impossible for us to assure the life of the Japanese people today."[3] The government's failure to take a hardline policy toward north China deeply disturbed the Army, its junior officers in particular, who favored subjugating the region by force.[4]

China in the late 1920s was troubled not only by the burgeoning struggle between the Communists and the Nationalists, but by warlords who controlled various parts of the country. The Japanese government's China policy at the time was divided between those who supported an attempted invasion and those who believed Japan's most important priority should be to protect its current rights and interests in the country. In early July 1927, Prime Minister Tanaka Giichi assembled officials from the cabinet, Foreign Ministry, the military, and diplomatic corps to China and convened the Far East

Conference to decide Japan's China policy. On July 7, the last day of the conference, the prime minister issued orders to his ministries concerning the unstable political situation in the country. The Prime Minister believed that Japan should not take sides with any political force in China. "The basis of Japan's policy toward China," he wrote, "should be to ensure peace in the Far East and to achieve the co-prosperity of Japan and China. [However,] . . . when it comes to measures that carry out this policy, Japan's strategy towards Interior China and Manchuria and Mongolia, of course, should be different."[5] The prime minister argued that the Japanese government should support Chinese leaders who were willing to acknowledge and "respect" Japan's special rights there and who would take measures to preserve political stability in Manchuria and Mongolia.[6]

The field officers in Manchuria immediately challenged Tanaka's directive. The assassination of Zhang Zuolin and the government's failure to punish the conspirators, as Navy Minister Okada Keisuke observed, demonstrated that the Kwantung army "was more powerful than the Japanese government in Tokyo."[7] In early 1931, the military and right-wing extremists in Japan continued to promote the idea that Manchuria and Mongolia were "Japan's lifeline, militarily and economically," and argued that it was necessary to impose a military solution to the north China issue.[8] Therefore, the Manchurian Incident not only served the Kwantung army's goal of subjugating Manchuria, it also consolidated the military's role in determining Japan's foreign policy.

At the time Japan seized Mukden, Chiang Kai-shek was returning to Nanjing from directing the Nationalist Army's third campaign of "encirclement and extermination" against the communists. Zhang Xueliang, son of the assassinated warlord, had already ordered his troops to withdraw from Manchuria. Ultimately, Chiang did not send troops to support north China, nor did he order Zhang to resist.[9] To Chiang, eliminating the communists remained his most pressing task. Instead of contesting the Japanese move militarily, he opted to bring the issue to the League of Nations.

However, as Warren Cohen observes, the fall of 1931 turned out to be an unfortunate time for China to try to obtain any aid from the Western democracies, which were reeling under the impact of the Great Depression.[10] In the United States, President Herbert Hoover's administration was focusing its energies entirely on the economic crisis that had overtaken the country, even though Secretary of State Henry Stimson was concerned that Japan's actions in Manchuria would challenge the principle of the Open Door in China.[11] At this point, the Western powers and the League of Nations were not ready or able to confront Tokyo. Neither the American nor British governments expressed the will to level political or economic sanctions against Japan.[12] Meanwhile, Josef Stalin's Soviet government, which was busy implementing the First Five-Year Plan, opted not to intervene.[13]

When Franklin Roosevelt became the U.S. president in March 1933, he largely adopted his predecessor's policy regarding the Sino–Japanese conflict in Manchuria. Economic recovery at home was his overriding concern, and he had no desire to become embroiled in East Asia's disputes. Over the next four years, he was content to ignore Japanese aggression as long as the Tokyo government respected America's rights and interests in Manchuria and did not seek to challenge the principle of the Open Door in China.

Roosevelt declined to confront Japan directly.[14] Another important reason behind the United States' failure to intervene in the Manchurian crisis was that America's most influential China experts, even those known for their pro-Chinese and anti-Japanese views, concluded that while Manchuria was a "vital interest" to Japan, American interests in the area were "insignificant." At this point, the United States lacked the political will and the military capability to challenge Japanese designs. Therefore, these officials contended that it was in the United States' best interest not to confront Japan and to tolerate a Japanese-dominated Manchuria.[15]

This American policy of appeasement only encouraged Japanese ambitions in China. In the absence of effective international economic or military sanctions, Japan appeared to be unstoppable. When a League of Nations commission chaired by Lord Lytton condemned it in 1933 as the aggressor during the Manchurian Incident, Japan walked out of the organization. Nevertheless, the United States did not alter its policy toward Japan's aggression in China. Even after the Marco Polo Bridge Incident in 1937, the Roosevelt administration remained unmoved to act.[16]

The Manchurian Incident proved to be the Munich moment of the Sino–Japanese War. Just as the war in Europe might have been averted had the Western democracies confronted Germany at the Munich conference, the Pacific War might also have been prevented had the West, led by the United States, not appeased Japan in Manchuria. Instead, the Western powers apparently ignored or failed to understand the implications of Mukden.

The conflict that began in Manchuria eventually escalated six years later into full-scale war between China and Japan. However, in 1931, it seems that neither the Kwantung army nor the Army Chief of Staff in Tokyo anticipated that China's struggle against Japan would be so determined. Kwantung army officers and military leaders in Tokyo predicted that Japan's conquest of Manchuria and the March 1932 establishment of Manchukuo would provoke an anti-Japanese backlash among the Chinese people, but they didn't anticipate the resilience of the Chinese resistance. Ultimately, the invasion aroused Chinese nationalism and mobilized the people against Japan. Nevertheless, the Japanese military leaders were initially confident that they would be able to put down Chinese resistance in relatively short order. In later years, the Japanese came to rely more heavily on large-scale military operations to crush Chinese resistance. Therefore, the Manchurian incident was crucial in leading Japan "onto the road of militarism, conquest, and ultimately, destruction."[17]

The Manchurian Incident, known as the Nine-Eighteen Incident in China, provoked unprecedented protests against Japan's aggression and also against the Nationalist government's non-resistance policy. On September 24, thirty-five thousand barge workers and tens of thousands of students in Shanghai spearheaded the first anti-Japanese demonstration. In the following days, students in all major Chinese cities launched strikes, protests, and anti-Japanese boycotts. The so-called "Resisting Japan and Saving the Country" movement soon spread throughout the country. Students from all over China poured into the capital of Nanjing demanding the government "stop the civil war [against the communists] and unite [with the communists] against Japan."

Nevertheless, Chiang Kai-shek believed that China should avoid full-scale hostilities with Japan while the country was divided by civil war and warlordism and was therefore unable to prepare fully for such a conflict.[18] He decided to appease Japan for the time being, a policy that lasted until his kidnapping by Zhang Xueliang in late 1936.

In 1936, in Japan and China, two events initiated by young army officers turned the tide of the Sino–Japanese conflict. On February 26, radical young officers in Japan staged a rebellion against the civilian government and briefly seized power in Tokyo. Although the coup was put down quickly, the military successfully increased its political clout in the government. After the February 26 Incident, Hirota Koki became Japan's prime minister. Under pressure from the armed forces, the Hirota cabinet met the military's demand to restore the policy by which only active-duty army generals and navy admirals were permitted to serve as army and navy ministers. This change provided the military, the army in particular, an institutional platform for intervening in Japan's politics.[19]

Under the Hirota government, the military attempted to establish a kind of "Second Manchukuo" in the five provinces of northeastern China (Hebei, Chahar, Suiyuan, Shanxi, and Shangdong), which they argued should be separated from China and placed under Japan's control. Japan's intensified aggression in China's northeast sparked further resistance from the Chinese people and aroused even more nationalist feeling against the Japanese.

Later that year, on December 12, the so-called Xian Incident altered not only the course of Sino–Japanese hostilities, but also the history of modern China. On that morning, two of Chiang Kai-shek's young generals, Zhang Xueliang and Yang Hucheng, kidnapped him. They demanded that he stop attacking the Communists and ally with them against the invading Japanese. The kidnapping of the Chinese head of state shocked the world. After communist intermediaries intervened, Chiang Kai-shek was eventually released and agreed to the generals' conditions. The civil war between the Communists and the Nationalists was ended temporarily, and the two groups cooperated to launch a United Front again Japan.

Meanwhile, the conflict in East Asia failed to attract the attention of the Western democracies. As historian Jay Taylor notes, Japan's subjugation of China did not seem to concern most Americans or their government.[20] The U.S. ambassador to the Nanjing government, Nelson T. Johnson, even suggested that "'efficient' Japanese management of Manchuria and North China . . . might open up important economic opportunities for American business."[21] It was clear that at this point, China's struggle against Japan did not impinge directly on the political and military interests of the West, the United States' in particular. Their economic interests in East Asia, especially in China, remained the only concern of most Western powers.

Yet another event in late 1936, the conclusion on November 25 of the German–Japanese Anti-Comintern Pact, had a profound impact on the course of the Sino–Japanese conflict. Nevertheless, before Japan and Germany officially established a military alliance during World War II, China was Germany's strategic partner in East Asia. China and Germany restored diplomatic relations that had been severed since the beginning of World War I, in 1921. Sun Yat-sen, the founding father of the Chinese

Nationalist Party and the Republic of China, was determined to use German experience to help the Chinese in building up their country militarily and economically. China, on the other hand, with its enormous market and abundance of strategic raw materials, provided an ideal partner for Germany's postwar economic recovery.[22]

Japanese historian Tajima Nobuo points out that in the early 1920s, Sun Yat-sen and Chiang Kai-shek proposed to the Soviets an alliance of China, Germany, and the Soviet Union against the capitalist countries of Britain, the United States, France, and Japan. This became a basic tenet of Nationalist China's foreign policy in the mid-1920s. Tajima further argues that this triple alliance was not simply the idea of Sun Yat-sen and Chiang Kai-shek, it was also embraced by officials in Germany and the Soviet Union. Notably, in the 1920s, the German Foreign Office was divided into a Pro-Western Faction, led by Foreign Minister Gustav Stresemann, and a Pro-Eastern Faction, controlled by Ago von Maltzan, assistant state secretary and head of the Eastern Department. Maltzan's faction contended that to confront Britain and the United States, Germany must pursue a new relationship with the Soviet Union. Further, within this group there were also diplomats who wanted to expand this policy to include East Asia and advocated a Sino–German–Soviet alliance.[23]

Beginning in 1921, the Nationalists invited German advisers to assist in China's military modernization. After the Nationalists established the Nanjing government in 1928, the Chinese and Germans established closer economic and military ties. The period between the late 1920s and the late 1930s marked a decade of German influence in China[24] and the early years of the Sino–Japanese War, especially, were a honeymoon era in their relations.

Sino–German cooperation, especially in military matters, reached its peak in the middle of the decade. In these years, Werner von Blomberg, German Minister of Defense, and his colleague Walther von Reichenau, chief of the Ministerial Office, proposed either a Eurasia bloc, including China, opposing Britain and the United States, or a Sino–German military alliance.[25] The German military missions played a key role in modernizing and equipping the Nationalist army. By the middle of the 1930s, Chiang Kai-shek's government became the most important foreign purchaser of German weapons. In 1936, 57.5 percent of German exports went to China.[26] The Nationalist government established two military academies in the capital city of Nanjing in which large numbers of German advisers acted as instructors. Some German advisers even operated with Chinese forces in the field. By the Battle of Shanghai in the summer of 1937, eighty thousand of Chiang Kai-shek's three hundred thousand troops had been trained and equipped by the Germans. They comprised the "spearhead" of Chiang's Central Army.[27]

After its defeat during World War I, Germany was stripped of its dependencies and special political rights in East Asia, but it continued to pursue its economic interests in the region. Absent political and strategic sources of friction, Germany and China were able to treat each other as equals. Germany remained neutral when Sino–Japanese hostilities commenced, but Berlin changed its China policy after the conclusion of the German–Japanese Anti-Comintern Pact in 1936 and following Japan's all-out invasion of China in 1937.

On July 7, 1937, while a Japanese unit was conducting field exercises at night near the Marco Polo Bridge, several artillery shells flew over their heads. The structure, once described by the Italian adventurer Marco Polo as "the most beautiful bridge in the world," is located ten miles southwest of Beijing. Under the Boxer Protocol of 1901, Japan, like many Western powers, was permitted to station troops outside Beijing. Following the incident, the Japanese commander immediately canceled the exercise and called the roll. When one soldier was unaccounted for, the commander contacted his battalion, which dispatched forces to the scene. The next morning, the Japanese attacked Chinese troops stationed in the city of Wanping and its surrounding areas. The Marco Polo Bridge Incident triggered a full-scale war between China and Japan.

Chiang Kai-shek immediately appealed to the League of Nations and the major Western powers for military intervention on China's behalf, but the United States and the European powers responded merely by insisting that the Japanese exercise restraint. In accordance with their interpretation of American neutrality laws, the U.S. government decided not to ship previously purchased military equipment to China, but it continued to allow limited sales of strategic materials to Japan.[28]

On the morning of July 28, Japanese troops launched an all-out attack against the Chinese army in Beijing and the Tianjin area, and by the next day they occupied nearly the entire region southwest of Beijing. The Japanese government referred to the military actions beginning on July 7 as the "North China Incident." The Chinese also used the expression "Lugouqiao (Marco Polo Bridge) Incident."

Uncertainty remains concerning the origin of the Marco Polo Bridge Incident, and various theories insist that either the Japanese or the Chinese communists planned it. Japanese historian Nagai Kazu contends that the Japanese army in the summer of 1937 did not rush into war at the Marco Polo Bridge without any preparation in advance. He points out that at the time the Japanese army was about to use military means to separate north China from the rest of the country. As early as 1933 the Japanese military had been conducting strategic research based on the premise that war with the Nationalist government over the control of north China was likely and that Japan would control the area.[29]

On September 23, 1936, Tashiro Kanichirō, commander in chief of the Japanese China Garrison Army, who also held the same position during the Marco Polo Bridge Incident, submitted to Terauchi Hisaichi, Minister of the Army, a "1936 Occupation Plan toward Occupied Territories in North China."[30] This document assumed that the Japanese army would occupy strategically important areas in north China, and it detailed the policies Japan should put in place during its conquest.[31]

According to the 1936 occupation plan, the basic goals of the occupation were to overthrow the existing [Chinese] government if it refused to cooperate with and obey the military and then create a pro-Japanese regime, and to obtain strategic resources for national defense through the establishment of a "Japan–Manchuria–China economic bloc."[32] Nagai argues that the theories behind the 1936 occupation plan were similar to those behind the "Manchurian Incident" and "advance southward." In other words, to prepare itself for possible future wars with the Soviet Union, and later the United States, the Japanese military wanted to make certain that they could secure important strategic and supply bases and obtain necessary military and industrial resources.[33]

If an occupation plan existed, naturally an operation plan should also have existed. In 1936, the "separation of north China from the rest of the country," the policy advocated by the army forces stationed in China, became Japan's official doctrine. The "1937 Operation Plan of the Imperial Army"[34] was the first yearly operation plan that was created under this new policy. Nagai points out that the basic structure of the 1937 operation plan coincided closely with the first section of the 1936 occupation plan. In other words, these two documents were formulated to cope with the same potential war.[35]

Although Nagai demonstrates that the Japanese army made occupation and operational plans for a "regional and limited war," such as the Marco Polo Bridge Incident initially provoked, he insists that he does not challenge the established theory among Japanese scholars that the military did not have plans for a full-scale war with China. Nevertheless, the military might have failed to realize that once they used force in north China, conflict could not be limited to the immediate area and would eventually escalate into a general war. Nagai believes that the Japanese military never appreciated the power of Chinese nationalism or the degree to which it would be inflamed by an incident like that at the Marco Polo Bridge. This was its strategic failure.[36]

On the other hand, although the Marco Polo Bridge Incident is generally considered the outbreak of a full-scale war between China and Japan, neither country declared war on the other at the time. The Sino–Japanese War is, in fact, often described as an "undeclared war." China eventually issued its declaration of war against the Axis after the beginning of the Pacific War on December 9, 1941. Japan, though, never declared war on China.

The most important reason that Japan did not declare war on China was that the government and the military feared that an official declaration of war would oblige the U.S. government to invoke its neutrality laws. American neutrality legislation not only prohibited the sale of weapons and strategic materials from the United States to belligerent countries but also prevented American private banks from providing them with loans.[37]

The Chinese did not openly declare war on Japan until the beginning of the Pacific War in December 1941. This decision was not only rooted in financial and economic concerns, but also in strategic imperatives. The Chinese worried that if the two countries entered a formal state of war, Japan would use its superior naval power to blockade China's trade and cut off its foreign sources of military supplies. The beginning of the Pacific War altered the Nationalist government's calculations. Chiang Kaishek then made every effort to forge an international military alliance against Japan by advocating simultaneous declarations of war on the Axis by China, the United States, Britain, and the Soviet Union. China's declaration of war on Japan was an important step towards the consolidation of the alliance. On December 9, after observing the reactions of the United States, Britain and the Soviet Union to the Japanese offensives launched over the previous two days, the Chinese government officially issued declarations of war against Germany, Italy, and Japan. At that point, China joined the Western democracies and established its role in a worldwide conflict between the Allied and the Axis nations.[38]

Japan's attack on north China in the summer of 1937 failed to discourage the Chinese from resisting the Japanese. In late August, the Communist Party held a Politburo conference at Luochuan in Shaanxi Province. There, the communists adopted the "Ten-Point Program for Resisting Japan and Salvaging the Nation," which aimed to mobilize all the military forces and people of China against Japan. The Ten-Point Program promised the Nationalist Party and the people of China that "the Chinese Communist Party firmly believes that we will be able to achieve our goal of defending our homeland and defeating the Japanese invaders through wholehearted, honest and decisive execution of these programs."[39] The communists articulated a strategy of guerrilla warfare against the enemy, and in late August, they began to commit their forces to the war of resistance. Based on the previous agreement between the Nationalists and Communists, the Red Army was reorganized as the Eighth Route Army of Chiang Kai-shek's National Revolutionary Army.

At the same time, near the end of July 1937, the Japanese government ordered the evacuation of Japanese residents in the Yangtze River Valley. Japanese battleships, crowded with civilians, forced their way to Shanghai. Tensions between Japanese and Chinese troops reached a breaking point. On August 13, the two armies clashed, and Japan opened a new front in Shanghai. The Japanese government now referred to the Sino–Japanese War as the "China Incident."

On August 14, Chiang Kai-shek issued a statement on "self-defense and resistance against Japan" and assumed the position of Commander in Chief of the Chinese Army, Air Force and Navy. In Shanghai, Chiang Kai-shek committed his elite forces, which had been trained and equipped by German advisers, to defend China's financial center. One of the important strategic reasons Chiang Kai-shek chose to fight the Japanese in Shanghai was to draw enemy troops away from north China. Chiang believed that in contrast to the north China plains, the streets and waterways of Shanghai would help slow Japan's advance. In addition to strategic concerns, Jay Taylor argues that the defense of Shanghai had psychological and political purposes. Most importantly, Chiang hoped that the fighting would impress the Western democracies, whose sympathy and assistance he hoped to win in his fight against Japan. The United States and major European powers maintained economic interests in the city, and large numbers of their own citizens resided there. Nevertheless, the powers' reactions were discouraging. Chiang could only hope to "build sympathy for the future."[40]

Although Chiang Kai-shek dispatched his German-trained elite divisions to Shanghai, and more than seventy German advisers served in the rear of the Chinese forces to supervise operations, the Nationalist army suffered terrible losses.[41] The Nationalists lost at least one-third of their more than three hundred thousand troops and ten thousand young officers. The accomplishments of a decade of German military training were reversed in a scant three months.[42]

Pursuing the demoralized Chinese forces from the Shanghai front, the Japanese army quickly approached the Nationalist capital of Nanjing. At this point, Chiang Kai-shek turned to Germany to mediate an end to hostilities. Germany, on one hand, did not want to see the Chinese driven into the arms of the Soviets. China's Non-aggression Pact with the Soviet Union that summer had alarmed Berlin. Neither did the Germans want to see their economic interests in the country harmed by the war. From an economic perspective, China was more important to Germany than Japan. In 1930, commerce between China and Germany was valued at 3.475 million Reichsmarks compared to 2.34 million Reichsmarks between Germany and Japan. In addition, the German oil industry was almost completely dependent on exports of bean products, especially soybeans, from Chinese Manchuria.[43]

Germany's ambassador to China, Oskar Trautmann, began to mediate between the Chinese and the Japanese in November. During the mediation, the Nationalist party's secretary general proposed to Trautmann a Non-aggression Pact and an economic cooperation agreement between China, Germany, and the Soviet Union.[44] In August, Chiang Kai-shek had signed a Sino–Soviet Non-aggression Pact with Stalin's government, and the Soviet leader had promised military assistance to the Nationalist government in its struggle against Japan. As John Garver argues, the non-aggression treaty "formed the basis for the close alignment and cooperation between those two countries during 1937–1939."[45] It seems quite clear that the Nationalist government was determined to pursue a triple alliance that would add Germany to the Non-aggression Pact. The forces in the Nationalist government that urged the formation of Sun Yat-sen's hoped-for alliance between China, Germany, and the Soviet Union were deep-rooted.

In the midst of Germany's mediation, Japanese troops captured Nanjing on December 13, 1937. According to the estimation of the postwar International Military Tribunal for the Far East, more than twenty thousand Chinese "men of military age" were killed and nearly twenty thousand women were raped in the following forty days, during what came to be called the "Rape of Nanjing."[46] At the postwar International Military Tribunal for the Far East, the violence committed by Japanese soldiers in Nanjing was described graphically:

> The Japanese soldiers swarmed over the city and committed various atrocities. According to one of the eyewitnesses they were let loose like a barbarian horde to desecrate the city. It was said by the eyewitness that the city appeared to have fallen into the hands of the Japanese as captured prey, that it had not merely been taken in organized warfare, and that the members of the victorious Japanese Army had set upon the prize to commit unlimited violence ... Soldiers went through the streets indiscriminately killing Chinese men, women, and children without apparent provocation or excuse until in places the streets and alleys were littered with the bodies of their victims.[47]

The events surrounding the "Rape of Nanjing," or the "Nanjing Massacre," and their interpretation have provoked a heated debate in China, Japan, and beyond in recent decades. The controversy arose first in Japan in the 1970s, and the Chinese joined the debate in the 1980s. Before the 1980s, the atrocities committed by Japan's Unit 731 in Manchuria, which conducted medical experiments on human subjects, and the Japanese "Three Alls" policy ("kill all, burn all, and loot all") received more attention in China as emblematic of Japanese wartime brutality. In recent years, however, Nanjing has become the focus of the Chinese communist government's campaign to promote patriotism.

The Rape of Nanjing occurred more than seven decades ago, yet Japanese historian Yoshida Takashi contends that, "the image of Nanjing as the site of particularly brutal atrocities is a more recent construction."[48] Yoshida further argues that the tragedy has gone through "continuous redefinition and reinterpretation" in China, Japan, and the world.[49] The memorialization of the Rape of Nanjing has served different purposes under different social and political conditions both domestically and internationally.

Debate over the Nanjing Massacre first garnered public attention in Japan in the early 1970s. At that time, the prevailing view in the country was that the massacre indeed happened. However, many "revisionists," including some conservative Japanese politicians concerned with issues of national pride, began to challenge, and even deny, this view. Outraged "progressives," critical of Japan's imperial past and its aggression, acted promptly to contest the revisionists and their denial of the atrocity.[50] Ironically, the revisionists and their vehement defense of Japanese behavior in Nanjing played an important role in introducing the debate to the public and exporting it beyond the borders of Japan.[51]

The debate over the Rape of Nanjing goes beyond whether it actually occurred. Disputes emerged, for instance, over whether the Chinese soldiers killed there should be counted as victims of the massacre, or what areas should be included in "Nanjing." These distinctions are important because the number of victims varies greatly depending upon how one defines these terms. In addition, the precise number of victims at Nanjing always occupies the center of the debate.[52]

After the fall of Nanjing, Germany's mediation between China and Japan continued. The Japanese at first rejected the possibility of a ceasefire. Then, after the seizure of the Nationalist capital, they requested, as a *quid pro quo* for a ceasefire, China's recognition of the puppet regime of Manchukuo, Chiang Kai-shek's collaboration in the struggle against the communists, Nationalist acceptance of demilitarized zones in the country, and war reparations. Chiang refused, contending that these conditions would make China subservient to Japan.[53] In a message to the Chinese people after the fall of Nanjing, Chiang called for continued resistance against Japan from the entire nation. At the end of his message, Chiang declared, "[w]ith the mandate I have received from the Party and the Government I can only go forward. Let us all go forward; let us never retreat. May you all encourage each other to stand firm in this hour of our nation's greatest peril."[54] Shortly afterward, Japan declared its intention to destroy the Nationalist regime.[55] Trautmann's mediation failed, and Germany subsequently changed its East Asian policy.

The appointment of Joachim Ribbentrop, a figure deeply sympathetic to Japan, as the new German foreign minister in February 1938 played an important role in reshaping Germany's diplomacy in East Asia. Ribbentrop's predecessors in the Foreign Office favored a pro-Chinese orientation and counseled neutrality during the Sino–Japanese crisis. Ribbentrop's pro-Japanese attitude, however, reflected Hitler's views. After he became foreign minister, the two overcame diplomatic and military skepticism and forged an alliance with Japan.[56] To Hitler and Ribbentrop, Japan was of greater use than China in tying down Soviet forces in East Asia. Moreover, a partnership with Tokyo would intimidate the Western powers.

Hitler announced unexpectedly in February 1938 that Germany would grant Manchukuo diplomatic recognition. In the following months, the German government not only withdrew its military advisers from China but also asked the Chinese to recall their military trainees from Germany. At the same time, it imposed an embargo on weapons exports to the Nationalist government. Finally, in June 1938, Hitler recalled his ambassador to China.[57]

Meanwhile, by mid-1938, its escalating war in China and simultaneous preparations for a possible conflict with the Soviet Union exceeded Japan's military capacities. The Japanese military leaders' preoccupation at this point became how to end the "China Incident." An alliance with Germany, they hoped, would help to conclude the conflict with China soon.[58]

Further, in mid-1939, the Kwantung army and the Soviet Union fought a large-scale but undeclared war along the Manchurian–Mongolian frontier as each nation came to the aid of their allies, Manchukuo and Mongolia, in a border dispute. The Japanese army suffered serious losses at the Battle of Nomonhan. Historian Ernst Presseisen contends that this defeat made it clear to the Kwantung army that "Japan could never hope to eliminate Russia's influence in Asia without the aid of an ally."[59]

In addition, on June 14, the Japanese army blockaded the British and French Concessions in Tianjin (Tientsin) after Japan accused the British of harboring anti-Japanese resistance fighters. The blockade soured Japan's already tense relationship with the two Western powers. The final straw came on July 26, when the U.S. government informed the Japanese that it intended to terminate the 1911 Japanese–U.S. Treaty of Commerce and Navigation. These mounting tensions between Japan and the Western powers in East Asia convinced the Japanese army of the necessity of a military alliance with Germany.

However, Germany also secretly approached the Soviet Union while pursuing an alliance with Japan. On August 23, 1939, the Soviet–German non-aggression pact shocked the world and caught Japan completely by surprise. Hitler abandoned the idea of an alliance with Japan, opting instead to reach an accommodation with the Soviet Union. Germany thus betrayed the spirit of the Anti-Comintern Pact with Japan and Italy. German–Japanese relations continued to deteriorate for the rest of 1939 and early 1940 and did not improve until German military victories in Western Europe that spring "set the tide in the other direction."[60]

The worsening of Sino–German relations and German–Japanese negotiations in the summer of 1938 caused China's military disposition against Japan to erode dangerously, and the absence of the German military mission invited further Japanese aggression in China. Although the Chinese did not receive any aid from the Western democracies, their early partnership with the Soviet Union paid important dividends at a crucial moment in the Sino–Japanese conflict.

After the departure of the German advisers, the Soviet Union became China's new military patron. Chiang Kai-shek concluded that Soviet assistance would be vital to China's war effort against Japan, especially at a moment when the Western powers and Germany showed no inclination to provide the Nationalists with military aid. Meanwhile, Stalin's generosity to the Nationalists was largely self-serving and based on the premise that China would provide a useful counterweight to Japanese military assets on the Soviet Union's eastern borders.

It seems that Stalin had first decided to aid China after the Germans signed the Anti-Comintern Pact with the Japanese in November 1936.[61] Along with the conclusion of the Sino–Soviet Non-aggression Pact, in 1938 and 1939 the Soviet Union signed three agreements with the Nationalist government that provided for a total of $250 million in loans to support China's fight against Japan. Additionally, between late 1937 and early 1939, the Soviets dispatched more than sixty thousand tons of equipment into northwest and southwest China. The Soviet aid proved to be vitally important to the Chinese. With advanced weapons, in March 1938, Nationalist troops won a decisive victory over the Japanese in Taierzhuang, in Shandong province. The Japanese lost two of their best divisions.[62]

The Soviet Union provided the Chinese Nationalists not only with materiel but also military personnel and advisers. Approximately fifteen hundred Soviet military advisers and two thousand Soviet pilots were deployed to China during this period. The first Soviet advisers arrived in China in June 1938, right after the last German group left. In addition, along with the arrival of thousands of pilots, the Soviets sponsored the establishment of aviation schools and an air base in Xinjiang and Sichuan. The joint Sino–Soviet effort once again achieved important successes. On April 29, 1938, Soviet and Chinese pilots destroyed several dozen Japanese aircraft at Wuhan, "the largest pre–World War II aerial battle."[63]

However, despite the important role played by its military support in major battles, Soviet assistance never went beyond materiel aid and very limited commitments of personnel. Stalin never intended to involve his country in a direct conflict with Japan on China's behalf, a commitment that Chiang Kai-Shek desperately sought. Nevertheless, Chiang appreciated that in contrast to the caution of the Western nations, the Soviets did provide concrete help to his people.

Sino–Soviet cooperation between 1937 and 1939 benefited both nations. The fighting in China tied down approximately one million Japanese troops in the interior of the country. This helped the Soviet army significantly during the fighting between Soviet and Japanese forces along the Manchurian–Mongolian border in the late 1930s. The Japanese army, after the border clashes, and especially following its disastrous defeat at Nomonhan in 1939, concluded that the Soviet Union was an enemy with which it did not want to tangle further. As a result, John Garver contends, "China's war of resistance made a direct and important contribution to keeping the Soviet Union out of a war with Japan."[64]

Before Nomonhan, different elements within the Japanese military entertained plans concerning the future and direction of Japan's expansion. Japan's reversal at Nomonhan ultimately discredited the *hokushin-ron* (advance northward) option, favored by the army and ultranationalists, who urged the invasion and conquest of the Korean Peninsula, Manchuria, Mongolia, and Siberia. Proponents of this option identified the Soviet Union as Japan's most important potential enemy. Defeat at Nomonhan gave added momentum, however, to the *nanshin-ron* (advance southward) option, associated with senior navy admirals, which urged a thrust into Southeast Asia to secure its natural resources. *Nanshin-ron* put Japan on a path towards confrontation with the United States and the European imperial powers and led directly to the war in the Pacific.[65]

After the Chinese Nationalists' unexpected victory during the air battle of Wuhan in late April, the city eventually fell to the Japanese. Wuhan at the time was Chiang Kai-shek's headquarters and the de facto capital of wartime China. Although Chiang relocated the Nationalist capital officially to Chongqing in China's southwestern Sichuan Province following the Japanese capture of Nanjing, he remained in Wuhan in his capacity as commander-in-chief of Chinese forces to direct military operations. Nevertheless, on October 25, 1938, after a spirited Nationalist defense lasting four-and-a-half months, the city fell to the enemy. The Battle of Wuhan was one of the longest, biggest, and most important battles of the Sino–Japanese War.

Despite heavy Chinese losses, many Chinese historians contend that the suffering at Wuhan was worthwhile strategically. The Japanese paid a tremendously high price during the attack, siege, and capture of the city and, as a result, decided by the end of the year not to press their advance into southwest China. Instead, they decided to focus their resources on securing the north.[66] Historian Immanuel Hsü argues that the fall of Wuhan brought to an end the "first stage of the Sino–Japanese War".[67] Thereafter, the war in China became deadlocked.

In Europe, a week after the conclusion of its non-aggression pact with the Soviet Union, Germany invaded Poland on September 1, 1939. Britain and France declared war on Germany two days later, plunging Europe into conflict. As a result, the political and diplomatic commitment of Britain and France to Southeast Asia declined markedly because of the outbreak of the war.

Germany's initial victories in the European war during the fall of 1939 and spring of 1940 inspired Chiang Kai-shek and his Nationalists to approach Nazi Germany and once again explore the possibility of an alliance between China, Germany, and the Soviet Union. Perhaps such a triple alliance would turn the tide of the Sino–Japanese War in China's favor.

At the same time, within the German government, there was a movement afoot to restore Germany's traditional friendship with the Chinese. Pro-Chinese figures, such as Ernst von Weizsäcker, State Secretary at the Foreign Office, Georg Thomas, head of the Defense Economy and Armament Office in the Defense Ministry, Hjalmar Schacht, former Minister of Economics and President of the Reichsbank, and Hermann Göring, commander-in-chief of the air force, believed that because the German government had given up the alliance with Japan, it was no longer necessary to distance themselves from

China. Nonetheless, these officials ended up taking a wait-and-see attitude as the wars in Asia and Europe raged.[68]

Meanwhile, Germany's victories in Europe also encouraged the Japanese. Military leaders in Tokyo decided again that the time was again right to pursue an alliance with the Nazis. The fall of the Netherlands and France in May and June 1940 further encouraged the Japanese, who believed that they now were in a position to absorb the Dutch East Indies and French Indochina into their sphere of influence. To break the deadlock of war in China, Japan needed to advance into Southeast Asia to obtain much needed strategic raw materials, especially oil.

The German government at this point was also willing to pursue an alliance with Japan as a means to discourage the United States from intervening in the European conflict.[69] After Germany occupied the Netherlands, Ribbentrop in fact urged the Japanese to join the Nazi's war against the European powers in exchange for a free hand in the Netherlands East Indies.[70] Japan was more than happy to take advantage of Nazi victories and the power vacuum in Southeast Asia. As a first step, on June 17, 1940, the Japanese blockaded the French Indochina route, through which the French government had been sending weapons and supplies to China. A week later, on the June 23, the Japanese began to advance into northern French Indochina. Then, on July 12, Japan blockaded the Burma Road, another important supply route by which the British had been sending aid to Chiang Kai-shek. Closing these Western supply routes, the Japanese believed, would decisively weaken China's ability to fight. On the other hand, the British government's decision, under Japanese pressure, to close the Burma Road further provoked anti-British and anti-American sentiment in the Nationalist government. The voices urging an alliance with Germany and the Soviet Union grew more insistent.[71]

However, the Nationalists' dream of establishing a triple alliance between China, Germany, and the Soviet Union disintegrated when, on September 27, 1940, Japan signed the Tripartite Pact with Germany and Italy. The new agreement served the needs of the signatories in a number of ways. The Nazi regime needed the Japanese to keep the Americans preoccupied in the Pacific and distract them from the European conflict. Japan, on the other hand, believed the alliance with Italy and Germany would prevent the United States from intervening in the Sino–Japanese War. Under the terms of the pact, the Germans acknowledged Japan's control over the former European colonies in Southeast Asia, and with Southeast Asia's petroleum resources secured, Japan was less vulnerable to America's economic sanctions.

The conclusion of the Tripartite Pact also ended America's hopes for a compromise with Japan and made it clear to U.S. officials that China's struggle against Japan was indeed crucial to U.S. security.[72] The Tripartite Pact was thus an important turning point in Sino–American relations during the Sino–Japanese conflict. As Warren Cohen points out, "nothing the Chinese or their friends in the United States could have done could have convinced Americans of their stake in the outcome of the Sino–Japanese war as effectively as Japan's decision to ally with Nazi Germany."[73] The Tripartite Pact not only made China "unmistakably an ally" of the Western democracies, which were struggling against fascism themselves, but also made the country "the principal beneficiary of the new Axis Alliance."[74] The United States, anxious that the new alliance would weaken China in its struggle against Japan, increased its support to Chiang Kai-shek's government. Although the U.S. government granted the Chinese $45 million in purchase credits during 1939 and 1940, it provided $95 million in credits to the Nationalist government in the six months following the conclusion of the Tripartite Pact. In May 1941, China became eligible for Lend Lease assistance. However, the Roosevelt administration declined to cut off American oil exports to Japan.[75]

The Tripartite Pact also made Chiang Kai-shek more valuable to the Soviets. Although Soviet aid to China shrank between 1939 and 1941, Stalin began to expand his support to China. However, the Chinese did not enjoy the increased Soviet aid for very long. On April 13, 1941, the Soviet Union and Japan signed a Neutrality Pact, and it became more apparent to Chiang that it would be impossible for the Soviets to enter the Sino–Japanese conflict in support of China. As Garver argues, the change in Soviet policy altered the country's position from one of siding with China against Japan to one of allying with Japan to enfeeble and dismember China.[76]

The pact between the Soviets and the Japanese did not diminish China's will, nor compromise its ability, to continue resisting Japan's occupation. Meanwhile, China's new relationship with the United States offered Chiang many possibilities. He concluded that the neutrality pact would further encourage Japan's southern strategy, which he believed would distract it from its embroilment in China and lead eventually to a Japanese confrontation with the United States.[77] On July 28, Japan marched into southern French Indochina, an action that greatly irritated the United States. President Franklin Roosevelt responded by freezing Japanese financial assets in the United States and imposing an oil embargo on the country.

At the same time, the Soviet Union had been fending off the German attack since June 22. Chiang Kai-shek identified the German–Soviet War as an opportunity to urge the Soviet Union to join China's struggle against Japan. Chiang fully expected to establish a united front with the United States, Britain, and the Soviet Union against the Axis powers.[78]

On December 7, 1941, the Japanese attack on Pearl Harbor precipitated the Pacific War. The following day the United States and Britain declared war on Japan, and on December 9, China declared war on Japan, Germany, and Italy. Nationalist China was now officially a member of emerging alliance to defeat the Axis Powers. On December 11, immediately after Hitler declared war on the United States, the U.S. government declared war on Nazi Germany. The war between Japan, the United States, and the Western Allies now bridged the two regional conflicts in East Asia and Europe. This has prompted some historians argue that December 1941 marked the true beginning of World War II. In reality, neither Germany's invasion of Poland nor Japan's attack on Pearl Harbor started World War II. That war had its origins in the great powers' direct and indirect involvement in the Sino–Japanese conflict that had begun with the 1931 Mukden Incident. The Western appeasement of Japan in 1931 encouraged Japanese ambitions in China, and later Southeast Asia, and ultimately contributed to the outbreak of the conflict in the Pacific. Nevertheless, the beginning of the Pacific War opened a new chapter of the war in East Asia.

Until Pearl Harbor, China fought continually against Japan, most of the time alone. Nevertheless, it was an article of faith among historians for decades after the war ended that Chiang's war effort was hobbled by his regime's incompetence, corruption, and preoccupation with fighting Mao Zedong's communist movement rather than confronting the invading Japanese. This interpretation was once a widely accepted truth about twentieth century Chinese history,[79] and was reinforced by popular accounts such as Barbara Tuchman's *Stilwell and the American Experience in China*. Consequently, Nationalist China itself was often depicted as "an unworthy ally for the West."[80] In recent years, however, revisionist accounts of China's place in the military and diplomatic history of World War II have proliferated. British historian Rana Mitter, for instance, argues that China's role in World War II has not been properly appreciated.[81] Western scholars, and even the government of the People's Republic until the early months of Xi Jinping's regime, have reevaluated the Nationalists' war effort and Chiang's conduct and reputation as wartime leader. Revisionist historians, such as Jay Taylor, praise Chiang for his "determination, courage, and incorruptibility."[82] They show more understanding of Chiang's policies and the factors underlying China's early defeats during the Sino–Japanese War. Hans van de Ven contends, for example, that China simply possessed neither the industrial base nor the bureaucratic and institutional infrastructure to wage a modern war against an advanced nation like Japan.[83] Merely surviving and refusing to capitulate was a major accomplishment.

Imperial Japan in the 1930s proved to be too powerful a military opponent for China and too formidable a rival for even the Western industrial nations to confront directly. Even the United States chose to pacify Tokyo after the 1931 Manchurian Incident rather than oppose its aggression. Between 1931 and 1941, Chiang Kai-shek worked relentlessly to acquire diplomatic support and material assistance for his war against the invading Japanese from whomever would offer it. His search required him to solicit aid from a variety of potential patrons—fascist, communist, and democratic—as the stability of the international system eroded and the world careened towards war. Time and again Chiang saw his diplomatic overtures rebuffed, his momentary alliances overturned, and China abandoned as the great powers pursued their increasingly complicated agendas with one another. Yet, he held his government and nation together while China became a diplomatic and military theater for the proxy struggles waged by the great powers. Indeed, the degree to which the Sino–Japanese War became internationalized in the 1930s leads to the conclusion that World War II did not begin in 1939 in Europe; it began in East Asia in 1931.

Notes

1. September 19, 1931, "Urgent and Top Secret, no. 630, Consul General Hayashi Hisajiro in Mukden (Shenyang) to Foreign Minister Shidehara Kijūrō," Diplomatic Record Office of the Ministry of Foreign Affairs of Japan, Japan Center for Asian Historical Records (hereafter JACAR; this digital archive may be found at http://www.jacar.go.jp), reference no. B02030185200, 0015.

2. Akira Iriye, *The Origins of the Second World War in Asia and the Pacific* (New York: Longman, 1987), 1.
3. Kojima Shinji, *Kindai nitchū kankeishi danshō* [*Fragments of the History of Modern Chinese–Japanese Relations*] (Tokyo: Iwanami Shoten, 2008), 145.
4. Fujiwara Akira, "Nihon rikugun to taibei senryaku" ["The Japanese Army and Its Strategies toward the United States"], in *Nichi-Bei kankeishi- kaisen ni itaru 10 nen (1931–41nen)* [*The History of Japanese–American Relations: 10 Years to the Outbreak of the [Pacific] War (1931–41)*], Vol. 2, ed. Hosoya Chihiro, Saitō Makoto, Imai Seiichi, and Rōyama Michio (Tokyo: Tokyo Daigaku Shuppankai, 1971), 75–76.
5. July 7, 1927, "Orders Concerning General Policies toward China. Foreign Minister Tanaka Giichi to the Foreign Ministry, the Ministries of Army, Navy and Finance, and the consuls in China," JACAR, B02030037900, 0009-0013.
6. Ibid.
7. Yale Candee Maxon, *Control of Japanese Foreign Policy: A Study of Civil–Military Rivalry, 1930–1945* (Westport, CT: Greenwood Press, 1973), 73–74.
8. Kojima Shinji and Maruyama Matsuyuki, *Chūgoku kin-gendaishi* [*History of Modern China*] (Tōkyō: Iwanami Shoten, 1986), 138.
9. Jay Taylor, *The Generalissimo: Chiang Kai-shek and the Struggle for Modern China* (Cambridge: Belknap Press of Harvard University Press, 2011), 92–93.
10. Warren Cohen, *America's Response to China: A History of Sino–American Relations*, 5th ed. (New York: Columbia University Press, 2010), 116.
11. Iriye, *The Origins of the Second World War*, 16.
12. Ibid., 19.
13. Kojima, *Kindai nitchū kankeishi danshō*, 139.
14. Iriye, *The Origins of the Second World War*, 27–28.
15. Cohen, *America's Response to China*, 116–118.
16. Cohen, *America's Response to China*, 128.
17. Immanuel C. Y. Hsü, *The Rise of Modern China*, 6th ed. (New York, Oxford: Oxford University Press, 2000), 548.
18. Taylor, *The Generalissimo*, 94.
19. Sadō Akihiro, Komiya Kazuo, and Hattori Ryūji, *Jinbutsu de yomu kindai Nihon gaikōshi: Okubo Toshimichi kara Hirota Kōki made* [*Understanding Modern Japanese Diplomatic History through Personalities: From Okubo Toshimichi to Hirota Koki*] (Tōkyō: Yoshikawa Kōbunkan, 2009), 304.
20. Taylor, *The Generalissimo*, 117.
21. Ibid.
22. Guo Hengyu, "Sun Zhongshan yu Deguo" [Sun Yat-sen and Germany]," *Guoshiguan guankan* [*Journal of the Academia Historica*] no. 23 (1997): 83.
23. Tajima Nobuo, "*Nitchū Sensō to Nichi-Doku-Chū-So kankei*" ["The Sino–Japanese War and the Relationship between Japan, Germany, China and the Soviet Union"], in *Kokusai kankei no naka no Nitchū Sensō* [*The Sino-Japanese War in International Relations*], ed. Nishimura Shigeo, Ishijima Noriyuki and Tajima Nobuo (Tōkyō: Keiō Gijuku Daigaku Shuppankai, 2011), 33–35.
24. William C. Kirby, *Germany and Republican China* (Stanford, CA: Stanford University Press, 1984), 3.
25. Tajima, "*Nitchū Sensō to Nichi-Doku-Chū-So kankei,*" 38.

26. Bernd Martin, "The Role of German Military Advisers on the Chinese Defense Efforts against the Japanese, 1937–1938," in *Resisting Japan: Mobilizing for War in China, 1935–1945*, ed. David Pong (Norwalk, CT: EastBridge, 2008), 60; Tajima, "*Nitchū Sensō to Nichi-Doku-Chū-So kankei*," 38.
27. Martin, "The Role of German Military Advisers," 59.
28. Taylor, *The Generalissimo*, 145–146.
29. Nagai Kazu, *Nitchū Sensō kara sekai sensō e* [*From the Sino-Japanese War to World War*] (Kyōto: Shibunkaku Shuppan, 2007), 38–39.
30. September 23, 1936, "Military Secret, no. 36, from Tashiro Kanichirō, commander in chief of the Japanese China Garrison Army, to Terauchi Hisaichi, Minister of Army: Report Concerning the Preparation of Secret Documents," JACAR, C01002726200.
31. Ibid., 0740.
32. "Report Concerning the Preparation of Secret Documents," JACAR, C01002726200, 0743.
33. Nagai, *Nitchū Sensō kara sekai sensō e*, 59–60.
34. [n.d.] "Operation Secret, Orders Concerning Imperial Army's Operation Plans in 1937," JACAR, C11110932800.
35. Nagai, *Nitchū Sensō kara sekai sensō e*, 52.
36. Ibid., 96–97.
37. Katō Yōko, *Mosakusuru 1930-nendai: Nichi-Bei kankei to Rikugun chūkensō* [*Stumbling in the 1930s: US–Japanese Relations and the Backbone of the Army*] (Tokyo: Yamakawa Shuppansha, 1993), 68–71; *Manshū Jihen kara Nitchū Sensō e* [*From the Manchurian Incident to the Sino-Japanese War*] (Tokyo: Iwanami Shoten, 2007), 232–233.
38. Tsuchida Akio, "Nitchū Sensō to Chūgoku sensen mondai" ["The Sino-Japanese War and the Issue Concerning China's Declaration of War"], in *Kokusai kankei no naka no Nitchū Sensō* [*The Sino-Japanese War in International Relations*], ed. Nishimura Shigeo, Ishijima Noriyuki, and Tajima Nobuo (Tōkyō: Keiō Gijuku Daigaku Shuppankai, 2011), 374.
39. Mao Zedong, "For the Mobilization of all the Nation's Forces for Victory in the War of Resistance, August 25, 1937," in *Selected Works of Mao Tse-tung*, Vol. 2 (Beijing: Foreign Languages Press, 1967), 23–29.
40. Taylor, *The Generalissimo*, 147.
41. Tajima, "*Nitchū Sensō to Nichi-Doku-Chū-So kankei*," 40.
42. Kirby, *Germany and Republican China*, 222–223.
43. Chen Renxia, *Zhong De Ri sanjiao guanxi yanjiu (1936–1938)* [*The Study of the Triangular Relations between China, Germany and Japan: 1936–1938*] (Beijing: Sanlian shudian, 2003), p.33.
44. Tajima, "*Nitchū Sensō to Nichi-Doku-Chū-So kankei*," 40.
45. John Garver, *Chinese–Soviet Relations, 1937–1945: The Diplomacy of Chinese Nationalism* (New York, Oxford: Oxford University Press, 1988), 18.
46. John Pritchard, ed., *The Tokyo War Crimes Trial*, Vol. 20 (New York: Garland Publishing, 1981), 49606, quoted in Takashi Yoshida, "A Battle over History," in *The Nanjing Massacre in History and Historiography*, ed. Joshua A. Fogel (Berkeley: University of California Press, 2000), 71.
47. Pritchard, *The Tokyo War Crimes Trial*, 49604–5, quoted in Yoshida, "A Battle over History," 70.
48. Yoshida Takashi, *The Making of the "Rape of Nanking": History and Memory in Japan, China and the United States* (New York: Oxford University Press, 2006), 4.

49. Ibid.
50. Fogel, *The Nanjing Massacre*, 71.
51. Yoshida, *The Making of the "Rape of Nanking,"* 5–6.
52. Ibid., 6, 181.
53. Stephen G. Craft, *V.K. Wellington Koo and the Emergence of Modern China* (Lexington: The University Press of Kentucky, 2004), 126.
54. Chiang Kai-shek, compiled by Chinese Ministry of Information, "After the Fall of Nanjing," in *The Collected Wartime Messages of Generalissimo Chiang Kai-Shek, 1937–1945*, Vol. 1 (1943) (New York: The John Day Company, 1943, 1944, 1945, and 1946) 51.
55. Craft, *V.K. Wellington Koo*, 127.
56. Frank William Iklé, *German–Japanese Relations: 1936–1940* (New York: Bookman Associates, 1956), 68.
57. "Germany Colluded with Japan: Germany Recognized 'Manchukuo,'" February 20, 1938, 191; "Germany Decided Not to Accept Military Trainees from China and Japan during the Conflict," March 3, 1938, 233; "Germany Withdrew Its Military Advisers in China," May 21, 1938, 484; "German and Italian Leaders Met in Roma and Decided to Strengthen Their Cooperation with Japan; Hitler Secretly Imposed an Arms Embargo on China," May 3, 1938, 442; "Germany Recalled Ambassador Oskar P. Trautmann," June 26, 1938, 598, in Zhu Huisen, Lai Min, and He Zhilin, eds., *Zhonghua Minguo shishi jiyao chugao: 1938 [First Edition of the Records of Historical Events of the Republic of China, 1938]* (Taipei: Guo shi guan, 1989).
58. Ernst L. Presseisen, *Germany and Japan: A Study in Totalitarian Diplomacy, 1933–1941* (The Hague: Martinus Nijhoff, 1958), 191–192; Yoshii Hiroshi, *Shōwa gaikōshi [The Diplomatic History of the Showa Era]*, 3rd ed. (Tokyo: Nansōsha, 1984), 85–86.
59. Presseisen, *Germany and Japan*, 216–217.
60. Iklé, *German–Japanese Relations*, 197.
61. Garver, *Chinese–Soviet Relations*, 16.
62. Ibid., 37–39.
63. Ibid., 40–41.
64. Ibid., 50.
65. Nagai, *Nitchū Sensō kara sekai sensō e*, 386; Mizushima Kunika, *Nitchū Sensō to Nomonhan Jiken: Taiheiyō Sensō e no michi [The Sino-Japanese War and the Nomonhan Incident: The Road to the Pacific War]* (Tōkyō: Daiichi Shobō, 2007), 4.
66. Stephen MacKinnon, *Wuhan 1938: War, Refugees, and the Making of Modern China* (Berkeley: University of California Press, 2008), 2.
67. Hsü, *The Rise of Modern China*, 584.
68. Tajima Nobuo, "Introduction," in *Kokusai kankei no naka no Nitchū Sensō [The Sino-Japanese War in International Relations]*, ed. Nishimura Shigeo, Ishijima Noriyuki, and Tajima Nobuo (Tōkyō: Keiō Gijuku Daigaku Shuppankai, 2011), 14.
69. Iklé, *German–Japanese Relations*, 150.
70. Ibid., 152.
71. Tajima, *"Nitchū Sensō to Nichi-Doku-Chū-So kankei,"* 42.
72. Garver, *Chinese–Soviet Relations*, 117–118.
73. Cohen, *America's Response to China*, 135.
74. Ibid.
75. Ibid., 136.
76. Garver, *Chinese–Soviet Relations*, 118.

77. Tajima, "Introduction," 17.
78. Ibid., 17–18.
79. Flemming Christiansen, "Review of Hans J. van de Ven, *War and Nationalism in China, 1925–1945*," *Bulletin of the School of Oriental and African Studies, University of London* 68, no. 1 (2005): 159–160.
80. Rana Mitter, *Forgotten Ally: China's World War II, 1937–1945* (Boston: Houghton Mifflin Harcourt, 2013), 420.
81. Mitter, *Forgotten Ally*, 4.
82. Taylor, *The Generalissimo*, 2–3.
83. Hans J. van de Ven, *War and Nationalism in China, 1925–1945* (New York: Routledge, 2012), 295.

Bibliography

Coble, Parks M. *Facing Japan: Chinese Politics and Japanese Imperialism, 1931–1937*. Cambridge, MA: Council on East Asian Studies, Harvard University, 1991.

Eastman, Lloyd E. *Seeds of Destruction: Nationalist China in War and Revolution, 1937–1949*. Stanford, CA: Stanford University Press, 1984.

Fogel, Joshua A., ed. *The Nanjing Massacre in History and Historiography*. Berkeley: University of California Press, 2000.

Garver, John W. *Chinese–Soviet Relations, 1937–1945: The Diplomacy of Chinese Nationalism*. New York, Oxford: Oxford University Press, 1988.

Iriye, Akira. *The Origins of the Second World War in Asia and the Pacific*. New York: Longman, 1987.

Kirby, William C. *Germany and Republican China*. Stanford, CA: Stanford University Press, 1984.

Mitter, Rana. *Forgotten Ally: China's World War II, 1937–1945*. Boston: Houghton Mifflin Harcourt, 2013.

Peattie, Mark R., Edward J. Drea, and Hans J. van de Ven, eds. *The Battle for China: Essays on the Military History of the Sino-Japanese War of 1937–1945*. Stanford, CA: Stanford University Press, 2011.

Taylor, Jay. *The Generalissimo: Chiang Kai-shek and the Struggle for Modern China*. Cambridge: Belknap Press of Harvard University Press, 2011.

CHAPTER 5

FORGING ALLIANCES: THE AXIS

RICKY W. LAW

When Britain and France opened hostilities against Germany in September 1939 over Germany's assault on Poland, the war was geographically confined and threatened less of the world than World War I did in 1914. To deter the Western democracies from standing up for Eastern Europe and to avoid a two-front war in case they did, Adolf Hitler had taken care to conclude a non-aggression pact with Joseph Stalin in late August 1939. The rest of the continent stayed neutral, and so did isolationist United States. Combat should be limited to Europe because Germany no longer had colonies overseas. Meanwhile in East Asia, the Second Sino–Japanese War was settling into a pattern of stalemates within China. But in just over two years, conflagration would roll across the globe, on land, at sea, and in the air. First, Italy entered the war in June 1940 and spread the fighting and German military operations to the Mediterranean. A year later, Germany led several allies in its invasion of the Soviet Union. Finally, in December 1941, the Japanese attacks on Pearl Harbor and Western possessions in Asia and the subsequent German and Italian declarations of war on the United States merged the distant wars in Europe, North Africa, Asia, and the Pacific into one worldwide confrontation.

Indeed, what made World War II a global conflict was the Axis alliance of Japan, Germany, and Italy. And what largely made the Rome–Berlin–Tokyo Axis— purposefully with Berlin at the center—were the decisions and actions of Germany. How did the peculiar Tripartite Alliance come into existence? The unorthodox strategic partnership required radical regimes, such as Fascist Italy, militarist Japan, and particularly Nazi Germany, that were willing to upend conventions. Yet, the three co-belligerents' related but uncoordinated campaigns also exposed and exacerbated the fragility of their bonds. From 1933, Germany under Hitler assiduously and simultaneously cultivated relations with Italy and Japan. In late 1936, Berlin reached separate accords with Rome and Tokyo. Hitler's reckless unilateralism in 1939 almost broke the Axis, but German military successes in 1940 drew Japan, Italy, and smaller European satellite states to tighter orbits around Germany. Until mid-1942, the Axis made impressive advances on multiple fronts. But when the Allies counterattacked, the Axis states crumpled one by one. What had made the Axis possible, namely its members' discrete territorial ambitions, turned out to be its fatal flaw, for Germany, Italy, and Japan prioritized fighting their own distinct wars over supporting their allies.

German–Italian Rapprochement, 1919–1936

Germany's road to cooperation with Italy was neither straight nor smooth. In World War I, Italy left the Triple Alliance with Germany and Austria-Hungary to join the Entente powers against its former partners. After the war, the Treaty of Saint-Germain rewarded Italy for its defection with the Austrian regions of South Tyrol and Istria. The territories rounded Italy's Alpine frontier, but many Italians felt that the compensation was too meager for Italy's sacrifices and postwar stature. Some violent irredentists, nationalists, anti-communists, and anti-liberals soon coalesced around the charismatic Benito Mussolini into the Fascist movement. In October 1922, the Fascists were handed the reins of government after staging a "March on Rome." Henceforth, Mussolini gradually consolidated his position to build a Fascist dictatorship.

The Fascist path to power could serve as a model for right-wing groups in Germany, but authoritarianism and expansionism did not cross borders effortlessly.[1] The March on Rome inspired Hitler to launch his Beer Hall Putsch in November 1923. The coup attempt failed, and Hitler was arrested, convicted, and imprisoned. For all Mussolini's dissatisfaction with the postwar settlement, Italy as a beneficiary of the Versailles order mostly adhered to international norms. It played a leading role in multilateral instruments in the 1920s, including the League of Nations and the Locarno and the Kellogg-Briand Pacts. To Germans, Italy was a pillar upholding the very system that humiliated Germany and enforced Germany's hated treaty obligations. Many German nationalists also resented Italy for forcibly Italianizing the ethnic Germans in South Tyrol. But uncommon among German rightists, Hitler supported trading South Tyrol for Italian friendship. In *Mein Kampf*, written during his stint in prison, Hitler argued, "I not only regard a reconquest of the South Tyrol by war as impossible, but that I personally would reject it."[2] In his worldview, Germany could neutralize France through collaboration with Italy and Britain. Berlin, Rome, and London should make natural allies because of their compatible spheres of influence: continental Europe for Germany, the Mediterranean for Italy, and overseas for Britain.[3]

Hitler's accommodating rhetoric toward Italy and admiration for Mussolini would have meant little without the world economic crisis that paralyzed German democracy and brought the Nazi Party mass support. But the appointment of Hitler as chancellor in 1933 did not immediately lead to German–Italian rapprochement and even caused a scandal. Although Italy and Germany could act in concert to challenge the Versailles order, they schemed to exploit the other's quarrel with France for a strategic free hand.[4] Even more damaging, Austria flared up as a flashpoint between Berlin and Rome. The Austrian-born Hitler, now at Germany's helm, would accept nothing short of a German annexation of Austria. In both the opening page of *Mein Kampf* and his first Reichstag speech, Hitler emphasized the blood ties that bound Germany and Austria.[5] But Mussolini had staked his prestige on preserving independent Austria as a client state that was too weak to reclaim South Tyrol.[6] So when Austrian Nazis attempted a putsch in July 1934, just one month after the first meeting of the two dictators, Mussolini felt so personally insulted that he excoriated Hitler in the press and ordered troops to the Austrian border.[7]

Neither Germany nor Italy wanted an armed confrontation, so for the time being both regimes backed away from Austria to pursue opportunities elsewhere. Still, Italian–German relations did not necessarily improve. In March 1935, Hitler brazenly broke the Versailles Treaty by announcing the rearmament of Germany. Britain and France reacted timidly out of self-interest and domestic politics. It was Mussolini who gathered the British and the French prime ministers for a conference in Stresa to denounce German unilateralism and treaty violation. Possibly to parade Fascist military prowess and to answer Nazi misbehavior, Italy attacked Abyssinia in October 1935.[8]

Mussolini's bid to assert and project Italian power backfired terribly. Instead, the war weakened and isolated his country and necessitated reconciliation with Hitler. One week into the campaign, France and Britain led the League of Nations to punish Italy with arms and economic sanctions. Germany had left the League in 1933 and so did not have to follow its policies. Hitler exploited this moment of Italian vulnerability to rehabilitate bilateral relations by sending supplies to Italy.[9] Prolonging the conflict would not only oblige Mussolini to Hitler and lure him away from the Anglo–French circle, but it would also distract attention from German transgressions. In March 1936, with Britain and France preoccupied with Italy, Germany remilitarized the Rhineland. Unlike the Stresa Conference the previous year, this time no meeting was convened even to mouth criticisms of Germany. In July 1936, with Italy dependent on Germany and unable to bolster Austria, Mussolini had no choice but to accept the Austro–German Agreement, whereby "Austria has acknowledged herself to be a German state."[10] Thus, Hitler emerged the real winner in Abyssinia. The conflict enabled him to extract concessions from Austria without alienating Italy, and to plant the seed of German–Italian rapprochement in the rift between the victors of World War I.

Also in July 1936, Rome and Berlin took another major step toward cooperation through intervention in the Spanish Civil War. The two dictators adopted a common cause when they independently agreed to back the insurrection led by Francisco Franco. Hitler assured Mussolini that Germany respected Italy's claim on the Mediterranean and would engage in Spain only to combat Bolshevism.[11] By flattering Mussolini that Spain lay within the Italian sphere and was thus Italy's responsibility, Hitler goaded Mussolini into escalating his involvement in Spain and so deepening Italian reliance on Germany.[12] Italy's poorly concealed activities in Spain further antagonized other European powers from the Soviet Union to the liberal democracies.

By October 1936, only Germany remained a possible partner. Mussolini dispatched his son-in-law and foreign minister, Galeazzo Ciano, to confer with Hitler. Germany and Italy concluded an agreement to honor each other's territorial interests in Central Europe or the Mediterranean. On November 1, 1936, Mussolini proclaimed the formation of the Rome–Berlin Axis.

German–Japanese Rapprochement, 1919–1936

Later in the month, Berlin and Tokyo also formalized their convergence by signing the Anti-Comintern Pact. As with Italy, Germany's path to collaboration with Japan was laden with twists and obstacles. The two countries were enemies in World War I. In August 1914, soon after war broke out in Europe, Japan as Britain's ally declared war on Germany.[13] In short order and with little bloodshed, Japan captured Germany's colonies in China and the Pacific. The war hollowed all major European powers and so elevated Japan's stature relative to the West. After the war, Japan as a great power helped restore international order by taking part in negotiating the Versailles Treaty and leading the League of Nations. Japan received from Germany a few submarines and nominal reparations as part of the peace settlement. Because territorial annexations were frowned upon in the postwar Wilsonian atmosphere of self-determination, the victorious powers were instead tasked with guiding former possessions of the Central Powers toward independence. Japan's control of the ex-German colonies of the Marshall, Caroline, and Mariana Islands was officially recognized as the South Pacific Mandate of the League of Nations, although Japan was not permitted to fortify the strategic archipelagos.

The Versailles Treaty ended hostilities and reestablished relations between Germany and Japan, but each country had far more pressing diplomatic priorities than bilateral interactions. The two sides shared an enemy only briefly and coincidentally when German *Freikorps* militiamen and Japanese troops fought the Bolsheviks in Russia. The Weimar Republic in its initial years had to battle for survival. Whatever diplomatic capital it could spare was spent on lightening the burden of the Versailles Treaty. Improving ties with faraway Japan hardly registered in German officialdom, especially because Germany and China were building a mutually beneficial partnership.[14] Germany's status as a state without colonies gave it an edge in China as the preferred source of expertise in modernization and industrialization. The two cash-strapped countries also developed a brisk barter trade. Meanwhile, Japan invested time and effort foremost to maintain its positions in China and vis-à-vis the United States.[15] Having finally achieved its long cherished goal of joining the great powers, Japan diligently played its part in the League of Nations and multilateral agreements such as the Washington Naval Treaty and the Nine-Power Treaty.[16] Bilateral Japanese–German ties occupied such a low priority in

Tokyo and Berlin that it took the two governments until 1927 to sign a treaty of commerce and navigation to replace the one abrogated by war.[17]

With official attention lacking, individuals and organizations in civil society in Japan and Germany acted as caretakers of German–Japanese relations. Japanese scholars and merchants returned to Germany soon after the war to resume their studies or to explore commercial prospects. At the same time, former German prisoners of war in Japan reclaimed their perches in academia and business in the country. Few Germans visited Japan, but some of those who did, including Nobel laureates Albert Einstein and Fritz Haber, were welcomed enthusiastically and spoke highly of Japan upon their return. Haber became an especially energetic and influential advocate of closer German cooperation with Japan. He launched the Japan Institute to encourage scholarly and economic exchange. Several other voluntary associations were founded in both countries with his endorsement. In addition, the 1920s saw the birth of popular international tourism, facilitated by the reopening of the Trans-Siberian Railway and surplus capacities on ocean liners. One also got a glimpse of the possibilities created by technology when in 1929 the airship *Graf Zeppelin* flew nonstop from Germany to Japan and in 1930 Berlin and Tokyo connected via live transmissions on telephone and radio.

The world economic crisis triggered fundamental transformations in Japanese–German relations. The Versailles system that both countries had sought to accommodate began to disintegrate. Elected politicians in Germany and in Japan seemed incapable of resolving the crises of the times, so fringe ideas and drastic measures gained more adherents. Many Japanese opinion makers became admirers of Hitler and cheered the ascendancy of Nazism. Without prompting from either government, they used the media to urge closer ties with the Third Reich. In Germany, the rise of Hitler enhanced the influence of loyally Nazi but amateurish foreign policy thinkers who made exceptions in Nazi ideology for the Japanese and who espoused the heterodox position of favoring Japan over China.[18]

Despite the more favorable conditions for a strategic realignment, German–Japanese rapprochement did not come early or easily. In 1932, in one of its last diplomatic acts at the League of Nations, the Weimar Republic contributed to the Lytton Commission report that criticized the Japanese seizure of Manchuria from China. Japan responded to the mild rebuke by abruptly quitting the organization.[19] The appointment of Hitler as chancellor led to several incidents that attracted negative coverage in the Japanese press in the first half of 1933. Nazi hooligans felt empowered to harass foreigners, including Japanese expatriates, and to abuse Germans of Jewish ancestry. Antisemitism had little purchase in Japan. The media was especially sympathetic to luminaries familiar to the Japanese, including Einstein and Haber. Talks by German nationalists of recovering former German colonies elicited harsh criticisms from Japanese officials and commentators. Hitler must also first consolidate his position in Germany and Europe before he could reorient Germany's posture toward East Asia. For several years, traditionalists who preferred China or non-commitment in East Asia retained control of the Foreign Office and the War Ministry. Most important, Hitler desired an alliance with Britain far more than one with Japan. Only after an understanding with

London no longer seemed likely or imminent did Hitler allow Joachim von Ribbentrop to pursue in earnest, behind the Foreign Office, an arrangement with Tokyo.[20] In Japan, institutionalists in the Foreign Ministry likewise held reservations about the repercussions of an agreement with Germany, pushed vociferously by the army officer Ōshima Hiroshi and other Japanese admirers of Hitler and Nazism.[21] But by the mid-1930s, Japan's room for diplomatic maneuvers had shrunk significantly. Its aggression toward China and withdrawal from the League of Nations alienated the West. Its suppression of communists antagonized the Soviet Union. Last, the Foreign Ministry and civilian rule overall had been undermined by a series of coup attempts and assassinations perpetrated by radicalized officers. The convergence of these factors enabled the two regimes to conclude the Anti-Comintern Pact on November 25, 1936.

The Axis Made and Nearly Unmade, 1937–1939

With the German–Italian and the German–Japanese agreements in 1936, and the Italian accession to the Anti-Comintern Pact in November 1937, the Rome–Berlin–Tokyo Axis was beginning to take shape. Still, growing pains plagued the alliance. Although Germany had hoped to keep working with China while building an ideological partnership with Japan, the Second Sino–Japanese War from July 1937 forced Germany to choose between the combatants. After Hitler purged traditional conservatives from the Foreign Office and the War Ministry in early 1938, Germany withdrew its military advisers from China and downgraded its diplomatic representation there to side with Japan. By March 1938, Nazis in Austria had deteriorated order to such an extent that Hitler decided that the moment to annex his homeland had arrived. Italian troops were still fighting in Spain, so Mussolini could only ask Hitler for time to soothe Italian sensibility. Hitler gave Mussolini one day's notice before Germany abolished Austria. By September 1938, Hitler was preparing to invade Czechoslovakia to seize the Sudetenland, a region with a large population of ethnic Germans. Neville Chamberlain failed to change Hitler's mind but managed to convince Mussolini to mediate through the Munich Conference. The Axis appeared to work brilliantly—Germany bloodlessly acquired Sudetenland while Mussolini was feted as a peacemaker merely for enabling Germany. But Hitler secretly resented Mussolini for meddling and depriving him of his war. He was determined that he would not be dissuaded from going through with the next conflict.[22]

The year 1939 saw both the consolidation and near-disintegration of the Axis, all because of German actions. In March, in utter contempt of the Munich Agreement, Germany occupied Bohemia and Moravia as a protectorate and reduced Slovakia to a client state. The invasion significantly enhanced Germany's strategic position, but Mussolini was outraged not just by another one-day notice from Hitler but also because

Hitler had promised to honor the Munich Agreement that Mussolini had brokered. So, Mussolini decided to counteract, rather than complement, German aggression by invading Albania in April—having also given minimal forewarning to Berlin. To other powers, Italy and Germany might appear to build on each other's expansion, but neither had consulted with its ally before taking action. Successive Axis transgressions at last roused Britain and France to guarantee the independence of Poland, Romania, Greece, and Turkey. These pledges seemingly encircled and isolated Germany and Italy. In May, Berlin and Rome reinforced the Axis through the Pact of Steel.[23] The two signatories agreed to help defend each other's "living space" and "immediately come to its assistance as an ally and support it with all its military forces" should either get into a war—with the crucial understanding that neither country would initiate such a war for a few years.[24]

Mussolini might have believed that the Pact of Steel would preclude further German unilateralism, but Hitler treated the agreement as Italian backing in his push for war against Poland in autumn 1939.[25] His faithlessness and disregard for his allies would almost break the Axis. As Warsaw refused to give in to German demands, Hitler needed a scheme to isolate Poland and deter the West from intervention. In late August, Berlin and Moscow concluded the non-aggression pact and a secret partition of Eastern Europe. Tokyo and Rome had not been informed of the negotiations and were as shocked by the pact as anyone.[26] The bombshell could not have landed at a worse time in Japan. Its Kwantung Army had been fighting the Red Army in escalating skirmishes along the Manchurian border. The clashes culminated in late August in the Battle of Khalkhin Gol that ended in a rout of the Japanese forces. Thus, just as Japanese soldiers were being killed by Soviet troops, Japan's ally, Germany, was reconciling its differences with Japan's enemy, the Soviet Union. The military disaster and Germany's public betrayal toppled Prime Minister Hiranuma Kiichirō. Tokyo vigorously protested the non-aggression pact and renounced the Anti-Comintern Pact.

Rome reacted just as negatively to Nazi–Soviet collusion. The non-aggression pact eliminated the threat of a two-front war for Germany, but it jeopardized Italy because it emboldened Hitler to drag Italy into a war through the Pact of Steel. Once war broke out in September, Mussolini vacillated between joining and repudiating Hitler. It was the exhaustion of the Italian armed forces, in combat since 1935, that forced Mussolini to stay out. Italy attempted to justify its inability to abide by the Pact of Steel by presenting Germany with an unrealistic list of supplies as preconditions for Italian belligerency. When the Red Army invaded Poland in mid-September, as prescribed in the secret protocol of the Nazi–Soviet pact, Italians were shocked and dismayed. Hardcore Fascists and pious Catholics alike fumed about Germany's connivance with the Soviet subjugation of eastern Poland. In late September, Berlin further aggravated Rome by signing a friendship and boundary treaty with Moscow. Mussolini learned of it "through the press, and then from the ambassadors."[27] Never could Mussolini have dreamed that, after making a career of anti-communism, he would one day call Stalin his ally's collaborator.

By late 1939, Hitler might well have bent the Axis to its breaking point through his insistence on war despite Italy's unpreparedness and the conclusion of the Nazi–Soviet pact without heeding Italian and Japanese sensitivity. Italy and Japan justly felt betrayed by Germany's disregard for its allies and volte-face vis-à-vis the Soviet Union. Germany thus entered World War II alone. Italy awkwardly declared "non-belligerency." Japan denounced Germany's shirking of its commitment to combat international communism. The Anti-Comintern Pact and Steel Pact rang hollow. After the Soviet Union invaded Finland in November 1939, Italy wanted to send help but Germany enraged Mussolini by turning back a trainload of Italian volunteers and equipment for fear of irritating Stalin. German–Italian relations were so strained that Ciano gave a speech in December 1939 to condemn German bad faith in invading Poland because Italy and Germany had agreed to avoid war for a few years as the premise of the Pact of Steel. He also decried Germany's habit of keeping its intentions secret from Italy and presenting them as fait accompli.[28] In a goodwill gesture to the West, Ciano highlighted Italy's potential as a mediator. In January 1940, Arita Hachirō, an opponent of Tokyo's rapprochement with Rome and Berlin, became the Japanese foreign minister. The next month, he signaled Japan's openness in remarks inviting foreign investors to return to China. It is not entirely inconceivable that creative, energetic Allied diplomacy might have persuaded Italy or Japan to distance themselves from Germany.

The Axis in Triumph, 1940–1942

Yet, somehow, the Axis not only endured, but within the year Italy, Germany, and Japan cemented their bonds with a three-way military alliance. The strength of German arms acted as the binding agent of the fractured Axis and drew other states to revolve around it—the Axis can be said to rise and fall with German martial prowess. Hitler and Stalin's deal, so upsetting to Italy and Japan, spared Germany from another two-front war. Italian non-belligerency, although ignominious, also freed Germany to focus on only one theater of war at a time. Hitler took advantage of the strategic realignment first to crush Poland and then to conquer Denmark and Norway. In late May 1940, through a combination of generalship, Allied missteps, and audacity, Germany managed to cut off the bulk of the French army and the British Expeditionary Force. The prospect of a swift, total German victory over the Western democracies presented lucrative opportunities to those who could choose to join the right side at the right time.

To be sure, the contradictions plaguing the Axis were not resolved, but only overlooked by Germany's partners seeking to profit from German military exploits. Foremost, South Tyrol flared up again. Ever since the German annexation of Austria, ethnic Germans in South Tyrol had been restless and agitating for the return of South Tyrol to German Austria. The conquest of Poland opened the possibility of transplanting these ethnic Germans to the incorporated territories in Eastern Europe. The South Tyrolese resented this proposed solution, for they wanted the transfer of their land rather than the population. Some of them equated impending migration to Greater Germany with legal immunity in Italy. They indulged in lawlessness and caused a number of incidents. Italy was particularly incensed that Germany imposed delays that slowed the pace of resettlement but somehow managed to evacuate eighty thousand ethnic Germans by sea just before the Soviets marched into Estonia, Latvia, and Lithuania in October 1939.

Moreover, communication between Rome and Berlin remained shoddy. Meetings on the ministerial level, between Ribbentrop and Ciano, accomplished little without the dictators' approval. Even when Hitler and Mussolini did meet, discussions were conducted in German and often dominated by a monologue by Hitler. Because the Germans from Hitler on down distrusted the Italians, if not Mussolini, few detailed military plans were ever shared. Thus, in April 1940, Italy learned of the invasion of Norway and Denmark at the same time the Scandinavian countries did. Ciano complained in his diary that Hitler always sent "the usual letter, in the usual styles, announcing what he had already done."[29] On May 10, another such missive arrived to reveal that the German offensive in the west had begun. Germany hid the operation from Italy so well that Ciano heard nothing relevant at the German embassy the night prior. Mussolini had every reason to feel slighted by Hitler, but his greed overshadowed his grievance when Germany unexpectedly routed the Allied armies.

The stunning lightning German victory over French and British forces opened unprecedented vistas of expansion for Germany's collaborators and secured their allegiance to Germany. On May 30, Mussolini finally resolved to join the war on Germany's side. Italy would wage what he called a "parallel war"—distinct from Germany's—against the Allies in the Mediterranean. But it took until June 10, when the roads to Paris lay wide open, for Italy to enter hostilities. Time ran out for Italy to make discernable gains before France sued for an armistice. Still, the capitulation of France and likely invasion of Britain left a vacuum in North Africa and the Middle East that looked ripe for exploitation, even by Italy's unprepared armed forces. The view from Japan looked even more enticing. The "orphaned" Dutch, French, and British colonies in Southeast Asia seemed ready for the taking. Time was of the essence for Tokyo, too. If the war ended before Japan made advances, the colonies could become part of a new German empire in peace negotiations.[30] So, in September 1940, the Italian army pushed from Libya into Egypt and Japan occupied northern French Indochina. With the benefits of triumphant German arms very much in mind, Rome and Tokyo found it easy to forgive Berlin's disrespect and betrayal. On September 27, Germany, Japan, and Italy concluded the Tripartite Pact, an economic and military alliance for mutual defense.[31]

In the spirit of the agreement, the rest of 1940 and 1941 saw a measure of coordination among the Axis. At sea, some Italian submarines operated in the North Atlantic from bases in German-occupied France while some U-boats prowled the Mediterranean. Farther afield, a few German commerce raiders camouflaged as merchantmen slipped through the British blockade to disrupt Allied shipping. Roaming in the Indian and the Pacific Oceans, these warships received support from and found refuge in Japanese-held territories. Some also disguised themselves as Japanese ships for security because the Allies wanted to avoid provoking Japan. Japanese assistance to Germany paid off handsomely in November 1940 when a raider captured a British steamer carrying mail that included a detailed report on British defenses in Asia.[32] A copy submitted to Japan went on to play a significant role in Japan's operational planning for overrunning Southeast Asia. Like Germany, Japan saved itself from a potential two-front war through a neutrality pact with the Soviet Union in April 1941.

The Axis made impressive gains in this period. On October 7, 1940, four days after a Hitler–Mussolini meeting, Germany marched into Romania to secure its oil fields and to forestall further Soviet intrusion into the Balkans. But Mussolini was angered not just by the lack of forewarning but also because he considered the Balkans in the Italian sphere. In reaction, Mussolini escalated his "parallel war" by attacking Greece in late October. Mussolini protested, "Hitler always faces me with a *fait accompli*. This time I am going to pay him back in his own coin. He will find out from the papers that I have occupied Greece."[33] Unfortunately for Italian independence and reputation, however, Greece repelled the aggressors and even counterattacked into Albania. By early 1941, the Italian positions in both the Balkans and North Africa had become untenable. Hitler summoned a chastened Mussolini in January to face the inevitable. Germany would have to step in to rescue Italy from more setbacks in Greece and Libya. In preparation for the campaign, Hitler drew Hungary, Slovakia, Romania, and Bulgaria into the Tripartite Pact between November 1940 and March 1941. On April 6, 1941, Germany and its new allies launched simultaneous attacks against Greece and Yugoslavia. No central organ coordinated the multinational forces. Hitler simply decreed that he would assume personal command of the whole Axis operation: "I reserve for myself the overall direction of this campaign in so far as it concerns the strategic objectives of Italian and Hungarian forces participating in accordance with the general plan."[34] By April 23, Germany's Balkan campaign was over. Germany took eighteen days to finish what Italy had tried to accomplish for three months, conquering Greece and even seizing Yugoslavia as a bonus. German intervention salvaged Italy's military positions but dealt Fascist prestige a serious blow and weakened Mussolini's position vis-à-vis Hitler. The remaining traces of balance between the two regimes were lost.

In the second half of 1941, the Axis states took on two powerful enemies in their indulgent quests for parallel wars. On June 22, Hitler unleashed Operation Barbarossa, his long-cherished invasion of the Soviet Union to conquer "living space." Like several other nations, Italy had heard of preparations for the campaign, but Germany repeatedly denied such "rumors" to its ally. So, when the attack began, Italy was as shocked as Soviet border guards. In fact, Italy was so ill prepared that when the familiar letter from Hitler arrived, Mussolini was vacationing on the Adriatic. Unlike Italy, Romania and Finland had been recruited by Germany to take part in the invasion because both countries suffered from Soviet expansionism.[35] Meanwhile, Tokyo's relations with Washington deteriorated markedly after Japan occupied all Indochina in July and the United States responded with an oil embargo and asset freeze. Japan and the United States entered intense negotiations but could not find common ground between their conflicting demands. Japan would not give up its territorial annexations and alliance with Germany. The United States refused to recognize Japanese hegemony in Asia. By late autumn, the Japanese leadership concluded that war against the United States might be inevitable. Without disclosing its intentions, Tokyo requested and received assurances from Berlin that Germany would intervene should war break out between Japan and the United States. Japan had to take such precaution because the Tripartite Pact as a defensive alliance was not necessarily triggered by an Axis offensive. On December 7, in a scheme hatched and executed in secrecy worthy of the Axis tradition, Japan attacked Pearl Harbor and Allied assets across Southeast Asia. As promised, days later Germany and Italy declared war on the United States.[36] At last, the Rome–Berlin–Tokyo Axis had common enemies.

Axis expansion reached its greatest extent in summer 1942. In Europe, the German-led coalition army rolled toward the Caucasus. In North Africa, German–Italian forces charged into Egypt, aiming for the Suez Canal and oil-rich Middle East. In Asia and the Pacific, Japan, although having lost the Battle of Midway, continued pushing into Burma and the Solomon Islands. The Axis even scored spectacular feats in technology, endurance, and propaganda. In July, an Italian aircraft flew from the Eastern Front to northern China and on to Japan, and then returned safely to Europe. In August, a Japanese submarine sailed from Malaya to France and back, carrying important cargoes each way. In light of these developments, Hitler and Ambassador Ōshima Hiroshi may well be excused for dreaming of the German and the Japanese armies converging in India.[37]

The Axis in Defeat, 1942–1945

But that scheme remained purely fanciful. By the end of 1942, the overextended Axis had suffered a series of irreversible setbacks. First, the breakthroughs in aviation and navigation accomplished little. The long-distance Japanese submarine sank enroute to Japan after striking a British mine off Singapore. The transcontinental Italian flight, which Japan had wished to keep secret, but which Italy exploited for propaganda, was not repeated because Tokyo refused to risk embarrassing Moscow by violating Soviet air space so publicly. Then, on November 4, Erwin Rommel's armies were routed by British Commonwealth forces at El Alamein. The British counterattacked so rapidly that the Afrika Korps had to leave behind some Italian units. On November 8, Anglo-American forces landed on the Moroccan and Algerian coasts. They then advanced into Tunisia and threatened to encircle Axis troops in Africa. On November 15, Japan was defeated in the Naval Battle of Guadalcanal and thus prevented from resupplying its position on the island. Finally, on November 19, the Red Army unleashed a massive offensive around Stalingrad, which had almost been captured by the German Sixth Army, with allied Hungarians, Italians, and Romanians guarding the flanks. The Soviet attack devastated these weaker units. When the envelopment closed on November 22, almost three hundred thousand Axis troops had been trapped, never to break out again. Stalingrad thus sent chills up spines not only in Berlin, but also in Budapest, Rome, and Bucharest. The tide of war had now turned.

In spring 1943, the Axis conducted fighting withdrawals in Eastern Europe and North Africa. The moment had arrived for the alliance to concentrate its strength in a single theater, but which one? As the fronts collapsed over winter, Mussolini had already twice through proxies tried to convince Hitler to make peace with the Soviet Union or at least adopt defensive postures to free up soldiers for the west. At the same time, Tokyo, too, instructed Ōshima to bring Hitler to reason regarding a separate peace with Moscow.[38] By February, Allied forces were squeezing the Italians and Germans into a corner in Tunisia and seemed poised to attack Italy soon. At a summit in April, Mussolini was supposed to propose treating with Stalin, as many Italian and German officials hoped, but he was instead subjected to a monologue by Hitler on a renewed German offensive in Russia. Granted, the Italian and the Japanese proposals in all likelihood did not stand much of a chance. But the fact remained that Hitler never allowed anything, even his allies, to stand in the way of his crusade against Judeo-Bolshevism. Even though Hitler admired Mussolini, he never consulted Mussolini in military matters. Instead, Hitler listened at times to the Romanian strongman Ion Antonescu, a Slavophobe who favored coming to terms with the West.

The Axis underwent disasters and fundamental transformations in mid-1943. In early May, 270,000 Germans and Italians surrendered in North Africa in what Winston Churchill touted as "Tunisgrad." On July 5, Hitler launched his armored attacks toward Kursk. On July 9, the Allies began landing in Sicily. Only after the German charge had grounded to a stop by July 13 did Hitler relent and transfer troops to Italy. Hitler then summoned Mussolini for a meeting, where Mussolini's top associates wanted him to extricate Italy from the war. But Hitler once again lectured Mussolini in German, and Mussolini said little beyond requesting more aid. Mussolini's failure to undo the Axis sealed his own fate. The Fascist Grand Council voted on July 25 to restore power to the king, who promptly had Mussolini arrested. To reassure Germany, the new government under Pietro Badoglio pledged to carry on the war, but in secret it began negotiations with the Allies.[39] In any case, Hitler distrusted Badoglio and sent troops into Italy and its occupation zones. Italy surrendered in September and declared war on Germany the next month.

Thus, the Axis stopped functioning—to the extent that it ever had—as a meaningful institution, but it did not disappear and even underwent a revival of sorts. Just after the Italian capitulation, Hitler had Mussolini liberated and installed as the reluctant head of the Italian Social Republic (also called Republic of Salò), a rump state in northern Italy dominated by fanatical Fascists and enforced by the SS (*Schutzstaffel*). Mussolini was reduced to a puppet of Hitler and subjected to the humiliation of seeing Germany annex South Tyrol and deport Italians of Jewish ancestry. Still, the influx of German troops stiffened defense and tied down substantial Allied resources, and so fulfilled the original purpose of the alliance. Only after the complete submission of Rome to Berlin did the Axis acquire a united front and purpose.

With Italy sidelined, only Germany and Japan fielded significant forces upholding the Axis. Germany's former Pacific colonies, which Japan had covertly militarized, proved their strategic worth as American forces fought bloody battles for their capture. Since mid-1943, German–Japanese naval collaboration intensified. A few Japanese and German submarines rendezvoused at sea to exchange cargoes and passengers, notably Subhas Chandra Bose, who traveled from Germany to Japan to seek support for his Free India movement.[40] Several German and Japanese submarines completed the journey between occupied France and East Indies. They ferried from Europe to Asia blueprints and parts of advanced technology, including radar and jets, and from Asia to Europe raw materials such as tungsten and rubber. Germany operated from a base in Penang an increasing number of U-boats and a couple of requisitioned Italian submarines in the Indian Ocean, where they achieved some success against Allied shipping. But these small victories merely betrayed the struggles confronting the Axis, namely the great distances that hindered strategic coordination and the overbearing Allied naval supremacy that drove U-boats from the North Atlantic to find refuge elsewhere.

As the Red Army stormed into Central Europe in 1944, the smaller Axis states began to peel off and seek an exit from the war on sufferable peace terms. Whereas Hungary and Romania had been persecuting Jews to gain favors from Germany, now their surviving Jews might be used as bargaining chips with the Allies. Hungary signaled its willingness to surrender to the Allies and was invaded in March by Germany. The Nazis immediately began to round up Hungarians of Jewish ancestry and deport them to Auschwitz. After Stalingrad, Romania scaled back its participation in the Holocaust and even resisted German pressure to deport the Jews within its prewar borders. And Japan never followed Germany in systematically persecuting the Jews in areas it controlled. Under the pressure of repeated setbacks and looming defeat, Germany and Japan, too, suffered a leadership shake-up in July 1944. On July 20, Hitler was shaken by an assassination and putsch attempt by high-ranking army officers. The same week, Prime Minister Tōjō Hideki was ousted, just before assassination plots were to be put into action. In late August, in a replay of Italy, the Romanian king arrested Antonescu and declared war on Germany. Days later, Slovak nationalists rose up against the pro-Nazi regime, triggering German intervention. Bulgaria, which did not join the campaign against the Soviet Union, surrendered and declared war on Germany in early September when the Red Army entered its territory. Shortly afterward, Finland concluded an armistice with the Soviet Union and began expelling German troops. From then on, what remained of the European Axis was held together at German gunpoint.

Germany's surrender in May 1945 left Japan the only belligerent state of the Tripartite Alliance, but some minor cooperation lingered on. In the East Indies, a few Italian and German submarines joined Japanese service and might even have been partially operated by their original crews. Some German agents in China entered contract labor with Japan to provide military intelligence and propaganda. Such detritus of the Axis did little to delay the inevitable Japanese defeat in August, hastened by the obliterations of Hiroshima and Nagasaki. In an ironic twist, in May 1945, the United States captured a shipment of uranium oxide from a surrendered German submarine bound for Japan.[41] The material might have been consumed by the Manhattan Project, conceived partly by former citizens of Axis countries such as Albert Einstein, Enrico Fermi, and Leó Szilárd.

Conclusion

Could the Axis have won? During the war, this specter was granted some credence, at least in the United States, to motivate its population to fight an enemy an ocean away. *Why We Fight*, a wartime documentary, warned American viewers that Germany and Japan aimed to divide the world between themselves and impose their tyrannical new order. After the war, scholarly works and popular media alike entertained the question in "what if" examinations of World War II.[42] An Axis victory served as the setting of fictional alternate histories, such as *The Man in the High Castle* or *Fatherland*. But like many hypothetical questions, it is ultimately unanswerable. To begin with, "winning" must be defined. Had the Axis confined its quarrel with Britain and France only, the prospect of winning or an eventual advantageous settlement may indeed seem conceivable. Once the Soviet Union was attacked, the path to victory narrowed significantly. Even if Japan had joined the German invasion in 1941, given the size of Siberia and Japan's previous lackluster performance against the Red Army, it looks improbable that the outcome would have differed greatly, especially after German-led forces failed to defeat the Soviet Union by the winter of 1941–1942. Japanese hostilities against Moscow could disrupt the flow of American Lend-Lease aid, much of which was unloaded in Vladivostok. But when the Axis declared war on the United States in December 1941, its defeat was but a matter of time. The fact remains that Axis "achievements" came mostly from expanding the conflict and collecting an ever-growing list of enemies through surprise attacks.

If the Axis could not win, a more historical query should focus on the causes of its failure. Some pilots, sailors, and submariners performed daring tasks to build bridges in the air, at sea, and underwater to connect Berlin and Rome with Tokyo. But the amount of goods moved by these risky exploits was dwarfed by any of the convoys from the United States, made safe by Allied countermeasures that sank more of the same Axis submarines and required greater sacrifices from their crews.

These feats embodied the main problem plaguing the Axis—the lines of transportation between Europe and Asia that no ceremonies trumpeting Axis solidarity or exhortations invoking fighting spirit could shorten. For some time, the Axis used the Trans-Siberian Railway to ferry cargoes, personnel, and intelligence. For instance, in spring 1941, Foreign Minister Matsuoka Yōsuke traveled by train from Asia to Europe. Hitler suggested at their meeting that Japan pounce on Allied colonies and he pledged German support for Japan in a war against the United States. On the return leg, Matsuoka signed the neutrality pact with Moscow to free Japan for its southward advance. But when Germany invaded the Soviet Union, the rail link was severed and, from then on, most Axis traffic was forced to submerge. Even at their greatest extents, the German and the Japanese armies never came close to aiding each other. Instead of the constant, routine traffic among the Allies, the Axis had to rely on extraordinary stunts by a few airmen and seamen.

If physical exchange was limited, Axis leaders could still communicate in person or through messages and envoys, although these channels suffered from their own ills. Between 1934 and 1944, Hitler and Mussolini met seventeen times.[43] These summits resolved little because they were wasted on propagandistic festivities in peacetime and Hitler's monologues during the war. Hitler as the center of gravity of the Axis also had individual meetings with the leaders of Finland, Romania, Hungary, Vichy France, and Spain. But the European Axis heads never congregated in one place to formulate a common strategy, and distance prevented Hitler from meeting any Japanese official above the foreign minister. The Axis alliance was mostly a collection of bilateral ties between Germany and its collaborators. By contrast, the Allies met often and jointly agreed on documents such as the Atlantic Charter, the Casablanca Declaration, the Cairo Declaration, or the Potsdam Declaration.

Short of personal conferences, the Axis maintained contact through the airwaves. During the war, Ōshima Hiroshi transmitted numerous coded, confidential messages to keep Tokyo informed of political and military affairs in Germany. Unfortunately for the Axis, American signal intelligence could decipher his reports and supply the same information to Allied leaders. His meticulous descriptions of German defenses on the Atlantic coast proved to be of singular worth in the Allied preparation for D-Day. Even some interpersonal conversations could not escape hostile infiltration. Richard Sorge, an undercover German Comintern agent posing as a journalist, ran a spy ring in Tokyo to obtain Axis secrets.[44] In autumn 1941, Sorge informed Moscow that Japan would not attack the Soviet Union, thereby freeing the Red Army to transfer troops and equipment to the west.

Japan's decision not to join Germany reveals another Achilles heel of the Axis—the absence of a uniform strategy or even a common adversary until December 1941. For the Axis to stand a chance, it needed to concentrate all its firepower on one target, because Germany or Japan alone could not vanquish the Soviet Union or the United States, not to mention Italy's struggles against British Commonwealth forces. But the Tripartite partners did not fight a synchronized campaign against a single foe. Instead, Berlin, Rome, and Tokyo each fought its own parallel war to secure its destiny in Eastern Europe, the Mediterranean, or Southeast Asia. While Germany was gearing up for its invasion of the Soviet Union in spring 1941, Italy embarked on its independent but disastrous campaign in the Balkans that ultimately required German intervention. Although easily triumphant in Yugoslavia and Greece, Germany had to push back Barbarossa by about a month and depleted its airborne units in its assault on Crete. The paratroops could have helped encircle more Soviet units, and the delay might have cost Germany the chance to capture Moscow. Just when German troops froze outside Moscow in December 1941 and needed help most, Japan threw its resources not into assisting its allies but attacking the world's greatest industrial power and turning it against the Axis. Also, Germany must have been bitter that Japan observed its neutrality vis-à-vis the Soviet Union so diligently that it dared not disrupt American Lend-Lease aid to Vladivostok.

The minor states, too, held dear their own priorities. Finland as a co-belligerent took up arms against the Soviet Union only to recover land lost in the Winter War in 1940.[45]

As such, it declined to advance beyond its old boundary. Romania also fought to reverse Soviet expansion and to acquire compensation for territories lost to Hungary. Bulgaria joined the Axis in exchange for Greek and Yugoslav land and even declared war on the Allies, but it refused to participate in hostilities against the Soviet Union for historical reasons. The Axis states' discrete territorial ambitions that made the alliance possible turned out to be an irreparable structural flaw in the foundation. Fundamentally, the Tripartite Pact was constructed as a defensive deterrent to potential enemies and was not supposed to be triggered by its own acts of aggression. When its members each waged and became consumed by its own parallel war, the Axis lost all its strategic value. To make matters worse, the Axis reliance on surprise attacks to overwhelm foes, especially those superior in number or resource, precluded genuine coordination or even sharing of plans within the alliance.

The absence of a concerted military strategy mirrored the Axis responses to Nazi racism, itself riddled with inconsistencies. The concession by "Aryans" that they needed help from Latin, Slavic, and even Asian allies undermined the Nazi racial worldview. As long as German arms prevailed, the Axis states could obfuscate the contradiction with verbal constructs such as "honorary Aryans" and "compatible" spheres of influence. But even German domination of Europe did not bring about an unobstructed implementation of Nazi racist and genocidal policies. For Hitler, the war and the Holocaust were two aspects of the same goal—conquering "living space" necessitated depopulating Eastern Europe. Thus, Germany and Romania began mass-shooting Soviet Jews behind the frontline soon after Barbarossa began. The expected victory over the Soviet Union in autumn 1941 prompted Germany to begin preparing for the "Final Solution" to deport, detain, and destroy European Jews. Even after death camps became operational, the implementation of the genocide still depended on individual Axis regimes. Croatia, Slovakia, and Romania turned out to be reliable partners in the crime. Still, Slovakia halted deportations once it learned of the gassing. Romania targeted mostly the Jews in its occupied areas and preserved its "own" Jews. Bulgaria and Hungary also gave up Jews in annexed regions but balked at surrendering their own nationals. Hungarians of Jewish ancestry remained shielded until the German takeover in 1944. Italy did not pass antisemitic legislation until 1938.[46] Its military even protected Jews fleeing their Croatian tormenters.[47] Only after the German occupation in 1943 were Italians of Jewish ancestry deported. Finland did not participate in the Holocaust. Nor did Japan, which admitted some Jewish refugees from Europe and did not persecute the Jews in the Greater East Asia Co-prosperity Sphere.[48] Of course, at the same time Japan was imposing its own racism across occupied Asia while force-feeding slogans about Pan-Asian solidarity and liberation from Western imperialism to the peoples it subjugated.

The divergent attitudes toward race manifest a last weakness that fractured the Axis—the ideological fissures among its members. During the war, the Allies portrayed the Axis as belonging to the same evil system. Since then, scholars have been debating to what extent the Axis shared an ideology, namely fascism. The Axis regimes each had its proponents of fascism, but not all Axis states can be considered fascist or even authoritarian. On one end of the spectrum was Finland, which did not implement a dictatorship. On the other end, Nazi Germany and Fascist Italy were certainly fascist regimes. Most scholars agree that National Socialism and Fascism shared features such as animosity toward democracy and communism, irredentism, glorification of violence and masculinity, nationalism, and charismatic leadership. But the degree to which Hitler outdid Mussolini in authority, genocide, war, and oppression can also seem to place Nazi Germany in a category of its own. Japan exhibited some traits of generic fascism but not others.[49] Wartime Japan expanded territorially and suppressed dissent, but its power was not backed by an ideological mass movement and its leadership exuded anything but charisma. Some junior officers radicalized Japanese politics through attempted coups and assassinations, but they did not take power. The minor Axis states likewise reacted to but were not run by fascists. In Hungary, the Arrow Cross replaced the conservative government only when Germany invaded in 1944. In Romania, Hitler even assisted Antonescu in crushing the Iron Guard in a power struggle. Ultimately for Hitler, having a reliable ally outweighed ideological consistency.

That Hitler alone exercised absolute power meant that the other Axis states could be challenged from within by alternative sources of legitimacy. When enemy troops began to appear on Axis borders, the regimes dropped out of the alliance one by one. The first to fall was Mussolini, who never fully controlled the military and had to compete with the king and the pope for influence. When the Allies invaded Italy, the king removed Mussolini. Antonescu suffered a similar fate when the Red Army was poised to attack Romania in 1944. Separation of power gave Hungary and Finland some room to explore a separate peace while still answering to Hitler. Finland succeeded in withdrawing from the war, while Hungary was taken over by its erstwhile ally. For Japan, the war came to an end when Emperor Hirohito spoke in favor of submitting to the Allies to break a deadlock among political and military leaders. Only Hitler remained in command until enemy soldiers were standing on his crumpling state, a telling end to the power binding the Rome–Berlin–Tokyo Axis.

NOTES

1. Aristotle A. Kallis, *Fascist Ideology: Territory and Expansionism in Italy and Germany, 1922–1945* (New York: Routledge, 2000).
2. Adolf Hitler, *Mein Kampf*, trans. Ralph Manheim (Boston: Houghton Mifflin, 1943), 628–629. Hitler expressed similar views in his so-called second book, see Adolf Hitler, *Hitler's Second Book: The Unpublished Sequel to* Mein Kampf, ed. Gerhard L. Weinberg, trans. Krista Smith (New York: Enigma Books, 2003), chapter XV.
3. Eberhard Jäckel, *Hitler's World View: A Blueprint for Power*, trans. Herbert Arnold (Cambridge: Harvard University Press, 1981), 29, 38; Hitler, *Mein Kampf*, 625.
4. F. W. Deakin, *The Brutal Friendship: Mussolini, Hitler and the Fall of Italian Fascism* (New York: Harper & Row, 1962), 5–6; Denis Mack Smith, *Mussolini* (New York: Vintage, 1983), 42; MacGregor Knox, *Common Destiny: Dictatorship, Foreign Policy, and War in Fascist Italy and Nazi Germany* (Cambridge: Cambridge University Press, 2000), 124.

5. Hitler, *Mein Kampf*, 3; Adolf Hitler, *My New Order: Hitler's Own Sequel to* Mein Kampf, ed. Raoul de Roussy de Sales (New York: Reynal & Hitchcock, 1941), 157.
6. Benito Mussolini, *Mussolini as Revealed in His Political Speeches (November 1914–August 1923)*, ed. and trans. Barone Bernardo Quaranta di San Severino (London: J. M. Dent, 1923), 125; Benito Mussolini, *My Rise and Fall, Volume I* (New York: Da Capo Press, 1998), 131; Mack Smith, 182.
7. Richard Lamb, *Mussolini as Diplomat: Il Duce's Italy on the World Stage* (New York: Fromm International, 1999), 105–106.
8. Elizabeth Wiskemann, *The Rome-Berlin Axis: A Study of the Relations between Hitler and Mussolini*, new and revised ed. (London: Collins, 1966), 57–58; Documents on German Foreign Policy (DGFP), series C, vol. IV, no. 545 (Washington, DC: Government Printing Office, 1954).
9. Klaus Hildebrand, *The Foreign Policy of the Third Reich*, trans. Anthony Fothergill (Berkeley: University of California Press, 1973), 35.
10. DGFP, series D., vol. I, no. 153.
11. Galeazzo Ciano, *Ciano's Diplomatic Papers*, ed. Malcolm Muggeridge, trans. Stuart Hood (London: Odhams Press, 1948), 43–48.
12. Stanley G. Payne, *The Franco Regime, 1936–1975* (Madison: University of Wisconsin Press, 1987), chapter 8; Robert H. Whealey, *Hitler and Spain: The Nazi Role in the Spanish Civil War, 1936–1939* (Lexington: University Press of Kentucky, 1989); Paul Preston, *Franco: A Biography* (New York: Basic Books, 1994), chapter IX.
13. Frederick R. Dickinson, *War and National Reinvention: Japan in the Great War, 1914–1919* (Cambridge: Harvard University Asia Center, 1999), chapter 2.
14. William C. Kirby, *Germany and Republican China* (Stanford: Stanford University Press, 1984).
15. Ian Hill Nish, *Japanese Foreign Policy in the Interwar Period* (Westport: Praeger, 2002).
16. Thomas W. Burkman, *Japan and the League of Nations: Empire and World Order, 1914–1938* (Honolulu: University of Hawai'i Press, 2008).
17. Akira Kudō, *Japanese-German Business Relations: Cooperation and Rivalry in the Inter-War Period* (London: Routledge, 1998).
18. Ricky W. Law, *Transnational Nazism: Ideology and Culture in German-Japanese Relations, 1919–1936* (New York: Cambridge University Press, 2019).
19. Christopher Thorne, *The Limits of Foreign Policy: The West, the League and the Far Eastern Crisis of 1931–1933* (New York: G. P. Putnam's Sons, 1973); Jessamyn R. Abel, *The International Minimum: Creativity and Contradiction in Japan's Global Engagement, 1933–1964* (Honolulu: University of Hawai'i Press, 2015).
20. John P. Fox, *Germany and the Far Eastern Crisis 1931–1938: A Study in Diplomacy and Ideology* (Oxford: Clarendon Press, 1982).
21. Carl Boyd, *The Extraordinary Envoy: General Hiroshi Ōshima and Diplomacy in the Third Reich* (Washington, DC: University Press of America, 1980). Japanese names in this chapter are rendered with the surname first, followed by the given name.
22. Christian Goeschel, *Mussolini and Hitler: The Forging of the Fascist Alliance* (New Haven: Yale University Press, 2018).
23. Mario Toscano, *The Origins of the Pact of Steel* (Baltimore: Johns Hopkins Press, 1967).
24. DGFP, series D, vol. VI, nos. 341 and 426; Ciano, *Papers*, 284.
25. H. James Burgwyn, *Italian Foreign Policy in the Interwar Period, 1918–1940* (Westport: Praeger, 1997), 194.

26. Galeazzo Ciano, *The Ciano Diaries 1939–1943: The Complete, Unabridged Diaries of Count Galeazzo Ciano, Italian Minister for Foreign Affairs, 1936–1943*, ed. Hugh Gibson (Garden City: Doubleday, 1946), 126.
27. Ibid., 152.
28. Lamb, 268–269; Wiskemann, 226–227; Ray Moseley, *Mussolini's Shadow: The Double Life of Count Galeazzo Ciano* (New Haven: Yale University Press, 1999), 89–90.
29. Ciano, *Diaries*, 234.
30. Jeremy A. Yellen, *The Greater East Asia Co-prosperity Sphere: When Total Empire Met Total War* (Ithaca: Cornell University Press, 2019), 25–45.
31. Ken Ishida, *Japan, Italy and the Road to the Tripartite Alliance* (Cham, Switzerland: Palgrave Macmillan, 2018).
32. August Karl Muggenthaler, *German Raiders of World War II* (Englewood Cliffs, NJ: Prentice-Hall, 1977), 39.
33. Mussolini, quoted in Ciano, *Diaries*, 300.
34. Adolf Hitler, *Hitler's War Directives 1939–1945*, ed. H. R. Trevor-Roper (London: Sidgwick and Jackson, 1964), 64; Burkhart Mueller-Hillebrand, *Germany and Its Allies in World War II: A Record of Axis Collaboration Problems* (Frederick, MD: University Publications of America, 1980), 106.
35. David Stahel, ed., *Joining Hitler's Crusade: European Nations and the Invasion of the Soviet Union, 1941* (Cambridge: Cambridge University Press, 2018).
36. Klaus H. Schmider, *Hitler's Fatal Miscalculation: Why Germany Declared War on the United States* (Cambridge: Cambridge University Press, 2021).
37. Carl Boyd, *Hitler's Japanese Confidant: General Ōshima Hiroshi and MAGIC Intelligence, 1941–1945* (Lawrence: University Press of Kansas, 1993), 72.
38. Boyd, *Hitler's Japanese Confidant*, 93.
39. Friedrich-Karl von Plehwe, *The End of an Alliance: Rome's Defection from the Axis in 1943* (New York: Oxford University Press, 1971).
40. Hans-Joachim Krug, et al., *Reluctant Allies: German–Japanese Naval Relations in World War II* (Annapolis: Naval Institute Press, 2001).
41. William J. Broad, "Captured Cargo, Captivating Mystery," *The New York Times*, December 31, 1995: 22; Carl Boyd and Akihiko Yoshida, *The Japanese Submarine Force and World War II* (Annapolis: Naval Institute Press, 2013), 165; Wolfgang W. E. Samuel, *American Raiders: The Race to Capture the Luftwaffe's Secrets* (Jackson: University Press of Mississippi, 2004), 114–115; Joseph Mark Scalia, *Germany's Last Mission to Japan: The Failed Voyage of U-234* (Annapolis: Naval Institute Press, 2000).
42. Dennis E. Showalter and Harold C. Deutsch, eds., *If the Allies Had Fallen: Sixty Alternate Scenarios of World War II* (New York: Skyhorse Publishing, 2012); Gavriel Rosenfeld, *The World Hitler Never Made: Alternate History and the Memory of Nazism* (New York: Cambridge University Press, 2005); Bevin Alexander, *How Hitler Could Have Won World War II: The Fatal Errors That Led to Nazi Defeat* (New York: Three Rivers Press, 2001).
43. Santi Corvaja, *Hitler and Mussolini: The Secret Meetings* (New York: Enigma Books, 2001).
44. Chalmers Johnson, *An Instance of Treason: Ozaki Hotsumi and the Sorge Spy Ring*, expanded ed. (Stanford: Stanford University Press, 1990).
45. Olli Vehviläinen, *Finland in the Second World War: Between Germany and Russia* (New York: Palgrave, 2002).

46. Meir Michaelis, *Mussolini and the Jews: German–Italian Relations and the Jewish Question in Italy* (New York: Oxford University Press, 1978).
47. Jonathan Steinberg, *All or Nothing: The Axis and the Holocaust 1941–1943* (New York: Routledge, 1990).
48. Meron Medzini, *Under the Shadow of the Rising Sun: Japan and the Jews during the Holocaust Era* (Boston: Academic Studies Press, 2016).
49. Reto Hofmann, *The Fascist Effect: Japan and Italy, 1915–1952* (Ithaca: Cornell University Press, 2015).

Bibliography

Abel, Jessamyn R. *The International Minimum: Creativity and Contradiction in Japan's Global Engagement, 1933–1964*. Honolulu: University of Hawai'i Press, 2015.

Alexander, Bevin. *How Hitler Could Have Won World War II: The Fatal Errors That Led to Nazi Defeat*. New York: Three Rivers Press, 2001.

Boyd, Carl. *The Extraordinary Envoy: General Hiroshi Ōshima and Diplomacy in the Third Reich*. Washington, DC: University Press of America, 1980.

Boyd, Carl. *Hitler's Japanese Confidant: General Ōshima Hiroshi and MAGIC Intelligence, 1941–1945*. Lawrence: University Press of Kansas, 1993.

Boyd, Carl, and Akihiko Yoshida. *The Japanese Submarine Force and World War II*. Annapolis: Naval Institute Press, 2013.

Broad, William J. "Captured Cargo, Captivating Mystery." *The New York Times*, December 31, 1995: 22.

Burgwyn, H. James. *Italian Foreign Policy in the Interwar Period, 1918–1940*. Westport: Praeger, 1997.

Burkman, Thomas W. *Japan and the League of Nations: Empire and World Order, 1914–1938*. Honolulu: University of Hawai'i Press, 2008.

Ciano, Galeazzo. *The Ciano Diaries 1939–1943: The Complete, Unabridged Diaries of Count Galeazzo Ciano, Italian Minister for Foreign Affairs, 1936–1943*. Edited by Hugh Gibson. Garden City: Doubleday, 1946.

Ciano, Galeazzo. *Ciano's Diplomatic Papers*. Edited by Malcolm Muggeridge. Translated by Stuart Hood. London: Odhams Press, 1948.

Corvaja, Santi. *Hitler and Mussolini: The Secret Meetings*. New York: Enigma Books, 2001.

Deakin, F. W. *The Brutal Friendship: Mussolini, Hitler and the Fall of Italian Fascism*. New York: Harper & Row, 1962.

Dickinson, Frederick R. *War and National Reinvention: Japan in the Great War, 1914–1919*. Cambridge: Harvard University Asia Center, 1999.

Documents on German Foreign Policy, 1918–1945. Washington, DC: Government Printing Office, 1954.

Fox, John P. *Germany and the Far Eastern Crisis 1931–1938: A Study in Diplomacy and Ideology*. Oxford: Clarendon Press, 1982.

Goeschel, Christian. *Mussolini and Hitler: The Forging of the Fascist Alliance*. New Haven: Yale University Press, 2018.

Hildebrand, Klaus. *The Foreign Policy of the Third Reich*. Translated by Anthony Fothergill. Berkeley: University of California Press, 1973.

Hitler, Adolf. *Hitler's Second Book: The Unpublished Sequel to Mein Kampf.* Edited by Gerhard L. Weinberg. Translated by Krista Smith. New York: Enigma Books, 2003.
Hitler, Adolf. *Hitler's War Directives 1939–1945.* Edited by H. R. Trevor-Roper. London: Sidgwick and Jackson, 1964.
Hitler, Adolf. *Mein Kampf.* Translated by Ralph Manheim. Boston: Houghton Mifflin, 1943.
Hitler, Adolf. *My New Order: Hitler's Own Sequel to Mein Kampf.* Edited by Raoul de Roussy de Sales. New York: Reynal & Hitchcock, 1941.
Hofmann, Reto. *The Fascist Effect: Japan and Italy, 1915–1952.* Ithaca: Cornell University Press, 2015.
Ishida, Ken. *Japan, Italy and the Road to the Tripartite Alliance.* Cham, Switzerland: Palgrave Macmillan, 2018.
Jäckel, Eberhard. *Hitler's World View: A Blueprint for Power.* Translated by Herbert Arnold. Cambridge: Harvard University Press, 1981.
Johnson, Chalmers. *An Instance of Treason: Ozaki Hotsumi and the Sorge Spy Ring.* Expanded ed. Stanford: Stanford University Press, 1990.
Kallis, Aristotle A. *Fascist Ideology: Territory and Expansionism in Italy and Germany, 1922–1945.* New York: Routledge, 2000.
Kirby, William C. *Germany and Republican China.* Stanford: Stanford University Press, 1984.
Knox, MacGregor. *Common Destiny: Dictatorship, Foreign Policy, and War in Fascist Italy and Nazi Germany.* Cambridge: Cambridge University Press, 2000.
Krug, Hans-Joachim, Yōichi Hirama, Berthold J. Sander-Nagashima, and Axel Niestlé. *Reluctant Allies: German–Japanese Naval Relations in World War II.* Annapolis: Naval Institute Press, 2001.
Kudō, Akira. *Japanese–German Business Relations: Cooperation and Rivalry in the Inter-War Period.* London: Routledge, 1998.
Lamb, Richard. *Mussolini as Diplomat: Il Duce's Italy on the World Stage.* New York: Fromm International, 1999.
Law, Ricky W. *Transnational Nazism: Ideology and Culture in German–Japanese Relations, 1919–1936.* New York: Cambridge University Press, 2019.
Mack Smith, Denis. *Mussolini.* New York: Vintage, 1983.
Medzini, Meron. *Under the Shadow of the Rising Sun: Japan and the Jews during the Holocaust Era.* Boston: Academic Studies Press, 2016.
Michaelis, Meir. *Mussolini and the Jews: German–Italian Relations and the Jewish Question in Italy.* New York: Oxford University Press, 1978.
Moseley, Ray. *Mussolini's Shadow: The Double Life of Count Galeazzo Ciano.* New Haven: Yale University Press, 1999.
Mueller-Hillebrand, Burkhart. *Germany and Its Allies in World War II: A Record of Axis Collaboration Problems.* Frederick, MD: University Publications of America, 1980.
Muggenthaler, August Karl. *German Raiders of World War II.* Englewood Cliffs, NJ: Prentice-Hall, 1977.
Mussolini, Benito. *Mussolini as Revealed in His Political Speeches (November 1914–August 1923).* Edited and translated by Barone Bernardo Quaranta di San Severino. London: J. M. Dent, 1923.
Mussolini, Benito. *My Rise and Fall, Volume I.* New York: Da Capo Press, 1998.
Nish, Ian Hill. *Japanese Foreign Policy in the Interwar Period.* Westport: Praeger, 2002.
Payne, Stanley G. *The Franco Regime, 1936–1975.* Madison: University of Wisconsin Press, 1987.

Plehwe, Friedrich-Karl von. *The End of an Alliance: Rome's Defection from the Axis in 1943.* New York: Oxford University Press, 1971.

Preston, Paul. *Franco: A Biography.* New York: Basic Books, 1994.

Rosenfeld, Gavriel. *The World Hitler Never Made: Alternate History and the Memory of Nazism.* New York: Cambridge University Press, 2005.

Samuel, Wolfgang W. E. *American Raiders: The Race to Capture the Luftwaffe's Secrets.* Jackson: University Press of Mississippi, 2004.

Scalia, Joseph Mark. *Germany's Last Mission to Japan: The Failed Voyage of U-234.* Annapolis: Naval Institute Press, 2000.

Schmider, Klaus H. *Hitler's Fatal Miscalculation: Why Germany Declared War on the United States.* Cambridge: Cambridge University Press, 2021.

Showalter, Dennis E., and Harold C. Deutsch, eds. *If the Allies Had Fallen: Sixty Alternate Scenarios of World War II.* New York: Skyhorse Publishing, 2012.

Stahel, David, ed. *Joining Hitler's Crusade: European Nations and the Invasion of the Soviet Union, 1941.* Cambridge: Cambridge University Press, 2018.

Steinberg, Jonathan. *All or Nothing: The Axis and the Holocaust 1941-1943.* New York: Routledge, 1990.

Thorne, Christopher. *The Limits of Foreign Policy: The West, the League and the Far Eastern Crisis of 1931-1933.* New York: G. P. Putnam's Sons, 1973.

Toscano, Mario. *The Origins of the Pact of Steel.* Baltimore: Johns Hopkins Press, 1967.

Vehviläinen, Olli. *Finland in the Second World War: Between Germany and Russia.* New York: Palgrave, 2002.

Whealey, Robert H. *Hitler and Spain: The Nazi Role in the Spanish Civil War, 1936-1939.* Lexington: University Press of Kentucky, 1989.

Wiskemann, Elizabeth. *The Rome-Berlin Axis: A Study of the Relations between Hitler and Mussolini.* New and revised ed. London: Collins, 1966.

Yellen, Jeremy A. *The Greater East Asia Co-prosperity Sphere: When Total Empire Met Total War.* Ithaca: Cornell University Press, 2019.

CHAPTER 6

GERMAN VICTORIES, 1939–1940

EUGENIA C. KIESLING

WHILE the passage of time has opened archives and allowed specialist historians to develop nuanced interpretations of Germany's military victories in the opening campaigns of World War II in Europe, distance also dilutes popular understanding. Twenty-first-century readers will mostly understand the campaigns in Poland, Scandinavia, the Low Countries, and France from September 1939 to June 1940 through the clichés of the immediate postwar years—gallant Polish hussars, brave but helpless Scandinavians, defensive French generals, and the inevitability of a second world war to redress the Treaty of Versailles. Above all, there is the widespread belief that the German army swept all before it with modern weapons, totalitarian efficiently, and the magic of "blitzkrieg."

This chapter will explore the 1939–1940 campaigns not as demonstrations of superior German operational skill but as manifestations of a general European failure to think through the consequences of diplomatic decisions and military planning. Miscalculations led the Allied nations into unwanted war and costly initial defeats, and Germany's "Thousand Year Reich" lasted only twelve years. The idea that superior cognitive processes, rather than military hardware or doctrine, explained Germany's defeat of France appeared even before the war ended. In his bitter 1943 memoir of France's "strange defeat," historian, soldier, and patriot Marc Bloch castigated France's sclerotic high command, concluding that the German army moved faster than its French adversary because its officers and men thought faster. Behind French military inertia, Bloch argued, lay a general lack of commitment to the national cause, a deficiency he blamed on the government of the Third Republic and on an educational system that failed to inculcate patriotic fervor in a people divided by class and politics.[1]

Inspired by Bloch's attribution of French failure to intellectual lethargy, this essay will argue that, if the French army thought too slowly, the German army's initial successes came at the cost of failure to think rigorously about the consequences of its actions. Indeed, far from "concentrating the mind," as Samuel Johnson famously said of the prospect of being hanged, the prospect of imminent European war sparked among both statesman and strategists various mixtures of resignation and wishful thinking.

If operating in the twin pressure cookers of national and international politics allows national leaders little opportunity for careful reflection, historians have less excuse for letting enthusiasm shape their analysis of military operations. Laudatory descriptions of "blitzkrieg" reflect fantasies of how a brilliant victory ought to look rather than the reality of a semi-mechanized army grappling uncertainly with new weapons and operational techniques. Ultimately, of course, the stunning successes of 1939–1940 tempted Germany's leaders to further adventures in North Africa and the Soviet Union. Here, too, the reality of ultimate defeat would be mitigated in much of the literature by the emphasis on the tactical and operational successes achieved by General Erwin Rommel's Afrika Korps and in the initial German drives on Moscow and Leningrad.[2]

The myth that Germany went to war in 1939 with a revolutionary "Blitzkrieg" doctrine has persisted because it has satisfied many constituents. During the war, Germany profited from the fear instilled by visions of inexorable armor–air force combined arms team, while the defeated found an explanation for their own failures.[3] For NATO forces facing the threat of a Soviet invasion of western Europe, Germany's alleged expertise at *Blitzkrieg* served as reassurance that small, agile, and technologically superior forces could "fight outnumbered and win."[4] To audiences more interested in admiring tank warfare than in examining military theory, the word *Blitzkrieg* remains evocative of military success, but the sensationalism of the discussion undermines our ability to grasp what actually happened in Poland, Scandinavia, and France.

Blitzkrieg and the Myth of German "Totalitarian War"

National Socialism claimed to gain strength through the "coordination" (*Gleichaltsung*) of German political, social, and economic life, but salient among the defects of the "totalitarian" state was a failure to integrate political and military planning.[5] The *Oberkommando der Wehrmacht* (OKW), created in 1938 to issue military directives in Adolf Hitler's name, was not a vehicle for integrated military planning but the Führer's tool for dominating military policy and marginalizing the professional soldiers.[6] Military spending was driven by Hitler's whims, without analysis of the needs of the depressed German economy or adequate understanding of military doctrines and planning.[7] Institutional competition, rather than strategic calculation, drove the apportionment of resources among the army, navy, and air force.[8] Unbridled military spending created economic dislocation and spurred Hitler to go to war years before the *Wehrmacht* was ready.[9] So glaring were the deficiencies in German armament, that historian A. J. P. Taylor mistakenly offered them as "decisive proof that Germany was not planning general war, and probably not planning war at all."[10] Taylor apparently could not understand that leaders could prepare for war so badly.

If Hitler used rearmament to boost Germany's international status, the army's leaders, only some of them enthusiastic National Socialists, exploited National Socialism for their own institutional ends. They appreciated Hitler's determination to liberate Germany from the shackles of Versailles but would have preferred a moderate rate of expansion consistent with maintaining a high level of training. Viewing the destruction of Poland as a long-term aspiration rather than an immediate objective, they were shocked at the Führer's insouciant attitude toward war against England and France.[11] Hitler's bellicosity drove General Ludwig Beck to retire from the post of army Chief of Staff, albeit without voicing his concerns in public. His replacement, the more aggressive General Franz Halder, thought that a coup d'état might be necessary to avert a war over Czechoslovakia and, in the fall of 1939, contemplated shooting Hitler if necessary to prevent a premature invasion of France.[12] So little did German war planning match any abstract idea of "totalitarian" coherence that Hitler never informed the army of the secret clause in the Molotov-Ribbentrop Pact of 23 August 1939 providing for Soviet control of eastern Poland. In mid-September, the generals would be surprised by orders to relinquish to Soviet troops territory already purchased with German blood.[13]

The *Wehrmacht* did not enter the war committed to new military doctrine. The language of famous, anonymous *Time* magazine correspondent who described the fighting in Poland as "no war of occupation, but a war of quick penetration and obliteration—*Blitzkrieg*—lightning war" was dramatic rather than technical, unwittingly combining two contradictory military ideas with whose respective merits the German high command was still wrestling.[14] Depending on the operational plan, the penetration of an enemy front could be the first step in the envelopment and destruction of an enemy army or the beginning of a paralyzing thrust into the enemy's rear area. The first method, the combination of penetration and envelopment, was classic German military practice, as demonstrated in Prussia's historic victories of encirclement (*Kesselschlachten* or "cauldron battles") at Königgratz (1866) and Sedan (1870). The architect of those victories, Field Marshal Count Helmut von Moltke, called the doctrine of decision through the destruction of the enemy army *Vernichtungsgedanke* ("the annihilation idea").[15] Commitment to *Vernichtungsgedanke* caused the German high command to view the nascent mechanized forces as tools to help infantry and its supporting artillery overcome defensive firepower to re-create the great cauldron battles of the past. Charles Messenger's claim in *The Blitzkrieg Story* that "by mid-1936 Germany was already shaping the tools for blitzkrieg" would have been more accurate had he replaced "blitzkrieg" with "*Kesselschlacht*."[16]

An alternative to *Kesselschlacht*, first proposed by British theorist J. F. C. Fuller and his protégé, B. H. Liddell Hart, that armored forces could stun enemy armies by rapid and deep attacks on command centers and lines of supply, rendering their physical destruction unnecessary, interested some German soldiers—most famously Colonel Heinz Guderian.[17] In advocating the use of tanks to execute the infiltration tactics developed by the *Reichswehr* during the Great War, Guderian and his ilk were out-numbered—and decisively out-ranked—by the traditionalists. As a result, the German campaign against Poland was a demonstration not of new doctrine but of the power of modern technology to enhance traditional German concepts of *Vernichtungsgedanke*. In particular, the *Luftwaffe*'s mission in Poland was not direct support of German armor, a mission to which only thirty-six Henschel 123 biplanes were permanently assigned, but to destroy the Polish air force and interdict the movement of troops and supplies.[18] Descriptions of *Luftwaffe* aircraft as "on-call artillery support" far exaggerated German military capabilities in 1939.[19]

Allied Strategy and Diplomacy

The appeasement policies of Britain and France grew from ghastly memories of 1914–1918 and from the expectation that a policy of trust and cooperation toward Germany would engender reciprocal trust and cooperation. Popular opinion in France and Britain supported the rectification of certain putative injustices inflicted upon Germany by the Versailles Treaty while the German people, although generally supportive of rearmament as part of the National Socialist government's project to restore Germany's status among nations, were unenthusiastic about actual war.[20] Appeasement failed in the 1930s not because appeasement is necessarily a flawed policy but because Hitler's rapacity went beyond what Prime Ministers Neville Chamberlain and Édouard Daladier were willing to concede.[21] But belief in the feasibility of mollifying Hitler diverted western policy makers from making more serious efforts to thwart Hitler's bellicose intentions.[22]

Discounting the likelihood of war helped the Allies to minimize painful and expensive preparations to fight one. Alliances were crucial to Polish, French, and British hopes, but hope was more evident than rigorous geopolitical calculation.[23] Poland had little faith in existing non-aggression pacts with Germany and the Soviet Union and, although spending a higher percentage of its gross domestic product on armaments than any country other than the Soviet Union (far less than Germany, however, in absolute terms), was indefensible without help.[24] Moreover, until 1936, most of Poland's defenses faced eastward toward the Soviet Union, and little was done to rectify the balance thereafter.[25] None of Poland's neighbors were eager to take its side against Germany, and the geographical situation worsened in March 1939, when the German occupation of Czechoslovakia extended the Germano–Polish frontier.[26] Moreover, Germany's economic power in Eastern Europe and the Soviet commitment to deliver raw materials blunted the threat of economic blockade. Although French and British military leaders agreed that an isolated Poland was indefensible, Britain's Foreign Office declined to urge Poles to negotiate with Germany over the status of the "Polish Corridor" or to make aid to Poland contingent on Polish reconciliation with neighboring Rumania or the Soviet Union.[27]

As Poland's situation deteriorated, French and British leaders reiterated disingenuous promises. They responded to Germany's invasion of Czechoslovakia in March 1939 with an empty "guarantee" of the integrity of Poland instead of urging Polish leaders to reassess their relations with Germany in light of the *Wehrmacht*'s new threat to Poland's southern border. In May 1939, French Chief of Staff General Maurice Gamelin reinforced that guarantee with a pledge, wholly irreconcilable with his army's existing plans and capabilities, for an eastward attack fifteen days after a German invasion of Poland. Britain and Poland reacted to news of the Russo–German Non-Aggression Pact by signing a mutual assistance pact, wishful thinking even for statesmen unaware of the pact's secret provision for Soviet occupation of eastern Poland.[28]

But only wishful thinking allowed Poland to take any stock in Anglo–French promises. Although Germany's western defenses were weak, France's army lacked offensive capabilities. It would respond to the German invasion of Poland with a tentative gesture into the Saar before withdrawing to the fortifications of the Maginot Line, and General Maurice Gamelin was mostly pleased at completing his mobilization without German interference.[29] Nor did the British army, compared by A. J. P. Taylor to "an expensive motor-car beautifully polished, complete in every detail, except that there was no petrol in the tank," entertain any offensive intentions.[30] Regardless of their obligations to Poland, France and Britain intended to employ against Germany a "long-war strategy" comprising a defensive posture on the Continent, economic pressure, and the gradual mobilization of superior military resources. The Poles expected a British bombing offensive against German industry, a plausible component of a long-war strategy, but British and French leaders feared Germany retaliation against their own cities and justified their inaction by citing Hitler's incredible promise that the *Luftwaffe* would attack only military targets. The British appraisal of Poland's situation can be summed up by a July 28, 1939 report by the Chiefs of Staff to the Committee of Imperial Defence concluding that, "the fate of Poland will depend on the ultimate outcome of the war." In other words, Poland fit into the long-war strategy only in the sense that it would take a long war to liberate it from the agony of German occupation.[31]

Such meaningless alliances represented a strategy of resolving strategic impasse through cognitive dissonance, simultaneously knowing both how bad the situation was and that, somehow, it would work out. For Britain and France, the only alternative to cognitive dissonance was to acknowledge strategic impotence, tacitly encouraging Hitler to continue his predation in Eastern Europe. Poland had to pretend also, rather than undermining the last shreds of deterrence by admitting her diplomacy, to be a charade and her armed forces out-classed.[32] A British journalist arrived in Katowice, Poland at the end of August 1939 to find, "officials genuinely cheerful and confident that in the approaching war . . . the Poles would give the hated Germans a good hiding."[33] It would have required impossible political courage for Poland's leaders to have revised their policies by seeking to come to terms with the Czechs before the Munich agreement eviscerated Czechoslovakia's defensive strength or, afterwards, with the Germans.

The French long-war strategy, which doomed Poland to short-term extinction, required resources from a coalition of allies. The ideal alliance system comprising Britain, Russia, and the United States was unattainable due to American isolationism, western loathing of Soviet communism, and British repugnance at the prospect of another continental bloodbath.[34] The replacement alliances with Poland, Czechoslovakia, Rumania, and Yugoslavia were manifestations of cognitive dissonance. They were supposed to raise French status and provide counterweights to Germany, not to create embarrassing demands for their actual defense. Another problem about which France could not think objectively was the decision of Belgium, crucially situated for French defense policy, to adjure her alliance of 1920 in favor of neutrality in October 1936.[35] Although French war plans always envisioned fighting in Belgium in cooperation with the Belgium Army, Belgium neutrality prevented coordinated planning and even led General Maurice Gamelin to pretend that French assistance to Belgium in event of a German invasion was not automatic, a pretense that threatened to become a policy.[36]

Britain had a natural strategic interest in protecting the Channel coast, but public discussion of commitments to France conflicted with efforts at appeasement and would arouse public debate about enlarging the army for service on the Continent.[37] The five-division British Expeditionary Force was smaller than Gamelin wanted, and it lacked badly needed mechanized troops. But Gamelin could not beg for British tanks without implying lack of confidence in his own army, while British soldiers embraced the fiction that France's large, well-prepared army required only minimal support.[38]

Western diplomacy was even less forthright in dealing with Scandinavian nations.[39] Nothing could be done for indefensible Denmark, but neutral Sweden was an important supplier of iron ore for German rearmament and a potential battleground in various Franco–British scenarios. Proposals to land an expeditionary force at Narvik and seize the Swedish iron mines at Galliwäre, or, even more fantastically, to traverse Sweden to assist the Finns against the Soviet Union in the Winter War, did nothing to shift Sweden from its pro-Axis tilt.[40] Hitler would have been delighted to see England and France at war on behalf of Finland against the hated Soviet Union, and fantasies of Western aid prolonged Finnish resistance until March 1940.

If distance rendered Allied attacks on Sweden or aid to Finland chimerical, Norway was the target of various Anglo–French schemes including mining Norwegian territorial waters to interdict German ore imports from Sweden and hiring Norway's merchant navy to supplement Allied shipping. But coordinated planning was unlikely given that the western Allies saw Norway as a diversionary battleground rather than a strategic partner. As Germany's threats to France and Britain became more urgent, the desire for a diversion increased. By the end of March 1940, British and French plans to sow naval mines in Norwegian territorial waters had "all but hypnotized" Norway's leaders, completely distracting them from Germany's plans.[41] So unclear was Norway's strategic position that, informed on April 9, 1940 that his nation was at war, King Haakon asked, "Against whom?"[42]

Military Factors

The relative importance of geographic realties, alliance structures, semi-rigid military organization, and contingent military plans in explaining Germany's victories over Poland, Norway, and France varied from country to country, but each defeated nation put faith in military arrangements whose flaws were evident to anyone willing to look.

Poland's geographical situation was hopeless and her allies useless. Absent funds, modern industry, and an efficient procurement system, the Polish Army was equipped mostly with Great War weapons and lacked heavy artillery, tanks, trucks, radio communications, and modern aircraft.[43] But Poles had nothing to gain by acknowledging the futility of bringing a horse-drawn army to a (marginally) mechanized war. Instead, as one participant put it, "we trusted our courage and the justice of our cause."[44] Short of declaring the *levée en masse* and guerrilla war, what could Poland do? And an air of imperturbability was essential to reassuring France and Britain that they backed a viable cause. For their part, Allied leaders eschewed penetrating questions; their confidence that the Poles had resilience, if not tanks, eased the guilt of leaving them in the lurch.[45]

The best explanation—other than geography—for the military outcome of Germany's "three-week war" against Poland is the effectiveness of the *Luftwaffe*. Dispersal to air fields around the country saved Poland's air force from being destroyed on the ground by the *Luftwaffe*'s initial attack, but, Poland, whose aviation budget was only one-tenth that of the *Luftwaffe* and whose aircraft were necessarily fewer and less capable, could not compete in the air.[46] Thus German troops enjoyed great freedom of movement while Polish soldiers could not dig in to stop German ground attacks without inviting destruction from the air.[47]

The New Times reporter's catchy neologism notwithstanding, Germany's military success owned nothing to novel military doctrine. Instead, the conventional thinking behind *Wehrmacht* operations stands out in the army's victory report of September 24, 1939, which boasted that Germany's "counter-attack" against Poland had required a mere eight days to *encircle* the bulk of the Polish army and ten more days to destroy them.[48] As historian of blitzkrieg Robert M. Citino unintentionally concedes in *Blitzkrieg to Desert Storm: The Evolution of Operational Warfare*, the German invasion of Poland produced a "fantastic *Kessel*."[49] Moltke would have been delighted by this demonstration of double envelopment.

If "blitzkrieg" is misleading in describing the German victory over Poland, it has no meaning in reference to Scandinavia. For Messenger, *Weserübung* ("Operation Weser") was "a different type of blitzkrieg," one involving "speed and surprise" and aircraft, paratroopers, and naval forces instead of tanks; Citino calls it "a blitzkrieg of a sort . . . a blitzkrieg by sea and air." Blitzkrieg implies the efficient coordination of different arms, but John Kiszely notes that planning for the operation did not include unity of command among the army, navy, and air forces.[50] Moreover, this blitzkrieg without tanks was so slow that Norway held out longer than either Poland or France.[51] Henrik O. Lunde more accurately treats the campaign as a collection of raids executed with vigor and remarkably good luck.[52]

Indeed, *Weserübung* was an improvised operation, and Kiszeley's observation that it, "in many ways, succeeded beyond expectations" suggests how low those expectations were.[53] Many generals expected *Weserübung* to fail, and some apparently hoped that failure would undermine Hitler's government.[54] Given Norway's geography, the OKW planned neither for *Kesselschlacht* nor penetration but the simultaneous capture of six widely scattered coastal objectives from Oslo to Narvik. Success had to be immediate because the *Kriegsmarine* lacked the capability to provide long-term fire support or maintain supply lines. Because the sea and airborne landing forces lacked tanks and heavy weapons, sheer surprise (and treason on the part of Vidkun Quisling's supporters) had to obviate Norwegian resistance.[55]

If OKW had a theory of victory, it was not *Vernichtungsgedanke* but decapitation, the seizure of the Norwegian government in the small hours of April 9, using by a naval flotilla led up the Oslo Fjord by the modern heavy cruiser *Blücher* and infantry deposited by the *Luftwaffe* at Oslo's Fornebu Airfield.[56] The navy withdrew after *Blücher*'s destruction by torpedoes fired from an antique coastal fortress, and fog delayed the landings at Fornebu.[57] By noon, when Oslo was occupied, Norway's government and gold supply had been evacuated. King Haakon VII eventually established a government in London, and Britain acquired a major strategic asset in the one thousand ships of Norway's merchant marine.[58] German planners had overestimated the effectiveness of their surprise attack and failed to anticipate that Quisling's collaboration would stiffen resistance.

Outside of Oslo, unexpected resistance delayed several of the landings, supply ships failed to arrive with needed fuel and weapons, and the Royal Navy inflicted serious losses on the supporting naval forces, which had both immediate tactical and long-term strategic effects on the *Kriegsmarine*. The *Kriegsmarine*'s withdrawal left the invasion force dependent on the *Luftwaffe*, now unexpectedly responsible for providing the ground forces with supplies and tactical air support. When German infantry attacks stalled, planes strafed and bombed Norwegian defenses and towns. Norwegian forces, however unprepared for war, fought so tenaciously that an article in the *Völkischer Beobachter* complained that Norwegian resistance "not only shows a complete lack of feeling for justice but borders on insanity."[59]

The German invasion led to the resurrection of Allied plans for major landings in Norway. As proposed in January 1940 and supported by Chief of the Imperial General Staff General William Edmund Ironside, the largely British operation would have required months of preparation and posed intractable problems of air support. Little had been accomplished before Finland's surrender, at which point all assets allocated to Norway were diverted elsewhere. Although the *Wehrmacht*'s presence in Norway greatly reduced the likelihood of a successful Anglo–French operation, it sparked an automatic reflex to send help.[60] Unprepared British, French, and Polish troops, many of them poorly trained British territorials, and miscellaneous light arms and equipment were haphazardly stowed in an improvised landing fleet. Planning and coordination were absent at every level. A comprehensive study of the campaign concludes that execrable intelligence, lack of airpower, poor relationships between army and navy, and complete absence of strategic purpose doomed the resulting operations to "ignominious failure" six weeks later.[61] Absent from this list is relations with the Norwegians, with whom the Anglo–French forces made little effort to cooperate and from whom they ultimately attempted to conceal their intentions of abandoning the campaign.[62] But the most pernicious defect was the glaring role of cognitive dissonance and wishful thinking.[63]

Excessive optimism led Britain and France to tactical defeat in Norway, but Germany did not accurately calculate the strategic consequences of their victory. The *Kriegsmarine* lost most of its surface fleet while Britain acquired Norway's merchant fleet, including invaluable oil tankers.[64] German leverage on neutral Sweden increased, but the defense of Norway against possible Allied invasion would tie down hundreds of thousands of German soldiers throughout the war.[65]

NAVIES

Cognitive dissonance was strongly at work in the *Kriegsmarine*. Thanks to the Versailles Treaty, the Germans had no significant legacy fleet to constrain their thinking, and geography suggested a concentration on land and air power with only defensive naval forces. Admiral Erich Raeder, head of the *Reichsmarine* (renamed the *Kriegsmarine* under National Socialism) from 1928, rightly discounted his fleet's ability to match the Royal Navy in open battle and favored a strategy based on commerce raiding with cruisers and submarines. Hitler, however, instructed Raeder to propose a capital-ship building program to bring about naval parity with Great Britain. Plan Z (four aircraft carriers, ten battleships, three battle cruisers, three heavy cruisers, and supporting ships), promulgated in 1939 for completion in the late 1940s, appeared too late to alter the naval balance with Great Britain, but diverted attention and resources from constructing U-boats, Germany's most effective naval weapon.

Because Plan Z greatly increased the navy's resource requirements, it drew Raeder's attention to the vulnerability of iron ore supplies from Sweden and led him to entertain the idea that Germany needed naval bases on the coast of Norway. After he gained Hitler's interest in the project, its scope expanded until Norway, and Denmark in passing, were to become permanent components of the German empire. *Weserübung* provided a showcase for innovation and daring on the part of Germany's naval forces, but few vessels survived to enjoy the operation's success.

The Royal Navy's vast size and global responsibilities brought challenges far more complex than those of the *Kriegsmarine*. The Norwegian campaign demonstrated how incompletely it had thought through the challenges of contemporary sea control, especially given the growing capabilities of land-based aircraft. The failure of the Royal Navy to prevent the much smaller *Kriegsmarine* from conveying Germany's invasion force to Norway stemmed largely from lack of intelligence. The separate German invasion elements took advantage of darkness and heavy weather to conceal their movements, while their dispersion helped to mask their intentions. Especially unnerving to the Royal Navy was uncertainly about the location of the battleships *Scharnhorst* and *Gneisenau*, which were assigned to escort the Narvik and Trondheim elements but posed a potential threat to all British naval and commercial shipping. As the British played this game of nautical blind man's bluff, every friendly capital ship was an asset to be hoarded and every enemy vessel a significant threat in and of itself. German acquisition of airfields in Denmark and southern Norway intensified the aerial menace, driving the Royal Navy to safer northern waters.

Tentative handling of the Home Fleet in novel situations had helped the Germans to maintain their foothold in Scandinavia, but the Royal Navy proved superior when fighting under more familiar conditions. In the two battles at Narvik on April 10 and April 14, Home Fleet destroyers sank ten modern German destroyers and a submarine.[66] Superior resources and advantageous geography would give the Royal Navy time to adapt to contemporary challenges while Germany's less realistic naval ambitions proved chimerical.

France

Studies of the 1940 campaign tend to emphasize French flaws in doctrine, leadership, training, and morale and note that German's risky attack through the Ardennes exploited these intangible French weaknesses while capitalizing on German strengths. But few French weaknesses could not have been ameliorated by a high command willing to tackle them explicitly, and closer analysis cuts Germany's alleged advantages down to a size that French soldiers might well have found manageable.

France was far stronger than Poland or Norway and, in many respects, began the war with a promising military situation. In particular, the long-war strategy, which France shared with Britain, was a sensible response to Great War experiences and accurately anticipated the actual course of World War II. French predictions were marred only by the fatal flaw that the German offensive culminated on the English Channel rather than against fortifications in Belgium. To collapse so comprehensively in May–June 1940 required unforced errors. Given French resources, Germany's victory was an anomaly, and an ephemeral one, in an age of industrial war.

Fortunately, our understanding of French defense policy has moved well beyond William Shirer's remark that the Maginot Line had been built in the wrong place. In the event, the Maginot Line achieved its intended purpose of channeling any German attack into Belgium by barring the direct route into Alsace-Lorraine. Confining the war to Belgian soil was a basic element of the long-war strategy, but an effective defense of Belgium entailed military consultations precluded by Belgian neutrality.[67]

France did not lose because she built the Maginot Line nor because money spent on fortifications was not available for tanks. Misunderstandings of the armor balance between France and Germany have long been corrected; France had more tanks than Germany and some French models were superior in quality.[68] France did not fall for lack of armored divisions, of which the French Army had two kinds. The *Divisions Légères Mechaniques* (DLM, Mechanized Light Divisions) were structurally comparable to the German Panzer division but performed traditional cavalry roles reconnaissance, screening, and exploitation.[69] Heavier tanks were formed in the *Divisions Cuirassées de Réserve* (DCR) or reserve armored divisions, created from 1936 to combat the German Panzer divisions. Tactical studies of the 1940 campaign reveal the vulnerabilities of German tanks to French tanks and anti-tank guns and emphasize the extent to which German infantry and artillery were called upon to compensate for the deficiencies of the Panzer forces.[70] The overall ineffectiveness of French armor units in 1940 is best explained in terms of training and preparation rather than technology or doctrine. Weaknesses in training were concealed under a superficial veneer of institutional confidence.[71]

But the main French answer to tanks was the anti-tank gun, a reasonable calculation given that most of the German vehicles employed in 1940 were vulnerable even to the obsolescent Hotchkiss 25mm anti-tank gun while the modern APX 47mm model 1937 could stop any existing German tank. But the army failed to think through the requirement of its doctrine, neither building the required number of guns nor acknowledging that non-existent guns would not defeat actual tanks. And many units received their weapons without sufficient time for training in their use.[72]

Anti-aircraft guns were scarcer than anti-tank guns, and most were of smaller calibre than desired.[73] In the distribution of these vital assets, the class B reserve divisions, including those defending the Ardennes sector, were particularly disadvantaged. The role of cognitive dissonance is especially glaring here, for, in his role as commander of French anti-aircraft forces, Marshal Phillipe Pétain had reassured his compatriots that the Maginot Line would be defended by "a veritable forest" of anti-aircraft guns. The forest was never planted, but the French army acted as if it had been.[74]

The real forests of the Ardennes were also supposed to contribute to the defense of France. In 1934, Pétain had claimed that the region could be rendered impassable simply by cutting down trees to block its few and difficult roads. "Could be rendered impassable" appears to have been interpreted as "is impassable" even though the trees remained standing. The French high command did not welcome criticism of its assumptions about the defense of the Ardennes. A May 1938 map exercise conducted by the region's commander, General André Prételat, in which German mobile forces reached the Meuse in a mere sixty hours did not convince Gamelin of the need to re-evaluate the penetrability of the Ardennes, while an inquiry by Deputy Pierre Taittinger about vulnerabilities he had observed while on an inspection trip to the region infuriated General Charles Huntziger.[75] In his excellent study of Sedan, Robert A. Doughty describes Huntziger's attitude as, "reflecting more confidence than was due," but the general's vocal expressions of confidence helped him to disguise and ignore weaknesses in the position he had to defend.[76] French commanders did little to fortify the Ardennes sector, and, even after months of the Phoney War, French reservists at Sedan still seemed to be "flabby civilians."[77] Warnings from more astute observers that the German victory in Poland presaged a new kind of war met confident rejoinders about French courage at Verdun in the Great War.[78]

Hitler's decision not to attack France immediately after victory in Poland offered Gamelin time for wishful thinking; perhaps Hitler had changed his mind or, as French intelligence reports suggested, a disgruntled German population might soon overthrow him.[79] Even after he undertook more urgent war planning in the spring of 1940, Gamelin maintained a distant approach, never visiting the likely front after mid-March. While one might argue that the commander-in-chief had to avoid distraction with tactical details, this degree of aloofness suggests a pathological degree of cognitive dissonance.

Refusal to face reality sharpened after the campaign began. Determined to fight the Germans in Belgium, Gamelin made no significant effort to discover what the Germans might be doing elsewhere. That aerial reconnaissance on Second Army's front in the Ardennes on May 10 found "no indications of armored vehicles" reassured high command that the main German effort would be where their plans required it to be, in the Gembloux Gap. What should have been increasingly alarming reports of German mechanized activities over the course of the next three days and a cogent intelligence analysis by General Alphonse Georges' staff identifying the Ardennes as the site of the main German effort did not disturb French complacency. French premises about the axis of the German advance and the impenetrability of the Ardennes were too fundamental to be reconsidered.[80]

If the Maginot Line was not in the wrong place, many French soldiers were. Thirty infantry divisions were positioned behind the Maginot Line, serving no purpose if the fortifications did their job of channeling the German attack through Belgium. To meet that German move, Gamelin shifted significant motorized and mechanized resources into central Belgium and moved his reserve force, General Henri-Honoré Giraud's 7th Army, from a central location reserve at Reims to the far-left flank. Gamelin' reorganization left the Ardennes sector only weakly protected and, in Martin Alexander's words, "stuck the necks of the Allies into the hanging noose of Germany's Manstein Plan."[81]

But even that error need not have been fatal. There were French soldiers available to hold Sedan—given effective air support. German planners were clearly concerned about the possibility of air attack on forces moving through the Ardennes, but the French air force was not thinking along those lines. Prételat's report about his May 1938 map exercise had warned that, "*given the current state of our air force* [original emphasis], it is not capable of intervening even in a minor way against the German transport columns," drew no reaction from the French high command. Although the 1938 air rearmament plan shifted the emphasis of French aircraft production from long-range bombers to fighters, air force leaders continued to value strategic bombing as the surest source of institutional autonomy.[82] Officially, that autonomy ended on February 26, 1940 with the transfer of all French air units to the control of land theaters, but the ground commanders who were now expected to exercise "authority over the objectives and scope of air operations" had never grappled with practical issues such as the relative importance of the pursuit role preferred by the aviators and the ground support missions needed by the army—or the command and control arrangements necessary for interservice cooperation. Nor was there an efficient system for collecting and analyzing air reconnaissance reports. And the soldiers had little desire to unleash the air force on French civilians. General Alphonse Georges, commander-in-chief of the northeast front, reacted to the German attack with an order restricting air activities to reconnaissance and pursuit missions and later, in keeping with Gamelin's own preference for a war without bombing, authorized bombing missions only if they avoided hitting built-up areas.[83]

The French army made no real effort to harness airpower close to air support, and the air force had other goals than fighting the Germans. As Faris Kirkland argues, its primary missions in the interwar period were, "securing independence from the army, improving career opportunities, and preserving the status of the regular air force." In pursuit of these objectives, senior aviators had kept personnel numbers too low to man the aircraft available and resisted the acquisition of additional new planes lest expansion reduce the promotion chances of existing pilots. When the war started, the average age of French pilots was far higher than that of the Germans, and too many excellent modern aircraft were still in their packing cases.[84] Few French combat aircraft were ready in the Ardennes sector on May 12, 1940 to take advantage of the fact that German movements had created "the hitherto biggest known traffic jam in Europe."[85]

Compared to French errors, German doctrine explains little about the outcome of the 1940 campaign. Manstein's "Sickle Cut" Plan to move Army Group A through the Ardennes was operationally daring in conception, but still merely a modern version of Moltke's *Vernichtungsgedanke*. To the extent that the Germans had a comprehensive plan out all, it was not to paralyze the French army but to destroy it in a *Kesselschlacht*, a project that exceeded OKH expectations thanks largely the French army's unexpected mistakes. Guderian's XIXth Corps executed a campaign of paralyzing deep penetration only by acting against the instructions of Panzer Group von Kleist's commander. Kleist's decision to stop the armored forces on May 16 refutes any claim of German commitment to a doctrine of paralysis.

Blitzkrieg fiction emphasizes close coordination of aircraft and armored forces with the *Luftwaffe*'s JU-87 Stuka serving as "flying artillery" in the place of horse-drawn guns unable to keep pace with the Panzers. In fact, the German army of 1940 lacked the means for direct front-line coordination between air and ground forces. The iconic example of aerial support of Panzer operations in France was *Fleigerkorps* 2's "rolling raid" in support of Guderian's XIX Corps' crossing of the Meuse River. A series of small bomber sorties, meticulously planned in advance rather than orchestrated at the front, struck selected targets at a pace calculated to maintain continuous pressure on the French defenders. The operation occurred despite an order from Kleist and *Luftflotte* 3 General Hugo Sperrle reducing the air support to a single, twenty-minute bomber attack.[86] In another example of German indiscipline at the highest levels, the bombers executed the original plan, but neither the single attack ordered by Kleist and Sperrle, nor Guderian's "rolling raid," fits the blitzkrieg myth of tight tactical cooperation between air and ground units. Moreover, as the crux of the German invasion plan, the Meuse crossing benefited from air assets normally unavailable to Guderian's armored corps.[87] Given the vulnerability of the slow Stuka, the myth of German air-ground coordination would never have emerged had the French Air Force devoted more resources to providing fighter protection to the army.[88]

Like the employment of *Luftwaffe*, the German victory over France resulted from relatively straightforward employment of conventional ideas by troops who were better trained and led than their adversaries. If their commanders had not resolved all the intellectual challenges of modern war, at least, as Marc Bloch insisted, they thought faster and reacted better to the unexpected.

Internal Explanations of Defeat

Everywhere, a natural response to defeat was to blame internal subversion. Such farfetched reports as Marta Korwin-Rhodes' claim that German sympathizers undermined Poland's economic and social life by hoarding the country's small change suggest an undercurrent of fear incommensurate with the magnitude of actual fifth-column activities.[89] Poland had a small, ethnic German population, whose "liberation" was the ostensible reason for Hitler's invasion. In writing that, "invasion is simplified when one has such good friends in the country invaded," English eyewitness Clare Hollingworth represented a wide-spread opinion, but actual instances of sabotage were few. Historian R. M. Douglass is surely correct in arguing, however, that even unfounded rumors played a role in inciting panic.[90] Poland's problem was not fifth-columnists, but despair. Because the government had played down both the risk of war and dire weaknesses of Poland's strategic situation, the population was stunned by the Germans unexpected military superiority and the ruthlessness with which it was employed.

Like the largely fictitious German supporters in Poland, Vidkun Quisling, head of Norway's "National Union" Party, has received more attention than his actions deserved. Quisling met with Hitler in December 1939 for conversations that encouraged Hitler to believe that German forces might find a sympathetic welcome in Norway.[91] Rather than hastening Norway's fall, a German effort to install Quisling as head of state after the invasion stiffened Norwegian opposition. While the commander of the Narvik garrison was a member of Quisling's party, his rapid capitulation reflected incompetence rather than treason.[92]

In France, as in Poland and Norway, the German advance was accompanied by rumors of treason which, although rarely justified, naturally undermined public confidence.[93] After the armistice, in an exercise in self-justification and an effort to ingratiate itself with the Germans, the Vichy government indicted Popular Front leaders for the invented "crimes" of fomenting a war against Germany and failing to make France militarily ready. Although the infamous Riom trials of 1942–1943 proved more embarrassing to the prosecution than to the defendants, they hinted at the possibility of blaming some Frenchmen—rather than the Germans—for the disaster of 1940.

By the war's end, two internal explanations, both confusingly subsumable under the label *decadence*, competed to explain the fall of France. Looking from the French left, Marc Bloch attributed his nation's defeat largely to the failures of its "ruling class" and the fracturing of Republican values and institutions, while right-wing historians blamed the Popular Front government for pacifism, communism, a weak parliamentary government, and failure to rearm."[94] But many of the alleged internal weaknesses enumerated by historian Jacques Chastenet—inertia among the citizens, pacifist propaganda, parliamentary hostility to "every adventure," and faith in the League of Nations—had vanished by the beginning of the Phoney War.[95]

William D. Irvine trenchantly describes the dangers of assessing French morale in hindsight. Had the *Wehrmacht* lost the war, posterity would doubtless have joined Hitler in blaming German citizens for lack commitment to the Fatherland. Had France won, "historians of modern France would be explaining the 'victory of 1940' in terms of the amazing resilience of a democratic regime."[96] Although the large French Communist Party found its anti-fascism complicated by the Russo–German Treaty of August 1939, loyalty to *la patrie* trumped class tensions as workers toiled in the armaments factories under conditions that brought great profits to industry, a point made for the vital aircraft industry by Herrick Chapman.[97]

Explanations based on national morale might be less prevalent if historians attended more carefully to the whole campaign, rather than focusing on its stunning opening moves. French soldiers played a vital, if unheralded, defensive role during the largely British evacuation from Dunkirk. Because the crushing defeat in the north left hundreds of thousands of Frenchmen under arms, the French government's request for an armistice was, in strictly military terms, premature.[98] If internal factors were largely responsible for the fall of France, the culprit was not national decadence but the decisions of a small clique of French leaders.

In fact, military defeat need not have led to complete capitulation. French Premier Paul Reynaud suggested to General Maximé Weygand, summoned from Beirut on May 19 to replace Gamelin, the withdrawal of the Third Republic's government and remaining military assets to French North Africa. After occupying metropolitan France, the German army would have had to deal with popular resistance without the infrastructure and the façade of legitimacy provided by Marshal Pétain's Vichy government.[99] With the French government still in the war, the Allies would have access to France's global empire, colonial troops, navy, merchant marine, and the many aircraft already flown by their pilots to North Africa.

Reynaud envisioned a drastic change in strategy but lacked the influence to impose it upon a nation that looked for succor in crisis to men like Marshal Pétain, appointed Deputy Prime Minister on May 18, and Weygand. The septuagenarian field marshal, touted as the heir to the "secrets of Marshal Foch," ordered army to hold firm while he hoped for a battlefield miracle or a *deus ex machina* in the form of Royal Air Force (RAF) bombers. As the military catastrophe worsened, Weygand and Pétain sought not to continue the war but to "save the army" and prevent political instability, goals best served by an immediate armistice with Germany. The cabinet's decision to authorize

Pétain to inquire about possible peace terms represented a tacit abdication of civilian leadership to a soldier who viewed curtailment of democratic institutions as a potential benefit of defeat. Preference for collaboration over resistance reflected both military conservatism and French political divisions. Diffuse and un-hierarchical resistance movements of workers and farmers threatened social stability. Whatever government would emerge from a resistance victory would not represent France's traditional elites. While some French citizens rallied to Brigadier General Charles de Gaulle's improvised "Free French" government in London, the bulk of the population accepted the war's end with relief and accepted the authoritarian government of Vichy as a condign punishment for the failure of the Third Republic.

Conclusion

Cognitive dissonance is a prerequisite for enthusiasm about *Blitzkrieg* because any positive evaluation of German military prowess must clash with knowledge of the brutality of German methods. Historians of *Blitzkrieg* generally shrug off German crimes with the phrase "war is hell" or attribute victories to the "professional" tradition of the *Wehrmacht* as distinguished from the savage amateurism of the National Socialist Party and the armed thugs of its Schutzstaffel (SS).[100] In military fantasy, blitzkrieg's paralyzing armored rapier spared civilians from the bloodshed and destruction inherent in wars of attrition. In fact, however, although the early campaigns lacked the systematic slaughter of civilians later induced by Hitler's genocidal mentality, a relatively weak army, and an air force only moderately prepared for close air support could not achieve rapid victories without ruthlessness.

Although Hitler assured the Reichstag on September 1, 1939 that the *Luftwaffe* would confine itself to military targets, bombs struck civilian areas in Warsaw the very next day. In another example of cognitive dissonance, British leaders rejected evidence the *Luftwaffe* had bombed and strafed Polish cities and towns because they were unwilling to live up to their treaty obligations with Poland.[101] Thus, any picture of a clean, "professional" blitzkrieg in Poland begins with disingenuous Allied acceptance of Hitler's propaganda.[102]

Because the period of German ascendency reflected contingent circumstances, it was also ephemeral. Methods employed successfully in Poland, Scandinavia, and France failed against Russia where geography added strategic depth to the superiority of defensive firepower. In 1943, when the Allies began the gradual reconquest of Europe, they rediscovered the high price of offensive warfare against armies prepared to defend their conquests and their homelands. In the end, the early flash of offensive success notwithstanding, Germany lost World War II for the same reason it lost World War I, insufficient military manpower and productive capacity to win a war of attrition against the coalition that German aggression had aroused. It is as an exception to this general pattern of strategically attritional warfare in World War II that the misleading ease of Germany's early victories demands explanation.

Each of those early German victories illustrates human unwillingness or inability to imagine what a war will look like. Poland, France, and Britain obviously wore blinders while analyzing the strategic balance in 1939, while Germany's misconceptions proved in the long run to be the worst of all. No nation's plans would have would have withstood the question "if we do this, what bad outcomes are likely?" But that question is one war planners rarely ask.

Notes

1. Marc Bloch, *Strange Defeat: A Statement of Evidence Written in 1940*, trans. Gerard Hopkins (New York: Norton, 1968), 48, 157, and *passim*.
2. Consider Allan R. Millett and William Murray's observation that, "Military historians have rightly given due credit to the *awesome* operational capabilities of the [German forces invading the Soviet Union]" (emphasis added), Allan R. Millett and Williamson Murray, eds., *Military Effectiveness*, Vol. I: *The First World War* (Boston: Unwin Hyman, 1988), 17. In praising the *Wehrmacht's* performance at the operational level of war, World War II historians are using a concept not generally employed until the 1980s.
3. Matthew Cooper, *The German Army 1933-1945: Its Political and Military Failure* (London: Macdonald and Jane's, 1978); Karl-Heinz Frieser and J. T. Greenwood, *The Blitzkrieg Legend: The 1940 Campaign in the West* (Annapolis, MD: Naval Institute Press, 2005).
4. The phrase appears, among other places, in the title of F. W. Mellenthin, R. H. S. Stolffi, with E. Sobik, *NATO Under Attack: Why the Western Alliance Can Fight Outnumbered and Win in Central Europe Without Nuclear Weapons* (Durham, NC: Duke University Press, 1984).
5. Len Deighton, *Blitzkrieg: From the Rise of Hitler to the Fall of Dunkirk* (New York: Ballantine, 1982), 270; Karl Dietrich Bracher, *The German Dictatorship: The Origins, Structure, and Effects of National Socialism*, trans. Jean Steinberg (New York: Praeger, 1970).
6. Geoffrey P. Megargee, *Inside Hitler's High Command* (Lawrence: University Press of Kansas, 2000), 63, 68; Adam Tooze, *The Wages of Destruction: The Making and Breaking of the Nazi Economy* (New York: Penguin, 2006), 329-330.
7. Charles Messenger, *The Blitzkrieg Story* (New York: Charles Scribner's Sons, 1976), 88.
8. Megargee, *Inside Hitler's High Command*, 30, 63.
9. Tooze, *The Wages of Destruction*, 249-268, 293-304.
10. A. J. P. Taylor, *The Origins of the Second World War*, 2nd ed. (Greenwich, CT: Fawcett, 1961), 211.
11. Megargee, *Inside Hitler's High Command*, 38-39, 52; Williamson Murray, *The Change in the European Balance of Power, 1938-1939: The Path to Ruin* (Princeton: Princeton University Press, 1984), 135-137.
12. Gordon A. Craig, *The Politics of the Prussian Army 1640-1945* (London and New York: Oxford University Press, 1955), 499-501; Joachim Fest, *Plotting Hitler's Death: The Story of the German Resistance*, trans. Bruce Little (New York: Henry Holt and Company, 1996), 124; Megargee, *Inside Hitler's High Command*, 77.
13. Megargee, *Inside Hitler's High Command*, 75.
14. The article appeared in the September 25, 1939 issue of *Time*. Military history might have had a very different image of German doctrine had that *Time* correspondent borrowed the

label "nutcracker tactics" offered by William L. Shirer in a radio address on September 16, 1939, William L. Shirer, *This is Berlin: Radio Broadcasts from Nazi Germany* (Woodstock, NY: Overlook Press, 1999), 84; Messenger, *Inside Hitler's High Command*, 90–91.
15. Frieser, *Blitzkrieg Legend*, 6, 11, 353. "Annihilation" is the obvious but problematic translation of "*Vernichtung*." Where "annihilation" implies obliteration, *Vernichtung* ought to be understood as eliminating an army's ability to affect military events as in Napoleon's encirclement of the Austrians army at Ulm in 1805 and German envelopments of Soviet armies in the summer and fall of 1941.
16. Messenger, *Inside Hitler's High Command*, 93.
17. Azar Gat, *British Armour Theory and the Rise of the Panzer Arm: Revising the Revisionists* (New York: St Martin's Press, 1999); Heinz Guderian, *Achtung-Panzer! The Development of Armoured Forces Their Tactics and Operational Potential*, trans. Christopher Duffy (London: Arms and Armour, 1992), 192, 196.
18. Messenger, *Inside Hitler's High Command*, 143.
19. Robert M. Citino, *The Path to Blitzkrieg: Doctrine and Training in the* Germany Army, *1920–1939* (Boulder, CO: Lynne Riener, 1999), 1.
20. Tooze, *Wages of Destruction*, 164.
21. Jeffrey Record, *The Specter of Munich: Reconsidering the Lessons of Appeasing Munich* (Washington, DC: Potomac Books, 2006). See Piotr S. Wandycz, *The Twilight of French Eastern Alliance 1926–36: French–Czechoslovak–Polish Relations from Locarno to the Remilitarization of the Rhineland* (Princeton: Princeton University Press, 1988), 12–14.
22. Peter Jackson, *France and the Nazi Menace: Intelligence and Policy Making 1933–1939* (Oxford: Oxford University Press, 2000), 395. Eugen Weber, *The Hollow Years: France in the 1930s* (New York: Norton, 1994),14.
23. This chapter does not deal with Czechoslovakia, which no longer existed when Germany invaded Poland in September 1939.
24. Steven Zaloga and Victor Madeg, *The Polish Campaign 1939* (New York: Hippocrene, 1985), 11.
25. Halik Kochanski, *The Eagle Unbound: Poland and the Poles in the Second World War* (Cambridge, MA: Harvard University Press, 2012), 76. On Polish distrust of Germany, see M. Norwid Neugebauer, *The Defence of Poland, September 1939*, first published in London in 1940 and excerpted at http://felsztyn.tripod.com/germaninvasion/id11.html.
26. Zaloga and Madeg, *The Polish Campaign*, 20–21; Kochanski, *The Eagle Unbound*, 44.
27. Azar Gat, *A History of Military Thought from the Enlightenment to the Cold War* (Oxford: Oxford University Press, 201), 748.
28. Stalin's refusal to see the Molotov-Ribbentrop Pact as Hitler's way of avoiding a two-front war while availing himself of Soviet resources is an unparalleled example of wishful thinking.
29. Martin S. Alexander, *The Republic in Danger: General Maurice Gamelin and the Politics of French Defence, 1933–1940* (Cambridge: Cambridge University Press, 1992), 316.
30. Taylor, *English History*, quoted in Nicholas Bethell, *The War Hitler Won, September 1939* (London: Allen Lane, 1972), 85; Brian Bond, *France and Belgium 1939–1940* (Newark: University of Delaware Press, 1975), 46; Bethell, *The War Hitler Won*, 122.
31. A. J. P. Taylor, *English History 1914–1945* (Oxford: Oxford University Press, 1965); Shirer, *This is Berlin*, 75.
32. Bethell, *The War Hitler Won*, 91.
33. Clare Hollingsworth, *Front Line* (London: Jonathan Cape, 1990), 13.

34. William K. Keylor, "France and the Illusion of American Support," in *The French Defeat of 1940 Reassessments*, ed. Joel Blatt (Providence, RI: Berghahn Books, 1998), 233–238.
35. Alexander, *The Republic in Danger*, 186–191.
36. Alexander, *The Republic in Danger*, 193.
37. Peter Dennis, *Decision by Default: Peacetime Conscription and British Defence 1919–39* (London: Routledge & Kegan Paul, 1972); Michael Howard, *The Continental Commitment: The Dilemma of British Defence Policy in the Era of Two World Wars* (London: Prometheus, 1989).
38. For the argument that the French army saw confidence as a crucial military asset, see Eugenia C. Kiesling, *Arming Against Hitler: France and the Limits of Military Planning* (Lawrence: University Press of Kansas, 1996), 171–172, 176–186.
39. In addition to somehow distracting Germany from France and assuaging a populace disgusted by the Phoney War, operations in Finland would pit France against it true, Bolshevik, enemy rather than Germany. François Kersaudy, *Churchill and de Gaulle* (New York: Atheneum, 1983), 18–19. See Alistair Horne, *To Lose A Battle: France 1940* (New York: Little, Brown, 1969), 167–170.
40. The idea of attacking Sweden from Narvik originated with the British Admiralty in September 1939, found a vociferous supported in the new First Lord Winston S. Churchill, and became intertwined with in a proposal by French premier Edouard Deladier to send British troops across Sweden to support Finland from the Soviets. Kersaudy, *Churchill and de Gaulle*, 15–24.
41. "[A]ll but hypnotized," Kersaudy, *Churchill and de Gaulle*, 61. It is possible to compile a timeline of various British schemes for intervention in Scandinavia from John Kiszely, *Anatomy of a Campaign: The British Fiasco in Norway, 1940* (Cambridge: Cambridge University Press, 2017), but the difficulty of the task demonstrates the extraordinary confusion of British planning.
42. Kersaudy, *Churchill and de Gaulle*, 67–68.
43. Zaloga and Madeg, *The Polish Campaign*, 11.
44. Marta Korwin-Rhodes, *The Mask of Warriors: The Siege of Warsaw, September 1939* (New York: Libra, 1964), 10.
45. Alexander, *The Republic in Danger*, 288.
46. Most of Poland's air assets were distributed for the direct support of army units with a Bomber Brigade (containing the modern medium bombers) and Pursuit Brigade held back as the "dispositional air force," Zaloga and Madeg, *The Polish Campaign*, 30.
47. Williamson Murray, *Luftwaffe* (Baltimore: Nautical and Aviation Publishing Company of America, 1985), 32.
48. "Counter-attack" Shirer noted, was a lie, and, despite such claims (and of Werner von Brauchitsch's formal announcement of the campaign's end in an Order of the Day of 20 September 1939), the fighting continued until October 6. Shirer, *This is Berlin*, 89, 93.
49. Robert M. Citino, *Blitzkrieg to Desert Storm The Evolution of Operational Warfare* (Lawrence: University Press of Kansas, 2004), 28.
50. Whether conventional *blitzkrieg* is a combined arms or a joint operation depends on whether the air assets belong to the army or to a separate air force.
51. Messenger, *The Blitzkrieg Story*; Citino, *Blitzkrieg to Desert Storm*, 38.
52. Henrik O. Lunde, *Hitler's Pre-emptive War: The Battle for Norway, 1940* (Havertown, PA: Casemate, 2009), 545–546.

53. Kiszley's identifies "a sense of purpose, thoroughness and professionalism" in German staff work, but he is comparing the German to their "hopelessly amateur" British foes. Kiszley, *Anatomy of a Campaign*, 85.
54. Lunde, *Hitler's Pre-emptive War*, 67–68; John W. Wheeler-Bennett, *The Nemesis of Power: The German Army in Politics 1918-1945* (New York: St. Martin's Press, Inc., 1954), 494.
55. Major Vidkun Quisling, leader of the Nasjonal Samling, saw an alliance with Hitler's Germany as Norway's only bulwark against Bolshevism. Kersaudy, *Churchill and de Gaulle*, 40–42.
56. Kiszley points out that the Germans keep their intentions secret from their own diplomats in Oslo and Copenhagen rather using the threat of war to exert diplomatic pressure. Kiszley, *Anatomy of a Campaign*, 85.
57. Kersaudy, *Churchill and de Gaulle*, 71.
58. Kersaudy, *Churchill and de Gaulle*, 121.
59. Quoted in Shirer, *This is Berlin*, 240; Megargee, *Inside Hitler's High Command*, 79.
60. Kiszely, *Anatomy of a Campaign*, 49
61. Kiszely, *Anatomy of a Campaign*, 299.
62. Kiszely, *Anatomy of a Campaign*, 282.
63. As noted at the time by Liddell Hart; Kiszely, *Anatomy of a Campaign*, 288.
64. Kersaudy, *Churchill and de Gaulle*, 121.
65. Weinberg, *A War at Arms*, 119; Kersaudy, *Churchill and de Gaulle*, 226.
66. Thomas Kingston Derry, *The Campaign in Norway* (London: H. M. Stationary Office, 1952), 43–46.
67. Bond, *France and Belgium*, 48.
68. The seminal work on the subject is R. H. S. Stolfi, "Equipment for Victory in France in 1940," *History* (1970): 1–20.
69. Jeffrey A. Gunsberg, "The Battle of the Belgium Plain, 12–14 May 1940: The First Great Tank Battle," *Journal of Modern History* 56 (1992): 207–244.
70. Frieser, *Blitzkrieg Legend*, 40–42; Doughty, *Breaking Point*.
71. Kiesling, *Arming Against Hitler*, 167–172.
72. For a different assessment of the anti-tank gun situation in one specific situation, see Doughty, *Breaking Point*, 117–118.
73. Doughty, *Breaking Point*, 118.
74. Kiesling, *Arming Against Hitler*, 177.
75. Kiesling, *Arming Against Hitler*, 178; Doughty, *Breaking Point*, 197–108.
76. Doughty, *Breaking Point*, 107–108, Ernst R. May, *Strange Victory: Hitler's Conquest of France* (New York: Hill and Wang, 2000), 389–390.
77. Frieser, *Blitzkrieg Legend*, 144–152; Horne, *To Lose A Battle*, 331.
78. Paul Reynaud, *In the Thick of the Fight: The Testimony of Paul Reynaud*, trans. James D. Lambert (New York: Simon and Schuster, 1955).
79. May, *Strange Victory*, 287. Reports of domestic unrest in Germany had an important role in French evaluations of the German–Polish crisis in August 1939, see Jackson, *France and the Nazi Menace*, 357. That they continued after the fall of Poland suggests the German people's lack of enthusiasm for military adventures.
80. Doughty, *Breaking Point*, 94–100. See also May, *Strange Victory*, 420.
81. Alexander, *The Republic in Danger*, 308. See also Horne, *To Lose A Battle*, 164–165, 264; Donald W. Alexander, "Repercussions of the Breda Variant," *French Historical Studies* 8 (1974): 459–488.

82. Faris Kirkland, "French Air Strength," *Air Power History* 40 (1993): 33. French Air Force leaders defended strategic bombing with optimistic assertion that "repeated bombardment incursions, even when not accompanied by effective destruction, will rapidly render moral results," see Anthony Christopher Cain, *The Forgotten Air Force: French Air Doctrine in the 1930s* (Washington, D.C.: Smithsonian Institution Press, 2002), 121.
83. Horne, *To Lose A Battle*, 265. Both the British and French theater air commanders discouraged the use of fighters in ground attack roles, see May, *Strange Victory*, 398.
84. Faris R. Kirkland, "The French Air Force in 1940: Was it Defeated by the Luftwaffe or by Politics?" *Air University Review* 36 (1985): 101–117. Cf., Kirkland, "French Air Strength." Frieser points out that only 242 of 932 French bombers assigned to the metropole were available for operations on May 10, see Frieser, *Blitzkrieg Legend*, 179.
85. Frieser, *Blitzkrieg Legend*, 116.
86. Heinz Guderian, *Panzer Leader* (Boston: Da Capo Press, 2001), 98, 102; Frieser, *Blitzkrieg Legend*, 154; Doughty, *Breaking Point*, 135.
87. May, *Strange Victory*, 429; Murray, *Luftwaffe*, 41.
88. The vulnerability of the Stuka was clearly demonstrated on May 12, when French pilots flying American-made Curtiss fighters destroyed one group of twelve Stukas and routed a second without loss to themselves, see Horne, *To Lose A Battle*, 289.
89. Korwin-Rhodes, *The Mask of Warriors*, 7.
90. Clare Hollingworth, *The Three Weeks of War in Poland*, cited in Kochanski, *The Eagle Unbound*, 68; R. M. Douglass, *Orderly and Humane: The Expulsion of the Germans after the Second World War* (New Haven: Yale University Press, 2012), 43; Kochanski, *The Eagle Unbound*, 70; Douglass, *Orderly and Humane*, 44.
91. Paul M. Hays, *Quisling: The Career and Political Ideas of Vidkun Quisling 1887–1945* (Bloomington: Indiana University Press, 1972), 173; Perry, 17.
92. Adam R. A. Claasen, *Hitler's Northern War: The Luftwaffe's Ill-Fated Campaign, 1940–1945* (Lawrence: University Press of Kansas, 2001), 73; Derry, 41.
93. Horne, *To Lose A Battle*, 119.
94. Robert Frankenstein, *Le Prix du rearmament français 1935–39* (Paris: Publications de la Sorbonne, 1982) demonstrates that, far from bearing the responsibility for French military deficiencies in 1940, the Popular Front government was largely responsible for the gains of the late 1930s.
95. Jacques Chastenet, *Déclin et Chute* (Paris: Librairie Hachette, 1962), 357; Jean-Baptiste Duroselle's 1979 *La décadence, 1932–1939* was published in an English translation in 2004 with the less evocative title *France and the Nazi Threat: The Collapse of French Diplomacy 1932–1939* (New York: Enigma Books. 2004).
96. William D. Irvine, "Domestic Politics and the Fall of France in 1940" in *The French Defeat of 1940 Reassessments*, ed. Joel Blatt (Providence, RI: Berghahn Books, 1998), 99.
97. Herrick Chapman, *State Capitalism and Working-Class Radicalism in the French Aircraft Industry* (Berkeley: University of California Press, 1991), 223.
98. Frieser, *Blitzkrieg Legend*, 316.
99. Philip Bankwitz emphases Reynaud's reluctance to order rather than suggest a retreat toward North Africa, see Philip C. F. Bankwitz, *Maximé Weygand and Civil-Military Relations in Modern France* (Cambridge, MA: Harvard University Press, 1967), 305–306. Robert Paxton tellingly refers to the prospect of continued French resistance as "Hitler's nightmare" and to German occupation of France as a "liability," see Robert O. Paxton,

Vichy France: Old Guard and New Order 1940-1944 (New York: Columbia University Press, 1972), 6-8.
100. For the falsity of that distinction, see Isabel V. Hull, *Absolute Destruction: Military Culture and the Practices of War in Imperial Germany* (Ithaca, NY: Cornell University Press, 2006).
101. Bethell, *The War Hitler Won*, 122-127.
102. Murray, *Luftwaffe*, 32.

Bibliography

Alexander, Martin. *The Republic in Danger: General Maurice Gamelin and the Politics of French Defence, 1933-1940*. Cambridge: Cambridge University Press, 1992.

Bloch, Marc. *Strange Defeat: A Statement of the Evidence Written in 1940*. Translated by Gerard Hopkins. New York: Norton, 1968.

Cain, Anthony Christopher, *The Forgotten Air Force: French Air Doctrine in the 1930*, Washington, D.C.: Smithsonian Institution Press, 2002.

Cooper, Matthew. *The German Army 1933-1945: Its Political and Military Failure*. London: Macdonald and James, 1978.

Derry, Thomas Kingston. *The Campaign in Norway* London: H. M. Stationary Office, 1952.

Doughty, Robert A. *The Breaking Point: Sedan and the Fall of France, 1940*. Mechanicsburg, PA: Stackpole, 1990.

Frieser, Karl-Heinz, and J. T. Greenwood, *The Blitzkrieg Legend: The 1940 Campaign in the West*. Annapolis, MD: US Naval Institute Press, 2005.

Horne, Alistair. *To Lose A Battle: France 1940*. New York: Little, Brown, 1969.

Kiesling, Eugenia C. *Arming Against Hitler: France and the Limits of Military Planning*. Lawrence: University Press of Kansas, 1996.

Kochanski, Halik. *The Eagle Unbound: Poland and the Poles in the Second World War*. Cambridge, MA: Harvard University Press, 2012.

Murray, Williamson R. *The Change in the European Balance of Power, 1938-1939: The Path to Ruin*. Princeton: Princeton University Press, 1984.

Paxton, Robert O. *Vichy France: Old Guard and New Order 1940-1944*. New York: Columbia University Press, 1972.

Petrow, Richard. *The Bitter Years: The Invasion and Occupation of Denmark and Norway, April 1940-May 1945*. New York: Morrow, 1974.

Weinberg, Gerhard. *A War at Arms: A Global History of World War II*. Cambridge: Cambridge University Press, 1994.

Zaloga, Steven, and W. Victor Madej. *The Polish Campaign, 1939*. New York: Hippocrene, 1985.

CHAPTER 7

THE BATTLE OF BRITAIN: BRITAIN AND THE BRITISH EMPIRE ALONE

ANDREW STEWART

THE summer of 1940 remains a defining moment in the history of World War II. The German invasion of Denmark and Norway and then the subsequent attack on the Low Countries and France, ending with the humiliating armistice signed at Compiegne on June 22, 1940, confirmed the devastating triumph of Adolf Hitler's military strategy. It also represented the culmination of four years of often daring political and military moves that had brought much of Western Europe under his control. The German leader now waited for the next logical step from his only remaining regional opponent and an approach by the British government to sue for peace. As it slowly became clear to him that this inexplicably would not happen, the German High Command was instructed to devise another plan that would complete the victory. If he was to win the war in the West and be free to turn his attention to deal with what he perceived to be the military and ideological menace of the Soviet Union, he would have to defeat a people for whom he had once professed great admiration.[1]

The period that followed, specifically from July 10 until October 31, which is commonly referred to as "The Battle of Britain," is described in great detail in a significant body of literature and still features strongly in popular memory. This period has been described as having been a "Year of Defiance," one which played a critical role in shaping the eventual outcome of the wider war, and remains even now a reference point and rallying cry during periods of perceived national emergency.[2] The decision to fight on through 1940 was hugely significant and the ultimately successful defeat of admittedly half-hearted German attempts to invade the country halted their opponent's momentum. It also, and more crucially, provided the time required for the global anti-Nazi alliance to emerge and grow strong enough to eventually prevail nearly five years later.

During the inter-war years, a combination of short-sighted military under-spending and ill-considered diplomatic appeasement had blighted British strategic planning. In this environment, dominated by what one Whitehall civil servant termed "the policy of the ostrich," even questions of home defense were not given any serious level of consideration.[3] In fact, prior to the war's outbreak it is debatable how many British political and military leaders actually believed that the possibility of an invasion by the German military was realistic.[4] Despite the overwhelming defeat that had been inflicted upon the Poles in September 1939, the prime minister, Neville Chamberlain, still concluded that his German counterpart would not now turn westwards as, "whether successful or unsuccessful [this] would entail such frightful losses as to endanger the whole Nazi system."[5] Indeed, he went so far as to state that there was unlikely to be a "complete and spectacular victory" in the war, an assessment strongly influenced by "experts," such as the military thinker Basil Liddell Hart, who confidently forecast that the defensive positions of the Maginot and Siegfried Lines were too strong to be attacked successfully. There were also the doubtful assurances given to Chamberlain by colleagues within his own cabinet that, in military terms, "our hand is a better one to play than that of the enemy."[6]

It was only in late October that an initial review had been conducted in Whitehall in which the potential for a German invasion was first considered in detail. A further meeting on the same subject followed but only after another month had passed.[7] The conclusion was that as long as Britain's naval and air forces remained intact there was no credible threat.[8] This sense of optimism, one which had little basis of supporting fact, continued until, in the first week of April 1940, Chamberlain told the Conservative Party that Hitler had missed the opportunity to attack.[9] Almost immediately this assessment was shown to be far from accurate as a new German offensive was first directed against Norway and Denmark before switching to engulf the Low Countries and France. The weeks that followed highlighted the depth and breadth of the flawed thinking which had become embedded amongst those tasked with the country's political and military leadership.

With the prime minister's resignation just five weeks later Winston Churchill, who on the war's outbreak had been appointed once again as First Lord of the Admiralty, now dramatically took charge and was tasked with leading the British people through whatever dangers lay ahead. A forceful critic of the government's inter-war defense policies, nobody knew better how this desperate position had been reached. On taking power he had quickly concluded that the traditional British political system was inappropriate to tackle the "the Nazi villains," hence his decision to form a coalition of what he believed to be the best men drawn from all three of the country's main political parties.[10] As he told the House of Commons just days after he became prime minister, within this administration of men and women of every party and of almost every point of view, "one bond unites us all—to wage war until victory is won, and never to surrender ourselves to servitude and shame, whatever the cost and agony may be."[11] The centralized form of political control he established would remain in place for the war's duration, a response to a grave national crisis, much as the national government had been when it had been formed nearly a decade before to tackle the global economic collapse. The subsequent actions taken by Churchill, many of which were criticized in the postwar years, saw him re-organize an apparatus that was not suited to the type of conflict being waged by Germany, a total war which required the mobilization of the entire resources of the nation. The team he assembled around him and the approach he implemented proved to be critical steps in helping safeguard the country's future.

As he took power in May 1940, there was a great deal for the new prime minister to reflect upon as he tried to balance a series of complicated strategic calculations. With the situation on the Continent deteriorating rapidly, there were many difficult decisions to be made relating to his principal European partner as the French military position came under intense pressure. The "impregnable" Maginot Line was actually incomplete and its northern flanks were left hopelessly exposed to German forces which swept easily through the Ardennes region and rapidly crossed the mighty River Meuse, creating a huge bulge in the Allied lines. On the evening of May 26, Lord Gort, commanding the ten divisions of the British Expeditionary Force (BEF), which had been sent to France the previous September, reached the conclusion that his deteriorating military position could not be saved and put into effect an operation to evacuate his remaining troops through the Dunkirk bridgehead.[12] While this marked the effective collapse of the Anglo–French alliance that had been formally established with the 1904 *Entente Cordiale*, it also represented one of the bravest and most decisive actions taken by a senior British military commander.

As the evacuation got underway—by May 29 more than twenty-five thousand men had been saved—the Germans resumed their attack and were pressing hard all around the contracting perimeter, leaving many observers in London to conclude that few additional men would be saved. With most of the remaining British units and the majority of the French forces all now inside a final perimeter and the *Luftwaffe* beginning intensive attacks against the beachhead, 47,310 more men were taken off the beaches in a single day for the loss of three destroyers sunk and several others damaged. The next day, May 30, saw a lull, mainly because of argument and confusion in the German High Command and, with Panzer units being withdrawn in preparation for the next stage in the battle for France, another 52,823 Allied personnel were evacuated. The rate at which troops were being rescued continued to increase despite a decision on June 1, in the face of the growing loss of ships, to halt daylight operations and the Germans breaking through the perimeter and forcing a further contraction of the defenses. The following day, with the French now entirely manning these defenses and the beach area having been reduced to only two miles in length, before dawn and after dark 26,256 men were evacuated, including the last British units to leave. On the night of June 3, 26,175 French troops were evacuated, the final Allied forces to escape from the Dunkirk pocket. When the last ship left at 0340 hours on June 4, there were still forty thousand men left for the Germans to capture whilst one hundred thousand British troops remained in France in areas still free of German occupation, most of whom would eventually manage to leave from other ports and make it home.

Operation *Dynamo* represented a vital event in the war to that point and, in typically British fashion, the evacuation of the BEF, which became commonly referred to as the "Miracle of Dunkirk," was hailed almost as a victory. Churchill himself had thought maybe one-quarter of the forces could be saved but the bulk of those British troops who had survived the withdrawal through the Low Countries had been rescued; a total of 198,315 Britons were amongst the 338,226 Allied troops rescued between May 26 to June 4, leaving 68,111 men killed, missing, wounded, or captured. Saving this considerable force was a huge psychological victory, but it was still achieved at a considerable cost. The evacuation fleet of 693 British ships lost six destroyers, eight personnel ships, a sloop, five minesweepers, seventeen trawlers, a hospital ship, and 188 lesser vessels and small craft all sunk, and an equal number damaged. Of perhaps greater significance in terms of what was to follow, Fighter Command lost 106 aircraft and, potentially critically, eighty pilots were killed. It was the equipment losses suffered by the British Army which, however, offered the most breath-taking and telling indicator of the scale of the defeat that had been suffered. According to one inventory completed in December 1940, this included 710 tanks and armored cars, 1,810 carriers, 3,075 artillery pieces or heavy guns, 523 anti-aircraft guns, sixty-four hundred anti-tank rifles, 11,330 machine guns, sixteen hundred mortars, three hundred thousand rifles, seventy-six thousand tons of ammunition, and five hundred thousand tons of general stores and supplies.[13] What this meant was that while the British Army had been largely saved from utter destruction, it was left without almost anything with which to fight.

There was, however, a large body of troops and the roll-call on the first day of July produced a total figure which was just in excess of 1.5 million men now concentrated in Britain and preparing to fight.[14] This included forty-two thousand men from the Dominions whose presence highlighted the importance of the long-established British imperial network.[15] Although largely overlooked now, the first months of the war had seen many "headline" examples of the contribution of "The Empire at War" and the mobilization of its resources.[16] As *The Times* noted in early January 1940, "every week in the columns . . . announcements are made of contributions to the prosecution of the war from distant parts of the Colonial Empire. Often each is too small for conspicuous mention, but in the aggregate they represent a wonderful expression of loyalty to the British Sovereign and to the ideals of freedom and justice of which the United Kingdom, the British Commonwealth of Nations, India, and the Crown Colonies are at all times, and now more than ever, the resolute defenders."[17] Included among these were fishermen from Newfoundland, arriving in Britain to join the Royal Navy and serve in a minesweeping flotilla. It was also revealed that one in every two hundred of the Maltese population had volunteered for maritime service. There were also prominent media references to the role played by the mule transport units from India and Cyprus in supporting the BEF and which were subsequently amongst those evacuated back to Britain.[18]

The greatest support inevitably came from the largest of the Imperial "partners"—Canada, Australia, New Zealand, and the Union of South Africa—who had all declared war in September 1939 in support of Britain, but this was limited. To help the Royal Navy conduct its global maritime role, even this group could initially muster no more than a handful of destroyers, cruisers, and a few other smaller vessels.[19] Of these, the Royal

Canadian Navy provided the largest contribution with a force which consisted of thirteen ships and 1,774 officers and men.[20] In terms of air forces, the combined available strength was less than ten thousand trained men, but most were needed for domestic training purposes; by August 1940 the Royal Air Force (RAF) included only 134 men from New Zealand, 112 Canadians, thirty-seven Australians, and twenty-five South Africans.[21] In addition, however, the first overseas Royal Canadian Air Force (RCAF) Headquarters had been established in January 1940 and it expanded rapidly—so much so that by the summer's end there were four designated Canadian squadrons in Britain responding to attacks by the *Luftwaffe*.[22]

The most visible support was on the land and, while some Australian and New Zealand troops reached Britain in June 1940, the largest contribution was once again made by Canada. After the losses of World War I, the country's leader, William Lyon Mackenzie King, had initially been reluctant for political and personal reasons to commit large numbers of troops to fight in Europe for a second time. Faced by increasingly hostile domestic opinion, he was eventually forced to concede to the sending of an expeditionary force, and, in December 1939, this force began to disembark at Scottish ports. By the following February additional arrivals meant there were twenty-five thousand , commanded by General Andrew McNaughton, who had served as an artillery officer in the Great War, were helping guard Britain.[23] Plans were also made to include some of these men both in the proposed expedition to assist Finland and as part of operations in Norway, but both came to nothing.[24] As the situation in France worsened, the Canadian division was again readied to secure the port of Calais and keep the coast road to Dunkirk open to allow troops from the BEF to be evacuated if necessary. They were never sent and, instead, eventually landed in Brittany in June to help establish a proposed fighting redoubt, but the rapid final collapse of the Allied position led to them returning hurriedly to England.[25] With their equipment still largely intact, they were now "considered the strongest individual unit in the British Army."[26] This meant that throughout the summer months of 1940 they were given a key role in which they were viewed as a strategic reserve and positioned to move rapidly toward the site of any German landing.

With the rump of the British Army's manpower rescued and increasing contributions arriving from overseas, the defense of Britain was further bolstered by the creation of a new and vast citizen militia. The establishment of the Local Defence Volunteers (LDV), later to be renamed as the "Home Guard," was announced in a radio broadcast on May 14 by the Secretary of State for War, Anthony Eden.[27] He had only been appointed two days before and the speech reportedly came as something of a surprise, even to some of his colleagues. Nonetheless, it provoked an instant and overwhelming popular response with queues forming at police stations almost immediately as tremendous numbers of men rushed to join.[28] A militia had been mobilized during both the Napoleonic wars and World War I, but the LDV quickly became the largest British civilian army ever created and would eventually grow in size to almost one million men.[29] Although the "Stand Down" broadcast from King George VI was made in December 1944, it was not formally disbanded for another twelve months.

The LDV's main purpose was to help defeat a potential German parachute attack and many of those who joined, certainly in 1940, did so to "keep our country safe."[30] Restrictions meant that those involved were supposed to be British, male, aged between 17 and 65, and of reasonable physical fitness; fitness levels varied, at times quite dramatically, and many who were much younger tried and, in some cases, succeeded in joining upe. It was also intended as an unpaid commitment and one which would not require anybody to leave their jobs. Even if many of the new recruits realized their probable fate if an attack came, morale remained high, even with the haphazard nature of their establishment and the difficult conditions they faced. As Churchill put it, it would be possible "to take one with you," and there was apparently no shortage of his countrymen, and women, who seemed prepared to take him at his word and make the ultimate sacrifice if Britain was attacked. This was despite the fact that there was little equipment available. It was only at the end of June, with the arrival of five hundred thousand rifles which had been purchased from American stocks, that the situation began to improve.

On June 18, 1940 a newly formed French government, under the leadership of the aging Marshal Philippe Pétain, immediately requested an armistice with Germany. On hearing the news, Churchill was prompted to deliver one of his most celebrated speeches to a packed House of Commons:

> What General Weygand called the Battle of France is over. I expect that the Battle of Britain is about to begin. Upon this battle depends the survival of Christian civilisation. The whole fury and might of the enemy must very soon be turned against us. Hitler knows that he will have to break us in this island or lose the war. Let us therefore brace ourselves so that if the British Commonwealth and Empire last for a thousand years men will still say, "this was their finest hour."[31]

With a seemingly substantial body of troops, although not much in the way of equipment for them, the task of organizing and conducting the defense lay with General Sir Edmund Ironside. Appointed on September 3, 1939 as Chief of the Imperial General Staff (CIGS), in May he had changed role and replaced General Walter Kirke as Commander-in-Chief Home Forces, bringing with him his considerable military experience and some more explicit knowledge of current German military capabilities. He recorded in his diaries his expectation that his opponent would begin his attack by launching an intensive bombing campaign targeted at breaking public morale. This would be supported by air attacks on ports and shipping, followed by assaults on the RAF and supporting industries.[32] Only when this had been completed would an invasion by air and sea follow. He identified the recently demonstrated German ability to effectively maneuver forces, the *Blitzkrieg* which had proven so devastating during the French campaign, as the most critical factor. Consequently, his plan sought to obstruct movement and deny the advancing forces access to key nodal points across Britain. On June 25, he delivered to his senior colleagues on the Chiefs of Staff Committee his general concept which would form "General Headquarters (GHQ) Operations Instruction No.

3." This called for the establishment of what was termed as a "crust" of troops along the coast to meet the first invaders with static strong points to the rear. Defensive barriers were to run northwards from the south coast, surrounding major cities and culminating in the potentially decisive "GHQ Stop-line" blocking any advance toward London and the Midlands. In reality, this was little more than a continuous ditch and a line of antitank obstacles running down from Yorkshire to England's southern coast which was intended to delay the enemy until the Canadian and British mobile columns could be brought into action.[33] How long these positions would have held out against any enemy attack was far from certain.

These plans, with an emphasis on strong beach defenses and stop-lines scattered across the country and intended to delay and wear down the enemy's attack, were not well received by the committee. Indeed, there were serious doubts about how this approach might work against an invading force which was now well experienced in rapidly assembling and concentrating its forces against its opponents' weakest and most vulnerable points.[34] Many other senior observers shared these concerns that the country's defenses appeared not to be getting stronger but weaker. The desperate situation facing Lieutenant-General Andrew "Bulgy" Thorne, who had been appointed on June 8 as commander of XII Corps, was fairly typical. He was responsible for the defense of Kent, Sussex, and parts of Hampshire and Surrey, but the force he led had little artillery, no tanks, and almost no ammunition.[35] Eden visited him at the end of the month and wrote back to Churchill that, "there is no anti-tank regiment or anti-tank gun in the whole of this Corps area."[36] He also noted that there was no armor, tangible air power, or any other means of repelling a German attack. Sir Alec Cadogan, the senior civil servant in the Foreign Office whose diary portrays so effectively the atmosphere and events of the wartime years, provided his own record of Eden's post-visit report. As he put it, this made it appear, "that the Germans can take a penny steamer to the coast and stroll up to London."[37] Another senior officer, dug in along the cliffs above Dover harbor, when discussing with his commander the question of how to repel German tanks, was told they would be using "beer bottles filled with petrol with a piece of rag sticking out which we would have to light with a match."[38]

Ironside's plan had made his position untenable and on July 19 he was promoted to Field Marshal and placed on the retired list. His replacement was General Sir Alan Brooke, who had overseen the BEF's II Corps in France and led the subsequent, and hastily cancelled, plans to establish a redoubt in Brittany. The new commander was under no illusions on what to expect; likely the last senior British officer to be evacuated from occupied Europe, he had recorded in his diary that the Germans were the "most wonderful soldiers."[39] Brooke now had to defend more than two thousand miles of coastline of which eight hundred were readily assailable by a seaborne attacker. This area was twice the size of the frontier which the joint Dutch, Belgian, French, and British armies had proven unable to hold in May. His first move was to revise Ironside's existing plan changing emphasis to the mobility of his forces and with a strategy based around attacking the beach landings, from land, air, and sea, before the Germans could get themselves established.[40] His assessment was that he needed at least six months to prepare yet he was now required to make dramatic improvements and turn the position around in only a few short weeks.

By the first week of August just four divisions were fully equipped with vehicles and equipment and Brooke was not convinced that people, even at the highest levels, genuinely understood that invasion was a real threat and that the land forces available to him were at this stage still hopelessly inadequate. Conducting an initial round of rapid inspections, he found the general state of training to be poor as was typified by the Canadian troops he observed. In mid-August the authorities in Ottawa were advised that all its units had completed "dawn attack exercises" with armored and air cooperation and were prepared for the anticipated German attack.[41] An exercise involving 1 and 3 Canadian Infantry Brigades plus supporting artillery, which took place in Ashdown Forest on the hills of the Weald between London and the south coast, suggested otherwise. The post-exercise conference conducted by General McNaughton accepted the "battle" had not been entirely positive and referred to the discussion as an opportunity to bring out lessons but the combat effectiveness of the troops under his command seemed highly questionable.[42] In his subsequent report he was much more critical, highlighting that previous instruction and training had been forgotten with bunching of troops and vehicles which would have led to considerable casualties and no sense of understanding about even basic principles such as how to find cover. The "men stood around in the sun" and showed a lack of urgency with little initiative on the part of leaders and a reliance on there being reinforcements available to help them push forward. These troops were part of the critical mobile reserve and their apparent lack of readiness seemed to confirm Brooke's worst fears. The reality was that the British general was faced with a position in which he had to take risks with only very limited resources and, if the Germans had got ashore and followed their plan, a British counterattack would have had almost insurmountable obstacles to overcome. Nonetheless, as he wrote afterwards, he believed that while his forces would have faced "a desperate struggle and the future might well have hung in the balance . . . I certainly felt that given a fair share of the fortunes of war we should certainly succeed in finally defending these shores."[43]

The principal source for optimism came with his entirely accurate assessment of the critical role that would be played by the German air force in determining the outcome of what was to follow. On August 1, Hitler issued his Directive No.17 "for the conduct of air and sea warfare against England." This called for an intensification of the war in the air but also made it clear that a successful offensive by the *Luftwaffe* was a prerequisite for the launching of any seaborne invasion. This was not lost on the British defenders; the assessment provided by the intelligence section for VII Corps represented the commonly held view, until such a point as air superiority had been achieved an invasion was unlikely.[44] As the aerial "Battle of Britain" gathered momentum the real invasion effort finally began on August 13 with *Adlertag*, the "Day of the Eagle." This marked the opening phase of the *Luftwaffe*'s efforts to defeat its British counterpart with sustained attacks directed against the RAF and their ground installations, as well as the country's aircraft industry. In addition to targeting air stations and factories, some of the 1,485 German aircraft who flew over Britain that day damaged five key radar stations, although it soon became clear that the critical role they played was not fully understood and these were largely abandoned as targets.[45]

During the first three days of combat, the Germans lost 190 aircraft, a figure that was only slightly higher than British casualties in the air and on the ground, but the crucial addition was the almost complete loss of aircrew. For the RAF, its pilots were mostly saved and able to fly again as soon as a replacement aircraft could be found for them. By August 18, German losses were already approaching four hundred aircraft, an entirely unsustainable figure, yet in many respects the decisive date for the Germans came five days later when they made a fatal mistake that changed the course of the battle. During a proposed night raid against aircraft manufacturing facilities, some bombers missed the target and jettisoned their bombs over populated areas in the city of London killing nine civilians.[46] Berlin was also then "inadvertently" bombed two nights later. This proved a turning point, as the focus of the German attack now began to shift. The airfields continued to be targeted but there were further limited raids against London and progressively Hitler redirected *Luftwaffe* missions to concentrate on Britain's cities rather than the key strategic targets, the destruction of which was a precondition for the launch of any invasion.[47] The direction of the offensive was now irreparably broken, and, notwithstanding the efforts of the German airmen, it never recovered.

Whilst the failings in German strategy and the apathy of Hitler and his senior commanders were key to the outcome, it would later become clear that the British did enjoy two other significant advantages. The role of intelligence gathered from signals intercepts—designated as ULTRA—during this period continues to provoke popular debate. One view is that "better grade intelligence came from prisoners, captured documents and improved air reconnaissance."[48] According to the official historian, limited information from *Luftwaffe* messages had begun to be produced on May 22, but this was of no operational value to the Commander-in-Chief, Fighter Command, Air Chief Marshal Hugh Dowding, with there even being some suggestion that he only became aware of its existence in the October.[49] It does seem, however, even though it was lacking in real detail and taking up to 48 hours to decrypt, this source did offer confirmation that the German leader has made air superiority a pre-requisite for the launching of any invasion. This alone would have offered a crucial advantage, not least because it enabled a better coordinated use of the resources available and allowed Churchill to adopt an often-bullish approach to the summer's events. While Brooke, who may also not have known about the available intelligence, appeared to have doubted the readiness of the men on the ground, his political commander knew that the key battle would actually be fought in the skies above Britain.

It is difficult to underestimate the extent of the role played by the British prime minister throughout the summer months. Aside from providing direction, and at times resolution, he motivated the population, helping to overcome the uncertainty and fear that inevitably emerged amongst some. At the very height of the threat in August just a week after the *Luftwaffe* had begun its attacks, he told a packed House of Commons:

> The British nation and the British Empire, finding themselves alone, stood undismayed against disaster. No one flinched or wavered; nay, some who formerly thought

of peace, now think only of war. Our people are united and resolved, as they have never been before. Death and ruin have become small things compared with the shame of defeat or failure in duty. We cannot tell what lies ahead. It may be that even greater ordeals lie before us. We shall face whatever is coming to us.[50]

Despite his dismissal, even Ironside was inspired to record later that Churchill created an environment whereby no "Britisher ... (wanted) to hand down such an inheritance (defeat and Nazi rule) to his descendants."[51] This was true in the air, at sea, and among the often overlooked ground forces, who all readied themselves for the onslaught that now seemed inevitable.

The decisive point came on the afternoon of September 7, a sunny late, summer weekend which, unbeknown at the time, was also the first day of the Blitz, the period of sustained bombing of British cities which continued through to the following May. Home Forces were already at a high state of alert as intelligence indicated that the Germans were creating new aerodromes and gun emplacements in France, moving bomber groups from Norway, removing inhabitants from French coastal towns, and nearing the completion of several weeks spent gathering barges between Le Havre and Ostend.[52] The overall assessment was that invasion preparations were approaching completion with a force of fifty thousand German troops now trained and ready to cross the English Channel. The weather and tides were also estimated to be at their most favorable during the three-day period of September 8 to September 10. Brooke had long believed that it would be the following week that would be critical, as his assessment pointed to this providing the best opportunity for German action. Daily observations on British morale noted that most of those questioned also anticipated an invasion taking place imminently but these also revealed there was great confidence that this would fail.[53]

As the *Luftwaffe*'s bombing from the air intensified, and with London in flames as 337 tons of bombs were dropped during the course of the first twenty-four hours of the attack, there seemed to be credible evidence that the invasion had begun. At 8pm in the evening, the decision was taken to issue the previously arranged "Cromwell" alert to military commands around the country. Troops along the south and east coasts of England and scattered units elsewhere around the country were mobilized in response to the "invasion imminent" message. The men were placed on four hours' notice to move and guards posted throughout the night with roadblocks manned by nervous sentries as church bells were mistakenly rung to alert the public to a threat which was not there. Although these measures were gradually withdrawn, a heightened state of alert continued until September 19, with another being issued three days later. Once this had passed, although it was not immediately recognized as such by those most intimately involved, the period of crisis and the direct threat of Britain being invaded was at an end, certainly for that summer.

Ironside was quite correct in his subsequent assessment, which he shared with the official historian writing the postwar account of Britain's defense of its shores, about what had happened during the summer of 1940.[54] For him, the Germans missed the opportunity that their success in France had presented to them and were too slow to take advantage of their opponent's weakness. The evidence confirms that there was no real enthusiasm for an attack. During a conversation in early June between Hermann Göring, commander of the *Luftwaffe*, and one of his senior commanders General Erhard Milch, the latter suggested that airborne divisions be used immediately to seize a bridgehead and capture airfields in southern England. Although he would later claim that he would have done so if he had had more men available, Göring said it could not be done.[55] This view was almost universally shared amongst the senior German military and political leaders who, like Hitler, had hoped that the British would look at what had happened on the continent of Europe and make terms. Indeed prior to the summer of 1940, Germany had never actually developed any really substantial plan for the invasion of Britain.[56] When something was hastily produced, the newly proposed *Sealion* operation required that the Royal Navy be deterred, the RAF defeated, and the *Kriegsmarine* and the *Luftwaffe* therefore had to succeed in accomplishing several complex goals before any attempted landing could be considered. While the most obvious was the destruction of British airpower, there was also a need to create mine-free corridors across the Channel and seal off the Dover Strait and the western entrance of the Channel with German minefields, as well as tying up British naval forces in the North Sea and the Mediterranean to prevent them from trying to break up the attempted landings.[57] Add to this the huge logistic build-up and the time spent training troops for a role that had not previously been considered and it is not difficult to see why Hitler remained indifferent about the prospects of any military action. As he himself noted, he was "quite water-shy" and he once remarked, "On land I am a Lion, but on water I don't know where to begin."[58] With the exception of the attack on Norway, the results of which were far from convincing, there was no real precedent for this kind of proposed operation and German military power was best configured for fighting on mainland Europe. As such, it was not really surprising when the operation was postponed indefinitely on October 12, 1940, a decision that was soon confirmed by British intelligence, allowing Brooke to switch his planning to the following year.

Churchill, with his potential, albeit limited, access to intelligence, remained much more sanguine about the potential longer-term risks. Even before the threat passed and only days after the country's assorted defenders had "stood to" expecting the worst, he felt sufficiently confident to push through a decision to send to North Africa the Australian and New Zealand troops who had been helping defend the country. He also gave orders that two tank battalions should be sent with them, a critical resource to lose from the defense of Britain's shores. This was in part based upon indications of an imminent Italian attack into Egypt and his reading of the available information, but it was also a clear statement of defiance and another signal to both domestic and international observers that the country was not defeated.[59] These forces were moved to Egypt over the following months and played a key role in Operation *Compass*, the largely successful attack by British Commonwealth forces which very nearly cleared Axis forces out of Libya.

Back in Britain, Canadian forces assumed an ever-greater role in garrisoning the country. During the final months of 1940, further reinforcements continued to arrive and in December, with the successful concentration of a second division and its equipping, it was now possible to establish an entirely Canadian corps which remained central to the GHQ Reserve force and retained the key role of rushing to the location of any German landings. For the military planners, the anticipation was that Hitler would almost certainly try to attack once again in the spring of 1941 and throughout the winter huge efforts were undertaken to strengthen defenses, manufacture more military equipment, and train more men. Exercises were held with ever greater frequency so that the defending forces would be at peak levels of readiness. These continued throughout 1942 but the invasion never came. The German leader's focus lay with the Soviet Union and his strategy for dealing with Britain centered on deception and fixing his opponent with the threat of military operations. This, ultimately, would reveal itself to be a grave miscalculation.

For Churchill, his leadership of the defense of his country in the face of a seemingly overwhelming and unstoppable German threat was a great personal triumph and it played a significant part in strengthening what, throughout the summer of 1940, had been an uncertain political position. It had, however, been a narrow victory for him and the people he led, if victory is the correct word, decided as much by the unwillingness of his German opponent to attempt one of the most difficult of military activities, a contested amphibious landing. When various retired military commanders carefully scrutinized the plans many years after the war's end, the eventual outcome of their simulation was that in the initial phases the Germans would have succeeded in establishing a bridgehead and would have had some significant success on land.[60] The attacking force would not, however, have been able to keep the Royal Navy out of the Straits of Dover nor gain air superiority, and without these critical elements the plan was always in some jeopardy. Unable to consolidate their position and failing to guarantee the essential sea lines of communication to support the operation, the exercise ultimately concluded that the invasion force had little choice but to withdraw back across the Channel. In the summer of 1940 this outcome was much less certain.

Acknowledgments

I am grateful to David Steeds and Professor Ashley Jackson for reading draft versions of this chapter and the helpful comments and suggestions they provided.

Notes

1. "Hitler letter hoping for "cordial relationship" with Britain for sale," *Daily Telegraph*, March 2, 2010.
2. "Britain's Year of Defiance," *BBC History Magazine* (2010); Richard Grayson, "WW2 has Become a Rallying Point for Leavers. It Need Not Have Been So," *LSE Brexit 2020* (Blog Post), January 31, 2020.

3. Sir Harry Batterbee to Malcolm MacDonald, January 7, 1938, DO35/543, The National Archives, London (hereafter 'TNA').
4. The potential threat of invasion is perhaps best examined in Collier, *The Defence of the United Kingdom*, 1–76, 175–182.
5. Chamberlain to Hilda Chamberlain, October 15, 1939, cited in Robert Self, *Neville Chamberlain: A Biography* (Aldershot: Ashgate Publishing, 2006), 395.
6. Cited in Self, *Neville Chamberlain*, Chamberlain to Liddell Hart, March 8, 1937; Ibid., Chamberlain to Hore-Belisha, October 29, 1937; "War Policy," September 12, 1939, Hankey Papers (HNKY 11/1), Churchill Archives Centre, Cambridge; Ibid., "War Appreciation," September 29, 1939.
7. War Cabinet Meeting (39)65, October 30, 1939, CAB65/1, TNA.
8. COS (39)125, November 18, 1939, CAB80/5, TNA.
9. Richard Overy, *The Origins of the Second World War* (London: Routledge, 2008), 2.
10. Roy Jenkins, *Churchill* (London: Macmillan, 2001), 476–479; Peter Fleming, *Operation Sea Lion* (London: Macmillan, 1975), 135–147.
11. "Statement to the House of Commons by Winston Churchill, May 13, 1940," *Hansard* 360: cc1501–1525.
12. Another extremely well covered episode of World War II, the official accounts remain definitive in terms of providing the chronology and details of events: Major L. F. Ellis, *The War in France and Flanders* (London: HMSO, 1953), 171–248. The official dispatch, "The Evacuation of the Allied Armies from Dunkirk and the Neighbouring Beaches" (Supplement to the *London Gazette*, no. 38017, Thursday July 17, 1947): 3295–3318 is another key source. Three other important texts are: Ronald Atkin, *Pillar of Fire: Dunkirk 1940* (Edinburgh: Birlinn Limited, 1990); Walter Lord, *The Miracle of Dunkirk* (London: Allen Lane, 1983); and, more recently, Hugh Sebag-Montefiore, *Dunkirk: Fight to the Last Man* (London: Penguin Books, 2006). For a concise and reflective German view there is also Karl-Heinz Frieser, *The Blitzkrieg Legend: The 1940 Campaign in the West* (Annapolis, MD: Naval Institute Press, 2005), 291–314.
13. "Losses in France and Norway of certain major items of equipment, consequent upon the withdrawal of the Expeditionary Forces—May and June 1940," December 24, 1940, Nuffield Papers (G502/32), Nuffield College, University of Oxford.
14. Ibid., "Strength of Troops (All Ranks) in the UK, Iceland and Faroes, 1.7.40," n.d. (G510/18, 40.1 pt.1).
15. Andrew Stewart, "The Battle for Britain," *History Today* 65, no. 6 (June 2015): 19–26.
16. Ashley Jackson, "The Empire/Commonwealth and the Second World War," *The Round Table* 100, no. 412 (February 2010): 65–70.
17. "The Colonies in the War," *The Times*, January 13, 1940.
18. "The Empire at War," *The Times*, January 1, 1940; "First Colonials in France," *The Times*, January 10, 1940.
19. Miss Y. Streatfield, "Relative strengths of each of the Dominion Armed forces at the outbreak of war, September 1939," n.d. (1945?), CAB101/275, TNA.
20. "Canada's War Effort," *The Journal of the Royal United Services Institution* 85, no. 544 (November 1941): 664.
21. "Relative strengths of each of the Dominion Armed forces . . . ," CAB101/275, TNA; Adam Claasen, *Dogfight: The Battle of Britain* (Barnsley: Pen and Sword Aviation, 2013), 186. Approximately one-fifth of the pilots and gunners who took part in the subsequent Battle of Britain were not British.

22. Royal Canadian Air Force, *The RCAF—The First Four Years* (Toronto: Oxford University Press, 1944), 6–34; Mathias Joost, "The Other Canadians in the Battle of Britain," *The Royal Canadian Air Force Journal* 1, no. 4 (Fall 2012): 39.
23. Vincent Massey, *What's Past Is Prologue: The Memoirs of the Right Honourable Vincent Massey* (Toronto: Macmillan, 1963), 318; "Dominion Men," *Time*, January 1, 1940; J. L. Granatstein, *The Generals: The Canadian Army's Senior Commanders in the Second World War* (Toronto: Stoddart, 1993), 59–61.
24. By the summer of 1940, Canadian forces were also playing a role in the defense of Newfoundland, Iceland, and the West Indies, freeing up British troops for service elsewhere; Lester Pearson, *Memoirs, 1897–1948: Through Diplomacy to Politics* (London: Victor Gollancz, 1973); Colonel C.P. Stacey, *Six Years of War: The Army in Canada, Britain and the Pacific* (Ottawa, Ontario, Canada: Authority of the Minister of National Defence | Roger Duhamel, Queen's Printer and Controller of Stationery, 1966), 165; Stacey, *Six Years of War—The Army in Canada, Britain and the Pacific*, 258–263.
25. Ibid., 263–269, 279–283.
26. "Memorandum of conversation with General Crerar, the new Canadian Chief of Staff, Ottawa," July 25, 1940, Canada, U.S. Legation and Embassy Ottawa, General Records—Chancery, Box 60 (National Archives, Maryland), RG84.
27. S. P. Mackenzie, *The Home Guard* (Oxford: Oxford University Press, 1995), 33–51.
28. David Carroll, *Dad's Army: The Home Guard 1940–1944* (Stroud: The History Press, 2002), 2–9; Charles Graves, *The Home Guard of Britain* (London: Hutchinson and Co., 1943), 13–16.
29. Brian Lavery, *We Shall Fight on the Beaches: Defying Napoleon and Hitler, 1805 and 1940* (London: Conway, 2009), 330–339; Bill Mitchinson, *Defending Albion: Britain's Home Army 1908–1919* (Basingstoke; Palgrave Macmillan, 2005), 52–75.
30. Earl of Avon, *The Eden Memoirs*, Vol. 3: *The Reckoning* (London: Cassell and Co. Ltd., 1965), 103.
31. "War Situation: Statement by the Prime Minister Winston Churchill, 18 June 1940," *Hansard*, 362: cc51–64; John F. Burns, "Seventy Years Later, Churchill's "Finest Hour" Yields Insights," *New York Times*, June 17, 2010.
32. Colonel Roderick Macleod and Denis Kelly, eds., *The Ironside Diaries 1937–1940* (London: Constable, 1962), 356–360.
33. COS (40)193, June 25, 1940, CAB79/4, TNA.
34. Macleod and Kelly, eds., *The Ironside Diaries*, 380.
35. Donald Lindsay, *Forgotten General: A Life of Andrew Thorne* (Salisbury: Michael Russell, 1987), 140.
36. Earl of Avon, *The Eden Memoirs*, Vol. 3, 119.
37. David Dilks, ed., *The Diaries of Sir Alexander Cadogan* (London: Cassell and Company, 1971), 308.
38. Brigadier J. O. E. Vandeleur, *A Soldier's Story* (Aldershot: Gale and Polden Ltd, 1967), 68.
39. Diary, May 23, 1940, cited in Alex Danchev and Daniel Todman, eds., *War Diaries 1939–1945: Field Marshal Lord Alanbrooke* (London: Phoenix Press, 2002), 67–68.
40. COS (40)247, August 5, 1940, CAB79/5, TNA.
41. Stacey, *Six Years of War—The Army in Canada, Britain and the Pacific*, 234–235.
42. "Inter-Brigade Exercise, 17 Jul 1940," Operations Canadian Forces—England, A. G. L. McNaughton Papers, Library and Archives Canada, Ottawa, MG30, E133; Series III, Vol.227; Ibid., "Memorandum—Conference on Two-Sided Exercise held on 17 Jul 1940."

43. Diary, July 29 and September 15, 1940, cited in Danchev and Todman, eds., *Field Marshal Lord Alanbrooke*, 96, 108.
44. Stacey, *Six Years of War—The Army in Canada, Britain and the Pacific*, 292.
45. Overy, *The Origins of the Second World War*, 79.
46. Edwin P. Hoyt, *Hitler's War* (New York: Da Capo Press, 1990), 164–165; Martin Gilbert, *The Second World War* (London: Fontana Paperbacks, 1990), 120–121.
47. Overy, *The Origins of the Second World War*, 115.
48. Andrew Lycett, "Breaking Germany's Enigma Code," *BBC History*, February 17, 2011.
49. F. H. Hinsley, *British Intelligence in the Second World War*, Vol. 1: *Its Influence on Strategy and Operations* (London: HMSO, 1993), 166–168; John Ray, *Battle of Britain—New Perspectives* (London: Arms and Armour Press, 1994), 59.
50. "War Situation: Statement to the House of Commons by the Prime Minister Winston Churchill, August 20, 1940," *Hansard* 364: cc1132–274.
51. Macleod and Kelly, eds., *The Ironside Diaries*, 358.
52. COS (40)300, September 7, 1940, CAB79/5, TNA.
53. "Daily Observations by Home Intelligence, Monday, September 16, 1940, No.101," HO199/436, TNA.
54. Ironside to Basil Collier, May 1, 1954, CAB106/1205, TNA.
55. David Irving, *Göring: A Biography* (London: Harper Collins, 1990), 290.
56. Hans Umbrit, "Plans and Preparations for a Landing in England," in *Germany and the Second World War*, Vol. 2: *Germany's Initial Conquests in Europe*, ed. K. A. Maier et al. (Oxford: Clarendon Press, 1991), 366–373.
57. Hugh Trevor-Roper, ed., *Hitler's War Directives* (London: Sidgwick and Jackson, 1964), 34.
58. Norman Rich, *Hitler's War Aims* (London: Andre Deutsch Ltd., 1973), 53.
59. COS (40)302, September 9, 1940, CAB79/6, TNA.
60. Richard Cox, *Sea Lion: Hitler Invades Britain* (London: Thornton Cox, 1974), 7–9.

Bibliography

Atkin, Ronald. *Pillar of Fire: Dunkirk 1940*. Edinburgh: Birlinn Limited, 1990.
Bader, Douglas, Group Captain RAF (Ret.). *Fight for the Sky*. New York: Doubleday and Co., 1973.
Bekker, Cajus. *The Luftwaffe War Diaries*. Translated and edited by Frank Ziegler. New York: Doubleday and Co., 1966.
Bell, P. M. H. *Twelve Turning Points of the Second World War*. London: Yale University Press, 2011.
Butler J. R. M. *Grand Strategy, September 1939–June 1941*. London: HMSO, 1957.
Calder, Angus, *The People's War: Britain 1939–1945*. New York: Pantheon Books, 1969.
Calvocoressi, Peter, and Guy Wint. *Total War: The Story of World War II*. New York: Pantheon Books, 1972.
Churchill, Winston. *The Second World War*, Vol. 2: *Their Finest Hour*. Cambridge, MA: Houghton Mifflin Co., 1949.
Collier, Basil. *The Defence of the United Kingdom*. London: HMSO, 1957.
Frieser, Karl-Heinz. *The Blitzkrieg Legend: The 1940 Campaign in the West*. Annapolis, MD: Naval Institute Press, 2005.
Lord, Walter. *The Miracle of Dunkirk*. London: Allen Lane, 1983.

Middlebrook, Martin, and Chris Everitt. *The Bomber Command War Diaries: An Operational Reference Book, 1939–1945*. London: Penguin Books, 1990.

Overy, Richard. *The Battle of Britain*. London: Penguin Books, 2004.

Parker, R. A. C. *The Second World War: A Short History*. Oxford: Oxford University Press, 2001.

Richards, Denis. *Royal Air Force 1939–1945*, Vol. I: *The Fight at Odds*. London: HMSO, 1953.

Roberts, Andrew. *The Storm of War: A New History of the Second World War*. London: Allen Lane, 2009.

Sebag-Montefiore, Hugh. *Dunkirk: Fight to the Last Man*. London: Penguin Books, 2006.

Wheatley, Ronald. *Operation Sea Lion: German Plans for the Invasion of England, 1939–1942*. Oxford: Oxford University Press, 1958.

CHAPTER 8

THE BATTLE OF THE ATLANTIC, 1939–1945

MARC MILNER

THE "Battle of the Atlantic" is a misnomer for a complex series of campaigns fought in the North and South Atlantic between the British declaration of war on Germany on September 3, 1939 and the final Nazi capitulation on May 8, 1945. It was therefore never a "battle" in the conventional sense, like Trafalgar or Midway. The war in the Atlantic consisted of a number of discrete campaigns over nearly six years in which German objectives, in particular, changed. Moreover, actual fighting between combatants was only part of the story. The Western alliance was primarily a global maritime one, and many of the bottlenecks affecting the development of Allied strategy in the war in the West had little to do with direct enemy action at sea.

The objectives of the two sides in the Atlantic war—the Allies and the Axis—were not symmetrical, nor was "victory" by either side zero-sum. In 1939, the sinews of war and many of the very basics of everyday life in Britain and France were drawn from overseas continents, colonies, and empires. This dependency provided Germany with a clear target to attack, which could, in theory, fatally weaken the two western powers. The defeat of France and the subsequent involvement of the United States simply increased the centrality of the North Atlantic to the Allied war effort. In contrast, Germany had no vital interests that spanned the globe, or even the Atlantic. Moreover, it soon possessed most of continental Europe to exploit by road, rail, and canals, systems that were not vulnerable to sea power.

As a result of this disparity in the role of the Atlantic between the two contending alliances, their strategies and purposes differed markedly. Allied military objectives in the Atlantic, such as the blockade of Axis Europe, securing their merchant ships, and projection of military power in the air and ashore on the Continent, were obtainable without direct attack on Germany's maritime interests in the European littoral. It was incumbent, therefore, on Germany to take the initiative in the Atlantic war as a way of weakening the Allies: only briefly, in the winter of 1940–1941, might a German victory at sea have determined the outcome of the war.

The initiative in the Atlantic fell primarily to the German navy, the *Kriegsmarine*, and to a much lesser extent the air force, the *Luftwaffe*. Both were woefully unprepared for a major naval war. In 1939, the *Kriegsmarine* was at least five years away from completion of its "Z Plan" to build a fleet to challenge Britain in European waters. And while the *Luftwaffe* possessed some excellent long-range maritime patrol aircraft, it was essentially a tactical air force built to aid the army. When Hitler precipitated war with Britain and France in 1939 by invading Poland, the Chief of the Staff of the *Kriegmarine*, Admiral Erich Raeder, protested that the war had come much to early: all his fleet could do was "die gallantly."[1]

German naval strategy during the Phoney War of 1939–1940 was, therefore, primarily one of harassment and containment of Allied naval forces through a war on shipping conducted largely by surface ships. In September 1939, several pocket battleships, built as oceanic commerce raiders, and disguised merchant ships fitted as raiders were already at sea. They were supported, in turn, by a fleet of purpose-built supply vessels capable of refueling and re-arming the raiders in remote areas. The most important, but little known, episode in this Phoney War was the sortie of the battlecruisers *Scharnhorst* and *Gneisenau* into the North Atlantic in late November 1939. After a perilous and secret passage of the North Sea the two raiders attacked the British northern patrols, sinking the Armed Merchant Cruiser (AMC) *Rawalpindi*. A massive effort by both the British and French fleets failed to find them and they returned safely to Germany.

The good news for the Allies in this period came the next month. In December 1939, three cruisers cornered and fought the pocket battleship *Admiral Graf Spee* off the River Plate in South America. *Graf Spee* had been attacking Allied shipping in the South Atlantic and transferring captured merchant seamen to its supply ships. The damaged raider took refuge in Montevideo, Uruguay, where it was entitled to shelter briefly. The unfolding drama was followed closely by the international media. When it was clear that *Graf Spee* had to leave but could not escape the waiting British cruisers, it was scuttled and burned to deny the British a victory. Many of the British seamen captured by *Graf Spee* were freed in February 1940 in the much-publicized British capture of the German supply ship *Altmarck*, which had taken refuge in a neutral Norwegian fjord. This all made for great historical writing, but none of it had any impact on the course of the war.[2]

The war at sea changed abruptly in April 1940 when Germany launched a successful naval and air assault on Norway. In addition to securing Germany's supply of iron ore, the occupation of Norway—under the protective umbrella of modern airpower—broke the Allied naval blockade and gave Germany ports on the Atlantic for the first time. The price was high, however, with the German surface fleet suffering heavy damage and significant losses.[3]

The fall of France at the end of June tipped the balance further in Germany's favor. Britain lost its greatest ally, and Germany obtained even better operational bases on the Atlantic. Not since 1805 had a British enemy controlled the European littoral from North Cape, Norway to the Iberian Peninsula. Once it became clear, following the *Luftwaffe*'s failure to defeat the Royal Air Force in the Battle of Britain in late September 1940, that immediate invasion was not possible, Germany had a clear and simple strategic objective in the war at sea: defeat Britain by severing its maritime communications.

This was much easier said than done. The Germans estimated that if they destroyed some 750,000 tons of British shipping per month for a year, then Britain would sue for peace. The figure was a guess: even the British were uncertain about their shipping needs. By one prewar estimate they needed forty-seven million tons of imports per year, but in 1940 these had yet to be winnowed down to essentials.[4] By 1942, Britain managed on less than half that amount. The Germans nonetheless applied all their resources to this attack over the winter of 1940-1941 in a comprehensive naval and air assault on shipping and British ports.

The British were better prepared to meet this German challenge than historians—who like to focus on combat—have allowed. The British had fought great maritime wars for centuries and understood how to manage (quite literally). While wartime propaganda lauded the fleet of escort vessels that closely guarded the merchant ship convoys as the first line of defense, in fact they were the very last line of a complex, global system of defense: the escort only fought if the system failed. Allied defense of shipping always relied on the covering actions of the main battlefleet. Its job was to keep the enemy's big ships at bay or destroy them if they came out, thus allowing the smaller vessels to guard the convoys against raiders. And if the enemy refused to come out, the British went after them in port. In the age of sail, this often meant raiding parties and fireships: by World War II, it meant airpower.

The secondary means of defending shipping was avoidance of the enemy. This was done through a combination of naval intelligence, which tracked enemy dispositions, and naval control of shipping (NCS). Naval intelligence gathered and collated every scrap of information on the movement of Allied and Axis naval and commercial vessels it could. NCS controlled the movements of Allied merchant ships, in much the same way modern air traffic control regulates the movement of aircraft. NCS worked closely with naval intelligence, mustering ships for convoys, and routing both convoys and independent ships away from known enemy deployments. Knowing where merchant ships were, where they were going, and when they went missing allowed naval authorities to check areas for raiders: that was how *Graf Spee* was found.[5]

In this system the close escort's primary job was—in the words of the Royal Navy's *Atlantic Convoy Instructions*—the "safe and timely arrival of the convoy," and that often meant just driving the enemy off long enough for the convoy to get away. It was assumed that the enemy would always be lurking, and that he could never be completely defeated: the ocean is vast. If the covering action of the main battle fleet, and the combination of naval intelligence and routing provided by NCS failed to keep convoys clear of danger, it was the escort's job to fight. If the enemy was destroyed in the process that was a bonus.

Surface raiders were the greatest threat to Allied shipping in the North Atlantic until well into 1941. The *Admiral Scheer* roamed the Atlantic in the fall of 1940, sinking the AMC *Jervis Bay* during one convoy battle on the Grand Banks of Newfoundland. The heavy cruiser *Hipper* roamed the North Atlantic in December, and in February left Brest after a short stay to join the battle cruisers *Scharnhorst* and *Gneisenau* in an attack on the main convoy routes. They were supported by very long-range Fokker-Wolf 200 aircraft and submarines operating from French bases. The British were never able to bring this powerful force to battle—not least because the Germans were not yet ready for a full-scale engagement. So, for months in the winter of 1941, powerful German warships "pulled the lion's tail" in the Atlantic. They disrupted shipping and deeply embarrassed the British, but they sank few ships: only 6.6 percent of shipping destroyed by Germany during the war was sunk by surface raiders of all kinds. By comparison, mines sank 10.3 percent, aircraft 15.9 percent, and unknown causes 12.3 percent.[6]

By the spring of 1941, the *Scharnhorst* and *Gneisenau* were safe in French ports: the beginnings of a powerful and modern squadron poised to challenge British domination of the Atlantic. In May 1941, the most modern and powerful battleship in the world, the *Bismarck*, and the heavy cruiser *Prinz Eugen*, left Norway to join them. *Bismarck*'s sister ship *Tirpitz* was due to enter service in the fall.

Bismarck and *Prinz Eugen* steamed into a much different operational environment in the spring of 1941. Long summer days in high latitudes and fairer weather made it much harder to hide from Allied patrols. So, too, did the advent of radar-equipped patrol aircraft. *Bismarck* and *Prinz Eugen* nonetheless achieved a dramatic success in breaking-out into the North Atlantic. In the Denmark Strait they met and defeated the British squadron sent to intercept them. The aging pride of the Royal Navy, the battlecruiser *Hood*—sleek, fast, elegant, and under-armored—was destroyed by one of *Bismarck*'s first salvoes. The brand-new battleship *Prince of Wales*, with workmen still aboard, was damaged but not before it struck *Bismarck* in the bow, causing serious flooding. That ended the cruise. *Prinz Eugen* was cut loose to roam the Atlantic while *Bismarck* headed for Brest. Air patrols eventually found *Bismarck* again. One fortuitous hit in its rudder by a torpedo from a British aircraft left *Bismarck* turning in aimless circles. On May 26 the British pounded *Bismarck* into a wreck and sent it to the bottom.[7]

The British remained vigilant for the return of the big ships in the North Atlantic until early 1942. Only after *Scharnhorst* and *Gniesenau* made their dramatic dash up the English Channel back to Germany in February, and Germany redeployed her surface fleet to Norway, did the danger from big ships in the broad Atlantic abate.

Increasingly Germany relied on its U-boat fleet to attack Allied shipping. By the end of the war, submarines accounted for roughly 60 percent of Allied merchant ship losses.[8] U-boat tactics by late 1940 were innovative and caught the British by surprise.[9] In 1939, it was assumed that submarines would operate submerged and inshore, as they had in 1917–1918 when oceanic convoys were introduced. So British anti-submarine (A/S) escort extended initially only to twelve degrees west and focused on defense against submerged attack. Outside the U-boat danger zone convoys in-bound to Britain (starting either in Canada or North Africa) were protected by cruisers and battleships against raiders, while west-bound convoys were dispersed west of twelve degrees. It was understood that submarines would not operate in the broad ocean because finding and attacking escorted convoys there was too difficult.

However, Admiral Karl Dönitz, commander of Germany's submarines, had developed a solution to both the search and the attack problems on the high seas. He deployed groups of U-boats in lines perpendicular to the convoy route and controlled them from headquarters ashore through high-frequency (H/F) radio. These "Wolf Packs" acted like a huge drift net to snare convoys. For the pack system to work, routine, daily two-way HF radio traffic was essential.[10] Once a U-boat made contact with a convoy it transmitted the convoy's position, course, and speed, and sent out a medium-frequency homing signal. When enough U-boats were assembled around the convoy, the Wolf Pack was turned loose to attack. The attack usually came at night, with U-boats operating independently on the surface like motor-torpedo boats, slipping inside the convoy at high speed to fire torpedoes.

The British were unprepared for these tactics in the winter of 1940–1941 and losses to some convoys were alarming. At the end of October, convoy SC 7 lost twenty-one of its thirty ships and HX 79 lost twelve of forty-nine: other heavy losses followed. The range of Allied naval and air anti-submarine escort expanded westward over the winter in response, and the Allies learned how to deal with the new German tactics. In March 1941, the British killed two of Germany's leading U-boat aces—Joachim Schepke and Gunther Prien—and captured the third, Otto Kretschmer. The next month they established bases in Iceland to push escorts even deeper into the Atlantic, and they opened "Western Approaches Command" in Liverpool to oversee A/S defense of convoys. Permanent escort groups and tactics were developed, and new equipment (such as radar and radio telephones for fast and efficient voice communications between escorts) introduced.

By May 1941, the only gap in trans-Atlantic A/S escort of convoys lay between Newfoundland (where Canadian escort stopped) and Iceland. That month the British asked the Royal Canadian Navy (RCN) to close the gap. The RCN was able to do so because Canada's large program of escort construction—begun the previous year—produced scores of Flower Class Corvettes in the spring of 1941. The corvette was not an ideal ocean escort vessel but it had the range necessary to allow the convoy system to function: that was the key.[11]

The gap in naval escort across the North Atlantic closed in June 1941 with the establishment of the Newfoundland Escort Force, but the limited ranges of land-based aircraft left a mid-Atlantic gap in air escort that was not closed for another two years. This "Black Pit" profoundly affected development of the battle until 1943.

Historians have said much of the apparent impunity with which U-boats attacked Allied shipping in the winter of 1940–1941, and it makes for good history. But there were never enough U-boats to achieve decisive results. Dönitz had wanted three hundred submarines for a war against Britain: in August 1940 he had twenty-seven and by February 1941 just twenty-one. Only about one-third were on station at a time: thirteen in August 1940 and a paltry eight in January 1941.[12] Historians typically draw a straight line between the dramatic convoy battles during this first U-boat "Happy Time" and a sharp decline in British imports over the winter of 1940–1941. But that decline in imports was the result of the closure of Britain's major ports (London and Southampton) by Luftwaffe bombers as part of the Blitz, and the subsequent temporary disruption as labor, rolling stock, and cargo handling equipment was shifted to west country ports.[13]

Fairer weather and longer days curtailed German submarine success in the spring of 1941. Merchant shipping losses over that year averaged about 250,000 tons per month, well short of Dönitz's objective. A faulty German torpedo contributed to this disappointing result. The Germans hoped that their new magnetic pistol, which detonated the torpedo under the ship's keel and broke it open, would produce a success rate of one ship for every torpedo fired. When the magnetic pistol failed, German submariners had to rely on their contact pistols, so it took an average of two torpedoes to sink each ship. This cut the theoretical "production" of each voyage in half.[14] Meanwhile, the British saved some three million tons of shipping by cutting down on imports, more efficient loading of ships,[15] and reducing port congestion, launched some 1.2 million tons of new shipping and ordered over seven million tons of new shipping from U.S. yards. The U-boat war in 1941 was therefore dramatic but not decisive. Germany's one chance to win the war by defeating Britain at sea failed.

From the summer of 1941 until the spring of 1943, German strategy aimed to embarrass Allied plans and forestall the development of the Second Front—the latter even more essential after the attack on Russia in June 1941. This failed as well.

The Allies struck back at the U-boats in 1941. In June, they captured U110 and all its coding and cipher books and equipment. Using these, the British broke the cipher for Atlantic U-boats and were soon reading German radio traffic with regularity and timeliness. This special intelligence, dubbed "Ultra," allowed convoys to be routed safely for the rest of the year, and may have saved three hundred Allied ships in late 1941.[16] The German attack on Russia, which began on June 22, and British success in North Africa also drew U-boats away from the North Atlantic as the year wore on. Hitler was paranoid about a British landing in Norway and then, as convoys to Russia began, it was necessary to attack them, too. Meanwhile, U-boats that redeployed into the Mediterranean were gone from the Atlantic forever. Submarines could ride the inbound current past British defenses in the Straits of Gibraltar in a single night, but the current was too strong to exit submerged and the nights were too short to clear the area on the surface.

The Allied situation in the North Atlantic in 1941 was also given an enormous boost by the active involvement of the United States Navy (USN) in the shooting war. The roots of that involvement lay in defense of shipping. In 1939, the United States proclaimed a neutral zone in the western Atlantic and acquired bases in various British colonies in 1941 as part of the destroyers-for-bases deal from which to police that zone. That much was public knowledge. But few outside of the USN knew that the Canadians and British ran an elaborate naval control of shipping and naval intelligence networks throughout the United States as part of Britain's global system. Ottawa was the regional center for all the information necessary to track and control Allied shipping in the western hemisphere north of the equator. It was linked to other regional centers and with the global naval control of shipping center in London. In 1941, steps were taken to integrate the USN into the system. A Canadian NCS liaison officer was appointed to Washington to help integrate the Americans into the British system, and the RCN supplied confidential books and special publications to the USN's emerging network of "Port Directors."[17]

When Churchill and Roosevelt met in Argentia in August 1941 to discuss what they might do jointly to further the Allied cause, some of the groundwork had already been laid. At Argentia, it was agreed that the USN neutrality zone would be expanded to include Iceland, that the USN would assume strategic control of the western Atlantic, and that in mid-September the USN would begin escorting convoys to and from Iceland. Ostensibly, these convoys would supply the new U.S. garrison in Iceland (which replaced the British and Canadians) and the island itself. In the event, the convoys were a legal fiction. A pool of American-flag ships was maintained at Halifax, Nova Scotia, to insert at least one into each regularly scheduled eastbound convoy. American ships returning Iceland just happened to join the westbound convoys.

So, in September 1941, the USN went off to war in the North Atlantic.[18] Its arrival allowed the Royal Navy to shift escorts to commence regular convoys to northern Russia.

By agreement, the USN's sleek destroyers, operating from the new American base at Argentia, Newfoundland, escorted the fast convoys between the Grand Banks of Newfoundland and Iceland. The Canadian navy, equipped with much slower corvettes, got the slow convoys. The latter, typically composed of less reliable and less well-maintained vessels, were restricted to 7.5 knots, and often made much less than that. They were incapable of evasive action in the event of attack and took days longer to cross the air gap to the safety of Iceland-based air support. It did not help that the RCN was in the throes of expansion, its crews were often new to the sea, and the RCN's basic equipment—including radio-telephones, signal lamps, secondary weapons, navigation equipment, and even foul weather gear—was not adequate for the task.

The result was a series of convoy battles in the fall of 1941 that went heavily against the Canadians. In September, slow convoy SC 42 lost fifteen ships in a week-long battle. SC 44 and SC 48 were attacked in the weeks to follow, and finally SC 52 was turned back to Canada in October when the Germans intercepted it in the Strait of Belle Isle (between Newfoundland and Labrador) and inflicted losses. British naval officers and historians later lamented the deplorable state of the RCN in the fall of 1941,[19] but the RCN and the British Admiralty knew that the system mattered more than the efficiency of individual escorts. Americans, it seems, drew their own lessons from their experience alongside the struggling Canadians.

The fall battles of 1941 also revealed a stark contrast between British and American conceptions of the purpose of convoy operations in the North Atlantic. The Royal Navy's (RN) "Western Approaches Convoy Instructions (WACIs)," issued in April, stated emphatically that "safe and timely arrival of the convoy" was the escort's principal task. The USN's "Escort of Convoy Instructions" issued in November put that dead last on the list of duties: the primary job of the USN escort was to sink subs. For its part, the RCN officially followed WACIs, but its men at sea inclined toward the American view and were often chastised for leaving their convoys to chase U-boats. There was, it seems, a distinct difference between the British and their North American cousins. For the British, the North Atlantic was a rear area, a line of communications. For the North American navies, the North Atlantic was primarily a war zone: fighting the Germans seemed to define the job.

Fortunately, by November, German withdrawals to the Mediterranean and Norway eased the crisis around the trans-Atlantic convoys just as Canadian reinforcements flooded in. Meanwhile, British forces in the eastern Atlantic inflicted a tactical defeat on the U-boats and their supporting long-range aircraft at the end of 1941. Indeed, they worked out the formula whereby the Wolf Packs would ultimately be beaten. New 10cm wavelength radar (Type 271) on escort vessels allowed the small target of U-boats awash on the surface to be detected, and ship-borne "High Frequency Direction Finding" (HF/DF) equipment allowed U-boat sighting reports to be plotted by the escort at sea. This provided good tactical intelligence and allowed sweeps by the escort to drive off U-boats and break contact. Support Groups, free of escort responsibility, were able to hunt U-boats while an auxiliary aircraft carrier provided local air support. All this worked superbly during the passage of convoy HG 76 in December. In exchange for two merchant ships, a destroyer and the auxiliary carrier, the British sank five U-boats, shot down four FW-200s long-range patrol aircraft, and drove off many shadowers. And just as it appeared that the exhausted naval escort might break while still seven hundred miles out to sea, new Very Long Range B-24 Liberators of the Royal Air Force arrived to drive of three of the final four U-boats. HG 76 was a signal British victory.[20]

The Atlantic war entered a new phase following the Japanese attack on Pearl Harbor on December 7, 1941: it opened the American eastern seaboard to U-boat attacks. What followed was a monumental American strategic blunder, perhaps America's greatest-ever naval defeat. It was redeemed only by America's enormous capacity to build ships faster than they could be lost.

As the U-boats pushed westwards into American waters in early 1942, the British urged the USN to introduce a system of convoys to defend shipping in its coastal zones. The Americans refused. In March 1942 the USN "Board on the Organization of East Coast Convoys" concluded that poorly escorted convoys simply concentrated targets: it was prudent to disperse shipping, and hunt submarines with the available forces.[21] This seems to be based on the USN's own experience with mid-ocean convoys in the fall of 1941. It failed to distinguish—as the Anglo–Canadians did—between mid-ocean operations in the face of Wolf Packs and inshore operations where attacks came from lone hunters in free-fire zones.[22]

In early 1942, the USN preferred to trust in "offensive" patrols by surface and air forces to hunt U-boats, while shipping sailed independently or at nicely spaced intervals along "protected lanes." The results were catastrophic. U-boats avoided the patrols and sank the shipping with impunity. In May and June 1942 alone, they sank over one million tons in U.S. waters—one-half their total score for 1941 in just two months. During 1942, nearly one-half of the more than sixteen hundred Allied ships lost globally were sunk in U.S. and Caribbean waters.[23]

British and Canadian frustration over the failure of the USN to introduce a convoy system arose in part because the two Commonwealth nations possessed the naval intelligence and the naval control of shipping infrastructure to make convoys happen in the U.S. zones. In fact, until the USN took control in July 1942, all oceanic routing of ships and convoys in the western hemisphere north of the equator—including U.S. waters—was done in Ottawa. It was sound organization that kept the Germans from success in the Canadian zone in 1942, not a dearth of targets. In fact, four hundred to five hundred ships per month plied waters off Canada, most following the Great Circle route between North America and Britain. The greatest losses in these waters in early 1942 came from ships of westbound convoys dispersed on the Grand Banks. When these convoys were escorted straight onto Halifax starting in March, losses in the Canadian zone plummeted. In the spring, the RCN introduced a system of coastal convoys which effectively eliminated easy targets inshore as well.

Not surprisingly, given their control of NCS and naval intelligence, it was the Canadians who started the first convoys in the American zones. In March, the RCN began the Boston to Halifax series. And in May, at the height of the carnage off the U.S. coast, the RCN began oil tanker convoys through the U.S. Eastern Sea Frontier to the Caribbean: these operated without loss.[24] The USN finally began to establish convoys in May.[25] As this system expanded, it reduced tonnage-sunk-per-U-boat-day-at-sea (Dönitz's basic measure of success), and forced U-boats to move further afield to less well-protected areas. Much of 1942 was therefore about extending the convoy system in the western hemisphere, and the progressive denial of operating areas for U-boats dependent upon surface maneuverability for both tactical and strategic success. Allied merchant shipping losses nonetheless peaked in 1942: 8.3 million tons, of which 6.1 million fell to U-boats. It could not be sustained. New ship construction surged past losses in the fall of 1942, as American industry gained momentum.

Expansion of the western hemisphere convoy system gradually forced most of the U-boat fleet, the small Type VIIs, back into the mid-ocean in late 1942; the only theater left where they could operate on the surface with impunity and hope to achieve decisive results. By August 1942, there were enough U-boats there to operate two large packs, and over the fall their numbers grew as the Atlantic war moved to its climax.

When the Germans returned in strength to the North Atlantic, they once again found a changed operational environment, this time to their advantage. Most of the USN destroyers were gone—off to fight in the Pacific—and Iceland was no longer an escort relay point. The Mid Ocean Escort Force, about two-thirds British or European navies in exile and one-third Canadian with one notionally American escort group, now protected convoys all the way between the Grand Banks and Ireland. Escorts could make the passage easily enough, but they needed a reserve of fuel for tactical purposes. This obliged convoys to stay perilously close to the most direct—and predictable—track. That was acceptable so long as U-boats were busy elsewhere. But until refueling at sea for small vessels expanded in late 1942, the mid-Atlantic convoy system lacked tactical flexibility. Worst still, since February, when the Germans introduced a new cipher for Atlantic U-boats, intelligence was no longer precise enough for really effective evasive routing. As summer gave way to fall, a crisis was looming.

In the fall of 1942, the new Wolf Packs fed primarily (although not exclusively) on the slow convoys, still largely escorted by Canadians. Although much more efficient than the previous year, the Canadians now lacked critical modern equipment, like 10cm radar and shipborne HF/DF, and their plodding convoys remained easy to find and easy to attack. The Germans also discovered that their first-generation radar detectors, "Metox," designed to alert them to air patrols in the Bay of Biscay, could also track the first-generation radars used by Canadian escorts. So Canadian radar transmissions often served as homing beacons for U-boats in the fall of 1942. As a result, some eighty percent of mid-Atlantic losses from July to December 1942 were suffered by Canadian-escorted slow convoys. It was a unique phase of the Atlantic war and one totally ignored by Anglo–American historians.[26]

This loss rate to slow convoys complicated an already complex situation by late 1942. In July, the Allies agreed to land in North Africa in early November in what became known as Operation TORCH. To assemble the escorts needed, oceanic convoys in the eastern and southern Atlantic were abandoned in late summer. As a result, U-boats sank a record amount of shipping in those theaters—virtually all of it British or British-controlled. British carrying capacity was also sharply reduced because of the routing of all shipping between Britain and the southern hemisphere through the convoy system of the western hemisphere. In short, Britain became utterly dependant on the main trans-Atlantic convoys as the only way in or out just as the Germans were driven to attack that route in force. The situation was further aggravated by the fact that the bulk of new merchant shipping was American while the vast majority of losses in 1942 were British. If all that was not bad enough, Operation TORCH soon placed an unexpectedly high demand on British supplies. The whole combination pushed Britain into its gravest import crisis of the war just as the battle in the North Atlantic built to a climax.[27]

It was fortunate for the Allies that naval the tactics, doctrine, and equipment to deal with Wolf Packs improved steadily through 1942. Air patrols synchronized their efforts more effectively with convoys, while white camouflage, higher patrol altitudes, and more effective fuses for depth charges contributed to increasingly successful air support. In August 1942, a few British Very Long Range (VLR) Liberators began operating again in the mid-ocean: a development noted with concern by the Germans. The 10cm radar and ship-borne HF/DF sets that made the defense of HG 76 the previous December so significant were now common among British escorts. Small escort aircraft carriers were supposed to help, but these were drawn off to the North African landings and the Russian convoys.

The looming climax in the North Atlantic led to the appointment of a new Commander-in-Chief, Western Approaches in November 1942, Rear Admiral Sir Max Horton. One of his first actions was to recommend that the struggling Canadian and American escorts in the mid-ocean be withdrawn for refit and retraining. In the event, only the Canadians were removed (in early 1943).[28] The situation in mid-Atlantic brightened for the Allies in late December when the Atlantic U-boat cipher, which they had stopped reading in February, was re-penetrated.

The good news about the restoration of Ultra intelligence was overshadowed by the increasing assault on Britain's one-remaining convoy link to the outside world and by the fact that unless British shipping losses from 1942 were made good Britain's already meagre import targets for 1943 would not be met. This would have a ripple effect on the whole Allied war effort, from rations for the British people, to British war production and, therefore, Allied military operations worldwide. Oil reserves were especially critical, with only a few weeks of steaming fuel left for the RN. The Allies now had plenty of new merchant ships available, but they were American-built and their employment was controlled by the U.S. Chiefs of Staff. In December, Winston Churchill appealed directly to Roosevelt to release ships to British control. Roosevelt spent the next four months in a futile struggle with his own senior officers to do that.[29] In the end, Roosevelt purchased ninety Liberty-type ten thousand-ton ships from Canada to cover-off America's commitment to Britain.[30]

As 1942 drew to a close, therefore, the Allies were in good shape, but Britain's situation was perilous. Losses to its merchant shipping during 1942 were unprecedented, and—ominously—now threatened the morale of the usually stoical British merchant seaman. As ships gathered in Iceland in November for renewal of the convoys to Russia there was genuine concern that the merchant seamen might not go. The Germans were aware of that, too. In November 1942 breaking the morale of Britain's merchant seamen became Dönitz's new target. He had wanted three hundred U-boats before starting a war with Britain: in the winter of 1943 the number of operational U-boats ranged from 403 to 435, with an average of over one hundred at sea each month, most in the Atlantic. When Dönitz became head of the *Kriegsmarine* in January 1943, he finally had the submarine fleet he always wanted, and a free hand to use it.

The Battle of the Atlantic climaxed in early 1943. In foul North Atlantic winter weather, the British proved no more adept at defending slow convoys than the Canadians had been, and bitter, protracted battles followed one another through January and February. Ultra failed again in late February when the Germans introduced a new rotor for their Engima encoding machine, and Allied losses skyrocketed. In the first three weeks of March, every North Atlantic convoy was located by the Germans, one-half were attacked and some twenty-two percent of shipping in those convoys sunk.[31]

Fortunately for the Allies, help was already on the way. In January 1943, at Casablanca, Roosevelt, Churchill, and their senior staffs met to determine their next moves. The war, at least in Europe, had turned in their favor. Axis forces in North Africa were on the run, and the Germans had suffered a shattering defeat on the eastern front at Stalingrad. Serious planning could now begin for a Second Front: a landing in France. But no build-up for that was possible until the problem of the Atlantic war was resolved. So, at Casablanca the Anglo–Americans finally gave the Atlantic top priority in the allocation of aircraft, destroyers, and escort carriers. By late March, just as Ultra intelligence was restored, Support Groups, one of them with a small aircraft carrier, began to reinforce convoys in the mid-ocean gap. VLR aircraft, enough to totally eliminate the "air gap" in the mid-ocean, were due to arrive in the spring.

In March 1943—in the depths of the crisis—the command architecture of the North Atlantic was also rationalized during a conference in Washington. By 1942, convoy operations (both naval and air) north of New York to the Grand Banks were almost entirely Canadian, and the balance of the route to the UK was a shared RN–RCN responsibility. But operational control west of the mid-ocean remained in American hands. The Canadians, in particular, grew increasingly restive under this arrangement, and increasingly obstructionist in their dealings with the American admiral notionally in command. For their part, the British disliked the fact that operational control over convoy battles switched from USN to RN authorities in the middle of the air gap: they wanted operational control over the mid-ocean. And so, the Allies met in Washington in early March to sort that out. As of April 30, 1943, the British assumed operational control over convoys east of the Grand Banks (forty-seven degrees west) and a new Canadian Northwest Atlantic command encompassed the area from the Gulf of Maine to the Grand Banks.[32]

The resolution of command issues was not fully implemented when resumption of Ultra intelligence and fairer spring weather at the end of March allowed the resources allocated at Casablanca to be applied with devastating results. It helped that Ultra also revealed the fragile state of morale in Germany's U-boats fleet. Dönitz's repeated admonitions to his captains to push home their attacks and not to fear Allied counter measures suggested that the time was ripe to counterattack. In April, aided by new Support Groups and the return of Canadian groups from their temporary exile for refitting and training, the British went on the offensive.

This took the form of deliberate confrontations forced on Dönitz's U-boats by the British. Good intelligence allowed selected convoys to be heavily reinforced and driven into waiting Wolf Packs. Superb radar, shipborne HF/DF, and increasingly effective air support allowed the close escort group to maintain a tight inner screen, while Support Groups and aircraft roamed the outer perimeter and hunted U-boats at leisure around the convoy.

Things did not always go well. A major battle developed around convoy ONS 5 in late April that nearly got out of control. A long, circuitous routing to the far north failed to get the convoy clear of several waiting packs, totaling some forty U-boats. By May 6, the convoy, somewhat broken by bad weather and beset by continuous attack, had lost eleven ships. The escort was running out of fuel and it appeared that ONS 5 might be annihilated. Then it steamed into fog on the Grand Banks and onto a glassy sea. As U-boats probed the murk trying to find the convoy, the escort (using its 10cm radar) sank six, depth-charged fifteen, and drove the packs off: two U-boats collided in the fog and also sank.[33]

In May 1943, a surge of British and Canadian VLR aircraft eliminated the air gap and more escort carriers arrived to join the battle. The U-boats were drawn into a battle of attrition they could not win. Forty-seven U-boats were sunk in May alone, bringing the total of German losses in the Atlantic during the first five months of 1943 to one hundred. At the end of May, Dönitz withdrew his battered packs: as far as the course of the war was concerned, the Battle of the Atlantic was over.[34]

The Atlantic war was not: it lasted until May 8, 1945. What followed the defeat of the Wolf Packs in the spring of 1943 was a series of campaigns initiated by the Germans in attempt to keep the Allies busy at sea and—at least until the summer of 1944—delay the opening of the Second Front in France. These all failed, but they made some dramatic history in the process.

The Allied anti-submarine offensive, begun in the mid-ocean in the spring of 1943, continued for the rest of the year. In the summer it was spearheaded by American "Hunter-Killer" groups built around escort carriers operating around the Azores and by Allied aircraft over U-boat transit routes in the Bay of Biscay. U-boats were still utterly dependent upon surface maneuverability for strategic and operational movements, and to keep their batteries charged for their brief underwater sprints. As a result, anti-submarine aircraft took an enormous toll of U-boats in 1943. Large land-based aircraft operating from bases in the UK, now directed by excellent 10cm radar and carrying acoustic homing torpedoes, swarmed the transit routes. U-boats on the surface could not match their firepower, while a dive in the presence of lumbering Sunderland flying boats or B-24 Liberators invited a shower of depth charges or a homing torpedo.

In the mid-North Atlantic, around the Azores and the approaches to the Mediterranean, USN Hunter-Killer groups built around small auxiliary carriers and directed by Ultra intelligence, sank U-boats with impunity. Here, too, aircraft swarmed the subs on the surface. Fighter aircraft swept the U-boat's decks of anti-aircraft gunners, then Avenger aircraft bracketed the U-boat with depth charges. If the sub was rash enough to try submerging a homing torpedo was dropped in its wake.[35]

An attempt by the U-boat fleet to renew the offensive in the mid-ocean in the fall, relying on heavier anti-aircraft armament and a new acoustic homing torpedo, was crushed. Air support for convoys was now too oppressive, while the Allies quickly developed counter measures for the German homing torpedo. The latter was first used on the night of September 19–20 in the opening stages of the battle for convoys ONS18/ON202, when HMS *Lagan* had her stern blown off. That night the Canadian destroyer *St Croix* became the first Allied warship sunk by the new German acoustic torpedo. Canadian scientists deduced immediately that the new weapon could be lured away by a pipe-noise maker towed astern of the escort. In three days, they designed, tested, and manufactured a solution. By the time the Canadian escorts of convoys ONS 18/ON 202 arrived in St John's, Newfoundland, fifty noise-makers were waiting on the wharf. The British took a little longer to figure it out, but the acoustic homing torpedo proved a manageable threat for the balance of the war.[36]

As a result of the defeat of the U-boats in 1943, Allied shipping losses plummeted. From January to May 1943, they averaged 450,000 tons per month. In the last half of the year, they dropped to approximately two hundred thousand tons, with only about forty thousand to sixty thousand tons accounted for by submarines. Meanwhile, with the fall of North Africa in March, then Sicily in August and the capitulation of Italy in September the Mediterranean opened to shipping again, with a tremendous savings in

Allied carrying capacity. Over the same period an enormous volume of new construction flowed from Allied shipyards—fourteen million tons in 1943, outstripping losses by about 11.5 million tons. The Allies now had far more shipping than they needed, and in late 1943, they abandoned many of their escort ship building programs.

The war did not end, of course, in 1943, and the Atlantic campaign continued. In December, the Germans stopped routine signaling while at sea, which sharply reduced both DF and Ultra intelligence on their positions. And while Dönitz tried to accelerate the building program for radically new types of submarines, a crash program of fitting schnorkel breathing tubes to the existing fleet was begun. The first U-boats sent to sea to trial the schnorkel in January and February, U264 and U406, were both sunk but both yielded survivors, including some scientists.[37] It is not clear if the losses delayed the widespread adoption of the device, but only a few schnorkels were in service when the Allies landed in France in June.

What followed in 1944 nonetheless was a major inshore campaign by schnorkel-equipped submarines in British waters, and a much smaller one in Canadian waters—one of the few places which U-boats operating primarily submerged could reach. The adoption of the schnorkel and fully submerged tactics by U-boats represented the beginnings of modern submarine and A/S warfare. While the Germans used the complex mixture of tides, rocky bottoms, and muddled temperature and salinity layers in inshore waters to avoid destruction, the Allies wrestled with ways of dealing with targets they now seldom saw. Very often the only confirmation of the presence of a U-boat was an attack. This allowed large numbers of naval and air forces to swarm the area and at the very least run the U-boat to exhaustion and force it to the surface. Only in 1945 with the increasing use of 3cm radar was it possible to detect the small schnorkel head of a submerged U-boat. Air power played a key role in keeping the U-boats down, but by the end of the war it had not managed to perfect a system for tracking and attacking submerged submarines.[38]

While the Canadians and British wrestled with the problems of inshore A/S warfare, the USN developed special skill at deep-ocean U-boat hunting which paid off in the spring of 1945. In April the last Wolf Pack of the war was deployed in the northwest Atlantic, and there was some fear that the Wolf Pack "Seewolf" was headed to the United States to launch V1 type weapons at American cities. The USN dispatched two small carriers and twenty destroyer-escorts to hunt the group down while it was still well out to sea. They sank five of the seven U-boats assigned to Seewolf: the other two surrendered at the end of the war.[39]

None of this post-1943 U-boat action had any appreciable impact on the course of the war. The U-boat fleet hung-on in hopes of better days, and they came perilously close to seeing them. At the end of the war in May 1945 there were twenty-five older schnorkel-equipped U-boats in and around the British Isles. They were held in check by over four hundred escort vessels and some eight hundred aircraft as the Allies struggled to deal with submarines which now seldom surfaced or sent out radio signals. Waiting in the wings were over one hundred of the radically new Type XXI and XXIII U-boats.

These were the predecessors of all postwar diesel electric submarines, designed to operate fully submerged, sleek and fast, with excellent underwater speed, sophisticated sonar targeting systems and weapons. The Type XXI had a ten-thousand-mile range and needed to "snort" only briefly to recharge its batteries. One Type XXI U-boat and one coastal Type XXIII variant made operational cruises in early May: neither was detected. The Type XXIII, U2336, sank two ships off Newcastle on May 7: the last merchant ships sunk by U-boats in the Atlantic war. What they might have accomplished had they attacked in numbers we will never know.[40]

Notes

1. Attributed to Admiral Raeder, see Tim Runyan and Jan M. Copes, *To Die Gallantly: The Battle of the Atlantic* (Boulder, CO: Westview, 1994), xiii.
2. The most informed and succinct—if dated—account of this first winter of the war remains Dan van der Vat, *The Atlantic Campaign: World War II's Great Struggle at Sea* (New York: Harper and Row, 1988), chapter 4.
3. See Cajus Bekker, *Hitler's Naval War* (Garden City, NY: Doubleday, 1974).
4. British merchant shipping is tackled superbly in C. B. A Behrens's much neglected *Merchant Shipping and the Demands of War* (London: HMSO and Longmans and Green, 1955).
5. The best discussion of the functioning and importance of NCS remains Marc Milner, "Naval Control of Shipping and the Atlantic War 1939–1945," *The Mariner's Mirror* 83, no. 2 (May 1992): 169–184.
6. See Table ZZ in Captain S. W. Roskill's British official history, *The War at Sea 1939–1945*, Vol. II: *The Offensive, Part II 1st June 1944–14th August 1945* (London: HMSO, 1961), 479.
7. The German contention that *Bismarck*'s crew scuttled the ship is made in Burkhard von Müllenheim-Rechberg, *Battleship Bismarck, A Survivor's Story* (Annapolis, MD: Naval Institute Press, 1980) makes the claim of scuttling in his account. It is a moot point because *Bismarck* was unable to maneuver and stranded well beyond range of German support.
8. For an exhaustively detailed reckoning of U-boat operations see Clay Blair's two massive tomes, *Hitler's U-Boat War, 1939–1942: The Hunters* (New York: Random House 1996) and *Hitler's U-Boat War, 1942–1945: The Hunted* (New York: Random House 1998).
9. For the origins of Wolf Pack tactics see Grand Admiral Karl Dönitz, *Memoirs: Ten Years and Twenty Days* (Annapolis, MD: US Naval Institute Press, 1990), chapter 3. For British attitudes toward the U-boat prior to 1939 see Stephen W. Roskill, *Naval Policy Between the Wars*, Vol. 2 (London: Collins, 1976), 224–226.
10. The most succinct account of how all this worked, and how Allied intelligence used it, remains W. A. B. Douglas and Jurgen Rohwer, "'The Most Thankless Task' Revisited: Convoys, Escorts, and Radio Intelligence in the Western Atlantic 1941–1943," in *The RCN in Retrospect 1910–1985*, ed. James A. Boutilier (Vancouver: University of British Columbia Press, 1982), 187–234.
11. The most succinct account of all Allied escort building programs is Peter Elliott, *Allied Escort Ships of World War II* (London: MacDonald & Jane's, 1977). For Canada's considerable shipbuilding effort see James Pritchard, *A Bridge of Ships: Canadian Shipbuilding*

during the Second World War (Montreal: McGill-Queen's University Press, 2011). The best account of the closing of the mid-ocean escort gap is in W. A. B. Douglas, Roger Sarty, and Micheal Whitby, et al., *No Higher Purpose: The Official History of the Royal Canadian Navy in the Second World War, 1939-1943*, Vol. II, Part 1 (St Catharines, ON: Vanwell Publishing, 2002), see chapter 3.

12. See Gunther Hessler's demi-official *The U-boat War in the North Atlantic 1939-1945* (London: HMSO, 1989), an authoritative work using captured German documents prepared under the auspices of the RN and USN by the former Chief of Staff of the U-boat command.
13. Martin Doughty, *Merchant Shipping and War* (London: Royal Historical Society, 1982).
14. For a discussion of the German torpedo problem seem Dönitz, *Memoirs*, 84-99. For a thorough analysis of German torpedoes see, Eberhard Rössler, *Die Torpedos der Deutschen U-Boote: Entwicklung, Herstellung, und Eigenschaften der deutschen Marine-Torpedos* (Hamburg, Berlin, Bonn: Verlag E.S. Mittler & Sohn, 2005).
15. Making better use of space and weight limits by, for example, shipping vehicles without their wheels and cabs fitted, or filling the empty space in ships laden with steel plate with light weight cargoes.
16. See David Kahn, *Seizing the Enigma: The Race to Break the German U-Boat Codes, 1939-1943* (Boston: Houghton Mifflin Company, 1991). For a more authoritative accounting of the Allied use of Ultra during the war see F. H. Hinsley, *British Intelligence in the Second World War*, Vols. 1-3 (London: HMSO, 1979-1988).
17. Milner, "Naval Control of Shipping."
18. The best account of this undeclared American war remains Patrick Abazzia, *Mr Roosevelt's Navy* (Annapolis, MD: Naval Institute Press Press, 1975).
19. The RCN's most trenchant critic was Captain Donald Macintyre, a veteran of the Atlantic war and one of its most accomplished escort commanders. His criticism of the Canadians as bungling and inept dominated the literature on the Atlantic war in the twentieth century. See especially his *U-Boat Killer* (London: Weidenfeld and Nicholson, 1956). For a corrective see Marc Milner, *North Atlantic Run: The Royal Canadian Navy and the Battle for the Convoys* (Toronto: University of Toronto Press, 1985).
20. Apart from memoirs and basic descriptions in Roskill's British official history, virtually nothing has been written on the UK-Gibraltar/Sierra Leone convoys.
21. See Milner, *North Atlantic Run*, chapter 4, for a discussion of the Anglo-American tension over convoys in early 1942. For a comprehensive analysis of the importance of the convoy as a strategy and the British view of shipping as a complex global system see Eric Grove, ed., *Defeat of the Enemy Attack on Shipping, 1939-1945: a Revised Edition of the Naval Staff History* (Aldershot: Naval Records Society, 1997).
22. The distinction between inshore and ocean escort operations against U-boats is laid out in Marc Milner, "Inshore ASW: The Canadian Experience in Home Waters," in *The RCN in Transition, 1910-1985*, ed. W. A. B. Douglas (Vancouver: University of British Columbia Press, 1988), 143-158.
23. See Appendix O of Roskill, *The War at Sea*, Vol. II for a list of ships and tonnage sunk by theaters.
24. Robert C. Fisher, "'We'll Get Our Own': Canada and the Oil Shipping Crisis of 1942," *The Northern Mariner* 3 (April 1993): 33-40. The Germans launched a major campaign in Canadian waters in 1942 which has escaped notice by Anglo-American historians

entirely. The most authoritative monograph on the campaign is Roger Sarty, *War in the St Lawrence: The Forgotten U-Boats Battles on Canada's Shores* (Toronto: Allen Lane, 2012).
25. Astonishingly, the best overall account of the 1942 campaign in U.S. waters remains S. E. Morison, *History of United States Naval Operations in World War II*, Vol. I (Boston: Little Brown and Co., 1947). The USN's records for the period are so difficult to use that historians have tended to rely on U-boat records as the basis for crafting narrative histories of the period, see for example Michael Gannon, *Operation Drumbeat: The Dramatic True Story of Germany's First U-Boat Attacks along the American Coast in World War II* (New York: Harper and Row, 1990), that focuses on the cruise of U123.
26. See Milner, *North Atlantic Run*, for a succinct account of the fall 1942 in the mid-ocean, and W. A. B. Douglas, et al., *No Higher Purpose* for a more detailed look, including the German use of Canadian radar to locate convoys.
27. The best discussion of the complex situation facing British imports in the fall of 1942 and the problems of getting aid from the Americans is Christopher M. Bell's recent *Churchill and Sea Power* (Oxford, UK: Oxford University Press, 2013), especially chapter 9.
28. The removal of the Canadians from the mid-ocean was unknown until Marc Milner began to publish in the 1980s, see his *North Atlantic Run*, chapters 7 and 8.
29. Bell, *Churchill and Sea Power*, chapter 9.
30. Pritchard, *A Bridge of Ships*, pp. 34–36.
31. Two complimentary books cover this period is great detail: Martin Middlebrook's *Convoy* (London: Allen Lane, 1976), tackles the human story of the brutal first weeks of March 1943, while Jurgen Rohwer's *Critical Convoy Battles of March 1943* (Annapolis, MD: Naval Institute Press, 1977), provides a detailed narrative of events with particular emphasis on the intelligence problems.
32. For the best scholarly account of the Washington Conference and the command problems that gave rise to it see, W. A. B. Douglas, et al., *No Higher Purpose*, chapter 11.
33. The most detailed account of the Atlantic in the spring of 1943 (with particular emphasis on the role of Ultra) is David Syrett's *The Defeat of the German U-Boats: The Battle of the Atlantic* (Columbia: University of South Carolina Press, 1994).
34. The role of airpower in the Atlantic war is sadly neglected, but it was critical to the victory of 1943. In that year aircraft were lethal killers of U-boats that still relied on surface maneuverability. A good introduction is provided by Alfred Price in *Aircraft versus Submarine* (London: Kimber, 1973), while the most modern account can be found in W. A. B. Douglas, *The Creation of a National Air Force: The Official History of the Royal Canadian Air Force*, Vol. II (Toronto: University of Toronto Press, 1986), section IV.
35. See William Y'Blood's *Hunter-Killer: U.S. Escort Carriers in the Battle of the Atlantic* (Annapolis, MD: Naval Institute Press, 1983) for an excellent account of these operations.
36. For a short account of the battle for ONS 18/ON 202 and the defeat of the German acoustic homing torpedo see Marc Milner, *The U-Boat Hunters: the Royal Canadian Navy and the Offensive Against Germany's Submarine* (Toronto: University of Toronto Press, 1994), 63–76.
37. For a pre-Ultra summary of this British operation see Roskill, Vol. III, part 2, 250–54. Dan van der Vat says a little about the Ultra role and implications, see his *The Atlantic Campaign*, 369.

38. Roskill, *The War at Sea*, Vol. III provides a cursory account of the inshore campaign in British waters in 1944–1945. For a more detailed account of the tactics and technology of the final year of the U-boat war see Milner, *The U-Boat Hunters*.
39. See Philip K. Lundeberg, "Operation *Teardrop* Revisited," in *To Die Gallantly: The Battle of the Atlantic*, ed. Tim Runyan and Jan M. Copes (Boulder, CO: Westview, 1994), 210–230. Lundeberg had worked on volume X of Morison's History of United States Naval Operations in World War II (1962), which deals with this operation, but at the time was unaware of Ultra.
40. For a discussion of the anticipated problems combating the Type XXI see Milner, *The U-Boat Hunters*.

Bibliography

Abbazia, Patrick. *Mr Roosevelt's Navy*. Annapolis, MD: Naval Institute Press, 1975.
Behrens, C. B. A. *Merchant Shipping and the Demands of War*. London: HMSO and Longmans and Green, 1955.
Bell, Christopher M. *Churchill and Sea Power*. Oxford: Oxford University Press, 2013.
Dönitz, Grand Admiral Karl. *Memoirs: Ten Years and Twenty Days*. Annapolis, MD: Naval Institute Press, 1990.
Douglas, W. A. B. *The Creation of a National Air Force: The Official History of the Royal Canadian Air Force*, Vol. II. Toronto: University of Toronto Press, 1986.
Douglas, W. A. B., Roger Sarty, and Michael Whitby, et al., *No Higher Purpose: The Official Operational History of the Royal Canadian Navy in the Second World War, 1939–1943*, Vol. III: Part 1. St Catharines, ON: Vanwell, 2002.
Doughty, Martin. *Merchant Shipping and War*. London: Royal Historical Society, 1982.
Gannon, Michael. *Operation Drumbeat: The Dramatic True Story of Germany's First U-Boat Attacks along the American Coast in World War II*. New York: Harper and Row, 1990.
Grove, Eric, ed. *Defeat of the Enemy Attack on Shipping, 1939–1945: A Revised Edition of the Naval Staff History*. Aldershot: Naval Records Society, 1997.
Hessler, Gunther. *The U-boat War in the North Atlantic 1939–1945*. London: HMSO, 1989.
Hinsley, F. H. *British Intelligence in the Second World War*, Vol. 1-3. London: HMSO, 1979–1988.
Kahn, David. *Seizing the Enigma: The Race to break the German U-Boat Codes, 1939–1943*. Boston: Houghton Mifflin, 1991.
Milner, Marc. *Battle of the Atlantic*. Stroud, Gloucestershire: Tempus Publishing, 2011.
Milner, Marc. *North Atlantic Run: The Royal Canadian Navy and the Battle for the Convoys*. Toronto: University of Toronto Press, 1985.
Milner, Marc. *The U-Boat Hunters: The Royal Canadian Navy and the Offensive Against Germany's Submarine*. Toronto: University of Toronto Press, 1994.
Morison, Samuel E. *History of United States Naval Operations in World War II*, Vols. I and X. Boston: Little Brown, 1947 & 1962.
Rohwer, Jurgen. *Critical Convoy Battles of March 1943*. Annapolis, MD: USNI Press, 1977.
Roskill, Captain S. W. *The War at Sea 1939–1945*, Vols. I–III. London: HMSO, 1956–1961.
Runyan, Tim, and Jan M. Cope. *To Die Gallantly: The Battle of the Atlantic*. Boulder, CO: Westview, 1994.

Smith, Kevin. *Conflict Over Convoys: Anglo–American Logistics Diplomacy in the Second World War*. Cambridge, UK: Cambridge University Press, 1996,

Syrett, David. *The Defeat of the German U-Boats: The Battle of the Atlantic*. Columbia: University of South Carolina Press, 1994.

Y'Blood, William. *Hunter-Killer: U.S. Escort Carriers in the Battle of the Atlantic*. Annapolis, MD: Naval Institute Press, 1983.

CHAPTER 9

THE AXIS INVASION OF THE SOVIET UNION, 1941–1943

JONATHAN A. GRANT

The end of the Cold War has led to a profound resurgence in the study of the Russian Front (1941–1945). No longer is this part of the war studied primarily to help NATO commanders learn how to repel a Soviet invasion across the North German plain. Instead, there is a growing recognition of how the self-serving recollections of captured German officers offered to Western interrogators skewed the first wave of Western historiography on the Russian Front.

On June 22, 1941, Nazi Germany launched Operation Barbarossa, the invasion of the Soviet Union. More than three million troops, thirty-six hundred tanks, six hundred thousand motorized vehicles, six hundred and twenty-five thousand horses, seven thousand artillery pieces, and twenty-five hundred aircraft from Nazi Germany invaded the Soviet Union with the expressed goal of destroying the Soviet regime. The Germans knew that they could not conquer and occupy all of the Soviet Union. Their plan was to destroy Red Army formations rapidly in a six-week campaign. By noon on June 22, the Germans had destroyed twelve hundred Soviet aircraft, mostly while they were sitting on the ground. In the first weeks of the war the Red Army lost twenty thousand tanks. More than twenty-seven million Soviet citizens died by 1945, and major cities such as Leningrad and Kiev were virtually reduced to rubble.

Did the Germans beat themselves, or was the war in the east unwinnable? Did the Soviets earn their victory, or did they simply get lucky thanks to the vastness and weather of Russia? Why did the Soviet Union not crack under the assault from the tremendous material and human losses?

Older scholarship, heavily influenced by the memoirs of defeated German generals, has explained the outcome of the war on the Eastern front as the result of a series of mistakes made by Hitler in opposition to his generals. For example, Hitler's decision not to press on directly to the Soviet capital in Moscow in 1941, and his fixation with taking the city of Stalingrad in 1942, led to disasters for the German army. In this view, the Germans could have achieved their victory and avoided defeat if only Hitler had listened to his generals. Meanwhile, as David Glantz observed, in these accounts the Red Army:

> remained a virtually featureless and colorless mass, devoid of structure or personality . . . the German school portrayed the Red Army as a fundamentally flawed colossus whose military ineptitude, particularly at lower command levels, was overcome only by Soviet exploitation of geographical factors, callous disregard for human losses, the Soviet Union's immense manufacturing capabilities, the Soviet soldier's capacity for suffering, and sheer weight of numbers . . . this school scorned Soviet combat performance and placed blame for ultimate German defeat squarely on the shoulders of Hitler's flawed strategy.[1]

Such is the position of R. H. S. Stolfi, who believes, based exclusively on German sources, that the Germans had beaten the Soviet field armies defending Moscow in June to July 1941, and therefore Germany could have defeated Soviet Russia by the end of October 1941. In this view, the fate of Barbarossa lay entirely in German hands to win or lose.[2] More recently, David Stahel has shown that Barbarossa possessed fundamental flaws from its conception such that the logistical difficulties and execution only compounded the problems of an unwinnable German plan.[3] In contrast, Stephen Fritz points to unexpectedly strong Soviet resistance playing a more decisive role in Germany's failure than Hitler's meddling.[4]

A German victory was not impossible, but the conception of Barbarossa revealed planning for a single campaign, not a war. The German General Staff's expectation of defeating the USSR in rapid fashion within six weeks was highly unrealistic, if not outright fantasy, and it represented a gross overestimation of their own logistical capabilities. The *Wehrmacht* had not devised a war-winning strategy. Regardless of the vastly larger territory and war potential of the Soviet Union, the Germans expected to crush the Soviet Union with forces hardly stronger than they had available in France in 1940.[5] Besides wildly optimistic assumptions, the plan also suffered from a lack of alternatives. In the absence of a fallback plan, everything had to go exactly according to plan for the Germans to succeed. If the initial invasion failed, the Germans would find themselves in a huge war of attrition with a vastly larger opponent. In that sense, Barbarossa had deep, fatal flaws from its inception.[6]

The German plan called for the destruction of the bulk of the Red Army by the time German troops arrived on the Dvina-Dnepr River lines, yet German planners understood that upon reaching this point their forces would hit the limits of the range for their motorized logistical system. Beyond this, the railroads would have to assume decisive importance.[7] The USSR had fifty-one thousand miles of railroads and apparently 850,000 miles of roads on the map, but only forty thousand miles were hard surfaced, all-weather roads.[8] Although German planners knew about the differences in railroad gauge between the Soviet and German track and anticipated using their railroad troops to convert and extend the German gauge, they also counted on capturing vast quantities of Soviet rolling stock and locomotives and quickly turning those captured assets to their advantage in order to continue the drive deeper into Soviet territory.

The Soviets confounded that German assumption through their rapid and extensive evacuation of trains and self-demolition of their railway materials as they retreated. This unexpected Soviet countermove meant that by the end of August 1941, the Germans had captured only about five hundred operational locomotives. Consequently, Soviet scorched earth policies placed tremendous, unexpected strain on the overextended German railways to commit twenty-five hundred locomotives and two hundred thousand railcars to support the advance, and the Germans were forced to expend time and troops for the conversion of the captured rail network to the narrower German gauge rather than taking advantage of the existing, broader Russian gauge.[9]

The scale of Soviet prisoners and booty taken by the Germans in the enveloping operations against the pockets at Bialystok-Minsk and Smolensk made those battles seem like crushing victories, but strategically the Germans had failed to strike the decisive blow. By June 30, the 2nd and 3rd Panzer Groups had encircled the Minsk pocket, in the process bagging over 417,000 Soviet soldiers. That huge haul overshadowed deficiencies in the German victory as large numbers of Red Army soldiers managed to escape. Despite suffering enormous losses at Smolensk, by July 16, the Soviets continued to hold the line and made good those casualties with new troops.

Even though their battlefield casualties were decidedly lower, German losses in men and equipment proved critical as their war aim of breaking Soviet resistance had not been achieved by Smolensk. The Germans needed a decisive victory, whereas on the other side the Soviets needed only to survive Smolensk and go on maintaining a stout resistance to frustrate German strategy. The Barbarossa plan had assumed that Smolensk would be the culmination of the campaign, but the Red Army had not been decisively beaten and its resistance was growing in intensity.[10]

The Battle of Smolensk should be understood not as a smashing German victory, but as a self-inflicted German strategic defeat. By this point, as Army Group Center's mobility declined and armored losses rose, the Soviets were deploying new armies. According to Stahel, unbeknownst to the Germans, Smolensk turned out to be "a fundamental and ruinous defeat"[11] for Germany because the Germans lost the ability to win the war at that point.

The failure to destroy the Red Army at Smolensk subsequently condemned Germany to a massive war of attrition and positional warfare more like World War I. In that kind of war, neither Germany nor the Soviet Union could be dealt a quick, knockout blow. Instead, Germany now had to contend with fighting a far different war than the campaign for which they had planned. The Red Army deserves some credit for this outcome, as at Smolensk for the first time in the war the Soviets had stopped Army Group Center cold during July and August, thereby forestalling an easy advance to Moscow.[12]

Following the Battle of Smolensk, Hitler's decision to turn his forces south into Ukraine rather than proceeding directly toward Moscow has engendered much debate in assessing the causes for German defeat. Even in the planning stages for Barbarossa, Hitler and his generals held sharply different views regarding the importance of Moscow as an objective. German generals such as Heinz Guderian, Fedor von Bock, and Franz Halder considered Moscow the key objective and logical concluding point for the invasion. Hitler, on the other hand, never considered Moscow the primary target, and he would approve the release of armored forces to aid an infantry march on Moscow only when Smolensk and the northern theater had been secured.[13]

The German transport and supply problems, coupled with fierce Soviet resistance, render the entire Moscow debate superfluous. The impracticalities of Barbarossa rendered Moscow out of reach within the time set by the Germans.[14] In the assessment of some scholars, Hitler displayed better military judgment than his generals on this point. The large Soviet formations in the south posed a potent threat to the flanks of any German thrust in the center toward Moscow, and destruction of the Red Army in the field was crucial to the rapid defeat of the Soviet Union. The Soviet South-Western Front in Ukraine had constituted the strongest of all Soviet military districts at the outset of the invasion. As Army Group Center had advanced, its southern flank became increasingly vulnerable because of fierce Soviet resistance against Army Group South.

Throughout June, Rundstedt's Army Group South had struggled to advance against vigorous Soviet counterattacks and, by early July, it still lagged behind Army Group Center. As Army Group South fell behind, Army Group Center acquired unexpected difficulties covering its exposed southern flank.[15] Even more importantly, the tough Soviet resistance in the center due to a fierce Soviet counterattack at Yelnia precluded a quick German strike up the gut.[16] In part, Hitler turned south from Smolensk because his forces could not advance in the direction of Moscow.[17]

The turn to the south led to another massive German encirclement, this time at Kiev. Although Kiev constituted the biggest German operational success to date, destroying six hundred thousand Red Army troops, it had been a slow, hard slog for the Germans. Once again, as had been the case with Minsk and Smolensk, German operational success did not translate into strategic victory even though it proved to be the *Wehrmacht*'s "greatest set-piece battle of World War II."[18] The *Wehrmacht* found itself in deep trouble in fall 1941 thanks to a fundamental flaw, namely the failure to resolve the problem of armor–infantry cooperation. Inability to coordinate the fast-moving panzers with slow moving infantry resulted in the escape of many encircled Red Army soldiers and left the panzer spearheads lacking in infantry support. The German lack of planning for armored personnel carriers for the infantry contributed mightily to this problem.[19]

If we accept the counter-factual argument that the Germans could have taken Moscow,[20] it seems highly unlikely that they could have held it for very long or that the Soviet state would have collapsed upon its loss based on historical studies of the Soviet home front. While much has been made of the panic in the city at the prospect of German advance on October 16, the disturbances in Moscow at that time stemmed not from anti-Sovietism, but from a breakdown in order caused by the factory evacuations. As factories were dismantled and transported to the east for reassembly, workers lost their jobs and benefits. In turn, the workers vented their frustrations in attacks on departing managers as acts of chastisement of those considered thieves and traitors to the fatherland. The panic in Moscow was connected in popular imagination with a sense of betrayal and moral outrage, not anti-Sovietism or a fear that the war was lost.[21] Approximately one million Muscovites volunteered for the defense of their city.[22]

Given how Stalin had regained mastery of his system after the opening weeks of the campaign and the massive mobilization of soldiers and material underway, it seems highly unrealistic to expect that the capture of Moscow would have brought about the collapse of the Soviet Union or broken Soviet will to resist. As of October 3, even Hitler did not expect that Stalin would capitulate or the Soviet Union would collapse if the Germans took Moscow.[23] A rapid German armored thrust would have lacked the necessary infantry support to occupy the city. Moreover, Soviet resistance in the capital would have been fierce and no doubt would have inflicted heavy losses on any German occupation force. German experience later at Stalingrad would seem to bear this out.[24] Besides offering staunch resistance, the Soviets had also made preparations to evacuate Moscow if necessary, and the region around Gorkii some 250 miles east of Moscow possessed useful connections as a potential rail hub to support Soviet defenses.[25]

Whereas older scholarship tended to blame Hitler for the German defeat, more recent scholarship equally points to Soviet mistakes, especially those committed by Stalin, as of crucial importance in enabling German successes. For example, on the evening of June 22, 1941, Stalin and Defense Commissar S. K. Timoshenko issued Directive No. 3 for a general counteroffensive against the Germans, and in the next several days they stubbornly insisted that the forward fronts implement this disastrous directive. Many of the early Soviet defeats should be laid at the feet of the inexperience of the Soviet field commanders who had survived Stalin's purges but lacked practical experience or confidence.[26]

During the Battle of Kiev, Georgi Zhukov, Soviet Chief of the General Staff, properly understood the German threat of cutting the rear of Kirponos's South-Western Front. Accordingly, Zhukov wanted Kirponos to pull his front back behind the Dnepr, which would have meant the abandonment of Kiev. Stalin relieved Zhukov of his command and had Timoshenko prepare a large-scale offensive all along his front. Stalin's refusal to allow Kirponos to retreat until it was too late did more to ensure a Soviet disaster than any German action.[27]

Stalin's penchant for general offensives served to weaken Soviet forces by dissipating their strength. A prime example was the Moscow counteroffensive launched December 5, 1941. This Soviet counteroffensive produced very good results around Moscow and it could have destroyed Army Group Center if Stalin had not expanded the scope too much by turning it into a general offensive all along the front on January 7, 1942.[28] Zhukov's Operation Mars, an offensive to destroy Army Group Center in November 1942, also proved a costly Soviet mistake.[29]

The Battle of Stalingrad conventionally stands as an alternative decisive turning point.[30] Even though the Soviets had defeated Barbarossa in 1941, the Germans still managed to grab the strategic initiative in summer 1942. In spring 1942, Stalin erroneously believed that the Germans would try again for Moscow, but Hitler headed south in a quest for economic targets, especially the oil fields in the Caucasus. German Operation Blau (Blue) unfolded as a main offensive conducted by Army Group South, attacking south of Kursk and then dividing into two groups. Group A would drive across the Don

River near Rostov and southward into the Caucasus while Group B advanced eastward into the Don River bend toward Stalingrad.[31]

The summer campaign was about protecting German oil supplies from Romania through a Crimean operation, then pushing into the Caucasus to deprive Soviets of their oil while taking it for Germany. Geographically and psychologically, Stalingrad did mark a turning point. The summer offensive in 1942 pushed the German advance to its ultimate furthest extent, and at the time, the Soviet victory there was immediately seen in the West as a turning point for the entire World War II.[32] Granted, Hitler's chances of victory over the Soviet Union were slim. Nevertheless, the stakes were extremely high, and the German seizure of the oilfields would have been a blow to the Soviets.[33] Stalingrad also served as a turning point in the sense that, after its defeat there, the *Wehrmacht* never again generated a series of victories.[34]

The role of non-German forces on the Eastern Front also merits attention. Conventionally, the place of non-German troops, especially Romanians,[35] as an asset or a liability comes up in the literature in discussion of the Soviet counteroffensive at Stalingrad. Half of the new divisions arriving in the south for Operation Blau were non-German, and these foreign troops served to cover the mightily overstretched front.[36] The Soviets launched their counteroffensive on November 19, 1942, by attacking the weaker Romanian units on the German flanks, thereby successfully cutting off the German spearheads in the city. Hitler blamed the Stalingrad disaster on his allies, and many historians have accepted the validity of that point.

Yet Hitler's allies made a significant contribution to the German military operations. Certainly the Romanians and Hungarians were highly vulnerable at Stalingrad because they lacked heavy anti-tank weapons. Nonetheless, the Germans should shoulder the blame for their allies' armament deficiencies because German pledges to equip their allies had been fulfilled halfheartedly with obsolete weapons. Moreover, Germany's allies had to hold much larger sections of the front than should have been expected, and generally the non-German contributions to Barbarossa proved highly significant in enabling German forces to concentrate their initial strikes in central Russia. Out of two thousand kilometers of front, Finnish and Romanian forces covered over one-half, nearly twelve hundred kilometers, and non-Germans provided one soldier out of four who invaded in 1941. Hitler could not have launched the summer offensive in 1942 without covering his flanks with Hungarian, Italian, and Romanian troops, and non-German forces helped prevent the Eastern Front from totally collapsing after Stalingrad.[37]

A final interpretive question regarding Stalingrad concerns whether the German Sixth Army could have broken out if only Hitler had allowed them to do so. Most German accounts assert that Sixth Army and the 330,000 German troops caught in the Soviet encirclement could have broken out on their own. However, given the German logistical and supply problems, it seems highly improbable that the German forces trapped in Stalingrad possessed enough fuel, ammunition, and transport to manage a breakout on their own. Meanwhile, Soviet counterattacks foiled German efforts to break in by driving relief forces back one hundred kilometers.[38] The role of German airpower also figures into the discussion, with scholars generally taking the view that the attempt by *Luftflotte 4* to supply the cutoff German forces through the Stalingrad Airlift turned into an unmitigated disaster.[39]

The myth of an apolitical, purely professional German army that fought valiantly and honorably for its country with no knowledge or participation in the crimes of the Nazi state is no longer sustainable. The myth, fostered by German commanders Erich von Manstein's *Lost Victories* and Heinz Guderian's *Panzer Leader* memoirs, published after the war, had obvious motive to redirect any responsibility for the crimes away from the Army and onto Hitler.

Manstein did not merely pass on the Commissar Order, which called for the immediate execution of Jews and Communists, he actively enforced that order after taking command of the Eleventh Army in Crimea. Tellingly, Manstein also issued orders on his own initiative on November 20, 1941, calling on soldiers to deliver harsh punishment to Jews, and he received regular reports on executions from Einsatzgruppe D, one of the SS killing units tasked with murdering Jews. Manstein's troops also cooperated with the Einsatzgruppe by supplying fuel, drivers, and military police to cordon off areas. The most egregious example was the massacre of eleven thousand Jews at Simferopol in November 1941. More than two thousand German soldiers took part in the action. Manstein also ordered the shooting of thirteen hundred people at Eupatoria as a reprisal.[40]

Manstein's actions were typical. The expectation of a methodical exploitation of the population by the German Army had featured in the prewar planning for the campaign as reflected in supposed distinctions between organized requisitioning and wild plundering. The German army anticipated pillaging the Soviet population to compensate for inadequate supply. The despoiling of the population began immediately with the German invasion as the panzer groups themselves carried out widespread looting and pillaging among the civil population to sustain the supply for their attacks.[41]

Hitler's apparent indifference to conventional operational planning in the conception of Barbarossa had less to do with a failure of strategic imagination than a radically different conception of how to undertake a racist war of annihilation to eradicate "Jewish Bolshevism."[42] To that end, the murderous orders predated the campaign and predefined the *Wehrmacht*'s victims while justifying such actions in advance as part of the German right to exact revenge against "partisans" and the right to conquer living space leading to the final occupation of the agriculturally and industrially developed parts of the Soviet Union. Commissars were to be shot, war prisoners deprived of their protected status under international law, the civilian population deemed suspected partisans, and Jews handed over to the Einsatzgruppen.[43]

The German army assisted the Einsatzgruppen by marking and registering Jews; providing the killing units with supplies and transport; and sometimes assembling, guarding, and even shooting the victims.[44] Although the Einsatzgruppe C pulled the triggers at Babi Yar, killing 33,771 Jews near Kiev on September 29–30, 1941, local army commanders had helped plan and organize that massacre in retaliation for Soviet bombings in occupied Kiev.[45]

The Holocaust in occupied Belorussia also revealed the active hand of the *Wehrmacht*.[46] In western Belorussia the *Wehrmacht* was initially responsible for the ghettos until the establishment of civil administration two months later. *Wehrmacht* units in occupied Belorussia were cognizant of Einsatzgruppen activities from the very start of the campaign. Common German soldiers, too, showed themselves capable of murderous actions against Jews. The 354th Infantry Regiment of 286th Security Division conducted its own shootings of Jews in Minsk in July 1941. The 727th Infantry Regiment, under 707th Infantry Division, took part in hunting Jews and executing them as part of a predetermined system in mid-October 1941. On the basis of a standing regimental order, if soldiers found any Jews outside their place of residence, they were to regard them as "partisans" and act accordingly.[47]

From October to November 1941, the first annihilation actions against the ghettos happened under *Wehrmacht* control, and by the end of November 1941 some twenty thousand Jews had been executed by army units under Major General von Bechtolsheim. Lastly, Wilhelm Kube, the head of civil administration in occupied Belorussia filed a written complaint on July 31, 1942, that Army Group Center had liquidated ten thousand Jews without consulting him. The nature of Kube's complaint was that the extermination of those Jews had been planned under his direction, but the army had killed them before his systematic operation could do the job. Such a litany of actions demonstrated that these were not the isolated directives from a few fanatic company commanders, but in fact part and parcel of German policy. At all levels of military command, from commanders to common soldiers, the German Army took part in a racist program of annihilation during the occupation in Belorussia from June 22, 1941, to July 1, 1942.[48]

The mass deaths of three million Soviet POWs also directly resulted from German war aims in the east. The seizure of the Soviet food supply served as a major war aim, and the *Wehrmacht* command used mass starvation as a means to that end. Aware that Soviet POWs were starving to death, General Eduard Wagner, the General Quartermaster of the Army, ordered a drastic reduction in their rations with the simple reasoning that, "Non-working war prisoners . . . are supposed to starve. Working prisoners may be fed from army rations in individual cases."[49] The *Wehrmacht* did not implement the pre-invasion Hunger Plan of May 1941 to use Soviet collective farms to starve millions, but rather starved populations where it seemed useful, and consequently the POW camps witnessed death on an unprecedented scale.[50]

Although German mistakes played a role when accounting for the final victory of the Red Army, other factors cannot be ignored to understand the resiliency of the USSR. To understand the achievement of Soviet victory in the war, one must consider the changes and developments in Soviet society and government which took place in the late 1920s and 1930s as Stalin initiated the centrally planned command economy to build socialism. The Soviets had initiated that mobilization, a kind of war mobilization in time of peace, beginning with the First Five-Year Plan (1928–1932). By 1941, then, the Soviets had had more than a decade of experience with crash military-industrial and labor mobilization in which whole industrial enterprises had been created from scratch.[51]

Under the immediate crisis and pressure brought on by the German onslaught, the Soviets responded in a manner consistent with their system and what they knew how to do. The idea for rapid physical redeployment of factory workers and industrial plants by disassembling them, relocating them via rail transport, reassembling them well to the east, and then resuming production at break-neck speed occurred immediately to Soviet leaders. Such actions caught the Germans completely off guard.

As early as June 24, 1941, the State Committee for Defense created a Council for Evacuation to relocate plants eastward to the Urals and Siberia. Southwestern Front's delay of Army Group South's advance into Ukraine gained precious time for disassembling factories and evacuating them east. Using almost 1.5 million railcars, the Soviets transferred in total 1,523 factories including 1,360 related to armaments, to the Volga River, Siberia, and Central Asia between July and November 1941,[52] and the Soviet Union out-produced Germany in tanks in 1941, with the newer T-34 and KV-1 tanks comprising sixty-six percent of these.[53]

From the outset the Soviet Union was fully mobilizing for a long war. As a specific example, equipment and seven thousand personnel from the Kirov Works in Leningrad were relocated to Cheliabinsk.[54] Soviet factories in the Urals and Caucasus produced 4,500 tanks, three thousand aircraft, fourteen thousand guns and over fifty thousand mortars before active operations resumed in May 1942.[55] Thanks to Soviet industrial mobilization, the margin by which the Soviet Union out-produced Germany only grew larger, even though the Soviets operated off a smaller resource base of coal and steel and with a less skilled workforce. The USSR produced more weapons in 1942 than it had in 1941, and in 1943 the gap widened further. Soviet plants produced three aircraft for every two German planes, and almost double the number of tanks, while in artillery the Soviets out produced the Germans three-to-one.[56]

The mass mobilization of soldiers proved another area where the Stalinist system excelled. Indeed, the Soviet rates of military mobilization were historically unprecedented. Whereas prewar German estimates had postulated an enemy of approximately three hundred divisions, by December the Soviets had fielded twice that number. On June 22, 1941, the Supreme Soviet had drafted most of its reservists born between 1905 and 1918 into the ranks of the Red Army while an emergency labor decree conscripted all able-bodied men aged eighteen to forty-five years and women eighteen to forty years who were not already working, to build defenses. In July 1941 no fewer than thirteen new field armies appeared and in August another fourteen came into service. Even with the disaster of the surrender of the Bialystok/Minsk pocket, the Soviets managed to replace their losses and even dramatically expand the size of the Red Army.[57]

From June to December 1941, Soviet armed forces lost 3,138,000 KIA, MIA, and POWs plus another 1,336,000 lost from wounds or illness. These losses were offset by ten million men enlisting during the first eight months of the war.[58] This allowed the Red Army to lose more than one hundred divisions in battle and continue the struggle.

The question of the motivations on the part of Soviet soldiers and civilians is one that has only begun to be explored. Were the harsh German occupation policies primarily responsible for driving potential German allies into the arms of the Soviet cause, or did the Soviet system generate its own bases of support? Why did Red Army soldiers fight so hard, and simultaneously why did millions surrender in 1941? As Robert Thurston has posed the question, how much did Soviet surrenders or collaboration with the Germans stem from hatred of the Soviet system and how much from more strictly military or wartime difficulties?[59]

The fierceness of Soviet resistance from the first days of the invasion, before the ruthlessness of German occupation policies became widely known, speaks in favor of internal factors as primary in motivating the Soviets to fight. Even from the first two days of the invasion, panzer groups in Army Group Center reported that the Soviet soldiers were fighting tenaciously and to the death. As Soviet command and control broke down over larger Soviet fighting formations, Soviet soldiers fought on in a host of smaller actions where they ambushed German supply columns from selected defensive positions. The large numbers of Soviet soldiers who surrendered did so in small groups. Thus, hundreds of thousands of Soviets surrendered, but not in mass surrender as whole divisions or armies. Thus, the capture of millions of Soviet soldiers in 1941–1942 testified neither to superior German generalship, nor anti-Stalinist sentiment. Rather, leadership failures and lack of training made Soviet officers wholly unprepared to lead their troops out of encirclement.[60]

Average Soviet citizens fought for the USSR for a variety of reasons. From the very start, Soviet propaganda took as its central theme the defense of the motherland, and this theme deeply resonated among the population. Additionally, Stalin played a significant role in bolstering Soviet morale and the psychological mobilization in 1941–1942.[61] Circumstances, nationality, and social group shaped the degree of support offered to the Soviet cause, but the state and Stalinism did not always figure prominently in people's decision to fight. Ukrainians and Belorussians did not fight with the same levels of determination as ethnic Russians, nor did peasants volunteer to the same degree as urbanites. The Soviet state had the most difficulty mobilizing rural, non-Russian minorities.

Coercion was less important and Soviet patriotism more important as a factor in maintaining Soviet military resistance. However, Soviet patriotism should not be equated with support for the Stalinist system. Motherland, home, and family functioned as key elements of Soviet patriotism, and the Soviet system converted ethnic Russian nationalism and imperial Russian patriotism into the mix with belief in the socialist experiment.[62]

Given the peasant hostility to forced collectivization under Stalin, the Germans possibly could have undermined Soviet loyalty if they had returned the land to the peasants. By the end of 1941, more than thirty-six hundred Belarusians were serving the Germans in over fifty-five gendarmerie posts throughout the region, and by the end of 1942, the number of volunteers whom the Germans recruited to indigenous auxiliary units increased almost tenfold. However, true volunteers probably only comprised about fifteen percent because many POWs were compelled to "volunteer" simply to escape the horrible camp conditions and hunger. In the majority of cases, Belarussians came to consider the Germans a greater evil than the Soviets partisans for whom they could feel affinity based on familiarity of language and sharing a similar background. In this case, harsh German occupation policies helped shore up Soviet patriotic resistance.[63] A similar pattern unfolded in German-occupied Ukraine.[64]

The mobilization of women provided additional power to Soviet resistance. Uniquely in World War II, Soviet women participated in combat.[65] Out of eight hundred thousand women in the Soviet armed forces, 310,000 volunteered, but even more (490,235) were conscripted. Female conscripts and female volunteers shared common demographics; that is, they were young, single, urban, students or working-class, ethnic Russians.[66] According to Anna Krylova, the phenomenon of female combat volunteers grew out of the socialist transformation of Stalinist society in the 1930s as part of the overthrow of traditional gender roles, and young Soviet women volunteered as an expression of their liberated Soviet womanhood.[67]

Krylova's point holds for the self-conceptions of the female volunteers, but as Roger Reese has noted, the Soviet state exhibited little enthusiasm for a dramatic reordering of gender roles in Soviet Society. As part of its mobilization planning at the time of the First Five-Year Plan, the Soviet government only expected to have to mobilize women in the factory to replace men who would be called up for military service. It did not plan to call up women, and therefore had not conducted a peacetime registration of women for the draft. Truly, the ideology of women's equality made the conscription of women easier to conceive, but the government only reluctantly arrived at that policy during the war.[68]

The military campaigns of the Eastern Front cannot be understood properly as a discrete and separate subject from the Holocaust.[69] The war on the Eastern Front requires an integrated study of the military, ideological, and economic dimensions, and only such an approach can begin to apprehend the multiple facets of the conflict.[70] A central question in this regard concerns the connection between German battlefield fortunes and the unfolding of the Final Solution.[71]

Was it the perception of German success or the perception of failure on the battlefield that accelerated the Holocaust? Did the German failed offensive against Moscow and the failure of *Blitzkrieg* generally by winter 1941–1942 serve as the catalyst for the beginning of the barbarization of the war in the east with the Wannsee Conference flowing from German military setbacks? A modified version of the military failure thesis pushes the timeline back to fall 1941 when "the expectation of a short, victorious campaign proved false, the extermination program was immediately set in motion with the *Wehrmacht* extensively involved."[72]

In contrast, the "euphoria of victory" interpretation sees the dramatic German military successes in the summer of 1941 as the prompt for Hitler to initiate actions to expand extermination in the east.

By late August 1941, although the decision to kill all the Jews in Europe had not yet been taken, the murder of all Jews in the Soviet Union was underway. By mid-September, with the apparent improvement of the military situation after the collapse of the Soviet pocket at Kiev and the cutting off of Leningrad, Hitler approved the decision to deport German Jews to the east, thereby truly beginning the process leading to the Final Solution. Military success emboldened the radicalization of Jewish policy, and by mid-October 1941 no European Jews were to be allowed to escape physical destruction.[73] Both interpretations can agree on mid-September 1941 as the key time, but the "euphoria" camp has the better reasoning. Historians in the twenty-first century seem to have a much clearer vision of the Barbarossa sputtering to a halt by fall 1941, whereas German commanders at the time still perceived Kiev as a triumph over the Soviets.

The failure of the German *Blitzkrieg* by fall 1941 meant that the Soviet Union would not be knocked out, but it did not yet signal ultimate Soviet victory. The Germans regained the initiative in summer 1942 until Stalingrad. Indeed, the seasonality of the combat fortunes reflected the relative equality of strength of the opposing sides from 1941 to 1943 and their continued military effectiveness. The Germans took the initiative and launched offensives in summer that waned in fall, while the Soviets launched offensives in winter that waned in spring. The rough equilibrium would not be altered, nor could the Soviets ultimately win victory over the Germans until the Red Army could undertake a successful summer offensive of its own. The Red Army finally managed that achievement in summer 1943.

There remains much to be done on the German side to break free of postwar myths and to craft rigorous studies unencumbered by the flawed conventional wisdom recycled from the first pro-German memoirs. On the Soviet side, too, there is plenty to discover about the "forgotten battles," especially the numerous failed Soviet offensives and counteroffensives in 1941 and 1942.[74] Such studies undoubtedly will put to rest the myth of German's unbroken series of victories in the east until Moscow and redraw the picture of Soviet lulls in 1942–1943.

Notes

1. David M. Glantz, "The Red Army at War, 1941–1945: Sources and Interpretations," *Journal of Military History* 62, no. 3 (1998): 596–597.
2. R. H. S. Stolfi, *Hitler's Panzer's East, World War II Reinterpreted* (Norman: University of Oklahoma Press, 1991), ix; Russel H. S. Stolfi, review of *Barbarossa: Hitler's Invasion of Russia, 1941* by David M. Glantz, *Journal of Military History* 66, no. 3 (2002): 888–889.
3. David Stahel, *Operation Barbarossa and Germany's Defeat in the East* (Cambridge: Cambridge University Press, 2009).
4. Stephen Fritz, *Ostkrieg: Hitler's War of Extermination in the East*, (Lexington: University Press of Kentucky: 2011), 87.
5. Fritz, *Ostkrieg*, xxiii.
6. Stahel, *Barbarossa*, 249, 259, 444–447.
7. Stahel, *Barbarossa*, 134–135.
8. Earl F. Ziemke and Magna E. Bauer, *Moscow to Stalingrad: Decision in the East* (Washington, DC: Center of Military History United States Army, 1987), 14.
9. Stahel, *Barbarossa*, 248; David M. Glantz & Jonathan House, *When Titans Clashed, How the Red Army Stopped Hitler* (Lawrence: University of Kansas Press, 1995), 73.
10. Glantz and House, *Titans*, 53; Stahel, *Barbarossa*, 345, 348; Fritz, *Ostkrieg*, 120.
11. Stahel, *Barbarossa*, 259.

12. Glantz and House, *Titans*, 58; Fritz, *Ostkrieg*, 123–126; Chris Bellamy, *Absolute War, Soviet Russia in the Second World War: A Modern History* (London: Macmillan, 2007), 245–248.
13. Fritz, *Ostkrieg*, 113, 153; Stahel, *Barbarossa*, 189.
14. Geoffrey P. Megargee, *War of Annihilation, Combat and Genocide on the Eastern Front, 1941* (Lanham, Md: Rowman and Littlefield, 2006), 80–81; Robert M. Citino, *Death of the Wehrmacht, The German Campaigns of 1942* (Lawrence: University of Kansas Press, 2007), 42–47
15. David M. Glantz, *Colossus Reborn, The Red Army at War, 1941–1943* (Lawrence: University of Kansas Press, 2005), 16; Stahel, *Barbarossa*, 170, 209; Fritz, *Ostkrieg*, 132–134.
16. Bryan I. Fugate and Lev Dvoretsky, *Thunder on the Dnepr, Zhukov-Stalin and the Defeat of Hitler's Blitzkrieg* (Novato, CA: Presidio Press, 1997), 168–193.
17. Fritz, *Ostkrieg*, 126; 129; Bellamy, *Absolute War*, 245.
18. David Stahel, *Kiev 1941: Hitler's Battle for Supremacy in the East* (Cambridge: Cambridge University Press, 2012), 4.
19. Mary Habeck, *Storm of Steel, The Development of Armor Doctrine in Germany and the Soviet Union, 1919–1939* (Ithaca, NY: Cornell University Press, 2003), xvii.
20. Stolfi, *Panzers East*, 181–188.
21. Rebecca Manley, *To the Tashkent Station, Evacuation and Survival in the Soviet Union at War* (Ithaca, NY: Cornell University Press, 2009), 107–110; Mikhail M. Gorinov, "Muscovites' Moods, 22 June 1941 to May 1942," in *The People's War, Responses to World War II in the Soviet Union*, ed. Robert W. Thurston and Bernd Bonwetsch (Urbana: University of Illinois Press, 2000), 122–127.
22. Roger R. Reese, *Why Stalin's Soldiers Fought, The Red Army's Military Effectiveness in World War II* (Lawrence: University of Kansas Press, 2011), 117.
23. Fritz, *Ostkrieg*, 148, 155.
24. Glantz, *Colossus*, 17.
25. Megargee, *War of Annihilation*, 82.
26. Glantz and House, *Titans*, 51, 64.
27. Stahel, *Barbarossa*, 362–363, 440; Evan Mawdsley, *Thunder in the East, the Nazi-Soviet War, 1941–1945* (London: Hodder Arnold, 2005), 80.
28. Glantz and House, *Titans*, 91.
29. David M. Glantz, *Zhukov's Greatest Defeat, the Red Army's Epic Disaster in Operation Mars, 1942* (Lawrence: University of Kansas Press, 1999).
30. Citino, *Death of the Wehrmacht*, 3, 301.
31. Glantz and House, *Titans*, 105–106, 110.
32. Joel S. A. Hayward, *Stopped at Stalingrad, The Luftwaffe and Hitler's Defeat in the East, 1942–1943* (Lawrence: University of Kansas Press, 1998), xv–xvii; Geoffrey Roberts, *Stalin's Wars, From World War to Cold War, 1939–1953* (New Haven: Yale University Press, 2006), 119.
33. Fritz, *Ostkrieg*, 197, 273; Geoffrey Roberts, *Victory at Stalingrad*, (London: Pearson, 2002), 5.
34. Rolf-Dieter Müller and Gerd R. Übererschär, *Hitler's War in the East 1941–1945: A Critical Assessment* (New York: Berghahn, 2002), 126.
35. Mark Axworthy, Cornel Scafeș, and Cristian Craciunoiu, *Third Axis Fourth Ally, Romanian Armed Forces in the European War, 1941–1945* (London: Arms and Armour Press, 1995); Olga Kucherenko, "Reluctant Traitors: The Politics of Survival in Romanian-occupied Odessa," *European Review of History* 15, no. 2 (2008): 143–155; Alexander Statiev, "The Ugly

Duckling of the Armed Forces: Romanian Armour 1919–41," *The Journal of Slavic Military Studies* 12, no. 2 (1999): 220–244.
36. Fritz, *Ostkrieg*, 236; Citino, *Death of the Wehrmacht*, 153.
37. Rolf-Dieter Müller, *The Unknown Eastern Front: The Wehrmacht and Hitler's Foreign Soldiers*, trans. David Burnett (London: I.B. Tauris: 2012), 255–56; see also Alexander Statiev, "When an Army Becomes 'Merely a Burden': Romanian Defense Policy and Strategy (1918–1941)," *The Journal of Slavic Military Studies* 13, no. 2 (2000): 82; Axworthy, *Third Axis*, 101–118.
38. Glantz and House, *Titans*, 134, 140; Bellamy, *Absolute War*, 537–539.
39. Hayward, *Stopped*, 314, 322; Wiliamson Murray, *Luftwaffe* (Baltimore: Nautical and Aviation Publishing, 1985), 143–154; Richard Muller, *The German Air War in Russia* (Baltimore: Nautical and Aviation Publishing, 1992), 86–101.
40. Ronald Smelser and Edward J. Davies II, *The Myth of the Eastern Front, the Nazi-Soviet War in American Popular Culture* (Cambridge: Cambridge University Press, 2008), 97–99.
41. Stahel, *Barbarossa*, 195.
42. Robert Gellately, *Lenin, Stalin, and Hitler, The Age of Social Catastrophe* (New York: Alfred A. Knopf, 2007), 413–428; Megargee, *War of Annihilation*, 33.
43. Hannes Heer and Klaus Naumann, eds., *War of Extermination: The German Military in World War II, 1941–1944* (New York: Berghahn Books, 2000), 2–5; Michael Berkowitz, "The Nazi Equation of Jewish Partisans with 'Bandits' and Its Consequences," *European Review of History* 13, no. 2 (2006): 311–333; Bellamy, *Absolute War*, 23–27.
44. Stahel, *Barbarossa*, 403.
45. Fritz, *Ostkrieg*, 102–104; Megargee, *War of Annihilation*, 95–96.
46. Fritz, *Ostkrieg*, 96–97.
47. Hannes Heer, "Killing Fields, The Wehrmacht and the Holocaust in Belorussia, 1941–1942," in *War of Extermination: The German Military in World War II, 1941–1944*, ed. Hannes Heer and Klaus Naumann (New York: Berghahn Books, 2000), 55–68, 72–73.
48. Ibid.
49. Christian Streit, "Soviet Prisoners of War in the Hands of the Wehrmacht," in *The German Military in World War II, 1941–1944*, ed. Hannes Heer and Klaus Naumann (New York: Berghahn Books, 2000), 81–82; See also Fritz, *Ostkrieg*, 166–173.
50. Timothy Snyder, *Bloodlands, Europe Between Hitler and Stalin* (New York: Basic Books, 2010), 162, 172, 175–178.
51. Lennart Samuelson, *Tankograd, The Formation of a Soviet Company Town: Cheliabinsk 1900s–1950* (London: Palgrave Macmillan, 2011), 128–133, 176–181; Mark Harrison, "Industry and Economy," in *The Soviet Union at War, 1941–1945*, ed. David R. Stone (Barnsley: Pen and Sword, 2010), 26; John Barber and Mark Harrison, *The Soviet Home Front 1941–1945, A Social and Economic History of the USSR in World War II* (London: Longman, 1991), 3–10; Sonia Melnikova-Raich, "The Soviet Problem with Two 'Unknowns': How an American Architect and a Soviet Negotiator Jump-Started the Industrialization of Russia, Part I: Albert Kahn," *The Journal of the Society for Industrial Archeology* 36, no. 2 (2010): 57–80.
52. Glantz and House, *Titans*, 68, 71–72; Bellamy, *Absolute War*, 220–221.
53. Stahel, *Barbarossa*, 228.
54. Samuelson, *Tankograd*, 188–189, 197.
55. Glantz and House, *Titans*, 191.

56. Richard Overy, *Russia's War, A History of the Soviet War Effort: 1941–1945* (New York: Penguin, 1997), 155.
57. Stahel, *Barbarossa*, 199, 377.
58. Fugate and Dvoretsky, *Thunder*, 347.
59. Robert W. Thurston, "Cauldrons of Loyalty and Betrayal: Soviet Soldiers' Behavior, 1941 and 1945," in Thurston and Bonwetsch, *People's War*, 235–237.
60. Reese, *Stalin's Soldiers*, 74, 309–310; Thurston, *People's War*, 239–241, 250.
61. Barber and Harrison, *Soviet Home Front*, 68, 72; Catherine Merridale, *Ivan's War, Life and Death in the Red Army, 1939–1945* (New York: Picador, 2006), 96–97.
62. Reese, *Stalin's Soldiers*, 14–15, 103–104, 141, 306.
63. Olga Baranova, "Nationalism, Anti-Bolshevism or the Will to Survive? Collaboration in Belarus under the Nazi Occupation of 1941–1944," *European Review of History* 15, no. 2 (2008): 122–124; Barber and Harrison, *Soviet Home Front*, 99–104; Snyder, *Bloodlands*, 179, 184–186.
64. Karel C. Berkhoff, *Harvest of Despair, Life and Death in Ukraine under Nazi Rule* (Cambridge: The Belknap Press of Harvard University Press, 2004), 20, 114–140.
65. Reina Pennington, *Wings, Women, War: Soviet Airwomen in World War II* (Lawrence, Kansas: University of Kansas Press, 2001); Susanne Couze and Beate Fiesler, "Soviet Women as Comrades-in-Arms: A Blind Spot in the History of the War," in Thurston and Bonwetsch, *People's War*, 211–234.
66. Reese, *Stalin's Soldiers*, 257–258; Reina Pennington, "Women," in Stone, *Soviet Union at War*, 93–120.
67. Anna Krylova, "Stalinist Identity from the Viewpoint of Gender: Rearing a Generation of Professionally Violent Women-Fighters in 1930s Stalinist Russia," *Gender and History* 16, no. 3 (2004): 628; Anna Krylova, *Soviet Women in Combat, A History of Violence on the Eastern Front* (Cambridge: Cambridge University Press, 2010), 14.
68. Reese, *Stalin's Soldiers*, 265, 281, 283.
69. Gerhard Weinberg has also made this point for the war as a whole. See Gerhard Weinberg, *A World at Arms, a Global History of World War II*, 2nd ed. (Cambridge: Cambridge University Press, 2005), 267, 299–305.
70. Fritz, *Ostkrieg*, xxii.
71. Megargee, *War of Annihilation*, xiv.
72. Heer and Naumann, *War of Extermination*, 6, 70.
73. Fritz, *Ostkrieg*, 181; Overy, *Russia's War*, 138–142.
74. Stahel, *Kiev*, 6; Glantz, *Colossus*, xvii.

Bibliography

Axworthy, Mark, Cornel Scafeș, and Cristian Craciunoiu. *Third Axis Fourth Ally, Romanian Armed Forces in the European War, 1941–1945*. London: Arms and Armour Press, 1995.

Barber, John, and Mark Harrison. *The Soviet Home Front 1941–1945, A Social and Economic History of the USSR in World War II*. London: Longman, 1991.

Bellamy, Chris. *Absolute War, Soviet Russia in the Second World War: A Modern History*. London: Macmillan, 2007.

Berkhoff, Karel C. *Harvest of Despair, Life and Death in Ukraine under Nazi Rule*. Cambridge, MA: Belknap Press of Harvard University Press, 2004.

Citino, Robert M. *Death of the Wehrmacht, The German Campaigns of 1942*. Lawrence: University of Kansas Press, 2007.
Fritz, Stephen. *Ostkrieg: Hitler's War of Extermination in the East*. Lexington: University Press of Kentucky, 2011.
Fugate, Bryan I., and Lev Dvoretsky. *Thunder on the Dnepr, Zhukov-Stalin and the Defeat of Hitler's Blitzkrieg*. Novato, CA: Presidio, 1997.
Gellately, Robert. *Lenin, Stalin, and Hitler, The Age of Social Catastrophe*. New York: Alfred A. Knopf, 2007.
Glantz, David M. *Colossus Reborn, The Red Army at War, 1941–1943*. Lawrence: University of Kansas Press, 2005.
Glantz, David M. "The Red Army at War, 1941–1945: Sources and Interpretations." *Journal of Military History* 62, no. 3 (July 1998): 595–617.
Glantz, David M. "Russel H. S. Stolfi, Barbarossa: Hitler's Invasion of Russua, 1941." *Journal of Military History* 66, no. 3 (July 2002): 888–889.
Glantz, David M. *Zhukov's Greatest Defeat, the Red Army's Epic Disaster in Operation Mars, 1942*. Lawrence: University of Kansas Press, 1999.
Glantz, David M., and Jonathan House. *When Titans Clashed, How the Red Army Stopped Hitler*. Lawrence: University of Kansas Press, 1995.
Habeck, Mary. *Storm of Steel: The Development of Armor Doctrine in Germany and the Soviet Union, 1919–1939*. Ithaca, NY: Cornell University Press, 2003.
Hayward, Joel S. A. *Stopped at Stalingrad, The Luftwaffe and Hitler's Defeat in the East, 1942–1943*. Lawrence: University of Kansas Press, 1998.
Heer, Hannes, and Klaus Naumann, eds. *War of Extermination: The German Military in World War II, 1941–1944*. New York: Berghahn, 2000.
Krylova, Anna. *Soviet Women in Combat, A History of Violence on the Eastern Front*. Cambridge: Cambridge University Press, 2010.
Kucherenko, Olga. "Reluctant Traitors: The Politics of Survival in Romanian-occupied Odessa." *European Review of History* 15, no. 2 (2008): 143–155.
Manley, Rebecca. *To the Tashkent Station, Evacuation and Survival in the Soviet Union at War*. Ithaca, NY: Cornell University Press, 2009.
Mawdsley, Evan. *Thunder in the East, the Nazi-Soviet War, 1941–1945*. London: Hodder Arnold, 2005.
Megargee, Geoffrey P. *War of Annihilation, Combat and Genocide on the Eastern Front, 1941*. Lanham, MD: Rowman and Littlefield, 2006.
Melnikova-Raich, Sonia. "The Soviet Problem with Two 'Unknowns': How an American Architect and a Soviet Negotiator Jump-Started the Industrialization of Russia, Part I: Albert Kahn." *Journal of the Society for Industrial Archeology* 36, no. 2 (2010): 57–80.
Merridale, Catherine. *Ivan's War, Life and Death in the Red Army, 1939–1945*. New York: Picador, 2006.
Müller, Rolf-Dieter. *The Unknown Eastern Front: The Wehrmacht and Hitler's Foreign Soldiers*, translated by David Burnett. London: I. B. Tauris, 2012.
Müller, Rolf-Dieter, and Gerd R. Übererschär. *Hitler's War in the East 1941–1945: A Critical Assessment*. New York: Berghahn, 2002.
Overy, Richard. *Russia's War, A History of the Soviet War Effort: 1941–1945*. New York: Penguin, 1997.
Pennington, Reina. *Wings, Women, and War: Soviet Airwomen in World War II Combat*. Lawrence: University of Kansas Press, 2001.

Reese, Roger R. *Why Stalin's Soldiers Fought, The Red Army's Military Effectiveness in World War II*. Lawrence: University of Kansas Press, 2011.

Roberts, Geoffrey. *Stalin's Wars, From World War to Cold War, 1939-1953*. New Haven, CT: Yale University Press, 2006.

Roberts, Geoffrey. *Victory at Stalingrad*. London: Pearson, 2002.

Samuelson, Lennart. *Tankograd, The Formation of a Soviet Company Town: Cheliabinsk 1900s-1950*. London: Palgrave Macmillan, 2011.

Smelser, Ronald, and Edward J. Davies II. *The Myth of the Eastern Front, the Nazi-Soviet War in American Popular Culture*. Cambridge: Cambridge University Press, 2008.

Snyder, Timothy. *Bloodlands, Europe Between Hitler and Stalin*. New York: Basic Books, 2010.

Stahel, David. *Kiev 1941: Hitler's Battle for Supremacy in the East*. Cambridge: Cambridge University Press, 2012.

Stahel, David. *Operation Barbarossa and Germany's Defeat in the East*. Cambridge: Cambridge University Press, 2009.

Statiev, Alexander. "The Ugly Duckling of the Armed Forces: Romanian Armour 1919-41." *The Journal of Slavic Military Studies* 12, no. 2 (1999): 220-244.

Stolfi, R. H. S. *Hitler's Panzer's East, World War II Reinterpreted*. Norman: University of Oklahoma Press, 1991.

Stone, David R., ed. *The Soviet Union at War, 1941-1945*. Barnsley: Pen and Sword, 2010.

Thurston, Robert W., and Bernd Bonwetsch, eds. *The People's War, Responses to World War II in the Soviet Union*. Urbana: University of Illinois Press, 2000.

Weinberg, Gerhard. *A World at Arms, a Global History of World War II*, 2nd ed. Cambridge: Cambridge University Press, 2005.

Ziemke, Earl F., and Magna E Bauer. *Moscow to Stalingrad: Decision in the East*. Washington, DC: Center of Military History, United States Army, 1987.

CHAPTER 10

THE MIDDLE EAST DURING WORLD WAR II

HAKAN GÜNGÖR AND PETER GARRETSON

WHILE the impact of World War I was more influential than World War II in the Middle East, by establishing most of its countries and borders and laying the foundation for future states, the role of World War II in the Middle East warrants further exploration. Military historians have extensively researched the battle of El Alamein and the importance of Germany's General Erwin Rommel. The impact of the conflict on Palestine (the future State of Israel) has also been exhaustively documented. Most World War II studies on the Middle East, largely emphasize the military component and the minutiae of the North African campaigns stretching from Operation Torch in Northwest Africa, to the battle of El Alamein in Egypt. Scholarship addressing the importance of social, political, and economic factors during this period have not been given their due. This chapters examines these factors and explains how they changed during the global conflict.

The four largest countries of the Middle East—Egypt, Turkey, Iran, and Iraq—have had an outsized impact on the region's history, particularly through social, political, and economic change. Turkey and Iraq were nations created by World War I. All four nations have been major world civilization centers. World War II centralized and strengthened all four states—economically and politically. Iran and Iraq were targeted by Germany as major sources of oil, and their conquest would have significantly advanced Axis war aim. Strategically, Turkey and Egypt provided the Allies with the best access routes to that oil from the region. Despite the importance of Middle Eastern oil it provided less than ten percent of the oil needed by the Allies. Meanwhile, the United States provided ninety percent of Allies' oil. More than this, all four nations were seen as important to the Allied war effort, as evidence by Britain intervening directly in the domestic politics of Egypt, Iraq, and Iran. Apart from oil production, significant economic change occurred in all four countries. They all experienced economic growth, but also soaring inflation, political unrest, and even food riots. The impact of World War II on the Middle East was greater than most histories—international, regional, or national—have been willing to admit.

Egypt during World War II

After World War I, Egyptian politics was dominated by a three-way competition for power between the British, the King Faruq and the Egyptian Parliament. The British made some concessions after the Italian forces invaded Ethiopia in 1935. Concerned with the Italian threat to Egypt and the Sudan, from the west in Libya, the south-east in Ethiopia and Italian East Africa, Britain signed the Anglo–Egyptian Treaty of 1936. With the outbreak of World War II, Britain emerged as the most influential member of the governing triangle. Meanwhile, both Faruk and the Parliament were greatly weakened and lost much of their legitimacy in the eyes of most Egyptians. In 1940, Italy belatedly declared War on Great Britain, presenting a security threat to Egypt and Sudan. It soon escalated when the Italian offensives in Egypt and the Sudan ground to a halt, and were replaced by the much more serious threat of General Rommel's German army.

In June 1942, Germany, under Rommel, launched a major offensive attack that forced the surrender of the British garrison in Tobruk. By the summer, Rommel's forces were poised to threaten Cairo and British interests in the entire region, including Palestine and access to oil from Iran and Iraq. On the eastern front, German forces were bearing down on Stalingrad and the Caucasus. If victorious, they could have turned south to attack Iraq and Iran via Turkey. By October, British forces, under General Bernard Montgomery, decisively defeated Rommel at al-Alamain. In January 1943, Soviet troops forced the surrender of German soldiers holding Stalingrad, causing the war to shift in favor of the Allies. As a result the Germans retreating from both fronts. Because these campaigns are, to most, common knowledge, they will not be dealt with further here. However, the broad international context needs to be clear to understand the particular instance of Egypt. Each of the four major countries of the Middle East reacted differently and individually to the shifting strengths of the world powers.

In Egypt, the most significant development was the February Fourth Incident of 1942. Britain, while defending Egypt from invasion by Rommel's forces, expressed alarm at the pro-Axis activities throughout Egypt, especially within the government and its supporters. Because the Egyptian prime minister was seen as sympathetic to the Axis powers, the British urged that he be replaced by their preferred choice Mustafa al-Nahas. King Faruq baulked at this suggestion, causing the stalemate to reach a climax on February 4. The British ambassador to Egypt, Sir Miles Lampson (later Lord Killearn) had arranged an audience with King Faruq at his official residence, Adbin Palace. Lampson ordered British forces to surround the palace before his meeting and issued an ultimatum. The ambassador offed Faruq two options: abdication or a government more aligned to British interests, with Nahas as prime minister and a suitable cabinet. Faruq backed down, appointed Nahas, and the British had, in effect, carried out a coup, but a more subtle one than an earlier one in Iraq. Both led to only quasi-independence in the two countries. The British role in Egypt increased significantly, but this led to the discrediting of the Egyptian monarchy and parliament, laying the foundation for the overthrow of the monarchy in 1952. Furthermore, the weakening of these two institutions opened the door to the increased influence of the Islamist Muslim Brothers whose prestige rose steadily in the 1940s, both politically and militarily, as they built up their paramilitary forces. This antecedent opened up the way for the creation of the Arab League in the last months of the war, with Egypt and Iraq playing important roles as two of its founding members, promoting a regional Arab identity and priorities for most of the countries of the Middle East.

Egypt had the largest economy in the Middle East during the war. Britain was particularly aware of the major economic dislocations that took place during World War I, which led to riots and major unrest that seriously threatened the colonial regimes. British officials were determined to avoid these threats as much as possible during World War II, especially food shortages that led to famine. Despite recognizing the potential problem, they failed to prevent major food riots in Egypt in 1942. By establishing the Middle East Supply Center (MESC)[1] the Allies helped avert many of these earlier issues. To respond to shortages of shipping, as a result of German victories during the Battle of the Atlantic, the MESC mandated import substitution to address shortages. The MESC and other measures encouraged the production of local foodstuffs so that they would not have to be imported from Europe or the United States. Before World War II, trade between and among the core countries of the Middle East amounted to seven percent of trade, whereas in 1943 it had risen to thirty-three percent. These advances marked the first tentative step toward greater regional economic integration in the Middle East. Because of these policies, many agriculturalists in the Middle East greatly benefited financially. This monetary wealth stands in stark contrast to World War I, when most were hoarding and/or facing famine. Further research is needed on these economic topics throughout the Middle East,.

The MESC in particular strengthened and set in motion various economic dynamics that had significant long-term impacts. The MESC strengthened the role and power of several central governments, not just Egypt but also Iran, Syria, Iraq, and Sudan. The administration of licenses for imports and exports were widely used to encourage import substitution. These measures had a major impact on agriculture, industry, and trade throughout the Middle East. They also provided increased opportunities for corruption, especially in Egypt and Iraq. British and American control of shipping and shipping priorities secured initial leverage.

In many, if not most countries, the strengthening of central administrations, exercised through a broad array of regulatory and advisory committees, led to the push independent nation states in the postwar period. Many of the committees regulating production of goods and their import and export were incorporated into the bureaucracies of these independent states, and such institutions remain present today. Thus, the Middle East inherited economic controls from World War II that strengthened existing and future nation-states, rather than encouraging stronger regional entities or encouraging decentralization, arguably a more democratic process. However, this process was somewhat different in Iraq, Turkey, and Iran.

Iraq during World War II

There are two significant parallels in the impact of World War II on Egypt and Iraq; for both countries, World War II proved to be a turning point, based on the treaties that they signed before the war and the military intervention Britain carried out during the war. Britain's 1930 treaty with Iraq made it the first country to gain independence under the mandate regime set up by the peace treaties after World War I. This nominal independence was limited by the British continuing indirect rule and maintaining bases in Iraq, creating resentment from many Iraqis (as they were in Egypt). A significant shift for came in came in 1941.

During the 1930s, a group of high-ranking Iraqi officers, often referred to as the "Golden Square," were Pan Arab nationalists increasingly opposed to British control. They supported a like-minded lawyer and politician, Rashid Ali al Gaylani, whose followers looked to the Germans and Italians to help fund their anti-British goals. In early April 1941, Rashid Ali, supported by his military allies, carried out a successful coup and took over the Iraqi government. The British acted swiftly, first to stop German influence and second to secure their Iraqi oil. The British sent troops from India to secure Basra and the south of Iraq, but were unable to quickly send troops to Baghdad or the key air force base nearby in Habbaniya, located in central Iraq. They were able to relieve their air base after sending a flying column from Transjordan in May 1941. By the end of the month, the Habbaniya and Basra forces converged on Baghdad, forced an armistice, and returned a pro-British government to Iraq. However, the conflict was a close call and troops had had to be cobbled together from India and the Arab Legion of Jordan; all during the hottest summer in a quarter of a century, in an area widely known for its extreme temperatures and vicious sandstorms. Consolidation of British power in Iraq allowed them to assist subsequent campaigns in Syria and Iran. Intelligence played a key role in both campaigns, although it was not always occurred—there were many "scares" predicting possible German threats from 1941 to 1944 that failed to materialize.

This consolidation of the British military hold on Iraq and its defeat of the major nationalist forces in Iraq caused resentment within the elite class and a majority of ordinary Iraqi civilians (mirroring a similar pattern in Egypt). It led to a significant growth of anti-British resentment and undermined the legitimacy of the British and the Iraqis who supported them. Many scholars draw a direct line from 1941 to the 1958 coup and the overthrow of the monarchy in that year. The pro-British Nuri al-Said's return to power combined with the removal of the nationalists and many in the military provided the opportunity for the emergence of new, younger political forces including the Communist party, the Shi'as, and the Kurds. In particular, Mulla Mustafa Barzani was able to consolidate his position in northern Kurdish Iraq and emerge as the foremost leader of the Kurds in Iraq and, increasingly, throughout the Middle East. He would then go on in 1946 to play a key role in the Kurdish Mahabad Republic, a significant highpoint in Kurdish history.

Great Britain depended heavily on Iraq and Iran. At the beginning of World War I, about seventy-five percent of British oil came from these nations. During World War II, the loss of its oil would have forced Britain to turn to the United States for more of this increasingly vital energy source. If the British lost access to Middle Eastern oil, it would have to purchase American oil in dollars, a currency that was increasingly in short supply in their treasury. During World War II, in 1941, although only five percent of oil was coming from the Middle East (mostly from Iran and Iraq), nearly thirteen million tons were produced there that did not need to be imported from the United States.[2] After the Italian declaration of war against Great Britain in 1940, the Allies took measure to ensure that the Axis powers would not gain free access to Middle Eastern oil. Furthermore, Allied intelligence sources indicated that the Germans were known to be eyeing Iraq and Iran as potential sources needed for growing German energy demands. Thus, as German influence in Iraq grew, the British, largely because of British Prime Minister Winston Churchill's insistence, took action to protect their existing oil imports from the south of Iraq and those expected from the large reserves located in northern Iraq in and around Kirkuk and Mosul.

Economic dislocation spawned shortages and rampant inflation. In 1939 the production index measured 100, by 1943 it had risen to 773. During the same period, the cost of living rose about sixfold, but salaries only rose by twenty-five percent. Furthermore, between 1939 and 1945, the index for foodstuffs rose from one hundred to 655 while the general index number (which besides foodstuffs, included clothing, fuel, light, rent, and other items) rose from one hundred to 590. The impact was greatest on the poor and lower classes, leading to food riots and widespread unrest, furthering anti-British sentiment and opposition to the pro-British Iraqi ruling elite. The serious economic disruptions led to greater British intervention in the economy, and greater overall centralized control until the end of the war and postwar period. This, as in Egypt, encouraged and reinforced a more centralized, authoritarian state.

Turkey in World War II

The Middle East was one of the main battlegrounds in World War I, and many nation states were created in the region after this Great War. Turkey was one of the major nation states which rose from the ashes of the Ottoman Empire. Many Turkish leaders from 1939 to 1945 had experienced the dissolution of the Ottoman Empire in World War I, and thus they worked hard to avoid entering the Second World War. During the war, the Turkish government's primary objective was to maintain national sovereignty. While Ismet İnönü, who succeeded Mustafa Kemal Atatürk in 1938, continued to uphold an authoritarian single-party amidst economic stagnation, and was well aware that the Turkish army had long outdated military equipment. Thus, there was no serious internal pressure against İnönü's policies.[3]

Although Turkey did not have any serious internal challenges, it faced pressure from external powers who sought the country as an ally. Both the Allies and the Axis forces courted Turkey during the 1930s and World War II. Despite being faced with these propositions, Turkey maintained good relations with both the Axis and Allies until 1944. After the Turkish War of Independence (1922), Atatürk, the founder of Turkey, sought a "zero problem" policy in Turkish international affairs.[4] Without making concessions to any state, Atatürk pursued friendship agreements with European powers and the Middle Eastern states. One of the immediate threats to Turkish unity and sovereignty came from the Soviet Union. To diffuse this threat from its northern neighbor Atatürk signed an non-aggression pact with the Soviet Union in 1925, and he renewed it in 1935.[5]

In September 1939, Şükrü Saraçoğlu, Turkey's foreign minister, visited Moscow to renew the friendship agreement. However, his visit turned out to be fruitless. The Soviet government did not sign a friendship agreement because General Secretary Stalin had already negotiated a non-aggression pact with Germany. Thus, the Soviets did not see Germany as a danger, but as a friend who might even help them to get control of Bosporus and the Dardanelles' Straits. Simultaneously, Italy emerged as a serious threat in the Balkans, which worried Turkey in 1939. In response, France and the United Kingdom sought an alliance with Turkey. The Italian invasion of Albania in 1939 confirmed Turkey's apprehensions. The Turkish government made clear that it was eager for a mutual assistance pact with the Soviet Union, which would secure the Balkans and the Black Sea region. However, the Soviets did not respond to this desire after they signed the Nazi–Soviet pact in 1939.[6]

To deter the Soviets and secure the eastern Mediterranean, Turkey signed the Tripartite Treaty with France and the United Kingdom in May 1939. The Tripartite Agreement declared that these powers would provide aid to each other in the event of an act of aggression leading to war in the Mediterranean. However, Turkish negotiators put an extra article in the agreement, stating that Turkey would not be held liable if war should break out between its allies and the USSR.[7] Turkey distinctly stipulated that in no case would it become an agent against the Soviet Union. But this did not mean that Turkey committed itself to becoming a satellite of the Soviet Union. However, when the Nazi–Soviet pact of August 1939 was signed, Turkish leaders took this to be a threat to their security. This agreement finally confirmed popular suspicions of Soviet intentions, which were to annex the straits and parts of eastern Turkey.

As for Germany, many influential Turkish leaders were cautious because their memories of what collaboration with this country had meant for them in World War I remained vivid. Nonetheless, they maintained diplomatic relations with Adolf Hitler and signed the Non-aggression Pact in June 1941. Even pro-German Turks suspected that a German victory might be more difficult to adjust to and be more of a threat to Turkish independence, than an Anglo–French victory. However, much excitement was aroused in Turkey because of the hatred and fear of the Soviets, and Germany's victories against Russia after Operation Barbarossa in 1941. When Germany invaded the Soviet Union in June 1941, Turkey again proclaimed its neutrality, which benefited Turkey in two ways: the country received planes, funds, and special training equipment from the British, and continued its trade with Germany.[8]

Like Britain and Germany, the United States preferred a neutral Turkey, and motivated the İnönü administration to remain that way. In 1941, President Roosevelt announced that the defense of Turkey was vital to the security of the United States,[9] because he thought that a neutral Turkey was far more beneficial from a military and economic perspective. A weak Turkey would require serious investments of money and military equipment. Although Turkey never militarily engaged in the war, the country accepted substantial aid from the Allied powers after the Soviet Union cemented their success against Germany. Financially, Turkey struggled, despite the increasing economic unrest and shortages of goods, Turkey slowly acted to prevent the Axis powers from getting the vital materials they desired.[10] This policy worsened the economic crisis at home.

World War II had a tremendous impact on the Turkish internal economy. To manage this serious economic situation, the government took major measures. The İnönü administration increased the authority of the police, established martial law, and expanded the army. Turkey was unofficially forced to declare a mobilization. In the face of this situation, the number of Turkish soldiers reached one million in the middle of the war. With limited resources, Turkey struggled to provide necessary food to its soldiers.[11] In addition, Turkish military equipment was outdated, mostly surplus from the Great War, and lacked the funds to purchase new equipment. In 1938, the general budget allocated 30.31 percent to civil defense, while in 1941 this rate increased to 55.44 percent.[12]

The İnönü administration allocated more than one-half of the general budget to civil defense during the war. These shifting budgetary priorities impacted industry, agriculture, public structures, and many other institutions operating in the country negatively In the meantime, because the workers in industry and in the agricultural sector had to join the army, production decreased while national consumption increased. Furthermore, the war fostered corruption in the economic sphere. Unwanted developments, such as inflation, famine, profiteering, and black marketing became rampant. The state tried to cope with the situation by issuing more decrees. The Turkish government enacted the National Protection Law (*Milli Korunma Kanunu*) on January 18, 1940 to stabilize the economy. This measure failed to achieve economic recovery and the situation worsened. The İnönü administration endeavored to meet the immense military expenditures and resuscitate the economy. Thus, the Turkish Parliament levied new taxes on individuals, such as the Capital Tax (*Varlık Vergisi Kanunu*) of November 11, 1942. All of these measures proved unsuccessful and failed to remedy Turkish economic problems resulting from the war.[13]

The İnönü administration found it was increasingly difficult to hold the home front together. Discontent among the Turks increased due to the constant economic deterioration from the beginning of the war, as well as censorship of the local press. In addition, İnönü had to deal with foreign powers in order to maintain neutrality. In 1943, Churchill put more pressure on Turkey to wage war on the Axis powers, and on August 2, 1944, İnönü finally broke off diplomatic relations with Germany. Turkey's token declaration of war on Germany and Japan followed on February 23, 1945. Although Turkey declared war against the Axis powers, the country never deployed armed forces against them. The declaration of war was made to meet "the deadline for a seat at the San Francisco meeting of the United Nations founders."[14]

IRAN IN WORLD WAR II

During and immediately following World War II, Reza Shah declared neutrality because he saw the British and the Russians as immediate threats to his country's sovereignty. Although the Shah benefited from good economic relations with Germany, he also feared Hitler's expansionist policy. Neither side aligned closely with the interests of Iran.[15] Iranian oil was vital to the British war effort. Persia's oil production was 8.4 tons in 1940.[16] This was evidenced by the anti-British revolt in Iran, and with Germany's advance in the western desert campaign and launching Operation Barbarossa against the in the USSR in June 1941. In the summer and fall of 1941, as the German army advanced deep into the Soviet Union the British and Soviets invaded Iran on the pretext of Shah's refusal to expel German advisors from Iran. The Allies' major intentions in were to open a supply line to the Soviet Union. The supply line meant to protect Iranian oil fields from falling into Hitler's hands, and put an end to German intelligence operations in Shah's country. The Allies asked the Shah to join the war on their side, but upon his rejection, a joint British and Soviet invasion of Iran started on August 25, 1941.[17]

The British–Soviet invasion of Iran in August 1941 caught Turkey off guard. The Turks would have been happy to see a German victory over their mutual enemy, the Soviet Union. Although the Allied Powers used German fifth column activities and German advisers to the Iranian government as the reason of the invasion, the Allies wanted a secure supply route for British and American supplies to the Soviet Union and aimed to dominate Iran militarily. Aside from securing the supply route, Churchill wanted to maintain a hold over Turkey. He believed the invasion of Iran would encourage Turkey to stand firm against allowing German troops passage into Syria and Palestine.[18]

Great Britain knew that the Iranian invasion would cause anxiety in Turkey, so the Allies approached the Roosevelt administration, requesting they inform Turkey that the United States approved this invasion. Thus, Secretary of State Cordell Hull stated that Iran's territorial integrity would be respected. Following this statement, the British and Soviet ambassadors told the Turks that they guaranteed the territorial integrity of Turkey. Despite this promise to maintain Turkish sovereignty, the invasion of Iran caused harsh criticism of the Allies in the Turkish media. Yunus Nadi of the newspaper, *Cumhuriyet*, stated, "it has absolutely no basis in legality and is nothing but a straightforward act of aggression and invasion."[19]

The newspapers claimed that after Iran, Turkey would be the next country to be confronted with British and Russian demands. However, the Turks were more cautious than the Persians in their dealings with the Allies and the Axis powers, and managed to avoid invasion by any of the Great Powers. When the Allied powers invaded Iran in 1941, several thousand Germans were there, including the advisers to the Shah's government. Following the German attack on Russia in June 1941, the Shah received telegrams from the Soviets and the British requesting him to drive the Germans out of Iran. Failing to fulfill the Allies' request, Iran was invaded on August 25, 1941. The Soviet–British forces rapidly took over the entire country and forced Reza Shah to relinquish his power in favor of his son, Mohammed Reza Pahlevi.

Following the invasion, the Allied powers started to use the transportation system and other facilities in Iran against the Axis powers. Iran, the Soviet Union, and Great Britain signed the Tripartite Agreement on January 29, 1942. With this agreement, the two Allies acknowledged "the territorial integrity, sovereignty, and political independence of Iran, and to defend Iran from German aggression. Iran...agreed to cooperate with the Allies in the war effort, putting its resources at their disposal."[20] Furthermore, the Allies agreed to leave Iran no later than six months after a signed armistice with Germany. Although Iran was under British military control, American troops were partially in charge of the railroad and the transportation of troops.

The amount of military supplies that passed through Iran to the Soviet Union was astonishing and showed the important role that Iran played in the Allies final victory. Although Iran and Turkey declared war on Germany, it did not militarily engage in the war. After the Iranian declaration of war on Germany in September 1943, Stalin, Churchill, and Roosevelt met in the capital of Iran, for the Teheran Conference, at the end of November 1943. At the conference, the United States, the Soviet Union, and the United Kingdom recognized the assistance that Iran gave during the war against the common enemy, particularly by facilitating the transportation of supplies from the United States and the United Kingdom to the USSR.[21]

In 1942, food riots broke out in Iran and the Allied powers feared the possibility of civil war. In response, the United States, the Soviet Union, and the United Kingdom provided food supplies, including grain, to Iran. When the Allies met in Teheran in 1943, the food crisis had turned into a full-blown financial crisis, which had to be addressed at the Conference. The Allied powers realized the Iranian economy had experienced severe inflation during the war, so they decided to assist Iran in overcoming this economic difficulty. They agreed that they would provide economic assistant to the Iranian Government. Although the Allies had economically assisted the Persians, in 1944 Tehran became one of the most expensive cities in the world. The cost of living soared over one thousand percent above figures preceding the war.[22] After the war, the Allies were in accord with the Shah's regime that any economic problems facing Iran at the end of hostilities should receive full consideration by international agencies such as the International Monetary Fund and the World Bank.[23]

The independence and territorial integrity was one of the Shah's main concerns that the Allies addressed at Tehran Conference. The three powers reaffirmed their desire for the maintenance of the sovereign independence and territorial integrity of Iran. The government of Iran found this text acceptable.[24]

The invasion of Iran, meant the Iranian government relinquished some control over its citizens. Like Turkey, Iran had strict press censorship. After Reza Shah abdicated in favor of his son, Muhamad Reza Pahlavi, the press was partially liberated. The growth of the Iranian press after 1942 was fascinating, and in complete contrast with Turkey. More than 150 newspapers and journals opened during the first two years of the occupation, as those who wanted to voice their grievances started a newspaper.[25] One of the other features of the occupation was the increase in political activity. After the new Shah declared a real constitutional government, politicians exiled by Reza Shah returned and became active again. Out of the several parties which were founded after 1942, the only lasting party was the Tudeh (Masses) party, which liberals had formed. Although the majority of the party members were liberals, Communists were in control, especially in the territories occupied by Red Army. Tudeh was more organized, and it emphasized its Marxist ideas in the 1944 election in which the party only managed to gain only eight seats out of more than 130 in the parliament. The Soviet Union sought to influence and control the Iranian economy.

By the end of 1943, rivalries emerged over Iranian oil resulting in many American and British companies sending representatives to negotiate with the Iranian government for oil concessions. The Soviets did not stay out of the game. In 1944, the Soviet government sent its delegations to Teheran seeking concessions for oil and other mineral deposits in northern Iran. Concerned with the Allies' requests, Iran declared that it would stop negotiations for concessions until the Allied troops had left its soil. After this announcement, the Iranian parliament passed a law stopping any Iranian official from even talking about oil concessions until every single foreign military force had left its soil.[26] Shortly after the law passed, the Tudeh party and its newspapers launched a campaign supporting oil concessions for the Soviets. Furthermore, the newspapers attacked the new Shah's government for its anti-Russian attitude. While the Soviet government continued negotiations with the Iranian government, the Soviet newspapers criticized the presence of American troops in Iran without a treaty agreement. In fact, this was later considered by some scholars the beginning of the U.S. confrontation with the USSR, not just in Iran but worldwide[27] (otherwise known as the Cold War).

The Soviet army took control in northern Iran and prevented the Persian government officials from collecting taxes. The Soviet-backed Tudeh party had more authority than government officials did. Witnessing the Central government's weakness, the Azerbaijanis formed the Azerbaijan Democrat party in 1945 to obtain autonomy. The Soviets did not want Azerbaijan to secede from Iran; they just wanted to use the Azerbaijan Democrat party against the central government. However, relations between the Azerbaijan Democrats and Teheran worsened in December 1945, and the party announced the creation of an Azerbaijan government. Following this declaration, Azerbaijani Turkish was introduced as the official language, and banks were nationalized. Seeing Azerbaijan as a propitious example, the Kurds established an independent republic with its center at the town of Mahabad. Although the Kurdish state did not last long, it underscored the weakness of the central government.[28] The invasion of Iran caused many troubles for Iranians. In addition to the change in government, the economic and food crisis challenged the everyday lives of most Iranians. Furthermore, the Red Army's presence in northern Iran split the country in two.

Overall, World War II had a substantial effect on the military, economic status, and politics of all four countries. Because, all four countries were militarily weak, foreign powers took advantage of them. Only Turkey escaped significant foreign intervention or invasion. Politically, all suffered from British intervention, but Turkey suffered the least. The Soviet Union and the United State only seriously impacted Iran, while affecting Turkey less so. Economically, all were significantly affected by the MESC, and experienced a sharp spike in inflation and food shortages. World War II in the Middle East was responsible for laying the foundation for the Cold War competition over the Middle East, in which the United States would play a major role, while the other major powers played, in varying degrees, lesser roles.

Notes

1. See Martin W. Wilmington, *The Middle East Supply Centre* (London: University of London Press, 1971).
2. Andrew Roberts, *The Storm of War: A New History of the Second World War* (New York: HarperCollins, 2011), 129.
3. I. C. B. Dear and M. R. D. Foot, "Turkey," in *The Oxford Companion to World War II* (New York: Oxford University Press, 1995), 1127.
4. Selim Deringil, *Turkish Foreign Policy during the Second World War* (New York: Cambridge University Press, 1989).
5. Edward Weisband, *Turkish Foreign Policy, 1943–1945: Small State Diplomacy and Great Power Politics* (Princeton: Princeton University Press, 1973), 3.
6. Deringil, *Turkish Foreign Policy*, 7.
7. Dear and Foot, "Turkey," 1127.
8. Lewis V. Thomas and Richard N. Frye, *The United States and Turkey and Iran* (Cambridge: Harvard University Press, 1951), 91–92.
9. Ibid., 93–94.
10. Ibid., 92–93.
11. Osman Sönmez, "II. Dünya Savaşı Sırasında Türkiye'nin İktisadi Politikası," PhD diss., (Selçuk Üniversitesi, 1992), 1–13.
12. Cemil Koçak, *Milli Şef Dönemi, (1938–1945)* (Ankara: Yurt Yayınları, 1986), 247.
13. Hakan Güngör, *Turkish–American Relations in World War II: Survival of Turkish Neutrality* (Ankara: Gece Akademi, 2019), 73–77.
14. Thomas and Frye, *The United States and Turkey and Iran*, 99.
15. Fariborz Mokhtari, *In the Lion's Shadow: The Iranian Schindler and His Homeland in the Second World War* (Stroud, Gloucestershire: The History Press, 2012), 33.
16. I. C. B. Dear and M. R. D. Foot, "Persia," in *The Oxford Companion to World War II* (New York: Oxford University Press, 2011), 874.
17. Dear and Foot, "Persia," 874.
18. Deringil, *Turkish Foreign Policy*, 126.
19. Ibid., 127.
20. Thomas and Frye, *The United States and Turkey and Iran*, 230.

21. "Declaration of The Three Powers Regarding Iran," December 1, 1943, FRUS, *The Conferences at Cairo and Tehran 1943* (United States Government Printing Office Washington: 1963), 646–647. [Accessed 10.31.2014] http://digital.library.wisc.edu/1711.dl/FRUS.FRUS1943CairoTehran.
22. Thomas and Frye, *The United States and Turkey and Iran*, 232.
23. "Declaration of The Three Powers Regarding Iran," December 1, 1943, FRUS, *The Conferences at Cairo and Tehran 1943* (United States Government Printing Office Washington: 1963), 647.
24. Louis G. Dreyfus, Jr., "The Minister in Iran (Dreyfus) to the Secretary of State," December 3, 1943, FRUS, *The Conferences at Cairo and Tehran 1943* (United States Government Printing Office Washington: 1963), 650. [Accessed 10.31.2014] http://digital.library.wisc.edu/1711.dl/FRUS.FRUS1943CairoTehran.
25. Thomas and Frye, *The United States and Turkey and Iran*, 232.
26. Ibid., 235.
27. Ibid., 235.
28. Ibid., 236–237.

Bibliography

Cooper, A. *Cairo in the War, 1939–1945*. London: Hamish Hamilton Press, 1989.

Foot, M. R. D. "Persia." In *The Oxford Companion to World War II*. Edited by I. C. B. Dear, and M. R. D. Foot. New York: Oxford University Press, 2011.

Deringil, Selim. *Turkish Foreign Policy during the Second World War*. New York: Cambridge University Press, 1989.

Güngör, Hakan. *Turkish–American Relations in World War II: Survival of Turkish Neutrality*. Ankara: Gece Akademi, 2019.

Lenczowski, G. *Russia and the West in Iran, 1918–1948: A Study in Big Power Rivalry*. Ithaca: Cornell University Press, 1949.

Millspaugh, A. C. *Americans in Persia*. Washington, DC: The Brookings Institute, 1946.

Roberts, Andrew. *The Storm of War: A New History of the Second World War*. New York: HarperCollins, 2011.

Skrine, C. *World War in Iran*. London: Constable Press, 1962.

Thomas, Lewis V., and Richard N. Frye. *The United States and Turkey and Iran*. Cambridge: Harvard University Press, 1951.

Vatikiotis, P. J. *The Modern History of Egypt*, Rev. ed. London: Frederick A. Praeger Publishers, 1980.

Wilmington, Martin W., *The Middle East Supply Centre*. London: University of London Press, 1971.

CHAPTER 11

PEARL HARBOR AND JAPAN ASCENDANT

SIDNEY PASH

JUST days before the Japanese attack on Pearl Harbor, Stanley Hornbeck, the State Department's resident Far Eastern expert, wagered with odds of five-to-one that Japan would not go to war against the United States in the near future. At the same time, half a world away, General Douglas MacArthur predicted with equal certainty that if war came to the Philippines his newly augmented air and ground forces would smash the Japanese. General George C. Marshall and Secretary of War Henry Stimson, men of outstanding talent and ability, shared both Hornbeck's view that Japan would shrink from war and MacArthur's confidence that if war came, the United States had little to fear from Japan.[1]

The profound shock that Hornbeck, MacArthur, Stimson, and Marshall experienced on December 7 had, within six months, morphed into something akin to desperation as an ascendant Japan overran the Philippines, Wake, and Guam and battered the already depleted U.S. Navy in the February 1942 Battle of the Java Sea. While buoyed by James Doolittle's April 1942 raid on the Japanese home islands and the U.S. Navy's tactical victory the following month in the Battle of the Coral Sea, Americans had little to celebrate. For the British, who drew strength from the U.S. entry into the war, the conflict's opening months, which saw the loss of Hong Kong, Malaya, Singapore, and Burma, and the sinking of HMS *Repulse* and *Prince of Wales*, were equally traumatic. The Dutch, meanwhile, already under German occupation at home, suffered more ignominy with Japan's rapid conquest of the East Indies.

The Japanese decision for war and the string of near uninterrupted triumphs that followed the attack on Pearl Harbor were at best vaguely understood by contemporary observers. Some two generations of historical enquiry, however, have produced well-grounded scholarship that highlights the importance of Japanese and American diplomatic blunders, Japan' decision to join the Axis Alliance in September 1940, Tokyo's drive to create the Greater East Asian Co-Prosperity Sphere, a Japanese-led Asian autarkic bloc, and Washington's relentless pursuit of economic sanctions and military deterrence. Decades of rivalry, mistrust, and the impact of the war in Europe, meanwhile, fatally exacerbated Japanese–American tensions and precluded successful diplomatic engagement. Japanese military superiority, short-lived as it was, has also been the subject of inquiry and here too, a consensus of sorts has emerged which stresses a combination of factors, foremost among them a staggering Allied underestimation of Japanese intentions and capabilities.[2]

However well-grounded, the consensus on these topics is worthy of reexamination. On closer inspection, for example, it is apparent that the Roosevelt administration practiced a remarkably successful containment strategy that sought to secure the long-term objective of protecting the Open Door and the short-term imperative of disrupting the Axis. This successful strategy broke down only in the summer of 1941 when policymakers abandoned containment in favor of a strategy that used draconian economic sanctions in an effort to force Japan from China and the Tripartite Pact.

The sobering and sometimes humiliating defeats that Japan wrought on the Western Allies likewise may be reexamined in light of new historical evidence and fresh perspectives. While the Western powers were clearly caught off guard by Japan's audacious assaults, this alone fails to explain Tokyo's early triumphs. The crusade to liberate Asia from Western colonial oppression and the need to secure Southeast Asian raw materials drove officers and men alike during the opening months of the conflict. This élan, combined with meticulous Japanese planning, training, and superior equipment, were every bit as important as the early element of surprise. Especially after the disastrous autumn of 1941 gave way to the even more terrifying winter of 1942.

The Coming of the War

More than a generation of American foreign policy in Asia pivoted around the Open Door as every administration, beginning with Theodore Roosevelt, worked to protect American access to the fabled China market. Built by two presidents and nurtured by four more, American containment worked to restrain Japan by maintaining a balance of power in Asia and through the use of military deterrence, diplomatic engagement, and on occasion, economic coercion. Overall, this program proved startlingly successful, especially given the phenomenal growth of Japanese military power, the waning of Anglo–French strength in Asia after 1914, the temporary collapse of Russian military might after the autumn of 1917, and the continued inability of successive Chinese administrations to protect the Middle Kingdom.

In the aftermath of Tokyo's stunning victory in the 1904–1905 Russo–Japanese War, President Theodore Roosevelt began Washington's decades long effort to contain Japanese expansion on the Asian mainland by supporting a Russo–Japanese balance of power in Northeast Asia. Although Roosevelt saw Japan fighting to protect the Open Door and applauded its February 1904 preemptive strike on the Russian Fleet at Port Arthur, he grew less sanguine as the war, and Japanese victories, continued.

While an idealist in a great many ways, the president was a foreign policy realist who understood that a balance of power in Northeast Asia would go a long way toward containing the victorious Japanese. To achieve this balance, the president worked to end the war in the summer of 1905 before Russia collapsed to preserve what the historian Raymond Esthus called the "line of friction . . . in Manchuria" between St. Petersburg and Tokyo.[3]

In addition to preserving the balance of power, the president used military deterrence to moderate Japanese foreign policy. In 1907, acting on the advice of the Army–Navy Joint Board, Roosevelt dispatched the Great White Fleet to Japan as part of its around the world cruise. A year later, once again on the urging of American war planners, Congress agreed to fund a major American naval base at Pearl Harbor, Hawaii. While significant, the balance of power and deterrence were not the president's sole or even his most successful method for containing Japan.[4]

Roosevelt pursued diplomatic engagement gradually and in response to a series of crises that threatened Japanese–American relations following the outbreak of war between Japan and Russia. In 1905, while in Tokyo on Roosevelt's behalf, Secretary of War William Howard Taft concluded a secret executive agreement that recognized Japanese hegemony over Korea and Manchuria in return for Tokyo's recognition of American control in the Philippines. Roosevelt turned again to engagement during the waning months of his second term when Japan's ambassador to the United States, Kogorō Takahira, and Secretary of State Elihu Root negotiated an agreement whereby Tokyo agreed to respect the Open Door and Washington recognized Japan's control over South Manchuria.[5]

President Roosevelt unhesitatingly accepted the Open Door and successfully limited Japanese expansion in Asia by rebuilding the Far Eastern balance of power and by combining military deterrence with diplomatic engagement. His policy was not perfect, yet when placed next to that of his immediate successor, Roosevelt's mistakes seem small in comparison. Unlike Roosevelt, William Howard Taft oversaw a spectacularly unsuccessful containment policy that convinced many Japanese that Washington was "spurring China on to an anti-Japanese policy." Woodrow Wilson, by contrast, mended fences and contained Japanese expansion despite the ravages of world war and revolution. Wilson resisted military deterrence during a 1913 war scare prompted by anti-Japanese legislation in California and instead relied heavily on diplomatic engagement, especially in 1915, after Japan issued the infamous Twenty-One Demands to the Chinese government, and again during the 1917 Lansing–Ishii talks. However short-lived and controversial, Lansing–Ishii signaled a Japanese willingness to support the Open Door in China in return for America's limited recognition of Japanese spheres of influence in Manchuria. Despite these notable accomplishments, the Wilson administration also added a new element to American containment when it introduced economic sanctions into Japanese–American diplomacy. Amid World War I, in an effort to temper Japanese wartime expansion, the War Trade Board refused Japan export licenses for steel plate, critical to the Japanese shipbuilding industry. While this decision may have influenced Tokyo to dispatch Ishii to Washington, it did far more harm than good as it convinced the next generation of policymakers that economic sanctions could bend Japan to America's will.[6]

While economic deterrence did little to improve Japanese–American ties, the bruising fight between Japanese and American negotiators at Versailles over Tokyo's determination to secure wartime gains and Washington's equally clear desire to limit Japanese expansion, poisoned relations. Secretary of State Robert Lansing, once the advocate of compromise, had grown weary of Japanese threats not to join the League of Nations and E. T. Williams, who served as chief of the State Department's Division of Far Eastern Affairs from 1914 to 1918, compared the Japanese to the defeated Germans, "whom the Japanese leaders openly admire." In Japan, meanwhile, the army's newest war plans designated America as its number two hypothetical enemy behind only the Soviet Union, while the navy, alarmed by America's wartime buildup, stepped up its planning as well. Ominously, the navy soon designated the United States as its most likely opponent.[7]

If Versailles signaled a new low point in Japanese–American relations, then the 1921–1922 Washington Conference breathed new life into the relationship and inaugurated the most successful period to date in the United States' long containment of Japan. At Washington, the Warren G. Harding administration ended the ongoing Anglo–American–Japanese naval building program and the Anglo–Japanese Alliance, won renewed Japanese support for the Open Door, and arranged for Japan to return Shantung province to China. Calvin Coolidge remained committed to engagement and disarmament and at the 1930 London Conference his successor, Herbert Hoover, achieved further meaningful reductions in Anglo–American–Japanese naval strength. While successful in limiting Japanese military power and continental expansion, these presidents did little to improve American–Japanese relations and Americans' deep affection and sense of mission in China increased throughout the decade as the Nationalist Party, purged of its Communist partners after 1927, unified the nation. In Japan, meanwhile, disarmament undermined both civilian and navy moderates who, after the London Conference, proved utterly powerless to restrain army firebrands who saw Chinese nationalism as an existential threat.[8]

With the end of the Northern Expedition, the military campaign to unify China, Chiang Kai-shek's Nationalist government initiated a campaign to end the unequal treaties, old agreements entered into between the Qing Dynasty and the various imperial powers. While moderate Japanese governments negotiated with Nanking over the future of South Manchuria, powerful elements within the Army General Staff, War Ministry, and Kwantung Army maintained that Japan must detach Manchuria from Chinese control. During the latter half of 1931, the Japanese Kwantung Army seized Manchuria and the following year created Manchukuo, a Japanese puppet state led by the last Qing emperor, Henry Puyi.[9]

These actions convinced American policymakers that Japan sought hegemony in East Asia and that traditional diplomatic instruments would not restrain Tokyo. History, however, convinced them that American economic and military deterrence could reorient Japanese diplomacy and these twin beliefs, in Japanese duplicity and thirst for expansion on the one hand, and vulnerability on the other, served as the Franklin D. Roosevelt administration's Far Eastern diplomatic polestar for nearly a decade.[10]

The president's containment policy took shape soon after inauguration day when Stanley Hornbeck refused Chinese overtures for U.S.-mediated Sino–Japanese peace talks. Hornbeck maintained that successful talks would reward Japanese aggression and encourage, rather than limit future conquests. This same opposition to traditional diplomatic engagement led Secretary of State Cordell Hull to reject a Japanese proposal to conclude a non-aggression pact the following year. Until Pearl Harbor, the administration opposed the kind of diplomatic agreements that Wilson and Theodore Roosevelt had successfully used to bolster American containment. Rather than diplomatic engagement, the administration used a varied aid program of commodity credits and arms sales to strengthen China while simultaneously increasing American naval strength to deter Japanese expansion.[11]

With the outbreak of the Second Sino–Japanese War in the summer of 1937 the administration redoubled its containment efforts. Once it became clear that China would continue to resist Japanese expansion the State Department rejected both Japanese and Chinese requests to mediate an end to the fighting and extended ever more generous aid to Nanking. Clearly influenced by the supposed success of the World War I steel embargo, Washington also unveiled a multifaceted economic sanctions policy that began with the 1938 Moral Embargo, in which the administration requested exporters to cease doing business with Japan, to the less well known but far more effective preclusive purchasing program. Officially designated as a preparedness measure in which the United States stockpiled strategic raw materials, the program attempted to deny Japan, Germany, and Italy critical raw materials by either preclusively purchasing the materials or, if need be, by simply outbidding the Axis.[12]

While these sanctions clearly alarmed Japan, America unsheathed its Sword of Damocles only in the summer of 1940 when Congress approved the 1940 Export Control Act, which required importers to secure an export license for products that the administration placed on a new export control list. In response to Japan's decision to join the Axis Alliance and occupy Northern French Indochina in September of 1940, as well as its continued aggression in China, the administration gradually refused Tokyo licenses so that by the summer of 1941 only oil and cotton remained widely available. The reason for this apparent anomaly is clear; policymakers feared that an oil embargo would trigger an attack on the oil rich Dutch East Indies and British Borneo and that would draw England, which after the fall of France in June 1940 was waging a lone struggle against Germany, into war with Japan. Japan then would receive oil as long as the Roosevelt administration feared for England's survival in its lone struggle against Nazi Germany. This fear, which dominated American foreign policy for more than a year, vanished on June 22, 1941, with the German invasion of the Soviet Union.[13]

Despite Germany's overwhelming early successes, American policymakers immediately recognized that the German invasion freed England from the threat of a cross-Chanel invasion for at least one year. They further reasoned that as long as the Nazi–Soviet war continued Japan would not go to war with either the United States or England. The conviction that Japan would not go to war, regardless of the severity of American economic sanctions, led the United States, British, and Dutch governments to freeze Japanese assets and end all trade with Japan following Tokyo's takeover of Southern French Indochina in late July 1941.[14]

The assets freeze and trade embargo, which represented an existential threat, immediately produced a new and extraordinary effort on the part of Prime Minister Fumimaro Konoe to stave off war. After securing the approval of Emperor Hirohito, Navy Minister Koshirō Oikawa, and perhaps most importantly, War Minister Hideki Tojo, Konoe worked for some two months to arrange a meeting with President Roosevelt to reopen the flow of imported oil. While historians on both sides of the Pacific continue to debate the likely results of a summit, the president's closest advisors opposed the meeting owing to their conviction that Japan could not be trusted, and that economic sanctions and military pressure were better guarantors of American safety. Anxious to gain additional time for military preparations, however, the administration carried on preliminary negotiations regarding the summit's location and agenda before finally rejecting the proposal in mid-October.[15]

The decision to reject the summit proposal did not end Japanese–American efforts to avoid war. Over a month earlier, on September 6, with prospects for a summit growing dim, the Konoe cabinet agreed to begin hostilities against the United States, Britain, and the Dutch Empire in mid-October should negations fail. Once Washington made it clear that the summit would never occur, however, Konoe resigned rather than lead Japan to war. He had surmised correctly that his successor would not be bound by the September 6 decision, thereby giving peace advocates additional time.[16]

As Konoe had guessed, the new government, led by Hideki Tojo, decided, with the emperor's support, to continue negotiations for an additional month. Rather than attempt to arrange a leader's summit, however, the Tojo cabinet forwarded two peace plans to its Washington embassy and dispatched the veteran diplomat Saburō Kurusu to Washington to assist Ambassador Kichisaburo Nomura, a former admiral and foreign minister, who during his tenure in Washington remained something of a well-meaning diplomatic ingénue.[17]

The Tojo cabinet's first plan contained sweeping concessions including a pledge to withdraw from Indochina and the bulk of China on conclusion of the Sino–Japanese War. The plan, however, also called on Washington to end aid to China while peace talks were underway and refused to renounce the Axis Pact, and so was a complete non-starter in Washington where civilian and military officials continued to question Japanese motives. U.S. Army intelligence officials, for example, convinced that a Japanese withdrawal from China would imperil both Tokyo's civilian moderates and the West's vulnerable Asian colonies, had already informed the president, Hull, Stimson, and Marshall not to seek "a cessation of hostilities in China." While Tokyo's comprehensive settlement was dead on arrival, other, more viable options remained.[18]

In early November, for example, Harry Dexter White, a Treasury official best known for his passionate support of preclusive purchasing, produced a comprehensive peace plan in which Japan abrogated the Axis Alliance and withdrew from China in return for a Japanese–American non-aggression pact and substantial American financial support. The plan, which protected long term American interests such as the Open Door and secured short term imperatives, including disrupting the Axis, won varying degrees of approval from State Department Asian expert Maxwell Hamilton, as well as General Leonard T. Gerow, Director of Army War Plans, and Admiral Harold Stark, Chief of Naval Operations. In the end, however, this plan also fell victim to the conviction that economic and military deterrence would protect the United States and its allies far more effectively than diplomatic engagement.[19]

In addition to White's plan, American diplomats also had two modus vivendi or temporary agreements to consider. On November 20, perhaps influenced by White's plan, which Hull forwarded to the president two days earlier, FDR resurrected an earlier idea to provide Japan "some oil and rice now more later" in return for a pledge not to support its Axis partners in the event the United States entered the European war. That same day, Nomura and Kurusu also presented a Japanese modus vivendi which was remarkably similar to Roosevelt's. Like FDR, the Tojo cabinet focused on restoration of trade in return for a Japanese pledge not to strike Western colonies in Asia. In the final weeks of peace then, Hull and his associates had three workable alternatives to choose from but in the end, they rejected all three.[20]

The widely held belief that Japan's policy of continental expansion was immutable, that Washington could not trust Japanese assurances, and that a compromise peace was unnecessary, helped determine Hull's decision. Had the Allies suffered a devastating defeat in the Middle East or the Russian Front or had the American public or the U.S. military given the secretary a compelling reason to change course he might have embraced either modus vivendi, but in the final weeks of peace nothing occurred to change Hull's mind. German setbacks in the Atlantic, Middle East, and Russia all augured well for Washington and while British and Dutch diplomats encouraged Hull to pursue a modus vivendi, they did not push back when he announced his decision to reject the temporary agreement. Marshall and Stark likewise would have welcomed additional time to prepare but neither man pressed Hull to accept a modus vivendi. The American public, meanwhile, had come to accept not only the possibility of war with Japan but the idea that the fight would prove "relatively easy." These issues, along with constant harassment from leading administration interventionists, led Hull to reject compromise and instead issue an American plan for a comprehensive settlement that was so extreme that upon reading its terms Foreign Minister Shigenori Tōgō concluded, incorrectly, that the U.S. had decided on war. Even Hamilton believed that the so-called Hull note must have appeared to Tokyo as an American ultimatum. With no diplomatic breakthrough, the Pearl Harbor strike force, which set sail on November 25, continued to its target to start the war that neither Tokyo nor Washington sought.[21]

JAPAN ASCENDANT, DECEMBER 1941 TO MAY 1942

During the first six months of the Pacific War, as Japan sought to secure Dutch and British oil and the sea lanes connecting the home islands to Southeast Asia, the Imperial Japanese Army and Navy were all but unbeatable. Between December 1941 and May 1942, Japanese forces swept the Western powers from the Dutch East Indies, Malaya, Singapore, Burma, and the Philippines, as well as the lonely islands of Guam and Wake. To be sure, the Allied powers underestimated the Japanese military, but the underestimation concerned capabilities rather than raw numbers. The War Department produced remarkably accurate estimates of the number of Japanese troops and amount of equipment available for offensive operations in Southeast Asia. Their estimates of Japanese capabilities, however, were less prescient. While the cause for this fatal underestimation will never be explained with certainty, the fundamental misreading of Japanese military history presents the most compelling explanation.[22]

Just three years after the Japanese surrender on the deck of the USS *Missouri*, General Sherman Miles, the head of U.S. Army Intelligence at the time of the Pearl Harbor attack, described how American war planners viewed their enemy in the months leading up to Pearl Harbor. "Japan's war record was not impressive," he noted, and the ongoing war in China, four years long in the summer of 1941, "indicated a low rating for Japanese military prowess." History, Miles explained, provided "[n]o better measure" of Japanese capability. "We had no reason to doubt our yardstick's . . . accuracy. Yet it was wholly false."[23]

While persistent Western racism no doubt shaped the collective American, British, and Dutch (ABD) yardstick, race alone cannot explain the failure of Allied intelligence. As John Dower noted in his 2010 *Cultures of War: Pearl Harbor/Hiroshima/9-11/Iraq*, "racial blinders alone do not adequately account" for the catastrophe at Pearl Harbor and Japan's success early in the war. To better understand Japan's early, unprecedented, and from the ABD standpoint, wholly unexpected victories, a brief examination of the war's opening months is in order.[24]

Japanese strategy during the war's first six months was determined by the need to secure oil and the sea lanes home. Since August, with the start of the Western oil embargo, Japan had begun to cannibalize its sizeable petroleum reserves with the result that the entire stock would run out by the end of 1942. Operations on oil-rich Borneo began on December 16 when Japanese forces landed in British Sarawak on the northern coast with follow on attacks further up the coastline at Brunei, Jesselton, and Dutch Borneo in January. By mid-February, the rising-sun flag flew over the entire island. The rapid conquest of Borneo was neither the product of Western racism nor a fundamental underestimation of Japanese capabilities, as British authorities had all but written off the island well before the Japanese landings began. Instead, Borneo's sheer size (the island is three times the size of Honshu, Japan's main home island) combined with a lack of air assets and ground troops doomed the Anglo–Dutch forces.[25]

Allied efforts to save the rest of the archipelago were no more successful despite the sizeable assets at their disposal. On Java, the main island in the Dutch East Indies, one hundred thousand mostly indigenous troops, eight combat air squadrons, and a fleet, which on paper was near Japan's equal, awaited the enemy. In late February, the allied flotilla composed of U.S., British, Dutch, and Australian ships attempted to block a Japanese invasion force steaming for Java with disastrous consequences. Commanded by Dutch Admiral Karel Doorman, the allied force suffered from the advanced age of its ships, the low morale of many of its crew, and command and control difficulties exacerbated by the lack of a common language and codebook. In the February 27–28 Battle of the Java Sea, Doorman, and over two thousand men under his command, perished in the face of superior Japanese night fighting capabilities, withering naval gun fire, and the equally lethal Long Lance torpedo. Dutch resistance on Java collapsed within two weeks while Sumatra, the target of a successful Japanese airborne landing in mid-February and seaborne invasion the following month, surrendered on March 28. Superior planning and execution, combined with control of the seas and the skies surrounding the islands, enabled Japan to conquer an empire three hundred years in the making in just over three months.[26]

Dutch East Indies oil, however valuable, would prove useless if the Japanese could not transport their hard-won prize safely to the distant home islands. British bases in Malaya and Singapore, as well as the U.S.-controlled Philippines, threatened to interdict the flow of oil home and so the Japanese military had to simultaneously undertake equally risky assaults against these British and American colonies. Although impressive on paper, the eighty thousand British and Commonwealth troops in Malaya were, on the whole, hastily assembled and untrained in jungle warfare. Adding to these problems, the decision to deploy the III Indian Corps, the anchor of British defense on the Malay Peninsula, to protect both RAF airfields and invasion beaches stretched the defenders too thin. The British also lacked an adequate number of air assets and troops and wrestled, until December 6, 1941, over whether to implement Operation Matador, which called for an advance into southern Thailand in order to preempt a Japanese invasion of northern Malaya. While not unique, the British forces also suffered from a tragic underestimation of Japanese military capabilities so great that the enemy was considered no better than the Italian or Afghan armies. Japanese forces, however, had begun planning for jungle warfare in 1940 and by the time staff officers completed their plans for the Malayan operation, Tokyo had assembled a balanced force of infantry, artillery, armor, and aircraft which, when combined, produced the greatest defeats in the history of British arms.[27]

The campaign against Malaya and Singapore began hours before the assault on Pearl Harbor when Japanese forces landed at Kota Bharu on the northeast Malayan coast. The defense of Malaya, already handicapped by indecision over Matador, as well as the decision to send precious men and machines to Singapore, Burma, and North Borneo, suffered irreparable harm on December 10 when Indochina-based aircraft sank the battlecruiser *HMS Repulse* and the battleship *HMS Prince of Wales*, both of which were operating in the South China Sea in an effort to block Japanese landings along the exposed Malayan coastline. The following day, as troops poured ashore at multiple points Japanese aviators established an effective air-umbrella over the war zone and, while the fight for Malaya continued into January, British ability to effectively resist had ended.[28]

However horrific, the British defeat in Singapore the following month dwarfed the Malayan debacle. While hard-headed realists recognized the island's vulnerability, those entrusted with safeguarding the colony had, by 1941, begun to equate Singapore with Gibraltar, Britain's impregnable Mediterranean fortress. As war enveloped Europe in September 1939 the British Chiefs of Staff concluded that Singapore could hold out for six months without relief. Two years later, Prime Minister Winston Churchill maintained that the garrison would hold out for a year. In the end, his forces capitulated on February 15, 1942, just one week after the Japanese landed on the island.[29]

Separated from Malaya by the kilometer-long Straits of Johor some eighty-five thousand men defended Britain's island fortress from fewer than forty thousand Japanese. While a myth soon developed that Singapore fell because its shore batteries could only fire at ships at sea, rather than at the Japanese troops coming ashore from Malaya, the truth by now is more familiar to the reader. As in Malaya, deficiencies in equipment and training and a series of command blunders, including the failure to anticipate the location of the main enemy landing, coupled with Japanese command of the sea and the skies surrounding the island, doomed the British, Indian, and Commonwealth forces. In the end, the vulnerability of Singapore's reservoirs and collapsing morale compelled Sir Arthur Percival, commander of Commonwealth forces, to surrender.[30]

Singapore's capture did not end Britain's imperial nightmare as Burma, the gateway to India, fell the following month. Advancing from Thailand, the numerically inferior Japanese continued to exploit their opponents' lack of experience in jungle warfare, reliable intelligence, and deficiencies in equipment to seize Burma's valuable raw materials and further isolate China from the outside world. As in Malaya and Singapore, the Japanese soon gained control of the air and while Chinese troops came to Burma's aid and reinforcements poured in following Singapore's fall, deprived of air cover, they could not stem the Japanese advance. While pockets of Burma remained outside of Japanese control, with the fall of Rangoon in March and Mandalay in May Japanese forces had accomplished their mission.[31]

The Japanese were no less successful against the United States military during the war's opening months and, by May 1942, Pearl Harbor, Wake, Guam, Bataan, and Corregidor were seared into the American lexicon. At Pearl Harbor, the United States Navy lost four battleships with another ten vessels seriously damaged while the Army Air Force suffered 165 aircraft destroyed, mostly on the ground. Nine separate hearings examined the cause of the debacle and the Joint Congressional Investigation into the Pearl Harbor Attack, the final and most authoritative investigation, concluded that a series of errors, including the now familiar underestimation of Japanese intentions and capabilities, as well as command blunders both in Honolulu and Washington, led to the disaster.[32]

For several months after Pearl Harbor the Japanese fleet remained the master of the Pacific and the best the U.S. Navy could accomplish were a series of pinprick raids against targets on the Marshall Islands and New Guinea. On April 18, however, sixteen Army B-25 bombers launched from the carrier USS *Hornet* struck Tokyo and targets in five other cities. While the raids clearly raised morale, they did not alter the balance of power in the Pacific and consequently, distant American outposts remained indefensible. Guam, the American base in the Northern Mariana Islands fell on December 9 after a brief struggle. Wake, the second major American possession taken by Japan, was protected by fewer than five hundred, primarily Marine Corps personnel, but nonetheless waged a heroic two-week fight. On December 11, Wake's defenders, aided by Marine Corps aircraft, repulsed the first Japanese invasion, sinking two destroyers and damaging another three cruisers in the process. Despite this victory, Wake's ultimate salvation depended on a relief expedition which Admiral William S. Pye, Acting Commander in Chief of the Pacific Fleet, cancelled on December 23, 1941, out of concern for the safety of the relief force. Hours later, Wake's garrison capitulated.[33]

Three thousand miles west of Wake Island, a very different and far greater defeat was playing out in the Philippines. Where Wake was considered indefensible, reinforcements, combined with the dispatch of B-17 bombers, had seemingly all but transformed the Philippines into a forward projection of American military power. Secretary of War Henry Stimson confidently informed President Roosevelt in October 1941 that Philippine-based airpower promised, "to stop Japan's march to the south and secure the safety of Singapore." Less than two weeks later, Army Chief of Staff General George C. Marshall concluded that U.S. forces in the Philippines "would[soon] have a deterrent effect on Japanese operations." In a November 15 interview intended to clarify the "deterrent effect," for Tokyo, Marshall assured a group of newsmen that Philippine based B-17s would "set the paper cities of Japan on fire." Within a month, however, the vaunted B-17 fleet lay shattered on the tarmac, most having never flown a sortie.[34]

With his air forces all but destroyed, General MacArthur had to rely on ground forces, which when fully mobilized reached 150,000 men, to defeat the invaders. While impressive on paper, his forces suffered from the same deficiencies in training, equipment, and lack of air cover and control of the seas that doomed the Dutch and British. Consequently, American and Filipino forces could not beat back the Japanese landings on Luzon and the day after Christmas MacArthur declared Manila, the Philippine capital, an open city.[35]

By this time, American and Filipino forces were in retreat to defensive positions on the Bataan Peninsula. Having decided to defeat the invaders on the beaches, however, MacArthur's forces were in no position to implement War Plan Orange-3 (WPO-3), the strategic retreat to Bataan and the island fortress of Corregidor, and consequently twice the number of troops, plus an estimated ten thousand civilians, withdrew up the peninsula. MacArthur had hoped that his forces would resist for upwards of six months, but disease, hunger, and the relentless Japanese cut that time by one-half. The end of the fighting on April 7, however, did not end the nightmare for the defenders as some six hundred Americans and at least ten thousand Filipino soldiers perished in route to prisoner of war camps. Thousands more died soon after arriving. After securing the Bataan Peninsula, which lay just north of Corregidor, the Japanese subjected the island to weeks of relentless shelling before making a successful landing on May 5, which forced General Jonathan Wainwright, who succeeded MacArthur after the latter left the Philippines for Australia, to surrender three days later. Unknown to Wainwright, Corregidor's fall marked the apogee of Japanese expansion as three thousand miles to the south, in the vast expanse of the Coral Sea, the United States Pacific Fleet turned back a Japanese invasion force headed for Port Moresby, New Guinea, the gateway to Australia.[36]

THE GREATER EAST ASIA CO-PROSPERITY SPHERE, 1942

Between December 1941 and May 1942, as the Japanese military fought to gain mastery over their Western opponents, Japanese bureaucrats, intellectuals, and policymakers labored both to justify and to rule Tokyo's burgeoning empire. Japan's traditional prewar empire, with the exception of Taiwan, was centered in Northeast Asia and was built during the heyday of the so- called New Imperialism. Imperialism, however, became an anathema after World War I and so successive Japanese administrations, beginning with the 1931 seizure of Manchuria and subsequent creation of Manchukuo, couched expansion in anti-imperial language, careful to justify military conquest as facilitating the legitimate, anti-colonial ambitions of the Asian peoples. Prime Minister Konoe's proclamation of a New Order in East Asia, in which Japan as senior partner worked with Manchukuo and China to defeat communism and stabilize Asia, was reiterating a near decade old theme that Japan would eschew territorial aggrandizement and instead lead China in a regenerative crusade. In June 1940, just after the Franco–Dutch collapse in Europe, and with the same fate apparently awaiting England, Foreign Minister Hachirō Arita expanded the New Order when he announced Japan's intention to create a Greater East Asian Co-Prosperity Sphere to encompass the vast Western colonial empire in Asia. Although expansion was always intended to benefit Japan first and foremost, the notion that His Majesty's military would employ force to liberate Asians from centuries of Western domination was both potent and real.[37]

While the Japanese military was phenomenally successful in sweeping Western forces from Asia and Japanese civilian and military intellectuals were reasonably successful in justifying expansion both at home and within Southeast Asia, the military and the civilian bureaucracies were spectacularly unsuccessful in creating a New Order that benefited either the home islands or the newly conquered peoples. The Co-Prosperity Sphere's architects were as thorough as the military when it came to prewar planning, but the exigencies of war and the rapidity and scope of Japanese conquests soon undercut their plans. To be sure, in Burma and the Dutch East Indies, nationalists initially welcomed the Japanese but even before the war turned against Japan, the people of the Co-Prosperity Sphere did. When Tokyo secured, for example, "close to a million tons of rice," in Vietnam, Japanese authorities inadvertently set in motion a policy which led to mass starvation and fomented the largest anti-Japanese insurgency within Southeast Asia. In the Philippines, meanwhile, where close to two hundred thousand eventually fought against the invaders, resistance organizations formed even before the fall of Bataan and Corregidor, clearly demonstrating that for Japan, winning an empire was easier than ruling it.[38]

Resistance within the empire proved the least of Japan's worries as victories were few and far between after the conquest of the Philippines. When the Tojo cabinet led Japan to war in December 1941, driven by the need to secure oil and the vision, real for some and manufactured for others, of freeing Asians from Western colonialism, it had no way of knowing that the war would bring only ruin. Superior planning, training, and equipment allowed Japan to win an empire, but after May 1942, Western material abundance, advances in technology, and the bravery and skill of their fighting men and women meant that for Japan, victory was short-lived.

Notes

1. Roberta Wohlstetter, *Pearl Harbor: Warning and Decision* (Stanford: Stanford University Press, 1962), 264; Cordell Hull Papers, Library of Congress, Box 75, Joint Board Minutes, November 3, 1941; Henry Stimson Diary, Sterling Library, Yale University, no. 35, 62 and 150; Michael S. Sherry, *The Rise of American Airpower: The Creation of Armageddon* (New Haven: Yale University Press, 1987), 102 and 107.
2. The reader wishing to study the historiography of the origins of the Pacific War would do well to read such enduring classics as Paul W. Schroeder, *The Axis Alliance and Japanese-American Relations, 1941*(Ithaca: Cornell University Press, 1958); Herbert Feis, *The Road to Pearl Harbor: The Coming of the War Between Japan and the United States* (New York: Atheneum, 1962); Dorothy Borg and Shumpei Okamoto, *Pearl Harbor as History: Japanese-American Relations, 1931–1941* (New York: Columbia University Press, 1973); and Waldo H. Heinrichs, *Threshold of War: Franklin D. Roosevelt and American Entry into World War II* (New York: Oxford University Press, 1988). The reader should also consult equally significant, and just as readable translated Japanese works, especially James William Morley, ed., *Taiheiyo senso e no michi: kaisen gaiko shi*, trans. David A. Tutus (New York: Columbia University Press, 1994). Japan's rapid advance during the war's opening months may best be understood by reading J. F. C. Fuller, *The Second World War: A Strategical and Tactical History, 1939–1945* (London: Eyre and Spottiswoode, 1948); John Toland, *The Rising Sun: The Decline and Fall of the Japanese Empire* (New York: Random House, 1970); Ronald H. Spector, *Eagle Against the Sun: The American War with Japan* (New York: Vintage Books, 1985); John Keegan, *The Second World War* (London: Hutchinson, 1989).
3. Raymond A. Esthus, *Theodore Roosevelt and Japan* (Seattle: University of Washington Press, 1966), 54–55, 62.

4. Howard K. Beale, *Theodore Roosevelt and the Rise of America to World Power* (Baltimore: Johns Hopkins University Press, 1956), 328–333; Charles E. Neu, *An Uncertain Friendship: Theodore Roosevelt and Japan, 1906–1909* (Cambridge: Harvard University Press, 1967), 227; Akira Iriye, *Pacific Estrangement: Japanese and American Expansion, 1897–1911* (Cambridge: Harvard University Press, 1972), 163; Albert C. Stillson, "Military Policy without Political Guidance: Theodore Roosevelt's Navy," *Military Affairs* 25, no. 1 (Spring 1961): 23.
5. Walter LaFeber, *The Clash: Japanese-American Relations Throughout History* (New York: W.W. Norton, 1997), 85–86; Thomas A. Bailey, "The Root Takahira Agreement of 1908," *The Pacific Historical Review* 9, no. 1 (1940): 19–35; Sidney Pash, *The Currents of War: A New History of Japanese-American Relations, 1899–1941* (Lexington: University Press of Kentucky, 2014), 19.
6. Philander Knox Papers, Library of Congress, Container 14, 2290–2299, Ohl to Knox, April 10, 1911; Raymond Esthus, "The Taft–Katsura Agreement: Reality or Myth?" *The Journal of Modern History* 31, no. 1 (March 1959): 48; Charles E. Neu, "1906–1913," in *American–East Asian Relations: A Survey*, ed. Ernest R. May and Charles E. Thomson Jr. (Cambridge: Harvard University Press, 1972), 158–160; La Feber, *The Clash*, 105–106; E. David Cronon ed., *The Cabinet Diaries of Josephus Daniels, 1913–1921* (Lincoln: University of Nebraska Press, 1963), 64–68; Robert Lansing, *The War Memoirs of Robert Lansing* (Indianapolis: Bobbs-Merrill, 1935), 283, 298–302; Robert Lansing Papers, Seeley Mudd Library, Princeton University, Box 2, Folder 4, Lansing–Ishii Agreement; Ibid, Box, 2, Folder 4, Memorandum of Lansing–Koo Conversation, November 12, 1917.
7. Jeffrey J. Safford, "Experiment in Containment: The United States Steel Embargo and Japan, 1917–1918," *Pacific Historical Review* 39, no. 4 (November 1970): 440–442, 445–447; Pash, *Currents of War*, 52; Akira Fujiwara, "The Role of the Japanese Army," in Borg and Okamoto, 189; Akira Iriye, *After Imperialism: The Search for a New Order in the Far East, 1921–1931* (Cambridge: Harvard University Press, 1965), 36.
8. Pash, chapter 2, *passim*.
9. Nobuya Bamba, *Japanese Diplomacy in a Dilemma: New Light on Japan's China Policy, 1924–1929* (Vancouver: University of British Columbia Press, 1972), 357–358; Michael Barnhart, *Japan and the World since 1868* (London: Edward Arnold, 1995), 86–87; Foreign Relations of the United States (hereafter *FRUS*), 1930, 2, (Washington, DC: United States Government Printing Office, 1945), 308; Ibid., 303–308; Chihiro Hosoya, "Characteristics of the Foreign Policy Decision-Making System in Japan," *World Politics* 26, no. 3 (April 1974): 360; Hiroharu Seki, "The Manchurian Incident," *Japan Erupts: The London Conference and the Manchurian Incident, 1928–1932*, trans. Marius B. Jansen, ed. James William Morley (New York: Columbia University Press, 1984), 137.
10. Cordell Hull, *The Memoirs of Cordell Hull*, Vol. I (London: Hodder and Stoughton, 1949), 117; Joseph Grew, *Ten Years in Japan* (New York: Simon and Schuster, 1944), 7.
11. Franklin D. Roosevelt Papers, Franklin D Roosevelt Library, Hyde Park, NY, President's Secretary's File 26, Hornbeck memorandum, May 9, 1933; Hull, Memoirs, I, 277–278; Frederick Leith-Ross, *Money Talks* (London: Hutchinson, 1968), 205–207; Henry Morgenthau Diary, Franklin D. Roosevelt Library, Diary number 10, 180; John Morton Blum, *Roosevelt and Morgenthau* (Boston: Houghton Mifflin, 1970), 104–107; Allan Seymour Everest, *Morgenthau, the New Deal and Silver* (New York: King's Crown Press, 1950), 113–118.

12. William L. O'Neill, *A Democracy at War: America's Fight at Home and Abroad in World War II* (New York: Free Press 1993), 60; Everest, *Morgenthau*, 120–121; John Morton Blum, *From the Morgenthau Diaries*, Vol. 1: *Years of Urgency* (Boston: Houghton Mifflin, 1965), 58–63.
13. FRUS, *Japan, 1931–1941*, 2, 222–223, 232–235, 238–260, passim; Pash, *Currents of War*, 171–172.
14. United States Archives and Records Administration, Washington DC, War Plans Division (hereafter WPD), Folder, "May–September 1941," General Leonard T. Gerow to General George C. Marshall, July 7, 1941; Ibid, Gerow to Marshall, July 16, 1941; FRUS, 1941, 4, 267–277; Pash, *Currents of War*, 179–183.
15. Heinrichs, 161; Alexander L. George and William E. Simons, et al., *The Limits of Coercive Diplomacy*, 2nd ed. (Boulder: Westview Press, 1994), 73–74; For the debate on the probable outcome of a summit see Pash, *Currents of War*, 203–205.
16. Nobutaka Ike, *Japan's Decision for War: Records of the 1941 Policy Conferences* (Stanford: Stanford University Press, 1967), 133–134; Roger B. Jeans, *Terasaki Hidenari: Pearl Harbor and Occupied Japan, A Bridge to Reality* (Lanham MD: Lexington Books, 2009), 73.
17. Jun Tsunoda, "The Decision for War," in *The Final Confrontation*, ed. James William Morley (New York: Columbia University Press, 1994); Ike, 201, 210–211; J. Garry Clifford and Masako Rachel Okura, *The Desperate Diplomat: Saburo Kurusu's Memoir of the Weeks before Pearl Harbor* (unpublished draft in author's possession).
18. Tsunoda, *Decision for War*, 254; Morley, *Final Confrontation*, 368–369; *Pearl Harbor Attack Hearings before the Joint Committee on the Investigation of the Pearl Harbor Attack*, Vol. 12–14. (Washington DC: U.S. Government Printing Office, 1946,, 1357–1358.
19. Pash, 229–231.
20. *Pearl Harbor Attack*, Vol. 12–14, 1109; Justus D. Doenecke and John E. Wilz, *From Isolationism to War, 1931 to 1941* (Wheeling, IL: Harlan Davidson, 2003), 159; Ike, *Japan's Decision*, 200, 210–211; *International Military Tribunal for the Far East* (Washington, DC: Library of Congress Photoduplication Service, 1974), 26,082–26,083.
21. Pash, *Currents of War*, 234–250.
22. For Japanese victories over the British see Alan Warren, *Britain's Greatest Defeat: Singapore 1942* (New York: Hambledon Continuum, 2007) and Christopher Bayly and Tim Harper, *Forgotten Armies, the Fall of British Asia, 1941–1945* (Cambridge: Harvard University Press, 2005). The Dutch defeat is best explored in Bill Yenne, *The Imperial Japanese Army: The Invincible Years, 1941–1942* (Oxford, UK: Osprey Publishing, 2014), chs. 18–24 and Jeffery Cox, *Rising Sun, Falling Skies: The Disastrous Java Sea Campaign of World War II* (Oxford, UK: Osprey, 2014). American defeats are detailed in Spector, *Eagle Against the Sun*, chs. 5–7; For an analysis of Japanese intentions and capabilities see WPD 4510, War Department Strategic Estimate, October 1941.
23. Sherman Miles, "Pearl Harbor in Retrospect," *The Atlantic*, July 1948, http://www.theatlantic.com/magazine/archive/1948/07/pearl-harbor-in-retrospect/305485/.
24. John W. Dower, *Cultures of War: Pearl Harbor/Hiroshima/9-11/Iraq* (New York: W.W. Norton, 2010), 50.
25. Ian W. Toll, *Pacific Crucible: War at Sea in the Pacific, 1941–1942* (New York: W.W. Norton, 2012), 234–235; Ashley Jackson, *The British Empire and the Second World War* (London: Bloomsbury, 2006), 440; Francis Pike, *Hirohito's War: The Pacific War 1941–1945* (London: Bloomsbury, 2015), 293–295; Paul S. Dull, *A Battle History of the Imperial Japanese Navy, 1941–1945* (Annapolis, MD: Naval Institute Press, 1978), 41–42.

26. Theodore Friend, *The Blue Eyed Enemy: Japan Against the West in Java and Luzon, 1942-1945* (Princeton: Princeton University Press, 1988), 71; John Grehan and Martin Mace, *Disaster in the Far East, 1940-1942: The Defense of Malaya, Japanese Capture of Hong Kong, and the Fall of Singapore* (Barnsley, UK: Pen and Sword, 2015), 459; Dull, *A Battle History*, 73-88. For information on the Japanese airborne assault on Sumatra see Gene Eric Salecker, *Blossoming Silk Against the Rising Sun: US and Japanese Paratroopers at War in the Pacific in World War II* (Mechanicsburg, PA: Stackpole Books, 2010), chapters 4 and 5 passim; Adrian R. Martin and Larry W. Stephenson, *Operation Plumb: The Ill-Fated 27th Bombardment Group and the Fight for the Western Pacific* (College Station: Texas A&M University Press, 2008), 138.

27. T. R. Moreman, *The Jungle, The Japanese, and the British Commonwealth Armies at War, 1941-1945* (London: Frank Cass, 2005), 18-25; Ong Chit Chung, *Operation Matador: World War II Britain's Attempt to Foil the Japanese Invasion of Malaya and Singapore* (Singapore: Times Academic Press, 1977), 134-135.

28. Evan Mawdsley, *December 1941: Twelve Days that began a World War* (New Haven: Yale University Press, 2011), 163; Duncan Redford, *A History of the Royal Navy: World War II* (London: I. B. Tauris, 2014), 178-181.

29. Timothy Hall, *The Fall of Singapore 1942* (New York: Routledge, 2015), 11; Pash, *Currents of War*, 177.

30. Karl Hack and Kevin Blackburn, *Did Singapore Have to Fall? Churchill and the Impregnable Fortress* (New York: Routledge, 2003), 53, 94-95; Louis Allen, *Singapore 1941-1942* (London: Frank Cass, 1977), 187-188, 211.

31. Alan Warren, *Burma 1942: The Road from Rangoon to Mandalay* (London: Bloomsbury, 2011), x, 144-146; Roy Conyers Nesbit, *The Battle for Burma* (Barnsley, UK: Pen and Sword, 2010), 44, 51, 54.

32. Thorough studies of the Pearl Harbor attack include Gordon Prang, Donald Goldstein, and Katherine Dillon, *Pearl Harbor: The Verdict of History* (New York: McGraw Hill, 1986) while the best source for the various Pearl Harbor studies remains the *Pearl Harbor Attack: Hearings before the Joint Committee on the Investigation of the Pearl Harbor Attack*, 39 vols. (Washington, DC: U.S. Government Printing Office, 1946).

33. Spector, *Eagle Against the Sun*, 149-151 and 153-155; Toll, *Pacific Crucible*, 228-231; Gregory J. W. Urwin, *Facing Fearful Odds, the Siege of Wake Island* (Lincoln: University of Nebraska Press, 2002), xvi, 194; Bill Sloan, *Given up for Dead: America's Heroic Stand at Wake Island* (New York: Bantam, 2003), 145-146; R. D. Heinl Jr., *The Defense of Wake* (Bennington, VT: Merriam Press, 2001; originally published Washington DC: Division of Public Information, U.S. Marine Corps, 1947), 87-90.

34. Pash, *Currents of War*, 223-226.

35. Louis Morton, *War in the Pacific: The Fall of the Philippines* (Washington, DC: US Government Printing Office, 1953), 23-29, 100, 130-144; Gerald Astor, *Crisis in the Pacific: The Battles for the Philippine Islands by the Men who Fought Them* (New York: Dell, 2002), 27, 38-41, 88, 92.

36. Donald J. Young, *The Battle of Bataan: A Complete History*, 2nd ed. (Jefferson, NC: McFarland and Co., 2009), 5; Astor, *Crisis in the Pacific*, 106-107; Kevin C. Murphy, *Inside the Bataan Death March: Defeat, Travail, and Memory* (Jefferson NC: McFarland and Co., 2014), 134-135; Spector, *Eagle Against the Sun*, 156-163.

37. Yenne, *The Imperial Japanese Army*, 51, 306; Peter Duus, et al., *The Japanese Wartime Empire, 1931-1945* (Princeton: Princeton University Press, 1996), xii-xxvii; Chihiro

Hosoya, "Retrogression in Foreign Policy," in *The Dilemmas of Growth in Prewar Japan*, ed. James William Morley (Princeton: Princeton University Press, 1971), 88–91.
38. Duus et al., *The Japanese Wartime Empire*, xxvii; Bruce F. Johnston, *Japanese Food Management in World War II* (Stanford: Stanford University Press, 1953), 108; Spector, *Eagle Against the Sun*, 465–468; Daniel B. Schirmer and Stephen Rosskamm Shalom, *The Philippines Reader: A History of Colonialism, Neocolonialism Dictatorship, and Resistance* (Boston South End Press, 1987), 69–70.

BIBLIOGRAPHY

Barnhart, Michael. *Japan and the World since 1868*. London: Edward Arnold, 1995.

Borg, Dorothy, and Shumpei Okamoto, eds. *Pearl Harbor as History: Japanese–American Relations, 1931–1941*. New York: Columbia University Press, 1973.

Feis, Herbert. *The Road to Pearl Harbor: The Coming of the War Between Japan and the United States*. New York: Atheneum, 1962.

Grehan, John, and Martin Mace. *Disaster in the Far East, 1940–1942: The Defense of Malaya, Japanese Capture of Hong Kong, and the Fall of Singapore*. Barnsley, UK: Pen and Sword, 2015.

LaFeber, Walter. *The Clash: Japanese–American Relations Throughout History*. New York: W.W. Norton, 1997.

Morley, James William, ed. *The Final Confrontation: Selected Translations from Taiheiyo senso e no michi: kaisen gaiko shi*. Translated by David A. Tutus. New York: Columbia University Press, 1994.

Pash, Sidney. *The Currents of War: A New History of Japanese–American Relations, 1899–1941*. Lexington: University Press of Kentucky, 2014.

Spector, Ronald H. *Eagle Against the Sun: The American War with Japan*. New York: Vintage Books, 1985.

Yenne, Bill. *The Imperial Japanese Army: The Invincible Years, 1941–1942*. Oxford, UK: Osprey Publishing, 2014.

CHAPTER 12

THE UNITED NATIONS AND THE GRAND ALLIANCE

DAVID B. WOOLNER

On January 1, 1942, less than a month after the devastating Japanese attack on Pearl Harbor, Franklin D. Roosevelt (FDR), Winston Churchill, and representatives from twenty-four other nations at war with one or more of the Axis powers gathered in the White House. They were there to sign a common pledge—what Franklin Roosevelt called a "Declaration by United Nations"—through which they agreed to adhere to the principles of the Atlantic Charter, to make no separate armistice or peace with the Axis, and to employ their full military and/or economic resources in the common struggle to see the Axis powers defeated.[1] The Declaration represented the first official use of the term "United Nations," a phrase coined by Franklin Roosevelt that would go on to become the official name of the Allied forces fighting the Axis and eventually the official name of the "United Nations Organization" that would draft the UN Charter and form the body known as the United Nations.

FDR's interest in creating an organization that would carry on the wartime cooperation that was vital to world peace was long-standing, and the need to create a grand coalition to defeat the forces of fascism and militarism in World War II provided the opportunity for FDR to work toward the creation of a new world body and to put his ideas into practice. This effort first manifested itself in January 1941 with FDR's call for a world founded on four fundamental human freedoms—freedom of speech and expression, freedom of worship, freedom from want, and freedom from fear. The quest for the Four Freedoms established a common set of values that would help inspire the generation locked in the struggle against the Axis that theirs was a fight for basic human rights, for all peoples—"everywhere in the world." These fundamental rights were further articulated eight months later in the Atlantic Charter, which was drawn up by Churchill and Roosevelt during their first wartime summit meeting off the coast of Newfoundland in August 1941. The charter signaled the rights of all peoples to choose the form of government under which they will live, and identified the need to secure improved labor standards, economic advancement, and social security for all. It also dedicated the

United States and its allies to what was referred to as a "permanent system of general security"—or to borrow a phrase that has now become commonplace—the creation of a new postwar international order, centered around the establishment of what would become the United Nations. It was the attainment of these goals that in essence became the war aims of the United States.[2]

There was another development during the fateful weeks that followed the Japanese attack on Pearl Harbor that was equally important to the defeat of the Axis and the establishment of world peace, however, and that was the creation of the "Grand Alliance." Technically speaking, the "Grand Alliance" and "United Nations" both refer to the association of nations that was brought together to defeat the Axis. But in practice the two appellations came to embody two separate, and at times, quite different, entities, with the Grand Alliance most often referring to the military coalition among Great Britain, the United States, and the Soviet Union, or the "Big Three," while the "United Nations" refers to the much broader affiliation of anti-Axis powers represented in the January 1, 1942 declaration. Viewed from this perspective, the two entities represented two separate wartime realities: the concentration and exercise of geo-political power among the Big Three—often guided by the precepts of national interest—versus a more expansive and inclusive interpretation of the exercise of power, based the concept of collective security and international cooperation. In this sense, the Grand Alliance and the United Nations also represent two separate visions for the future: the first placing a greater emphasis on the perpetuation of Great Power prerogatives; the second placing a greater emphasis on the democratization of power and the reduction—or repurposing—of those prerogatives.

Not surprisingly, it was Winston Churchill who came up with the phrase "Grand Alliance," in a conscious attempt to tie the Big Three's efforts to defeat the Axis with the alliance that would defeat Louis XIV in the 1701–1714 War of the Spanish Succession under the leadership of his ancestor, the First Duke of Marlborough. For Churchill, World War II was as much about restoring the glory of Great Britain and the British Empire as it was about the defeat of the Axis. And while the British prime minister certainly embraced FDR's Four Freedoms and helped craft the Atlantic Charter, with its call to "respect the right of all peoples to choose the form of government under which they will live," he did so with the clear understanding that the terms of the charter did not apply to the British Empire, but only to states currently occupied by the Germans. Joseph Stalin, the Soviet premier, interpreted the terms of the charter regarding self-determination in the same way, noting, as he said later, that the practical application of the charter "must necessarily adapt itself to the circumstances, needs, and historic peculiarities of particular countries."[3]

Nor was the United States immune from such equivocations. All three of the major powers, in fact, understood that the high principles articulated in the charter would not necessarily apply in all circumstances, but might have to be adapted to the changing conditions of the war. Roosevelt himself said as much, when he cautioned the American people in his last state of the union address not to forget that the Atlantic Charter does "not provide rules of easy application to each and every one of this war-torn world's tangled situations." FDR also assumed that the Big Three plus China would play a special role in maintaining world peace, what he sometimes referred to as the "trusteeship of the powerful" for the well-being of the less powerful. But, unlike his Russian and British counterparts, who viewed their Great Power status in more nationalistic terms, FDR saw the Atlantic Charter as a turning point; as the moment at which the United States, under his leadership, laid the foundation for the new postwar world order that was incompatible with British Imperialism and the closed socio-economic regime imposed on the Soviet Union.[4]

THE ARCADIA CONFERENCE

Both the Declaration by United Nations and the Grand Alliance came into being during the lengthy visit Winston Churchill made to the White House shortly after the Japanese attack on Pearl Harbor. Churchill arrived on December 22 and would remain in Washington—with the exception of a brief visit to Ottawa, Canada, and a short stay in Florida—until mid-January 1942. His sojourn at the White House marks the first of the many wartime planning conferences that would take place between Great Britain and the United States now that the Americans were fully in the war. Churchill's arrival also signaled the formal beginning of the Grand Alliance. Prior to this, a *de facto* alliance among the three powers had already emerged, made manifest through Roosevelt's initiation of secret staff talks among the American, British, and Canadian Chiefs of Staff in January 1941 (the ABC-1 Talks), followed by the establishment of the Lend Lease program in March—which would provide war materiel to both Great Britain and the Soviet Union before the year was out—and the Atlantic Charter Conference in August.

The U.S. entry into the war made this tacit alliance explicit, and at this first Washington Conference, also known by its code name, Arcadia, the Allies established the mechanism through which the Anglo–American alliance would operate: the Combined Chiefs of Staff (CCOS). Comprised of the soon-to-be constituted U.S. Joint Chiefs of Staff and the British Chiefs of Staff—and established in Washington at the insistence of FDR—the CCOS advised Churchill and Roosevelt on military strategy, and implemented the decisions taken by the two leaders. The conference also reaffirmed the Germany First strategy established during the ABC-1 talks and set up the ill-fated ABDA (American–British–Dutch–Australian) Command under General Archibald Wavell, which soon disintegrated as Singapore and the Dutch East Indies fell to Japanese forces. The British also proposed continuing their policy of closing the ring around Germany, through maximum aid to the USSR and through a possible invasion of North Africa, together with bombing, blockade, and subversion.[5]

These basic understandings on strategy would not last, however, as the tensions between the overall purposes of a war waged on behalf of the "Grand Alliance" versus a war waged on behalf of the "United Nations" began to emerge. One the first and most dramatic manifestations of the tensions between these two separate visions for the war can be seen in the ordering of signatories to the Declaration by United Nations. Both Churchill and Roosevelt—along with the Soviet and Chinese ambassadors to Washington—agreed that the first four powers listed for signature under the declaration should be the United States, China, the Union of Soviet Republics, and the United Kingdom of Great Britain and Northern Ireland—what FDR by this point was beginning to call "the Four Policemen." Thereafter, Churchill favored listing the four British dominions plus India under the United Kingdom, after which the remaining signatory nations would be listed in alphabetical order. But FDR found this so distasteful that he insisted—as illustrated by his edits to the initial hand written draft that the two leaders had drawn up —that the British Dominions and India should incorporated into the alphabetical list (see Figure 12.1).

It was FDR who also insisted that India should be added to the list as a separate nation, even though India was not an independent dominion like Australia or Canada. Listing India "boosted her constitutional status," as one Roosevelt administration official put it, which was in keeping with FDR's deep-seated antipathy for colonialism and determination that the war serve as a catalyst for change.[6] Like many of his colleagues in Washington—and a majority of the U.S. public—FDR had no intention of fighting a war to save the British or other European Empires. He was particularly hostile to the idea of a French return to Indochina, and on a number of occasions even informed Queen Wilhelmina of the Netherlands—whom he regarded as a special friend due to his Dutch ancestry—that she should grant self-government to the Dutch East Indies.[7] FDR understood that immediate independence for the European colonies would not necessarily be possible, as this might cause widespread disorder and conflict. But there can be no doubt as to his conviction that imperialism was a thing of the past. To facilitate its orderly demise, FDR favored the establishment of trusteeships, preferably international trusteeships under the auspices of the postwar United Nations Organization, whereby the orderly transfer of governmental responsibility would occur over a period of years, as was the case when his administration granted "commonwealth" status to the Philippines in 1934 with the promise of full independence in 1946.[8]

The differences over how to list the British dominions on the United Nations Declaration raises another important aspect of the war: the evolving relationship among the dominions and Great Britain under the auspices of the Grand Alliance, versus the changing nature of the bilateral relationship between the dominions and the United States under the auspices of the United Nations.

Given Great Britain's proximity to Europe, and the extent to which the United States carried out the war in the Pacific on its own, British involvement in World War II is most often remembered through its participation in the European conflagration. This is not to say, as Ashley Jackson points out in his seminal work, *The British Empire and the Second War*, that some of the war's important imperial landmarks—such as the Canadian forces raid on Dieppe in 1942, the fall of Singapore, or the imperial make-up of the "British" forces fighting in North Africa—are not recognized, but these events tend to be recalled in isolation or, as in the case of North Africa, viewed primarily as an extension of the European conflict.[9]

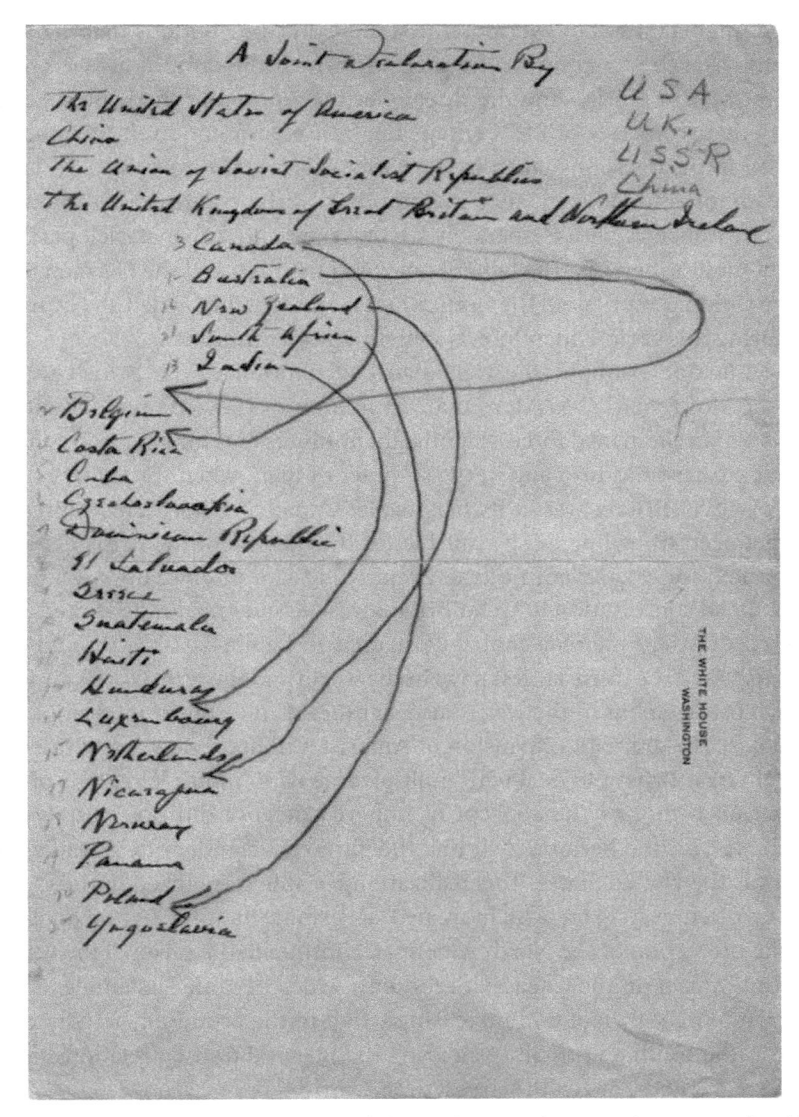

FIGURE 12.1 Draft of the signature page of the Declaration by United Nations edited by FDR. Courtesy of the FDR Presidential Library.

This parochial view belies the reality that existed at the time, however. Certainly, from the perspective of London—where Trafalgar Square is often referred to as "the Hub of Empire"—the war was a global struggle, involving not only imperial forces fighting alongside British Tommies, but also disparate British battles and strategic concerns that formed one part of an interconnected whole.[10] To a large extent, in fact, Great Britain's imperial responsibilities and imperial strategic vision determined where and how the British fought the war.[11]

It is also important not to overlook the significant contributions that the dominions made to the overall war effort or the extent to which the dominions viewed the outbreak of the war in Europe and the threat Germany posed to the United Kingdom as a threat to their own way of life. Perhaps the best manifestation of this phenomenon can be seen in the decisions taken in the various dominion capitals to declare war on Germany almost immediately after the outbreak of the conflict. The dominions also supplied Great Britain with desperately needed men and war materiel, particularly in the critical months between the fall of France in June 1940 and the German invasion of the Soviet Union a year later. The notion that Great Britain carried the burden of war "alone" during this period, therefore, is something of a misnomer.

To take but one example, the Canadian contribution to the British war effort is nothing short of remarkable. More than 1.5 million of Canada's population of twelve million served in the armed forces. Significant numbers of Canadian troops had arrived in Britain by Christmas 1939 and in the summer of 1940, when the threat of a German invasion of Great Britain was at its height, the Canadian First Army represented the largest organized front-line force available for the defense of the British Isles. Canada also accounted for one-seventh of the Empire and Commonwealth's war production and its financial contribution to Great Britain was second only to the United States and, in fact, exceeded the American contribution on a per capita basis. By the end of the war, Canada possessed the third-largest navy in the world and the fifth-largest air force.

Canada's involvement in the war is also significant in terms of its relations with the United States. The dramatic expansion of American military power and the increasing inability of Great Britain to deal with multiple threats in multiple regions of the world meant that even though the concept of imperial defense did not entirely disappear during the war, it soon became clear that the ultimate defender of Canadian territorial integrity was the United States. This realization became formalized in the Ogdensburg Agreement of August 1940, which created a Permanent Joint Board on Defense to oversee the protection of the North American continent. The onset of the war also had a significant impact on the Canadian economy, which became less and less dependent on trade with Great Britain and increasingly tied to the economic activity of its giant neighbor to the south, eventually rendering the bilateral trading relationship between the United States and Canada the largest in the world.[12]

The political ramifications of these changes are equally important. Thanks in part to the significance of its war effort, Canada was much more assertive than the other dominions in demanding a voice over the deployment of its forces. Canada's military and economic stature—which included involvement in the top-secret effort to develop the atomic bomb—also meant that, as the war progressed, the United States tended to see Canada as more of an independent entity rather than a self-governing extension of Great Britain. In recognition of this change, the two countries agreed in November 1943 to elevate the status of their legations to embassies and change the rank of their representatives from minister plenipotentiary to ambassador, rendering Leighton McCarthy, Canada's representative in Washington, the first Canadian ambassador to any country in the world.

To a certain extent, this pattern was repeated in the dominions of Australia and New Zealand. As was the case with Canada, both countries made significant contributions to the British war effort over the first two years of the conflict. Australian troops, for example, made up a significant portion of the British forces fighting in the Western Desert and other areas of the Middle East. New Zealand also supplied troops, and both countries remained a vital source of food, raw materials, and arms. At the start of the war, ninety-seven percent of New Zealand's food exports, for example, went to Great Britain.

But the expansion of the war to the Pacific in December 1941 also altered the economic and security relationship between the two Pacific dominions and Great Britain and the United States. On the one hand, the outbreak of the war in September 1939 and willingness of the Australia and New Zealand to support the British struggle against the Axis strengthened the bonds of Empire. On the other hand, the rapid advance of the Japanese in the spring of 1942 and inability of the British government to provide adequate security for Australia and New Zealand meant that this role was increasingly usurped by the United States. More than twenty thousand Americans service personnel were stationed in New Zealand between 1942 and 1945, and within six months of the Japanese assault on Pearl Harbor, Australia became the main American base for the war in the Far East. In the economic sphere, war in the Pacific dramatically expanded the level of trade between the two Dominions and the United States, as Washington—like London—began to look toward Australia and New Zealand as a significant source of supply for the war effort.

This same duality can be seen operating in other parts of the British Empire. Thanks in large part to the loss of Malaya and the fall of Singapore and Rangoon, India became the frontline in the British war against Japan, and as such, one of the most important staging areas of the war, along with Egypt. It was also the wellspring of the Indian army, an all-volunteer force which made up a significant portion of the multi-national Fourteenth Army, that would go on to fight the Japanese in Burma under the command of British General Sir William Slim. As was the case in other parts of the Empire, the onset of the war in the Pacific led to a significant expansion of India's military and economic capacity. Between 1941 and 1945, for example, India produced millions of dollars' worth of guns, ammunition, armored vehicles, aircraft supplies, and textiles that were dedicated to both the British and American war efforts. And the Fourteenth Army, which at the time represented the largest army in the world, would go on to kill more Japanese soldiers than any other Allied formation in the war. In this sense, the war enhanced India's stature and strengthened the military and economic ties between London and the sub-continent.[13]

But to Indian nationalists, the war provided a unique opportunity to press for independence, or at the very least a significant increase of their role in governing India. By 1939, Indian officials and members of the Indian Civil Service were already helping man the political structures of the Raj at all levels. This was in keeping with the Government of India Act that was passed by the British Parliament in 1935, which facilitated this expansion, and was designed to ultimately lead to India being granted full status as a dominion. Senior members of the most prominent Indian political party, the Indian National Congress, and other nationalists, remained dissatisfied with these arrangements, however, and once war broke out, leading members of the party insisted that they would only support the war effort if the British would agree to immediate independence. Two years of wrangling followed, highlighted by sporadic outbreaks of civil disobedience, and increasing harsh countermeasures by the British. These tensions would explode into a full-scale political crisis in the spring of 1942, when members of the Congress Party, and other nationalists, led by Mahatma Gandhi, renewed their demands for what Gandhi called "an orderly British withdrawal from India" at the very moment when a Japanese invasion of the country became a real possibility after the fall of Singapore and Rangoon. Unable or unwilling to meet this demand—in part because of the perilous situation that existed on the borders with Burma, and in part because of the intransigence of Winston Churchill—London instead offered immediate independence upon the cessation of hostilities. And when this offer was rejected, amidst much recrimination on all sides, Gandhi and the Congress Party decided to launch its "Quit India" movement. Furious at what Churchill and many of his contemporaries regarded as a betrayal, the British government in India used its emergency powers to suppress the nationalist movement, ban the Congress Party, and arrest its leadership—including Gandhi—for the duration of the war.[14]

The events in India provide yet another example of how the outbreak of World War II fundamentally altered the conditions of empire, and in in this case, signaled its demise. Taken together, the evolving conditions of the war in these far flung regions, coupled with the Roosevelt administration's determination to move the world away from the bonds of Empire and precepts of colonialism, helped lay the basis for the new, multilateral world that FDR sought via the Declaration by United Nations. As such, even though the war in many respects marks the highpoint of the British Empire, it also hastened its decline, as by 1945 Great Britain's financial and economic exhaustion made it impossible for the country to sustain it.[15]

THE UNITED NATIONS, THE GRAND ALLIANCE, AND THE SOVIET UNION

Many of the same dynamics that became manifest in the evolving relationship between Great Britain and the United States under the auspices of the Grand Alliance versus the United Nations were also present in the triangular relationship between London, Washington, and Moscow. Never one to accord ideology much weight, FDR tended to regard the Union of Soviet Socialist Republics (USSR) in the same way he viewed Russia, as a continental power largely devoid of colonial ambitions that was driven by the same fears and ambitions as Europe's other leading states. As such, FDR was never all that concerned about the spread of communism, or the messianic rhetoric found in Marxism. He regarded Nazism and Japanese militarism as far more dangerous, in part because they were being put forward by governments bent on world conquest, and in part because he remained convinced that the American people would never wholeheartedly embrace communism, a political and economic philosophy that was completely alien to American culture and experience. This is not to say that FDR had any illusions about Joseph Stalin or the nature of the Soviet regime. FDR fully understood that Stalin was an oppressive ruler and that his "dictatorship was as absolute as any other dictatorship in the world."[16] But Stalinist Russia, focused inward and more concerned about her external security than with spreading Bolshevik ideology, could also serve as a counterweight to both German and Japanese expansionism. Moreover, it could also serve as a counterweight to British imperialism, which, in so far as FDR was concerned, represented an even greater threat to his vision for the future than Russia's demands for the security of its border regions.[17]

It is for this reason that FDR made the decision—once it became clear that the Soviet Union would not only survive the German onslaught, but would emerge from the war, like the United States, as a superpower—to try to develop an independent relationship with Joseph Stalin. Here, his goal was to try to overcome Soviet suspicions of the outside world and draw it into the postwar system of peace and security FDR hoped to establish in the United Nations.

Churchill's relationship with the Soviet premier, on the other hand, was based more on the traditional prerogatives of Great Power diplomacy, and the British prime minister's desire to use his working relationship with Stalin to come to an understanding about British and Soviet "spheres of influence" in Southeastern Europe and the Eastern Mediterranean. As evidenced by Churchill's so-called percentages agreement with Stalin of October 1944—which granted the Soviet Union a ninety percent influence in Romania in exchange for Great Britain retaining a ninety percent influence in Greece—there was an element of *realpolitik* in these negotiations; a recognition that there was very little, if anything, the Anglo–Americans could do to prevent the Soviet Union from extending its power westward into Poland and other parts of Eastern Europe.[18]

Churchill was also much more of an anti-communist than Roosevelt, but like FDR, firmly believed—even as late as the Yalta Conference in February 1945—that Stalin was a man with whom the West "could do business." As he said to the House of Commons roughly two weeks after the close of the Yalta conference, "The impression he brought back from the Crimea is that Marshal Stalin and the Soviet leaders wish to live in honorable friendship and equality with the Western democracies." He was confident that Stalin would live up to his promises. Indeed, he knew "of no other government . . . which stands to its obligations more solidly than the Russian Soviet Government."[19]

In private, however, Churchill was less sure about the outcome of Yalta, and as it became more and more clear that the Soviets had no intention of even fashioning the pretense of democracy in Poland—which not only disturbed his sympathy for the Polish people, but also proved politically embarrassing to his standing at home—he began to pressure FDR to try to bring the Soviet dictator to heel. By this point, Churchill's own ability to pressure Stalin on these questions was severely limited by the precepts of the percentages agreement, and Churchill's reluctance to do anything that might jeopardize the understanding he had achieved with Stalin over Greece.

FDR certainly shared Churchill's disquiet about Poland in the weeks and months following Yalta, but he refused to allow the Polish question to stand in the way of his larger objectives, which included the establishment of the United Nations Organization and the maintenance of Great Power cooperation in the wake of the defeat of the Axis powers. Nor was FDR alone in thinking this way. The U.S. Joint Chiefs of Staff shared this view and even as late as April 2, 1945, continued to argue that "the maintenance of Allied unity . . . must remain the cardinal and over-riding objective of our politico-military policy with Russia." Indeed, the Chiefs even went so far as to insist that "the instances of Russian refusal to cooperate . . . while irritating and difficult to understand if considered as isolated events are of relatively minor moment." They would only assume real importance "if their occurrence should cause our government to adopt retaliatory measures in kind, and these in turn should be followed by further Russian measures, and thus lead to a break in Allied unity."[20]

As these comments make clear, like Churchill, FDR and his military advisors also harbored something of a *realpolitik* view of the Soviet Union. But unlike the British, their over-arching aim in trying to maintain the wartime cooperation of the Soviets stemmed more from a desire not just to maintain the peace and avoid another, even more cataclysmic war, but also from a desire to use this cooperation as a means to promote the American "United Nations" agenda for the postwar world.

This was especially true in FDR's case. Perhaps the best example of this can be found in the terms by which FDR tried to secure Soviet participation in the war against Japan in February 1945. Disappointed over China's ability to wage war against Japan, and cognizant of the fact that it was vitally important to minimize the ability of the Japanese to withdraw large numbers of troops from the Asian mainland to help defend the Home Island against the expected American invasion, FDR and his military chiefs viewed Russian participation in the Pacific war—which would prevent such a withdrawal—as critical. FDR also recognized that Soviet support in the war against Japan might also translate into Soviet support for Chang Kai-shek's Nationalist regime, and equally important, serve to bolster Washington's ability to contain Japanese power in the future—without recourse to the European colonial powers.

His private conversations with Stalin over the future of China and Korea during the Yalta conference make this eminently clear. Hence, in what could be described as a reversal of President Nixon's much-heralded overture to Beijing in the 1970s, FDR hoped to enlist Stalin's support in achieving the twin goals of building up a strong, unified, and reasonably democratic China, on the one hand, and eventually removing the European colonial regimes he found so antithetical to his democratic principles, on the other. In these conversations, FDR informed Stalin that there were certain "elements among the British, who, out of imperial considerations, desire a weak and disunited China in the post-war period." FDR secured Stalin's agreement to conclude a pact of friendship and alliance with the nationalist government of China and suggested that the United States, the Soviet Union, and China should manage the trusteeship of Korea. The president estimated that this would lead to full independence for Korea within a period of twenty-five to thirty years—a time frame significantly shorter that the fifty years first articulated in the Cairo Declaration of 1943. He also insisted that there should be no British participation in this effort, to which Stalin wryly responded by saying, "Churchill will kill us." FDR also made it clear that he fully expected to establish a trusteeship in Indochina and had no interest "in giving it back to the French" as preferred by the British, undoubtedly out of the latter's concern for the "implications" this might have for their control over Burma. FDR's frequent observation that France "had done nothing" to improve the lot of the native population indicates that he continued to view colonialism as a form of shameless exploitation. Moreover, even though FDR still insisted, although less strenuously, that he favored "international" as opposed to "national" trusteeships, his determination that "we must find a formula to resolve the relations between the White and Yellow races"—one that would ultimately lead to independence for peoples in the Far East—remained steadfast.[21]

FDR was well aware of the many challenges associated with attempting to cooperate with the Soviet Union, but as was the case in his decision to extend recognition the Bolshevik regime in November 1933, he hoped that Soviet–American cooperation in 1945 would serve as a counterweight to Japanese power in Asia—a goal that had taken on new importance given the relative weakness of China after seven long years of war. Moreover, there can be little doubt that FDR's forward-thinking geopolitical considerations in pursuit of Soviet–American cooperation had as much to do with his desire to counter British imperialism as with the need to maintain a strong front against Japan. Viewed from this perspective, his conversations with Stalin on the Far East at Yalta represent an effort to enlist Soviet support for his United Nations vision, and what were essentially American interests in the Pacific region after the war.[22]

THE UNITED NATIONS, THE GRAND ALLIANCE, AND LATIN AMERICA

Although Latin America remained relatively isolated from the fighting that took place in World War II, the global nature of the struggle rendered it impossible for the region not to be significantly influenced by the conflict. From a strategic perspective, the war heightened the importance of maintaining the security of the Panama Canal—an area of obvious concern to the United States—but also maintaining the security of such areas as the northeast corner of Brazil, which, due to its proximity to West Africa, was viewed as a potential bridgehead for Axis forces in the event that Nazis gained control of the French colonial possessions along the west coast of the African continent following the fall of France. The invasion of North Africa by Anglo–American forces in November 1942 brought the Axis threat to northeastern Brazil to an end, but the area remained important as an air transit hub for the ferrying of aircraft and other supplies to the Mediterranean, European, and Soviet theaters during the war. Because of the importance of maintaining the flow of goods and commodities from the New World to the Old, Latin America also played an important role in the Battle of the Atlantic, and, along with the Caribbean, served as the location of a number of important British and American naval facilities.

Of all the regions of the world, Latin America, particularly South America, perhaps represents the most dramatic example of how World War II facilitated American displacement of British influence and interests. Having developed strong economic and cultural links to such countries as Brazil, Chile, and Argentina, South America had long been regarded as part of what was called Great Britain's "informal empire." British capital had financed most of the major economic development projects in the region, and up until the outbreak of the war in September 1939, Great Britain remained the primary trading partner of most of the major states of the continent.

This not to say that the United States had little or no interest in the vast territory that lay south of its border. On the contrary, America's focus on the region and articulation of the Monroe Doctrine in 1823 made it quite clear that United States regarded the Western Hemisphere as an area falling under an American sphere of influence. But it is important to remember that the success of the Monroe Doctrine depended in large part on the acquiescence of the British Government and the presence of the Royal Navy. Hence, even though the United States may have felt it possessed a special prerogative to maintain the territorial status quo in Latin America, this did not stop the British from developing close financial and economic ties to the region—and considerable political sway along with it.

By the early twentieth century, however, direct U.S. intervention in the region became more pronounced. This was especially true in Central America, the Caribbean, and the northern reaches of South America. In addition to the construction of the Panama Canal—which included the creation of the U.S.-backed state of Panama in 1903—a number of other military incursions occurred in the first decades of the twentieth century. These, along with the exploitative polices of such corporations as the United Fruit Company, tarnished America's reputation.

In an effort to reverse this trend, Franklin Roosevelt committed his administration to what he termed "the Good Neighbor Policy." Through it, FDR and his secretary of state, Cordell Hull, signaled their intention to move away from the more heavy-handed and interventionist policies of the past and instead take an approach toward U.S.–Latin American relations that was based on mutual respect and international cooperation. The shift to the Good Neighbor Policy first became apparent at the Pan-American Conference of December 1933 in Montevideo, the capital of Uruguay. Here, under FDR's and Hull's leadership, the United States signed the Montevideo Convention on the Rights and Duties of States, which declared, "no state has the right to intervene in the internal or external affairs of another." The Good Neighbor Policy would also find expression in Cordell Hull's push for freer trade, which under the 1934 Reciprocal Trade Agreements Act would see trade agreements signed with nearly a dozen Latin American countries by the close of the 1930s.

Meanwhile, in the wake of Hitler's decision to rearm and repudiate the Versailles Treaty in March 1935 and the subsequent Italian invasion of Abyssinia in October, FDR and Hull added a new dimension to the Good Neighbor Policy—the preservation of peace and security in the Western Hemisphere. The result was the Inter-American Conference for the Maintenance of Peace held in Buenos Aires in December 1936, specifically called by FDR "to determine how the peace of the American Republics may best be safe guarded." The 1936 conference, which FDR addressed as part of his "Good Neighbor Cruise" of Latin America in the fall of that year, committed the Latin American republics to consult with one another whenever the peace of the Western Hemisphere was threatened.

As the international situation continued to deteriorate in Europe and Asia, further Pan-American gatherings were held in Lima, in 1938, where the Latin American Republics agreed to resist "all foreign intervention or activity," and in Panama in 1939, as well as Havana in 1940. In Panama, the Latin American Republics agreed to adhere to the three hundred mile "Neutrality Zone" established by FDR in response to the outbreak of war; while at Havana, just weeks after the conquest of the Netherlands and the fall of France, the American states agreed to the "no transfer" principle, by which it was understood that there should be no change in sovereignty or transfer of territory anywhere in the Western Hemisphere as a result of the European war.

Following the U.S. entry into the war, the cooperation that had been established between the United States and the Latin American republics under the Good Neighbor Policy continued. No less than nine of the original twenty-six nations that signed the United Nations Declaration on January 1, 1942 came from Latin America, and by 1945, all had done so, including Argentina, which, despite pressure from Washington, had remained neutral for most of the war.

The Good Neighbor Policy vastly improved U.S.-Latin American relations, and coupled with the strong relationship that the Roosevelt administration established with Canada, was held up by the Roosevelt administration as an example international cooperation among sovereign states that stood in sharp contrast to the aggressive foreign policies of Italy, Germany, and Japan in the prewar years. It was FDR's hope that this example might help avert the onset of World War II, and although this was not the case, the principles established in the Good Neighbor Policy provided FDR with a model for how his United Nations vision might work. In keeping with these principles, the Good Neighbor Policy would find new life in the establishment of the Organization of American States in 1948, which continues to foster neighborly relations among the nations of the Western Hemisphere to this day.

In sharp contrast with Washington's largely successful expansion of U.S. political, economic, and strategic influence in the region in the 1930s and 1940s, British relations with Latin America underwent a precipitous decline during the course of the war. Part of this was due to the vast increase in U.S. military and economic power that naturally occurred as a result of the conflict, but much of it also came about as a direct result of U.S. wartime foreign economic policy. The cash and carry provisions of 1939 Neutrality Act, for example, not only brought British investment in the region to an abrupt halt, but also made it necessary for the British government to sell off most of its overseas assets, including its significant holdings in Latin America. Moreover, even though Winston Churchill referred to the establishment of Lend Lease as "the most unsordid act" in an address at the Mansion House in London in the fall of 1941, in practice the United States used its policy of wartime aid to Britain not only as a means to try to force London to abandon the Ottawa System of Imperial Preference—where, under the terms of the Mutual Aid Agreement negotiated in the wake of Lend Lease, the United States demanded its demise—but also as a means to limit British gold and dollar reserves.[23] The net effect of this use of Lend Lease—which was driven largely by FDR's Treasury Secretary, Henry Morgenthau Jr., and the parochial, anti-British sentiment of many members of the U.S. Congress—was a severe curtailment in British trade with Latin America. American business interests quickly took advantage of this development. By 1945, Great Britain took only twelve percent of South America's exports, and provided a mere four percent of its imports.[24] Viewed in this light, the pursuit of FDR's United Nations vision, which included the promotion of freer trade, can also be seen—particularly in the case of Central and South America—as an extension of U.S. national interests.

The Grand Alliance and the Establishment of the United Nations Organization

While the war continued to rage in the months after Pearl Harbor, officials within the U.S. State Department under the leadership of Secretary of State, Cordell Hull, and Under Secretary of State, Sumner Welles, quietly carried out work on the crafting of a new international organization—which by mid-1943 FDR was referring to privately as the United Nations Organization.

These initial efforts—which included significant conversations with officials in the British Foreign Office and consultation with the Kremlin—came to a head in October 1943 at the Moscow Conference of Foreign Ministers, where Hull, the British foreign secretary Anthony Eden, the Soviet foreign minister Vyacheslav Molotov, and the Chinese ambassador to Russia Foo Ping-sheung, issued a document called the Four Power Declaration. Here, all four parties agreed on the necessity of "establishing at the earliest possible date a general international organization, based on the principle of the sovereign equality of all peace-loving states, and open to membership by all such states, large and small, for the maintenance of international peace and security." As the *New York Times* reported at the time, the Moscow Declaration represented the "first formal undertaking by the United Nations 'Big Four' that they would work together not only in war but in peace" and this was widely heralded in the *Times* and elsewhere as major step toward the creation of a new international organization.

Following the successful conclusion of the Moscow Conference, FDR, Churchill, and Stalin met at Tehran, where FDR further elaborated on his vision for the postwar organization, including his concept that the "Four Policemen"—the United States, Britain, China, and the USSR—must play a leading role in such a body. It was also at Teheran where FDR first sketched out his vision for the United Nations on a simple piece of paper. Here we can see the outlines of the basic structure of the new organization with the forty nation states of the General Assembly focused primarily on "freedom from want," through worker rights (represented by the ILO or International Labor Organization), health, agriculture, and food. In the center we see the organization's Executive administration, or secretariat, and to the right the Security Council, where, as indicated by the circle on the right, the world's four—and later five—"policemen," Britain, France, the United States, China, and Russia would work together to maintain global peace (see Figure 12.2).

The understandings achieved at Tehran cleared the way for the 1944 Dumbarton Oaks conference where the details of the new organization were negotiated among the Big Four; followed by the Yalta conference, where the twin issues of the number of Soviet seats in the General Assembly and the question of the veto powers among the five permanent members of the Security Council were resolved. Having achieved these understandings, the members of the United Nations coalition gathered in San Francisco in April 1945 to craft the final language of the United Nations Charter.

For most observers, the creation of the United Nations—along with the establishment of the World Bank and International Monetary Fund—mark the start of what we refer

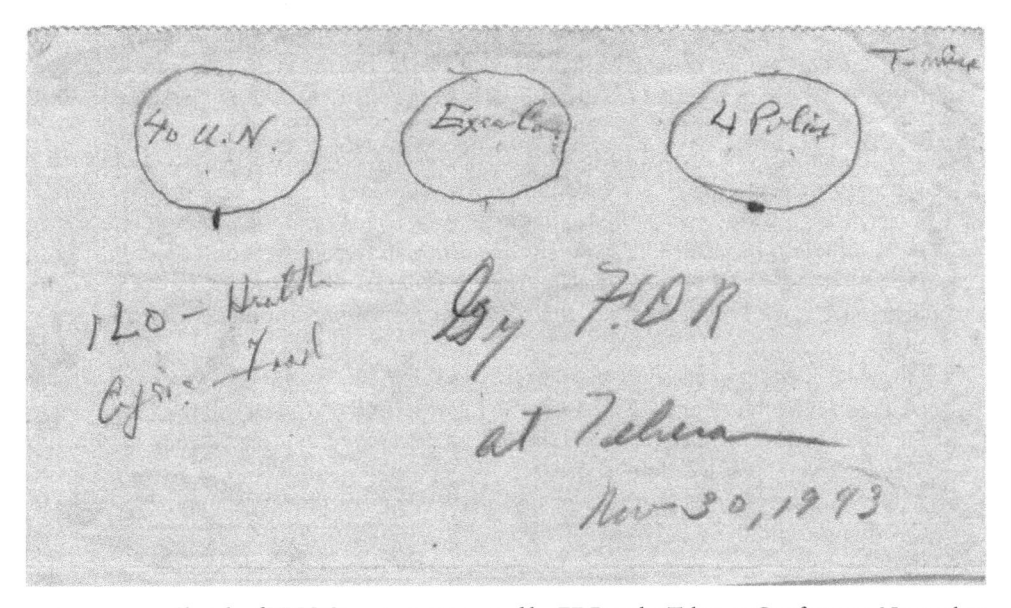

FIGURE 12.2 Sketch of UNO Structure as penned by FDR at the Teheran Conference, November 30, 1943. Courtesy of the FDR Presidential Library.

to as the multilateral postwar order. The emergence of this postwar structure also marks the beginning of the globalization of the world's economy. And while it is certainly true that the United States benefited enormously from these developments, it is also important to remember that FDR's determination to reject unilateralism and embrace freer trade and the free movement of capital stemmed from an equally strong desire to move the world away from imperialism and the destructive tenets of economic nationalism that helped precipitate the Great Depression and the concomitant rise of fascism in the 1930s. Viewed from this perspective FDR's efforts to use the war as a means to set the world on a more prosperous and peaceful path proved successful. Yet it is also true that many of the impulses behind the creation the Grand Alliance have survived—particularly in the Western world, where the close transatlantic security ties that developed between Great Britain and the United States during the war have re-emerged in the form of the NATO alliance after the war. In this sense, it seems reasonable to argue that the world we live in today is very much a reflection of the attempts to reconcile tensions between these two formidable institutions: the Grand Alliance and the United Nations.

Notes

1. Declaration by United Nations, January 1, 1942, Grace Tully Papers, Box 6, FDR Library, Hyde Park, New York.
2. David B. Woolner, "FDR and the Creation of the Postwar International Order," in *American Mosaic, Festschrift in Honor of Cornelis A. van Minnen*, ed. William E. Leuchtenburg (Amsterdam: VU University Press, 2017), 34–35.
3. Warren F. Kimball, *Forged in War: Roosevelt, Churchill and the Second World War* (New York: William and Morrow, 1997), 100; Townsend Hoopes and Douglas Brinkley, *FDR and the Creation of the U.N.* (New Haven: Yale University Press, 1997), 40.
4. David B. Woolner, *The Last 100 Days: FDR at War and at Peace* (New York: Basic Books, 2017), 14–15.
5. The Joint Chiefs of Staff, which replaced the Army Navy Board, were established in February 1942, a few weeks following the Arcadia Conference. For more, see Mark A. Stoler, *Allies and Adversaries: The Joint Chiefs of Staff, the Grand Alliance, and U.S. Strategy in World War II* (Chapel Hill: University of North Carolina Press, 2000), 64–65.
6. David Bercuson and Holger Herwig, *One Christmas in Washington: The Secret Meeting Between Churchill and Roosevelt that Changed the World* (Toronto: McArthur & Co., 2005), 219–220.
7. Lloyd Gardner, "FDR and the Colonial Question," in *FDR's World: War, Peace and Legacies*, ed. David B. Woolner, et al. (New York: Palgrave Macmillan, 2008), 127–128.
8. Fredrik Logevall, *Embers of War: The Fall of an Empire and the Making of America's Vietnam* (New York: Random House, 2013), 47–48.
9. Ashley Jackson, *The British Empire and the Second World War* (London: Hambledon Continuum, 2006), 1.
10. Ibid.
11. Ibid., 5.
12. This remains true today.

13. I. C. B. Dear, *The Oxford Companion to World War II* (Oxford: Oxford University Press, 2000), 557–564; Tarak Barkawi, *Soldiers of Empire: Indian and British Armies in World War II* (Cambridge: Cambridge University Press, 2017), 192–226; Jackson, *The British Empire*, 2
14. Dear, *The Oxford Companion to World War II*, 557–564.
15. Jackson, *The British Empire*, 21–22.
16. Franklin Roosevelt Address to the American Youth Congress, February 10, 1940, Master Speech File, Box 50, FDR Presidential Library, Hyde Park, NY.
17. Woolner, *The Last 100 Days*, 137.
18. Under the terms of the percentages agreement, which came in the form of a note that Churchill passed across the table to Stalin, the prime minister proposed that the Soviets would retain ninety percent influence in Romania and that Great Britain would hold the same figure for Greece. The two powers would split Hungary and Yugoslavia fity–fifty, while the Russians would retain a seventy-five percent influence—and Great Britain a twenty-five percent interest—in Bulgaria (Woolner, *The Last 100 Days*, 51).
19. David Reynolds, *From World War to Cold War: Churchill, Roosevelt, and the International History of the 1940s* (New York: Oxford University Press, 2006), 240; Churchill to the House of Commons, February 19, 1945, in Robert Rhodes James, ed. *Winston Churchill: His Complete Speeches*, Vol. VII (New York: Chelsea House, 1974).
20. Woolner, *The Last 100 Days*, 204.
21. Foreign Relations of the United States, Diplomatic Papers, *The Conferences at Malta and Yalta, 1945* (Washington: US Government Printing Office, 1955), 770, 984.
22. Yalta Briefing Papers, Political Memoranda for the Yalta Conference, February 1945, The Far East, Harry Hopkins Papers, Group 24, Containers 169–171, FDR Library; Woolner, *The Last 100 Days*, 119.
23. Randall B. Woods, *A Changing of the Guard: Anglo–American Relations 1941–1946* (Chapel Hill: University of North Carolina Press, 1990), 93–100. Here we should that the United States did not hold the USSR to same standard—a fact which drove the British to distraction and which places the competitive nature of the Anglo-American relationship in a clear light.
24. Jackson, *The British Empire*, 94.

Bibliography

Barkawi, Tarak. *Soldiers of Empire: Indian and British Armies in World War II*. Cambridge: Cambridge University Press, 2017.

Dallek, Robert. *Franklin Roosevelt and American Foreign Policy, 1932–1945*. New York: Oxford University Press, 1995.

Gardner, Lloyd C. "FDR and the Colonial Question." In *FDR's World: War, Peace and Legacies*, edited by David B. Woolner, et. al. New York: Palgrave Macmillan, 2008.

Gardner, Lloyd C. *Spheres of Influence: The Great Powers Partition of Europe from Munich to Yalta*. Chicago: Ivan R. Dee, 1993.

Gilbert, Martin. *Winston S. Churchill: Road to Victory, 1941–1945*. Boston: Houghton Mifflin, 1986.

Hoopes, Townsend, and Douglas Brinkley. *FDR and the Creation of the U.N.* New Haven: Yale University Press, 1997).

Jackson, Ashley. *The British Empire and the Second World War*. London: Hambledon Continuum, 2006.

Kimball, Warren F. *Forged in War: Roosevelt, Churchill and the Second World War*. New York: William and Morrow, 1997.

Kimball, Warren F. *The Juggler: Franklin Roosevelt as Wartime Statesman*. Princeton: Princeton University Press, 1991.

Logevall, Fredrik. *Embers of War: The Fall of an Empire and the Making of America's Vietnam*. New York: Random House, 2013.

Louis, William Roger. *Imperialism at Bay*. Oxford: Oxford University Press, 1986.

Packwood, Allen. *How Churchill Waged War: The Most Challenging Decisions of the Second World War*. Philadelphia: Frontline Books, 2018.

Reynolds, David. *From World War to Cold War: Churchill, Roosevelt, and the International History of the 1940s*. New York: Oxford University Press, 2006.

Reynolds, David, and Vladimir Pechatnov. *The Kremlin Letters: Stalin's Wartime Correspondence with Churchill and Roosevelt*. New Haven: Yale University Press, 2018.

Schlesinger, Stephen C. *Act of Creation: The Founding of the United Nations*. Boulder: Westview Press, 2003.

Stoler, Mark A. *Allies and Adversaries: The Joint Chiefs of Staff, the Grand Alliance, and U.S. Strategy in World War II*. Chapel Hill: University of North Carolina Press, 2000.

Woods, Randall B. *A Changing of the Guard: Anglo-American Relations 1941–1946*. Chapel Hill: University of North Carolina Press, 1990.

Woolner, David B. *The Last 100 Days: FDR at War and at Peace*. New York: Basic Books, 2017.

Woolner, David B., Warren F. Kimball, and David Reynolds, eds. *FDR's World: War Peace and Legacies*. New York: Palgrave Macmillan, 2008.

CHAPTER 13

THE AIR WAR: GERMANY AND ITALY

M. HOUSTON JOHNSON V

Air power did not win World War II. Despite cataclysmic predictions from Giulio Douhet, H. G. Wells, and others that in future conflicts waves of bombers would paralyze industrial economies and undermine nations' morale, airpower advocates' greatest hopes—and fears—did not come to pass. Instead, aviation played a supporting role in overall strategy; success in the air represented a necessary, although not sufficient, condition to achieve victory. As the war progressed, military and civilian leaders came to understand that virtually all their assumptions regarding military aviation were either obsolete or inaccurate, while aviators struggled to adapt to wartime conditions. The rapid pace of technological development further complicated matters, creating a fluid environment calling for flexibility, adaptability, and vision.

Nowhere were these conditions more apparent than in Europe. Germany relied on tactical air power in its invasions of Poland, France, and the Low Countries. After the fall of France, combat between Britain and Germany took place almost exclusively in the skies. Fighting in the Mediterranean and North Africa similarly demonstrated each side's commitment to air power. First the Germans and then the Soviets used tactical air power to great effect over the vast Eastern front. Most significantly, strategic bombing dominated the air war over Germany and Italy.

British and American air power advocates led the way in developing bombing doctrine during the interwar era, viewing strategic attacks as a way to demonstrate air forces' value while promoting those forces' autonomy from other service branches. Allied efforts never proved capable of ending the war alone, but they served as the focal point of British and American efforts in the West for four years and played an important role in setting the stage for both the Normandy invasion and eventual victory. More ambiguously, the bomber offensive raised unsettling questions about the morality of modern conflict. British night area bombing, and Americans' de facto embrace of its daylight equivalent by 1944, resulted in hundreds of thousands of civilian deaths. While strategic bombing hindered the German war effort, the majority of the deaths bombing caused did little to aid Allied victory, underscoring the difficulties weighing the ethics and efficacy of Allied air strategy.

Background Conditions

As World War II loomed, issues including air forces' command structures, the tactics and strategy each embraced, technological development, and aircraft production capabilities suggested the outlines of the conflict to come. The central question each nation addressed was whether air forces merited independence, or if they should be placed within the command structure of another branch—fundamentally, whether ground commanders should have operational control over air units.

In Britain and the United States, air advocates argued that suborning air forces to ground commanders hamstrung the former by limiting their operational flexibility. Advocates argued that operational independence provided air leaders the freedom to decide whether to use their forces directly in support of ground troops, or to engage the enemy behind the battle line. In both countries advocates embraced strategic bombing, sharply distinguishing their goals from those of the other combatant powers. A focus on strategic attacks expanded air forces' purview far beyond the battlefront and offered powerful evidence supporting autonomy. The Royal Air Force (RAF) achieved that goal, winning its independence even before the end of World War I. U.S. air forces remained within the Army command structure until 1947, although a reorganization in 1941 granted the newly renamed Army Air Forces (USAAF) greater freedom. In both countries, air advocates successfully freed military aviation from army operational control, enabling greater flexibility and vision in the coming war.

In Germany and the Soviet Union, air forces remained subservient to ground commanders. The *Luftwaffe* achieved independence in 1935, although with leadership largely comprised of army officers. The *Luftwaffe*'s conservative commanders viewed tactical support for ground forces as the service's primary role, particularly as blitzkrieg doctrine matured. Similarly, Soviet leaders viewed aircraft as tactical tools, leading the Red Air Force to organize largely along close support lines. Neither country established a strategic bombing doctrine, which had significant implications for both forces' capabilities and technological development.

Organizational and command structures influenced tactics and strategy. In Germany, the *Luftwaffe*'s focus on close air support reflected the service's de facto subservience to the *Wehrmacht* and the latter's commitment to fast, armored attack. The *Luftwaffe* developed dive-bombers, heavy attack fighters, and medium bombers to serve those ends. Those aircraft provided able service in early *Blitzkrieg* attacks, but sharply limited German air strategy as the war progressed. The Soviet Air Force exhibited analogous limitations, but the nature of war on the Eastern front, particularly in its earlier defensive phases, generally played to the Soviets' strengths. In Britain and the United States, air force leaders embraced a less-restrictive operational framework. Air leaders worked to free their tactical and strategic planning from Army oversight. This granted leaders greater operational flexibility and promoted the development of a greater range of aircraft types. Four-engine, heavy bombers offer the best example, planes that would play a key role in the aerial offensives to come.

The path of the European air war also reflected the dynamic technological context shaping military aviation during the 1930s, an era that witnessed the revolutionary transition from biplane to monoplane designs. All the combatant nations embraced this change, but did so at different times, with significant implications for wartime capabilities. France, for instance, embarked upon an ambitious building program in the early 1930s, creating arguably the world's most capable contemporary air force. Unfortunately, the French saw their biplanes become obsolete in only a few years as other nations perfected new monoplane designs. Germany, in contrast, began the transition in the late 1930s; by the eve of war, the *Luftwaffe* fielded a fleet of advanced fighters and bombers. The British and Soviet revolutions fell approximately a year behind the German, and the United States followed shortly thereafter. As a result, Germany possessed the most technologically advanced air force in the world in 1939, but the Allies were poised to regain the advantage during the critical 1940–1942 period.

Success in the air war also depended on nations' ability to produce aircraft in sufficient quantities to gain and hold control of the skies. In this respect, Germany fell short. The German leadership, most notably Herman Goring, consistently underestimated Allied production figures and overestimated German production capabilities. As a result, Germany entered the war with only a thin production advantage over the British— 8,295 versus 7,940 in 1939—an advantage that disappeared quickly as the British ramped up production and the Germans lost large numbers of aircraft in their continental offensives and the Battle of Britain.[1] *Luftwaffe* leadership continued to underestimate aircraft needs until at least 1944 as Germany's combat commitments expanded, resulting in an almost constant shortage of combat-ready planes. With Soviet and later American entry into the war the Germans fell hopelessly behind, a condition exacerbated by Goering's unwillingness to admit his mistakes to Hitler.

THE EARLY WAR IN THE WEST

The German invasion of Poland on September 1, 1939, offered military leaders their first opportunity to assess the nature of contemporary air combat. The German *Blitzkrieg* attack benefitted from a concentrated *Luftwaffe* campaign that quickly won air superiority and provided valuable close air support to German ground forces. While the quick German victory appeared to confirm the *Luftwaffe*'s strength and the quality of German strategy and tactics, on closer inspection the Polish campaign suggested several looming problems for German air forces. First, the *Luftwaffe* leadership concluded its existing aircraft were adequate for future offensives. Contemporary German fighters like the Messerschmitt Bf-109 were equal or superior to contemporary Allied aircraft, but the reliance on slow and vulnerable dive-bombers like the Junkers JU-87 Stuka and the lack of a long-range heavy bomber hamstrung German efforts moving forward. Second, the *Luftwaffe* High Command saw little need to increase production quotas, even in the face of almost eighteen percent losses in Poland.[2] British production had already surpassed Germany's in the fall of 1939, and more difficult air battles ahead would demonstrate the egregious short-sightedness of this conclusion.

German actions in France in the spring of 1940 confirmed the existing pattern. The *Luftwaffe* again achieved a convincing victory, although German forces were fortunate to face a French Air Force suffering from poor leadership and tactics, inferior aircraft, and low morale. British forces fought ably, but they struggled to come to terms with the new reality of air war. Many British aircraft deployed to France—most notably the infamous Fairley Battle—were unable to cope against advanced German fighters. Even modern designs like the Hawker Hurricane suffered from fitment with antiquated, wooden, fixed-pitch propellers that sharply limited their performance. British tactics, too, failed to measure up to the German exemplar. British fighters flew in three-plane "vic" formations, limiting their operational flexibility. German fighter pilots, in contrast, utilized the "finger-four" formation, with two sets of wingmen providing mutual support. RAF commanders and pilots worked to redress the shortcomings, but those gains came too late for the Battle of France.

Unfortunately for the *Luftwaffe*, success in France reinforced the dangerous lessons of the Polish campaign. Despite losing more than thirty-five percent of their forces, the High Command saw no need to expand the *Luftwaffe*'s size, increase production targets, or develop new aircraft types. Overconfident from his successes, Goering went so far as to mandate that all work stop on projects without short-term benefit to the war effort. This stalled work on jet engine development that might have played a crucial role during the Allied bombing offensive in coming years.[3]

German oversights quickly became apparent as the fighting moved beyond its continental origins. During the Battle of Britain, the *Luftwaffe*'s lack of a long-range, single-engine fighter and a four-engine, heavy bomber hamstrung the German offensive. Whereas the Germans had been able to dictate the terms of battle in Poland and France, they found themselves struggling to mount a long-distance air campaign against British forces that could rely on radar, new fighters like the Supermarine Spitfire, ever-increasing production numbers, and the luxury of fighting over its own territory. German frontline strength had declined by almost one-half since the beginning of the Battle of France, and commanders were forced into a disadvantageous battle of attrition.

THE EASTERN FRONT

The war in the East encompassed Germany's greatest aerial triumphs during World War II, but ultimately broke the power of the *Luftwaffe*. Paralleling the *Wehrmacht*'s progress on the ground, the *Luftwaffe* achieved tremendous victories in the summer and fall of

1941, but found itself undermined by poor leadership at the highest levels, an inability to maintain operational readiness in the harsh local conditions, and an ever-growing numerical disadvantage in the skies. The Soviets, in contrast, rebounded from disastrous early engagements to perfect new organizational structures, strategies, and tactics that, combined with new aircraft designs, impressive production figures, Lend Lease aid, and creative logistical and maintenance solutions, gave the Red Air Force a decisive edge by the latter stages of the war.

German preparations for war against the Soviet Union reflected the lessons drawn from the previous two years of fighting. The *Luftwaffe* achieved great success supporting ground offensives across the continent, while struggling with the strategic offensive against Britain. Goering and the *Luftwaffe* High Command thus focused preparations on using their forces to support the armored ground offensive. Hitler, too, had become convinced that the *Luftwaffe* could only achieve decisive results when working in close concert with ground commanders, forestalling any calls to reevaluate German strategy.[4] As Operation Barbarossa began, the *Luftwaffe* focused on destroying Soviet aircraft and winning air superiority over the battlefield. As they had over Poland and France, German pilots achieved tremendous early success. On the first day of fighting, the *Luftwaffe* destroyed 1,811 Soviet aircraft while losing only thirty-two of their own. By early October the Soviets had lost more than five thousand aircraft—more than the total *Luftwaffe* force at the onset of the offensive.[5]

German leaders embraced several key, erroneous assumptions about the opposition. First, Goering and the High Command dramatically underestimated Soviet production capabilities. German intelligence estimated Soviet production at five thousand planes annually, when it fact it was double that number and growing rapidly.[6] German production remained at pre-war levels through 1942, a situation that combined with logistical problems to leave the *Luftwaffe* dangerously short of planes and parts. Second, *Luftwaffe* leaders exhibited a lack of foresight regarding their strategic goals, eschewing plans to interdict Soviet supply lines or to engage in ongoing attacks behind enemy lines. Finally, German leaders dismissed the quality of Soviet forces. While obsolete aircraft dominated Red Air Force squadrons in the summer of 1941, the Soviets were in the midst of a dramatic transition to more modern designs. German victories in the summer and fall of 1941 had the effect of speeding this transition—particularly because thousands of Soviet aircraft were destroyed on the ground, leaving their pilots alive to continue fighting. By 1942, the majority of Soviet frontline aircraft were at least close to parity with their German counterparts, while Soviet numerical superiority continued to increase. These conditions augured well for the Soviets moving forward, a fact the Germans began to digest in the spring of 1942.

Red Air Force doctrine reflected Stalin's overriding influence. Like the rest of the Soviet military, the Air Force suffered from the late-1930s purges, though in the Air Force's case that damage was mitigated by the emergence of a talented group of aircraft designers who would flourish during the war, and Stalin's desire that the Air Force assume a narrow, close support role. These limited objectives simplified Soviet tactics and strategy, particularly following a reorganization effort in the winter of 1941–1942.

Moving forward, air army commanders served directly under army group commanders at the front, facilitating tactical integration and air-ground coordination; the Soviets also expanded the Air Force command structure to serve that goal. Both air and ground commanders, moreover, agreed on the need for operational flexibility, particularly to build up forces in preparation for major offensives and speed the transfer of aircraft to critical areas of the front. This flexibility and adaptability combined with ever increasing numerical superiority over the *Luftwaffe* to give the Red Air Force key advantages as the war progressed.[7]

The Red Air Force also distinguished itself by allowing women to fly combat missions, a role closed to them in all other combatant nations. Beginning in October of 1941, the Soviets deployed three all-female air regiments—one each of fighters, bombers, and night bombers. These units were particularly noteworthy, as women—all volunteers—commanded the units, chose and trained the ground personnel, and served with distinction in a variety of combat air roles. Between their activation in early 1942 and the end of the war, these women flew more than thirty thousand combat missions and more than thirty achieved the status of Hero of the Soviet Union.[8]

Throughout the war, Soviet forces benefited from superior logistics and maintenance, particularly during the harsh Russian winters. Soviet aircraft were less complicated to build and easier to maintain than their German counterparts; the Soviets also designed aircraft and support vehicles for use on rough terrain and during severe weather conditions. The cold proved a dangerous enemy for German forces. With aircraft often standing in the open in temperatures that could drop to −50 degrees Fahrenheit, German mechanics sometimes resorted to building fires under their planes' engines to get them started. *Luftwaffe* leaders undermined their forces by failing to provide air units with adequate cold weather equipment, sufficient spare parts, and engineering aid to improve airfields. Admittedly, some of these difficulties reflected the logistical challenges faced by all German forces. The combination of rain and unimproved roads made supplying both the *Wehrmacht* and *Luftwaffe* a nightmare during the summer months, while the winter cold affected trucks and drivers just as it did planes and pilots. Regardless, for the duration of the war, only about fifteen percent of *Luftwaffe* vehicles were operational at any given time, a crushing disadvantage for a force already suffering numerical shortcomings.[9]

By the spring of 1943 the outcome of the air war was no longer in doubt. During the winter of 1942–1943 the Red Air Force completed its reorganization efforts while continuing to introduce new, modern aircraft designs. Soviet leadership agreed that all frontline aircraft should be equipped with radios, a key development moving forward. The Soviets also solidified their numerical superiority. In 1942, Germany produced 15,409 aircraft for use in all fronts. The Soviets produced 25,240 for the eastern front alone, in addition to lend-lease aid, which totaled more than twenty-five thousand aircraft by the war's end.[10]

The combination of new aircraft, streamlined command structure, and numerical superiority proved decisive. By the time German forces at Stalingrad surrendered, the

Red Air Force was in a position to dictate the terms of battle. German planes could still win air superiority over a battlefield, as they did during the first day of the offensive at Kursk, but such victories were temporary exceptions to the larger rule. From the spring of 1943 until the end of the war the *Luftwaffe* found itself playing an ever-narrower close support role, desperately trying to stem the Soviet advance. Outnumbered more than four-to-one, unable to mount offensives against airfields or supply columns in the Soviet rear, and unable to prevent Red Air Force aircraft from dominating the skies during Soviet offensives, German pilots fought a losing battle against the Russian advance.

The Mediterranean

The Mediterranean theater, often overshadowed by the campaigns in Western Europe and the Soviet Union, served as an important crucible for British and American air forces. Facing both Italian and German opposition in Malta, Sicily, Italy, and North Africa, the Allies developed close air support doctrine, laying the groundwork for key aspects of the air offensive against Germany.

The Italian Air Force exhibited inconsistent quality as the war began. During the 1930s, the Regia Aeronautica served as a preeminent example of Mussolini's modernist vision for Italy. By the onset of World War II, however, the majority of Italian aircraft were obsolete. As the war progressed, Italy steadily introduced new, more modern monoplane fighters, although they suffered from Italy's failure to produce a sufficiently powerful engine like the Rolls-Royce Merlin, and from inferior armament. Inadequate production numbers, low serviceability rates, and inconsistent leadership also undermined the Regia Aeronautica's fighting ability.

For the British and Americans, fighting in the Mediterranean provided the opportunity to develop a general air strategy and perfect tactics that would underlie operations in Western Europe following the D-Day invasion. British leaders entered the fighting without any method to coordinate the activities of air and ground units, a startling oversight in the wake of German combined-arms success in Poland, France, and the Low Countries. After Pearl Harbor, U.S. commanders too grappled with these issues as they contemplated their invasion of North Africa. The Mediterranean presented the Allies with a unique opportunity to overcome these obstacles in a theater of subordinate importance for the Germans.

The first challenge facing Allied air forces was the need to formulate a general air strategy—a strategy for coordinating the use of strategic and tactical assets to support offensive and defensive action. The British led this effort, passing their lessons on to the Americans in modified form as the war progressed. Central to British air strategy was the realization of the necessity of establishing and maintaining air superiority over the battlefield. Aircraft could not "hold" territory in the same way that ground forces did;

maintaining air superiority necessitated an ongoing commitment to deploying aircraft over the battlefront. To accomplish this goal, British strategy focused on creating command structures allowing for the flexible utilization of air units, communication between air and ground commanders, and the balanced use of fighter, fighter-bomber, and bomber aircraft in tactical and strategic roles.

The British placed a central air headquarters in charge of air forces. The headquarters worked closely with ground commanders, but it remained independent of ground commanders' chain of command. This structure promoted cooperation while allowing air commanders freedom to deploy their forces across the front as they saw fit. At times this resulted in fewer British aircraft appearing over the battlefront in favor of interdiction raids on supply lines, airfields, and other targets behind the front lines, targets often overlooked by ground commanders concerned with immediate engagements with the enemy. As British strategy matured, it encompassed a multifaceted approach to air warfare including offensive fighter sweeps to maintain air superiority or attack enemy airfields close to the front, almost continuous armed reconnaissance patrols over the battlefront to establish as complete a view of the front as possible and deny such a view to the enemy, close air support sorties in direct support of ground operations, and bomber attacks behind the battle line focusing on communications, supplies, and airfields.[11]

U.S. forces embraced a broadly similar system, organized around Tactical Air Commands (TACs), which supported an Army but maintained an independent chain of command. As they gained experience, U.S. commanders diverged from British practice, often displaying a more flexible approach that facilitated greater coordination between ground and air units. American forces perfected the use of forward air controllers (FACs) in Italy, whereby a light aircraft would orbit over the battlefront to direct accurate and timely air attacks on enemy troops and armor. U.S. forces also assigned FACs to ride in radio-equipped tanks during armored assaults to maximize the value of close support strikes.[12]

By the eve of the Normandy invasion, both the U.S. and Britain had made significant strides. The USAAF's publication of *Field Manual 100-20* in July 1943 highlighted those lessons. Clearly establishing that "land power and air power are coequal interdependent forces," the *Manual* emphasized, "the gaining of air superiority is the first requirement for the success of a major land operation . . . control of available air power must be centralized and command must be exercised through the air force commander."[13] These dictates would guide Allied strategy over France and Germany following the Normandy invasion with great success, although tactical aviation often remained in the shadow of the strategic offensive.

Allied commitment of air units to the Mediterranean also bled German units from other theaters. Hitler withdrew key German air units from the Eastern Front in the fall of 1941 to meet the British challenge in Sicily, and maintained significant German air strength in the Mediterranean theater even as the *Luftwaffe* suffered tremendous losses in the Eastern front in 1942 and 1943. This diffusion of German strength aided both the Soviets and Western allies and hindered a *Luftwaffe* already short of aircraft.

Strategic Bombing

Strategic bombing represents the most widely explored and most controversial aspect of the European air war. British and American strategic attacks formed a centerpiece of Allied actions against Germany from the fall of France until the D-Day invasion. After June 1944, the Allies expanded their bombing campaign in an effort to weaken the Nazi regime. The origins of Allied doctrine trace to the interwar period, when both British and American air power advocates argued that strategic bombing had the potential to achieve victory independent of ground forces; these arguments informed Allied efforts for the duration of the conflict and, at least in the United States, formed the focal point of support for the creation of an independent air force. Allied bombing resulted in hundreds of thousands of civilian deaths across Europe, in addition to tremendous material destruction. The morality of bombing—or lack thereof—must stand at the center of any discussion of the Allied campaigns; likewise, any discussion of strategic attacks must interrogate the extent to which Allied bombing materially aided the war effort.

In the years between the world wars, British and American air power advocates embraced strategic bombing as the centerpiece of their doctrinal focus. Wary of committing ground troops to a continental conflict in the aftermath of World War I, British bombing supporters argued that long-range air attacks would allow their forces to project power without recourse to a large standing army. Hugh Trenchard, Chief of the Air Staff from 1919 until 1930 and Britain's most vocal advocate for strategic bombing, argued that a properly formulated campaign against key military and economic targets would disrupt enemy infrastructure, reducing the war-making capacity of that nation and undermining the enemy's ability to respond in kind. More importantly, bombing would undermine enemy morale, throwing society into chaos and, ideally, undermining the enemy government. By the eve of World War II, British doctrine facilitated the creation of the semi-autonomous RAF Bomber Command, though many challenges remained. The RAF had no systematic method for identifying and prioritizing targets and no tactical guidelines governing how bombers should assemble and proceed to their targets, while RAF crews consistently struggled with navigation and target acquisition.[14]

American bombing advocates emphasized using pinpoint attacks to undermine an enemy's economy and obviate the need for ground battles. Unlike the RAF, American air forces were part of the Army command structure during the interwar period. Air power advocates chafed at this subservience and struggled to define a role for aviation that would justify status as an independent service. General William "Billy" Mitchell led the effort to create American doctrine, arguing that scientifically applied air power could revolutionize conflict and remove the need for traditional ground offensives. Mitchell's outspoken advocacy for air power eventually resulted in his court martial and banishment, but his ideas motivated a small but significant group of like-minded officers who carried forward Mitchell's vision in the 1930s through the Air Corps

Tactical School. The Tactical School refined strategic doctrine through the creation of "industrial web theory," which suggested that pinpoint attacks on critical intersections of an enemy's industrial web—targets like transportation infrastructure, gas and oil, and communications—could undermine the war effort and crush civilian morale in the process. With growing support from figures like General George C. Marshall and President Roosevelt and new technologies like the Boeing B-17 "Flying Fortress" heavy bomber and Norden bombsight, the U.S. Army Air Service entered World War II ready to prove strategic bombing's value.[15]

German leaders, in contrast, largely eschewed a focus on strategic attacks. The German experience in the Spanish Civil War appeared to support these conclusions, as strategic attacks had not been decisive in the way that air power advocates had forecast. Although Hitler and Goering did intend the *Luftwaffe* to have strategic capability, the High Command's lukewarm support for long-range bombing scuttled any large-scale program like those engendered by Britain and the United States. Ironically, German leaders' lack of interest in bombing also blinded them to the need for concentrated air defenses, an oversight they would struggle to overcome for the duration of the war.[16]

Early Allied bombing efforts left much to be desired. As the war began, the British remained steadfast in the belief that unrestricted bombing attacks—particularly those that intentionally targeted civilians—were barbaric. German attacks on British cities during the Blitz furthered that belief. Within the year, however, British bombers engaged in similar attacks on German cities, and eventually expanded those efforts to encompass a wide-ranging area bombing campaign.

The British transition from daylight attacks on military targets to nighttime area bombing reflected Bomber Command's operational limitations. In 1940, the RAF had neither the hardware nor the personnel capable of mounting pinpoint daylight raids. The British were developing heavily armed four-engine bombers like the Short Sterling, Handley-Page Halifax, and Avro Lancaster, but these designs would not appear in numbers until 1942. Early in the war Bomber Command relied on two-engine designs like the Vickers Wellington and Handley-Page Hampton, aircraft that lacked the bomb load and defensive armaments to mount worthwhile daylight attacks.

Those weaknesses became readily apparent in early raids; in one representative example German air defenses destroyed fifteen of twenty-four Wellingtons attacking submarine pens at Wilhelmshaven.[17] Bomber Command responded by turning to nighttime raids, although its crews lacked the necessary skills to find their targets, not to mention attack them successfully. These weaknesses came to light following the publication of a Statistical Section bombing survey in August of 1941. The so-called Butt Report related that only one-in-five bombers on an assigned mission flew within five miles of the intended target; on moonless or hazy nights that proportion dropped to one-in-fifteen.[18]

Recognizing the need to address these shortcomings, the British engaged in a thorough overhaul of their bomber force during the next year. A change in leadership precipitated these developments; in February 1942, Sir Arthur Harris assumed leadership of Bomber Command. A passionate proponent of strategic attacks, "bomber"

Harris threw his full support behind expanding the campaign against Germany. By 1942, new heavy bombers dramatically increased British forces' combat radius and payloads. Scientists also perfected new electronic navigation systems to help guide bombers to their target cities. Additionally, Bomber Command instituted a policy of prefacing the main bomber stream with "pathfinder" aircraft. These light bombers, crewed with expert pilots and navigators, flew ahead of the attacking force and dropped small incendiary bomb loads to mark the target for their compatriots. These advances significantly increased the results achieved by Bomber Command while fostering momentum for area bombing, a startling reversal of opinion from eighteen months prior.

The U.S. contribution to the bombing offensive began in 1942 as the Eighth Air Force deployed to Britain. American strategy reflected the overriding influence of the Air Corps Tactical School, focusing on daylight strategic attacks against vital economic centers. Army Air Force leaders hoped that a concentrated air offensive, in concert with British attacks, would bring Germany to its knees and—hopefully—obviate the need for a Continental invasion. Eighth Air Force commander Ira Eaker began operations slowly. American bombers first flew in anger on July 4, 1942 and did not attack a target in Germany until January of 1943.

As operations accelerated, U.S. forces struggled with myriad obstacles. The buildup of Allied forces in North Africa, the Mediterranean, and the Pacific stripped crewmen and planes from the Eighth Air Force. American pilots and bombardiers struggled to find targets, and they displayed disappointing bombing accuracy. The weather proved tremendously frustrating, sharply limiting missions and hindering accurate bombing. More worryingly, U.S. bombers suffered distressing losses, particularly when attacking targets without fighter escort. By early 1943, Eighth Air Force bombers were averaging an eight percent loss rate, an unacceptable pace when considering a twenty-five-mission tour. Leaders like Curtis LeMay attempted to address these issues by perfecting new combat formations and instituting a system whereby the most experienced pilots and bombardiers would lead missions; the lead bomber would aim for the bomber group, which would drop its bombs when the lead plane did. These efforts bore limited fruit, but U.S. bombers continued to struggle with both accuracy and losses as the *Luftwaffe* expanded its air defenses.[19]

Through the middle of 1943, Allied attacks achieved only token results. The formalization of Allied cooperation in the Combined Bomber Offensive—first discussed at the Casablanca Conference in January of 1943 and implemented the following June—signaled the expanding intent of the RAF and USAAF but did little to change conditions in the skies over the Continent. British and American bombing efforts did assist the Soviets on the Eastern front, giving weight to U.S. and British promises to aid the USSR during the critical years of fighting in the east. The ever-increasing pace of Allied attacks also forced the *Luftwaffe* to commit escalating resources to the west.[20]

As Allied attacks increased, the Germans engaged in a concomitant expansion of their air defense network, although they did so reactively. The German leadership invested heavily in anti-aircraft guns—deploying almost thirteen thousand around industrial zones by June of 1940—but lacked similar airborne resources.[21] Until 1943, the Germans stationed only two fighter squadrons in the west, although these pilots acquitted themselves well against British fighter sweeps and daylight bombing raids. As the British transitioned to nighttime attacks and American forces expanded their efforts, *Luftwaffe* leaders were forced to respond. In March 1941, General Hubert Weise united control over Germany's air defense regions and established a dedicated night-fighter organization that integrated control over radar instillations, searchlight batteries, anti-aircraft artillery, and night fighters. The British responded with new tactics, including dropping "window"—small metal strips designed to reflect radar energy and cloud the scopes of the German radars— but German defenses held their own and occasionally won air superiority until the middle of 1944.[22]

The *Luftwaffe* also increased their daytime air defenses; from the initial two squadrons, fighter forces in the west grew to more than sixteen hundred aircraft by the beginning of 1944. German pilots learned to attack American bombers head-on to take advantage of the B-17s and B-24s lack of forward-facing defensive guns—although later versions of both bombers redressed this shortcoming. German fighters also deployed rockets and aerial mortars that allowed them to remain outside the range of American guns while lobbing fire into the bomber formations. German advances devastated the Eighth Air Force, resulting in a temporary bombing halt in 1943.[23]

By the spring of 1944, the Allies regained the advantage, one they would hold for the remainder of the war. Allied success emerged from a series of key changes. In the closing months of 1943, P-51 Mustang fighters began arriving in Britain, for the first time offering U.S. forces a fighter that could escort bombers all the way to Berlin and equal or better the German opposition. Deployed in significant numbers by early 1944, the Mustang changed the balance of power in the air war. That same January, Carl Spaatz succeeded Ira Eaker as commanding general of U.S. strategic air forces in Europe. Spaatz benefited from Eaker's work and a new influx of bombers and crews, immediately expanding the scope and pace of U.S. raids. Spaatz brought with him General James "Jimmy" Doolittle, who took control of the Eighth Air Force and enacted widespread changes to prevailing tactics and strategy. Most significantly, Doolittle allowed U.S. fighters to pursue the German opposition beyond the immediate vicinity of the bomber stream, which dramatically increased kill totals and inflicted lasting damage to the *Luftwaffe*.[24]

Early 1944 also witnessed a dramatic increase in U.S. and British attacks, culminating in the "Big Week" attacks of late February. Between the 19th and the 25th, U.S. forces flew thirty-eight hundred bomber sorties and dropped almost ten thousand tons of bombs— more than during the entire first year of operations. Combined with aggressive fighter escort, the attacks devastated the *Luftwaffe*. The Germans lost 2,121 planes in February, and a further 2,115 in March.[25] Although it is too simplistic to suggest the Big Week defeated the *Luftwaffe*, the offensive highlighted the effects that new fighters, new leadership, and new tactics had on the air war. Big Week combined with Spaatz and Doolittle's commitment to counterforce attacks against German fighters and ever-increasing U.S. aircraft production to spell the end of *Luftwaffe* air superiority. U.S. raids on the German aircraft industry also bore fruit, and although German reorganization of that industry led to increasing production numbers by the summer of 1944, the *Luftwaffe* was never able to regain air superiority.

Big Week and its aftermath also opened the door for the Normandy invasion, as Eisenhower and his commanders viewed Allied air superiority as a necessary precondition for the attack. Ironically for U.S. air power advocates, the *Luftwaffe*'s defeat resulted not from pinpoint attacks against the industry itself, but rather from using heavy bombers to lure German fighters into the open where long-range escort fighters could dispatch them.[26]

For the remainder of the war, the Allied forces enjoyed air superiority, using their dominance to bludgeon German targets with strategic attacks and dispatch fighter-bombers on tactical strike missions across Europe. Between May and September 1944 Eisenhower assumed direct control over all air forces, using strategic as well as tactical aircraft to support the D-day invasion. Between the reactivation of the combined bombing offensive in the middle of September and the end of conflict, U.S. and British bombers engaged in by far the heaviest attacks of the war, dropping three quarters of the total European wartime bomb tonnage. Spaatz and his commanders focused their attacks on transportation and, increasingly, oil. The latter proved particularly damaging to the Germans; during 1944 Allied attacks reduced German oil production by approximately three quarters.[27]

During the same period tactical aircraft expanded their activities in both close-support and armed reconnaissance roles. American and British commanders built on the lessons learned during the Mediterranean and North African campaigns, using air superiority to support ground troops, attack German transportation infrastructure and airfields behind the battle line, and engage in roving patrols designed to destroy trucks, troop concentrations, and other targets of military value. The effect was to dramatically hinder German forces' mobility while undermining morale.[28]

American and British commanders hoped that the expanded bombing campaign would bring Germany to its knees. Spaatz, in particular, focused on increasing the weight of U.S. attacks, even at the expense of accuracy. While U.S. bombers had at times engaged in de facto area bombing since 1942—often using British radio guidance systems to attack targets obscured by clouds—in the closing stages of the war Spaatz demonstrated a willingness to trade accuracy for speed and destructive power. U.S. commanders remained committed to precision attacks whenever possible, but the desire to achieve victory through airpower created a willingness to compromise those principles in practice.[29]

During the offensive, Allied aircrew experienced their own challenges and terrors in the skies over Europe. Both British and American strategic forces suffered combat-related causalities totaling more than fifty percent of their respective aircrew strengths. The Allies lost more than eighteen thousand aircraft; approximately eighty-one thousand crewmen lost their lives. Cold temperatures, low visibly, fog and clouds, and high winds resulted in a significant number of non-combat crashes—Bomber Command, for instance, suffered 2,681 accidents in 1943 and 1944 alone. Crewmen also had to face hours aloft in unpressurized, freezing conditions, wind howling past open windows.

Flight times for missions to German targets frequently exceeded ten hours, and crewmen had to endure that time in temperatures that could approach −60 degrees Fahrenheit. Over enemy territory, Allied aircrews faced fighters and flack, which, particularly during the early years of the war, resulted in devastating loss rates. Fighter pilots dealt with similar conditions, lacking the camaraderie of bomber crews, but with more freedom to control their own fate against enemy fighters and with the ability to maneuver to avoid flack. Despite these challenges, Allied crewmen exhibited remarkably good morale for the duration of the war. The volunteer forces performed their duties consistently and well, generally displaying bravery, competence, and pride in their accomplishments.[30]

When surveying the Allied bombing efforts, questions of morality and effectiveness stand at the center of any analysis. While estimates vary considerably, British and American attacks killed at least 350,000 Germans, most of them civilians.[31] Allied bombs destroyed cultural landmarks like the monastery at Monte Cassino, ravaged infrastructure in German cities, and displaced—"de-housed" in British parlance—millions of Germans and Italians. These effects raise serious questions about the morality of Allied actions, particularly when measuring those effects against the military gains bombing achieved.

The question of intention is central any such debate. In this respect, significant differences emerge between British leaders and their American counterparts. Although the British entered the war frightened by the specter of "terror bombing," the Blitz and their inability to launch successful daylight raids quickly pushed Bomber Command to embrace nighttime area bombing. Arthur Harris led this charge and, for the duration of the war, remained an ardent supporter of "morale bombing" designed to disrupt and demoralize the German population by targeting population centers. Harris and his supporters saw civilians as legitimate targets, in so far as they believed that undermining civilian morale offered a path to victory.[32]

American commanders did not intentionally target civilians. Pre-war American doctrine emphasized strategic air power's ability to aid victory with minimal loss of life. That doctrine guided early U.S. efforts in Europe, but as the war progressed a combination of weather-related difficulties, mounting evidence of German crimes, and pressure to maximize results conspired to push American Commanders to embrace—or at least tacitly approve—de-facto area attacks. American commanders, however, remained uncomfortable with the implications of doing so, and consistently stove to emphasize the military nature of U.S. attacks. Even when Roosevelt and Eisenhower pressured their commanders to launch a "death blow" against Berlin in early 1945, Spaatz and Doolittle diligently worked to identify military targets in the city and avoid haphazard attacks on the civilian population.[33]

Both British and American actions must be understood in the context of the larger war effort. The Allied commitment to unconditional surrender highlighted the necessity of prosecuting the war to the bitter end. For men like Arthur Harris, undermining German morale represented a legitimate and potentially productive strategy. The American expansion of the strategic air war following the Normandy invasion also derived from leaders' desire to end the conflict as quickly as possible. It seems clear that few, if any, Allied air leaders sought to kill Germans purely out of hatred. In the end, the Allied bombing campaign against Germany expanded the definition of total war and embraced actions that would have been almost unthinkable only a few years before. While specific attacks—Dresden serving as the most visible example—were reprehensible, it is difficult to conclude that either the British or Americans engaged in a fundamentally immoral program. U.S. attacks on Japan, however, offer a caveat to that statement. The expansion of the European air war opened the door for American commanders like Curtis LeMay to engage in systematic attacks against the Japanese civilian population and, ultimately, atomic warfare. Those actions are harder to defend and owed their origins to changing perceptions of moral acceptability originating in the skies over Germany.[34]

Questions of morality aside, strategic bombing did contribute to Allied victory in substantial ways. Although neither British nor American attacks had a significant effect on German war-making capability until 1944, in the final year of the conflict strategic attacks severely damaged German industry, transportation, resource production, and military forces. British contributions are more difficult to assess than their American counterparts. British area bombing disrupted Germans' lives through property destruction, population dispersal, lost productivity, and damage to transportation infrastructure. These effects, however, paled in comparison to the damage wrought by U.S. daylight attacks. Perhaps more importantly, British attacks forced the *Luftwaffe* to respond by pouring resources into air defense networks, night fighters, and anti-aircraft artillery.[35]

The American bombing campaign took longer to mature than its British counterpart, but ultimately bore more fruit. Most significantly, the U.S. offensive destroyed the *Luftwaffe* as an effective fighting force and won air superiority over Europe. Allied air superiority made possible the Normandy invasion, and it granted Allied ground and air forces tremendous advantages during the final year of war. Control of the skies opened the door for an aggressive tactical aviation campaign that supported Allied ground operations, destroyed German armor, troops, and transport vehicles, interdicted supply routes behind the battle line, and undermined the morale of German soldiers and pilots alike. U.S. attacks also disrupted German transportation infrastructure and manufacturing. Although German industrial production increased steadily until the middle of 1944, U.S. bombing forced its dispersal, which, combined with ongoing attacks to transportation infrastructure, capped German production and made it difficult for the *Wehrmacht* and *Luftwaffe* to deploy men and material. Even more damaging were American attacks on German oil supplies and refining capacity. Spaatz's aggressive targeting of petroleum resources choked off German access to fuel by the fall of 1944, limiting both air and ground forces' effectiveness. By 1945, *Luftwaffe* commanders found themselves forced to use teams of draft animals to tow aircraft to takeoff positions, such was the shortage of aviation fuel. Although U.S. strategic attacks failed to end the war on their own, the aerial offensive ultimately did much to validate Air Corps Tactical School strategy, particularly aspects of the industrial web theory.[36]

Allied bombing also forced Hitler to transfer *Luftwaffe* forces from the East at crucial points in the campaign against the Soviet Union. In early 1943 the *Luftwaffe* deployed approximately forty-three percent of its fighters in the west; by October of 1944 that number had risen to eighty-one percent. This played a key role in Germany's loss of air superiority on the eastern front. The increasing resources needed to counter the Allied bombing campaign also stripped finances, manpower, industrial capacity, and resources from other aspects of the war effort. By 1944, German industry was producing four thousand new anti-aircraft guns a month, while anti-aircraft weapons consumed one-fifth of German's total ammunition production. Fully one-half of the German electronics industry focused on anti-aircraft production, and almost nine hundred thousand Germans labored in the anti-aircraft service. These massive commitments stripped capabilities from other sectors, limited research and development on new weapons systems—jet aircraft and strategic bombers among others—and severely constrained German efforts to optimize resource allocation. Fundamentally, U.S. and British embrace of a general air strategy denied Germany the same opportunity, paving the way for Allied air superiority and the resulting benefits for Allied forces on the ground and aloft.[37]

Conclusion

In an October 1945 press conference, the Vice-Chairman of the U.S. Strategic Bombing Survey (USSBS), Henry Alexander, summarized the group's findings, concluding that "Allied air power was decisive in the war in Europe."[38] The USSBS certainly had an interest in highlighting aviation's, particularly strategic bombing's, contribution to Allied victory. Alexander's conclusions, nonetheless, stand up to scrutiny. Although air power did not prove transformative in the way many pre-war thinkers envisioned, strategic and tactical air forces played a critical role in the defeat of Germany. Most significantly, the British and American embrace of a general air strategy undermined the German war effort, aided the Soviet cause, and made possible the Allied invasion of western Europe in the spring of 1944. Although the *Luftwaffe*'s early successes in Poland, France, and the Soviet Union appeared to demonstrate the strength of Germany's air forces, in fact the limited, tactical nature of those operations signaled the *Luftwaffe*'s failure to adopt a sufficiently broad strategy. As the Soviets blunted the German advance in the east and the western Allies ramped up their strategic offensives, German leaders found themselves forced into a reactive position, without the freedom and resources necessary to redress their shortcomings. By 1944, the *Luftwaffe* lost air superiority in both theaters with devastating consequences.

Airpower's decisive contributions to victory, however, in no way suggest that air forces won the war. While air superiority and its associated benefits formed a necessary precondition for victory in World War II, it was not sufficient for success. The total nature of World War II required combatants to apply the full weight of their industrial economies and use those resources in the air, on the ground, and at sea. All did so, but with sharp differences in emphasis. The British and Americans distinguished themselves by embracing air power as one of the primary instruments for winning the war. Both adopted a general air strategy, granted their air forces' status co-equal—or close to co-equal—status with ground- and sea-based forces, and provided their air commanders the freedom to develop and apply strategies and tactics adequate to the wartime challenges their forces faced. Combined with Allied superiority in research and development and greater industrial capacity, the result was an Allied triumph in the skies over Europe, and a significant aid to overall victory.

Notes

1. Richard Overy, *The Air War, 1939-1945* (Washington, DC: Potomac Books, 2005), 21.
2. Walter J. Boyne, *Clash of Wings: World War II in the Air* (New York: Simon & Schuster, 1994), 40-41.
3. Ibid., 54.
4. Overy, *The Air War*, 47.
5. Boyne, *Clash of Wings*, 143-145.
6. Overy, *The Air War*, 49.
7. Ibid., 53-54. See also Von Hardesty and Ilya Grinberg, *Red Phoenix Rising: The Soviet Air Force in World War II* (Lawrence: The University Press of Kansas, 2012).
8. See Reina Pennington, *Wings, Women, and War: Soviet Women in World War II Combat* (Lawrence, Kansas: The University Press of Kansas, 2001).
9. Boyer, *Clash of Wings*, 149.
10. Ibid., 161; Overy, *The Air War*, 56.
11. Ian Gooderson, *Air Power at the Battlefront: Allied Close Air Support in Europe, 1943-45* (Portland, OR: Frank Cass, 1998), 22-24; Overy, *The Air War*, 67.
12. Ibid., 40-53.
13. *United States Army Air Force Field Manual 100-20*, quoted in Boyne, *Clash of Wings*, 188.
14. Tami Davis Biddle, *Rhetoric and Reality in Air Warfare: The Evolution of British and American Ideas About Strategic Bombing, 1914-1945* (Princeton, NJ: Princeton University Press, 2002), 69-127.
15. Ibid., 128-175; Mark Clodfelter, *Beneficial Bombing: The Progressive Foundations of American Air Power, 1917-1945* (Lincoln: University of Nebraska Press, 2010), 7-102.
16. Overy, *The Air War*, 13.
17. Boyne, *Clash of Wings*, 289.
18. Richard Overy, *The Bombers and the Bombed: The Allied Air War Over Europe, 1940-1945* (New York: Viking, 2013), 68.
19. Clodfelter, *Beneficial Bombing*, 103-147; Biddle, *Rhetoric and Reality in Air Warfare*, 203-208; Boyne, *Clash of Wings*, 303-307.
20. Boyne, *Clash of Wings*, 314.
21. Overy, *The Bombers and the Bombed*, 51.
22. Ibid., 77-79; Boyne, *Clash of Wings*, 296-302.
23. Overy, *The Air War*, 76-81; Boyne, *Clash of Wings*, 314-315.
24. Overy, *The Bombers and the Bombed*, 171-185.

25. Boyne, *Clash of Wings*, 336–338.
26. Overy, *The Bombers and the Bombed*, 182–194; Boyne, *Clash of Wings*, 335–338.
27. Overy, *The Bombers and the Bombed*, 194–195.
28. Gooderson, *Air Power at the Battlefront*, 57–226.
29. Clodfelter, *Beneficial Bombing*, 148–183; Conrad Crane, *Bombs, Cities, & Civilians: American Airpower Strategy in World War II* (Lawrence: University Press of Kansas, 1993), 105–120.
30. See Mark K. Wells, *Courage and Air Warfare: The Allied Aircrew Experience in the Second World War* (London: Frank Cass, 1995) and John C. McManus, *Deadly Sky: The American Combat Airman in World War II* (Novato, CA: Presidio Press, 2002).
31. Overy, *The Bombers and the Bombed*, 304–307.
32. Biddle, *Rhetoric and Reality in Air Warfare*, 289–292.
33. Crane, *Bombs, Cities, and Civilians*, 105–119; Ronald Schaffer, *Wings of Judgment: American Bombing in World War I* (New York: Oxford University Press, 1985), 80–106.
34. Biddle, *Rhetoric and Reality in Air Warfare*, 289–301; Crane, *Bombs, Cities and Civilians*, 93–142; Schaffer, *Wings of Judgment*, 80–189.
35. Overy, *The Bombers and the Bombed*, 217–230.
36. Biddle, *Rhetoric and Reality in Air Warfare*, 270–288; Overy, *The Bombers and the Bombed*, 217–230.
37. Overy, *The Bombers and the Bombed*, 217–230; Overy, *The Air War*, 82–84; Biddle, *Rhetoric and Reality in Air Warfare*, 286–288.
38. Quoted in Biddle, *Rhetoric and Reality in Air Warfare*, 273–274.

Bibliography

Beck, Earl R. *Under the Bombs: The German Home Front, 1942–1945*. Lexington: University Press of Kentucky, 1986.

Biddle, Tami Davis. *Rhetoric and Reality in Air Warfare: The Evolution of British and American Ideas About Strategic Bombing, 1914–1945*. Princeton, NJ: Princeton University Press, 2002.

Boyne, Walter J. *Clash of Wings: World War II in the Air*. New York: Simon & Schuster, 1994.

Clodfelter, Mark. *Beneficial Bombing: The Progressive Foundations of American Air Power, 1917–1945*. Lincoln: University of Nebraska Press, 2010.

Corum, James S. *The Luftwaffe: Creating the Operational Air War, 1918–1940*. Lawrence: University Press of Kansas, 1997.

Crane, Conrad. *Bombs, Cities, & Civilians: American Airpower Strategy in World War II*. Lawrence: University Press of Kansas, 1993.

Fredrich, Jörg. *The Fire: The Bombing of Germany, 1940–1945*. New York: Columbia University Press, 2006.

Gooderson, Ian. *Air Power at the Battlefront: Allied Close Air Support in Europe, 1943–45*. Portland, OR: Frank Cass, 1998.

Hardesty, Von, and Grinberg, Ilya. *Red Phoenix Rising: The Soviet Air Force in World War II*. Lawrence: University Press of Kansas, 2012.

McManus, John C. *Deadly Sky: The American Combat Airman in World War II*. Novato, CA: Presidio Press, 2000

Overy, Richard. *The Air War, 1939–1945*. Washington, DC: Potomac Books, 2005.

Overy, Richard. *The Bombers and the Bombed: The Allied Air War Over Europe, 1940–1945.* New York: Viking, 2013.

Pennington, Reina. *Wings, Women, and War: Soviet Women in World War II Combat.* Lawrence: University Press of Kansas, 2001.

Schaffer, Ronald. *Wings of Judgment: American Bombing in World War II.* New York: Oxford University Press, 1985.

Sherry, Michael S. *The Rise of American Air Power: The Creation of Armageddon.* New Haven, CT: Yale University Press, 1987.

Wells, Mark K. *Courage and Air Warfare: The Allied Aircrew Experience in the Second World War.* London: Frank Cass, 1995.

CHAPTER 14

NORTH AFRICA AND ITALY

DOUGLAS PORCH

Two myths inform the traditional verdict on the Mediterranean theater in World War II. The first is that, on the strategic level, it was an "encounter theater" into which Germany, and subsequently the United States, were drawn by flailing allies. The second myth follows invariably from the first, that the Mediterranean offered a wasteful peripheral distraction on the margins of the two "decisive" Eastern and Western fronts in Northern Europe. In the view of U.S. Army Chief of Staff George C. Marshall, the decision to enter the Mediterranean taken at the June 1942 Washington Conference was "fundamentally unsound," a "prestige" strategy that simply reinforced British Prime Minister Winston Churchill's "dalliance" in the Mediterranean, and his reluctance to take the war to northern Europe.[1] Many postwar historians endorsed Marshall's verdict by pointing out the relatively low number of German forces in North Africa and Italy and the grinding, inconclusive, and protracted nature of much of the fighting there. This included in particular the Western Desert prior to Bernard Montgomery's breakthrough victory at El-Alamein in November 1942; Tunisia where Vichy French prevarication allied with Anglo-American operational and tactical ineptitude to produce a bloody and entirely avoidable eight-month campaign; the dreary slog up the Italian peninsula from September 1943; and finally Anvil-Dragoon in August 1944, an operation launched too late to support Overlord or to trap many Germans in the south of France, whose only benefit was to allow the French a walk-on role in the liberation of their own country. Not only did Dragoon starve Overlord and Italy of resources, but also pre-empted an Anglo-American advance through the Balkans which might have forestalled the Soviet occupation of Eastern and Southeastern Europe. They cite Churchill's imperial focus and his "baleful" influence over U.S. President Franklin Roosevelt, whose "vacillation" offered the principal reason that the two Western allies persisted in such a "wasteful peripheral strategy" whose main beneficiary was Stalin.[2]

Like most myths, these two contain a kernel of truth. Hitler was never interested in the Mediterranean as a German strategic focus. He was drawn there by Mussolini's "parallel war" and intervened initially to rescue his Axis partner from defeat in Greece and North Africa in early 1941, and to seal his southern flank for Barbarossa, Germany's June

1941 attack on the Soviet Union. But although he never committed enough troops in North Africa to make a difference, his decision to intervene in the Mediterranean forced him to commit significant resources—roughly fifty divisions in aggregate plus considerable *Luftwaffe* assets by 1943–1944—to garrison Greece and the Balkans, Italy, and southern France against actual and potential Allied incursions and to divert troops to counterinsurgency operations to secure his lines of communications.

In the summer of 1942, Roosevelt decided to commit to Operation Torch, the Anglo–American invasion of French North Africa scheduled for November. On the strategic level, U.S. engagement in the Mediterranean offered a down payment on Stalin's demand for a "second front," although the Soviet Dictator failed to see it that way.[3] It emphasized Roosevelt's intention to prioritize the European over the Pacific theater, preempted any Axis attempt facilitated by Vichy to seize the shoulder of Africa, promised to bring the French back into the war on the Allied side, and open direct shipping lanes to the USSR and India. Roosevelt viewed the large army favored by Marshall with its promise of titanic, casualty-heavy clashes in a premature land campaign on the European continent, as an outdated concept. Instead, he favored, "an air–sea machinery-based war, with a remarkably small land army, all things considered."[4]

On the operational and tactical level, however, almost everything about Torch was daringly experimental. Amphibious assaults against fortified targets had enjoyed no success to date.[5] And although the Allies had made improvements since the failed Dakar expedition of September 1940, in the shadow of the Dieppe "fiasco," even Marshall's staff rated Torch's chances of success at no better than fifty percent.[6] And indeed, Torch revealed significant operational, logistical, and command-and-control problems—the assault was delayed by inexperience, loading problems, poor coordination, and navigation errors which meant that troops were sometimes landed on the wrong beaches. High surf, especially on the Moroccan coast, knocked many of the new Higgins boats out of control and drowned their heavily laden soldiers. Those craft that made it to the beaches were stranded by the tide and could not return to the transports to ferry supplies. Smaller harbors were easily captured, but they proved too shallow to bring in supplies and reinforcements. Troops who landed could not advance for lack of supplies, equipment, and heavy weapons, leaving them vulnerable to counterattack. These logistical problems were complicated by French shelling and occasional strafing runs by French aircraft.[7]

Fortunately, the Anglo–Americans had surprise on their side. The French represented by commander-in-chief of Vichy French forces Admiral Jean-François Darlan, and land forces commander in North Africa General Alphonse Juin, had split on whether the Allies or the Axis posed the greater threat, and hence from which directions an invasion might emanate. Nor did the French believe the Anglo–Americans capable of mounting an amphibious assault before the spring of 1943 at the earliest, when weather conditions would be more favorable. As a result, Juin had ordered units guarding the Moroccan coast to take up winter quarters in the interior. For these reasons, the French dismissed leaks from some of those involved in an espionage network created by American Minister in North Africa Robert Murphy, because they believed the Allies incapable of mounting an invasion of such magnitude less than a year after the United States had entered the war. Without strategic intelligence of their own, the French were forced to rely on Axis intelligence services, that detected the approaching Allied flotillas, but believed them destined to support Malta, or to land behind Axis forces in Egypt.[8]

Although "resistance" in French North Africa was not large, its existence played important role in at least two ways: without the assurance that the French in North Africa awaited liberation, the operation might never have left the drawing board.[9] Second, by November 1942, many army commanders were unsure if they could count on their subordinates to resist an Anglo–American invasion. While resistors in Algiers briefly detained both Darlan and Juin, the delayed French response was largely the result of unsuccessful maneuvers by Admiral François Darlan and Vichy Premier Pierre Laval to harness the Allied invasion to negotiate an easing of the conditions of the German occupation in France.[10] The French reaction to Torch was also complicated by a command system intentionally muddled to insure that no single commander could order French North Africa to defect to the Allies. As a result, the defense of Algiers, Oran, and Casablanca was badly synchronized with Vichy, that had failed to delineate authority between army and navy, and between the military commanders and the governor general of Algeria, and residents general in Tunisia and Morocco. The result of this command vacuum was "a succession of orders and counter-orders" that increased confusion that basically "created competition among several headquarters, thus several commanders, each with a modicum of authority and all independent in the hierarchy of rank and functions in the chain of command," writes French historian Robin Leconte.[11] As a consequence of these confused and shattered lines of authority, many local French commanders were left isolated and on their own. The result was that French resistance to Torch was piecemeal and sporadic, succeeding only in Tunisia where it was bolstered by the rapid reinforcement of Axis troops.[12]

With the conflict for the moment deadlocked in Northern Europe in 1942, and the Soviets demanding a second front, both Churchill and Roosevelt looked to the Mediterranean as the place where the Anglo–Americans could engage the Axis at a relative advantage. Both leaders were navalists, having served as First Lord of the Admiralty and Assistant Secretary of the Navy respectively. Both nurtured a keen awareness of the mobility and strategic flexibility that navies brought to a global war.[13]

The assumption of decision-makers at the time, and of many historians since, has been that Churchill converted the American president to his views on the centrality of the Mediterranean to Allied success. However, in an innovative view that lifts Mediterranean revisionism into the realm of grand strategy, Andrew Buchanan argues that Roosevelt was already convinced of the Mediterranean's importance. For Roosevelt, the Mediterranean provided an opening into Europe in 1942–1943, a location where U.S. troops could engage in the European theater while evading the inordinately high risks of a cross-Channel invasion in 1942 or 1943. Furthermore, far from mortgaging U.S. policy to British imperial interests, the Mediterranean became the setting for Roosevelt's Grand Strategic vision for a U.S.-imposed postwar order.[14]

If the Mediterranean became such an important stepping-stone to the success of Allied strategy, how does one explain the theater's reputation at the time as a costly strategic diversion, and the perpetuation of this unfavorable verdict into the postwar years? Denunciations of Roosevelt's decision to engage in the Mediterranean can be traced in part to the fact that U.S. military leaders felt that they should have a major say on strategic priorities. However, in the view of Marshall and others, at the Washington Conference of June 1942, Roosevelt was persuaded by Churchill to surrender U.S. strategic autonomy to British imperial interests.[15]

Torch also helped to promote the view that the Mediterranean was a highly politicized theater riven by political, ethnic, and religious divisions that complicated military operations. Indeed, from the beginning, the results of Torch were criticized as being at odds with Allied war goals because it allowed a clutch of former Vichy collaborationists to retain power in French North Africa. While the controversial "Darlan deal"—the November 1942 imposition of Admiral Darlan to lead the break-away French—was advertised as a pragmatic decision to quell French resistance to Torch, it was hotly condemned at the time in both Washington and London.[16] In this way, Vichy's *ancien régime* in North Africa received a new lease on life from the liberating Americans, complete with its discriminatory, antisemitic legislation and racist practices that betrayed Allied principles set out in the Atlantic Charter and the Four Freedoms. This came as a great disappointment to many of France's imperial subjects who initially had viewed the Anglo–Americans as a liberating army. Nor could Darlan deliver his sailors, neither at Toulon where the High Seas Fleet scuttled rather than sail to Allied controlled harbors, nor in Tunis, where French Resident General Vice-Admiral Jean Esteva allowed Axis troops and the *Luftwaffe* to pour unhindered into Tunisia.

With Torch, France became represented by three separate political entities. The fear that the "Darlan deal" might also portend further compromises between the Western Allies and other unsavory Nazi or fascist leaders sourced the unconditional surrender policy declared at the January 1943 Anfa conference. Yet, this declaration was violated barely eight months later when the Western Allies initiated secret talks with the Italian government in the summer of 1943, which culminated on September 3, 1943, with an armistice.[17] In its essentials, the surrender of Italy resembled the "Darlan deal" redux. Like Charles de Gaulle in the French case, anti-fascist exiles like Count Carlo Sforza initially were passed over in favor of the retention of the monarch King Victor Emmanuel and of a discredited military leader Marshal Pietro Badoglio to head the new regime. As in French North Africa, the democratic principles of the Atlantic Charter were suspended in favor of the status quo shorn of its most notorious fascist elements.

The controversy that surrounded many of Roosevelt's seemingly pragmatic wartime decisions, together with the confusion over the policy of "unconditional surrender", combined to make the Mediterranean appear a theater where the ideals of the Western powers were compromised by the requirement to negotiate with dubious characters like Darlan and Badoglio. This, combined with the postwar pedestal upon which American military leaders like Eisenhower and Marshall were placed, served to sanctify their seemingly principled military stances over the sordid, politically motivated arrangements green lighted by the American President. An anti-New Deal spirit especially on the right played a role in these postwar assessments. The opinions expressed in the memoirs of Eisenhower and those of other military leaders like the staunchly anti-communist General Albert Wedemeyer, were endorsed in the writings of Secretary of State Cordell Hull, who enjoyed a fraught relationship with FDR, as did Secretary of War Henry Stimson, a conservative Republican who generally backed his military commanders in their disputes with their Commander-in-Chief, although some of these were the very men who had championed Washington's policy of Vichy accommodation and opposition to Charles de Gaulle's Free French.[18] Postwar memoirs, especially those of Churchill, who portrayed himself as the seasoned European schooling his naïve American partner, lent credence to the perception that the British had hijacked American strategy and policy in the Mediterranean to serve Churchill's nostalgically imperial vision.

In the shadow of the Cold War, the deceased Roosevelt was condemned in anachronistic fashion for having failed to foresee at Yalta the stranglehold that the devious Stalin planned to clamp on Central and Eastern Europe.[19] This judgment seems especially imbalanced as, apart from Yugoslavia, the Mediterranean offered a theater where the communists were notably unsuccessful in their attempts to seize power, in part because of the overwhelming Anglo–American presence there, the rebuilding of a French army, the nurturing by the Anglo–Americans of a democratic republic in Italy, and the establishment of U.S. postwar dominance in the region. Without U.S. intervention in the Mediterranean that began with Torch, it is entirely possible that Greece and Italy, perhaps even France, might have been dominated at war's end by communist regimes that had emerged from the European resistance phenomenon.[20]

A further reason that the perception of the Mediterranean as a British priority gained the upper hand was that neither Roosevelt nor Churchill clearly articulated what strategic advantage a "dalliance" in the Mediterranean was meant to achieve. As Buchanan points out, Roosevelt's process of foreign policy formulation was notoriously opaque, often back channel, which gave the impression of being ad hoc and opportunistic. Roosevelt might not tip his hand until the last minute, precisely to avoid open and prolonged clashes over policy and strategy with Marshall and Stimson, whose strategic vision was restricted to militarized notions of mass and concentration of force. In contrast, Roosevelt realized that the collapse of France, the erosion of British power, and Italy's wobbly status in the Axis had created a dynamic environment in the Mediterranean rich with strategic opportunity for the United States to backstop a stable postwar world order. The Middle Sea offered a channel into Europe's heartland susceptible to intervention by a maritime power, a viable second front, and the best chance of victory for whoever was able to dominate it. However, Roosevelt's *modus operandi* allowed his critics and subsequently some historians to postulate an eleventh-hour kidnap of American strategy by the wily Churchill.[21]

One of the ironies of this British-centric interpretation is that, while American military leaders chaffed that Roosevelt had enlisted them to fight for what they saw as British priorities, according to British historian Simon Ball, British military leaders too were just as clueless as were the Americans about the Mediterranean's strategic purpose. For London's generals and admirals, the war in the Mediterranean appeared improvised on the fly, practically empty of strategic and political purpose.[22]

Strategic confusion in the Mediterranean was matched only by the challenges of organizing a political foundation for realizing goals there. To American soldiers, the political complexities of Mediterranean seemed daunting—factious Frenchmen and mercurial Italians, its shores awash in exiles and insurgents of various political stripes. French North Africa offered multi-racial and multi-religious boil of majority Muslims, Jews, European settlers, and a significant population of refugees that teetered on the cusp of conflagration. This perpetuated the postwar assessment prominent in the American military that while Anglo–American policy in the Mediterranean claimed to be informed by broad democratic principles proclaimed in the Atlantic Charter, in practice, it appeared opportunistic and operationally driven, and sought to entrench the status quo rather than upend it.

One consequence of Mediterranean engagement was to open that sea to postwar U.S. naval dominance. As a consequence of Torch, Toulon became the cemetery of the French High Seas Fleet. In the view of Thomas Vaisset and Philippe Vial, *le sabordage* became the metaphor for Vichy's moral bankruptcy.[23] Moreover, for a nation that nurtured pretentions to global power, stripped of its navy, France was no longer even a Mediterranean power. By 1945, the French navy had lost sixty-five per cent of its 1940 tonnage, while French naval air had been virtually wiped out. The French navy was fourteen times smaller than the United States Navy, and eight times smaller than the Royal Navy. Even the Italian navy was larger. Only fifty-five percent of the French ships remaining in the war could be considered modern. And only after the liberation of Tunisia, in May 1943, did the French navy gain access to its unique small overseas shipyard in Bizerte. The Toulon scuttle removed most of the best ships in the French inventory. At war's end, Darlan's navy of 1940 was one-third of what it had been in September 1939, even though it had hardly fired a shot in anger except at the Anglo–Americans. Its losses had been largely self-inflicted.[24] But, as a consequence, and because of Darlan's equivocal behavior in November 1942, France saw its prestige among the Anglo–Americans plummet, and its clout in the alliance diminished to the status of courtesy power.[25]

The reaction of the Italian fleet was more ambiguous. Many Italian naval officers were shocked and shamed by the announcement of the September 1943 armistice between Badoglio and the Allies. Ships at Taranto followed orders to sail to Malta. But only after it was realized that battleship *Roma* on its way to surrender had been sunk by a German glider bomb, and not by the British, did that portion of the fleet at Tirreno set sail for Bizerte. A handful of Italian captains scuttled and were executed by the Germans. A few captains preferred to be interned with their ships in the Balearic Islands. In all, the Allies recouped only about one-half of the Italian fleet.[26] The disappearance of the Mediterranean's two major navies opened a sea power vacuum in the Mediterranean that the American Navy would fill. But the process of this transformation appeared incomprehensible to American and British sailors, who were not forced to make such confusing choices in a fluid political landscape.

While enticing the French empire out of neutrality, bouncing Italy out of the war, and keeping Spain neutral offered significant accomplishments of the Mediterranean strategy and diplomacy, both Allied governments vastly overestimated the strategic advantages that would accrue to them by a French return to belligerency and the Italians switching sides. This, too, has contributed to the unfortunate reputation of the Mediterranean among contemporaries and historians. Pre-war U.S. defense policy had been anchored in the French army and the Royal Navy. As a consequence, the fall of France in 1940 threw Washington into a complete funk, as U-boats ran amok in the Caribbean and alarmists began to fear a pox of Nazi-backed regimes in Latin America.[27] For those like Roosevelt who remembered France as the pillar of the victorious World War I coalition, France's subsequent contribution to the Allied victory must also have proved a disappointment.[28] French North Africa was poor in human resources and lacked an industrial infrastructure. If anything, the French military situation had been further degraded by Torch and the subsequent Tunisian campaign. Indeed, *l'armée d'Afrique* that Harold Macmillan witnessed on parade in Tunis on May 20, 1943 to mark the conclusion of the Tunisian campaign (November 1942–May 1943) resembled a ragged, penurious vestige of France's glorious military past. Many of the soldiers were barefoot and armed with weapons that had been obsolete in 1914. "One realized what a brave show they had put up during all these months with such poor equipment and material," the future British prime minister concluded.[29]

Rearming the eleven—later reduced to eight—French divisions agreed to at the Anfa Conference in January 1943, was in part the reward for French performance in Tunisia despite their poor equipment. French rearmament was also made necessary by the shift of seven U.S. and British divisions back to Britain at the conclusion of Husky in August 1943. The breakthrough on the Gustav Line in May 1944, achieved largely by the French Expeditionary Corps (CEF) under Juin, offered a tribute to the professionalism, tenacity, iron discipline, adaptability, and rusticity of the CEF, sixty percent of whom were North African Muslims.[30] But it also showcased the limitations of attempting to fashion a modern military *levée* out of an underdeveloped, largely illiterate colonial population with low to non-existent technical, mechanical, and administrative skills. Only a limited number of slots for Muslims existed in the officer crops. Europeans and, once Vichy discriminatory legislation was abrogated in 1943, North African Jews were enlisted to serve as cadres and in supply and support roles required of the modern mass army insisted upon by the Americans. Attempts to enlist women from the North African settler population to serve in communications, as ambulance drivers, and in other technical specialties encountered stiff opposition because it transgressed strict Mediterranean gender norms. As a result, instead of the eleven divisions to include three armored divisions approved at Anfa, the French initially were able to muster only five infantry and two armored divisions.[31]

The Italian surrender also failed to produce its hoped-for strategic dividend. Unfortunately, the fecklessness and cowardice of Badoglio and King Victor Emmanuel III negated potential Italian aid in seizing Rome and advancing Allied armies up the Italian boot. Because they were left confused, leaderless, and without orders, rather than switch sides, most Italian soldiers surrendered meekly and were marched off to brutal captivity in Germany. Unfortunately, in the process of arranging the Italian surrender, the Allies also underestimated the German response to the Italian volte-face. German Mediterranean commander Albert Kesselring managed to convince Hitler to mount a forward defense on a line running from the Tyrrhenian Sea to the Adriatic between Naples and Rome. So, rather than surge to the Alps, or at least the Pisa–Rimini line, the Allied campaign in Italy became a desperate improvisation, with progress up the peninsula frozen during the winter of 1943–1944. This became a source of impatience, frustration, and recriminations in the Allied camp, hardly surprising as the decision had been made in August 1943 to reduce the Mediterranean to a secondary theater and shift the focus of the war to Northern Europe.

No one trusted the Italians. For this reason, the Germans had finalized plans to disarm the Italian army and occupy the country from July 25, even before secret negotiations between the Italians and the Anglo–Americans had been initiated. Therefore, one interpretation is that it was the Germans who betrayed the Italians, not vice-versa. The Anglo-Americans also distrusted the Italians, and with good reason. Badoglio's miscalculation in September 1943 was to believe that Italy could exit the war without direct conflict with the Germans, an attitude that stemmed from an ambivalence in Rome over the wisdom of concluding an armistice with the Allies. Badoglio and the King had little confidence in the armed forces commanders, several of whom opposed abandoning their Axis ally. The two Italian leaders also prioritized their own safety and feared that a call for popular national defense would ignite a revolution. Therefore, on the eve of Salerno, they simply fled to Brindisi in the company of the three armed forces ministers. Because resistance by Italian troops to the Germans was leaderless, fragmented, uncoordinated, and often non-existent, the Germans were not pressed in the Eastern Mediterranean. Because of the premature transfer of Allied divisions to the United Kingdom, the Salerno invasion was undertaken by a dangerously diminished Allied force. As a consequence, the strategic initiative in Italy passed to Kesselring.[32] Nevertheless, the Italian surrender proved to be a significant event that, in Churchill's words, left Hitler "utterly alone," while Germans were forced to replace Italian soldiers and fight their battles solo in France, Italy, Yugoslavia, and Greece.

Unlike French North Africa, which as a result of the Darlan deal continued to be governed for better or worse by French officials, the collapse in Italy on September 8, 1943 created a governance vacuum. This was filled north of Monte Cassino by a spontaneously organizing Resistance that, popular mythology holds, was the progenitor of the Italian Republic born of the 1946 referendum, and south of that line by the Allies. One consequence may have been that, together with other factors, it accentuated the historical north–south divide that contributed to the difficulties of forging an Italian identity.[33] The Civil Affairs Corps activated on March 1, 1943, had been dispatched to Sicily as part of Husky with orders to govern through coalitions drawn from priests and local notables, in short, the very elite that had underpinned fascist rule, as well as—many alleged—organized crime.[34]

Known as the Allied Military Government of Occupied Territories (AMGOT), experience in Sicily quickly revealed that the primary focus of civil affairs—minimize civilian disruption in battle zones by reconstituting the carabinieri under the supervision of Allied military police and enforcing a rationing system established by the Fascists—proved desperately inadequate. There were not enough civil affairs officers to replace a fascist administration that largely imploded, often amidst the looting of local records that aimed to destroy evidence of property ownership, tax files, or felony convictions. The Allied invasion of the Italian mainland also precipitated a humanitarian crisis, the cumulative result of war damage, German depredations and sabotage, indiscriminate Allied requisitions, a lack of electric generating capacity that caused shops and factories to close creating widespread unemployment, the destruction of the Italian merchant marine on the North Africa run, and an agricultural economy consisting of small hill farms that in the best of times were inadequate feed the population in the south. The Allies initially had factored in no provisions to sustain the Italian population, and so had to scramble and improvise, no mean feat given a dearth of shipping.[35]

The arrival of Allied, especially U.S., soldiers paid in occupation script sent inflation through the roof, forced many women whose soldier husbands were dead or in POW camps into prostitution to survive, created a lawless atmosphere behind the lines where any piece of Allied equipment not chained down was liable to be stolen, and saw a resurgence of organized crime, which had largely been suppressed by the Fascists.[36] The mishandling of the Italian surrender followed by the implosion of governance, combined with the lack of charisma and success of the Allied command team of Generals Harold Alexander, Mark Clark, and Oliver Leese, created a simmering stalemate that recalled the trench deadlock and chateau generalship of World War I's Western Front. For those on the ground, the heroism of the fighter became an expendable commodity. The betrayal of the Darlan deal and subsequent bickering between Giraudists and Gaullists in Algiers, combined with the fiasco of the Italian surrender and the misery and disorder behind the lines in Italy, meant that the Allied "liberation" narrative failed to find traction in the Mediterranean.

While wartime impatience with the lack of progress on the ground in Italy was understandable, to transpose that frustration into a negative historical verdict on the Mediterranean in general and Italy in particular, would be to misjudge the Mediterranean's role in the stability of postwar Europe. Buchanan makes the argument that, although Italy ceased to be the focus of Allied military operations after Husky (the invasion of Sicily), Italy's transformation from a fascist state into a successful democracy and Allied partner remained among Roosevelt's priorities. Italy's shift to co-belligerent status and its declaration of war on Germany in October 1943, gave Italy a unique status and allowed it to become the vehicle through which the American President confirmed America's ascendency in the Western Alliance, and eclipsed British dominance in the Mediterranean. An Allied Control Commission (ACC) established on November 10, 1943, under Eisenhower and Allied Force Headquarters (AFHQ), became responsible for direct military rule in frontline areas and indirect oversight of the Italian government established at Brindisi. The ACC soon acquired a large bureaucracy initially to oversee emergency relief, food distribution, and the reconstitution of local government and police. But its role increasingly became more political to include press censorship, labor relations, and the "defascistization" of Italian politics, administration, and the legal system. Growing pressure to include political parties came to a head with the capture of Rome in June 1944, which, at Allied insistence, was followed by the King's abdication and the establishment of a multi-party government under Ivanoe Bonomi.[37]

Nor was political transformation limited to the Mediterranean's northern shore. If Torch returned France to the war, it also deepened the tensions that would erupt in the War for Algerian Independence (1954–1962) and the civil–military crisis that was to roil France from 1958 to 1961. Following their 1940 defeat, French professional soldiers had turned inward, blamed defeatist French conscripts and a "decadent" Third Republic for their battlefield humiliation in 1940, and increasingly saw the empire and *l'armée d'Afrique*—the military force that historically garrisoned French North Africa—as a refuge from modernism and change.

The post-Torch challenge in French North Africa became to carry out a mobilization, and to build a coherent military force, with an army and a population whose divisions were deepened by the war. Most professional soldiers remained politically and emotionally loyal to Marshal Pétain and his National Revolution. Yet, this pro-Vichy officer corps was to lead a liberation that would terminate the government that, in their view, had restored their "honor," largely by shifting blame for defeat onto the shoulders of *la troisième* and the republic's combat-shy constituents. For this reason, Torch and the resumption of the war produced a schizophrenia among a deeply antisemitic and anti-Muslim settler population in French North Africa nostalgic for the National Revolution.[38] In this way, neither the Anfa military upgrade, nor the heroic performance of the CEF in Italy served to heal the civil–military rift caused by 1940.

While in North Africa, Roosevelt had been at pains to reassure the French that he had no intention of upsetting the colonial status quo, by its very presence, by the power of its military, Torch had rattled France's North African empire. Because of French dependence on U.S. arms, equipment, and basic necessities, French legitimacy in North Africa was undermined and questioned by many of its Muslim subjects. Above all, through the wide diffusion of the Atlantic Charter of August 1941 and Roosevelt's "Four Freedoms," not to mention the overwhelming power of Anglo-American arms that had bested the formidable Wehrmacht in Tunisia, the United States had rattled North Africa's imperial and racial order. The December 11, 1942 mobilization of reservists found a lack of enthusiasm to liberate France, even within the settler population. Meanwhile, Algerian nationalists exploited unequal pay and service conditions imposed on Muslims, not to mention Vichy's stripping North African Jews of French citizenship, to argue that independence, not the acquisition of French citizenship, should become the objective of Algerian Muslims.

Torch was the decisive moment of that transition. Nationalism may not have been the only game in town among the very diverse indigenous population of French North Africa. But the incoherent French response to Torch, and the subsequent quarrels between Giraudists and Gaullists that played out in North Africa from the summer of 1943, helped to make it so. This Franco–French war joined the 1940 defeat, and the presence of a liberating Anglo–American army, to erode French prestige among the colonized. At Constantine in Eastern Algeria on December 12, 1943, de Gaulle promised to open positions in the army, the administration, commerce, and banks to Muslims. But by then, many North African Muslims were no longer interested in equality. By May 1945, when the Sétif rebellion erupted in Eastern Algeria—the opening skirmish in the War of Algerian Independence according the nationalist narrative—nationalism had become a mass movement throughout the Maghreb.[39]

One real pay-off of Torch for the Allies only became apparent on the Liberation of France. If the post-Overlord war in Northern Europe was in contrast relatively friction free on a political level, it is thanks in part to the experience gained, compromises reached, and precautions taken in the Mediterranean. The governments of Belgium and Holland had surrendered in 1940 and transferred their established governments to a London exile. Therefore, there were no legitimacy battles to be fought out in the Low Countries upon liberation. Any distant prospect of a communist insurrection emerging in Germany had been taken care of by the Nazis. Like Italy and Greece, who would govern France, however, posed a potential problem for the Allied liberators. The 1940 armistice, followed by Torch and the growth of robust resistance movements, proliferated a panoply of dissident factions. However, the gradual takeover of the Provisional Government of the French Republic (GPRF) in Algiers by Charles de Gaulle, and the nominal unification of resistance groups in the Conseil national de la Resistance on May 27, 1943, engineered by Jean Moulin, all but settled the issue of government transition in France, even though Washington did not officially recognize the France's provisional republic (GPRF) until October 1944.

The liberation of Corsica by French forces in September–October 1943 had witnessed a communist-directed putsch characterized by the seizure of two hundred municipalities, the supplanting of the police by communist partisans, the creation of "conseils de préfecture," and the organizing of large demonstrations in Ajaccio. Corsica served as the blueprint for Jacques Duclos, leader of the *Parti communist français clandestine,* to spearhead a "national insurrection" through the occupation of prefectures and sub-prefectures, town halls, police commissariats, and post offices with the goal of substituting communists for Vichy representatives.[40]

Duclos' plans for a communist putsch in France upon Liberation misfired for several reasons. Alerted by Corsica, the Gaullists prepared countermeasures: resistance groups were placed under the military command of Gaullist General Pierre Koenig, the hero of Bir Hacheim in 1942. The Gaullist Jacques Chaban-Delmas was inserted as the national military delegate into the *Comité d'action militaire* (COMAC) responsible for naming official resistance heads and coordinating with the regional military delegates and other resistance groups. The Gaullists also appointed a network of "Republican commissars" seamlessly to replace Vichy officials upon liberation. Behind these Gaullist measures stood the implied threat of AMGOT, and a repetition of the Darlan deal that conceivably could envisage a scenario by which the Allies might simply recognize in situ Vichy officials.

Finally, the presence on French soil of a rehabilitated French army introduced by Operation Anvil in August 1944, backed by U.S. divisions, also offered a mechanism to balk communist plans to seize power through the "amalgamation" of *Forces françaises de l'intérieur* (FFI) into regular units from September 1944 as a way to disperse and control them. But, as in Italy where Palmiro Toglietti returned from Moscow with orders to join the Badoglio government, the ultimate brake on communist-induced disorder was provided by Joseph Stalin. French communist leader Maurice Thorez, who had deserted to Moscow in 1939, returned to France in November 1944 to drive a stake into the "1917 model" of "national insurrection" and disarm the patriotic militias, even though it cost both the Italian and French communists parties their quasi-hegemonic control of the working class movement.[41] Decelerating the radical political dynamic of antifascist liberation movements in southern Europe proved a major accomplishment of Washington's Mediterranean strategy.[42]

But the transformative nature of the political events in the Mediterranean that would include the eventual conquest of Yugoslavia by Tito's communist partisans, the brewing civil war in Greece, the rise of nationalism in the Levant and North Africa, and the confirmation of Zionism as a potent political force in Palestine, had been masked by a quasi-military stalemate there. From the perspective of 1943, it is easy to see why the Mediterranean would become Europe's pivotal theater, without which it would have been impossible for the Western Alliance to transition from Dunkirk to D-Day.[43]

The fact that Anvil/Dragoon coincided with the Allied breakout of the Normandy beachhead, caused many to view it as a belated bookend, an afterthought whose postponement had gutted it of strategic purpose. In fact, eight to ten German divisions had been stationed in southern France, divisions that might have bolstered the German defenses in Normandy. Anvil/Dragoon prodded the Germans to abandon their occupation of France and retreat to the Vosges mountains, but not before 131,250 German soldiers had been killed, captured, or incarcerated in the "Atlantic pockets" in southwestern France—that is, more troops than Hitler had lost at either Stalingrad or who had surrendered at Tunis in May 1943. Above all, the seizure of Marseilles and Toulon, that included a bag of fifty-seven thousand German POWs against light losses by French and U.S. forces, balked Hitler's plan to deny those important port cities to the Allies. Without the supplies funneled through those important Mediterranean harbors, estimated as meeting one-third of Allied needs, the Allies could not have supported three armies in Northern Europe through the winter of 1944–1945. And without three Allied armies in Northern Europe in December 1944, George Patton might not have been able to staunch Hitler's Ardennes offensive.[44]

Attrition formed a final military advantage of the Mediterranean strategy. Hitler's decision to reinforce his bombastic Axis partner's "parallel war" offers a case study of strategic overextension, as Churchill and Roosevelt had recognized. Simon Ball argues that German commanders continued to imagine well into 1943 that they could inflict an operational defeat in either Tunisia or Sicily so overwhelming that the Allies might be stunned into strategic inactivity.[45] However, fixated on the Eastern Front, Hitler was unable to fold the Mediterranean into a geostrategic vision, however twisted, with a global strategy to match. Axis commanders were slow to prioritize theaters, and to acknowledge their rapidly diminishing combat power in the Mediterranean.

In theory, the Axis should have been able to operate in all three-dimensions of Mediterranean combat. In practice, because the Axis partners frequently failed to cooperate, their operational capabilities rapidly eroded. The Italian navy was a wasting asset as it lacked integrated air power that would have allowed it to operate out of range of land-based aircraft. The Axis decision to mount a major effort on the southern shore of the Mediterranean severely stretched and exposed its lines of communication. The Italian navy was increasingly depleted in the course of ferrying supplies to North Africa by Malta-based British aircraft and submarines. The Germans attempted to substitute air power for their lack of sea power, in particular in Crete in 1941, and again in Tunisia in the winter/spring of 1942–1943. For instance, the *Luftwaffe* had committed forty percent of its bomber force to the Mediterranean, even as fighting raged at Stalingrad. One-third of *Luftwaffe* losses were inflicted in the Mediterranean, making it a mere shadow of its former self. In September 1943, the Mediterranean became the graveyard the Axis with Italy's exit from the war.[46]

The Mediterranean's unfortunate reputation emerges principally from the sluggish progress of the Italian campaign, which tied down over a million Allied personnel, not to mention air and naval assets.[47] So long as the fighting played out on the southern shore of the Mediterranean, the Allies held the advantage. Conversely, there can be no doubt that, on the tactical level, the fighting in Italy was bitter, frustrating, and difficult. One reason that combat in Italy was compared to the static fronts of World War I, was that, in the aftermath of Salerno, the *Wehrmacht* had been reduced to an infantry army fighting a dogged rearguard defensive campaign, simply staving off defeat in the hope that victory might be snatched elsewhere. Furthermore, the notion that Italy post-September 1943 represented an expenditure of Allied resources for scant strategic benefit comes from the fact that contemporaries at the time, and many historians since, have considered the Italian campaign as a standalone, rather than view it in the broader context of the strategic picture of the Mediterranean in the last two years of the war. By 1944, one-fifth of German troop strength was tied up in Italy. And this is multiplied if one factors in roughly twenty Germans divisions in Greece and the Balkans, and a further ten stationed in southern France. German losses in Italy amounted to sixty thousand killed, 163,000 wounded, and 357,000 captured.[48] The Italian campaign of 1943–1945 was half as costly in casualties for the Allies than was the shorter campaign in Northwestern Europe from June 1944 to May 1945.[49]

Seen from this perspective, it was Hitler, not Churchill and Roosevelt, who poured resources into Italy and its surrounding countries for scant political or military benefit. Hitler should have taken Erwin Rommel's advice and withdrawn to the Alps, and that way economized divisions that might have been deployed to greater strategic benefit from a German perspective to the Eastern Front and Normandy. At the same time, the Mediterranean bought time for the Allies to identify their best commanders and to learn to fight in a theater where losses and setback were not debilitating as had been those in the trenches of the Great War, in France in 1940, or on the Eastern Front from June 1941. Italy and Corsica also supplied important bomber bases for attacking Germany, and Rumanian oil at Ploesti.

Once the Allies had committed to the Mediterranean, they had to continue to apply pressure there. One view is that operations in the Mediterranean were incremental. The commitment of military assets and the creation of bases created a momentum in the Mediterranean that was difficult to redirect. In this view, although Mediterranean operations passed the culminating point of success, the Allies continued to press offensive operations there even though they paid increasingly diminished dividends. But at what point did this happen? Some believed that once the southern shore of the Mediterranean was cleared, ships could pass safely through the Mediterranean without the need for further offensives on the northern shore. This certainly conformed to the view that the Mediterranean's principal strategic benefit to the Allies was as a shipping channel.

But other views held that Sicily had to be occupied for sea passage to become truly secure. And once Sicily was conquered, the Italians indicated a desire to switch sides. The Allies simply could not turn their backs on the important political and strategic opportunity to crack the Axis. And once Italy was invaded, the German defenders at Monte Cassino, in Greece and the Balkans and Southern France had to be pressured and threatened to lock their divisions into the Mediterranean front, and not shift them to the East or Northwestern Europe where they might have made a difference.

But this interpretation of incremental Allied engagement stands in contrast to Buchanan's thesis that Roosevelt's goal was not merely to conquer the Mediterranean, but to transform Europe into a constellation of modern liberal democracies, beginning in the Mediterranean. From a global war perspective, the notion, current into the twentieth-first century, that the Mediterranean was an opportunistic and incremental theater of marginal strategic impact, that competed for resources with more strategically lucrative fronts, can no longer stand close scrutiny.

The Mediterranean reinforced Roosevelt's "Europe first" strategy. It offered a place where the Western Allies could learn to fight at diminished risk and at a strategic advantage. It bought time for Roosevelt to build up U.S. military might, and hence increase American influence in the postwar reconfiguration of Europe. It seriously attrited Axis resources, and even provided the lever that pried the Axis apart. For better or worse, the Mediterranean campaign initiated the political transformation of the region. Andrew Buchanan has argued that the Mediterranean was central to Roosevelt's vision of building a stable, liberal, democratic postwar European order, one that avoided the risks and dangers of a premature engagement in Northern Europe. Axis leaders proved unable to concoct a similar comprehensive strategic vision for the Mediterranean. They simply threw good money after bad and committed too many resources in tactical reactions to Allied initiatives in a theater in which they were poorly configured operationally and tactically to compete.

Notes

1. Michael Simpson, "Superhighway to the World Wide Web: The Mediterranean in British Imperial Strategy, 1900-45," in *Naval Policy and Strategy in the Mediterranean: Past, Present and Future*, ed. John B. Hattendorf (London: Frank Cass, 2000), 64.
2. Albert C. Wedemeyer, *Wedemeyer Reports!* (New York: Henry Holt, 1958), 330. Among the historians who express this view, see John Ellis, *Brute Force: Allied Strategy and Tactics in the Second World War* (New York: Viking, 1990), xx, 289, 292-293; Robert W. Love, *History of the U.S. Navy*, Vol. 2: *1940-1941* (Harrisburg, PA: Stackpole, 1992), 87; John Keegan, *The Second World War* (London: Penguin, 1989), 368; Dominick Graham and Shelford Bidwell, *Tug of War: The Battle for Italy, 1943-1945* (New York: St. Martin's, 1986), 403. Other verdicts along these lines are cited by Andrew Buchanan, *American Grand Strategy in the Mediterranean during World War II* (Cambridge: Cambridge University Press, 2014), 6. Claire Miot also discusses the historiographical debate surrounding Anvil/Dragoon: "Le débarquement de Provence, une opération inutile," in Jean Lopez and Olivier Wieviorka, *Les Mythes de la seconde guerre mondiale* (Paris: Perrin, 2013), 245-260.
3. Sean McMeekin, *Stalin's War. A New History of World War II* (New York: Basic Books, 2021), 441.
4. Phillips Payson O'Brien, *The Second Most Powerful Man in the World: The Life of Admiral William D. Leahy, Roosevelt's Chief of Staff* (New York: Dutton, 2019), 203-209, 227; Buchanan, American Grand Strategy in the Mediterranean during World War II, 281.
5. The two successful Allied amphibious landings to date at Guadalcanal and Diego Suarez (Madagascar) had been unopposed. Although Operation Jubilee, the August 19, 1942 assault on Dieppe, and Operation Agreement, the equally failed attack on Tobruk by the New Zealand, Rhodesian, and British troops barely a month later on September 13-14, 1942, were undertaken against allegedly second-class opposition, both had failed.
6. Dakar had demonstrated the need for a communications ship better to coordinate operations. Specialized landing craft developed and used in Torch included the landing craft personnel (LCP) with a ramped version (LCPR), landing craft vehicle (LCV), landing craft mechanized (LCM), landing craft support (LCS), and the landing ship tank (LST), an adaptation of Lake Maricumbo tankers capable of carrying twenty-one tanks to shore. Vincent P. O'Hara, *Torch: North Africa and the Allied Path to Victory* (Annapolis, MD: Naval Institute Press, 2015), 27-29, 49-50.
7. George F. Howe, *United States Army in World War II. The Mediterranean Theater of Operations, Northwest Africa: Seizing the Initiative in the West* (Washington, DC: Center of Military History, 1991), 123-127, 134-137.
8. On intelligence assessments, see F. H. Hinsley, *British Intelligence in the Second World War. Its Influence on Strategy and Operations*, Vol. 2 (New York: Cambridge University Press, 1981), 479, 482; O'Hara, Torch, 75-79; John Patch, "Fortuitous Endeavor. Intelligence and Deception in Operation TORCH," *Naval War College Review* 61, no. 4 (Autumn 2008): 78-81, 83, 85, 93.
9. Buchanan, *American Grand Strategy*, 45.
10. Bernard Costagliola, *Darlan. La collaboration à tout prix* (Paris: CNRS éditions, 2015), 248.
11. Robin Leconte, "Face au débarquement allié de novembre 1942: La Division de Marche de Constantine, entre obeisance et résistances aux ordres," in *Militaires en résistances en France et en Europe*, ed. Claire Miot, Guillaume Piketty, Thomas Vaisset (Villeneuve d'Ascq: Presses universitaires du Septentrion, 2020), 71.

12. Howe, *Northwest Africa: Seizing the Initiative in the West*, 108–109.
13. Buchanan, *American Grand Strategy in the Mediterranean during World War II*, 9.
14. Buchanan, *American Grand Strategy in the Mediterranean during World War II*, 7, 11.
15. George F. Howe notes that Marshall continued to insist that Roosevelt's decision for Torch was merely provisional, so that on 25 July 1942, the President was forced to insist that Torch "very definitely... should be undertaken at the earliest possible date ... (as) this operation was our principal objective... President Roosevelt's action amounted to a modification of the Combined Chiefs of Staff's recommendation so drastic as to be almost a rejection." *The United States Army in World War II. The Mediterranean Theater of Operations. Northwest Africa: Seizing the Initiative in the West* (Washington, D.C., Center of Military History United States Army, 1993), 13–14.
16. Carlo d'Este, *Eisenhower. A Soldier's Life* (New York: Henry Holt, 2002), 356.
17. Unconditional surrender was not invoked on the rather slender logic that Mussolini had been removed and imprisoned and the fascist party disbanded. Elena Agarossi, *A Nation Collapses. The Italian Surrender of September 1943* (Cambridge: Cambridge University Press, 2000), 27–32, 65–66, 75, 128–129.
18. This is brilliantly laid out in Michael S. Neiberg, *When France Fell. The Vichy Crisis and the Fate of the Anglo-American Alliance* (Cambridge, Massachusetts: Harvard University Press, 2021).
19. Russell Frank Weigley, *The American Way of War: A History of United States Military Strategy Policy* (Bloomington and Indianapolis: Indiana University Press, 1973), 332.
20. This does not let Roosevelt off the hook. Sean McMeekin faults the American President for making far too many political concessions to Stalin and for continuing Lend-Lease aid which allowed for the extension of Soviet influence into Eastern Europe and Asia. *Stalin's War*.
21. Buchanan, *American Grand Strategy in the Mediterranean during World War II*, 8, 10, 269–270.
22. Simon Ball, "The Mediterranean and North Africa, 1940–1944," in *The Second World War*, Vol. I: *Fighting the War*, ed. John Ferris and Evan Mawdsley (Cambridge: Cambridge University Press, 2015), 358.
23. Philippe Vial, ed., "L'histoire d'une revolution. La Marine depuis 1870," *Études marines* 4 (March 2013): 76; Thomas Vasset and Philippe Vial, "Toulon 27 novembre 1942. Rien qu'une défaite, ou plus qu'une défaite?" 8, 11. Unpublished manuscript communicated by the authors.
24. Thomas Vasset and Philippe Vial, "Toulon 27 novembre 1942. Rien qu'une défaite, ou plus qu'une défaite?" 2. Unpublished manuscript communicated by the authors.
25. Thomas Vaisset and Philippe Vial, "Louis Jacquinot Ministre de la Marine, le "Colbert de la Libération?" in *Louis Jacquinot, un indépendant en politique*, ed. Olivier Dard, Julie Bour, Lydiane Gueit-Montchal, and Gilles Richard (Paris: Presses de l'université Paris-Sorbonne, 2013), 113–114, 121, 124; Vial, "L'histoire d'une revolution," 74–78; Vasset and Vial, "Toulon 27 novembre 1942," 6.
26. Agarossi, *A Nation Collapses*, 100–101.
27. Neiberg, *When France Fell*, 9–16.
28. Général André Beaufre, *Mémoires, 1940–1945* (Paris: Presses de la Cité, 1965), 288–289.
29. Macmillan, *War Diaries*, 89.
30. Julie Le Gac, *Vaincre sans gloire. Le corps expéditionnaire français en Italie (novembre 1942–juillet 1944)* (Paris: Les Belles Lettres/Ministère de la défense-DMPA, 2013), 68.

31. The CEF in Italy consisted of four divisions: 3rd Algerian Infantry Division, 2nd Moroccan Infantry Division, 4th Moroccan Mountain Division, and the 1st Motorized Infantry Division, which was the old 1st Free French Division. Armée B under General Jean de Lattre de Tassigny that would take part in Anvil as the First French Army consisted of the 9th Colonial Infantry Division and the 1st and 5th Armored Divisions. The 2nd Armored Division under General Philippe Leclerc de Hautcloque was constituted to participate with the American army in Normandy and subsequent campaigns. Belkacem Recham, *Les Musulmans algériens dans l'armée française (1919-1945)* (Paris: L'Harmattan, 1996), 234.
32. Agarossi, *A Nation Collapses*, 127–131.
33. Agarossi, *A Nation Collapses*, 133–138.
34. Buchanan, *American Grand Strategy in the Mediterranean during World War II*, 122–123. For the general concept of the development of civil affairs, see Hilary Fotitt and John Simmonds, *France 1943–1945* (Leicester: Leicester University Press, 1988), 20.
35. Between August 1943 and March 1944, the United States provided 414,000 tons of civilian relief. Buchanan, *American Grand Strategy in the Mediterranean during World War II*, 193.
36. On AMGOT in Italy, see Stanley Sandler, *Glad to See Them Come and Sorry to See them Go: A History of U.S. Army Tactical Civil Affairs/Military Government, 1775–1991* (No place: no publisher, no date); C. R. S. Harris, *Allied Military Administration of Italy, 1943–1945* (London: HMSO, 1957); Paul Ginsbourg, *A History of Contemporary Italy: Society and Politics, 1943-1988* (London: Penguin, 1990); George C. S. Benson and Maurice Neufel, "American Military Government in Italy," in *American Experiences in Military Government in World War II*, ed. Carl J. Frederich (New York: Reinhart, 1948); Norman Lewis, *Naples '44* (London: Collins, 1978).
37. Buchanan's interpretation was that this was a deliberate attempt to diminish Churchill's role in Italy. *American Grand Strategy in the Mediterranean during World War II*, 135, 140–157.
38. Le Gac, *Vaincre sans gloire*, 51, 90–91, 117, 123, 505–506.
39. Levisse-Touzé, *L'Afrique du nords dans la guerre 1939–1945*, 343–354, 368–369; Le Gac, *Vaincre sans gloire*, 105–106, 108.
40. Philippe Buton, *Les lendemains qui déchantent. Le Parti communiste français à la Libération* (Paris: Presses de la Foundation Nationale des Sciences Politiques, 1993), 27–34.
41. Buton, *Les lendemains qui déchantent*, 12–13, 81–89, 180–184.
42. Buchanan, *American Grand Strategy in the Mediterranean during World War II*, 277.
43. Douglas Porch, *Path to Victory. The Mediterranean Theater in World War II* (New York: Farrar, Straus and Giroux, 2004); Porch, *Path to Victory*, 662.
44. Porch, *Path to Victory*, 664.
45. Ball, "The Mediterranean and North Africa, 1940–1944," 381.
46. Ball, "The Mediterranean and North Africa, 1940–1944," 381, 383, 388.
47. David Kennedy, *Freedom from Fear* (Oxford: Oxford University Press, 1999), 556.
48. John Ellis, *Brute Force: Allied Strategy and Tactics in the Second World War* (New York: Viking, 1990), 255.
49. There were 312,000 casualties in Italy, against 766,294 in Northwestern Europe. See Graham and Bidwell, *Tug of War*, 403.

Bibliography

Agarossi, Elena, *A Nation Collapses. The Italian Surrender of September 1943*. Cambridge: Cambridge University Press, 2000.

Ball, Simon. *Bitter Sea. The Struggle for Mastery in the Mediterranean, 1935–1945*. New York: Harper Press, 2009.

Buchanan, Andrew. *American Grand Strategy in the Mediterranean during World War II*. Cambridge: Cambridge University Press, 2014.

Ehlers, Jr., Robert S. *The Mediterranean Air War. Airpower and Allied Victory in World War II*. Lawrence: University Press of Kansas, 2015.

Graham, Dominick, and Bidwell Shelford. *Tug of War: The Battle for Italy, 1943–1945*. New York: St. Martin's Press, 1986.

Howe, George F. *United States Army in World War II. The Mediterranean Theater of Operations, Northwest Africa: Seizing the Initiative in the West*. Washington, DC: Center of Military History, 1991.

Leconte, Robin. "Face au débarquement allié de novembre 1942: La Division de Marche de Constantine, entre obeisance et résistances aux orders." In *Militaires en résistances en France et en Europe*, edited by Claire Miot, Guillaume Piketty, and Thomas Vaisset. Villeneuve d'Ascq: Presses universitaires du Septentrion, 2020, 67–82.

Le Gac, Julie. *Vaincre sans gloire. Le corps expéditionnaire français en Italie (novembre 1942–juillet 1944)*. Paris: Les Belles Lettres/Ministère de la défense-DMPA, 2013.

Levisse-Touzé, Christine. *L'Afrique du nords dans la guerre 1939–1945*. Paris: Albin Michel, 1998.

McMeekin, Sean. *Stalin's War. A New History of World War II*. New York: Basic Books, 2021.

Macmillan, Harold. *War Diaries. Politics and War in the Mediterranean January 1943–May 1945*. London: Macmillan, 1984.

Metzger, Chantal. *Le Maghreb dans la guerre 1939–1945*. Paris: Armand Colin, 2018.

Neiberg, Michael S. *When France Fell. The Vichy Crisis and the Fate of the Anglo-American Alliance*. Cambridge, Massachusetts: Harvard University Press, 2021.

O'Hara, Vincent P. *Torch: North Africa and the Allied Path to Victory*. Annapolis, MD: Naval Institute Press, 2015.

Porch, Douglas, *France at War 1939–1945*, 2 vols. Cambridge: Cambridge University Press, forthcoming.

Porch, Douglas. *Path to Victory. The Mediterranean Theater in World War II*. New York: Farrar, Straus and Giroux, 2004.

CHAPTER 15

EASTERN EUROPE IN WORLD WAR II

DEBORAH S. CORNELIUS AND JONATHAN A. GRANT

As Europe headed for war it became almost inevitable that the Eastern European countries of Poland, Romania, and Hungary would be drawn into the conflict. Given that each of the Eastern European countries viewed the spread of communism from the Soviet Union as the most immediate threat, the central question became whether they would enter the German orbit as occupied countries, client states, or allies. Poland would first bear the brunt of Nazi and Soviet attack and occupation, whereas Romania and Hungary would gradually move into the German sphere of influence.

This chapter addresses the respective roles of Poland, Romania, and Hungary in the war and their contributions to the war effort. Why did these countries fight and for whom? In the cases of Romania and Hungary, did Hitler skillfully and cynically manipulate them or did they opportunistically and purposefully play their own game? How much did domestic policy and ideology harmonize with Nazi genocidal racism or generate resistance to it?

As Hungary and Romania became allied with Germany, each had its own motivations for joining the alliance and for participation in the war, often at variance from those of Nazi Germany. Occasionally termed German satellites or puppet states, in actuality Hungary and Romania exerted considerable independence in internal and occasionally external affairs. Their participation changed over time, but in almost all cases Hungarian and Romanian leaders based their decisions on their own perceptions of national interests, and at times they were at odds with German wishes.

Undoubtedly, Germany had plans to harness the region economically and make it subservient to the Reich. By 1939 the German plan to chain the countries of Eastern Europe to the German economy had proved largely successful. The new economic policy, the *Neuer Plan*, was designed to support Nazi preparation for war by overcoming difficulties of armament and lack of foreign currency. The system was well suited to intensify economic relations with the agrarian countries of Eastern Europe, which had suffered from the financial crisis along with Germany. German economic expansion meant a new orientation to the countries south and east of Germany.

The *Neuer Plan*, based on bilateral trade agreements, conceived a complete economic reorganization of the area, demoting Hungary and Romania to the level of sectors of the German war economy. Germany would buy as much as possible from states without requiring currency in exchange for German products. Instead of currency, Germany established the values of the trade in Reich Marks and credited a country's account established in Germany. Eastern European countries could use these accounts only for purchases in Germany as the funds were not transferable. Germany concentrated its imports on those needed for the military, foodstuffs, and raw materials such as Romanian oil.[1] Great Britain and France made clear they had no interest in engaging in trading with Eastern European countries, and during the 1930s Germany became the one country willing and able to take their products. For instance, French financing of Romanian rearmament in February 1936 withered in part thanks to French unwillingness to accept large quantities of Romanian products as payment.[2]

In 1939 the Germans increased their economic demands on Hungary, making clear their intention to turn the country into a raw material and food supply base for the German economy. To avoid complete dependence, Hungary turned to Great Britain, offering to sell the entire 1939 wheat surplus, but Britain refused. The British ambassador in Budapest, Sir Geoffrey Knox, reported that there was no sense in helping Hungary because it was bound to fall into German hands. Germany then took over the promise to buy the entire wheat surplus.[3] Poland figured differently in Hitler's plans. According to Timothy Snyder, the real design of Nazi agricultural policy was the creation of an eastern frontier empire by taking fertile land from Polish and Soviet peasants, who would be starved, assimilated, deported, or enslaved.[4]

Territorial revision worked as another tool of German manipulation of the Eastern European countries. Although Germany had initiated the dismemberment of Czechoslovakia by taking the Sudetenland in September 1938 by means of the Munich Agreement, Hungary and Poland participated as well. In an attachment signed by the four powers at Munich (Germany, Italy, Britain, and France), the question of transferring Czechoslovakian lands to meet Polish and Hungarian claims were to be settled within three months by negotiation with the Czechoslovak government. If the problems could not be settled within three months, the four powers would meet again. The Poles, not willing to wait, issued an ultimatum to Czechoslovakia for the immediate surrender of Teschen, and the Czech government agreed.[5]

The First Vienna Award, declared on November 2, 1938, in the Belvedere Palace, returned most of the Hungarian-inhabited areas on the southern boundary of Czechoslovakia to Hungary. The mood of the Hungarians was one of national jubilation; the population shouted revisionist slogans—Everything back! On to Transylvania.[6] The first Vienna Award raised the prospect of the redrawing of the national borders in Eastern Europe and therefore served as a powerful tool for Germany in keeping alliances or gaining new allies.

Although Hungary and Romania used anti-Jewish legislation to woo German support, Budapest and Bucharest, not Berlin, determined the treatment of their own Jewish populations. The timing of Hungarian Anti-Jewish legislation (First, Second, and Third Jewish Laws of 1938, 1939, 1941) demonstrated Hungary's willingness to cooperate with Nazi Germany to get territorial compensation. In 1938 and 1939 Hungary passed laws limiting Jewish civil rights, supposedly for economic reasons. The laws set quotas on the number of Jews permitted in the professions and in business and the Second Law also defined Jews by race instead of just religion, altering the status of those who had formerly converted from Judaism to Christianity. In 1939, Hungarian Jews were excluded from service in the armed forces and had to serve in forced labor battalions instead. Thirty-five thousand to forty thousand forced laborers, mostly Jews or of Jewish origin, served in the Hungarian Second Army, which fought in the USSR.

Antisemitism had long been strong in Romania. Forced to grant citizenship to all Jews and equal rights to minorities according to terms of the peace treaty after World War I, Romanian politicians in the 1930s attempted to drive Jews out of educational institutions and the more important branches of economy. By 1939, more than one-third of Romanian Jews had been deprived of citizenship.[7]

POLAND

The German invasion of Poland, begun on September 1, 1939, proved a hard-fought affair. Although perceptions of Poland's combat performance during the 1939 Campaign have long been shaped by the romantic myth of medieval Polish cavalry lancers futilely charging modern German tanks, such a view is no longer sustainable. The Polish army deployed close to the German border and far from natural defensive areas, such as the Vistula, with the goal of purposefully tying down German armies in anticipation of a French attack. Because the Poles expected help from their Western allies, they planned to fall back, thereby luring the Germans further to the east. On the seventeenth day, in coordination with the French attack as stipulated by the military convention, the Poles would counterattack with their reserve army group.[8]

Considering that Germany invaded Poland on September 1, 1939, followed by British and French declarations of war against Germany on September 3, and the Soviet invasion and occupation of eastern Poland on September 17, the Polish defeat owed more to the lack of action by the Western allies and the stab in the back from the Soviet Union than crushing German Panzer brilliance.[9] Matthew Palmer has exploded the myth of German Panzer invincibility through a detailed analysis of the operations of the German 4th Panzer Division in the Polish campaign. Palmer shows that when 4th Panzer Division's 341 tanks confronted an under-strength Polish cavalry brigade supported by a single armored train on September 1, the Poles succeeded in knocking out over one hundred tanks and another fifty armored cars with their cannon and anti-tank rifles. In this initial engagement at Mokra, Polish forces drove 4th Panzer back to its start line while inflicting thirty percent casualties. Only the Polish planned withdrawal from Mokra enabled the Germans to take the town the next day. By September 9, the 4th Panzer had sustained tank losses of sixty percent. Overall, the Germans lost fourteen hundred tanks in Poland by September 16, and 850 of these were damaged beyond repair.[10]

In the air, the Poles shot down 564 German aircraft out of three thousand (285 destroyed, 279 damaged) while losing 325 planes (out of 433 total combat aircraft). All told, Poland managed to hold out for five weeks in 1939, but in the process the Poles took one hundred thousand military deaths while killing sixteen thousand German troops. In addition, the Germans took roughly four hundred thousand Polish POWs and the Soviets another two hundred thousand.[11]

Nevertheless, Poland did not formally surrender, and Polish armed resistance transformed into underground formations participating in acts of violence, sabotage, and military intelligence. As John Connelly has pointed out, "Poles spoke not of 'collaboration,' or 'resistance' but rather-as befitted people living in a state of war-of 'treason' on the one hand and of 'underground' or 'conspiracy' on the other."[12] The Nazi intention to reduce the Poles to peonage and physically destroy the Polish intelligentsia did not leave much room for Polish collaboration.

In the context of Nazi-occupied Europe, the Germans' hesitance to seek out Poles for acts of collaboration proved an outlier. Only after defeat at Stalingrad, did Governor General Hans Frank float the idea to court Poles as possible auxiliaries against advancing Soviets, but Heinrich Himmler and Hitler vetoed his proposal. Most likely the Poles would not have responded favorably to such an offer as they were, by then, "irrevocably alienated by the Nazi excesses and atrocities."[13]

The brutal Nazi rule generated an active Polish resistance consisting of several underground organizations including the Peasant Battalions (Bataliony Chłopskie, 160,000 members), the National Armed Forces (Narodowe Siły Zbrojne, eighty thousand to one hundred thousand members) the People's Army (Armia Ludowa, a Soviet-backed partisan force, ten thousand to thirty thousand members), and the Home Army (Armia Krajowa or AK), numbering approximately 350,000 members.[14] After 1941, Polish underground resistance tied down roughly five hundred thousand German troops with occupation patrols and disrupted transports to the Eastern Front. Official German figures record Polish resistance prevented one out of eight *Wehrmacht* transports from making it to the Eastern Front. According to Polish records, resistance destroyed or temporarily put out of action 6,930 locomotives, derailed 732 German military transports, and damaged 19,058 railway wagons.[15]

The advance of Soviet forces from the east in 1944 raised the prospect of the AK pursuing coordinated military action with the Soviets against the Germans, but also posed the challenge of Poland simply replacing Nazi rule with new Soviet masters. In January 1944, Soviet forces had crossed the prewar Polish border, and by July of that year they were approaching Vilnius, Lublin, and Lviv. AK forces rose up in each of these cities as part of "Operation Storm" (Burza in Polish) developed in March 1944. The AK forces, fighting with limited weapons and supplies, suffered high casualties. Nevertheless, they obtained victory through coordination with Soviet forces. Having used the Polish fighters to their advantage, Soviet authorities quickly disarmed AK units after the battle and dissolved the AK while establishing pro-communist Polish entities. For example, in Lublin the Soviets proclaimed the "Polish Committee for National Liberation" because Stalin sought to eliminate the influence of the AK and the London Government in postwar Poland.[16]

The Warsaw uprising led by the AK turned into a catastrophe for the city. Operation Storm had not pertained to Warsaw originally, but Soviet advances to the outskirts of the capital in July prompted the AK to add the city to its plans on July 21, 1944. On July 30 the Soviet Second Tank Army was on the Vistula. Although AK forces in Warsaw possessed minimal arms and supplies including just thirty-nine heavy machineguns, 130 light machineguns, twenty-four hundred rifles, twenty-eight hundred pistols, twenty-one British anti-tank guns, and about thirty-six thousand grenades, on August 1, 1944, the Warsaw uprising began with the Poles hoping to take control of their capital before the Red Army did so.

With no expectation of the Soviets providing material support, roughly twenty thousand AK fighters rose up against thirteen thousand to twenty thousand German troops and police. The first day of the uprising cost the Poles ten percent of their forces. Meanwhile, Soviet Second Tank Army came up against five German tank divisions and was forced onto the defensive, and by August 4 the Soviet forces had lost two-thirds of their 810 tanks in heavy fighting just east of Warsaw. Also at that time, August 4, major German reinforcements arrived in the city.[17]

As fighting raged, block-by-block and house-to-house, the Germans executed orders to destroy the entire city. An estimated 150,000 to two hundred thousand Poles died in Warsaw by the time the Germans put down the uprising on October 2. The Soviet forces nearby never entered the struggle as Stalin let the Germans eliminate the potential Polish opposition to pave the way for Soviet control in postwar Poland.[18] The Warsaw Uprising left the city in rubble. Over the course of World War II, Warsaw lost 720,000 people or roughly a sixty percent casualty rate. The devastation of Warsaw was comparatively worse than Dresden or Hiroshima.[19]

Hungary and Romania

Lacking any territorial designs on Poland, the Hungarians rebuffed Hitler's attempts to involve Hungary in military actions against that country in 1939. A long tradition of friendship and sympathy existed between Hungary and Poland, and Hungary was determined to follow a policy of neutrality. The government refused passage to German troops, sheltered large numbers of Polish refugees (one hundred thousand), and also allowed Polish soldiers to move on to France. Hungary's neutral position surprised the British government because it indicated that Hungary remained an independent country.[20] However, already by December 1939 Hungarian Prime Minister Pal Teleki understood that Hungary would have to fight on Germany's side to get Transylvania back from Romania.[21]

Romania became a revisionist power as a result of Soviet provocations and German connivance. Taken by surprise on June 26, 1940, the Romanian government received a Soviet ultimatum: Molotov demanded the return of Bessarabia, but also the Ukrainian inhabited northern Bukovina. The Romanian government panicked. The German ambassador advised the government to give in without a struggle as unbeknownst to Romania, Germany had conceded Bessarabia to the Soviets in the Secret Protocol of the Nazi–Soviet Non-Aggression Pact.[22]

The Romanian General Staff feared if war broke out on the eastern border, Hungary and Bulgaria would begin simultaneous invasions. The government accepted the Soviet ultimatum and, on June 28, Soviet troops crossed the border. The loss of territory inflicted a stunning blow to the Romanian political and military leadership. On June 29, King Carol's government announced that Romania openly expressed its friendship for Germany, hoping that German protection could prevent further Soviet demands and block Bulgaria and Hungary from demanding the return of their territories. Two days later Romania terminated English and French guarantees. Both Bulgaria and Hungary began efforts to attain the return of territories granted Romania in the post-World War I peace treaties.[23]

The Soviet annexations from Romania opened the door for territorial revisions, and Hitler now walked through it. Up to this point Hitler had refused to satisfy Hungary's territorial claims on Romania, but now Hungary and Romania were mobilizing their troops and a Hungarian–Romanian war appeared imminent as Hungary deployed twenty-three divisions on the Romanian border. Hitler, concerned about the possibility of a joint Soviet–Hungarian move against Romania which would threaten the Romanian oil fields that supplied ninety-four percent of German imports in 1940,[24] offered Germany's services as mediator. This German pressure forced the Bucharest leadership to take the first steps toward negotiations with Hungary on territorial revision.[25]

Ultimately, Hitler's granting of Transylvania to Hungary drove Romania and Hungary into the German camp. The new Hungarian–Romanian border was presented to the delegates of Hungary and Romania on August 30, 1940, at the Belvedere. In accordance with the decision, Hungary reclaimed forty percent of Transylvania (forty-three thousand square kilometers). The Second Vienna Award, termed the *Viennese Dictat* by the Romanians, shocked both parties. When the Romanian foreign minister, Mihail Manoilescu, saw the new borders he fainted.[26]

The Romanian reaction to the decision was so violent that it fatally weakened the position of the bumbling, corrupt Romanian king. After the collapse of King Carol's government on September 6, he called on General Ion Antonescu to form a new government. Antonescu forced the King to abdicate and was then appointed president of the Council of Ministers by the new King, the nineteen-year-old Michael. Known for his personal integrity, Antonescu enjoyed widespread public support, but he had no tolerance for parliamentary government. He soon took over complete control of the country.[27]

Under Antonescu, the country made a complete turn toward Nazi Germany. Antisemitic measures increased, usually under the guise of "Romanianization." Antonescu blamed the failure of Romanian foreign policy primarily on the Jews and demanded that the country be "purified" of all alien elements. Many Romanians shared his view that a people's strength depended on its racial purity. Antonescu thus shared an ideological affinity with Hitler, including linking anti-Bolshevism and antisemitism.[28] His principal foreign policy aim, which he announced openly, was to return to Romania all the territories annexed by foreign powers during 1940, not only Bessarabia and northern Bukovina, but northern Transylvania as well. He committed Romania to fight with the Axis, stating: "Either we triumph with the Axis, or we fall with it."[29]

Hungary, paying the price for regaining northern Transylvania, had signed another substantial economic agreement with Germany. The government also permitted German training troops to pass through Hungarian territory by rail to the Romanian oil fields, a decision which brought a protest from Britain. On November 20, 1940, Hungary joined Germany, Italy, and Japan in the Tripartite Pact, effectively putting an end to Hungarian neutrality. General Antonescu signed the pact for Romania three days later.

While Hungarian and Romanian leaders tried to play off German interests in the region for their own foreign policy ends, the Germans sought to use their mediating position between Hungary and Romania to gain support for the German war effort.[30] Hitler had seemingly achieved an incredible diplomatic balancing act by bringing Hungary and Romania into the Axis camp and channeling their mutual antagonisms into competition for Germany's favor.

The German invasion of the Soviet Union ultimately brought Romania and Hungary actively into the war. On June 22, 1941, Germany launched Operation Barbarossa. Hitler had not informed his allies of the plans and did not expect their participation. Antonescu was the first to be told of the plan on June 12 at a meeting with Hitler in Munich. Hitler had been extremely impressed with Antonescu at their first meeting, seeing him as someone he could trust. Antonescu explained his plans to cooperate with Germany and insisted that the Second Vienna Award be revised because Antonescu believed "the road to Transylvania lies through Russia" and loyal cooperation with Hitler.[31] Although Hitler made no promises, Antonescu believed that he had made a commitment to alter the terms of the Award. After recovering Bessarabia and Bukovina, Antonescu insisted that Romanian units continue to fight side-by-side with the Germans to defeat the Soviet Union.

The Romanians made an enormous contribution to Operation Barbarossa. Romanian Third and Fourth Armies, designated as "Army Group Antonescu," comprised 325,685 men.[32] As detailed by Mark Axworthy, the total number of troops involved on the Eastern Front with the Romanian Third and Fourth Armies exceeded the Italian contribution and ranked second only to that of Nazi Germany itself. Every first-line Romanian division served at the front in the first year of the German invasion of the Soviet Union. The main site of Romanian action was the siege of Odessa 1941, where Romania took heavy casualties. For example, Romanian 4th Army lost 4,599 officers out of 4,821. While Romanian forces on the Eastern Front amounted to twelve percent of the German total between August and September 1941, they suffered disproportionately higher losses by accounting for thirty percent of the casualties. Romania losses totaled ninety-eight thousand since crossing the Dniester River. Not surprisingly, given the magnitude of Romanian sacrifice, by end of 1941 Romanians felt they had earned their Transylvanian reward from Germany.[33]

During the "euphoria of victory" in the summer 1941, Antonescu embarked upon the ethnic cleansing of the territories retaken from the Soviet Union. Specifically, between July and October 1941 Romanian authorities systematically murdered roughly 280,000 to 380,000 Jews in the territories of Bessarabia, Bukovina and Transnistria. Of the twenty-five thousand Romani who were deported to concentration camps in Transnistria, eleven thousand died. Half of the 320,000 Jews living in Bessarabia, Bukovina, and Dorohoi district in Romania were murdered within months of the entry of the country into the war during 1941. Even after the initial killings, Jews in Moldavia, Bukovina, and Bessarabia were subject to frequent pogroms, and were concentrated into ghettos from which they were sent to Nazi concentration camps, including camps built and run by Romanians.[34] Antonescu's regime ordered the shooting of thousands of more Jews in Transnistria in December 1941 and January 1942.[35]

Hungarian political leadership had no intention of joining Hitler's campaign. Hungary had no claims against the Soviet Union and its army was ill prepared. Hitler himself did not consider Hungarian participation necessary or desirable.[36] All this changed on June 26 when three unidentified planes dropped bombs on the Hungarian city of Kassa. Local military authorities concluded that Soviet planes were responsible, although this has never been substantiated. Nonetheless, describing the attack on Kassa as an act of unprovoked aggression, Hungary joined the war against the USSR.[37]

Expecting a short war, the military leadership dispatched the Carpathian Group consisting of sixty thousand to seventy thousand troops across the Hungarian frontier on July 1.[38] The Hungarian formations included the Rapid Corps, or Mobile Corps, placed under the German command of Army Group South. The Rapid Corps participated in German encirclements of the large Soviet forces west of the Dniester River. Even though the Rapid Corps was completely worn down by the end of August, the Hungarian force had performed well under the German 1st Panzer Group.[39]

Due to the failure of the Barbarossa campaign in 1941, Hungary and Romania had to increase their military contribution on the Eastern Front in 1942 with disastrous results thanks to the debacle at Stalingrad. Hungarian participation in Operation Barbarossa in 1941 had been voluntary, but Hitler wrote to Miklos Horthy, Regent of Hungary, at the end of December demanding more military support. For spring 1942, Horthy agreed to mobilize an army of two hundred thousand Hungarian troops in addition to forty thousand occupation troops and thirty-seven thousand for labor battalions constituted as Hungarian Second Army. Hungary had one-half as many divisions as Romania on the Eastern Front in spring/summer 1942 in anticipation of German assault on Stalingrad.

By the end of 1942, Hungary had provided 250,000 troops to the Eastern Front and in the process had committed three-quarters of its weapons, vehicles, and aircraft. The Second Army's two hundred thousand troops at Voronezh, near Stalingrad, suffered forty thousand dead, thirty-five thousand wounded, and another sixty thousand became Soviet POWs by January 1943. The Romanian losses to the Third and Fourth Armies during the Soviet Stalingrad counter-offensive amounted to 155,010, more than one-quarter of all Romanian troops on the front. By April 1943, Hungarian and Romanian armies had sustained overall losses in excess of one-half of their mobilized fighting forces on Eastern Front.[40]

In the second half of 1942, Romania and Hungary stopped trying to curry favor with Germany and began asserting more autonomy. In summer of 1942 Antonescu made a fundamental change in policy. The Romanians refused German requests that the remaining Jewish population of Romania be sent to death camps in Poland. He also reversed the policy of deportation to Transnistria. The reasons are not clear, but there was strong internal opposition, including pressure from King Michael and the Queen Mother. Antonescu may have been concerned about Romania's fate at an eventual peace settlement.[41]

After Miklós Kállay became the Hungarian prime minister, the German government on October 17, 1942 ordered that Jews be completely shut out of economic and cultural life, that they wear the yellow star, that deportations begin, and that three hundred thousand Jews be sent to the Ukraine. Kállay and Horthy rejected the German demands. The Hungarian government flatly rejected the request to force Jews to wear a distinguishing mark or to prepare for deportation. On the matter of sending three hundred thousand Jews to the Ukraine, Kállay said Jews could be usefully employed on work projects in Hungary. In any case, the Jewish Question was an internal affair, and Hungary would not brook any interference from outsiders.[42]

As a consequence of the Axis defeat at Stalingrad, Hungarian–Romanian rivalry turned into competition for Allied favor as each country put out peace feelers with the hope of dominating Transylvania in postwar Europe. Motivated by concerns that ending up on the losing side would doom Hungary to reduced borders as had happened with World War I, the Hungarians moved first. In the fall of 1942, even before the defeat at Stalingrad, Hungarian envoys in Turkey conveyed to the U.S. government that the Hungarian army would not resist an Anglo–American invasion.[43]

Meanwhile, Antonescu told his closest supporters in January 1943, "Germany has lost the wider war. We must make every effort to ensure that we don't lose our own war."[44] Indeed, Romanians talked about war not with the USSR, but with Hungary, as the troops considered fighting for Germans as the means for restoring Transylvania to Romania.[45] Romanian security services reported in early 1943 that, "Romanian soldiers, when asked why they are fighting, say that they are fighting only for the recovery of Transylvania."[46]

In September 1943 meeting in Turkey, the British secretly informed the Hungarians of preliminary conditions for Hungary to switch sides and join the Allies. The change of sides would occur only after the Anglo-Saxon powers reached Hungary's borders. However, because the Anglo–American forces never reached the Hungarian borders the agreement remained moot.[47] On October 2, 1943, the Romanian military attaché in Ankara delivered Antonescu's message to the British indicating Romania's willingness to cooperate with any Anglo–American forces landing in the Balkans. Antonescu even offered Romanian assistance to the Western Allies in the form of oil, gold, money, and trained pilots to avoid a Soviet occupation of Romania.[48]

Ultimately, Romania succeeded in switching sides whereas Hungary endured German occupation. In either case, both countries experienced hard fighting and significant losses. Between January and April 1943, some two thousand Romanian POWs petitioned Soviet military authorities to join fight for "liberation of Romania." Eventually they constituted the Tudor Vladimirescu Division in which ten thousand Romanians fought under Soviet command in the battle for Transylvania in early September 1944.[49] Having fielded the second-largest Axis force on the Continent in 1943–1944, Romania ultimately provided the fourth-largest Allied army in 1944–1945, and it suffered the third-highest Allied casualties during that period.[50]

In contrast, Hungary was subjected to German invasion and occupation. Around one hundred thousand *Wehrmacht* and SS troops, amounting to almost ten divisions, marched into Hungary on March 19, 1944.[51] Soon thereafter mass deportations of Jews to German death camps began. SS Colonel Adolf Eichmann arrived in Hungary to oversee the large-scale deportations. Between May 15 and July 9, Hungarian authorities deported 437,402 Jews. All but fifteen thousand of these Jews were sent to Auschwitz-Birkenau, and ninety percent of those were immediately killed. Under the dual pressures of foreign and domestic protests, combined with German defeats and the Allied landing at Normandy, in early July 1944 Regent Horthy finally had the deportations halted. By taking action, he saved the lives of some two hundred thousand Jews from Budapest.[52] In late August, Horthy refused Eichmann's request to restart the deportations.[53]

World War II cost the lives of roughly some 6.2 percent of Hungary's population of 14.5 million, or approximately nine hundred thousand persons. These included an estimated 340,000– 360,000 soldiers and about five hundred thousand Jews. Some six hundred thousand wound up in Soviet captivity, while three hundred thousand surrendered to the Anglo-Saxon powers.[54] In the last year of the war one out of ten Hungarians was killed.[55]

Conclusion

The collapse of communism in the Eastern Bloc and the Soviet withdrawal from the region by 1990 removed the Communist censorship and has opened the way for reconsideration of the consequences and the roles of Poland, Hungary, and Romania in World War II. Considerations of collaboration and resistance now extend beyond the period of Nazi dominance to include Soviet occupation as well, and consequently scholars increasingly include the processes of Sovietization up to 1948 as the appropriate end point for studies of World War II.

Although the formal sovereignty of Poland, Romania, and Hungary was restored after World War II, the Soviet Union assumed political dominance over them through economic and political Sovietization. The wartime experiences of the Eastern European societies and especially the traumas inflicted on certain sectors of those societies under Nazi German occupation greatly facilitated Sovietization. Thus, strong continuities run through the wartime years of German conquest and the immediate postwar years of the developing Soviet Bloc.[56]

Notes

1. György Ránki, *Economy and Foreign Policy, the Struggle of the Great Powers for Hegemony in the Danube Valley, 1919–1939* (Boulder, CO: Columbia University, 1983), 146.
2. Nicole Jordan, *The Popular Front and Central Europe: The Dilemmas of French Impotence, 1918–1940* (Cambridge: Cambridge University Press, 1992), 108–135.
3. Deborah S. Cornelius, *Hungary in World War II: Caught in the Cauldron* (New York: Fordham University Press, 2011), 100–101.
4. Timothy Snyder, *Bloodlands: Europe Between Hitler and Stalin* (New York: Basic Books, 2010), 19.
5. Cornelius, *Hungary in World War II*, 103.
6. Ibid., 91.
7. Holly Case, *Between States: The Transylvanian Question and the European Idea during World War II* (Stanford, CA: Stanford University Press, 2009), 182–183; Cornelius, *Hungary in World War II*, 73–75, 106–109.
8. Michael Alfred Peszke, "The Forgotten Campaign: Poland's Military Aviation in September, 1939," *Polish Review* 39, no. 1 (1994): 65, 71.
9. D. G. Williamson, *Poland Betrayed: The Nazi–Soviet Invasions of 1939* (Mechanicsburg, PA: Stackpole, 2011), 167.
10. Matthew S. Palmer, "The Grand Delusion: The Creation and Perseverance of the September Campaign Mythos," *Journal of Slavic Military Studies* 30, no. 1 (2017): 65–67, 73.
11. Peszke, "The Forgotten Campaign," 65, 69, 71; Walter M. Drzewieniecki, "The Polish Army on the Eve of World War II," *Polish Review* 26, no. 3 (1981): 63; Brian Porter-Szücs, *Poland in the Modern World, Beyond Martyrdom* (Chichester: Wiley Blackwell, 2014), 198–199; Jozef Garlinski, *Poland in the Second World War* (London: Macmillan, 1985), 25.
12. John Connelly, "Why the Poles Collaborated So Little—and Why That is No Reason for Nationalist Hubris," *Slavic Review* 64, no. 4 (Winter 2005): 774.
13. Joseph Rothschild and Nancy M. Wingfield, *Return to Diversity* (Oxford: Oxford University Press, 2008), 21.
14. Porter-Szücs, *Poland in the Modern World*, 217–218.
15. Patrick G. Zander, *Hidden Armies of The Second World War: World War II Resistance Movements* (Santa Barbara, CA: Praeger, 2017), 142; István Deák, *Europe on Trial: The Story of Collaboration, Resistance, and Retribution during World War II* (Boulder, CO: Westview, 2015), 149.
16. Porter-Szücs, *Poland in the Modern World*, 222, 225; Zander, *Hidden Armies*, 147.
17. Włodzimierz Borodziej *The Warsaw Uprising of 1944*, trans. Barbara Harshav (Madison: University of Wisconsin Press, 2006), 61, 63, 67, 70–78; Zander, *Hidden Armies*, 150.
18. Zander, *Hidden Armies*, 148, 150, 152.
19. Porter-Szücs, *Poland in the Modern World*, 228.

20. Cornelius, *Hungary in World War II*, 114; Ignác Romsics, "Hungary," in *Joining Hitler's Crusade: European Nations and the Invasion of the Soviet Union, 1941*, ed. David Stahel (Cambridge: Cambridge University Press, 2017), 84.
21. Case, *Between States*, 70.
22. Barbara Jelavich, *History of the Balkans, Twentieth Century*, Vol. 2 (Cambridge: Cambridge University Press, 1983), 222.
23. Cornelius, *Hungary in World War II*, 124.
24. Mark Axworthy, Cornel Scafeș, and Cristian Craciunoiu, *Third Axis, Fourth Ally, Romanian Armed Forces in the European War, 1941–1945* (London: Arms and Armour Press, 1995), 19.
25. Case, *Between States*, 71; Cornelius, *Hungary in World War II*, 126–127; Dennis Deletant, "Romania," in *Joining Hitler's Crusade: European Nations and the Invasion of the Soviet Union, 1941*, ed. David Stahel (Cambridge: Cambridge University Press, 2017), 60.
26. Case, *Between States*, 70; Cornelius, *Hungary in World War II*, 130.
27. Cornelius, *Hungary in World War II*, 131; Case, *Between States*, 72.
28. David Stahel, "Introduction," in *Joining Hitler's Crusade: European Nations and the Invasion of the Soviet Union, 1941*, ed. David Stahel (Cambridge: Cambridge University Press, 2017), 9.
29. Denis Deletant, *Hitler's Forgotten Ally: Ion Antonescu and His Regime, Romania 1940–44* (New York: Palgrave Macmillan, 2006), 54.
30. Case, *Between States*, 74–75.
31. Axworthy, Scafeș, and Craciunoiu, *Third Axis*, 49.
32. Stahel, "Introduction," 9.
33. Axworthy, Scafeș, and Craciunoiu, *Third Axis*, 57–58, 71–72, 118.
34. Vladimir Solonari, "An Important New Document on the Romanian Policy of Ethnic Cleansing during World War II," *Holocaust and Genocide Studies* 21, no. 2 (Fall 2007): 268–269; Mariana Hausleitner, "Romania in the Second World War: Revisionist out of Necessity," in *Territorial Revisionism and the Allies of Germany in the Second World War*, ed. Marina Cattaruzza, Stefan Dyroff, and Dieter Langewiesche (New York: Berghahn, 2013), 186.
35. Dennis Deletant, "Romania," 73.
36. Romsics, "Hungary," 87.
37. Cornelius, *Hungary in World War II*, 147–150.
38. Romsics, "Hungary," 101.
39. Stahel, "Introduction," 10.
40. László Borhi, "Secret Peace Overtures, the Holocaust, and Allied Strategy vis-à-vis Germany: Hungary in the Vortex of World War II," *Journal of Cold War Studies* 14, no. 2 (Spring 2012): 29, 35; Cecil D. Eby, *Hungary at War, Civilians and Soldiers in World War II* (University Park: Pennsylvania State University Press, 1998), 19–21; Cornelius, *Hungary in World War II*, 184; Romsics, "Hungary," 102; Case, *Between States*, 68, 78; Deletant, "Romania," 77.
41. Deletant, *Hitler's Forgotten Ally*, 212.
42. Cornelius, *Hungary in World War II*, 245.
43. Borhi, "Secret Peace Overtures," 31, 34.
44. Quoted in Axworthy, Scafeș, and Craciunoiu, *Third Axis*, 119.
45. Case, *Between States*, 80.
46. Ibid., 82.

47. Cornelius, *Hungary in World War II*, 256–258.
48. Borhi, "Secret Peace Overtures," 41.
49. Case, *Between States*, 86.
50. Axworthy, Scafeş, and Craciunoiu, *Third Axis*, 9.
51. Borhi, "Secret Peace Overtures," 67.
52. Romsics, "Hungary," 104.
53. Cornelius, *Hungary in World War II*, 298, 310.
54. Romsics, "Hungary," 106.
55. Borhi, "Secret Peace Overtures," 31.
56. Rothschild and Wingfield, *Return to Diversity*, 20.

Bibliography

Axworthy, Mark, Cornel Scafeş, and Cristian Craciunoiu. *Third Axis Fourth Ally, Romanian Armed Forces in the European War, 1941–1945*. London: Arms and Armour Press, 1995.

Borhi, Laszlo. "Secret Peace Overtures, the Holocaust, and Allied Strategy vis-à-vis Germany: Hungary in the Vortex of World War II." *Journal of Cold War Studies* 14, no. 2 (Spring 2012): 29–67.

Borodziej, Włodzimierz. *The Warsaw Uprising of 1944*. Translated by Barbara Harshav. Madison: University of Wisconsin Press, 2006.

Case, Holly. *Between States, The Transylvanian Question and the European Idea during World War II*. Stanford, CA: Stanford University Press, 2009.

Cornelius, Deborah S. *Hungary in World War II, Caught in the Cauldron*. New York: Fordham University Press, 2011.

Romsics, Ignác. "Hungary." In *Joining Hitler's Crusade: European Nations and the Invasion of the Soviet Union, 1941*, edited by David Stahel, 79–106. Cambridge: Cambridge University Press, 2017.

Snyder, Timothy. *Bloodlands: Europe Between Hitler and Stalin*. New York: Basic Books, 2010.

Williamson, D. G. *Poland Betrayed: The Nazi-Soviet Invasions of 1939*. Mechanicsburg, PA: Stackpole, 2011.

CHAPTER 16

THE EASTERN FRONT, 1943–1945

DAVID R. STONE

From 1941 to 1943, Stalin's Soviet Union and the Red Army survived Nazi Germany's onslaught and began to roll back the tide of German conquest. From 1943 to 1945, the Soviets went from survival to triumph, smashing the *Wehrmacht*, occupying Berlin, and imposing a new Soviet system on eastern Germany. Our understanding of how the Soviet Union achieved this has changed fundamentally over the years since 1945. In the early postwar years, Soviet secrecy, the accessibility of captured German generals, and the ideological strictures of the Cold War produced a picture in the West of Soviet victory that minimized the positive achievements of the Soviets. German generals blamed Hitler for German strategic mistakes, and attributed Soviet victories to massive material and human resources, along with a willingness to spend lives on a horrific scale. The increasing availability of Soviet sources, beginning with official histories and memoirs in the 1950s and 1960s, and expanded by the opening of Soviet archives at the end of the 1980s, has fundamentally changed this understanding. The Soviet regime was willing to spend lives, but it was also capable of mobilizing economic resources. The Red Army's high command proved adaptable and capable of learning under the most trying circumstances. The Soviet Union, despite its ostensible technical backwardness, outproduced Nazi Germany in vital categories of war material, and its equipment was generally better suited to the conditions of the Eastern Front. Nazi Germany was not simply defeated by dark masses of bestial Soviet conscripts but was beaten at its own game.

The war on the Eastern Front from 1943 to 1945 had a fundamentally different nature and operational rhythm from the war up to that point. The German formula of mobile warfare, destroying enormous Soviet formations in vast battles of encirclement, had begun to show its limits in 1942. By 1943, the Germans were no longer capable of the stunning victories they had achieved in the early days of the war in the East. Despite this different nature, the later stages of the war in the East have been relatively neglected by scholars, particularly those working in the West. The campaigns of the first eighteen months of the Soviet–German War—Barbarossa, the German assault on Moscow in late 1941, the Soviet winter counteroffensive, the German drive on the Caucasus, and its culminating battle at Stalingrad—have generally consumed more attention than the subsequent thirty months.

The nature of fighting fundamentally changed in the later years of the war as strategic initiative shifted to the Soviets. Until the Battle of Kursk in summer 1943, the Soviets found it nearly impossible to achieve substantial gains against prepared German defenses, or to engage in successful offensives without the benefit of bad weather to reduce German operational mobility. Soviet tactical and operational successes, which did occur and were occasionally substantial, took place under specific, advantageous circumstances. They involved the stubborn defense of fixed positions, as in 1941 at Odessa and in 1942 at Sevastopol and then Stalingrad. They also took the form of counteroffensives against overextended and exhausted Axis troops whose offensives had culminated at the limits of their logistical support. At Moscow in December 1941, at Stalingrad in November 1942, and then finally at Kursk in August 1943, the Soviets launched devastating counterattacks, but against German forces which were ill-prepared to defend as a result of their own failed offensives.

After Kursk, the strategic dynamic was fundamentally different. Beginning with the lengthy Soviet pursuit after Kursk, the pattern of the war became one of Soviet offensives employing superiority in manpower, armor, and artillery to break through German defenses and exploit those breaches to recapture huge swaths of occupied territory. The most successful Soviet offensives encircled and annihilated sizable German formations; the least successful achieved meager gains, won territory without inflicting significant casualties, or surrendered ground to German counterattacks. As the war progressed after summer 1943, the *Wehrmacht* increasingly found itself having to withdraw in response to Soviet offensives to avoid wholesale destruction, abandoning territory to preserve fighting men. Once a Soviet offensive exhausted its reserves of men and supplies, the retreating Germans engaged in sharp counterattacks to reclaim some lost ground and inflict losses on the Soviets. Over time, the Soviet offensives became steadily more ambitious, the German counterattacks less effective, and the overall Soviet superiority more pronounced. After Kursk, the Germans were never in a position to carry out a major offensive against the Soviets, only to counterpunch against overextended Soviet advances. When Germany did manage to accumulate reserves for a major offensive, Adolf Hitler deliberately chose to expend those resources in the Ardennes against the Western Allies in December 1944, not against the Soviets.

At the level of high command and grand strategy, the German war effort by 1943 had already been set into deeply pathological patterns, with Adolf Hitler convinced of his own genius and the timidity or even active hostility of his own generals. The *Oberkommando der Wehrmacht* (OKW), Hitler's operational staff, which was generally responsible for the war outside the Eastern Front, remained in the politically reliable but strategically deferential hands of the subservient Wilhelm Keitel. The *Oberkommando des Heeres* (OKH), running the war in the East, was headed as it had been since December 1941 by Hitler himself. His Chief of Army General Staff Kurt Zeitzler was a competent administrator and planner, but he lacked the will or combat record to stand up to Hitler's whims. As a result, Hitler's ongoing resistance to tactical withdrawals and to the surrender of territory to gain time and preserve troops hindered the German war effort through the end of the war.[1]

By contrast, Stalin had, by mid-1943, grown to trust the professional competence of his generals and benefited from a skilled and efficient high command, *Stavka*, to run the war. The Soviet General Staff ran smoothly under the competent and thoroughly professional leadership of Aleksandr Vasilevskii and his deputy for operations Aleksei Antonov. A vicious winnowing by the hard school of war had finally produced Soviet Front (army group) commanders of real skill. These Soviet Fronts, which could number as many as a dozen at any one time, were coordinated in larger operations by *Stavka* representatives, notably Georgi Zhukov, the most successful Soviet commander of the war. Although the Soviet high command never fully solved the problem of properly uniting the actions of its Fronts and their constituent armies, performance was far better than it had been in 1941 and 1942 and improved steadily until final victory.

A similar pattern took place at the operational and tactical level. At odds with a picture of Germany as a society far ahead of the Soviet Union in its industrial and economic development, the German military was demechanized by the end of the war. The Soviet Union substantially outproduced Germany in tanks while manufacturing comparable numbers of aircraft. The Soviets also benefited from the industrial resources of their British and American allies, an asset Hitler entirely lacked. By the end of the war, German infantry marched on foot in advance and retreat, and Germany's losses of men and material to Soviet encirclements were largely attributable to lack of motorized transport to evacuate troops and supplies faster than Soviet armor and infantry (riding in Lend Lease trucks) could advance. The Anglo–American bombing campaign against Germany had an often-neglected effect on the Eastern Front of compelling the German high command to pull fighter aircraft and anti-aircraft guns away from the war against the Soviets to defend German cities. This gave the Soviets a critical margin of superiority in the air and in armored warfare that made the German position on the Eastern Front increasingly untenable.[2]

Although German generals after the war blamed their defeat on mindless Soviet hordes or Hitler's counterproductive interference in operational matters, Soviet commanders grew increasingly sophisticated in their ability to conduct mechanized warfare. Soviet intelligence and counterintelligence improved markedly over the course of the war, and in particular the Soviets became masters of misdirection to conceal their strategic and operational intent from Hitler's generals. In addition, Soviet supply and logistical capability to support large and geographically ambitious offensives was quite impressive. A detailed account of the operations of a Soviet tank army, for example, shows how it could begin an offensive close to its nominal strength of four hundred tanks, have most of them disabled or destroyed with a matter of days, and almost as quickly build back to near full strength through repairs and replacements, all while advancing three hundred kilometers in two weeks.[3]

Despite that, German tactical and operational skill continued to inflict serious losses on the Soviets, far out of proportion to German casualties. Unless the Soviets could achieve wholesale encirclements of large German formations, they routinely lost three to five times as many men as the Germans did in each successive campaign. Nonetheless, the Germans could ill-afford their lost manpower, entangled as they were in a simultaneous struggle against the Western Allies as Germany's own allies were successively driven out of the war. Even the vast Soviet population did not prevent manpower shortages by the end of the war, but the Soviet Army pulled manpower from partisan groups, liberated populations, and freed prisoners-of-war and conscript labor as it rolled west. After cursory training, this manpower was pressed into service to fill out depleted formations. The last two years of the war were thus an increasingly frantic German attempt to stave off complete disaster.

The Kursk Counteroffensive

The long road to Berlin began with the high-water mark of the German offensive at Kursk. July 12, 1943 marked a fundamental change in the war in the east. Operation *Citadel*, the German offensive against the vast Kursk salient, had begun a week before. Progress had been slow and costly against well-entrenched Soviet positions, but it had been progress, nonetheless. Konstantin Rokossovskii's Central Front to the north and Nikolai Vatutin's Voronezh Front to the south both defended stubbornly, constantly feeding in reserves to halt German breakthroughs. On both flanks of the salient, though, German fortunes took a sharp turn for the worse on July 12. To the south, the German II-SS Panzer Corps smashed into the Soviet 5th Guards Tank Army. Although the Germans wrecked the Soviet tank force, their own advance was blunted and their limited stock of manpower and equipment further drained. Far more serious was the northern sector, where German advances had been more limited, enabling a more rapid Soviet turn to the offensive. The Soviets began Operational *Kutuzov*, breaking through German forward defenses with the Western and Bryansk Fronts. The Germans had expended much of their armor in the *Citadel* offensive, and this lack of armor to counter the new Soviet attacks combined with overwhelming Soviet material superiority compelled the *Wehrmacht* to halt its northern offensive pushing south toward Kursk to defend their positions. German resistance to the *Kutuzov* counteroffensive prevented any major Soviet breakthroughs and forced the Soviets to commit their armor far earlier than they had preferred, but the pressure made it clear the Kursk offensive could not continue. On July 13, Hitler told Army Group commanders Erich von Manstein and Günther von Kluge that mounting German losses and the Allied invasion of Sicily compelled an end to *Citadel*. On July 25, Hitler further acquiesced to pressure from his generals and agreed to the evacuation of the German salient north of Kursk. By August 5, Soviet troops had liberated Orël and by August 18, Bryansk.[4]

The failed German offensive at Kursk and the subsequent Soviet riposte forced many participants in the war into a fundamental reassessment. Soviet partisans, who had primarily served to bolster morale and assure Soviets under occupation that governmental authority remained and would return, now became increasingly effective at interdicting German rail transport, and recruited more manpower as Soviet victory seemed increasingly likely.[5] After the disaster of Stalingrad and the subsequent retreat from the Volga, Hitler's allies had begun seriously rethinking their commitment to the war. The Romanian army, numerically the most significant of the German allies in the East, had been devastated by the Soviet counteroffensive at Stalingrad and its nine remaining divisions were incapable of serious additional effort, in part because of German failure to deliver sufficient armor to the Romanians or enable them to produce tanks for themselves. The Finns avoided offensive actions in 1943 to ease a deal with the Soviets to enable Finland to leave the war intact.[6]

Hitler's agreement to halt the Kursk offensive as a concession to the changing balance of forces on the Eastern Front did nothing to halt Soviet momentum. Operation *Kutuzov* was the first of a series of Soviet offensives stretching the length of the front and leaving the Germans no respite to consolidate their positions and construct a coherent defense. Soviet superiority in men and material, now allied to intermittent, but nonetheless improving, operational and tactical skill, enabled the continuing exploitation of the failure of *Citadel*. On July 17, five days after Operation *Kutuzov*, a matching Soviet counteroffensive south of the Kursk salient drove across the Mius River. After this drew German reserves to the Mius, another subsequent offensive, Operation *Rumiantsev*, broke out of the southern face of the Kursk salient on August 3. German resistance was fierce, and Soviet breakthroughs generally required the early use of large, armored formations, spending tanks to crack German defenses instead of using them to exploit breaches through deep penetrations behind German lines. Nonetheless, the German commanders at the front were pressing a reluctant Hitler to permit tactical withdrawals, and they found that their local counterattacks slowed but could not halt the Soviet advance. The devastated industrial center of Kharkov fell to the Soviets on August 28. By early September, Hitler had no choice but to endorse a withdrawal in the south to the general line of the Dnepr River. While this sacrificed territory, it preserved German fighting formations intact and prevented catastrophic losses.

Stalin's pattern in the war's first two years had been to rush to try to convert local successes into broad offensives along the entire length of the Eastern front, dissipating any temporary advantage the Soviets might have and ending in expensive failure. In mid-1943, Stalin was still learning to trust the judgment of his military professionals, and he repeated his earlier mistakes by overestimating the possibilities of exploiting success at Kursk. Throughout the Soviet advance, continuing shortfalls in operational coordination, combined with excessively ambitious offensives, meant losses far greater than those sustained by the Germans. The Soviets did not simply pursue the retreating Germans along the southern sector of the Eastern Front, but also attacked north of the Pripet Marshes in terrain more suitable for German defenses. While the Soviets did manage to make some headway, taking Smolensk in September 1943, the gains were nowhere near as dramatic as in the southern sector and cost the Soviets heavily. A massive Soviet effort in October 1943 to destroy German positions in Belorussia, anticipating the later and much more successful Operation *Bagration*, ended in abject failure and enormous casualties. This offensive was essentially expunged, like other unsuccessful Soviet offensives before, from later celebratory Soviet narratives of the war.[7]

The Soviets pursued the withdrawing Germans across eastern Ukraine, reaching the Dnepr River in September 1943. Where possible, they seized isolated bridgeheads, hoping to ease their subsequent task of forcing the wide river where the Germans enjoyed high ground on the Dnepr's western bank. Initial Soviet attacks out of those bridgeheads during October achieved little because the logistical demands of bringing up men and material necessarily forced a halt to major operations. The German 1st Panzer Army retained a foothold in the vast Dnepr bend, where the river swings far to the east before flowing back west to empty into the Black Sea. The German struggle to maintain this eastern bulwark drew attention and resources away other sectors. In the far south, Soviet spearheads swept past the Perekop isthmus connecting mainland Ukraine to the Crimean Peninsula, cutting off land communications with the German Seventeenth Army.

More importantly, the fighting southeast of Kiev in the Dnepr bend distracted the German high command from a concealed Soviet buildup of forces in difficult terrain around a bridgehead at Liutezh, just north of Kiev. Through October, the Soviets built up men and supplies in preparation for a renewed offensive. At the beginning of November 1943, Vatutin's 1st Ukrainian Front broke out of the bridgehead, and within two days had isolated Kiev and retook the city on November 6. Manstein carried out counterattacks that temporarily halted further Soviet advances but never came close to Kiev. The German situation in the east cried out for tactical withdrawals to a more defensible line, but Hitler blocked any such efforts, leaving Manstein to improvise local counterattacks. Manstein's highly effective troops achieved some successes, but they lacked the mass to make them truly decisive. Soviet mobile formations pushed west from Kiev toward Lvov and Kovel.[8]

By January 1944, Soviet troops had pushed three hundred kilometers past Kiev to the west Ukrainian town of Kovel. Even as the Soviets streamed west across northern Ukraine, the Germans, still retained two substantial footholds in southern Ukraine on the Dnepr: one just north of the Black Sea and the other, far more vulnerable, at Korsun south-east of Kiev. Hitler refused to permit withdrawal to a more defensible position, so the Soviets were able to spring a trap. On January 24, Ivan Konev's 2nd Ukrainian Front attacked from the south-east and Vatutin's 1st Ukrainian two days later from the northwest to pinch off the Korsun salient. By January 27, the German flanks had collapsed and within a week, Soviet forces had linked up behind Korsun, trapping two German corps. While Manstein attempted to break through to the Korsun pocket in early February, the Soviets worked to collapse and destroy it. After the failure of Manstein's initial relief effort, the nearly fifty thousand surrounded Germans launched a breakout on the night of February 16–17. It quickly devolved in a disorganized mob attempting to rush through Soviet positions to safety inside German lines. Surprisingly, well over one-half of the encircled Germans managed to escape, but at a cost of nearly all their supplies and heavy weapons. Soviet and German losses in this battle, contrary to much of the rest of the war in the East, were roughly equal. Further pursuit through early spring 1944 drove Germany forces out of Ukraine entirely, with numerous formations only narrowly escaping encirclement and destruction. The long pursuit after Kursk finally hit its high-water mark with a failed invasion of Romania in April–May 1944, creating a momentary lull in the relentless Soviet drive west.[9]

Over the second half of 1943 and early 1944, the precipitate Soviet advance from the Don to the Dnepr across the full breadth of Ukraine had recaptured ground, but it cost the Soviets casualties far greater than the Germans they pursued, often in a ratio of as much as five-to-one. While young men from the liberated population could be pressed into service in the advancing Red Army, the industrial resources of eastern Ukraine had been wrecked by the back-and-forth movement of the fronts. The Germans, by contrast, had lost a great deal of territory which had not been of particular benefit to them. On the other hand, while their manpower losses had been far less than the Soviets, they also had less margin to absorb those losses. By fall 1943, Germans divisions in Army Group South were approaching an average of only one thousand effective troops. The Soviets could not yet achieve the encirclement and wholesale destruction of large German formations, but over time the steady attrition of German mechanized and motorized support and increasingly critical shortages of fuel combined to force technological regression on the *Wehrmacht*. Small units of heavy German armor could inflict terrible losses on Soviet attacking formations, but there were never enough of these to halt the advance. Extracting Army Group South from Ukraine intact required the steady transfer of equipment and effective formations from Army Group Center and Army Group North, a borrowing that left the Germans desperately short of heavy equipment north of the Pripet Marshes by summer 1944. This staved off disaster in Ukraine, but it left German troops in Belorussia and the Baltic dangerously shorthanded.

In the first half of 1944, the Soviets took advantage of the weakened position of German troops in the north. At the beginning of the year, Hitler's forces were still dug in on the outskirts of Leningrad. Although in early 1943 the Soviets had managed to open a precarious land corridor to Leningrad, further attempts through the rest of 1943 to widen that lifeline had achieved few results at high cost. On January 14, 1944, however, the Leningrad and Volkhov Fronts broke out of both Leningrad itself and a beachhead further west on the Baltic shore. Weather slowed the Soviet advance, but Stalin nonetheless achieved his central purpose of removing the immediate threat to Leningrad. Army Group North withdrew rather than risk encirclement.[10]

The Soviets completed the process of securing Leningrad by driving Finland from the war. Finland had balked at Soviet peace feelers in late 1943 and early 1944, so in June the Finns faced the full impact of Soviet wrath. After painstaking and thorough accumulation of massive quantities of men and machines, Leonid Govorov's Leningrad Front attacked into the constricted space of the Karelian Isthmus. Soviet performance was far superior to that during the 1939–1940 Winter War, and by June 21, Govorov has reached Vyborg and Kirill Meretskov's Karelian Front attacked north of Lake Ladoga. Hurried

German reinforcements only temporarily halted the Soviet advance, which reached the old border in mid-July. By September, Finland accepted an armistice to escape Soviet occupation.

OPERATION *BAGRATION*

The Soviet pursuit of the Germans after the Battle of Kursk had produced a year of almost uninterrupted westward advance through Ukraine to the Carpathians and the pre-war Soviet border. That advance had, however, largely been confined to the southern sectors of the front, where space and relatively open terrain permitted rapid maneuver. North of the Pripet marshes, Soviet advances had been far more moderate against steady German resistance in Belorussia. The result was a geographic anomaly: the German front lines in Belorussia extended east like a giant shelf of rock hanging out in empty air—what the Soviets termed a "balcony." Despite the natural target this enormous salient seemed to present for Soviet attack, skilled Soviet deception operations and German failure to understand available intelligence led the German high command to expect that further Soviet offensives would exploit their point of greatest advance in western Ukraine, on the south side of the Pripet marshes, rather than attacking the Belorussian salient to the north. Beginning in April 1944, the Soviet General Staff began preparing the massive Operation *Bagration* to crush Army Group Center. Previously, Army Group Center had been able to employ elastic tactics and mobile defenses to prevent Soviet breakthroughs. The forthcoming offensive, employing huge Soviet armored formations against German armies essentially stripped of tanks and motor vehicles, turned mobility against the Germans. The Allied landings in Normandy likewise prevented the Germans from concentrating their scarce aviation and armor against the looming Soviet threat.

Four full Soviet Fronts were involved in the operation, and they enjoyed overwhelming superiority in manpower and, particularly, in equipment. Vasilevskii coordinated the 1st Baltic and 3rd Belorussian Fronts on the northern flank of the salient while Zhukov managed the 1st and 2nd Belorussian Fronts to its southern flank. Although the assault amassed four thousand tanks, it began with widespread attacks by Soviet partisans in German rear areas against rail communications. *Bagration* is where Soviet partisan warfare came into its own. The combination of Belorussia's terrain of forests and marshes and the ongoing strain on the German logistical system and railroad net allowed massive and coordinated partisan attacks to prevent the *Wehrmacht* from reinforcing or evacuating its beleaguered infantry divisions. The real offensive began on June 22, 1944, the third anniversary of Barbarossa, with a two-pronged encirclement of Vitebsk in the northeastern corner of the salient followed by attacks around the rest of the perimeter. Soviet armored formations quickly broke through toward Minsk, which was taken on July 2–3. Lacking mechanized transport and with railroads paralyzed by partisan attack, German infantry divisions were bypassed by Soviet armored advances and then crushed by pursuing infantry. Soviet air superiority aided in the interdiction of any German efforts to respond to the Soviet advance. The speed of Soviet advance was remarkably rapid, enabled by growing stocks of Lend Lease trucks to maintain supply, and took Vilnius by mid-July and reached the outskirts of Warsaw in only five weeks.[11]

Bagration shattered the German army in the east, wrecking thirty divisions and essentially completing the liberation of pre-war Soviet territory. On July 17, 1944, Stalin marched nearly sixty thousand German prisoners through Moscow in a display of the scope of his victory. The combination of German losses and the successful Allied landings in Normandy made any possibility of salvaging an acceptable peace settlement increasingly remote; nonetheless, elements among the German officer corps tried to find an exit from Germany's desperate situation with a failed assassination attempt on Hitler on July 20, 1944.

Pursuit across Belorussia brought the Soviets to Polish territory, and then to the Vistula River and the outskirts of Warsaw. The status of Poland had been bitterly contested between the Western allies, the Polish government-in-exile and its Home Army inside the country, and finally Stalin and his own puppet Polish government. The presence of the Soviet Army in the heart of Poland challenged the Polish Home Army to take steps to liberate Poland itself rather than see Warsaw freed by foreign troops. Home Army planning had not intended on an uprising in Warsaw, as supplies were short and the risk of devastation too great. Circumstances changed, however, as the German armies in the east seemed to be collapsing and the failed July 20 assassination attempt on Hitler suggested that an end to the war might be near. The imperative of staking a claim on the future of postwar Poland was too overwhelming to resist. Persuaded by local Home Army generals that circumstances were propitious, Home Army commander Tadeusz Bór-Komorowski ordered armed revolt with only days left to prepare. As the Soviets approached Warsaw and lead units entered the city's suburbs on the east bank of the Vistula, the Home Army began an uprising on August 1, 1944. The Home Army's forty thousand fighters managed to seize temporary control of much of Warsaw, but their crippling lack of heavy weapons and supplies, given that Warsaw had never been intended as a center for resistance, meant that the Germans quickly began rolling back Home Army control and leveling the city. The headlong Soviet advance westward halted on the Vistula, and the *Wehrmacht* wiped out the Warsaw uprising in two months of vicious fighting.

Debate has raged ever since about Stalin's intentions. There is no doubt that Soviet troops were exhausted and short on supplies after their race across Eastern Europe. Operation *Bagration* had advanced five hundred kilometers in five weeks, and ran up against the substantial barrier of the Vistula. The Home Army's uprising was rushed and enjoyed little chance of success. On the other hand, advancing Soviet forces broadcast calls for a Polish uprising as they approached Warsaw. The Soviets barred use of their airfields for British and American airdrops of supplies to Warsaw until German victory was assured. While internal Soviet documents on the decisions at Warsaw are still inaccessible, it is clear that both the Home Army and Stalin saw the Warsaw Uprising as primarily about the status of postwar Poland. The Home Army had already attempted to preempt Soviet liberation of Vilnius and L'viv to strengthen its postwar claims, a motive equally clear in the Warsaw Uprising. Stalin saw little benefit to assisting anti-Soviet Polish forces, which would certainly contest his postwar plans, and likely shed few tears as the Germans did him the favor of annihilating them.[12]

By the late summer of 1944, *Bagration* had not only wrecked Army Group Center, but the efforts to halt the headlong Soviet advance through Belorussia to Poland weakened German defenses elsewhere. The Soviet offensive push resumed in the south, where remnants of the Romanian and Hungarian armies had now been incorporated under German command in an effort to hold the Soviets in western Ukraine. Still expecting a Soviet attack through Kovel, southeast of Warsaw and anchoring the hinge of the German frontline where it turned south toward the Black Sea, the German High Command weakened Army Group North Ukraine. Taking advantage of this, the Soviet 1st Ukrainian Front struck at Lvov in mid-July, forcing the Germans past the Bug River to new defenses on the Vistula. The Soviets then followed with an attack to take Romania out of the war. Although the spring 1944 offensive against Romania had failed badly, the equation had changed dramatically by late summer. When the Soviet southern offensive opened on August 20, 1944 and smashed through Romanian defenses, Romania's King Michael carried out a coup to oust Marshal Antonescu and appeal to the Allies for peace. Romania switched sides, depriving Hitler of his chief source of oil as well as badly needed manpower, although poorly trained and equipped. The German 6th Army and almost twenty German divisions were pocketed and destroyed west of Kishinev by a pincer attack from the Soviet 2nd and 3rd Ukrainian Fronts. Bulgaria, an Axis ally which had not participated in the war against the Soviet Union, broke with Germany on September 8 and joined the Allies, but this did not spare it Soviet occupation. Soviet troops also moved into Yugoslavia. Although part of Yugoslavia was liberated by Yugoslav partisans without appreciable Soviet support, the Red Army did take Belgrade on October 20, 1944.[13]

As German defenses in the Balkans collapsed, the Soviets seized key mountain passes through the Carpathians. In October, fearing the implications of Soviet invasion, Admiral Miklós Horthy desperately attempted to pull Hungary out of the war. Germany quickly quashed this, seizing the opportunity to deport Hungary's previously protected Jewish population to extermination camps. The German countercoup was a pyrrhic victory, however, as Hungarian forces, never eager to fight for the Germans under the best of circumstances, lost all effectiveness. The geographical advantage of the Carpathian barrier, however, allowed the Germans to slow the Soviet advance toward Budapest.

Bagration also enabled Soviet offensives against Army Group North. In late July, Ivan Bagramian's 1st Baltic Front broke through to the Baltic coast and briefly cut land contact to the German troops in Estonia and Latvia. Although the Germans restored communications, a renewed Soviet offensive in early October severed the connection for good and isolated two German armies. As a result of Hitler's ongoing reluctance to abandon territory no matter the gains in efficiency, a surprisingly large number of German divisions remained in the Baltic states for months, contributing little to the German war effort besides tying down some Soviet formations. The Soviets then pushed west into East Prussia, an event of major political significance. Soviet occupation of German soil, combined with widespread atrocities by vengeful Soviet soldiers, notably mass rape of hundreds of thousands, perhaps millions of women, drove a wave of refugees west ahead of the advancing Red Army.[14]

From the Vistula to Berlin

By the end of 1944, Germany's position looked increasingly desperate. The last-ditch Ardennes offensive failed to inflict more than a temporary reverse on the Allies, and Romania's defeat and switch to the Allied side had cut off an important source of fuel. German manpower reserves were exhausted. Nonetheless, Hitler continued to hope for a decisive strategic victory or a breakdown of the Allied coalition to rescue the Third Reich, just as the death of Russia's Empress Elizabeth in 1762 had saved Frederick the Great's Prussia from certain destruction in the Seven Years' War. The speed of Allied advance on both fronts had indeed slowed after the headlong Anglo–American breakout across northern France and the Soviet advance to the Vistula. Terrain finally worked in Germany' favor, as the Eastern Front grew increasingly narrow as it approached Berlin. On the eastern approaches to the German capital, German defenses grew denser, and the enormous Soviet mechanized forces had less room in which to maneuver. The Allied advance slowed in the southern sector of the Eastern Front as well. Hitler pushed scarce reserves into the defense of Hungary, his sole remaining ally. After a slow and costly advance, Soviet armored offensives had managed to break through north and south of Budapest in December, but only completed the encirclement of the city on December 27, trapping a half-dozen Axis divisions. Still hopeful that the tide of war might turn, Hitler expended much of his remaining armor in futile attempts to break through to the city. Even after Budapest fell on February 13, Hitler expended his last armor reserves in a quixotic offensive west of the city at Lake Balaton in early March.

The Soviets had not previously engaged in a major winter offensive against prepared German defenses, but this very fact provided an important avenue for strategic surprise. Hitler expected the next Soviet blows to come on the flanks of the Soviet advance in East Prussia and Silesia. Stalin instead gambled on a massive winter assault along the Vistula directly into the center of the German line. At the same time, he played on the ambition of two of his best operational commanders. The narrower front no longer required Zhukov to continue his role in coordinating the operations of multiple Soviet Fronts, and in late 1944, he had taken direct command of the 1st Belorussian Front. This placed him alongside Konev's 1st Ukrainian Front just to his south. Stalin engineered a subtle, and then open, competition between the two men, hoping to speed the advance to Berlin and at the same time undercut Zhukov's burgeoning reputation as the key engineer of Soviet victory. On January 12, 1945, Konev's troops attacked west into Silesia, and two days later Zhukov followed, along with Rokossovskii's 2nd Belorussian Front. German defenses on the Vistula collapsed, and Warsaw fell to the Soviets in the first week of the offensive. Soviet mobile forces raced ahead to the Oder River, covering four hundred kilometers in two weeks and bypassing German strongpoints for later reduction.

While this Soviet offensive had been pushed in part to alleviate the pressure of Germany's Ardennes offensive, it also created important facts on the ground for the inter-allied conference at Yalta from February 4–11, 1945. In discussions on the future status of Germany and Eastern Europe, as well as potential Soviet participation in the final attack on Japan, U.S. President Franklin Roosevelt and British Prime Minister Winston Churchill had relatively few cards to play. Soviet divisions occupied Eastern Europe, including the bitterly contested Poland, and sat on the Oder River barely forty miles from Berlin. The Western allies, by contrast, remained stalled on the western bank of the Rhine. Roosevelt's Manhattan Project had yet produced no operational atom bombs, and he desperately needed Soviet assistance for the war against Japan. As even enormous American manpower reserves grew scarce, Roosevelt dreaded the possibility of a bloody invasion of the Japanese home islands without the assistance of Soviet troops to at least tie down Japanese forces in Manchuria. All this allowed Stalin to drive a favorable bargain while his army prepared for the final push to Berlin.

After the precipitous rush from the Vistula to the Oder, the Soviet advance halted, as Stalin and his generals determined that their overextended troops needed to rest and refit. Zhukov and Konev entertained the possibility of attempting to force the Oder off the march, not waiting for reinforcements and supplies, to take advantage of German disorganization. These discussions went nowhere; although it was tempting to storm into Berlin before the German army could consolidate its defenses, long supply lines and the defensive barrier of the Oder River compelled caution. At the same time, the drive directly on Berlin had achieved enormous successes, but left substantial German forces intact and threatening Soviet flanks in East Prussia to the north and Silesia to the south. The result was that the Soviet advance paused for several weeks roughly along the line of the Oder River, tantalizingly close to Berlin, and the Soviets shored up the flanks of their advance. The Western allies were still mired on the far side of the Rhine, so the Soviet high command expected to have time to consolidate its positions and prepare carefully for the next offensive, not needing to run the risk of a precipitate drive to Berlin.

The German strongpoints bypassed in the headlong advance of the Soviet winter 1944–1945 offensive presented Stalin and his generals with a dilemma. While these enclaves lacked real offensive punch, devoid of armor and fuel, they often sat astride key road and rail junctions and hindered further Soviet advance. The Soviet high command decided to eliminate them in preparation for the final assault on Berlin. Posen, an important communication junction, was strongly defended and held out for a month before finally falling on February 23. On the southern flank of the Soviet drive west, Soviet forces had reached the outskirts of Breslau in late January. On February 8, Konev's 1st Ukrainian Front reopened its offensive and pushed well west of Breslau while leaving the city still in German hands. By February 13, a Soviet ring closed around the city with some thirty-five thousand German soldiers trapped inside. The German high command even flew reinforcements into doomed Breslau, which managed to withstand a major Soviet attack at the beginning of April and hold out until Germany's final defeat. On the Baltic, the fortress-city of Königsberg was isolated in January and left to wither for almost three months. In early April, Vasilevskii took command of a bloody storm of the city. The precise motive for this attack is difficult to determine, given the real possibility of simply leaving it until the imminent German capitulation.[15]

The hopelessness of resistance became increasingly clear to the *Wehrmacht*, although not yet to Hitler himself. Perhaps 1.5 million German soldiers were killed in 1945 when defeat was already inevitable. As the pointlessness of the war became apparent, vaunted German discipline finally began to break down, and thousands of public executions of deserters attested to efforts by soldiers to save themselves by flight away from the Eastern Front. German civilians streamed west ahead of the advancing Soviet formations, hoping to escape retribution for the violence that German soldiers had inflicted on millions in Eastern Europe. Hitler seemed resigned to bringing the German people with him into destruction. Some within Germany, however, began to act to limit the harm the end of the war might bring. Available manpower and resources were directed east, in hopes of keeping as much of Germany as possible under the presumably more benign occupation of the Western powers. Others began to argue that policy needed to be directed to preserving lives and economic resources for rebuilding after the war, to no avail. To be sure, many accounts of efforts to alleviate suffering were little more than postwar self-justifications, as in the particular case of Hitler's architect and economic manager, Albert Speer.

The cumulative effect of attrition, allied material superiority, and breakdown in German morale finally produced an increasingly rapid advance by the Western allies past the Rhine and into the heart of Germany by March 1945. This convinced Stalin that he himself needed to speed his own timetable, despite unfavorable circumstances. The terrain on the Oder River was particularly bad for offensive action, as a Soviet forced crossing would put them into marshy ground overlooked by the commanding Seelow Heights east of Berlin.

After amassing over two million men and an astounding collection of material on the Oder, early on the morning of April 16, 1945 the Soviet offensive by three Fronts— from the north, the 2nd Belorussian under Rokossovskii, the massive 1st Belorussian under Zhukov, and the 1st Ukrainian under Konev—swept across the river toward the Seelow Heights. The ambitious Soviet night attack proved costly and unsuccessful; the German 9th Army was well-prepared in positional defenses. Initial Soviet artillery barrages fell on deserted German front lines, and the marshy ground between the Oder and the heights bogged down the Soviet advance. Zhukov committed his armored reserves, intended to race to Berlin, simply to gain the Heights. Only on April 17–18, well behind schedule and at the cost of heavy losses, was Zhukov able to consolidate his control of the Heights and press west to Berlin. Desperate German rear-guard attacks on advancing Soviet tank columns inflicted serious losses, but German shortages of manpower and ammunition were too dire to halt the Soviet advance.

By April 21, Zhukov's advance units had reached Berlin's outer ring road northeast and east of the city, and the bulk of the German 9th Army was surrounded in a pocket southeast of the city. Zhukov's slog directly west toward Berlin, whatever its profligate expenditure of Soviet lives, drew German defenders away from the northern and southern approaches to Berlin. In particular, Konev's breakthrough southeast of Berlin was so successful that he convinced Stalin to allow his troops to turn north and race Zhukov for Berlin. Konev's lead tank armies were in Berlin's suburbs by April 22, and within another two days, the city was entirely cut off. On April 25, in a moment of great symbolic but little military significance, Konev's troops met advancing Americans at Torgau on the Elbe River, bringing the Eastern and Western Fronts together.

Further resistance was pointless, but Hitler had long since lost connection with the realities of the war. He continued to coordinate resistance from his Berlin bunker, planning illusory maneuvers by non-existent formations, through his April 20 birthday and until his April 30 suicide. Soviet troops clawed their way into the center of Berlin and the Reichstag, the symbolic heart of the Nazi regime, against fanatical resistance by the remnants of the *Wehrmacht*. Eighty thousand Soviet troops died in the final offensive against Berlin, along with the old men and young boys pressed into last-ditch German service. Uncounted German civilians died in the ruins of Berlin, and Soviet soldiers throughout German territory carried out mass rapes in an orgy of vengeance. Berlin finally ceased resistance on May 2, and isolated groups of soldiers and civilians infiltrated through Soviet lines west to relative safety in the hands of the Western allies.[16]

The Soviet Army, which occupied the eastern half of Europe, was transformed almost beyond recognition from the force which Hitler had confronted in 1941. The Soviet military at the time of *Barbarossa* was essentially annihilated in the first six months of the war. The sole exception was the high command, which went through a harsh winnowing process. Talent was recognized and promoted, even when pulled from Soviet prison camps, and the generals who kept their positions and rose to the top through four hard years were skilled professionals. They commanded an army with huge material resources and extensive experience in coordinating all the branches of a modern mechanized force on a grand scale. Their human material was crude but effective. High casualty rates had killed and crippled many experienced rank-and-file soldiers, but those who had survived were as tough and skilled in their own way as the generals who commanded them, and they provided a vital glue for the raw conscripts the Soviets had to rely on to make up their manpower shortages. Although the Soviet Union lacked the atom bomb in 1945, its conventional military power was formidable, and provided Stalin an important tool in the Cold War already beginning to take shape as the war in Europe came to a close.

Notes

1. Geoffrey P. Megargee, *Inside Hitler's High Command* (Lawrence: University Press of Kansas, 2000).
2. Philips Payson O'Brien, *How the War was Won: Air–Sea Power and Allied Victory in World War II* (Cambridge: Cambridge University Press, 2015), 360–363.

3. Igor Nebolsin, *Stalin's Favorite: The Combat History of the 2nd Guards Tank Army from Kursk to Berlin*, Vol. 1: *January 1943–June 1944*, trans. and ed. Stuart Britton (Havertown, PA: Casemate, 2015).
4. David M. Glantz and Jonathan M. House, *The Battle of Kursk* (Lawrence: University Press of Kansas, 1999), 151–254; Robert M. Citino, *The Wehrmacht Retreats: Fighting a Lost War, 1943* (Lawrence: University Press of Kansas, 2012), 198–237; Dennis E. Showalter, *Armor and Blood: The Battle of Kursk: The Turning Point of World War II* (New York: Random House, 2013), 182–279.
5. Edgar M. Howell, *The Soviet Partisan Movement, 1941–1944* (Bennington: Merriam Press, 1999 [original edition 1956]), 79–128; Leonid Grenkevich, *The Soviet Partisan Movement, 1941–1944* (London: Frank Cass, 1999), 223–272; Alexander Hill, *The War Behind the Eastern Front: The Soviet Partisan Movement in North-West Russia 1944* (London: Frank Cass, 2005), 120–163. For a skeptical view of partisan effectiveness, see Bogdan Musial, *Sowjetische Partisanen 1941–1944: Mythos und Wirklichkeit* (Paderborn: Ferdinand Schöningh, 2009).
6. Richard DiNardo, *Germany and the Axis Powers* (Lawrence: University Press of Kansas, 2005) 174, 181–183; see also Henrik O. Lunde, *Finland's War of Choice: The Troubled German-Finnish Coalition in World War II* (Newbury: Casemate, 2011), and the essay collection Jonathan R. Adelman, ed. *Hitler and His Allies in World War II* (New York: Routledge, 2007).
7. David M. Glantz, with Mary Elizabeth Glantz, *Battle for Belorussia: The Red Army's Forgotten Campaign of October 1943–April 1944* (Lawrence: University Press of Kansas, 2016).
8. Rolf Hinze, *Crucible of Combat: Germany's Defensive Battles in the Ukraine, 1943–44* (Solihull: Helion, 2009), 142–179.
9. Anton Meiser, *Die Hölle von Tscherkassy* (Schnellbach: Bublies, 2000); Douglas E. Nash, *Hell's Gate: The Battle of the Cherkassy Pocket, January–February 1944* (Southbury: RZM Imports, 2002); David M. Glantz and Harold S. Orenstein, trans., *The Battle for the Ukraine: The Red Army's Korsun'-Shevchenkovskii Operation, 1944 (The Soviet General Staff Study)* (London: Frank Cass, 2003). Niklas Zetterling and Anders Frankson, *The Korsun Pocket: The Encirclement and Breakout of a German Army in the East, 1944* (Philadelphia: Casemate, 2008); Hinze, *Crucible*, 26–141. Gregory Liedtke, "Lost in the Mud: The (Nearly) Forgotten Collapse of the German Army in the Western Ukraine, March and April 1944," *JSMS* 28 (2015): 215–238.
10. David M. Glantz, *The Battle of Leningrad, 1941–1944* (Lawrence: University Press of Kansas, 2002), 259–470.
11. Gerd Niepold, *Battle for White Russia: The Destruction of Army Group Centre June 1944*, trans. Richard Simpkin (London: Brassey, 1987); David M. Glantz and Harold S. Orenstein, trans., *Belorussia 1944: The Soviet General Staff Study* (London: Frank Cass, 2001); C. J. Dick, *From Defeat to Victory: The Eastern Front, Summer 1944* (Lawrence: University Press of Kansas, 2016), 89ff.
12. Most authors have admired the heroism of the Home Army, but many have been skeptical of their chances of success. Jan M. Ciechanowksi, *The Warsaw Uprising of 1944* (Cambridge: Cambridge University Press, 1974) and, to some degree, Włodzimierz Borodziej, *The Warsaw Uprising of 1944* (Madison: University of Wisconsin Press, 2006) see the uprising as lacking realistic hopes of achieving its goal. Norman Davies, *Rising '44: The Battle for Warsaw* (New York: Viking, 2003) takes a more romantic view of the subject. See also Alexandra Richie, *Warsaw 1944: Hitler, Himmler, and the Warsaw Uprising* (New York: Farrar, Strauss and Giroux, 2013). For an early presentation of the anti-Stalin

interpretation of Soviet inaction, see Richard C. Lucas, "Russia, the Warsaw Uprising, and the Cold War," *Polish Review* 20, no. 4 (1975): 13–25. For initial conclusions on Soviet decisions, see Irina Mukhina, "New Revelations from the Former Soviet Archives: The Kremlin, the Warsaw Uprising, and the Coming of the Cold War," *Cold War History* 6, no. 3 (August 2006): 397–411.

13. Rolf Hinze, *To the Bitter End: The Final Battles of Army Groups North Ukraine, A, Centre, Eastern Front 1944–45* (Solihull: Helion, 2005).
14. Prit Buttar, *Battleground Prussia: The Assault on Germany's Eastern Front 1944–45* (Botley: Osprey, 2010), 46–114.
15. Christopher Duffy, *Red Storm on the Reich: The Soviet March on Germany, 1945* (New York: Atheneum, 1991); Richard Hargreaves, *Hitler's Final Fortress: Breslau 1945* (Barnsley: Pen & Sword, 2011).
16. A. Stephan Hamilton, *Bloody Streets: The Soviet Assault on Berlin, April 1945* (Solihull: Helion, 2008); A. Stephan Hamilton, *The Oder Front 1945: Generaloberst Gotthard Heinrici, Heeresgruppe Weichsel and Germany's Final Defense in the East, 20 March–3 May* (Solihull: Helion, 2017).; Tony Le Tissier, *The Battle of Berlin 1945* (New York: St. Martin's, 1988), later revised as Tony Le Tissier, *Race for the Reichstag: The 1945 Battle for Berlin* (London: Frank Cass, 1999).

Bibliography

Adelman, Jonathan R., ed. *Hitler and His Allies in World War II.* New York: Routledge, 2007.
Barnett, Corelli, ed. *Hitler's Generals.* London: Weidenfeld and Nicolson, 1989.
Bialer, Seweryn, ed., *Stalin and His Generals: Soviet Military Memoirs of World War II.* New York: Pegasus, 1969.
Die Ostfront 1943/44: Der Krieg im Osten und an den Nebenfronten. Stuttgart: Deutsche Verlags-Anstalt, 2007.
Erickson, John. *The Road to Berlin.* Boulder: Westview, 1983.
Fritz, Stephen G. *Endkampf: Soldiers, Civilians, and the Death of the Third Reich.* Lexington: University Press of Kentucky, 2004.
Fritz, Stephen G. *Ostkrieg: Hitler's War of Extermination in the East.* Lexington: University Press of Kentucky, 2011.
Glantz, David M. "American Perceptions of Operations on the Eastern Front during World War II." *Journal of Soviet Military Studies* 1 (1988): 110–128.
Glantz, David M. *The Battle of Kursk.* Lawrence: University Press of Kansas, 1999.
Glantz, David M. *Colossus Reborn: The Red Army at War, 1941–1943.* Lawrence: University Press of Kansas, 2005.
Glantz, David M. "The Soviet-German War, 1941–1945." In *World War II in Europe, Africa, and the Americas, with General Sources: A Handbook of Literature and Research,* edited by Lloyd E. Lee and Robin Higham, 157–178. Westport, CT: Greenwood, 1997.
Glantz, David M., and Jonathan House. *When Titans Clashed: How the Red Army Stopped Hitler,* 2nd ed. Lawrence: University Press of Kansas, 2015.
Hardesty, Von, and Ilya Grinberg. *Red Phoenix Rising: The Soviet Air Force in World War II.* Lawrence: University Press of Kansas, 2012.
Hill, Alexander. *The Red Army and the Second World War.* Cambridge: Cambridge University Press, 2017.

Hürter, Johannes. *Hitler's Heerführer: Die deutschen Oberbefehlhaber im Krieg gegen die Sowjetunion 1941/42*. Munich: Oldenbourg, 2007.

Istoriia Velikoi Otechestvennoi voiny Sovetskogo Soiuza, 1941-1945, 6 vols. Moscow: Voenizdat, 1960-1965.

Kershaw, Ian. *The End: The Defiance and Destruction of Hitler's Germany, 1944-1945*. New York: Penguin, 2011.

Mawdsley, Evan. *Thunder in the East: The Nazi-Soviet War, 1941-1945*. London: Hodder, 2007.

Müller, Rolf-Dieter, and Gerd R. Ueberschär. *Hitler's War in the East 1941-1945: A Critical Assessment*. Oxford: Berg, 1997.

Shukman, Harold, ed., *Stalin's Generals*. London: Weidenfeld and Nicolson, 1993.

Smelser, Ronald, and Edward J. Davies, II. *The Myth of the Eastern Front: The Nazi-Soviet War in American Popular Culture*. Cambridge: Cambridge University Press, 2008.

Velikaia otechestvennaia voina 1941-1945: Voenno-istoricheskii ocherki, 4 vols. Moscow: Nauka, 1998.

Wette, Wolfram. *The Wehrmacht: History, Myth, Reality*. Cambridge: Harvard University Press, 2006.

Yelton, David K. *Hitler's Volkssturm: The Nazi Militia and the Fall of Germany, 1944-1945*. Lawrence: University Press of Kansas, 2002.

Ziemke, Earl R. *Stalingrad to Berlin: The German Defeat in the East*. Washington, DC: US Government Printing Office, 1968.

Der Zusammenbruch des Deutschen Reiches 1945: Die militäriche Niederwerfung der Wehrmacht. Munich: Deutsche Verlags-Anstalt, 2008.

CHAPTER 17

FROM D-DAY TO THE ELBE

PETER MANSOOR

In a speech to the French people in October 1940, British Prime Minister Winston Churchill said, "Good night then: Sleep to gather strength for the morning. For the morning will come. Brightly it will shine on the brave and true, kindly upon all who suffer for the cause, glorious upon the tombs of heroes. Thus will shine the dawn."[1] Dawn came nearly four years later, but only after immense preparations and a massive mobilization of manpower and resources in both Great Britain and the United States.

The allied invasion of Normandy on D-Day, June 6, 1944—the beginning of what Allied Supreme Commander Gen. Dwight Eisenhower termed the "Great Crusade"—was the climax of more than two years of planning and preparations to launch Allied forces into Northwest Europe in what would clearly be the decisive campaign for the western Allies in World War II.[2] It was the most complicated military operation ever planned and executed in the history of warfare. Victory was not foreordained. The invasion was but the first act of a long campaign to liberate France and the Low Countries, engage and destroy German forces in decisive battle, and overrun the Third Reich. Its success enabled the United States and Great Britain to share power in postwar Germany with the Soviet Union.

Planning and Preparations for the Cross-Channel Attack

Planning for a return to the Continent began shortly after the United States entered the war. Operation Bolero was designed to deploy U.S. forces to Great Britain in preparation for an invasion of the mainland. However, the failure of the Canadian raid on Dieppe in August 1942 showed just how difficult a full-scale invasion would be, especially one aimed at taking a major port on D-Day.[3] Furthermore, the Allies diverted most of the available forces to launch Operation Torch, the invasion of North Africa, in

November 1942. In reality, the time was not right in 1943 to launch a full-scale invasion of Europe: the Battle of the Atlantic was still raging, Allied airmen had yet to gain superiority over the skies of Europe, and American troops had not yet been tested in battle against the *Wehrmacht*. Nevertheless, U.S. military leaders fumed at the seemingly endless diversion of resources to the Mediterranean, even though they were themselves responsible for sending scarce ships, planes, and troops to shore up the American position in the Pacific. American military leaders also understood that the materiel required to support a cross-Channel attack would not be ready until the spring of 1944, and they therefore concurred with follow-on operations against Sicily and mainland Italy.[4]

At the Casablanca Conference in January 1943, the Combined Chiefs of Staff agreed to establish a group to begin preliminary planning for an invasion of France, Operation Overlord. Two months later they appointed Lt. Gen. Frederick Morgan as the Chief of Staff to the Supreme Allied Commander (Designate), or COSSAC. Morgan and his staff gathered data and intelligence and conducted an analysis of the various options open to the Allies.[5]

The most important decision was where to invade. The site had to be near a port to allow the Allies to open up a logistical lifeline to the sea, close enough to Great Britain to allow single engine fighters and fighter-bombers to support the landing, but remote enough to enable its isolation from German reinforcements moving toward the area from other parts of France. The planners rejected the easily assessable area around the Pas de Calais because that area was also obvious to the Germans and therefore heavily defended. Furthermore, the Pas de Calais was vulnerable to counterattack from three different directions. Brittany was another option that the planners rejected, as it was too far away from the airfields in Great Britain and Allied strategic objectives in France. Instead, the planners selected Normandy. The Cotentin Peninsula was remote enough to be isolated from enemy reinforcements, the port of Cherbourg could be seized fairly quickly, and it was close enough to Great Britain to enable Allied airpower to operate effectively over the area.[6]

The next most important decision was when to invade. At the Tehran Conference in November 1943, President Franklin Roosevelt and Soviet Premier Joseph Stalin prevailed on Churchill to accept an invasion of France in May 1944, a date later postponed by a month to allow for more landing craft production. Regarding the specific date, there were several factors to consider. A full moon was required to illuminate navigational landmarks for the transport crews piloting airborne troops to their destinations, and a low but rising tide near dawn would enable Allied troops to land without hitting the obstacles emplaced by the Germans in the surf. These conditions aligned only a few times each season. The invasion was therefore scheduled for June 5.[7]

The Dieppe fiasco suggested that the invasion would have to come and be supported over open beaches. This realization brought with it considerable logistical difficulties. Men and supplies would have to download into smaller landing craft and then move to beaches for debarkation onto the shore. Consequently, the Allies required landing craft in far greater numbers than the planners had initially envisaged. A worldwide shortage of such craft and the demands of the Pacific war represented major hurdles. Only in 1944 did the Allies dispose of sufficient landing craft to make the invasion possible; indeed, most of the landing craft used in the Normandy landings were built in the six months before the invasion.[8]

The Allies came up with inventive solutions to the problems of downloading supplies onto the beaches. Some landing craft, such as the Landing Ship Tank, or LST, had doors that opened in the bow to allow vehicles to drive directly onto the shore. The worldwide shortage of such craft prompted Churchill to lament, "How it is that the plans of two great empires like Britain and the United States should be so much hamstrung and limited by a hundred or two of these particular vessels will never be understood by history."[9] The Allies also created artificial harbors, nicknamed "Mulberries," that were to be installed on or adjacent to the invasion sites. The artificial harbors included breakwaters, piers, and landing facilities to speed up the offloading of supplies and equipment. This was an impressive engineering achievement, but it came at a cost. The Mulberries used thirty thousand tons of steel and three hundred thousand cubic meters of concrete; furthermore, only one of the two ports functioned as designed, as a massive storm that blew in on June 19 destroyed the Mulberry off of Omaha Beach.[10]

Eisenhower and his ground forces commander, British Gen. Bernard Montgomery, arrived in London in December 1943 and got their first look at COSSAC's plan for the Normandy invasion, which they rejected as insufficient. They added forces and expanded the objective area, which now encompassed landing beaches from north of Caen to the Cotentin Peninsula. Forces consisted of six infantry divisions and three airborne divisions, backed by massive air and naval armadas. Immediate invasion objectives were to secure a lodgment area on five beaches—Utah, Omaha, Gold, Juno, and Sword from west to east—and then advance inland to seize the crucial road center at Caen and the port of Cherbourg.

The Allies used deception effectively to confuse the Germans as to the location and timing of the invasion. The overall name for the deception plan was Bodyguard, which on the Western front was divided into two parts. Fortitude North was meant to lure the Germans into believing the Allies would invade Norway, while Fortitude South would make them believe that the main invasion of France would occur in the Pas de Calais. Deception operations included a variety of ruses such as the positioning of fabricated equipment (inflatable rubber tanks, plywood artillery, etc.) in the open (to allow German aircraft to film it); controlled leaks of false information through diplomatic channels via neutral countries; misleading wireless traffic, which supposedly came from units of the nonexistent First U.S. Army Group, or FUSAG (notionally commanded by none other than Lt. Gen. George S. Patton Jr.); and most importantly, the use of captured German agents (most of them housed in prison) to send false information to German intelligence. Fortitude was so successful that Hitler and the German General Staff regarded the Normandy invasion, when it came, as a strictly secondary operation. As a result, German mobile reserves were largely unable to affect the Normandy landings on D-Day, the infantry divisions of the German Fifteenth Army remained anchored to the Pas de Calais until the decision in Normandy was beyond doubt, and the *Wehrmacht* kept more than three hundred thousand troops in Norway until the war's end.[11]

For the invasion to succeed, the Allies needed to isolate Normandy to delay the arrival of German reinforcements while Allied forces established themselves ashore. In January 1944, the Deputy Supreme Allied Commander, Air Marshal Arthur Tedder, sent Solly Zuckerman, a pioneer in operations research, to join the Overlord planning group in London. Heeding the lessons of North Africa and Italy, Zuckerman argued for the interdiction of the rail lines leading to Normandy. Zuckerman's targeting methodology sought to knock out marshaling yards and repair facilities to achieve maximum effect. The Germans could easily repair damaged rail lines but could not quickly fix rail centers and repair facilities.[12]

Eisenhower agreed with Zuckerman's analysis and sought direction over all Allied air assets, including the heavy bomber fleets, beginning on April 1, 1944, to implement an air campaign against French rail networks. U.S. and British bomber commanders opposed the plan, preferring instead to target German cities and oil facilities. But the issue was so important that Eisenhower wrote a note that if he were not given control of the bombers, he would "take drastic action and inform the Combined Chiefs of Staff that, unless the matter is settled at once, I will request relief from this command."[13] Eisenhower won his point with the Combined Chiefs of Staff, who gave him direction over the bomber fleets.

Beginning in early April, air strikes precipitated a sharp drop in French railway traffic. Military train capacity northern France fell by more than fifty percent by early May. In late May, attacks by fighter bombers on the Seine River bridges further accelerated the isolation of Normandy. Across northern France, the French rail network was paralyzed. By mid-May the system was operating at only a third of its capacity before the bombing began, and by D-Day the French rail network was operating at just ten percent capacity. Normandy had been successfully isolated from German reinforcements.

Destruction of the French rail transportation network forced the German army in Normandy to fight without sufficient quantities of armor, artillery, ammunition, and fuel.[14]

German Army Group B, under the command of Field Marshal Erwin Rommel, knew the invasion was coming. Upon taking command in January 1944, Rommel threw his not inconsiderable energies into putting teeth into the Atlantic Wall. German engineers and conscripted labor laid millions of mines, built concrete and steel fortified bunkers, and installed beach defenses and obstacles. "Rommel asparagus" (poles with wire strung between them) sprouted across French fields to destroy Allied gliders.[15] But Rommel differed with his superior, Field Marshal Gerd von Rundstedt, as to how best to defend against an Allied invasion. Von Rundstedt believed that he should retain a large, centrally located armored reserve near Paris to move to the site of any landing and deliver a crushing blow against the Allied forces. Rommel, mindful of his experiences in North Africa, argued that superior Allied air power would prevent such a mobile defense from succeeding. He contended that the *Wehrmacht* must stop the invasion on the beaches. Once the Anglo–American forces were established ashore, German forces would be unable to throw them back into the sea. Above both commanders hovered Hitler's baleful influence; typically, he kept the strings of military control firmly within his grasp.

Neither Rundstedt nor Rommel had authority to move the armored reserve without the Führer's consent.[16]

D-Day

As D-Day approached, sunny May weather gave way to the worst Channel storm in twenty years. However, the Allies enjoyed the advantage of having ships in the Atlantic report on incoming weather. At 3:30am on June 5, with Allied troops already on their ships for more than twenty-four hours, meteorologist Group Captain James Stagg briefed a narrow invasion window opening on June 6. Eisenhower weighed the risks and then gave the order to proceed with the invasion.[17] Eisenhower then penned a note accepting total blame if the invasion resulted in disaster.[18] As it turned out, his decision was inspired in more ways than one. The next available window of favorable moon and tides was June 19–21, which just happened to coincide with the most ferocious Channel storm in more than a century.

On the eastern flank of the beachhead, the British 6th Airborne Division had the mission of destroying the bridges across the Dives River and capturing intact those across the Orne River and its associated canal to protect the eastern flank against German counterattacks. Major John Howard and D Company, 2nd Battalion, Oxfordshire and Buckinghamshire Light Infantry, seized the bridge at Benouville on the Caen Canal and a nearby bridge over the Orne River in a daring glider-borne assault just after midnight. The small force held the bridge until reinforced by commandos early in the afternoon, and supported by tanks and naval gunfire, repulsed counterattacks by elements of the 21st Panzer Division during the day.[19] The main force of British paratroopers was badly scattered in the night drop; nevertheless, the British paratroopers accomplished all the missions assigned to them, including the destruction of the Merville gun battery overlooking Sword Beach.

Over western Normandy, where a low bank of clouds impeded navigation, conditions were less satisfactory. Many planes got lost, and other aircraft were greeted by heavy flak, which caused inexperienced pilots to veer off course and scattered American paratroopers across a wide swath of the Cotentin Peninsula. This miscalculation proved to be of some advantage; reports of paratroopers everywhere confused the Germans and delayed their response to the seaborne landings. Inspired leadership along with thousands of individual acts of bravery enabled the American airborne forces to achieve their purpose of preventing German reinforcements from moving toward Utah Beach and seizing the causeways that separated it from the interior of the Cotentin Peninsula.[20]

Medium and heavy bombers and naval ships offshore were supposed to pummel enemy defenses before the assault troops landed, but the fire support plan largely failed the test of combat. During the preparations for Overlord, U.S. Army Chief of Staff Gen. George C. Marshall transferred Maj. Gen. Charles Corlett to London to assist with planning. Corlett was the highly successful commander of the U.S. 7th Infantry Division whose plan for the invasion of Kwajalein just four months before the Normandy invasion resulted in the capture of the island at minimal cost to his forces. In London, Corlett was received with disdain by Allied commanders and their staffs, who viewed operations in the Pacific as strictly "Bush League stuff."[21] Lt. Gen. Omar Bradley ignored his recommendations for heavy, longer, and more accurate shore bombardment. As a result, American forces debouched onto the shore of France with inadequate fire support; for example, the landings on Omaha Beach were supported by a dozen destroyers and cruisers but only a single battleship, the USS Arkansas, commissioned in 1912 with twelve-inch guns, insufficient for the task of destroying German Atlantic Wall fortifications.[22]

The British landings fared better. The key objectives were to seize Caen and the nearby Carpiquet aerodrome. Landings by the British 3rd Division on Sword Beach began at 7:25am against weak resistance. By the afternoon the Germans were ready to launch a counterattack in this area on the eastern flank of the allied landings. The 21st Panzer Division attacked from Caen toward Sword Beach, but Allied fighter bombers, naval gunfire, and British tanks and anti-tank guns halted the German advance by nightfall. Nevertheless, the attacks prevented British forces from seizing Caen, which would not all to the allies for another six weeks.[23]

Two brigades of the Canadian 3rd Division landed in the center of the British zone. The preliminary bombardment proved ineffective and rough weather hampered landing operations. Several assault companies took heavy casualties, but the Canadians nevertheless cleared most of the coastal defenses on Juno Beach within two hours of landing. Traffic jams developed on the narrow beachfront and the subsequent push inland achieved mixed results. Although only one unit had reached its D-Day objective by nightfall, the Canadians had succeeded in pushing further inland than any other division. In succeeding days, they would perform yeoman's work in stopping German armored counterattacks aimed at throwing the Allied invasion back into the sea.[24]

Despite some opposition, British forces broke through German defenses on Gold Beach. They had significant assistance from the 79th Armoured Division, equipped with specialty tanks known as Hobart's "Funnies." Vehicles such as the Sherman flail tank and Churchill Crocodile tank, among others, proved their worth on D-Day. They cleared minefields, bridged ditches, laid trackway across sand, and provided flamethrower support to infantry attacking strongpoints.[25] By midnight the British 50th Division had penetrated six miles inland and linked up with Canadian forces. British troops reached Arromanches at 8:00pm and cleared it an hour later. Engineers soon went to working constructing an artificial harbor that would prove critical in supporting the logistics of the Allied forces ashore.[26]

At the other end of the invasion area, the American assault on Utah Beach was highly successful. Utah Beach was a great tidal flat protected only by reinforced concrete fortifications the Germans had emplaced above the dunes. Medium bombers attacking the area came in under the cloud cover and dropped their loads to excellent effect. The final bomb runs wrecked the key German fortification overlooking the area where the first troops would mistakenly land due to the effects of the offshore tide. Once on the beach, Brig. Gen. Teddy Roosevelt, the son of President Teddy Roosevelt and a distant cousin of President Franklin D. Roosevelt, quickly realized he was in the wrong place. "We'll begin the war from here," Roosevelt remarked. Troops of the 4th Infantry Division quickly overcame remaining German resistance on the beach and advanced inland to link up with the Screaming Eagles of the 101st Airborne Division.[27]

If nearly everything went right on Utah Beach, almost nothing went right on Omaha Beach. Omaha Beach was dominated by steep bluffs on which German forces were heavily entrenched. The heavy bombers attacking Omaha Beach flew at high altitude above the overcast. They had to drop their loads blind, based on a time-distance calculation. To avoid hitting the invasion flotilla, the bombers delayed releasing their loads by several seconds, a critical mistake. The bombardment completely missed the German defenses above the beach and as Corlett predicted, the naval shore bombardment was too limited and too inaccurate.[28] The German defenses remained largely intact.

The Germans put up a stiff resistance that devastated the attacking soldiers of the 1st and 29th Infantry Divisions. Landing craft disgorged weary and seasick infantrymen onto the fire-swept shore of France. More than one thousand died before ever reaching the foot of the bluffs. Tanks fitted with special swimming gear were launched too far from shore, and all but five designated to land on Omaha Beach ended on the bottom of the Channel. The carefully prepared but critically flawed plan for the invasion of Omaha Beach was in danger of failing. The situation was rescued by courageous destroyer captains who maneuvered their vessels to within a few hundred yards of shore—thereby risking beaching them in the shallow water—to engage enemy fortifications with their deck guns, and by infantry commanders who found gaps in the German defenses and led their soldiers off the beach in a difficult climb up the bluffs to take the enemy pillboxes and entrenchments from behind. "Bloody Omaha" had cost the Americans nearly twenty-five hundred dead, more than twice the body count from the Marine invasion of Tarawa six months earlier.[29]

The German reaction to the Allied landings was too slow and haphazard to stop the momentum of the assault once the beach defenses collapsed. The OB West panzer reserve could not move without Hitler's sanction, and that did not come soon enough to make a difference on D-Day. The counterattack by the 21st Panzer Division failed to throw the Allies back into the sea. When the Panzer Lehr Division began to move the next day, it was exposed to constant air attacks on its way to Normandy.

On June 6, 1944, the Allies landed 155,000 men and established a shallow beachhead in Normandy. They had needed only half a day to penetrate an Atlantic Wall that Hitler and his legions had taken four years to build.[30] The assault divisions had suffered twelve thousand casualties, with two-thirds suffered by American forces—a down payment on the one-half million American men who would be killed or wounded in Europe. The allies would now pour reinforcements ashore and expand the lodgment area as the battle for the liberation of France began in earnest.

The Normandy Campaign

The extensive damage to the French rail and road network made German attempts to reinforce their lines in Normandy difficult. Allied fighter bombers prevented movement by day, and the Germans could only move so far during the short summer nights. French partisans added to German problems. The 2nd SS Panzer Division (Das Reich) took nearly two weeks to arrive in Normandy from its base in southern France, a journey that without opposition would normally have taken just two days. After a French partisan killed one of their battalion commanders, the Waffen SS soldiers, true to their Eastern front traditions, exacted revenge against the French citizenry by killing 642 inhabitants of Oradour-sur-Glane and razing the village to the ground.[31]

The Allies raced against weather and time to build up their forces and establish a solid lodgment area. The Mulberry Harbors helped—for a while. But the weather again failed to cooperate. A ferocious Channel storm that blew in from June 19–22 destroyed the Mulberry off of Omaha Beach and damaged the other near Gold Beach. British engineers were able to restore the functionality of the artificial harbor at Arromanches. From D+4 until October 31, the British landed 220,000 men, forty thousand vehicles, and 628,000 tons of supplies over the remaining Mulberry, christened "Port Winston."[32] But despite the carefully crafted logistical plan for the Normandy invasion, until the port of Antwerp was opened most of the supplies sent to Allied forces in Northwest Europe were landed over the open beaches.[33]

Two distinct battles developed. In the west, the Americans fought their way through hedgerow barriers in the *bocage* to capture Cherbourg and then to expand the lodgment area to the south. In the east, the British battered their way toward the open ground beyond Caen, where they hoped to fight a mobile battle. Both efforts involved a massive application of firepower to exhaust the Germans in a bloody battle of attrition. British commanders in particular realized that they commanded the last viable ground forces of the empire, with no replacements or reinforcements in the offing. They therefore moved carefully, applying massive amounts of firepower in lieu of more risky ground maneuver whenever possible.

Throughout the battles in eastern Normandy, outnumbered panzer and panzergrenadier forces held their own against their British opponents. Montgomery made repeated attacks against Caen, an objective he had planned to capture in just two days. These constant, repetitive attacks served a useful purpose. They drew German armor piecemeal into an enormous battle of attrition that steadily wore away the enemy's reserve forces. But this was not Montgomery's plan, despite his postwar protestations to the contrary.[34]

In the west the Americans made greater headway against fierce resistance. They liberated Cherbourg on June 27, but the Germans had carried out such effective demolitions that the port remained unusable for two months. With Cherbourg in their hands, the Americans attacked to break through German defenses in western Normandy. Here they ran up against the worst of the *bocage*; virtually every field and village offered heavy cover to the defenders. The Germans were able to dig into the hedgerows and use them as mini-fortresses to stymie allied advances. American losses were heavy, but their formations did something that no other army in Normandy managed: they learned from their mistakes and figured out a way to attack successfully through the difficult hedgerow country.[35] Slowly, but inexorably, the Americans drove the Germans back.

By the end of June, the Allies had twenty-five divisions in France with another fifteen awaiting transport in Great Britain. The Germans had just fourteen divisions in the area, and none of them had their full complement of equipment and troops. Through Ultra intelligence, the Allies were well-aware of the diminishing German strength.[36] In the second half of July, they launched two offensives to break out from Normandy. Goodwood, a British operation involving three armored divisions, proved indecisive and resulted in massive losses of British armor, but it drew further German reinforcements to the Caen sector.

A week after U.S. forces seized St. Lô, Bradley launched Operation Cobra. The plan called for an intense aerial bombardment of a narrow front. The use of heavy bombers to pulverize the German front lines, Bradley believed, would open the way for his armored divisions to drive deep into the German rear. Although the poorly executed bombing resulted in hundreds of friendly casualties, including U.S. Army Ground Forces commander Lt. Gen. Lesley J. McNair, who was in Normandy as an observer, it pulverized the German defenders. Three infantry divisions then attacked to open the way for two armored divisions and a motorized infantry division. American forces poured through the resulting gap and quickly reached Avranches, the gateway to the Brittany Peninsula. Bradley then activated Patton's Third Army, thus finally putting the best Allied operational commander into battle.[37]

Once Avranches fell the Americans could either drive west into Brittany or swing east behind the German forces in Normandy. Unfortunately, Bradley missed the operational possibilities that an eastward advance would provide. He instead followed plans made months ahead of time to capture the Brittany Peninsula and its ports, despite the fact that German demolitions at Cherbourg indicated that those ports would likely be useless for months to come.

Hitler, however, recognized the threat. He ordered his panzer divisions to counterattack toward Avranches to cut off American forces. Fortunately, Bletchley Park was once again up to the task of divining German intentions. Ultra decoded enemy signals concerning the counterattack and American commanders massed artillery and airpower to pulverize the attacking German formations. The 2nd Battalion, 120th Infantry Regiment played a crucial role in the fighting. The battalion occupied a crucial piece of high ground, Hill 317, just east of the city of Mortain. Although surrounded by German forces, the soldiers of this unit held their positions and called in devastating artillery strikes against the Germany spearheads arrayed below them.[38]

As the Germans attacked at Mortain, American spearheads finally turned east. Despite the growing danger, Hitler persisted in reinforcing failure. The 5th Panzer Army, 7th Panzer Army, and Panzer Group Eberbach were in danger of being encircled; if the

Allies destroyed these forces, they would have devastated German fighting power in the West. Yet neither Bradley nor Montgomery could take advantage of the opportunity. Bradley ordered Patton's forces to halt at Argentan to await the British and Canadians, attacking from the north. Bradley preferred, in his words, "a solid shoulder at Argentan to the possibility of a broken neck at Falaise."[39] His risk aversion led him to pass up an opportunity for a major victory that could very well have ended the war by the end of 1944. Anglo–American forces failed to close the gap at Falaise until upwards of forty thousand German troops had escaped the pocket, although air strikes and artillery destroyed most of their vehicles and heavy equipment.[40]

Breakout and Pursuit

As Allied armies surged across France, logistics became the limiting factor in their advance. In their planning for the Normandy invasion, the Allies assumed a relatively steady advance. Allied forces were to reach Avranches by D+20, Le Mans by D+40, and the Seine River by D+90. In such a scenario, they would require fuel and ammunition in relatively equal amounts. But through the end of July the relatively stationary battle in Normandy consumed more ammunition and less fuel than predicted. To account for this reality, at the beginning of August, Allied logisticians increased ammunition allocations at the expense of fuel—at precisely the moment when the campaign turned mobile in a fashion the planners had never expected. After the success of Operation COBRA, the allies advanced far more rapidly than even the most optimistic pre-D-Day predictions. Between D+49 and D+79, the Allies occupied the ground they had planned on taking between D+15 and D+90. In the next nineteen days (August 25 to September 12), they advanced from the D+90 to the D+350 phase line. Fuel now became the critical commodity to sustain the allied offensive. The real problem was the lack of a usable port. By the end of October 1944, ninety percent of the supplies landing in France still arrived over the beaches of Normandy and had to be moved from there to a front line that was quickly disappearing eastward.[41]

On August 15, Allied forces initiated Operation Dragoon, the invasion of southern France. After pushing Army Group G out of southern France, American and French forces advanced to the Vosges Mountains, where they would fight until the final offensive into Germany.[42] Along the way French forces seized the ports of Toulon and Marseilles, which helped alleviate the supply situation. Approximately thirty percent of all supplies sent to France after the invasion came through the ports of southern France, thereby validating Eisenhower's insistence that this operation was essential to Allied operations in northwest Europe.[43]

Paris fell to Free French forces on August 25. By early September Montgomery had captured Brussels. Patton, meanwhile, was heading toward Metz. German forces, defeated and in disarray, streamed back toward the Reich. All was not well, however. British forces seized Antwerp in early September with its port facilities intact, but they failed to clear the Scheldt Estuary that connected the port to the Channel. Furthermore, Montgomery's failure to take the Scheldt Estuary allowed the German 15th Army, until now defending the Pas de Calais, to escape certain destruction.[44] U.S. and British forces were able to close up to the West Wall fortifications and even penetrate them in a few places, but lacked the logistical capacity for more than one more major offensive before they had to pause to restore their lines of communication from the Channel ports to the front along the German frontier.

Disagreements on the way ahead plagued the Allied high command. On September 1, Eisenhower assumed control over ground operations, supplanting Montgomery, who had performed this role since D-Day. Chafing at being eclipsed and wary of the capabilities of senior American commanders, Montgomery argued for a powerful, single thrust through the Low Countries and into Germany, commanded, of course, by the British field marshal himself. Bradley argued for greater support for the U.S. First and Third Armies; the latter army, under the hard-driving Patton, currently heading toward the Saar industrial basin. But Montgomery had geography on his side; the Ruhr Valley was a more crucial objective, and the launching sites for the German V-1 and V-2 rockets were in his zone. Meeting in Brussels on September 10, Eisenhower and Montgomery more or less ironed out their disagreements—at least for the moment. Eisenhower would allow Montgomery to defer the opening of the Scheldt Estuary to gain a bridgehead across the lower Rhine River.[45] While the American advance would not be halted completely, the bulk of the remaining supplies would support the 21st Army Group's bold, but ultimately futile, bid to end the war in 1944.

Operation Market-Garden, the largest airborne assault in history, entailed a massive drop by three airborne divisions along a sixty-mile corridor to seize bridges across numerous water barriers in Holland, including the bridge across the Rhine River at Arnhem. Ground forces were to quickly advance through the airborne carpet, envelop the West Wall, and exploit into the Ruhr industrial region. Even if successful, it probably would not have achieved its objectives due to the weakness of the Allied logistical situation in September 1944, a weakness largely of their own making. Additionally, Ultra intelligence and the Dutch underground both indicated the presence of panzer formations in the Arnhem area, which made success problematical at best.[46]

On September 17 the first wave of British and American paratroopers and gliderborne forces dropped into Holland. They were able to take some of their objectives, but German resistance and blown bridges delayed the advance by the British XXX Corps long enough to doom the British 1st Airborne Division, fighting for its existence north of the Rhine River. Lightly armed paratroopers found themselves up against elements of the 9th and 10th SS Panzer divisions that had recently moved to the area to refit. On September 26, Montgomery ordered the remnants to withdraw. Out of ten thousand men dropped into Arnhem, only 2,163 reached Allied lines south of the Rhine River.[47] Market-Garden had failed—"a bridge too far" in the words of Lt. Gen. Frederick "Boy" Browning, the commander of the Allied First Airborne Army.[48] Hopes of an early end to the war quickly faded.

THE BROAD FRONT STRATEGY

The Allied offensive slowed to a crawl as logistical realities caught up with British and American forces that had outrun their supply system. The wrecked French railroad and road network now worked against the Allies as they struggled to bring supplies forward from the beaches in Normandy. U.S. forces besieged Brest in an attempt to open another port, but when they finally dislodged the German defenders, the facilities were so thoroughly wrecked that the port remained unusable until after the end of the war.[49] Upon Eisenhower's insistence Montgomery finally turned his full attention to opening the Scheldt Estuary, but by then the Germans had had plenty of time to prepare their defenses. A task that could have been easily accomplished in early September took two months of bitter and costly fighting. Not until mid-November did British and Canadian forces finish clearing the Scheldt and opening the way to Antwerp. The first transports finally docked at Antwerp in early December 1944, just before the Germans launched their major counteroffensive in the Ardennes Forest.[50]

Hampered by poor weather and constrained logistics, the Allies had difficulty coming to an agreement on the strategy to be used in defeating German armies in the West. Montgomery continued to argue for a single thrust advance led by the British Twenty-first Army Group, while American commanders argued for support for their forces as well. Eisenhower decided to support all the army groups more or less equally, a decision based on the limited logistical capabilities available until Antwerp was open.[51] This "broad front" strategy succeeded in keeping the Allies together as they inched their way toward Germany. Dismal weather and swollen rivers made movement difficult. The West Wall provided the *Wehrmacht* with defensive fortifications that inhibited the Allied advance. An American offensive to seize Aachen was successful, but it did not lead to a major breakthrough.

To continue the pressure against German forces, Bradley ordered the First U.S. Army, under the command of Lt. Gen. Courtney Hodges, to attack through the Hürtgen Forest. The dense pine forest negated the American advantages in mobility, artillery, and airpower that had enabled the rapid advance across France. There were other options—such as attacking through the Losheim Gap in the northern part of the Ardennes Forest—but Bradley and Hodges failed to recognize them. They opted instead for a frontal assault into the teeth of German defenses, designed to protect the staging areas for the upcoming Ardennes counteroffensive. Only belatedly did American leaders realize that any advance across the Roer River would be jeopardized if the Germans chose to destroy the dams upriver to the east of the Hürtgen Forest, thus flooding and cutting off any units on the east side. The seizure of the dams became the ex post facto excuse for the decision to fight the battle, which cost U.S. forces more than thirty-one thousand casualties for little gain.[52] The Roer River dams remained in German hands until February 1945.

The Battle of the Bulge

Even as Allied armies hammered against the West Wall, Hitler dreamed of launching a massive counteroffensive to turn the tide of the war in Europe. He selected the Ardennes—the scene of the *Wehrmacht*'s greatest triumph in 1940—as the location for the attack. The goal was the vital port of Antwerp, the seizure of which would destroy a vital Allied logistical base and encircle the British 21st Army Group.

On December 16 the Germans struck thinly defended American lines in the Ardennes Forest underneath a thick blanket of clouds that grounded Allied aircraft. German forces achieved total surprise. The main effort, the Sixth SS Panzer Army in the north, met stiff resistance along Elsenborn Ridge and at the town of St. Vith. One unit, Kampgruppe Peiper, broke through the American lines, but was unable to reach the Meuse River as American engineers blew the bridges it needed to cross the Ambleve River.[53] Along the way Joachim Peiper's Waffen SS troops massacred several hundred American soldiers and Belgian civilians near Malmedy.[54]

The Fifth Panzer Army encircled two regiments of the U.S. 106th Infantry Division, which capitulated in the largest surrender of American troops since the fall of Bataan. A regiment of the 28th Infantry Division sacrificed itself in the Belgian town of Clervaux and elsewhere to delay the German advance long enough to allow reinforcements to reach the front. The 82nd Airborne Division moved north toward St. Vith, while the 101st Airborne Division fortified the Belgian town of Bastogne, a crucial communications hub. The defense of encircled Bastogne did much to delay the German advance toward the Meuse River.[55]

By Christmas Eve, elements of the German Fifth Panzer Army had reached the outskirts of Dinant on the Meuse River, but the next day the U.S. 2nd Armored Division counterattacked and savaged the German formations, now out of fuel. Patton's Third U.S. Army relieved the U.S. forces at Bastogne and the crisis passed. Over the next several weeks counterattacks drove the Germans out of the Bulge. By the end of January German forces had abandoned all their gains and much of their equipment. The battle was a disaster for the *Wehrmacht*, which squandered the last German armored reserves—reserves stripped, for the most part, from the Eastern Front, and now unavailable to slow the final Soviet drive to Berlin.[56]

The Bulge also brought about another serious crisis in the Allied high command. The German assault split the 12th Army Group, hindering control of the largest assemblage of American forces in Northwest Europe. To ease the burden, Eisenhower made the difficult decision to place the forces on the northern side of the Bulge (the First and Ninth U.S. Armies) under Montgomery's command, leaving Bradley in charge of the forces on the southern shoulder consisting mainly of Patton's Third U.S. Army. Montgomery tidied up the organization of forces and brought a degree of order to the chaos that had resulted from the German attack. Then, having made a substantial contribution to victory, he threw away any goodwill he had created by taking public credit for stemming the

German tide and once again raising the issue of designating himself as the commander of all Allied ground forces. Given the fact that the Bulge was the largest battle in the history of the U.S. Army, Eisenhower was furious. He considered cabling the Combined Chiefs of Staff and demanding either Montgomery's or his own relief from command. Faced with having Eisenhower's and his disagreements laid before the Combined Chiefs of Staff, which would almost certainly have led to his dismissal, Montgomery backed down and sent a note of apology to the Supreme Commander.[57] Churchill, with a better understanding of the political situation than his battlefield commander, declared before Parliament on January 18 that the credit for turning back the German counteroffensive belonged to the Americans.[58] The crisis passed.

Overrunning the Third Reich

Continued pressure over the wet, cold, and miserable winter wore away the remaining strength of the *Wehrmacht* and brought Allied forces to the west bank of the Rhine River. The Twenty-first Army Group executed an attack by two armies to clear the Rhineland in its zone. On February 8 the First Canadian Army kicked off Operation Veritable, with forces attacking from Nijmegen to the southeast along the west bank of the Rhine River. This movement was supposed to be coordinated with an attack by the Ninth U.S. Army (Operation Grenade) to the northeast across the Roer River. But the Germans, who still controlled the Roer River dams, released a flood that delayed the American attack by two weeks. The Canadians made slow headway against stiff resistance until the waters receded. On February 23 the Ninth U.S. Army crossed the Roer River and the advanced picked up pace. By the March 10 the Allied armies had cleared the west bank of the Rhine of German forces, setting the stage for the final assault into Germany.

By early March British and American troops had battered their way into the Rhineland. The British Twenty-first Army Group held the western bank of the Rhine River between Düsseldorf and Nijmegen, where Montgomery ordered a pause to prepare for a massive assault. American forces moved more quickly. On March 7 the 9th Armored Division reached the Rhine River at Remagen, where it seized intact the Ludendorff Railroad Bridge. The First U.S. Army now poured reinforcements across the Rhine River and expanded the bridgehead. Not to be outdone, Patton's Third U.S. Army cracked German defensive positions in the Eifel. After surrounding nearly one hundred thousand German troops, Patton's forces crossed the Rhine River at Oppenheim on the night of March 22.

Following two weeks of intense preparations, Montgomery launched his blow, Operation Plunder. Against five weak divisions, the British used an artillery bombardment of thirty-three hundred guns, the air support of Allied strategic and tactical air forces, and a landing by two airborne divisions. Allied forces quickly crossed the Rhine and soon broke out into the open.[59] The British advance, combined with rapid exploitation by the Americans south of the Ruhr, put the Germans in a hopeless position. On

April 1 the Allied forces met, encircling the Ruhr industrial region. Within the wreckage of Germany's industrial heartland lay more than three hundred thousand soldiers of Field Marshal Model's Army Group B. The troops surrendered, while Model committed suicide in lieu of capture.[60] Nothing remained in western Germany except a few pockets of fanatical Nazis to hinder the advance of Anglo–American forces into the heart of the Third Reich.

The major question remaining was whether the Allies would race the Soviets to Berlin. Eisenhower decided against the move. The Soviet juggernaut, situated on the Oder River only forty miles from the German capital, was better positioned to seize it. Taking Berlin would cost the Allies tens of thousands of additional casualties and leave them in possession of territory that would end up in the Soviet zone of occupation by agreements already reached by the Big Three at Yalta. It was more important, Eisenhower figured, to seize ports on the North Sea and the Baltic and prevent the Germans from establishing a national redoubt in Bavaria.[61] Indeed, the former objective was crucial; although the Allies had already agreed on the postwar occupation of Germany, Denmark was up for grabs. In the event Montgomery's forces reached Lübeck on the Baltic coast to the east of the Jutland peninsula a day before the Red Army, leaving Denmark in the hands of the Western Allies.[62]

Conclusion

Historians have since debated the reasons for Allied victory. Some argue that the German army was technically and tactically superior to American, British, Canadian, and French forces. German leaders were more competent, they could maneuver their forces more adeptly than Allied commanders, and German soldiers were better trained and disciplined on the battlefield. The Allies, these historians argue, won the war through the application of materiel superiority that overwhelmed the *Wehrmacht* in a relatively unskilled manner.[63]

More recent scholarship has challenged this thesis. The German army had significant flaws beyond the lack of materiel wherewithal, notably poor intelligence, an insufficient ability to mass fires, and logistics that still largely relied on railroads, horses, and wagons. When comparing the *Wehrmacht* with Allied forces in a more holistic manner, the Allied forces come out ahead. The American army, in particular, was adaptable to the combat environments in which it fought and by the end of the Normandy campaign was more than a match for the Germany army. Far from rumbling their way to victory, Allied forces developed an impressive degree of combat effectiveness that contributed a great deal to the Allies' ultimate triumph.[64]

However fashioned, success in the campaign for Northwest Europe was but one element of Allied victory in the largest and most destructive war in human history. For the troops involved in the Great Crusade, in the end that contribution was achievement enough.

Notes

1. Winston Churchill, "Sleep to Gather Strength for the morning," radio broadcast, October 19, 1940, http://www.ibiblio.org/pha/policy/1940/1940-10-19a.html.
2. Dwight Eisenhower, *Crusade in Europe* (New York: Doubleday & Company, 1948).
3. C. P. Stacey, *Official History of the Canadian Army in the Second World War*, Vol. 1: *Six Years of War: The Army in Canada, Britain and the Pacific* (Ottawa: Queen's Printer and Controller of Stationery, 1955), 397–401.
4. Jim Lacy, *Keep From All Thoughtful Men: How U.S. Economists Won World War II* (Annapolis: Naval Institute Press, 2011), chapters 9 and 10.
5. General Sir Frederick Morgan, *Peace and War: A Soldier's Life* (London: Hodder Stoughton, 1961).
6. Gordon A. Harrison, *Cross-Channel Attack* (Washington: Center of Military History, 1951), 56–57.
7. Ibid., 188–190.
8. Olivier Wieviorka, *Normandy: The Landings to the Liberation of Paris*, trans. M. B. DeBevoise (Cambridge, MA: Belknap Press of Harvard University Press, 2008), 96–105.
9. Winston Churchill to Gen. George C. Marshall, April 16, 1944, quoted in Winston S. Churchill, *The Second World War* (New York: Houghton Mifflin, 1951), Vol. 5: *Closing the Ring*, 514.
10. Wieviorka, *Normandy*, 107.
11. Craig Bickell, "Operation Fortitude South: An Analysis of Its Influence on German Dispositions and Conduct of Operations in 1944," *War & Society* 18, no. 1 (May 2000): 91–121.
12. Solly Zuckerman, *From Apes to Warlords, 1904–46: An Autobiography* (New York: Harper & Row, 1978), 217–219.
13. Forest C. Pogue, *Supreme Command* (Washington: Center of Military History, 1953), 125.
14. Williamson Murray, *The Luftwaffe, 1933–1945: Strategy for Defeat* (London: George Allen & Unwin, 1985), 267–272; Williamson Murray and Allan R. Millett, eds., *A War to Be Won: Fighting the Second World War* (Cambridge, MA: Harvard University Press, 2000), 327; Rebecca Grant, "The War on the Rails," *Air Force Magazine*, August 1, 2007, https://www.airforcemag.com/article/0807rails/.
15. Steven Zaloga, *D-Day Fortifications in Normandy* (New York: Osprey, 2005).
16. Williamson Murray, "Field Marshall Erwin Rommel's Defense of Normandy During World War II," *World War II* 21, no. 3 (June 2006), reprinted at https://www.historynet.com/field-marshall-erwin-rommels-defense-of-normandy-during-world-war-ii.htm.
17. Eisenhower, *Crusade in Europe*, 250.
18. Stephen E. Ambrose, *Eisenhower: Soldier, General of the Army, President-Elect, 1890–1952* (New York: Simon & Schuster, 1983), 309. Eisenhower kept the note in his wallet and never made it public.
19. Stephen Ambrose, *Pegasus Bridge: June 6, 1944* (New York: Simon & Schuster, 1985).
20. Harrison, *Cross-Channel Attack*, 288–289.
21. Geoffrey Perret, *There's a War to Be Won* (New York: Random House, 1991), 299.
22. At Kwajalein Corlett's 7th Infantry Division was supported by no fewer than six battleships.
23. Andrew Stewart, *Caen Controversy: The Battle for Sword Beach 1944* (Tulsa: Helion, 2014).
24. Marc Milner, *Stopping the Panzers: The Untold Story of D-Day* (Lawrence: University Press of Kansas, 2014).

25. Richard Doherty, *Hobart's 79th Armoured Division at War: Invention, Innovation and Inspiration* (Barnsley, UK: Pen and Sword, 2012).
26. Simon Trew, *D-Day Landings: Gold Beach* (Stroud, UK: The History Press, 2011).
27. Joseph Balkoski, *Utah Beach: The Amphibious Landing and Airborne Operations on D-Day, June 6, 1944* (Mechanicsburg, PA: Stackpole, 2005). Roosevelt would be awarded the Medal of Honor for his exceptional leadership on D-Day.
28. Williamson Murray, "Needless D-Day Slaughter," *Military History Quarterly* 15, no. 3 (Spring 2003), 26–30.
29. Adrian R. Lewis, *Omaha Beach: Flawed Victory* (Chapel Hill: The University of North Carolina Press, 2003).
30. Stephen Ambrose, *D-Day: June 6, 1944: The Climactic Battle of World War II* (New York: Simon & Schuster, 1994), 576–579.
31. Max Hastings, *Das Reich: The March of the 2nd SS Panzer Division Through France, June 1944* (New York: Henry Holt, 1982).
32. Assistant Chief of Staff G-4, SHAEF, "Mulberry 'B,'" 'D+4—D+147 1944, 10 June to 31 October," http://www.ibiblio.org/hyperwar/ETO/Overlord/MulberryB/.
33. Roland G. Ruppenthal, *Logistical Support of the Armies*, Vol. 2: *September 1944–May 1945* (Washington: Office of the Chief of Military History, 1959), 53.
34. Carlo d'Este, *Decision in Normandy: The Unwritten Story of Montgomery and the Allied Campaign* (New York: E. P. Dutton, 1983), 77–78, 249–250.
35. Michael Doubler, *Closing with the Enemy: How the GIs Fought the War in Europe, 1944–1945* (Lawrence: University Press of Kansas, 1994).
36. Ralph Bennett, *Ultra in the West: The Normandy Campaign of 1944–45* (New York: Scribner, 1980).
37. James Carafano, *After D-Day: Operation Cobra and the Normandy Breakout* (Mechanicsburg, PA: Stackpole, 2008).
38. Alwyn Featherston, *Saving the Breakout: The 30th Division's Heroic Stand at Mortain, August 7–12, 1944* (Novato, CA: Presidio, 1993); Mark J. Reardon, *Victory at Mortain: Stopping Hitler's Counteroffensive* (Lawrence: University Press of Kansas, 2002).
39. Omar Bradley, *A Soldier's Story* (New York: Henry Holt, 1951), 377.
40. Martin Blumenson, *The Battle of the Generals: The Untold Story of the Falaise Pocket—The Campaign that Should Have Won World War II* (New York: William Morrow, 1993).
41. Steve Waddell, *United States Army Logistics: The Normandy Campaign, 1944* (Westport, CT: Praeger, 1994).
42. Jeffrey J. Clarke and Robert Ross Smith, *Riviera to the Rhine* (Washington: U.S. Army Center of Military History, 1993).
43. Ruppenthal, *Logistical Support of the Armies*, Vol. 2, 124.
44. Charles Perry Stacey, *Official History of the Canadian Army in the Second World War*, Vol. 3: *The Victory Campaign: The Operations in North-West Europe 1944–1945* (Ottawa: The Queen's Printer and Controller of Stationery, 1960), 301–303.
45. Eisenhower, *Crusade in Europe*, 306–307.
46. Antony Beevor, *The Battle of Arnhem: The Deadliest Airborne Operation of World War II* (New York: Viking, 2018), 50.
47. Cornelius Ryan, *A Bridge Too Far* (New York: Simon & Schuster, 1974), 591.
48. Ibid., 9.
49. Martin Blumenson, *Breakout and Pursuit* (Washington: Office of the Chief of Military History, 1961), 655.

50. Mark Zuehlke, *Terrible Victory: First Canadian Army and the Scheldt Estuary Campaign: September 13–November 6, 1944* (Vancouver: Douglas & McIntyre, 2007).
51. Roland G. Ruppenthal, "Logistics and the Broad-Front Strategy," in *Command Decisions*, ed. Kent Roberts Greenfield (Washington: Office of the Chief of Military History, 1960), chapter 18.
52. Charles B. MacDonald, *The Siegfried Line Campaign* (Washington: Office of the Chief of Military History, 1963), 493.
53. Janice Giles, *The Damned Engineers* (Boston: Houghton Mifflin, 1970).
54. Danny S. Parker, *Fatal Crossroads: The Untold Story of the Malmedy Massacre at the Battle of the Bulge* (Boston: Da Capo Press, 2012).
55. S. L. A. Marshall, *Bastogne: The Story of the First Eight Days* (Washington: Infantry Journal Press, 1946); Peter Schrijvers, *Those Who Hold Bastogne: The True Story of the Soldiers and Civilians Who Fought in the Biggest Battle of the Bulge* (New Haven: Yale University Press, 2014).
56. Charles B. MacDonald, *A Time for Trumpets: The Untold Story of the Battle of the Bulge* (New York: William Morrow, 1985), 617–618.
57. Rick Atkinson, *The Guns at Last Light: The War in Western Europe, 1944–1945* (New York: Henry Holt, 2013), 473; Eisenhower, *Crusade in Europe*, 356–357; Russell Weigley, *Eisenhower's Lieutenants: The Campaign of France and Germany, 1944–1945* (Bloomington: Indiana University Press, 1981), 542–544.
58. Winston Churchill, *The Second World War*, Vol. 6: *Triumph and Tragedy* (Boston: Houghton Mifflin, 1953), 281–282.
59. Stephen L. Wright, *The Last Drop: Operation Varsity, March 24–25, 1945* (Mechanisburg, PA: Stackpole, 2008); Tim Saunders, *Operation Plunder* (Barnsley, UK: Pen and Sword, 2006).
60. Derek S. Zumbro, *Battle for the Ruhr: The German Army's Final Defeat in the West* (Lawrence: University Press of Kansas, 2006).
61. Stephen E. Ambrose, *Eisenhower and Berlin, 1945: The Decision to Halt at the Elbe* (New York: W.W. Norton, 1967).
62. Forrest C. Pogue, *The Supreme Command* (Washington: Center of Military History, 1954), 449–451.
63. Two of the more salient works are Martin van Creveld, *Fighting Power: German and U.S. Army Performance, 1939–1945* (Westport, CT: Greenwood Press, 1982) and John Ellis, *Brute Force: Allied Strategy and Tactics in the Second World War* (New York: Viking, 1990).
64. Three of the salient works are Keith E. Bonn, *When the Odds Were Even: The Vosges Mountains Campaign, October 1944–January 1945* (Novato, CA: Presidio, 1994); Peter R. Mansoor, *The GI Offensive in Europe: The Triumph of American Infantry Divisions, 1941–1945* (Lawrence: University Press of Kansas, 1999); and Richard Overy, *Why the Allies Won* (New York: W. W. Norton, 1996).

Bibliography

Ambrose, Stephen. *Citizen Soldiers: The U.S. Army from the Normandy Beaches to the Bulge to the Surrender of Germany*. New York: Simon & Schuster, 1997.

Ambrose, Stephen. *D-Day: June 6, 1944: The Climactic Battle of World War II*. New York: Simon & Schuster, 1994.

Ambrose, Stephen. *Eisenhower and Berlin, 1945: The Decision to Halt at the Elbe.* (New York: W.W. Norton, 1967.
Ambrose, Stephen. *Eisenhower: Soldier, General of the Army, President-Elect, 1890–1952.* New York: Simon & Schuster, 1983.
Ambrose, Stephen. *Pegasus Bridge: June 6, 1944.* New York: Simon & Schuster, 1985.
Astor, Gerald. *The Bloody Forest: Battle for the Huertgen: September 1944–January 1945.* Novato: Presidio, 2000.
Atkinson, Rick. *The Guns at Last Light: The War in Western Europe, 1944–1945.* New York: Henry Holt, 2013.
Balkoski, Joseph. *Beyond the Beachhead: The 29th Infantry Division in Normandy.* Mechanicsburg, PA: Stackpole, 1989.
Balkoski, Joseph. *Omaha Beach: D-Day, June 6, 1944.* Mechanicsburg, PA: Stackpole, 2004.
Balkoski, Joseph. *Utah Beach: The Amphibious Landing and Airborne Operations on D-day, June 6, 1944.* Mechanisburg, PA: Stackpole, 2005.
Beevor, Antony. *The Battle of Arnhem: The Deadliest Airborne Operation of World War II.* New York: Viking, 2018.
Beevor, Antony. *D-Day: The Battle for Normandy.* New York: Viking Penguin, 2009.
Bennett, David. *Magnificent Disaster: The Failure of Market Garden, The Arnhem Operation, September 1944.* Drexel Hill, PA: Casemate, 2008.
Bennett, Ralph. *Ultra in the West: The Normandy Campaign of 1944–45.* New York: Scribner, 1980.
Blumenson, Martin. *The Battle of the Generals: The Untold Story of the Falaise Pocket—The Campaign that Should Have Won World War II.* New York: William Morrow, 1993.
Blumenson, Martin. *Breakout and Pursuit.* United States Army in World War II series. Washington: Office of the Chief of Military History, 1961.
Blumenson, Martin. *The Duel For France, 1944: The Men And Battles That Changed The Fate Of Europe.* Boston: Houghton Mifflin, 1963.
Bonn, Keith E. *When the Odds Were Even: The Vosges Mountains Campaign, October 1944—January 1945.* Novato, CA: Presidio, 1994.
Bradley, Omar. *A Soldier's Story.* New York: Henry Holt, 1951.
Brown, Anthony Cave. *Bodyguard of Lies.* New York: Harper & Row, 1975.
Caddick-Adams, Peter. *Snow and Steel: The Battle of the Bulge, 1944–45.* New York: Oxford University Press, 2014.
Carell, Paul. *Invasion—They're Coming! The German Account of the Allied Landings and the 80 Days' Battle for France.* New York: E. P. Dutton & Co., 1963.
Carafano, James. *After D-Day: Operation Cobra and the Normandy Breakout.* Mechanicsburg, PA: Stackpole, 2008.
Churchill, Winston S. *The Second World War.* Vol. 5: *Closing the Ring.* New York: Houghton Mifflin, 1951.
Clarke, Jeffrey J., and Robert Ross Smith. *Riviera to the Rhine.* United States Army in World War II series. Washington: U.S. Army Center of Military History, 1993.
Cole, Hugh M. *The Ardennes: The Battle of the Bulge.* United States Army in World War II series. Washington: Office of the Chief of Military History, 1965.
Cole, Hugh M. *The Lorraine Campaign.* United States Army in World War II series. Washington: Office of the Chief of Military History, 1950.
Crookenden, Napier. *Dropzone Normandy: The Story of the American and British Airborne Assault on D-Day 1944.* New York: Scribner, 1976.

Delaforce, Patrick. *Churchill's Secret Weapons: The Story of Hobart's Funnies*. Barnsley, UK: Pen and Sword, 2008.

D'Este, Carlo. *Decision in Normandy: The Unwritten Story of Montgomery and the Allied Campaign*. New York: E. P. Dutton, 1983.

Doherty, Richard. *Hobart's 79th Armoured Division at War: Invention, Innovation and Inspiration*. Barnsley, UK: Pen and Sword, 2012.

Doubler, Michael. *Closing with the Enemy: How the GIs Fought the War in Europe, 1944–1945*. Lawrence: University Press of Kansas, 1994.

Eisenhower, Dwight. *Crusade in Europe*. New York: Doubleday & Company, 1948.

Eisenhower, John S. D. *The Bitter Woods: The Battle of the Bulge*. New York: G. P. Putnam's Sons, 1969.

Ellis, John. *Brute Force: Allied Strategy and Tactics in the Second World War*. New York: Viking, 1990.

Ellis, L. F. *Victory in the West*. Vol. I: *The Battle of Normandy*. History of the Second World War series. London: HMSO, 1962.

Ellis, L. F. *Victory in the West*. Vol. II: *Defeat of Germany*. History of the Second World War series. London: HMSO, 1968.

Featherston, Alwyn. *Saving the Breakout: The 30th Division's Heroic Stand at Mortain, August 7–12, 1944*. Novato, CA: Presidio, 1993.

Fenelon, James M. *Four Hours of Fury: The Untold Story of World War II's Largest Airborne Invasion and the Final Push into Nazi Germany*. New York: Scribner, 2019.

Giles, Janice. *The Damned Engineers*. Boston: Houghton Mifflin, 1970.

Harrison, Gordon A. *Cross-Channel Attack*. United States Army in World War II series. Washington: Office of the Chief of Military History, 1951.

Hart, Russell A. *Clash of Arms: How the Allies Won in Normandy*. Norman: University of Oklahoma Press, 2004.

Hartcup, Guy. *CODE NAME MULBERRY: The Planning, Building and Operation of the Normandy Harbours*. Newton Abbot, UK: David & Charles, 1977.

Hastings, Max. *Armageddon: The Battle for Germany, 1944–1945*. New York: Alfred A. Knopf, 2004.

Hastings, Max. *Das Reich: The March of the 2nd SS Panzer Division Through France, June 1944*. New York: Henry Holt, 1982.

Hastings, Max. *Overlord: D-Day and the Battle for Normandy*. New York: Simon & Schuster, 1984.

Hesketh, Roger. *Fortitude: The D-Day Deception Campaign*. New York: Overlook, 1999.

Keegan, John. *Six Armies in Normandy: From D-Day to the Liberation of Paris, June 6th–August 25th, 1944*. London: Johnathan Cape, 1982.

Kershaw, Robert. *It Never Snows In September: The German View of Market-Garden and the Battle of Arnhem, September 1944*. New York: Sarpedon, 1990.

Lacy, Jim. *Keep From All Thoughtful Men: How U.S. Economists Won World War II*. Annapolis: Naval Institute Press, 2011.

Levine, Alan. *From the Normandy Beaches to the Baltic Sea: The Northwest Europe Campaign, 1944–1945*. New York: Praeger, 2000.

Lewis, Adrian R. *Omaha Beach: Flawed Victory*. Chapel Hill: The University of North Carolina Press, 2003.

MacDonald, Charles B. *The Battle of the Huertgen Forest*. Philadelphia: J. B. Lippincott, 1963.

MacDonald, Charles B. *The Last Offensive*. United States Army in World War II series. Washington: Office of the Chief of Military History, 1973.
MacDonald, Charles B. *The Mighty Endeavor: The American War in Europe*. Oxford: Oxford University Press, 1969.
MacDonald, Charles B. *The Siegfried Line Campaign*. United States Army in World War II series. Washington: Office of the Chief of Military History, 1963.
MacDonald, Charles B. *A Time for Trumpets: The Untold Story of the Battle of the Bulge*. New York: William Morrow, 1985.
Macintyre, Ben. *Double Cross: The True Story of the D-Day Spies*. New York: Crown, 2012.
Mansoor, Peter R. *The GI Offensive in Europe: The Triumph of American Infantry Divisions, 1941–1945*. Lawrence: University Press of Kansas, 1999.
Marshall, S. L. A. *Bastogne: The Story of the First Eight Days*. Washington: Infantry Journal Press, 1946.
Marshall, S. L. A. *Night Drop*. New York: Little Brown, 1962.
McManus, John C. *The Americans at D-Day: The American Experience at the Normandy Invasion*. New York: Forge, 2004.
McManus, John C. *The Dead and Those About to Die: D-Day: The Big Red One at Omaha Beach*. New York: NAL Caliber, 2014.
McManus, John C. *September Hope: The American Side of a Bridge Too Far*. New York: NAL, 2012.
Miller, Edward G. *A Dark and Bloody Ground: The Hurtgen Forest and the Roer River Dams, 1944–1945*. College Station: Texas A&M Press, 1995.
Millett, Allan R. "The United States Armed Forces in the Second World War." In *Military Effectiveness*, Vol. 3: *The Second World War*, edited by Allan R. Millett and Williamson Murray, 45–89. Boston: Unwin Hyman, 1988.
Milner, Marc. *Stopping the Panzers: The Untold Story of D-Day*. Lawrence: University Press of Kansas, 2014.
Montgomery, Field Marshall The Viscount Montgomery of Alamein. *Normandy to the Baltic*. Boston: Houghton Mifflin, 1948.
Morgan, General Sir Frederick. *Peace and War: A Soldier's Life*. London: Hodder Stoughton, 1961.
Murray, Williamson. *The Luftwaffe, 1933–1945: Strategy for Defeat*. London: George Allen & Unwin, 1985.
Murray, Williamson. "Needless D-Day Slaughter." *Military History Quarterly* 15, no. 3 (Spring 2003): 26–30.
Murray, Williamson, and Allan R. Millett. *A War to Be Won: Fighting the Second World War*. Cambridge, MA: Harvard University Press, 2000.
Neillands, Robin. *The Dieppe Raid: The Story of the Disastrous 1942 Expedition*. Bloomington: Indiana University Press, 2005.
O'Keefe, David. *One Day in August: The Untold Story Behind Canada's Tragedy at Dieppe*. Toronto: Knopf Canada, 2013.
Overy, Richard. *Why the Allies Won*. New York: W. W. Norton, 1996.
Parker, Danny S. *Fatal Crossroads: The Untold Story of the Malmedy Massacre at the Battle of the Bulge*. Boston: Da Capo Press, 2012.
Perret, Geoffrey. *There's a War to Be Won*. New York: Random House, 1991.
Pogue, Forrest C. *The Supreme Command*. United States Army in World War II series. Washington: Office of the Chief of Military History, 1954.

Powell, Geoffrey. *The Devil's Birthday: The Bridges to Arnhem, 1944*. London: Buchan & Enright, 1984.
Prados, John. *Normandy Crucible: The Decisive Battle that Shaped World War II in Europe*. New York: NAL, 2011.
Reardon, Mark J. *Victory at Mortain: Stopping Hitler's Counteroffensive*. Lawrence: University Press of Kansas, 2002.
Ruppenthal, Roland G. *Logistical Support of the Armies*. Vol. 2: September 1944–May 1945. United States Army in World War II series. Washington: Office of the Chief of Military History, 1959.
Rush, Robert. *Hell in Hürtgen Forest: The Ordeal and Triumph of an American Infantry Regiment*. Lawrence: University Press of Kansas, 2001.
Ryan, Cornelius. *A Bridge Too Far*. New York: Simon & Schuster, 1974.
Ryan, Cornelius. *The Longest Day: June 6, 1944*. New York: Simon & Schuster, 1959.
Saunders, Tim. *Operation Plunder*. Barnsley, UK: Pen and Sword, 2006.
Schrijvers, Peter. *Those Who Hold Bastogne: The True Story of the Soldiers and Civilians Who Fought in the Biggest Battle of the Bulge*. New Haven: Yale University Press, 2014.
Speidel, Hans. *Invasion 1944: Rommel and the Normandy Campaign*. Chicago: Henry Regnery, 1950.
Stacey, Charles Perry. *Official History of the Canadian Army in the Second World War*, Vol. 3: *The Victory Campaign: The Operations in North-West Europe 1944–1945*. Ottawa: The Queen's Printer and Controller of Stationery, 1960.
Stewart, Andrew. *Caen Controversy: The Battle for Sword Beach 1944*. Tulsa: Helion, 2014.
Symonds, Craig L. *Neptune: The Allied Invasion of Europe and the D-Day Landings*. Oxford: Oxford University Press, 2014.
Toland, John. *Battle: The Story of the Bulge*. New York: Random House, 1959.
Trew, Simon. *D-Day Landings: Gold Beach*. Stroud, UK: The History Press, 2011.
Van Creveld, Martin. *Fighting Power: German and U.S. Army Performance, 1939–1945*. Westport, CT: Greenwood Press, 1982.
Waddell, Steve. *United States Army Logistics: The Normandy Campaign, 1944*. Westport, CT: Praeger, 1994.
Weigley, Russell F. *Eisenhower's Lieutenants: The Campaign of France and Germany, 1944–1945*. Bloomington: Indiana University Press, 1981.
Whiting, Charles. *Battle of Hurtgen Forest*. Conshohocken, PA: Combined, 2000.
Whitlock, Flint. *If Chaos Reigns: The Near-Disaster and Ultimate Triumph of the Allied Airborne Forces on D-Day, June 6, 1944*. Havertown, PA: Casemate, 2011.
Wieviorka, Olivier. *Normandy: The Landings to the Liberation of Paris*. Trans. M. B. DeBevoise. Cambridge, MA: Belknap Press of Harvard University Press, 2008.
Wright, Stephen L. *The Last Drop: Operation Varsity, March 24–25, 1945*. Mechanisburg, PA: Stackpole, 2008.
Zaloga, Steven. *D-Day Fortifications in Normandy*. New York: Osprey, 2005.
Zaloga, Steven. *The Devil's Garden: Rommel's Desperate Defense of Omaha Beach on D-Day*. New York: Stackpole, 2013.
Zuckerman, Solly. *From Apes to Warlords, 1904–46: An Autobiography*. New York: Harper & Row, 1978.
Zuehlke, Mark. *Holding Juno: Canada's Heroic Defence of the D-Day Beaches: June 7–12, 1944*. Vancouver: Douglas & McIntyre, 2006.

Zuehlke, Mark. *Juno Beach: Canada's D-Day Victory—June 6, 1944.* Vancouver: Douglas & McIntyre, 2004.

Zuehlke, Mark. *Terrible Victory: First Canadian Army and the Scheldt Estuary Campaign: September 13–November 6, 1944.* Vancouver: Douglas & McIntyre, 2007.

Zuehlke, Mark. *Tragedy at Dieppe: Operation Jubilee, August 19, 1942.* Vancouver: Douglas & McIntyre, 2013.

Zumbro, Derek S. *Battle for the Ruhr: The German Army's Final Defeat in the West.* Lawrence: University Press of Kansas, 2006.

CHAPTER 18

THE LAND WAR IN ASIA: CHINA, BURMA, AND INDIA

ALAN JEFFREYS

At the onset of the war in South-East Asia, the China–Burma–India theater (CBI) was created under an American command led by Lieutenant General Joseph "Vinegar Joe" Stilwell, who was responsible for supporting the airlift to China and for reopening land communications to China with the reconquest of Northern Burma. In March 1942, he was also made Chief of Staff to Chiang Kai-shek in his role as Supreme Allied Commander of the China theater. These conflicting command structures in CBI continued throughout the war and were further impeded by the animosity that arose between Stilwell and Chiang. Stilwell even had fundamental differences of opinion with the only other U.S. general in CBI, General Claire Chennault, head of the American air force in China.[1] Stilwell became Deputy Supreme Allied Commander, South-East Asia Command (SEAC) in 1943 but found it equally difficult to get on with his British allies: General William Slim, commander of Army, was one of the few generals who could work with Stilwell. At the same time, Stilwell commanded Northern Combat Area Command, with the American and Chinese forces fighting in North Burma, which took up most of his time and energy.[2] Both as Chief of Staff of the China theater and deputy command of SEAC, he continued to have direct communication with General George C. Marshall, the U.S. Army Chief of Staff and continued to use this channel to argue against SEAC positions that, as Deputy Supreme Commander, he had been party to. The problems of the unwieldy command structures of the CBI and South-East Asia Command theaters were never truly resolved.[3]

The Chinese role in World War II has been somewhat overlooked but this omission has been remedied with the publication of a number of important English language historical studies by Rana Mitter and Hans van de Ven. China was one of the big four Allies, along with Britain, the United States, and the USSR. More than fourteen million Chinese died during the war, of whom two million were battlefield casualties. China's role has now been documented with the opening up of the archives, and that has meant that a more nuanced perspective is now available both in the West and, more importantly, in China. Historians of China have examined both the Nationalist and Communist contribution to the war.[4] A multitude of museums in China have sprung up to commemorate the war; a war that has political resonances to the present day in the region, demonstrated by China marking the seventieth anniversary of victory over Japan with a military parade.[5]

A historiographical study of this theater has shown the difficulty of studying the CBI, epitomized by the continuing use of the nickname "Constant Bickering Inside." Maochun Yu commented that there is a lack of good quality scholarship and what there is very much due to the political situation in China, Burma (Myanmar), India, the United Kingdom, and the United States. Thus, in China, the domination of the Communist ruling party discouraged looking at the role of Chiang Kai Shek and the Nationalist Party, even though the Nationalists and their warlord allies undertook most of the fighting against the invading Japanese forces since 1937. In Burma and India, the nationalist narrative has dominated and in India it is only very recently that the military and social history of the war in India has been re-published, researched and documented.[6] In the UK, the colonial history of India and Burma has not proved a popular subject to study at universities and, as such, World War II studies have generally remained Eurocentric. Similarly, studies by American scholars have been more interested in the Vietnam War than South-East Asia in this period. As a result, much that has been produced in the early years after the war has been very partisan. Indeed, no volume exists that looks at the theater in equal measure from the point of view of the three main Allies: American, British, and the Commonwealth (African and Indian troops); Chinese forces, as well as nationalist forces, such as the Indian National Army and the Burma Defence Army under Aung Sang Sun; and the Japanese occupation forces.[7] However, research in this area has gained momentum in more recent decades. For example, this has meant a complete reassessment of Stilwell's abilities as a commander. Previously depicted as the straight-talking American hero, he is now presented as rather incompetent and out of his depth as an army commander. Indeed, in his chapter, Maochun Yu understandably conforms to this partisan view and reflects only on the American and Chinese historical work on CBI, as the topic is indeed huge and published in different languages.

In Japan, academic work has been undertaken but there is considerably less interest in the war there than in any other of the major belligerents.[8] Therefore, as a continuation of partisanship, but also due to available space, this chapter will mainly look at the new research on the campaigns in Burma fought by the British and Indian armed forces trained in India and their role in the defeat of Japan.

The Burma campaign of 1942–1945 has been called the "Forgotten War." However, a huge bibliography has been produced since the end of World War II. The second edition of *The Burma Campaign Memorial Library: Descriptive Catalogue and Bibliography*, published in 2001, listed 1,034 publications on the campaign. Even at the time, the troops were not forgotten at home.[9] The campaign from the Japanese point of view has been magisterially told by Louis Allen, an intelligence officer during the war, who served at the South-East Asia Translation and Interrogation Centre in Delhi for the last two years of the war.[10] The most forgotten aspects of the campaign are undoubtedly that during the last two years of the war, with the reconquest of Burma, it was a largely Indian Army campaign. This chapter will chart this aspect of the war. Equally forgotten is the African contribution, who provided about one-quarter of the troops in Burma with two West African divisions, one East African division, and a West African brigade. Their role has largely been ignored by historians with the exception of a history of the 81st West African Division, written by a former officer in the Division, and the pioneering work on African soldiers undertaken by David Killingray and others.[11]

The Japanese army invaded Burma on December 11, 1941, after the successful invasion of Malaya (Malaysia) and Singapore. The defeat of the British, Indian, and Australian forces in Malaya and Singapore in February 1942, commanded by Lieutenant General Arthur Percival, earmarked the end of the British Empire in South and South-East Asia, as well as the Australians looking to the United States as their main ally rather than Britain after 1942. The defeat even foresaw the end of the Indian Army as the protector of British rule in India.[12] The Japanese forces of two divisions, reinforced later by the Guards Division, crushed the defending forces of one Indian Corps of two Divisions, one Australian Division, and the very unlucky British 18th Division, who practically embarked to walk straight into prisoner of war camps, spending three-and-one-half years in the very harsh conditions of the camps on the Burma–Thailand Railway. A similar number of civilian internees (American, Australian, Canadian, and British, but mainly Dutch from the Dutch East Indies) endured over three years in camps across the Chinese mainland and South-East Asia with fourteen thousand internees dying in captivity.[13]

The retreat from Burma was the longest retreat in British military history. The Japanese forces had invaded to protect the advances in South-East Asia and prevent American supplies getting to China over the Hump. They defeated British, Indian, Chinese, and American (in the form of the air force unit—the American Volunteer Group, also known as the Flying Tigers) armed forces. However, Burma had been a backwater prior to the war, with only British garrison battalions and various paramilitary imperial units such as the Burma Military Police and the Burma Frontier Force. The regular forces comprised four battalions of the Burma Rifles in 1939. The onset of the war resulted in the expansion of the regiment to eight battalions. This rapid expansion was an important factor in the lack of fighting efficiency of the regiment despite being well-led, as the officers all spoke the relevant languages, having come from the civil service, police, or were forestry officials, many of whom were university-educated.[14] They were reinforced by the partially trained 17th Indian Infantry Division that had originally undertaken training for the Middle East, but two of the brigades were sent to Malaya, and later comprised the 16th, 48th and 63rd Indian Infantry Brigades. However, all these units together still did not amount to a viable military force. The main issue was undoubtedly the rapid expansion of the armed forces both in Burma and India, in addition to the lack of training prior to the Japanese invasion. The lack of equipment was another severe handicap as well as being equipped for a different theater. For example, 16th

Indian Infantry Brigade had vehicles painted in desert colors with sun compasses for navigation in the Middle East.

Lieutenant General Thomas Hutton was appointed by General Sir Archibald Wavell, Commander-in-Chief (C-in-C) India, to take over command of Burma Army and replace the retiring Lieutenant General Sir Donald Macleod as General Officer Commanding (GOC) Burma. The defending forces at Moulmein were overwhelmed by the advancing Japanese 55th Division. Wavell and Hutton wanted the defending forces to keep as much distance between the enemy and Rangoon as possible, but the speed of the Japanese advance meant that 17th Indian Division was forced to retreat all the way back to the bridge over the Sittang River. The bridge was of vital importance to both armies because it was only one hundred miles from Rangoon, a vital supply link both for the Burma Road to China, as well as for reinforcements and supplies for the Burma campaign. The divisional commanding officer, Acting Major General John "Jackie" Smyth ordered the demolition of the bridge before two brigades were able to cross the river. The disaster at Sittang Bridge sealed the fate of the defending forces. It marked the beginning of the end of the campaign for the Allied forces, although reinforced by the battle-hardened 7th Armoured Brigade from the Middle East and the Chinese Fifth and Sixth Armies, nominally under the command of Stilwell but whose divisional commanders were reluctant to take action unless agreed by Chiang Kai-shek. The Allied forces were under-equipped and under-trained, and the long retreat became inevitable despite the formation of the Burma Corps (Burcorps) on March 19, 1942, commanded by Lieutenant General William "Bill" Slim.[15] The Chinese forces covered the road north toward Mandalay and Burcorps took over Western Burma. However, unrelenting Japanese pressure and the withdrawal of the Royal Air Force (RAF) from Burma meant that, with a few exceptional actions where the Japanese forces were bettered, the retreat continued until May when the last remnants of the defending forces entered Imphal, India.

Historical studies of the retreat have mostly been written by veterans and high-ranking officers, such as Smyth and Hutton (both fired during the campaign), to protect their reputations.[16] A re-assessment of the campaign is much needed.[17] It is worth noting that all the army commanders at the initial stages of the Japanese invasion—Hutton, Percival (GOC Malaya Command) and Stilwell—were all staff officers with no experience of field command and this is demonstrated in their conduct of operations. Stilwell and the remnants of the 38th Chinese Division retreated to India rather than China. They underwent training at Ramgarh and fought extremely well under Stilwell's command later in Northern Burma, but the divisional commander, Major General Sun Li-jen, was never again trusted by Chiang Kai-shek.

The next encounter with the Japanese in the Burma campaign was even more disastrous. The ill-fated First Arakan campaign was the remainder of the cancelled ambitious "Anakim" offensive to invade Burma and recapture Rangoon. It consisted of a limited offensive into the Arakan region, clearing the Mayu peninsula overland with an amphibious operation to take Akyab Island, although this part of the plan was cancelled due to the lack of equipment and troops. The 14th Indian Division, commanded by Major General Wilfrid Lloyd, launched the attack on both sides of the Mayu Ridge on the September 21, 1942. The advance was very slow due to the supply lines and to avoid exposing the flanks to Japanese counterattacks. However, it meant that Japanese reinforcements were given time to arrive, and British forces encountered well-defended bunkers. On January 7, 1943, a company of the 1st Battalion Royal Inniskilling Fusiliers reached Donbaik at the end of the peninsula and unsuccessfully attacked the position held by one Japanese company. Another attack launched by the whole battalion two days later supported by field and mountain artillery similarly failed. A series of attacks with increasing strength on the position were made over the next two months. On February 1, the 47th Indian Infantry Brigade, which had relieved 55th Brigade, attacked Donbaik along with eight tanks, an additional one-and-a-half field batteries and a Light Anti-Aircraft battery but was equally unsuccessful. The British and Indian forces had encountered Japanese defensive bunkers for the first time, to which they had no response.[18] The abortive attacks on Donbaik and other positions gave time for the Imperial Japanese Army to mount a counteroffensive. In stark contrast, the Japanese forces managed to clear the Kaladin Valley and both the east and west flanks of the Mayu range combined with encircling attacks on Rathedaung and Donbaik. It took less than a month, pushing back numerically superior Commonwealth troops in demoralizing confusion. In addition, the command situation was still in array. At one point Lloyd had five brigades under his command, with Eastern Army commanded by Lieutenant General Noel Irwin. Slim, XV Corps commander, recommended a corps command in the Arakan but Irwin refused. Eventually Lloyd was replaced by Major General Cyril Lomax and Slim formed a corps command, but it was too late. The First Arakan attack was an utter disaster undertaken by partially trained and demoralized troops, as well as untrained reinforcements, with an inefficient command structure. Morale was also undermined by the huge numbers of soldiers affected by malaria and disease and the problems of evacuation of the sick and wounded back to base hospitals. In addition, the military situation was hampered by the Quit India movement of 1942 in response to the failure of the Cripps Mission, when Sir Stafford Cripps led an unsuccessful British mission to India to try and persuade Indian nationalist politicians to support the war in return for promises of full autonomy after the war. This meant that large numbers of troops were required to act as "Aid to Civil Power."[19] This, in combination with the Bengal Famine of 1943–1944, which killed an estimated three million Indians, meant that much of India was at its lowest ebb during this period.[20]

Military morale, however, was improved both in India and the UK, by the First Chindit operation, Operation Longcloth. Brigadier Orde Wingate, under the patronage of Wavell, was given command of 77th Indian Infantry Brigade to undertake irregular operations behind the lines, destroying railway lines. It was described as a long-range penetration group based on tactics Wingate had developed in Palestine before the war, but also during the Ethiopian campaign with Gideon Force supporting Emperor Haile Selassie's return to power in May 1941. The initial attack on February 13, 1943, surprised Japanese forces but the Chindits encountered fierce resistance. By May 26, the remainder of the brigade made its way back to Imphal. The operation was notable for the fact that British and Commonwealth forces had got the better of the Japanese forces in the jungle, dispelling the myth of Japanese "supermen." It was widely publicized at the time as a huge success story in contrast to the disastrous First Arakan campaign. However, it has remained controversial, as only two-thirds of the force returned to India and one-half of these were not fit enough for duty again.

During the war, India was the base and provided supplies for the campaigns in the Middle East and South-East Asia. General Headquarters (GHQ) India directed campaigns in the Middle East at the beginning of the war and South-East Asia up until 1943 when South-East Asia Command was formed under the command of Admiral Lord Louis Mountbatten with General Stilwell as his deputy. From this period onward, India was responsible for training units and formations for the jungle war in Burma. As a result of the Infantry Committee convened by Wavell in June 1943, training divisions were set up where recruits undertook two months training in jungle warfare after their basic training at the regimental training centers. Jungle warfare schools were also established to train units and instructors. For the first time, a comprehensive doctrine was available for fighting the Japanese, the jungle, and disease. This was encapsulated in the training pamphlet produced by GHQ India entitled *The Jungle Book*. Lessons were also learned and disseminated from the Australian and American experience of fighting the Japanese in New Guinea and the Pacific. The returning C-in-C India, General Claude Auchinleck, ensured that jungle warfare training was the main focus of all training in India.[21]

This training organization was a continuation of the pre-war Indian Army that was built upon throughout the war. In addition, Indian Army formations in North Africa and Italy trained for desert and mountain warfare respectively and continued to learn the lessons from their experiences. In India, a training structure was in place for all levels of training from recruits and officer cadets to combined operations for amphibious operations.[22] Thus, the Indian Army had developed "a more comprehensive training organisation than any other country at that time."[23]

The majority of troops in the reconquest of Burma in 1944–1945 were from the Indian Army who provided three Indian Corps of eight infantry divisions, along with the two British infantry divisions, two West African divisions, and one East African division. In numerical terms, the Fourteenth Army comprised about 340,000 Indian, one hundred thousand British, and ninety thousand African troops. Indian Army divisions comprised three infantry brigades, consisting of usually one British Army battalion, one Indian Army, and often one battalion from the Gurkha regiment or another Indian Army battalion. The Indian army was officered by mainly British officers and a small number of Indian officers at the beginning of the war, but, by 1945, Indian officers numbered over fifteen thousand.

By 1944, the Fourteenth Army, and indeed the Indian Army as a whole, was well-trained, and capable of defeating the Japanese in the jungle. The *jawans* of the rapidly expanded Indian Army had become seasoned soldiers by the time the Imperial Japanese Army made its main attack, Operation U-GO, in the spring of 1944. The prime objective was the speedy capture of Imphal by the Japanese Fifteenth Army, under General Renya Mutaguchi, to forestall the imminent Allied invasion of Burma. There was no plan to march on Delhi. The Japanese forces were focused on defending the perimeters of their empire evidenced by the fact they only had three weeks of supplies with them. Fourteenth Army commander, General "Bill" Slim, and IV Corps Commander, Lieutenant General Geoffrey Scoones, had decided to fight a defensive battle at Imphal due to the terrain and the all-weather airfields at Imphal and Palel. The successful defense of Imphal relied on IV Corps and 221 RAF Group.

The historiography of the Battles of Kohima and Imphal continues unabatedly in favor of the fighting at Kohima where the larger percentage of British troops such as the 4th Battalion, the Royal West Kent Regiment, and the 2nd British Division fought. Imphal, where the majority of defending troops were part of the Indian Army, has only very recently found two modern interpretations of the battle that does justice to their role in the battle, as the last good history of the battle was written back in 1962.[24] This bias toward Kohima, with barely any mention of the Indian Army, started with the publication of the Winston Churchill's memoirs with only two pages devoted to the battles of Kohima and Imphal.[25] Churchill's low opinion of the Indian Army has affected the subsequent historiography of not only the Indian Army but also the Battles of Kohima and Imphal.[26]

The advance of the Japanese 33rd and 15th Divisions began on March 9, 1944. To the north, the 31st Division was assigned the objective of Kohima to cut the Dimapur–Imphal Road. The Japanese offensive had been expected but not quite so soon, leaving the defending troops spread out over a wide area: the 17th Indian Division was in the Tiddim area, the 50th Indian Parachute Regiment were training near Kohima, one brigade of the 23rd Indian Division was near Ukrul, and the 20th Indian Division was in the Kabaw Valley. They all had to withdraw to concentrate under IV Corps to prevent Japanese infiltration. This withdrawal of large numbers of troops was in stark contrast to the early defeats of the British and Indian Armies in South-East Asia. Here they carefully conducted tactical fighting withdrawals rather than pell-mell retreats. The 17th Indian Division was not ordered to withdraw until March 13 and, as a result, they were cut off by the rapid advance of the Japanese 33rd Division. Two brigades of the 23rd Division were called in to help the division. In addition, the 5th and 7th Indian Divisions, after their successes in the Second Battle of Arakan, were transferred by air and train to the Imphal and Dimapur area. Slim's plan was to allow the Japanese forces to reach the edge of the Imphal plain and then destroy them using mobile strike forces supported by artillery, armor, and air support.

Initially, the advancing 31st Japanese Division was held up by two battalions of the 50th Parachute Brigade at Sangshak plus a battalion of the newly formed Assam Regiment at Jessami, providing the garrison at Kohima essential time to build up their inadequate defenses. This also allowed the 5th Indian Division, and particularly the 161st Indian Infantry Brigade, to arrive by air from Arakan. The Kohima area was less densely covered by jungle with Kohima Ridge about five thousand feet above sea level and a number of higher points along the ridge, which were all held at the start of the siege. The 161st Brigade was sent into action immediately, with orders to protect Kohima and keep the vital supply route to Dimapur open. The 4th Battalion, Royal West Kent Regiment, together with a battery of the 24th Mountain Regiment and the 2nd Field Company, Indian Engineers, joined the garrison of mainly non-combatants or exhausted units retreating from the Chindwin River. The garrison at Kohima consisted of about one thousand men, commanded by Colonel Hugh Richards, with the remains of the Assam Regiment, detachments of the paramilitary Assam Rifles, the Burma Regiment plus troops from the Reinforcement camp, non-combatant troops who had not been evacuated, and a battalion of untrained Nepalese State Forces.

The Japanese attacked Kohima on April 4. Indeed, if General Sato and the 31st Division had bypassed Kohima, they would have probably taken the lightly defended Dimapur, which was the base and railhead for the whole central front and thus of strategic importance, but his orders were to march on Kohima, to which he doggedly adhered. The remainder of the 161st Brigade were two miles away at Jotsoma, from where the formation provided decisive artillery support to the garrison, protected by two infantry battalions, as the artillery battery with the garrison was too restricted in space to use their guns and therefore acted as observation posts with wireless communication. One target was hit by thirty-five hundred rounds in the space of five hours.

By mid-April the general situation looked bleak. Nevertheless Mountbatten, Slim, and Scoones were not discouraged by the existing state of affairs as large-scale reinforcements were already on their way and, coupled with air supremacy, the air supply of formations could go ahead as planned. As Slim had requested, XXXIII Corps, comprising the 2nd Division, the 268th Indian Infantry Brigade, and two tank regiments, was transferred from the other side of India to join the fighting. The plan was to open up the Dimapur–Kohima–Imphal road and join forces with IV Corps with an immediate objective of relieving 161st Brigade and the garrison at Kohima. However, the Japanese had taken most of Kohima, with the defenders grouped around the Deputy Commissioner's bungalow and tennis court on Garrison Hill. Supplies were air-dropped by parachutes but due to the very small drop zone often fell into Japanese hands, with the RAF also providing support with canon-fire and pin-point bombing.

The siege was over on April 18, when the road was cleared by the 1st Punjab Regiment and the wounded and non-combatants were evacuated. The defenders had survived twenty-five Japanese attacks in fourteen days, although it should be remembered that the siege itself comprised only fourteen days out of a total of the sixty-four that it took to defeat the Japanese at Kohima. The garrison was finally relieved by 6th Brigade of the 2nd Division. General George Giffard, C-in-C of the Eleventh Army Group, saw this early defense of Kohima as the turning point in the Japanese attack, where a mixed group of trained and untrained troops successfully held off two Japanese regiments, the equivalent of two brigades, proving that their training and morale had improved considerably as compared to earlier battles in Burma. It took the 2nd Division and 33rd Indian Infantry Brigade until June to clear the area of Japanese troops who tenaciously held onto their bunkers and defensive positions along Kohima Ridge.[27]

Fighting around Imphal continued during this period at considerable intensity. The battle comprised hundreds of ambushes, attacks, and stalwart defense and hence renders it almost impossible for historians to chart them completely.[28] The

33rd Japanese Division was still fighting the 17th Indian Division to the south-west of Imphal at Bishenpur. On April 9, the Bishenpur–Silchar track, the last remaining overland communication to Imphal, was cut by the 33rd Japanese Division. The remaining defending forces comprising the 20th Indian Division at Shenan, together with the 5th Indian Division at Ukrul and the 23rd Indian Division in reserve, were all up against the advancing Japanese 15th Division.

The Japanese came closest to success on April 6, when they captured the commanding heights around Nunshigum, overlooking Imphal. The IV Corps was encircled. This was the nearest the Japanese army would get to Imphal (about six miles away). It was taken from a detachment of the 3rd and 9th Jat Regiments, but the remainder of the battalion retook the position. On April 11, the Japanese retook the position and the Allied counterattack followed two days later. The hill was reclaimed in a famous action by the 3rd Carabiniers and a battalion of the 17th Dogra Regiment, in which all the officers became casualties and the attacks were led by non-commissioned officers, after nearly two hours of bombing attacks by Vengeances and Hurricanes. The action at Nunshigum demonstrated that the importance of junior leadership during training had proved immensely effective. Thus, despite the best efforts of the Japanese, the basic plan of concentrating IV Corps in the Imphal Plain had been carried out without losing either the 17th or 20th Indian Divisions. Scoones now had 17th, 20th, 23rd, and 5th Indian Divisions under his command. By 1944, it was not unusual for an Indian division to be formed of almost entirely Indian units due to the manpower shortages in the British Army. For example, the 23rd Indian Division only had one British infantry battalion and one artillery unit, with the remaining all being Indian units.[29]

In May the counteroffensive plan for IV Corps was to attack Ukhrul and for the 17th Indian Division to cut the Tiddim Road to the rear of the 33rd Japanese Division. After regrouping, Scoones used the 5th and 23rd Indian Divisions for the counteroffensive against the Japanese forces. The 5th Indian Division advanced ten miles up the Imphal–Kohima road, the 20th Indian Division held the hills of Crete West and Scraggy and pushed twenty-three miles along the track to Ukhrul until they were relieved by the 23rd Indian Division, who pushed the Japanese out of the Shenan Area. The 17th Indian Division got the better of the Japanese 33rd Division, against whom they had fought in the 1942 retreat. On the night of June 5–6, the 2nd Division met up with troops of the 5th Indian Division, twenty-nine miles north of Imphal at Milestone 109. Although the Japanese forces refused to admit defeat and when the order was finally given to the Fifteenth Army to retreat to the Chindwin on July 9, the Japanese 15th and 31st Divisions were in complete disarray, only the 33rd Division kept its cohesion as a fighting force.

The Battles of Imphal and Kohima depended on air supply and the retention of the airfields at Imphal and Palel. Allied air superiority was maintained by short Spitfire fighters and long-range fighters—Mustangs and Lightnings. During April, transport squadrons provided continuous air supply to IV Corps, which received a daily average of nearly five hundred tons of supplies. The RAF, together with the USAAF and the Indian Air Force (IAF), were instrumental in winning the battles of Kohima and

Imphal. For example, air defense of Imphal was conducted by a day-to-day strength of seven squadrons: eighteen from the RAF and three from the IAF.[30]

During these battles, the British and Indian Armies achieved a crushing defeat on the Imperial Japanese Army. They inflicted 53,505 casualties on the Japanese Fifteenth Army, whose overall strength had been 84,280, in contrast to the 16,700 casualties in Fourteenth Army. The fighting bore out the importance of jungle warfare training, as well as air superiority, organized logistics, and good leadership. It demonstrated exactly what resolute jungle-trained troops, with confidence in themselves and their leaders, could achieve in battle. The actions at Kohima and Imphal highlighted the successful use of infiltration tactics and aggressive patrolling when fighting in dense jungle against the Japanese. It evidenced the benefits of tank, artillery, and air co-operation, and it showed the resolve of support units, all of which was made possible with thorough jungle warfare training.

The soldiers of the Fourteenth Army had grown considerably in confidence and were now neither afraid of the jungle nor the Japanese, and hence displayed increasing battlefield effectiveness with aggressive tactics in both defense and attack. The Fourteenth Army was by no means perfect by the summer of 1944, but it now had the upper hand over the Japanese. The divisions prepared for the next phase of the fighting and absorbed the lessons of the recent operations. The Indian Army was not only trained for jungle warfare but also for air-mobile, amphibious operations and for the open warfare. It fought in the central plains of Burma at the battles of Mandalay and Meiktila and the ensuing recapture of Burma. Similarly, medical advances included the standardized treatment of malaria, along with rigidly enforced health discipline and the adoption of mepacrine that played an important role toward achieving victory in South-East Asia.[31]

The second Chindit operation, Operation Thursday, began in March 1944. The formation had grown from a brigade in 1943 to almost the size of a small corps, comprised of six brigades of twenty-three thousand men acting as a long-range penetration force. It was predominantly a British formation with Gurkhas, West Africans, and Burma Rifles. Wingate disliked Indian Army officers and mistakenly thought Indian troops were of an inferior standard to his Chindits, and, with the exception of Gurkha battalions, would not countenance Indian Army battalions in his force. For a short period of time Wingate even commanded the 5307th Provisional Unit, an American infantry unit led by Brigadier General Frank Merrill and more commonly known as "Merrill's Marauders." Wingate had accompanied Winston Churchill to the Quebec Conference, where Wingate had convinced the Combined Chiefs of Staff that a long-range penetration force could make a decisive impact in the Burmese campaign. As a result, the Chindits were supported by the American No. 1 Air Commando, led by Colonel Cochrane, for troop lifts, air supply, and support with additional support from the RAF and USAAF.

The objective of the Chindits was threefold: to support Stilwell's advance into Myitkyina, encourage the Chinese forces from Yunnan to fight in northern Burma, and, as in the first operation, to attack the Japanese lines of communication. Five of the brigades were flown in and one went overland. Thence the brigades established strongholds from which columns would harass Japanese communications. This was Wingate's first field command above brigade level, and he was found lacking. However, Wingate died in an aircrash on March 24. He was replaced by Brigadier Lentaigne who had commanded the 1st and 4th Gurkhas in the retreat from Burma, and then commanded the 111th Brigade. Lentaigne, an Indian Army officer, was not a Wingate disciple and disagreed with many of his predecessor's views on long range penetration tactics. The strongholds were attacked by the Japanese, and these quickly became very attritional battles that the Chindits were neither trained nor equipped for. The Chinese forces advanced toward Myitkyina with the Chindit brigades supporting them, now commanded by Stilwell. They also attacked Mogaung under his orders, which was captured by Brigadier Mike Calvert's 77th Indian Infantry Brigade. However, as in the first Chindit operation, it was at a huge cost. The 77th Brigade had only three hundred men left fit to fight and the formation suffered 1,811 battle casualties throughout the operation. Stilwell unfairly questioned the Chindit commitment, ignoring the fact that the brigades had fought continuously for months on end and were used in roles for which they were untrained. Indeed, Stilwell was equally harsh on Merrill's Marauders, who took the south airfield at Myitkyina, and he oversaw the decimation of the unit. Once the Americans and Chinese joined forces, the Chindits were withdrawn and disbanded. A large volume of literature, and equally large controversy, has subsequently developed over the role of Wingate and the Chindits in both operations.[32]

Meanwhile the Fourteenth Army continued to press the Japanese forces further across the Chindwin valley and into central Burma. Slim's plan, Operation Capital, was to defeat the Japanese Burma Army on the Shwebo plain, but it was clear that the Japanese were not of the same mind and withdrew their forces over the Irrawaddy River. Thus, the plan was revised, Operation Extended Capital, with the IV Corps crossing the river at Nyaungu in radio silence and the XXXIII Corps to cross upstream north of Mandalay. The defending Japanese engaged in combat with what they thought was the main force at Mandalay, while the IV Corps sandwiched the Japanese at Meiktila using hammer-and-anvil tactics.[33] It was during these battles that the Indian Army fought the Indian National Army (INA) as a formation, rather than piecemeal as in earlier battles, such as Imphal. It had been formed mainly from Indian prisoners of war captured after the Fall of Singapore. The INA was headed by the nationalist politician Subhas Chandra Bose, and due to his persistence, the Second Nehru Division INA was allotted its own sector along the Irrawaddy. However, as a military organization it was flawed. The formation was overrun by the 7th Indian Division and was in retreat after just two days of fighting with the majority of the troops (eleven hundred) either deserting or surrendering. As Chandar Sundaram elucidates, the INA's real significance was not in its military capability but in its political impact on the British Empire and the forthcoming independence of India.[34] Operation Extended Capital was a complete success and the 14th Army advanced to Rangoon before the monsoon broke to achieve "the last and greatest Victory of the British Indian Army."[35]

The clash between Chiang and Stilwell culminated in 1944, when Stilwell insisted on his appointment to command the Chinese Army, prompting Chiang to demand his recall to the States. Stilwell was replaced by General Albert Wedemeyer when the command structure in China slightly improved. Unlike his predecessor, he no longer commanded the Chinese forces in Burma, as the CBI was divided into India–Burma and a separate China theater, with the two remaining Y Force divisions that had fought in Burma being brought back as reinforcements against the devastating Japanese Ichi-Go offensive (April–December 1944). As a result, U.S. supplies that were being flown over the "Hump" were now going to the Chinese divisions fighting in China rather than those in Burma as under Stilwell. Although relations between the Americans and the Chinese began to improve, it was at too late a stage of the war to be hugely beneficial. The Ledo Road, linking India with China, was opened on January 12, 1945, but the amount of material that could be transported along it was insignificant compared to the supplies coming in by air.

The victory in Burma was achieved by the Indian Army supported by the British, East African, and West African forces. The American and Chinese forces were also instrumental with the fighting in Northern Burma, alongside the combined air forces of the Royal Air Force, the United States Army Air Force, and the Indian Air Force. In addition, equipment was no longer in short supply in South-East Asia Command by the summer of 1944, in contrast to the previous low priority accorded to this theater. Thus, in conclusion, training, doctrine, improved logistics, air supply, medical advances and improved health discipline, artillery, tank and air support, high morale, and good leadership were all essential in the largest defeat, to date, of the Japanese forces on land during the war.

Notes

1. See Gerhard L. Weinberg, *A World at Arms: A Global History of World War II* (Cambridge: Cambridge University Press, 2005), 638.
2. The most recent biography is Jay Taylor, *The Generalissimo: Chiang Kai-shek and the Struggle for Modern China* (Harvard: Belknap Press of Harvard University Press, 2003). A reassessment of Stilwell and the CBI theater is long overdue, with historians still referring to Barbara Tuchman, *Sand Against the Wind: Stilwell and the American Experience in China, 1911–1945* (New York, MacMillan, 1971) and T. H. White, ed., *The Stilwell Papers* (New York: William Sloane Associates, 1948). See also the U.S. official history in Charles Romanus and Riley Sunderland, *China-Burma-India Theater*, 3 vols. (Washington, DC: Center of Military History United States Army, 1953–1959) and Jonathan Templin Ritter, *Stilwell and Mountbatten in Burma: Allies at War, 1943–1944* (Denton: University of North Texas Press, 2017). For a succinct historiographical interpretation of the Western consensus of the Chinese theater, see Hans van de Ven, "The Sino–Japanese War in History," in *The Battle for China*, ed. Mark Peattie, Edward Drea, and Hans van de Ven (Stanford: Stanford University Press, 2011), 448–452.
3. See Raymond Callahan, *Churchill and his Generals* (Kansas: Kansas University Press, 2007), 200–201.
4. See Rana Mitter, *China's War with Japan, 1937–1945: The Struggle for Survival* (London: Penguin Books, 2013); Mark Peattie, Edward Drea, and Hans van de Ven, eds., *The Battle for China: Essays on the Military History of the Sino-Japanese War of 1937–1945*

(Stanford: Stanford University Press, 2011); Hans van de Ven, *China at War: Triumph and Tragedy in the Emergence of the New China 1937–1952* (London: Profile, 2017) and S. C. M. Paine, *The Wars for Asia, 1911–1949* (Cambridge: Cambridge University Press, 2012).

5. See *The Economist*, February 7–13, 2015, 52.
6. The History Division of the Indian Ministry of Defence re-published eight volumes of the official histories of the Indian Armed Forces in during World War II in 2012 and a further four in 2014. See also Yasmin Khan, *The Raj at War: A People's History of India's Second World War* (London: Bodley Head, 2015); Srinath Raghavan, *India's Wars: The Making of Modern South Asia (1939–1945)* (London: Allen Lane, 2016); and Kaushik Roy, *India and World War II: War, Armed Forces, and Society, 1939–45* (New Delhi: Oxford University Press, 2016).
7. See Maochun Yu, "CBI: A Historiographical Review," in *A Companion to World War II*, ed. Thomas W. Zeiler and Daniel M. Dubois (Chichester: Wiley-Blackwell, 2013), 140–142.
8. See John Ferris and Evan Mawdsley, "Introduction to Volume 1," in *The Cambridge History of the Second World War*, Vol. 1, ed. John Ferris and Evan Mawdsley (Cambridge: Cambridge University Press, 2015), 13.
9. See Ashley Jackson, *The British Empire and the Second World War* (London: Hambledon Continuum, 2006), 351–352.
10. See Louis Allen, *Burma: The Longest War 1941–45* (London: J. M. Dent, 1984). See also Edward J. Drea, *Japan's Imperial Army: Its Rise and Fall, 1853–1945* (Kansas: Kansas University Press, 2009).
11. See John A. L. Hamilton, *War Bush: 81 (West African) Division in Burma 1943–1945* (Norwich: Michael Russell, 2001) and see also, for example, David Killingray and Martin Plaut, *Fighting for Britain: African Soldiers in the Second World War* (Woodbridge: James Currey, 2012).
12. See Indivar Kamtekar, "The Shiver of 1942," *Studies in History* 18, (2002): 82–83, 97, 99.
13. See Bernice Archer, *The Internment of Western Civilians under the Japanese 1941–1945: A Patchwork of Interment* (Hong Kong: Hong Kong University Press, 2008).
14. See James Lunt, "The Burma Rifles," *Journal of the Society for Army Historical Research* LXXVI, no. 307 (Autumn 1998): 202–207.
15. Slim has dominated the historiography of the Burma campaign. His memoir *Defeat into Victory* (London: Cassell, 1956) is essential reading. The most recent biography is Russell Miller, *Uncle Bill: The Authorised Biography of Field Marshal Viscount Slim* (London: Weidenfeld &Nicolson, 2013). Ronald Lewin, *Slim: The Standardbearer* (London: Leo Cooper, 1976) remains the best.
16. See Ian Lyall Grant and Kazuo Tamayama, *Burma 1942: The Japanese Invasion* (Chichester: Zampi Press, 1999). See also the many books published by Brigadier Sir John Smyth, for example, *Before the Dawn: A Story of Two Historic Defeats* (London: Cassell, 1957) and the unpublished memoir by Lieutenant General Sir Thomas Hutton, "Rangoon 1941–42: A Personal Record," Papers of Lieutenant General Sir Thomas Hutton, Imperial War Museum, 99/73/1.
17. The most recent study based on secondary sources is Alan Warren, *Burma 1942: The Road from Rangoon to Mandalay* (London: Continuum, 2011). As with the Fall of Singapore, the retreat from Burma was another signpost in the impending demise of the British Empire in South and South-East Asia. The huge exodus of civilians has been largely uncharted until recently. See Michael D. Leigh, *The Evacuation of Civilians from Burma: Analysing the 1942 Colonial Disaster* (London: Bloomsbury, 2014).

18. For more on bunkers see Tim Moreman, "'Debunking the Bunker': From Donbaik to Razabil, January 1943–March 1944," in *The Indian Army: Experience and Development*, ed. Alan Jeffreys and Patrick Rose (Farnham: Ashgate, 2012), 109–134.
19. See Andrew N. Buchanan, "The War Crisis and the Decolonization of India, December 1941–September 1942: A Political and Military Dilemma," *Global War Studies* 8, no. 2 (2011): 5–31.
20. See Bayly and Harper, *Forgotten Armies*, 282–291. See also Khan, *The Raj at War*, 200–216.
21. See Daniel Marston, *Phoenix from the Ashes: The Indian Army in the Burma Campaign* (Westport: Praeger, 2003) and Tim Moreman, *The Jungle, the Japanese and the British Commonwealth Armies at War, 1941–45* (London: Routledge, 2005).
22. See Alan Jeffreys, *The Approach to Battle: Training the Indian Army during the Second World War* (Solihull: Helion, 2017).
23. F. W. Perry, *The Commonwealth Armies: Manpower and Organisation in Two World Wars* (Manchester: Manchester University Press, 1988), 111.
24. See Sir Geoffrey Evans and Antony Brett-James, *Imphal: A Flower on Lofty Heights* (London: Macmillan, 1962); Hemant Singh Katoch, *The Battlefields of Imphal* (Abingdon: Routledge, 2016); and Raymond Callahan, *Triumph at Kohima-Imphal* (Lawrence: University Press of Kansas, 2017).
25. See Winston Churchill, *The Second World War*, Vol. V: *Closing the Ring* (London: Cassell, 1952).
26. See Raymond Callahan, "Did Winston Matter? Churchill and the Indian Army, 1940–45," in *The Indian Army, 1939–47*, ed. Alan Jeffreys and Patrick Rose (Farnham: Ashgate, 2012), 57–67. See also Cat Wilson, *Churchill on the Far East in the Second World War: Hiding the History of the "Special Relationship"* (Basingstoke: Palgrave, 2014).
27. A good recent history of Kohima is Fergal Keane, *Road of Bones: The Siege of Kohima 1944* (London: Harper Press, 2010)
28. See Jon Latimer, *Burma: The Forgotten War* (London: John Murray, 2004), 272.
29. See Lieutenant Colonel A. J. F. Doulton, *The Fighting Cock: Being the History of the 23rd Indian Division, 1942–1947* (Aldershot: Gale & Polden, 1951), Appendix A, 306–307. This drain on manpower was exacerbated by the Second Chindit Operation with one historian recently seeing the Chindits as "the single greatest waste of British Army manpower in the Second World War," see Alan Allport, *Browned Off and Bloody-Minded: The British Soldier goes to War, 1939–1945* (London: Yale University Press, 2015), 219–220.
30. See Peter Preston-Hough, *Commanding Far Eastern Skies: A Critical Analysis of the Royal Air Force air superiority campaign in India, Burma and Malaya 1941–1945* (Solihull: Helion, 2015).
31. See Mark Harrison, *Medicine & Victory: British Military Medicine in the Second World War* (Oxford: Oxford University Press, 2004), chapter 5.
32. See Callahan, *Triumph at Imphal-Kohima*, 137–149.
33. See Field Marshal Sir William Slim, *Defeat into Victory* (London: Cassell, 1956), 327.
34. See Chandar S. Sundaram, "The Indian National Army, 1942–1946: A Circumstantial Force," *A Military History of India and South Asia*, ed. Daniel P. Marston and Chandar S. Sundaram (Westport: Praeger, 2007), 127, 130. For Aung San and the Burmese Defence Army who changed sides in 1944 to become the Anti-Fascist People's Freedom League, see Bayly and Harper, *Forgotten Armies*, pp. 429–434.
35. See Graham Dunlop, "The Re-capture of Rangoon, 1945: The Last and Greatest Victory of the British Indian Army." In *The Indian Army, 1939–47*, ed. Alan Jeffreys and Patrick Rose (Farnham: Ashgate, 2012), 137–155.

Bibliography

Allen, Louis. *Burma: The Longest War 1941–1945*. London: J. M. Dent, 1984.

Barkawi, Tarak. *Soldiers of Empire: Indian and British Armies in World War II*. Cambridge: Cambridge University Press, 2017.

Bayly, Christopher, and Tim Harper. *Forgotten Armies: The Fall of British Asia, 1941–1945*. London: Allen Lane, 2004.

Callahan, Raymond. *Churchill and His Generals*. Kansas: University Press of Kansas, 2007.

Callahan, Raymond. *Triumph at Kohima-Imphal: How the Indian Army Finally Stopped the Japanese Juggernaut*. Kansas: University Press of Kansas, 2017.

Callahan, Raymond and Daniel Marston, *The 1945 Burma Campaign and the Transformation of the British Indian Army*. Kansas: University of Kansas, 2021.

Drea, Edward J. *Japan's Imperial Army: The Rise and Fall, 1853–1945*. Kansas: University of Kansas Press, 2009.

Dunlop, Graham. *Military Economics, Culture and Logistics in the Burma Campaign, 1942–1945*. London: Pickering & Chatto, 2009.

Jeffreys, Alan. *Approach to Battle: Training the Indian Army during the Second World War*. Solihull: Helion, 2017.

Jeffreys Alan, and Patrick Rose, eds. *The Indian Army, 1939–1947: Experience and Development*. Farnham: Ashgate, 2012.

Latimer, Jon. *Burma: The Forgotten War*. London: John Murray, 2004.

Lyman, Robert, *A War of Empires: Japan, India, Burma & Britain 1941-45*. Oxford: Osprey, 2021.

Marston, Daniel. *Phoenix from the Ashes: The Indian Army in the Burma Campaign*. Wesport, CT: Praeger, 2003.

Marston, Daniel. *The Indian Army and the End of the Raj*. Cambridge: Cambridge University Press, 2014.

Mitter, Rana. *China's War with Japan, 1937–1945: The Struggle for Survival*. London: Penguin, 2013.

Moreman, Tim. *The Jungle, the Japanese and the British Commonwealth Armies at War, 1941–45*. London: Routledge, 2005.

Paine, S. C. M. *The Wars for Asia, 1911–1949*. Cambridge: Cambridge University Press, 2012.

Peattie, Mark, Edward Drea, and Hans van de Ven, eds. *The Battle for China: Essays on the Military History of Sino-Japanese War of 1937–1945*. Stanford: Stanford University Press, 2011.

Preston-Hough, Peter. *Commanding Far Eastern Skies: A Critical Analysis of the Royal Air Force Superiority Campaign in India, Burma and Malaya 1941–1945*. Solihull: Helion, 2015.

Raghavan, Srinath. *India's Wars*. London: Allen Lane, 2016.

Romanus, Charles, and Riley Sunderland. *China–Burma–India Theater*. 3 vols. Washington, DC: Center of Military History United States Army, 1953–1959.

Slim, Field Marshal Sir William. *Defeat into Victory*. London: Cassell, 1956.

Spector, Ronald. *The Eagle and the Sun: The American War with Japan*. London: Viking, 1985.

Thorne, Christopher. *Allies of a Kind: The United States, Britain and the War Against Japan, 1941–1945*. London: Hamish Hamilton, 1978.

van de Ven, Hans. *China at War: Triumph and Tragedy in the Emergence of the New China 1937–1952*. London: Profile, 2017.

CHAPTER 19

THE PACIFIC WAR

KYLE P. BRACKEN

In December 1941, few Americans would have confidently predicted military victory over Imperial Japan. The attacks on Pearl Harbor and subsequent Allied possessions throughout Asia and the Pacific revived a feeling of uncertainty that had lingered in America since the early days of the Great Depression. During his address to Congress on December 8, President Franklin D. Roosevelt spoke to great applause of an "inevitable triumph" over Japan, but in that moment the future appeared bleak. In the following months Japanese naval, air, and ground forces tore through Burma, Malaya, Thailand, British North Borneo, Hong Kong, the Philippines, the Netherlands East Indies, Guam, Wake, and the Gilbert Islands with unprecedented rapidity. The success of the offensive exceeded even Japan's most optimistic expectations, and it left Allied leaders without the manpower or productive capabilities to stop it. Victory, then, became contingent on the Allies mobilizing wartime industry, outproducing their enemies, and harnessing the military and scientific peculiarities of waging war over the twenty-eight million square miles of the Pacific Ocean.

Despite the stunning emotional impact the Pearl Harbor operation had on the American public, the attacks disappointed Admiral Yamamoto Isoroku, commander of the Japanese Combined Fleet. In the strategic tradition of naval theorist Alfred Thayer Mahan, Yamamoto sought a single and decisive engagement that would damage the U.S. Pacific Fleet long enough for the Japanese to complete their conquest of East Asia and the Pacific. At the heart of this vision remained the elimination of the American battleships, the strategic symbol of naval power in the early twentieth century. The attack, which involved some four hundred carrier-based aircraft launched in two waves, succeeded in sinking or damaging dozens of ships, including all eight U.S. battleships. Aircraft parked wingtip-to-wingtip made lucrative targets for Japanese pilots, who raked the harbor throughout the morning, killing or wounding nearly thirty-five hundred American servicemen in the process.

The failure at Pearl Harbor, however, stood not with Yamamoto, but with the operation's commander, Admiral Nagumo Chūichi. Fearing he had lost the element of surprise, Nagumo disengaged without launching a third wave of attacks targeting fuel reserves and repair facilities. Additionally, none of the American aircraft carriers were present that morning, ensuring that the time that the U.S. needed to repair the Pacific Fleet's would not buy the Japanese as much time as they had hoped. This costly oversight ensured that Yamamoto would have to seek his grand, Mahanian victory elsewhere, and that the Americans would have to make carriers, not battleships, central to their overall strategy.

At the end of December, President Roosevelt and his military advisors met with British Prime Minister Winston Churchill and his staff in Washington to discuss the Pacific situation. Roosevelt confirmed, to Churchill's relief, that the United States intended to pursue a "Germany first" strategy that prioritized manpower and resources for the European war. Despite this qualification, the group did not fail to recognize that the deepening crisis in the Pacific demanded immediate attention, and in the first three months of 1942 some eighty thousand American GIs were sent to this "secondary" theater, nearly four times the number sent to Europe during the same period.[1]

In Washington, the delegations also laid the foundations for the American, British, Dutch, and Australian Command (ABDA), an organization charged with the seemingly impossible task of bringing the Japanese to a halt. British General Sir Archibald Wavell assumed the undesirable role of commanding ABDA for its brief existence in an attempt to maintain control of the "Malay Barrier," a resource-rich defensive line that ran from the British naval base at Singapore on the Malay Peninsula, through the Netherlands East Indies, Australian New Guinea, and finally to Australia itself. Wavell's attempts to slow the Japanese onslaught and deprive them of the region's oil, however, proved futile against the experienced and numerically superior foe. The British stronghold in Singapore fell on February 15, followed by Java and the Netherlands East Indies in the following weeks. In only a few months, ABDA's entire operational theater, except Australia, had fallen to the Japanese.[2]

Just as Singapore represented British colonial power in the Asia–Pacific world, United States influence in the Pacific hung on its naval base in the Philippines. After World War I, American strategists predicted that Japan would present the greatest military threat to the United States, and they drafted their war plans accordingly. During the 1920s and 1930s, War Plan ORANGE underwent several revisions as American and British attempts to stifle Japanese naval expansion became increasingly desperate, but it retained a basic assumption that Japan would eventually strike first against an American base in the Pacific. In this case, garrisons on Midway, Wake, Guam, and the Philippines would have to hold out until the Pacific Fleet could steam west from Hawaii and relieve them.

General Douglas MacArthur, commander of U.S. Army Forces in the Far East (USAFFE), did not care for ORANGE on the grounds that it was passive, restrictive, and hopelessly optimistic. Even before the battleship losses on December 7, it appeared increasingly unlikely that the navy could reach MacArthur before the Japanese overwhelmed his combined American and Filipino forces. Despite this reality, MacArthur did little to prepare for the Japanese before they invaded the Philippines island of Luzon on December 8. He failed to properly disperse his aircraft, resulting in heavy losses from aerial bombardment, and made few defensive preparations. When he finally ordered a withdrawal from Manila into the narrow Bataan peninsula in January, he neglected to consolidate ammunition, food, and medical supplies for the ensuing four months of fighting.

The defense of Bataan gained considerable media attention from an American population starved for good news, which they did not receive as the situation deteriorated and the Japanese bore down on the exhausted defenders. Lacking adequate supplies and reinforcements, the Bataan garrison surrendered on April 9 in the largest capitulation of American forces since the Civil War. Now prisoners of the Japanese, the seventy-eight thousand defenders marched more than sixty miles under the watchful eye of their captors, in what came to be called the Bataan Death March. Subjected to exhaustion, starvation, frequent beatings, and bayonetting, some six hundred Americans and as many as eighteen thousand Filipinos died on the trek, which was later declared a war crime by a postwar military tribunal.

MacArthur spent the first months of 1942 directing the Bataan defense from the island fortress of Corregidor. The general and his staff headquartered themselves inside the Malinta Tunnel, where they rode out daily aerial bombardments accompanied by assorted family members, diplomats, and Philippines president Manuel L. Quezon. President Roosevelt, however, was unwilling to lose a trusted general or suffer public and political scrutiny for abandoning the hero of Bataan, and he ordered MacArthur out of the Philippines and to safety in Australia. On the night of March 11, the general, his family, and key members of his staff left Corregidor, ultimately bound for Melbourne. Days later MacArthur assumed command of the newly formed Southwest Pacific Area (SWPA), vowing to return and liberate the Philippines from the Japanese.

With the Philippines in jeopardy, Australia remained the last point from which the Allies could stage future operations in the Pacific. MacArthur's arrival in late March came to the great relief of the Australian people as well as Prime Minister John Curtin, whose burgeoning relationship with the new SWPA commander ensured the cooperation of the Australian government and helped leverage MacArthur's position with Roosevelt and the Joint Chiefs of Staff (JCS). With the bulk of his operational area now in Japanese hands, MacArthur faced the challenge of maintaining the Malay Barrier and the string of airfields that connected Australia with Hawaii, the United States, and the Panama Canal Zone. Rather than defend the largely rural Australian continent, he chose instead to use the natural barrier afforded by the island of New Guinea to the north. The southeastern "tail" of the bird-shaped island, bisected by the jagged peaks of the Owen Stanley Mountains, created the "natural barrier" behind which the Allies could defend both New Guinea and Australia. Port Moresby, on the southern coast of Papua, New Guinea, afforded the Allies an advanced base and airdromes from which aircrews could attack targets as far as the northern Solomon Islands and the Philippines.[3]

Roosevelt's decision to give MacArthur command of SWPA offered a short-term solution to the war's greatest command dilemma. With the geographic nature of the Pacific War dictating a significant commitment of naval, ground, and air forces, the longstanding rift between the U.S. Army and Navy swirled around the issue of who would hold supreme command. MacArthur, never one to pass on an opportunity for public praise, naturally hoped for overall command of Allied forces in the Pacific, largely on the grounds that a failure to liberate the Philippines in a timely manner would damage relations between the United States and its island colony. Such a campaign, however, could never succeed without the U.S. Navy's aircraft carriers, which remained closely guarded by the Chief of Naval Operations and Commander-in-Chief of the United States Fleet, Admiral Ernest J. King. Careful not to ruffle the feathers of these two volatile personalities, the JCS formed a separate Pacific Ocean Area (POA) subdivided into northern, central, and southern sectors all under the command of Admiral Chester W. Nimitz. Despite the ultimate success of the Allies in 1945, the unconventional command arrangement complicated operations for the entire war.

In early 1942, however, MacArthur and Nimitz faced the mutual task of anticipating and halting Japan's next offensive. U.S. carrier forces under Vice Admiral William Halsey Jr. conducted some of the only offensive operations against the Japanese in early 1942, raiding Japanese garrisons by air in the Gilbert and Marshall Islands. The most significant of these raids occurred on April 18, when sixteen B-25 bombers flew from the deck of the carrier *Hornet* and bombed Tokyo, defying both the laws of physics and the boastful rhetoric of the Japanese. The attack, led by Lieutenant Colonel James Doolittle, became the first carrier-based bomber attack in history, and despite the minimal damage inflicted by the bombs, news of the raid offered Americans their first surge of optimism in months.

Eager to press their gains and cut off Australia from the United States, the Japanese launched Operation MO in early May, with the objectives of seizing Port Moresby in Papua as well as Tulagi in the Solomons. Supported by airfields in the Lae-Salamaua-Gona area of northern Papua, the Japanese 4th Fleet and its three carriers under Admiral Inoue Shigeyoshi attempted an amphibious assault on Port Moresby, with the additional hope of trapping and destroying any Allied carrier forces in the area. Nimitz, informed by intelligence warning of Japanese movements, sent the carriers *Lexington* and *Yorktown* under Admiral Frank "Jack" Fletcher to intercept the invasion force. The resulting Battle of the Coral Sea marked the first major carrier engagement of World War II, and the first in history in which aircraft ensured that the opposing fleets never met face to face.

Although both sides disengaged without gaining any discernible advantage, the Battle of the Coral Sea was effectively a tactical victory for the Allies. In exchange for the loss of *Lexington*, one destroyer, dozens of aircraft, and heavy damage to *Yorktown*, American and Australian planes had sunk the carrier Japanese *Shōhō*, damaged the light carrier *Shōkaku*, and shot down nearly one hundred enemy aircraft. Furthermore, the fight ensured the immediate security of Port Moresby by sea, later forcing the Japanese to pursue an overland campaign against the Australian garrison in New Guinea. But the governing lesson remained that carrier-based aircraft could succeed against fleet forces, and that Japan's Mitsubishi A6M "Zero" fighter still vastly outperformed any Allied competitor.

The failure in the Coral Sea placed future operations in New Guinea primarily in the hands of the Imperial Japanese Army (IJA), but it did not deter Admiral Yamamoto from aggressively seeking a fight with the U.S. Pacific Fleet. He first proposed the Midway operation in February 1942, and had it been suggested by anyone else in the Imperial Japanese Navy (IJN), it would likely have been rejected outright. The fifty-eight-year-old admiral, however, had achieved such great prestige within the Japanese military that the mere threat of his resignation kept his critics in check. Yamamoto planned to capitalize on the damage inflicted at Pearl Harbor and draw the weakened U.S. fleet into battle, and with the news that *Yorktown* remained sidelined for repairs the Combined Fleet enjoyed a four-to-two advantage in aircraft carriers.

Midway Atoll stood at the western end of the Hawaiian archipelago, roughly halfway between the North American and Asian continents. Threatening the small U.S. naval station on Midway, reasoned Yamamoto, would be enough to draw the American flattops out of Hawaii in response. Despite his existing numerical advantage, Yamamoto planned to deceive the opposing fleet with a diversionary assault on the Aleutian Islands in the northern Pacific with two of his carriers. The Americans, already devoid of battleships, would have no choice but to commit their forces on Japanese terms. Like Nimitz, Yamamoto was a champion of offensive carrier strategy, and it was by those means that he hoped to deliver the decisive blow that had eluded him the previous December.[4]

Nimitz, however, did have one element working heavily in his favor. On the same day that *Lexington* went down in the Coral Sea, U.S. Navy signals intelligence decrypted radio transmissions discussing an IJN "aviation conference" in the Central Pacific. The information came from Station Hypo in Hawaii, the same intelligence station that had informed Nimitz of the IJN's Coral Sea offensive. The concentration of four carriers suggested to Hypo's commander, Lieutenant Joseph J. Rochefort, that the Japanese were planning an offensive in the Central Pacific, but the objective, designated "AF," remained unclear. Rochefort became convinced the next day that the target was Midway when a Japanese scout plane passing near the island radioed that it was passing "AF."[5]

The intelligence did not convince Ernest King, who feared a renewed IJN effort against Port Moresby or New Caledonia, but Nimitz trusted Rochefort. Bordering on insubordination, Nimitz convinced King that Midway was the central objective of the proposed late May offensive, and despite his commander's insistence on caution, he planned to assemble as many of his carriers as possible to confront Yamamoto. With Halsey's two carriers, *Hornet* and *Enterprise*, and the rapidly repaired *Yorktown*, he sent his forces west in late May. With the additional aircraft stationed at Midway, Nimitz had four airstrips to deliver his planes against the approaching enemy.[6]

Admiral Nagumo, commanding the First Carrier Striking Force, remained unaware of the U.S. fleet's location when he ordered the first attack against Midway before dawn on June 4, and as a precaution held back one-half of his available carrier aircraft. This decision proved advantageous as American scout aircraft from Midway spotted the Japanese carriers shortly after the last planes had left their decks. In response, the U.S. carrier force turned southwest to intercept the Japanese while the entire air force on Midway roared off their runways to do the same.

The remaining crop of U.S. marine aviators on Midway met the Japanese over the island, but their inexperience and outdated aircraft resulted in heavy casualties. The Japanese bombers, however, failed to destroy the airfield and suffered greatly from accurate American anti-aircraft fire. After losing more than sixty percent of its aircraft, the Japanese strike force radioed back to Nagumo requesting his remaining planes. Then under attack from U.S. bombers, Nagumo reasoned that the Midway airstrip still posed a significant menace to his carriers, and he opted to rearm his planes for another strike. Japanese aircrews required little more than an hour to do this and, with no sign of the American carriers, the risk seemed minor.

At 7:28am, Nagumo received word of ten American ships approaching, which scouts soon identified as five cruisers and five destroyers. Under another attack from Midway-based bombers and torpedo planes, Nagumo faced the choice of whether to launch his available dive bombers against the American ships or wait until his returning fighters could refit and join the contest. He opted for the latter, having just observed the vulnerability of unescorted American dive bombers against his ships, and despite new reports that a carrier now appeared to accompany the U.S. ships. This decision proved the most decisive of the battle, as Nagumo's restraint was soon met by uncharacteristic aggression by his opponent.

Admiral Raymond A. Spruance delivered all of *Hornet* and *Enterprise*'s planes at the dangerously long distance of 150 miles, hoping to seize the initiative and knock out the Japanese flattops, which had begun moving northeast to maintain a safe distance while their planes rearmed. The move deceived most of Spruance's pilots, who found no ships at the reported location. Only one torpedo squadron from each carrier successfully located the Japanese fleet, but it scored no hits while losing all but four aircraft. *Yorktown*'s planes, sent by Admiral Fletcher ninety minutes after the others, had an easier time locating the Japanese carriers, and reached them roughly the same time as those from *Enterprise*.

Their torpedo bombers flew in just above deck level, drawing a swarm of Zeros. Leading *Yorktown*'s fighters through the suicidal gauntlet, Commander James Thach watched as the superior enemy fighters downed one plane after another. With the Zeros glistening all around, Thach noticed above him the first of *Yorktown*'s dive bombers, tightly formed and cascading down onto the enemy ships "like a beautiful silver waterfall." The Japanese had drawn in their air cover to contest the low-flying fighters and torpedo bombers, allowing the American dive bombers to engage unmolested with the carriers. They attacked with superb precision, landing four bombs through the deck of *Kaga* and setting her ablaze. The flagship *Akagi* took two more bombs while another struck *Soryu*, all detonating bombs and torpedoes that had been brought onto the flight decks to rearm the carriers' planes. Dive bombers and torpedo bombers from *Enterprise* and *Yorktown* attacked the fourth carrier, *Hiryu*, later in the day and left it sinking, but not before *Hiryu*'s planes dealt a crippling blow to *Yorktown*. After its repairs and heroic return to service after the Coral Sea engagement, *Yorktown*, abandoned and listing hard to its port side, sank two days later after being struck by two torpedoes from the Japanese submarine *I-168*.

Yamamoto had hoped to pursue the Americans, but without his large carriers and his only reinforcements far to the north near the Aleutian Islands, the Japanese Combined Fleet sailed west on the morning of June 5 toward the protection of its air bases on Truk and Rabaul. Having lost the *Yorktown*, Spruance sailed east to avoid a night engagement against a still superior Japanese battle fleet, and after failing to detect the Japanese fleet on the 5th, retired to the east on the 6th. At Midway the U.S. Navy proved that it could defeat the Japanese Fleet in a surface engagement, but not without revealing the inexperience of its own commanders, whose confusion grew as the battle unfolded. Still, having destroyed Yamamoto's heavy carriers they had wrestled the initiative from the Japanese and limited their offensive capabilities for the remainder of the war.[7]

Their early thrust had earned the Japanese a foothold in the northern Solomons, a tropical island chain to Australia's northeast that could be occupied to restrict shipping between the Commonwealth and the United States. Japanese strength in the Solomons began at Rabaul, a fortified harbor installation on the northernmost island of New Britain. In addition to offering safe anchorage for naval forces, Rabaul provided an air base from which Japanese air forces could survey the islands, harass Allied shipping, and if practicable, support a ground campaign against Australia. The naval defeat at Midway had slowed Japan's southerly advance, but it did not remove the IJN as a significant threat to Allied operations.

Eager to capitalize on the shift in momentum and assume a limited offensive by the end of 1942, the JCS outlined an offensive plan on July 2 aimed at neutralizing Rabaul. Admiral King, who had been advocating for a Pacific naval offensive, suggested isolating New Britain by pushing north through the Solomon Islands, while General MacArthur argued instead for a decisive strike at directly at Rabaul. The solution reached by the JCS was to divide command responsibility between MacArthur and Nimitz. In three phases, the July 2 memorandum outlined first the capture of Tulagi in the lower Solomons, the northern coast of Papua New Guinea, and Rabaul by the end of 1943. The first of phase fell under navy command in in the South Pacific Area (SOPAC), with the other two under army leadership in SWPA.

The first phase began on August 7, 1942 with landings by the American First Marine Division Tulagi-Gavutu and Guadalcanal, where the Japanese had begun constructing an additional airstrip. Despite the marines' growing reputation as amphibious warriors, Major General A. A. Vandegrift's men had received little training in ship-to-shore operations, and they had not trained as a division since leaving the States in December 1941. This might have mattered to the marines encountering stiff Japanese resistance on Tulagi, but those on Guadalcanal scampered down the ramps of their landing craft to find an island seemingly devoid of human life. By the end of the day, they had captured the airstrip, which they named Henderson Field after the marine aviator killed at Midway, and they dug in to await the enemy they knew remained concealed within the labyrinth of lush jungles and fetid swamps.

With the marines safely ashore, efforts to supply Guadalcanal and secure the surrounding air and sea quickly exposed Allied weaknesses. Commanding from his flagship *Saratoga*, Admiral Fletcher raised concerns about the vulnerability of his fleet with increasing reports of Japanese naval forces to the north. Fletcher had warned the amphibious forces commander, Admiral Richmond Kelly Turner, that his ships could not remain in the area for more than four days, and he opted to head for open sea on August 8. That night, Admiral Mikawa Gunichi took eight ships up "the slot" between Guadalcanal and nearby Savo Island and struck the withdrawing American forces in a masterful act of radar navigation and night gunnery. Fearing exposure to the American flattops, however, Mikawa prematurely broke off the attack before hitting the American transports and returned north. The engagement cost the Allies fifteen hundred sailors and six ships, and forced the skittish American fleet to the relative safety of open waters with the amphibious landing forces in close pursuit.[8]

The Allied campaign for Guadalcanal proceeded through October as a shoestring effort to sustain the marines and the "Cactus Air Force" flown into Henderson Field from New Caledonia, Australia, and New Guinea. Unprepared to fight at night, U.S. naval forces used daylight hours to ship in supplies under the veil of air cover. At night the unchallenged Japanese ships of the "Tokyo Express" lobbed shells onto the island while transports disgorged fresh reinforcements. The American marines withstood nightly bombardments, sometimes by a lone bomber they called "Washing Machine Charlie," who added sleep deprivation to a list of ailments that included skin infections, malaria, dysentery, hunger, and failing nerves. Before November the Japanese tried repeatedly to reclaim Henderson Field, but failed to dislodge the marines, who had been reinforced by the U.S. 164th Infantry in October.

The situation at sea began to improve for the U.S. Navy when Nimitz named Halsey to command in SOPAC, relieving Vice Admiral Robert L. Ghormley. A far more aggressive personality than his predecessor, Halsey opted to challenge the Japanese fleet. On October 26 at the battle of Santa Cruz, the strategy cost the Americans the carrier *Hornet* and inflicted little damage to the Japanese battle fleet. In an engagement on November 12–15, the Allies sank two battleships, three destroyers, and seven transports carrying reinforcements to Guadalcanal, but again at considerable loss. Ultimately, the naval actions succeeded in convincing Yamamoto to concede the contest for Guadalcanal and seek another fleet engagement at a more favorable time and place.[9]

In New Guinea, the Japanese had been grappling with Australian and Papuan forces since July, in an overland drive against Port Moresby. The action occurred high in the Owen Stanley Mountains along the Kokoda Trail, a merciless sixty-mile jungle path connecting Kokoda in the north with Owen's Corner to the south. The combatants exchanged ground throughout the summer and, following a failed attempt to invade Milne Bay to the east, the Japanese began withdrawing toward Buna-Gona and Sanananda. Bolstered by the U.S. 32nd Infantry Division in September, the Australians pursued the Japanese across the mountains. From well-concealed defensive positions, the Japanese withstood repeated Allied assaults before between November and January, but ultimately failed to hold the coast and critical surrounding airstrips.

The 1942 offensives, while ultimately successful, revealed the weaknesses of Allied forces in the Pacific. A clear lack of experience by senior leadership hindered operations throughout the year, as well as an insufficient knowledge of the operational area.

Soldiers and marines went ashore without accurate maps or protection against an epidemic of tropical diseases. Fighting an island war also required more fluid integration of air, ground, and naval forces to contend with enemy forces over varying terrain and under unpredictable weather conditions. Nevertheless, the Allies had soundly defeated the Japanese in Papua and the Solomons, dispelling myths of Japanese invincibility and establishing an invaluable foundation of confidence heading into the new year.[10]

Japan entered 1943 searching for its best course of action. The situation worsened for the Imperial General Staff following the disastrous Battle of the Bismarck Sea in March, when bombers of Major General George Kenney's U.S. Fifth Air Force attacked and destroyed eight transports carrying elements of the Japanese 51st Division destined for New Guinea. In April, during a desperate air offensive targeting Allied shipping and air bases, Admiral Yamamoto was killed when American fighters shot down his plane over Bougainville. Facing a divided command situation not dissimilar to that between MacArthur and Nimitz, the Japanese army and navy could not agree on how best to proceed. The navy insisted that a fleet engagement near the Marshall Islands could turn the tide in Japan's favor, but this hypothetical situation did not sit well with army leadership, who felt that such an expansive front could not be defended. Ultimately, they decided against conducting further air operations for most of the year and turned their attention toward protecting the naval bases at Rabaul and Truk.[11]

Allied strategy for the reduction of Rabaul in 1943 depended on expanding the reach of the air forces throughout the theater. In a complex serious of operations known as *Cartwheel*, MacArthur's Australian and American forces battled up the New Guinea coast while Halsey climbed the Solomon ladder. After the costly and time-consuming invasion of New Georgia in July, Halsey and his staff began considering ways to bypass and isolate enemy strongholds in favor of softer targets that could support airfields. This concept of "island-hopping" became a hallmark of the Allied strategy in the Pacific and pointed to an improvement in planning at the operational level.

In addition to the meticulous planning and preparation required to carry out *Cartwheel*'s complex combined maneuvers, the Allies had to address the incredible rates of disease plaguing ground forces. Malaria in particular, had run rampant during the Guadalcanal and Buna-Gona battles, disabling roughly seventy-five percent of all Allied troops with crippling body aches, chills, and nausea. In 1942, American and British scientists ramped up research on new anti-malarial substances, a project made urgent by the Japanese capture of Java and the only source of quinine in the Pacific. The favored drug was Atabrine, which in tests proved effective and minimally toxic in the proper doses. Shipping of Atabrine to SWPA and the South Pacific Area (SOPAC) became high priority in 1943, as the Allied infantry divisions navigated through jungles teeming with malarial mosquitoes.[12]

The effectiveness of Atabrine on the ground depended on how well individual units enforced malaria discipline. In late 1943, U.S. Sixth Army soldiers in New Guinea experienced a marked decrease in rates of infection after regularly administering Atabrine, while less disciplined units continued to suffer. During the bitter fight for Bougainville beginning in November, malaria control units accompanied combat forces, destroying mosquito populations through pesticide spraying and draining stagnant water near encampments. Combined with Atabrine, these measures decreased rates of first-time infection. The introduction of the miracle-pesticide dichlorodiphenyltrichloroethane (DDT) to the battlefield in 1944 added another weapon to the fight against insect-borne illness. Even in small quantities the inexpensive chemical eliminated mosquitoes and other insects in far greater numbers than its predecessors, and for longer periods of time. To disperse DDT over greater areas, the U.S. Army Air Forces and Royal Australian Air Force modified aerial smoke spraying tanks to apply it from the air. The multinational effort to combat malaria was perhaps the most important scientific development of the Pacific War. It allowed the Allies to concentrate on defeating their human enemies, while Japanese soldiers succumbed to the disease in droves through the end of the war.[13]

In August the JCS, feeling that the *Cartwheel* operations would make it strategically insignificant, decided to bypass Rabaul rather than attempt to capture it. Admiral King used the decision as an opportunity to initiate a drive into the Gilbert Islands of the Central Pacific, hoping to again draw the IJN into action. On November 20, the 2nd Marine Division assaulted tiny Betio Island in the Tarawa Atoll. Due to unanticipated tidal conditions many of the outdated Higgins landing craft became grounded on a coral reef, leaving the attacking marines to wade five hundred yards to shore under a murderous enemy fire. The nearly three thousand Japanese defenders fought to the death and in seventy-six hours killed nearly seventeen hundred marines. The blunder horrified and outraged the American public, and it offered a preview of what awaited American troops in the coral atolls of the Central Pacific.

In the final weeks of 1943, the Allied offensive began its gradual move north across the equator and into the heart of the Japanese empire, ushering in the war's most destructive period. By 1944, war production in United States had long eclipsed what Japanese factories could achieve. American GIs, supported by a surging U.S. war economy, went into action as the best-equipped fighting men in the world. The Japanese, by contrast, lost ships, planes, and pilots faster than they could replace them, and now faced a two-headed Allied push west across the Pacific. Allied landings in the Gilbert and Marshall Islands and the subsequent destruction of the naval base at Truk by the U.S. Navy stunned the Japanese in January and February 1944. With these actions, the Navy initiated a drive west across the Central Pacific while the Army, in a parallel advance, charged up the New Guinea coast. In April, MacArthur leapt four hundred miles to Hollandia-Aitape, bypassing an enemy stronghold at Wewak and expediting his timeline to return to the Philippines. In June and July, casualties mounted in bitter fights for the Mariana Islands, including over thirty thousand civilians on Saipan and Tinian.

On the islands the increasing recalcitrance of the Japanese only served to exacerbate racial tensions with the Americans and contributed to an escalating battlefield trend of trophy collecting and mutilation of enemy dead. In 1944, *Life* magazine featured a photograph of an American woman admiring a Japanese skull collected by her boyfriend in New Guinea. The image subsequently appeared in Tokyo newspapers, offering the Japanese people verifiable evidence of Americans' inherent savagery. American servicemen often cited the Bataan Death March, executions of American pilots, and

Japanese soldiers' unwillingness to surrender to justify own their actions, while the Japanese pointed to mounting civilian casualties from Allied strategic bombing in Europe and the Pacific. Propaganda helped circulate rumors and escalate the level of violence as the Americans pushed further into the heart of Japan's prewar empire. Following the midsummer fall of the Mariana Islands, the war entered its most destructive phase, during which more than one-half of the war's total deaths occurred.[14]

Following the U.S. Sixth Army ashore on Leyte in October, MacArthur announced to the people of the Philippines, "I have returned." Halsey's gargantuan naval force, wielding seventeen carriers, supported the equally enormous landing, which did not move with the same rapidity MacArthur had seen in New Guinea. Whereas the speed of MacArthur's advance through New Guinea had advanced the timetable for landings in the Philippines, September operations for the Palau Islands of Peleliu and Morotai encountered particularly ardent resistance. Combined with the stagnation of progress on Leyte in front of immovable Japanese troops, the late year engagements pushed back the entire operational timetable for early 1945.[15]

Initially surprised by the expedited timing of the Allied landing at Leyte, the IJN jumped at another opportunity to decisively smash the U.S. fleet. Unlike the concentrated attack force used in the Marianas, the Japanese returned to a plan to divide and deceive, similar to that used at Midway. In four separate formations, the Japanese battleships and carriers (still lacking planes and pilots after their earlier losses) converged on Halsey's 3rd Fleet, hoping to spread out the American flattops and catch the landing force unguarded. Halsey's aggressive style of leadership invited disaster at Leyte Gulf, as his pursuit of Ozawa Jisaburō's Northern Force left the American transports and supply ships open to attack by Kurita Takeo. Thanks to a heroic stand by a handful of destroyers, cruisers, and one escort carrier, the Americans fought off the attacking forces and destroyed Ozawa's carriers in the largest naval engagement in history.[16]

Victory during the Battle of Leyte Gulf came with great consequences for the Allies present and those participating in future operations. The U.S. carrier *Princeton* fell to Japanese planes on October 24, the first Allied carrier lost in two years. The most frightful confrontation, however, occurred the next day when Japanese planes slammed into American ships, sinking the carrier *St. Lo*. This first organized appearance of *kamikaze* attacks terrified American sailors who faced the suicide attacks for the remainder of the war. *Kamikaze* attacks, while rarely successful, caused incredible damage to ships, and inflicted horrendous casualties, taking an additional mental toll on sailors and mandating increased anti-aircraft protection on Allied ships.

In the first days of 1945, the JCS began planning for what they assumed would be an eventual invasion of the Japanese Home Islands. With MacArthur in charge of all ground forces and Nimitz at the head of all naval forces going forward, they proceeded in selecting islands closer to Japan to serve as air bases for bomber escorts. In February, two marine divisions clamored onto the tiny volcanic island of Iwo Jima to fight the most costly battle in the history of the U.S. Marine Corps. During the subsequent conquest of Okinawa in the Ryukyus, thousands of *kamikaze* aircraft rained onto American ships, sinking thirty-six and killing nearly five thousand sailors. Japanese defenders clung to one muddy ridge after another while the remnants of the IJN hurled themselves against the Allied landing forces. With American submarines additionally sinking thousands of tons of Japanese shipping per week, the war did not end but continued to claim lives at an ever-increasing rate.[17]

While the warring armies and navies competed for Okinawa with exceptional violence, Japan's cities absorbed simultaneous attacks. By capturing the Marianas the previous summer, the Allies had effectively opened a third front in the Pacific. From Guam, Saipan, Tinian, and the Philippines, the new B-29 "Superfortress" began bombing mainland Japan and exacting a heavier toll on Japanese industry and morale. General Curtis Lemay, the architect of the American bombing campaign in Europe, soon had B-29s flying regular bombing missions against Japan's cities, employing incendiary bombs that created infernos in neighborhoods built primarily of bamboo and wood. On the night of March 9–10, 1945, a particularly devastating incendiary attack destroyed sixteen square miles of Tokyo and killed more than one hundred thousand Japanese civilians. By the end of the war, the unrelenting air campaign accounted for as many as two hundred thousand deaths in Japan.[18]

Aerial bombing raids over Japan increased in tempo in the final months of the war with ever-increasing lethality. On July 16, 1945, at a secret test site in New Mexico, the United States conducted the world's first successful detonation of a nuclear weapon. President Harry S. Truman, who assumed the presidency in April 1945 when Roosevelt died, immediately approved the new weapon for service in the Pacific. In May 1945, a new air unit, the 509th Composite Group, shipped off for service in the Marianas. Under a shroud of secrecy, the 509th was charged with training to deploy the world's first nuclear weapons in combat.

On Monday August 6, the B-29 bomber *Enola Gay* took off from Tinian carrying one uranium-based atomic bomb called *Little Boy*. At 8:15am the bomber's crew dropped the device above its primary target, the Japanese city of Hiroshima. With a tremendous flash, the bomb detonated above the city with a force equivalent to sixteen kilotons of TNT and a core temperature matching the surface of the sun. In an instant, it leveled Hiroshima for a mile in every direction, and the ensuing firestorm killed as many as 150,000 Japanese civilians and servicemen. That evening President Truman announced the bomb's use in a radio address, claiming that if he did not receive Japan's unconditional surrender, "they may expect a rain of ruin from the air, the like of which has never been seen on this earth." After no surrender occurred, the Soviet Union invaded Manchuria in the early hours of August 9. That afternoon, the B-29 *Bockscar* dropped a second bomb on Nagasaki, prompting Emperor Hirohito's decision to surrender on the sole condition that the Imperial throne be preserved. The Allies accepted these terms, and a Japanese delegation signed the formal instrument of surrender aboard the USS *Missouri* on September 2.

Historians continue to debate the ethical dimensions of Harry Truman's decision to use nuclear weapons on the Japanese. While these discussions will never likely reach a consensus, the atomic bombings illustrate the war's scientific and destructive apex. The Allied war with Imperial Japan began as a decades-long exercise in military planning, evolved with the execution and improvisation of those plans, and the ended in a paradigm altering instant. The congruent roles of science, nature, and industry during the Pacific War are the conflict's most significant developments, ones which elucidate simultaneously the belligerents' efforts to better protect and destroy one another. The sum of these efforts was a war on a particularly violent trajectory that, in many ways, reached its logical conclusion in 1945.

NOTES

1. Ronald H. Spector, *Eagle Against the Sun: The American War With Japan* (New York: Vintage Books, 1985), 123, 143–144; Stephen R. Taaffe, *Marshall and His Generals: U.S. Army Commanders in World War II* (Lawrence: University Press of Kansas, 2011), 13. The Washington conference, codenamed "Arcadia" marked the first discussion of wartime strategy by British and American leadership. In addition to developments regarding the Pacific theater, the group established the Combined Chiefs of Staff and made plans for the European bombing campaign and North Africa campaigns of 1942.
2. Spector, *Eagle Against the Sun*, 127–128.
3. Douglas MacArthur, *Reminiscences* (New York: McGraw Hill, 1964), 152–154.
4. Craig L. Symonds, *The Battle of Midway* (New York: Oxford University Press, 2011), 97–101.
5. Ibid., 147, 182.
6. Ibid., 182–185.
7. Spector, *Eagle Against the Sun*, 170–177.
8. Richard B. Frank, *Guadalcanal: The Definitive Account of the Landmark Battle* (New York: Penguin, 1990), 83–123; Williamson Murray and Allan R. Millett, *A War to be Won: Fighting the Second World War* (Cambridge: The Belknap Press, 2000), 211.
9. Murray and Millett, *A War to Be Won*, 211–212.
10. Ibid., 200–206.
11. Hiroyuki Shindo, "The Japanese Army's Search for a New South Pacific Strategy, 1943," in *Australia 1943: The Liberation of New Guinea*, ed. Peter J. Dean (New York: Cambridge University Press, 2014), 82–84.
12. Mary Ellen Condon-Rall, "Malaria in the Southwest Pacific in World War II, 1940–1944," in *Science and the Pacific War: Science and Survival in the Pacific, 1939–1945*, ed. Roy M. Macleod (Boston: Kluwer Academic Publishers, 2000), 53–59.
13. Ibid., 60–66; Edmund Russell, *War and Nature: Fighting Humans and Insects with Chemicals from World War I to Silent Spring* (New York: Cambridge University Press, 2001), 134–135.
14. John W. Dower, *War Without Mercy: Race and Power in the Pacific War* (New York: Pantheon Books, 1987), 66, 71–73.
15. Russell F. Weigley, *The American Way of War: A History of United States Military Strategy and Policy* (New York: Macmillan Publishing, 1973), 302–304.
16. Ibid., 302–305.
17. Ibid., 307–309.
18. There is still considerable debate over the number of civilians killed during Operation Meetinghouse on March 9–10, 1945. Early estimates of eighty-eight thousand by the U.S. Strategic Bombing Survey have been considered conservative by historians who estimate

much higher numbers. Elise K. Tipton, *Modern Japan: A Social and Political History*, 3rd ed. (New York: Routledge, 2015) estimates the figure to be between seventy-five thousand and two hundred thousand.

Bibliography

Adams, Michael C. C. *The Best War Ever: America and World War II*. Baltimore: Johns Hopkins University Press, 1994.

Asada, Sadao. *From Mahan to Pearl Harbor: The Imperial Japanese Navy and the United States*. Annapolis, MD: Naval Institute Press, 2013.

Bennett, Judith E. *Natives and Exotics: World War II and Environment in the Southern Pacific*. Honolulu: University of Hawaii Press, 2009.

Bergerud, Eric. *Touched With Fire: The Land War in the South Pacific*. New York: Penguin Group, 1996.

Cameron, Craig M. *American Samurai: Myth, Imagination, and the Conduct of Battle in the First Marine Division, 1941–1951*. Cambridge: Cambridge University Press, 1994.

Collingham, Lizzie. *The Taste of War: World War II and the Battle for Food*. New York: Penguin Press, 2012.

Dean, Peter J. *MacArthur's Coalition: US and Australian Operations in the Southwest Pacific Area, 1942–1945*, Lawrence, Kansas: University Press of Kansas, 2018.

Dean, Peter J., ed. *Australia 1942: In the Shadow of War*. Port Melbourne, VIC: Cambridge University Press, 2013.

Dean, Peter J., ed. *Australia 1943: The Liberation of New Guinea*. Port Melbourne, VIC: Cambridge University Press, 2014.

Dean, Peter J., ed. *Australia 1944–45: Victory in the Pacific*. Port Melbourne, VIC: Cambridge University Press, 2016.

Dower, John W. *War Without Mercy: Race and Power in the Pacific War*. New York: Pantheon, 1986.

Drea, Edward J. *Japan's Imperial Army: Its Rise and Fall, 1853–1945*, Lawrence: University Press of Kansas, 2009.

Drea, Edward J. *MacArthur's ULTRA: Codebreaking and the War Against Japan, 1942–1945*. Lawrence: University Press of Kansas, 1991.

Frank, Richard B. *Guadalcanal: The Definitive Account of the Landmark Battle*. New York: Random House, 1990.

Frank, Richard B. *Tower of Skulls: A History of the Asia–Pacific War, July 1937–May 1942*. New York: W.W. Norton & Company, 2020.

Griffith, Thomas E., Jr. *MacArthur's Airman: General George C. Kenney and the War in the Southwest Pacific*. Lawrence: University Press of Kansas, 1998.

Heinrichs, Waldo, and Marc Gallicchio. *Implacable Foes: War in the Pacific, 1944–1945*. New York: Oxford University Press, 2017.

Holzimmer, Kevin C. *General Walter Krueger: Unsung Hero of the Pacific War*. Lawrence: University Press of Kansas, 2007.

Laakonen, Simo, Richard Tucker, and Timo Vuorisalo, eds. *The Long Shadows: A Global Environmental History of the Second World War*. Corvallis: Oregon State University Press, 2017.

Lacey, Sharon Tosi. *Pacific Blitzkrieg: World War II in the Central Pacific.* Denton: University of North Texas Press, 2013.
MacArthur, Douglas. *Reminiscences.* New York: McGraw-Hill Book Company, 1964.
MacLeod Roy M., ed. *Science and the Pacific War: Science and Survival in the Pacific, 1939–1945.* Boston: Kluwer Academic Publisher, 2000.
Miller, Edward S. *War Plan Orange: The U.S. Strategy to Defeat Japan, 1847–1945.* Annapolis, MD: Naval Institute Press, 1991.
Murray, Williamson, and Allan R. Millett. *A War to be Won: Fighting the Second World War.* Cambridge: The Belknap Press, 2000.
Overy, Richard. *Why the Allies Won.* New York: W. W. Norton & Company, 1996.
Powell, Alan. *The Third Force: ANGAU's New Guinea War, 1942–46.* South Melbourne, VIC: Oxford University Press, 2003.
Russell, Edmund, and Richard P. Tucker, eds. *Natural Enemy, Natural Ally: Toward and Environmental History of War.* Corvallis: Oregon State University Press, 2004.
Russell, Edmund. *War and Nature: Fighting Humans and Insects with Chemicals from World War I to Silent Spring.* New York: Cambridge University Press, 2001.
Sarantakes, Nicholas Evan. *Allies Against the Rising Sun: The United States, the British Nations, and the Defeat of Imperial Japan.* Lawrence: University Press of Kansas, 2009.
Schrijvers, Peter. *Bloody Pacific: American Soldiers at War with Japan.* New York: Palgrave Macmillan, 2010.
Spector, Ronald H. *Eagle Against the Sun: The American War with Japan.* New York: Vintage Books, 1985.
Symonds, Craig L. *The Battle of Midway.* New York: Oxford University Press, 2011.
Taaffe, Stephen R. *Marshall and His Generals: U.S. Army Commanders in World War II.* Lawrence: University Press of Kansas, 2011.
Tipton, Elise K. *Modern Japan: A Social and Political History.* 3rd ed. New York: Routledge, 2015.
Weigley, Russell F. *The American Way of War: A History of United States Military Strategy and Policy.* New York: MacMillan Publishing, 1973.

CHAPTER 20

THE AIR WAR AND CONFLICT TERMINATION IN THE PACIFIC

CONRAD C. CRANE

ANYONE trying to understand the end of World War II in the Pacific should start by reviewing American journals and newspapers during the period between V-E and V-J Days. In May 1945, *Newsweek* headlines called the conflict in the Pacific theater, "War Without Quarter" and proclaimed that the Japanese were, "Fanatical and Capable of Long Resistance." Kamikaze attacks received widespread publicity, as did the Japanese announcement that branded all their citizens as "suicide attackers." The expected invasion of the Home Islands was viewed with dread. Much can be gleaned from the front page of the May 30 *New York Times*. Headlines trumpet Marine advances on Okinawa against suicidal resistance. Another article notes that the Russians are planning to draft fifteen-year-olds. The first revelations about the fire raids on Japan appear, with Curtis LeMay's estimate that they had probably incinerated a million civilians. Except for Secretary of War Henry Stimson, who was surprised and appalled by the reports, no one else seemed to care about such carnage. Worse was expected soon.

Of all the areas of research and writing concerning World War II, there is none filled with more contention and controversy than that concerning the end of the war in the Pacific. As we move further away from the atmosphere of 1945, the actions taken by the Allied powers to force Japanese surrender appear more extreme. The vanquished find it easier to portray the victors as villains, while newer generations question the motivations leading to the obliteration of enemy cities.

Ironically, the first steps in the slide to total air war in the Pacific were taken by the Japanese, when they began bombing Chinese cities in 1937. The Western world was shocked by appalling pictures of a blackened, crying baby who had lost its mother in the destroyed rail yard in Shanghai that year, and of civilians trampled to death trying to get to air raid shelters in Chongqing in 1941. Those images increased international support for China while reinforcing impressions that the Japanese were especially brutal.

Some Americans flew with the International Squadron of mercenaries recruited to provide some viable defense with outdated fighters against waves of Japanese bombers. The Flying Tigers of the American Volunteer Group recruited by Claire Chennault joined the fight in December 1941. In June 1942, these pilots became a part of the 23rd Fighter Group of Chennault's China Air Task Force (CATF).[1]

By then another American airman, Lieutenant Colonel "Jimmy" Doolittle, had led a daring raid on Tokyo with Army B-25 bombers launched from the deck of the carrier *Hornet*. That April attack inflicted little damage on Japanese warmaking capacity but much on their pride, resulting in harsh reprisals against captured airmen and helping to accelerate risky naval operations that culminated in the decisive Battle of Midway. In the early stages of the war, Japanese airmen and aircraft, especially the nimble Zero fighter, had overwhelmed opposition in the Philippines, Malaya, and the Dutch East Indies, but pilot attrition and technological stagnation ensured they would eventually be overwhelmed by the Americans, who soon fielded great quantities of superior aircraft flown by better trained aviators. By the end of the war, the Japanese were reduced to committing novice airmen in outdated aircraft as flying bombs in suicide attacks on American ships, the fearsome *kamikazes*.[2]

Once the tide turned and the United States launched twin drives across the Pacific toward the Japanese homeland, airpower played a dominant role in the "triphibious warfare" that seized island footholds. Admiral Chester Nimitz made brilliant use of his carriers in supporting invasions and decimating the Japanese Navy. General Douglas MacArthur gave free rein to his innovative air commander, Major General George Kenney, as Southwest Pacific Area forces swept across New Guinea and into the Philippines. Initially Kenney commanded the Fifth Air Force, but eventually his organization became the Far East Air Forces (FEAF), adding the Thirteenth Air Force in 1944. Allied airmen from Australia and New Zealand contributed to the command as well. Other numbered air forces in the Pacific included the Seventh, which began supporting Nimitz but eventually came under FEAF in 1945, the Eleventh in Alaska and the Aleutians, the Tenth in India that provided essential support to General Bill Slim as he cleared Burma, and Chennault's Fourteenth in China which had grown from the CATF. These organizations all contributed to tactical and operational success in support of higher Army or Navy commanders.[3]

But air attacks directly on the Japanese homeland were always an assumed part of siege operations to bring victory, and the Army Air Forces (AAF) took full advantage of the command responsibilities divided between the Army and the Navy in the Pacific to establish its own independent operational element there, the Twentieth Air Force, which was kept under the direct control of the AAF commander, General Henry "Hap" Arnold. AAF planning about attacking Japan with B-29s from China began as early as March 1943, and after much prodding from Chennault and Chiang an operation that would be named Matterhorn was approved by the Joint Chiefs of Staff (JCS) in November with a target date of May 1, 1944. The Sextant Conference at Cairo in December 1943 also directed the capture of the Marianas Islands with B-29 operations to begin from bases there by December 1944, which was bound to set up competition between the two concepts. Those operations would both take advantage of the unique product of the Very Heavy Bomber program, the B-29 Superfortress, with its superior speed, long range, and increased bomb carrying capacity. Its innovative technology included a pressurized cabin and a sort of computerized gun control. But impatient to get the weapon into the war, Arnold deployed it before all testing was completed; so many technological deficiencies had to get worked out during combat. Among them were the propensities of the engines to catch fire, and for gunners' cupolas to pop out at high altitudes, often taking gunners with them.[4]

In an attempt to get the potentially war-winning aircraft into action against Japan as soon as possible, and to help keep a faltering China in the war, the JCS directed the implementation of Matterhorn. The logistics were daunting. Thousands of Chinese laborers were recruited to build airfields while aircraft, fuel, and munitions all had to be flown over the Himalaya Mountains, the infamous "Hump." Many key targets in the enemy homeland were still out of range of those bases, and early bombing results were poor. Still the threat of such raids proved enough of a potential nuisance that the Japanese Launched Operation Ichi-Go in April 1944 to neutralize any potential airfields in eastern China, and continued the offensive until the end of the year. Nothing is more effective at preventing air attacks than destroying the bases from which they are launched.[5]

The vulnerability of Japan to aerial bombardment, especially with incendiary munitions, was common knowledge. Air Corps Tactical School texts highlighted the destruction inflicted by earthquakes in 1924 upon Japanese cities to show how flimsy and flammable they were. President Roosevelt was an enthusiastic supporter of plans advanced by Chennault in late 1940 to furnish the Chinese with American bombers to burn down Japanese industry. Once the United States was drawn into the war, planners in Washington did not take long to focus on inflammable targets in Japan. By February 1942, Arnold's staff had already prepared target folders that included areas of Tokyo ranked in order of their vulnerability to incendiary attack. Strategic bombing objectives in the Pacific were also being examined by planners from the B-29 program as well as the Committee of Operations Analysts, a group of military and civilian experts on industrial intelligence and target selection that produced special studies for Arnold. From these efforts, Arnold prepared "An Air Plan for the Defeat of Japan," which he presented at the Quebec Conference in August 1943. He sent an outline of his views to the president which emphasized that only seventeen hundred tons of incendiaries could produce uncontrollable fires to destroy numerous key war industries in twenty major cities. But he never made these opinions known to his field commanders. The real impetus for the incendiary campaign would come from them.[6]

In December 1944, Chennault, now commanding the Fourteenth Air Force, persuaded General Albert Wedemeyer, commander of all American forces in the China–Burma–India (CBI) theater, to order an incendiary attack by B-29s on supplies in Hankow. Major General Curtis LeMay, commander of the XX Bomber Command executing Matterhorn in India and China since August, reluctantly complied, believing that it was not his mission to attack such a limited objective outside Japan. The operation was a resounding success, however, creating widespread fires that destroyed Hankow's utility as an enemy base. LeMay would not soon forget the results. Probably the most innovative air commander of the war, he had developed many of the most important tactics used in the American strategic bombing campaign in Europe, and he was renowned for his problem-solving capabilities.[7]

However, the Hankow raid was also notable because it was one of the few successes of early B-29 operations in the Pacific. At the same time that LeMay took over the logistically-constrained XX Bomber Command in the CBI, Major General Haywood "Possum" Hansell became commander of the XXI Bomber Command in the Marianas. Arnold expected the most important and effective aerial attacks on Japan to come from Hansell, one of the primary architects of early American plans for the air war and the precision bombing doctrine that shaped them. The XXI Bomber Command had better logistics, more secure bases, and was closer to Japan than the XX Bomber Command, and could concentrate its considerable firepower against the enemy's industrial heart. Arnold had high hopes that Hansell could finally exert decisive airpower against the enemy's homeland fortress and prove the worth of an independent air service, always a long-term goal for the AAF commander. He had staked a lot on the Very Heavy Bomber program, and it looked like his considerable investment was finally going to prove its worth.

But Hansell faced significant difficulties. Many of them were due to the many technological glitches in the weapons system that have already been mentioned. This resulted in a very high abort rate when aircraft could not finish missions, and many accidents that destroyed more B-29s than Japanese defenses. Crews were supposedly prepared to bomb primarily at night by radar-directed methods, but operators had received inadequate training in the United States because of a lack of equipment. Hansell planned to overcome this shortcoming by bombing visually by day in accordance with precision doctrine and Arnold's directives, but the shift in tactics required that all crews be retrained, a lengthy process. And no amount of training could prepare the crews for the weather over Japan, which made high-altitude precision bombing impossible most of the year.[8]

Extensive cloud fronts along the Japanese coast disrupted bomber formations and increased their vulnerability to enemy fighters. Even if planes arrived safely over the target, jetstream winds of more than 230 knots at bombing altitude created conditions that exceeded the capabilities of bombardiers and bombsights. Bombing tables were not designed to deal with the 550 knot ground speeds that tailwinds produced, and slow-moving B-29s fighting headwinds were sitting ducks hovering for anti-aircraft gunners. Wind speeds were highest from December to February, when XXI Bomber Command was trying to perfect their tactics, but still excessive in other months. And those periods with the fewest high winds compensated with increased cloud cover.[9]

As 1945 began, the number of targets destroyed by XXI Bomber Command remained low, and abort rates stayed high. B-29 crews were losing faith in their planes and their tactics. Their precision attacks had little effect on Japanese industry due to the woeful inaccuracy of high explosive bombs they were dropping from high altitude, as well as the dispersion of cottage industries throughout urban areas. Hansell seemed unable to produce timely improvements, and Arnold needed results quickly, not only to prove the worth of airpower and the B-29s, but also to keep from losing control of them to MacArthur or Nimitz, or even to Lord Mountbatten who commanded the CBI theater. The Japanese offensive in China had also made Operation Matterhorn untenable. Hansell did not help his cause by giving some pessimistic news interviews about his operations, which also contributed to Arnold losing faith in his abilities. So in January, the AAF commander decided to concentrate all B-29s in the Marianas under one commander, and as part of the reorganization he relieved Hansell and replaced him with the feisty and innovative LeMay.[10]

He began with a total shakeup of personnel, bringing over many of his people from China to replace key staff members and group commanders. Airfields on the Marianas were still incomplete, so he successfully lobbied Admiral Nimitz for increased engineering support. He set new training programs in motion, especially concerning radar, and General Lauris Norstad, Twentieth Air Force chief of staff under Arnold, procured some radar lead crews from Europe to help. LeMay established a better maintenance program that put more planes in the air and lowered the abort rate. To improve weather reports he tried breaking the Russian radio codes to better decipher their information, and delivered medical supplies to Mao Zedong in exchange for the right to set up a radio station in Yenan that reported on weather coming from China. Crew morale rose and aircraft performance improved, but the results of daylight precision attacks did not get much better.[11]

Wishing to exploit the psychological effects of the return to the Philippines in 1944, some planners on Arnold's staff recommended that the time was ripe for an incendiary assault on urban industrial centers that would further demoralize the Japanese people. But AAF targeting directives emphasizing pinpoint attacks on aircraft engine factories did not change. No leader in Washington showed any willingness to order area bombing of enemy cities, especially after the February public relations flap over Dresden that produced accusations in the press that the AAF was now adopting terror attacks. Both Hansell and LeMay believed that the Arnold desired continuation of precision bombing methods. LeMay began to query Norstad if the AAF commander ever went for a gamble. Norstad gave LeMay the impression that Arnold was fine with unorthodox approaches, but Norstad gave no indications he recommended such a course, even though he had prodded LeMay into a disappointing experiment with high-altitude incendiary bombing of Kobe in early February. Although uneasy, LeMay decided to switch his methods without informing Washington of the details. He claimed that he wanted to shield Arnold from any blame for possible failure, so he would have a free hand to put in a new commander, if necessary, to salvage the B-29 program.[12]

There is no evidence that LeMay feared any moral backlash from anyone in Washington concerning fire bombing, and he never seemed to worry much about ethical considerations, anyway. He may have been afraid, however, that AAF headquarters would disapprove his tactics if they found out he was about to risk such valued aircraft in dangerous and untried attacks at low altitude with reduced defensive armament. With the dismal results of the air campaign up to that time, LeMay felt he had nothing to lose by trying something new.

LeMay mounted one more test incendiary raid led by Brig. Gen. Thomas Power of the 314th Bomb Wing on February 25. They bombed Tokyo in a heavy snowstorm, and although weather severely limited the number of planes that reached the target, the results convinced Power to develop a plan for mass low-level fire bombing. Many others also claim credit for the idea, but Lemay had to make the final decision. There were many tactical reasons for his adoption of such a method. Planes at lower altitudes normally encountered winds of only twenty-five to thirty-five knots and fewer clouds. Scope definition of the ground on primitive radars was better, also. Such attacks took advantage of the Japanese lack of effective night fighters or low-level anti-aircraft fire. These factors all improved bombing accuracy. Additionally, low-altitude flying reduced engine strain and resulting fires. With the use of a bomber stream and the elimination of the need to fly in formation, or to climb to high altitudes, less fuel was needed and a greater bomb load could be carried. To increase it further, LeMay also removed all ammunition from the B-29s except that for the tail guns, which made some crews very nervous. Selected urban target areas contained numerous industrial objectives. One mission report emphasized, "It is noteworthy that the object of these attacks was *not* to bomb indiscriminately civilian populations. The object *was* to destroy the *industrial and strategic targets* concentrated in the urban areas." This wording could have been designed to counter any future criticism of the fire raids, or perhaps to strengthen the resolve or ease the troubled consciences of airmen who may have questioned the value of the missions or felt guilty about the stench of charred flesh that lingered in their bomb bays. The passage does highlight a key difference between British area bombing in Europe and the American campaign against Japan. Although their methodologies were similar, the primary objectives were not. While RAF Bomber Command also aimed to overwhelm the enemy's war economy, from 1942 on its main focus was on undermining the morale of the German populace, especially industrial workers.[13]

The different objective of the American area bombardment was not evident to people in targeted cities, particularly in Tokyo, during that first fire raid, codenamed Operation Meetinghouse, on the night of March 9, 1945. The selected zone of attack included six important industrial targets along with numerous smaller factories, railroad yards, home industries, and cable plants. But it also covered one of the most densely populated areas of the world, Asakusa Ku, with more than 135,000 people per square mile.[14] Despite the claims of the mission report quoted above, it appears that another consideration for this first raid of the new air campaign was to attack an especially dense urban area to provide the best possible chance for a spectacular success.

Before Operation Meetinghouse was over, between ninety thousand and one hundred thousand people were killed. Most died horribly as intense heat from the firestorm boiled water in canals and rolled molten glass down the streets. Panicked crowds suffocated in underground shelters or open parks, crushed unlucky victims who fell in the streets, or surged toward waterways to escape the rampaging flames. B-29 crews fought superheated updrafts from the conflagration that tore apart at least ten aircraft, and wore oxygen masks to avoid vomiting from the stench of burning flesh even five thousand feet above the inferno. Assigned by LeMay to observe the raid, Power sketched the growing conflagration, noting as they circled the city that smoke rose over twenty-five thousand feet and the glow from the fires was visible 150 miles away. When the attack ended, almost sixteen square miles of Tokyo were burned out, and over one million people were homeless. Survivors remembered that terrible night as "The Raid of the Fire Wind."[15]

The resort to the incendiary campaign marked the most radical leap in the escalation to total war in the Pacific, and represented the culmination of trends started in the air war against Germany. Although target selection, especially of transportation objectives, late in the European campaign showed less effort to avoid civilian casualties, LeMay's planning ignored such considerations even more. His intelligence officers and operations analysts advised him that massive conflagrations were essential to jump the fire breaks around factories, and residential tinder fed those flames. Noncombatant deaths were unavoidable in order to destroy the Japanese means to resist and forestall an invasion of Japan, which LeMay and other leaders feared would cost many American lives. The success of the new method at producing obvious results also restored the morale of LeMay's crews, and proved to them the worthiness of the B-29. While areas of industrial concentrations remained the primary target objectives, all Japanese were perceived as manufacturing something for the war effort, often in their homes.[16]

Whenever possible, targeted populations were warned to evacuate. LeMay saw this as a humane gesture that would disarm potential critics of his tactics at home and abroad, but he also intended to capitalize on the bonus of fear generated by his raids to disrupt industry and the social infrastructure without killing everyone. Refugees congested transportation networks and caused the Japanese government immense relocation problems. Leaflets dropped by American planes all over Japan showed a B-29 dumping incendiaries, with the names of eleven cities printed around the plane. The text emphasized that air attacks were only aimed at military installations, "to destroy all the tools of the military clique which they are using to prolong this useless war." It continued, "But, unfortunately, bombs have no eyes. So, in accordance with America's well-known humanitarian principles, the American Air Force, which does not wish to injure innocent people, now gives you warning to evacuate the cities named and save your lives." It concluded with the promise that at least four of the named cities would be attacked, but also noted that unnamed others could be hit as well. This psychological warfare campaign had significant impact. At its height, more than 6.5 million Japanese were involved in leaving their cities. Their government had been trying to get people to disperse from hard-to-defend urban areas, but the fire raids are what finally convinced one-seventh of the Japanese population to eventually flee to the countryside.[17]

George Kenney followed suit. Completely trusted by MacArthur, Kenney had a free hand to conduct Far East Air Forces operations, and he built upon LeMay's psychological warfare with his own. FEAF initially dropped leaflets on Kyushu that exploited the results of the B-29 raids, then followed with warnings to its three targeted cities seventy-two hours before the B-24 bombers arrived, proclaiming, "We want you to see how powerless the military is to protect you." Civilians were urged to evacuate, and also to overthrow their government, "to save what is left of your beautiful country." After the attacks, which did have industrial target objectives to include factories making rocket suicide planes, follow-up leaflets again urged regime change while comparing American might to feared forces of nature: "The military forces of Japan can no more halt the overwhelming destruction of the United States Air Force than the people can stop an earthquake." These campaigns to exploit civilian morale incorporated a scheme that had been proposed and rejected in Europe, another sign of the intensification of the war in the Pacific.[18] This use of psychological warfare made the generation of terror a formal, although secondary, objective of the fire raids. While no American leader would publicly admit it, AAF area attacks against Japan now resembled those that RAF Bomber Command had conducted against Germany. And LeMay's XXI Bomber Command was more efficient than the RAF, and flimsy Japanese cities were much more vulnerable than robust German ones.

After observing the results of the initial fire raids, LeMay wrote in April 1945 that he believed that he had the resources to destroy the enemy's ability to wage war within six months. When Arnold visited him in June, LeMay's staff described how their bombers could bring Japan to the brink of defeat by destroying all industrial facilities by October 1. By then the Navy was also contributing to the aerial assault with carrier-based attacks against industrial facilities along the coasts, and would soon begin shore bombardment of the targets by battleships as well. Arnold had already received a message that President Truman wanted to meet with the JCS to discuss how best to defeat Japan, and the AAF chief decided to send LeMay back to Washington to assist in presenting the air force position. LeMay's staff went with their commander, and repeated the briefing to the JCS that they had just given Arnold. Army Chief of Staff General Marshall slept through most of the presentation, and a frustrated LeMay came away convinced that leaders in Washington were fully committed to invading Japan just as they had invaded Europe.[19]

At about the same time, Norstad was chairing meetings in Washington between the Joint Target Group (JTG) and the United States Strategic Bombing Survey (USSBS) staff returned from Europe. In final reports to the Secretary of War in July, both teams agreed there was a large gap between the most important target system, Japanese transportation, and any other objective. Second in priority for the USSBS was ammunition reserves, followed by precision industrial targets and attacks on rice production. Attacks on urban industrial areas were last priority, and they were to be hit only if there was a less than one-third chance of hitting more precise objectives. The JTG was in general agreement, although they did place more emphasis on incendiary attacks on cities and less on other target systems. Both groups briefed their position to General Carl Spaatz, newly designated commander of the newly created U.S. Army Strategic Air Forces (USASTAF), which included the Eighth and Twentieth Air Forces. The former was to be redeployed from Europe and given B-29s to replace their B-17s and B-24s. He was being sent to the Pacific to take over the direction of most strategic air operations there, although MacArthur and Kenney retained control over their own heavy bombers. In accordance with his record of adherence to precision bombing, Spaatz agreed with the USSBS recommendations for his forces. He went to Guam with a directive to concentrate on, in order of priority, Japanese railways, aircraft production, ammunition supplies, and only then industrial concentrations and stores.[20]

However, there was little the new USASTAF commander could do to change the course of the air war in the Pacific. The fire raids had too much momentum. Ammunition dumps were filled just with incendiary clusters, and aircrew training and operations were designed for the night, low level attacks. Arnold used statistics covering the amount of bombs dropped and number of factories destroyed to demonstrate the power of the AAF, while data on civilian bombing casualties was ignored. Much attention was being paid to predictions of potential losses of American lives, however, and the devastating raids were tied into preparations for the impending invasion. The Twentieth Air Force was fully committed to the fire bombing of Japanese cities.

When Spaatz arrived in the Pacific, he quickly became convinced that the Japanese faced national suicide if they did not surrender immediately. Continued fire raids and the dropping of the atomic bombs helped bring some Japanese leaders to the same conclusion. Appalled by the destruction his airmen wrought on Japan, Spaatz wrote in his diary about the new weapon and the fire raids, "When the atomic bomb was first discussed with me in Washington I was not in favor of it just as I have never favored the destruction of cities as such with all inhabitants being killed." Washington directed him to continue bombing until surrender arrangements were completed. Spaatz canceled one raid due to weather, and when the press interpreted that as a ceasefire, President Truman ordered him to halt bombing to avoid a misperception that the resumption of bombing indicated a breakdown in negotiations. When the Japanese delayed, Truman ordered more bombing, and Arnold demanded a maximum effort to display the power of the AAF. Despite Spaatz's anxious queries, no cancellation was ordered, and more than one thousand planes hit Japan on August 14, some even after Japanese radio announced acceptance of the surrender terms.[21]

While AAF officers quibbled over the number of American lives saved by their bombing, all agreed with Prince Konoye's arguable claim, "Fundamentally, the thing that brought about the determination to make peace was the prolonged fire bombing by the B-29s." LeMay's air campaign had burned out 180 square miles of sixty-seven cities, killed at least three hundred thousand people, and wounded at least another four hundred thousand.[22] Hansell later posited that precision attacks on the Japanese electrical industry, using low-altitude attacks at night with new radars and tactics, would have destroyed Japan's ability to make war and brought it to the peace table "at less cost with fewer undesirable side effects." This alternative strategy would have taken fewer sorties and saved many civilian lives, although it would have taken more time (and perhaps cost more American lives). Hansell's clean and rational strategy also assumed that the Japanese would realize that they logically could not continue the war without electricity, and it would have lacked the strong component of psychological shock produced by the incendiary conflagrations. Yet one can only wonder what would have happened if another leader, like Spaatz, had commanded the B-29s. Would he have been more likely to expend additional time and effort to explore other alternatives before resorting to the extreme of the fire raids? Such a course would have been difficult, especially after Hansell's experience, and might have risked the loss of AAF operational control of the B-29s. Even Hansell concedes that after his relief from command, the chosen strategy of the fire raids was "decisively effective" and a "sound military decision," because of the time pressures that existed in the Pacific.[23]

Another possibility for the application of conventional bombing was the transportation targeting proposed by the USSBS. The Japanese rail network was especially vulnerable, with many critical bottlenecks at bridges and tunnels. The most promising commodities to target were food and fuel, and combined with the destruction of Japanese shipping, some analysts claimed that such a campaign would have forced Japanese surrender by itself. However, there are many reasons to question the USSBS data and conclusions, and the actual results of such a campaign are hard to predict. And while such a blockade would not have had the terrifying psychological impact of the incendiary campaign, it would not necessarily have been more humane. Just as many German civilians died from the hardships of the British naval blockade in World War I as were killed by the bombs of the Allied Combined Bomber Offensive in World War II.[24]

Spaatz was not the only leader troubled by the urban-area bombing. Aged and ill, poorly informed by his military subordinates, and preoccupied with the logistical and personnel problems of continuing the war, Secretary of War Stimson appears to have only realized the severity of the fire raids in late May, probably from press reports. Stimson complained that he had been misled by AAF leaders who had promised to restrict operations against Japan to precision bombing as in Europe. In his diary he wrote, "I am told it is possible and adequate. The reputation of the United States for fair play and humanitarianism is the world's biggest asset for peace in the coming decades." Discussing the topic later with President Truman, Stimson realized the validity of AAF arguments for fire bombing, but "did not want to have the United States get the reputation of outdoing Hitler in atrocities." He often agonized over sanctioning bombing raids and wondered about the lack of public protest. J. Robert Oppenheimer recalled that Stimson thought it was "appalling" that no Americans protested the heavy loss of life caused by the air raids against Japan. "He didn't say that the air strikes shouldn't be carried on, but he did think there was something wrong with a country where no one questioned that." As troubled as he was by bombing results, however, Stimson justified Hiroshima and Nagasaki with the same "Airpower Ethic" espoused by the most zealous airmen, claiming that in the long run the air attacks that ended the war saved more lives than they cost.[25]

In his exemplary study of the escalating air war between Germany and Great Britain in 1940, F. M. Sallagar notes that, "changes crept in as solutions to operational problems rather than as the consequences of considered policy decisions. In fact, they occurred almost independently of the formal decision making process."[26] For LeMay, the fire raids seemed to be the only way with the combat conditions and available resources in the Pacific that he could destroy the ability of Japan to wage war in a timely and efficient manner. As destructive as the incendiary campaign was, the course of the Pacific War may very well have been even more terrible without it. LeMay's urban area attacks hit their crescendo shortly before the dropping of the atomic bombs, and were an important component of the series of shocks that brought about the surrender. The accumulated destruction of the incendiary assault did much to destroy the Japanese infrastructure and economy, and to degrade the will of leaders and the populace to continue the war. If Hansell, or some other commander, had been allowed to pursue precision tactics, even if he had perfected them, the delayed and different effects of the air campaign might not have been terrible enough to be an important factor in the Japanese decision to surrender. If Prince Konoye is correct, than without the conflagrations like Operation Meetinghouse, the war in the Pacific might have been even longer and even bloodier.

However, the leap from precision bombing to the fire raids was more critical in the slide to total war in the Pacific than the resort to the atomic bomb. It was farther from Schweinfurt to Tokyo than from Tokyo to Hiroshima, both literally and figuratively. Once it became acceptable to drop incendiary bombs that burned one hundred thousand people to death in a single night, killing a similar number with a single bomb was not a hard decision. For American leaders considering the use of the new weapon, they had already crossed any perceived critical moral divide about the mass killing of civilians.

More people died in the fire raids than from the atomic bombs, but the terrible devastation and horrible casualties described so vividly in Hersey's *Hiroshima* in 1946 or caricatured in Nakazawa's comics of Barefoot Gen in the 1970s have commanded much more attention. The Manhattan Project was a truly monumental effort that could not have been accomplished by any other nation at the time. It was launched after a letter from Albert Einstein describing the possibility of the bomb was delivered to President Roosevelt on October 11, 1939. Project leaders actually made the decision to expand the program to full production the day before Pearl Harbor. There were two theoretical paths to build the new weapon, using either plutonium or uranium as the fissile material. While other competitors in the race to build the bomb wrestled with which expensive technique to pursue, the United States elected to do both. Brigadier General Leslie Groves managed extensive production facilities from Hanford, Washington to Oak Ridge, Tennessee, while J. Robert Oppenheimer led the team of scientists working at Los Alamos, New Mexico. They detonated a test of the more complex plutonium "Fat Man" bomb on July 16, 1945. The uranium "Little Boy" bomb was dropped in Hiroshima on August 6, 1945, and a Fat Man devastated Nagasaki three days later. The first raid by the *Enola Gay* went off basically without a hitch, but the second experienced many problems. Among them, the primary target, Kokura, was obscured by clouds and haze, and because of fuel tank problems *Bock's Car* had to make an emergency landing in Okinawa on its return. Contrary to the stories that have surfaced over the years, no members of the crews of the planes who dropped either bomb suffered a nervous breakdown or came out against their use. (An alcoholic pilot of an accompanying weather plane later did blame his problems on the bomb.) The airmen's sentiments are best expressed by the comment a crewman on the Nagasaki raid penned in his journal,

"Those poor Japs, but they asked for it." While they felt compassion for their victims, they also were and remained morally confident that their actions were justified.[27]

That position is not acceptable for critics of the Hiroshima and Nagasaki missions, troubled by what we now know in hindsight about the terrible suffering and death that resulted. The most intense controversy about the end of the war in the Pacific revolves around the question of whether the B-29s needed to cap the air war against Japan by dropping two atomic bombs in order to bring surrender. Some historians question the real motivations for using nuclear weapons, whether other approaches might have brought an early surrender, and why President Harry Truman did not pursue these so-called alternatives. Others debate the actual effects of the bombs on ending the war. Arguments about the necessity and impact of the devastation of Nagasaki have been particularly sharp.

This spirited debate over the morality and utility of these weapons is a relatively recent phenomenon. For the Cold War generation, the atomic bomb launched their conflict, but for the World War II generation, the nuclear detonations thankfully ended theirs. In a *Fortune* magazine poll taken in December 1945, fewer than five percent of those queried thought the bombs should not have been dropped. Anyone who wants to study or research the decision to use the atomic bomb should start by getting a feel for the atmosphere of the Pacific War in 1945, especially the increasing carnage of ground combat as American forces approached Japan. The land and sea campaign to take Okinawa claimed thirty thousand American, 110,000 Japanese, and 150,000 Okinawan lives. This heightened the fears of leaders all the way up to Truman, of even higher casualties in any invasion of the Home Islands, and inspired the sentiments in American servicemen so eloquently expressed in books like Paul Fussell's *Thank God For the Atomic Bomb*. These emotions were shared by Allies in the theater. Thousands of Allied and American POWs also would have been massacred or starved to death if the war had not ended so abruptly and early.[28]

Since early in the war, the American JCS had wrestled with the conflicting options of assault or siege to defeat Japan. Haunted by fears of war weariness at home and the specter of intensifying enemy resistance, the Navy and Army Air Forces supported a sea blockade and aerial bombardment while the Army insisted that only an invasion would accomplish military and political goals in a timely manner. In the end the JCS pursued these objectives and more. They clearly understood that Japan's defeat would result from the increasing application of a combination of military, psychological and political pressures upon the island nation. They developed a strategy using multiple means and ways. The JCS tightened the crippling blockade, launched a relentless aerial assault with conventional and atomic weapons, contributed to efforts to induce an early Japanese capitulation by clarifying the unconditional surrender formula, and strongly urged both Roosevelt and Truman to secure early Soviet entry into the war. A whole series of shocks was required to finally bring Japanese surrender; fire raids and the atomic bomb, diplomatic pressure, the inexorable island-hopping advance toward Japan, Russian entry, and the naval air and submarine campaign that along with aerial mining by the B-29s was strangling the home islands.[29]

Any monocausal explanation for the end of the war in the Pacific is bound to be insufficient and unsatisfactory. This has not prevented historians—especially those wanting to minimize the importance of atomic weapons—from making such arguments. For instance, some Japanese historians argue fervently that it was Soviet entry into the war that was the decisive factor that forced their nation's leadership to accept surrender.[30] In the twenty-first century, the historical consensus has moved away from revisionist interpretations. A good summary of the current position has been expressed by Donald Kagan, who answers those who decry America's failure to confront its "moral failings" about Hiroshima by writing, "An honest examination of the evidence reveals that their leaders, in the tragic predicament common to all who have engaged in wars that reach the point where every choice is repugnant, chose the least bad course. Americans may look back on that decision with sadness, but without shame."[31]

Gerhard Weinberg, the dean of American World War II historians, emphasizes the importance of the second atomic bomb, signifying that more could be coming, and the apparent American acceptance of keeping the Emperor, in convincing the peace faction to create the deadlock that forced him to break it. He discounts the arguments of some revisionists that more time should have been allowed after Hiroshima for Japanese leaders to ponder the new weapon before attacking Nagasaki. The resulting American occupation not only guaranteed the return of Japan to the civilized world, it also insured the position of the United States in the Pacific with secure bases that would be essential to fight the next war in Asia. (MacArthur's quick actions in late 1945 also averted a devastating famine.)[32] It is worth contrasting the relatively smooth transitions in Japan and the Philippines with the upheavals that erupted throughout the rest of the liberated Japanese empire. A comprehensive litany of the unintended consequences of the removal of Japanese authority includes the war in Korea and Communist revolts throughout Asia. One interesting postwar "What if" question to contemplate concerns Soviet plans to invade Hokkaido in September, aided by naval assets the U.S. had provided. Although the Soviets did not expect to do much more than gain a foothold, that would have created quite a political dilemma for Allied occupation. If Japanese surrender had been delayed long enough for the Soviets to establish a presence in the Home Islands, they could have demanded an occupation zone, and perhaps Japan would have ended up partitioned like Germany.[33]

Weinberg also deems historical interpretations that attribute the dropping of the atomic bombs to racial factors or the desire to intimidate the Soviets as "far-fetched fairy tales" for which he has never seen any evidence. A much more diplomatic dismissal is presented by Richard Frank in what is the best existing account of the end of the war and the impact of the atomic bomb. He is an accomplished lawyer as well as an historian, and he has brilliantly analyzed all the most recent evidence to make his case, including a very candid assessment of the few strengths and many weaknesses of American intelligence. Frank addresses every issue covered in this essay, from whether railroad attacks could have ended the war without an invasion (probably, but months later with the death of many more non-combatants), to the utility of the two atomic bombs (without them, the

Emperor's intercession would have been delayed, and the war dragged on.) He describes how revelations about the Kyushu buildup had Nimitz prepared to recommend against the landing there. For Frank, the whole casualty debate is a red herring. American leaders knew the public would not abide a large number of casualties, and he believes that once the size of the Japanese buildup on Kyushu was realized, the use of the bombs would have been inevitable. His analysis of Soviet intervention is especially detailed. He points out that more Japanese died as a result of Soviet captivity on the mainland than from both atomic bombs. Without Hiroshima, the Soviet offensive in Manchuria would have been delayed, with uncertain impact. That delay might have galvanized the Japanese Army to resist surrender even more, or it might have allowed time for leaders to evaluate a new American bombing campaign against food and transportation. Again the war would have ended later, with more Japanese deaths, and there definitely would have been Soviets in Hokkaido.[34]

The atomic bomb was not the only secret project designed to shorten the war in the Pacific theater, on both sides. With the president's backing, the AAF launched a program in 1942 to have Mexican freetailed bats burn down Japanese cities with small incendiary bombs. Project X-Ray was eventually taken over by the Navy and actually showed some promise before it was terminated in early 1944 in favor of the Manhattan Project. The Japanese ran programs in China to develop chemical and biological weapons, which often involved experiments on Chinese victims. The war ended before a plan could be attempted to deliver biological agents to the United States in balloons released into prevailing winds. Hundreds of paper balloon bombs were launched with conventional explosives, however, and Japanese submarines also launched seaplanes to drop incendiaries on forests in the American Northwest. If the war had continued, the United States had plans to use poison gas to assist the invasions and other chemicals to destroy the Japanese rice crop, which would have made famine conditions far worse. George Marshall even considered using nine atomic bombs in a tactical role to support landings in Kyushu.[35] No one can dispute that the war would have indeed become even more terrible if it had not ended in mid-1945. This was very evident to people on both sides who were alive at the time. Historians today, however, will continue to debate whether the war could have been ended differently than with the nuclear destruction of Hiroshima and Nagasaki, and the shadow those mushroom clouds cast over the future.

Notes

1. Martin Caidan, *The Ragged, Rugged Warriors* (New York: Bantam, 1979).
2. Carroll V. Glines, *The Doolittle Raid: America's Daring First Strike Against Japan* (New York: Orion, 1988).
3. Thomas E. Griffith, *MacArthur's Airman: General George C. Kenney and the War in the Southwest Pacific* (Lawrence: University Press of Kansas, 1998); Wesley Frank Craven and James Lea Cate, eds. *The Army Air Forces in World War II*, Vol. V: *The Pacific, Matterhorn to Nagasaki* (Chicago: University of Chicago Press, 1953), 742–748.

4. Craven and Cate, *The Army Air Forces in World War II*, Vol. V, 9–41; Kenneth P. Werrell, *Blankets of Fire: U.S. Bombers over Japan during World War II* (Washington, DC: Smithsonian, 1996), 55–74.
5. Craven and Cate, *The Army Air Forces in World War II*, Vol. V, 58–91; John Toland, *The Rising Sun* (New York: Bantam, 1971), 697–698, 706.
6. Lesson Plan for Conference on Air Operations Against National Structures, April 11, 1939, File 248.202A-25, Air Force Historical Research Agency, Maxwell AFB, Alabama; Memo, BG Martin Scanlon to MG Barney Giles, "Priorities: Japanese Objective Folder Material," February 19, 1942, File 360.02, Box 101, Henry H. Arnold Papers, Library of Congress, Washington, DC; "Air Plan for the Defeat of Japan," ABC 381 Japan (August 27, 1943), File ABC 384.5, Boxes 477–478, The Army Staff, RG 319, National Archives II, Suitland, MD; "Outline of presentation of views of Commanding General, AAF, on the role of the Air Forces in the defeat of Japan," February 22, 1944, Naval Aide's Files, Maproom Box 167, FDR Library, Hyde Park, NY.
7. Thomas M. Coffey, *Iron Eagle: The Turbulent Life of General Curtis LeMay* (New York: Crown, 1986), 127–128.
8. Ibid., 121; Werrell, *Blankets of Fire*, 124–137; Briefing, Pasco to Arnold, December 18, 1944, Box 41, Arnold Papers.
9. Msg, Hansell to Arnold, January 16, 1945; Memo, Lanasberg to Stearns, "Estimate of Possibilities of Visual Bombardment of Primary Targets," February 28, 1945; Memo, Seaver to Loughridge, "Ballistic Winds over Japan," March 1, 1945, File 762.912-1, AFHRA.
10. Craven and Cate, *The Army Air Forces in World War II*, Vol. V, 551–567; H. H. Arnold, *Global Mission* (New York: Harper and Brothers, 1949), 541; Haywood S. Hansell, Jr., *The Strategic Air War against Germany and Japan* (Washington: USGPO, 1986), 208–215; Coffey, *Iron Eagle*, 129–132, 144–145; St. Clair McElway, "A Reporter with the B-29s: II—The Doldrums, Guam, and Something Coming Up," *The New Yorker* (June 16, 1945): 32.
11. Letter, LeMay to Norstad, January 31 1945, Box B11, Papers of Curtis LeMay, Library of Congress; Curtis LeMay, with MacKinley Kantor, *Mission with LeMay* (Garden City, NY: Doubleday, 1965), 344–345, 368; Letter, Norstad to Spaatz, March 3 1945, File 519.9701-15, AFHRA; Coffey, *Iron Eagle*, 125–126.
12. Craven and Cate, *The Army Air Forces in World War II*, Vol. V, 568–576; Hansell, *The Strategic Air War*, 51; Coffey, *Iron Eagle*, 139–140, 147, 157; Werrell, *Blankets of Fire*, 142; for more on the flap over Dresden, see Conrad C. Crane, *American Airpower Strategy in World War II* (Lawrence: University Press of Kansas, 2016), 154–159.
13. Transcript of Interview of General Thomas Power by Kenneth Leish, July 1960, Box 9, Thomas R. Power Manuscript Collection, Syracuse University Library, Syracuse, NY; Werrell, *Blankets of Fire*, 152–154; Foreword to XXI Bomber Command Tactical Mission Report, Mission No. 40, Urban Area of Tokyo, March 10, 1945, prepared April 15 1945, Box 26, LeMay Papers; Tami Davis Biddle, "British and American Approaches to Strategic Bombing: Their Origins and Implementation in the World War II Combined Bomber Offensive," *Journal of Strategic Studies* 18, no. 1 (March 1995): 91, 117.
14. "Pacific Report #90," *The United States Strategic Bombing Survey*, Vol. X. (New York: Garland, 1976), 70–73.
15. Wilbur H. Morrison, *Point of No Return* (New York: Times Books 1979), 224; Lawrence Cortesi, *Target: Tokyo* (New York: Kensington Publishing, 1983), 233–274; Thomas R. Havens, *Valley of Darkness* (New York: W. W. Norton 1978), 178–181; Letter, LeMay to Arnold, March 11, 1945, with attached handwritten report, File 312.1-2/59, 1945 AAG,

Records of the Army Air Forces, RG 18, NAII; Leish Interview of Power; Harold H. Martin, "Black Snow and Leaping Tigers," *Harper's Magazine* 192 (February 1946): 151–153.

16. LeMay, with Kantor, *Mission with LeMay*, 351–352, 384; Morrison, *Point of No Return*, 225; XXI Bomber Command, "Analysis of Incendiary Phase of Operations Against Japanese Urban Areas," 39–40, Box 37, LeMay Papers.
17. Robert L. Gleason, "Psychological Operations and Air Power," *Air University Review* 22 (March–April 1971): 36–37; 20th AF Mission Reports 297–302, June 28–29, 1945, File 760.331, AFHRA; Havens, *Valley of Darkness*, 167.
18. Psychological Warfare Branch, U.S. Army Forces, Pacific Area, "Report on Psychological Warfare in the Southwest Pacific Area, 1944–1945," Record Group 4, Reel 617 of microfilm copy of Douglas MacArthur Archives at USMA Library, West Point, NY; Craven and Cate, *The Army Air Forces in World War II*, Vol. V, 698; Kuter to Anderson, August 15, 1944, Anderson diary, Papers of F. L. Anderson, Hoover Institution on War, Revolution and Peace, Stanford University, Stanford, California.
19. LeMay, with Kantor, *Mission with LeMay*, 373; Journal, "Trip to Pacific June 6, 1945 to June 24, 1945," June 13 entry, Box 272 and Msg, Arnold to Eaker, Anderson, and Norstad, undated, Truman File, Box 45, Arnold Papers; Coffey, *Iron Eagle*, 174–175.
20. Memo, Lovett to Stimson, July 31, 1945, with accompanying report, File Aircraft, Air Corps General, Records of the Office of the Secretary of War, RG 107, NAII; David R. Mets, *Master of Airpower* (Novato, CA: Presidio 1988), 298–299; Directive, Eaker to CG, US Army Strategic Air Forces, July 26 1945, Box 13, LeMay Papers; Crane, *American Airpower Strategy*, 182.
21. Msg, Spaatz to Eaker, August 2, 1945 and Diary entry, August 11, 1945, Box 21, Papers of Carl Spaatz, Library of Congress; Mets, *Master of Airpower*, 302–303; Barton Bernstein, "The Perils and Politics of Surrender: Ending the War with Japan and Avoiding the Third Atomic Bomb," *Pacific Historical Review* 46, no. 1 (1977): 16–17.
22. Craven and Cate, *The Army Air Forces in World War II*, Vol. V, 756; Wartime History, 20th Air Force (PIO Version), File 760.01, AFHRA.
23. Hansell, *Strategic Air War*, 74–93.
24. On the perceived vulnerability of Japanese transportation, look at "Pacific Report #53" in Volume VIII of the Garland reprint of the *United States Strategic Bombing Survey* and "Pacific Report #54" and "Pacific Report #55" in Volume IX; on the weaknesses and distortions of the USSBS, see Gian P. Gentile, *How Effective is Strategic Bombing?* (New York: NYU Press, 2001); Barton Bernstein, "Compelling Japan's Surrender Without the A-bomb, Soviet Entry, or Invasion: Reconsidering the US Bombing Survey's Early-Surrender Conclusions," *The Journal of Strategic Studies* 18, no. 2 (June 1995): 101–148; Martin Gilbert, *The First World War: A Complete History* (New York: Henry Holt and Company, 1994), 256n.
25. Diary of Henry L. Stimson, May 6, June 6, July 2, 1945, Yale University Library (microfilm); Noam Chomsky, *American Power and the New Mandarins* (New York: Pantheon, 1969), 167; Len Giovannitti and Fred Freed, *The Decision to Drop the Bomb* (New York: Coward-McCann, 1965), 36; Henry L. Stimson, with McGeorge Bundy, *On Active Service in Peace and War* (New York: Harper and Brothers, 1948), 630–633; for a good example of the press coverage of LeMay's May releases see page 1 of the May 30, 1945 *New York Times*.
26. F. M. Sallagar, *The Road to Total War* (New York: Van Nostrand Reinhold, 1975), 156–157.
27. John Hersey, *Hiroshima* (New York: A. A. Knopf, 1946); Keiji Nakazawa, *Barefoot Gen*, Vol. 1: *A Cartoon Story of Hiroshima* (San Francisco: Last Gasp, 2003), (the series contains at

least ten volumes); Gordon Thomas and Max Morgan Witts, *Enola Gay* (New York: Pocket Books, 1978). The best coverage of the development of the atomic bomb is Richard Rhodes, *The Making of the Atomic Bomb* (New York: Simon and Schuster, 1986) and Leslie R. Groves, *Now It Can Be Told: The Story of the Manhattan Project* (New York: Harper, 1962).

28. Paul Fussell, *Thank God for the Atomic Bomb and Other Essays* (New York: Summit Books, 1988); Stephen Harper, *Miracle of Deliverance: The Case for the Bombing of Hiroshima and Nagasaki* (London: Sidgwick and Jackson, 1985).
29. Charles F. Brower, IV, *The Joint Chiefs of Staff and Strategy in the Pacific War, 1943–1945* (New York: Palgrave Macmillan, 2012).
30. See, for example, Tsuyoshi Hasegawa, *Racing the Enemy: Stalin, Truman, and the Surrender of Japan* (Cambridge, MA: Belknap Press of Harvard University Press, 2005).
31. Donald Kagan, "Why America Dropped the Bomb," *Commentary* 100 (September 1995): 23.
32. Gerhard L. Weinberg, "The End of the Pacific War in World War II," in *Between War and Peace: How America Ends its Wars*, ed. Matthew Moten (New York: Free Press 2011), 220–236. For more details on the occupation, see John W. Dower, *Embracing Defeat: Japan in the Wake of World War II* (New York: W. W. Norton, 1999).
33. Ronald Spector, *In the Ruins of Empire: The Japanese Surrender and the Battle for Postwar Asia* (New York: Random House, 2007); Allan R. Millett, *The War for Korea, 1945–1950: A House Burning* (Lawrence: University Press of Kansas, 2005); Thomas B. Allen and Norman Polmar, *Code-Name Downfall: The Secret Plan to Invade Japan—And Why Truman Dropped the Bomb* (New York: Simon and Schuster, 1995), 250.
34. Richard Frank, *Downfall: The End of the Imperial Japanese Empire* (New York: Penguin Books, 1999).
35. Crane, *American Airpower Strategy*, 163, 179–182; Jack Couffer, *Bat Bomb: World War II's Other Secret Weapon* (Austin: University of Texas Press, 1992); Peter Williams and David Wallace, *Unit 731: Japan's Secret Biological Warfare in World War II* (New York: Free Press, 1989); Barton Bernstein, "Eclipsed by Hiroshima and Nagasaki: Early Thinking About Tactical Nuclear Weapons," *International Security* 15 (Spring 1991): 149–173.

Bibliography

Brower, Charles F., IV. *The Joint Chiefs of Staff and Strategy in the Pacific War, 1943–1945*. New York: Palgrave Macmillan, 2012.
Crane, Conrad C. *American Airpower Strategy in World War II: Bombs, Cities, Civilians, and Oil*. Lawrence: University Press of Kansas, 2016.
Craven, Wesley Frank, and James Lea Cate, eds. *The Army Air Forces in World War II*, Vol. IV: *The Pacific, Guadalcanal to Saipan*. Chicago: University of Chicago Press, 1950.
Craven, Wesley Frank, and James Lea Cate, eds. *The Army Air Forces in World War II*, Vol. V: *The Pacific, Matterhorn to Nagasaki*. Chicago: University of Chicago Press, 1953.
Frank, Richard. *Downfall: The End of the Imperial Japanese Empire*. New York: Penguin Books, 1999.
Griffith, Thomas E. *MacArthur's Airman: General George C. Kenney and the War in the Southwest Pacific*. Lawrence: University Press of Kansas, 1998.
Groves, Leslie R. *Now It Can Be Told: The Story of the Manhattan Project*. New York: Harper, 1962.
LeMay, Curtis, with MacKinley Kantor. *Mission with LeMay*. Garden City, NY: Doubleday, 1965.

Rhodes, Richard. *The Making of the Atomic Bomb*. New York: Simon and Schuster, 1986.
Sakai, Saburo, with Martin Caidan and Fred Saito. *Samurai!* New York: E. P. Dutton and Co., 1958.
Walker, J. Samuel. *Prompt and Utter Destruction, Third Edition: Truman and the Use of Atomic Bombs against Japan*. Chapel Hill: University of North Carolina Press, 2016.
Werrell, Kenneth P. *Blankets of Fire: U.S. Bombers over Japan during World War II*. Washington, DC: Smithsonian, 1996.

CHAPTER 21

HOME FRONTS AT WAR

JUDY BARRETT LITOFF

EXCEPT for the Americas and southern Africa, nearly every country involved in World War II came under sustained enemy attack that often blurred the lines between home front and battle front. Throughout much of the world, women and children were mobilized to an unprecedented degree as warring nations confronted rationing, the scarcity of agricultural and industrial goods, severe labor shortages, defending the homeland from bombings and air raids, maintaining the morale of civilians and the fighting forces, and the overall conversion to a wartime economy.

THE MAJOR ALLIED POWERS

The United States

One of the most striking features of the civilian experience of war in the United States is how radically it differed from that of the other major combatants. For millions of civilians throughout the world, fear, suffering, and hunger dominated their lives as they witnessed family members being raped and killed, saw their homes and towns destroyed, and observed the roundup of six million European Jews who were deported to horrific death camps. By contrast, the continental United States never came under enemy occupation and there remained relatively few civilian deaths from enemy action.[1] Moreover, the democratic process continued without interruption. While the exigencies of war forced the electoral process to be put on hold in Europe, Asia, Africa, and the Middle East, the United States held two presidential, three congressional, and hundreds of state and local elections.[2]

By the time of the Japanese attack on Pearl Harbor on December 7, 1941, American citizens had anticipated the nation's entry into World War II for many months. The United States had already adopted conscription, bolstered defense spending, and sent substantial goods to Great Britain and the Soviet Union.[3] With breathtaking speed, the United States converted its industries' military production. The War Production Board, established in 1942, set priorities and prohibited the production of "nonessential" civilian goods, such as automobiles and home appliances. The automobile industry quickly converted to the production of heavy war machinery. Newly constructed aircraft plants and shipyards turned out military airplanes and warships in record-breaking numbers. Although there were occasional wildcat strikes and a major coal strike by the United Mine Workers in 1943, the labor movement, as a whole, united solidly behind the war effort.

The mobilization of the nation's economy for war created an unprecedented demand for new workers. In response to this need, some 6.5 million women entered the work force. The proportion of women in the labor force increased from twenty-five percent at the beginning of the war to thirty-six percent at war's end—an increase greater than that of the combined previous four decades. The composition of the female labor force also changed as the number of married and older women who worked escalated.[4]

For the first time, women could find employment in heavy industry, such as shipyards and defense plants. In sharp contrast to the Depression years of the 1930s, when working women were criticized for taking jobs away from men, the woman war worker was highly lauded, and "Rosie the Riveter," the generic term used to describe women workers in America during World War II, became a national heroine.

As exciting as war work was for American women, they often faced exhausting schedules that included forty-hour plus workweeks, in addition to taking care of household chores, and, if they had children, finding appropriate child care arrangements. The Lanham Act of 1943 provided federal funds for thirty-one hundred child care centers that served about six hundred thousand children, but many more centers were needed. Unfortunately, private child care centers were often overcrowded, ill equipped, understaffed, and expensive.[5]

Widespread segregation and racial discrimination meant that African American women faced even tougher obstacles as war workers than their white counterparts. African American women were the last to be hired and the first to be fired as war workers. Still, new opportunities in manufacturing enabled black women to leave low-paying domestic work, one of the few jobs available to them prior to World War II, for better-paying factory positions.[6]

With the vast majority of the nation's resources going toward war production, shortages and rationing of consumer goods were very much a part of the home front experience. In response to food shortages, Americans planted millions of Victory Gardens. At the height of the war there were nearly twenty million gardens, yielding forty percent of all vegetables produced in the United States.[7]

Despite the need for agricultural workers, the wartime farm population declined by six million people as many farmers joined the military or sought more lucrative work in war industries. The resultant wartime agricultural labor shortage required the nation to look for new sources of agricultural labor. While farm workers were imported from Mexico and the Caribbean to help meet the shortages, and military personnel were furloughed to do emergency farm work, it was the millions of American women who came forward to avert an agricultural labor crisis.

The percentage of American women engaged in agricultural production rose from eight percent in 1940 to twenty-two percent in 1945. This included approximately three million nonfarm women, about one-half of whom were members of the Women's Land Army (WLA), established in 1943 by the Department of Agriculture and modeled after the British organization with the same name, to recruit mostly middle-class town and city women for farm jobs. Whether farm wives driving tractors, college women milking cows, housewives picking apples, or secretaries spending summer vacations harvesting vegetables, these workers responded with energy and ingenuity to the wartime need for farm labor as they performed crucial agricultural work.[8]

Geographic mobility was another distinguishing hallmark of the American experience of World War II. Approximately twenty percent of the U.S. population was on the move as one of the major demographic shifts in American history took place. The U.S. Census Bureau estimated that 15.3 million civilians moved, more than one-half of them across state lines. In addition, the sixteen million American citizens who served in the military traveled to distant posts around the nation and the world. These statistics, as startling as they are, actually underrepresent the amount of travel that occurred because many people moved multiple times during the war.[9] People who had barely ventured beyond the immediate vicinity of their hometowns crisscrossed the nation as they flocked to new job openings in shipyards and war plants located in cities like Detroit, Pittsburgh, Chicago, Los Angeles, and Seattle. Service wives who followed their husbands to their stateside military postings were also a part of this great migration.[10]

The United States emerged from World War II a much stronger and richer nation. However, for significant segments of the population, especially African Americans and the 120,000 Japanese Americans who were incarcerated at ten specially built prison camps, what the U.S. government called "relocation centers," the war represented an era when racism, discrimination, and prejudice remained a part of the American landscape. For the families of the four hundred thousand Americans who lost their lives, World War II represented an era of grave sacrifice. Yet overall, the war brought out the best in the American people as they joined together to meet the extraordinary challenges that helped lead to the defeat of the Axis powers and propelled the United States into the position of the world's leading political, military, and economic power in the immediate postwar era.

Great Britain

Even before the German invasion of Poland on September 1, 1939, Great Britain had begun to prepare for war. The Women's Voluntary Service (WVS), founded in 1938, could claim one million members by the end of 1941. Further preparation for war began in July 1939, when gas masks, with instructions for proper use, were issued to all British citizens.[11]

At the start of the war, a massive evacuation campaign was introduced to ensure the safety of children who lived in cities that were in danger of Nazi bombing, such as London, Birmingham, Liverpool, and Plymouth. Eventually, some three million children were evacuated to the countryside. Some evacuees were sent to distant Commonwealth countries. In addition, five thousand British children were evacuated to the United States through special private programs.[12]

Seeking shelter from nightly aerial bombings by the *Luftwaffe* during the Blitz, the German bombing offensive against Britain between September 1940 and May 1941, thousands of London families sought safety in the Underground. British citizens collected clothing and food for the needy, organized first aid courses, and lent a helping hand wherever they were needed.

Fears of a German invasion of Great Britain led to the creation of a Home Guard in May 1940, which consisted of 1.5 million volunteers who were ineligible for regular military service, usually because of age. The Home Guard defended the seacoast, airfields, factories, and military installations. Home Guardsmen also operated anti-aircraft guns and were credited with shooting down many *Luftwaffe* aircraft and V-1 and V-2 weapons. An additional 1.4 million Air Raid Wardens patrolled the streets during blackouts, helping people find the nearest shelter during bombing raids, and touring their sectors to check for fires, bombs, shrapnel and falling debris.[13]

The official mobilization of British women for war began in March 1941 when they were required to register their family occupations with the local Employment Exchange. This represented the first step toward the conscription of women, which began in December 1941 with the passage of the National Service Act, the first time in the history of Great Britain that women were conscripted. This legislation initially applied to unmarried women between twenty- and thirty-years-old. Later, it was extended to all married women. Once women were called up, they could choose between the military services, civil defense, or other vital war work.[14]

Shortages and rationing of food were very much a part of the British home front experience. Before the war, Great Britain, as an island, imported a great deal of foodstuffs. But German submarines patrolling the Atlantic Ocean disrupted this flow of supplies. Beginning in 1940, ration books were issued to all families, including the royal family.

To increase the much-needed food supply, the British Women's Land Army (WLA), originally established during World War I, was revitalized in June 1939. Initially women were encouraged to volunteer for the WLA, but the passage of the National Service Act in December 1941 allowed for the conscription of women into the Land Army. Despite its name, the WLA was a civilian organization under the control of the Ministry of Agriculture. "Land Girls," as they were affectionately called, came from a variety of walks of life and performed a wide range of vital agricultural jobs from milking cows to plowing and harvesting crops.[15]

Clothing, gasoline, furniture, nylon stockings, cigarettes, and a variety of other items were rationed. In response to these shortages, British citizens sometimes resorted to the black market. For British women, standing in long lines for hours at a time for scarce goods became a way of life. This posed a special problem for Britain's growing female labor force. Twelve-hour shifts were not uncommon, and married women with children faced exhausting schedules. Finding adequate child care arrangements remained a perennial problem throughout the war years. Despite these obstacles, by the end of the war in 1945, 44.5 percent of all females between the ages of fourteen and fifty-nine were part of the civilian labor force.[16]

The end of the war in Europe came on May 7, 1945, with Germany's unconditional surrender. Throughout Great Britain, the celebrations began immediately, although May 8 marked the official V-E Day. Prime Minister Winston Churchill, who had led Great Britain through the war years, spoke to cheering crowds from the balcony of the Ministry of Health in Whitehall. But many British citizens, exhausted after almost six years of war, found little to celebrate. News of the horrors and atrocities committed at Bergen Belsen and other concentration camps, and the challenges of caring for displaced people and returning prisoners of war, and coping with the more than 450,000 military and civilian British deaths caused a shadowy pall to fall over Britain. Shortages and rationing remained a problem and food rationing would not be completely lifted until 1954. Moreover, World War II and its aftermath confirmed that Great Britain was no longer the world power that it had once been. That role now belonged to the United States.

The Soviet Union

Scholars agree that the Soviet Union suffered the greatest civilian and military death toll of any warring nation. Official Soviet statistics place the total number of Soviet war-related deaths at 26.6 million. This number includes 8.7 million military deaths and 17.9 civilian deaths.[17] However, some scholars argue that these figures substantially underestimate the total number of war-related deaths, which they place as high as forty-two million.[18]

When Germany, initially an ally of the Soviet Union with the signing of the Nazi–Soviet Nonaggression Pact of August 1939, began its massive assault on the USSR on June 22, 1941, the citizens of that country quickly geared themselves for what they called the Great Patriotic War. Given the Soviet Union's history of shortages and coping with economic crisis, its citizens were better prepared to endure the material hardships associated with total war than most other warring nations.[19] Because major battles were fought on Soviet territory, the home front and battle front were often indistinguishable. During the nine-hundred-day siege of Leningrad between September 1941 and January 1944, the city's civilian population of nearly three million joined with Soviet soldiers to defend the encircled city. Hunger, malnutrition, starvation, and disease were all too common during the siege, and at least 640,000 lives were lost.[20] The Battle of Stalingrad (now Volgograd) between August 1942 and February 1943 included air raids and close quarters combat; it killed an estimated forty thousand civilians.[21]

The war resulted in hardship unequaled in Soviet history. The reduction of basic necessities, especially food, made an exceedingly unsatisfactory system of rationing, first introduced in 1941, mandatory for the urban population. Peasants, by contrast, received no rations and were forced to rely on inadequate local resources.[22]

In the early months of the war, vital defense plants and war machinery located in the path of the Nazi army were evacuated to interior areas. War-related industries, crops, and livestock that could not be moved in the short time available were burned or blown up so that they would not fall into Nazi hands. Still, large amounts of grain, livestock, and military equipment were confiscated by the Nazis and sent back to Germany.[23]

A greatly expanded Soviet work force included inexperienced young people, the elderly, and a preponderance of women. At the height of the war, women comprised fifty-three percent of the work force.[24] In addition, approximately one million Soviet women played a significant role in the Red Army and in Partisan units.[25]

The Soviet Union emerged victorious at the end of the war as its citizens joined in euphoric celebrations. But the cost of victory had been enormous, with a staggering loss of life, destruction of property, and economic and military upheavals. Unlike, Germany, Japan, France, Italy, and Great Britain, who witnessed new postwar governments, Joseph Stalin remained in power and sought a return to the prewar order.[26] By the late 1940s, however, the Soviet Union had experienced a remarkable economic and military recovery and posed a significant challenge to the United States as these two powerful nations became embroiled in a Cold War that would dominate global politics for the next four decades.

China

Beginning with the September 1931 Japanese invasion of Manchuria and the establishment of the puppet state of Manchukuo in February 1932, China and Japan became embroiled in a major conflict which did not end until fourteen years later with the Japanese surrender to the Allies in August 1945. However, not until July 1937, with the powerful Japanese assault on the eastern third of China, did full-scale war between the two countries begin. This long and devastating war, which resulted in twenty to thirty million civilian and military deaths, is known in China as the Chinese People's War of Resistance against Japanese Aggression.

Following the events of July 1937, there was a massive movement of Chinese refugees, armies, factories, industries, and universities to interior regions as part of Chiang Kai-shek's policy of "trading space for time." Inland cities saw their populations soar. Faculty and students from China's most prestigious eastern universities relocated to the National Southwest Associated University (Lianda) in Kunming.[27] Chongqing was transformed from a remote provincial city in Sichuan province with a population of just under five hundred thousand to the capital of Nationalist China with a population of more than one million. Relatively safe from a land attack, it was bombed more than two hundred times between February 1938 and August 1943. Although Chongqing was the most heavily bombed city in China, most cities faced aerial attacks from the Japanese.[28]

China's women made myriad wartime contributions. In addition to caring for homeless refugee children, women participated in fundraising drives, cared for the wounded, brought gifts and greetings to soldiers, and provided psychological and moral support for war-weary citizens.[29] Families were torn apart as they fled the invading Japanese army. Refugee children, in particular, posed a special problem. To address this problem, the Wartime Child Welfare Protection Association (WCWPA) was established in 1938 by activist women representing all political points of view. Headquartered in Chongqing for most of the war, the WCWPA housed and trained thirty thousand homeless refugee children. Women in occupied China accepted the occupation with resignation and adopted survival strategies that enabled them to help their families live with the enemy. Overt protests were rare, but active support for the Japanese was quite limited. Women often found themselves the victims of the Japanese, and some two hundred thousand Asian women were taken as "comfort women" to work in military brothels.[30]

In a desperate effort to prevent the advancing Japanese army from gaining control of Chinese assets, the Chinese army deliberately destroyed bridges, roads, railway tracks, and factories. This scorched-earth policy included the opening of the Yellow River dike at Huayuankou, which flooded seventy thousand square kilometers and resulted in eight hundred thousand civilian deaths.[31]

The burning of the wealthy provincial capital of Changsha, located in Hunan province, in November 1938 also resulted in great tragedy for the Chinese people. Steeped in rich cultural and historical tradition, Changsha became the home for many refugees fleeing from the north and east. Fearing that Japanese forces would overtake Changsha, Chiang Kai-shek made the decision to burn all its public and private buildings, including the huge rice warehouses, rather than allow them to fall into the hands of the enemy. At least twenty thousand people died and two hundred thousand were left homeless.[32]

Famine resulted in millions of additional deaths. For example, the Henan Famine of 1942–1943, caused by a combination of natural and man-made disasters, resulted in over three million deaths and another three to four million people were left homeless. What made this famine particularly tragic was that the area had already suffered from the 1938 Yellow River flood.[33]

From 1937 until the end of the war, an uneasy truce between the Chinese Nationalists and Chinese Communists existed. This United Front, established in September1937, brought an end to the ten-year civil war between the Communists and Nationalists. However, to suggest that the Communists and Nationalists faced no military, political, or ideological differences after 1937 misrepresents the complexity of their relationship. For example, as many as one-half million of Chiang Kai-shek's best-trained soldiers were used to blockade the Communist headquarters in Yan'an in northern China. Yet as imperfect as the United Front may have been, it prevented a full-fledge civil war between the Communists and Nationalists from breaking out during the years of the War of Resistance.[34]

In 1935, Chiang Kai-shek's Nationalist forces far outnumbered the small group of Communists who had just survived the Long March and settled in Yan'an. Life in Yan'an was simple and basic. Cave houses carved into the side of the hills served as homes for everyone. Manual labor was expected of all, even the top leaders.[35] However, by the last year of the war, the military and political position of the Communists had undergone a massive transformation. Mao Zedong was now recognized as the undisputed leader of the Chinese Communist Party (CCP), and a greatly expanded Red Army, led by inspiring generals, including Commander-in-Chief Zhu De, controlled significant portions of north China. The CCP received strong support from peasants and ordinary Chinese, while the Nationalist leadership was perceived as corrupt, decadent, and out of touch with the common people.[36]

The unconditional surrender of Japan in August 1945 brought an end to China's fourteen-year War of Resistance. But the cost of victory had been enormous. Twenty to thirty million military and civilian deaths resulted in a decline in China's overall population by eighteen million. One-quarter of China's population had been displaced. Bombed cities and towns had to be restored. Grief, exhaustion, and fear plagued the nation.[37]

Unfortunately, the end of the war did not bring about an end to China's suffering. The CCP emerged from the war far stronger than it had been fourteen years earlier. Almost immediately after the conclusion of the War of Resistance, China became embroiled in a devastating civil war that pitted Chinese against each other and wreaked devastating havoc on the nation for four more years. On October 1, 1949, Mao Zedong proclaimed the defeat of the Nationalists and officially established the People's Republic of China.

THE MAJOR AXIS POWERS

Japan

Most Japanese citizens date World War II from September 18, 1931, when Japanese troops invaded Manchuria and established the puppet state of Manchukuo in February 1932, until August 15, 1945, when Emperor Hirohito announced over the radio the unconditional surrender of Japan to the Allies. During this period, approximately three million Japanese civilians and military personnel died. Even today, the Japanese have still not agreed on what to call this conflict. It is variously referred to as the China Incident, the Japan–China War, the Pacific War, the Fifteen Year War, and, after Pearl Harbor, the Greater East Asia War.[38]

Prior to Pearl Harbor, the Japanese government emphasized the mobilization of its spiritual and physical resources for war. Extravagance, showy dress, cosmetics, and permanent waves were banned. The press and radio emphasized self-sacrifice for the war effort. School children underwent additional physical training. "Home honor" plaques signified that a man from that house was at war.[39]

As the war progressed, mobilization became more pronounced. Following the announcement of the Greater East Asia Co-Prosperity Sphere in August 1940, and the growing presence of Japan in East Asia, Japanese officials were hopeful that minerals and raw materials from this area could be used to support military and industrial development in the homeland. Nonetheless, Japan's deficiency of coal, iron, tin, rubber, and petroleum portended difficult times throughout the war years.[40]

The Japanese attack on Pearl Harbor on December 7, 1941 brought the war even closer to home. Food, clothing, and other basic necessities were in short supply. In addition to rice rationing, which had been introduced in April 1940, almost all major food items, including miso, soy sauce, fish, eggs, and tofu, were placed under ration controls in the months after Pearl Harbor. Making do with scarce supplies became the maxim for home front civilians. Slogans such as "Luxury is the enemy," "Saving is the road to victory," and "Deny one's self and serve the nation" became commonplace.[41] Industrial mobilization for war was also stepped up as the Japanese now had one million troops in China to support, as well as a large military presence in the Pacific that was facing the well-equipped United States Army, Navy, and Marines.

The work of previously established neighborhood associations, formed in the late 1930s and situated throughout Japan, took on new meaning as the war was brought home to Japanese families. These associations, under the control of the Home Ministry, carefully watched each other to make sure that citizens practiced air and fire defense drills and to ensure neighbors purchased the required allotment of government war bonds. Each association also made certain that friends and neighbors demonstrated enthusiasm for the war by contributing precious metals, such as gold rings, to the war effort and adhering to the rationing system and price controls enacted by the government. Despite all the efforts of the neighborhood associations, the black market became a common feature of life in war-torn Japan.[42]

After Pearl Harbor, the militaristic and nationalist indoctrination of the nation's schools intensified. Even elementary schools emphasized the importance of sacrifice for the nation. The Great Japan Youth Association, consisting of fourteen million members by June 1943, led to the further regimentation of Japanese youth. As the war wore on, students above the third grade made up a growing proportion of the labor force. Vacations and holidays were dedicated to war work. Education was further disrupted as school days and the school year were shortened to allow students to take on additional war work. By the end of the war, some three million students had been inducted into the labor force.[43]

From the earliest days of the war, Japanese women had formed volunteer associations to cheer on the men as they left for war. In February 1942, all these organizations were brought together in a unified organization, the Greater Japan Women's Association. All married and single women over twenty years of age were expected to join the organization, resulting in a membership of some twenty million, and reinforcing traditional views of Japanese women as homemakers and mothers.[44]

In Japan, unlike in the United States, Great Britain, and the Soviet Union, women as industrial laborers were an underused asset. By 1944, 1.4 million women had been added to the civilian labor force but this was just three percent more than in 1940. Traditional views of women and family prevailed even in the face of severe labor shortages as the Japanese armed forces swelled to 8.2 million men.[45] Only during the last year of the war, as Japanese defeats mounted and an Allied invasion appeared imminent, did the government begin to train women on how to defend the homeland. The Volunteer Military Service Law, adopted on June 23, 1945, conscripted women between the ages of seventeen and forty into the National Volunteer Combat Corps, an organization that was to assist the military in the event of an Allied invasion. During the final year of the war, the Japanese media produced powerful images of female strength and determination, even as women were expected to continue to perform their traditional roles as homemakers and mothers.[46]

By mid-1944, the effective Allied naval blockade and fire-bombing of Japanese cities made food and labor shortages acute. When American B-29 bombers began attacks on Japan in June 1944, the Japanese people had no effective way to defend themselves. In response to these bombings, the Japanese government relocated 450,000 students and their teachers to the countryside.[47]

In the spring of 1945, the bombing raids further intensified. On March 9–10, Tokyo was attacked by 325 B-29 bombers. More than one hundred thousand people died and one million people were left homeless. By the end of the war, more than sixty Japanese cities had been severely damaged by bombings. Because almost all of Japan's urban dwellings were made of wood and other flammable materials, little could be done to prevent these cities from going up in flames.[48]

By the spring of 1945, the spirit of the Japanese people was depleted, but it was not broken. While the bombing of Tokyo and other Japanese cities weakened morale, the majority were willing to continue to fight. The image of certain victory embraced by the Japanese media throughout the war did not wane.[49] Little did the Japanese people know that the United States had a powerful new weapon that would soon wreak havoc on the cities of Hiroshima and Nagasaki. The dropping of the atomic bombs on August 6 and 9 resulted in tens of thousands of deaths; by the end of 1945 the death toll stood at over two hundred thousand.

Recognizing that Japan was a defeated nation, Emperor Hirohito, in an unprecedented radio address to the nation on August 15, announced that Japan had agreed to an unconditional surrender to the Allies. This was the first time that the Japanese people had heard the voice of "the living god." Subsequently, the emperor renounced his divinity, exchanged his commander-in-chief's uniform for a western style suit, and embarked on an extensive tour of Japan to meet his subjects.[50] Japan continues to grapple with the legacy of the war years. Controversies concerning war responsibility, war guilt, the Yasukuni Shrine, and the meaning of defeat have not been resolved.

Germany

Some eighteen million German men served in the military, leaving families behind to cope with the daily challenges of a nation at war, especially in 1944–1945. Wives and mothers wrote detailed letters to their loved ones in which they discussed the problems associated with rationing (first introduced in 1939), air-raid alerts, the deterioration of living conditions, clearing rubble from bombing raids, standing in long lines for scarce household supplies, and bringing up children alone. Given these exhausting challenges, at war's end, most German women wanted to return to their traditional roles as wives and mothers.[51] The employment of women increased only slightly during the war years, from fourteen million in 1939 to 14.9 million in 1944.[52]

Despite the Nazi ideology that German men were to be the protectors of their women, by the end of the war approximately five hundred thousand women were classified as female *Wehrmacht* auxiliaries. The German military casualty rate during the last two years of the war necessitated that women take on auxiliary roles within the *Wehrmacht*. They served as searchlight operators and anti-aircraft auxiliaries; occasionally, they found themselves engaged in actual combat. Women were also hired to do office and communication work for the *Wehrmacht* that had once been staffed by men. A few women, most notably Hanna Reitsch, became test pilots, while others served as ferrying pilots for the *Luftwaffe*. In addition, thirty-seven hundred women served as SS prison guards (*SS-Helferin*) in Nazi concentration camps. Moreover, by the end of the war, four hundred thousand German women served as Red Cross nurses and nurses' aides.[53]

As the labor shortage mounted during the last two years of the war, elderly men on pensions were urged to go back to work on factories and farms. Hitler Youth between the ages of ten and fifteen helped farmers harvest their crops, collected scrap metal, and served as part-time anti-aircraft gunners.[54]

Throughout the final months of the war, Germany faced a massive refugee problem as some six million Germans fled westward in an effort to escape the plunder and ravage of the Red Army. Many died in the process. This refugee problem was compounded by the liberation of prisoners of war, concentration camp survivors, and forced laborers during the last weeks of the war. All total, the refugee population in Germany at the end of World War II totaled eleven million people.[55]

In both eastern and western Germany, invading armies inflicted drunkenness, vandalism, and violence on the local populations. Soviet soldiers killed and mutilated civilians and raped German women without regard for their age. Allied troops in western Germany also committed atrocities, including rape, against the local populations.[56]

At the end of the war in early May 1945, Germany had suffered six to eight million civilian deaths and 5.5 million military deaths.[57] Moreover, Allied strategic bombing had left many towns and cities in shambles. Survival amidst this rubble was first and foremost on the minds of German citizens. Rebuilding the German economy would be decades in the making.

Italy

Benito Mussolini was popular dictator during much of his reign, but his popularity, which had peaked in the 1930s, dramatically declined during the early 1940s as news of Italian military defeats in Greece, North Africa, and the Soviet Union proliferated. Rationing of food and other scarce products was quickly introduced, but many of these items found their way to the black market. The grim reality of war took on even greater meaning for home front Italians as Allied bombing of towns and cities intensified in 1943.

Life on the Italian home front is best understood if it is divided into two distinct periods: June 1940–June 1943 and July 1943–April 1945. Throughout both periods, peasants represented the largest occupational group in Italy in an economy centered on agricultural production. Poverty and heavy workloads characterized the daily lives of peasants. Fascist propaganda extolled women peasants as the "mothers of the nation and the guardians of the rural world, the most praiseworthy of Italian women." By mid-1943, some three million peasant women had joined the *Massaie Rurali*, the rural housewives' section of the *Fasci Femminilli*, the women's division of the National Fascist Party (PNF). Under the direction of the PNF, the *Massaie Rurali* produced pamphlets, calendars, a newspaper, short films, special radio programs, outdoor rallies, and technical training courses that emphasized the importance of farming, rural life, and motherhood.[58]

Fascist propaganda exalted the role of women as mothers and providing warriors for the regime. Large families were rewarded with government benefits while bachelors were saddled with special taxes. Yet despite these incentives to raise large families, women comprised over one-quarter of Italy's work force in the 1930s.[59]

As the nation reluctantly mobilized for war, new opportunities for working women emerged. The move from farm to factory was especially striking. Whether employed in factories or farms, professional work, such as teaching or secretarial work, working women faced the triple burden of how to balance motherhood, homemaking, and work responsibilities. Moreover, wherever women worked, they regularly faced long hours, low pay, and gender discrimination.[60]

Although Mussolini was an avowed anti-cleric, he recognized the importance of seeking the support of the Italian Catholic Church. Ninety-nine percent of Italians were Catholic, and the Church exerted a powerful influence over the nation. Mussolini understood the futility of taking on such an influential institution; therefore, he chose to work with the Catholic Church throughout his reign. In the 1930s, fascist rallies often began with morning Mass and the PNF employed twenty-five hundred priests to serve as chaplains to local fascist groups. Recent scholarship stresses the crucial role of the Catholic Church in buttressing the fascist regime. For the church it gained a concordant that granted sovereignty to Vatican City.[61]

Not until the summer of 1943 did significant opposition to Mussolini begin to take shape. Following Mussolini's forced resignation in July 1943 and his subsequent appointment as the puppet leader of German-occupied northern Italy in September, expressions of discontent with Mussolini could be heard throughout Italy. The Resistance movement that emerged, heavily dominated by Communists, sought to overthrow the fascist regime and expel the German invaders.[62]

The war in Italy officially ended on April 25, 1945, celebrated as Liberation Day of each year to commemorate the end of Nazi occupation and Fascist rule. At the end of the war, the Italian economy was in shambles and much of the country lay in ruins. Italy suffered almost one-half million military and civilian deaths and hundreds of thousands of others were left homeless. Despite the grim outlook, the Italian economy recovered with the help of American aid through the Marshall Plan. The war had discredited the Italian monarchy and lead to the establishment of a republic.[63]

Conclusion

The impact of the war that engulfed much of the world between 1939 and 1945 involved a great deal more than battles and military maneuvers. Global death statistics substantiate this assertion as home front causalities (forty-five million) far exceeded those of the battle front (fifteen million). Without question, World War II had a direct, far-reaching, and long-lasting influence on both home fronts as well as battle fronts.

Nonetheless, whether living in war ravaged Germany or the relative safety of the United States, home front civilians faced many similar challenges. Coping with family separations when loved ones were called to battle, struggling to make ends meet in the face of shortages and rationing, adjusting to jobs in the newly emerging war economy, finding appropriate child care arrangements, surviving the death of a loved one, maintaining the morale of civilians and the fighting forces, and planning for the postwar world were just a few of the many challenges shared by all home front citizens. Moreover, as millions of men went off to war, women and children, who were mobilized to on an unprecedented degree, were often required to assume new and unorthodox responsibilities.

For the United States, the experience of war propelled the nation into the world's leading political, military, and economic power in the immediate postwar era. According to historian Studs Terkel, for many Americans World War II was *"The Good War"*.[64] At the other end of the spectrum, Italy's refusal to address its Fascist past and ingeniously to place the blame of the entire era on one man alone—the dictator Mussolini—starkly differs from that of the United States. Given these and other varied interpretations of World War II, the topic of the long-lasting impact of home fronts at war will, in all likelihood, continue to engage the attention of historians.

Notes

1. "By the Numbers: World-Wide Deaths," The National World War II Museum, http://www.nationalww2museum.org/learn/education/for-students/ww2-history/ww2-by-the-numbers/world-wide-deaths.html (accessed January 21, 2015). An estimated ninety-three hundred Merchant Marines were also killed. "U.S. Merchant Marine in World War II," http://www.usmm.org/ww2.html (accessed on January 30, 2015).

2. Judy Barrett Litoff, "Home-Front Americans at War," in *Daily Lives of Civilians in Wartime Modern America: From Indian Wars to the Vietnam War*, ed. David S. Heidler and Jeanne T. Heidler (Westport, Connecticut: Greenwood Press, 2007), 68.
3. Litoff, "Home-Front Americans at War," 68–69.
4. Susan M. Hartmann, *The Home Front and Beyond: American Women in the 1940s* (Boston: Twayne Publishers, 1982), 77–78. An excellent documentary film on this topic is *The Life and Times of Rosie the Riveter* by Connie Field (Clarity Films, 1980). In 1996, this now-classic film was selected for preservation in the National Film Registry, Library of Congress.
5. See, for example, William M. Tuttle, Jr., *"Daddy's Gone to War": The Second World War in the Lives of America's Children* (New York: Oxford University Press, 1993), chapter 5, 69–90.
6. Karen Tucker Anderson, "Last Hired, First Fired: Black Women Workers during World War II," *Journal of American History* 69 (June 1982): 82–97.
7. Litoff, "Home-Front Americans at War," 72.
8. Judy Barrett Litoff and David C. Smith, "'To the Rescue of the Crops': The Women's Land Army of World War II," *Prologue* 25 (Winter 1933): 348–358.
9. Litoff, "Home-Front Americans at War," 74–77.
10. See, for example, Vance Packard, "Millions on the Move," *American Magazine* (October 1944): 34–36, 97; Vance Packard, "Soldiers' Wives Give Up Home and Job for Camp Life with Husbands," *Life* (October 12, 1942): 56–62; Barbara Klaw, *Camp Follower: Story of Soldier's Wife* (New York: Random House, 1943).
11. Jenny Hartley, ed., *Hearts Undefeated: Women's Writing of the Second World War* (London: Virago Press, 1994), 135–136; Penny Summerfield, *Women Workers in the Second World War* (London: Routledge, 1989), 117. For an in-depth examination of the Women's Voluntary Service, see James Hinton, *Women, Social Leadership and the Second World War: Continuities of Class* (New York: Oxford University Press, 2002); BBC, WW2 People's War: An Archive of World War Two Memories—Written by the Public, Gathered by the BBC, "Fact File: Women's Volunteer Groups, May 1938–1945," http://www.bbc.co.uk/history/ww2peopleswar/timeline/factfiles/nonflash/a6651894.shtml?sectionId=0&articleId=6651894 (accessed January 29, 2015).
12. BBC, WW2 People's War: An Anthology of World War Two Memories—Written by the Public, Gathered by the BBC, "Fact File: Evacuation, 1939–1944," http://www.bbc.co.uk/history/ww2peopleswar/timeline/factfiles/nonflash/a1057222.shtml?sectionId=1&articleId=1057222 (accessed January 29, 2015); Jocelyn Statler, ed. *Special Relations: Transatlantic Letters Linking Three English Evacuees and Their Families, 1940–1945* (London: Imperial War Museum, 1990).
13. For a detailed study of the Home Guard, see J. P. Mackenzie, *The Home Guard: A Military and Political History* (New York: Oxford University Press, 1995); BBC, WW2 People's War: An Archive of World War Two Memories—Written by the Public, Gathered by the BBC, "Fact File: Air Raid Precautions, April 1938–1945," http://www.bbc.co.uk/history/ww2peopleswar/timeline/factfiles/nonflash/a6651425.shtml (accessed January 29, 2015).
14. Summerfield, *Women Workers in the Second World War*, 34–35; Hartley, ed., *Hearts Undefeated*, 104.
15. Gail Braybon and Penny Summerfield, *Out of the Cage: Women's Experiences in Two World Wars* (London: Pandora Press, 1987), 152, 156, 167, 187–188. BBC, WW2 People's War: An Archive of World War Two Memories—Written by the Public, Gathered by the BBC, "Fact

File: Women's Land Army, June 1939–1950," http://www.bbc.co.uk/history/ww2peoples war/timeline/factfiles/nonflash/a6652055.shtml (accessed January 29, 2015).
16. Summerfield, *Women Workers in the Second World War*, 53, 196.
17. Michael Ellman and S. Maksudov, "Soviet Deaths in the Great Patriotic War: A Note," *Europe–Asia Studies* 46 (July 1994): 671–681.
18. Michael Haynes, "Counting Deaths in the Great Patriotic War: A Note," *Europe–Asia Studies* 55 (March 2003): 303–309.
19. John Barber and Mark Harrison, *The Soviet Home Front 1941–1945: A Social and Economic History of the USSR in World War II* (London: Longman, 1991), 77
20. "The 900-day Siege of Leningrad," http://www.saint-petersburg.com/history/siege.asp (accessed February 3, 2015).
21. British Pathe, "Battle of Stalingrad," http://www.britishpathe.com/gallery/ww2-bloodiest-battles (accessed February 2, 2015).
22. Barber and Harrison, *The Soviet Home Front*, 77–89.
23. Barber and Harrison, *The Soviet Home Front*, 127–137.
24. Barber and Harrison, *The Soviet Home Front*, 98.
25. Conze and Fieseler, "Soviet Women as Comrades-in-Arms," 228.
26. Barber and Harrison, *The Soviet Home Front*, 207, 209.
27. John Israel, *Lianda University: A Chinese University in War and Revolution* (Stanford: Stanford University Press, 1999).
28. Diana Lary, *The Chinese People at War: Human Suffering and Social Transformation, 1937–1945* (New York: Cambridge University Press, 2010), 87–89.
29. Li, *Echoes of Chongqing*, 21, 95.
30. Lary, *The Chinese People at War*, 68–70, 99–100.
31. Lary, *The Chinese People at War*, 60–62.
32. Lary, *The Chinese People at War*, 62–64.
33. Lary, *The Chinese People at War*, 124–126.
34. Judy Barrett Litoff and David Lux, "Memory, Museums, and Cultural Heritage: The Chinese People's War of Resistance against Japanese Aggression, 1931–1945," 2013 *Proceedings, Tourism and the Shifting Values of Cultural Heritage: Visiting Pasts, Developing Futures—International Conference, Taipei, Taiwan*, April 4–7, 2013, 1–12.
35. Lary, *The Chinese People at War*, 102.
36. Lary, *The Chinese People at War*, 148–149.
37. Lary, *The Chinese People at War*, 173–175.
38. Haruko Taya Cook and Theodore F. Cook, *Japan at War: An Oral History* (New York: The New Press, 1992), 11.
39. Thomas R. H. Havens, *Valley of Darkness: The Japanese People and World War II* (Lanham, MD: University Press of America, 1986), 11–33.
40. Cook and Cook, *Japan at War*, 171.
41. Cook and Cook, *Japan at War*, 174–177.
42. Cook and Cook, *Japan at War*, 171–175; Havens, *Valley of Darkness*, 37–43.
43. Cook and Cook, *Japan at War*, 172–173; Havens, *Valley of Darkness*, 139–142.
44. Cook and Cook, *Japan at War*, 172; Havens, *Valley of Darkness*, 58–59.
45. Havens, *Valley of Darkness*, 106–108.
46. Havens, *Valley of Darkness*, 188–191; David C. Earhart, *Certain Victory: Images of World War II in the Japanese Media* (Armonk, NY: M. E. Sharp, 2008), 179–180.
47. Havens, *Valley of Darkness*, 154, 163.

48. Cook and Cook, *Japan at War*, 340–341; Havens, *Valley of Darkness*, 176–180.
49. Havens, *Valley of Darkness*, 187; Earhart, *Certain Victory*, xi–xiv, 461–474.
50. Cook and Cook, *Japan at War*, 15, 403–406; John W. Dower, *Embracing Defeat: Japan in the Wake of World War II* (New York: W. W. Norton, 1999), 308–338. See also John W. Dower, *Japan in War and Peace: Selected Essays* (New York: W. W. Norton, 1993), 339–348, for a discussion of why, at the end of the war, the United States supported a conciliatory policy toward Emperor Hirohito.
51. Hester Vaizey, "Empowerment or Endurance? War Wives' Experiences of Independence During and After the Second World War in Germany, 1939–1948," *German History* 29 (March 2011): 57, 67; Ulrich Herbert, "Forced Laborers in the 'Third Reich'—an Overview," *International Labor and Working-Class History* 58 (Fall 2000): 192–218.
52. Karen Hagemann, "Mobilizing Women for War: The History, Historiography, and Memory of German Women's War Service in Two World Wars," *The Journal of Military History* 75 (October 2011): 1075; Jill Stephenson, *Women in Nazi Germany* (London: Longman, 2001), xvi, xvii, 55.
53. Campbell, "Women in Combat," 313–318; Hagemann, "Mobilizing Women for War," 1079–1082; Perry Biddiscombe, "Into the Maelstrom: German Women in Combat, 1944–45," *War & Society* 30 (March 2011): 61–89; Evelyn Zegenhagen, "German Women Pilots at War, 1939–1945," *Air Power History* 56 (Winter 2009): 10–27.
54. David K. Yelton, *Hitler's Home Guard: Volksstummann—Western Front* (Oxford: Osprey Publishing, 2006).
55. William L. Hitchcock, *The Bitter Road to Freedom: The Human Cost of Allied Victory in World War II Europe* (New York: The Free Press, 2009), 167, 250.
56. Hitchcock, *The Bitter Road to Freedom*, 160–161.
57. "By the Numbers: World-Wide Deaths," The National World War II Museum, https://www.nationalww2museum.org/students-teachers/student-resources/research-starters/research-starters-worldwide-deaths-world-war.html (accessed January 21, 2015).
58. Perry Wilson, *Peasant Women and Politics in Fascist Italy: The Massaie Rurali* (London and New York: Routledge, 2002), front matter, [n.p.], 171; Roger Absalom, "The Peasant Experience under Italian Fascism," in *The Oxford Handbook of Fascism*, ed. R. J. B. Bosworth (Oxford: Oxford University Press, 2009), 127–149.
59. Victoria De Grazia, *How Fascism Ruled Women, Italy, 1922–1945* (Berkley: University of California Press, 1992), 69–73, 166.
60. De Grazia, *How Fascism Ruled Women*, 166–200; Perry Wilson, "Women in Mussolini's Italy," in *The Oxford Handbook of Fascism*, ed. R. J. B. Bosworth (Oxford: Oxford University Press, 2009), 215–220.
61. David I. Kertzer, *The Pope and Mussolini: The Secret History of Pius XI and the Rise of Fascism in Europe* (New York: Random House, 2014), 178–179, 405; "*Pope and Mussolini* Tells the 'Secret History' of Fascism and the Church," Fresh Air—National Public Radio interview, January 27, 2014. http://www.npr.org/2014/01/27/265794658/pope-and-mussolini-tells-the-secret-history-of-fascism-and-the-church (accessed April 19, 2015).
62. Jane Slaughter, *Women and the Italian Resistance, 1943–1945* (Denver: Arden Press, 1997), 3.
63. Bosworth, *Mussolini's Italy*, 457; Alessandro Cavalli, "The Memory of Fascism and of the Anti-Fascist Resistance among Italian Youth," *European Review* 21 (2013): 501–506; "*Pope and Mussolini* Tells the 'Secret History' of Fascism and the Church," Fresh Air—National Public Radio interview, January 27, 2014. http://www.npr.org/2014/01/27/265794658/

pope-and-mussolini-tells-the-secret-history-of-fascism-and-the-church (accessed April 19, 2015).
64. Studs Terkel, *"The Good War": An Oral History of World War Two* (New York: Pantheon Books, 1984).

Bibliography

Barber, James, and Mark Harrison. *The Soviet Home Front 1941–1945: A Social and Economic History of the USSR in World War II*. London: Longman, 1991.
Bosworth, R. J. B. *Mussolini's Italy: Life Under the Fascist Dictatorship, 1915–1945*. New York: Penguin, 2006.
De Grazia, Victoria. *How Fascism Rule Women, Italy, 1922–1945*. Berkeley: University of California Press, 1992.
Gellately, Robert. *Backing Hitler: Consent and Coercion in Nazi Germany*. New York: Oxford University Press, 2001.
Hartley, Jenny, ed. *Hearts Undefeated: Women's Writing of the Second World War*. London: Virago Press, 1994.
Hartman, Susan. *The Home Front and Beyond: American Women in the 1940s*. Boston: Twayne, 1982.
Haruko, Taya Cook, and Theodore F. Cook. *Japan at War: An Oral History*. New York: New Press, 1992.
Havens, Thomas R. H. *Valley of Darkness: The Japanese People and World War II*. Lanham, MD: University Press of America, 1986.
Hinton, James. *Women, Social Leadership and the Second World War: Continuities of Class*. New York: Oxford University Press, 2002.
Kershaw, Ian. *"The Hitler Myth": Image and Reality in the Third Reich*. New York: Oxford University Press, 1987.
Koontz, Claudia. *Mothers in the Fatherland: Women, the Family and Nazi Politics*. New York: St. Martin's Press, 1987.
Lary, Diana. *The Chinese People at War: Human Suffering and Social Transformation, 1937–1945*. New York: Cambridge University, 2010.
Li, Danke. *Echoes of Chongqing: Women in Wartime China*. Urbana: University of Illinois Press, 2010.
Litoff, Judy Barrett, and David C. Smith. *Since You Went Away: World War II Letters from American Women on the Home Front*. New York: Oxford University Press, 1991.
Summerfield, Penny. *Women Workers in the Second World War: Continuities of Class*. New York: Routledge, 1989.
Tuttle, Jr., William M. *"Daddy's Gone to War": The Second World War in the Lives of America's Children*. New York: Oxford University Press, 1993.

CHAPTER 22

NEUTRAL POWERS IN A GLOBAL WAR

NEVILLE WYLIE

ONE of the many ways in which our understanding of World War II has changed in recent years has been the new sensitivity shown toward the experiences of neutral states and societies. The catalyst for this change was the campaign in the 1990s to recover the assets of concentration camp victims, which had been sold by the Nazis to neutral banks or salted away in neutral "safe havens."[1] Scholarly attention focused on the actions of neutral bankers, bureaucrats, and politicians who appeared to connive in Germany's despoliation of occupied Europe and subsequently obstructed the process of postwar restitution. The findings of this research have tended to foreground two aspects of wartime neutrality. On the one hand, they portrayed neutrality as a moral rather than merely a political choice. Although neutral politicians and officials explained neutrality as an act of political realism, they could not evade responsibility for the moral consequences of their actions. On the other hand, the new centrality of the Holocaust in our reading of neutrality inevitably emphasized the importance of the interactions between Nazi Germany and those neutrals—principally Switzerland and Sweden—best placed to alleviate the continent's suffering.

Our understanding of neutrality, and the war itself, has unquestionably been enriched by placing the neutrals in the spotlight, highlighting their response to the unfolding humanitarian tragedy, and exposing the role they played in Germany's overseas financial operations. At the same time however, the "normative" reading of neutrality has encouraged the rather parochial, European, outlook that had long marked scholarship on the subject and ignores the trend in historical writing that views the conflict as a global event.[2] This chapter seeks to recalibrate the debate. It does so by first broadening the geographical scope of analysis and addressing how neutral states faired outside Europe, as much as inside it. This approach leads to a depiction of neutrality as a global phenomenon and a purposeful political activity rather than simply a strategy of survival.[3] While the actions of the Allied and Axis powers were not morally equivalent, both were guilty of abusing neutral rights and undermining neutral sovereignty. Second, it directs our attention to those elements of neutrality that have been overlooked, or marginalized in recent writing, and in the process, reflects on the multiple ways in which the war impinged on neutral states and societies.

NEUTRALITY DURING THE PHONEY WAR

The importance of neutral states for the direction of the war reached its zenith during the so-called "Phoney War" (from the outbreak of war in September 1939 to the fall of France in June 1940), but it continued to affect the shape of the war until the winter of 1941–1942. During this period, the political choices of the European neutrals were dictated by the *absence* of great power patronage for any form of collective defense of neutral rights, and the persistence of local or regional political dynamics that remained in play despite the dramatic shifts in the balance of power brought about by the war. Of the two, it was the former, notably the behavior of the United States and the Soviet Union, that had the greatest impact on the neutrals' outlook. Both powers had historically championed neutral rights, but by 1939 neither was prepared to shoulder such responsibilities. In contrast to its Tsarist predecessors, who had sponsored "leagues of armed neutrality" in the eighteenth and nineteenth centuries, the Soviet regime refused to act as a counterweight to Nazi Germany or extend moral or political support to neutral states more generally. Indeed, as most states proclaiming neutrality in 1939 were opposed to Soviet ideological and political ambitions, Moscow's dramatic about face in the last days of peace, in concluding the Hitler–Stalin pact, essentially placed the Soviet Union in the position of malevolent neutrality, both with respect to the issues at stake in the war and the concept of neutrality itself. Its subsequent attack on Poland (September 17, 1939) and neutral Finland (November 30, 1939) only confirmed the long-held suspicions over Moscow's commitment to the political status quo; doubts which had, of course, already stymied western efforts to build a common front in defense of Czech, Romanian, and Polish independence before war broke out.[4]

Although it occupied a radically different political position, the United States proved to be equally non-committal toward European neutrality. Washington roundly condemned belligerent encroachments on its neutral trading and commercial interests, but its support for collective action in defense of neutrality was limited to the western hemisphere (it joined the Argentine Anti-War Pact of 1932). U.S. attitudes toward "neutrality" remained governed by a reading of its own national interests and "neutrality acts," and was little affected by any innate sympathy for or commitment to the broader rights claimed by the European neutrals. In the last resort, as Sumner Welles' mission to Europe in February 1940 demonstrated, Washington was too anxious to safeguard its own freedom of maneuver to risk aligning itself with any fledgling "neutral club" in Europe.[5]

Without great power patronage, the neutrals were left to ward off belligerent demands on their own. All indigenous attempts to promote a collective defense of neutral rights were stillborn. The Swedish government, mindful both of the delicacy of its own strategic position and the failure of the pre-war attempts to develop a regional collective bargaining position around the Oslo Pact, refused to offer the leadership necessary for a cohesive defense of the "northern" Scandinavian neutrals.[6] Rome briefly flirted with the idea of fostering a neutral "bloc" in southeastern Europe in early 1940, in the hope of containing German influence in the region, but it quickly abandoned the idea once it became clear that Italian interests were better served by cooperating with its northern neighbor, even in a region deemed to lie within Italy's "natural" sphere of influence.

What is striking about the conduct of neutral states in the first eighteen months of the war is the extent to which their policies were shaped by their own national agendas, and not solely by their reading of the unfolding conflict. Clearly, the invasion of seven neutral countries within a matter of months had a momentous impact on the political and strategic map of Europe. It could hardly do otherwise. But Russia's unprovoked attack on Finland, Germany's invasion of Denmark, Norway, Belgium, Holland, and Luxembourg, and Britain's "occupation" of Iceland were not viewed in quite the same heinous light as the Kaiser's violation of Belgian neutrality twenty-five years earlier.[7] While the law governing neutrality in wartime remained on the statute books, and a few states, such as Switzerland, professed to be guided by neutrality, the concept of neutrality had lost much of its force by 1939. Some western decision-makers felt genuine distaste in violating neutral rights, but governments of all hues showed little compunction in letting considerations of military necessity or convenience dictate policy.[8] So diminished had the status of neutrality come by 1939 that Italy (September 1939–June 1940) and Spain (June 1940–March 1942) dispensed with the term altogether, preferring instead to define themselves as "non-belligerents." Arguably, Finland (July 1941–May 1945) and Vichy France (June 1940–November 1942) adopted a similar position, even if they did not articulate it as such.[9]

Even those states declaring neutrality after 1939 were selective in their policies, and did not necessarily view it as the lodestar, guiding their foreign political relations or ambitions. The citizens of neutral states could afford to occupy very different positions toward the war than their belligerent counterparts. It was not uncommon for neutral observers to feel "neutral" toward, say, the Franco–British–German conflict, but distinctly partial toward Germany's "defence of European Christendom" after July 1941. Such views explain the attraction of service in Spain's Blue Division or the five Swiss Red Cross medical units that toured the eastern front administering aid to German wounded, but not their Soviet counterparts. It also explains the generosity shown to Goebbels's annual appeals for winter-clothing after December 1941. Here lay one of the neutrals' principal difficulties, for it was precisely their refusal to march to the belligerents' drumbeat that generated such friction in their relations with the belligerent powers. Winston Churchill's celebrated outburst against the neutrals on January 20, 1940 encapsulated the issue well. The derision provoked by Churchill's speech across neutral Europe reflected a natural aversion toward taking lessons from a largely discredited British politician, but it was also rooted in the belief that Churchill's concerns were simply not those of the rest of Europe.[10]

In retrospect, it is easy to fault neutral governments for failing to heed Churchill's warning and blithely "feeding the crocodile in the hope that it would eat them last."[11] But the agendas of European states were complex and could not be cast in shades of a single color. Belgian's decision to abandon its 1920 defense pact with Paris and "return" to "neutrality" in 1936 was not based on an ignorance of the potential menace posed by Nazi Germany, but was instead driven by the determinants of Belgium's national politics, and the looming danger of Flemish succession if the state's foreign-political alignment remained tied to the interests of the Francophone parties.[12] The dynamics in Scandinavia were different, but no less constraining. Here, for the most part, it was anxiety of Russia that framed the strategic calculus and shaped responses to the Anglo–German struggle. The fear was felt most acutely in Finland and Sweden, where the national elites had long viewed Germany as a vital bulwark to Russian influence.[13] Yet even in Norway, whose territory was not directly threatened by Soviet forces, Moscow's actions were a major determinant of national policy. The central paradox facing Norwegian policy makers lay in the fact that the force most likely to violate Norwegian neutrality—Britain's Royal Navy—was also the principal guarantor of Norwegian independence. Oslo was well aware of those in London who looked to the dispatch of an expeditionary force to Finland as a means of precipitating a "pre-emptive" occupation of the Norwegian iron ore fields. So, while the economic negotiations for Norway's war trade agreement with London may have been determined by Britain's blockade of Nazi Germany and its desire to secure access to Norway's merchant fleet, until the collapse of Finnish resistance in March 1940, the country's *strategic* position was determined by events further to the east. In the last resort, as the historian Patrick Salmon has observed, Norway's conundrum in 1939–1940 rested on the fact that the country had lost the strategic, economic, and political isolation that had previously kept it out of harm's way.[14]

The interplay of regional political undercurrents was even more pronounced in southeast Europe. Time and time again, the region's politicians strayed from the scripts handed down to them from the chancelleries in western and central Europe. In short, European geo-politics did not cohere with the region's political currents. Thus, while the collapse of Anglo–French military fortunes in the summer of 1940 undercut the position of western-leaning governments, opened the door to Italian belligerency in June 1940, and heightened German influence in Hungary, Romania, Bulgaria, and later Yugoslavia, it did not fundamentally change the nature of Balkan politics. Balkan maneuvering remained driven by the contest between those who had gained from the postwar territorial settlement, twenty years before, and those who had not. The European war merely recast the context within which regional politics were played out. Although external powers were intent on intervening in the region—Italy made its first military foray into the war by invading Greece in October 1940, and the British landed forces at Salonika to exploit Italian difficulties the following March—but it was ultimately the political instability of the region, and the danger this posed to German ambitions against Russia that prompted Berlin to dispense with its economic and political levers and use force to bring Balkan "neutrals" to heel in the spring of 1941.[15] Neither the declaration of war in September 1939 nor its opening campaigns were sufficiently transformative to eclipse the undercurrents of political life in Europe or alter the national interests of the neutral states.

Neutrality beyond Europe's Shores: The Case of Thailand

Given the centrality of the European neutrals to war's direction and tempo before the spring of 1941, scholars have rightly placed Europe center stage in historical research. But as the war became a global phenomenon over the course of 1941, so too did neutrality. The cases of Thailand, whose experience of neutrality throws up some interesting parallels with what was going on in Europe, and Brazil, whose actions as a neutral had a direct bearing on the fate of Spanish and Portuguese neutrality, are illustrative.

In many respects, the history of independent Thailand fitted the classic nineteenth-century European model of small, neutral states mediating tensions and rivalries of the Great Powers.[16] Perched between French Indochina to the east and Britain's colonial possessions to the south and west, Thailand functioned as a neutral buffer between the two European empires. Where it differed from the European case, though, was the extent to which levels of foreign interference not only co-existed with Thai neutrality but were in many respects an essential precondition for it. Although ostensibly independent, Thailand's ruling elite had become accustomed to operating within an environment of constrained sovereignty. Successive Thai monarchs not only hired the services of foreign advisers but over time oversaw the virtual submersion of Thai economic and financial interests into the British imperial system.[17] Foreigners' influence ensured that the major powers remained invested in the survival of an independent Thai state. The logic of Thailand's geo-political position, coupled with its economic dependency on British markets meant that when a series of coups ended monarchical government in 1932 and brought a military-backed government to power the following year, the new regime was careful to temper its nationalist rhetoric with a sober appreciation of the country's political and economic realities.

The conditioning of Thai leaders to operate within the context of constrained sovereignty goes some way to explaining the ease with which the country's leadership under Phibun Songkhram legitimized Thailand's claims to "independence" after Japanese forces entered the country on December 8, 1941. This was a conceptual model of neutrality that echoed the notion of "neo-neutrality" popularized by the influential Danish lawyer, Georg Cohn.[18] Where Cohn and Phibun's approaches diverged, however, was in the overarching influence exercised by Phibun's political ambitions and the manner in which these ambitions corroded the bases of neutrality. Although frequently labeled "pro-Japanese," Phibun might best be described as an opportunistic Thai nationalist. The change from "Siam" to "Thailand" in 1939 was emblematic of Phibun's wider goal of building an ethnically constituted Thai nation at home, and reconstituting Thai prestige abroad by "recovering" the territory "lost" to French Indochina, Malaya, and Burma.[19] As a consequence, his approach to neutrality had a distinctly "Balkan" flavor, with neutrality providing a framework in which Thailand could chart its own course between an expansionist Japan and the ailing European empires. The policy served Bangkok well in the twelve months after the summer of 1940, when Japanese support secured some of Thailand's territorial claims following an inconclusive border conflict with the French in Indochina. The price Tokyo exacted for such support was high; Phibun pledged Japan limited transit rights for its forces in southern Thailand in any subsequent operations against the British in Malaya and Singapore. But it is likely that at this stage, Phibun believed he could avoid repaying the debts. He certainly worked to this end by quietly encouraging British and American resolve in the face of Japanese expansion.

This policy began to unwind after the summer of 1941, as deteriorating U.S.–Japanese relations slowly closed down Thailand's room for autonmous action. With war looking increasingly imminent, Phibun publicly vowed to defend Thailand against all oncomers, but he worked feverishly with the Japanese military attaché in Bangkok to limit Japanese demands and restrict any Japanese military presence to the south of the country. By absenting himself from the capital on December 8, the Thai premier avoided having to answer Japan's ultimatum. The token resistance offered by Thai military units in the face of Japanese landings in the south provided, as Bruce Reynolds has observed, a "face-saving show of resistance" sufficient to keep Phibun's options open, should Japanese forces suffer a reverse at British hands.[20] It was only the swift collapse of western resistance that convinced Phibun to sign an alliance with Japan on December 21, 1941.

Phibun's subsequent declaration of war against Britain and the United States, on January 25, 1942 effectively brought Thailand's formal neutrality to an end.[21] Given the path the war took in Asia, it is likely that some political accommodation with Japan was inevitable, irrespective of the political complexion of the government in Bangkok.[22] The Japanese authorities showed scant regard for Thai interests and little sympathy with the concept neutrality in a conflict pitting "Asia" against "Europe." Nevertheless, it would be wrong to see the demise of Thai neutrality as preordained. The agreement to turn southern Thailand into a staging post for Japan's attack on Malaya arose from Phibun's determination to capitalize on French difficulties and press Thailand's claim over its former satellites in Laos and Cambodia. The Japanese–Thai alliance included a secret clause in which Phibun pledged assistance to Tokyo in return for Japanese support for Bangkok's territorial revisionism. Thailand's contribution to Japanese operations in Burma from May 1942, was likewise prompted by Phibun's determination to extend Thai control over Burmese territory. It was one of the many ironies of Phibun's premiership that not only did Tokyo refuse to acquiesce to the permanent annexation of Burmese territory—leaving Bangkok with only temporary administrative responsibility for its "new" territories—but the fighting brought Thai troops into conflict with elements of the Chinese Nationalist expeditionary force, and thereby added Nationalist China to Thailand's list of enemies. In short, Thailand did not begrudgingly abandon neutrality to ingratiate itself with the new regional hegemon. It discarded its neutrality in pursuit of a Thai supremacist agenda that ultimately proved incompatible with the political intentions of its new imperial masters in Tokyo. This was not so much a matter of "feeding the crocodile" but rather of donning the crocodile's clothes and joining in the feeding frenzy.

Global Connections: The Trans-Atlantic "Zone of Neutrality"

To understand Brazil's experience of neutrality, and its significance for the wider conflict, it is necessary to place Brazil within what might be usefully termed a trans-Atlantic "zone of neutrality," stretching from the shores of Latin America to the peaks of the Pyrenees. The importance of the eastern end of this zone—the Iberian Peninsula—has long been recognized. Indeed, in its quest to keep Spain neutral and German troops out of the peninsula, Britain was involved in nothing less than a struggle for its own survival.[23] Had Spain thrown in its lot with the Axis at any point in the twelve months after France's fall, British belligerency would have been seriously compromised. Its position in North Africa and the eastern Mediterranean would have unraveled, and its ability to draw succor from the Americas and its Empire in Asia, India, and southern Africa, gravely impaired.[24] Before turning to Brazil, therefore, it is important to consider the state of neutrality in Spain and Portugal.

Like Phibun, Spain's Francesco Franco had some outstanding debts to repay at the start of the war. Germany and Italy had invested blood and treasure in the nationalists' victory in the Spanish civil war by March 1939. Ideologically, there was a strong affinity to the fascist regimes too, particularly after Germany's attack on the Soviet Union assuaged Spanish qualms over Hitler's "ungodly" pact with Stalin and brutal subjugation of Catholic Poland. Historians continue to argue over the depth of Franco's commitment to the Axis, with some applauding him for deftly steering Spain out of Hitler's clutches by always setting the price for Spanish belligerency beyond Hitler's grasp, and others depicting the Caudillo as a frustrated expansionist and convinced ideologue, who only abandoned the dream of committing Spain to the war in the final months of the conflict.[25]

In contrast to Phibun's Thailand, circumstances never quite conspired to tip the balance of advantage decisively in favor of belligerency. With Spain's economy ravaged by the civil war, Franco had to look outside Europe for the food and raw materials necessary to stave off famine and coax Spanish industries back into life. Nowhere did the British play their economic cards quite as well as they did in Spain, where a mixture of blockade concessions and outright bribery kept the Spanish on a tight leash.[26] Even if Spanish belligerency was genuinely on offer in the wake of Germany's victories in the summer of 1940, the fact remains that for Hitler, a prostrate France had more to offer than an impoverished Spain and its inscrutable dictator.

The Führer came away from meetings with the French premier Marshall Pétain on October 22 and October 24, 1940 convinced that German interests were best served by maintaining the benevolent neutrality of Vichy's possessions in North Africa. By contrast, his discussions with Franco on October 23 were inconclusive. Not only did the two men not hit it off, but the potential benefits of bringing Spain into the war—blocking British access to the Mediterranean and threatening its sea routes across the Atlantic—came to look meager in comparison with the cost of meeting Spain's exorbitant economic demands, and courting Vichy enmity by agreeing to Spanish territorial designs in North Africa.

In many respects, Spain demonstrated the inherent elasticity of neutrality. Franco's closeness to the Axis bloc stretched the concept of "benevolent" neutrality to its limits. Spain was rightly regarded by the British as a "semi-hostile" state. In a speech on July 17, 1941, Franco talked of Hitler's war against Russia as, "the battle for which Europe and Christianity have so many years longed", and where "the blood of [Spanish] youth [would] mingle with that of our Axis comrades as an expression of firm solidarity."[27] Until September 1942, when the pro-Axis foreign minister Ramón Serrano Suner was finally replaced by General Juan Luis Beigbeder y Atienza and the term "nonbelligerency" dropped from official pronouncements in favor of "neutrality," Spain's conduct was firmly aligned with the interests of the Axis powers. German and Italian U-boats refueled and replenished their provisions in Spanish ports; Axis commercial interests were promoted and protected from British countermeasures. As late as November 1943, Franco willfully undermined Allied attempts to lock Germany out of the Spanish wolfram market, by injecting funds into the Spanish–German clearing account. Most dramatically of all, some 18,500 Spaniards joined the Blue Division to fight alongside their German comrades on the Russian front.[28]

Spain's concessions to the Axis were scarcely reciprocated in its relations with the Allies, but its support for the Axis was carefully calibrated. Far from being the harbinger of war, the dispatch of the Blue Division helped Franco appease the ideological zealots in the *falange* without committing Spain to full belligerency.[29] The majority of Spain's contributions to the Axis remained confined to the shadows, while its outward displays of pro-Axis sympathy took "acceptable" forms, such as the rapturous welcome shown to wounded German prisoners-of-war who passed through Barcelona as part of an Anglo–German exchange agreement in November 1943.

Finally, it is important to recognize that Franco was by no means the master of Spain's destiny. At home he was constrained by the need to mediate between the competing interests of his domestic backers (the *falange*, church and monarchy) while tackling the residual Republican "threat" in Spain and abroad. However much he might have admired Germany's military triumphs and yearned to capitalize on the opportunities these created, in the last resort, his country was in no position to embark on the path of war. Most studies on Britain's bribery of Spanish generals conclude that the money was probably ill-spent, as few officers genuinely relished the prospects of Spain entering the war.[30] There was, in short, a considerable degree of inertia in Spain that acted as a break on Franco's ambitions and restricted his policy options.

This was a situation that was discretely encouraged by Spain's neighbor, Portugal. Although the corporatist, authoritarian *Estado Novo* regime of Antonio Salazar enjoyed close political, cultural, and security relations with the Third Reich, Portugal's strategic interest clearly lay in keeping the Iberian Peninsula at peace. Portuguese neutrality might conceivably have survived Spain's entry into the war, but this was never a foregone conclusion and came to look even less certain after the neutral dominoes fell in quick succession in the Balkans over the spring of 1941. With a treaty of alliance with Britain dating back to 1373 and a colonial empire whose existence depended on its access to international sea-lanes, there were powerful reasons for Portugal to remain aloof from the conflict. Salazar's problem, however, lay in the fact that the key to the peninsula's future ultimately rested in Madrid. Lisbon had little influence over the course of events, while anyone turning up in Madrid preaching moderation was unlikely to receive a receptive audience. Salazar nevertheless moved quickly to strengthen Portuguese standing, updating the friendship and non-aggression pact of March 17, 1939 with an additional protocol on July 29, 1940 and tasking his ambassador in Madrid, Teotónio Pereira, to champion the cause of regional stability and autonomy. Pereira proved particularly effective in working across a broad spectrum of Spanish elite opinion and quietly mediating between the British embassy and the local authorities.[31] Although careful to distinguish Portugal's interests from those of Spain, there was sufficient common ground between the two for Lisbon to act as an informal shock-absorber for Anglo–Spanish relations, especially on economic and financial matters.[32]

The decisive issue for both Iberian governments, though, was not the ideological preferences of their leaders or the constraints imposed by their economic conditions, but the extent to which the peninsula figured in the belligerents' strategic calculations. The postponement of Hitler's invasion plans for the United Kingdom on September 17, 1940, and the consequent decision to starve Britain into submission had the effect of shifting the focus of Anglo–German relations from the skies above southern England to the Atlantic sea-lanes. The battle of the Atlantic was, as Churchill freely acknowledged, the one battle Britain could not afford to lose, and this naturally colored British willingness to pander Spanish and Portuguese sensitivities over their neutrality. As Britain's only deep-water port between England and West Africa capable of accommodating capital ships, the fate of Gibraltar was of paramount importance to the security of Britain's re-supply routes. Ensuring against its possible loss, by negotiating access to the Spanish and Portuguese Atlantic islands, or taking them by force, became a key element in British military planning after the summer of 1940. Thus, while the danger of German units crossing the Pyrenees remained a live issue—German operational planning for military operations against Gibraltar continued until May 1941—the most immediate threat to Iberian neutrality following the fall of France actually came from the Allies. Britain held forces in reserve to occupy the Spanish and Portuguese Atlantic islands throughout this period, only dispersing them in February 1942.[33]

While it is tempting to assume that any action against Spanish territory would lead inexorably to Spain's entry into the war, we should be wary of leaping too hastily to this conclusion. There are sufficient examples of states retaining their neutrality in such circumstances to give us pause for thought. Much, of course, would depend on the particular circumstances at the time, but in truth, the value of belligerency for Spain progressively declined over the second half of 1940 and into 1941, despite Franco's bellicose outbursts in support of Germany in July 1941. We should not discount the possibility of Franco reacting to an Allied seizure of the Canary Islands by claiming *force majeure* and limiting his retaliation to measures short of war. Although the Portuguese were always more committed to neutrality than their Spanish neighbors, it is significant that when Salazar was finally persuaded to grant the Allies' access to bases in the Azores islands in October 1943, he insisted that Portuguese neutrality remained intact. Even internally, Salazar framed his decision in terms of Portuguese neutrality, conjuring up the rather artful distinction between "slight" neutrality, as practiced in the Azores, and "greater" neutrality, which continued to govern policy on the mainland.[34]

Any evaluation of the strategic significance of the Spanish and Portuguese Atlantic archipelagos needs to be set within the context of the wider Atlantic theater, and events happening at the "western" edge of the trans-Atlantic zone of neutrality. Although Brazilian neutrality ostensibly lasted until August 1942, when a series of attacks on Brazilian merchant vessels led President Getulio Vargas to declare war on Germany, Brazil had already abandoned "strict" or impartial neutrality earlier that year when it severed diplomatic relations with the Axis in January and joined U.S. naval and air operations against German U-boat and blockade runners over the spring. The key issue shaping Brazilian neutrality, however, concerned the use of the air and port facilities in Brazil's north-east by the U.S. Pressure on Brazil mounted over 1940–1941 as Washington sought to strengthen hemispheric security in light of German military successes in western Europe. A secret agreement with PanAm saw the U.S. develop a string of airfields linking Miami with Brazil in late 1940; the following April, Brazil agreed to open two of its ports to U.S. warships. Over the first half of 1941, Washington worked on Vargas to have him agree to an Airport Development Programme, capable of expanding facilities in the north-east of the country to a level sufficient to deal with the burgeoning volume of air traffic to and from West Africa. Quite apart from the political implications of locking Brazil into America's regional security architecture, the ferrying of aircraft and material across north-east Brazil obliged Vargas to turn a blind eye to the use of Brazilian airspace and facilities for the benefit of one belligerent camp. More problematic, however, was Washington's request to allow the stationing of American troops on Brazilian soil to protect the bases from German attack. American concerns about the vulnerability of the "Brazilian bulge" had steadily mounted over the second half of 1941, and it became increasingly acute after its entry into the war, amidst fears that Hitler might react to his setback in Russia by redirecting German forces toward Iberia, Northwest Africa, and, ultimately, Latin America.

The way U.S.–Brazilian relations developed over this period helps situate Brazil within a broader reading of neutrality and non-belligerency. The stationing of U.S. troops in Brazil sits in a spectrum of belligerent relations with the neutral camp on military issues, ranging from the German–Swedish agreement of July 8, 1940 governing the transit of (unarmed) German troops across Swedish territory, to Salazar's agreement in

August 1943 granting the Allies' access to the Azores islands and Philbun's brief, and ultimately unsuccessful, attempt to square protestations of neutrality with the Japan's use of southern Thailand for its attack on Malaya. The protracted U.S.–Brazilian negotiations over the deployment of U.S. troops followed a path that would have been recognizable to neutral diplomats in Europe, with Brazilian negotiators seeking to extract maximum economic advantages and security guarantees, while avoiding any action that might justify Washington imposing a solution on its own terms, undermining Brazilian sovereignty and slighting its national pride.[35] In retrospect, Brazilian "neutrality" over 1941 reflected the position occupied by Europe's "non-belligerents"—Nationalist Spain and Vichy France—both of whom faced a strategic landscape that set strict limits on their field of action, regardless of the political ambitions of their leaders. Their fates were also intertwined, the decisions of one, affecting the policy options of the other. Vargas' concessions to Anglo–American security concerns in northeast Brazil essentially left London free to indulge Iberian neutrality and play the long-game in its negotiations over base-rights in the Azores.[36]

Neutrality in Total War

Brazil offers a good point of departure for exploring three additional angles in which the experience of neutral states bisected with the global conflict. The first involves the neutrals' place in war's cultural battleground. Even before the arrival of U.S. servicemen in northeast Brazil, Brazil had felt itself drawn into the orbit of an increasingly bullish U.S. cultural offensive directed at its near neighbors across Latin America.[37] How neutral states responded to the belligerents' cultural activities varied enormously, as did the level of sophistication shown by the belligerents in tailoring their "message" to neutral audiences. Within Europe at least, neutral societies appear to have withstood the tide of cultural propaganda fairly well, even if the authorities resorted to draconian censorship regulations to achieve this end.[38] Indeed, for all the grim forebodings of political and social dislocation that punctuated debate in the 1920s and 1930s, the social fabric of neutral states survived the war remarkably well. The Swiss were particularly stoic in this respect: Germany found its products and cultural events regularly boycotted by their cousins south of the Rhine, while in early 1941, the BBC was obliged to suspend its "Swiss" radio service after it became clear that the multilingual Swiss audience were affronted at the thought that they might be incapable of understanding the BBC's other language services. Edward Corse's study of the British Council underlines the difficulty such institutions had in striking the right chord in its cultural programs in neutral Europe. It was only through trial and error that it discovered that the Spanish would visit philatelic exhibitions in droves but that Swedes preferred lectures by English poets.[39] While more research is needed on the subject, it would appear that in competing for the neutral ear, the belligerents' propaganda activities acted as a major stimulus to the neutrals' own cultural nationalism and state-sponsored efforts to forge a cultural narrative around the policy of neutrality. This was not achieved with equal success, nor pursued with the equal vigor across the neutral world, but there is little doubt that for Switzerland, Ireland, and Sweden, and in rather different ways, Spain and Portugal, the countries' cultural experience during the war had a marked effect on their post war political trajectories.

The second area where Brazil, in common with the other neutral states, found itself in competition with the belligerents concerned the issues of domestic security and intelligence gathering. The large and commercially powerful *Auslandsdeutsche* community in Brazil was a cause for concern for anxious onlookers in Washington. Fortunately, although founding of the *Estado Novo* in November 1937 introduced many fascist trappings to Brazilian politics, any ideological symmetry with European fascism was skin-deep. The banning of foreign political organizations in 1938 substantially curtailed German political influence and its capacity to mobilize its supporters. Close surveillance of German cultural and commercial organizations allowed Brazilian security forces to identify and ultimately neutralize Axis intelligence networks by the spring of 1942.[40] With his mind set on hammering Brazil's colors to the Allied mast, Vargas had good reason to target these networks. Other neutral governments took a more nuanced stand on the affairs of the "secret world" and viewed the provision of intelligence gathering facilities as part of their broader relations with the belligerent powers.[41] There is ample evidence to suggest that as long as their own interests were not endangered by the activities of foreign intelligence organizations, most neutral governments were prepared to condone their presence and extract political and other advantage in return. This was clearly evident in Anglo–Swiss relations, where Berne traded access to intelligence facilities for concessions in Britain's blockade.[42] That these activities largely took place in the shadows meant that neutral governments had a degree of flexibility and freedom not found in other policy areas. The Irish and Turkish security services were clearly comfortable entertaining relations with the belligerents that went considerably beyond the limits set by their country's policy of neutrality.[43] In this area at least, neutral conduct was far from marginal to the outcome of hostilities.

Historians have probably written more on the neutrals' economic relations than any other subject. Early studies based their conclusions largely on the official trade statistics and tended to focus on either the strategic significance of this trade to the belligerents' war economies (principally Norwegian iron ore, Swedish steel and ball-bearings, Turkish chrome, Portuguese and Spanish wolfram, etc.) or on the neutrals' efforts to tailor their economic relations to changes in the broader military balance. Recent research has added nuance to these debates, but also exposed a picture of economic relations that is far more complex and multifaceted than was once assumed.[44] External trade was important, not least as it provided an easily identifiable indicator and reflected a century of thought and legislation on the role of neutrals in trade wars. But, in total war, the neutrals' economic significance extended beyond just trade receipts. Ireland's principal economic contribution to the British war economy took the form of Irish laborers working in the British Isles, not the output of its industries. Cross-border labor flows occupied an important element in the economic relations of other neutrals as well.[45]

The neutrals' financial activities have attracted particular attention, with some scholars suggesting that the Swiss were complicit in sustaining the German war machine in the final years of the war by keeping open credit lines to Berlin.[46] While Swiss banks occupied a significant place in overseas financial affairs, their insurance companies participated actively in the domestic German insurance market, especially the German War Insurance Association. Different mechanisms were at work in Switzerland's relations with the other camp. The slump in exports to Britain after June 1940 was largely off-set by Britain's secret purchases in the Swiss watchmaking and engineering sector and in the payments for "invisibles" (royalties, agency expenses, insurance premiums, and commissions). Far from being shut out of the Swiss market, by early 1943, Britain's annual expenditure on the Swiss account (£9.42m) exceeded its receipts (£1.9m) by a factor of nearly four.[47] In short, our understanding of neutral economic relations during the war has gone beyond a reading of crude trade statistics. In illuminating the breadth of neutral engagement with the belligerents' economic and financial needs, recent scholarship has gone a long way to explaining why the major powers were so often frustrated when they sought to translate their strategic or economic strength into political gains.[48]

The attention devoted to examining how the Nazis' commercial and financial interests developed outside the Reich has led to a deeper understanding of the Allied countermeasures, the "safe haven" program, and of the different national approaches to economic warfare.[49] What has become apparent is that the neutrals' resistance to Allied demands at the war's close was not simply a question of shamelessly protecting their business interests in the Reich. Instead, it was founded on a particular and traditional view of neutrality that gave neutrals not only the right, but also the duty to remain impartial in their relations with the warring factions. More than any other belligerent, the United States government came to judge this reading of neutrality as an anathema; morally and politically reprehensible in a war fought on behalf of democracy and freedom. Not everyone in the Allied camp shared Washington's zeal. Officials in London were clearly more disposed toward recognizing neutral rights and acknowledging their historical role within the European state system. Neutral governments were also suspicious of the motives behind Allied demands. The neutrals had long objected to the Allied "black listing" of neutral firms, not just as an assault on their economic sovereignty but out of fear that it was merely a screen to further Allied commercial interests. The demand for access to Nazi bank details in the closing months of the war was held in the same light. This was an aspect of Allied policy that was readily apparent to neutrals lying outside Europe, especially in Latin America, where Washington's campaign to deport Axis nationals quickly shifted from a "notion of removing subversive Germans [to] an unsentimental drive to commandeer market share from the Germans who remained."[50] To many neutral officials, then, Allied economic demands seemed to mask crude, capitalist, self-interest that made a mockery of their lofty political and moral claims.

Conclusion

A number of conclusions can be drawn by placing neutrality within a broader analytical and geographical framework. First, the exercise reminds us that the concept of neutrality was challenged from all sides over the course of the war. True, more neutral states succumbed to invasion from the Axis than from the Allies; but to those states anxious to remain outside the conflict, the demands made on them by the two sides could look and feel surprisingly similar. It is worth recalling that more lives were lost resisting the Anglo–Soviet invasion of neutral Iran in August 1941 than were lost defending Denmark from the *Wehrmacht* in April 1940 or resisting Japanese landings in southern Thailand in December 1941. And while historians typically describe British actions in Iceland after May 10, 1940 as an "occupation," Reykjavik had no hesitation in condemning the landings as an invasion, and vigorously protesting at the "flagrant violation" of Icelandic neutrality.[51] World War II was ultimately fought for noble ends—the images disgorged from Hitler's death camps left this in no doubt, as did the fates of former neutrals forced to live under Axis occupation. But for most of the war, neutral officials did not view events through a moral prism. They were, instead, entirely preoccupied with conducting the "nimble, if occasionally, unheroic diplomacy" required to protect their country's territorial integrity, economic sovereignty, and social fabric from the corrosive effects of global war.[52]

Second, while neutrals and belligerents alike talked in terms of neutral "credibility," in reality, the fate of neutral states had little to do with their perceived "credibility." Their interaction with the belligerents was too complex, too multifaceted, and too opaque for the concept of credibility to have any value beyond that of a rhetorical device. How, for instance, were belligerents to judge the credibility of Swiss neutrality: by its political institutions, the balance of its external trade, the public utterances of its politicians, or its strategic position as guardian of the Alpine passes? The experience of neutrals outside Europe should prompt us to avoid drawing too fine a distinction between "neutrality" and "non-belligerency." The status of non-belligerency was not unique to Germany's "fellow-travellers" in Rome, Madrid, Vichy, or Helsinki, but could equally be applied to neutrals such as Brazil or Thailand, who traversed a period of non-belligerency before entering the war. Moreover, as studies of the neutrals' place in the secret world suggest, neutrality did not prevent states from pursuing distinctly un-neutral policies. Neutrality could and did mean different things for different states; opening and closing opportunities, depending on the particular national context. Paul Moeyes arresting comparison of Dutch and Swiss neutrality after 1914 makes this point very well. Both states walked a tight-rope, but for the Dutch, neutrality was the tight-rope itself; one wrong move and Holland would tumble into the abyss of a world war. In contrast, for the Swiss, "neutrality was the safety net they could always fall back on; in the secure knowledge that it was there, they were less fearful and more robustly independent in finding their way to the other side." It was the very acceptance of Swiss neutrality that justified the "apparent carelessness with which the Swiss authorities ... indulged in un-neutral actions during the war years."[53]

Finally, by acknowledging the multiple ways in which neutrals engaged with the war, we can begin to see the neutrals as part of the war itself, and not just as bystanders. As the historian Maartje Abbenhuis rightly notes, neutrality "rarely correlates to a basic dichotomy between 'those at war' and 'those not at war' or those 'unwilling or unable to go to war.'"[54] Neutrality, as we have seen, was a defining feature of the Atlantic battle space. While in the northern Atlantic, Icelandic neutrality was ultimately deemed incompatible with British security, in the south, the battle of the Atlantic was fought out in what amounted to, for a time at least, a zone of neutrality stretching from the Iberian Peninsula, through the Spanish and Portuguese islands, to the northeast of Brazil. A similar note can be struck elsewhere: Sweden's experience of war was not solely set by its neutrality but was shaped by its position amongst the Scandinavian and Nordic countries. Neutral states then, while never entirely master of their own destinies, were nevertheless autonomous actors, whose actions influenced not just those around them but arguably, the wider direction of the war.

Notes

1. See Stuart Eizenstat, *Imperfect Justice: Looted Assets, Slave Labor, and the Unfinished Business of World War II* (New York: Public Affairs, 2004); Philippe Braillard, *Switzerland and the Crisis of Dormant Assets and Nazi Gold* (Abingdon: Routledge, 2014).
2. See, *inter alia*, Evan Mawdesley's *World War II: A New History* (Cambridge: Cambridge University Press, 2009).
3. In doing so it reflects writing on neutrality in other periods: Sandra Bott, Jussi M. Hanhimaki, Janick Schaufelbuehl, Marco Wyss, eds., *Neutrality and Neutralism in the Global Cold War* (Abingdon: Routledge, 2016). Leos Müller, Neutrality in World History (Abingdon: Routledge, 2019).
4. Zara Steiner, *The Triumph of the Dark: European International History, 1933–1939* (Oxford: Oxford University Press, 2011), esp. 359–413; Neville Wylie, "The Neutrals," in *The Origins of World War Two: The Debate Continues*, ed. Joseph Maiolo and Robert Boyce (Basingstoke: Palgrave, 2003), 176–189.
5. Jürg Martin Gabriel, *The American Conception of Neutrality after 1941*, 2nd ed. (Basingstoke: Palgrave, 2002), 36–41.
6. See Ger van Roon, *Small States in Years of Depression: The Oslo Alliance, 1930–1940* (Assen: Van Gorcum, 1989).
7. For the latter, see Isabel Hull, *A Scrap of Paper: Breaking and Making International Law during the Great War* (New York: Cornell University Press, 2014), chapter 2.
8. See Patrick Salmon, "British Attitudes towards Neutrality in the Twentieth Century," in *Neutrality in History*, ed. Jukka Nevakivi (Helsinki: SHS, 1993), 117–132; Christian Leitz, *Nazi Germany and Neutral Europe during the Second World War* (Manchester: Manchester University Press, 2001).
9. See essays in Neville Wylie, ed., *European Neutrals and Non-belligerents during the Second World War* (Cambridge: Cambridge University Press, 2001); Henrik O. Lunde, *Finland's War*

of Choice: The Troubled Finnish–German Coalition in World War II (Newbury: Casemate, 2011); Olli Vehviläinen, *Finland in the Second World War* (Basingstoke: Palgrave, 2002).
10. Patrick Salmon, "Norway," in *European Neutrals and Non-Belligerents*, ed. Neville Wylie (Cambridge: Cambridge University Press, 2001), 66; Johan Ostling, "The Rise and Fall of Small-State Realism," in *Nordic Narratives of the Second World War. National Historiographies Revisited*, ed. Henrik Stenius, Mirja Osterberg, and Johan Ostling (Lund: Nordic Academic Press, 2011), 127–148.
11. Winston S. Churchill, Radio address, January 20, 1940; Martin Gilbert, ed., *Winston S. Churchill: The Finest Hour* (London: Heinemann, 1983), 12–64, 301–307.
12. See Alain Colignon, "Belgium: Fragile Neutrality, Solid Neutralism," in *European Neutrals and Non-Belligerents*, ed. Neville Wylie (Cambridge: Cambridge University Press, 2001), 97–115.
13. See John Gilmour, *Sweden, the Swastika and Stalin: The Swedish Experience in the Second World War* (Edinburgh: Edinburgh University Press, 2010).
14. Patrick Salmon, *Scandinavia and the Great Powers* (Cambridge: Cambridge University Press, 1997), 317–355.
15. See Sheila Lawlor, "Greece, March 1941: The Politics of British Military Intervention," *The Historical Journal* 25, no. 4 (1982): 933–46.
16. See Maartje Abbenhuis, *An Age of Neutrals. Great Power Politics, 1815–1914* (Cambridge: Cambridge University Press, 2014).
17. By the early twentieth century, thirty-seven percent of Thai imports were drawn from British Empire sources, seventy percent of its rice crop was exported to British Malaya, and its entire currency reserve was held as sterling balances in London. Richard Aldrich, *The Key to the South. Britain, the United States and Thailand during the Approach to the Pacific War, 1929–1942* (Oxford: Oxford University Press, 1993), 7, 12.
18. G. Cohn, *Neo-Neutrality* (New York: Columbia University Press, 1939).
19. See, in general, Suwannathat-Pian Kobkua, *Thailand's Durable Premier: Phibun through Three Decades, 1932–57* (Kuala Lumpur: Oxford University Press, 1995), and E. Bruce Reynolds, "Phibun Songkhram and Thai Nationalism in the Fascist Era," *European Journal of East Asian Studies* 3, no. 1 (2004): 99–134.
20. E. Bruce Reynolds, "Anomaly or Model? Independent Thailand's Role in Japan's Asian Strategy, 1941–1943," in *The Japanese Wartime Empire, 1931–1945*, ed. Peter Duus, Ramon H. Myers, and Mark Peattie (Princeton: Princeton University Press, 2010), 243–272.
21. Discussion over sovereignty, independence, and autonomy did not end. Within a year of signing the alliance, tensions boiled over in anti-Japanese riots. Japan's grip on Phibun tightened, but Thailand used its treaty relationship with Tokyo to avoid the fate that befell the former European colonies, in succumbing to direct Japanese control, or Japan's puppet regimes in Manchukuo and occupied China.
22. See, in general, E. Bruce Reynolds, *Thailand and Japan's Southern Advance, 1940–1945* (New York: St Martin's Press, 1994).
23. Denis Smyth, *Diplomacy and the Strategy of Survival. British Policy and Franco's Spain, 1940–1941* (Cambridge: Cambridge University Press, 1986).
24. See, for example, Denis Smyth, "Franco and the Allies in the Second World War," in *Spain and the Great Powers in the Twentieth Century*, ed. Sebastian Balfour and Paul Preston (London: Routledge, 1999), 188–189.
25. See, *inter alia*, Paul Preston, *Franco* (London: Fontana, 1995) and David Wingeate Pike, *Franco and the Axis Stigma* (Basingstoke: Palgrave, 2008).

26. W. N. Medlicott, *The Economic Blockade*, Vol. 1 (London: HMSO, 1952), 509–548; W. N. Medlicott, *The Economic Blockade*, Vol. 2 (London: HMSO, 1959), 282–313.
27. Quoted Smyth, *Diplomacy and Strategy of Survival*, 230.
28. Paul Preston, "Franco and the Axis Temptation," in *The Politics of Revenge: Fascism and Military in Twentieth Century Spain*, ed. Paul Preston (London: Routledge 1995), 51–84; Juan José Díaz Benítez, "The Italian Naval War in the Mid-Atlantic: Blockade Runners and Submarines in the Canary Islands (1940–1943)," *The Mariner's Mirror* 1000, no. 2 (2014): 186–197.
29. Denis Smyth, "The Dispatch of the Spanish Blue Division to the Eastern Front: Reasons and Repercussions," *European History Quarterly* 24, no. 4 (1994): 537–553; Juan José Díaz Benítez, "The Spanish Support for the Third Reich in the Second World War: New Considerations about the *Etappenorganisation*," *The International Journal of Maritime History* 28, no. 3 (2016): 513–531.
30. David J. Dunthorn, *Britain and the Spanish Anti-Franco Opposition* (Basingstoke: Palgrave, 2000), 11–44.
31. See Samuel Hoare, *Ambassador on Special Mission* (London: Collins, 1946), 45.
32. Glyn Stone, *Spain, Portugal and the Great Powers, 1931–1941* (Abingdon: Palgrave, 2005).
33. Plans for sabotage continued though: see Marta Garcia Cabrera, "Operation Warden: British sabotage planning in the Canary Islands during the Second World War," *Intelligence and National Security* 35, no. 2 (2020): 252-268.
34. See Filipe Ribeiro De Meneses, *Salazar: A Political Biography* (London: Enigma, 2010), 275–288. Winston Churchill insisted that the deal did "nothing" to affect Portugal's "continued desire…, to continue their policy of neutrality on the European mainland and thus maintain a zone of peace in the Iberian Peninsula." *Hansard Parliamentary Debates, House of Commons* 392 (October 12, 1943): 717–718.
35. Joseph Smith, *Brazil and the United States: Convergence and Divergence* (Athens: University of Georgia Press, 2010).
36. For an assessment of how operational planning for Brazil and Azores overlapped, see Stetson Conn and Byron Fairchild, *The Framework of Hemisphere Defense* (Washington: Center of Military History, 1989/1960), 116–129.
37. For the activities of the U.S. Coordinator for Inter-American Affairs, see Antonia Pedro Tota, *The Seduction of Brazil: The Americanisation of Brazil during World War II* (Austin: University of Texas Press, 2009); Thomas C. Mills, "Mobilising the Americans for War: Jefferson Caffery in Brazil, 1937–1944," in *Diplomats at War: the American Experience*, ed. J. Simon Rofe and Andrew Stewart (Dortrecht: Republic of Letters, 2013), 27–45.
38. Interestingly, censorship in Ireland was particularly severe. See Robert Cole, *Propaganda, Censorship and Irish Neutrality in the Second World War* (Edinburgh: Edinburgh University Press, 2006); Clair Wills, *The Neutral Island. A Cultural History of Ireland During the Second World War* (London: Faber & Faber, 2014); Donal Ó. Drisceoil, *Censorship in Ireland 1939–1945: Neutrality, Politics and Society* (Cork: Cork University Press, 1996).
39. Edward Corse, *The Battle for Neutral Europe: British Cultural Propaganda during the Second World War* (London: Bloomsbury, 2012), 118, 183.

40. Stanley E. Hilton, *Hitler's Secret War in South America, 1939-1945: German Military Espionage and Allied Counter-Espionage in Brazil* (Baton Rouge: Louisiana State University Press, 1981), 4, passim.
41. See Neville Wylie and Marco Wyss, "Guardians of the 'Whispering Gallery'? Switzerland, Neutrality and the Clandestine War," in *Neutral Countries as Clandestine Battlegrounds, 1939-1968*, ed. André Gerolymatos and Denis Smyth (Lanham: Lexington, 2020), 135–152.
42. Neville Wylie, *Britain, Switzerland and the Second World War* (Oxford: Oxford University Press, 2003), 266–299.
43. See Eunan O'Halpin, "Small States and Big Secrets: Understanding Sigint Cooperation between Unequal Powers during the Second World War," *Intelligence & National Security* 17, no. 3 (2002): 1–16; Eunan O'Halpin, *Spying on Ireland: British Intelligence and Irish Neutrality during the Second World War* (Oxford: Oxford University Press, 2010); Paul McMahon, *British Spies and Irish Rebels. British Intelligence and Ireland, 1916-1945* (London: Boydell Press, 2011); Egemen Bezci, "Ankara. Rabbit-Warren of Spies," in *Neutral Countries as Clandestine Battlegrounds, 1939-1968*, ed. André Gerolymatos and Denis Smyth (Lanham: Lexington, 2020), 193–208.
44. See, for example, Eric Golson, "Did Swedish Ball Bearings Keep the Second World War Going? Re-evaluating Neutral Sweden's role," *Scandinavian Economic History Review* 60, no. 2 (2012): 165–182, and, in general, Neville Wylie, "Life in Pluto's Cave: Neutral Europe in the Second World War," in *A Companion to World War II*, ed. Thomas W. Zeiler and Daniel M. Dubois (New York: Wiley-Blackwell, 2012), 603–617.
45. Eric Golson, "Spanish Civilian Labour for Germany," *Revista de Historia Económica* 31, no. 1 (2013): 145–170; Eric Golson, "Swiss High Skilled Labour for Germany during the Second World War," *Revue Suisse d'histoire* 64, no. 1 (2014): 16–44.
46. Stuart E Eizenstat, ed., *U.S. and Allied Efforts To Recover and Restore Gold and Other Assets Stolen or Hidden by Germany During World War II. Preliminary Report* (Washington, 1997).
47. Treasury Memo. "Sterling Area Balance of Payments with Switzerland, April 1942–March 1943," Statistics Office, "Estimated Payments to Switzerland for "Invisibles," March 19, 1943. Bank of England Archive. London. OV6.270.
48. Michael Handel, *Weak States in the International System*, 2nd ed. (Abingdon: Routledge, 1990), 259.
49. See David A. Messenger, *Hunting Nazis in Franco's Spain* (Baton Rouge: Louisiana State University Press, 2014).
50. Max Paul Friedman, *Nazis & Good Neighbors. The US campaign against the Germans of Latin America in World War II* (Cambridge: Cambridge University Press, 2003), 4–5.
51. See Donald F. Bittner, *The Lion and the White Falcon: Britain and Iceland in the World War II Era* (Hamden, CT: Archon, 1983).
52. John Gilmour and Jill Stephenson, eds., *Hitler's Scandinavian Legacy* (London: Bloomsbury, 2013), 7.
53. P. Moeyes, "Neutral Tones: The Netherlands and Switzerland and Their Interpretations of Neutrality, 1914-1918," in *Small Powers in the Age of Total War 1900-1940*, ed. Herman Amersfoort and Wim Klinkert (Leiden: Brill, 2011), 84.
54. Maartje Abbenhuis, "Not Silent Nor Silenced: Neutrality and the First World War," in *Shaping Neutrality throughout the First World War*, ed. José-Leonardo Ruiz Sánchez, Inmaculada Coredo Olivero, and Carolina García Sanz (Seville: Editorial Universidad de Sevilla, 2016), 20.

Bibliography

Abbenhuis, Maartje. *An Age of Neutrals: Great Power Politics, 1815–1914*. Cambridge: Cambridge University Press, 2014.

Abbenhuis, Maartje. "Not Silent nor Silenced: Neutrality and the First World War." In *Shaping Neutrality throughout the First World War*, edited by José-Leonardo Ruiz Sánchez, Inmaculada Coredo Olivero, and Carolina García Sanz, 17–36. Seville: Editorial Universidad de Sevilla, 2016.

Aldrich, Richard. *The Key to the South. Britain, the United States and Thailand during the Approach to the Pacific War, 1929–1942*. Oxford: Oxford University Press, 1993.

Benitez, Juan José Díaz. "The Italian Naval War in the Mid-Atlantic: Blockade Runners and Submarines in the Canary Islands (1940–1943)." *The Mariner's Mirror* 1000, no. 2 (2014): 186–197.

Benitez, Juan José Díaz. "The Spanish Support for the Third Reich in the Second World War: New Considerations about the *Etappenorganisation*." *The International Journal of Maritime History* 28, no. 3 (2016): 513–531.

Bezci, Egemen. "Ankara. Rabbit-Warren of Spies." In *Neutral Countries as Clandestine Battlegrounds, 1939–1968*, edited by André Gerolymatos and Denis Smyth, 193–208. Lanham: Lexington, 2020.

Bittner, Donald F. *The Lion and the White Falcon: Britain and Iceland in the World War II era*. Hamden, CT: Archon, 1983.

Bott, Sandra, Jussi M. Hanhimaki, Janick Schaufelbuehl, and Marco Wyss, eds. *Neutrality and Neutralism in the Global Cold War*. Abingdon: Routledge, 2016.

Braillard, Philippe. *Switzerland and the Crisis of Dormant Assets and Nazi Gold*. Abingdon: Routledge, 2014.

Cohn, Georg. *Neo-Neutrality*. New York: Columbia University Press, 1939.

Cole, Robert. *Propaganda, Censorship and Irish Neutrality in the Second World War*. Edinburgh: Edinburgh University Press, 2006.

Colignon, Alain. "Belgium: Fragile Neutrality, Solid Neutralism." In *European Neutrals and Non-belligerents during the Second World War*, edited by Neville Wylie, 97–115. Cambridge: Cambridge University Press, 2001.

Corse, Edward. *The Battle for Neutral Europe. British Cultural Propaganda during the Second World War*. London: Bloomsbury, 2014.

Drisceoil, Donal O. *Censorship in Ireland 1939–1945: Neutrality, Politics and Society*. Cork: Cork University Press, 1996.

Dunthorn, David J. *Britain and the Spanish Anti-Franco Opposition*. Basingstoke: Palgrave, 2000.

Eizenstat, Stuart E. *Imperfect Justice: Looted Assets, Slave Labor, and the Unfinished Business of World War II*. New York: Public Affairs, 2004.

Eizenstat, Stuart E., ed. *U.S. and Allied Efforts to Recover and Restore Gold and Other Assets Stolen or Hidden by Germany During World War II. Preliminary Report*. Washington, 1997.

Fairchild, Conn, and Bryon Fairchild. *The Framework of Hemisphere Defense*. Washington: Center of Military History, 1989. (Originally published in 1960).

Friedman, Max Paul. *Nazis & Good Neighbors: The US campaign against the Germans of Latin America in World War II*. Cambridge: Cambridge University Press, 2003.

Gabriel, Jürg Martin. *The American Conception of Neutrality after 1941*. 2nd ed. Basingstoke: Palgrave, 2002.

Garcia Cabrera, Marta, "Operation Warden: British sabotage planning in the Canary Islands during the Second World War," *Intelligence and National Security* 35, no. 2 (2020): 252-268

Gilbert, Gilbert, ed. *Winston S. Churchill: The Finest Hour*. London: Heinemann, 1983.

Gilmour, John. *Sweden, the Swastika and Stalin: The Swedish Experience in the Second World War*. Edinburgh: Edinburgh University Press, 2010.

Gilmour, John, and Jill Stephenson, eds. *Hitler's Scandinavian Legacy*. London: Bloomsbury, 2013.

Golson, Eric. "Did Swedish Ball Bearings Keep the Second World War Going? Re-evaluating Neutral Sweden's Role." *Scandinavian Economic History Review* 60, no. 2 (2012): 165–182.

Golson, Eric. "Spanish Civilian Labour for Germany." *Revista de Historia Económica* 31, no. 1 (2013): 145–170.

Golson, Eric. "Swiss High Skilled Labour for Germany during the Second World War." *Revue Suisse d'histoire* 64, no. 1 (2014): 16–44.

Handel, Michael. *Weak States in the International System*. 2nd ed. Abingdon: Routledge, 1990.

Hilton, Stanley E. *Hitler's Secret War in South America, 1939–1945: German Military Espionage and Allied Counter-Espionage in Brazil*. Baton Rouge: Louisiana State University Press, 1981.

Hoare, Samuel. *Ambassador on Special Mission*. London: Collins, 1946.

Hull, Isabel. *A Scrap of Paper: Breaking and Making International Law during the Great War*. New York: Cornell University Press, 2014.

Lawlor, Shelia. "Greece, March 1941: The Politics of British Military Intervention." *The Historical Journal* 25, no. 4 (1982): 933–946.

Leitz, Christian. *Nazi Germany and Neutral Europe during the Second World War*. Manchester: Manchester University Press, 2001.

Lunde, Henrik O. *Finland's War of Choice. The Troubled Finnish–German Coalition in World War II*. Newbury: Casemate, 2011.

Mawdesley, Evan. *World War II: A New History*. Cambridge: Cambridge University Press, 2009.

McMahon, Paul. *British Spies and Irish Rebels: British Intelligence and Ireland, 1916–1945*. London: Boydell Press, 2011.

Medlicott, W. N. *The Economic Blockade*. 2 vols. London: HMSO, 1952, 1959.

Messenger, David A. *Hunting Nazis in Franco's Spain*. Baton Rouge: Louisiana State University Press, 2014.

Mills, Thomas C. "Mobilising the Americans for War: Jefferson Caffery in Brazil, 1937–1944." In *Diplomats at War: the American Experience*, edited by J. Simon Rofe and Andrew Stewart, 27–45. Dordrecht: Republic of Letters, 2013.

Moeyes, Paul. "Neutral Tones. The Netherlands and Switzerland and Their Interpretations of Neutrality, 1914–1918." In *Small Powers in the Age of Total War 1900–1940*, edited by Herman Amersfoort and Wim Klinkert, 57–84. Leiden: Brill, 2011.

Müller, Leos, *Neutrality in History*. Abingdon: Routledge, 2019.

O'Halpin, Eunan. "Small States and Big Secrets: Understanding Sigint Cooperation between Unequal Powers during the Second World War." *Intelligence & National Security* 17, no. 3 (2002): 1–16.

O'Halpin, Eunan. *Spying on Ireland: British Intelligence and Irish Neutrality during the Second World War*. Oxford: Oxford University Press, 2010.

Ostling, Johan. "The Rise and Fall of Small-State Realism." In *Nordic Narratives of the Second World War: National Historiographies Revisited*, edited by Henrik Stenius, Mirja Osterberg, and Johan Ostling, 127–148. Lund: Nordic Academic Press, 2011.

Preston, Paul. *Franco*. London: Fontana, 1995.

Preston, Paul. "Franco and the Axis Temptation." In *The Politics of Revenge: Fascism and Military in Twentieth Century Spain*, edited by Paul Preston, 51–84. London: Routledge 1995.

Pike, David Wingeate. *Franco and the Axis Stigma*. Basingstoke: Palgrave, 2008.

Reginbogin, Herbert R. *Faces of Neutrality*. Berlin: Lit Verlag, 2009.

Reynolds, E. Bruce. "Anomaly or Model? Independent Thailand's Role in Japan's Asian Strategy, 1941–1943." In *The Japanese Wartime Empire, 1931–1945*, edited by Peter Duus, Ramon H. Myers, and Mark Peattie, 243–272. Princeton: Princeton University Press, 2010.

Reynolds, E. Bruce. "Phibun Songkhram and Thai Nationalism in the Fascist Era." *European Journal of East Asian Studies* 3, no. 1 (2004): 99–134.

Reynolds, E. Bruce. *Thailand and Japan's Southern Advance, 1940–1945*. New York: St Martin's Press, 1994.

Salmon, Patrick. "British Attitudes towards Neutrality in the Twentieth Century." In *Neutrality in History*, edited by Jukka Nevakivi, 117–132. Helsinki: SHS, 1993.

Salmon, Patrick. "Norway." In *European Neutrals and Non-belligerents during the Second World War*, edited by Neville Wylie, 53–74. Cambridge: Cambridge University Press, 2001.

Salmon, Patrick. *Scandinavia and the Great Powers*. Cambridge: Cambridge University Press, 1997.

Smith, Joseph. *Brazil and the United States: Convergence and Divergence*. Athens: University of Georgia Press, 2010.

Smyth, Denis. *Diplomacy and the Strategy of Survival. British Policy and Franco's Spain, 1940–1941*. Cambridge: Cambridge University Press, 1986.

Smyth, Denis. "The Dispatch of the Spanish Blue Division to the Eastern Front: Reasons and Repercussions." *European History Quarterly* 24, no. 4 (1994): 537–553.

Smyth, Denis. "Franco and the Allies in the Second World War." In *Spain and the Great Powers in the Twentieth Century*, edited by Sebastian Balfour and Paul Preston. London: Routledge, 1999.

Steiner, Zara. *The Triumph of the Dark: European International History, 1933–1939*. Oxford: Oxford University Press, 2011.

Stone, Glyn. *Spain, Portugal and the Great Powers, 1931–1941*. Abingdon: Palgrave, 2005.

Suwannathat-Pian, Kobkua. *Thailand's Durable Premier: Phibun through Three Decades, 1932–57*. Kuala Lumpur: Oxford University Press, 1995.

Tota, Antonio Pedro. *The Seduction of Brazil: The Americanisation of Brazil during World War II*. Austin: University of Texas Press, 2009.

van Roon, Ger. *Small States in Years of Depression: The Oslo Alliance, 1930–1940*. Assen: Van Gorcum, 1989.

Vehviläinen, Olli. *Finland in the Second World War*. Basingstoke: Palgrave, 2002.

Wills, Clair. *The Neutral Island. A Cultural History of Ireland During the Second World War*. London: Faber & Faber, 2014.

Wylie, Neville. *Britain, Switzerland and the Second World War*. Oxford: Oxford University Press, 2003.

Wylie, Neville. "Life in Pluto's Cave: Neutral Europe in the Second World War." In *A Companion to World War II*, edited by Thomas W. Zeiler and Daniel M. Dubois, 603–617. New York: Wiley-Blackwell, 2012.

Wylie, Neville. "The Neutrals." In *The Origins of World War Two: The Debate Continues*, edited by Joseph Maiolo and Robert Boyce, 176–189. Basingstoke: Palgrave, 2003.

Wylie, Neville, ed. *European Neutrals and Non-belligerents during the Second World War.* Cambridge: Cambridge University Press, 2001.

Neville Wylie, and Marco Wyss. "Guardians of the 'Whispering Gallery'? Switzerland, Neutrality and the Clandestine War." In *Neutral Countries as Clandestine Battlegrounds, 1939–1968*, edited by André Gerolymatos and Denis Smyth, 135–152. Lanham: Lexington, 2020.

CHAPTER 23

WESTERN RELIGIOUS LEADERS, COMMUNITIES, AND ORGANIZATIONS BEFORE AND DURING WORLD WAR II

VICTORIA J. BARNETT

IN the western world, the actions of religious leaders, communities, and international organizations between 1939 and 1945 were shaped both by the aftermath of World War I and by political and cultural developments of the late nineteenth and early twentieth centuries. Post-Enlightenment trends toward modernity and secularization and the repercussions of the Industrial Revolution had altered the social standing and authority of religious leaders and their institutions throughout Europe. Church leaders believed they were under fire, threatened by new social and political movements that jeopardized their standing and influence. After 1918, they were alarmed by the rise of Communism and new ethnonationalist and fascist movements across Europe, especially those that became aligned with factions within the different Christian traditions. Within western Protestantism there were growing divisions between liberal theologians who embraced new interpretations of tradition and doctrine, and orthodox and fundamentalist theologians who viewed such developments (and modernity itself) as a threat to "Christian culture."

Among European and North American Jews, the emancipation laws of the eighteenth and nineteenth centuries had led to greater assimilation and integration in the political, cultural, and economic spheres. A related religious development was the emergence of Conservative and Reform Jewish traditions.[1] Especially in western Europe, some Jews embraced secularization. Nonetheless, Orthodox Jewish communities and culture continued to flourish, particularly in eastern Europe. Despite the greater possibilities open to them as a result of the emancipation laws, however, Jews throughout Europe continued to experience antisemitism, discrimination, and violence. One response was the Zionist movement, which emerged in the late nineteenth century and offered a new model for a transnational Jewish identity that could unify Jews everywhere.[2]

In Asia, Africa, and Latin America, nineteenth-century European and North American missionaries became actively involved in colonialist processes; such missionary activity often led to the suppression and marginalization of indigenous religions. The processes of conversion and Christianization in many colonized countries created elite Christian minorities among the local population, leading to new social classes and divisions. As anti-colonial movements began to emerge in the early twentieth century, some of the newer Christian churches that had been established by missionaries came under fire because of their alignment with colonial powers. These mission churches were often an amalgamation, incorporating traditions and cultural attitudes of indigenous religious traditions, including localized patterns of relationship to political authority, with western religious understandings and practices.

There was also an expanding network of religiously affiliated international organizations, primarily but not only within world Christianity. The international missionary movement did a great deal to forge international connections between the nations. In 1910, the World Missionary Conference in Edinburgh drew around twelve hundred delegates from around the world. Jews were not engaged in missionary activity, but international Jewish organizations were founded during the same era, and European and U.S. Jewish leaders became quite engaged in humanitarian and refugee issues. The U.S. Jewish Joint Distribution Committee was founded in 1914, but by the 1920s it had an active network of staff across Europe who worked with Jewish refugees across Europe who had fled the pogroms in the east. The World Jewish Congress was founded in 1936 in direct response to the events unfolding in Nazi Germany and had its central offices in Geneva.

By the early twentieth century, these international networks had become transnational organizations, convening representatives of different churches and in some cases different faiths. By the late nineteenth century, active interreligious relationships among Jews, Catholics, and Protestants were forming, primarily in the United States. During the 1920s, the "tolerance movement" in the U.S. united Jews and Christians in fighting prejudice against religious and racial minorities, leading to the founding of the National Conference of Christians and Jews in 1928. On the international front, the first meeting of the World Parliament of Religions, held in Chicago in 1893, drew around five thousand delegates from around the world representing the ten major world religions.

The Protestant ecumenical movement also emerged as a significant way for representatives of mainline Protestant churches to work together diplomatically and politically; internationally it would play a crucial role during World War II. In the United States, the Federal Council of Churches, representing the thirty-three largest Protestant denominations, was formally constituted in 1908. In Europe, ecumenism began to spread rapidly in the wake of World War I, propelled by the widespread commitment of church leaders in the different European nations to work cooperatively for peace.

The founding meetings of the European ecumenical movement were the 1925 Universal Christian Conference on Life and Work, convened in Stockholm, followed in 1927 by the World Conference on Faith and Order in Lausanne, Switzerland. During the 1930s these two conferences merged to become the World Council of Churches in Process of Formation, which had its offices in Geneva and eventually became the World Council of Churches in 1948. A related development in the wake of World War I was the founding of an internationalist pacifist organization, the International Fellowship of Reconciliation, which, while not formally affiliated with a specific religion, drew members primarily from Protestant churches and the "peace churches," such as the Quakers and Mennonites.

In the Roman Catholic world, the 1929 Lateran Treaties between the Holy See and the state of Italy established Vatican City as an independent state under the sovereignty of the Holy See. As the central authority for world Catholicism, the Vatican increasingly saw its task not only as providing moral authority over matters of church doctrine but representing the Catholic church in a turbulent political world in which the church, from its perspective, was all too often under attack. Particularly in Italy, the Vatican became a political player. This new phase of Vatican leadership was decisively shaped by Eugenio Pacelli, who served as apostolic nuncio to Germany from 1917 to 1930 and became Pope Pius XII in 1939. Coming from a family with a long history of service to the papacy, Pacelli understood himself as a diplomat and viewed his primary obligation as pope to be the guidance and preservation of the church in perilous times.

By the 1920s, then, there was an international network of religious leaders and organizations, and a growing sense among European and North American religious leaders that they held not only moral authority over their flocks but a larger global political responsibility. The agendas of most of these groups, even those dedicated to fostering international understanding among all peoples, were firmly western and Christian in their self-understanding, values, and leadership. The same was true of the early ecumenical networks in Asia, most of which had been founded by western missionaries. Although the five thousand participants in the 1893 World Parliament of Religions represented a genuine mix of different religions from all over the world, for example, its roster of speakers was seventy-three percent Christian. A growing number of representatives who attended ecumenical meetings came from Asia, the Middle East, Africa, and Latin America, but they were Christians from churches established by missionaries.

There was a backlash against these trends and developments, however, manifested in political instability, nationalism, and anti-colonialism. Although the colonial era would not end until after 1945, resistance against western Christian missionaries intensified in the early twentieth century, in conjunction with new anti-colonial movements and in some cases as the result of localized conflicts. The Japanese defeat of Russia in 1904 shocked western and eastern nations alike, and it generated new nationalist movements, some religiously aligned, in parts of Asia,. During the Japanese occupation of Korea, for example, Koreans were forced to become Shinto (a tradition in Japan) and the National

Christian Council of Korea (founded in 1904 by missionaries) was dissolved and forcibly merged with the Japanese National Christian Council, with preferential treatment given to mission churches willing to cooperate with Shinto leaders.[3]

Because most of the international religious networks of the early twentieth century were Christian and had historically close relations to colonial governments, modernization, and nation-building, anti-colonial movements were often tied to religious and pro-nationalist issues. This was especially true in the British Mandate of Palestine, where a primary goal of the Arab nationalist movement was a region that would be unified through Islam. Amin al-Husseini, the Arab nationalist who became Mufti of Jerusalem in 1921, viewed the fight against the British state and the Zionist movement as one battle, a position that subsequently led to his active support for Adolf Hitler during World War II.

Such developments were on the agenda of many early ecumenical conferences. Ecumenical leaders viewed their role not just as representatives of western Christianity but as mediators. In North Africa, Palestine, and Turkey, for example, where Islam was the majority religion, ecumenical leaders tried to forge new ties between Muslim leaders and the minority Eastern Orthodox and Coptic churches, as well as between the different Christian churches themselves.[4] The World Student Christian Federation (WSCF), founded in 1895 by the American missionary and ecumenist John Mott, began quite early to reach across interreligious lines, particularly in China, India, Burma, the Philippines, Japan, Ceylon, and Java. One of the organization's first mediation efforts was the 1895 Pacific Area Conference in California, where WSCF leaders invited religious representatives from China and Japan to discuss the Sino–Japanese conflict.

In Europe, the ecumenical and interreligious movements were vehemently opposed by the Roman Catholic Church and the Orthodox churches, both of which rejected ecumenism as doctrinally unsound. Catholic leaders, in particular, feared that interreligious work and ecumenism would open the door to syncretism and "indifferentism" (the view that all religions as equally valid, condemned as a heresy in the 1832 papal encyclical *Mirari Vos*, "On Liberalism and Religious Indifferentism"). There was backlash against ecumenism even within Protestantism itself, particularly in the United States, where, by the 1920s, an upsurge of religious fundamentalism led to strong tensions between mainline Protestants and the growing number of evangelical and fundamentalist churches.

In the aftermath of World War I, European Catholic and Protestant leaders were especially concerned about the newly uncertain political landscape for institutional churches. The Russian revolution—which had led to closings and desecrations of churches, and arrests and executions of clergy through Russia—sparked intensified fears about the spread of Communism. The Vatican and Catholic leaders throughout the world aligned with Franco during the Spanish Civil War of 1936–1939 to fight the anti-clerical Popular Front. In Europe, the backlash against modernity, accompanied by rising nationalist resentments, led to the rise of new nationalist and fascist movements, many of which used religious language or combined forms of religious traditionalism and orthodoxy with ethno-centric and nationalist ideologies. These groups also tended to be explicitly antisemitic, like the Protestant "German Christians" (*Deutsche Christen*) in Germany and the Legion of the Archangel Michael (known as the "Iron Guard" and aligned with the Orthodox Church) in Romania, both founded during the 1920s. In Italy, the Fascist movement, although anti-clerical, found support and eventually a cautious rapprochement with the Vatican, which hoped for a new church–state relationship that would combat Communism and restore the Church's influence.

The religious landscape was also shifting in China and Japan. In both countries, Christians remained the minority; moreover, because Christian communities had been founded there by a very diverse and wide variety of missionary enterprises from different countries and at different times, there was no unified "church" in either country. In China, Christians and religious groups in general came under attack in the 1920s, with a brief period of calm during the 1930s until Japan invaded China in 1937.[5] After the late nineteenth century, the Shinto tradition in Japan became characterized by reverence for collective notions of race, culture, nation, and state, as embodied by the Emperor and his family.[6] Shinto also increasingly marked a clear dividing line against the influence of western churches, thereby undergirding a new sense of nationalism.

Throughout the world, then, the early twentieth century was marked by a growing sacralization of collective national, ethnic, or political identities. Many of the newer political and ideological movements identified with a religious tradition. In Europe there was an additional factor: the fusion of traditional Christian antisemitism with the new ethno-nationalist religions. Throughout European history, the Jewish minority had suffered discrimination and persecution as a minority within a self-defined Christian culture. Traditional Christian teachings that blamed Jews collectively for the death of Christ and viewed conversion to Christianity as the necessary antidote to Jewish suffering had shaped attitudes and laws on both sides of the Atlantic. Although the changes brought about by the emancipation laws and increased assimilation seemed to have ushered in a new era, these sociopolitical developments had not led to the eradication of antisemitism, nor had they led churches to confront the theological antisemitism that remained firmly embedded in Catholic, Protestant, and Orthodox theologies, doctrines, and liturgies. In the United States, the interfaith movement involved only a minority of religious leaders, and it focused quite deliberately on uniting the different faiths around common social issues, not challenging anti-Jewish theological teachings. Only after 1945, in the wake of the Holocaust, did a serious internal process begin within different Christian churches that confronted the theological underpinnings of antisemitism and led churches to officially repudiate these teachings.

Once the Nazis came to power in Germany, the implications of this theological reality were international in scope and affected all Christians, both Protestant and Catholic. Antisemitism in Europe was not confined to extremist ethno-religious groups like the "German Christians" or the Iron Guard. While most Protestant and Catholic church leaders condemned these extremist groups for their ideological and racialized versions of Christianity, they continued to preach and defend theological antisemitism as part of Christian teachings.

The largest church in Germany in 1933 was the German Protestant Church; two-thirds of the German population were members of this church. There was widespread enthusiasm within the German Protestant Church when Adolf Hitler came to power, and prominent church leaders and theologians defended the anti-Jewish legislation. A minority of clergy in both the German Catholic and Protestant churches even became Nazi Party members. While Catholic and Protestant leaders worried about possible regime interference in church governance and institutions, they confined their concerns about Nazi anti-Jewish policies to the effects on church members who, because of Jewish ancestry, were considered legally "non-Aryan."

The leadership style that quickly emerged in German churches in response to Nazism ranged from cautious accommodation to open support. Although there were individual clergy and lay members who spoke out or resisted the Nazi regime, the only organized countermovement that arose was the Confessing Church in the German Protestant Church, which emerged initially as a movement in defense of "non-Aryan" clergy and in opposition to the "German Christian" attempts to nazify the German Protestant Church. Even the Confessing Church, however, had members who supported some aspects of National Socialism, although there was a more radical wing of the Confessing Church that gradually became more outspoken against regime measures.

During the 1930s, this pattern of cautious accommodation was shared by many church leaders outside Nazi Germany, particularly in the Vatican and among Protestant leaders whose churches had formal ties to German churches. In July 1933 the Vatican signed a concordat with Nazi regime leaders, hoping that this would permit Catholic churches in Germany to retain institutional independence, including governance over Catholic schools. As Nazi measures against regime opponents intensified, the Vatican's concern was about measures that threatened or restricted the church's existence and message. In framing its objections to Nazism, particularly in the 1937 papal encyclical *Mit brennender Sorge* ("With burning concern"), the Vatican emphasized the "anti-Christian" and "materialistic" nature of Nazism.

Within the German Protestant Church there was a bitter fight during the 1930s (the so-called Church Struggle) between the "German Christians," the Confessing Church, and "neutral" leaders for control of church governance and theological education. The Nazi regime dealt swiftly with church opponents who ventured beyond the boundaries of purely church interests and became critical of state policies. There was a mass arrest of Protestant clergy in Prussia in 1935 following a pulpit proclamation criticizing the state, for example, and the regime reacted strongly to the publication of a critical 1936 memorandum that Confessing Church leaders had sent to Hitler by arresting several of those involved and murdering one of them.[7]

Most Protestant church leaders abroad sought to retain ties to all three factions in the German Protestant Church, avoiding any statements or stands that might antagonize the regime and lead to repercussions for Christians in Germany. In addition to the German Protestant Church, there were smaller "free" Protestant churches in Germany, including Baptists and Methodists. Both these churches also included strong supporters of the new regime, which led to caution among their international colleagues, although at the 1934 International World Baptist Congress, which was held in Berlin, some of the North American representatives condemned the Nazi racial ideologies and anti-Jewish laws.

The responses of international ecumenical and interfaith organizations were much clearer than those of denominations abroad (e.g., U.S. Lutheran churches) and included early condemnations of Nazi anti-Jewish measures. The September 1933 ecumenical conference in Sofia, Bulgaria, passed a resolution condemning the Nazi racial laws, and ecumenical leaders in New York and London wrote their German Protestant Church counterparts to complain about anti-Jewish violence. In the United States, an interfaith refugee committee was formed in 1934 by Jewish, Catholic, and Protestant leaders. Interfaith clergy coalitions organized protest rallies in 1933 and supported boycotts of German goods in 1933 and a boycott of the Berlin Olympics in 1936. The November 1938 "*Kristallnacht*" pogroms in Germany and Austria drew vehement reactions from church leaders, particularly in the United States, where several national radio broadcasts included statements from leading Catholic bishops, as well as Catholic and Protestant clergy, and strong condemnations from European ecumenical leaders.

Such outspoken responses however were the exception. During the 1930s most Americans were concerned about the economic depression and had little interest in international engagement. Antisemitism was widespread, as were anti-immigration sentiments. Between 1933 and 1939, the number of antisemitic hate groups in the United States, many of them expressing open solidarity with Nazi Germany, grew dramatically. Jewish organizations in the United States feared that even their friends in the interfaith movement failed to understand the gravity of the situation in Europe and its implications for the United States. American Jews were deeply divided about how best to draw attention to what was happening in Europe without provoking greater antisemitism in the United States. Membership in the Zionist Organization of America reached its lowest point in 1931, but that would change dramatically in the fifteen years that followed. During the 1930s, the most active Jewish organization internationally was the Joint Distribution Committee, which became very active in refugee and humanitarian work and played a significant role after 1939.

While the focus of Jews everywhere was on the events unfolding in Nazi Germany, western church leaders and ecumenical circles were concerned about a variety of issues that included but were not confined to the situation in Nazi Germany. The international Protestant movements, as well as the Vatican, tended to lump together all the extremist movements—fascism, nationalism, Communism, and National Socialism—as "political religions" that seemed to be "anti-Christian" and above all threatened to bring about another European war. This was the lens through which they saw events in Nazi Germany. In 1938 the Danish ecumenist Hal Koch responded to developments in Russia, Germany, and Japan with a warning that "worldwide religion is becoming national, and nationalism assumes a religious character."[8] Reverend Everett Clinchy, the president of the National Conference of Christians and Jews in the United States, wrote in a 1935 pamphlet titled *Collective Lunacies* that, "if organized religion is to make a contribution to the solution of the problems that face the world order it must itself resist the intrusion of the tribal lunacies that obsess a large fraction of humanity today and keep itself free from the corrupting influences which everywhere about it are provoking war among the nations."[9]

As World War II began in 1939, there were international Catholic, Protestant, Jewish, and interreligious networks in place with several decades of experience in engaging on issues of common concern. These networks viewed the emergence of nationalist movements and their ethno-centric religious allies as a serious threat to world peace. At the same time, denominational Protestant and Catholic church leaders feared that their actions could have repercussions for Christians in Germany. Everywhere, there were religious lines of demarcation and alliances based not only upon doctrine and theology but on institutional interests and larger agendas. For many church leaders the overriding concern was about the effect that another European war would have on Christians everywhere and after 1941, there were similar worries about the future of Christians in Asia. In September 1939, then, international Christian leaders were focused more on their own constituencies than the plight of European Jews. In contrast, the situation had just become more threatening for Jews everywhere.

1939–1945

After the war began there were new restrictions in Nazi Germany on church publications and religious education, but in general the focus on the war effort meant less attention from Catholics and Protestants to the church–state tensions of the 1930s. Leaders of both churches offered unified support for the soldiers and the Fatherland. There was widespread conscription of Protestant clergy (and many enlisted). A provision of the 1933 concordat had exempted various categories of Catholic clergy from military conscription, but during the war some Catholic clergy and theological students were nonetheless called up.

The primary Nazi state measure during this period that provoked opposition from the German churches was the T-4 program (the "euthanasia" measures) that began in October 1939. The T-4 program, under which institutionalized patients with genetic, mental, or emotional disabilities were murdered, directly affected Catholic and Protestant institutions where many of the affected patients lived. Although leaders of both churches were opposed to and horrified by the measures, they followed the same approach they had tried throughout the 1930s, refusing to protest publicly and trying to work behind the scenes to stop the measures by contacting regime officials. Only after Bishop von Galen, the Catholic bishop of Münster, spoke out publicly in August 1941 was the program officially ended (although it continued behind the scenes); by 1941 approximately 250,000 patients had been murdered. The other Nazi state measure that confronted German churches was the September 1941 law that ordered all Jews, including people of Jewish descent who were Christians, to wear the yellow star; the first deportations of German Jews, including Christian "non-Aryans," followed in October

1941. In both churches, support for their "non-Aryan" members had always been ambivalent and minimal; by the beginning of the war, it was nonexistent. Five of the Protestant regional churches had already set up separate congregations for their "non-Aryan" members in 1939; following the September 1941 order, some churches barred people with stars from entering.

On the international front, the Vatican, Protestant churches, and the Protestant ecumenical movement had desperately hoped to prevent another European war. In 1939, as it became clear that Germany was moving toward war, there had been a flurry of exchanges between the Vatican and ecumenical leaders in Geneva and London about a possible joint Catholic–Protestant call for peace, facilitated by Cardinal Arthur Hinsley in England. Once war began, these church leaders were focused on stopping it. In the fall of 1939, the Vatican was contacted directly by a circle from within the German military opposition seeking a peace agreement with Great Britain. The opposition offered to overthrow the regime in exchange for British guarantees of a negotiated peace. This led to a protracted series of negotiations called the "Vatican exchanges" throughout 1940; after these conversations ended there were other attempts through 1943, with ongoing contacts between representatives of different German resistance circles and the Vatican, as well as with ecumenical leaders in Geneva and Anglican leaders in Great Britain. Some of the German resistance figures who were involved in these peace feelers had connections to the Confessing Church (notably Dietrich Bonhoeffer) or the German Catholic underground in Germany (notably the Bavarian Catholic lawyer Josef Mueller, who was an old friend of Eugenio Pacelli). In the absence of a successful coup, and given Nazi Germany's rapid and aggressive expansion, Allied leaders were dubious about the sincerity and viability of the peace feelers, and they viewed the engagement of international church leaders in these diplomatic efforts as naive. The Allied policy of "unconditional surrender" declared at the 1943 Casablanca conference, as well as the 1943 arrests of several of the key German resistance figures involved, including Bonhoeffer and Mueller, put an end to these attempts.

In the United States there was intense debate particularly in Protestant churches between isolationists who opposed U.S. involvement in the European war and interventionists who believed that U.S. involvement in the fight against Nazism was inevitable, a debate that was finally resolved by the Japanese attack on Pearl Harbor and the Axis declaration of war on the U.S. in 1941. Nonetheless some religious leaders remained outspoken about the morality and justification of tactics like the massive bombing of cities. Such debates were more pointed in Great Britain. After the extended German bombing of Britain in 1940, there were a few voices in the Anglican Church, notably that of Bishop George Bell of Chichester, who condemned the bombings of German cities, urging Allied leaders to draw a distinction between the German people and their leaders. Given the German bombings of British cities, it was an unpopular opinion that probably prevented Bell from being named to a higher post. Most of the Anglican leadership, including Archbishop of Canterbury Cosmo Lang (who served until 1942) and his successor William Temple, viewed the war on Germany as a just war that had to be won.

In the United States, Reform Rabbi Stephen Wise, the most prominent Jewish leader, had been an early activist in urging a decisive U.S. response to events in Nazi Germany, leading calls for boycotts of German goods and easing of immigration laws. In August 1942, World Jewish Congress secretary Gerhart Riegner informed western diplomats that the Germans had begun the mass murders of European Jews (through the "Riegner telegram"), and Wise urged the U.S. government to denounce the genocide. Nonetheless, U.S. military leaders remained focused on the military defeat of the Axis powers. As a result, some sectors of the Jewish community viewed Wise as a weak advocate and turned to more radical groups, such as the Committee for a Jewish Army of Stateless and Palestinian Jews and the Emergency Committee to Save the Jewish People of Europe, both founded by Lithuanian-born activist Peter Bergson (also known as Hillel Kook). Bergson engaged tirelessly in publicizing the plight of the European Jews and trying to mobilize American popular opinion.

The efforts of international Jewish organizations were devoted almost exclusively to refugee-related issues, including lobbying for changes in immigration laws and raising money to assist refugees with visas and resettlement. They were joined by the American Friends Service Committee (run by the Quakers), which was the leading organization trying to assist refugees. With the onset of war, however, the task of assisting refugees became immeasurably more difficult at both ends of the process. Emigration from Nazi Germany and Austria had been difficult but possible, but Germany banned Jewish emigration after 1939. As the German army marched across Europe, Jewish communities were immediately murdered, confined to ghettos, or deported to concentration camps. In Great Britain and especially the United States, the resources available for refugee organizations were sharply curtailed. As historian J. Bruce Nichols notes, once the war began religious refugee work became a "political orphan": the priority of the Allied governments was to win the war, and "religious groups were expected to conform to Allied military policy."[10]

European church leaders were more focused on the plight of the respective European churches (in many cases their own) that found themselves under German occupation. This confronted the Vatican in particular with immediate and crucial issues, for the invasion of Poland was brutal and German occupation forces dealt particularly harshly with Polish Catholic clergy. By the end of 1939 almost one thousand Polish clergy were in concentration camps. In desperation, Polish Catholic leaders contacted the Vatican, and Cardinal August Hlond went to Rome, where he urged the pope to speak out against the German atrocities. The papal reply would set the pattern for subsequent statements from the Holy See: there would be official impartiality with respect to the issues of the war. In his radio addresses, Pius XII condemned the sufferings of innocents, and there were reports on the Vatican radio about the conditions in Poland, but there was no explicit condemnation of Germany from the pontiff.

This would be the same approach three years later, when (via the Riegner telegram) knowledge of the mass deportations and murders of the European Jews had reached the Vatican and the heads of Protestant churches and ecumenical leaders. In addition to notifying western diplomats, Gerhart Riegner (who met weekly in

Geneva with Protestant ecumenical leaders) informed international church bodies, sending a detailed memorandum to the Vatican about the deportations and mass murders.

The responses of these religious leaders were strikingly different. Following the Riegner telegram, the papal message of December 1942 spoke only generally of the suffering of civilians across Europe, not explicitly of the murders of the European Jews. The ecumenical and Protestant statements in response to news of the genocide were far stronger. The only real Protestant counterpart to the Pope was the Archbishop of Canterbury, who was the spiritual leader of the world's Anglican and Episcopal churches. William Temple, who had become Archbishop of Canterbury in 1942, gave an impassioned speech in the House of Lords in March 1943 calling for immediate aid to Europe's Jews and the lifting of British immigration restrictions, warning of "a great moral danger in the paralysis of feeling . . . it is most important for our own moral health and vigor that we express horror at the persecution of the Jews, (which) . . . almost baffles imagination and leaves one horrified at the power of the evil that can show itself in human nature." In the United States, the Federal Council of Churches resolution passed on December 11, 1942, was even more explicit: "It is impossible to avoid a conclusion that something like a policy of deliberate extermination of the Jews in Europe is being carried out. The violence and inhumanity which Nazi leaders have publicly avowed toward all Jews are apparently now coming to a climax in a virtual massacre. We confess our own ineffectiveness in combating the influences which beget antisemitism in our own country, and urge our constituencies to intensify their efforts on behalf of friendly relations with the Jews." Finally, the Protestant ecumenical leaders in Geneva issued a joint memorandum with the World Jewish Congress in March 1943, which was sent to Allied governments, the Vatican, and the Intergovernmental Committee on Refugees in London, calling for the "immediate rescue" of Jewish communities across Europe.[11]

Given these other statements, the pope's reticence to speak more explicitly was controversial even at the time, and it has led to ongoing debate among scholars about the role of the Vatican and Pope Pius XII between 1933 and 1945. The Vatican made clear that it feared Nazi retaliation against the millions of Catholics throughout Europe who were now under German occupation. Pius XII himself approached the situation as a diplomat, believing that behind the scenes diplomacy would be more effective both in ending the war and helping Europe's Jews. In addition, there were Catholic religious monasteries, convents, and schools that hid Jews, although it is unclear whether this was with the knowledge or at the instigation of the Vatican. The most dramatic scene came in October 1943, when the Jews of Rome were rounded up by Nazi forces. Most of the Roman Jewish community was successfully hidden, primarily in convents and monasteries, but 1,015 were deported to their deaths. There was no public protest by the pope.

The debates about Pope Pius XII highlight the complexities of religious and moral leadership during World War II, particularly with respect to the persecution and genocide of the European Jews. All the international religiously affiliated organizations during this period were juggling multiple priorities: how to most effectively protect their institutions and members who were in the war zones or under German occupation, trying to lobby with their respective governments for greater policy influence, attending to public opinion in their respective countries, and responding to the humanitarian issues like the refugee crisis. Antisemitism was prevalent throughout western society and there was little solidarity with the European Jews. All too often, this meant that the "moral voice" was absent. The 1942–1943 protests against the genocide of the Jews are striking precisely because they are such isolated examples.

Nonetheless, religious leaders in Europe and in the United States viewed and addressed the events of the war in language that revealed their fears about how "total war" was eroding the moral underpinnings of western culture and society—language that was also used by Roosevelt and Churchill. In 1939, for example, Roosevelt had stressed the need for cooperation between the "seekers of light" (religious groups) and "seekers of peace" (governmental leaders). Once the United States entered the war, much of the country's religious leadership took up the charge, defending the war as a just one in defense of democratic values. The Protestant theologian Reinhold Niebuhr became a leading voice, founding the influential journal *Christianity and Crisis* in 1941 to combat the voices of isolationism and pacifism in the Protestant churches. The National Conference of Christians and Jews published a series of pamphlets titled "Why We Fight: Minister, Priest, Rabbi Discuss the Issues at Stake"; other religious bodies sponsored programs and films along similar lines. Roosevelt's "Four Freedoms" speech in January 1941 stressed freedom of worship as one of the essential freedoms under siege in the world. John Foster Dulles, a Protestant lawyer who had been a lay delegate to many international ecumenical meetings during the 1930s, convened a meeting of U.S. religious and community leaders in 1942 to write what eventually became his "Six Pillars of Peace" statement, which emphasized the role of Christian values in the fight against Nazis.

While similar documents emerged from European church and ecumenical circles during the war, they had a different tone. Europeans were directly affected by the events of the war—and the second European war had come very soon after the first, making them even more fearful of the political instability they saw everywhere, especially that of the various ideological movements, from Communism to ethno-nationalism. In particular, the churches were concerned about the radical ethno-nationalist Christian groups and churches that had aligned themselves with Nazism, not only in Nazi Germany but in Finland, Romania, Lithuania, and Ukraine. In 1940, Willem Visser 't Hooft, who headed the ecumenical offices in Geneva, described the purpose of the ecumenical efforts as "the war behind the war": a "war to stem the tide towards spiritual and moral nihilism," which he attributed equally to Nazism and Communism.[12] From the perspective of Geneva, Rome, and London, the war was not only a fight against Nazism but against the broader erosion and destruction of Christian values—to some extent, a battle against modernity itself. These church leaders, particularly the Vatican, viewed Nazism as an extreme manifestation of developments that could be traced back to the nineteenth century, and they feared that the physical and moral destruction wrought by the war would make it even more difficult to build a moral foundation for postwar civilization.

In this regard the ecumenical and Protestant documents echoed many of the concerns coming from the Vatican. In April 1940 Visser 't Hooft issued a letter, "The Ecumenical Church and the International Situation," in which he described Nazism and Communism as "anti-Christian" forces that would eradicate Christianity. The churches, he argued, were called to "confront in a wholly new manner that hardest of all tasks which it has faced since the times of the early Middle Ages, namely the reconversion of most of the Western world... The perspective with which the Church should approach the whole question of the postwar situation is that of a tremendous spiritual and missionary task rather than a task of a technical and political character."[13] British church leader William Paton's 1943 book, *The Church and the New Order*, affirmed this analysis, arguing for a church-led postwar renewal of European society that would explicitly restore Christian values.

There were no such statements about events in North Africa and the Pacific, which European and American church leaders tended to view as extensions of what was happening in Europe, but there were church diplomatic efforts in response to state measures that directly impacted western churches. Ties to churches in Africa and Asia were maintained by the respective denominational missionary organizations and the World Student Christian Federation, not the ecumenical movement (there were also a small number of Catholic missions in Asia). In 1941, however, when the Japanese government forced the Federation of Churches (founded by Protestant missionaries in 1911) to include all Christian churches, including the Catholic and Orthodox churches, until the end of the war in 1945, the situation was monitored by the respective churches to ensure that their clergy in Japan did not suffer adverse consequences.

In the North African countries under the governance of Vichy France (Morocco, Algeria, and Tunisia), there were about thirty concentration camps to which both foreign and local Jews were sent; when the German army briefly occupied Tunisia in 1942 they set up around forty detention and labor camps, imprisoning around five thousand Tunisian Jews. The longstanding relationships between Jewish and Muslim communities in North Africa led some Muslims to rescue their Jewish neighbors during the German occupation.

Western leaders viewed the Shinto tradition in Japan through the lens of the European dynamics, seeing patterns that were similar to the rise of religious European ethno-nationalism. After the defeat of Japan, General Douglas MacArthur ordered the dismantling of what the U.S. government labelled "State Shinto" and the emperor was ordered to renounce his claim to divinity. In Germany, a much longer process of debate about the churches' accountability for National Socialism began. Nazism had constituted a form of "religion" for many enthusiastic Germans (and the Protestant "German Christians" had embraced it as such) and the churches' compromises between 1933 and 1945 amounted to a sanctification or legitimization of the regime.

Conclusion

The international developments in the religious world in the nineteenth and early twentieth centuries were the foundation for the responses of religious leaders between 1939 and 1945. In many respects, the era of "total war" from 1939–1945 was an intense, violent phase of a much longer process. The challenges of colonialism, nationalism, church–state conflicts, and alliances continued to play out after 1945. The postwar era was a period of transition for international religious organizations like the ecumenical movement. The end of the colonial era, the Cold War, the establishment of the United Nations, and other international developments after 1945 led to a further expansion of international religious networks, often far more contentious in terms of political issues. It marked the beginning of the end for western Christian hegemony in international religious relationships.

Any deeper examination of the religious responses during World War II, however, must go beyond an analysis of the historical actions, priorities, and alliances of different religious communities during that era. National Socialism and the genocide of the European Jews raised deeply troubling historical and theological questions for Christians. In addition to challenging questions about their own religious traditions and beliefs in the wake of the catastrophe, Jews had to begin the painful process of lament, rebuilding, and the recovery of community. Between Christians and Jews, a new and difficult "post-Holocaust" era began. Over the decades since 1945, this has led to some real changes in theological understanding and interreligious relations.

Notes

1. Conservative Judaism acknowledges the binding nature of traditional teachings and values of Judaism but is open to the critical study of Jewish texts and the modernization of rituals and practices. Reform Judaism challenges the binding nature of many traditional rituals and practices, beliefs, and laws as it seeks to adapt Judaism to the modern world.
2. Zionism emerged as an international Jewish revival movement in the late nineteenth century; Austro-Hungarian journalist and activist Theodor Herzl founded political Zionism, which called for the establishment of a Jewish state.
3. See Ruth Rouse and Stephen C. Neill, *A History of the Ecumenical Movement, 1517–1948* (Philadelphia: Westminster Press, 1954), 389ff.
4. Rouse and Neill, *A History*, 394ff.
5. See Rouse and Neill, *A History*, 382.
6. Paul Brooker, *The Faces of Fraternalism: Nazi Germany, Fascist Italy, and Imperial Japan* (New York: Oxford University Press, 1991), 210.
7. See Victoria J. Barnett, *For the Soul of the People: Protestant Protest against Hitler* (New York: Oxford University Press, 1992), 83–85.

8. In Tine Reeh, "Hal Koch's International Network," in *International Religious Networks*, ed. Jeremy Gregory and Hugh McLeod (Woodbridge, Suffolk, UK and Rochester, NY: Published for the Ecclesiastical History Society by the Boydell Press, 2012), 268.
9. Victoria J. Barnett, "'Fault Lines': An Analysis of the National Conference of Christians and Jews, 1933–1948" (PhD diss. George Mason University, 2012), 106.
10. J. Bruce Nichols, *The Uneasy Alliance: Religion, Refugee Work and U.S. Foreign Policy* (New York: Oxford University Press, 1988), 53, 55.
11. All quotations are from Victoria Barnett and Franklin Sherman, "Jews and Christians: The Unfolding Interfaith Relationship: International Protests from Church Leaders," https://www.ushmm.org/research/about-the-mandel-center/initiatives/ethics-religion-holocaust/articles-and-resources/jews-and-christians-the-unfolding-interfaith-relationship/international-protests-from-church-leaders. Accessed May 2, 2021.
12. Klemens Von Klemperer, *German Resistance against Hitler: The Search for Allies Abroad, 1938–1945* (New York: Oxford University Press, 1992), 267–268.
13. Quoted in Victoria J. Barnett, "Communications between the German Resistance, the Vatican and Protestant Ecumenical Leaders," in *Religion im Erbe: Dietrich Bonhoeffer und die Zukunftsfähigkeit des Christentums*, ed. Christian Gremmels and Wolfgang Huber (Gütersloh: Kaiser, Gütersloher Verlagshaus, 2002), 67.

Bibliography

Barnett, Victoria J. "'Fault Lines': An Analysis of the National Conference of Christians and Jews, 1933–1948." PhD diss., George Mason University, 2012.

Barnett, Victoria J. *For the Soul of the People: Protestant Protest against Hitler*. New York: Oxford University Press, 1992.

Barnett, Victoria J. "Track-Two Diplomacy, 1933–1939: International Responses from Catholics, Jews, and Ecumenical Protestants to Events in Nazi Germany." Kirchliche Zeitgeschichte 27, no. 1 (2014): 76–86.

Bergen, Doris L. *Twisted Cross: The German Christian Movement in the Third Reich*. Chapel Hill: University of North Carolina Press, 1996.

Berkowitz, Michael. *Western Jewry and the Zionist Project, 1914-1933*. Cambridge: Cambridge University Press, 1997.

Boum, Aomar, and Sarah Abrevaya Stein, eds. *The Holocaust and North Africa*. Stanford: Stanford University Press, 2019.

Boys, Mary C. *Seeing Judaism Anew*. Lanham, MD: Rowman & Littlefield Publishers, 2005.

Breitman, Richard, and Allan J. Lichtman. *FDR and the Jews*. Cambridge, MA: The Belknap Press of Harvard University Press, 2013.

Brooker, Paul. *The Faces of Fraternalism: Nazi Germany, Fascist Italy, and Imperial Japan*. New York: Oxford University Press, 1991.

Burleigh, Michael. *Moral Combat: Good and Evil in World War II*. New York: HarperCollins, 2011.

Carter-Chand, Rebecca, and Kevin Spicer, eds. *Religion, Ethnonationalism, and Antisemitism in the Era of the Two World Wars*. Montreal: McGill University Press, 2022.

Chamedes, Giuliana. *A Twentieth Century Crusade: The Vatican's Battle to Remake Christian Europe*. Cambridge, MA: Harvard University Press, 2021.

Dorrien, Gary. *The Word as True Myth: Interpreting Modern Theology*. Louisville: Westminster John Knox, 1997.

Fackenheim, Emil L. *To Mend the World: Foundations of Post-Holocaust Jewish Thought*. Reprint. Bloomington: Indiana University Press, 1994.

Granick, Jaclyn. *International Jewish Humanitarianism in the Age of the Great War*. Cambridge: Cambridge University Press, 2021.

Gregory, Jeremy, and Hugh McLeod, eds. *International Religious Networks*. Woodbridge, Suffolk, UK and Rochester, NY: Published for the Ecclesiastical History Society by the Boydell Press, 2012.

Hanebrink, Paul A. *In Defense of Christian Hungary: Religion, Nationalism, and Antisemitism, 1890-1944*. Ithaca: Cornell University Press, 2006.

Hardacre, Helen. *Shinto: A History*. New York and London: Oxford University Press: 2016.

Helmreich, Ernst Christian. *German Churches under Hitler: Background, Struggle, and Epilogue*. Detroit: Wayne State University Press, 1979.

Hollinger, David A. *Protestants Abroad: How Missionaries Tried to Change the World but Changed America*. Princeton: Princeton University Press, 2017.

Hulsether, Mark. *Building a Protestant Left: Christianity and Crisis Magazine, 1941-1993*. Knoxville: University of Tennessee Press, 1999.

Marty, Martin E. *Pilgrims in Their Own Land: 500 Years of Religion in America*. Reprint. New York: Penguin Books, 1985.

Mazzenga, Maria, ed. *American Religious Responses to Kristallnacht*. New York: Palgrave Macmillan, 2009.

Motadel, David. *Islam and Nazi Germany's War*. Cambridge, MA: The Belknap Press of Harvard University Press, 2014.

Nichols, J. Bruce. *The Uneasy Alliance: Religion, Refugee Work and U.S. Foreign Policy*. New York: Oxford University Press, 1988.

Nirenberg, David. *Anti-Judaism: The Western Tradition*. New York: W. W. Norton, 2014.

Phayer, Michael. *The Catholic Church and the Holocaust, 1930-1965*. Bloomington: Indiana University Press, 2000.

Riegner, Gerhart. *Never Despair: Sixty Years in the Service of the Jewish People and the Cause of Human Rights*. Translated by William Sayers. Chicago: Ivan R. Dee, 2006.

Robert, Dana L., ed. *Converting Colonialism: Visions and Realities in Mission History, 1706-1914*. Grand Rapids, MI: Wm. B. Eerdmans Publishing, 2008.

Rouse, Ruth, and Stephen C. Neill. *A History of the Ecumenical Movement, 1517-1948*. Philadelphia: Westminster Press, 1954.

Rubenstein, Richard L. *After Auschwitz: History, Theology, and Contemporary Judaism*. 2nd ed. Baltimore: The John Hopkins University Press, 1992.

Sherman, Franklin, ed. *Bridges: Documents of the Christian-Jewish Dialogue*, Vol. 1: *The Road to Reconciliation (1945-1985)*. New York: Paulist Press, 2011.

Snoek, Johan M. *The Grey Book: A Collection of Protests against Anti-Semitism and the Persecution of the Jews issued by Non-Roman Catholic Churches and Church Leaders during Hitler's Rule*. Introduction by Uriel Tal. Assen: Van Gorcum & Comp., 1969.

Sorkin, David. *Jewish Emancipation: A History across Five Centuries*. Princeton: Princeton University Press, 2019.

Spicer, Kevin. *Antisemitism, Christian Ambivalence, and the Holocaust*. Bloomington: Indiana University Press, 2007.

Spitzer, Lee B. *Baptists, Jews, and the Holocaust: The Hand of Sincere Friendship*. Valley Forge, PA: Judson Press, 2017.

Ventresca, Robert A. *Soldier of Christ: The Life of Pope Pius XII*. Cambridge, MA: The Belknap Press of Harvard University Press, 2013.

Visser 't Hooft, Willem. *Memoirs*. Philadelphia: The Westminster Press, 1973.

Von Klemperer, Klemens. *German Resistance against Hitler: The Search for Allies Abroad, 1938–1945*. New York: Oxford University Press, 1992.

CHAPTER 24

SCIENCE AND TECHNOLOGY

RONALD E. DOEL AND KRISTINE C. HARPER

SCIENCE and technology profoundly influenced World War II, and the war profoundly influenced science and technology around the globe. Radar, proximity fuzes, penicillin, guided missiles, and nuclear weapons all emerged during the war. In this conflict, for the first time, more soldiers died from combat wounds than from infections. Aircraft and aviation—from the German lightning war at the start of World War II to the Allied strategic bombing campaigns that helped to end it—were crucial as warring states sought dominance. Access to oil, the increasingly dominant fuel of mid-twentieth century industries, inspired the Japanese to enter World War II. The concept of total war, involving the mobilization of entire societies to meet the industrial and technological demands of modern warfare, emerged in this period.[1] By the war's end, both the United States and the Soviet Union emerged as dominant global leaders, their scientific and technological infrastructures more robust and far less damaged than those in Western Europe and Japan—and the trajectory of the Cold War, which began less than two years after World War II ended in 1945, reflected wartime developments such as rockets, nuclear weapons, and advanced submarines.

Developments in both science and technology are treated in this chapter. While related and overlapping domains, they are distinct in their aims, practitioners, professional organizations, and institutional foundations. While scientists, working within their disciplines—physics, chemistry, biology, and more—seek to understand observed phenomena and to develop testable theories about how nature behaves, specialists in technology, including engineers and industrial scientists, focus on fashioning products that perform particular tasks: in the context of war, aircraft to rockets to munitions. Technological projects during World War II sometimes depended on scientific breakthroughs—the atom bomb is the clearest example—although many drew on routine scientific work. Although the Second World War is sometimes called the "physicists' war" because of atomic weapons (just as World War I became the "chemists' war" because of lethal battlefield agents including chlorine, phosgene, and mustard gas), many branches of science, including the environmental sciences, were intimately interwoven into wartime research.

Early Years of the War

In the decade preceding the outbreak of World War II, levels of scientific and technological achievement in the nation-states that later became the Allied and Axis powers were mixed. Germany, Britain, the United States, the Soviet Union, and Japan were all regarded as leading scientific nations, although their systems of support for research, and particular strengths, varied widely: in the Western democracies, much scientific work was pursued at public and private universities. By contrast, most Soviet scientific work took place in specialized research academies controlled by its imperial National Academy of Sciences, while much cutting-edge research in Germany emerged from similarly specialized (and government-supported) Kaiser Wilhelm Institutes (KWI).[2] Research strengths were similarly unequal in the 1930s: the Soviet Union and Germany excelled in theoretical physics, a field roiled by revolutionary breakthroughs in understanding the nature of matter and energy, while the U.S., with more limited mathematical training, excelled in experimental physics (although persecuted Jewish physicists fleeing Nazi Germany increased America's standing in theoretical physics).[3]

Industrial and technological output in these nations in the 1930s was similarly disparate. The United States had enjoyed tremendous industrial output in the decade following World War I, as the second industrial revolution led to enhanced steel production, the construction of skyscrapers, and the mass production of automobiles. But the Great Depression, beginning in 1929, had mothballed many manufacturing plants; major government-funded undertakings, such as Hoover Dam and the Tennessee Valley Authority, underscored federal faith in large-scale technological projects.[4] Britain, casting a wary eye at Germany, continued supporting its Navy—then the largest in the world—and steered funds to government science agencies tasked with military readiness.[5] While Japan, like Britain, steadily augmented its economic, industrial, and technological resources as it sought to maintain its expanding empire in China, Korea, and throughout the Pacific region in the mid- and late 1930s, it was Germany that most dramatically augmented its military capacity. Prohibited by the Versailles Treaty after World War I from manufacturing or importing aircraft, and barred from aviation-related research (the physicist Ludwig Prandlt, at the KWI for hydrodynamics, could not build wind tunnels crucial for his experimental-theoretical work), Germany rapidly expanded its tank and aircraft production after Hitler's rise to power in 1931. By 1935, German authorities had built some 365 military aircraft secretly, and by 1939, were producing over eight thousand per year.[6]

When Germany and the Soviet Union invaded Poland in September 1939, one of the first casualties was scientific internationalism: the open exchange of scientific publications and the global circulation of scientists. The outbreak of hostilities, which quickly escalated as Britain, France, Australia, New Zealand, India, and South Africa declared war on Germany, curtailed a meeting of the International Union of Geodesy and Geophysics in Washington, DC, as foreign delegates hurried back to their home cities. But scientific internationalism had already been eroding through the 1930s, as racially based "Aryan Science" took root in Germany and Western "bourgeois" science was repressed in the Soviet Union, particularly during the purges of 1937–1938, challenging turn-of-the-century optimism that science was immune from political ideology. What replaced internationalism during the war years was secrecy and scientific intelligence-gathering, as political, industrial, and military leaders increasingly understood that basic research could lead to useful wartime applications.[7] Neutral nations, including Switzerland and several Latin American countries, became prized exchange points for periodicals between what became the Allied and Axis powers. The war also made science and scientists more tightly bound within the political and social fabric of nation-states than ever before. In the U.S., Federal Bureau of Investigation director J. Edgar Hoover instructed his agents to assess the political loyalties of American scientists, and in Britain, leading scientists, highlighting state persecutions of scientists in Nazi Germany and the Soviet Union, argued that, "Science and democracy are no longer merely desirable goals; they are conditions of survival."[8]

The outbreak of major hostilities in Europe also inspired governments to invest more to build existing scientific capacity. Because American democracy "had the benefit of a long partnership with science, not a long record of hostility," as historian A. Hunter Dupree has observed—and because influential Department of War officials challenged the long-standing conviction that warfare was solely the business of professional military personnel—the U.S. swiftly established new scientific institutions tasked with producing wartime advances.[9] Increasing anxiety that relatively few scientists and engineers were involved in defense work, and that a wide gap remained between imagined weapons and the battlefield, led President Franklin D. Roosevelt in 1941 to replace the National Defense Research Council (which he had created just the year before) with the far more powerful Office of Scientific Research and Development (OSRD), the most highly integrated, centralized, and successful agency of its kind created during the Second World War.[10] Led by Vannevar Bush, a seasoned MIT engineer, the OSRD would ultimately spend some $450 million dollars (over $6.8 billion in 2021 dollars) on weapons research and development, the bulk of these funds dispersed to elite research universities including MIT, Caltech, Harvard, and Columbia. While the field of physics was a primary beneficiary—by early 1942, OSRD was spending four times more on physics than chemistry, particularly for radar—funds flowed also to medicine (mass-production of penicillin), mathematics (improved methods for deploying bombers and searching for enemy submarines), and the earth sciences (including the discovery of the deep sound channel in the oceans, crucial for long-range communication in the oceans and anti-submarine warfare, and the successful wave and weather forecast that allowed Allied forces to prevail in the D-Day landing in Normandy in 1944).[11] The OSRD also increased funding for training programs. Demand for physicists outstripped the annual production of universities nearly fourfold by late 1942, while the paucity of meteorologists led to a crash training program that produced some seven thousand new recruits, filling strategic observing and forecasting posts around the globe.[12]

Technological superiority, however, rather than advances in science or the numbers and quality of troops, favored Germany in the first years of World War II. Even before Germany defeated Belgium, Holland, Denmark, and France, and launched the aerial warfare campaign later known as the Battle of Britain, German submarines (U-boats) sought to weaken this island nation—whose food, raw materials, and armaments all arrived via the sea—by sinking merchant and passenger ships in the North Atlantic. What aided Germany in this distinct Battle of the Atlantic was the strength of its Enigma Code—a combination of highly effective codes and U-boat-based decryption devices known as Enigma Machines—which allowed German submarine commander Admiral Karl Dönitz to target vulnerable convoys bound for England or, before their defeat, France and the low-lying countries.[13] The challenge of defeating the U-boat campaign inspired interim solutions (including Roosevelt's Lend-Lease program), while the highly classified effort to crack the Enigma Code was assigned to a group of linguists, classicists, mathematicians and chess players at the Government Code and Cypher School in Bletchley Park, England. There, the highly gifted polymath Alan Turing, aided by captured German codebooks and Enigma devices, broke Enigma's naval code, and also led in designing a high-speed code-breaking machine while developing the concept of an electronic stored-program universal digital computer. Bletchley Park's efforts collectively shortened the war in England by two years.[14] Signals intelligence, like the broader realm of scientific intelligence, came to be a growing advantage for Allied nations. Navajo code-talkers, embedded within advancing troops in the Pacific, circumvented the great strengths of Japanese code-breakers when Allied forces took Iwo Jima and other strategic islands, and disaster was averted when Soviet forces held Stalingrad in 1943, preventing German authorities from acquiring an immense treasure of Allied scientific knowledge stored there.[15]

Air power, nevertheless, was singularly important in shaping the essential fabric and ultimate trajectory of World War II, both in the European and Pacific theaters. For Germany, Britain, and the U.S., aircraft production dominated the war economy, and by war's end, Allied air superiority would emerge as a key reason the Axis powers did not prevail.[16] The need to ferry aircraft from North America to Britain—and the limited ranges of World War II-era planes—helped bring the war to the far north, as the U.S. established air bases in Greenland and Iceland.[17] While German military leaders banked on defeating Britain in the Battle of Britain (the first major campaign in history fought entirely by aircraft)—just as Japan had hoped to cripple the U.S. Pacific Fleet in its attack on Pearl Harbor in December 1941—neither effort succeeded: German medium-range bombers and ground attack planes proved insufficient against British air defenses, and by not destroying U.S. aircraft carriers (several were absent from Pearl Harbor on that day), Japan failed to deliver a lethal blow. Two additional German aviation advantages— its development of the world's first jet-propelled military aircraft, the Messerschmitt, and its acquisition through espionage of the Norden bombsight (which made precision bombing from high-flying aircraft possible, and was one of the most closely guarded U.S. technological secrets)—failed to play a major role because the Messerschmitt became available only in 1944, too late to affect its aerial campaign, and Germany had no ability to mass-manufacture the Norden bombsight.[18] Germany reached the pinnacle of its wartime aircraft production in 1944, producing over thirty-nine thousand planes that year, but by then U.S. production of military aircraft far surpassed Germany's, with 96,318 aircraft rolling off assembly lines.[19] This unprecedented industrial output also had major societal consequences: many thousands of American women were recruited to factories to replace men drafted into military service. Rosie the Riveter became the symbol of women who, at least during the war years, found ways to actively participate in the second industrial revolution.[20]

WONDER WEAPONS

Not all wartime research projects focused on devices or systems that seemed fully within reach of successful completion before the likely end of combat. In three nations—Germany, Japan, and the United States—scientists and engineers proposed "wonder weapons" they believed might turn the tide of war in their nation's favor. In each of these instances, government and military leaders provided encouragement and resources—including, in the cases of Germany and Japan, slave laborers and captured enemy soldiers who served as involuntary medical test subjects. None of these weapons systems determined the outcome of the Second World War, but several came to profoundly affect global history, not just through 1945 but far into the Cold War era as well.

While Japan began working on advanced weaponry only in the summer of 1942, after captured U.S.–British radar sets convinced military officials of the importance of new science-based technologies, ideas for new breakthrough weapon systems were soon aired. One concept that briefly took hold was a "death ray": an idea to focus ultraviolet, X-ray and radio waves into a beam sufficiently concentrated and powerful that it could knock planes from the sky, or at a minimum incinerate their occupants.[21] Japanese physical science research lagged behind that of other scientifically advanced nations, however—World War II did not inspire a Big Science revolution in Japan, as it did in the West—but research involving bacteriological and biochemical agents, already well underway by the late 1930s, became an even greater priority for Japanese military leaders.[22] The scale of Japanese bacteriological research was staggering: backed by militarists, fervent scientists, medical specialists and veterinarians, thousands of top, talented investigators and technicians experimented with anthrax, plague, cholera, typhoid, and other contagious diseases in what became more than a dozen secret laboratories scattered across the home islands, the Asian mainland, and occupied territories and colonies. Because Japan's militaristic government maintained control over Korea and had savagely occupied China, human guinea pigs were readily available: thousands of Chinese, Koreans, Mongolians, and Soviets were sacrificed in barbaric experiments, and up to two hundred thousand people ultimately died.[23] Had World War II dragged on into 1946, Japanese leaders likely would have unleashed chemical and biological weapons in the Pacific theater.[24] Although a clear and deeply disturbing example of science divorced from moral and ethical boundaries during the war, Allied governments kept Japan's bacteriological weapons program secret after 1945, in part so that Western researchers could better learn about Japanese progress, and in part to conceal biological warfare programs secretly undertaken in other leading nations, including the Soviet Union, Germany, Britain, France (until its defeat in 1940), Canada, and the United States. Only the physicians and administrators involved in Germany's wartime biomedical experiments—evaluated in the Doctors Trial of 1946–1947, the first of the Nuremberg trials—were subject to criminal proceedings at war's end.[25]

In contrast to Japan, whose wartime scientific efforts were hindered by interservice rivalries and conflicting institutional claims, the decentralized structure of German science and industrial production, while frequently inefficient, also allowed bursts of creativity.[26] During the Second World War, German scientists and engineers pursued two distinct wonder weapons projects. The first involved guided missiles. An outgrowth of the spaceflight movement in Weimar Germany during the 1920s best symbolized by Fritz Lang's classic film *Frau im Mond* (Woman in the Moon), the German rocketry program began in earnest in the 1930s, when it gained military funding after Hitler's rise to power. Karl Becker, leader of the German rocketry effort, ardent Nazi supporter, and later head of Army Ordnance, believed that, "the surprise introduction of a radical new weapon could produce a stunning psychological blow against an enemy."[27] Genuine advances in rocket engineering between 1936 and 1941, Hitler's infatuation with rockets as terror weapons, and the availability of concentration camp slave labor made it possible for the rocketry program to remain a high priority of the German war machine. By the early 1940s, two types of guided missiles were in production: the winged V-1 "buzz bomb" targeted at London and Antwerp from bases in Northern France, the Netherlands, and Western Germany, and the V-2, a larger, more deadly guided missile fired from Peenemünde, on the Baltic island of Usedom. A massive facility, Peenemünde included an assembly line capable of producing three hundred V-2s per month, operated in part by an embedded concentration camp with six hundred Russian and French prisoners. After Allied aircraft bombed Peenemünde in 1943, V-2 production shifted to an underground facility in the Harz Mountains in Austria sustained by some four thousand prisoners (predominantly Russian, Polish, and French) working in dank, chilly tunnels. Working conditions for prisoners were horrific; at least twelve thousand workers at the Dora-Mittelwerk concentration camp facility in Austria were executed or died of malnutrition by April 1945.[28] Despite massive state investment, the V-2 program produced virtually no wartime benefit for Germany. While killing some five thousand Allied civilians, the total explosive load of all the Third Reich's Vengeance weapons, as historian Michael J. Neufeld has noted, "was scarcely more than a single large RAF air raid," and its psychological and material impact on London and Antwerp residents was slight. Still-primitive electronics and computers that limited aiming accuracy made guided missiles ineffectual during World War II, although this technological system would come to have profound importance for national defense (and ultimately space exploration) in future years and decades.[29]

German scientists also sought to create a new, unprecedented kind of weapon based on new insights about the structure of matter. In 1939, aware that recent breakthroughs in atomic physics indicated that nuclear fission—the splitting of large, unstable elements—could lead to a chain reaction that would release unimaginable energy in a short moment, a number of German university units and KWI began devoting research efforts to this phenomenon.[30] By autumn 1941, leading German physicists involved in this undertaking, including Werner Heisenberg, realized that the uranium isotope 235 (less stable than U-238 and thus most suitable for nuclear fission) could be produced by an ultracentrifuge, and thus a nuclear weapon was feasible. After the winter of 1941–1942, when the German Lightning War against the Soviet Union had ground to a halt, and Hitler's declaration of war against the U.S. increased the scope of Germany's wartime challenges, German Army Ordnance pressured the nation's science-technology project leaders to step up efforts.[31] Despite backing from Reich Minister of Armaments and War Production Albert Speer (who had advocated to fellow German leaders that a nuclear weapon could be of "great future potential"), Army leaders limited support for the uranium project, believing funds were better spent on its rocket program.[32] Allied authorities, fearing continued German progress, and aware that Heisenberg believed heavy water would work well to control the fission process, in 1943 bombed a Norwegian heavy water plant previously captured by the Germans. When the sixty scientists recruited for the code-named Alsos mission swept across war-ravaged Germany behind advancing Allied troops in spring 1945 to locate, apprehend, and interview German physicists, they realized how far German researchers were from completing a nuclear weapon.[33]

American physicists, similarly aware of the discovery of nuclear fission, and the potential for Germany to build an atomic weapon, had begun their own, ultimately successful, effort to create the bomb, simultaneously instituting the largest and most costly Big Science project undertaken during World War II. In contrast to Japanese bacteriological research and German work on rockets and atomic weapons, the U.S. effort to construct the atomic bomb was international in two distinct ways: Canadian, and especially British, scientists contributed directly to its design and manufacture, and several leading theoretical physicists who became vital to the effort, including Leó Szilárd, Enrico Fermi, and Eugene Wigner, were refugees who had fled persecution in Europe in the 1930s. Initial U.S. efforts to explore the prospects of atomic weapons proceeded more slowly than in Germany. In August 1939, Szilárd and Wigner drafted a letter for the most famous of all German refugee scientists, Albert Einstein, to send to President Franklin D. Roosevelt, warning of the potential development of "extremely powerful bombs of a new type." Even before Roosevelt, acting on advice from the director of the National Bureau of Standards, approved funding for an atomic bomb program in October 1941— what became known as the Manhattan Project—British scientists contributed their research to U.S. colleagues, aware that Britain could not undertake a bomb project on its own. Not until December 1942 did Fermi, working under the bleachers of Stagg Field at the University of Chicago, successfully test the world's first nuclear reactor. But by then construction had begun on two massive facilities to create fissionable fuel for atomic bombs: the U-235 separation plant at Oak Ridge, Tennessee, and the plutonium production plant at Hanford, Washington. Occupying a former ranch school in remote Los Alamos, New Mexico, nuclear physicist J. Robert Oppenheimer headed the team of physicists and engineers tasked with designing the weapon.[34] In July 1945, shortly before dawn, the atomic era began with the first secret (and successful) nuclear bomb test near Alamogordo, New Mexico. Even before then, atomic weapons development had stirred tremendous controversy within the United States and the Soviet Union. Eight Manhattan Project scientists, including Szilárd and James Franck, vehemently objected to using atomic weapons against Japan (arguing that Japan had no atomic bomb project, while the defeat of Germany had neutralized the threat of Hitler with the bomb). Their appeal—including a declaration that, "if we consider international agreement on total prevention of nuclear warfare as the paramount objective . . . [then introducing] nuclear weapons to the world may easily destroy all our chances of success"—did not gain support within the White House, occupied by Harry S. Truman after Roosevelt's death in April 1945.[35] And while Stalin displayed no emotion when Truman informed him at the Potsdam Conference on July 24—a week after the successful test—that the U.S. had "a new weapon of unusual destructive force," the Soviet leader, through British and American spies, was already well-informed about the Manhattan Project, and had begun laying the foundation for a crash program within the Soviet Union to secure its own atomic bomb.[36]

There is little doubt that use of atomic weapons against Japan hastened the end of World War II. On August 6, 1945, the B-29 bomber *Enola Gay* released an atomic bomb (using U-235) on Hiroshima. Three days later, a second bomb (plutonium-based) fell on Nagasaki. Together their explosive power equaled roughly forty thousand tons of TNT—about one-hundredth of the energy released by all weapons used in World War II. At least one hundred thousand civilians in each city died. Along with guided missiles, this "wonder weapon" profoundly influenced world history in subsequent years and decades. But it is also the case, as historian David Edgerton has noted, that atomic weapons "came too late to have anything except a minor impact on the outcome of the Second World War."[37] Equally perceptive is the assessment of historian Daniel J. Kevles that "[t]he atomic bomb only ended the war. Radar won the war."[38] Allied scientific and technological advantages on several fronts, in retrospect, turned the tide of the war by 1943: mass-produced penicillin and DDT gave Allied soldiers an edge in surviving infections and unsanitary living conditions, while the proximity fuze (allowing explosives to detonate with lethal force even without precisely striking their targets) greatly increased the effectiveness of strikes against planes, missiles, ships, and ground troops.[39] Advances in code-breaking allowed Allied forces to prevail in the Battle of Midway and kept Japan from establishing military bases near Hawaii; despite greatly increased aircraft production and kamikaze suicide missions, Japan could not stem its losses.[40] Operations Research (OR), allowing reliable calculation of the economic costs and benefits of particular weapons systems, provided Western nations a further strategic edge.[41] Even the availability of crucial natural resources such as oil and coal—and blunders by Axis military leaders—gave technological advantages to Allied forces. Oil, more vital in World War II than in any previous conflict, grew ever scarcer in Germany after its forces failed to reach oil fields in Azerbaijan; by March 1944, synthetic fuels became essential for fifty-seven percent of Germany's total oil supply and ninety-two percent of its aviation gasoline. The Japanese failure in 1941 to destroy fuel resources and tanks when it attacked Pearl Harbor, as historian Daniel Yergin has written, was "a strategic error with momentous reverberations" because all Pacific Fleet oil had to be transported from the mainland.[42] Even coal resources preferentially benefitted the Allies: the U.S. coal-fired economy largely produced American aircraft, tanks, weapons and munitions—the "sinews of war" central to Allied dominance in the last years of World War II.[43]

Radar, however, was crucial. The advantage of Allied radar was particularly evident in the aerial bombardment campaign against Germany—regarded as "the most important large-scale novelty in the mode of warfare conducted by Britain and the USA"—that ended the Second World War in the European theater.[44] Once radar allowed Allied aircraft to operate over German airspace with near impunity, U.S. forces began precision daytime bombing raids using B-24 and later B-29 Superfortress bombers, targeting factories and rail centers; by contrast, British RAF Lancasters and Halifaxes conducted night raids centered on residential districts where factory workers lived. Initially ineffective in shattering the morale of German citizens or limiting war production, the "firestorm" campaigns in winter 1945 (including the February 13–14, 1945 firestorm attack on Dresden and a similar U.S. attack on Tokyo in March) killed more than one hundred thousand citizens in both cities, grievously degrading Axis industrial capacity.[45] By war's end strategic bombing allowed British planes to drop more bombs on German cities in twenty-four hours than all the tonnage of explosives aimed at Britain by V-1 and V-2 missiles in all of 1944.[46] These policies and activities helped define the concept of "total war" and, like the atomic bombing of Japan, and fatal human biomedical experiments in Japan and Germany, raised questions about the erasure of moral boundaries in science and technology during wartime.

Legacy

Science and technology influenced the immediate postwar world no less profoundly than the war itself. This played out in many ways: in the elevation of atomic weapons as an element of foreign policy, in the determination of Allied powers to include scientific and technological resources in seeking wartime reparations from vanquished Axis nations, in renewed emphasis on scientific intelligence, and in maintaining robust state funding for continued research. In the aftermath of the atomic bombing of Hiroshima and Nagasaki in August 1945, causing Japan to surrender and the Second World War to end, government leaders as well as ordinary citizens became acutely aware of the power of science and technology to secure victory and to create once unimaginable destruction.

At war's end, leaders in the United States and the Soviet Union—the leading technologically advanced nations that had emerged victorious—were convinced that wartime gains in science and technology were key to national security. German achievements in jet propulsion and rocketry were prized for military aviation and as delivery systems for conventional and atomic weapons ("War has become vertical," declared U.S. General Henry Arnold), and in the closing days of the European campaign, American and Soviet troops vied with one another to seize technological assets.[47] Extending the long-established concept of wartime reparations—previously limited to factories and scientific laboratories—American authorities transported the German rocket pioneer Wernher von Braun and sixteen hundred additional specialists in ballistic missiles, sarin gas bombs, and weaponized bubonic plague who had served Hitler, Himmler, or Göring to U.S. military installations, denying them to the Soviets. Project Paperclip, as this operation became known, came under fire decades later for allowing numerous war criminals to circumvent screening applied to all other refugees seeking entry into the United States. Paperclip came to symbolize the ethical dilemma of balancing ethical standards versus surviving annihilation from a technologically superior enemy, but it was just one node in an expanding network of scientific intelligence-gathering practices nurtured in World War II that continued without interruption into the early Cold War.[48]

That Allied scientific advances had won the war both in Europe and the Pacific affected the practice of science and technology in other important ways. Government funding for scientific research (including the development of electronic computers and guided missiles) continued at levels similar to that during wartime, in sharp contrast to any prior era of peace.[49] The U.S. Department of Defense became the biggest single patron of American science after 1945, while the Kremlin, under Joseph Stalin, constructed new, isolated "cities of science" to enhance research in nuclear physics and other strategic fields.[50] While scientists sought to reinstate scientific internationalism— international scientific congresses resumed in the late 1940s, and the United Nations Educational, Scientific, and Cultural Organization (UNESCO) was created in November 1945—national security concerns created novel challenges distinct from those in the interwar years.[51] Secrecy involving new weapons systems also remained at wartime levels. Allied governments concealed information about wartime Japanese bacteriological experiments, initially (although wrongly) concerned that Japanese researchers were far ahead of Western projects. While Harvard President and governmental science advisor James B. Conant privately mused in 1946 that if biological warfare "is really a weapon like the Atomic Bomb shouldn't we have a public demonstration like the Bikini [atomic] test," White House and Pentagon officials kept details of Japanese wartime bacteriological work classified for decades.[52]

A separate issue facing Western democracies after World War II involved the new political power of science and technology, whose "sudden intrusion into the structure of the state," in the words of historian A. Hunter Dupree, "was a challenge to the resiliency of our institutions."[53] Despite postwar optimism that science could provide wondrous cures—a pamphlet by the British Association of Scientific Workers declared in 1947 that "when sufficiently large resources of finances, organization and scientists are used there are few problems of the control and exploitation of nature that cannot be solved, often with unexpected speed"—many elected officials grew suspicious about the loyalties of scientists as the Cold War began, and sought to hold them politically accountable.[54] By the end of the 1940s, even as rapid Soviet advances in atomic physics (including its successful atomic bomb test in 1949) undermined immediate postwar faith that democratic societies were required for successful techno-scientific achievements, Western democracies accepted that science served crucial state needs and required continued state support.[55]

Historians continue to debate key issues involving science and technology during World War II. While author Thomas Powers has declared that Werner Heisenberg and fellow German physicists deliberately slowed down the German atomic bomb project so as not to give this weapon to Hitler—a theme explored by Michael Frayn in his popular play *Copenhagen*—most historians of science, including Mark Walker and David Cassidy, have argued that mounting historical evidence instead suggests that Heisenberg had few ethical qualms about the project and its modest results in part reflected limited engineering advances.[56] New releases of previously classified documents also have led historians to conclude that Soviet efforts to infiltrate the U.S atomic weapons empire in 1944 and 1945 were more extensive (and successful) than previously understood: espionage by the American-born but Soviet-trained engineer George Koval, assigned to the Manhattan Project's Oak Ridge facility, accelerated the Soviet bomb program by several months.[57]

Other scholars exploring the practice and applications of science and technology during World War II have urged significant revisions to widely shared interpretations of their place in history and culture. The long-standing story of Britain as a fragile imperial power ill-prepared for World War II has been strongly challenged by historian of technology David Edgerton: for Edgerton, pre-war advances in British armaments in industrial and governmental laboratories, distinct from disinterested academics in university departments, made it "a pioneer of modern, technology focused warfare" with a military–industrial–scientific complex second to none.[58] An even broader challenge has come from Roy McLeod who argues that, rather than viewing the history of science as a story of steady progress interrupted by war, greater insights come instead from "reading history of science and war as parallel, often intersecting, and mutually dependent activities, rather than opposing narratives."[59] McLeod's reconceptualization, Carole Sachse and Mark Walker have observed, suggests that historians need to focus more on wartime scientific institutions that mediated between the sphere of military-state authority and the distinct sphere of scientists, to improve our understanding of how scientists used "the national political culture of war ... for their own professional ends."[60]

Other major issues remain poorly explored. The lives of "ordinary" scientists and technicians—those not directly involved in military projects—who labored amid the extraordinary challenges of the war years is inadequately investigated, as is the practice of signals intelligence within the Axis powers.[61] Science and technology developments in the entire Pacific theater, as well as in smaller states in Western and Eastern Europe, have received limited attention.[62] Further studies are needed of the effectiveness of heavy bombers in the Allied campaign against Germany in 1944 and 1945, along with—as Edgerton writes—the relative importance of tramp steamers versus tanks, refrigerated ships versus rockets, and oil versus atomic weapons.[63] Absent too are comprehensive assessments of the impacts wartime technologies had on global as well as local environments—including attempts to dispose of nuclear wastes on Eniwetok Atoll in the Pacific as the U.S. tested atomic weapons in the immediate aftermath of the Second World War—and the rise of the "One World" political movement in response to the existential threat posed by nuclear weapons.[64]

Notes

1. Ad Maas, "Introduction: Ordinary Scientists in Extraordinary Circumstances," in *Scientific Research in World War II: What Scientists Did in the War*, ed. Ad Maas and Hans Hooijmaijers (London: Routledge, 2009), 16.
2. Robert Kohler, *Partners in Science: Foundations and Natural Scientists, 1900–1945* (Chicago: University of Chicago Press, 1991); Loren R. Graham, *Science in Russia and the Soviet Union: A Short History* (New York: Cambridge University Press, 1993).
3. Charles Weiner, "A New Site for the Seminar: The Refugees and American Physics in the Thirties," in *The Intellectual Migration: Europe and America, 1930–1960*, ed. Donald Fleming and Bernard Bailyn (Cambridge, MA: Harvard University Press, 1969), 190–234.
4. Carroll Purcell, *The Machine in America: A Social History of Technology*, 2nd ed. (Baltimore, MD: Johns Hopkins University Press, 2007); Thomas P. Hughes, *American Genesis: A Century of Innovation and Technological Enthusiasm, 1870–1970* (Chicago: University of Chicago Press, 2004).
5. David Edgerton, *Britain's War Machine: Weapons, Resources, and Experts in the Second World War* (Oxford: Oxford University Press, 2011), 2–3, and David Edgerton, *Warfare State: Britain, 1920–1970* (Cambridge: Cambridge University Press, 2006), 1.
6. Walter E. Grunden, Yutaka Kawamura, Eduard Kolchinsky, Helmut Maier, and Masakatsu Yamazaki, "Laying the Foundation for Wartime Research: A Comparative Overview of Science Mobilization in National Socialist Germany, Japan, and the Soviet Union," *Osiris* 20 (2005): 85, also 93–97; Jonathan Zeitlin, "Flexibility and Mass Production at War: Aircraft Manufacture in Britain, the United States, and Germany, 1939–1945," *Technology and Culture* 36, no. 1 (1995): 46–79, on 52.
7. Mark Walker, "The Mobilisation of Science and Science-based Technology," in *Scientific Research in World War II*, ed. Ad Maas and Hans Hooijmaijers (London: Routledge, 2009), 19; Carola Sachse and Mark Walker, "Introduction: A Comparative Perspective," *Osiris* 20 (2005): 8–9; Ronald E. Doel, "Scientific Internationalism since 1940," in *Oxford Encyclopedia of the History of American Science, Medicine, and Technology*, ed. Hugh Richard Slotten, Ronald L. Numbers, and David N. Livingstone (New York: Cambridge University Press, 2018): 60–74; Pamela Spence Richards, *Scientific Information in Wartime: The Allied-German Rivalry, 1939–1945* (Westport, CT: Greenwood Press, 1994), 1.
8. Quoted in David E. H. Edgerton, "British Scientific Intellectuals and the Relations of Science and War in Twentieth Century Britain," in *National Military Establishments and the Advancement of Science: Studies in Twentieth Century History*, ed. Paul Forman

and José M. Sanchez-Ron (Dordrecht: Kluwer, 1996), 13. See also Ronald E. Doel, "Roger Adams: Linking University Science with Policy on the World Stage," in *No Boundaries: University of Illinois Vignettes*, ed. Lillian Hoddeson (Urbana: University of Illinois Press, 2004), 124–144; Richards, *Scientific Information in Wartime*.

9. A. Hunter Dupree, *Science in the Federal Government: A History of Policy and Activities*. Rev. ed. (Baltimore, MD: Johns Hopkins University Press, 1986), 381; Daniel J. Kevles, *The Physicists: The History of a Scientific Community in Modern America* (Cambridge, MA: Harvard University Press, 2001), 309, 314.

10. Carroll Purcell, *Technology in Postwar America* (New York: Columbia University Press, 2007), 4; Dupree, *Science and the Federal Government*, 371; Grunden et al., "Laying the Foundation," 80.

11. Kevles, *The Physicists*, 320, 348; Peter Neuschel, "Science, Government, and the Mass Production of Penicillin," *Journal of the History of Medicine and Allied Sciences* 48 (1993): 371; Kristine C. Harper, "Research from the Boundary Layer: Civilian Leadership, Military Funding, and the Development of Numerical Weather Prediction (1946–1955)," *Social Studies of Science* 33 (2003): 667–696; Ronald E. Doel, "Constituting the Postwar Earth Sciences: The Military's Influence on the Environmental Sciences in the USA after 1945," *Social Studies of Science* 33 (2003): 635–666.

12. Kristine C. Harper, *Weather by the Numbers: The Genesis of Modern Meteorology* (Cambridge, MA: MIT Press, 2008).

13. Philip Kaplan, *Grey Wolves: The U-Boat War, 1939–1945* (New York: Skyhorse Publishing, 2014); David Kahn, *Seizing the Enigma: The Race to Break the German U-Boat Codes, 1939–1943* (Boston: Houghton-Mifflin, 1991); Gary E. Weir, *An Ocean in Common: American Naval Officers, Scientists, and the Ocean Environment* (College Station: Texas A&M University Press, 2001).

14. B. Jack Copeland, "Alan Turing, 1912–1954," *The Essential Turing: Seminal Writing in Computing, Logic, Philosophy, Artificial Intelligence, and Artificial Life, "plus" The Secrets of Enigma* (Oxford: Oxford University Press, 2004), 1–3.

15. David Alvarez, *Allied and Axis Signals Intelligence in World War II* (Hoboken, NJ: Taylor and Francis, 2013): 14; Richards, *Scientific Intelligence in Wartime*, 91.

16. Zeitlin, "Flexibility and Mass Production at War," 46–79, 73.

17. Ronald E. Doel, Robert Marc Friedman, Julia Lajus, Sverker Sörlin, and Urban Wråkberg, "Strategic Arctic Science: National Interests in Building Natural Knowledge—Interwar Era through the Cold War," *Journal of Historical Geography* 44 (2014): 60–80.

18. Michael J. Sulick, *Spying in America: Espionage from the Revolutionary War to the Dawn of the Cold War* (Washington, DC: Georgetown University Press, 2012), 133–136.

19. Zeitlin, "Flexibility and Mass Production," 52.

20. William Chafe, *The American Woman: Her Changing Social, Economic, and Political Roles, 1920–1970* (New York: Oxford University Press, 1972).

21. Maas, "Introduction," 3; Morris F. Low, "The Useful War: Radar and the Mobilization of Science and Industry in Japan," in *Science and the Pacific War: Science and Survival in the Pacific, 1939–1945*, ed. Roy MacLeod (Dordrecht: Kluwer, 2000), 291–293.

22. Walter Grunden, *Secret Weapons and World War II: Japan in the Shadow of Big Science* (Lawrence: University of Kansas Press, 2005): 14.

23. Sheldon H. Harris, "The American Cover-Up of Japanese Human Biological Warfare Experiments, 1945–1948, in *Science in the Pacific War: Science and Survival in the Pacific, 1939–1945*, ed. Roy MacLeod (Dordrecht: Kluwer, 2000), 253–254.

24. Roy MacLeod, "Introduction," in *Science in the Pacific War: Science and Survival in the Pacific, 1939–1945*, ed. Roy MacLeod (Dordrecht: Kluwer, 2000), 6.
25. Walker, "The Mobilisation of Science," 20; Sheldon Harris, "The American Cover-Up"; Donald H. Avery, *The Science of War: Canadian Scientists and Allied Military Technology* (Toronto: University of Toronto Press, 1998), 230.
26. Sachse and Walker, "Introduction," 11.
27. Quoted in Michael J. Neufeld, *The Rocket and the Reich: Peenemünde and the Coming of the Ballistic Missile Era* (New York: Free Press, 1995), 275.
28. Yves Béon, *Planet Dora: A Memoir of a Holocaust and the Origins of the Space Age*, ed. Michael J. Neufeld, trans. Yves Béon and Richard L. Fague (Boulder, CO: Westview Press, 1997); Neufeld, *Rocket and the Reich*, 2, 211–212.
29. Neufeld, *Rocket and the Reich*, quoted on 273, 274; Michael J. Neufeld, *Von Braun: Dreamer of Space, Engineer of War* (New York: Knopf, 2007).
30. Walter E. Grunden, Mark Walker, and Masakatsu Yamazaki, "Wartime Nuclear Weapons Research in Germany and Japan," *Osiris* 20 (2005): 107–130.
31. Mark Walker, *German National Socialism and the Quest for Nuclear Power, 1939–49* (New York: Cambridge University Press, 1989), 14–17.
32. Grunden, Walker, and Yamazaki, "Wartime Nuclear Weapons Research," 114.
33. Mitchell Ash, "Denazifying Scientists—and Science," in *Technology Transfer out of Germany after 1945*, ed. Judt Matthias and Burghard Ciesla (Amsterdam: Harwood Academic Press, 1996), 61–80; Walker, *German National Socialism*; Samuel A. Goudsmit, *Alsos* (Woodbury, NY: American Institute of Physics Press, 1996); Walker, "Mobilisation of Science and Science-based Technology," 23.
34. Richard Rhodes, *The Making of the Atomic Bomb* (New York: Simon & Schuster, 1986); Kevles, *The Physicists*.
35. Kevles, *The Physicists*, 335; Alex Wellerstein, "Redactions: The Uncensored Franck Report," *Restricted Data: The Nuclear Secrecy Blog*, http://blog.nuclearsecrecy.com/2012/01/11/weekly-document-9-the-uncensored-franck-report-1945-1946/, accessed July 4, 2017.
36. David Holloway, *Stalin and the Bomb: The Soviet Union and Atomic Energy, 1939–1956* (New Haven, CT: Yale University Press, 1996); Sulick, *Spying in America*, 222–224.
37. David Edgerton, "Science and War," in *Companion to the History of Modern Science*, ed. R. C. Olby, G. N. Cantor, J. R. R. Christie, and M. J. S. Hodge (London: Routledge, 1990), 943.
38. Kevles, *The Physicists*, 308.
39. Edgerton, "Science and War," 934–945; Tom Schachtman, *Terrors and Marvels: How Science and Technology Changed the Character and Outcome of World War II* (New York: William Morrow, 2008).
40. Frank Cain, "The Role of Scientific Intelligence in the Pacific War," in *Science and the Pacific War: Science and Survival in the Pacific, 1939–1945*, ed. Roy MacLeod (Dordrecht: Kluwer, 2000), 271–272, 284.
41. Edgerton, "Science and War," 941–942.
42. Manfred Weissenbacher, *Sources of Power: How Energy Forces Human History*, Vol. 1 (Santa Barbara, CA: ABC Clio, 2009): xxi; Daniel Yergin, *The Prize: The Epic Quest for Oil, Money, and Power* (New York: Free Press, 2008), 326.
43. Howard Bucknell III, *Energy and National Defense* (Lexington: University Press of Kentucky, 1981), 138.
44. Edgerton, *Britain's War Machine*, 283.

45. Timothy Moy, *War Machines: Transforming Technologies in the U.S. Military, 1920–1940* (College Station: Texas A&M University Press, 2001), 164; Kenneth P. Werrell, "The Strategic Bombing of Germany in World War II: Costs and Accomplishments," *Journal of American History* 73 (1986): 702–713.
46. Edgerton, *Britain's War Machine*, 285.
47. Adrian R. Lewis, "The American Culture of War in the Age of Artificial Limited War," in *War and Culture in World History*, ed. Wayne Lee (New York: New York University Press, 2011), 187–218, on 198; John Gimbel, *Science, Technology, and Reparations: Exploitation and Plunder in Postwar Germany* (Stanford, CA: Stanford University Press, 1990).
48. Annie Jacobsen, *Operation Paperclip: The Secret Intelligence Program that Brought Nazi Scientists to America* (Boston: Little, Brown & Co., 2014); Ronald E. Doel and Allan A. Needell, "Science, Scientists, and the CIA: Balancing International Ideals, National Needs, and Professional Opportunity," *Intelligence and National Security* 12 (1997): 59–81; Douglas M. O'Reagan, "Science, Technology, and Know-How: Exploitation of German Science and Challenges of Technology Transfer in the Postwar World," PhD diss., University of California Berkeley, 2014; Richards, *Scientific Information in Wartime*.
49. Dupree, *Science in the Federal Government*, 373.
50. Stuart W. Leslie, *The Cold War and American Science: The Military–Industrial–Academic Complex at MIT and Stanford* (New York: Columbia University Press, 1993); Paul R. Josephson, *New Atlantis Revisited: Akademgorodok, the Siberian City of Science* (Princeton, NJ: Princeton University Press, 1997).
51. Ronald E. Doel, Dieter Hoffmann, and Nikolai Krementsov, "National States and International Science: A Comparative History of International Science Congresses in Hitler's Germany, Stalin's Russia, and Cold War United States," *Osiris* 20 (2005): 49–76.
52. Sheldon H. Harris, *Factories of Death: Japanese Biological Warfare and the American Cover-Up* (London: Routledge, 1994); James Conant to Roger Adams, September 19, 1946, Box 7, Papers of Roger Adams, University of Illinois archives.
53. Dupree, *Science in the Federal Government*, 369.
54. Quoted in David Edgerton, "British Scientific Intellectuals," 14; Jessica Wang, *American Science in an Age of Anxiety: Scientists, Anticommunism, and the Cold War* (Chapel Hill: University of North Carolina Press, 1999).
55. Sachse and Walker, "Introduction," 17; Michael A. Dennis, "Historiography of Science: An American Perspective," in *Science in the Twentieth Century*, ed. John Krige and Dominique Pestre (London: Harwood Academic Publishing, 1997), 1–26; Bruce L. R. Smith, *American Science Policy since WWII* (Washington, DC: Brookings Institution, 1990).
56. Thomas Powers, Stanley Goldberg, and Thomas Powers, "Declassified Files Reopen 'Nazi Bomb' Debate," *Bulletin of the Atomic Scientists* 48, no. 7 (1992): 32–40; Michael Frayn, *Copenhagen* (New York: Anchor Books, 1998); Mark Walker, *Nazi Science: Myth, Truth, and the German Atomic Bomb* (New York: Basic Books, 2001); David Cassidy, "New Light on *Copenhagen* and the German Nuclear Project," *Physics in Perspective* 4 (2002): 447–455.
57. Sulick, *Spying in America*.
58. Edgerton, *Warfare State*, 1.
59. MacLeod, "Introduction," 2.
60. Sachse and Walker, "Introduction," 9.
61. Maas, "Introduction," 1; Alvarez, *Allied and Axis*.

62. MacLeod, *Science and the Pacific War*; Matthew Farish, "Creating Cold War Climates: The Laboratories of American Globalism," in *Environmental Histories of the Cold War*, ed. John R. McNeill and Corinne R. Unger (New York: Cambridge University Press, 2013), 51–83.
63. Edgerton, *Britain's War Machine*, 290, 6.
64. Donald T. Fitzgerald, "The Machine in the Pacific," in *Science and the Pacific War: Science and Survival in the Pacific, 1939–1945*, ed. Roy MacLeod (Dordrecht: Kluwer, 2000), 71–81; J. R. McNeill, *Something New Under the Sun: An Environmental History of the Twentieth Century World* (New York: W. W. Norton, 2001); Martin J. Sherwin, *A World Destroyed: Hiroshima and its Legacies*, 3rd ed (Stanford, CA: Stanford University Press, 2003).

Bibliography

Alvarez, David. *Allied and Axis Signals Intelligence in World War II*. Hoboken, NJ: Taylor and Francis, 2013.

Avery, Donald H. *The Science of War: Canadian Scientists and Allied Military Technology*. Toronto: University of Toronto Press, 1998.

DiNardo, Richard Louis. *Mechanized Juggernaut or Military Anachronism? Horses and the German Army of World War II*. Mechanicsburg, PA: Stackpole Books, 2008.

Dupree, A. Hunter. "The Great Instauration of 1940: The Organization of Scientific Research for War." In *The Twentieth Century Sciences: Studies in the Biography of Ideas*, edited by Gerald Holton, 443–467 (New York: W. W. Norton, 1972).

Dupree, A. Hunter. *Science and the Federal Government: A History of Policy and Activities*. Rev. ed. Baltimore, MD: Johns Hopkins University Press, 1986.

Edgerton, David. *Britain's War Machine: Weapons, Resources, and Experts in the Second World War*. Oxford: Oxford University Press, 2011.

Edgerton, David. "British Scientific Intellectuals and the Relations of Science and War in Twentieth Century Britain." In *National Military Establishments and the Advancement of Science: Studies in Twentieth Century History*, edited by Paul Forman and José M. Sanchez-Ron, 1–35. Dordrecht: Kluwer, 1996.

Edgerton, David. "Science and War." In *Companion to the History of Modern Science*, edited by R. C. Olby, G. N. Cantor, J. R. R. Christie, and M. J. S. Hodge, 934–945. London: Routledge, 1990.

Edgerton, David. *Warfare State: Britain, 1920–1970*. Cambridge: Cambridge University Press, 2006.

Ellis, John, and Courtland Moon. "Project Sphinx: The Question of the Use of Gas in the Planned Invasion of Japan." *Journal of Strategic Studies* 12 (1989): 303–323.

Grunden, Walter. *Secret Weapons and World War II: Japan in the Shadow of Big Science*. Lawrence: University of Kansas Press, 2005.

Grunden, Walter E., Yutaka Kawamura, Eduard Kolchinsky, Helmut Maier, and Masakatsu Yamazaki. "Laying the Foundation for Wartime Research: A Comparative Overview of Science Mobilization in Nazi Socialist Germany, Japan, and the Soviet Union." *Osiris* 20 (2005): 71–106.

Harper, Kristine C. *Weather by the Numbers: The Genesis of Modern Meteorology*. Cambridge, MA: MIT Press, 2008.

Harris, J. P. "The Myth of Blitzkrieg." *War in History* 2 (1995): 335–352.

Holloway, David. *Stalin and the Bomb: The Soviet Union and Atomic Energy, 1939–1956*. New Haven, CT: Yale University Press, 1996.

Jacobsen, Annie. *Operation Paperclip: The Secret Program that brought Nazi Scientists to America*. Boston: Little, Brown & Co., 2014.

Kennedy, Paul. *Engineers of Victory: The Problem Solvers Who Turned the Tide in the Second World War*. New York: Random House, 2013.

Kevles, Daniel J. *The Physicists: The History of a Scientific Community in Modern America*. Cambridge, MA: Harvard University Press, 2001.

MacLeod, Roy, ed. *Science and the Pacific War: Science and Survival in the Pacific, 1939–1945*. Dordrecht: Kluwer, 2000.

Maas, Ad, and Hans Hooijmaijers, eds. *Scientific Research in World War II: What Scientists Did in the War*. London: Routledge, 2009.

Mindell, David A. *Between Human and Machine: Feedback, Control, and Computing before Cybernetics*. Baltimore, MD: Johns Hopkins University Press, 2004.

Moy, Timothy. *War Machines: Transforming Technologies in the U.S. Military, 1920–1940*. College Station: Texas A&M University Press, 2001.

Neufeld, Michael J. *The Rocket and the Reich: Peenemünde and the Coming of the Ballistic Missile Era*. New York: Free Press, 1995.

Rhodes, Richard. *The Making of the Atomic Bomb*. New York: Simon & Schuster, 1986.

Sachse, Carole, and Mark Walker, eds. "Politics and Science in Wartime: Comparative International Perspectives on the Kaiser Wilhelm Institute." *Osiris* 20 (2005).

Smith, Bruce L. R. *American Science Policy since World War II*. Washington, DC: Brookings Institution, 1990.

Sulick, Michael J. *Spying in America: Espionage from the Revolutionary War to the Dawn of the Cold War*. Washington, DC: Georgetown University Press, 2012.

Walker, Mark. "The Mobilisation of Science and Science-based Technology during the Second World War." In *Scientific Research in World War II: What Scientists Did in the War*, edited by Ad Maas and Hans Hooijmaijers, 13–30. London: Routledge, 2009.

Walker, Mark. *Nazi Science: Myth, Truth, and the German Atomic Bomb*. New York: Basic Books, 2001.

Weinberg, Gerhart L. *A World at Arms: A Global History of World War II*. 2nd ed. New York: Cambridge University Press, 2005.

CHAPTER 25

THE ENVIRONMENTAL IMPACT

CHARLES CLOSMANN

WORLD War II profoundly transformed global environments. More than any previous military conflict, the war that engulfed the globe between 1939 and 1945 devastated landscapes, consumed vast amounts of natural resources, and disrupted ecological relationships for years to come. The war also accelerated scientific and economic developments that were occurring before the war began, with serious long-run consequences for humans and their physical surroundings. At the same time, however, the effects of war on the environment could be unpredictable, and even beneficial. On the one hand, the residents of major cities devastated by bombs rebuilt quickly after the war, sometimes constructing greener, more livable urban spaces. On the other hand, the construction of military bases across the South Pacific permanently altered island habitats and wiped out some endangered species of birds. A conflict in which belligerent nations deployed the vast power and technology of modern states, World War II changed the environment in complex ways that scholars are still attempting to understand.[1]

Through the late-2010s, relatively few military historians have explored the environmental consequences of World War II. Tradition surely explains part of this. From the time of Thucydides, military historians were fascinated most by battle tactics, the decisions of great generals, and troop movements, among other features of military conflict. Historians who focused on such battle-related military history paid relatively little attention to the natural environment. When military historians studied environmental factors, it was usually when terrain or weather represented obstacles or advantages on the battlefield. Natural environments rarely figured into their thinking as an actor; rather, it was more often a backdrop.[2]

Until about the year 2000, scholars in the burgeoning field of environmental history have also neglected this topic. Defined here as the study of the historical relationship between human societies and their physical surroundings, environmental history originated in the activist climate of the 1960s and 1970s, and it focused on a perceived "ecological crisis" created by rapid population growth, pollution, and dwindling natural resources, among other things. Enough problems existed during times of peace to draw the attention of historians in this field, without having to consider war.[3] Another possibility for the lack of attention to World War II's environmental consequences also exists. If the landscapes of Europe and Japan—including cities like Hiroshima and Nagasaki—could rebuild so quickly after the war, perhaps there just was not much to interest scholars.[4]

Yet while historians showed little interest in this topic until the 2000s, scholars from other fields began to take interest earlier, in the 1980s and 1990s. Alarmed by the effects of Agent Orange on Vietnam, oil fires in the Persian Gulf wars, and other events, scientists started to explore the complicated nexus of warfare and the environment. A movement that matured during this era, modern environmentalism also inspired researchers to ask questions not only about the effects of military operations on people, but also the long run effects on flora, fauna, and ecosystems. Scholars now began to see the material effects of war, and especially twentieth-century war, as a crucial force for ecological change and a threat to sustainability. They also recognized that the quest for resources, such as forests, petroleum, and soil, could itself be a casus belli.[5]

Most of the scholars who began to investigate this topic agreed that World War II marked a decisive change in the relationship between war and the environment.[6] Scientist/activist Arthur H. Westing pioneered this view. Concerned about the impact of modern warfare on a crowded planet, Westing stated:

> With the Earth's natural resources already insufficient to provide an adequate standard of living for all, it becomes especially important to reduce to the extent possible all unnecessary depredations of the global environment. One obvious place to do this is with the environmental depredations that are associated with warfare.[7]

In *Warfare in a Fragile World* (1980), Westing accumulated mountains of data to chronicle how World War II and other twentieth-century conflicts devastated cities, farms, and island ecosystems, sometimes for years.[8] In a subsequent work, *Environmental Hazards of War* (1990), Westing noted that modern technology enabled the belligerent powers of World War II to deliver blast explosives and other munitions in massive quantities, some fifteen million kilograms per day.[9]

Other scholars also emphasized the tangible effects of warfare and agreed that World War II altered global environments in important ways. Focusing on timber resources, Richard P. Tucker noted that World War II had much more devastating effects on forests than World War I. He also demonstrated how accelerated harvesting of wood for war in North America and scientific investigations of hardwoods in tropical regions paved the way for permanent increases in timber production after 1945.[10] Historian John McNeill concurred that World War II brought unprecedented exploitation of resources and new ways of thinking about defense priorities. For instance, McNeill has demonstrated how World War II encouraged the America public to believe that the United States needed bases around the world to ensure its national interests. In the aftermath of World War II, the United States constructed hundreds of bases and thousands of smaller installations around the world, sites that have eventually covered over two million acres of land. Such facilities have left behind toxic chemicals, nuclear radiation, and other environmental hazards.[11]

To McNeill's point, environmental historians have recently emphasized the enormous marshalling of resources that occurred in the United States. In the spirit of President Roosevelt's 1940 call to make America an "arsenal of democracy," the United States authorized the massive expansion of shipyards, armaments plants, oil refineries, mines, and military training grounds across the country. These installations produced vast quantities of air and water pollution, with effects that were often ignored during the time of war.[12] This total war campaign also led to the expansion of cities like Houston, New Orleans, Los Angeles, and Seattle.[13]

Several factors explain why scholars have agreed that World War II marked a decisive event in global environmental history. Above all, they have focused on the measurable consequences of war, things like hectares of forests destroyed, alterations in plant communities on small islands, and the volume of rubble created by aerial bombing of major cities. Such effects were dramatic and global in scope, and they left relatively little room for disagreement that World War II inflicted massive damage on the environment.[14] As noted above, they have also emphasized the vast transformation of society—and environment—that accompanied the preparations for war.[15]

Where some disagreements exist, they concern the more indirect or less tangible environmental effects of World War II. For instance, while scholars agree that cities destroyed by Allied bombing rebuilt quickly after the war, they are more divided about the quality of wastewater systems constructed in the wake of conflict. Scholars who study so-called, "militarized landscapes" also disagree about the legacy of World War II. Peter Coates et al. define such landscapes as sites that have been modified by the military to achieve its goals, while reflecting both evidence of human culture and the physical transformation of the land. They can include a variety of former World War II sites, many of which involved training and logistics, rather than actual combat.[16] The research in this field has increasingly examined not only the material scale and other tangible features of these sites, but also the representational discourses surrounding militarized landscapes. Geographer Rachel Woodward, for example, has explored the British military's claims to environmental sensitivity on military installations, claiming that such proclamations are intended to give the Army a hard-to-criticize image.[17] In contrast, Coates et al. portray such claims by Britain's Ministry of Defense (MOD) in a more positive light.[18] Recent work on militarized landscapes has also emphasized the great diversity of interactions between human communities, nature, and military activities at sites across the globe.[19]

In any event, some of the sharp debates in the field of militarized landscapes concern the period after World War II.[20] Regarding the environmental effects of combat and the marshalling of resources during times of war, there is less disagreement.[21] A few examples, focusing on the material effects of warfare on rural landscapes, cities, forests, and the home front, illustrate this point.

Landscapes of Destruction

Combat inflicted unprecedented destruction on the land during World War II. Nowhere was the destruction more widespread or shocking than in the former Soviet Union. Here, the gigantic size of German and Soviet forces engaged, and the vicious, ideological nature of the war, guaranteed not only massive loss of life (some thirty million Soviet citizens died in the war), but also enormous environmental destruction. Germany attacked the Soviet Union in 1941 with 148 divisions of German troops, and tens of thousands of Finns, Romanians, and other forces. In support of this army of over three million soldiers, the Germans also deployed thousands of artillery pieces, tanks, airplanes, trucks, and horses. More than two million Soviet troops and thousands of tanks and aircraft opposed the German *Blitzkrieg*.[22] German troops quickly outdistanced their supply lines in the summer and fall of 1941, forcing the *Wehrmacht* to strip the countryside of all food and supplies. Retreating Soviet troops also engaged in a brutal "scorched earth" campaign to deny their enemy food, fuel, and capital stock. A series of special administrative groups, including the Council for Evacuation under Lazar Kaganovich, also rushed to save factories and farms from the advancing Germans.[23]

Based upon prewar plans that emphasized development in the Soviet East, and especially Siberia, these special task forces relocated over one thousand factories, countless animals, stores of grain, and other materials to locations east of the Urals.[24] In the Ukraine and other parts of the Soviet Union's western regions, they harvested all remaining crops as they retreated, leaving nothing behind for the Germans or their own citizens. The Soviets burned or dynamited almost everything else.[25] Agricultural and industrial production collapsed: In 1940, the Soviet Union harvested some forty-three million tons of grain in the territories occupied by German troops; two years later this figure fell to less than twelve million. The production of iron, steel, and cement also declined sharply in the so-called Occupied Eastern Territories, as did the generation of electricity at power plants.[26] In the Baltic States, combat and timber cutting left much of the region's forests "burned out and cut over," according to geographer Allan Rodgers.[27] In other parts of the Soviet Union, the war forced twenty-five million people from their homes and left behind destroyed farms, burned villages, and ruined factories.[28]

Much of the landscape recovered after the war. Nature did much of the work, regreening many ruined fields, but the Soviet people also painstakingly rebuilt houses, farms, and factories. Except where battlefields have been commemorated, many former sites of bloody combat showed relatively little evidence of destruction.[29] Yet some environmental problems persisted due to postwar Soviet policies. Determined to rebuild industry quickly after the war, Soviet planners immediately launched another Five Year Plan (1946–1950) with the help of Lend Lease funds from the United States and reparations from Germany. The Soviets prioritized reconstruction and not cleaning up the oil, gas, and chemical wastes dispersed haphazardly during the war. This Stalinist policy mirrored peacetime practices of ignoring environmental concerns like pollution in the interest of rapid industrialization.[30]

Other Soviet policies also profoundly altered the environment. When Soviet officials moved factories and other facilities to Siberia during the war, they opened this vast land to mines, factories, and other gigantic installations in the postwar years. Here, enthusiastic Soviet planners built huge hydroelectric plants along the Angara and Ob rivers, while also harvesting the oil and gas of the Tiumen region. Once again, they adopted careless methods of waste disposal and paid little attention to ecosystems. During the Cold War, they also stored some twenty-six tons of nuclear waste at Mayak, some of which eventually leaked into the Techa River, a tributary of the Ob and the source of drinking water for thousands of people. The Mayak complex became the most radioactive place on earth, and the site of a deadly nuclear explosion in 1957. The cleanup of this devastated region will be an enormous, massively expensive task.[31]

Paradoxically, World War II in the Soviet Union also benefited some features of the environment. Finland transferred huge forested areas and several damaged pulpwood facilities to Soviet Karelia when the war ended. Soviet workers rebuilt the paper mills, but because the Soviet Union had relocated much of the local population, production from these mills was not needed in the region; rather, the Soviets shipped it to locations elsewhere in European Russia.[32] A sixty-mile-wide empty strip on the border between Russia and Finland now became a refuge for wolves, bears, and other rare animals.[33]

The existence of such a greenbelt underscores key lessons about the environmental history of the Soviet Union. First, this history illustrates how plans made for warfare, activities conducted to support war, or policies carried out after war has ended, often have more enduring environmental effects than combat itself.[34] Indeed, the Soviet's relocation of industrial plant east of the Urals more profoundly affected ecosystems than the great battles of Moscow or Kursk. Second the environmental history of the "Great Patriotic War," cannot be understood without considering Stalinist policies of the 1930s, 1940s, and 1950s. For example, the Soviets relocated industrial capacity to Siberia not only to avoid capture by the Germans, but also to open up the Soviet East for development.[35] Finally, this history is extraordinarily complex. For every case of the reckless disposal of toxic wastes or the destruction of river watersheds in Siberia, there undoubtedly exist forests saved from the axe or fragile ecosystems preserved.[36]

World War II also devastated great cities across the globe.[37] In Europe, American and British bombers attacked over one hundred German cities, killing about six hundred thousand people, obliterating urban landscapes, and leaving about one million people homeless. During Operation Gomorrah, bombers attacked Hamburg over seven days in July and August of 1943, dropping thousands of pounds of incendiaries and conventional explosives, killing over forty-two thousand people, and destroying about seventy-five percent of buildings in the city.[38] Targets included military installations, like dockyards, in addition to factories and civilian apartment blocks in outlying areas. The Allies intended not only to inflict massive destruction and loss of life, but also to destroy the morale and fighting spirit of the German people.[39] Bombing and field artillery left some forty percent of all homes in German cities badly damaged or destroyed, and, depending upon how a city was constructed (from wood, stone, or concrete), anywhere from fifty to ninety percent of all structures. By 1945, government officials estimated that Berlin counted some fifty-five million cubic meters of debris, followed by Hamburg with thirty-six million cubic meters, and Dresden with about twenty-five million cubic meter of debris.[40]

The bombing raids also smashed urban infrastructures, including underground water and sewer systems. In Hamburg, the attacks destroyed about twenty-two hundred miles of water pipes and thirteen hundred miles of sewer lines, along with lift stations, electric pumps, and other equipment. Constant raids also prevented repair and maintenance, such that by the end of the war, Hamburg's water supply leaked over thirty-three percent of all water pumped through the system. About two hundred thousand people had also settled outside the city, in areas that lacked proper water and sewer systems.[41] In Frankfurt am Main, aerial bombing created hundreds of breaks in the city's water lines, damage which resulted in the loss of about fifty-five percent of all water in the city's water supply network.[42]

The U.S. Air Force singled out Japanese cities for special treatment. Working in tandem, civilian and military officials from the Air Force and from research teams at Harvard and the National Research Defense Committee, developed new incendiary weapons for attacks on Japan. Military planners encouraged the research teams to produce bombs that would quickly destroy the wooden buildings that characterized most Japanese cities. Using these weapons, the Air Force launched a spectacular raid on Tokyo in March, 1945, an attack that killed more than seventy thousand people, destroyed about seventy percent of the city's buildings, and left about one million people homeless. In total, the United States conducted sixty-two such firebomb attacks on Japanese cities. The United States concluded its brutal air war on Japan with the dropping of atomic bombs on Hiroshima and Nagasaki, raids that instantly killed thousands of people and wiped out large portions of both cities.[43]

The big cities of Japan and Europe rebuilt in short order. Immediately after the war, workers in Hamburg cleared the streets and filled canals with debris, while in Berlin, Munich, and other cities, laborers shoveled rubble into craters or created new park space with bricks and stones. Similar efforts occurred in Warsaw, Rotterdam, and several Japanese cities.[44]

Remarkably, nature and the urban landscapes of Hiroshima and Nagasaki also rebounded. Scientists reported that vegetation near the explosion sites appeared within days and that small animals exposed to the blasts, such as mice, rabbits, and insects, showed no abnormalities. In Hiroshima, wildflowers, vines, and other luxuriant vegetation overran the ruined buildings and charred bones scattered about the landscape, and by 1950 residents had built new houses and other buildings.[45] In fact, urban environments and residents often proved remarkably resilient during the war, although this could vary widely from city to city.[46]

At the same time, the devastation of Hamburg, Tokyo, and other great cities also caused more indirect and enduring changes to the urban landscape. The bombing raids blasted away buildings, bridges, transportation arteries, and other structures, clearing out densely packed cityscapes and leaving a "tabula rasa" for urban planners and developers. Even before the war ended, European experts began planning for the reconstruction and renewal of large cities. Urban planners drew upon criticisms of the city that long predated the war. According to this critique, big cities were unhealthy places, crowded and polluted sites that lacked parks, and that failed to provide light, air, and recreation for the working classes. Sharing this critique, urban planners generally proposed one of three visions for restoring the vitality of cities: modernist designs of planners associated with the Congress of Modern Architecture, older visions of decentralized "garden cities", and ideas from the "city beautiful" movement. Incidentally, planners in other parts of the world, including Japan and the United States, shared similar critiques and similar visions for urban renewal.[47]

Even in the midst of war, some planners promoted these visions of urban renewal. In 1944, Nazi Minister of Armaments Albert Speer called planners and architects together outside Berlin to discuss the rebuilding of Germany. The draft "Wriezen Protocols," as they were called, advocated small, decentralized settlements, a balance of industry and residential housing, and communities that blended harmoniously with local topographical features. Such communities were to reconcile commercial and industrial activities with the need for flood control, electricity, water supplies, and the disposal of sewage.[48]

The reality of postwar urban renewal was far more complicated. Politicians, developers, and experts rarely carried out these utopian visions of decentralized, "greener" cities. Instead, a variety of urban renewal schemes flourished across Europe, Japan, and the United States, depending upon local circumstances. In Germany, cities such as Cologne, Frankfurt, and Munich more often reflected a hodge-podge of rebuilt, older historic buildings beside modern glass structures and/or modern buildings clad in traditional materials. In some cases, cities built broad new esplanades or avenues where bombing had cleared out the landscape; in other cases, cities left old streets in place, a policy that also made rebuilding easier after the war. Suburbs developed according to their own needs, and cityscapes often reflected painful tradeoffs between property owners, developers, and city governments.[49]

The urgent need for new housing also shaped this process. In 1948, and again in 1949, publishers of *Der Städtetag*, a periodical dedicated to urban issues, called for the immediate construction of new housing.[50] It is hardly surprising that German cities rebuilt quickly, in a chaotic form that preserved some features of older urban centers along with scores of hastily constructed residential blocks. This urgency to rebuild also characterized efforts in Japan and other devastated regions.[51]

World War II also altered the urban environment in more subtle ways. While some German cities quickly restored water and sewer systems after the war, this does not seem to have been the case everywhere. Engineers associated with Hamburg's City Water Department have described in detail how city workers struggled for years to repair and extend the supply of drinking water to the inner city and to outlying districts.[52] In fact, the influx of refugees to regions outside the city also resulted in massive environmental and public health problems. Often crowded twenty people to a small house, refugees lacked access to sewer lines and sewage treatment systems, conditions that caused massive pollution in local streams and that would not be alleviated for years.[53] Some engineers have pointed out that the outbreak of war also discouraged the use of "sewage farming," a method of wastewater treatment that involved recycling human waste on farmland. Pioneered by Nazi Germany's Ministry of Agriculture during the 1930s, "sewage farming" was intended not only to provide irrigation and fertilizer to farmland, but also to cleanse the domestic sewage of big cities like Hamburg and Leipzig. After the war, this technology no longer enjoyed widespread support, in part because the increase in Germany's suburban population reduced the amount of farmland available for this technology. Overall, World War II delayed the construction of wastewater treatment systems that might have reduced the horrific pollution that plagued major streams like the Rhine and Elbe.[54]

MARSHALLING RESOURCES FOR WAR

World War II also encouraged the exploitation of natural resources to unprecedented levels. Although this was true for several important natural resources, it was especially true for forests. Because several major powers, including especially Great Britain and Japan (once the war began) controlled vast overseas forests, the exploitation of timber resources also spread throughout the world. It should also be noted that the exploitation of forests could have complicated, long-term consequences.[55]

The destruction and overharvesting of French woodlands was especially severe. Covering about twenty-five million acres during the twentieth century, these forests barely sufficed to meet France's domestic timber needs even during times of peace. When Germany overran France in 1940, it acquired forests that were still recovering from the devastation of World War I. The intense shelling, burning, and other effects of combat destroyed about one million acres of French woodlands during the war, while forest fires burned another five hundred thousand acres. German officials also demanded a fifty percent increase in timber production, with severe implications for France's post war recovery. Arthur Westing has argued that such acute deforestation would have required the French people to reduce timber harvesting by twenty percent annually for five years after the war, just to allow the country's woodlands to recover.[56] More positively, Richard Tucker asserts that American experts believed French forests had survived the war in relatively good condition.[57]

During the war, French forests also served other purposes. For example, the Vichy Regime deployed—both literally and figuratively—the image of young men working in the forest as a source of national regeneration. Vichy Minister for Public Instruction Jacques Chevalier also encouraged the naming of one particular oak for Marshall Pétain, the supposedly stolid leader of the Vichy government. Yet, at the same time, the French resistance movement contested such claims on the meaning of the nation's woodlands, hiding out in the woods and extolling their own work as foresters to create a separate, oppositional sense of national identity. During war, the forest could serve as more than just a vital resource.[58]

Timber harvesting for war had even more profound consequences in other parts of the world. Cut off from sources of timber in Europe, Great Britain harvested millions of board feet of conifers from Canada's Pacific Northwest, wood destined for the construction of airplanes, hangars, packaging, lifeboats, and other equipment. The United States also vastly increased harvesting of wood in the region. The country's use of wood for shipping materials increased from 5.5 billion board feet in 1941, to 16.5 billion by 1943. During World War II, the United States, Great Britain, and other countries exploited timber because it was cheap and easily transported to mills and factories.[59] Forestry officials and private lumber companies also replanted millions of trees, not only conserving forests for future use, but also accelerating the creation of monoculture forests in Oregon, Washington, and British Columbia. By 1945, the frantic campaign to exploit North American forests had created a modern, efficient forest industry, one that would be even more productive in the years to come.[60]

In other parts of the globe, tropical forests became embroiled in war. During 1939 and 1940, the British dramatically increased the harvesting of teak and other hardwoods in Burma, West Africa, and India, among other places. Japanese occupation forces also exploited woodland resources, immediately instituting draconian forestry decrees when they overran Southeast Asia. In Burma, they combined four Japanese forest companies into one—the Nippon Burma Timber Union—to cut as much hardwood as possible. Yet the Japanese never came close to achieving their production goals, even with local workers. In the Philippines, for example, combat had destroyed too many mills, labor troubles persisted under Japanese rule, and many areas remained under the control of local guerrilla forces. In the end, the material damage to tropical forest was relatively limited on a global scale, despite severe deforestation in some parts of Southeast Asia and the Pacific. At the same time, however, Allied forestry experts had conducted extensive surveying of tropical woodlands in Latin America and Africa, efforts that opened these areas up for exploitation in later years.[61]

The warring powers also drew upon other resources during the war. In Japan, government agencies encouraged civilians to make do with less, substituting unfamiliar products for well-known sources of food, fuel, and sustenance. Desperate for fertilizer, Japanese farmers scoured the woods for leaves, fallen branches, and other materials that could be used as compost or fuel. Under the pressure of war, the Japanese also killed millions of songbirds for food, in addition to household pets, animals in the Tokyo Zoo, and other creatures. To fuel their warships, Japanese scientists experimented with new sources of energy, exploring the use of orange peel, soybeans, and pine needles.[62] In Germany, the National Socialist regime built upon practices dating to World War I and encouraged housewives to salvage bones, rags, kitchen scraps, and other refuse, practices that continued for years after the war.[63] During the war, Americans also engaged in a variety of recycling and salvage campaigns as part of their own massive effort to support their armed forces.[64]

Scholars remain divided about the long-term consequences of such war time salvaging, especially in Germany. Ruth Oldenziel and Heike Weber, for instance, have argued that practices of reusing rags, paper, and other materials lasted for one to three decades after the war, in part because wartime activities had become so routine for German housewives (who had to carry out these measures).[65] Oldenziel and Weber's assertion challenges an influential belief among some scholars that the 1950s and 1960s represented a period when newly affluent Europeans abandoned recycling practices. According to this school of thought (pioneered by historian Christian Pfister, who coined the term "Das 1950er Syndrom"), fuel and packaging were cheaper than ever, and Europeans embraced a new economy that encouraged consumption. Hence, they quickly rejected wartime measures that no longer seemed to make sense.[66] Oldenziel and Weber also call attention to the ways that women, children, and other groups were forced to take over the salvaging of materials (presumably glass, rags, metal, and other materials) from Jewish-owned firms, and how, after the war, modern practices of consumption coexisted with older traditions of salvaging and reusing resources.[67]

Warfare also impacted ocean resources, and especially fisheries. Just prior to the war, Japanese trawlers expanded the harvest of tuna and crabs, mostly in an effort to earn hard currency on world markets. The Japanese also stepped up their whale harvest, sending their factory ships into Antarctic waters in search of these creatures. While such efforts done in preparation for war negatively impacted marine resources, the direct effects of combat were more complex, sometimes even beneficial. Once naval warfare began in the Pacific, Japan's overseas fishing efforts completely ended: combat, shortages of hemp and other materials, and the fact that many fishermen entered the military made fishing almost impossible. Valuable marine fish enjoyed a respite from overfishing until at least the late 1940s.[68] Warfare also benefited the marine environment off the continental shelf of Europe, where a halt in commercial fishing allowed populations of haddock, plaice, and hake to increase threefold from the start to the end of the war. Well into the 1970s, sunken ships, abandoned mines, and other wreckage off the coasts of Sweden and Canada discouraged fishing in these regions. At the same time, however, hundreds of sunken merchant vessels and warships created an environmental hazard, littering the ocean floor and leaking millions of cubic meters of oil. The British also dumped surplus chemical munitions off the coasts of Scotland and Ireland after the war, while authorities in the Baltic region discarded German weapons near the island of Bornholm. Overall, the complex impact of World War II on the marine environment demands further study.[69]

Other actions taken in the name of war have accelerated environmental changes. In some cases, research into the development of chemicals to control pests evolved in conjunction with the development of chemical warfare agents.[70] This was certainly true in Germany, where scientists at the chemical conglomerate I. G. Farben worked on the production of both insecticides and other chemicals during the 1930s. By the 1940s, German chemists had developed over one hundred toxic substances, including the poison gases tabun and sarin, and the insecticide Zyklon B, which was later used to murder Russians, Jews, and other groups during the Holocaust.[71]

In the United States, scientists with the Bureau of Entomology and Plant Quarantine began experimenting with the insecticide DDT to shield soldiers from typhus. Later, in the Pacific theater of war, the Chemical Warfare Service sprayed DDT on islands to control malaria, a campaign that saved countless lives.[72] (Incidentally, the development of aerosol spraying of insecticide was itself an innovation driven by military necessity.)[73] Impressed by the results from early tests with DDT, some entomologists called for a "total war" against insect enemies that were attacking crops on the home front. In so doing, they continued the use of language that metaphorically linked the Japanese enemy, one form of "pest," with the insect enemy, another form of "vermin." Such metaphorical language linking insect and human enemies helped not only encourage a war of annihilation against mosquitoes and other pests, but also to dehumanize the Japanese. After 1945, the "war" on insects continued unabated with the relatively careless deployment of DDT and other newly developed chemicals on a massive scale.[74]

Finally, the new scientific breakthroughs associated with the war encouraged some experts to think beyond older ideas of conservation (focused on saving resources), and to envision an early form of environmentalism. Shocked by the vast amounts of pollution created by new technologies and the destructive potential of modern weapons, experts like Aldo Leopold and Rachel Carson embraced a new, more pessimistic way of thinking about the relationship between humans and nature.[75]

Militarized Landscapes

Civilian and military authorities in the United States and other nations needed places—militarized landscapes—to test DDT, incendiaries, and other modern weapons. In the United States, for example, the military's Chemical Warfare Service experimented with incendiary gel weapons in Alabama, Florida, and Utah, sites where they constructed buildings designed to match exactly, down to the curtains and furniture, the kinds of structures targeted for firebombing in Germany and Japan.[76] Scientists in the United States also developed and stored atomic weapons at Los Alamos, New Mexico; Hanford, Washington; and Oak Ridge, Tennessee, all of which suffered from radiation pollution to one degree or another.[77]

Many other types of militarized landscapes also existed during World War II. Such sites have included barracks, parade grounds, airfields, prisoner of war camps, and myriad other places that helped the Allied and Axis forces carry out a "total war." Many such sites still exist as military installations, although many have also been repurposed in one way or another for civilian use. Whether for weapons testing or less immediately violent purposes, militarized landscapes have inspired critical appraisal and considerable debate among scholars of war and the environment.[78]

For example, that British experiments with anthrax on Scotland's Gruinard Island during World War II have created a legacy of distrust among residents of the mainland. In the 1970s, Scottish activists fiercely criticized the government for disregarding the health of local citizens and the quality of the local environment. Even after Britain's MOD conducted clean-up operations in the 1980s, the site remained contaminated with anthrax spores and the source of continuing uncertainty and resentment.[79] Similar controversies have erupted in other locations, such as the Epynt plateau in Wales, where the British military expelled the local population to establish a base in the middle of the war. More controversial was the military's decision to retain this site after the war, action that inspired the anger of Welsh nationalists and the Campaign for Nuclear Disarmament in the 1990s.[80] The British military has made efforts to placate local activists, extolling its own role in protecting local ecosystems, flora, and fauna on these kinds of sites, something that Coates, Pearson et al. have generally praised.[81] Geographer Rachel Woodward is more critical of such claims. Not only does the rhetoric of military environmentalism portray conservation and military aggression as consistent, but it also depicts them as moral equivalents. She points, for instance, to Ministry of Defence (MOD) claims that artillery shell craters in England's Otterburn Training Area have created watery habitats for insects and valuable feeding grounds for birds.[82]

Epilogue: Militarism, Sprawl, and the Sunshine State

A revealing example of the history of militarized landscapes, and the environmental legacy of World War II more generally, exists in Florida. During World War II, over one million soldiers, sailors, and airmen trained in Florida, forever altering the social and economic makeup of the state. Between 1940 and 1943, airfields, encampments, barracks, and navy bases sprang up overnight as the United States government sought to take advantage of Florida's sunny weather and strategic location. Many of these sites, including MacDill Field in Tampa and the extensive navy facilities in Jacksonville, have remained important installations after the war.[83]

The presence of so much military activity in Florida has transformed the environment in crucial ways. Among other things, the experience of serving at Florida's military bases attracted millions of immigrants to the Sunshine State in the 1950s and 1960s, new residents who wanted to enjoy the state's weather, beaches, and other amenities. Such a massive influx of people put extraordinary pressure on Florida's ecosystems, and especially its coastal wetlands, forests, and aquifers. Much research remains to be done on this topic, and especially the way that Floridians have blithely accepted and supported the military presence.[84]

The example of Florida highlights major themes from the environmental history of World War II. First, the long run effects of warfare (especially things "done in the name of war") have often had more profound environmental consequences than combat itself. Patterns of sprawl, pollution, and habitat loss in Florida demonstrate this clearly. Second, the environmental consequences of World War II have often depended upon much broader factors such as pre-war and postwar patterns of forestry, industrial development, and urban planning, issues which also shape the environment.[85] Finally, military sites and activities are ubiquitous, a constant presence in many parts of the world with enormous potential to transform ecosystems for better or worse. Hence, the environmental history of warfare is likely to draw the attention of historians, geographers, and other scholars for years to come.

Notes

1. Charles E. Closmann, ed., *War and the Environment: Military Destruction in the Modern Age* (College Station: Texas A&M University Press, 2009); J.R. McNeill, *Something New Under the Sun: An Environmental History of the Twentieth-Century World* (New York: W. W. Norton & Company, Inc., 2000), 344–347; Richard P. Tucker and Edmund Russell, eds., *Natural Enemy, Natural Ally: Toward an Environmental History of War* (Corvallis, OR: Oregon State University Press, 2004); Arthur H. Westing, *Warfare in a Fragile World: Military Impact on the Human Environment* (London: Taylor & Francis, 1980), 128–143; Thomas Robertson, Richard P. Tucker, Nicholas B. Breyfogle, and Peter Mansoor, eds., *Nature at War: American Environments and World War II* (Cambridge: Cambridge University Press, 2020), eBook.com Online Reader format.
2. My evidence for the lack of research by military history specialists derives from a review of selected tables of contents for the *Journal of Military History*. Scanning selected tables of contents from 2009 through 2021, I found only a handful articles with an environmental focus. The most common environmental themes concerned disease and chemical warfare. For evidence of the way that military historians have often portrayed the environment, see Edmund Russell and Richard P. Tucker, "Introduction," in *Natural Enemy, Natural Ally*, eds. Tucker and Russell, 1–14. See also Charles E. Closmann, "Introduction: Landscapes of Peace, Environments of War," in *War and the Environment*, ed. Closmann, 1–9. See also Simo Laakkonen, Richard P. Tucker, and Timo Vuorisalo, eds., *The Long Shadows: A Global Environmental History of the Second World War* (Corvallis, OR: Oregon State University Press, 2017).
3. Regarding the lack of research on warfare by environmental historians, see Closmann, "Introduction: Landscapes of Peace, Environments of War," in *War and the Environment*, ed. Closmann, 1–9; and Russell and Tucker, "Introduction," in *Natural Enemy, Natural Ally*, eds. Tucker and Russell, 1–14. Another important work in the history of war and the environment, in addition to those noted above, is Edmund Russell, *War and Nature: Fighting Humans and Insects from World War I to Silent Spring* (Cambridge: Cambridge University Press, 2001). The phrase "ecological crisis" comes from Lynn White Jr., "Historical Roots of our Ecological Crisis," *Science* 155, no. 3767 (1967): 1203–1207, https://doi.org/10.1126/science.155.3767.1203. Other literature in the field of environmental history is enormous, and no attempt to summarize that literature will be made in this essay. A few important texts include Roderick Nash, *Wilderness and the American Mind* (New Haven: Yale University Press, 1967); Donald Worster, *Nature's Economy: A History of Ecological Ideas* (Cambridge: Cambridge University Press, 1977); and William Cronon, *Changes in the Land: Indians, Colonists, and the Ecology of New England* (New York: Hill and Wang, 2003).

4. See Jeffry M. Diefendorf, "Wartime Destruction and the Postwar Cityscape," in *War and the Environment*, ed. Closmann, 171–192; and Ferenc M. Szasz, "The Impact of World War II on the Land: Gruinard Island, Scotland, and Trinity Site, New Mexico as Case Studies," *Environmental History Review* 19, no. 4 (Winter 1995): 15–30, https://doi.org/10.2307/3984690.
5. Closmann, "Introduction: Landscapes of Peace, Environments of War," in *War and the Environment*, ed. Closmann, 1–9; McNeill, *Something New Under the Sun*, 345–347; Russell and Tucker, "Introduction," in *Natural Enemy, Natural Ally*, eds. Tucker and Russell, 1–14. See also Westing, *Warfare in a Fragile World*; Arthur H. Westing, ed., *Environmental Hazards of War: Releasing Dangerous Forces in an Industrialized World* (London: Sage Publishers, 1990); Arthur H. Westing, ed., *Herbicides in War: The Long-term Ecological and Human Consequences* (London: Taylor & Francis, 1984); Seth Shulman, *The Threat at Home: Confronting the Toxic Legacy of the U.S. Military* (Boston: Beacon Press, 1992), 61–112; J. P. Robinson, *The Effects of Weapons on Ecosystems* (New York: United Nations Environmental Programme, Pergamon Press, 1979).
6. Closmann, "Introduction: Landscapes of Peace, Environments of War," in *War and the Environment*, ed. Closmann, 1–9; McNeill, *Something New Under the Sun*, 345–347; Russell and Tucker, "Introduction," in *Natural Enemy, Natural Ally*, eds. Tucker and Russell, 1–14; Westing, *Warfare in a Fragile World*; Westing, ed., *Environmental Hazards of War*; Shulman, *The Threat at Home*, 61–112; Robinson, *The Effects of Weapons on Ecosystems*.
7. Westing, *Warfare in a Fragile World*, 1–43, esp. 13–14.
8. Ibid.
9. Westing, ed., *Environmental Hazards*, 1–9; Russell, *War and Nature*, 104–106, 119–144.
10. Richard P. Tucker, "The World Wars and the Globalization of Timber Cutting," in *Natural Enemy, Natural Ally*, eds. Tucker and Russell, 110–141.
11. J. R. McNeill and David S. Painter, "The Global Environmental Footprint of the U.S. Military, 1789–2003," in *War and the Environment*, ed. Closmann, 10–31.
12. See various chapters in Robertson, Tucker, Breyfogle, and Mansoor, eds., *Nature at War*. Regarding Roosevelt's speech, see Julian E. Zelizer, *Arsenal of Democracy: The Politics of National Security—From World War II to the War on Terrorism* (New York, NY: Basic Books, 2010), 1–2.
13. Robertson, Tucker, Breyfogle and Mansoor, eds., *Nature at War*.
14. For evidence of how scholars have approached the consequences of World War II, see various chapters in Tucker and Russell, eds. *Natural Enemy, Natural Ally*, and Closmann, ed. *War and the Environment*. See also chapters in Laakkonen, Tucker, and Vuorisalo, eds. *The Long Shadows*.
15. Robertson, Tucker, Breyfogle, and Mansoor, eds., *Nature at War*.
16. Peter Coates, Tim Cole, Marianna Dudley, and Chris Pearson, "'Defending Nation, Defending Nature?' Militarized Landscapes and Military Environmentalism in Britain, France, and the United States," *Environmental History* 16, no. 3 (July 2011): 456–491, esp. 458, https://www.jstor.org/stable/23049827.
17. Rachel Woodward, "Khaki Conservation: An Examination of Military Environmentalist Discourses in the British Army," *Journal of Rural Studies* 17, no. 2 (April 2001): 201–217, esp. 207, https://doi.org/10.1016/S0743-0167(00)00049-8.
18. Coates et al. "'Defending Nation, Defending Nature?'" 456–491.
19. Robertson, Tucker, Breyfogle, and Mansoor, eds., *Nature at War*. See also Simo Laakkonen, J.R. McNeill, Richard P. Tucker, and Timo Vuorisalo, eds., *The Resilient City*

in *World War II: Urban Environmental Histories* (Cham, Switzerland: Palgrave Macmillan, 2020), accessed August 25, 2022, https://link.springer.com/content/pdf/10.1007/978-3-030-17439-2.pdf.
20. Ibid., and Woodward, "Khaki Conservation," 201–217.
21. For evidence of how scholars have approached the consequences of World War II, see various chapters in Tucker and Russell, eds. *Natural Enemy, Natural Ally*, and Closmann, ed. *War and the Environment*. See also chapters in Laakkonen, Tucker, and Vuorisalo, eds. *The Long Shadows*.
22. Paul Josephson, Nicolai Dronin, Ruben Mnatsakanian, Aleh Cherp, Dmitry Efremenko and Vladislav Larin, *An Environmental History of Russia* (Cambridge: Cambridge University Press, 2013), 112–131.
23. Ibid., 112–115, and Sanford R. Lieberman, "The Evacuation of Industry in the Soviet Union during World War II," *Soviet Studies* 35, no. 1 (January 1983): 90–102, https://www.jstor.org/stable/151494.
24. Josephson et al. *Environmental History of Russia*, 112–115; and Lieberman, "The Evacuation of Industry," 90–102, esp. 112–115.
25. Josephson et al. *Environmental History of Russia*, 112–131.
26. Ibid., 112–115, esp. 115.
27. Allan Rodgers, "Changing Locational Patterns in the Soviet Pulp and Paper Industry," *Annals of the Association of American Geographers* 45, no. 1 (March 1955): 85–104, esp. 100, 10.1111/j.1467-8306.1955.tb01484.x.
28. Josephson et al. *Environmental History of Russia*, 116–128, 130–131, esp. 115.
29. McNeill, *Something New Under the Sun*, 344–345; and Laakkonen, Tucker, and Vuorisalo, "The Long Shadows," in *The Long Shadows*, ed. Laakkonen, Tucker, and Vuorisalo, 3–14.
30. Josephson et al. *Environmental History of Russia*, 116–128, 130–131.
31. McNeill, *Something New Under the Sun*, 343–344; Josephson et al. *Environmental History of Russia*, 130–131.
32. Rodgers, "Changing Locational Patterns," 101.
33. Simo Laakkonen, "War—An Ecological Alternative to Peace? Indirect Impacts of World War II on the Finnish Environment," in *Natural Enemy, Natural Ally*, ed. Tucker and Russell, 175–194.
34. Ibid., 175–194; McNeill, *Something New Under the Sun*, 341–347; and Laakkonen, Tucker, and Vuorisalo, ed., *The Long Shadows*.
35. Important works on the environmental history of the Soviet Union include Stephen Brain, *Song of the Forest: Russian Forestry and Stalinist Environmentalism, 1905-1953* (Pittsburgh: University of Pittsburgh Press, 2011); Josephson et al. *Environmental History of Russia*, and Douglas Weiner, *Models of Nature: Ecology, Conservation and Cultural Revolution in Soviet Russia* (Pittsburgh: University of Pittsburgh Press, 2000). For McNeill's general conclusion, *Something New Under the Sun*, 344.
36. Josephson et al. *Environmental History of Russia*; Brain, *Song of the Forest*; Laakkonen, Tucker, and Vuorisalo, eds., *The Long Shadows*.
37. Simo Laakkonen, Richard P. Tucker, and Timo Vuorisalo, "Hypotheses: World War II and its Shadows," in *The Long Shadows*, ed. Laakkonen, Tucker, and Vuorisalo, 315–332.See also Laakkonen, McNeill, Tucker, and Vuorisalo, eds., *The Resilient City*.
38. Jeffry M. Diefendorf, "Wartime Destruction and the Postwar Cityscape," in *War and the Environment*, ed. Closmann, 171–192.

39. Russell, *War and Nature*, 130–144; Diefendorf, "Wartime Destruction," in *War and the Environment*, ed. Closmann, 171–192.
40. Diefendorf, "Wartime Destruction," 171–192. See also Tony Judt, *Postwar: A History of Europe since 1945* (New York: Penguin Press, 2005), 81–86, 235–236.
41. Alfred Meng, *Geschichte der Hamburger Wasserversorgung* (Hamburg: Medien-Verlag Schubert, 1993), 291–313; Wilhelm Drobek, "Das Wasser einer MillionenStadt," *Hamburger Echo*, December 9, 1950.
42. K. S. Watson, "The Water Supply in Frankfurt, Germany," *Water & Sewage Works* 93, no. 7 (July 1946): 261–266.
43. Russell, *War and Nature*, 119–144.
44. Diefendorf, "Wartime Destruction," in *War and the Environment*, ed. Closmann, 171–192. See also William M. Tsutsui, who notes that Tokyo recovered quickly after the great bombing raids, with shacks and market stalls emerging just days later. See William M. Tsutsui, "Landscapes in the Dark Valley: Toward an Environmental History of Wartime Japan," *Environmental History* 8, no. 2 (April 2003): 294–311, esp., 296.
45. Tsutsui "Landscapes in the Dark Valley," 294–311, esp., 296–297.
46. See also Laakkonen, McNeill, Tucker, and Vuorisalo, eds., *The Resilient City*. Regarding Munich, see Thomas J. (Tom) Arnold, "Gaining Strength from Nature: Surviving War in Munich," in *The Resilient City*, eds. Laakkonen, McNeill, Tucker, and Vuorisalo, 127–150.
47. Diefendorf, "Wartime Destruction," in *War and the Environment*, ed. Closmann, 171–192, esp., 181.
48. Ibid., 171–192, esp., 181.
49. Ibid., 171–192.
50. "Wir brauchen Wohnungen, Wohnungen, Wohungen" 5 *Der Städtetag* (May 1949), page numbers not recorded; "Heimat den Heimatlosen," *Der Städtetag* 8 (August 1949), page numbers not recorded.
51. Diefendorf, "Wartime Destruction," in *War and the Environment*, ed. Closmann, 171–192.
52. Wilhelm Drobek, "Die Wasserversorgung der Freien und Hansestadt Hamburg, Sonderdruck aus GWF," *Das Gas und Wasserfach* 95, no, 10, 20, 22 (1954), complete page numbers not recorded, probably 1–15.
53. Regarding overall conditions in Hamburg, see *Hamburg und seine Bauten: 1929–1953* (Hamburg: Hoffman und Camp Verlag, 1953), 315–316.
54. H. Rohde, "Sewage Treatment Progress in Germany," *Water & Sewage Works* 101, no. 4 (April 1954): 176–179; Hendrik Seeger, "The History of German Waste Water Treatment," *European Water Management* 2, no. 5 (October 1999): 51–56.
55. Greg Bankoff, "Woods for War: The Legacy of Human Conflict on the Forests of the Philippines, 1565–1946," in *War and the Environment*, ed. Closmann, 32–48; J. R. McNeill and David S. Painter, "The Global Environmental Footprint," in *War and the Environment*, ed. Closmann, 10–31; Richard P. Tucker, "The World Wars and the Globalization of Timber Cutting," in *Natural Enemy, Natural Ally*, ed. Tucker and Russell, 110–141; J. R. McNeill, "Woods and Warfare in World History," *Environmental History* 9, no. 3 (July 2004): 388–410. See also McNeill, *Something New Under the Sun*, 344–347.
56. Westing, *Warfare in a Fragile World*, 51–53.
57. Tucker, "The World Wars and the Globalization of Timber Cutting," in *Natural Enemy, Natural Ally*, ed. Tucker and Russell, 110–141.

58. Chris Pearson, "'The Age of Wood': Fuel and Fighting in French Forests, 1940–1944," *Environmental History* 11, no. 4 (October 2006): 775–803.
59. McNeill, "Woods and Warfare in World History," 388–410.
60. Tucker, "The World Wars and the Globalization of Timber Cutting," in *Natural Enemy, Natural Ally*, ed. Tucker and Russell, 110–141.
61. Ibid., 388–410; Bankoff, "Woods for War," in *War and the Environment*, ed. Closmann, 32–48; Tucker, "The World Wars and the Globalization of Timber Cutting," in *Natural Enemy, Natural Ally*, ed. Tucker and Russell, 110–141.
62. Tsutsui, "Landscapes in the Dark Valley," 294–311.
63. Ruth Oldenziel and Heike Weber, "Introduction: Reconsidering Recycling," *Contemporary European History* 22, no. 3 (August 2013): 347–370, https://www.jstor.org/stable/43299390.
64. See Robertson, Tucker, Breyfogle, and Mansoor, eds., *Nature at War*.
65. Oldenziel and Weber, "Reconsidering Recycling," 347–370.
66. Ibid., 347–370, esp., 368; Frank Uekötter, "Umweltbewegung zwischen dem Ende der nationalisozilistischen Herrschaft und der 'ökologischen Wende': Eine Literaturbericht," *Historische Sozialforschung* 28 no. 1, 2 (2003): 270–289, http://www.jstor.org/stable/20757983. The term "Das 1950er Syndrom" comes from Christian Pfister, *Das 1950er Syndrom: Der Weg in die Konsumgesellschaft* (Berne: Haupt, 1995).
67. Oldenziel and Weber, "Reconsidering Recycling," 347–370, and Chad Denton, "'Récupérez!' The German Origins of French Wartime Salvage Drives, 1939–1945," *Contemporary European History* 22, no. 3(August 2013): 399–430, https://www.jstor.org/stable/43299392.
68. Tsutsui, "Landscapes in the Dark Valley," 294–311.
69. Westing, *Warfare in a Fragile World*, 144–182.
70. Edmund Russell, "Mobilizing for War," in *Natural Enemy, Natural Ally*, ed. Tucker and Russell, 142–174, esp. 144.
71. Ibid., 154–166.
72. Ibid., 142–174.
73. Randall Latta and L. D. Goodhue, "Aerosols for Insects," in *The Yearbook of Agriculture, 1943–1947* (Washington, DC: United States Department of Agriculture, U.S. Government Printing Office, 1947), 623–627.
74. Russell, "Mobilizing for War," in *Natural Enemy, Natural Ally*, ed. Tucker and Russell, 142–174, esp., 157 and 160.
75. Thomas Robertson, "Total War and the Total Environment: World War II and the Shift from Conservation to Environmentalism," in *Nature at War*, ed. Robertson, Tucker, Breyfogle and Mansoor, 325–358.
76. Russell, *War and Nature*, 104–108.
77. Szasz, "The Impact of World War II on the Land," 15–30.
78. Coates et al. "Defending Nation, Defending Nature?" 456–491; Chris Pearson, "Researching Militarized Landscapes: A Literature Review on War and the Militarization of the Environment," *Landscape Research* 37, no. 1 (February 2012): 115–133, https://www.tandfonline.com/doi/abs/10.1080/01426397.2011.570974.
79. Szasz, "The Impact of World War II on the Land," 15–30.
80. Coates et al. "Defending Nation, Defending Nature?" 456–491.
81. Chris Pearson, Peter Coates, and Tim Cole, "Introduction: Beneath the Camouflage: Revealing Militarized Landscapes," in *Militarized Landscapes: From Gettysburg to*

Salisbury Plain, ed. Chris Pearson, Peter Coates, and Tim Cole (London: Continuum, 2010), 1–20.
82. Woodward, "Khaki Conservation," 201–217.
83. Joe Crankshaw, "Military Activity isn't New to Florida," *Stuart News/Port St. Lucie News*, February 11, 2003; Lewis N. Wynne, *Florida at War* (Dade City, Fla: Saint Leo College Press, 1993), 1–8.
84. Jack E. Davis and Raymond Arsenault, eds. *Paradise Lost? The Environmental History of Florida* (Gainesville, Fla: University Press of Florida, 2005).
85. Closmann, ed. *War and the Environment*; McNeill, *Something New Under the Sun*, 344–347; Tucker and Russell, eds. *Natural Enemy, Natural Ally*; Pearson et al. *Militarized Landscapes*.

Bibliography

Bennett, Judith A. *Natives and Exotics: World War II and Environment in the South Pacific*. Honolulu: University of Hawai'i Press, 2009.

Closmann, Charles E. *War and the Environment: Military Destruction in the Modern Age*. College Station: Texas A&M University Press, 2009.

Diefendorf, Jeffry M. *In the Wake of War: The Reconstruction of German Cities after World War II*. New York: Oxford University Press, 1993.

Josephson, Paul, Nicolai Dronin, Ruben Mnatsakanian, Aleh Cherp, Dmitry Efremenko, and Vladislav Larin. *An Environmental History of Russia*. Cambridge: Cambridge University Press, 2013.

Laakkonen, Simo, Richard Tucker, and Timo Vuorisalo, eds., *The Long Shadows: A Global Environmental History of the Second World War*. Corvallis, OR: Oregon State University Press, 2017.

McNeill, J. R. *Something New Under the Sun: An Environmental History of the Twentieth-Century World*. New York: W.W. Norton & Company, Inc., 2000.

Oldenziel, Ruth, and Heike Weber. "Introduction: Reconsidering Recycling." *Contemporary European History* 22, no. 3 (August 2013): 347–370. https://www.jstor.org/stable/43299390.

Pearson, Chris, Peter Coates, and Tim Cole, eds., *Militarized Landscapes: From Gettysburg to Salisbury Plain*. London: Continuum, 2010.

Robertson, Thomas, Richard P. Tucker, Nicholas B. Breyfogle, and Peter Mansoor, eds., *Nature at War: American Environments during World War II*. Cambridge, Cambridge University Press, 2020. eBook.com Online Reader format.

Russell, Edmund. *War and Nature: Fighting Humans and Insects with Chemicals from World War I to Silent Spring*. Cambridge: Cambridge University Press, 2001.

Tucker, Richard P., and Edmund Russell, eds., *Natural Enemy, Natural Ally: Toward an Environmental History of War*. Corvallis, OR: Oregon State University Press, 2004.

Westing, Arthur H. *Warfare in a Fragile World: Military Impact on the Human Environment*. London: Taylor & Francis, 1980.

CHAPTER 26

MEDICINE AND DISABILITY

JOHN M. KINDER

"War is a gluttonous and capricious feeder. It demands the full strength of men for its food. But so vicious and profligate are its habits that many who approach it as sacrifices are merely mauled, bled, and thrown aside half devoured." So wrote Keith Wheeler, an American war correspondent who was shot at the Battle of Iwo Jima and later penned a book about the men he met while recovering in hospital. That Wheeler lived to tell the tale was, as the author acknowledged, mere luck—an inch or two in any direction and the bullet would have undoubtedly killed him. However, his case (and millions like it) also testified to the power of military medicine to undo the effects of war's violence.[1]

Any discussion of medicine in World War II will no doubt devolve into a tangle of generalizations—and rightfully so. There were simply too many people involved, too many contradictory forces at work, for a single author to cover the medical dimensions of the conflict in their entirety. By most estimates, more than seventy-five million people perished during World War II, the vast majority of them civilians. Tens of millions of men and women returned home permanently disabled, their bodies and minds forever marked by war's traumas. Following the war, all the major belligerent nations produced multivolume medical histories (sometimes thousands of pages long) in an effort to make sense of the slaughter. Read today, works like the *Medical Services of the R.A.N. and R.A.A.F.* (1961) and the *United States Army Dental Service in World War II* (1952) convey a remarkable note of hopefulness, a belief that the lessons learned in a half-decade of savage fighting will translate into a healthier future for postwar generations. Even so, they remain catalogues of injury, disease, and suffering. Flipping through the seemingly endless descriptions of ruptured organs and deranged minds, one cannot help but wonder how anyone survived the carnage intact.

Yet survive they did, in many cases because of the remarkable courage and ingenuity of the men and women charged with their care. Government-sponsored histories aside, World War II spawned countless memoirs, published diaries, and firsthand accounts of doctors in uniform.[2] Although the experiences of individual physicians and medics inevitably varied, two themes run throughout postwar medical testimony. Perhaps the most jarring is a pronounced awe at humans' capacity to unleash violence on each other.

All wars are, by their very nature, bloodbaths, but World War II subjected combatants and civilians to hitherto unimagined butchery. At the same time, survivors marveled at the human body's capacity to endure amidst the most terrible of conditions. Thanks to the development of new medicines, surgical techniques, and evacuation procedures, frontline soldiers were less killable than at any previous time in world history. Broadly speaking, then, the history of medicine in World War II is best understood as part of a larger human project: the struggle to reconcile the frailty of the human body to the life-ending dangers of the technological world.

Its historical implications notwithstanding, World War II medicine is significant in its own right. To begin with, the threat of injury and disease was one of the few things all uniformed troops had in common. Bodily damage was the *lingua franca* of World War II, the language that all troops understood (and, often, their chief way of communicating with their adversaries). As a result, medical personnel were a persistent presence throughout the war, from the airbases of Britain to the jungles of Southeast Asia. More than any other war preceding it, World War II was a biopolitical conflict, a war in which all sides attempted to marshal the forces of life and death to serve the needs of the state.[3]

Furthermore, medicine—like all wartime resources—was not equally distributed during the war, nor was it equally available on all sides. In World War II, the most successful armies (e.g., the United States) had not only the greatest stores of drugs, wound dressings, and blood plasma, but also the most thorough means of maximizing their effect. Indeed, a common sign of an army's impending defeat in World War II (the Germans in the Soviet Union, the Japanese in the South Pacific) was the rapid decline of much-needed provisions of medical supplies. A fighting force without medicine faced the same fate as one without food or weapons: destruction, capture, and defeat.

No less important, the field of wartime medicine was as expansive and diverse as the war itself. Although medics were typically expected to deal with a common set of injuries (wounds, burns, broken bones), the practice of medicine in World War II evolved in response to a wide array of medical emergencies and fighting environments. In this sense, the term "military medicine" functioned largely as an umbrella under which more specialized fields—aviation medicine, desert medicine, tropical medicine, naval medicine—came to flourish.

Ultimately, medicine played a dual role in World War II and its aftermath. On the one hand, medical personnel extended the lives of millions of people. Advances in wound treatment, sulfa drugs, and emergency evacuation allowed sick and severely wounded combatants to survive and, in some cases, recover from injuries that would have proved fatal just a few years earlier. On the other hand, medicine was deployed as a tool of oppression, torture, and genocide. In the United States, psychiatrists and military higher-ups wielded medicine as an instrument for reshaping not only the makeup of the armed forces but the postwar world as well. Psychiatric discharges for homosexuality, alcoholism, "troublemaking," and other perceived ailments tarred some veterans as "undesirable" for life. In fascist Germany and imperial Japan, concentration camp and frontline surgeons performed ghastly medical procedures on civilian and military prisoners—sometimes out of a proclaimed desire to better their craft, sometimes under the cloak of race science, and sometimes simply for their own pleasure. After the war, the victorious armies grappled with questions about the ethical use of medical knowledge derived from torture and murder victims.

Put simply, medicine in World War II was not relegated to the science of healing. Surgeons, psychiatrists, and other medical personnel functioned as important cogs in the production of death and suffering on a global scale.

Narrating Military Medicine: Omission, Exception, and Advancement

In retrospect, military medicine—a term that encompasses everything from antimalarial campaigns to facial reconstruction surgery—occupies a curious place within the written history and public memory of World War II. The war was, by any measure, the most destructive military conflict the world has ever known. In perhaps the first (and only) truly total war of modern history—and, due the development of atomic weapons, most likely the last—military tactics once deemed criminal attained a newfound sense of moral legitimacy. Both Axis and Allied forces carried out "strategic" bombing campaigns against military bases, arms factories, and civilian centers previously considered off-limits according to the rules of "civilized" warfare. Cultural monuments were looted and destroyed; landscapes reshaped by metal and fire; cities razed to the ground; populations eradicated. Whatever sense of moderation that had once held war's violence in check was gradually, and then with astonishing rapidity, abandoned.[4]

Against this backdrop, the story of military medicine in World War II is typically narrated in one of two ways—if it is presented at all. A surprising number of general histories of World War II ignore the issue of medicine, beyond citing injury statistics and rates of disease. Several factors are to blame for such omissions. Popular histories of the war often focus on matters of combat and strategy—in other words, what many readers perceive to be the "real" war. Likewise, relatively few military historians have the background and inclination to grapple with medical issues, a dimension of war studies notorious for its faulty statistics, inscrutable jargon, and dense archival records. For some historians of World War II, it would seem, analyzing medicine in depth simply is not worth the effort.

When military medicine is discussed at length, it is often presented as a matter of *exception*, adjacent to and yet somehow set apart from the central narrative of the war.[5] For students of military history, this should come as no surprise. Since the nineteenth century, the realm of medicine has attempted to separate itself from warfare, even as the two have become inextricably intertwined. According to the Geneva Conventions, World War II-era hospital ships and medics were off-limits from intentional attack. Medical personnel wore brassards indicating their non-combatant status, and hospital buildings and vessels were frequently adorned with large red crosses. In a conflict of such immense scale, no one fully expected medical personnel to escape the war unscathed. Accidents were inevitable, and thousands of doctors, nurses, and medics were killed in aerial attacks, ground assaults, and naval battles. Moreover, in numerous cases, both medical personnel and wounded troops were targeted for attack. During the battle of Tobruk in 1941, Axis forces bombed several Australian medical buildings. Shortly thereafter, an Australian infantry unit fired upon a German medical post (unintentionally, according to Canberra); the next day, an Australian lorry was bombed in reprisal.[6]

Despite the relative frequency of such attacks, postwar commentators nevertheless expressed outrage when war's most sacred commandment—do not touch the wounded and medical staff—had been violated. Among Western writers, Japan received the bulk of the criticism. In a conflict fueled by nationalism, religion, and racial hatred, Japanese forces bombed hospitals, bayoneted the wounded, and intentionally targeted enemy medical officers. But they were not alone. As the war dragged on, Allies fighting in Asia increasingly felt little need to recognize the medical realm's exceptional status. Writing in the *Atlantic Monthly* in 1946, the U.S. war correspondent Edgar L. Jones demanded, "What kind of war do civilians suppose we fought anyway? We shot prisoners in cold blood, wiped out hospitals, strafed lifeboats, killed or mistreated enemy civilians, finished off the enemy wounded, tossed the dying into a hole with the dead, and in the Pacific boiled the flesh off enemy skulls to make table ornaments for sweethearts." A major with the U.S. 5th Bomber command was more succinct: "You can't be sporting in a war."[7] Everything, including killing the already-injured, was fair game.

By far the most popular means of narrating the history of World War II medicine relies upon the concept of *advancement*, an insistence upon framing medical developments as evidence of technological and moral progress. Other military technologies—weapons, for example—are routinely cast as "advancements," some with long-term benefits for postwar generations. However, the progressive character of medical developments is rarely challenged. Indeed, for serious historians and World War II mythmakers alike, an ideology of advancement has dominated discussions of military medicine. Armed with a pharmacy of new drugs, better developed systems of casualty evacuation, and more enlightened approaches to soldiers' physical and mental injuries, warring armies were able to save the lives of millions of injured troops. Diseases and injuries that would have been fatal in earlier conflicts now resulted only in permanent disability; precious manpower that would have been lost for the duration of the conflict could be salvaged, if only temporarily. Developments in military medicine are among the few aspects of World War II that are held up as unassailably good. Historian Gerhard L. Weinberg echoes what has become the dominant refrain: "In a war which involved so many new types of weapons, many of them more deadly even than those which had caused such carnage in World War I, there was one field of endeavor in which great advances were made in the saving rather than the destruction of life: Medicine."[8]

As evidence, historians typically point to the introduction of new drugs designed to curb disease and eliminate that most dreaded of wartime scourges: infection. During World War II, physicians' arsenal included a host of new pharmaceuticals. The most groundbreaking were sulfonamide (sulfa) drugs, a category of anti-bacterial medicines credited with saving the lives of thousands of injured troops. Although toxic in large doses, sulfa drugs—administered either topically or orally—were used to treat everything from burns and tissue wounds to influenza, sore throat, and gonorrhea. In some armies, sulfa drugs were issued to soldiers heading into battle, and they were generally considered among the "basic" components (along with morphine, wound dressings, and splints) of medics' first aid kits.[9] Beginning in 1943, large numbers of wounded Americans were saved by a second, more powerful, "wonder drug" capable of fighting infection deep within the body. To many, the introduction of penicillin marked the dawn of a new era in modern warfare: moving forward, microscopic bacteria would no longer be an invisible killer.

World War II spawned other medical developments, some as important, if not quite as readily lauded, as antibacterial medications. Warring armies used airlifts and a strategy of "phased evacuation" (i.e., treating the most seriously injured near the front and carrying out more difficult procedures later) to speed wounded troops from the battlefield to the operating table. Surgical teams invented techniques for treating post-injury shock. Blood plasma—dehydrated, shipped in bags, and then rehydrated on the battlefield—worked wonders to extend wounded men's lives. Plasma could not fully replace whole blood, which spoiled easily and, unlike plasma, required typing. Nevertheless, the expansion of the blood bank model of blood plasma donation remains one of World War II's most significant, if overlooked, medical legacies. If nothing else, it allowed millions of anonymous donors to give something of themselves—quite literally—so that their wounded countrymen might live.[10]

An additional medical advance from the World War II era merits brief mention: a recognition of soldiers' limitations to endure the hardships and horrors of modern warfare. Throughout military history, a combatant's ability to keep fighting—to "soldier on" despite threat to body and mind—has been viewed as sign of individual courage, loyalty, or manliness. Although World War I had introduced much of the world to the phenomenon of "shell shock," a culture of brutishness continued to hold sway amongst many of the old breed that led both the Allied and Axis war efforts.[11] In August 1943, U.S. Army General George S. Patton famously assaulted a young psychiatric patient, slapping his face and calling him a "god-damned coward" after the man complained of weak nerves.[12] Yet studies by the U.S. Surgeon General's Office and other agencies confirmed what earlier generations of military psychiatrists had long suspected: that "the stress of war set limits to human endurance."[13] No matter how well trained, no matter how pumped full of propaganda, all uniformed troops had a breaking point. The only questions were, how long did individual combatants have before they broke down, and what measures, if any, could be taken to forestall the inevitable?

MEDICINE AND THE WAR SYSTEM

Histories of medical advancement during World War II frequently obscure a more significant development: the integration of medical science into the war system, the network of bureaucratic, commercial, and military structures that make modern war possible. Although experienced on an individual level, World War II was conceptualized, waged, and ultimately won on a mass scale. Warring nations not only had to mobilize millions of would-be heroes but also produce, transport, and manage massive supplies of food, weapons, and material—often from thousands of miles away or while enduring invasion at home. Within this context, an army's access to the latest drugs or technologies was far less important than its ability to put some kind of medical strategy—no matter how crude—into practice.

As one might expect, belligerents with the strongest industrial bases and transportation systems had a decided advantage. Troops from the United States, Great Britain, and Germany tended to have access to large caches of drugs and dressings, and, over the course of the war, the three nations developed highly sophisticated networks of evacuation and supply. By the war's end, American pharmaceutical manufacturers were pumping out more than seven thousand billion units of penicillin a year (up from twenty-one billion units in 1943).[14] Other warring parties, however, struggled to translate military-medical potential into reality. The Soviet Union, for example, suffered from shortages of medical equipment, instruments, and expertise from the very beginning. Recognizing the deficiency, Stalin's government attempted to ramp up production of new doctors, but it was too little, too late. In her study of wartime Soviet medicine, Mary Schaeffer Conroy concludes that Russian industry was simply "not ready for war on Soviet Soil." Although the Soviets eventually claimed victory in the Great Patriotic War, they paid a heavy price: twenty million dead, among them an unknown number of civilians killed in the typhus and typhoid epidemics that swept the country.[15]

Even if medical supplies were readily available, there was no guarantee that troops would use them. Take the case of malaria, for instance. In the South Pacific, malaria was a constant menace, with disease rates nearing one hundred percent on some jungle islands. When U.S. forces were cut off from sources of quinine, the primary treatment of malaria, scientists developed a synthetic alternative: Atabrine. Inexpensive to manufacture and distribute, it appeared to be the perfect answer to the military's dilemma. There was just one problem: the soldiers refused to take it. The little yellow pills tasted bitter and sometimes produced disturbing side effects, from nausea and vomiting to psychotic episodes. During one epidemic, medics were forced to inspect men's mouths to ensure that they had swallowed the pills. In the end, however, large numbers of soldiers and marines chose the tropical illness over the government-supplied medicine.[16] Whether they intended to or not, their refusal taught a powerful lesson, one that all medical planners had to learn at one time or another: military medicine cannot succeed without at least the tacit approval of the combatants themselves.

In no aspect of war was the relationship between medicine and the war system more intimate (and interdependent) than in the burgeoning field of air medicine. Although military aviation predated World War II, the conflict marked a turning point in the history of aerial warfare. The Allies' victory in the battle for air supremacy was a deciding factor—some might argue *the* deciding factor—in the defeat of Germany and Japan. Unfortunately, as physicians quickly discovered, long-term exposure to the upper air wreaked havoc on flyers' bodies and minds. The cabins of World War II-era planes were deafening and frigidly cold. Temperatures routinely dropped to fifty below zero °F, and airmen returned to base suffering from ailments normally associated with high-altitude mountaineers: frostbitten limbs, trench foot, and excruciating gas build-up in the blood (a condition better known as the "bends"). Oxygen deprivation caused men to vomit and slur their speech, and pilots attempting to pull out of steep dives progressively lost vision as blood was forced from the irises in their eyes. Worst of all was the mental anguish—the strained monotony punctuated by bursts of adrenaline and terror. Long-range bombing runs could last more than ten hours, during which time flight crews had little to do other than ponder the inevitable and struggle to remain awake. For the average airman, debilitating fatigue was normal, eventual psychiatric collapse a near certainty.[17]

Working with flight engineers, physicians developed new oxygen masks and inflatable "anti-G" flight suits designed to encourage blood flow during long sorties. They produced drugs to prevent motion sickness and personal protection against flak, bits of flying shrapnel that caused the highest percentage of airmen's injuries. In Australia, potential flyers were given Rorschach personality tests to screen for "defects of personality" alongside standard exams for night vision and hand-eye coordination. Before the war began, some nations developed special research committees to analyze the medical dimensions of air war. The most forward-thinking understood what has since become standard wisdom in aviation medicine: that healthy human bodies and minds are a necessary component of any air arsenal.[18]

The aerial theater notwithstanding, did medicine play a decisive role on the World War II battlefield? The simple answer is yes—and no. In a conflict where even relatively minor skirmishes could involve hundreds, if not thousands, of combatants, no single factor—not weather, not courage, not surprise, not innovation—was ever wholly decisive in determining victory or defeat. One of the most frustrating aspects of World War II, especially for those who seek to mythologize it, is the war's resistance to easy explanation. Historians cannot even agree when the war began: With the German invasion of Poland in 1939? The Japanese attack on China in 1937? Earlier still? That said, the availability of medical supplies and the implementation of sound medical practices was, without a doubt, a singular advantage to forces in the field. In the simplest terms: excess of medicine did not ensure victory in World War II, but it certainly helped.

As a test case, consider the U.S.–Japanese battle for the island of Guadalcanal (August 1942–February 1943). The terrain was a military doctor's worst nightmare. Jutting out of the southwestern Pacific like a steaming green rock, the former volcano was covered in dense rainforest and jagged peaks. Where the land had been cleared, razor-edged kunai grass stretched above men's heads. At midday, the heat was stifling, an effect exacerbated by near persistent humidity. Malaria was endemic on Guadalcanal as were skin-rotting fungal infections and plagues of dengue fever (sometimes called "breakbone fever"). Mosquitoes and centipedes bit men while they slept, and in the tropical muck, even a small scratch was likely to lead to painful, possibly fatal, infection.

The eleven thousand Marines who led the U.S. attack lacked the medical safety net of those who followed them. During the campaign's early days, food, salt tablets, and sulfa drugs were in short supply. In the hardest-hit units, ninety percent of Americans contracted malaria, a disease that, even though not usually fatal, had a devastating effect on fighting effectiveness and morale.[19] Yet American supply chains quickly recovered, and before the end of 1942, the U.S. military implemented remarkably efficient evacuation policies to transport wounded troops to rear base hospitals hundreds of miles away. The Japanese, by contrast, endured slow, painful extermination at the hands of the better-armed Americans and the pitiless, tropical environment. Cut off from shipping routes, Japanese soldiers on "Starvation Island" subsisted on whatever they could scrounge for food. Beriberi, a condition triggered by vitamin deficiency, was rampant, and by the battle's end, Japanese troops lacked even a semblance of preventive medicine. A 1944 report by a U.S. intelligence officer offered a sobering assessment: "Miserable, without shelter, soaked with rain, underfed, and with little hope of evacuation, the Japanese died in large numbers."[20]

Although historians disagree about the number of Japanese war dead on Guadalcanal—a consensus seems to be about thirty thousand—one thing is beyond question: that the vast majority of Japanese fighters died from disease and not from American firepower.[21] To reiterate, effective medicine did not necessarily make the difference between victory and defeat in World War II. It did, however, make victory more achievable and defeat less painful.

THE POLITICS OF WORLD WAR II MEDICINE

Medicine cannot be separated from the broader social and political culture in which it takes place. Its practice in World War II was no exception. When pressed, military physicians of all nations touted their scientific objectivity and benign mission. In a world of politics gone mad, their goal was to heal, to save lives irrespective of ideology. Frontline medics, in particular, demonstrated an astonishing willingness to sacrifice their safety to help their fellow countrymen. Yet, in mending the sick and comforting the wounded, World War II-era physicians were inevitably enlisted to reaffirm dominant— and, in the eyes of state ideologues, commonsensical—ideas about race, gender, sexuality, and nation.

In the United States, the line between medicine and social engineering was frequently blurred. Physicians helped the military screen for homosexuals, "perverts," and other sexual bogymen deemed unworthy of wartime participation.[22] They also lent their medical expertise to the broader culture of racial segregation. Although the United States military encouraged African American participation in the war effort—even going so far as to release a film, *The Negro Soldier* (1944), to spur minority enlistment—the entire U.S. medical enterprise was corrupted by systemic racism. Some white doctors treated African American patients with disdain or refused to treat them altogether.

The racist logic of American medicine even extended to bodily fluids. After initially refusing donations from African Americans, U.S. blood banks separated plasma based upon the racial origins of the donors, a practice that was not only costly but also inherently wasteful. (As physicians well knew, there was no such thing as "white" and "black" blood.) Worst of all, by acceding to the practice, American doctors lent credence to the very sort of pseudo-scientific race theories spouted by the United States' fascist enemies.[23]

In imperial Japan, doctors pursued even darker paths, carrying out deliberately cruel experiments on Chinese and Russian prisoners. At the headquarters of the notorious Unit 731 in Manchuria, some prisoners were intentionally infected with plague in an effort to jumpstart Japan's biological warfare program. Others were locked in pressure chambers "to see how much the body can withstand before the eyes pop from their sockets." Still others were dissected while still alive and without anesthesia. Numbers remain sketchy, but thousands of prisoners, including infants, died in the medical experiments, their corpses—or, at least, select body parts—preserved in glass jars for future study. Although Japan's medical war crimes are now a matter of national scandal, the scope of physicians' cruelty was largely kept secret in the aftermath of World War II. In exchange for their findings, the occupying U.S. Army shielded some of the worst medical offenders from prosecution. Future U.S. physicians would come to regret the devil's bargain (much of the data proved worthless). Still, as *New York Times* writer Nicholas Kristof pointed out in 1995, Uncle Sam proved a powerful ally. The head of Unit 731 lived until 1959, and his colleagues rose to high ranks in the postwar Japanese government and medical establishment.[24]

Nowhere was the physician's creed to "do no harm" more debased than in Adolf Hitler's Nazi Germany. Doctors had occupied a prominent place in the regime even before the war, lending credibility to the dictator's antisemitic fantasies and staking their professional reputations on the rise of the Third Reich. During the war itself, Nazi doctors not only cared for the wounded (again, often valiantly) but also assumed a second task: experimenting on POWs and concentration camp victims. Decades later, the Nazis' crimes remain startling in their sadistic cruelty: men, women, and children were infected with disease, exposed to bitter cold, and butchered on the operating table; potential mothers were sterilized with X-rays; male Jews had their genitals burned by caustic chemicals. Some Nazi doctors invoked military goals to justify their brutality. But such niceties mattered little. Concentration camps did not fall under the normal penal code, and doctors were given free reign over the human "guinea pigs" in their charge. More than sideline collaborators, many Nazi doctors were active agents of genocide, in some cases helping to develop the technical means that made the "Final Solution" possible.[25]

And yet, as was the case in Japan, few German physicians were forced to answer for their crimes. Although a handful of high-profile Nazi doctors were convicted in the Nuremburg Trials of 1945–1946, some former concentration camp physicians, including the notorious Josef Mengele, escaped to South America to live out their lives in relative safety. Many more resumed their prewar middle-class identities with little hit to their professional reputations. Most disturbing of all, a cadre of German doctors was spirited away to the United States as part of Operation Paperclip, a secret plan to collect Nazi scientists, physicians, and experimental data (no matter how it was obtained) for use in the brewing war against the Soviet Union. Among the new immigrants was Hubertus Strughold, an aviation physician enlisted to conduct research for the Air Force and NASA. For his contributions to the American space program, he was eventually dubbed the "Father of Space Medicine." Only after Strughold's death in 1986 did the public learn what the U.S. government had long tried to keep secret: that during the war, as a member of the *Luftwaffe*, the beloved Dr. Strughold had carried out deadly oxygen deprivation experiments on epileptic children.[26]

After the Battle

At the end of World War II, the dead numbered in the tens of millions. Countless more suffered the ravages of hunger, injury, and disease. Across war-torn Europe and Asia, public health facilities were in ruin, basic medical equipment (drugs, dressings, syringes) nearly impossible to obtain. The victors provided some relief, but the task was overwhelming. In newly defeated Germany, Berliners—so confident of world domination a few years earlier—survived on fewer than one thousand calories a day.[27] Epidemics of typhoid, dysentery, and venereal disease, spread by the Allies and Axis alike, decimated civilian populations. Among the most vulnerable were survivors of the newly liberated Nazi concentration camps. Many ex-inmates looked like human skeletons and could barely stand upright because of years of starvation and torture. Frequently, their bodies were riddled with the long-term effects of chronic diarrhea, tuberculosis, and pneumonia. Forced into crude holding centers (sometimes at the same place where they had spent years in captivity) or left to wander the countryside, camp survivors died by the thousands throughout the early postwar period, as did another of World War II's most iconic casualty groups: the irradiated civilian victims of the U.S. atomic bomb attacks on Hiroshima and Nagasaki in August 1945.

As is usually the case, disabled military veterans of World War II benefited more from postwar recovery efforts than their injured civilian counterparts. During World War I, all the belligerent nations had adopted *rehabilitation* in some form or another as the philosophical backbone of disabled veterans' policy. Rehabilitation was touted as a decidedly "modern" approach to the problem of disabled vets. Rather than consign permanently injured troops to lives of dependency, bolstered by meager pensions or dreary old soldiers' homes, rehabilitation promised to elevate disabled vets to futures of manly productivity. At its heart, rehabilitation was premised on the notion that the social consequences of disability (exclusion, poverty, stigma) were avoidable; with adequate training and expert supervision, severely disabled men might even rise on the economic ladder—a final bonus for their loyal service to the state. Although World War I-era rehabilitation programs failed to live up to their lofty promises, rehab specialists were confident that the bulk of World War II disabled vets would be able to reintegrate into postwar society.[28] However, rehabilitation (indeed, expansive disabled veteran policy of any kind) was a luxury few World War II belligerents could afford, let alone hope to put into practice. A brief survey of Axis and Allied programs reveals a spectrum of approaches to the problem of the disabled veteran—most of which failed.

At one end of the spectrum was Japan, a nation with a long tradition of venerating disabled veterans. Known as *hakui no yūshi* ("heroic figures in white") because of the flowing robes they often wore in public, Japan's veteran-disabled expected preferential treatment and state support at war's end. However, U.S. occupying forces quickly dismantled veterans' programs. The reasoning behind the decision was stark: disabled veterans' special privileges were the product of an aggressively militaristic culture that had no place in postwar Japan. Disabled veterans were forced to sell their possessions and beg on the street. Tens of thousands banded together in "inpatient associations" to protest the occupying force's policies. Over time, the Japanese Ministry of Health and Welfare managed to restore some care programs, a move that drove a wedge between disabled veterans and civilians. Even so, to many, Japanese postwar disability policies smacked of victor's justice. If nothing else, they represented a final indignity to those who sacrificed so much for so little.[29]

Occupied Germany, at one time a world leader in disability rehabilitation, followed similar patterns. With the fall of the Third Reich, federal disability policy was one of the first items on the postwar chopping block. Eager to quash all remnants of Nazi-era militarism, Allied occupiers slashed veterans' pensions and disability benefits.[30] Although military veterans made up four-fifths of the nation's population of disabled people (compared to about five percent in the United States), lingering associations with Nazi war crimes made it difficult to portray disabled vets in a heroic light, a strategy commonly used by veterans and their allies to demand recognition from the state. Within a decade of the war's end, however, circumstances had changed. Public sentiment insisted that disabled German veterans deserved rehabilitation and preferential treatment. Because the Allies had outlawed veterans-only associations, German vets joined more inclusive advocacy groups, such as the 1.5-million-member Association of War Disabled, War Survivors, and Social Pensioners. By the 1950s, a growing cohort of survivors, activists, and artists was working to expand government recognition of war-disabled people to include, among other previously overlooked populations, female victims of wartime rape.[31]

In the Soviet Union, disability policy was shaped as much by internal politics as by the needs of war's survivors. By the most conservative estimates, some 2.6 million Soviet veterans were classified as "war invalids" (the actual number was no doubt much higher). Joseph Stalin believed that the state had an obligation to support disabled troops, if only to prevent them from rebelling, as they had in the past. At the same time, government censors made it their mission to erase the most disturbing aspects of the Great Patriotic War, including the bodily toll borne by Soviet troops. References to war disability were virtually taboo, and postwar vocational training programs prioritized rebuilding the national workforce above the rehabilitation of individual vets. As was the case elsewhere, physical wounds were privileged over psychological ones, and veterans' hospitals were often shabby and understaffed. Over time, the burden of caring for the Soviet war-disabled was pawned off on local communities. Some battle-scared vets were even forced to resettle to rural areas or were exiled to forced labor colonies to live out their days toiling for the state.[32]

Of all the conflict's major participants, only the United States was primed to tackle the problem of the disabled veteran on a national scale.[33] Three factors were especially advantageous. First, the United States' economy and industrial base emerged from the war virtually unscathed (if anything, they were stronger in 1945 than they were when the war began). Second, the United States' new population of disabled veterans was relatively small: in four years of fighting, only about 678,000 U.S. personnel sustained nonfatal injuries, less than five percent of the 16.1 million Americans who served in the armed forces (although more than one million suffered debilitating psychiatric trauma).[34] Third, the United States had the experience and technical knowledge necessary to put rehabilitation into practice. Thought to be an experiment in the 1910s–1920s, rehabilitation was at the heart of U.S. relief programs during World War II. As a pair of rehab boosters wrote in 1945, "The measures developed for the care of veterans of the First World War were largely palliative and experimental in nature. Today's provisions are based on the experiences and modifications of the twenty-five intervening years."[35] Not only were disabled vets eligible for extensive physical reconstruction and vocational training, but they also benefited from the Servicemen's Readjustment Act of 1944 (better known as the "GI Bill"). The GI Bill extended a number of rehabilitation's rewards—job training, university education, and so forth—to all honorably discharged service personnel.[36] America's disabled veterans were not the "Greatest Generation," as they are sometimes called; but they had access to more resources, facilities, and support networks than any previous cohort of disabled vets in military history.[37]

Still, Americans' lingering anxieties about war disability—and the limitations of military medicine—were not easily quelled. Newspapers printed lurid accounts of disabled veterans languishing in government hospitals or panhandling for change. Men with disfigured faces were publicly shunned, and disabled veterans remained potent icons of antiwar dissent. In an especially telling move, the U.S. Army banned *Let There Be Light*, John Huston's 1946 poignant documentary about shell-shocked GIs, out of concerns for future military recruitment. The ban would not be lifted until the 1980s.

Legacies

In the twenty-first century, the world is still grappling with the mixed legacies of medicine in World War II. On the one hand, the deployment of preventive medicine, military surgery, combat psychiatry, and other treatment regimens prolonged the lives of millions of combatants (if only to fight another day). The war years spurred the introduction of novel techniques for treating mental trauma and wound infection—techniques that would be applied, with increasing success, to civilian populations at war's end. Most optimistic of all, medicine promised something that not even the atomic bomb could deliver: the hope that war was not a death sentence. More than any other technology, medicine leveraged the modernist fantasy that, with enough technical know-how, all mistakes could be undone.

Unfortunately, World War II left behind more disturbing legacies as well. Reflecting on Nazi doctors, psychiatrist Robert Jay Lifton laments, "Psychologically speaking, nothing is darker or more menacing, or harder to accept, than the participation of physicians in mass murder." Their "experiments, in their precise and absolute violation of the Hippocratic oath, mock and subvert the very idea of the ethical physician, of the physician dedicated to the well-being of patients."[38] From today's perspective, it is tempting to hold up the Nazi doctors and other torturers as aberrational figures— sick minds that perverted an otherwise noble and benign profession. But in a war that led to the deaths of some seventy-five million soldiers and civilians—a war in which men and women were roasted alive in bomb attacks, poisoned by nuclear radiation, and systematically slaughtered on both sides of the conflict; a war in which millions of injured troops were quickly patched-up and sent back into the field of battle, in which the deranged and the psychologically broken were abandoned and ignored, in which physicians actively prolonged the conflict by implementing novel means of keeping the injured from dying—it is necessary to ask whose well-being was served by military medicine in World War II.

Put another way: is it even possible to commit mass murder on an international scale without the participation of physicians? If the twentieth century—a period defined by a relentless parade of wars, mass killings, and bloody conflicts—is any indication, the answer is a resounding no.

Notes

1. Keith Wheeler, *We Are the Wounded* (New York: E. P. Dutton & Company, 1945), 11.
2. Representative English-language examples of this genre include Gordon Stifler Seagrave, *Burma Surgeon* (New York: W. W. Norton, 1943); Alexander R. Griffin, *Out of Carnage* (New York: Howell, Soskin, 1945); Jan K. Herman, *Battle Station Sick Bay: Navy Medicine in World War II* (Annapolis, MD: Naval Institute Press, 1997); and Robert J. Franklin, *Medic! How I Fought World War II with Morphine, Sulfa, and Iodine Swabs* (Lincoln: University of Nebraska Press, 2006).
3. On the concept of biopolitics, see, Thomas Lemke, *Biopolitics: An Advanced Introduction*, trans. Eric Frederick Trump (New York: New York University Press, 2011).
4. Chris Hables Gray, *Postmodern War: The New Politics of Conflict* (New York: Guilford Press, 1997), 110.
5. On the significance of exceptionality, see Giorgio Agamben, *Homo Sacer: Sovereign Power and Bare Life*, trans. Daniel Heller-Roazen (Stanford: Stanford University Press, 1998); Mary L. Dudziak, *War Time: An Idea, Its History, Its Consequences* (New York: Oxford University Press, 2012).

6. Allan S. Walker, *Medical Services of the R.A.N. and R.A.A.F.* (Canberra: Australian War Memorial, 1961), 510–511.
7. Quoted in John W. Dower, *War Without Mercy: Race and Power in the Pacific War* (New York: Pantheon, 1986), 64, 67.
8. Gerhard L. Weinberg, *A World at Arms: A Global History of World War II* (New York: Cambridge University Press, 1994), 584.
9. Albert E. Cowdrey, *Fighting for Life: American Military Medicine in World War II* (New York: Free Press, 1994), 53, 203. For a wartime take on the significance of sulfa drugs, see E. M. K. Geiling, "Chemotherapy," in *Medicine and the War*, ed. William H. Taliaferro (Chicago: University of Chicago Press, 1944).
10. Rob Wallace, "Medical Innovations: Charles Drew and Blood Banking," National World War II Museum, May 4, 2020, https://www.nationalww2museum.org/war/articles/medical-innovations-blood-banking.
11. On the history of shell shock and other psychiatric casualties, see Ben Shephard, *A War of Nerves: Soldiers and Psychiatrists in the Twentieth Century* (Cambridge: Harvard University Press, 2003).
12. Quoted in Cowdrey, *Fighting for Life*, 139.
13. Cowdrey, *Fighting for Life*, 151.
14. Ibid., 187.
15. Mary Schaeffer Conroy, *Medicines for the Soviet Masses during World War II* (Lanham, MD: University Press of America, 2008), 42, 39–46.
16. Cowdrey, *Fighting for Life*, 40, 63.
17. Ibid., 226–238; Walker, *Medical Services*, 324–338.
18. Walker, *Medical Services*, 324–338.
19. Cowdrey, *Fighting for Life*, 63.
20. Quoted in Ibid., 66.
21. On the number of Japanese troops who died on Guadalcanal, see Richard Frank, *Guadalcanal: The Definitive Account of the Landmark Battle* (New York: Random House, 1990); Stanley Coleman Jersey, *Hell's Islands: The Untold Story of Guadalcanal* (College Station: Texas A&M University Press, 2008).
22. In his path-breaking book, *Coming Out Under Fire: The History of Gay Men and Women in World War II* (New York: Plume, 1991), Allan Bérubé notes that military screening exams developed by psychiatrists "listed three possible signs for identifying male homosexuals . . . 'feminine bodily characteristics,' 'effeminacy in dress and manner,' and a 'patulous [expanded] rectum.'" Quoted in Margot Canaday, *The Straight State: Sexuality and Citizenship in Twentieth-Century America* (Princeton: Princeton University Press, 2009), 147.
23. Cowdrey, *Fighting for Life*, 110–112, 170–171.
24. Nicholas Kristof, "Unmasking Horror," *New York Times*, March 17, 1995. See also Sheldon H. Harris, *Factories of Death: Japanese Biological Warfare, 1932–1945, and the American Cover-up*, revised edition (New York: Routledge, 2002); Jing Bao Nie et al., eds., *Japan's Wartime Atrocities: Comparative Inquiries in Science, History, and Ethics* (New York: Routledge, 2010).
25. On German physicians' complicity in the Holocaust, see Robert Jay Lifton, *The Nazi Doctors: Medical Killing and the Psychology of Genocide* (New York: Basic Books, 2000).
26. Annie Jacobsen, *Operation Paperclip: The Secret Intelligence Program that Brought Nazi Scientists to America* (New York: Little, Brown, 2014); Eric Lichtblau, *The Nazis*

Next Door: How America Became a Safe Haven for Hitler's Men (New York: Houghton Mifflin, 2014).
27. Cowdrey, Fighting for Life, 289.
28. On the rise of rehabilitation and the history of disabled veterans in general, see David A. Gerber, *Disabled Veterans in History*, revised edition (Ann Arbor: University of Michigan Press, 2012); Beth Linker, *War's Waste: Rehabilitation in World War I America* (Chicago: University of Chicago Press, 2011); John M. Kinder, *Paying With Their Bodies: American War and the Problem of the Disabled Veteran* (Chicago: University of Chicago Press, 2015).
29. Fujiwara Tetsuya, "Disabled War Veterans during the Allied Occupation of Japan," trans. Ruselle Meade, *SOAS Occasional Translations in Japanese Studies* 3 (2012), http://www.soas.ac.uk/jrc/translations/. See also Lee K. Pennington, *Casualties of History: Wounded Japanese Servicemen and the Second World War* (Ithaca: Cornell University Press, 2015).
30. James M. Diehl, *The Thanks of the Fatherland: German Veterans after the Second World War* (Chapel Hill: University of North Carolina Press, 1993), 3.
31. Carol Poore, *Disability in Twentieth Century German Culture* (Ann Arbor: University of Michigan Press, 2007), 158, 162, 172–74, 153.
32. Sarah D. Phillips, "'There Are No Invalids in the USSR!': A Missing Soviet Chapter in the New Disability History," *Disabilities Studies Quarterly*, 29, no. 3 (2009); http://dsq-sds.org/article/view/936/1111. See also Mark Edele, *Soviet Veterans of World War II: A Popular Movement in an Authoritarian Society, 1941–1991* (Oxford: Oxford University Press, 2008).
33. This is not to suggest that other nations failed to carry out significant, even successful, rehabilitation programs. For example, Great Britain and several Commonwealth nations (e.g., Canada, Australia, New Zealand) allotted substantial public resources to the rehabilitation of disabled vets.
34. David A. Gerber, "Heroes and Misfits: The Troubled Social Reintegration of Disabled Veterans in *The Best Years of Our Lives*," in *Disabled Veterans in History*, ed. David A. Gerber (Ann Arbor: University of Michigan Press, 2000), 73.
35. Wilma T. Donahue and Clark Tibbitts, "The Task before the Veteran and Society," *Annals of the American Academy of Political and Social Science* 239 (May 1945): 2.
36. See Stephen R. Ortiz, *Beyond the Bonus March and GI Bill: How Veteran Politics Shaped the New Deal Era* (New York: New York University Press, 2010); Nancy Beck Young, "'Do Something for the Soldier Boys': Congress, the G.I. Bill of Rights, and the Contours of Liberalism," in *Veterans' Policies, Veterans' Politics: New Perspectives on Veterans in the Modern United States*, ed. Stephen R. Ortiz (Gainesville: University Press of Florida, 2012), 199–221.
37. Tom Brokaw, *The Greatest Generation* (New York: Random House, 1998).
38. Lifton, *The Nazi Doctors*, 4.

Bibliography

Conroy, Mary Schaeffer. *Medicines for the Soviet Masses during World War II*. Lanham, MD: University Press of America, 2008.

Cowdrey, Albert E. *Fighting for Life: American Military Medicine in World War II*. New York: Free Press, 1994.

Gerber, David A., ed. *Disabled Veterans in History*, revised edition. Ann Arbor: University of Michigan Press, 2012.

Kinder, John M. *Paying With Their Bodies: American War and the Problem of the Disabled Veteran*. Chicago: University of Chicago Press, 2015.

Lifton, Robert Jay. *The Nazi Doctors: Medical Killing and the Psychology of Genocide*. New York: Basic Books, 1986.

Nie, Jing Bao et al., eds., *Japan's Wartime Medical Atrocities: Comparative Inquiries in Science, History, and Ethics*. New York: Routledge, 2010.

Phillips, Sarah D. "There Are No Invalids in the USSR!": A Missing Soviet Chapter in the New Disability History." *Disability Studies Quarterly* 29, no. 3 (2009). https://dsq-sds.org/article/view/936/1111.

Shephard, Ben. *A War of Nerves: Soldiers and Psychiatrists in the Twentieth Century*. Cambridge: Harvard University Press, 2003.

Taliaferro, William H. *Medicine and the War*. Chicago: University of Chicago Press, 1944.

Tetsuya, Fujiwara. "Disabled War Veterans during the Allied Occupation of Japan." Translated by Ruselle Meade. *SOAS Occasional Translations in Japanese Studies* 3 (2012).

Walker, Allan S. *Medical Services of the R.A.N. and R.A.A.F.* Canberra: Australian War Memorial, 1961.

Weinberg, Gerhard L. *A World at Arms: A Global History of World War II*. New York: Cambridge University Press, 1994.

CHAPTER 27

THE HOLOCAUST

JAN-RUTH MILLS

The National Socialist German Workers Party (Nazi) regime murdered more than six million Jews during World War II with the cooperation of its Axis allies and local collaborators. The *Schutzstaffel* (SS, *Defense Force*), *Wehrmacht*, (German Armed Forces), *Sicherheitspolizei* (SD, Security Police), and *Ordnungspolizei* (Order Police), with local assistance, shot to death more than two million Jews in occupied Poland, the Baltic states, and the former Union of Soviet Socialist Republics (USSR).[1] While the use of Zyklon B (cyanide gas) to murder nearly one million Jews at the Nazi Death Camp Auschwitz has become a symbol of the Holocaust, Jews were also murdered in occupied Poland through the use of gas vans at Chełmno, as well as through the use of exhaust fumes at Treblinka, Bełżec, and Sobibór.[2]

Hundreds of thousands were beaten or starved to death in concentration camps or eliminated through "extermination by labor" in camps situated all over the Third Reich (primarily Germany and Austria)[3] and occupied Europe.[4] In the last months, thousands more died on "death marches" from camps in the East to the Reich as the Allies advanced.[5]

Why did the Third Reich embrace the Final Solution of genocide? How did its policies evolve from forced emigration, to expulsion, to extermination? Certainly, Hitler's decisions and the expression of his ideological goals in public and private motivated his subordinates in the decision-making process that led to genocide.[6] However, no written order from Hitler to exterminate the Jews has been found.[7]

In practice, the mass murder of Jews resulted from the radicalization of Nazi policies by officials in the expanding bureaucracy who accelerated violence in response to conditions on the Eastern Front. The German invasion of the Soviet Union served as the catalyst for an undefined moment when genocide presented itself as a solution in a variety of local problems. The investigation of local decisions explains the seeming passivity of some *Wehrmacht*, SS, or Order Police leaders and units where others showed murderous initiative and willing collaboration to exterminate Jews.[8]

Nevertheless, larger Nazi goals could only be developed and implemented by the leadership in Berlin. A popular understanding of *Lebensraum* (living space), is that Hitler planned to transform the conquered lands in the east into an agricultural zone by eradicating or enslaving the unwanted peoples to clear the way for resettlement by ethnic Germans. Hitler's plans included the creation of autarky, which required developing an internal market to the east to consume the Reich's future industrial bounty. Hitler's obsession with creating a "Jew-free" German economy meant that, like German Jewish civilians, the millions of Jews living in the conquered territories could not continue to live, even as slaves.[9] As conceived by Adolf Hitler, Hermann Göring, Heinrich Himmler, Reinhard Heydrich, and other leaders of the regime Jews had to be physically removed.

Lebensraum required the largest forced demographic shift ever imagined or attempted.[10] While the specific methods of extermination would be developed later, the goal of a Jew-free economy in the Reich linked those plans to the treatment of Jews in Germany before the war. Between 1933 and 1939, the goal of anti-Jewish policies and actions was to force Jews to emigrate by destroying their social and economic existence.[11] In support of the violence, the liberal legal tradition of equality under the law was gradually eroded through the extreme execution of existing laws until a new Criminal Code transformed the police into a weapon against the state's enemies, making the courts themselves subservient to police justice.[12] The first phase of violence against Jews began in 1933, with boycotts and attacks on Jewish-owned businesses.[13]

Antisemitism also became state policy with the passage of laws intended to limit Jews' access to employment and education. The Law on the Restitution of the Professional Civil Service called for non-Aryans, specifically Jews, as well as communists, to be fired.[14] Laws limiting Jewish public-school attendance and practice in legal professions followed, along with a prohibition on Jewish doctors treating patients under the national insurance program.[15]

In 1935, the *Reichstag* passed the Nuremberg Laws. These included the Reich Citizenship Law, which defined Jews as biologically separate from other Germans and rendered them subjects of the Third Reich rather than citizens. The Law for the Protection of German Blood and Honor, which prohibited marriage or sex between Aryans and Jews, was also part of the Nuremberg Laws.[16] In addition to humiliating them, these laws were intended to force Jews to emigrate.[17]

In August 1938, Heydrich, whom Himmler had appointed as head of the *Sicherheitsdienst* (Secret Service) named Adolf Eichmann (an SS member who had worked in the SD's Jewish Office in Berlin working on ways to persecute, expel, and plunder Jews) to establish the Central Office for Jewish Emigration in Vienna. Eichmann developed innovative, efficient processes to prepare the paperwork for Jews forced to leave their homeland. In exchange for their citizenship, property rights, and money, Jews received a passport that expired after only fourteen days. Therefore, they had only two weeks to secure a visa from a foreign country. The office was financed by the property extorted from the Jews it served.[18] Eichmann's office processed fifty thousand Jews for emigration, leaving most nearly penniless.[19]

As Germany prepared to annex Czechoslovakia, the German economy faced a looming financial crisis brought on by massive military spending. Actually convinced that Jews ran the Reich's economy, the regime instigated new measures in 1938 to strip

Jews of their economic resources. After April 1938, all Jews in the Reich had to register their assets.[20] To keep the Reich from bankruptcy, new measures forced Jews to convert assets into government bonds and live off the interest.[21] Another policy required that the Nazi party approve the sale of Jewish businesses. Major banks, corporations, and the wealthy competed for larger firms which sold at rock-bottom prices, while Jewish small-business owners, long the target of boycotts and vandalism, were pressured to sell to Aryan neighbors looking for a good deal. As Adam Tooze explains, analysis of this registry of Jewish assets revealed an important fact; the miniscule Jewish minority in Germany never held a dominant role in the German economy.[22]

From spring 1938, Jews were targeted with a third phase of violence, and anti-Jewish viciousness increased, culminating in the pogrom known as *Kristallnacht*.[23] The violence began with scattered attacks on Jews across the Reich on November 9, purportedly in response to the death of a German diplomat shot in Paris by a Jewish refugee from Poland.[24] Hearing about the scattered violence, Hitler seized the opportunity. The SA, SS, Gestapo, Nazi Party members, and their supporters attacked synagogues, Jewish orphanages, homes, and businesses throughout the Reich. Hundreds of Jews committed suicide. At least ninety-one Jews were murdered, for which no one was ever brought to trial. Functioning in support of the regime, German courts increasingly declined to prosecute crimes motivated by ideology: hatred of Jews was justification enough for violence, even for murder. Over thirty thousand Jews were sent to concentration camps where they were held until they agreed to apply to emigrate.[25] Over one thousand Jews in concentration camps did not survive or died later of wounds.[26]

The Nazi government nullified any insurance claims filed by Jewish policy-holders if they filed for damage to businesses and homes. Not only could Jews not receive compensation for their damages, but the government charged the Reich's Jews one billion Reichmarks in atonement for the damage done to their communities, forcing them to sell any remaining stocks, real estate, and even government bonds.[27]

Clearly, both the war and the extermination of the Jews were Hitler's goals. On January 30, 1939, in a speech to the Reichstag, Hitler declared to the German public that if "international finance Jewry" started another world war, it would mean the "annihilation of the Jewish race in Europe."[28] Also a matter of public record are notes from Hitler's diplomatic meetings with foreign statesmen before and during the war that reveal his intent to murder Jews. On January 21, 1939, in a meeting with the Czechoslovakian foreign minister, Hitler said that the Jews of Germany were to be destroyed. Although he told a foreign statesman after *Kristallnacht* that the Jewish question was a European problem,[29] two years later, on November 28, 1941, he told the Grand Mufti of Jerusalem, Mohammed Amin al-Husseini, that the *Wehrmacht*'s planned offensive to reach the Middle East through the Caucasus had the singular aim of destroying the Jews living there.[30]

Hitler's intent on blaming all the Jews in the world for the war to justify their murder can be seen in his frequent postdating of the Reichstag speech referenced above to September 1, 1939, the day Germany invaded Poland. For example, on September 30, 1942, in a speech at the *Sportspalast*, Hitler postdated the Reichstag speech to the first day of the war, saying that Jews had laughed then at his "prophecy," but now that they had brought many other nations into the conflict, the Jews would soon stop laughing everywhere.[31]

Brutal as the war in central and eastern Europe was, circumstances behind the front were exacerbated by the Reich's plans for the conquered territory to be resettled and exploited by the ten million ethnic Germans living under Soviet control (including those in the Baltic states, occupied by the Soviets after June 1940). Hitler called these ethnic Germans *Volksdeutsche*, signifying a kinship of "blood" and "race."[32]

A few weeks after the war began, Hitler appointed Himmler to take charge of what might be considered this mirror project of the Final Solution—identifying the ethnic Germans to be resettled as a benefit of the *Lebensraum* created by genocide. The Nazi understanding and propaganda about ethnic "Germanness" called for the eradication of Jews, Sinti, Roma, and the handicapped, and also for the relocation and the improvement of the social status of *Volksdeutsche* in the east. *Volksdeutsche*, in general, but especially those willing to join a *Selbschutz* (Self-Defense Force) unit and take part in war crimes, benefited from the theft of Jewish property, homes, and businesses.[33]

As many as three hundred thousand Jews fled or were forced across the new Soviet border immediately after the invasion of Poland, until the Soviets threatened to retaliate by keeping *Volksdeutsche* from crossing to the west.[34] Within a few weeks, one hundred thousand *Volksedeutsche* were listed as potential *Selbstschutz* units, which were eventually integrated into the Ordinary Police.[35] After Poland surrendered, SS regiments and Einsatzgruppen, under Theodor Eicke and Reinhard Heydrich, assisted by the Selbstschutz, conducted systematic terror in the "Intelligentsia Operation," a murder campaign directed against the leaders of Polish society. Nazi violence targeted Polish nationalist organizations, teachers, clergy, former officials and military officers, and especially Jews.[36]

After annexing western Poland, Germany planned to settle one million *Volksdeutche* there, expelling the unwanted population of approximately six hundred thousand Jews and 8.9 million Poles, into new German colonies in central and southern Poland. The largest colony, the General Government, established in October 1939, contained the Polish cities of Warsaw, Krakow, Radon, and Lublin, where twelve million Polish citizens (1.5 million of them Jews) lived.[37] Despite the immensity of these goals, the Nazis made few concrete plans until weeks into the war.[38]

The policy of Ghettoization of the Jews developed in fits and starts. Heydrich ordered his security chiefs to concentrate Jews in urban areas to facilitate their later deportation to a potential Jewish reservation on September 21, 1939.[39] Conditions for Jews in the 1,150 ghettoes—which were eventually established in occupied Poland and the USSR, the largest of which were in Łódz and Warsaw—varied as to how they were established and maintained, whether sealed or open. However, all processes were brutal.[40] This lack of regulation from Berlin suggests that ghettoes emerged as a temporary measure resulting from failed efforts at expulsion.[41]

Himmler's plans to clear the annexed territories first to make room for settlements conflicted with Hitler's orders to Eichmann to transport Jews from the Reich. Both plans raised the objections of Governor General Hans Frank, who resisted further Jewish deportees being dumped in the General Government. In addition, train schedules prioritized troop transports from east to west in preparation for the invasion of France and then east for the invasion of the Soviet Union.[42] Although the Lublin district would remain the intended dumping ground for Jews expelled from the Reich, the expulsion plans continued in starts and stops until Himmler was able to assert his authority over them.

By 1941, the Germans had transported roughly 308,000 Poles and Jews from the annexed territories to the General Government, and by the end of 1942 an additional fifty-seven thousand unwanted peoples had arrived. These numbers were far short of the original goal.[43] Even before the invasion of France, however, Hitler revealed his ambivalence about the various expulsion schemes. On March 12, 1940, he told a Swedish visitor that deportation would never be a solution to the "Jewish question."[44]

The evolution of extermination policies followed the outbreak of the war. Victory in Poland also occasioned the intensification of programs on the German home front to murder the unwanted and weak. The Nazis' continual erosion of the previously accepted legal and behavioral norms and limits made these actions possible.[45] The struggle so central to Nazi ideology was not merely physical. Military dominance would also determine the inherent moral superiority of the victor, and this conviction overthrew ethical and moral tenets to care for the vulnerable, sick, and poor, and re-cast charity as a policy damaging to society by increasing degeneracy.[46]

After the passage of the 1933 Law for the Prevention of Hereditarily Diseased Progeny, four hundred thousand Germans were sterilized. A "health court" determined whose physical or emotional abilities cost too much: blindness, alcoholism, mental illness, "moral retardation," or being "work-shy," could be deemed a threat to future generations.[47] Five thousand women died from botched, hasty sterilizations, but no surgeons were held to account while the women themselves were blamed for moving too much during the procedure.[48] The use of gas to murder began through experiments on the disabled and elderly. These so-called "useless eaters" among "Aryan" Germans and Austrians were scrutinized for their worthiness to exist within the "people's community" based on their ability to contribute economically and the expense of their healthcare to the state.[49]

Henry Friedlander identified these murders the as the first step toward the Final Solution that would eventually target Jews, Sinti, and Roma for extermination.[50] In October 1939, Hitler signed off on a program known as Aktion T4 (predated to September 1, 1939 to associate it with the war) authorizing the murder of people with disabilities. Aktion T4 provided the model and training ground for eventual mass murder and genocide, establishing the method of selecting victims, the techniques of gassing them, and the policy of burning the bodies to hide the crimes. Between 1939 and 1945, up to six thousand children were murdered in special wards where they were taken after doctors identified them to be unfit for life. Six hospitals in the Reich were equipped to use carbon monoxide gas to kill people with mental disabilities. About forty medical professionals worked in each ward and, between 1939 and 1941, the medical records kept by health care professionals revealed that 70,273 adults were gassed.[51]

In Germany, Hitler claimed to have ended the euthanasia program in August 1941. That event seemingly exemplified the effectiveness of public protest and of the influence of Catholic bishop Clemens August Graf von Galen in speaking out against euthanasia.[52] In reality, this was one of Hitler's many alleged compromises.[53] The murder of disabled children and adults continued in secret in the Reich itself, at Hadamar, Germany, and at Hartheim Castle, in Austria. At the latter, slave laborers from the Dachau camp system, as well as camps associated with Mauthausen, especially Gusen I and II, were murdered once they became "useless eaters," unable to work.[54] Murders for similar reasons continued at concentration and death camps until the end of the war, part of a program known as 14 F 13 and initiated at Sachsenshausen in April 1941.[55]

The euthanasia program in Poland in 1939 provided the training ground for the systematic mass shootings that escalated after 1941. The procedure of selecting victims among mentally disabled Poles that began at several locations directly after the invasion suggests coordination from a central authority rather than a coincidence of local initiatives. Once a hospital was taken over, patients were placed in three categories reflecting the seriousness of their illness, their ability to work, and whether they were ethnic Germans, Polish Christians, or Polish Jews. After sending the lists to Berlin, murders-by-fatal-shooting were carried out in secret, beginning on September 10, a month before Hitler authorized Aktion T4 in Germany.

In October, patients taken to Fort VII, near Poznan, were killed in a sealed bunker into which carbon monoxide was introduced. The murders in Poznan were under the direction of SS-*Obersturmführer* Herbert Lange with an SS *Sondercommando* (Special Unit) composed of fifteen Security Police and sixty Order Police, as well as Polish prisoners from Fort VII.[56] A total of seventy-seven hundred patients were murdered.[57] After December, Herbert Lange's unit used gas vans, and Lange then used this technique later while commanding the first death camp at Chełmno.[58]

After the fall of France in May 1940, expulsion continued to be the Nazi regime's expressed goal for the Jews. Hitler approved a plan to deport the Jews in occupied Europe to Madagascar. However, Britain's decision to continue to fight made traversing British waters en route to the Indian Ocean island militarily imprudent. For similar reasons, the Germans abandoned the possibility of transporting Jews to a German colony in Central Africa.[59] According to Eichmann's postwar testimony, Hitler intended to hold four million Jewish hostages in Madagascar to influence U.S. President Franklin Roosevelt.[60]

Like the territorial solutions in Poland, conditions and the climate of Madagascar rendered the plan genocidal. However, once the Madagascar plan was abandoned, a memo of Eichmann's indicated that the Nazi leadership considered emigration an "initial solution." A "final solution" was to remove Jews not only out of the occupied territories and the Reich, but also its allies and satellites, including the French colonies in North Africa.[61]

In January 1941, Hitler repeated in his *Sportspalast* speech the 1939 threat against Jews, should Germany engage in another world war. He was in part expressing his anger over America's Lend Lease Act in support of Britain, which he saw as more evidence of an economic if not military coalition against Germany. Any resistance to Nazi rule magnified the supposed "world Jewish conspiracy," which he saw as Germany's main enemy.[62] Similar antisemitic convictions informed Field Marshall Wilhelm Keitel's orders to retaliate against Jews for resistance not only in the East, but also in occupied Western Europe and the Balkans.[63]

With the German invasion of the Soviet Union in June 1941, the *Wehrmacht*'s murderous fulfilment of the Commissar Order to kill the political leaders of the Soviet state quickly resulted in the targeting by both the *Wehrmacht* and Einsatzgruppen of Jewish civilians as racial representatives of Judeo-Bolshevism. Pacification and reprisals against alleged "plunderers" and "saboteurs" justified the execution of Jews and other civilians, including women and children.[64] In the first five weeks following the invasion of the Soviet Union, mass shootings established that murdering thousands of civilians was logistically possible. By summer's end, the total annihilation of the Jewish population in the East entered the realm of possibilities, marking an important step toward the eventual attempt to annihilate the Jews of Europe.[65]

By the end of 1941, an estimated two million Soviet prisoners of war were murdered or starved to death along with five hundred thousand to eight hundred thousand Jews.[66] One explanation for the murders in summer 1941 is an inability to feed the massive number of POWs and racially undesirable civilians under German control, but this does not explain why the murder of Soviet POWs peaked before 1942, when conditions on the eastern front did not improve.[67] Saul Friedländer points out that the act of selecting victims by any criteria argues against this motive, as everyone needs to eat—Soviet POWs no more or less than Jewish women and children.[68]

In the USSR, as elsewhere, the Nazi concept of justice impacted events through the politicization of German martial law. Deaths resulting from criminal orders from above,[69] as they are now considered, would not have been violations of the German criminal code on the German home front because they were motivated by Nazi ideology. Furthermore, on Hitler's orders, the *Wehrmacht* was not to prosecute soldiers for war crimes against civilians, although civilians caught committing crimes were to be shot or put down with collective violence against whole communities.[70] Despite some qualms about the atrocities, the *Wehrmacht* leadership refrained from attempts to bring under military jurisdiction the SS and Security Police in the forward operational zones. Instead, army leadership demonstrated a willingness to reframe martial law to conform to the regime's concept of political and racial justice, which called for mass murder of the regime's ideological and biological enemies. In the rear operational zones, the SS and Security Police were ultimately under Himmler's authority as *Reichsführer* of the SS and the German Police.[71]

When *Wehrmacht* leadership became concerned that indiscriminate violence might threaten discipline, they were unable to use a moral argument to control troops under their jurisdiction, having used a moral argument to justify war crimes. The troops knew that an order that was not backed up by punishment was not meant to be followed. Although disobedience for other infractions was brutally executed, the men accepted more readily their officers' brutality because they were able to act out brutally on the civilian population. Participating in atrocities while enduring harsh discipline themselves also enhanced their sense of camaraderie.[72]

Within the SS, Himmler's subordinates knew that fervor and adaptability were as important as his orders, and by August 1941 all units under his command knew shooting Jews was a priority.[73] This structure reflects Himmler's insistence that the SS be a voluntary organization of racial elites willing to follow Hitler.[74] Although Himmler accepted into the SS[75] *Volksdeutsche* in occupied territories, who were hoping to avoid military service by volunteering for the Order Police, these enlisted men had been vetted for their political reliability as well as their racial suitability.[76] Officers and men under Himmler, when not attached to *Wehrmacht* units in the forward zones of operation, were under a disciplinary court system (SS Arbitration and Honor Court)[77] separated by Hitler's order from the German military on November 27, 1939.[78]

Far from restricting violence, the SS "Honor Law" gave SS men permission to use arms freely, limiting only violence against *Volksgennossen*, or folk-comrades. While SS punishment battalions existed, as did assignments to concentration camps where the duty was intended to "re-barbarize" the offender, expulsion from the SS was considered the most extreme consequence.[79] Even convictions for homosexuality, an obsession of Himmler's which was to be punished by death in both the SS and police after 1941, did not always result in execution. In winter 1945, the sentence was a transfer to the front, which still did not absolutely guarantee death.[80]

Not all paramilitary units under Himmler's command performed with equal murderous zeal during two waves of mass shootings in the Baltics and former USSR in summer of 1941. Both Himmler and Heydrich frequently visited the *Einsatzgruppen*, *Waffen*-SS, and other paramilitary organizations to encourage an escalation of the mass shootings of Jews, but the response was not uniform, even between the two SS brigades that reported directly to Himmler.[81] Despite the common claim to have been "just following orders," not a single paramilitary member was prosecuted for failing to participate in the mass shootings. Nor did serious consequences follow if commanders in the field fell short of the initiative shown by those who included women and children in mass shootings at the end of July.[82]

Himmler, concerned about the effect on the perpetrators' morale after a day of shooting thousands of men, women, and children, contemplated the long-term consequences of stress on his men.[83] In addition to provisions to reassign to other duties those reluctant to pull a trigger, Himmler insisted that pleasant evenings of music and comradery should follow days of extermination.[84]

Even as the military planned its war of annihilation in January 1941, Hitler tasked Heydrich—via separate communications from both Himmler and Göring—to prepare a comprehensive solution for the "European Jewish problem" to be acted on after victory over the USSR.[85] Hitler gave a speech on July 16, when victory in the USSR was assumed, expressing his desire for the total elimination of communists, Jews, and other unwanted people in order to create a "Garden of Eden" for Germans. Also in mid-summer, Hitler wanted to ask every country in Europe to rid themselves of Jews and authorized Heydrich to submit his plan for the Final Solution.[86]

Heydrich's first draft of the "Final Solution" was unanimously accepted by the Secretaries of State gathered at the Wannsee Conference on January 20, 1942.[87] The transfer of experts from the T4 program to develop the gas chambers at death camps in the fall of 1941 directly connected the T4 program to the Final Solution.

Heydrich's plan outlined the deportation of the Jews of Europe to the General Government as a stopping place en route to their final, albeit unspecified, destination in the soon-to-be occupied eastern Soviet Union. Used as forced labor, Jews would be separated by sex to build roads and other construction projects. According to the plan, most would die, but any survivors were to be considered the most dangerous because of their ability to resist, demonstrating the Nazis' belief that Jewish lives were analogous to germ cells. Although the plan did not expressly state they would be murdered, Christopher Browning concludes that, as all the functionaries present at Wannsee knew that Jews were being shot en masse, all understood the intent was the total extermination of the eleven million Jews within the Nazis' grasp.

The only contentious discussions were legal ones regarding whether to deport half-Jews and Jews in mixed marriages.[88] The argument was not over the morality of murder but rather over whom could be murdered under current German laws; the undermining of the Western liberal tradition was complete, as was the subversion of German civil, criminal, and martial law to a radical campaign to put Germany, and those defined as Germans, first.

Eichmann, who was present at Wannsee, testified at his trial that, up to that point, the killing method had not been determined, but in the post-conference afternoon soirée they discussed the use of gas.[89] In a meeting in Paris that May, Heydrich, who believed Jews were behind the increased resistance activity all over occupied Europe, assured his listeners that, while gas vans were insufficient for the job, "'bigger, more perfect and numerically more productive solutions' meant that a 'death sentence' had been passed on the 'entirety of the European Jews.'"[90] Equally important for the project was Eichmann's expertise in arranging deportations. As head of the Gestapo's Office of Jewish Affairs, he coordinated his subordinates and local officials as they arrested, detained, and loaded Jews onto transports. In all, nine hundred thousand German Railway (*Reschsbahn*) employees, in cooperation with the French and other national rail systems all over Europe, worked together to transport whole Jewish communities to their deaths.[91]

The best-known death camp was at Auschwitz in Upper Silesia, southwest of Chełmno in annexed Poland. In September 1941, experiments with Zyklon B (prussic gas) killed Soviet POWs and sick Polish workers. By March 20, 1942, Jews from Silesia were murdered in two farmhouses converted into gas chambers at a second camp, Auschwitz-Birkenau.[92] Also a permanent slave-labor camp, Auschwitz-Birkenau continued to exploit prisoners and operate as a transit-camp, sending Jews to labor camps, but after transports of stateless Jews from Western Europe began arriving in June 1942, Himmler ordered that Jews incapable of work should be murdered immediately.[93] By March 1943, the two gas chambers and a total of five crematoria were murdering and cremating 4,756 people in a twenty-four-hour period.[94] In all, of the 1.1 million European Jews who arrived at Auschwitz, 865,000 were killed on arrival, as well as ten thousand

Poles.[95] Non-Jewish Poles and other racial and political enemies of the Reich were swept into the extensive slave labor system from the start of the war, but Jews were targeted for murder wherever they were—regardless of the value of their labor—simply because they were Jews.

The regime's genocidal plans for other peoples in the East cannot be doubted. However, the ferocity of the murder of the Jews of Poland in the operation known as Aktion Reinhard demonstrated that the destruction of the European Jews was an end in itself, even where ethnic cleansing of other peoples was a stated goal and where the opportunity existed to murder them as well.

Frustrations with the pace of deportations to occupied Poland in the spring of 1941 created the impetus to find a "solution" there, a matter made all the more urgent when Galicia was incorporated into the General Government in August 1941. In October 1941, Odilo Globočnik, who had served under Eichman in Vienna, sought permission from Himmler to construct a gassing facility to murder the 320,000 Jews in the Lublin district. A few weeks later construction began on permanent gas chambers at Bełżec. The death camp at Sobibór may also have been prepared late in 1941. Construction on a third camp, Treblinka, near Warsaw, began in May 1942.[96] In the spring of 1942, in addition to the operation of these three death camps in the General Government, and Auschwitz and Chełmno in annexed Poland, there was a second wave of shooting deaths throughout the occupied East.[97]

When Heydrich was assassinated in Prague in the first week of June 1942 by the Czech resistance, the regime held Jews responsible for his death. The following July, Himmler demanded that most of the European Jews be dead by the end of the year. In Heydrich's honor, the deportations from the Warsaw Ghetto to Treblinka were named Operation Reinhard, although the title is used to refer to the gassings in all three death camps in the General Government. By October 1943, Odilo Globočnik, who, with Eichmann, remained a central figure in its execution, declared Aktion Reinhard complete.[98] During this period, two million Jews were murdered by gas or bullet in the General Government, but while most murders were previously believed to be concentrated over a thirteen-month period, in actuality as many as 1.47 million people were killed in a 105-day period, from July 22, 1942 to November 4, 1942 according to an analysis of 480 train deportations from 399 Polish ghettoes and towns to Treblinka, Bełżec, and Sobibór. All three camps operated simultaneously in October and November, concentrating on different areas of the General Government, one district at a time. Half-a-million people were killed in August and September, with a minimum of 1.32 million killed in a ninety-two-day period.[99]

The closure of these camps was previously understood to be a response to the Warsaw Ghetto Uprising in April 1943, the Uprising in Treblinka in August 1943, and the Revolt at Sobibór in October 1943.[100] However, the fact that most Jews in Poland were dead by the previous December suggests that the camps were closed because they ran out of Jewish victims in Poland. Jews from other parts of Europe would continue to be transported to their deaths in Auschwitz, where four hundred thousand Jews from Hungary would be murdered in the summer of 1944. Mass shootings would continue until the end of the war. However, the speed with which the Jews of the General Government were killed reveals for scholars a genocide with a kill rate[101] that remains unsurpassed, even by the genocide in Rwanda in July 1994.

To this day, the Holocaust should be the focus of study for what it can reveal about the tenuousness of civilization and the importance of the rule of law over people and institutions. As Yehuda Bauer explains:

> The very unprecedentedness of the Holocaust—that is, its specificity regarding the character of both the perpetrator and the victim—makes it of universal importance, because the ethnic or national or racial groups that could be future victims are as specific as the German Nazis and the Jews. Although the Holocaust has no precedent, it could become one.[102]

Notes

1. Geoffrey Megargee, *War of Annihilation: Combat and Genocide on the Eastern Front, 1941* (Lanham, MD: Rowman & Littlefield, 2006); Jan Tomasz Gross, *Neighbors: The Destruction of the Jewish Community in Jedwabne, Poland* (London: Arrow, 2003).
2. Henry Friedlander, *The Origins of Nazi Genocide: From Euthanasia to the Final Solution* (Chapel Hill: University of North Carolina Press, 1995), 287.
3. "The Moscow Conference, October 1943" *The Avalon Project Yale Law School*, http://avalon.law.yale.edu/wwii/moscow.asp. Also Gerhard L. Weinberg, *A World at Arms: A Global History of World War II* (Cambridge, UK: Cambridge University Press, 1994), 621
4. Michael Thad Allen, *The Business of Genocide: the SS, Slave Labor, and the Concentration Camps* (Chapel Hill: University of North Carolina Press, 2002).
5. Deborah E. Lipstadt, *History on Trial: My Day in Court with David Irving* (New York: Ecco, 2005).
6. Gerhard L. Weinberg, "Ignored and Misunderstood Aspects of the Holocaust," *Historical Reflections/Réflexions Historiques* 39, no. 2 (2013): 7–13; Yehuda Bauer, *Rethinking the Holocaust* (Boulder: University Press of Colorado, 2013), 4.
7. Eberhard Jäckel, *Hitler in History* (Hanover, NH: University Press of New England, 1984), 46.
8. Gerhard Weinberg, "The Holocaust Seventy-five Years after it Ended: A Panoramic View of Achievements and Challenges in Research and Interpretation," in *Search and Research—Lectures and Papers*, ed. Dan Michman and Yaron Pasher (Jerusalem: Yad Vasehm, 2019).
9. Adam J. Tooze, *The Wages of Destruction: The Making and Breaking of the Nazi Economy* (New York: Penguin Books, 2008), 10, 658.
10. Gerhard L. Weinberg, *Visions of Victory: The Hopes of Eight World War II Leaders* (New York: Cambridge University Press, 2005), 14, 8.
11. Richard Evans, *The Third Reich in Power* (New York: Penguin, 2005), 575.
12. Robert Gellately, *Backing Hitler: Consent and Coercion in Nazi Germany* (Oxford: Oxford University Press, 2013), 37.
13. Shlomo Aronson, *Hitler, the Allies and the Jews* (Cambridge: Cambridge University Press, 2004), 4.

14. Christoph Kreutzmüller, Jane Paulick, and Jefferson S. Chase, *Final Sale in Berlin: The Destruction of Jewish Commercial Activity, 1930–1945* (New York: Berghahn Books, 2017), 95, 154, 7.
15. Ian Kershaw, *Hitler 1889–1936: Hubris* (New York: W. W. Norton, 1999), 473.
16. Norman J. W. Goda, *The Holocaust: Europe, the World, and the Jews 1918–1945* (Boston: Pearson, 2013), 82.
17. Aronson, *Hitler, the Allies*, 4.
18. Robert Gerwarth, *Hitler's Hangman, The Life of Heydrich* (New Haven: Yale University Press, 2011), 124.
19. Deborah Dwork and Robert Jan van Pelt, *Holocaust: A History* (New York: W. W. Norton, 1990), 98.
20. Tooze, *The Wages*, 277, Aronson, *Hitler, the Allies*, 6.
21. Götz Aly and Jefferson S. Chase, *Hitler's Beneficiaries: Plunder, Racial War, and the Nazi Welfare State* (London: Verso, 2016), 44–45.
22. Tooze, *The Wages*, 276.
23. Aronson, *Hitler, the Allies*, 6; Tooze, *The Wages*, 277.
24. Goda, *The Holocaust*, 77–79.
25. Tooze, *The Wages*, 277; Peter Longerich, *Heinrich Himmler* (Oxford: Oxford University Press, 2012), 424, 853.
26. Gerwarth, *Hitler's Hangman*, 128.
27. Aly and Chase, *Hitler's Beneficiaries*, 46.
28. Quoted more fully in Goda, *The Holocaust*, 103. See also http://avalon.law.yale.edu/imt/2322-ps.asp.
29. Jäckel, *Hitler in History*, 49.
30. Weinberg, *A World at Arms*, 302; Jeffrey Herf, "Haj Amin al-Husseini, the Nazis and the Holocaust: The Origins, Nature and Aftereffects of Collaboration," *Jewish Political Studies Review* 26, no. 3/4 (2014): 13–37.
31. "Chancellor Adolf Hitler's Address at the Opening of the Winter Relief Campaign," UNC, Chapel Hill, www.ibiblio.org/pha/policy/1942/420930a.html; Christopher Browning and Jürgen Matthäus, *The Origin of the Final Solutions: The Evolution of Nazi Jewish Policy September 1939–March 1942* (Lincoln: University of Nebraska Press, 2004), 392.
32. Doris L. Bergen, "Instrumentalization of 'Volksdeutschen' in German Propaganda in 1939: Replacing/Erasing Poles, Jews, and Other Victims," *German Studies Review* 31, no. 3 (2008): 447.
33. Doris L. Bergen, "The Nazi Concept of 'Volksdeutsche' and the Exacerbation of Anti-Semitism in Eastern Europe, 1939–45," *Journal of Contemporary History* 29, no. 4 (1994) 570.
34. Goda, *The Holocaust*, 106; Browning and Matthäus, *Origins*, 30.
35. Longerich, *Himmler*, 420.
36. Longerich, *Himmler*, 430.
37. Bergen, "Instrumentalization of 'Volksdeutschen,'" 459.
38. Browning and Matthäus, *Origins*, 26.
39. Eberhard, *Hitler in History*, 50; Longerich, *Himmler*, 439–440; Aronson, *Hitler, the Allies*, 26.
40. Goda, *The Holocaust*, 115.
41. Browning and Matthäus, *Origins*, 36.
42. Goda, *The Holocaust*, 108–115.

43. Longerich, *Himmler*, 440–444; Aronson, *Hitler, the Allies*, 24.
44. Jäckel, *Hitler*, 50.
45. Omer Bartov, *Germany's War and the Holocaust: Disputed Histories* (Ithaca: Cornell University Press, 2003), 3–4.
46. Richard J. Evans, *The Coming of Third Reich* (New York: Penguin, 2004), 35.
47. Goda, *The Holocaust*, 152–153.
48. Goda, *The Holocaust*, 152.
49. Weinberg, *A World at Arms*, 95–96.
50. Friedlander, *The Origins of Nazi Genocide*, 22.
51. Goda, *The Holocaust*, 155–156.
52. Eugen Kogon, Hermann Langbein, and Adalbert Rückerl, *Nazi Mass Murder: A Documentary History of the Use of Poison Gas* (New Haven: Yale University Press, 1994), 32–34.
53. See Nathan Stoltzfus, *Hitler's Compromises: Coercion and Consensus in Nazi Germany* (New Haven: Yale University Press, 2016).
54. Kogon, Langbein, and Rückerl, *Nazi Mass Murder*, 34.
55. Goda, *The Holocaust*, 156.
56. Tadeusz Nasierowski, "In the Abyss of Death: The Extermination of the Mentally Ill in Poland During World War II," *International Journal of Mental Health* 35, no. 3 (2006): 50–51.
57. Longerich, *Himmler*, 431.
58. Longerich, *Himmler*, 547. Browning and Matthäus, *Origins*, 188.
59. Weinberg, *A World*, 173.
60. Aronson, *Hitler, the Allies*, 26.
61. Longerich, *Himmler*, 511.
62. Aronson, *Hitler, the Allies*, 8.
63. Waitman W. Beorn, "A Calculus of Complicity: The 'Wehrmacht,' the Anti-Partisan War, and the Final Solution in White Russia, 1941–42," *Central European History* 44, no. 2 (2011): 313.
64. Browning and Matthäus, *Origins*, 260.
65. Browning and Matthäus, *Origins*, 284; Longerich, *Himmler*, 520.
66. Browning and Matthäus, *Origins*, 244, 260.
67. Browning and Matthäus, *Origins*, 244.
68. Friedländer, *Years of Persecution*, 208.
69. Friedländer, *Years of Persecution*, 259.
70. Longerich, *Himmler*, 522; Beorn, "A Calculus of Complicity," 311.
71. Gerwarth, *Hitler's Hangman*, 185.
72. Omer Bartov, *Hitler's Army: Soldiers, Nazis and War in the Third Reich* (New York: Oxford University Press, 1994), 65–70.
73. Browning and Matthäus, *Origins*, 283.
74. Manfred Wolfson, "Association, Constraint and Choice in the SS Leadership," *The Western Political Quarterly* 18, no. 3 (September 1965): 551–568.
75. Browning and Matthäus, *Origins*, 230.
76. Browning and Matthäus, *Origins*, 230.
77. Wolfson, "Association, Constraint and Choice," 560.
78. Browning and Matthäus, *Origins*, 25; Gerwarth, *Hitler's Hangman*, 148.
79. Wolfson, "Association, Constraint and Choice," 562.

80. Geoffrey J. Giles, "The Denial of Homosexuality: Same-Sex Incidents in Himmler's SS and Police," *Journal of the History of Sexuality* 11, no. 1/2 (2002): 257.
81. Browning and Matthäus, *Origins*, 257.
82. Browning and Matthäus, *Origins*, 282; Martin Cüppers, *Wegbereiter der Shoah: die Waffen-SS, der Kommandostab Reichsführer-SS und die Judenvernichtung 1939–1945* (Darmstadt: Wissenschaftliche Buchgesellschaft, 2005).
83. Longerich, *Himmler*, 547.
84. See Christopher R. Browning, *Ordinary Men: Reserve Police Battalion 101 and the Final Solution in Poland* (New York: Harper Perennial, 2017).
85. Tooze, *The Wages*, 465; Gerwarth, *Hitler's Hangman*, 182.
86. Browning and Matthäus, *Origins*, 426.
87. Tooze, *The Wages*, 467.
88. Browning and Matthäus, *Origins*, 411–414.
89. Browning and Matthäus, *Origins*, 413.
90. Quoted in Gerwarth, *Hitler's Hangmant*, 274.
91. Goda, *The Holocaust*, 239; Lewi Stone, "Quantifying the Holocaust Hyperintense Kill Rates during the Nazi Genocide," *Science Advances* 5, no. 1 (January 2, 2019): 2–3; Maïa de la Baume, "French Railway Formally Apologizes to Holocaust Victims," *New York Times* (January 25, 2011).
92. Browning and Matthäus, *Origins*, 358; Longerich, *Himmler*, 548; Goda, *The Holocaust*, 242.
93. Longerich, *Himmler*, 572.
94. Goda, *The Holocaust*, 242.
95. Goda, *The Holocaust*, 241–242.
96. Longerich, *Himmler*, 545–566; Goda, *The Holocaust*, 218.
97. Browning and Matthäus, *Origins*, 275.
98. Goda, *The Holocaust*, 238.
99. Stone, "Quantifying the Holocaust," 3–7.
100. Goda, *The Holocaust*, 237.
101. Stone, "Quantifying the Holocaust," 2.
102. Bauer, *Rethinking*, 74.

Bibliography

Allen, Michael Thad. *The Business of Genocide: The SS, Slave Labor, and the Concentration Camps*. Chapel Hill: University of North Carolina Press, 2002.

Aly, Götz, and Jefferson S. Chase. *Hitler's Beneficiaries: Plunder, Racial War, and the Nazi Welfare State*. London: Verso, 2016.

Aronson, Shlomo. *Hitler, the Allies and the Jews*. Cambridge: Cambridge University Press, 2004.

Bauer, Yehuda. *Rethinking the Holocaust*. New Haven, Yale University Press, 2001.

Browning, Christopher. *Ordinary Men: Reserve Police Battalion 101 and the Final Solution in Poland*. New York: Harper Perennial, 2017.

Browning, Christopher, and Jürgen Matthäus. *The Origin of the Final Solutions: The Evolution of Nazi Jewish Policy September 1939–March 1942*. Lincoln: University of Nebraska Press, 2004.

Friedlander, Henry. *The Origins of Nazi Genocide: From Euthanasia to the Final Solution*. Chapel Hill: University of North Carolina Press, 1995.

Gellately, Robert. *Backing Hitler: Consent and Coercion in Nazi Germany*. Oxford: Oxford University Press, 2001.
Gerwarth, Robert. *Hitler's Hangman, The Life of Heydrich*. New Haven: Yale University Press, 2011.
Goda, Norman J. W. *The Holocaust: Europe, the World, and the Jews 1918–1945*. Boston: Pearson, 2013.
Gross, Jan Tomasz. *Neighbors: The Destruction of the Jewish Community in Jedwabne, Poland*. London: Arrow, 2003.
Longerich, Peter. *Heinrich Himmler*. Oxford: Oxford University Press, 2012.
Megargee, Geoffrey. *War of Annihilation: Combat and Genocide on the Eastern Front, 1941*. Lanham, MD: Rowman & Littlefield, 2006.
Weinberg, Gerhard. *A World at Arms: A Global History of World War II*. Cambridge: Cambridge University Press, 1994.

CHAPTER 28

THE HUMANITARIAN IMPULSE

HILLARY SEBENY

INTERNATIONAL humanitarian law developed rapidly through the catastrophic wars of the twentieth century, and along with it came increasingly sophisticated international efforts and organizations aimed at alleviating human suffering in wartime. Vulnerable groups worldwide, including prisoners of war, populations targeted by Nazi genocide or Japanese aggression, and civilians contending with the effects of bombing, malnutrition, and displacement, presented an enormous challenge to relief agencies and governments hoping to alleviate their suffering. Despite the unprecedented scale of destruction brought on by World War II, many humanitarian efforts achieved remarkable success. Although the majority of aid was ultimately directed toward Western nations, and especially European nations, the intergovernmental organizations that emerged from the wartime humanitarian impulse helped define the role of relief work and human rights in the post-1945 world.

By the late 1930s, an international acceptance of the necessity of humanitarian relief had largely emerged through the twin disasters of World War I and the Great Depression. The Wilsonian inventions of the League of Nations and its attendant Fourteen Points had prompted the creation of organizations like the High Commission on Refugees (HCR), and had led to relief efforts, such as Herbert Hoover's Committee for Relief in Belgium and American Relief Agency (aimed at alleviating famine in the Russian Civil War). Interwar treaty-making, such as the Kellogg–Briand Pact, signified a growing tendency among many nations to regulate the conditions under which war could be legally or morally waged. After 1929, the Great Depression, especially, drew attention to domestic relief within nations affected by the market collapse, as evidenced in British and American responses to the crisis and the American return to isolationism. The weaknesses of the League of Nations, however, and its attendant organizations like the HCR, prevented international solutions to many of the global crises of the late 1930s.

As war first broke out in East Asia, and subsequently enveloped the globe at the close of the decade, millions around the world suddenly found themselves in desperate need of assistance. While the Allied governments, jointly, were often slow to react to a variety of problems, such as the necessity of providing asylum to European Jews, or in supplying food to starving populations, hundreds of both official and private organizations worldwide met a great many challenges throughout the course of the war. These included such independent groups as the International Committee of the Red Cross, as well as relief agencies administered by religious groups, and dozens of social organizations. By 1943, the foundations for Allied cooperation in the United Nations Relief and Rehabilitation Administration (UNRRA) had been laid, to be cemented in the mission of the United Nations two years later. The genesis of the United Nations, and its subsidiaries like the World Health Organization, signaled another major shift in the codification of humanitarian law and the distribution of aid, this time toward larger, coordinated international responses.

Analysis of the worldwide humanitarian reaction to the war's crises has become a subject of renewed scholarly interest. Two-thirds of World War II's casualties were noncombatants, what Richard Bessel has described as "unnatural deaths," those caused by mass murder, forced labor, disease, starvation, and other disasters to befall civilians and POWs around the world.[1] The global response to these situations, this humanitarian impulse to alleviate suffering, rose above divisions of religion, ethnicity, and nationality, to varying degrees of success, and ultimately helped shape the way the world responds to such crises today.

Background

Much of the history of international law seems to follow a pattern: extreme violence gave way to new efforts at restricting inhumane behavior, only to find that the next era of destruction forced the creation of still better guidelines. Within Europe, the period after the Thirty Years' War saw some of the continent's first efforts at restricting behavior during war, leading to an extended period of limited warfare that would only be upended by the Napoleonic Wars. The Congress System and intervening decades of regional conflicts gave way to the establishment of the International Committee of the Red Cross in 1863 and the signing of the first Geneva Conventions in 1864, and the Hague Conventions in 1899 and 1907, respectively. Within the United States, the first established laws of war emerged in 1863 with Abraham Lincoln's issuance of the Lieber Code, aimed at ensuring humane treatment for prisoners of war during the American Civil War.

Yet humanitarian efforts have also long existed outside the treaty-making and state activity that shapes international law. One cause that fueled many nineteenth-century humanitarian endeavors originated in English opposition to the slave trade and the abolition movement promoted by early evangelical churches and traditional peace churches, such as the Society of Friends. The distinct connections between abolitionists and more modern practices of humanitarianism provided a model for aid motivated by religious conviction, which would continue throughout the nineteenth century and into the chaotic twentieth century.

This model of aid motivated by theological constructs was perhaps best exemplified and systematized in a recognizably modern form by Henri Dunant, the Swiss founder of the International Committee of the Red Cross (ICRC). Dunant, a devoted Calvinist, established the ICRC in 1863 as an organization independent of official state or church strictures, a structure that sociologist Shai M. Dromi has characterized as the genesis of independent humanitarian endeavors.[2] As Dunant and his cofounders envisioned it, the ICRC would work alongside militaries during times of war or crisis, yet would not work in subordination to them, allowing the Red Cross and subsequent similar groups to tailor their work specifically to humanitarian needs. The ICRC worked to publicize the Geneva Conventions, codified the following year, to ensure that nations around the world were aware of humanitarian workers' independence from other actors on the battlefield.[3]

From its inception, the Red Cross aimed to frame the ethics of war within Christian theology, while also emphasizing the Calvinist impulse for charity to exist outside the auspices of the state. The particular strain of its Calvinist doctrine argued that its sixteenth-century foundational texts had no need of nineteenth-century updates, and harbored skepticism of the role of government going beyond a simple separation of church and state. In this Swiss Reformed view, charity and social work was the purview and duty of the willing church community. Adapting to modernity was unnecessary, particularly because the state and modernity were perceived as the source of contemporary warfare and suffering. Thus, the group strove to remain politically neutral and to refrain from criticizing belligerents in a given conflict, to better promote the ICRC's broader aim of humanitarian organizations operating strictly under what they saw as the universal moral value of preserving human life.[4] As the number of national offshoots of the Red Cross grew in the late nineteenth century, the Calvinist religiosity of the group also waned in the expanding universal and eventually secular appeal of humanitarian rights. Ottoman Red Cross workers in the 1870s even substituted a Muslim crescent for the cross in their insignia, and the organization is today known as the International Red Cross and Crescent.[5] Thus, despite its strictly religious origins, the Red Cross and its promotion of international law ultimately created the structures necessary to promote a notion of humanitarian aid and responsibility that transcended one religion and became a more universally accepted ethic.

Despite these advances, World War I presented a global catastrophe for which many nations were entirely unprepared. As in centuries past, existing legal protections and relief institutions were proven inadequate when the war left its mark in humanitarian crises of an unprecedented scale. The use of chemical weapons in combat, abuses of prisoners of war, attacks on civilian populations, the widespread effects of hunger and disease, and a global refugee crisis presented a litany of challenges to traditional humanitarian organizations led by specific religious organizations and even larger organizations like the Red Cross. The rise of massive relief operations conducted by technocrats and experts, like Hoover, and the failure to adequately prosecute war criminals, led to a wider understanding after the Armistice that new legal structures and nongovernmental organizations would be needed to continue relief and organize it in the future.

Amidst the rise of secular and institutional ideals in postwar restructuring, the language of humanitarian work, too, changed from a position of dispensing charity in the name of "humanitarian rights" toward an argument for universal human rights.[6] Although these rights were conceived as universal, their dispensation in the post-1918 world was often biased toward Western peoples. Many of the imperial inequities that persisted after the Treaty of Versailles were reflected in the amount and types of aid that non-Western nations received in the Great War's aftermath, and in the ways that dispensation of aid continued into World War II.

In the sphere of international law, existing agreements were refined and amended in the 1920s, while new laws were codified. In 1922, the United States, Great Britain, Japan, France, and Italy signed the Washington Naval Treaty, which set limits on tonnage for the construction of new ships and temporarily halted their construction altogether. The Geneva Conventions were updated to include greater protections for prisoners of war, and the Hague Conventions were amended in 1925 to establish a ban on the use of chemical and biological weapons in combat. The Declaration of the Rights of the Child, promoted by Eglantyne Jebb, the English humanitarian who founded the Save the Children Fund, was adopted by the League in 1924, providing a moral groundwork for international reconciliation in the postwar era.[7]

Yet the Versailles Conference and the newly established League of Nations marked a new era in international, intergovernmental methods of dealing with problems persisting after the peace. Civil war in the new Soviet Union, genocide in Armenia, and disease and starvation affecting dozens of nations continued to demand complex solutions. The problem of refugees, especially, posed an enormous problem to the international community, as the breakup of old empires and the tumult of the Armenian genocide and Russian Revolution left millions stateless and without the necessary documentation to move across borders and to new homes abroad.

So, in 1922, Norwegian polar explorer Fridtjof Nansen, the head of the League's High Commission on Refugees, devised a solution. The Nansen Passport, as it came to be known, aimed to facilitate the movement of refugees through the identity and travel certificate, and by 1926, forty nations recognized the Nansen Passport in accepting refugees for asylum. The major limitation of the Nansen Passport, however, proved to be its inability to distinguish individual refugees from their national classifications, a problem that would be highlighted in the struggles of German and Austrian Jews fleeing their homelands in the 1930s.[8]

Not all humanitarian organizations and efforts to emerge in the post-Armistice world were entirely new, however, and many had the benefit of gaining expertise during World War I to refine their operations. Herbert Hoover's Committee for Relief in Belgium, which had operated from 1915 through the war's end, was directly responsible for the successes of his American Relief Agency in Central and Eastern Europe in the early 1920s.[9] This process of learning and refining humanitarian efforts can be seen as contiguous with the work of international organizations and relief agencies through World

War II and beyond. Without these learning processes, the global response to World War II would have seen far fewer successes.

The limitations of the spirit of internationalism and institutions like the League of Nations, however, came into sharp relief against the persistence of nationalism in many regions throughout the 1920s and 1930s. It would take another worldwide conflict to more firmly cement the notions of universal human rights and dignity and to prove the efficacy and dedication of humanitarian activists and organizations, both religious and secular, in the face of an even greater global challenge.

Global Crisis and Refugees

Perhaps the most widely discussed aspects of the humanitarian response to the war concern refugees. The problem of refugees and resettlement in the interwar era had been alleviated, but not eliminated, through international efforts such as the High Commission on Refugees, and the outbreak of hostilities created new refugee populations in each country the war touched. The Japanese invasion of Manchuria in 1931 and the ensuing second Sino–Japanese War marked not only the first hostilities, but also the first humanitarian crises of what would become World War II. The conflict between Japan and China in the 1930s provided a preview of the problems that would face the rest of the world by the end of the decade, particularly violence against civilians, the global refugee crisis, and the disastrous consequences of widespread famine.

Despite the Japanese seizure of Manchuria in 1931 and gradual incursions into Mongolia, large-scale organized Chinese military resistance did not begin until after the Imperial Army had crossed the Great Wall. After the 1937 Marco Polo Bridge incident, Chinese forces (largely Chiang Kai-Shek's Nationalist forces at this early point in the war) began contesting Japanese conquest. The imperial Japanese army forged a trail of brutality throughout China, most notoriously in the December 1937 atrocities that have become known as the Rape of Nanjing. But the Sino–Japanese conflict also created a persistent refugee problem within China, leaving thousands more homeless or orphaned with each passing month.

After Nanjing, the Yellow River became a focal point of both Chinese and Japanese war plans in early 1938, and the Nationalist forces hoped that a strategic breach of the Yellow River's dikes in the Henan province would prevent Japanese advances into the region. Chiang's forces detonated explosives on Yellow River dikes in June of that year, completely flooding the surrounding plains and devastating the livelihoods and food supply of peasant farmers in the Henan Province. Nearly one million people perished in the 1938 flood, and perhaps as many as ten million were left homeless, weakening the Nationalists' support among the province's peasants and intensifying China's internal conflict between Chiang's forces and the Communists.[10]

By July 1938, the city of Wuhan held nearly half a million refugees as a result of the chaos triggered by the flooding, many of whom were children. The International

Committee of the Red Cross conducted relief operations in the city and sponsored orphanages, but locally based humanitarian efforts became especially noteworthy in Wuhan, thanks to the work of socially prominent women like Song Meiling (the wife of Chiang Kai-Shek) and Shi Liang. Shi's organization, the Warfare Child Welfare Committee, ultimately became the model for social welfare programs in both mainland China and Taiwan after the war.[11]

Meanwhile, in Europe, refugee crises that had begun with the Nazi rise to power in Germany, and had worsened because of the Spanish Civil War, grew even more dire as an increasing number of Jewish refugees attempted to leave Germany. A somewhat ecumenical effort driven by organized American Jewish, Quaker, Catholic, and various Protestant relief efforts attempted to raise domestic concern for the plight of German Jews. This alarm grew more dire after Germany's March 1938 Anschluss of Austria, leading to President Roosevelt's appointment of James McDonald as the head of the President's Advisory Committee on Political Refugees in May of that year. McDonald had previously served as the High Commissioner for Refugees from Germany in the League of Nations, and his appointment allowed FDR to bypass the domestically unpopular League.[12]

Although FDR and McDonald were unable to move State Department immigration quotas, Roosevelt proposed an international conference on German and Austrian Refugees to be held in France at Evian-les-Bains in July 1938. McDonald realized the European refugee problem was too vast to be solved by private organizations, but little was accomplished at the meeting, save for the creation of the Intergovernmental Committee on Refugees, which would attempt to negotiate with Germany on the issue, as well as an offer from the Dominican Republic to accept one hundred thousand refugees (more than the tiny nation's government could plausibly handle).[13] The massive *Kristallnacht* pogrom in November 1938 prompted FDR to announce the creation of fifteen thousand new visitors' visas for German and Austrian refugees.[14]

After war broke out in Europe in 1939, relief agencies were often cut off from access to German-occupied territories. The British naval blockade of the European continent, supported by the United States and coupled with American neutrality legislation, hobbled many attempts to provide humanitarian intervention to civilians and would-be refugees in the months between the war's outbreak and America's entry to the conflict. Attempts at legislating a program similar to Britain's Kindertransports or even alleviating the strict immigration quota system failed within the United States, and American antisemitism was particularly pronounced in the late 1930s. Gallup polling from May 1939 had even indicated that fully one-fifth of Americans would support or be sympathetic to a campaign against Jews in the United States.[15]

Intense debate continues as to whether Allied governments did enough to aid Jewish populations trying to flee Nazi persecution. Groups such as the American Friends Service Committee continued to lobby on behalf of refugees, although the closure of American consulates in belligerent nations complicated the process. Aid workers in cities like Lisbon and Casablanca became instrumental in securing passage for Jewish refugees. After the Nazi seizure of most of mainland Europe was complete in the summer of 1940, humanitarian groups that had once been allowed to work outside the strictures of the British blockade were effectively barred from doing so by Secretary of State Cordell Hull. The peace churches and Herbert Hoover led a public campaign in favor of breaking the blockade for humanitarian purposes, but the State Department ended the discussion by arguing that there would be no way to even ensure that the Nazi occupiers allowed fair distribution of humanitarian aid and resources.[16] After Pearl Harbor and the United States' entry to the war, the last possibility of escape was dashed for most of Europe's refugees.

Prisoners of War

Despite the existence of the Geneva Conventions, prisoners of war suffered even greater injustice in many arenas of the conflict than they had during the Great War. For imprisoned combatants, the conditions and legality of treatment by their captors varied wildly on different fronts of the war. Many nations, such as the United States and the Commonwealth countries, tended to follow the guidelines established for POWs by the Geneva Conventions. Other nations, such as Nazi Germany, tended to ignore the Geneva Conventions when their prisoners were members of groups considered racially inferior—and the brutality of the Eastern Front extended to POWs held by both the Germans and the Soviets.

Within the European theater, Anglo–American prisoners held by Axis forces and vice-versa (and here the British designation also entails combatants from Commonwealth nations) were generally overseen by the International Committee of the Red Cross. The Allies welcomed this oversight in the hope that if their fair treatment of the large number of German POWs in captivity was broadcast, their own troops would receive the same consideration. All concerned nations in this situation were signatories to the Geneva Convention, so the Germans could not object to their prisoners' legal status, as would be the case with Soviet prisoners because the USSR was not party to that convention. The Red Cross undertook scheduled inspections of camps every three months, reporting on conditions using a scale that ranged from "very good" to "inadequate," although this scale was somewhat relative—conditions that might be considered unsatisfactory in the early months of the war could often be considered much better in 1945.[17] Poor material conditions for Allied POWs in German hands increased after the onset of the German war against the Soviet Union, but the number of criminal actions against Allied prisoners was relatively limited.[18]

Additionally, there were a number of Red Cross-sanctioned POW exchanges throughout the war. For example, the first Anglo–Italian prisoner exchange took place in 1942, with a second in 1943. After the Italian exit from the war, the British forces moved on to exchanges with the Germans that continued from late 1943 through 1944. However, the trials of ex-POWs did not end after their repatriation; many former prisoners were regarded with suspicion within Britain and Australia after their return, so the Red Cross also took care to advocate for their fair treatment upon their homecoming. The process of welcoming home repatriated POWs worked somewhat better in Britain than Australia, as these men continued to be treated as dishonorable within Australia, an unusual break with British military policy at the time.[19]

The fate of Italian prisoners provides perhaps the most useful example in illustrating the extreme variation in legal and humanitarian considerations toward POWs during the war. More than one million Italian troops were taken prisoner in locations as far flung as North America, Australia, Russia, North Africa, and India, and the Italian surrender in 1943 made many Italians prisoners of their former German allies. These German-held prisoners did not receive the considerations that their Anglo–American counterparts did, and they were often regarded as traitors by their captors. When German food supplies ran drastically short in the final months of the war, Anglo–American POWs frequently received augmented rations provided by the Red Cross to fill in the gap; Italian POWs rarely received the same dispensation from the Germans. And while the United States and the Soviet Union had completed their repatriation of Italian prisoners by 1946, Italians held by the British were the last to be returned home, some as late as 1947, largely due to the economic benefits of their labor.[20]

Economic considerations often drove Soviet treatment of their prisoners of war, as well. While possibly hundreds of thousands of German POWs died in Soviet hands, and the 1940 massacre of Polish POWs in Katyn stand out as examples of Soviet war crimes, more often than not Soviet-held POWs were subjected to harsh conditions as a result of the rapid deterioration of the entire Soviet home front. Whereas German forces targeted Eastern European Jews and Soviet POWs as subhuman groups undeserving of quarter, the Soviets often, although not consistently, made an effort to treat prisoners as fairly as possible. Prisoners were put to work to alleviate the economic burden of the war effort, and encouraged to grow their own food for subsistence, but the nationwide lack of food and adequate protections from climate led to many POW deaths. For many Eastern European Jewish POWs in Soviet hands, they received similar treatment to captives of other Eastern nations, yet they were often kept laboring in captivity for months, or years, after the end of the war, particularly in the case of Hungarian Jews.[21]

The legal and humanitarian issues surrounding POWs become more complicated by the internment of civilians in many nations. In addition to the vast system of Nazi concentration camps throughout Germany and occupied Europe, civilians of Japanese descent in the United States were forced into internment camps by President Roosevelt's Executive Order 9066, and throughout the Pacific civilians were imprisoned by occupying Japanese forces. Within the United States, one of the major efforts on behalf of imprisoned Japanese Americans came in the form of legal challenges to the system of internment camps. In *Korematsu v. United States* (1944), Fred Korematsu deliberately disobeyed the executive order to report for internment, challenging its constitutionality as a violation of his Fifth Amendment rights, but the Supreme Court ruled against him. Another case, regarding the legality of curfew laws for Japanese Americans, *Hirabayashi v. United States* (1943), was brought by Gordon Hirabayashi with the support of the Friends Service Committee and was also decided in the government's favor.

Japanese-held prisoners (both combatants and civilians) in the Pacific were often subject to brutal conditions, and their treatment of POWs frequently failed to adhere to Geneva Convention guidelines. Scholarship on civilian internment, however, has shown that Japanese attitudes toward civilian prisoners often failed to follow a monolithic policy and depended largely on circumstance. Prior to the outbreak of war, Japan had been signatory to a Red Cross-backed 1934 Tokyo Draft Convention guaranteeing fair conditions for civilians captured either in enemy territory or who lived in enemy-occupied territory. The start of hostilities prevented this convention from being properly codified, but during the early years of the war, Japanese forces often adhered to these standards in British colonial territories in Asia, especially if Japanese prisoners were promised reciprocal treatment. However, many civilians were blocked from receiving Red Cross supplies or medical treatment, a condition that worsened after the tide of the war turned in 1943.[22] After this point, starvation increasingly became the most serious problem facing many civilians, POWs, and even Japanese soldiers in their empire's territories. The problem of famine, however, proved more widespread than just occupied territories and has increasingly drawn attention as perhaps the most destructive element of World War II.

Famine and Food Policy

Hunger, even more than violence, was responsible for the majority of fatalities worldwide during the war. Famine and malnutrition affected combatants, civilians, and prisoners of war alike, and as many as twenty million people died as a result of starvation and malnutrition during World War II.[23] In many situations, especially in areas under Nazi occupation, famine was a deliberately engineered ideological pursuit. For other nations, starvation and malnutrition emerged from the colonial structures that prioritized Western nations over subjugated peoples; in many other cases, famine was the unhappy accident of ecological disaster and the strictures of war.

Nazi food policies aimed to reroute food away from occupied and conquered territories for the benefit of the war effort, and wherever the German armies marched, devastating and often fatal hunger typically followed, but this was no mere byproduct of limited resources. The Nazi push for *Lebensraum* (living space) led directly to German economic planners' desire for continually more agricultural production across thousands of miles of territory. These planners hoped to permanently end Germany's food supply problems by starving "useless eaters" in the Eastern European populations that Nazi ideology identified as racially subhuman. These goals, concretely outlined in Nazi agricultural secretary Herbert Backe's Hunger Plan, and in the more shockingly grandiose General Plan East, were never completely realized, yet nonetheless contributed millions to the war's number of "unnatural deaths." Regions like Ukraine, recently devastated by Stalinist famine, were hit especially hard by German hunger policies, and the extreme violence and scorched-earth tactics seen on the Eastern Front exacerbated the suffering of millions in the Soviet East.

In Asia, Chinese populations had been among the first to experience widespread famine, caused by both the invading Japanese forces and ecological disaster. Like a number of other nations, China suffered the misfortune of environmental conditions intensifying human suffering in an already-costly conflict. Beginning after the Japanese incursion into Manchuria in 1931, attempts by Chiang Kai-Shek's Nationalist government to implement flood control measures over the Huai River area actually exacerbated the subsequent damage caused by irregular weather patterns, a problem that continued after the escalation of war with Japan in 1937. Problems in Henan worsened further still in 1943, when famine caused by lingering effects of the Yellow River flood and amplified by war killed as many as two million citizens. The 1943 famine became so dire that reports of widespread cannibalism emerged from the area, as the people of Henan suffered due to both ecological disaster and excessive taxation enforced by the Nationalists to feed the army.

The failure of the Nationalist government to address the suffering in Henan and other regions enabled the Chinese Communist forces to step in and attempt to alleviate the crisis. Rather than seizing land from property holders, as they had in earlier years, Mao's plan to win the loyalty of the peasantry involved reducing rents, improving agricultural output, and granting the peasants greater access to farming profits. Various schemes, including assigning Communist soldiers to assist in harvests and reducing the amount of food requisitioned by troops, not only lessened rural Chinese suffering but would also later endear Mao's forces to the population.[24]

Japanese control of most of the world's rice-producing lands by 1942 did little to alleviate the food shortages and malnutrition that had developed throughout those rice-producing lands in Southeast Asia, Indochina, and the Indian subcontinent. The rice requisitioned by the Japanese to feed its far-flung forces and home islands left very little for the occupied territories. Although it had not been as deliberate or motivated by ideology like the German Hunger Plan, at least seven million people in the region starved to death during the war.[25] The American navy's success in disrupting Japanese shipping lanes by 1943 put further stress on the Japanese Empire's vast geography and the nutritional needs of the home islands and troops in the field. The American naval strategy of allowing Japanese island garrisons to "wither on the vine" not only affected imperial Japanese troops, but the natives of the islands, and Allied prisoners of war as well. So it came to pass that in the final two years of war, Japan controlled virtually the entire world's supply of rice, but their troops and prisoners suffered starvation, malnutrition, and its accompanying diseases, including beriberi (often caused by drinking water contaminated by corpses) and pellagra. Here, too, cannibalism became a frequent recourse for the starving.[26]

Allied food policies and hunger relief suffered their own failures and complications. Between 1942 and early 1945, much of Europe, the Mediterranean, and the Soviet Union remained in some way restricted from access to hunger relief due to Nazi occupation or the Allied naval blockade. British Prime Minister Winston Churchill had argued against any break in the blockade out of fear that the Germans could not be trusted to fairly allocate food resources, yet relief organizations argued that, by allowing occupied lands to starve, the Allied language of humanitarianism against Nazi atrocity would be called into question.

The situation was especially dire in Greece, where fourteen percent of the nation's population died of hunger-related conditions. Due to a historic dependence on imported food and the exacerbating effects of Nazi plunder, food shortages in Greece became so desperate that the Allies were forced to make an exception to their own blockade of occupied Europe. The International Committee of the Red Cross, along with numerous British and American groups, including the Oxford Committee for Famine Relief (Oxfam), demanded a break in the blockade in the summer of 1941. When Churchill relented and agreed to break the blockade for the sake of the Greeks, food shipments began to arrive in the first half of 1942. However, the Germans did eventually weaponize the aid, preventing the distribution of food to areas of heavy partisan activity.[27] This would be the only exception to the naval blockade.

As in World War I, the majority of humanitarian funds from Allied nations were directed toward Europe. British food policy largely left colonial possessions to fend for themselves in securing adequate food supplies and market controls to stabilize prices, leading to widespread suffering in India. Colonial neglect, coupled with ecological conditions that destroyed the 1942 rice harvest in Bengal, left rural Indians with no hope for food by the end of 1942. The following year, colonial officials began to take note of the famine, and local charities and relief organizations were unable to keep up with the desperate need throughout Bengal. While the Indian government's Food Department eventually established a rationing system that covered the entire nation by early 1945, the Churchill government repeatedly refused pleas for aid to India, rejecting a Canadian offer of ten thousand tons of wheat in 1943, and later prohibiting India from applying for United Nations aid.[28] The horrors resulting from the unequal distribution of Allied famine relief are only now coming into scholarly focus, having been overshadowed for decades by the debate over the Allied nations' response to the Holocaust.

THE INTERNATIONALIZATION OF RELIEF AND THE HOLOCAUST

Within the British–American alliance, while private sector or religious organizations often worked on behalf of refugees seeking asylum, the official response of the Roosevelt administration has often been interpreted as indifference or antisemitism. More recently, however, some scholars have attempted a more nuanced look at the frequent changes in FDR's public positions on Jewish persecution. Broadly put, Roosevelt's response to the crisis that escalated throughout the 1930s and exploded in the early 1940s depended largely on either his domestic political situation or the successes of Allied forces abroad. Although he entered office vocally opposed to Nazi antisemitism, the pressures of re-election and American public opinion kept the president quieter in the mid-to-late 1930s. After 1939, the gradually increasing pressures of neutrality, American entry to the war, and blockade prevented large-scale action on behalf of threatened civilians.[29]

When the Roosevelt administration officially signaled a change to refugee policy in 1944, most Holocaust victims had already been killed. This major change in American policy arrived with the creation of the War Refugee Board in 1944. While the efficacy of any method of refugee assistance in 1942 or 1943 was dubious at the height of the Holocaust's killing efforts, and a low point in many Allied military efforts, the Roosevelt administration had finally acknowledged the ongoing crisis and officially pledged relief efforts. The previous lack of support for those seeking refuge in the United States, however, could not be undone, as most of the organized genocide conducted in the death camps or mass shootings had slowed by 1944. Treasury Department official Josiah DuBois noted the Roosevelt administration's failure to act sooner, and as 1943 drew to a close, he drafted a memo titled "Report to the Secretary on the Acquiescence of this Government in the Murder of Jews." DuBois blamed former Assistant Secretary of State Breckenridge Long and members of his staff, who had been motivated by antisemitism to intentionally slow the visa application process and create a refugee backlog, condemning thousands of European Jews by denying them a chance at rescue. The administration reacted to DuBois's report by creating the War Refugee Board in January 1944. In James McDonald's view, the War Refugee Board had several major advantages over the previous efforts: first, that it streamlined the refugee process into a single agency; that the agency had direct access to power as it was overseen by the Secretaries of War, State, and the Treasury; also, that its existence signaled a kind of "psychological warfare" emboldening those who wished to help imperiled Jews and warning those who wished to persecute them.[30]

This streamlining visible in the establishment of the War Refugee Board extended to other forms of aid as well. At the outset of World War II, the humanitarian response to suffering had been often fractured, led by numerous independent agencies within individual countries, such as the various religious organizations that had lobbied on behalf of refugees. The establishment of the War Relief Control Board in 1942 was an attempt to organize individual charities under a larger government umbrella, in an effort to prevent fraud and oversee the consolidation of regional groups into larger, national organizations. The licensing power of the War Relief Control Board and the consolidation process oversaw 235 relief groups that had existed in 1939 shift to just eleven in 1942, with Americans ultimately donating more than one billion dollars to charities throughout the war.[31]

The United States' gradual process of broadly organizing humanitarian agencies was by no means unique (as can be seen in the establishment of the Council of British Societies for Relief Abroad). This dynamic shift across the Allied world led to the 1943 establishment of the United Nations Relief and Rehabilitation Administration (UNRRA), a non-governmental, international agency encompassing relief efforts from religious, private, and governmental organizations. Yet even in naming the UNRRA, one can observe the late-war shift of many humanitarian objectives—rescue, now all but impossible for threatened populations, had been reoriented as relief (rehabilitation would come later).

The UNRRA's beginnings marked a wider change in Allied and international understanding of humanitarian responsibilities as a social and essentially human obligation. This also necessitated the waning of individual organizations' geopolitical significance, especially religious organizations like the American Friends Service Committee or private efforts like Hoover's hunger relief. However, these smaller organizations continued to play a pivotal role in UNRRA efforts, especially due to the personal relationships and warm feelings that had persisted among many nations that had benefitted from their World War I and post-1918 work. Not all welcomed the new UNRRA, though—the French, in particular, bristled at the United States' eagerness to seize the reins of global leadership through the organization.[32]

When the war drew to a close in 1945, the UNRRA conducted operations throughout devastated nations, and to alleviate a variety of needs—disease control, famine relief, aid for displaced persons (DPs), and general social reconstruction. The problem of DPs proved the stickiest for the UNRRA; many nations disagreed with the organization's conception of the nation-state and its lack of consideration of local politics in its repatriation of displaced persons. The official mandate and composition of the UNRRA prohibited the group from working within Germany and on behalf of German DPs, and so the massive expulsion of ethnic Germans from territory that had been seized by the Third Reich or subject to its brutality went largely unaddressed. Once again, aid funds were largely directed at Europe and the West, preventing complete rehabilitation of colonial territories in Africa, Asia, and the Pacific world. Additionally, the UNRRA's seemingly simultaneous promotion of the competing interests of the West and the Communist East also eventually drew condemnation from some in the United States, and some DPs from Communist nations were even repatriated against their will.[33]

Despite these shortcomings, however, the UNRRA achieved many successes in postwar relief. More than $4 billion in food, medical, and industrial aid was distributed globally by the organization, and it briefly helped bridge the ideological chasm between the Western Allies and the Communist Eastern Bloc before the deepening of Cold War divides. By feeding Soviet citizens in desperate need, the internationalist spirit that would be enshrined in the United Nations got an early start, although it proved to be short-lived.[34] The UNRRA malaria relief program in Greece built upon the humanitarian inroads that had begun during the break in the Allied naval blockade to administer medical relief badly needed after the widespread destruction in that nation, and this spirit would live on in the creation of the World Health Organization. So, even though the UNRRA was merged into the United Nations structure in 1945 and would operate for only about two years after the war's end, the pursuit of impartially distributed aid and the organization of global health initiatives continues to survive. The United Nations charter ensured that the issue of human rights, then, became enshrined in international humanitarian law, rather than as a motivation for humanitarian action.[35]

Although the influence of World War II is most pronounced in the post-1945 international order led by the United Nations, it is important to recognize the continuities from the aftermath of the Great War, as well. The operating procedures of the League of Nations' High Commission on Refugees persist in many ways, such as the dependence on the assistance of former refugees to deal with governments on a local level.[36] This is but one example of the ways in which international humanitarian law and assistance might be better served by a twentieth-century-wide perspective of continuity, rather than separating the responses to World War I and World War II on a comparative basis.

The precedents set by postwar trials and international law have proven useful in prosecuting war criminals in the decades since 1945, but other aspects of the international response to the horrors of World War II have left a markedly murkier legacy. The efficacy of the Allied nations' refugee policies remains a perpetual subject of debate, and our understanding of the extent of famine and ecological disaster in colonial possessions and non-Western nations continues to lag behind studies of European calamities, especially. Additionally, thanks to such programs as the International Tracing Service, the impulse to provide closure and information for families affected by the Holocaust allows wartime efforts to live on in a certain way. Yet as ethnic cleansing, famine, and disregard for international law continue to generate calamities throughout the globe, the study of what went wrong, and what went right, in World War II's humanitarian efforts remains as relevant as ever.

Notes

1. Richard Bessel, "Unnatural Deaths," in *The Oxford Illustrated History of World War II*, ed. Richard Overy (New York: Oxford University Press, 2005), 322–323.
2. Shai M. Dromi, "Soldiers of the Cross: Calvinism, Humanitarianism, and the Genesis of Social Fields," *Sociological Theory* 34, no. 3: 169–219.
3. Ibid., 203, 206–207.
4. Ibid., 210.
5. Ibid., 212–213.
6. Bruno Cabanes, *The Great War and the Origins of Humanitarianism* (New York: Cambridge University Press, 2014), 300.
7. Ibid., 292–298.
8. Ibid., 182–186.
9. Ibid., 302.
10. Micah S. Muscolino, *The Ecology of War in China: Henan Province, the Yellow River, and Beyond, 1938–1950* (New York: Cambridge University Press, 2014), 1–2, 22; Diana Lary, "Drowned Earth: The Strategic Breaching of the Yellow River Dyke, 1938," *War in History* 8, no. 2 (2001): 201–207.
11. Steven Hugh Lee, "The Japanese Empire at War, 1931–1945," in *The Oxford Illustrated History of World War II*, ed. Richard Overy (New York: Oxford University Press, 2005), 46–47.
12. Strictly Confidential Minutes of PACPR, May 16, 1938, in Richard Breitman, Barbara McDonald Stewart, and Severin Hochberg, *Refugees and Rescue: The Diaries and Papers*

of James G. McDonald, 1932–1945 (Bloomington: Indiana University Press for the United States Holocaust Memorial Museum), 129–131.

13. See editorial notes, Breitman, Stewart, and Hochberg, *Refugees and Rescue*, 138–139.
14. Robert Dallek, *FDR and Foreign Policy, 1932–1945* (New York: Oxford University Press, 1979), 18–19, 168–169.
15. Richard Breitman and Allan J. Lichtman, *FDR and the Jews* (Cambridge, MA: Belknap Press of Harvard University Press, 2013), 144–149.
16. Andrew Preston, *Sword of the Spirit, Shield of Faith: Religion in American War and Diplomacy*, (New York: Anchor, 2012), 290–294.
17. Vasilis Vourkoutiotis, "What the Angels Saw: Red Cross and Protecting Power Visits to Anglo–American POWS, 1939–1945," *Journal of Contemporary History* 40, no. 4 (2005): 689–691.
18. Ibid., 705–706.
19. Seumas Spark, "Dishonourable Men? The Australian Army, Prisoners of War and Anglo–German POW Repatriations in the Second World War," *Australian Historical Studies* 45 (2014): 242–265.
20. Bob Moore, "Enforced Diaspora: The Fate of Italian Prisoners of War During the Second World War," *War in History* 22, no. 2 (2015): 174–175, 188–189.
21. George Barany, "Jewish Prisoners of War in the Soviet Union During World War II," *Jahrbücher für Geschichte Osteuropas* 31, no. 2 (1983): 161–209.
22. Felicia Yap, "International Laws of War and Civilian Internees of the Japanese in British Asia," *War in History* 23, no. 4 (2016): 416–438.
23. Lizzie Collingham, *The Taste of War: World War II and the Battle for Food* (New York: Penguin Press, 2012), 1.
24. Ibid., 258–261.
25. Stephen Porter, "Humanitarian Politics and Governance: International Responses to the Civilian Toll in the Second World War," in *The Cambridge History of the Second World War*, ed. Michael Geyer and Adam Tooze (Cambridge: Cambridge University Press, 2015), 505.
26. Collingham, *Taste of War*, 298–300.
27. Collingham, *Taste of War*, 166–168.
28. Ibid., 141–151.
29. This is one of the primary arguments of Breitman and Lichtman's *FDR and the Jews*.
30. See editorial notes on Josiah DuBois meeting with FDR, and James McDonald, Address to the National Conference for Palestine, Chicago, November 19, 1944, *Refugees and Rescue*, 315–317.
31. An official summary of the War Relief Control Board's activities can be found in Joseph E. Davies, *Voluntary War Relief During World War II: A Report to the President by the President's War Relief Control Board* (Washington, DC: United States Government Printing Office, 1946).
32. Laure Humbert, "French Politics of Relief and International Aid: France, UNRRA and the Rescue of European Displaced Persons in Postwar Germany, 1945–47," *Journal of Contemporary History* 51, no. 3 (2016): 632–634.
33. Ibid., and Jessica Reinisch, "'We Shall Rebuild Anew a Powerful Nation': UNRRA, Internationalism and National Reconstruction in Poland," *Journal of Contemporary History* 43, no. 3 (July 1, 2008): 451–476.

34. Andrew Harder, "The Politics of Impartiality: The United Nations Relief and Rehabilitation Administration in the Soviet Union, 1946–1947," *Journal of Contemporary History* 47, no. 2 (2012): 347–369.
35. Katerina Gardikas, "Relief Work and Malaria in Greece, 1943–1947," *Journal of Contemporary History* 43, no. 3 (2008): 493–508.
36. Cabanes, *The Great War and the Origins of Humanitarianism*, 157–158.

Bibliography

Barany, George. "Jewish Prisoners of War in the Soviet Union During World War II." *Jahrbücher Für Geschichte Osteuropas* 31, no. 2 (1983): 161–209.

Breitman, Richard. "The Allied War Effort and the Jews, 1942–1943." *Journal of Contemporary History* 20, no. 1 (January 1, 1985): 135–156.

Breitman, Richard, and Allan J. Lichtman. *FDR and the Jews*. Cambridge, MA: Belknap Press of Harvard University Press, 2013.

Cabanes, Bruno. *The Great War and the Origins of Humanitarianism, 1918–1924*. New York: Cambridge University Press, 2014.

Cameron, Lindsey. "The ICRC in the First World War: Unwavering Belief in the Power of Law?" *International Review of the Red Cross* 97, no. 900 (December 2015): 1099–1120.

Cohen, G. Daniel. "Between Relief and Politics: Refugee Humanitarianism in Occupied Germany 1945–1946." *Journal of Contemporary History* 43, no. 3 (July 1, 2008): 437–49.

Collingham, Lizzie. *The Taste of War: World War II and the Battle for Food*. New York: Penguin Books, 2012.

Dallek, Robert. *Franklin D. Roosevelt and American Foreign Policy, 1932–1945: With a New Afterword*. 2nd ed. New York: Oxford University Press, 1995.

Dromi, Shai M. "Soldiers of the Cross: Calvinism, Humanitarianism, and the Genesis of Social Fields." *Sociological Theory* 34, no. 3 (September 1, 2016): 196–219.

Feingold, Henry L. *Bearing Witness: How America and Its Jews Responded to the Holocaust*. Syracuse, NY: Syracuse University Press, 1995.

Feingold, Henry L. *The Politics of Rescue: The Roosevelt Administration and the Holocaust 1938–1945*. New Brunswick, NJ: Rutgers University Press, 1970.

Friedman, Saul S. *No Haven for the Oppressed: United States Policy Toward Jewish Refugees, 1938–1945*. Detroit: Wayne State University Press, 1973.

Gardikas, Katerina. "Relief Work and Malaria in Greece, 1943–1947." *Journal of Contemporary History* 43, no. 3 (July 1, 2008): 493–508.

Giannakopoulos, Georgios. "A British International Humanitarianism? Humanitarian Interventions in Eastern Europe (1875–1906)." *Journal of Modern Greek Studies* 34, no. 2 (September 28, 2016): 299–320.

Hamerow, Theodore S. *Why We Watched: Europe, America, and the Holocaust*. New York: W. W. Norton & Company, 2008.

Harder, Andrew. "The Politics of Impartiality: The United Nations Relief and Rehabilitation Administration in the Soviet Union, 1946–7." *Journal of Contemporary History* 47, no. 2 (April 2012): 347–369.

Humbert, Laure. "French Politics of Relief and International Aid: France, UNRRA and the Rescue of European Displaced Persons in Postwar Germany, 1945–47." *Journal of Contemporary History* 51, no. 3 (July 1, 2016): 606–634.

Kraus, Hertha. *International Relief in Action, 1914–1943*. Scottdale, PA: The Herald Press, 1944.
Láníček, Jan. "What Did It Mean to Be Loyal? Jewish Survivors in Post-War Czechoslovakia in a Comparative Perspective." *Australian Journal of Politics & History* 60, no. 3 (September 2014): 384–404.
Lary, Diana. "Drowned Earth: The Strategic Breaching of the Yellow River Dyke, 1938." *War in History* 8, no. 2 (April 2001): 191–207.
Lee, Steven Hugh. "The Japanese Empire at War, 1931–1945." In *The Oxford Illustrated History of World War II*, edited by Richard Overy. New York: Oxford University Press, 2005.
Lipstadt, Deborah E. *Beyond Belief: The American Press and The Coming Of The Holocaust, 1933–1945*. Reprint ed. New York: Touchstone, 1993.
Looking toward the Post-War World: Statement of the Friends Conference on Peace and Reconstruction Held at Wilmington, Ohio, August 31–September 4, 1942. Philadelphia, Pa., 1942.
Ludi, Regula. "More and Less Deserving Refugees: Shifting Priorities in Swiss Asylum Policy from the Interwar Era to the Hungarian Refugee Crisis of 1956." *Journal of Contemporary History* 49, no. 3 (July 1, 2014): 577–598.
McDonald, James G. *Refugees and Rescue: The Diaries and Papers of James G. McDonald, 1935–1945*. Edited by Richard Breitman, Barbara McDonald Stewart, and Severin Hochberg. Bloomington: Indiana University Press, 2009.
Medoff, Rafael. *Blowing the Whistle on Genocide: Josiah E. DuBois, Jr. and the Struggle for a U.S. Response to the Holocaust*. West Lafayette, IN: Purdue University Press, 2008.
Medoff, Rafael. *The Deafening Silence/American Jewish Leaders and the Holocaust*. New York: Carol Pub Group, 1986.
Medoff, Rafael. *FDR and The Holocaust: A Breach of Faith*. Washington: The David S. Wyman Institute for Holocaust Studies, 2013.
Moon, Claire. "Human Rights, Human Remains: Forensic Humanitarianism and the Human Rights of the Dead." *International Social Science Journal* 65, no. 215–216 (March 1, 2014): 49–63.
Moore, Bob. "Enforced Diaspora: The Fate of Italian Prisoners of War during the Second World War." *War in History* 22, no. 2 (April 2015): 174–190.
Morse, Arthur D. *While Six Million Died: A Chronicle of American Apathy*. New York: Random House, 1968.
Muscolino, Micah S. *The Ecology of War in China: Henan Province, the Yellow River, and Beyond, 1938–1950*. Studies in Environment and History. Cambridge: Cambridge University Press, 2014.
Novick, Peter. *The Holocaust in American Life*. Boston: Mariner Books, 2000.
Overy, Richard, ed. *The Oxford Illustrated History of World War II*. New York: Oxford University Press, 2015.
Park, Yoosun. "Making Refugees: A Historical Discourse Analysis of the Construction of the 'Refugee' in US Social Work, 1900–1957." *British Journal of Social Work* 38, no. 4 (June 1, 2008): 771–787.
Porter, Stephen. "Humanitarian Politics and Governance: International Responses to the Civilian Toll in the Second World War." In *The Cambridge History of the Second World War*, edited by Michael Geyer and Adam Tooze. Cambridge: Cambridge University Press, 2015.
Power, Samantha. *A Problem From Hell: America and the Age of Genocide*. 2nd ed. New York: Basic Books, 2013.

Reid, Fiona, and Sharif Gemie. "The Friends Relief Service and Displaced People in Europe After the Second World War, 1945-48." *Quaker Studies* 17, no. 2 (March 2013): 223–243.

Reinisch, Jessica. "Introduction: Relief in the Aftermath of War." *Journal of Contemporary History* 43, no. 3 (July 1, 2008): 371–404.

Reinisch, Jessica. "'We Shall Rebuild Anew a Powerful Nation': UNRRA, Internationalism and National Reconstruction in Poland." *Journal of Contemporary History* 43, no. 3 (July 1, 2008): 451–476.

Rieffer-Flanagan, Barbara Ann. "Is Neutral Humanitarianism Dead? Red Cross Neutrality: Walking the Tightrope of Neutral Humanitarianism." *Human Rights Quarterly; Baltimore* 31, no. 4 (November 2009): 888–915.

Rubinstein, W. D. *The Myth of Rescue: Why the Democracies Could Not Have Saved More Jews from the Nazis*. New York: Routledge, 1997.

Shephard, Ben. "'Becoming Planning Minded': The Theory and Practice of Relief 1940–1945." *Journal of Contemporary History* 43, no. 3 (July 1, 2008): 405–419.

Snowden, Frank. "Latina Province, 1944–1950." *Journal of Contemporary History* 43, no. 3 (July 1, 2008): 509–526.

Spark, Seumas. "Dishonourable Men? The Australian Army, Prisoners of War and Anglo-German POW Repatriations in the Second World War." *Australian Historical Studies* 45 (May 2014): 242–265.

Steinert, Johannes-Dieter. "British Humanitarian Assistance: Wartime Planning and Postwar Realities." *Journal of Contemporary History* 43, no. 3 (July 1, 2008): 421–435.

Taylor, Melissa Jane. "Bureaucratic Response to Human Tragedy: American Consuls and the Jewish Plight in Vienna, 1938–1941." *Holocaust and Genocide Studies* 21, no. 2 (September 21, 2007): 243–267.

Toscano, Alberto. "The Tactics and Ethics of Humanitarianism." *Humanity: An International Journal of Human Rights, Humanitarianism, and Development* 5, no. 1 (January 28, 2014): 123–147.

Tsilaga, Flora. "'The Mountain Laboured and Brought Forth a Mouse': UNRRA's Operations in the Cyclades Islands, c.1945–46." *Journal of Contemporary History* 43, no. 3 (July 1, 2008): 527–545.

Voluntary War Relief during World War II: A Report to the President by the President's War Relief Control Board. Washington, 1946.

Weindling, Paul. "'For the Love of Christ': Strategies of International Catholic Relief and the Allied Occupation of Germany, 1945–1948." *Journal of Contemporary History* 43, no. 3 (July 1, 2008): 477–492.

Wilson, Joan Hoff, and Oscar Handlin. *Herbert Hoover: Forgotten Progressive*. Prospect Heights, IL: Waveland Press, 1992.

Wylie, Neville. "Prisoner of War Relief and Humanitarianism in Canadian External Policy During the Second World War." *Journal of Transatlantic Studies (Edinburgh University Press)* 3, no. 2 (September 2005): 239–258.

Wyman, David. *The Abandonment of the Jews: America and the Holocaust, 1941-1945*. New York: Pantheon, 1986.

Wyman, David S. *Paper Walls: America and the Refugee Crisis, 1938–1941*. Boston: The University of Massachusetts Press, 1968.

Yap, Felicia. "International Laws of War and Civilian Internees of the Japanese in British Asia." *War in History* 23, no. 4 (2016): 416–438.

CHAPTER 29

RENDERING JUSTICE

MICHAEL S. BRYANT AND
JAMES BURNHAM SEDGWICK

A comprehensive account of German and Japanese war crimes during World War II would fill several library shelves. The transcripts of the International Military Tribunal (IMT) at Nuremberg alone are forty-two thick volumes, and this trial dealt only with a limited spectrum of Nazi wrongdoing. Similarly, the crimes of the Japanese, while commanding less attention than their German counterparts, are neither less appalling nor their trial records less voluminous. In fact, investigations by the Tokyo IMT extended over a longer time period, stretching from the late 1920s and Japanese penetration into Manchuria to the final desperate months of Japan's war in the spring and summer of 1945. German and Japanese atrocities became objects of criminal prosecution by military, national, and international courts in the immediate postwar period.

GERMANY

In the early years of the war, reports of German atrocities drew public condemnations from Allied governments that hinted at future judicial punishment but never clearly warned of trials. From early on, the Allies were determined to avoid the fiasco that had occurred after World War I, when little was done to hold German and Turkish perpetrators legally accountable. At no time during World War I was an international agency created to document German crimes and offer recommendations for future action by Allied policymakers. It was widely believed in the decades after World War I that lack of Allied planning on the war crimes question weakened the will to prosecute German war criminals.[1] During World War II, by contrast, the British and Americans sought to coordinate their statements on German war crimes. Churchill and Franklin D. Roosevelt issued separate but complementary warnings about punishing German reprisal shootings in the fall of 1941. These statements energized the Allied exile governments in London, who issued their own joint declaration on January 13, 1942, at St. James's Palace, London, stating that a "principal" aim of the war was the prosecution of German war criminals.[2] The United States and Great Britain, however, were at first reluctant to make public announcements of future trials for fear they could lead to retaliation against their POWs in German custody. Eventually they changed their minds: by late 1942 the Anglo–Americans began to threaten the Germans with judicial punishment.

The USSR issued its own threat, insisting that an international court should prosecute the Nazi leadership while lower-ranking German war criminals were tried in national criminal courts. In November 1943, the Soviets, British, and Americans issued the Moscow Declaration, which provided that German war crimes suspects would be returned to the scenes of their alleged crimes after the war for trial by the newly reconstituted governments. Further, it stated that major war criminals whose crimes "had no geographical location" would be punished by a joint decision of the Allies. What form the "joint decision" would take remained unstated. Although the Allies would later decide to try the major war criminals in an international tribunal, in October 1943 that decision had not yet been made.

In August 1942 the British proposed to Roosevelt that a fact-gathering commission might be established to document Nazi atrocities. The proposed commission would forward the results of its investigations to the governments whose citizens were the victims. The report would include the names of suspected perpetrators, and only crimes arising from official policy would be considered. The affected governments would then decide whether to prosecute the accused. By early October 1942 the Americans had agreed with the proposal to establish the United Nations War Crimes Commission (UNWCC), which came into being in the fall of 1943.

By 1943, the United States, Great Britain, and the USSR were all warning of future judicial punishment for Nazi war criminals. As far as the top Nazi leaders were concerned, however, the British initially favored summary execution. From the summer of 1942, Foreign Office legal advisers urged Prime Minister Winston Churchill to avoid trials of the leading Nazis due to the difficulties involved in creating an international court and the inevitable charge of "victor's justice" it would invite. Sir John Simon stated his view to the War Cabinet in September 1944 that judicial proceedings of top Nazis were "quite inappropriate."[3] In late November 1943, at a meeting of Stalin, Churchill, and Roosevelt in Teheran, Stalin suggested—perhaps in jest—that fifty thousand German officers be liquidated after the war. While in his memoirs Churchill claimed to be deeply offended by this suggestion,[4] at Yalta (in February 1945) Churchill raised the possibility of shooting German war criminals without trial.[5]

Soviet and U.S. officials would ultimately reject this proposal. However, there was at least one high-ranking figure within the American government who favored it—Secretary of the Treasury Henry Morgenthau Jr. Morgenthau urged that a list of Nazi leaders be given to the military with instructions to turn them over for execution by a UN firing squad. Morgenthau reserved trials by Allied military commissions only for lower-ranking war crimes suspects charged with offenses "against civilization." If found guilty by the commission, the convicted would be executed absent extenuating circumstances.[6] An opponent of Morgenthau's proposal was the Secretary of War, Henry Stimson, who only days after the Morgenthau memorandum authored a categorical rejection of it. Stimson argued that the Nazi leaders should be afforded a trial in an international court, in which they would enjoy U.S.-style legal rights—notification of the charge and the right to defend themselves. The accused would be charged with "offences against the laws of the Rules of War." Lower-ranking suspects would be sent back to the scenes of their crimes for trial by national military commissions as stipulated by the Moscow Declaration.[7]

By the early fall of 1944 Lieutenant Colonel Murray Bernays, the head of the War Department's Special Projects Office, had added a crucial element to Stimson's trial proposal. Specifically, Bernays tackled the question of how the Allies should deal with the administrative challenges of prosecuting thousands of German war crimes suspects individually. His solution was to identify as "criminal organizations" the leading Nazi agencies implicated in war crimes. Thereafter, anyone belonging to these organizations could be charged with conspiracy for crimes perpetrated by their various members.[8] After Roosevelt's death on April 12, 1945, his successor, Harry Truman, endorsed this plan. At the UN's founding conference in San Francisco, U.S. representatives shared it with their British and Soviet counterparts. The international tribunal would consist of judges from Great Britain, the United States, France, and the USSR. In addition to trying individual defendants, the Americans proposed prosecuting Nazi agencies as criminal organizations. Once an organization was convicted, everyone who had joined it voluntarily "would ipso facto be guilty of a war crime."[9] The British and Soviets agreed to the American proposal, as did the French shortly thereafter.

Alongside Stimson's and Bernays's proposals, the year 1944 produced a third seminal contribution to the Allied war crimes program: the notion of "aggressive war." On November 28, 1944, Colonel William Chanler, the deputy chief of the War Department's Civil Affairs Division, sent Stimson a memorandum outlining the case for putting the Nazi leadership on trial for violating the Kellogg–Briand Pact of 1928. Signatories to the Pact had agreed to renounce war as an instrument of national policy, as well as to settle disputes through peaceful mediation. For Chanler, Kellogg–Briand was binding international law for all countries that had signed it—meaning that Germany's invasions of other countries were criminally punishable.[10]

On August 8, 1945, the Allies produced a charter setting forth the charges against the major war criminals. The "London Charter," as it is called, would become the cornerstone of the indictment against the major war criminals. Article 6 (a) defined "Crimes against Peace" as "planning, preparation, initiation or waging of a war of aggression" or "in violation of international treaties." Article 6 (b), "War Crimes," embraced "murder, ill-treatment or deportation to slave labor . . . of civilian population of or in occupied territory, murder or ill-treatment of prisoners of war . . . , killing of hostages, plunder of public or private property, wanton destruction of cities, . . . or devastation not justified by military necessity." Article 6 (c), "Crimes against Humanity," was among the most innovative of the substantive charges, condemning inhumane acts—"murder, extermination, enslavement, deportation"—inflicted on civilians.[11]

Article 6 also embodied Bernays's conspiracy approach to Nazi crimes, insofar as it charged the Nazi leaders with participating in a "Common Plan or Conspiracy" to commit each of the crimes listed.[12]

The indictment of the major Nazi war criminals was signed on October 6, 1945. The final list of defendants was the outcome of Allied negotiations in London during the previous summer. It included:

- Prominent members of the Nazi Party/government: Hermann Göring, Rudolf Hess, Joachim von Ribbentrop, Robert Ley, Wilhelm Frick, Baldur von Schirach, Fritz Sauckel, Martin Bormann, Franz von Papen, Albert Speer, Constantin von Neurath, Baldur von Schirach, Artur Seyss-Inquart, Fritz Sauckel, Ernst Kaltenbrunner, and Walter Funk
- Leading military commanders: Wilhelm Keitel, Karl Dönitz, Erich Raeder, and Alfred Jodl
- Leaders in the civilian administration of Eastern Europe: Alfred Rosenberg and Hans Frank
- Leaders of the German economy/industry: Hjalmar Schacht and Gustav Krupp von Bohlen und Halbach
- Prominent propagandists: Julius Streicher and Hans Fritzsche

Three of the defendants listed in the indictment were ultimately unavailable for trial: Robert Ley, Gustav Krupp von Bohlen und Halbach, and Martin Bormann. Thus, when the international military tribunal began its formal sessions on November 20, 1945, only twenty-one of the twenty-four defendants were present in the courtroom. In addition to the twenty-four named defendants, the indictment asked the tribunal to criminalize a handful of Nazi and German governmental organizations: the Reich Cabinet, the leadership corps of the Nazi Party, the SS, the SD, the Gestapo, the SA, and the General Staff and High Command of the German Armed Forces (OKH).

The procedural law applied at the trial was a mixture of Anglo–American and continental European law. Superior orders were inadmissible as a defense but could be used in mitigation of guilt. Similarly, the judges deemed the defense of *tu quo que* ("you too") inconsistent with Article 18 of the Charter, and Allied prosecutors strove to exclude it during the trial. Their efforts notwithstanding, some of the defense counsel successfully argued *tu quo que*, such as Admiral Karl Dönitz's defense counsel, Otto von Kranzbühler. Kranzbühler obtained an interrogatory completed by U.S. Admiral Chester Nimitz, Commander in Chief of the U.S. Pacific Fleet during the war, which he successfully offered into evidence. Dönitz was charged with war crimes in connection with the German U-boat practice of unrestricted submarine warfare and failing to rescue the crews of torpedoed vessels. In his interrogatory, Nimitz answered that the United States pursued a similar policy against the Japanese. Nimitz's statement carried significant weight for the American judge, Francis Biddle, who expressed reservations about convicting Dönitz for doing what the Americans had done in the Pacific. Although Dönitz was convicted on other counts and was sentenced to a ten-year prison term, the tribunal absolved him of responsibility for breaches of the law of submarine warfare largely on the strength of the Nimitz interrogatory.[13]

The IMT judges agreed with the prosecution that a conspiracy to wage aggressive war did indeed exist as early as November 1937. They chose this date because of the "Hossbach Memorandum," a document the Americans had found in the summer of 1945. It consisted of notes taken by a Hitler adjutant, Colonel Friedrich Hossbach, at a meeting in the Reich Chancellery on November 5, 1937. At the meeting Hitler unveiled his "last will and testament": he would seek "living space" for the German people and "overthrow" Austria and Czechoslovakia.[14] The prosecution argued that the Hossbach memo decisively proved the existence of a conspiracy to commit crimes against peace. The IMT agreed not only with the prosecution's interpretation of the memo but with its argument that Germany's union with Austria and annexation of Czechoslovakia were the opening gambits in a plan to wage aggressive war.[15] The judges refused, however, to recognize a conspiracy to commit war crimes and crimes against humanity as alleged in Count 1 of the indictment.[16]

The indictment had requested that the tribunal declare certain agencies of the Nazi state to be criminal organizations. According to the judges, mere membership was not sufficient to convict a defendant of belonging to a criminal organization. To convict, it had to be shown the defendant either knew of the "criminal purposes or acts of the organization" or personally contributed to them. The judges then declared the Nazi leadership corps, SS, SD, and Gestapo to be "criminal organizations." They declined to grant the prosecution's request regarding the SA, Reich Cabinet, and General Staff.[17]

On October 1, 1946, the tribunal announced its verdict. It found all the defendants save Hjalmar Schacht, Franz von Papen, and Hans Fritsche guilty of one or more of the four counts. Twelve of them were sentenced to death by hanging (Göring, Ribbentrop, Keitel, Kaltenbrunner, Rosenberg, Frank, Frick, Streicher, Sauckel, Jodl, Seyss-Inquart, and Bormann), three to a life term in prison (Hess, Funk, and Raeder), and four to prison terms ranging from ten to twenty years (Donitz, Schirach, Speer, and von Neurath). After confirmation by the Allied Control Council for Germany, the sentences were executed: those condemned to death were hanged, those sentenced to prison terms were interned in Berlin's Spandau prison. (The exception was Hermann Göring, who cheated the hangman by committing suicide in his jail cell.)[18]

Article 22 of the IMT Charter provided for a series of Nazi war crimes trials to be prosecuted by the tribunal—the first at Nuremberg and subsequent trials at locations the tribunal would later determine. Due to logistical difficulties, the decision was made to allow each zone of occupation to prosecute its Nazi offenders. The legal basis of these "subsequent" trials was a law passed on December 20, 1945 by the Allied Control Council. Called "Control Council Law No. 10," the decree authorized each of the four zones to arrest war crimes suspects and try them in "appropriate tribunals." While the Soviets did little to implement Law No. 10, policies were different in the western zones. The French conducted a high-profile trial under Law No. 10 in their military tribunal at

Rastatt, targeting the German industrialist Hermann Röchling. The British meanwhile were holding their own trials based not on Law No. 10 but on a British executive decree (the Royal Warrant of June 14, 1945), which contained no charges for crimes against humanity or peace; rather, they tried their accused for violations of the laws of war. The cases involved a congeries of defendants, ranging from *Wehrmacht* General Nikolaus von Falkenhorst (who planned and commanded the invasion of Denmark and Norway), *Luftwaffe* Field Marshall Albert Kesselring (charged with ordering the execution of 335 civilians and inciting the killing of others in Italy), and *Luftwaffe* General Kurt Student (charged with mistreating and in some cases murdering POWs in Crete) to concentration camp guards from Bergen-Belsen and Ravensbrück. In Belgium, Denmark, Greece, the Netherlands, Norway, Poland, Russia, and Yugoslavia, numerous war criminals were also hauled into court.[19]

The bulk of these trials were conducted under national military decrees or domestic law. The most ambitious of the trial programs explicitly based on Law No. 10 were the American National Military Tribunals at Nuremberg. There was considerable overlap in the language and definitions of Law No. 10 and the IMT Charter. At other points, Law No. 10 modified the Charter's provisions in significant ways. Perhaps the most consequential of the revisions was the insertion of language enabling the Allies to charge Nazi offenders with crimes against humanity whether or not they were connected to aggressive warfare—a charge that could not be sustained under the IMT Charter.[20]

Most of the accused war criminals indicted and tried by the Americans at Nuremberg were already in U.S. custody; others were delivered to them by the British, French, and Poles for prosecution. This was especially true for the first of the U.S. trials, the "medical case" (*U. S. v. Karl Brandt et al.*),[21] in which the Americans' decision to devote an entire trial to medical atrocities prompted the British to send them SS and military doctors and other health care personnel in British custody. The U.S. medical case was illustrative of the Americans' approach of centering prosecution on a specific occupational group complicit in Nazi crimes. The defendants were grouped into five categories:

- German professionals: doctors and lawyers (Cases 1 and 3: thirty-nine defendants)
- SS and Police (Cases 4, 8, and 9: fifty-six defendants)
- Industrialists and Financiers (Cases 5, 6, and 10: forty-two defendants)
- Military leaders (Cases 7 and 12: twenty-six defendants)
- Government Ministers (Cases 2 and 11: twenty-two defendants)[22]

Unlike the IMT, which was a single integrated trial, the American subsequent tribunals comprised several trials running concurrently and involving different court members. These courts were staffed with three or more American lawyers appointed by the U.S. military governor.[23]

Three of the subsequent American trials were devoted to the role of German businesses in the crimes of the Third Reich. The trials targeted forty-two defendants, nearly half of whom were high-ranking corporate officers of the I. G. Farben chemical cartel. The remaining defendants were officers of the Krupp and Flick coal and steel firms. In *U.S. v. Flick* (Case No. 5), six defendants were charged with participating in the Nazis' slave labor program by using forced workers in their mines and factories, as well as spoliation in France and the USSR. Friedrich Flick and his co-defendants argued that they were ensnared in a situation of duress, wherein they faced grave retaliation from the Nazis for refusal to use slave labor in furtherance of the war effort. Remarkably, Military Tribunal IV agreed with some of the defendants on most of the slave labor charges. In the Tribunal's view, a genuine situation of necessity existed to exonerate them from the charge. Flick and another co-defendant, however, were ineligible for the defense and were convicted.[24]

Another business-focused case, *U.S. v. Alfried Krupp von Bohlen und Halbach et al.* (Case No. 10), followed the Flick trial in yielding uneven results. From 1943 until the war's end, Alfried Krupp was the owner of Krupp enterprises, a major supplier of armaments to the German military. Krupp and eleven of his underlings were charged with crimes against peace for their role in planning and waging aggressive war and conspiracy to wage aggressive war. After the prosecution had rested, the defense moved for an acquittal on these two charges, which the Military Tribunal granted on the rationale that the evidence failed to prove the defendants were fully aware of Hitler's aggressive plans. On the charges of spoliation and forced labor, six of the accused—including Krupp—were convicted, while the other four were acquitted.[25]

The principle expressed in the Tribunal's verdict that arms manufacturers could not be found guilty of aggressive war as a matter of law reappeared in the trial of I. G. Farben's corporate officers. Military Tribunal IV acquitted all the defendants of the charge of planning and waging aggressive war and conspiracy to plan and wage aggressive war. Only five of the twenty-four defendants were convicted of enslavement and mistreatment of POWs, deportees, and concentration camp prisoners.[26]

In addition to professional men and industrialists/financiers, the Americans prosecuted twenty-five German military leaders. One of these trials embraced twelve army commanders charged with war crimes during the German occupation of Yugoslavia, Albania, and Greece (*U.S. v. List et al.*). All were accused of killing thousands of Yugoslav and Greek civilians under an order providing for the execution of one hundred civilian hostages for every German soldier killed by guerrillas. The primary issue was the permissibility of reprisals against civilian hostages under the law of war.[27]

The Military Tribunal presiding over the *List* trial held that hostage-taking was allowed prior to 1945. It made clear its lack of sympathy with the rule yet added in a caveat that, "it is not our province to write international law as we would have it—we must apply it as we find it." The judges believed an occupying army under the law of war could take hostages to ensure the peace and even shoot them if occupation troops were attacked. However, the judges imposed qualifications on the hostage rule, insisting that hostages could only be taken if there was a connection between the assailants and the population from whom the hostages were drawn.[28] The court found that the Germans failed to satisfy these preconditions. It convicted List and seven others of war crimes and crimes against humanity, handing out prison terms from life to as few as seven years. Two of the defendants were acquitted, while two others were unavailable for prosecution.[29]

The second of the military cases tried by the Americans at Nuremberg, *U.S. v. Wilhelm von Leeb et al.*, involved thirteen high-ranking German military leaders charged with participating in Hitler's plans to wage wars of aggression. Many of the defendants were present at conferences in which Hitler had communicated his intention to attack other countries and as a result were convicted by the IMT. Prosecutors at the *Leeb* trial must have thought that proving the generals' attendance would produce the same results. Although not all of them had attended the meetings, they had all either known about or actively contributed to preparing for the invasions. However, Military Tribunal V acquitted the defendants of the aggressive war charge, holding that mere knowledge of the Führer's plans to wage aggressive war was not enough to convict. To sustain the charge, the prosecutors had to show not only that the accused knew of Hitler's intentions but were "in a position to shape or influence the policy" of waging aggressive war. Because no such proof had been offered, Leeb and his co-defendants could not be found guilty of the charge.[30]

At the same time as the IMT and subsequent trials in Nuremberg, the U.S. Army held its own trials of Nazi war criminals. Because most of these trials were held at the site of the former concentration camp at Dachau, they are collectively called the "Dachau trials" and form the third major war crimes program of the United States in Europe. Until the spring of 1945 the U.S. Army did not plan on significant investigations of war crimes unless the victims were American soldiers. This changed after liberation of the concentration camps by the U.S. Army, when pressure mounted to investigate and try these cases.[31]

On July 8, 1945, the U.S. Joint Chiefs of Staff instructed the European Theater Commander, Dwight Eisenhower, to investigate and arrest persons suspected of war crimes, waging wars of aggression, and persecutions on racial, religious, or political grounds. Shortly thereafter, Eisenhower issued an order to commanders of the 3rd and 7th Armies, instructing them to establish special military government courts to prosecute war crimes committed before May 9, 1945. The Dachau trial program focused on four categories of war crimes, described as violations of the Hague and Geneva Conventions:

- attacks on U.S. airmen and soldiers,
- killing of U.S. soldiers by the 1st SS Panzer Division during the Ardennes offensive,
- murder of ill Eastern European workers at the Hadamar mental hospital, and
- atrocities committed in Nazi concentration camps in Germany.

Several military commission trials of German civilians involved in murderous attacks on American airmen occurred as early as the summer of 1945.[32] The first U.S. Army trial of concentration camp war criminals occurred from November 15, 1945 to December 13, 1945 at the site of the Dachau camp (*U.S. v. Martin Gottfried Weiss et al.*), in which army prosecutors charged forty camp personnel with acting "in pursuance of a common design" to commit war crimes on Allied civilians and POWs. The accused were a motley assortment of camp staff, from the commandant and deputy commandant to medical officers, orderlies, guards, and prisoner functionaries. The "common plan or design" charge was a version of the conspiracy allegation leveled at accused Nazi war criminals at both the IMT and the subsequent trials. Common plan was easier to prove than conspiracy: the prosecution did not have to show an actual meeting or agreement between the conspirators to commit criminal acts but the existence of a "community of intention," which required only that participants in the common plan knew of the illegal acts committed in the camp *and* actively encouraged them through their own behavior.[33]

The appalling conditions in the camps were enough to ensure conviction of all forty of the defendants at the *Weiss* trial. Thirty-six received death sentences (a handful were commuted on review to hard labor for life), while the others received prison terms from life to hard labor for ten years.[34]

U.S. v. Martin Weiss, as the first of the American concentration camp trials, received the designation of "parent case." There followed a succession of trials at Dachau of other crimes committed in the camp during the war, as well as in the sister camps of Buchenwald, Flossenbürg, Mühldorf, and Mauthausen. The *Weiss* trial established important precedents for these subsequent prosecutions. In addition to the doctrine of a "common plan/design" to commit war crimes, the first of the concentration camp cases implied that mere presence as a staff member raised a presumption of involvement in war crimes.

Like the Americans at their successor trials in Nuremberg, the Polish provisional government in 1945 created a special court to adjudicate the crimes of the Nazi government, the "Supreme National Tribunal for Trials of War Criminals" (*Najwyzsy Trybunal Narowdowy*, or NTN). Its legal foundation, the Decree of August 31, 1944, enabled the authorities to prosecute and punish by death anyone who helped the Germans murder, mistreat, or deport Polish civilians or POWs during the German occupation of Poland. At trial the Polish prosecutors would argue, and the NTN would accept, that reference to "murder" in the Decree covered genocide, a new term coined only in 1943 by the Polish jurist Raphael Lemkin. The NTN is thus distinguished by its willingness two years before adoption of the UN Genocide Convention to charge Nazi war criminals with that offense. (Neither the Nuremberg nor Tokyo tribunals ever charged their defendants with genocide.) Among its defendants were Arthur Greiser, the governor of the Wartheland (the part of Poland annexed to Germany); Amon Göth, the commandant of the Płaszów concentration camp in Kraków; and Rudolf Höss, the leading commandant of Auschwitz. These former Nazis were convicted of murder and genocide and hanged. In sum, between 1944 and 1951 the Poles convicted eighteen thousand people of war crimes, of whom five thousand were German.[35]

No Allied country in the European theater suffered more casualties at German hands than the Soviet Union. The unbridled devastation of war on the eastern front may explain why the Soviets convened war crimes trials already in the summer and fall of 1943. They took place in three cities—Krasnodar, Krasnodon, and Maripol. The most notable was the trial by military court of eleven Soviet citizens at Krasnodar, accused of treason and collaboration with German *Einsatzgruppen* units in northern Caucasus. All the defendants were convicted; eight were sentenced to death, three to terms of hard labor from three to twenty years. The first public trial of German war criminals followed in December 1943 in Kharkov (Ukraine), where three Gestapo agents were charged with massacring Soviet "civilians" (i.e., Jews). All three of the accused were convicted and hanged on December 19, 1943. At the urging of Great Britain and the United States, after Kharkov Stalin deferred public trials of Nazi defendants until the end of the war. The Soviets continued, however, to prosecute Germans in secret proceedings, as well as to conduct military trials of suspected Soviet collaborators with the Nazis.[36]

The Soviets resumed public trials of accused German war criminals after the war in Bryansk, Kiev, Leningrad, Minsk, Riga, Smolensk, and Velikiye Luki. Some of the Soviet efforts to punish Nazi crimes became entangled with Stalin's political agendas, as when sixteen members of the Polish underground were indicted for collaboration and war crimes. In June 1945, they were subjected to a show trial, which ended with the conviction of three of them. They received sentences ranging from four months to ten years in prison.[37]

JAPAN

The Asia-Pacific sphere lacked the totemic evil of a Nazi holocaust. Yet, the war fought "without mercy"[38] produced terrifying levels of violence and atrocities that demanded redress. During the so-called Rape of Nanking (December 1937–February 1938), Japanese soldiers raped, terrorized, or killed tens of thousands of Chinese civilians. "Death Marches" in Bataan (April–May 1942), Sandakan (March–June 1945), and other occupied territories drove thousands of Allied personnel and associates to early graves. Forced labor on the Burma–Thailand Railway worked thousands of local civilians, as well as Australian, British, and Dutch POWs, to death. Massacres in Manila, Singapore, and Java killed hundreds of thousands. Innumerable women and girls were forced into sexual slavery as so-called "comfort women." Japanese military units used humans for target practice. Doctors performed grotesque medical experiments and developed bacteriological weapons. Almost every Allied power—and millions of civilians beside—held stakes in rendering justice for victims of Japan's scourge. Accountability was carefully planned and meticulously investigated. War crimes operations were extensive. Then, they were "studiously ignored,"[39] as one prosecutor lamented, and promptly forgotten.

At least, that is the standard narrative. In truth, the Asian trials have been under-researched but never forgotten. Contemporary observers diligently followed the trials. Millions attended court sessions, media outlets reported on proceedings, governments monitored progress, and experts assessed their legal and historical importance. Perpetrator groups listened in shame, resentment, or denial. Victim communities faithfully remember court findings or lament their omissions. Only academics and public educators in the West still undervalue war crimes operations in the Asia-Pacific, and even that is changing. The International Military Tribunal for the Far East (IMTFE or Tokyo IMT) forms a lone exception. As in Europe, where "Nuremberg" dominates popular and scholarly imaginations, "Tokyo" prefigures all assumptions about justice in Asia, obscuring the thousands of other courts held throughout the region by dozens of governments.

The Allied powers condemned Axis abuses during the war. They promised international retribution. Primarily responding to German violations, Allied statements, such as the 1942 Inter-Allied Joint Declaration and 1943 Moscow Declaration, held implications for Asia. At the Cairo Conference in December 1943, Britain, China, and the U.S. specified Allied intent to also "punish" Japan's "aggression."[40] The final and clearest censure came on July 26, 1945, when Britain, China, the United States—and subsequently the USSR—issued the Potsdam Declaration, which promised "stern justice" for all war criminals. On September 2, the Japanese government unconditionally accepted Potsdam's terms.[41] The Allies entered postwar Japan with the full intent and authority to hold its leaders and soldiers accountable.

Trials require more than the will to prosecute; they also require evidence and laws. During the war, the Allies established domestic and international investigative bodies to build a legal and evidentiary framework for punishing war criminals. Officials compiled lists of criminals from the Japanese elite—including, controversially, Emperor Hirohito[42]—down to frontline soldiers and prison guards. In June 1943, for instance, Australia organized a commission of inquiry into massacres, POW mistreatment, labor camps, torture, and other Japanese crimes in the South Pacific. The three resulting Webb Reports (1943, 1944, and 1945) gained wide public attention, which stiffened Allied determination to punish Japan. The reports also amassed evidence for future trials, including over eight hundred witness affidavits.[43] Starting in October 1945, the Dominion Office in London exchanged war criminal lists with Australia, Burma, Canada, India, and New Zealand. The lists included so-called "major" "Class A" criminals accused of conspiring to lead Japan into war, "minor" criminals accused of "Class B" (conventional war crimes and crimes against humanity), and "Class C" (command responsibility for planning, permitting, or failing to stop violations) crimes.[44] The first Commonwealth list had more than two hundred alleged war criminals on it.[45] National level evidence gathering contributed to a wider international effort. In May 1944, the UNWCC set up a Far Eastern Sub-Commission (FESC) headquartered in Chongqing, China.[46] By focusing on combatant status only, Allied policy excluded Indochinese, Indonesian, Korean, Micronesian, Malayan, New Guinean, Taiwanese, Thai, and other victim communities not considered sovereign contributors to the war effort.[47]

Legal frameworks were needed to turn evidence gathering into accountability. Each country involved in the international project formulated domestic protocols to try Japanese war criminals (see Table 29.1). Most national laws empowered military rather than civilian courts. Planning for Tokyo internationalized war crimes laws. In December 1945, American, British, and Soviet representatives met in Moscow to give complete authority over "the implementation of the Terms of Surrender" (including war crimes) to the Supreme Commander for the Allied Powers (SCAP).[48] In January 1946,

Table 29.1 Allied War Crimes Operations in the Asia-Pacific (by Country), 1945–1951[a]

Country	Cases Tried	Accused Tried	Accused Convicted	Death Sentences Passed	Death Sentences Per Convictions
United States and the Philippines	546	1,578	987	68	6.9%
The Netherlands	448	1,038	969	236	24.4%
Britain and Dominions (excluding Australia)*	306–533	920–930	776–811	279–287	28.4%–32.7%
Australia	592	924	644	148	23.0%
Nationalist China	605	883	504	149	29.7%
Communist China**	Unavailable	unavailable	unavailable	unavailable	Unavailable
France	39	230	198	63	31.8%
USSR***	Unavailable	unavailable	unavailable	unavailable	Unavailable

* Statistics for British war crimes operations vary
** Statistics for Communist Chinese trials have not yet been properly tabulated
*** Proper statistics for Soviet trials have also never been calculated

[a] Philip R. Piccigallo, *The Japanese on Trial: Allied War Crimes Operations in the East, 1945–1951* (Austin: University of Texas Press, 1979); R. John Pritchard, "The Gift of Clemency Following British War Crimes Trials in the Far East, 1946–1948," *Criminal Law Forum* 7, no. 1 (February 1996): 15–50.

SCAP issued a Tokyo Charter almost identical to the Nuremberg Charter.[49] The Allies planned a comprehensive network of trials to hold Japan accountable, undertaking exhaustive fact-finding missions in difficult postwar circumstances. Putting plans into action proved even more difficult, and the inevitable shortcomings poisoned the trials' legacy. National legislation included:

- U.S. Presidential/Executive Orders 9324 (March 1943), 9547 (May 1945), and 9660 (November 1945)[50]
- The Netherlands' Extraordinary Penal Law Decree (December 1943)
- The French *Ordonnance relative à la répression des crimes de guerre* (August 1944)
- The British War Office's Royal Warrant outlining Regulations for the Trial of War Criminals (June 1945)
- Canada's War Crimes Regulations (August 1945)
- The Australian War Crimes Act (October 1945)
- The Republic of China's Law Governing the Trial of War Criminals (October 1946)[51]

Allied war crimes operations in Asia represent one of history's most substantial judicial endeavors. Over millions of square kilometers of land and sea, on isolated atolls, in dense jungles, and in bustling metropolises, a dozen countries conducted hundreds of civilian and military trials to bring thousands of war criminals to justice. Haunted by the conflict's devastated landscapes, blood-soaked memories, and uncertain futures, trial participants sought to make sense of the war and its aggressors. Justice offered hope and closure for families in despair and ruined states. The trials and their legacies cannot be understood without appreciating both the courts' lofty promises and the gritty realities faced by their organizers. Postwar exigencies made "success" almost impossible and amplified every difficulty. The lingering impression of "failure" diverts attention from the enormously ambitious scope of trials in the region.

Statistically, the United States and its Philippine protectorate contributed the most to war crimes trials in the Asia-Pacific sphere. In October 1945, American authorities became the first to try Japanese criminals. The sensational trial of General Yamashita Tomoyuki in Manila included massive media coverage, graphic testimony, colorful characters, resonant defense narratives, packed spectator galleries, marquee atrocities, the pioneering application of legal concepts (specifically "command" or "negative" responsibility), a guilty verdict, and accompanying death sentence. The case even saw an unsuccessful defense appeal to the U.S. Supreme Court, in part because the Yamashita judgment endorsed a very broad interpretation of command responsibility. The prosecution case rested on what Yamashita should have known, rather than what he knew. The allegation felt hollow given the fractured lines of communication in the Philippines under Yamashita's command.

U.S. administrators also oversaw courts in Yokohama, where a simple soldier named Tsuchiya Tatsuo became the first war criminal tried on Japanese soil. Following an unconvincing defense of "superior orders," Tsuchiya was sentenced to life imprisonment in December 1945.[52] The Yokohama commission ultimately prosecuted more cases than any other Allied court. The U.S. established similar commissions in the South Pacific[53] and China. Taken together, U.S. courts painted a grim image of Japan's atrocities, from cannibalism and vivisection to POW mistreatment and civilian slave labor. Including post-independence Philippine courts, the U.S. war crimes prosecution program in Asia tried 546 cases and 1,578 accused between 1945 and 1949.[54]

With huge Indonesian territories, the Netherlands formed the second largest contributor to courts in the Asia-Pacific sphere. Beginning in September 1946, the Dutch ran military commissions in Jakarta/Batavia (on Java), Khuntien/Pontianak (on Dutch Borneo), Medan (on Sumatra), Ambon Island, and Makassar (on Sulawesi/Celebes Island). Most Dutch trials involved POW mistreatment, especially that of forced labor. Other cases involved mass murder and violence against civilians, including sexual slavery. Dutch trials ran through 1949, until resistance to ongoing colonial rule made trial administration untenable. All remaining criminals were moved to Tokyo in 1950. Dutch authorities tried 448 total cases involving 1,038 accused war criminals.[55]

Like the Netherlands, British imperial holdings left a lot of ground to cover in the postwar era. Beginning in February 1946, Britain convened twelve military courts in Singapore, Yangon/Rangoon, Hong Kong, Malaya, and Sabah/British North Borneo. By its last trial in December 1948,[56] Britain had brought hundreds of cases and over nine hundred accused to trial.[57] Canada and New Zealand contributed investigators and lawyers to British investigation efforts, normally in cases involving crimes against citizens of their respective countries. Between November 1945 and May 1951, Australia also operated its own independent tribunals in Wewak (New Guinea), Morotai, Labuan, Darwin, Rabaul (New Britain), Singapore, Hong Kong, and Manus Island. Australia completed fewer cases than Britain (296), but it tried at least as many accused (924). Together, Britain, Australia, and other dominions tried 592 cases and 1,844 accused.[58]

No country suffered more under Japanese domination than China. Even fighting a devastating civil war, Chinese authorities proved determined to hold Japanese war criminals accountable. They also pursued justice for "collaborators" in the Japanese-endorsed Wang Jingwei regime. Ground-level conditions complicated judicial ambitions. From Chongqing, Guomindang/Nationalist China under Chiang Kai-shek (Jiang Jieshi) set up tribunals in Beijing, Guangzhou, Hankou, Northeast Xuzhou, Zhuzhou, Henan, Hunan, Shanxi, Hebei, Suiyuan, and Taiwan. These trials began in April 1946 and prosecuted the accused for conspiracy to commit aggression, conventional war crimes, and "enslaving, crippling, or annihilating the Chinese Nation" through torture, starvation, massacres, narcotization, bacteriological attacks, and other violations again civilians.[59] When the Communist threat closed down courts in Guangzhou, Hankou, and Beijing in 1948, the remaining Guomindang cases moved to Shanghai, where they continued until Chiang's regime collapsed in 1949. Despite all these pitfalls, Nationalist China tried 605 cases and 883 individuals.[60]

The Chinese Communist Party (CCP) also hungered for justice. Upon winning the civil war in 1949, Mao Zedong and his closest associates, such as Zhou Enlai and Liu Shaoqi, turned their attention to war criminals—both Nationalist (i.e., from the civil war) and Japanese. As a People's Republic of China (PRC) spokesperson said on February 5, 1949, "These war criminals [Nationalist and Japanese] have to be arrested; even if they flee to the remotest corners of the globe, they must be arrested."[61] To prevent communist access to wartime intelligence, British and America authorities repatriated many alleged Japanese war criminals before CCP victory. Nevertheless, during peace talks with exiled Guomindang, the CCP negotiators forced opponent leaders to hand over hundreds of alleged "war criminals." Little is known about the ensuing CCP proceedings. Although they did try some Japanese war criminals, PRC policies focused more on Nationalist "traitors."

France and the Soviet Union made relatively modest contributions to the Asia-Pacific war crimes regime. Despite substantial territories in the region—particularly in Indochina—France fixated more on Axis criminality in Europe. The Vichy collaboration government's wartime policies also complicated matters. Technically, Vichy "invited" Japan into Indochina, a fact which undercut French allegations of Japanese aggression. Moreover, the Vichy "invitation" meant Japan's occupation of the territory proved less violent than in other regions. Finally, violent Indochinese resistance to colonialism in the region diverted French attention. French trials compensated for their limited number by issuing the region's harshest war crimes verdicts, including sentencing almost one-third of all convicted war criminals to death (31.8 percent, or sixty-three of 198). The United States, in contrast, meted out capital sentences in only 6.9 percent of its cases (sixty-eight of 987).[62] In total France charged 230 accused in thirty-nine trials between the war's close and March 1951.[63]

The Soviet Union also played a comparatively limited role in prosecuting Japanese war criminals. Because it did not officially declare war on Japan until August 1945, the USSR had fewer actionable grievances. Other than the Tokyo IMT, Soviet investigators seriously pursued only one case: proceedings against Unit 731, Japan's secret biological warfare division. In late 1949, twelve Japanese were tried in Khabarovsk for bacteriological warfare and human experimentation. Although it was an important historical moment, the court largely evolved into a propaganda tool against other Allies, especially U.S. occupation forces in Japan. Nevertheless, Khabarovsk shed light on crimes that remained otherwise hidden for decades, thanks in part to a deliberate cover-up by U.S. authorities. France and the USSR punched below their weight, but both countries made valuable contributions to rendering justice in Asia.[64]

International cooperation anchored Allied war crimes operations in the Asia-Pacific sphere. Australia, Britain, China, France, the Netherlands, the Philippines, and the U.S. ran independent trials, but they shared resources and a commitment to justice. Organizers welcomed prosecution teams from other jurisdictions into their courts. Legal and investigative teams collaborated throughout the region. This spirit or necessity of international cooperation brought thousands of Japanese war criminals to justice.

Allied trials in Asia were extensive, but also incomplete. Omissions tend to outweigh accomplishments in historiography and memory. High stakes international endeavors rarely live up to expectations because expectations are unattainably high. Sea changes in global politics conspired against positive trial legacies. In the later 1940s, cold war tensions shifted Allied policy from punishment to revitalization in Japan. Many Japanese were released without trial. Some, including convicted criminals, returned to prominence in Japanese society. Shigemitsu Mamoru, for example, was sentenced to seven years in prison by the Tokyo IMT. He became foreign minister in 1954, only four years after (early) parole. Kishi Nobusuke was held, but never tried, until his release in 1948. Kishi became prime minister in December 1956. Kaya Okinori, who was sentenced to life by the IMTFE, was paroled in 1955 and became Japan's minister of justice in 1963.[65] Meanwhile, decolonization exposed Allied hypocrisies in the region. The British in Malaya, the French in Indochina, and the Dutch in Indonesia violently resisted anticolonial movements while criminalizing Japanese imperialism in courts. Instability, logistical difficulties, and double standards undermined trial conduct and credibility. Nevertheless, Asia-Pacific war crimes operations proved substantial. All told, they tried twenty-two hundred cases and over five thousand accused. This massive case load speaks to commitment rather than apathy and omission.

On May 3, 1946, nine judges from nine countries (Australia, Britain, Canada, China, France, the Netherlands, New Zealand, the Soviet Union, and the United States) gathered to try twenty-eight Japanese war leaders in an improvised courtroom inside the former War Ministry Building in Tokyo. Judges from India and the Philippines arrived later, making the Tokyo IMT a court heard before eleven judges from eleven countries. The accused represented a cross-section of an alleged conspiracy that led

Japan into an illegal and inhumane war. Each was defended by American and Japanese attorneys, who clashed in court with prosecution lawyers from all participating countries—including British-administered Burma and the Netherlands East Indies. The judges formed a motley cast from different backgrounds, ethnicities, personalities, legal traditions, and value systems. Despite presenting a unified public face, internal dissonance and divergent opinions plagued the judicial team behind the scenes. In addition to legal professionals, the court formed an enormous institutional structure including hundreds of translators, file clerks, stenographers, administrators, security personnel, photographers, researchers, and custodians. The IMTFE created its own complex legal and social world amid the rubble of a devastated but recovering postwar society. After two-and-a-half years of operation, the majority verdict on November 4, 1948 sentenced seven to death, sixteen to life in prison, one to twenty years' imprisonment, and another to seven years in jail. None were acquitted.[66] Two defendants died during the trial, and one was found mentally unsound. Since its inception, criticism of the IMTFE has set a negative tone that dominates assessments of all war crimes courts in the Asia-Pacific region.

Because Occupation forces were largely American, the IMTFE has often been labelled an American trial, a misconception largely unchallenged by scholars until the past decade or so.[67] In truth, the court required support from all Allied powers. It became an international military tribunal in both name and operation. Issued on January 19, 1946, the Tokyo Charter[68] constituted a multilateral institution within a global framework. As the Asian component of an international judicial project, the IMTFE reinforced Nuremberg principles by examining three general charges, all of them imported from the London Charter, including "common plan" and "conspiracy" to commit "crimes against peace," "conventional war crimes," "crimes against humanity," and other "inhuman acts."[69]

The prosecution subdivided these general charges into fifty-five specific counts.[70] As in Nuremberg, these charges opened Tokyo to legal criticism. Contemporaries questioned holding individuals responsible for state actions, especially on *ex post facto* (retroactive) grounds. Unprecedented charges like "crimes against peace" and "crimes against humanity" proved controversial. This criticism peaked when the court hanged an accused found guilty *only* of committing "crimes against peace," something not done by Nuremberg judges.[71] The concept of "negative" or "command" responsibility also drew fire by punishing leaders because they *should* have known about and prevented crimes committed by others. Using the largely Anglo–American concept of "conspiracy" to criminalize aggressive war also felt inappropriate in an international tribunal.[72] Few doubted the horrors unleashed by Japan or the culpability of its leadership, but legal scholars and political experts resisted the creation of "new" laws to deal with the problem.[73] Tokyo benefited by having Nuremberg law for precedent, but the tribunal struggled to force Japan's convoluted political history into a rubric custom-made for the Nazi-German context.[74]

More substantive challenges to IMTFE legitimacy strike at the very essence of all war crimes prosecutions. The arbitrary or "political" selection of defendants causes problems. The immunity of Emperor Hirohito remains divisive.[75] Amnesty for bacteriological warfare, sexual slavery, state-sanctioned drug trafficking, industrial collusion,[76] and abuses of the dreaded *kempeitai*, or secret police, rankles. Like any large collection of individuals, trial participants included social misfits, inveterate alcoholics, unprofessional workers, inexperienced jurists, incompetent staffers, political operators, philanderers, and bullies. Judges drew ire for poor attendance records, apparent disinterest, and uneven treatment of attorneys. Many judges lacked experience in international law. Several had pre-existing connections to the case. When coupled with lax evidentiary rules, improvised procedures, logistical difficulties, and emotionally jarring crimes, Tokyo justice struggled to live up to its lofty expectations.

In-court controversies, such as former Prime Minister Tōjō outmaneuvering chief prosecutor Joseph B. Keenan on the stand, or Australian President of the Tribunal William F. Webb's surly treatment of defense attorneys like Owen Cunningham, undercut the trial's reputation. Dissents by judges Henri Bernard (France), Radhabinod Pal (India), and B. V. A. Röling (the Netherlands) publicized disfunction. The IMTFE seems less fair than it was, a negative perception that poisons attitudes toward other Asia-Pacific courts which mostly stuck to accepted legal spheres. The IMTFE was not even then the only IMT convened in Japan. In 1948 and 1949, Admiral Toyoda Soemu and Lieutenant-General Tamura Hiroshi were also tried before SCAP-administered international courts.[77] Yet Tokyo's profile casts a wide shadow of controversy over all other courts in the arena.

The IMTFE embodies the failings of war crimes trials *in toto*: debatable precedent, selectivity, political interference, lax rules of evidence, racial overtones, prosecutorial bias, exclusionary power structures, double-standards, disruptive personnel, melodrama, and the like. The tribunal also showcased the era's best attributes: international cooperation, genuine commitment to justice, transformative aims, detailed investigations, dedicated participants, ground-breaking legal concepts, public accountability, didactic value, individual responsibility, deterrent potential, mountains of evidence, and a global profile. Post-World War II courts occupied an emotionally ripe period unconducive to impartial justice. The only scholar to publish a book-length exploration of all Allied war crimes operations in the Asia-Pacific, Philip Piccigallo, captures the "near impossible" task at hand. Court organizers contended with "rapid demobilization and repatriation of ex-POWs, witnesses and evidence scattered literally throughout the world, wholesale destruction of key documents by Japanese," not to mention "incredible difficulties in identifying, locating and apprehending suspects in Japan proper and East Asia."[78] In this context, the array of courts that did function and were effective and warrant recognition. The IMTFE and its confreres should be remembered as flawed but vital parts of history.

Conclusion

By drawing plans during the war to handle war crimes when the conflict was over, forming agencies to document Axis crimes during the war, and ensuring that suspects were delivered for punishment, the Allies avoided the failures that plagued the post-World War I settlement. In so doing, they introduced a whole new set of challenges and contingencies. The trials held in Europe and Japan undoubtedly invited charges of "victors' justice": the judges and prosecutors were appointed by the victors, and the defendants were all nationals of the defeated countries. The tribunals themselves were not independent bodies but creations of the victorious nations. In particular, the IMTFE and the military commissions presiding over the trials of Yamashita and other prominent defendants have often been accused of procedural irregularities stemming from Allied anger toward the Japanese and their desire for revenge. These criticisms aside, the trial programs in Europe and Japan were momentous developments in the history of the law of war. For the first time, international rather than national courts applied international penal law to the war crimes of political and military leaders. They pioneered new international crimes—crimes against peace and crimes against humanity—never previously recognized under international law, and if the Allies made themselves vulnerable to the *ex post facto* criticism, their willingness to charge these offenses meant that they would gain increasing acceptance as international customary law in the seven decades after 1945. The jurisprudence of the Allied courts set forth legal doctrines that persist till the present day, such as the liability of heads of state, command responsibility, rape as a crime against humanity, and rejection of the superior orders defense. Finally, both the crimes committed during the war and their judgment afterward fostered a moral revulsion against extreme forms of state criminality in the postwar era, leading by the 1990s to ad hoc tribunals and, in an effort to establish a fair, permanent, and independent judicial body, an international criminal court. However imperfect, Nuremberg, Tokyo, and their associated courts changed forever international criminal justice.

Notes

1. Consider, for example, criminologist Sheldon Glueck's allegation that Allied disunity contributed to the failure to prosecute German war crimes after World War I. Sheldon Glueck, *War Criminals: Their Prosecution and Punishment* (New York: A. A. Knopf, 1944), 32, 39.
2. U.S. Department of State, *Foreign Relations of the United States: Diplomatic Papers 1941* (Washington, DC: Government Printing Office, 1960), I:445ff.
3. Michael R. Marrus, *The Nuremberg War Crimes Trial 1945–46: A Documentary History* (Boston/New York: Bedford Books, 1997), 23.
4. Winston S. Churchill, *The Second World War*, Vol. 5: *Closing the Ring* (New York: Bantam Books, 1962), 319–320.
5. Martin Gilbert, *Winston S. Churchill, 1941–1945: Road to Victory* (London: William Heinemann, 1986), 1201–02.
6. Henry Morgenthau Jr., "Memorandum for President Roosevelt," in Marrus, *Nuremberg War Crimes Trial*, 24–25.
7. Henry L. Stimson, "Memorandum Opposing the Morgenthau Plan," in Ibid., 26–27.
8. Michael S. Bryant, *Confronting the "Good Death:" Nazi Euthanasia on Trial, 1945–53* (Boulder, CO: University Press of Colorado, 2005), 67.

9. "Memorandum of Conversation of E. R. Stettinius Jr. and S. Rosenman with V. Molotov and A. Eden in San Francisco," in Marrus, *Nuremberg War Crimes Trial*, 35–37.
10. "Document 24: Memorandum on Aggressive War by Colonel William Chanler," in *The American Road to Nuremberg: The Documentary Record*, ed. Bradley F. Smith (Stanford, CA: Hoover Institution Press, 1982), 69–74. Chanler's proposal to charge the Nazis with aggressive war was likely influenced by the Soviet jurist A. N. Trainin, who had suggested Nazi leaders might be prosecuted in an international tribunal for conspiracy to wage aggressive war, or crimes against peace, as well as with violations of the law of war.
11. Charter of the International Military Tribunal, in *Trial of the Major War Criminals before the International Military Tribuna* (Nuremberg, Germany: International Military Tribunal, 1947), I: 11.
12. Ibid., I: 12.
13. Telford Taylor, *The Anatomy of the Nuremberg Trials: A Personal Memoir* (New York: Alfred A. Knopf, 1992), 409, 567, 593.
14. Reproduced in J. Noakes and G. Pridham, ed., *Nazism: A History in Documents and Eyewitness Accounts 1919–1945* (New York: Schocken Books, 1983–1984), 2: 685.
15. Judgment, *Trial of the Major War Criminals*, I: 186; Marrus, *Nuremberg War Crimes Trial*, 127–128.
16. Judgment, *Trial of the Major War Criminals*, I: 226, 253.
17. Ibid., 255 ff.
18. Telford Taylor, "Nuremberg Trials: War Crimes and International Law," *International Conciliation* 450 (1949): 271.
19. Ibid., 255–256.
20. Bryant, *Confronting*, 75.
21. See, e.g., Paul Julian Weindling, *Nazi Medicine and the Nuremberg Trials: From Medical War Crimes to Informed Consent* (New York: Palgrave, 2004).
22. Taylor, "Nuremberg Trials," 279.
23. Ibid., 275.
24. Ibid., 306.
25. Ibid., 311–12.
26. Ibid., 313–16; Cassese, *International Criminal Law* (Oxford: Oxford University Press, 2003), 139.
27. Taylor, "Nuremberg Trials," 321–322; Beate Ihme-Tuchel, "Fall 7: Der Prozeß gegen die 'Südwest-Generale' (gegen Wilhelm List und andere)," in *Der Nationalsozialismus vor Gericht: Die alliierten Prozesse gegen Kriegsverbrecher und Soldaten 1943–1952*, ed. Gerd R. Ueberschär (Frankfurt: Fischer, 1999), 145.
28. Taylor, "Nuremberg Trials," 323. The judgment can be found in "The Hostage Case," in *Trials of War Criminals before the Nürnberg Military Tribunals* (Washington, DC: Government Printing Office, 1950), vol. XI.
29. Taylor, "Nuremberg Trials," 324–325.
30. Ibid., 326–328.
31. Gary Bass, *Stay the Hand of Vengeance: the Politics of War Crimes Tribunals* (Princeton, NJ: Princeton University Press, 2000), 29–31, 151 ff.
32. See, e.g., the trial by U.S. military commission of eleven German civilians at Darmstadt on July 25, 1945, accused of killing three US POWs (*U. S. v. Joseph Hartgen, Friedrich Wust, Margarete Witzler, et al.*).

33. "Trial of Martin Gottfried Weiss and 39 Others," in *Law Reports of Trials of War Criminals*, ed. The United Nations War Crimes Commission (London: His Majesty's Stationery Office, 1949), VI: 14.
34. Ibid., 8.
35. David M. Crowe, *The Holocaust: Roots, History, and Aftermath* (Boulder, CO: Westview, 2008), 423–424.
36. Ibid., 425–427.
37. Ibid., 427.
38. John W. Dower, *War without Mercy: Race and Power in the Pacific War* (New York: Pantheon Books, 1986).
39. Christmas Humphreys, *Via Tokyo* (London: Hutchinson & Company, Ltd., 1948), 82.
40. Britain, China, and the United States attended the Cairo Conference. International Military Tribunal for the Far East (IMTFE), "The Cairo Conference," *Exhibits*, Volume 1, Exhibit No. 1, E. H. Northcroft Papers—MB 1549, Macmillan Brown Library, University of Canterbury, Christchurch, New Zealand, Box 221. Hereafter, "Northcroft Papers."
41. IMTFE, "The Potsdam Declaration", *Annexes to Judgment*, Volume I, Annex No. A-1, 1-4, Northcroft Papers, Box 322; and IMTFE, "Instrument of Surrender", *Annexes to Judgment*, Volume I, Annex No. A-2, 11-15, A-1, 1-4, Northcroft Papers, Box 322.
42. Australia placed Hirohito #7 on their original list of war criminals. "No. 1 Australian List: Japanese Major War Criminals" (n.d.). Archives New Zealand, Wellington, New Zealand. EA2 1946-31B 106-3-22 Part 1.
43. For records of the Webb Reports, see Series Numbers A10943, A11049, and A10950 of the National Archives of Australia (NAA), Canberra, Australia.
44. Dominion Office, London to Governments of Canada, Australia, New Zealand, South Africa (October 25, 1945), London, UK: Indian Office Records, British Library, Asia, Pacific and Africa Collections (Previously Oriental and India Office Library). IOR/L/PS/12 458-0180 Telegrams India Foreign Office, Japanese War Criminals—Major War Crimes—October 1945–December 1947.
45. "Restricted: Perpetrators." General Headquarters, Allied Forces Pacific, Office of the Theatre Judge Advocate, War Crimes Branch (13 October 1945), Imperial War Museum and Archives, Duxford, United Kingdom. FO 648, Box 155, Folder 4.
46. M. E. Bathurst, "The United Nations War Crimes Commission," *The American Journal of International Affairs* 39 (1945): 565–570; and Egon Schwelb, "The United Nations War Crimes Commission," *The British Yearbook of International Law* 23 (1946): 364–376.
47. Herbert Bix, *Hirohito and the Making of Modern Japan* (New York: Harper Collins Publishers, 2000), John Dower, *Embracing Defeat: Japan in the Wake of World War II* (New York: W.W. Norton & Company, 1999).
48. This Moscow Conference should not be confused with the November 1943 Moscow Declaration mentioned earlier, which stated that the official objective of the Allied forces was to try war criminals.
49. IMTFE, "Special Proclamation, Establishment of an International Military Tribunal for the Far East", *Annexes to Judgment*, Volume I, Annex No. A-4, 16–18, Northcroft Papers, Box 322.
50. Executive Order 9324 in March 1943 amended the U.S. Manual for Courts-Martial. Executive Order 9547 provided U.S. representation in preparing and prosecuting Axis leaders, their principal agents, and accessories. Executive Order 9660 granted special

powers to the Chief of Counsel in prosecuting Japan's leaders, their principal agents, and accessories. Executive Order 9679 amended No. 9547.
51. United Nations War Crimes Commission, ed. *Law Reports of Trials of War Criminals*, Volumes I–XV (London: His Majesty's Stationary Office, 1947–49).
52. Timothy P. Maga, *Judgment at Tokyo: The Japanese War Crimes Trials* (Lexington: University Press of Kentucky, 2001), 1–2 and 8–20.
53. The Marianas, Marshall, Gilbert, Palau, Bonin, and Caroline Island groups. For U.S. trials in Guam, see Maga, *Judgment at Tokyo*, 93–119.
54. Piccigallo, *The Japanese on Trial*, 34–95.
55. Piccigallo, *The Japanese on Trial*, 174–184.
56. For rare insight into the decision to stop British trials see Pritchard, "The Gift of Clemency," 15–50.
57. Statistical discrepancies exist regarding British war crimes prosecutions in Asia. Some accused were tried more than once. R. John Pritchard counts 533 British cases with 930 accused and 776 convictions, including 287 death sentences and 220 executions. Philip Piccigallo calculates that the British brought 306 cases and 920 accused to trial, convicting 811, passing 279 death sentences, and executing 265. Piccigallo, *The Japanese on Trial*, 120; and Pritchard, "The Gift of Clemency," 15–16.
58. Piccigallo, *The Japanese on Trial*, 96–142.
59. Republic of China, Law Governing the Trial of War Criminals (October 24, 1946), Article II.
60. Piccigallo, *The Japanese on Trial*, 158–73.
61. "Peace Terms Must Include the Punishment of Japanese War Criminals and Kuomintang War Criminals—Statement by the Spokesman for the Communist Party of China, February 5, 1949", in Mao Tse-Tung (Zedong), *Selected Works of Mao Tse-Tung*, Volume IV, (Peking: Foreign Languages Press, 1961), 336. See also: Adam Cathcart and Patricia Nash, "'To Serve Revenge for the Dead': Chinese Communist Responses to Japanese War Crimes in the PRC Foreign Ministry Archive, 1949–1956," *The China Quarterly* 200 (December 2009): 1053–1069.
62. China sentenced 29.7 percent (149 of 504) of those convicted to death. The Dutch percentage was 23.3 percent (236 of 969), and the Australian was 23.0 percent (148 of 644). British estimates vary from Pritchard's 28.4 percent to Piccigallo's 32.7 percent, see note #58 above.
63. Piccigallo, *The Japanese on Trial*, 201–208.
64. "Japanese Plan to Invade Russia: Report of Evidence To Soviet Court," *The Press* (December 31, 1949), 7; "Japanese Use of Germs in War: Report of Evidence At Russian Trial: U.S. Said To Have Been Menaced," *The Press* (December 28, 1949), 5; "Russian Allegations of Bacteriological Warfare," *The Times* (February 3, 1950), 3; "Russian Trial of Japanese: Charges of Using Germ Warfare," *The Press* (December 30, 1949), 5; "12 Japanese On Trial: Use of Germs In War Alleged: Accused Appear Before Russian Court," *The Press* (December 27, 1949), 5; "Use of Germs In War: Japanese Gaoled By Soviet Court," *The Press* (January 3, 1950), 7.
65. Kenneth G. Henshall, *A History of Japan: From Stone Age to Superpower*, (London: Macmillan Press, 1999), 156 and R. John Pritchard, "The International Military Tribunal for the Far East and its Contemporary Resonances (Nuremberg and the Rule of Law: A Fifty-Year Verdict)," *Military Law Review* 149 (1995): 25–35.

66. The IMTFE issued verdicts on Araki Sadao, Doihara Kenji, Hashimoto Kingorō, Hata Shunroku, Hiranuma Kiichirō, Hirota Kōki, Hoshino Naoki, Itagaki Seishirō, Kaya Okinori, Kido Kōichi, Kimura Heitarō, Koiso Kuniaki, Matsui Iwane, Minami Jirō, Mutō Akira, Oka Takazumi, Ōshima Hiroshi, Satō Kenryō, Shigemitsu Mamoru, Shimada Shigetarō, Shiratori Toshio, Suzuki Teiichi, Tōgō Shigenori, Tōjō Hideki, Umezu Yoshijirō. Nagano Osami and Matsuoka Yōsuke died. Ōkawa Shumei was deemed mentally unfit. IMTFE, *Individual Accused in Judgment*, Volume I, A–K, Northcroft Papers, Box 325; IMTFE, *Individual Accused in Judgment*, Volume II, M–U, Northcroft Papers, Box 326; IMTFE, "Findings on Counts of the Indictment," *Judgment*, Chapter IX, Northcroft Papers, Box 321; and IMTFE, "Verdicts," *Judgment*, Chapters X, Northcroft Papers, Box 321.

67. See for instance Aleksandra Babovic, *The Tokyo Trial, Justice, and the Postwar International Order* (Singapore: Palgrave Macmillan, 2019); James Burnham Sedgwick, "A People's Court: Emotion, Participant Experiences, and the Shaping of Postwar Justice at the International Military Tribunal for the Far East, 1946–1948," *Diplomacy & Statecraft* 22, no. 3 (September 2011), 480–499; Yuki Takatori, "'America's' War Crimes Trial? Commonwealth Leadership at the International Military Tribunal for the Far East, 1946–48," *Journal of Imperial & Commonwealth History* 35, no. 4 (2007): 549–68; Kerstin von Lingen, ed., *Transcultural Justice at the Tokyo Tribunal: The Allied Struggle for Justice, 1946–48* (Leiden: Brill Publishing, 2018).

68. The "Tokyo Charter" went through several iterations. In April 1946, it was amended to include judges from India and the Philippines. Justice Northcroft underlined the change in his copy. See IMTFE, "Charter of the International Military Tribunal for the Far East," in *Charter, Indictment, Japanese Constitution*, Northcroft Papers, Box 337. For the original January text, see IMTFE, "Special Proclamation, Establishment of an International Military Tribunal for the Far East," *Annexes to Judgment*, Volume I, Annex No. A-4, 16–18, Northcroft Papers, Box 322. For the final version: IMTFE, "Charter of the International Military Tribunal for the Far East," *Annexes to Judgment*, Volume I, Annex No. A-5, 19–29, Northcroft Papers, Box 322. Hereafter, "IMTFE Charter."

69. IMTFE Charter.

70. IMTFE, "Indictment", *Annexes to Judgment*, Volume I, Annex No. A-6, 29–131, Northcroft Papers, Box 322. See also "Summary of Indictment" in *Charter, Indictment, Japanese Constitution*, Northcroft Papers, Box 337.

71. Michael Biddiss, "Victors' Justice? The Nuremberg Tribunal," *History Today* 45, no. 5 (1995), 43.

72. Justice Pal's dissent accused the prosecution of ignoring "French, German, Dutch, Spanish, Chinese, and Japanese and Russian legal orders . . . I cannot accept this." Radhabinod Pal (India), "International Military Tribunal for the Far East: Judgment of the Honourable Mr. Justice Pal, Member from India" (July 30, 1948), 1007, Northcroft Papers, Box 332a-c. The prosecution, in turn, hired experts to prove that "conspiracy" was universal to all legal systems.

73. Egon Schwelb gives a contemporary explanation of why "crimes against humanity" proved controversial. Egon Schwelb, "Crimes Against Humanity," *British Year Book of International Law* 23 (1946): 178–226.

74. For more see James Burnham Sedgwick, "Brother, Black Sheep, or Bastard? Situating the Tokyo Trial in the Nuremberg Legacy, 1946–1948," in *The Nuremberg Trials and Their Policy Consequences Today*, ed. Beth Griech-Polelle (Baden-Baden, DE: Nomos Verlaggesellschaft, 2009), 63–76.

75. For a rich account of Hirohito's immunity (and life) see Bix, *Hirohito and the Making of Modern Japan*. See also David Bergamini, *Japan's Imperial Conspiracy* (New York: Morrow, 1971); Arnold C. Brackman, *The Other Nuremberg: The Untold Story of the Tokyo War Crimes Trials* (New York: Morrow, 1987); Richard H. Minear, *Victors' Justice: The Tokyo War Crimes Trial* (Princeton, NJ: Princeton University Press, 1971).
76. Many believe *Zaibatsu* companies should have been held more accountable. The term translates literally as "financial clique," was usually applied to large conglomerates intricately linked to Japanese imperialism. *Zaibatsu* maintained very close ties with political powers in Japan. During the U.S. Occupation of Japan, the large corporations were nationalized and dissolved.
77. "High Japanese Indicted: Admiral and General Will Be Tried on War Crimes Charges" *New York Times*, (October 20, 1948), 3. See also Ann Marie Prévost, "Race and War Crimes: The 1945 War Crimes Trial of General Tomoyuki Yamashita," *Human Rights Quarterly* 14, no. 3 (August 1992): 330–335.
78. Piccigallo, *The Japanese on Trial*, 13.

Bibliography

Babovic, Aleksandra. *The Tokyo Trial, Justice, and the Postwar International Order. New Directions in East Asian History*. Singapore: Palgrave Macmillan, 2019.

Bazyler, Michael. *Holocaust, Genocide, and the Law: A Quest for Justice in a Post-Holocaust World*. New York: Oxford University Press, 2016.

Boister, Neil, and Robert Cryer. *The Tokyo International Military Tribunal: A Reappraisal*. Oxford: Oxford University Press, 2008.

Boister, Neil, and Robert Cryer. *Documents on the Tokyo International Military Tribunal: Charter, Indictment and Judgments*. Oxford: Oxford University Press, 2008.

Brackman, Arnold C. *The Other Nuremberg: The Untold Story of the Tokyo War Crimes Trials*. New York: Morrow, 1987.

Bryant, Michael S. *Nazi Crimes and their Punishment 1943–1950: A Short History with Documents*. Indianapolis/Cambridge: Hackett Publishing Co., Inc., 2020.

Cohen, David, and Yuma Totani. *The Tokyo War Crimes Tribunal: Law, History, and Jurisprudence*. New York: Cambridge University Press, 2018.

Crowe, David M. *War Crimes, Genocide, and Justice: A Global History*. New York: Palgrave MacMillan, 2014.

Dower, John W. *War without Mercy: Race and Power in the Pacific War*. New York: Pantheon Books, 1986.

Finder, Gabriel N., and Alexander V. Prusin. *Justice behind the Iron Curtain: Nazis on Trial in Communist Poland*. Toronto: University of Toronto Press, 2018.

Hirsch, Francine. *Soviet Judgment at Nuremberg: A New History of the International Military Tribunal after World War II*. New York: Oxford University Press, 2020.

Kochavi, Arieh J. *Prelude to Nuremberg: Allied War Crimes Policy and the Question of Punishment*. Chapel Hill: University of North Carolina Press, 1998.

Maga, Timothy P. *Judgment at Tokyo: The Japanese War Crimes Trials*. Lexington: University Press of Kentucky, 2001.

Marrus, Michael R. *The Nuremberg War Crimes Trial, 1945–46: A Brief History with Documents*. Boston/New York: Bedford/St. Martin's, 2018.

McCormack, Timothy, Toshiyuki Tanaka, and Gerry J. Simpson, eds. *Beyond Victor's Justice: The Tokyo War Crimes Trial Revisited*. Leiden: Martinus Nijhoff Publishers, 2011.

Minear, Richard H. *Victors' Justice: The Tokyo War Crimes Trial*. Princeton, NJ: Princeton University Press, 1971.

Noakes, J., and G. Pridham, eds. *Nazism: A History in Documents and Eyewitness Accounts 1919-1945*. New York: Schocken Books, 1983-1984.

Piccigallo, Philip R. *The Japanese on Trial: Allied War Crimes Operations in the East, 1945-1951*. Austin: University of Texas Press, 1979.

Takeda, Kayoko. *Interpreting the Tokyo War Crimes Trial: A Sociopolitical Analysis*. Ottawa: University of Ottawa Press, 2010.

Taylor, Telford. *The Anatomy of the Nuremberg Trials: A Personal Memoir*. New York: Knopf, 1992.

Totani, Yuma. *Justice in Asia and the Pacific Region, 1945-1952: Allied War Crimes Prosecutions*. New York: Cambridge University Press, 2015.

Totani, Yuma. *The Tokyo War Crimes Trial: The Pursuit of Justice in the Wake of World War II*. Cambridge, MA: Harvard University Asia Center, 2008.

Ueberschär, Gerd, ed. *Der Nationalsozialismus vor Gericht: Die allierten Prozesse gegen Kriegsverbrecher und Soldaten 1943-1952*. Frankfurt: Fischer, 1999.

Von Lingen, Kerstin, ed. *Debating Collaboration and Complicity in War Crimes Trials in Asia, 1945-1956*. Cham: Palgrave Macmillan, 2017.

Von Lingen, Kerstin, ed. *Transcultural Justice at the Tokyo Tribunal: The Allied Struggle for Justice, 1946-48*. Leiden: Brill, 2018.

Von Lingen, Kerstin, ed. *War Crimes Trials in the Wake of Decolonization and Cold War in Asia, 1945-1956: Justice in Time of Turmoil*. Cham: Palgrave Macmillan, 2016.

Weindling, Paul Julian. *Nazi Medicine and the Nuremberg Trials: From Medical War Crimes to Informed Consent*. New York: Palgrave, 2004.

Wilson, Sandra, R. B. Cribb, Beatrice Trefalt, and Dean Aszkielowicz. *Japanese War Criminals: The Politics of Justice after the Second World War*. New York: Columbia University Press, 2017.

CHAPTER 30

CULTURAL RESPONSES TO TOTAL WAR, 1930S–1945

ANNIKA A. CULVER

BROADLY characterizing the arts produced from 1931 until 1945 by individuals under global wartime regimes—democratic, totalitarian, or authoritarian—is daunting, and risks triteness, oversimplification, or omission. Moreover, the arts cover multifaceted disciplines, including painting, photography, film, literature, music, drama, architecture, and sculpture.

World War II began in stages at different times for different countries, and it went far beyond Europe for participating empires. Some Asianists situate the global conflict's first salvos in the Japanese Kantô Army's 1931 invasion of Manchuria, whereas others indicate that Japan's large-scale conflict with China beginning in 1937 preempts the Pacific War (1941–1945). Following the 1931 Manchurian Incident, imperial Japan's flourishing proletarian literature and arts movement encountered persecution, with 95 percent of leftists denouncing earlier political affiliations.[1] Europeanists note the Spanish Civil War (1936–1939), composed of clashes between supporters of fascism and socialism, as an arena where Hitler tested new weaponry before his troops invaded Poland to initiate Europe's "hot" war. This moment coincides with Surrealism's rise as a global art movement with Japanese offshoots, with anxieties presaging war in cultural fields described by Walter Benjamin and other Frankfurt School intellectuals. In the 1939–1940 "Phoney War," Germany's rapid defeat of Poland without retaliation indicated Britain and France's complacent war-weary attitudes. Between 1940 and 1941, the German military occupied northern and southern Europe before its disastrous June incursion into the Soviet Union. Within areas under Nazi control, increased persecution of cultural producers with Jewish backgrounds or leftist affiliations prompted a "brain drain" of intellectuals fleeing to the United States or Great Britain, while others experienced deportation, internment, and extermination.

After imperial Japan's devastating 1941 attack on the U.S. naval base at Pearl Harbor, American entry into global hostilities reinvigorated the Allied conflict. Before total war with the Axis powers, the United States had experienced more than a decade of economic devastation during the Great Depression, which engendered increased government support of the arts. The arrival of total war at different times for developed nations, which often possessed empires, had a significant impact on the arts as cultural producers responded by fleeing into exile, privately creating critical work, or supporting wartime regimes. The multifaceted term "total war" could refer to operational strategy, mass mobilization of soldiers plus civilians, and wartime effects on the home front. Total war also pertains to different societies at varying points during wartime, and it is expressed in culturally specific ways intersecting with political regimes running countries or dominating regions. Here, it refers to an entire society's mass mobilization, with all resources geared toward war, including cultural production.[2]

World War II's totality affected major nations as primary actors: Germany, France, Japan, China, the Soviet Union, Great Britain, and the United States. The war precipitated complex conditions for artists, broadly construed. Canvas or paper became scarce with rationing; international trade in European art supplies steeply declined; and by 1943, these shortages of supplies even prevented Japanese artists in far-off Manchukuo from painting. As the war progressed, bombardment destroyed display venues, while certain themes were prohibited or encouraged in literature, art, theaters, or film. Censorship, by political authorities or artists, led to the production of works building morale against enemies or supporting totalizing state goals. Many studies challenge paradigms of collaboration versus resistance or tacit support by individuals under repressive authoritarian wartime regimes. "True" collaboration or resistance was rare, with multifaceted spectra of adherence to state (or commercial) directives for cultural policies.

Politics and the Arts in the 1930s

Early twentieth-century European and Asian arts movements interconnected through swift train transportation into wartime. Flows of goods, peoples, and ideas spread diverse art forms throughout Eurasia, while Europeans and Americans increasingly traveled to such cultural centers as London, Paris, New York, and Berlin. After boarding ships in Japan, Japanese artists or literati began European journeys by train from continental Dairen and traveled overland to Europe via the Soviet Union until Stalin's 1933 border closure. Ship voyages from Asia proceeded through the Suez Canal, docked in Marseilles or Naples, and continued by train to Berlin or Paris, reaching London over the English Channel via ferry. Relatively easy transcontinental transit deteriorated in the 1930s because of sealed borders blocking Trans-Siberian routes to Europe, instability in northeast China, and depression-era economic strictures. Economic devastation and war worsened, and often halted, transnational creative exchanges.

The October 1929 New York Stock Exchange crash that sparked the Great Depression affected all global economies; seismic economic and political instability prompted developed nations and empires with colonies to flirt with forms of socialism, such as rightwing fascism in Italy, Germany, Nationalist China, Japan, and Manchukuo;

left-wing totalitarianism in the Soviet Union and Communism in China; or centrist liberalism in the U.S. New Deal and progressive Parliamentarianism in Great Britain. Only the Soviet Union avoided economic ruin, through totalitarian Five-Year Plans, while Great Britain, France, and Japan relied upon colonial economies.

State intrusion into cultural activities in fascist or totalitarian countries began in 1925 for Mussolini's fascist Italy, Stalin's Soviet Union in 1932, and Hitler's Germany in 1933. A censorship regime also arose in imperial Japan (an authoritarian constitutional monarchy since 1868) following the 1925 Peace Preservation Act, banning attacks against the imperial system after 1928. Such censorship laws affected left-wing activists, but extended to writers and filmmakers in influencing work, publication or display venues, and personal associations. Leftist persecution tightened after the 1931 Manchurian Incident initiated Asia's Fifteen Year War. In a progressive United States, the government coopted proletarian culture by funding Depression-era cultural producers in the 1930s-era "Cultural Front," a movement of politically left-oriented artists and intellectuals.[3] The U.S. government sponsored writers and artists under the Works Progress Administration's Federal Project Number One (1935–1943), while private commercial interests motivated Hollywood filmmakers. In the 1930s, economic concerns motivated choices in style and political affiliation for artists everywhere.

By the early 1930s, modernist forms dominated cultural production in imperial capitals.[4] The avant-gardes, as radical derivatives of modernism, assumed an anti-establishment, often radical, political orientation, opposing the market or state's bourgeois values.[5] However, expressions of global modernism in the arts and film transcended political lines: in 1933, Nazi propaganda minister Josef Goebbels praised Soviet film director Sergei Eisenstein's *Battleship Potemkin* (1925). Early Soviet films influenced American and German film into the early 1930s. Although cultural propaganda predates the 1930s, this era marks growing interest in appropriating the arts for political agendas by polities soon involved in World War II, culminating in heightened politicization of cultural atmospheres during a time of total war.

Philosopher Walter Benjamin's 1936 essay, "The Work of Art in the Age of Mechanical Reproduction," presciently highlights infinitely reproducible photography and film for propaganda purposes in authoritarian regimes manipulating sensory perceptions to achieve "simultaneous collective experience."[6] He examines Nazi mass rallies filmed at Nuremberg (1933–1938), but also cites Italian fascism's aestheticization, noting: "The logical result of Fascism is the introduction of aesthetics into political life ... All efforts to render politics aesthetic culminate in one thing: war."[7] Literary scholar Andrew Hewitt indicates Benjamin's grasp of the "totalitarian potential of the medium of film."[8] Besides film and photography, early twentieth century posters, postcards, stamps, illustrated magazines, and other media rapidly and cheaply disseminated politicized visual cultures, through consumer advertising, didactic public service posters, and propaganda. Official and unofficial propaganda forms advertised ideas serving political purposes of regimes from communist to fascist in the 1930s and 1940s. During World War II, ideologues and national leaders believed the arts were inextricably tied to spiritual welfare and morale, and they felt that cultural activities needed strict control and the proper channeling and fostering by the government to represent a polity's wartime needs in effectively mobilizing the populace.

State involvement in the arts coincided with cultural production hidden until peacetime by individuals privately retaining works or engaging in what German writer Frank Thiess called "inner emigration," contrasting with exiled German writers fleeing Nazism, such as Thomas Mann.[9] The seeds of global conflict sprouted early amidst the aestheticization of politics by didactic leaders-Mussolini in the early 1920s, Stalin and Hitler in the early 1930s, Mao's Yenan-based Chinese communists in the mid-1930s, and Manchukuo's literature and film-besotted propagandists Mutô Tomio and Amakasu Masahiko in the late 1930s.

Fascist Italy, 1922–1943

World War I destabilized working-class Italians by heightening pre-existing class divisions and economic distress. Mussolini's nationalistic fascism of the late teens promised regaining Italian glory through irredentism, or the return of all Italian-speaking areas to Italy, and the assuaging of social conflict through an economic policy of paternalistic corporatism. After usurping power from a moribund monarchy in a 1922 coup, the Italian fascist leader proclaimed that art should serve populist social revolution and the state. In 1925, he held a Congress of Fascist Culture in Bologna, where participants wrestled with expressing Fascism in cultural activities. This endeavor succeeded in architecture, such as the classically inspired modernist Palazzo della Civiltà Italiana, built in 1936 for the Esposizione Universale Roma, and in film, with Mussolini and his son Vittorio's 1937 establishment of Cinecitta film studios to reinvigorate Italian cinema through propaganda films. The writer Filippo Tommaso Marinetti attempted to persuade Mussolini to promote Futurism as the regime's "official" art form, but he instead allowed diverse modernisms. In 1938, the German Degenerate Art Exhibition was scheduled to tour Italy, but Marinetti convinced Mussolini to refuse to host it because Hitler viewed the Futurists as degenerate. As a result, Mussolini vigorously criticized Italian fascists who attempted to import Hitler's aesthetic ideologies.

Mussolini's original control over cultural endeavors evinced his desire to resurrect ancient Rome's magnificence, presaging Hitler's Third Reich (also inspired by Italian fascism). Besides film and architecture, he remained distant from state manipulation of the arts for political ends, in contrast to Germany's politicized cultural consolidation of the mid-1930s onwards. Mussolini's interpretation of fascist culture and political influence in the arts was populist, paradoxically allowing multiple styles to flourish despite uneven or arbitrary censure.[10] Fascist Italy lacked enthusiasm for Germany's genocidal encroachment upon the arts, which by the 1930s had purged Jews from cultural activities.

Pragmatic collaboration and Mussolini's complex attitude toward the arts marked the artist Georgio De Chirico's wartime career. He attained fame in the late 1910s with his metaphysical paintings, and then evolved into a heralded Surrealist icon until his

1920s-era "excommunication" by theorist Andre Breton. By the late 1930s, he assumed a neo-Baroque style unrelated to Surrealism. Since the 1920s, De Chirico's deserted classical squares of solitary faceless figures seemingly reflected Mussolini's empty promises, with later paintings evincing political equivocation. While in New York exile (1935–1938), he painted the enigmatic Romanesque series, "Visits to the Mysterious Baths," revealing vulnerable men positioned in empty landscapes (evoking Italian colonialism in Ethiopia after the 1935–1936 invasion) with naked counterparts apparently overseen by a colonial government functionary.

Surprisingly, De Chirico returned home after German-influenced antisemitism had penetrated Italy, potentially endangering his Jewish wife. After officials made antisemitic pronouncements and deported some Italian Jews to concentration camps, the couple fled to Paris. In exile, and during Vichy France's German occupation, De Chirico painted public commissions for Italy's fascist regime—including a 1942 portrait of Mussolini's daughter.[11] The artist's wartime collaboration reveals the complexities in defining Fascist Italy's cultural policies.

THE SOVIET UNION, 1928–1945

While Italy represents the first time a twentieth century dictatorial government manipulated the arts for political aims following economic distress, the Soviet Union presaged imperial Japan's concern with left-wing cultural production and Nazi Germany's mid-thirties art purges. Usurping power in 1928 following Lenin's death, Stalin began exerting complete control over the arts to consolidate the Soviet regime; cultural policy directives burgeoned from 1932 to 1953, with allegiance to the Communist Party line deeply influencing the arts in a cultural system that continued beyond his tenure.[12] In 1932, Stalin presided over arts amalgamation under a unified system of creative associations for cultural producers, policies that preceded Goebbels's 1933 institution of the Reichskammer system and Mutô's similar 1938 Manchukuo-based program. All official art needed to express Socialist Realist aesthetics and political norms as decreed by the Communist Party's Central Committee.

In Soviet propaganda and poster art, Socialist Realism co-opted earlier religious iconography to appeal to illiterate populations by depicting a heroic proletariat and godlike Stalin, a policy that instructed them in state values.[13] Its leading proponent was Alexander Gerasimov, known for quasi-hagiographic official portraits of Stalin that garnered him a 1941 Stalin Prize, who ruled over the Union of Artists of the USSR with dictatorial proprietorship. Philosopher Boris Groys diverges from earlier studies on the semi-canonization of martyred avant-garde artists and their persecution and objectively assesses Socialist Realism by focusing on its appealing qualities.[14] Stalin's ensuing cult of personality caused a proliferation of his image in art and propaganda. As war overshadowed Europe in 1939, pictorial representations of Stalin reached their apex, with 147 official depictions, plunging to forty-nine in 1941, when Hitler attacked Russia, and reaching a low of twenty-one in 1942, but recovering to fifty-three in 1945 after peace.[15] However, Soviet art failed to become a wartime propaganda force until 1941, when Hitler abrogated the two nation's neutrality pact with his invasion. From 1941 onwards, Russian artists, including Gerasimov, like their Japanese and German counterparts, traveled to the front to accumulate material and depicted the conflict in sketches detailing important battles and generals' feats. Since wartime requisitioning limited access to canvas, artists chose subjects with historical significance. Vasili Nikolaevich Yakovlev painted a portrait of heroic Marshal, later General, Georgi Zhukov, to commemorate Operation Bagration after the June 1944 Allied D-Day invasion. His stance evokes portraits of the French dictator Napoleon, in a striking blue uniform against a plain background, emphasizing power and resolve by pressing his hand against a map.

Former art curator Igor Golomstok argues that totalitarian regimes like Stalin's Soviet Union, Hitler's Germany, Mussolini's Fascist Italy, and Mao's Communist China favored iconographic paintings and sculptures that symbolized political ideals.[16] Golomstok's 1950's experiences as an education guide for Moscow's Pushkin Museum of Fine Arts informed his ideas, where he noticed that children visiting the Museum failed to distinguish between Soviet and Nazi art. These both used aesthetic forms evoking Western realist traditions, while their epic paintings and monumental sculptures captured the totalism of a dictatorial regime, with classical Greco-Roman Antiquity inspiring architecture and other arts.[17]

Nazi Germany, 1933–1945

Nazi Germany's statist control over the arts is well-represented in scholarly literature and public interest.[18] A November 2013 discovery of "degenerate art" seized in the thirties and housed by Cornelius Gurlitt, the son of a Nazi art dealer, reinvigorated art historical inquiry into the Third Reich and highlighted phantoms haunting World War II's artistic legacies. Three hundred allegedly confiscated works appeared in the 1937 NSDAP-sponsored degenerative art exhibition in Munich, before it traveled to Berlin.[19] Prior to this, Hitler created the Dresden-based "Chamber of Horrors" to show spectators art forms the regime wished to eliminate, while Jewish, homosexual, and Marxist socialist cultural producers fled or were sent to concentration camps. Displaying "degenerate art" created by Jews or leftists, it provided counterexamples for German artists to shun. Party members like Gurlitt confiscated exhibited pieces and later documented them as "lost" during air raids, while "purchasing" more art at bargain prices.

Nazi Germany's political leaders envisioned themselves as cultural elites, and also engaged in plundering where personal tastes influenced art-looting during the conflict.[20] From 1937 to 1944, Hitler selected all artworks exhibited at the Haus der Deutschen Kunst built to showcase art in Munich for the "Great German Art Exhibition," and he created coteries of artists and sculptors resembling earlier royal courts.[21] Hitler viewed the arts as inseparable from politics, with culture serving to attain his Aryan "superstate" and the arts veiled ruthless goals for absolute power.[22] German art under the Nazis ritualistically reproduced the regime's racialist politics in quasi-religious depictions and enactments of themes emphasizing a utopian future.[23]

Such ideas stemmed from Hitler's own experiences in the teens and twenties as a failed artist competing amidst anti-realist avant-garde production.[24] In the interwar Weimar Republic (1919–1933), antiwar painter Otto Dix, expressionist Emile Nolde, and others depicted fractured planes, deformed bodies, overt sexuality, and tortured visages in riotous colors to emphasize capitalism's ravages upon individuals.[25] These painters' amorphous modernisms soon conflicted with the emergent racialist politics of fascist Nazism arising in mid-1920s Germany. For Nazis envisioning a post-World War I Aryan political utopia, portrayals of a whole national body were ideal, mirroring a Third Reich modeled after ancient Rome. These ideologies issued out of early amalgamations of politics and culture dating from the regime's beginnings.

One of Hitler's targets was artwork by Georg Grosz, whose 1925 portrait of poet Max Herrmann-Neisse, a leading cabaret critic, encapsulates satirical realism by Berlin-based Weimar-era artists who boldly depicted painful human frailties and parodied capitalists. In 1933, before Hitler's assumption of power, Grosz's strong anti-Nazi sentiments and Communist party membership motivated his permanent emigration to New York City, where he returned to teach at the Art Students League after serving as visiting professor in 1932. Artists producing works labeled "degenerate"—also describing their left-wing political orientation or Jewish background—fled to New York or London, invigorating the arts scenes there.

Hitler's regime soon affected Germany's cultural arenas. On March 13, 1933, his propaganda minister Joseph Goebbels launched the Reich Ministry of Popular Enlightenment and Propaganda to take charge of Nazi party propaganda. However, it soon became an organization guiding the arts to foster aesthetic visions communicating Nazi ideals. It supervised the Nazification of the arts, which eventually forced all German artists to join the Reich Chamber of Fine Arts, part of the Cultural Ministry headed by Goebbels.[26] Much of this consolidation was predicated upon racial and "aesthetic" purity. In 1935, under Hitler's orders, Goebbels' began steady "de-Jewification" of the arts. By 1938, the Reich Chamber system even influenced arts organizations in wartime Manchukuo. However, Nazi Germany is unique in purging a religious minority from the cultural world, where Jews represented a considerable proportion.

The Reich Chamber system, run by Goebbels, a failed writer serving Hitler, who had been an unsuccessful artist, extended to literature, where Hitler's seminal 1925 text *Mein Kampf* was proposed as literary model. The regime's infamous book burnings began in 1933, which prompted many of Germany's leading writers, including Thomas Mann and Bertholdt Brecht, to flee to U.S. or British exile. Leftist or Jewish avant-garde writers and cultural producers, like Walter Benjamin in 1941, progressively fled from areas occupied by or at war with Nazi Germany or joined resistance movements in France and Great Britain.

Most representative "Nazi" artists and writers remain obscure, excepting a notable architect and film director. British film-maker Peter Adam, who grew up in Germany under Hitler, views Nazi-sanctioned art as solely interpretable through the lens of Auschwitz, and he focuses on the political import of cultural production under the Nazis.[27] Nazi works reproduced in original art magazines such as *Art in the German Reich* reveal painting, sculpture, the Autobahn, architecture, and film as multifaceted arenas for authoritarian involvement. Albert Speer, chief Nazi Party architect from 1934 to 1942, and Minister of Armaments and War Production from 1942 to1945, promoted neo-classical architecture and joined Hitler's trusted inner circle of artists and staff. In 1933–1934, he served as Nazi Party Commissioner for Artistic and Technical Presentation of Party Rallies and Demonstrations, and as Hitler's official Third Reich architect from 1934 to 1942, best known for archetypal monumentalism in Nuremberg's parade grounds at the Zeppelinfeld Stadium.

In film, Leni Riefenstahl remains a controversial figure who admired Hitler and cultivated close relationships with key Nazi officials to opportunistically further her art and engaged in postwar historical revisionism to avoid prosecution and to sanitize her reputation.[28] Her filming of the 1936 Berlin Olympics exemplifies Nazi-sponsored film, which also featured Speer's architecture modifying a modernist stadium with stone creating a "traditional" appearance. Riefenstahl's notable films include *Triumph of the Will* (1935) and *Olympia* (1938), which premiered for Hitler's forty-ninth birthday. Riefenstahl's and Speer's collaborations with the Nazi regime tainted their later careers, while Speer's deep political leadership within the Nazi party resulted in more than two decades of imprisonment.

As Nazi Germany invaded Poland in September 1939, initiating World War II in Europe, the arts assumed great significance for the regime, where Goebbels increasingly emphasized their propaganda import via the Reichskammer system. According to German art historian Berthold Hinz, themes in Nazi art shifted from "genre painting" to "ideational" (symbolic) or "feudal" (warlike) painting during the early thirties into late wartime.[29] Total war themes showcased ideal multigenerational families now headed by women, powerful heroic *Wehrmacht* soldiers, and mythological stories from Germany's ancient past.

THE SPANISH CIVIL WAR, 1936–1939, AND VICHY FRANCE, 1940–1945

Until 1940, when the Nazis overran Paris, the city harbored artists across the ideological spectrum who had benefitted from Léon Blum's progressive socialist Popular Front since 1936. Chronicled in his *Strange Defeat* (1940), historian Marc Bloch details why France so readily capitulated, with ruling elites, politicians, and the military lacking a unified national policy and misunderstanding the pace of modern warfare.[30] Intellectuals were slow to understand the Nazi regime's burgeoning threat, previously revealed in military strength on Spain's battlefields. In 1936–1939, Hitler sent prototypical German tanks and planes to arm pro-Franco forces during the Spanish Civil War, a conflict between leftist Republicans supported by an international coalition and General Franco's fascist dictatorship upheld by the Spanish aristocracy and Catholic church. Spain's civil war polarized the French public and provided openings for antisemitic and fascist politics to take root, predating German occupation and sowing seeds for the "Vichy Syndrome," which historian Henry Rousso defines as "the complex of heterogenous symptoms and manifestations revealing, particularly in political, cultural, and social life, the existence of traumas engendered by the Occupation, especially those linked to internal divisions."[31]

Salvador Dali, briefly part of Breton's Parisian Surrealist group, left Spain for Paris during the conflict. His work reveals equivocal politics contrasting with leftist Pablo Picasso, whose art he emulated since the mid-twenties, but who suffered Nazi censorship under later occupation. In 1929, Dali wrote the script for Luis Buñuel's Surrealist film, *An Andalusian Dog*, and joined Breton's group. But, in 1934, Breton denounced and expelled him for not formally renouncing Hitler's fascism. From 1937 onwards, Dali painted nightmarish works evoking the Spanish Civil War's horrors, while Picasso's iconic 1937 work *Guernica* revealed early aerial bombing campaigns' grotesque effects on civilian populations. Dali distanced himself from Communism and professed apolitical Surrealism, but to avoid wartime Europe, moved to New York in 1940 where the Julian Levy Gallery sold his lucrative artworks. "The Face of War" (1940-1941) vividly captures Dali's unease with Europe's situation immediately after he began his American exile, and it conjures memories of Spain's civil war in skull-like depictions of eye sockets and mouths harboring exponentially smaller skulls. Surrealist films by Dali's compatriot Buñuel also reveal equivocating politics. *The Golden Age* (1930) criticizes Italian Fascism and the Catholic Church, where feces deface the fictional Republic's cornerstone. During a Paris screening, the fascist League of Patriots and antisemitic youth vandalized the theater's screen and art gallery. Yet, Buñuel's "ethnographic surrealism" in *Land Without Bread* (1933) seemingly advocates extermination of the Hurdanos, an impoverished, marginal people in an area historically populated by Jews forcibly converted by Spain's Inquisition.[32]

In 1936, to flee the Spanish Civil War, Buñuel left for Switzerland and Paris, where he served the leftist Republican government in exile, and in 1938, moved to the U.S. to work for Warner Brothers. He later transferred to New York to aid Iris Barry, film curator at the Museum of Modern Art, who persuaded him to join a government committee investigating propaganda and produce an abridged version of Riefenstahl's "Triumph of the Will" to demonstrate Nazi propaganda's effectiveness. After 1941, out of MOMA, he served the Office of the Coordinator of Inter-American Affairs. However, his career floundered in 1942 when his American citizenship application was threatened by earlier Communist party affiliations (1931-1935) mentioned in Dali's popular autobiography published that year. The controversy (and near-murderous confrontation with his rival Dali) prompted Buñuel's 1944 resignation from MOMA and his return to Hollywood.

In 1940, after barely two months of conflict, France fell easily, as if occupation were preferable to protracted war, with some rushing to aid the German invaders. Spanish artists driven into exile sometimes joined French counterparts, often Jewish, fleeing German troops. Favored destinations remained London, soon engulfed in the Blitz, and New York, free of a wartime climate until late 1941. According to Rousso, an "intractable collective malaise" plagued French memories of the 1940–1944 German occupation under the Nazis.[33] Artists and writers wondered how they could continue to be productive in such an atmosphere, while some served the occupying regime and others resisted.

After the cultural establishment's minimal resistance to "Aryanization" of the Parisian art world, "normalcy" quickly reestablished itself under the Vichy Regime, while Nazi strictures against "degenerate art" considerably relaxed in France, although artists needed to register as "French" and not Jewish before exhibiting works.[34] The Musée National d'Art Moderne, under the collaborationist Ministry of Education and Youth, staged its inaugural exhibition on August 6, 1942, omitting art by Picasso, Jewish members of the École de Paris, or abstractionists, while "Neoimpressionism, Symbolism, French-style Cubism, and particularly Fauvism were well represented (a lone Tanguy stood for French Surrealism."[35] In Paris' famed entertainment world, theaters, revues, operas, and nightclubs operated as usual—further highlighting a strange "normalcy" under the Nazis.[36] Artists, writers, and others were forced into a spectrum of complex choices between collaboration and resistance.

On August 25, 1944, French Forces of the Interior, popularly known as the Resistance, the 2nd French Armored Division (including exiled Spanish Republicans), and the U.S. 4th Infantry division liberated Paris. Upon Germany's surrender, General Charles De Gaulle arrived from London to lead the city, garnering international respect for the Resistance. Collectively, the French population, including artists and other cultural producers, now faced consequences for collaboration, resulting in the postwar "Vichy Syndrome." This "syndrome" of collective memory mirrors that of cultural figures from Japanese-occupied China and Manchukuo in the postwar period and evokes interesting parallels.

IMPERIAL JAPAN, MANCHUKUO, AND OCCUPIED CHINA, 1931–1945

Studies on wartime cultural mobilization by Americanists and Europeanists often omit imperial Japan, or essentialize Japan and neglect Manchukuo's key role in cultural endeavors for Japan's wartime empire whose experience mirrors European nations and the U.S. imperial acquisitions after the 1898 Spanish American War. They overlook Japanese art circles' cosmopolitan character and early twentieth-century interactions between Asia and Europe, continuing into the European outbreak of World War II. For European-focused scholars, war began in Europe in 1939, not with the 1931 Manchurian Incident that is recognized by most Asianists. Their studies indicate lack of dialogue with Asianists or Japan specialists, while failing to highlight the importance of empire and colonies for Japan like other European empires.

Japan and the United States achieved modernization and unification rapidly in the mid-nineteenth century and established empires by century's end, touching in waters surrounding Taiwan (Japanese since 1895) and the Philippines (an 1898 U.S. purchase). For both nations, the early twentieth century ushered in the growth of cities attracting millions from rural areas and overseas. Since the 1880s, and notably in the 1920s to early thirties, Japanese and Americans traveled to such European capitals as Berlin and Paris to learn from "authentic" cultural centers, and they absorbed knowledge to create unique interpretations. Global interconnectivity for Japan's arts appears within the leftist avant-garde Constructivist group MAVO, whose leader, Maruyama Tomoyoshi, interacted with artists in 1920s Weimar-era Berlin but experienced persecution in 1930s Japan.[37] Although European contemporaries occasionally viewed Japanese artists and writers as parvenus, they influenced Europe's art and literary worlds through innovation, pioneering optimism, and daring exoticism. The Japanese surrealist movement in literature and art evinces considerable interaction between Asians and Europeans.[38] Japanese artists and writers traveled throughout the empire, and gained inspiration in Taiwan, Korea, Okinawa, and northeast China—continuing into wartime and even onto the battlefield. After 1928, Chiang Kai-Shek's military unification of China below the Great Wall prompted Japanese nationalists' fear of a strong united neighbor. The northeast China-based Kantô Army assassinated the region's warlord Zhang Zuolin to cut Manchuria off from China proper, but Emperor Hirohito condemned their 1928 plot. The 1931 invasion succeeded and resulted in Manchukuo's 1932 establishment as Japan's client state. From 1933–1937, by sacrificing Manchuria to the Japanese, Chiang's Tang'gu Truce maintained tenuous peace between China and Japan. Since the 1920s, Japanese art and literature had flourished in colonial Dairen within southeastern Manchuria, and throughout Manchukuo after 1932.[39] This region influenced arts in domestic Japan from the 1920s into 1940s, when artists and writers targeted international audiences beyond East Asia. Avant-garde photographer Fuchikami Hakuyô, influenced by Soviet photographic realism, led the Manchurian Photographic Arts Association exhibiting abroad in wide-ranging venues like Chicago and Paris in the 1930s, and created propaganda photography for Manchukuo during wartime.[40] Surrealist artist Fukuzawa Ichirô studied in Paris from 1924 until his 1931 Tokyo return, where he invigorated Japan's art world with new interpretations of Surrealism. His characteristic work "Oxen" (1936), produced after a 1935 Manchukuo sojourn, depicts paper-machéd livestock foregrounding juxtaposed scenes of toil and pleasure, to reflect proletarian social themes popular among socially concerned cultural producers worldwide during the Great Depression.[41]

From 1919–1932, before Japan began "official" hostilities in China, writers inspired by Lu Xun's vernacular writings and May Fourth protests against Japanese imperialism in China mobilized literature to "awaken" and save their nation. After the Manchurian invasion, anti-Japanese literature and art proliferated amongst leftwing Chinese cultural producers in popular essays, "proletarian" woodblock prints, and cartoons in diverse media.[42] Yet, Chiang's civil war against communists since his 1927 Shanghai Purge dampened leftwing political participation and forced cultural censorship. His military campaign against the Jiangxi Soviet (1927–1934) prompted the 1934–1935 Long March, pushing communists into exile at Yan'an in Shanxi province, where discourses of resistance developed to establish the communists' legacy as sole effective fighters against Japan. By 1937, imperial Japan's aggression prompted most Chinese cultural producers to flee areas under occupation if collaboration or enduring the regime proved impossible. After 1938, some escaped to Chungking, a heavily bombed mountain-ringed Republican capital stymying Japanese troops, or to Hong Kong, falling to Japan in late December 1941.

The collaborationist Wang Jingwei regime (1938–1944) sponsored Greater East Asian Writers Congresses and fostered the arts under Japanese-inspired official organizations and exhibitions. For imperial Japan, a mutual pan-Asianist culture amalgamated occupied countries harboring disparate languages and cultures. After 1940, Manchukuo modeled a template for the Greater East Asian Co-Prosperity Sphere's cultural construction through multiple empire-wide writers' conferences. Intriguingly, in Wang's 1943 address to the Greater East Asian Conference, he calls Manchukuo a leading "friend" to China above all of imperial Japan's occupied nations, and he frames the Greater East Asian Co-prosperity Sphere as a bulwark against Anglo-American colonialism and wartime "aggression." Through the arts, Manchukuo's multi-ethnic culture showcased ideological and cultural construction of Pan-Asianist aims for conquered Chinese and Southeast Asian territories. Kawabata Yasunari wrote how imperial Japan's success in Manchukuo was crucial as a Pan-Asianist model.[43] However, Chinese women writers there defied artificial collaboration versus resistance paradigms by engaging in passive resistance while adhering to surface acceptance of state philosophies and wartime arts sponsorship.[44] Painful collaborationist legacies persisted into contemporary China, with objective investigation only arising by the 1990s and 2000s. In Manchukuo, Japanese authorities Ishiwara Kanji and propagandist Mutô Tomiô promoted a new utopian multiethnic culture and used neo-Confucian ideals to bolster the state's political functioning. These ideas were disseminated via literary endeavors and popularization of "national policy films" produced by the Manchurian Film Association founded in 1937 and headed by controversial bureaucrat Amakasu Masahiko after 1939.[45] Mutô adopted Nazi-inspired cultural consolidation to further state war aims after the Second Sino–Japanese War's 1938 entrenchment.[46] Like Nazi Germany or the Soviet Union, he intended to build a portfolio of iconic works expressing national ideals. Beginning in 1931 with the Manchurian Incident and intensifying after outbreaks of the second Sino–Japanese (1937) and Pacific (1941) wars, Japanese cultural production became an important wartime propaganda force throughout the empire. Since 1931, domestic Japanese directors, producers, companies, and bureaucrats collaborated to produce propagandistic films supporting Japan's war aims.[47] The Cabinet Information Bureau's manipulation of media images, photographs, and art shows how the Pacific War was represented as a "certain victory" to the home front in mobilizing audiences to fight against Western powers.[48] Historian Louise Young describes Manchukuo's important ideological role: "Like total war, total empire was made on the home front. It entailed the mass and multidimensional mobilization of domestic society: cultural, military, political, and economic."[49] Officially sponsored exhibitions in Tokyo like *Teiten* featured war art, and after 1938, joint exhibitions were also held in Manchukuo's capital Shinkyô (contemporary Changchun). Officials emulated art as propaganda, and by the early 1940s, even the Japanese Army engaged in art debates.

Cultural producers were deemed crucial to war efforts so the military sent artists and writers to the front, including "pen brigades" traveling throughout wartime China and southeast Asia, like popular fiction writers Kikuchi Kan and Yoshiya Nobuko, and formerly proletarian author Hayashi Fumiko.[50] Newspaper journalists wrote riveting battle accounts; although censored and later banned, Ishikawa Tatsuzô's "Soldiers Alive," a 1938 serialized story of a squadron heading to Nanking, portrays troops as human but capable of horrific atrocities.[51] Of Japan's "war record" artists, Fujita Tsuguharu gained international renown for iconic documentary realism in a 1938 painting of a Mitsubishi Zero fighter plane's shadow overflying Suzhou, "Pearl Harbor on 8 December 1941," and a monumental 1943 canvas featuring the suicidal Attack on Attu in Alaska.[52] To continue wartime cultural production, artists carefully disguised critique, objectively recorded battles, or enthusiastically propagated "colonial liberation" or "Greater East Asian Co-Prosperity." Imperial Japan's wartime legacies lasted deep into the postwar, but attenuated by 1960, following riots against renewing the U.S.—Japan Security Treaty, after which Prime Minister Ikeda Hayato's "Double Income Plan" ushered in the Economic Miracle.

THE UNITED STATES AND GREAT BRITAIN, 1939–1945

In late 1941, after over a decade of Depression-generated economic turmoil and wariness toward foreign military involvement, the U.S. joined the Allied struggle against the Axis Powers as a relative latecomer to the European and Asian conflict. Its political isolationism extended into the arts, leading to blasé attitudes toward developments on the European continent despite exiled emigrés' knowledge of the Nazi threat. From 1939–1940, Britain expressed war-weariness engendered by WWI's painful memories, and rode out the Phoney War before German bombardment brought the Blitz from September 1940 until May 1941. Although government mechanisms to mobilize the arts for war existed since the 1930s, the Anglo–American cultural world responded slowly to global conflict. Commercial concerns also motivated these choices.

From the 1920s into late 1930s, in Hollywood, competition and collaboration existed amongst German and American actors and filmmakers transiting between Berlin and Los Angeles (L.A.), including Marlene Dietrich and Leni Riefenstahl. Films leniently portrayed Nazi Germany from 1933 until 1939, when Warner Brothers courageously broke embargos against anti-Nazi film. American studies scholar Thomas Doherty notes how "Germany was a lucrative market to cultivate and exploit, or a business rival to co-opt and crush."[53] To the American cultural establishment, German belligerency appeared gradually, with rare films like producer Mike Mindlin and sponsor Cornelius Vanderbilt, Jr.'s (IV) sensationalistic documentary *Hitler's Reign of Terror* (1934) illuminating Nazi threats amidst public scorn after release. In 1936, the L.A. film industry produced its only anti-Nazi feature film: *I Was a Captive of Nazi Germany*. Hollywood avoided political engagement or worked with Hitler's representatives to allow films' continued screening in Germany due to high profits and huge market shares for American movies.[54] Hollywood "appeased" German censors before American entry into WWII. As the 1930s progressed, the industry found itself in a moral dilemma where largely Jewish film moguls, some with German roots, weighed political considerations against continued profit.[55] However, after 1941, it wholeheartedly supported the U.S. war effort by making movies with pro-American wartime themes. Newspapers and other media enlisted popular culture for propagandistic aims once war began for the Americans. In the early forties, Donald Duck appeared in hundreds of cartoons lampooning antics by Hitler and the Nazis, or Japanese and their emperor. Historian John Dower notes that while Nazis are portrayed as brutish but cruel humans, racist stereotypical depictions of treacherous buck-toothed Japanese seem bestial.[56] These cartoons appeared between newsreels and feature films to entertain American viewers and provide moments of levity, with capers entertaining viewers distraught by hard news of battlefront coverage.

Marxist critics exiled from the European conflict viewed American popular culture as disseminating indigenous cultural totalitarianism, and they attacked mindless mass consumption of ideas spread by Hollywood's culture industry. Deeply critical of homogenous cultural conformity engendered by American capitalism, Theodor Adorno and Max Horkheimer wrote diatribes from L.A.'s exclusive Pacific Palisades area labeled "Weimar by the Sea" for its German or Austrian Jewish émigré intellectuals. Their 1944 privately-circulated essay, "The Culture Industry: Enlightenment as Mass Deception," whose title puns Germany's Reich Ministry for Mass Enlightenment, criticizes the culture industry's uniformity in late capitalist "liberal" nations like the U.S. for spawning characters like Donald Duck.[57] Adorno and Horkheimer view "culture as publicity" where, "[t]he blind and rapidly spreading repetition of words with special designations links advertising with the totalitarian watchword."[58] Films and pulp fiction engaged in consumerist political messaging, while the culture industry disseminated generic ideas uniformly consumed by the masses without reflection.

Despite intellectuals' criticisms of popular culture as propaganda, sentimental images created by easily recognizable artists effectively garnered American mass support for the war. Norman Rockwell, whose wartime career reveals intersections between propaganda and advertising, characterizes successful U.S. home front cultural production.[59] As a beloved *Saturday Evening Post* illustrator, his May 29, 1943 cover "Rosie the Riveter" energized women's contributions to the war effort by inspiring them to assume traditionally male workplace roles.[60] Against the fluttering backdrop of an iconic stars and stripes, a young woman's foot treads upon Hitler's 1925 manifesto *Mein Kampf* as she defiantly eats her ham sandwich during lunch break. Muscular arms stained by grease cradle a weapon-like blowtorch on her lap, and shows how the Nazi threat inspires daily toil to build more armaments and planes. The 1994–1995 exhibit "Powers of

Persuasion: Poster Art of World War II" at the U.S. National Archives showcased the raw impact of Rockwell's images. His poster of a small-town worker standing up at a town hall meeting, captioned "Save Freedom of Speech," urged citizens to purchase war bonds—evoking public service posters in Britain, Japan, and even Manchukuo. These popular artworks with proletarian themes suggest earlier 1930s Works Progress Administration (WPA) depictions and persuaded ordinary Americans to assume patriotic behaviors supporting the war like invest in war bonds, collect scrap materials, and curb "loose talk."

Governments in Great Britain and the United States enlisted war artists, like Japan and the Soviet Union, and built upon systems of pre-existing officially sponsored art organizations arising before the conflict. Writers also served as journalists at the front, while media newsreels and fictional filmic representations of heroic military service, spy dramas, or home fronts, like *Mrs. Miniver* (1942), further supported Allied wartime ideological aims. In 1940, Britain's Ministry of Information headed the Crown Film Unit, which made documentaries like *Britain Can Take It* (1940) to galvanize popular morale against the Blitz, with *Listen to Britain* (1942) further detailing home front civilian efforts. In 1939, Great Britain's Ministry of Information created the War Artists Advisory Committee (WAAC), a government body under Sir Kenneth Clark's leadership as director of London's National Gallery. From 1939–1945, cognizant of British artists' key propaganda impact in WWI, WAAC commissioned around six thousand works of art from over four hundred artists to boost morale, record the war, and develop a cohesive British cultural patriotism. According to the National Maritime Museum, war art played an influential role: "official war art served the purposes of commemoration, instruction, documentation and propaganda as well as raising morale at home and at the front."[61] The U.S. Army's most renowned war artist was Ed Reep, whose paintings cite American Surrealism, European Expressionism, and the prismatic, lonely atmosphere of contemporary Edward Hopper, known for his iconic painting "Nighthawks" (1942). Reep's "Morning After" (1944) portrays complex grief after friends perished in a German bombing raid destroying an underground movie theater. Reep and artists serving the U.S. Army, Navy, or Marine Corps, *Yank*, *Life Magazine*, or Abbott Laboratories depicted the conflict and showcased American contributions.[62] These images generated constellations of aid for those who served and supported broader home front mobilization aims.

Conclusion

World War II ended on August 15, 1945 when American atomic weapons and the Soviet invasion of Manchukuo imparted a "twin shock" prompting Japan's Emperor, through his Prime Minister and Cabinet, to surrender to the Allies.[63] The twentieth century's most brutal total war caused sixty million dead, with nearly half being civilians.[64] In its immediate aftermath, survival initially superseded reflection upon collaborationist legacies for individuals serving Axis powers' wartime regimes.[65] The postwar period marked rebuilding in Europe and Asia, and for the United States, a "return to normalcy" with economic prosperity, while Britain suffered rationing and shortages into the 1950s. Veterans resumed lives and professions, including cultural production.

Many Germans and Japanese attempted to erase or "forget" wartime roles after concerns for survival slowly dissipated, while Chinese experienced continuation of an earlier civil war between Nationalists and Communists, and Maoist cultural ideologies reemerged after 1949 Liberation when the arts again served political aims. German artists within the Nazi regime's official Reich Chamber system of arts organizations quickly distanced themselves from wartime pasts, and repudiated support for a genocidal regime or quietly buried earlier roles. In Italy, Mussolini's earlier lack of control over artistic endeavors allowed less complicated postwar political situations for artists, with some, like Di Chirico, working in interdisciplinary media beyond painting, while formalistically copying earlier themes.

In Japan, artists and writers resumed cultural activities after the United States allowed limited expansion of freedoms prior to the 1947 "Reverse Course" when Cold War anxieties necessitated renewed surveillance over revived socialist and communist groups allegedly harboring pro-Soviet intellectuals.[66] Some with left-wing orientations or proletarian sympathies were lauded for expressing anti-imperialist or antiwar sentiments during wartime. In 1945, Ishikawa's "Living Soldiers" was finally published in full as a critically antiwar work, with the journalist lauded as a postwar hero for realistic depictions of the imperial Army in China despite a 1938 arrest. In fine art, Fukuzawa's "Defeat in War" (1948) captured the immediate postwar atmosphere surrounding Japan's defeat, and it evoked a 1935 painting citing oppression of Manchukuo's Chinese workers. It depicts naked men heaped without national distinction within a barren desert landscape, crushed and embracing each other, pressing those below into a greening earth. However, after Japan's 1952 Allied Occupation ended in 1952, the Korean War (1950–1953) energized fears of the Soviet Union while invigorating the Japanese economy. Cold War rhetoric buried reflection upon imperial Japan's war years. Artistic endeavors revived slowly, and in 1954, the avant-garde *Gutai* group arose under Yoshihara Jirô to gain ascendance with performance art and outdoor installations.[67] In 1955, primed by earlier American military procurements during the Korean conflict, Japan's economy began a sustained rise dubbed the "Economic Miracle."

In the Soviet Union, artists, writers, and filmmakers initially focused on survival in the brutal war's aftermath leaving over twenty-six million Russian dead, but works soon emerged memorializing the conflict.[68] In 1946, Yakovlev completed a bombastic, Napoleon-inspired portrait of General Zhukov mounting a rearing white stallion to commemorate successful command over the Red Army in Europe, and later, the August 1945 invasion of Japanese-occupied northeast China. Stalin now attended a bipolar world featuring the U.S. as a key capitalist opponent and strongest nuclear-armed world power, in decades of rivalry where the arts continued to serve the Soviet Union. After Stalin's 1953 death, a period of liberalization known as the "Thaw" began under

Krushchev. In experimenting with abstractionism, artists moved away from official Socialist Realism, with works termed "Nonconformist Art."

Sustained political influence upon official art worlds continued into the postwar for major powers that fought in World War II. By the late 1940s, the U.S. government viewed American Abstract Expressionism as a cultural beacon for democracy, with the U.S. Information Service funding European 1950s-era exhibition tours in cultural struggles against Soviet totalitarianism—upholding Jackson Pollack as its most prominent practitioner.[69] Cold War concerns soon affected artists' cultural production in the United States, Soviet Union, communist China, and Japan, while individuals everywhere envisioned a brighter future in a world of increasing global cultural interactions fostered by international organizations including the United Nations, and initiatives like the U.S. Institute of International Education's Fulbright program.

Notes

1. Donald Keene, *Dawn to the West: Japanese Literature of the Modern Era—Fiction* (New York: Holt, Reinhart, and Winston, 1984), 184.
2. Historians claim multiple interpretations of "total war," but space limitations prevent discussion of an extensive historiography. An excellent study arising from five global conferences on total war to focus specifically on World War II is Roger Chickering, Stig Förster, and Bernd Greiner, eds., *A World at Total War: Global Conflict and the Politics of Destruction, 1937–1945* (Cambridge, UK: Cambridge University Press, 2010). Chickering and Förster discuss a theory of total war in their Introduction, 1–18.
3. Michael Denning, *The Cultural Front: The Laboring of American Culture in the Twentieth Century* (New York: Verso Books, 1996).
4. Raymond Williams, *The Politics of Modernism: Against the Rise of the New Conformists* (New York: Verso Books, 2007).
5. Peter Bürger, *The Theory of the Avant-Garde* (Minneapolis: University of Minnesota Press, 1984).
6. See Walter Benjamin, *Illuminations: Essays and Reflections* (New York: Schrocken, 1969), 217–252. Walter Benjamin, "The Work of Art in the Age of Mechanical Reproduction," trans. Harry Zohn, https://www.marxists.org/reference/subject/philosophy/works/ge/benjamin.htm.
7. The context is Mussolini's invasion of Ethiopia. In his epilogue, Benjamin quotes Marinetti, eerily predicting World War II in Europe. Benjamin, *Illuminations: Essays and Reflections*, 252.
8. Andrew Hewitt, *Fascist Modernism: Aesthetics, Politics, and the Avant-Garde* (Stanford: Stanford University Press, 1996), 170.
9. H. R. Kleineberger, "The 'Innere Emigration': A Disputed Issue in Twentieth-Century German Literature," *Monatshefte* 57, no. 4 (April–May 1965), 171.
10. Matthew Affron and Mark Antliff, *Fascist Visions: Art and Ideology in France and Italy* (Princeton, NJ: Princeton University Press, 1997).
11. Barbara McCloskey, *Artists of World War II (Artists of an Era)* (Westport, CT: Greenwood Press, 2005), 100.

12. Matthew Cullerne Bown, *Art Under Stalin* (London: Phaedon Press, 1991).
13. Victoria E. Bonnell, *The Iconography of Power: Soviet Political Posters Under Lenin and Stalin* (Berkeley: University of California Press, 1997).
14. Boris Groys, *The Total Art of Stalinism: Avant-Garde, Aesthetic Dictatorship, and Beyond*, trans. Charles Rougle. New York: Verso Books, 2011.
15. Jan Plamper, *The Stalin Cult: A Study in the Alchemy of Power* (New Haven: Yale University Press, 2012), 228.
16. Igor Golomstock, *Totalitarian Art in the Soviet Union, the Third Reich, Fascist Italy, and the People's Republic of China*, trans. Robert Chandler (New York: Overlook TP, 2012).
17. Kanan Makiya, "What Is Totalitarian Art? Cultural Kitch from Stalin to Saddam," *Foreign Affairs* (May/June 2011), http://www.foreignaffairs.com/articles/67734/kanan-makiya/what-is-totalitarian-art, accessed January 1, 2015.
18. Excellent, although older texts on Hitler's regime include Telford Taylor, *Sword and Swastika: The Wehrmacht in the Third Reich* (London: Victor Gollancz Limited, 1953), Alan Bullock, *Hitler: A Study in Tyranny* (London: Odhams Press Limited, 1952), and Erich Fromm, *Escape From Freedom* (New York: Farrar and Rinehart, 1941).
19. The exhibition "Degenerate Art: The Attack on Modern Art in Nazi Germany" that ran March 13 to September 1, 2014 in New York City's Neue Gallerie, offered a complete historical overview of the phenomenon, with analyses on postwar restitution, and was the latest exhibit on degenerate art since the 1991 Los Angeles County Museum of Modern Art exhibition. http://www.neuegalerie.org/content/degenerate-art-attack-modern-art-nazi-germany-1937, accessed on January 1, 2015.
20. Frederic Spotts, *Hitler and the Power of Aesthetics* (New York: Overlook Books, 2003).
21. Ines Schlenker, *Hitler's Salon: The "Grosse Deutsche Kunstausstellung" at the Haus der Deutschen Kunst in Munich, 1937–1944* (New York: Peter Lang Academic International Publishers, 2007).
22. Spotts, *Hitler and the Power of Aesthetics*.
23. Eric Michaud, *The Cult of Art in Nazi Germany (Cultural Memory in the Present)* (Stanford: Stanford University Press, 2004).
24. For Hitler-centered studies, see Klaus Backes, *Hitler und die bildende Kuenste: Kulturverständnis und Kunstpolitik im Dritten Reich* (Ostfildern: DuMont Reiseverlag, 1992) and O. K. Werckmeister, "Hitler the Artist," *Critical Inquiry* 23 (1997): 270–297.
25. Dresden's Zwinger Museum houses phenomenal collections of Otto Dix's massive oil paintings.
26. Alan Steinweis, *Art, Ideology, and Economics in Nazi Germany: The Reich Chambers of Music, Theater, and the Visual Arts* (Chapel Hill: University of North Carolina Press, 1993)
27. Peter Adam, *Art of the Third Reich* (New York: Harry N. Abrams, 1992), 9.
28. Steven Bach, *Leni: The Life and Work of Leni Riefenstahl* (New York: Vintage Books, 2008).
29. Berthold Hinz, *Art in the Third Reich*, trans. Robert Kimber and Rita Kimber (New York: Pantheon Books, 1979), 163.
30. Marc Bloch, *Strange Defeat: A Statement of Evidence Written in 1940* (New York: W. W. Norton, 1999).
31. Henry Rousso, *The Vichy Syndrome: History and Memory in France Since 1944* (Cambridge: Harvard University Press, 1994), 18–19.
32. See James F. Lastra, "Why Is this Absurd Picture Here? Ethnology/Equivocation/Buñuel," *October* 89 (Summer 1999): 51–68, http://www.jstor.org/stable/779139, accessed January 1, 2015.

33. Rosemarie Scullion, "Unforgettable: History, Memory, and the Vichy Syndrome," *Studies in 20th Century Literature* 23, no. 1 (January 1, 1999): 11.
34. Michele C. Cone, *Artists Under Vichy: A Case of Prejudice and Persecution* (Princeton: Princeton University Press, 1992).
35. Hilton Kramer, "Art and Politics in the Vichy Period," *The New Criterion* (March 1992), https://newcriterion.com/issues/1992/3/art-politics-in-the-vichy-period, accessed June 1, 2015.
36. Alan Riding, *And the Show Went On: Cultural Life in Nazi-Occupied Paris* (New York: Vintage Books, 2011).
37. Gennifer Weisenfeld, *MAVO: Japanese Artists and the Avant-Garde, 1905–1931* (Berkeley: University of California Press, 2001).
38. Annika A. Culver, "'Between Distant Realities': The Japanese Avant-Garde, Surrealism, and the Colonies, 1924–1943," PhD diss., University of Chicago, 2007.
39. Annika A. Culver, "The Making of a Japanese Avant-Garde in Colonial Dairen, 1924–1937" *History Compass* 2, no. 2 (March 2007): 347–361.
40. Kari L. Shepherdson-Scott, "Fuchikami Hakuyō's Evening Sun: Manchuria, Memory, and the Aesthetic Abstraction of War," in *Art and War in Japan and Its Empire, 1931-1960*, ed. Ming Tiampo, Louisa McDonald, and Asato Ikeda (Boston: Brill: Leiden, 2012).
41. Annika A. Culver, *Glorify the Empire: Japanese Avant-Garde Propaganda in Manchukuo* (Vancouver: University of British Columbia Press, 2013), 67.
42. Eclectic art activities of China's avant-garde cultural producers via the lens of *Shidai manhua* [Modern Sketch] appear in John Crispi, "China's *Modern Sketch* 1: The Golden Era of Cartoon Art, 1934–1937," https://visualizingcultures.mit.edu/modern_sketch/index.html.
43. Culver, *Glorify the Empire*, 188.
44. Norman Smith, *Resisting Manchukuo: Chinese Women Writers and the Japanese Occupation* (Vancouver: University of British Columbia Press, 2007). Mei Niang and Wu Ying worked within official channels but wrote stories showcasing dark and depressing narratives of social dissipation or moral debauchery in a supposedly "bright" utopia under imperial Japanese auspices.
45. Specialized studies on film in Manchuria and Occupied China include Michael Baskett, *The Attractive Empire: Transnational Film Culture in Imperial Japan* (Honolulu: University of Hawaii Press, 2008).
46. See "The Manchukuo Publicity and News Bureau's War of Words and Images: Mutô Tomio and the Discourse of Culture, 1938–1943," in Culver, *Glorify the Empire*, 134–167.
47. Peter High, *The Imperial Screen: Japanese Film Culture in the Fifteen Years' War, 1931–1945* (Madison: University of Wisconsin Press, 2003).
48. David Earhart, *Certain Victory: Images of World War II in the Japanese Media* (Armonk, NY: M. E. Sharpe, 2009), xiii.
49. Louise Young, *Japan's Total Empire: Manchuria and the Culture of Wartime Imperialism* (Berkeley: University of California Press, 1998), 13.
50. Hiromi Tsuchiya Dollase, "Kawabata's Wartime Message in *Utsukushii tabi* [Beautiful Voyage]," in *Negotiating Censorship in Modern Japan*, ed. Rachel Hutchinson (London: Routledge, 2013), 74.
51. Ishikawa Tatsuzô, *Soldiers Alive*, trans. Zeljko Cipris (Honolulu: University of Hawaii Press, 2003). The serialized novel appeared in 1938, but publication ended after four issues

when it was banned and its author arrested. Documenting in grim detail, Ishikawa was imbedded as a journalist with a regiment retreating from the September 1937 attack on Shanghai, marching toward Nanking by November, and committing the massacre in December 1937 after defeating the city.

52. Asato Ikeda, Aya Louisa McDonald, Ming Tiampo, *Art and War in Japan and Its Empire, 1931–1960* (Leiden: Koninklijke Brill, 2012).
53. Thomas Doherty, *Hollywood and Hitler, 1933–1939* (New York: Columbia University Press, 2013), 17.
54. Doherty, *Hollywood and Hitler, 1933–1939*, 73.
55. Ben Urwand, *The Collaboration: Hollywood's Pact with Hitler* (Cambridge, MA: Harvard University Press, 2013).
56. John Dower, *War Without Mercy: Race and Power in the Pacific War* (New York: Pantheon Books, 1987), 181–202.
57. Max Horkheimer and Theodor W. Adorno, "The Culture Industry: Enlightenment as Mass Deception," in *Dialectic of Enlightenment: Philosophical Fragments* (Stanford: Stanford University Press, 2002), 94–136; Theodor Adorno and Max Horkheimer, "The Culture Industry as Mass Deception," https://www.marxists.org/reference/archive/adorno/1944/culture-industry.htm, accessed on December 28, 2014.
58. Quoted in Ibid.
59. See Susan E. Meyer, *Norman Rockwell's World War II: Impressions from the Home Front* (USAA Foundation, 1991).
60. http://www.saturdayeveningpost.com/2013/07/01/art-entertainment/norman-rockwell-art-entertainment/rosie-the-riveter.html, accessed on January 2, 2015.
61. National Maritime Museum blog, https://www.iwm.org.uk/partnerships/mapping-the-centenary/projects/war-artists-at-sea, accessed June 5, 2015; http://www.rmg.co.uk/whats-on/events/war-artists-at-sea, accessed on January 1, 2015.
62. Airing in May 2000, a PBS television documentary series "They Drew Fire," featured contributions from Reep and others. See a web gallery of representative works at http://www.pbs.org/theydrewfire/gallery/index.html, accessed January 1, 2015.
63. Asada Sadao, *Culture Shock and Japanese–American Relations: Historical Essays* (Columbia, MO: University of Missouri Press, 2011), 174–206.
64. Statistics quoted from the National World War II Museum in New Orleans, http://www.nationalww2museum.org/learn/education/for-students/ww2-history/ww2-by-the-numbers/world-wide-deaths.html.
65. McCloskey, *Artists of World War II*, 101.
66. Kazu Kaido and David Elliott, ed., *Reconstructions: Avant-Garde Art in Japan, 1945–1965: An Exhibition* (New York: Museum of Modern Art, 1985, digitized in 2009).
67. See Alexandra Munroe, *Japanese Art After 1945: Scream Against the Sky* (New York: Harry Abrams, 1996); Doryun Chong, Michio Hayashi, Fumihiko Sumitomo, and Kenji Kajiya, eds., *From Postwar to Postmodern, Art in Japan, 1945–1989 (MoMa Primary Documents)* (New York: MOMA, 2012).
68. Michael Ellman and S. Maksudov, "Soviet Deaths in the Great Patriotic War: A Note-World War II," *Europe–Asia Studies* (July 1994), 677.
69. Eve Cockcroft, "Abstract Expressionism, Weapon of the Cold War," *Artsforum* 15, no. 10 (June 1974): 39–41, https://www.msu.edu/course/ha/240/evacockroft.pdf and http://www.independent.co.uk/news/world/modern-art-was-cia-weapon-1578808.html.

Bibliography

Adam, Peter. *Art of the Third Reich*. New York: Harry N. Abrams, 1992.

Adorno, Theodor W., and Horkheimer, Max. "The Culture Industry: Enlightenment as Mass Deception." In *Dialectic of Enlightenment: Philosophical Fragments*, 94–136. Stanford: Stanford University Press, 2002.

Adorno, Theodor W., and Horkheimer, Max. "The Culture Industry as Mass Deception." https://www.marxists.org/reference/archive/adorno/1944/culture-industry.htm, 1944.

Affron, Matthew, and Mark Antliff. *Fascist Visions: Art and Ideology in France and Italy*. Princeton, NJ: Princeton University Press, 1997.

Asada, Sadao. *Culture Shock and Japanese–American Relations: Historical Essays*. Columbia: University of Missouri Press, 2011.

Bach, Steven. *Leni: The Life and Work of Leni Riefenstahl*. New York: Vintage Books, 2008.

Backes, Klaus. *Hitler und die bildende Kuenste: Kulturverständnis und Kunstpolitik im Dritten Reich*. Ostfildern: DuMont Reiseverlag, 1992.

Baskett, Michael. *The Attractive Empire: Transnational Film Culture in Imperial Japan*. Honolulu: University of Hawaii Press, 2008.

Benjamin, Walter. "The Work of Art in the Age of Mechanical Reproduction." *Illuminations: Essays and Reflections*, 217–252. New York: Schrocken, 1969.

Bloch, Marc. *Strange Defeat: A Statement of Evidence Written in 1940*. New York: W. W. Norton, 1999.

Bohm-Duchen, Monica. *Art and the Second World War*. Farnham, Surrey: Lund Humphries, 2013.

Bonnell, Victoria E. *The Iconography of Power: Soviet Political Posters Under Lenin and Stalin*. Berkeley: University of California Press, 1997.

Bürger, Peter. *The Theory of the Avant-Garde*. Minneapolis: University of Minnesota Press, 1984.

Chickering, Roger, Stig Förster, and Bernd Greiner, eds. *A World at Total War: Global Conflict and the Politics of Destruction, 1937–1945*. Cambridge, UK: Cambridge University Press, 2010.

Chong, Doryun, Michio Hayashi, Fumihiko Sumitomo, and Kenji Kajiya, eds. *From Postwar to Postmodern, Art in Japan, 1945–1989 (MoMa Primary Documents)*. New York: MOMA, 2012.

Cockcroft, Eve. "Abstract Expressionism, Weapon of the Cold War." *Artsforum* 15, no. 10 (June 1974): 39–41.

Cone, Michele C. *Artists Under Vichy: A Case of Prejudice and Persecution*. Princeton: Princeton University Press, 1992.

Cullerne Bown, Matthew. *Art Under Stalin*. London: Phaedon Press, 1991.

Culver, Annika A. "'Between Distant Realities': The Japanese Avant-Garde, Surrealism, and the Colonies, 1924–1943." PhD diss., University of Chicago, 2007.

Culver, Annika A. *Glorify the Empire: Japanese Avant-Garde Art in Manchukuo*. Vancouver: University of British Columbia Press, 2013.

Culver, Annika A. "The Making of a Japanese Avant-Garde in Colonial Dairen." *History Compass* 5, no. 2 (March 2007): 347–361.

Culver, Annika A. "Manchukuo and the Creation of a New Multi-Ethnic Literature: Kawabata Yasunari's Promotion of 'Manchurian' Culture." In *Sino–Japanese Transculturation: Late Nineteenth Century to the End of the Pacific War*, edited by Richard King, Cody Poulton, and Katsuya Endo, 189–207. Lanham, MD: Lexington Books, 2012.

Denning, Michael. *The Cultural Front: The Laboring of American Culture in the Twentieth Century*. New York: Verso Books, 1996.
Doherty, Thomas. *Hollywood and Hitler, 1933–1939*. New York: Columbia University Press, 2013.
Dower, John. *War Without Mercy: Race and Power in the Pacific War*. New York: Pantheon Books, 1987.
Earhart, David. *Certain Victory: Images of World War II in the Japanese Media*. Armonk, NY: M. E. Sharpe, 2009.
Golomstock, Igor. *Totalitarian Art in the Soviet Union, the Third Reich, Fascist Italy, and the People's Republic of China*. Translated by Robert Chandler. New York: Overlook TP, 2012.
Groys, Boris. *The Total Art of Stalinism: Avant-Garde, Aesthetic Dictatorship, and Beyond*. Translated by Charles Rougle. New York: Verso Books, 2011.
Hewitt, Andrew. *Fascist Modernism: Aesthetics, Politics, and the Avant-Garde*. Stanford: Stanford University Press, 1996.
High, Peter. *The Imperial Screen: Japanese Film Culture in the Fifteen Years' War, 1931–1945*. Madison: University of Wisconsin Press, 2003.
Hinz, Berthold. *Art in the Third Reich*. New York: Pantheon, 1979.
Ikeda, Asato, Aya Louisa McDonald, and Ming Tiampo, eds. *Art and War in Japan and Its Empire, 1931–1960*. Leiden: Koninklijke Brill, 2012.
Ishikawa, Tatsuzô. *Soldiers Alive*. Translated by Zeljko Cipris. Honolulu: University of Hawaii Press, 2003.
Kaido, Kazu, and David Elliott, eds. *Reconstructions: Avant-Garde Art in Japan, 1945–1965: An Exhibition*. New York: Museum of Modern Art, 1985 (digitized in 2009).
Kramer, Hilton. "Art and Politics in the Vichy Period." *The New Criterion* (March 1992). http://www.newcriterion.com/articles.cfm/Art-politics-in-the-Vichy-period-4518.
Lastra, James F. "Why Is this Absurd Picture Here? Ethnology/Equivocation/Buñuel." *October* 89 (Summer 1999): 51–68. http://www.jstor.org/stable/779139.
McCloskey, Barbara. *Artists of World War II (Artists of an Era)*. Westport, CT: Greenwood Press, 2005.
Meyer, Susan E. *Norman Rockwell's World War II: Impressions from the Home Front*. San Antonio, TX: USAA Foundation, 1991.
Michaud, Eric. *The Cult of Art in Nazi Germany (Cultural Memory in the Present)*. Stanford: Stanford University Press, 2004.
Munroe, Alexandra. *Japanese Art After 1945: Scream Against the Sky*. New York: Harry Abrams, 1996.
Plamper, Jan. *The Stalin Cult: A Study in the Alchemy of Power*. New Haven: Yale University Press, 2012.
Petropolos, Jonathon. *Art as Politics in the Third Reich*. Chapel Hill: University of North Carolina Press, 1999.
Riding, Alan. *And the Show Went On: Cultural Life in Nazi-Occupied Paris*. New York: Vintage, 2011.
Rousso, Henry. *The Vichy Syndrome: History and Memory in France Since 1944*. Cambridge: Harvard University Press, 1994.
Schlenker, Ines. *Hitler's Salon: The "Grosse Deutsche Kunstausstellung" at the Haus der Deutschen Kunst in Munich, 1937–1944*. New York: Peter Lang, 2007.
Spotts, Frederic. *Hitler and the Power of Aesthetics*. New York: Overlook Books, 2003.
Steinweis, Alan. *Art, Ideology, and Economics in Nazi Germany: The Reich Chambers of Music, Theater, and the Visual Arts*. Chapel Hill: University of North Carolina Press, 1993.

Urwand, Ben. *The Collaboration: Hollywood's Pact with Hitler*. Cambridge, MA: Harvard University Press, 2013.
Weisenfeld, Gennifer. *MAVO: Japanese Artists and the Avant-Garde, 1905–1931*. Berkeley: University of California Press, 2001.
Werckmeister, O. K. "Hitler the Artist." *Critical Inquiry* 23 (1997): 270–297.
Williams, Raymond. *The Politics of Modernism: Against the Rise of the New Conformists*. New York: Verso Books, 2007.
Young, Louise. *Japan's Total Empire: Manchuria and the Culture of Wartime Imperialism*. Berkeley: University of California Press, 1998.

CHAPTER 31

POSTWAR SETTLEMENTS AND INTERNATIONALISM

REGINA GRAMER AND YUTAKA SASAKI

Due to its character as a "total war" in which participants, victorious and defeated nations alike, had mobilized their resources to the fullest extent, World War II created a unique necessity, as well as opportunity, to establish a new peaceful postwar world order. The unprecedented violence, destruction, and global reach of the war spurred the search for new international rules and institutions, and it resulted in one of history's most comprehensive global reorganizations.[1] In the realm of politics, the creation of multilateral organizations such as the United Nations signaled a renewed momentum toward great power cooperation and away from balance-of-power politics. In the realm of economics, negotiations over an open system of non-discriminatory trade and finance culminated in the Bretton Woods agreements providing an alternative to bilateral trade and imperial preference systems. And in the realm of international security, an entirely new notion emerged as nation states conceptualized and pursued national security in the form of economic prosperity and reconstruction as well as disarmament, reparations, and occupation. The dual crises of the Great Depression and World War II sparked a new awareness of a precariously interdependent world, a renewed pursuit of decolonization and global development, and an unprecedented re-integration of aggressor nations, in this case Germany and Japan, into a reconstructed postwar liberal capitalist order. Together, these new norms and institutions are often referred to as "liberal international order" or "liberal multilateralism."[2]

Until the collapse of the Soviet Union in 1991, World War II was invariably considered a mere prelude to the Cold War, in particular with regard to its aftermath, the creation of a new postwar international order. The results of the diplomatic negotiations at the Yalta and Potsdam conferences, and the creation of the United Nations and the Bretton Woods system were typically evaluated from the vantage point of Cold War stability, irrespective of scholars' political positions.[3] So imminent was the threat of nuclear annihilation and so omnipresent was the pain of East–West division that World War II studies had, in the eyes of at least one eminent U.S. diplomatic historian, as late as 2001 not yet liberated itself from "Cold War colonization."[4] This is ironic in at least two respects. For one, new post-Cold War scholarship increasingly employs a global, i.e. post-colonial, lens to the study of World War II—"arguably the only global war in history."[5] And for the other, decolonization is the operative concept to understand both the unique characteristics of World War II's postwar settlements as well as the new developments in post-Cold War scholarship on 1940s internationalism.

Expanded views of the Cold War, challenging its bipolarity and emphasizing its embeddedness in broader historical developments such as globalization, actually help to accentuate the unique and unprecedented characteristics of the settlements of World War II.[6] What was new was, above all, the challenge to restore peace after a genocidal war. It was Adolf Hitler's conquest through "demographic revolution"[7] that made World War II different from World War I and any other prior war, even though the Big Three never discussed the Holocaust, Jewish refugees, or Palestine at Potsdam.[8] New, too, was the response to restructure and rebuild the defeated enemy countries. American postwar planners insisted not only on Germany's and Japan's unconditional surrender, but also on their disarmament, occupation, and regional reintegration.[9] Also new was the global and multifaceted nature of wartime anti-colonialism, whether it took the form of military conquest as in the case of the Greater East Asia Co-Prosperity Sphere; American, Soviet, and Chinese opposition to British, Dutch, and French imperialism; or Latin American initiatives for its hemispheric security and state-led developmentalism.[10]

This is not to argue against any continuity. Anti-colonialism, for instance, had been on the agenda at the Versailles Peace Conference in 1919.[11] The United Nations clearly followed in the footsteps of the failed League of Nations, in particular with regard to principles of collective security, multilateralism, and self-determination.[12] And, American power was preeminent at the end of both world wars, along with its pursuit of an open world economy and a global democratic order.[13] The leaders of World War II carefully looked back to the failures of the World War I settlement as they planned for a new world order after 1945. They were focused more directly on state-level social welfare than on individual human rights.[14]

BLUEPRINTS FOR THE POSTWAR WORLD ORDER: THE ATLANTIC AND PACIFIC CHARTERS

The first important statement by the Allied powers for the creation of a new world order was the Atlantic Charter issued by U.S. President Franklin D. Roosevelt and British Prime Minister Winston Churchill on August 14, 1941. The principles of the Atlantic Charter stipulated no territorial aggrandizement, national self-determination, free and equal access to trade for all nations, freedom from fear and want, and the establishment of a wider and permanent system of general security. The Charter represented "an American effort to insure [sic] that Britain signed onto its liberal democratic war aims,"[15] and became the lodestar for the postwar world, in part because its principles were applied to the defeated Axis powers as well.

The principles enunciated in the Atlantic Charter reflected the liberal internationalist ideals championed by Woodrow Wilson's Fourteen Points as well as part of the Franklin Roosevelt's Four Freedoms (freedom of speech, expression, and worship, and freedom from want and fear).[16] Even though the statement at that time was no more than a press release by the leaders of a belligerent nation (Britain) and a neutral power (the U.S. had not entered the war at this point), it was incorporated into the "Declaration by United Nations" signed by representatives of twenty-six nations (including the Soviet Union and China) on January 1, 1942, thus providing the basic framework of war and peace aims of the United Nations. Given that the Atlantic Charter was deemed relatively innocuous at that time, it may come as a surprise that the question of its universal applicability turned into a hotly disputed issue, even between Roosevelt and Churchill.[17]

One of the most important questions regarding the postwar world involved "territorial settlements," including not only the mandatory territories (enemy colonial territories) entrusted by the League of Nations to Japan and Italy after World War I, but also colonies ruled by the major Allied powers of the United Kingdom and France. The United States took the position that all dependent peoples should eventually be allowed to exercise the right of sovereignty to decide on the body politic under which they would live. Like Woodrow Wilson, President Roosevelt viewed competition for overseas markets and raw materials as a fundamental cause of war, and he feared the continued existence of colonial empires as a potential cause of future wars.[18] Following his strong anti-colonial views, Roosevelt preached "the gospel of independence," especially to the officials of the British government, including its Prime Minister, Winston Churchill, an ardent defender of the British Empire. When Churchill visited the United States within two weeks after the Pearl Harbor attack in late 1941, for example, Roosevelt urged Churchill to make a promise of Indian independence by establishing a timetable for it.[19] The American president was a gradualist, advocating for the eventual independence of colonial peoples only after "a period of tutelage" by the "parent" states sanctioned by a new international organization. This approach was crystalized by the doctrine of "trusteeship," under which non-self-governing territories were administered by a soon-to-be-created trusteeship council of a new international organization.[20]

Anti-colonialism was an essential, if contested and inconsistent, aspect of postwar planning, not only from the Anglo–American perspective.[21] The Chinese leader Chiang Kai-shek, for instance, urged President Roosevelt as early as January 1942 to push the British and Dutch to extend the principles of the Atlantic Charter to their own colonies. Eager to bolster its own full independence, China specifically supported immediate independence for India, Korea, and Indochina. Advocating on behalf of Asian nationalism, the Chinese government issued the Pacific Charter in the summer of 1942.

Designed to complement the Atlantic Charter, the Pacific Charter called for a complete defeat of Japan, positive national self-government, and racial equality. Having fought Japanese aggression four years longer than the United States, China needed material and political support from the United States for ending colonialism in Asia. However, both leaders did not have each other's full support and failed to lock in decolonization during their wartime meetings. While President Roosevelt worked toward his idea of an international trusteeship for both Korea and Indochina, Chiang pursued an immediate independence for Korea and Chinese "big brother" status over Indochina.[22]

When Roosevelt and Churchill met in Casablanca, Morocco, in January 1943, they formally announced that the Allies would seek "unconditional surrender" of the Axis powers, meaning that no peace terms would be discussed until after they surrendered without any conditions attached. This formula was adopted mainly because of the lesson of the armistice of 1918 in which the Germans, having approached President Wilson, succeeded in obtaining a peace settlement on the basis of the Fourteen Points.[23]

The Cairo Conference in November 1943 dealt with war strategies and postwar settlements in Asia. The fact that Chiang Kai-shek was invited to meet with Roosevelt and Churchill clearly signaled that Roosevelt wanted China to play a major role in postwar Asia. Churchill, on the other hand, feared that Roosevelt would bolster China to push back on British imperial holdings in Asia. In October 1943, the Soviet Union had supported the inclusion of China as one of the four major powers. Roosevelt sought to include China as a junior partner in an American-led peace in the Pacific and to show that this was not a racial war, as Japanese war-time propaganda alleged.[24] Roosevelt and Chiang, however, could not agree on a strategy for Korea's independence and missed their chance to strategize on the decolonization of Indochina.[25]

Arguably, the most important summit meeting up to that time took place in Tehran, Iran, between November 28 and December 1, 1943. Franklin Roosevelt, Winston Churchill, and Joseph Stalin met for the first time, discussing not only the coordination of their military strategy against Germany and Japan, but also important issues concerning postwar arrangements. During the Tehran Conference, Roosevelt successfully enlisted the support of Stalin for the termination of French colonial rule in Indochina, as well as his trusteeship scheme. One night during this conference, Churchill, sensing that the president's scheme for international trusteeship would be applied throughout the colonial world, including the British Empire, reacted to it sharply by remarking that "nothing would be taken away from England without a war."[26]

At Tehran the "Big Three" agreed that Germany was to be partitioned into Allied zones of occupation, that the German–Polish border would be moved to the Oder and Neisse rivers to compensate Poland for the loss of territory due to the annexation of Poland's eastern border into the Soviet Union, and that the Soviet Union would acquire the Kurile Islands and Southern Sakhalin from Japan in exchange for a Soviet declaration of war against Japan.[27] Moreover, Roosevelt privately discussed with Stalin the creation of an international organization designed to maintain "international security and peace." This prospective international organization was to be dominated by the Four Policemen: the United States, Great Britain, the Soviet Union, and China.[28]

NEW ECONOMIC ORDER, NEW POLITICAL ORDER

Regarding a new economic order, negotiations between American and British officials began as early as 1941. Led by Harry Dexter White, the U.S. Treasury Department discussed competing visions and schemes of postwar economic arrangements with British policy experts under the leadership of Sir John Maynard Keynes. By the end of 1943, a broad consensus on principles and technical positions had emerged; that is, an open multilateral trading system coupled with measures to ensure employment stability.[29]

At the same time, the discussion on the prospective postwar international order to maintain security and peace of the world was also in progress. In the Moscow Conference held in October 1943, U.S. Secretary of State Cordell Hull secured the consent of the foreign ministers of the United Kingdom, the Soviet Union, and China to jointly sign a declaration to create "a general international organization, based on the principle of the sovereign equality of all peace-loving states, and open to membership by all such states, large and small, for the maintenance of international peace and security."[30] In July 1944, forty-four nations convened for two weeks at Bretton Woods, New Hampshire to address the economic cause of World War II. The world economy had collapsed due to the deterioration of the balance of trade, which led each state to resort to devaluate its own currency. Not only had the Axis powers created closed trading blocks, but Great Britain's imperial preference system had created its own sterling block. Therefore, especially in the eyes of American planners, the postwar economic order was to be based on the free flow of trade and capital, and currency stability in a multilateral open economy.[31] Negotiations mainly took place between the American delegation led by White and the British delegation led by Keynes. While Keynes developed an ambitious plan involving new mechanisms for both the orderly adjustment of exchange rates and the mobilization of credit to protect debtor nations from deflation, White aimed for a more modest relief fund with limited obligations for creditor nations.[32] The agreements at Bretton Woods reflected a compromise between two objectives. The first objective was to establish a stable system of exchange rates for the expanding global economy. The second objective was to promote full employment, social welfare, and national economic health without resorting to inflation and currency depreciation. To achieve these twin objectives, the conferees agreed to establish the International Monetary Fund, the International Bank for Reconstruction and Development, and the International Trade Organization. Overall, the agreements at Bretton Woods conformed to White's plan, which clearly reflected the imbalance of power between the United States as creditor nation and Great Britain as debtor nation. Instead of the new international currency Keynes had proposed, the U.S. dollar became the lead currency; that is, the only gold convertible currency with all other currencies pegged against the dollar. Nevertheless, the Bretton Woods agreements were a unique, if forgotten, blend of laissez-faire economics and welfare-state interventionism.[33]

Beginning in the late 1930s, Latin American policymakers were instrumental in working closely with U.S. officials to map out a development-friendly international order. During the Bretton Woods negotiations, policymakers from China, India, the Philippines, and eastern Europe also supported the idea of state-led development. China, which had brought the second-largest delegation after the United States, submitted a formal alternative to the Keynes and White plans. Receiving the fourth-largest quota and voting share in the Bretton Woods institutions, China took on the role of championing the development goals of the less-industrialized countries. Thus, the Cold War did not so much initiate as undermine the international development agenda hammered out at Bretton Woods.[34]

To draft the charter of the United Nations, representatives of the United States, Great Britain, the Soviet Union, and China, joined by the delegates from thirty-four other nations, met at Dumbarton Oaks in Washington, DC, from August 21st through October 7th, 1944. Elaborately planned by the U.S. Department of State, the conference was composed of the Anglo–American–Soviet phase (August 21–September 28) and the Anglo–American–Chinese phase (September 29–October 7). Conversations were kept informal and exploratory, especially during the Chinese phase in order not to undermine the fragile Anglo–American agreements.[35] The Dumbarton Oaks Proposals named collective security as the major purpose of the organization, "to take collective measures for the prevention and removal of threats to the peace and the suppression of acts of aggression or other breaches of the peace, and to bring about by peaceful means adjustment or settlement of international disputes which may lead to a breach of the peace."[36]

The proposed Security Council was composed of representatives of the United States, Great Britain, the Soviet Union, China, and "in due course" France.[37] It reflected Roosevelt's conception of "the Four Policeman," assuming the continuation of war-time cooperation among the United States, Great Britain, the Soviet Union, and China. Unresolved were the voting system of the Security Council and the question of the membership for individual Soviet republics. Regarding the veto power of the permanent members of the Security Council, the Soviet Union insisted on blanket veto power and the United States opposed it. It was agreed that this matter was to be settled at the Yalta Conference.[38]

The subject of trusteeship was completely omitted from discussion at the Dumbarton Oaks conference even though the U.S. Department of State had drafted a "Declaration by the United Nations on National Independence" in early 1943 to establish an "International Trusteeship Administration" for the purpose of transitioning colonial peoples toward independence.[39] British officials had objected to the goal of "independence" and sought to avoid any binding international accountability for the colonial powers.[40] British opposition was so strong that both governments did not issue a joint statement on the colonial question. After the Dumbarton Oaks conference, the American position on trusteeship shifted as well due to pressure from the Navy and War Departments. To protect American security interests in the Japanese mandated islands, trust territories were to be classified as either "non-strategic" or "strategic" areas, with the latter coming under the supervision of the Security Council rather than the General

Assembly or Trusteeship Council of the proposed new international organization. This proposal was submitted to the other major powers prior to the United Nations conference at San Francisco.[41]

The second summit meeting of the Big Three was held in Yalta from February 4 to 11, 1945. In this one-week conference on the Crimean Peninsula, Roosevelt, Churchill, and Stalin made several important decisions regarding the execution of the war, as well as the shape of the postwar world. Stalin renewed his pledge to go to war against Japan a few months after the German surrender. As a quid pro quo, Roosevelt agreed to give Stalin a "sphere of influence" in the Far East; the Soviets were allowed to annex the Southern part of Sakhalin Island and the Kurile Islands (located off the coast of Hokkaido), to control the operation of the Manchurian railroads, and to use Dairen and Port Author ports on the Liaotung Peninsula.[42] As for the treatment of a defeated Germany, the three leaders agreed to unconditional surrender and dismemberment. The Big Three planned to hold supreme authority and allocate a French zone of occupation. Germany was to assume responsibility for reparations in kind "to the greatest extent possible" to be discussed by an Allied reparations commission in Moscow.[43]

The Polish question dominated discussions at Yalta. The three leaders agreed to move the Polish–Soviet border westward to the Curzon line, with Poland receiving territorial compensation from the eastern part of Germany.[44] The formation of a Polish government was contentious. The Soviets recognized the provisional government in Lublin while the British and Americans urged the provisional government in London, composed mostly of anti-Soviet Polish exiles, to create a unified Polish government.[45] While Churchill advocated free elections, Stalin prioritized establishing a Soviet-friendly Polish government first and free elections later.[46] Neither Roosevelt nor Churchill openly challenged Stalin's demands for the sake of great-power cooperation.[47] In the Allied declaration on the future of Poland, the United States and Great Britain essentially surrendered Poland to Soviet control, according to one historian.[48]

The trusteeship question remained unresolved at Yalta. Churchill argued forcefully against any outside interference or change to the British Empire.[49] It was decided that the planned members of the Security Council would consult each other before the United Nations organizing conference. The three leaders agreed that territorial trusteeship would only apply to existing League of Nations mandates, territory to be detached from the enemy, and any other territory that may voluntarily be placed under trusteeship.[50] One can argue that Roosevelt retreated from the Atlantic Charter principles by not insisting to include all colonial holdings in trusteeship deliberations, while Churchill relented in failing to exclude British League of Nations mandates, notably Tanganyika.[51]

Regarding the formation of the United Nations, the three leaders agreed to call for a conference to start in San Francisco on April 25, 1945.[52] The controversy over the veto power of the permanent members of the Security Council in voting procedures appeared resolved for the time being.[53] While the permanent members of the Security Council would retain veto power on "nonprocedural (or substantive) matters," a permanent member involved in a dispute could not veto "procedural matters."[54]

On June 26, 1945, after two months of tense negotiations, fifty nations signed the United Nations Charter in San Francisco, officially signaling the birth of a new international organization to succeed the defunct League of Nations. It was, from its inception, an international organization whose real powers resided, to the dismay of the colonized and developing countries, in the victorious Big Powers.[55] In this sense, the United Nations Charter institutionalized the wartime alliance of the Great Powers, including its abandonment of liberating colonized peoples.[56]

For one, the representatives of the United States, the Soviet Union, the United Kingdom, China, and France accepted the American proposal to divide trusteeship territories into "strategic" and "non-strategic" trusts with the former reporting to the Security Council, not to the proposed General Assembly's Trusteeship Council.[57] For the other, declaring "independence" for Europe's colonial possessions remained controversial. While China and the Soviet Union favored the term "independence," the British opted for the term "self-government" in the proposed statement of the general policy vis-à-vis non-self-governing territories to forestall a rapid dissolution of the British Empire. The United States backed the British position, arguing that self-government was one form of independence.[58] In the end, the word "independence" was not inserted in Article 73 on non-self-governing territories, although, with the backing of the U.S. delegation, it found its way into Article 76 dealing with the objectives of the trusteeship system. Even though the U.S. delegation was more focused on improving its anti-imperialist image than actually dismantling colonialism,[59] one can argue that it helped to legitimize decolonization in the long run.[60]

The issue of Great Power "veto" right turned contentious again. While the "smaller" nations, who did not belong to the Security Council, were interested in weakening the veto power of the Great Powers, the Soviet Union pursued "absolute veto power" to block issues from even reaching the Security Council. After difficult negotiations, Stalin agreed with the U.S. position to hold firm on veto power, but to give up on "absolute veto power."[61] A group of nations, including New Zealand and Australia, demanded for the Security Council to secure the concurrence of the General Assembly in enforcement action, including the use of armed forces, and for the General Assembly the right to discuss and make recommendations on any matters "within the sphere of international relations."[62] In opposition, the Great Powers cited the ineffectiveness of the Council of the League of Nations to justify the Security Council's sole enforcement authority. A compromise was reached with a new formulation for Article 10 of the Charter: "The General Assembly has the right to discuss any questions or any matters within the scope of the Charter or relating to the powers and functions of any organs provided for in the Charter."[63] Hence, even though the General Assembly's right of discussion was expanded, the power of the Security Council, as laid out in the Dumbarton Oaks proposal, remained in force.

The right of collective self-defense created another conflict between the Great Powers and the "smaller" nations. Shortly before the San Francisco conference, the Latin American nations had adopted the Act of Chapultepec stipulating collective self-defense in case of aggression against any one of them. They thus challenged the power of the Security Council to veto any action by a regional block, as set out in the Dumbarton Oaks proposal. The U.S. delegates faced the formidable dilemma of keeping Latin America committed to the new international organization while not eroding the Security Council's global reach.[64] After much deliberation, the U.S. delegation proposed a new concept of self-defense, which departed from the Dumbarton Oaks proposal and formulated an "inherent right of individual or collective self-defense." After securing approval from the Latin delegations and the Big Five, the proposed amendment was embodied in two separate articles (namely Articles 51 and 52) of the United Nations Charter. The wording of Article 51 made clear that the regional arrangements should operate independently only in self-defense and in the event of failure of the Security Council to act, thereby making the right of collective self-defense explicitly "inherent" without impairing the idea of global security.[65] Article 52 provided the legal basis for the creation of major regional security pacts, including NATO, SEATO, CENTO, and the Warsaw Pact, all of which were established in the early Cold War.[66]

Even though the participant nations of the San Francisco conference were united in their hope to avoid another catastrophic world war, they had different objectives and values in participating in the new international organization. The Soviet Union regarded the UN as a useful vehicle for guaranteeing Russian prestige and hegemony in the Eastern Europe, especially through the use of veto power. Great Britain and France welcomed the United Nations as an organization that could buttress collective security through the participation of the United States, while at the same time viewing it as an useful supplement to traditional diplomacy. China viewed the UN as an international organization that could enhance its prestige by following the lead of the United States. For the "smaller" nations, the UN could serve as a means to exert its collective influence based on the notion of "sovereign equality" of all participant nations. Finally, the United States regarded the UN as an organization that could serve as a means to spread liberal internationalism through its determined leadership. Thus, far from being an organization that could function as a highly centralized "world government," the newborn international organization was in fact "a mirror image of the prevailing system of nation-states."[67]

The last meeting of the Big Three, which took place at Potsdam, outside Berlin, from July 17 to August 2, 1945, underscored the power of white Americans, Britons, and Russians to set the terms of the peace.[68] The only non-whites present were Filipino waiters employed by the Americans and Central Asian soldiers in Red Army uniforms. With Germany having signed an unconditional surrender on May 8, 1945 and with the war with Japan entering its final phase, the discussion focused mainly on the postwar settlements for Germany and Poland, and the Allied strategy to end the war in the Pacific theater.

The Allied powers agreed on the general goals of postwar German demilitarization, denazification, democratization, and economic decentralization "for the purpose of eliminating the present excessive concentration of economic power as exemplified in particular by cartels, syndicates, trusts and other monopolistic arrangements."[69] However, how and when to exact reparations became a major issue. While British and

American diplomats considered German economic recovery essential for European reconstruction, and hence prioritized recovery over reparations, Soviet diplomats wanted to exact reparations prior to German recovery and indeed had already started to strip the eastern zone of Germany of all removable industrial capital equipment (i.e., reparations in kind).[70] The Americans then proposed for each occupying power to exact reparations from its own zone. This zonal reparations scheme resulted in "the abandonment of four-power cooperation in Germany"[71] and, intentionally or not, in the eventual division of Germany.[72] In the long run, the Big Three envisioned the Germans "to take their place among the free and peaceful peoples of the world."[73]

Regarding Poland, the Big Three agreed to move its western border to the Oder–Neisse line to compensate for the concession of the eastern border area to the Soviet Union. The rift over the Polish Provisional Government, however, grew. Based on their understanding of Yalta, that the Soviet Union would allow for free elections, the United States and Great Britain had recognized the new government in Warsaw just before the Potsdam Conference. Stalin, on the other hand, did not act in accordance with the "Declaration of Liberated Europe" issued at Yalta. The U.S. delegation strongly objected to the pro-Soviet governments installed in Rumania, Hungary, and Bulgaria, as well as in Poland.[74] On the other hand, President Truman knew he needed to respect Soviet security concerns in Eastern Europe to not jeopardize U.S.–Soviet cooperation for the successful launching of the United Nations and the control of Germany.[75]

In the Far East, American and Soviet strategic interests clashed as well. Stalin sought Soviet participation in the postwar occupation of Japan in order to forestall any future Japanese military threat.[76] Truman, by contrast, initially pursued Soviet support in defeating Japan, but, given the increasing tension in Europe and Soviet unilateral actions in the Far East, he wanted to avert a joint occupation.[77] After learning about the successful detonation of "a powerful new weapon" on July 16, Truman concluded that the United States could defeat Japan without the help of the Soviet Union.[78] On July 24, Truman told Stalin that his country developed a new bomb, "far more destructive than any other known bomb," and planned to use it against Japan; Stalin reportedly encouraged Truman matter-of-factly to do so.[79] This brief conversation was the most dramatic moment of the Potsdam Conference, the starting point of the arms race between the United States and the Soviet Union.

On July 26, 1945, the United States, the UK, and China issued the so-called Potsdam Declaration, calling for unconditional surrender of Japan to avoid "the inevitable and complete destruction of the Japanese forces and just as inevitably the utter devastation of the Japanese homeland."[80] They clarified, though, that Japan shall not be "destroyed as [a] nation,"[81] and ultimately be granted to rejoin the international community. Projecting to end the postwar occupation of Japan as soon as a peaceful government was restored, they granted the option to retain the emperor institution. The Japanese Premier Suzuki declined to accept unconditional surrender and the stated goals of "liberal integrationism."[82] According to the recollection of the U.S. Secretary of State Byrnes, "There was nothing to do but use the bomb."[83]

The Soviet Union was not invited to co-sign the Potsdam Declaration, as Truman believed the U.S. would be able to defeat Japan without Soviet support.[84] While no detailed discussions of the amount of Japanese reparations were conducted during the Potsdam Conference, the Potsdam Declaration required Japan to pay reparations. As in the case of Germany, the Allies intended for reparations not to undermine economic recovery and international trade.[85] Edwin Pauley, head of the U.S. presidential reparations mission, emphasized "Japan should be left enough export industry to make possible the imports which she must have."[86] To be sure, Japanese officials found the U.S. reparations program too harsh.[87]

Conclusion

The surrender of the Axis forces in Italy on May 2, Nazi Germany on May 8, and Imperial Japan on September 2, 1945, brought World War II to its official end. The United States had started to plan for a new postwar order on September 16, 1939, a mere two weeks after the outbreak of war in Europe.[88] Postwar planning was inspired by the principles of liberal internationalism and the lessons drawn from the failed settlements after World War I.[89] The United Nations, the Bretton Woods system, and the Tokyo and Nuremberg Trials, were all characteristic embodiments of liberal internationalism; they institutionalized a new era of multilateral governance whose greatest accomplishment was the avoidance of a third world war. It has often been pointed out that postwar planners had neither anticipated the level of physical destruction of World War II, nor the emerging Cold War. It is also true, however, that the Big Three did not make the prevention of the unprecedented human cost of this total war a priority in their settlements; this concerns not only the victims of genocide and expulsion, but also the victims of mass rape and strategic bombing.[90]

Moreover, the limitations of postwar planning were all too clear regarding decolonization. As for the Indo–China conflict, the United States abandoned international administration and, with British support, recognized the restoration of French sovereignty. In the case of Korea, instead of the projected independence there emerged permanent division. In the aftermath of the sudden collapse of the Japanese empire, the United States and Soviet Union sent troops to the Korean Peninsula and the thirty-eighth parallel became the demarcation line between American and Soviet forces.[91] While the United States continued to oppose European imperialism, it also wanted to avoid the establishment of pro-communist governments in Asia. The Western fear of revolutionary nationalism was reinforced by the victory of the Chinese communists led by Mao Zedong in Mainland China in 1949 and its perceived domino effect in Asia. Choosing anti-communism over anti-colonialism, the United States ended up acting as an "imperial proxy" as it became involved in the Korean and Vietnam Wars.[92]

Even though the Soviet Union quickly veered away from the Bretton Woods arrangements and the Soviet–American rivalry undermined collective governance, post-Cold War research reaffirms the progressive and global elements of wartime negotiations. The Bretton Woods Conference, for one, was a truly multilateral affair, the first large-scale multilateral North–South dialogue on global finance and governance, a meeting of colonial, anti-colonial, and postcolonial minds which, absent any Cold War divide, introduced a "new form of Southern agency,"[93] however limited its reach.

At a time of resurgent protectionism and nationalism, the settlements of World War II face multiple challenges today. It remains to be seen whether "The New Atlantic Charter," issued by President Joseph Biden and Prime Minister Boris Johnson on June 10, 2021, can create the momentum necessary to address the increasingly urgent long-term consequences of World War II and its liberal multilateralist settlement.[94] Substantiating the widespread concern over the sustainability of global economic growth, the International Monetary Fund has identified income inequality as "the defining challenge of our time."[95] While the United States has violated WTO rules and acted as an "illiberal hegemon," the Bretton Woods institutions have been undermined further.[96] China, the new motor of the global economy, has been building parallel financial institutions and may develop its own power block due to its obvious underrepresentation in the International Monetary Fund.[97] The United Nations has been struggling to address major conflicts and challenges—among them the rise of armed conflict, climate change, cybercrime, and global economic instability.[98] Russia's 2022 invasion of Ukraine has revived the long-standing issue of how to limit the use of veto power by the members of the five permanent members of the Security Council. Absent any global war, almost 70.8 million individuals were forcibly displaced worldwide by the end of 2018,[99] a record number projected to grow to 117 million in 2023,[100] and topping the sixty million persons displaced during and immediately after the end of World War II.[101] The postwar liberal international order has indeed forestalled a third world war, but not the social crisis of a world at war.

Notes

1. G. John Ikenberry, *After Victory: Institutions, Strategic Restraint, and the Rebuilding of Order after Major Wars*, new ed. (Princeton: Princeton University Press, 2019), 163.
2. G. John Ikenberry, "A World Economy Restored: Expert Consensus and the Anglo-American Postwar Settlement," *International Organization* 46 (December 1992): 289–290; G. John Ikenberry, "Liberal Internationalism 3.0: America and the Dilemmas of Liberal World Order," *Perspectives on Politics* 7 (March 2009): 76–80.
3. Gabriel Kolko, *The Politics of War: The World and United States Foreign Policy, 1943–1945* (New York: Random House, 1968); John L. Gaddis, *The United States and the Origins of the Cold War, 1941–1947* (New York: Columbia University Press, 1972).
4. Warren F. Kimball, "The Incredible Shrinking War: The Second World War, Not (Just) the Origins of the Cold War," *Diplomatic History* 25 (Summer 2001): 349.
5. Ibid., 348.
6. Allen Hunter, ed., *Rethinking the Cold War* (Philadelphia: Temple University Press, 1998), 7; Oscar Sanchez-Sibony, *Red Globalization: The Political Economy of the Soviet Cold War from Stalin to Khrushchev* (Cambridge: Cambridge University Press, 2014), 245–253.

7. Gerhard L. Weinberg, "World War II: Comments on the Roundtable," *Diplomatic History* 25 (Summer 2001): 495–496.
8. Michael Neiberg, *Potsdam: The End of World War II and the Remaking of Europe* (New York: Basic Books, 2015), 253–254.
9. Patrick J. Hearden, *Architects of Globalism: Building a New World Order during World War II* (Fayetteville: University of Arkansas Press, 2002), 229–284.
10. Gary R. Hess, "War and Empire: The Transformation of Southern Asia," in *A Companion to World War II*, Vol. I, ed. Thomas W. Zeiler, with Daniel M. DuBois (West Sussex: Wiley-Blackwell, 2013), 124–140; Eric Helleiner, *Forgotten Foundations of Bretton Woods: International Development and the Making of the Postwar Order* (Ithaca: Cornell University Press, 2014); Kevin M. Kruse and Stephen Tuck, eds., *Fog of War: The Second World War and the Civil Rights Movement* (New York: Oxford University Press, 2012).
11. Erez Manela Dunwalke, *The Wilsonian Moment: Self-Determination and the International Origins of Anticolonial Nationalism* (New York: Oxford University Press, 2007).
12. M. Patrick Cottrell, "Lost in Transition? The League of Nations and the United Nations," in *Charter of the United Nations: Together with Scholarly Commentaries and Essential Historical Documents*, ed. Ian Shapiro and Joseph Lampert (New Haven: Yale University Press, 2014), 91–106.
13. Ikenberry, *After Victory*, 117–162.
14. Samuel Moyn, *The Last Utopia: Human Rights in History* (Cambridge: The Belknap Press of Harvard University Press, 2010); Samuel Moyn, "Die neue Historiographie der Menschenrechte," *Geschichte und Gesellschaft* 38 (2012): 545–572.
15. Ikenberry, *After Victory*, 173.
16. For an emphasis on the human security implications of the Atlantic Charter, see Elizabeth Borgwardt, *A New Deal for the World: America's Vision for Human Rights* (Cambridge: The Belknap Press of Harvard University Press, 2005).
17. Theodore A. Wilson, *The First Summit: Roosevelt and Churchill at Placentia Bay*, rev. ed. (Lawrence: The University of Kansas Press, 1991), 226–227; Lloyd C. Gardner, "The Atlantic Charter: Idea and Reality, 1942–1945," in *The Atlantic Charter*, ed. Douglas Brinkley and David R. Facey-Crowther (New York: St. Martin's Press, 1994), 459–460.
18. Wm. Roger Louis, *Imperialism at Bay, 1941–1945: The United States and the Decolonization of the British Empire* (Oxford: Oxford University Press, 1977), 3.
19. Warren F. Kimball, *The Juggler: Franklin Roosevelt as Wartime Statesman* (Princeton: Princeton University Press, 1991), 133; David F. Schmitz, *The Sailor: Franklin D. Roosevelt and the Transformation of American Foreign Policy* (Lexington: University Press of Kentucky, 2021), Chapter 6.
20. Louis, *Imperialism at Bay*, 3.
21. Gardner, "The Atlantic Charter," 45–81.
22. Xiaoyuan Liu, *Recast All Under Heaven: Revolution, War, Diplomacy, and Frontier China in the 20th Century* (New York: Continuum, 2010), 39–84.
23. Warren F. Kimball, *Forged in War: Roosevelt, Churchill, and the Second World War* (New York: William Morrow and Company, 1997), 188–191; Gaddis Smith, "Unconditional Surrender," in *Encyclopedia of U.S. Foreign Relations*, Vol. 4, ed. Bruce W. Jentleson and Thomas G. Paterson, (New York: Oxford University Press, 1997), 232.
24. Kimball, *Juggler*, 129, 131; Christopher Thorne, *The Issue of War: States, Societies, and the Far Eastern Conflict of 1941–1945* (New York: Oxford University Press, 1985), chapters 5, 6.
25. Liu, *Recast All Under Heaven*, 64–67.

26. Kimball, *Juggler*, 143.
27. Tsuyoshi Hasegawa, *Racing the Enemy: Stalin, Truman, and the Surrender of Japan* (Cambridge, MA: Harvard University Press, 2005), 25.
28. Ruth B. Russell, *A History of the United Nations Charter* (Washington, DC: Brookings Institution, 1958), 154–156.
29. Ikenberry, "A World Economy Restored," 289–321.
30. Russell, *A History of the United Nations Charter*, 134.
31. Ikenberry, "A World Economy Restored," 297-298, 305–308.
32. Benn Steil, *The Battle of Bretton Woods: John Maynard Keynes, Harry Dexter White, and the Making of New World Order* (Princeton: Princeton University Press, 2013), 123–154.
33. Ikenberry, "A World Economy Restored," 294–295 ; Thomas McCormick, "The Long American Century, 1870–2000: Hegemony and the Cycles of Capitalism" (unpublished paper), 17–18.
34. Helleiner, *Forgotten Foundations of Bretton Woods*, 1–28, 184–200, 258–277.
35. Russell, *A History of the United Nations Charter*, 392–394, 411–416; Robert C. Hilderbrand, *Dumbarton Oaks: The Origins of the United Nations and the Search for Postwar Security* (Chapel Hill: The University of North Carolina Press, 1990), 229.
36. Russell, *A History of the United Nations*, 1019; Harley A. Notter, *Postwar Foreign Policy Preparation 1939–1945* (Washington, D.C.: GPO, 1949), 611–612.
37. Great Britain and the Soviet Union supported a permanent security council seat for France after it had formed a new postwar government, while the United States had reservations. Russell, *A History of the United Nations Charter*, 1022; Hilderbrand, *Dumbarton Oaks*, 122–123.
38. Ibid., 183–228; Russell, *A History of the United Nations Charter*, 445–455.
39. Ibid., 85–88; Notter, *Postwar Foreign Policy Preparation*, 109–110, 470–472.
40. Louis, *Imperialism at Bay*, 231–232, 243–258; Russell, *History of the United Nations Charter*, 88–91.
41. Louis, *Imperialism at Bay*, 366–377, 482–484; Hilderbrand, *Dumbarton Oaks*, 174–175; Russell, *A History of the United Nations Charter*, 573, 576–581.
42. U.S. Department of State, *Foreign Relations of the United States, The Conferences at Malta and Yalta* (Washington, DC: GPO, 1955), 378–379, 768–769. At the time, the U.S. military planners believed that a Soviet entry of war against Japan was imperative to avoid a possible very costly war against Japan. It should be noted that the Soviet annexation of the Kurile islands has continued to be a major unresolved diplomatic issue between Russia and Japan, hampering the conclusion of a peace treaty between the two countries even today.
43. Ibid., 611–623, 969–971.
44. Ibid., 667–668, 974.
45. Russell, *A History of the United Nations Charter*, 482–484.
46. FRUS, *The Conferences at Malta and Yalta*, 669–671, 779–781, 973.
47. Kimball, *The Juggler*, 170–171.
48. S. M. Plokhy, *Yalta: The Price of Peace* (New York: Penguin Books, 2010), 249–251.
49. FRUS, *The Conferences at Malta and Yalta*, 844; Louis, *Imperialism at Bay*, 457–458.
50. Ibid., 459–460; FRUS, *The Conferences at Malta and Yalta*, 859, 944–945.
51. James P. Hubbard, *The United States and the End of British Colonial Rule in Africa, 1941–1968* (Jefferson: McFarland, 2014), 20–21.
52. FRUS, *The Conferences at Malta and Yalta*, 971.

53. Ibid., 665–667, 943-944.
54. Ibid., 661. This proposal was already sent to the British and Soviet Governments for consideration in late 1944.
55. Townsend Hoopes and Douglas Brinkley, *FDR and the Creation of the U.N.* (New Haven: Yale University Press, 1997), 184–188, 204.
56. Mark Mazower, *No Enchanted Palace: The End of Empire and the Ideological Origins of the United Nations* (Princeton: Princeton University Press, 2009), 28–65.
57. Russell, *History of the United Nations Charter*, 833–834.
58. Ibid., 813–818.
59. Ibid., 830–832; Stephen C. Schlesinger, Act of Creation: The Founding of the United Nations: A Story of Superpowers, Secret Agents, Wartime Allies and Enemies, and Their Quest for a Peaceful World (Boulder, CO: Westview Press, 2003), 235.
60. Ibid., 235–236; Harold K. Jacobson, "Mandates and Trusteeships," in *Encyclopedia of U.S. Foreign Relations*, Vol. 4, ed. Bruce W. Jentleson and Thomas G. Paterson (New York: Oxford University Press, 1997), 103.
61. Schlesinger, *Act of Creation*, 216–218.
62. Russell, *History of the United Nations Charter*, 750-751, 754-755.; Schlesinger, *Act of Creation*, 193–200.
63. Russell, *History of the United Nations Charter*, 755–775.
64. Hoopes and Brinkley, *FDR and the Creation of the U.N.*, 192–195; Russell, *A History of the United Nations Charter*, 559–566.
65. Russell, *A History of the United Nations Charter*, 688–706.
66. Hoopes and Brinkley, *FDR and the Creation of the U.N.*, 197–198; Schlesinger, *Act of Creation*, 191–192.
67. Hoopes and Brinkley, *FDR and the Creation of the U.N.*, 206–208.
68. Neiberg, *Potsdam*, 159.
69. United States Department of State, *Documents on Germany, 1944–1985* (Washington, DC: Department of State Publication 9446, 1985), 58.
70. Neiberg, *Potsdam*, 183–204.
71. Bruce Kuklick, *American Policy and the Division of Germany: The Clash with Russia over Reparations* (Ithaca and London: Cornell University Press, 1972), 141–166.
72. FRUS, *Conference on Berlin (The Potsdam Conference) 1945*, Vol. II, 1504–1506; Hearden, *Architects of Globalism*, 256; Carolyn Woods Eisenberg, *Drawing the Line: The American Decision to Divide Germany, 1944–1949* (Cambridge: Cambridge University Press, 1996).
73. FRUS, *Conference on Berlin (The Potsdam Conference) 1945*, Vol. II, 1502; Hearden, *Architects of Globalism*, 253–254.
74. Hearden, *Architects of Globalism*, 310–311; FRUS, *Conference on Berlin (The Potsdam Conference) 1945*, Vol. II, 643–644.
75. Melvyn Leffler, *A Preponderance of Power: National Security, the Truman Administration, and the Cold War* (Stanford: Stanford University Press, 1992), 34–35 .
76. *Memoirs by Harry Truman*, Vol. 1: *Year of Decisions* (New York: Doubleday & Company, 1955), 265; Tsuyoshi Hasegawa, "The Soviet Factor in Ending the Pacific War: From the Neutrality Pact to Soviet Entry into the War in August 1945," in *The End of the Pacific War: Reappraisals* (Stanford, CA: Stanford University Press, 2007), ed. Hasegawa, 204–205; David Holloway, "Jockeying for Position in the Postwar World: Soviet Entry into the War with Japan in August 1945" in Ibid., 183.

77. Hearden, *Architects of Globalism*, 280–283.
78. Sean L. Malloy, *Atomic Tragedy: Henry L. Stimson and the Decision to Use the Bomb against Japan* (Ithaca: Cornell University Press, 2008), 133–134.
79. FRUS, *Conference on Berlin (The Potsdam Conference) 1945*, Vol. II, 379. This account is based on the memoir of Secretary of State James Byrnes who recalled: "I was surprised at Stalin's lack of interest." James Byrnes, *Speaking Frankly* (New York: Harper & Brothers, 1947), 263. For a variety of interpretations of Stalin's apparent lack of response, see David Holloway, *Stalin and the Bomb: The Soviet Union and Atomic Energy, 1939–1956* (New Haven: Yale University Press, 1994), 117–118.
80. FRUS, *Conference on Berlin (The Potsdam Conference) 1945*, Vol. II, 1475.
81. Ibid., 1476.
82. Akira Iriye, *Power and Culture: The Japanese and American War 1941–1945* (Cambridge, MA: Harvard University Press, 1981), 253–254.
83. Byrnes, *Speaking Frankly*, 263.
84. Hasegawa, "The Soviet Factor in Ending the Pacific War," 214–218.
85. Iriye, *Power and Culture*, 262–263; Hearden, *Architects of Globalism*, 283.
86. Edwin Pauley, "Report on Japanese Reparations to the President of the United States November 1945 to April 1946, ", 7. https://catalog.hathitrust.org/Record/007426500, accessed on August 7, 2018.
87. Aiko Ikeo, ed., *Japanese Economics and Economists since 1945* (New York: Routledge, 2000), 145–146.
88. Stewart Patrick, *The Best Laid Plans: The Origins of American Multilateralism and the Dawn of the Cold War* (Lanham: Rowman and Littlefield, 2009), 46.
89. Tony Smith, *Why Wilson Matters: The Origin of American Liberal Internationalism and Its Crisis Today* (Princeton: Princeton University Press, 2017), 8–22.
90. John Cooper, *Raphael Lemkin and the Struggle for the Genocide Convention* (New York: Palgrave Macmillan, 2008); Yuki Tanaka and Marilyn B. Young, eds., *Bombing Civilians: A Twentieth-Century History* (New York: The New Press, 2009); Nicola Henry, *War and Rape: Law, Memory, and Justice* (New York: Routledge, 2011).
91. *Memoirs by Harry S. Truman*, Vol. II: *Years of Trial and Hope*, 316–317.
92. Wm. Roger Louis (with Ronald Robinson), "The Imperialism of Decolonization," *The Journal of Imperial and Commonwealth History* 22, no. 3 (1994): 467.
93. Giles Scott-Smith and J. Simon Rofe, eds., *Global Perspectives on the Bretton Woods Conference and the Post-War World Order* (Cham: Palgrave Macmillan, 2017), 1–11.
94. The White House Briefing Room, "The New Atlantic Charter," June 10, 2021, https://www.whitehouse.gov/briefing-room/statements-releases/2021/06/10/the-new-atlantic-charter/, accessed June 14, 2020.
95. IMF Strategy, Policy, and Review Department, *Causes and Consequences of Income Inequality: A Global Perspective*," SDN/15/13 (June 2015), 4, https://www.imf.org/external/pubs/ft/sdn/2015/sdn1513.pdf, accessed June 18, 2015.
96. Gideon Rose, "The Fourth Founding: The United States and the Liberal Order," *Foreign Affairs* 98 (January/February 2019): 10–21; Douglas A. Irwin, "The False Promise of Protectionism: Why Trump's Trade Policy Could Backfire," *Foreign Affairs* 96 (May/June 2017): 45–56.
97. China's voting power in the IMF is currently set at 3.81 percent (measured in voting shares as percentage of total votes), slightly above Italy which weighs in at 3.16 percent. https://www.imf.org/en/About/executive-board/members-quotas, accessed June

23, 2015; George Soros, "A Partnership with China to Avoid World War," *The New York Review of Books* LXII (July 9, 2015): 4–8.
98. Institute for Economics and Peace, *Global Peace Index 2020*, https://www.economicsandpeace.org/wp-content/uploads/2020/08/GPI_2020_web-1.pdf, accessed June 14, 2020; Commission on Global Security, Justice and Governance, *Confronting the Crisis of Global Governance* (June 2015) https://www.stimson.org/wp-content/files/file-attachments/Commission_on_Global_Security_Justice%20_Governance_0.pdf, accessed June 14, 2020; Dimitris Bourantonis, *The History and Politics of UN Security Council Reform* (New York: Routledge, 2005).
99. UN High Commissioner for Refugees (UNHCR), *UNHCR Global Trends: Forced Displacement in 2018* (June 19, 2019), https://www.unhcr.org/globaltrends2018/, accessed June 20, 2019.
100. UN High Commissioner for Refugees (UNHCR), Global Appeal 2023, https://reporting.unhcr.org/globalappeal2023/pdf, accessed January 11, 2023.
101. John Twigg, "World War II," in *Encyclopedia of Disaster Relief*, ed. K. Penuel and Matt Statler (Thousand Oaks: Sage Publications, 2011). Although one can find significantly higher estimates, the number of Chinese refugees alone, for instance, may have reached more than eighty million in World War II. Cf., Rana Mitter, *Forgotten Ally: China's World War II, 1937–1945* (New York: Houghton Mifflin Harcourt, 2013), 5.

Bibliography

Eisenberg, Carolyn Woods. *Drawing the Line: The American Decision to Divide Germany, 1944–1949*. Cambridge: Cambridge University Press, 1996.

Hasegawa, Tsuyoshi, ed. *The End of the Pacific War: Reappraisals*. Stanford, CA: Stanford University Press, 2007.

Hearden, Patrick J. *Architects of Globalism: Building a New World Order during World War II*. Fayetteville: University of Arkansas Press, 2002.

Helleiner, Eric. *Forgotten Foundations of Bretton Woods: International Development and the Making of the Postwar Order*. Ithaca: Cornell University Press, 2014.

Hoopes, Townsend, and Douglas Brinkley. *FDR and the Creation of the U.N.* New Haven: Yale University Press, 1997.

Ikenberry, G. John. *After Victory: Institutions, Strategic Restraint, and the Rebuilding of Order after Major Wars*. New ed. Princeton: Princeton University Press, 2019.

Kimball, Warren F. *The Juggler: Franklin Roosevelt as Wartime Statesman*. Princeton: Princeton University Press, 1991.

Liu, Xiaoyuan. *All Under Heaven: Revolution, War, Diplomacy, and Frontier China in the 20th Century*. New York: Continuum, 2010.

Louis, Wm. Roger. *Imperialism at Bay, 1941–1945: The United States and the Decolonization of the British Empire*. Oxford: Oxford University Press, 1978.

Neiberg, Michael. *Potsdam: The End of World War II and the Remaking of Europe*. New York: Basic Books, 2015.

Plokhy, S. M. *Yalta: The Price of Peace*. New York: Penguin Books, 2010.

Russell, Ruth B. *A History of the United Nations Charter*. Washington, DC: Brookings Institution, 1958.

Schmitz, David F. *The Sailor: Franklin D. Roosevelt and the Transformation of American Foreign Policy.* Lexington: University Press of Kentucky, 2021.

Scott-Smith, Giles, and J. Simon Rofe, eds. *Global Perspectives on the Bretton Woods Conference and the Post-War World Order.* Cham: Palgrave Macmillan, 2017.

CHAPTER 32

REINTEGRATING VETERANS AND DEMOBILIZING POPULATIONS

R. M. DOUGLAS

Considered from the widest perspective, World War II was a demographic conflict. Adolf Hitler's aim was not merely the conquest of *Lebensraum*, but the reconfiguration of the population map of central and eastern Europe through a vast program of forced migrations and mass killings of which even the Holocaust was but a single component.[1] Although internal divisions within the Japanese government precluded the drawing up of any coherent program of war aims, influential figures within official and military circles in Tokyo were also contemplating enormous changes in the Pacific in which large-scale colonization and displacement of existing populations featured prominently.[2] In the end, though, it was a different kind of demographic factor that made the Allied victory all but inevitable. With around two-thirds of the world's population under its banner in 1942, the human, no less than the material, resources available to the anti-Axis coalition were so overwhelming that it is difficult to perceive any possible route to victory for Germany, Japan, and Italy, as long as the Allies were determined to fight to a finish.[3]

Defeating the Axis, all the same, required a huge personnel mobilization effort on the Allies' part. In a war characterized by superlatives—the bloodiest and most economically costly conflict in human history, extending over the greatest territorial field of hostilities—it was predictable that at its close the task of putting the machinery into reverse would also be the largest and most complicated such operation ever attempted. The process of demobilization was far more fraught with difficulty and lasting in its consequences than merely giving the tens of millions of surviving servicemen, and millions of servicewomen, a civilian "demob" suit and a travel warrant to their homes. For some, especially in eastern Europe, the ferocity of the fighting had erased their places of origin from the map, leaving them with no home to which to return. Others were unable to go back because of shifts in territorial boundaries and the forcible population transfers that often accompanied them. For others again, the death of family members or loved ones, the disappearance of economic opportunities, or the transformation of the political or ethnic complexion of the places from whence they came rendered the idea of return impractical or impossible. The demobilization process would, therefore, see the realization of significant changes in the population geography of the world that had been years in the making.

Nor was that all. Coping with the population problems caused by the war was not just a logistical matter, but a political, economic, and social one as well. Especially in Europe, policymakers were keenly aware of how disillusionment and anger on the part of ex-servicemen had fueled extremisms of the left and right during the inter-war years. The uncertain future of captured enemy forces, who could neither be kept unproductive in detention facilities for long periods nor given free rein to rebuild the dangerous economic potential of the aggressor countries, was another potential source of instability. Lastly, the presence of tens of millions of uprooted civilians—expellees, refugees, and displaced peoples—added yet a third volatile element to the mix. To many sober observers, the sheer scale of the problem of demobilization, demilitarization, and re-integration was itself a first-order crisis that, if mishandled, might sow the seeds of yet another world war.

Captivity Changes Face

For one group of servicemen—Allied prisoners in the hands of the Axis—the end of the war brought swift liberation, even if the future of many remained shrouded in doubt. The Free French government, which had begun planning the return of its prisoners, deportees, and refugees as early as November 1943, distinguished itself in this regard, bringing home its POWs at a peak rate of two hundred thousand a week. By mid-July 1945, some 950,000 French military detainees, and more than one-half a million civilians, had been repatriated from Germany.[4] The two hundred thousand British and Commonwealth prisoners, and ninety-five thousand Americans, held by the Nazis were also quickly returned to their homelands, albeit sometimes by highly circuitous routes, as were around 180,000 Western POWs who survived Japanese captivity.[5]

It was a different matter for the largest single group of Allied POWs, the 2,800,000 Red Army servicemen who, greatly against the odds, had lived through the murderous ordeal of Nazi incarceration.[6] More than three million of their comrades had already perished at the Germans' hands, the majority in the seven months following the launch of Operation Barbarossa in June 1941.[7] The status of the survivors was in many respects an unenviable one, for Joseph Stalin was by no means the only Soviet officeholder to regard capture by the enemy as tantamount to treason. Alexandra Kollontai, the USSR's ambassador to Sweden, expressed a commonly held view when she declared during the war: "The Soviet Union does not recognize Soviet POWs. We consider Soviet soldiers who fell into German hands deserters."[8] Nonetheless, the often-expressed contention in

Western literature that returning POWs were swiftly dispatched to the GULAG or the grave has recently been found suitable for revision. The casualty rate was especially high among officers, whose "betrayal" was considered particularly unforgiveable. But even among the seventy-six Soviet generals who were captured by the Germans, only thirteen were executed upon their return to the USSR, some of whom, like the notorious Alexei Andreevich Vlasov, had collaborated with the enemy on a most serious scale. The largest single cohort among the captured general officers were those who, following their liberation, were found innocent of wrongdoing and restored to their places in the army.[9] Of the enlisted men, more than one-half were returned to military service after a brief examination in so-called "filtration" camps; some, freed from German control in late 1944, were back on the front lines in time to participate in the final assault on Berlin six months later. While some 340,000 former POWs were assigned to labor battalions after V-E Day and not formally demobilized until the autumn of 1946, only a minority of the rank-and-file suffered serious adverse consequences from the screening process.[10]

It is undeniable that Soviet ex-POWs remained the objects of suspicion decades after the conflict came to an end. Many experienced official discrimination, partly in anticipation of future purges. Over time conditions for most did improve, less because of the repeal of adverse laws than the discontinuance of their enforcement. Not until around the time of Khrushchev's Secret Speech of 1956, though, were ex-POWs given the benefit of a "silent amnesty." As late as the Gorbachev era, many Soviet citizens continued to adhere to the belief that war captives were traitors and should be treated as such. Even after the end of the Soviet Union itself, ex-prisoners had to attest to their former POW status on official documents, and they were finally put on the same legal footing as other veterans only in 1995, by which time most of them were dead.

When it came to the Axis prisoners in their own hands, the end of the war posed acute legal and logistical problems for the Western Allies. While the conflict was under way, the Anglo–Americans had, as a general rule, adhered to the terms of the 1929 Geneva Convention in respect of the Axis prisoners of war they had captured. Article 11 of the Convention unambiguously imposed upon detaining powers the obligation of feeding POWs on a scale "equal in quantity and quality to that of [the captors'] depôt troops," as well as the provision of adequate accommodation, clothing, footwear, and medical care.[11] Prisoners were also entitled to receive payment for any labor required of them, to benefit from recreational facilities, and to bring complaints before a protecting power or the International Committee of the Red Cross. Lastly, the Convention required the prompt repatriation and release of POWs at the conclusion of hostilities.[12]

There was no possibility of the Allies adhering to these commitments after the Axis surrender. In a world that had suffered profound economic dislocation and physical damage as a result of the war, maintaining tens of millions of enemy prisoners on such a standard would have imposed severe strain on the victors' limited resources. But the chief objection was political, not practical. After the Axis powers had conducted themselves with such unprecedented barbarity, neither the Allied leaders nor their peoples were willing to see the perpetrators obtain more favorable conditions than many, if not most, of their victims, merely because of a formal legal commitment. Winston Churchill had already, in February 1944, signaled the Western Allies' intended approach to this matter when he told the House of Commons that, "Unconditional surrender means that the victors have a free hand. It does not mean that they are entitled to behave in a barbarous manner ... [but] if we are bound, we are bound by our own consciences to civilisation."[13]

Accordingly, in a series of coordinated moves, Washington and London devised a pair of new categories for the millions of Axis servicemen who would fall into their hands at the end of the war.[14] Drawing on a Nazi precedent whereby the 3,700,000 Italian soldiers captured by the Germans after 1943 were reclassified as "military internees" (*italienische Militärinternierte*) to facilitate their exploitation as forced labor, the European Advisory Commission and the U.S. Combined Chiefs of Staff ruled that Axis troops who delivered themselves into Allied hands on or after V-E Day were to be classified as "disarmed enemy forces" (the U.S. term) or "surrendered enemy personnel" (the British one). Whereas Axis captives already in Anglo-American camps would continue to benefit from the provisions of the Geneva Convention, those detained after the surrender would enjoy no legal protection or standards of treatment other than those the Allies themselves found it convenient to provide. A threadbare justification was offered for this policy, on the basis that inasmuch as the Axis governments would no longer exist after the war, neither would any legitimate Axis armed forces. In reality, however, this unilateral jettisoning of the Geneva Convention was only one example of a general resolve on the part of all the Allies that any international legal instruments standing in the way of their plans for the postwar world were, as a matter of policy, to be considered as no longer having effect.

A similar feat of legal legerdemain briskly disposed of the 1907 Second Hague Convention's requirement that prisoners were to be repatriated to their homelands "as speedily as possible" upon the conclusion of peace. Once again following in the footsteps of Adolf Hitler, who in 1940 had concluded an armistice rather than a final settlement with Vichy France, in part to facilitate his exploitation of French POW labor, the Allies contended that the continued detention and exploitation of Axis prisoners was legitimate until such time as a peace conference was convened. The breakdown in relations between the superpowers signified by the indefinite suspension of the Council of Foreign Ministers' meetings in 1947 made clear that this would not occur within the foreseeable future.

While self-interest and sharp legal practice was thus not entirely absent from the Anglo-American stance on prisoners, some allowance can be made for the logistical mistakes made at the outset, for the number of people who required to be dealt with turned out to be prodigious. More than 7,500,000 German servicemen were in the hands of the Western Allies north of the Alps by V-E Day, with another 3,150,000— among them, Frenchmen from Alsace and Moselle, the so-called *malgré-nous*, who had been dragooned into the *Wehrmacht* after the annexation of 1940—in the custody of the Soviets, and around 1,400,000 in detention in Italy. The continuation of the war for more than a week after Hitler's death had made it possible for 1,800,000 members of the *Wehrmacht* to surrender to the Anglo-Americans rather than the USSR, a tactic that ultimately spared many of their lives.[15] The question of how to feed and accommodate this enormous body of detainees had been the subject of little advance planning, and the initial Allied response, especially in the U.S. occupation zone, was chaotic. Because of the failure of the British authorities—who pleaded troop shortages and transportation difficulties—to live up to previous agreements to divide the number of surrendering Germans equally, the U.S. military government quickly found itself with five million former *Wehrmacht* and *Volkssturm* (militia) personnel, including some members of the women's armed-forces auxiliaries (*Wehrmachthelferinnen*), on its hands, rather than the three million it had bargained for. (Another 371,000, to whom full POW status had already been granted, were in camps in the United States.) To relieve the pressure, more than one million prisoners in American custody were herded into an improvised network of twenty-three "Prisoner of War Temporary Enclosures," known to their inmates as *Rheinwiesenlager* ("Rhine meadow camps"). The largest of these, at Remagen, had a peak population of nearly 170,000 by April 1945; its near neighbor, Sinzig, contained almost 120,000. These pens consisted simply of barbed-wire corrals hastily set up in open fields close to the banks of the River Rhine, where German soldiers, exposed to the elements except for the fortunate few in possession of pup-tents, spent up to six months in detention between April and September 1945. A significant number of unnecessary deaths, perhaps as many as forty thousand, resulted from disease, malnutrition, hypothermia, and occasional physical maltreatment by the U.S. guards, although the record-keeping apparatus of these establishments, which was as shambolic as every other aspect of their operations, precludes any definitive count.[16]

The greatest difficulties affecting Allied handling of German military detainees, however, arose not from administrative or logistical shortcomings but the entanglement of the prisoner-of-war question with the victors' manpower requirements and with the process of denazification. The designation by the British of some 2,400,000 POWs on German soil as surrendered enemy personnel, and by the Americans of a further 1,600,000 as disarmed enemy forces (in addition to the more than three million already in Soviet hands) not only partially relieved the Allies of the burden of providing for their welfare according to international standards, but also opened up the possibility of using them as forced laborers for an indeterminate period. The USSR was the first to press for the exploitation of German and Hungarian POWs as "reparations in kind," but the Western Allies proved apt pupils. The Big Three agreed at the Yalta Conference to make use of German labor for this purpose, and the POW detention facilities thus became, in effect, massive depositories of manpower from which withdrawals, and even temporary loans from one country to another, might be made as the Allies found convenient. It was of a piece with this policy that the first groups to be released *en masse* in the early summer of 1945—elderly *Volkssturm* detainees, members of the *Hitlerjugend*, and women—were those whose labor services were least valuable. In the same way, the camps also became impromptu remand centers for hundreds of thousands of military personnel suspected of war crimes. The process of screening was often extremely slow, further delaying the winding-down of a network of detention facilities that proved to be ill-adapted to the purposes for which it was now being used.

For the Soviet Union, considerations of international law did not enter into the equation. Any theoretical difficulty arising from that quarter was made to disappear by categorizing most Axis captives as "war criminals" who could, after drumhead judicial procedures or by means of mere declaration, be convicted of offences against the Soviet state and sentenced to prison terms covering the period for which their services might be required. Ex-enemy prisoners were retained firstly as manpower assets whose combined labor power, according to one calculation, contributed approximately one billion man-days to the task of Soviet reconstruction; secondly for the purpose of weakening the countries of the defeated Axis; and lastly as hostages and bargaining-chips that could be used in the context of Cold War diplomacy.[17] In addition to the German POWs, by far the largest national group, about 640,000 Japanese, more than five hundred thousand Hungarians, close to two hundred thousand Romanians, and some seventy thousand Italians became prisoners of the USSR.

In the Pacific theater, the demilitarization of the Japanese armed forces was not nearly as straightforward as American publicists later claimed it to be. The army's Field Service Code of January 1941 declared that surrender was unacceptable under any circumstances. Tokyo during the war maintained the fiction that no Japanese POWs existed, even when officially notified of prisoners' names by Allied governments or the Red Cross. Instead, families of captured servicemen were provided with boxes purporting to contain the bones of their lost relatives. This absurd pretense collapsed when the nearly thirty-nine thousand Japanese prisoners in Allied hands on V-J Day were forced to return home, startling relatives who, in many cases, had been mourning them for years.[18]

This cohort, however, paled into insignificance in comparison to the 7,200,000 Imperial servicemen in uniform at the end of the war, with whom the Allies now had to deal. Approximately half that number were distributed across Japan's former overseas colonies and occupied territories, extending from northeast China to the Philippines. Nearly as many civilian personnel and their dependents accompanied them. Almost one-quarter of a million of these expatriates died in Manchuria during the winter of 1945–1946 before they could be repatriated. A large contingent, totaling somewhere between two and three million, was retained by the Soviets, Chinese, British, Dutch, and Americans as forced labor, some for years after the surrender. Controversially, tens of thousands of Japanese servicemen were rearmed and, in violation of international law, employed by British military authorities to repress nationalist agitation or re-impose colonial order in Vietnam, Indonesia, and Malaya during the first year of peace. Several hundred were killed in action on behalf of the Allies while so doing; others volunteered to assist one or other of the contending factions in the Chinese Civil War.[19] Nearly all the Japanese captives in Western hands were transported back to Japan by the autumn of 1947, and most of the survivors still detained by the USSR and China made their way home in 1949, although some continued to be held as late as 1956.[20] Hundreds of thousands of "Japanese Surrendered Personnel" simply disappeared, their fate remaining unclear to the present day.[21]

The same was true of many of the German prisoners in the USSR. Recent recalculations of the data suggest that one in three POWs in Soviet hands—one million men in total—did not survive the experience. As Frank Biess cautions, however, their deaths seem to have been chiefly due to local food shortages, Soviet maladministration at all levels, and a lack of medical care, rather than any purposeful program of mass killing.[22] The mortality rate of the sixty thousand Italian soldiers in the USSR was still higher.[23] Of the German prisoners in Western hands, those detained by the French fared worst, partly as a result of using them for hazardous, and probably illegal, duties like mine clearance. At least 16,500 died, by far the highest proportion of deaths among any cohort held by the Western powers.[24]

The release of the German POWs occurred in waves, according to a seemingly haphazard process reflecting the Allies' immediate manpower needs more than anything else. The Rhine meadow camps were quickly liquidated, and large numbers of their inmates discharged to civilian life. At the end of 1945, the total number of German POWs had halved from V-E Day, and was to halve again by the close of the following year.[25] Mere caprice often dictated how long a given prisoner would spend in detention. Instead of liberating all their POWs, for example, the United States lent eight hundred thousand of them to the French government for up to an additional year's labor service as part of what the *New York Times* described in an editorial in December 1947 as "a modern slave system" that had "become a dark blot on our victory and our civilization."[26] Pressure of this kind may have impelled the Western Allies firstly to commit to, and then to accomplish, the liberation of all remaining German POWs by the end of 1948. Predictably, the Soviet Union lagged behind, with the last captives of the USSR not being returned to their homeland until January 1956.

Demobilization and Reintegration

That the process of demobilizing the enormous Allied armies was sometimes chaotic ought to surprise no one. The remarkable thing was that it was accomplished with so little serious disruption to the societies and economies into which tens of millions of ex-servicemen and women were rapidly decanted. To be sure, the major combatants had the benefit of recent experience upon which to draw. A badly botched demobilization scheme in Britain after the Great War provided object-lessons in what to avoid, while even in the United States the "veteran problem" had loomed so large between the wars that an eighth of the federal budget was being spent on it as late as 1932. Among the major military forces, the Red Army was perhaps best placed to deal with the challenge, in light of the fact that during the interwar era, one-half of its conscripts were returned to civilian life each year.[27]

The most contentious aspect of the various demobilization arrangements was the establishment of a set of priorities for discharge. The United States and Britain opted for points-based systems, with the American version being much more complex. The

Department of Defense allocated points for time in uniform, decorations, dependent children, and service overseas, whereas in the British armed forces only two factors counted for most veterans: age and date of enlistment. The Soviets, for their part, set in place a simple age-based system. Regardless, the Anglo–Americans found it necessary to jettison aspects of their respective schemes in the face of intense pressure from servicemen and their families.

The belated discovery by some British forces, especially those serving in Asia with the Royal Air Force, that the official system required a higher points total of certain military trades produced a wave of "demob strikes" early in 1946.[28] Similar, although less serious, discontent in the United States was fueled by the expedited release of members of especially valuable occupational categories like coal miners. In the face of a rising political crisis on both sides of the Atlantic, policymakers soon came to prioritize speed of discharge over practically every other consideration. The British government returned nearly two million servicemen to civilian life in the first half of 1946, and almost as many in the second. In the same year, U.S. releases were running at a peak rate of twenty-six thousand a day. For both countries, the demobilization process had been virtually completed by the beginning of 1947. The USSR took somewhat longer, as was to be expected in view of the sheer size of the Red Army, but the number of Soviet servicemen and women in uniform had fallen from more than eleven million on V-E Day to a little under three million three years later. The last birth cohort called up during the war, however, had to wait until 1950 before they could resume their civilian lives.

For one uniformed group, demobilization came especially quickly, and was not always welcomed. Around 490,000 women had worn uniform as members of the Soviet armed services during the war, along with 415,000 Britons and 266,000 American servicewomen.[29] Almost all were rapidly disposed of, notwithstanding the wishes of many to continue their military careers. Because few women in uniform could claim overseas service, adjustments were made to the points-based systems to ensure that releases in their case did not fall behind those of the men. In the U.S. army, women required one-half the points accumulated by male veterans to qualify for discharge. Additionally, priority was assigned to married women.[30] By December 1946, in consequence, fewer than ten thousand officers and enlisted women remained in the U.S. Women's Army Corps.[31]

Discharging servicemen and women to civilian life was only the first, and in many respects the less complicated, of a two-part process of reintegration. Fortunately, robust postwar labor markets, with certain isolated and temporary exceptions, addressed veterans' most pressing requirement: gainful employment. This was as well inasmuch as welfare provisions for ex-servicemen and women often left much to be desired in terms of legal entitlements and actual delivery on promises made. The United States went furthest of all with its adoption, more than a year before the war ended, of the Servicemen's Readjustment Act, later to become famous as the "G.I. Bill of Rights." Applying to the great majority of those who had served in any capacity, the G.I. Bill achieved greatest fame for the educational subsidies it provided—which, in the event, were taken up by only one-half of those who qualified. Less well remembered, but equally appreciated at the time, was the Bill's provision of low-interest guaranteed loans for veterans seeking to buy their own homes, as well as an allowance of $20 a week for up to a year for ex-servicemen and women seeking jobs.

British and Soviet veterans had to make do with considerably less generous forms of recognition of their services. While some limited welfare benefits were available to British soldiers, most received a tax-free cash gratuity based on rank and length of service and the famous civilian "demob suit," which came in a limited choice of patterns. Despairing of the task of devising an equivalent that would be acceptable to most servicewomen, the War Office provided female veterans with a ration book containing "points" valid for the purchase of civilian clothing of their own choice and a cash payment in lieu.

Red Army troops fared worst of all, a situation that was only partly compensated for by the opportunities for pillage enjoyed by many who had served abroad. A Soviet equivalent to the G.I. Bill did exist, but its terms were parsimonious. Discharged soldiers were entitled to a new uniform (but no civilian clothes), a pair of shoes, free transportation home, and a golden handshake calculated on the basis of rank and period of service. Regional governments were instructed to attend to the veterans' housing, fuel, and employment needs. The norm specified that they were to be given a job within a month of resuming civilian life. Even delivering on these meager promises, though, proved beyond the state's ability, or will. In the Republic of Bashkiria, Mark Edele notes, "only one demobilized person in a thousand received a head of cattle, twelve in a thousand a pair of shoes, and six in a thousand one piece of clothing."[32] Essentially left to fend for themselves, Soviet veterans depended on families, informal networks with former comrades, the black economy, and the assistance of religious organizations, both Orthodox and Moslem, whose existence, somewhat paradoxically, Stalin was still tolerating.

In the end, most ex-servicemen and women, regardless of their nationality, were constrained to rely on themselves most of all for their own reintegration into civilian society. For many of both sexes who had undergone traumatic wartime experiences, this was to prove a lifelong struggle. Some revealed themselves to have particularly serious difficulties, and these were not always the most predictable groups. Contrary to the postwar image, fueled by popular books and films, of prisoner-of-war life being an adventure-filled round of escape attempts and playful baiting of one's captors, a U.S. study decades after the war found that more than two-thirds of former POWs suffered at one time or another from the symptoms of post-traumatic stress disorder.[33] Little recognition, and less by way of effective treatment, were accorded to the millions from all the combatant countries who were undergoing deep and lasting war-related psychological distress. Self-medication using alcohol or drugs, the support of an empathetic spouse, and the passage of time were the only resources available to the overwhelming majority of those who found the challenges of returning to civilian life to be all that, or more than, they could handle.

Addressing One Forced-Migration Catastrophe...

A question that generated still greater official concern was what was to be done with the so-called "displaced persons," or DPs—the millions of forced laborers, concentration-camp inmates, refugees, stateless people, and other individuals who for one reason or another had been compelled to leave their homelands during the war. An early calculation on behalf of Supreme Headquarters Allied Expeditionary Forces (SHAEF) suggested that there were 11,332,700 of these scattered across Europe, with nearly eight million present in Germany itself. Suspiciously precise though this figure may have been, it was probably not far from the truth. The largest single category among the DPs, at around six million, consisted of the foreign workers brought to Germany to work in war industries. Of these, Soviet and Polish citizens made up slightly more than one-half, with contingents from France, Yugoslavia, Italy, the Netherlands, and Belgium also contributing significantly to the total.[34] Swelling the DP count were the 475,000 concentration-camp survivors, the great majority of whom were non-German.[35] But by no means were all people categorized as DPs victims of Nazi oppression. Significant numbers had thrown in their lot with the Germans during the war; many of these were, for good reason, anxious not to be repatriated to their homelands. To be sure, there were innumerable others among the DP population whose anti-Nazi sentiments were unimpeachable and who also desired, for equally cogent if considerably less disreputable considerations, not to return.

Responsibility for dealing with the DPs was initially assigned to the United Nations Relief and Rehabilitation Administration (UNRRA), at the time of its creation in November 1943 the largest international agency in the world's history. With the backing of the four great powers and forty smaller states, UNRRA was endowed with a $2 billion fund, although it wound up spending nearly twice that much. Its unwieldiness and persistent bureaucratic disorganization, however, led to its mandate to work on behalf of DPs being transferred to a smaller, cheaper, and more nimble entity, the Provisional Committee of the International Refugee Organization (IRO), a body that lost its "provisional" designation when the IRO proper, the precursor of today's United Nations High Commissioner for Refugees, came into being at the end of 1946. Unlike its stance with respect to UNRRA, the Soviet Union refused to participate in the IRO because of its dissatisfaction over the fact that the new organization failed to co-operate in compulsorily repatriating citizens of areas like eastern Poland and the Baltic states that had been annexed by the USSR during the currency of the Nazi–Soviet pact. In reality, Moscow had few legitimate complaints to make about the stringency with which the rules on mandatory repatriation were applied. As early as September 1944, the British government had agreed to return all citizens whose homes lay within the USSR's borders of September 1, 1939, regardless of their wishes or of the human cost involved. Of the two million Soviet DPs, properly so called, a remarkable ninety-eight percent had been transported home by December 1945.

Fortunately, the DP problem never threatened to bear out the overheated concerns ventilated in innumerable newspaper stories and official planning documents about hordes of brutalized vagabonds roaming the European continent, strewing havoc in their wake and resisting all efforts either to persuade them to go home or to integrate them in postwar society. While crimes of violence perpetrated by DPs did occur and received far more than their share of lurid coverage in the press, Ulrich Herbert points out that DPs' rate of criminality did not exceed that of the Germans beside whom most of them lived, although both indices were admittedly much higher than during the prewar years.[36] The physical health of the displaced persons proved to be astonishingly good, only one percent of those in Germany and Austria requiring any immediate medical care at all in the summer of 1945. And a great many DPs proved not only eager to return to their places of origin, but in many cases returned on their own initiative by hitching rides, traveling by bicycle, or walking. By September 1945, one-half of the European DPs were already home.[37] A similar picture unfolded in the former Pacific theater, with more than one million Korean forced laborers returning expeditiously to their homeland, along with around sixty thousand workers from mainland China and Formosa.[38]

Likewise, the "hard-core" DPs, who continued to occupy UNRRA-established camps as late as 1950, presented less of a problem than expected. After the forcible return to the USSR of forty thousand collaborationist Cossack troops and their families produced a wave of state killings and mass suicides, accompanied by an equally grisly spectacle when twenty-seven thousand pro-German Yugoslavs were promptly executed by the Tito régime, the Western powers progressively abandoned their rigid stance on compulsory repatriation in the first half of 1946. The beneficiaries were in the end successfully resettled. Around one million of the DPs found new homes outside Europe, taking advantage of the developed countries' increasingly acute postwar labor shortage. All in all, then, and notwithstanding the inefficiency and expense of UNRRA's initial attempts to come to grips with the question, the solution of the displaced-person problem can be regarded as a qualified success.

... And Creating Another

The truly gross population movements occasioned by the end of the war occurred partly as a result of the reversal of the brutal forced migrations perpetrated by the Axis powers during the conflict itself, but to a much greater extent by the mass expulsions—often little less inhumane—perpetrated by the Allies in its aftermath. Soon after the conquest of Poland, more than three-quarters of a million gentile Poles had been driven out of their homes to the so-called *Generalgouvernement*, their places—literally, in view of the appropriation of their real property—being taken by approximately the same number of ethnic Germans, or *Volksdeutsche*, relocated from central and eastern Poland, the Baltic, and Romania, to the now-expanded *Reich*.[39] As many Polish citizens from the territories invaded by Stalin on September 17, 1939 were deported to the Soviet Union, forcibly inducted into the Red Army, or transferred to forced-labor or prisoner-of-war camps during the same period.[40] In northern Yugoslavia, some eighty thousand inhabitants of Slovenia were deported into neighboring Croatia as part of one of Heinrich Himmler's lesser-known but more vicious colonization schemes.[41]

The ambitions of the greater and the lesser Allies, however, extended far beyond undoing the brutal forced migrations perpetrated by Germany and its satellites during the first three years of the war. Rather, from the beginning of the war, coerced population transfers were seen as a vital tool with which to create a more nationally and ethnically homogeneous—and hence, it was hoped, a more stable—Europe. The official rationale, though, was by no means purely forward-looking. Correctly perceiving that the driving out of entire populations under the desperate conditions that were certain to prevail immediately after the war would inevitably lead to great suffering for those affected, policymakers saw the use of this expedient as a form of collective punishment that would cause ordinary Germans in the future to think twice about backing militarist or expansionist régimes. Frankly appealing to the doctrine of *tu quoque*, proponents of mass expulsions cited examples of Nazi crimes as evidence of both the effectiveness and the acceptability of such conduct. As the *Economist* editorialized in 1940, "Hitler, by the very brutality of his methods, is creating precedents which, used with discretion, may solve a host of European problems once an Allied victory has been secured."[42]

As events showed, discretion proved to be the chief element lacking in Allied wartime schemes for a wholesale redrawing of the demographic profile of central Europe. Aligning itself with the head of the Czechoslovak government-in-exile, Edvard Beneš, who had been pressing since the beginning of the war for a radical solution to the problems arising from the fact that close to one-third of his fellow citizens were neither Czech nor Slovak, the British government committed itself in July 1942 to "the general principle of the transfer to Germany of German minorities in Central and South-Eastern Europe after the war in cases where this seems necessary and desirable."[43] From the outset, moreover, the British made clear that there was to be no question of exempting non-Nazis or even proven anti-fascists from the scope of this decision. As Frank Roberts, a senior Foreign Office functionary, noted three months later, any concessions of this kind "might lead to an unwelcome limitation of our right to make considerable transfers of population because we may want (and the Americans may propose) to use this remedy on a large scale without reference to 'guilt' and it seems important that we should keep our hands free to do so."[44]

Having admitted the principle, the Western Allies found it impossible to resist its extension beyond what they had initially contemplated. Stalin's refusal to consider returning the eastern half of Poland that he had invaded in collaboration with Adolf Hitler in September 1939 for a time threatened the stability of the wartime Grand Alliance. His proposal, however, that a restored Poland should be allowed to compensate itself by occupying an area of eastern Germany more or less equivalent in size to the territories it had lost, enabled the Big Three to avoid a mutually damaging confrontation. It was understood that this solution must also involve the expulsion of the eight or nine million people living beyond the "Oder–Neisse line" that would constitute the new German–Polish frontier, bearing in mind that otherwise around one-quarter of the population of postwar Poland would be German-speaking. Yet a third cohort was included when in 1945 the Big Three greenlighted the request of the Soviet-influenced Hungarian government to rid itself of its half-million-strong German minority. The cumulative result of these decisions, however, was that, as the *New York Times* soberly noted, the Allies were committed to the driving-out of a group of people that was "roughly equal to the total number of immigrants arriving in the United States during the past forty years."[45]

When the expulsion operation commenced in the spring of 1945, the results were predictably disastrous. Initial efforts on the part of the postwar Polish and Czechoslovak governments to stampede their Germanophone populations to the border through the use of internment, extra-judicial executions, forced marches, or deprivation of the means of existence proved less effective than had been hoped; they did, on the other hand, produce scenes of utter chaos within Germany itself.[46] By the time of the Potsdam Conference these had become so grave that the Big Three demanded a temporary moratorium on further displacements until such time as an "orderly and humane" process could be set in place. When the ban was lifted, the experience of the "organized expulsions" were to show that this was a contradiction in terms. The overwhelming majority of the expellees consisted of women, children, and the elderly, whose vulnerability to abuse was particularly great. A vast network of detention facilities—in many cases including former concentration camps like Auschwitz, Theresienstadt, and Majdanek—was created as a component of the deportation process, in which, as a series of confidential reports by the International Committee of the Red Cross recorded, conditions varied from unsatisfactory to lethal.[47] Women and girls (and also some men and boys) were subjected while in the camps, on the expulsion trains, and on the roads, to a wave of sexual violence that, being sustained for longer, may very well have exceeded in scope the better-known depredations of the Red Army in eastern Germany during the late spring and summer of 1945. The suffering continued for a considerable time after the expellees had arrived at their destinations. Having given rise to the single largest man-made refugee crisis in history, the Allies found it necessary to proceed to the further resolution that no international aid of any kind was to be extended to the displaced population, so as to prevent a situation whereby the lion's share of such relief would wind up going to Germans.

Given the disorder in which the operation was carried out, any statistical data are subject to wide margins of error. Estimates of the number of expellees (including those who fled for their own safety from the approaching Red Army in early 1945 but were prevented from returning to their homes after V-E Day) range from twelve million to fourteen million. They included hundreds of thousands of German-speakers from Yugoslavia and Romania whose removal was never sanctioned by the Great Powers but were forced out nonetheless by the postwar régimes in Belgrade and Bucharest. The total of those who lost their lives is an equally contentious matter, depending in part on varying definitions of what constitutes an "expulsion-related" death, but according to the most conservative estimates must nonetheless be numbered in the hundreds of thousands.[48]

Beyond the human costs, perhaps the most remarkable aspect of the German expulsions was the sheer recklessness of those who authorized them and carried them out. The depositing of millions of penniless, embittered and rootless people in a devastated country that was unable to house, feed, or find work for them and whose indigenous population viewed the newcomers with considerable disapprobation could hardly have been better calculated to create the preconditions for another world war.[49] As a result of the operation, and notwithstanding the considerable territorial losses it had incurred, Germany emerged as the only major European country with a substantially larger population in the aftermath of the war than at its beginning. So alarmed by this fact was the postwar French government, whose acquiescence to the displacements had not been sought by the Big Three, that in 1947 Prime Minister Georges Bidault publicly offered to accept as immigrants to France a substantial number of expellees as the only means, as he saw it, of preventing this element from destabilizing the peace of Europe and the world.[50] The fortuitous advent of the *Wirtschaftswunder*, as well as (notwithstanding the noisy fulminations of some of their more hot-headed representatives) the sobriety and realism of the expellees themselves, rescued the Allies from the worst consequences of their own injudiciousness.[51] So fortunate an outcome was, however, neither guaranteed nor even likely.

The scale of the German expulsions has overshadowed the other forced migrations that occurred in the immediate aftermath of the European war. Cumulatively, the number of people affected was significant. An agreement on an "exchange" of populations between Poland and the USSR (in reality a linked pair of involuntary displacements) caused close to one million Poles, and about one-half million ethnic Ukrainians, to lose their homes.[52] Although Edvard Beneš hoped to follow his expulsion of Czechoslovakia's Germanophone population with a similar exile of the eight hundred thousand Hungarian-speakers in Slovakia, opposition on the ground in both countries, combined with increasing disillusionment on the part of the Great Powers with the idea of population transfers, prevented more than a small proportion of the program from being fulfilled. A pair of exchanges between Czechoslovakia and the Soviet Union was on an even smaller scale, involving some tens of thousands of people. Other than in central Europe, the most important displacements took place in Istria and Dalmatia. While the ruling Tito régime did not adopt a formal policy of expulsion, the unleashing of state terror, including large-scale massacres, induced as many as 250,000 Italians to flee across the new border. The creation of "facts on the ground" proved almost as effective in bringing about the desired objective in these districts as the Great Powers' more frankly acknowledged approach had done.

By the end of the 1940s, the short-lived but intense vogue for mass coercive population transfers as a means of addressing the problems arising from ethnic and linguistic heterogeneity had begun to wane. Efforts by the expelling states to colonize the cleared areas with members of the dominant ethnicities, though absorbing a great deal of time, effort, and resources, were far less successful than hoped; to this day, many of the most badly affected districts of central Europe continue to bear visible signs of the disruption and economic retardation they experienced in the postwar quinquennium.[53] The Great Powers, for their part, discovered, as an American post-mortem ruefully recorded, that "a tremendous economic and social burden ha[d] been transferred" to their shoulders, an experience that few of their leaders were anxious to repeat.[54] Not until the early 1990s would the violent break-up of Yugoslavia provide a grim coda to an episode that reflects no credit on any of its authors and serves to complicate, though not to contradict, the popular image of the conflict of 1939–1945 as constituting, from the Allies' perspective, a "Good War."

Conclusion

Credit must be given to the Allies, in their approach to the problems of demilitarization, demobilization, and re-integration, for avoiding a repeat of at least some of the errors committed in the aftermath of the Great War. However many gaps remained in the systems they created, considerable efforts were made to anticipate future conditions and to address them notwithstanding the existence of acute material and political constraints. Enlightened measures like the G.I. Bill have been widely copied in the decades since the war, and they have proven how effective imaginative and forward-thinking policy can be.

In their handling of the displaced-person crisis, too, the Allies could look back on their record with a measure of satisfaction. Although UNRRA deserves most of the criticism it attracted during its operational lifetime, conditions for the DPs and for Europe as a whole would have been infinitely worse if it had not existed. While it is true that a great many DPs relieved the Allied authorities of a serious problem by taking the initiative to "re-place" themselves, relying on their own wits and resources, a combination of official benevolence and the improvisation of administrators and relief workers who learned on the job alleviated a great deal of suffering that otherwise was certain to arise.

Nothing of the kind can be said, however, for the Allies' involvement in the postwar expulsion of the ethnic Germans, a fundamentally misconceived and inhumane policy whose ill effects continue to reverberate to the present day. Firstly, and most obviously, it represented an undeclared continuation of hostilities against a vulnerable civilian population, producing a death toll that leaves even the ghastly body-count in a later and better-known exercise in the forcible transfer of populations in the former Yugoslavia in the shade. Secondly, it inflicted irreparable economic and cultural harm on the lands affected by it, the effects of which are all too evident to the present day. Thirdly, it failed to bring about the political stability that was its principal officially stated justification, instead poisoning relations between postwar Germany and its eastern neighbors and requiring other entities, like NATO and the EU, to accomplish the task whose difficulty it aggravated. Most seriously of all, perhaps, it weakened the international human rights system to a far greater and more damaging extent than is generally realized. The Allies' adoption of legal short-cuts at Nuremberg and Tokyo has been the subject of an immense volume of criticism in the years since the war—whether justified or not is beyond the scope of this essay. But there can be no doubt that the official exclusion by *fiat* of the expellees from the ambit of human-rights law for a period of years after the war, and the need to adjust or interpret postwar instruments ranging from the 1948 Genocide Convention to the Rome Statute of the International Criminal Court so as to continue to maintain the operation's legality, has had a lasting and entirely harmful impact upon the architecture of human rights in general. In any drawing-up of the balance sheet of the Allies' handling of the challenges confronting them in the immediate postwar era, it is regrettable that this episode will have to figure so prominently at the head of the debit column.

Notes

1. M. Burleigh, *Germany Turns Eastwards: A Study of* Ostforschung *in the Third Reich* (Cambridge: Cambridge University Press, 1988); G. Aly & S. Heim, *Vordenker der Vernichtung: Auschwitz und die deutschen Pläne für eine neue europäische Ordnung* (Hamburg: Hoffmann & Campe, 1991).
2. Hoi Sik Jang, "Japanese Imperial Ideology, Shifting War Aims and Domestic Propaganda during the Pacific War of 1941–1945," PhD diss., State University of New York at Binghamton, 2007.
3. M. Harrison, "The Economics of World War II: An Overview," in *The Economics of World War II: Six Great Powers in International Comparison*, ed. M. Harrison (Cambridge: Cambridge University Press, 1998), 7, table 1.2.
4. C. Lewin, *Le retour des prisonniers de guerre français: naissance et développement de la FNPG, 1944–1952* (Paris: Publications de la Sorbonne, 1986), 61–64.
5. A. J. Kochavi, *Confronting Captivity: Britain and the United States and their POWs in Nazi Germany* (Chapel Hill: University of North Carolina Press, 2005), 1; R. Foregger, "Soviet Rails to Odessa, British Ships to Freedom," *Journal of Slavic Military Studies* 8, no. 4 (1995): 844–860.
6. The precise number of Soviet prisoners is a matter of dispute, arising out of discrepancies and omissions in both the Soviet and German records. The figures given here are indicative rather than definitive, and they represent those most commonly accepted at present by scholars in the field.
7. C. Streit, *Keine Kameraden: Die Wehrmacht und die Sowjetischen Kriegsgefangenen, 1941–1945* (Bonn: Dietz, 1991), 136.
8. Quoted in M. Edele, *Veterans of the Second World War: A Popular Movement in an Authoritarian Society, 1941–1991* (Oxford: Oxford University Press, 2008), 102.
9. A. A. Maslov, *Captured Soviet Generals: The Fate of Soviet Generals Captured in Combat 1941–45* (Abingdon, Oxon: Routledge, 2011), 310–317.
10. P. V. Polian, *Deportiert nach Hause: Sowjetische Kriegsgefangene im „Dritten Reich" und ihre Repatriierung* (Munich: Oldenbourg, 2001), 167–170.
11. That is, troops at base camps. "Convention of July 27, 1929, Relative to the Treatment of Prisoners of War," *League of Nations Treaty Series* 118, no. 1–4 (1931–1932): 361 *et seq.*

12. Although the USSR was not a party to the Geneva Convention, it announced on November 25, 1941 its recognition of the Fourth Hague Convention (1907), which imposed substantively similar obligations. G. Ginsburgs, "The Nuremberg Trial: Background," in *The Nuremberg Trials and International Law*, ed. G. Ginsburgs & V.N. Kudriavtsev (Dordrecht: Martinus Nijhoff, 1990), 10.
13. 397 *H.C. Deb.* 5s., cols. 698-9 (February 22, 1944).
14. "Minutes of the Seventh Formal Meeting of the European Advisory Commission, Lancaster House, London, July 25, 1944, 6 p.m.," Annex 2, art. 2 (b). United States Department of State, *Foreign Relations of the United States: Diplomatic Papers, 1944: General* (Washington, DC: Government Printing Office, 1966), 257.
15. R. Bessel, *Germany 1945: From War to Peace* (New York: HarperCollins, 2009), 125.
16. R. Overmans, "Die Rheinswiesenlager 1945," in *Ende des Dritten Reiches, Ende des Zweiten Weltkriegs*, ed. H.-E. Volkmann (Munich: Piper, 1995), 259–291. Suggestions by the Canadian pseudohistorian James Bacque that the U.S. and French military authorities presided over the death, through starvation and exposure, of more than eight hundred thousand German military prisoners have been comprehensively discredited. J. Bacque, *Other Losses: An Investigation into the Mass Deaths of German Prisoners of War at the Hands of the French and Americans after World War II* (Boston: Little, Brown, 1989); G. Bischof and S. E. Ambrose, eds., *Eisenhower and the German POWs: Facts against Falsehood* (Baton Rouge: Louisiana State University Press, 1991); A. Frohn, "Das Schicksal deutscher Kriegsgefangener in amerikanischen Lagern nach dem Zweiten Weltkrieg: Eine Auseinandersetzung mit den Thesen von James Bacque," *Historisches Zeitschrift* 111, no. 2 (1991): 466–492.
17. A. Hilger, "Sowjetische Gewahrsamsmacht und Deutsche Kriegsgefangene 1941–56: Zum Verhältnis von Völkerrecht und Nationalem Interesse in Stalinismus," *Militärgeschichtliche Zeitschrift* 62, no. 2 (2003): 395–422; S. Kamer, A. J. Kay, and B. Stelzl-Marx, "In Stalin's Custody: The Soviet Camp System for Prisoners of War during and after World War II," *Contemporary Austrian Studies* 17, no. 1 (January 2009): 121–134.
18. U. A. Straus, *The Anguish of Surrender: Japanese POWs of World War II* (Seattle, WA: University of Seattle Press, 2003), 29, 38–39, 234–239.
19. S. Connor, "Side-Stepping Geneva: Japanese Troops under British Control, 1945–7," *Journal of Contemporary History* 45, no. 2 (April 2010): 389–405; H. Kobayashi, "The Post-War Treatment of Japanese Overseas Nationals," in *Japanese Prisoners of War*, ed. P. Towle, M. Kosuge, and Y. Kibata (London: Hambledon & London, 2000), 168–169.
20. S. I. Kuznetsov and D. M. Glantz, "The Situation of Japanese Prisoners of War in Soviet Camps (1945–1956)," *Journal of Slavic Military Studies* 8, no. 3 (September 1995): 612–629.
21. According to Igarashi, ninety thousands of these servicemen, captured in Manchuria and held in a network of twelve hundred Siberian camps, died while in Soviet captivity; Kobayashi offers a lower estimate of fifty thousand. Y. Igarashi, "Belated Homecomings: Japanese Prisoners of War in Siberia and their Return to Post-War Japan," in *Prisoners of War, Prisoners of Peace: Captivity, Homecoming and Memory in World War II*, ed. B. Moore and B. Hatley-Broad (Oxford: Berg, 2005), 105; Kobayashi, "The Post-War Treatment," 170.
22. F. Biess, *Homecomings: Returning POWs and the Legacies of Defeat in Postwar Germany* (Princeton, NJ: Princeton University Press, 2006), 5.
23. B. Moore, "Enforced Diaspora: The Fate of Italian Prisoners of War during the Second World War," *War in History* 22, no. 2 (April 2015): 188.

24. S. P. MacKenzie, "The Treatment of Western Prisoners in World War II," *Journal of Modern History* 66, no. 3 (September 1994): 503; N. Ferguson, "Prisoner Taking and Prisoner Killing in the Age of Total War: Towards a Political Economy of Military Defeat," *War in History* 11, no. 2 (April 2004): 186, table 4.
25. Bessel, *Germany 1945*, 202.
26. *New York Times*, December 11, 1947.
27. R. Dale, *Demobilized Veterans in Late Stalinist Leningrad: Soldiers to Civilians* (London: Bloomsbury, 2015), 19.
28. A. Allport, *Demobbed: Coming Home after the Second World War* (New Haven, CT: Yale University Press, 2009), 41–47.
29. The frequently quoted figure of eight hundred thousand servicewomen having participated in the "Great Patriotic War," derived from early Soviet official sources, has recently been revised downwards. R. D. Markwick and E. C. Cardona, *Soviet Women on the Frontline in the Second World War* (Basingstoke, Hants.: Palgrave Macmillan, 2012), 150.
30. M. M. Hampf, *Release a Man for Combat: The Women's Army Corps in World War II* (Köln: Böhlau, 2010), 85–86.
31. M. E. Treadwell, *The Women's Army Corps* (Washington, DC: Government Printing Office, 1954), 743.
32. Edele, *Soviet Veterans*, 74.
33. T. Childers, *Soldier from the War Returning: The Greatest Generation's Troubled Homecoming from World War II* (Boston: Houghton Mifflin Harcourt, 2009), 270.
34. U. Herbert, *Hitler's Foreign Workers: Enforced Foreign Labor in Germany under the Third Reich* (Cambridge: Cambridge University Press, 1997), 462, table 40.
35. M. Spoerer and J. Fleischhacker, "Forced Laborers in Nazi Germany: Categories, Numbers, and Survivors," *Journal of Interdisciplinary History* 33, no. 2 (Autumn, 2002): 194, table 7.
36. Ibid., 377.
37. B. Shephard, *The Long Road Home: The Aftermath of the Second World War* (New York: Knopf, 2011), 84.
38. J. Dower, *Embracing Defeat: Japan in the Wake of World War II* (New York: Norton, 1999), 48–54.
39. I. Heinemann, *Rasse, Siedlung, deutsches Blut: Das Rasse- und Siedlungshauptamt der SS und die rassenpolitische Neuordnung Europas* (Göttingen: Wallstein, 2003), 230.
40. P. Ahonen, G. Corni et al., eds., *People on the Move: Forced Population Movements in Europe in the Second World War and its Aftermath* (London: Bloomsbury, 2008), 23–26.
41. M. Mazower, *Hitler's Empire: How the Nazis Ruled Europe* (New York: Penguin, 2008), 203–204.
42. *The Economist*, February 17, 1940.
43. A. Eden, "Anglo-Czechoslovak Relations," July 2, 1942, quoted in D. Brandes, *Der Weg zur Vertreibung 1938–1945: Pläne und Entscheidungen zum "Transfer" der Deutschen aus der Tschechoslowakei und aus Polen* (Munich: Oldenbourg, 2001), 168.
44. F. K. Roberts to P. B. Nichols, October 6, 1942, FO 371/30835, quoted in R. J. Hoffmann, K. Heißig, and M. Kittel, eds., *Odsun: Die Vertreibung der Sudetendeutschen: Dokumentation zu Ursachen, Planung und Realisierung einer 'ethnischen Säuberung' in der Mitte Europas 1848/49–1945/46*, Vol. II (Munich: Sudetendeutsches Institut, 2010), 344.
45. *New York Times*, December 16, 1945.

46. B. Nitschke, *Vertreibung und Aussiedlung der deutschen Bevölkerung aus Polen (1945–1950)* (Munich: Oldenbourg, 2004); T. Staněk, *Verfolgung 1945: Die Stellung der Deutschen in Böhmen, Mähren und Schlesien (außerhalb der Lager und Gefängnisse* (Vienna: Böhlau, 2002).
47. R. M. Douglas, *Orderly and Humane: The Expulsion of the Germans after the Second World War* (New Haven, CT: Yale University Press, 2012), ch. 5 *passim*.
48. M. Beer, *Flucht und Vertreibung der Deutschen: Voraussetzungen, Verlauf, Folgen* (Munich: Beck, 2011), 127–134.
49. A. Kossert, *Kalte Heimat: Die Geschichte der deutschen Vertriebenen nach 1945* (Berlin: Siedler, 2008); P. Ther, *Deutsche und polnische Vertriebene: Gesellschaft und Vertriebenenpolitik in der SBZ/DDR und in Polen 1945–1956* (Göttingen: Vandenhoeck & Ruprecht, 1998); I. Connor, *Refugees and Expellees in Post-War Germany* (Manchester: Manchester University Press, 2007).
50. Telegram from Georges Catroux, French Ambassador, Moscow, to the Ministère des Affaires étrangères, March 17, 1947, 178QO/107, reel P9709, MAE papers, Centre des Archives diplomatiques, La Courneuve, Paris.
51. A. Demshuk, *The Lost German East: Forced Migration and the Politics of Memory, 1945–1970* (Cambridge: Cambridge University Press, 2012).
52. C. Gousseff, "Evacuation *versus* Repatriation: The Polish–Ukrainian Population Exchange, 1944–6," in *The Disentanglement of Populations: Migration, Expulsion and Displacement in Post-War Europe, 1944–9*, ed. J. Reinisch and E. White (Basingstoke, Hants.: Palgrave Macmillan, 2011), 91–111.
53. T. D. Curp, *A Clean Sweep? The Politics of Ethnic Cleansing in Western Poland, 1945–1960* (Rochester, NY: University of Rochester Press, 2006); D. W. Gerlach, *The Economy of Ethnic Cleansing: The Transformation of the Czech-German Borderlands after World War II* (Cambridge: Cambridge University Press, 2017); E. Glassheim, "Ethnic Cleansing, Communism, and Environmental Devastation in Czechoslovakia's Borderlands, 1945–1989," *Journal of Modern History* 78, no. 2 (March 2006): 65–92; H. Service, *Germans to Poles: Communism, Nationalism and Ethnic Cleansing after the Second World War* (Cambridge: Cambridge University Press, 2013); G. Thum, *Uprooted: How Breslau became Wrocław during the Century of Expulsions* (Princeton, NJ: Princeton University Press, 2011).
54. Prisoners of War and Displaced Persons Branch, "Memorandum to Major General Keating—Subject: Sudeten Transfers," December 13, 1946, Office of Military Government, Records of the Civil Administration Division, PW & DP Branch: Records Relating to Expellees in the U.S. Zone, 1945–49, RG 260/390/42/26/1-2, box 187, "Agreements Expellees" file, National Archives and Records Administration, College Park, MD.

Bibliography

Childers, Thomas. *Soldier from the War Returning: The Greatest Generation's Troubled Homecoming from World War II*. Boston, MA: Houghton Mifflin, 2009.

Edele, Mark. *Soviet Veterans of the Second World War: A Popular Movement in an Authoritarian Society, 1941–1991*, New York: Oxford University Press, 2008.

Hitchcock, William I. *The Bitter Road to Freedom: A New History of the Liberation of Europe*. New York: Free Press, 2008.

Moore, Bob, and Hatley-Broad, Barbara, eds. *Prisoners of War, Prisoners of Peace: Captivity, Homecoming and Memory in World War II*. Oxford: Berg, 2005.

Naimark, Norman M. *Fires of Hatred: Ethnic Cleansing in Twentieth Century Europe*. Cambridge, MA: Harvard University Press, 2001.

Shephard, Ben. *The Long Road Home: The Aftermath of the Second World War*. London: Bodley Hill, 2010.

CHAPTER 33

THE MEMORY AND COMMEMORATION OF WAR

BRIAN M. PUACA AND SHIZUE OSA

Leaders from around the world gathered in the small French town of Ouistreham on June 6, 2014, to commemorate the seventieth anniversary of D-Day. U.S. President Barack Obama attended the festivities, as did Russian president Vladimir Putin. Also present was German chancellor Angela Merkel, who received an invitation for the ceremonies from French president François Hollande. While in France for these events, Merkel said she considered the postwar German–French reconciliation to be "something of a miracle." Her recognition of this lengthy collaboration between the two countries dating back to the 1950s, however, papered over the long-lasting memories of trauma and resentment that existed across the Rhine deep into the twentieth century.

Merkel's political mentor, Helmut Kohl, never received an invitation to attend the D-Day commemorations during his sixteen years as chancellor. Despite his strong commitment to NATO and European integration, Kohl was conspicuously absent at the D-Day commemorations held in 1984 and 1994. It has taken decades for European countries to come to terms with their wartime past, and as the D-Day commemorations reveal, only recently have Germany's neighbors worked through the traumatic memories of occupation, exploitation, and collaboration and been able to reconcile fully with their former enemy.

That very same month witnessed continued anti-Japanese protests in China over disputed islands in the East China Sea. At the center of this outpouring of rage were Chinese memories of Japanese atrocities committed during World War II. Perhaps making the protesters even more frustrated—and sustaining their fury—was the belief that the Japanese had refused to acknowledge their wartime past in an open and honest fashion. Despite decades of controversy in Japan over the depiction of World War II in history textbooks, many argue that the country continues to minimize its own responsibility for the war and avoid difficult discussions of responsibility and guilt.[1] As anti-Japanese protests in China (and elsewhere in East Asia) demonstrate, these memories of the past continue to exert significance influence on social and political relations more than seventy-five years later.

Despite the fact that the small number of men and women who personally experienced the war is decreasing every day, the memory of the conflict continues to exercise great influence on the contemporary world. Perhaps more accurately, there are many memories of World War II within each nation that cooperate, compete, and coexist.[2] Scholarly examinations of memory occur on three different levels: the individual, collective, and official (or institutional).[3] All memory—individual, collective, and official—is selective, constructed, and defined as much by what is remembered as by what is not.

While the events of World War II have long since passed, the memory of the conflict is ever present and constantly changing. In all the nations touched by the war, the ways that it is remembered and commemorated has changed significantly since 1945. As the collective memory of these nations has changed over time due to a variety of factors, so too have the official memories of the war. These stages of memory are highly dependent on internal national dynamics and vary from country to country. Political developments, legal proceedings, economic challenges, military engagements, news coverage, popular media products and even tourism can provoke dramatic changes in the way the war is remembered.[4]

All countries affected by the war have grappled with some aspect of remembering it, and none have experienced the same postwar developments regarding memory and commemoration of the conflict. Germany and Japan, the leading members of the Axis powers, have had to wrestle with the crimes they committed during the war as well as the suffering experienced by their populations as the conflict neared its end. France endured foreign occupation and faced difficult questions of resistance, compliance, and collaboration. Even before the fighting ended, Charles de Gaulle of the Free French sought to forge a collective memory that emphasized resistance to German occupation as the norm, not the exception. China's war with Japan would be followed by the continuation of the Chinese Revolution that played an important role in supplanting memories of World War II for a generation. Only in the 1980s would official and popular interest in World War II lead to a flurry of memorialization projects.

These countries are representative in the way that they highlight the interplay of collective and official memories, the evolution of how the past has been remembered, and the continuing relevance of World War II to national identity in the twenty-first century. Collective memory is permanently in flux, and despite many similar experiences—be it victory, defeat, occupation, resistance, or collaboration—there is no single, shared memory of World War II.

The Axis

The experiences of the two major Axis powers, Germany and Japan, reveal a great deal about the ways in which the war has been remembered (or not remembered) in those nations that experienced defeat in 1945. How has Germany mastered its past?[5] In the 1950s, the West German Government both offered reparations to the State of Israel and began war crime trials for perpetrators of the Holocaust. In Japan, successive governments have refused to apologize for Japanese war of aggression and war crimes, despite the negative impact on foreign relations with the Republic of Korea, China, and other East Asian nations.

While both countries share a history of wartime aggression and militarism, rapid territorial acquisition, occupation of conquered populations, catastrophic destruction, and ultimate defeat, their memory and commemoration of the war differs greatly. Likewise, few would dispute that each nation's memory has undergone dramatic changes since 1945. The question then is why the memory culture of Germany is so different than that of Japan regarding its involvement in World War II.

Despite important differences in their memory cultures, the legacy of the war has profoundly impacted the foreign and military policy of both countries regarding the use of force. In the case of Japan, the postwar Constitution renounced the sovereign right to wage war and efforts by successive Japanese prime ministers to modify this prohibition has sparked fierce debate and been unsuccessful. While its national elites and wider public remained fiercely divided over the issue of war crimes committed by Japanese, there is a strong memory of Japanese victimhood and remembrance of the loss of life from the conventional and atomic bombing of the county.

Germany has not renounced the right to wage war and the armed forces have constitutional basis in contrast to Japan's "self-defense force." Despite their alliances with the United States, both countries have been reluctant to send to troops to fight abroad, even when sanctioned by the United Nations. Although there existed strong currents of memory of victimhood in Germany, especially regarding expulsion of Germans from a number of Eastern European countries, the legacy of culpability for the Holocaust has muted public commemoration of victimhood.[6]

Although the focus in this chapter will be on Federal Republic (West Germany) there existed a significant divergence in the way German Democratic Republic (GDR) commemorated the war. In the GDR there existed a greater willingness to publicly commemorate the war, but by embracing a Marxist–Leninist framework of class struggle that saw Nazism as the final stage of monopoly capitalism. The GDR disowned any responsibility for the war crimes committed by the Nazi regime, maintaining the German proletariat were among the victims. Although there existed a reluctance to fully acknowledge the extent of German culpability for the Holocaust in West German state, the essential antisemitic character was widely acknowledged. The GDR minimized the antisemitic nature of the Holocaust and instead focused on Communist martyrs. For instance, when the GDR administered the Buchenwald concentration camp it offered scant commemoration of the Jewish victims who perished.

Germany (or West Germany, for much of this period) has experienced several stages of memory since 1945 that indicate an ongoing process of engagement with the past and an explicit recognition of the connections between World War II and the present.[7] As Wulf Kansteiner convincingly argues in his analysis of postwar German memory, the

Germans immediately confronted their wartime past under the watchful eyes of the occupation powers.[8] New German and Allied news outlets devoted so much attention to the Third Reich and its brutality that Nazi crimes played an important role in the construction of a new postwar German identity.[9]

Yet with the heating up of the Cold War and a shift in Allied fears toward the Soviet Union, frank discussions of German responsibility and guilt vanished from public discourse at the end of the 1940s. The shift in memory culture that comes at this time has less to do with the creation of a new democratic German state and more to do with the interests of the western occupation powers in securing a stable and reliable partner in an increasingly antagonistic Cold War world.

This silence regarding German responsibility in the 1950s, however, does not mean that the war simply disappeared from view. Political and social elites concentrating primarily on reconstruction and rehabilitation frequently discussed the war and placed emphasis not on German guilt, but on German suffering.[10] This memory of German victimhood was most prevalent in homes, private groups, and local communities.[11] The persecution of minorities in Germany, most notably the Jews, went largely unobserved as the country concentrated instead on the sacrifices of soldiers and civilians who had perished at the hands of foreign powers and those who had been forcibly driven from their homes at the close of the war.[12] The 1950s saw a rich and vibrant memory culture, but one that was highly selective about the themes and experiences it wished to include.

West Germany's collective memory of the war faced challenges from several internal groups during the 1960s and 1970s. Several judicial trials related to war crimes reawakened interest among some Germans for a discussion of the Third Reich and the country's difficult past. The perception among many younger Germans that the country continued to be run by former Nazis fueled a broader discontent among students. This frustration, coupled with other political, social, and cultural concerns, culminated in the student movement of the late 1960s.

These young Germans demanded an open and honest reckoning with the Nazi past and considered a critical self-appraisal of their parents' actions as a prerequisite for this process to begin. The student movement, however, was short-lived and had only limited impact on the country's collective memory. The decade that followed saw most Germans—including political elites—return to an uncomfortable quiet about the war. Only a few determined groups, among them a new generation of professional historians and a handful of idealistic filmmakers, remained preoccupied with the Third Reich and memories of the war.

It was not until the 1980s that West Germany truly engaged in a process of *Vergangenheitsbewaeltigung*, or "overcoming the past." Indeed, the collective memory of the war, steered by chancellor Helmut Kohl's refashioning of the nation's official memory, came to be dominated by the principles of acceptance, reconciliation, and responsibility. In his view, the crimes of the Third Reich could not be allowed to dominate the country's collective memory; rather, the Nazis and the war should be normalized and integrated into the nation's past, thereby allowing Germans the opportunity to craft a more positive national identity. Despite constant criticism from political opponents,

Kohl built new monuments and museums to facilitate an official reconceptualization of the German past.[13] Additionally, the 1980s saw professional historians engage in a vigorous debate about the Third Reich and its meaning in the contemporary West German state (the Historians' Controversy), as well as popular television and film productions, most notably the broadcast of the U.S. miniseries *Holocaust*, that all contributed to these debates about memory and the country's wartime past.[14]

The Germans have continued to engage with their wartime past since the 1990s, and they have consistently received praise and even admiration from other nations for their willingness to discuss, debate, and acknowledge their actions during World War II. The changes in the memory culture of West Germany in the 1980s and 1990s have facilitated the creation of a new, more positive national identity that is shaped by a recognition of Germany's crimes during the war. Indeed, these changes in the memory landscape of West Germany prompt one to think that Helmut Kohl's efforts were largely successful. Seeing their chancellor participate in international commemorations recognizing the sacrifices and suffering of Europeans in World War II, few could dispute that Germany has become a "normal" nation once again.[15]

While Germany has become a trusted friend and ally of its former enemies, Japan continues to instill feelings of anxiety and resentment among its neighbors. The Japanese government's reluctance to engage openly with its overseas actions in World War II plays a large role in this climate of distrust, as memories of the war continue to shape politics, diplomacy, and cultural attitudes in East Asia. The resistance to grappling with the war crimes committed by Japanese during the war has greatly damaged Japan's image in East Asia and, to a lesser extent, on the international stage.

While August 15 has become the official day of commemoration of the end of the Pacific War in postwar Japan, this date was fixed in the popular memory primarily because of domestic politics. It was one day earlier, on August 14, 1945, that the Japanese government accepted the surrender terms contained in the Potsdam Declaration. On the following day, the regime used its administrative machinery to summon the people of Japan, including those in the colonies, to gather around the radio. The voice of the Showa Emperor and the role he played would henceforth be associated with the end-of-the-war image. Newspapers appearing on August 15 contained photos of teary-eyed people on bended knee in the open space in front of the Imperial Palace. However, these pictures were taken the previous day. The tearful prayers of those pictured were actually supplications for a Japanese victory.[16]

It was the imperial government that selected the arbitrary date of "the 15th of August" as a day of remembrance for lamenting the war dead. The date cemented itself as a media event following the San Francisco Peace Treaty in the summer of 1952, and the National Memorial Service for War Dead has been held on this day since 1963. Conducting war memorial events on August 15 also ensured that these events would coincide with the various media reports, television programs, and school undertakings that occur around the 15th, not to mention the traditional Buddhist custom of Bon. Focusing attention on the 15th allowed other important days to be selectively forgotten, most notably V-J Day (August 14, 1945), Japan's formal surrender (September 2, 1945) and the Victory Day of Anti-Japanese Aggression War (September 3, 1945) celebrated by the former Soviet Union and Republic of China.[17]

Selecting a date to commemorate the end of the war is but one of the many difficult issues when it comes to Japan's collective memory of the war. What was the starting point for the war? Against whom was the war fought? Where was the war fought? To understand the past as history, it is necessary that clear terms be coined by responsible authorities. In relation to this point, successive Japanese politicians and bureaucrats have avoided explicit language, using instead terms like "that war" and "this war."

For the people living in the Asia Pacific region and the former colonies of Japan, "the 15th of August" is a day to commemorate liberation and victory. In particular, around 1990 there was an emergence of pan-national commemorations, taking into account the people's voices and collaborative projects. People began to empathize with the victims of the human rights violations that were not provided for under postwar international law. Perhaps the most notable such example of these unrecognized victims were the comfort women, who were women forced into sexual slavery by the Japanese military in the areas they controlled before and during the war. Given that "the 15th of August" can also be considered a memorial day that reflects relationships in East Asia, there continues to be a need to establish a stable, common, and pan-national understanding of the date.

On the other hand, it is important to ascertain the kind of memories that are associated with "the 15th of August." The memories of war endorsed and circulated by the media, citizens' movements, and public education around "the 15th of August" have focused on the civilian deaths and the damage wrought by the war because scores of civilians were incinerated in their homes by the nuclear bombings, and many more fell victim to the devastating air raids in the closing stages of the war. In the context of the new Cold War world, fingers were not pointed at those responsible for this destruction, and the rights and wrongs of the war were not questioned. Instead, a discourse of peace emerged in postwar Japanese society in the form of an antiwar movement, a key aim of which was the total abolition of nuclear weapons.[18]

Hiroshima became a keyword around the world, and from the 1970s—a decade rocked by anti-Vietnam War protests—it became an important theme in peace education, a theme that encapsulated Japan's national memory of the war. The 1970s also saw the emergence of publications aiming to convey the message of Hiroshima to future generations. The *Barefoot Gen* was a manga about a boy called Gen who was exposed to the Hiroshima bombing.[19] There are various scenes showing the death of entire families, streets littered with corpses, and the disposal of the dead. The manga vividly depicts atomic bomb survivors staring into the abyss of death, people's prejudice toward survivors, and the poverty and social discrimination subsequently faced by those who bore the after-effects of the bombing.

Furthermore, this decade witnessed greater efforts to commemorate the wartime air raids that had devastated Japan (once again as a means to oppose the Vietnam War). In a single night during the Tokyo air raids (March 10, 1945), around one hundred thousand people perished. This movement was in opposition to the historical perspective that lionized the Imperial Navy and it also stood in opposition to the former army staff's opinion on war.[20] The movement recorded testimonies of the air raids, which took place repeatedly up until August 14 (after the nuclear bombing) and targeted more than 430 areas throughout Japan, including Nagoya (March 12), Osaka (March 15), and Kobe (March 17). It developed into a nationwide grassroots anti-war movement.[21]

Beginning in the late 1970s, there were also full-fledged efforts to pass on memories to future generations. Survivors of the Hiroshima and Nagasaki bombings took on the role of communicating in the public arena their personal experiences, the grief of losing one's family in an instant, and their worries about the continuing after-effects of the blasts. Political and educational leaders deemed elementary and junior high school excursions to be apt opportunities for peace education, thereby increasing the number of visits to Hiroshima. From the late 1980s, the air raids commemoration movement started promoting investigations of air raids on regional cities based on U.S. official documents, and the war memories of local areas were incorporated into regional studies at elementary and junior high schools.

The memory of the fighting that took place on Japanese soil is concentrated on the Battle of Okinawa. Commemorating the day on which the fierce fighting ended there in 1945, Okinawa Prefecture has its own war memorial day—"the 23rd of June." From the late 1980s and through the 1990s, there were many history books published by local governments in Okinawa that included sections on war not found in history books published by local governments on the mainland. The collected accounts of Okinawan residents' experience of the fighting provide a stark contrast to the official memory of the war in Japan. In March 1945, the U.S. forces in the Pacific landed in Okinawa, and intense fighting ensued. The death toll among civilians exceeded that of U.S. and Japanese soldiers. There were also frequent occasions when Japanese soldiers treated residents as the enemy, and scores of civilians were gunned down as a result.

The Okinawan prefectural administration erected the Cornerstone of Peace in 1995 to mark the fiftieth anniversary of the Battle of Okinawa. This monument was inscribed with the names of all those who lost their lives in the battle, including American soldiers, Japanese soldiers, and Koreans who were forcibly brought to the island. The monument consists of black granite screens bearing a startling number of names of the lost, many of which are traditional Okinawan girls' names like Kama and Ushi, and people who share the same family name. It is thus unlike any other space for mourning and reflecting on war.[22]

On the other hand, as awareness of Japanese wartime crimes spread during the 1990s, there was a change in the exhibits of museums around the country. Among the efforts to uncover the war experiences among local residents that took place to mark the fiftieth anniversary of the war, there was an increasing focus on exhibiting the experience of retreat, the experience of soldiers on the battlefield, and the atrocities perpetrated by the Japanese forces, which form an important part of the memory of war among Japan's neighbors in Asia.

These years also saw the experiences of comfort women emerge as an international gender and human rights concern. It has not proven easy to establish an official and permanent exhibition hall of contemporary history, but the Osaka International Peace

Center (Peace Osaka) was established as an official prefectural establishment in 1991. The exhibits focus on testimonies of the Osaka air raids, but there is also a permanent exhibit detailing the experiences of the Sino-Japanese War as per the center's founding principle which states: We must never forget the terrible atrocities wrought upon the people of China and other places in Asia and the Pacific where the war was fought, and also on the Koreans and Taiwanese who lived under Japanese colonial rule.[23]

The collective memory of World War II in Japan has remained a contentious battlefield in the twenty-first century, as several new controversies have emerged. The attempt during the 1990s to convey memories of the battlefield increased the potential for a new and pan-national way of remembering war. At the same time, school textbook accounts and museum displays became increasingly politicized. Regarding the screening of school textbooks, critics led by Ienaga Saburō put pressure on the Ministry of Education (MOE) to revise accounts about Japan's prewar aggression, actions against civilians in China, the Battle of Okinawa, and the forced transportation of Koreans and Chinese.

The MOE's decision to address these difficult issues in textbooks published in the mid-1990s prompted a backlash from Japanese conservatives. For example, there was a move by historical revisionists, involving various media, to delete references to comfort women in textbooks. The accounts about the comfort women were ultimately removed from all officially screened junior high school textbooks in 2008.[24] High school textbooks also became a target in 2014. In 2013, there was a movement that aimed to remove *Barefoot Gen* from schools on account of its critique of nuclear weapons, and there were calls in April 2015 to remove the exhibits on wartime atrocities from the Osaka International Peace Center as part of its renewal.[25]

France and China

Whereas the defeated Axis nations have worked to come to terms with their memories of guilt and responsibility, those countries occupied by Germany and Japan have also faced significant challenges confronting the past. The countries of East Asia occupied by the Japanese have engaged in the same sort of selective memory and mythmaking as their European counterparts. Yet in this case, as is also true of Europe, it has often been a surplus of memory, rather than a shortage of it, that has been the greatest hurdle.[26]

Whereas the western European countries have relied largely on silence and omission to craft their foundational myths, the nations of East Asia have used multiple memories and myriad traumas as weapons against their former enemies. Thus, once again, the examples of France and China illustrate not only the selectivity of memory and its construction, but its manipulation and national specificity as well.

It is safe to say that by V-E Day in May 1945, French mythmaking related to the war was already well underway. Having been carved into two parts by the Germans in

1940—an occupied portion in the north and the Vichy state in the south—the French had to grapple with a variety of wartime experiences after the country's liberation. None was more difficult than the question of collaboration. Who had collaborated and how should guilt be apportioned? So, too, did the French struggle with recognizing and commemorating its resistance to the Germans. Who had taken the greatest risks? Who had sacrificed the most?

Thorny questions such as these would not—indeed, could not—be debated openly and honestly in French society after 1945. Instead, collective memory in France embraced a myth created by Charles de Gaulle that was too simple and comforting to resist. The creation of a nation of resisters, rallying to the support of their endangered *patrie* (homeland), was a political myth of necessity for de Gaulle as he sought to unify the nation after the trauma of war and occupation. Although his initial time in power ended in 1946, the myth he helped to create would outlive him, only coming under serious criticism after his decade as president ended in 1969 and his death one year later.

The memory of the war has evolved significantly in France since 1945. Perhaps the most influential work on French memory of the war is Henry Rousso's *The Vichy Syndrome*.[27] Rousso, who draws on the work of Sigmund Freud, conceives of France's troubled collective memory as a kind of psychological impairment. Rousso's book is particularly effective in illuminating the relationship between official and collective memory in the immediate postwar era, as well as the willingness of most French men and women to collude with the construction of a mythical past. This highly selective and carefully constructed memory could not last forever, and, as Rousso argues, caused great controversy; it ultimately collapsed in the face of challenges from a variety of social actors.

The Vichy Syndrome surfaced with the liberation of France in 1944 and was already afflicting the nation before the war's end. The first stage of the syndrome lasted for a decade and witnessed the French making initial efforts to address the difficult legacies of the war. The incomplete and highly selective nature of postwar purges and the instability of the newly created Fourth Republic certainly did not provide much support for this process. Nor did the political rhetoric, represented most visibly by Charles de Gaulle, which spoke of a France as a "nation of resisters." Rousso ably illustrates the tensions between the collective memory of the postwar era and the efforts of elites to recast this into a more cohesive and less traumatic shared conception of the nation's wartime past. Indeed, to engage in an honest reckoning of the country's defeat, occupation, and collaboration with the enemy would only undermine efforts at rebuilding and national unity. By the mid-1950s, Rousso argues that these elite efforts to reshape the nation's collective memory had been largely successful.

The death of de Gaulle in 1970 facilitated a remarkable transformation of the memory landscape in France. It was only at this point, Rousso asserts, that a frontal assault on the mythical memory of the war was possible. The challenge to the collective memory of France that took place in the early 1970s came from several sources. Certainly the spirit of the student movement that briefly shook de Gaulle's grip on power in 1968 prompted a reassessment of France's wartime past. Inspired by the idealism and iconoclasm of the Parisian students, several young filmmakers turned a critical eye toward the war and shattered the comfortable memory that de Gaulle had spent twenty-five years building.

Most notably, Marcel Ophuls released his documentary, *The Sorrow and the Pity*, in France in 1971 after its international premiere more than two years earlier.[28] The delay was caused by French authorities unhappy with his portrayal of the resistance. Charles de Gaulle is virtually absent in the film, and many resisters come across as opportunists. Just as shocking was the film's depiction of widespread petty collaboration among the French. But perhaps most disturbing of all was Ophuls' interview with collaborators who acted out of ideological conviction and felt no compunction about their actions.

Building on this assault on the Gaullist myth, director Louis Malle released his *Lacombe Lucien* three years later.[29] Malle's film unnerved so many because his collaborator is a wayward young man who chooses to side with the Gestapo out of a sense of adventure and desire for personal reward.[30] Furthermore, the film reminded viewers that antisemitism was not imported by the Germans and that there was a deep antipathy toward the Jews among the French that their enemies capitalized upon after the armistice. And as if this were not enough of an affront to France's collective memory of the war, a young American historian of modern France, Robert Paxton, published his detailed study of Vichy France. In it, Paxton used a wealth of archival evidence to explore the antisemitic and explicitly collaborationist policies of Vichy, thereby devastating key parts of the Gaullist myth.[31]

The last several decades have not seen France finally come to terms with its wartime past. Indeed, the opposite seems to have occurred as the French have remained obsessed with Vichy since the mid-1970s. Public debates surrounding the trials of Lyon Gestapo chief Klaus Barbie in the late 1980s and Vichy officials Paul Touvier and Maurice Papon in the early 1990s reopened old wounds that many French thought had been closed forever. While this fascination with the Dark Years has receded, controversies continue to emerge from time to time that illustrate the deep tensions in France's collective memory that exists just beneath the surface.

In 2012, in a speech observing the seventieth anniversary of the Vel d'Hiv roundup, French president François Hollande spoke of the deportation of French Jews as a crime committed "in France by France." Yet he then said that "the Vel d'Hiv crime was also committed against France, against its honor, against its values, against its principles." In this moment, many observers argued that Hollande was using intentionally vague language to suggest that the Vichy regime was guilty while a separate and distinct France—a nation of resisters—stood apart from these crimes. More than forty years after the General's death, the legacy of his comfortable myth of two Frances continued to influence official memory and shape the nation's conception of the war.

Rousso's work has continued to be the basis for the study of French wartime memory more than three decades after publication. Scholars in the field continue to use his model as a way to approach French memory, even as they seek new interpretations and engage different themes.[32] Drawing on Rousso's innovative work, Richard Golsan has sought to discern changes in memory in the past thirty years and sees the legal trials beginning in the late 1980s as a "Second Purge."[33] Robert Gildea explores the efficacy of political myths coming from the World War II related to France's empire, the United States, and German people.[34] Focusing on the creation of museums in France to commemorate the country's wartime past, Henning Meyer suggests that an attempt to create universal meanings out of local tragedies signaled a shift toward a "decentralized" memory and a break with the national framework that had been so dominant for decades.[35] Nevertheless, he acknowledges that even as the collective memory of an event such as the massacre at Oradour links to a broader global victim culture, local memories still play a significant role.

In contrast to France, China never surrendered, although broad swaths of the population came under enemy occupation by Japanese forces. The toll of death, destruction, and turmoil engendered by the conflict is difficult to fully imagine. By war's end, millions of Chinese soldiers and civilians had died. After coming to power in 1949. the Chinese Communist Party (CCP) has carefully managed—and manipulated—the memory of World War II and used it as a means to legitimate its control. But even within an authoritarian society, there remained divergent memories in a country as vast and populous in China. Moreover, the official memory of the war underwent considerable change over time.

The CCP through the 1970s focused little attention to forging a memory of World War II as central event in China's history. Part of this reflected the greater importance accorded to commemorating the Chinese Revolution and promoting a world view that embraces class as more important than nationalism. To commemorate the war also meant focusing on the role of the Nationalist regime that had done the bulk of the fighting. For instance, the defenders of Nanjing massacred along with civilians were Nationalists. Lingering trauma also contributed to the reticence to memorialize, and even remember, the war.

As the Cold War wound down in the 1980s, the CCP attitude changed dramatically. It now saw the war as central to national identity and sought to bring attention not only to heroic resistance of Chinese people, but also the war crimes committed by the Japanese aggressors. The reputation of the Nationalists underwent a dramatic rehabilitation that acknowledged their role in fighting the Japanese. The CCP was also tapping into a significant interest within segments of Chinese society that sought to document the history of the period.

The Chinese government built a series of museums to provide public cultural spaces for remembering and reflecting on the war against Japan. Following criticism against Japan in 1982 over the manner in which Japanese textbooks portrayed the war, the Chinese government opened the Nanjing Massacre Memorial Hall by Japanese Forces of Aggression in Nanjing in 1985, the Museum of the War of Chinese People's Resistance against Japanese Aggression near Beijing in 1987 (the place where the Sino-Japanese War began), and the September 18th History Museum in Shenyang in 1991 to commemorate the Mukden Incident that occurred there.

However, a certain length of time is necessary before war memories based on people's testimonies and experiences can be used for exhibition. Even in the case of the Nanjing Massacre, which was investigated by the International Military Tribunal for the Far East

(1946–1948), it was not until the 1980s that official attempts in China to document the testimonies of residents began in earnest. Those museums have undergone renovations in the new millennium—the Beijing museum in 2005 and the Nanjing museum in 2007—each adding extensive testimonies of local victims. In the case of the former, the new exhibits focus on the various participants in the anti-Japanese National United Front who fought with the Nationalists. In the case of the latter, there was the installation of a new memorial hall featuring exhibits of the atrocities committed, including a wall inscribed with the names of victims.

The relatively well-known atrocities of the Japanese army, such as the Three Alls Policy (Burn All, Kill All, Loot All) and the Nanjing Massacre, are merely the tip of the iceberg when it comes to the horrors of war being taught to the next generation in China. Toward the end of the Asia–Pacific War, the government of the Republic of China encouraged the documentation of war crimes committed by the Japanese army, having been inspired to do so by the movement to try Nazi war criminals.

These records were subsequently referred to in local history-gathering projects that developed from the 1980s onward. For example, there was a case involving an operation conducted by the Japanese army in Yunnan, a province occupied by the Japanese. The operation involved making the area a no-go zone to test the effectiveness of germ warfare.[36] This operation was a classified military secret. Therefore, a grassroots movement and pan-national research were also required to determine how the community could recover the information and form a societal record and memory of the war damage for future generations. An investigation into the Japanese bombing of Chongqing was conducted in earnest from the 1990s onward as a result of a grassroots movements in Japan and China.[37]

From the late 2000s onwards, there was a slew of class-action lawsuits by Chinese victims of Japanese atrocities and by Japanese citizens suing over the damages caused by the American bombing campaign in 1945. These suits failed in the Japanese courts which have seldom granted restitutions damage caused by American bombings or for war crimes committed by the Japanese government concerning atrocities brought by Chinese. Nonetheless, the cases generated significant media attention in Japan and East Asia.

It is also worth mentioning the investigation into a Japanese atrocity in Taiwan. Having joined in the chemical arms race after World War I, the Japanese forces in Taiwan dropped mustard gas bombs in an attempt to quell the rebellion of the Wushe (an aboriginal people in Taiwan). Investigations into this incident have proceeded since the 2000s following a change in historical awareness in Taiwan.

Conclusion

Despite the diversity of national experiences and the various internal dynamics that have shaped memories of the war in these countries, several trends can be seen. The first of these has to do with the nature of memory itself and how it is constructed. It is clear that memories of World War II continue to evolve and are carefully and selectively constructed by both elites and the general population. As a result, it is valuable to examine changes in collective memory as moving through distinct stages, usually determined by a combination of external and internal developments. So, too, it is apparent that these memories matter greatly as they continue to shape national identity in the present. One such example comes from a September 2014 speech given by German chancellor Merkel, who alluded to the war in saying that it was the Germans' "national and civic duty to fight anti-Semitism" as she spoke about attacks on Jews in Germany resulting from the Gaza conflict.

A second trend is the universal allure of victimhood and the unifying effects of a memory concentrating on shared suffering. In every example, including those nations deemed to have been the instigators of World War II, the people have chosen to view themselves as victims. This memory narrative has been fundamental to rebuilding efforts through providing a sense of unity in the aftermath of unprecedented destruction. This particular development reminds one of the political power inherent in the ability of elites to shape a collective memory that suits their objectives. In the German and Japanese cases, the people suffered at the hands of external forces as well as groups of internal enemies that could be remembered selectively and incompletely. Japan's collective memory of the atomic bombings of Hiroshima and Nagasaki is unique regarding the weapons used by the enemy, but it is representative of the larger narrative of victimization and civilian suffering present in all these nations.

A third and final trend is the importance of national and regional considerations when analyzing memory. In each of these cases, national political, social, and cultural developments played a crucial role in shifting memories of the war. Perhaps just as importantly, regional factors have contributed to the ways in which these nations remembered World War II. Germany openly confronted its past in the 1980s, which was undoubtedly part of its grander ambitions for the European project. Japan, on the other hand, has a strong relationship with the United States and relies on the superpower for security, thus reducing the need for regional cooperation and closer ties with neighbors. This has meant that Japan has not needed to seek the same sort of reconciliation in East Asia that Germany has sought out in Europe. At the same time, this close alliance with the United States had a significant impact on what was remembered—and what was forgotten—about the bombing of Japanese cities and the use of nuclear weapons.

Notes

1. On the history textbook controversy in Japan, see Claudia Schneider, "The Japanese History Textbook Controversy in East Asian Perspective," *Annals of the American Academy of Political Science* 617 (May 2008): 107–122. See also Yoshiko Nozaki, *War Memory, Nationalism, and Education in Postwar Japan, 1945–2007* (New York: Routledge, 2008).
2. On the false dichotomy between vernacular and official memory, see Alon Confino, "Collective Memory and Cultural History," *American Historical Review* 102, no. 5 (December 1997): 1386–1403.

3. See Richard Ned Lebow, "The Memory of Politics in Postwar Europe," in *The Politics of Memory in Postwar Europe*, ed. Richard Ned Lebow, Wulf Kansteiner, and Claudio Fogu (Durham, NC: Duke University Press, 2006), 8–16.
4. Betram M. Gordon, *War Tourism: Second World War France from Defeat and Occupation the Creation of Heritage* (Ithaca: Cornell University Press, 2018).
5. Particularly helpful on how historians have debated Germany's past is Charles Maier, *The Unmasterable Past* (Cambridge, MA: Harvard University Press, 1998).
6. Ian Buruma, The Wages of War: Memories of War in Germany and Japan. New York: Farrar Straus Giroux, 1994.
7. As might be expected, dramatic differences existed in how East and West Germany chose to remember the war. This is most visible both in how the two states conceptualized the victims of the war, as well as how they apportioned responsibility. See Jeffrey Herf, *Divided Memory: The Nazi Past in the Two Germanies* (Cambridge, MA: Harvard University Press, 1997).
8. Wulf Kansteiner, "Losing the War, Winning the Memory Battle," in *The Politics of Memory in Postwar Europe*, ed. Richard Ned Lebow, Wulf Kansteiner, and Claudio Fogu (Durham, NC: Duke University Press, 2006), 102–146. See also Wulf Kansteiner, *In Pursuit of German Memory: History, Television and Politics After Auschwitz* (Athens, OH: Ohio University Press, 2006).
9. Kansteiner, "Losing the War," 107.
10. Robert Moeller, *War Stories: The Search for a Usable Past in the Federal Republic of Germany* (Berkeley: University of California Press, 2001), 16. See also Norbert Frei, *Adenauer's Germany and the Nazi Past: The Politics of Amnesty and Reintegration* (New York: Columbia University Press, 1996); Jeffrey Olick, *In the House of the Hangman: The Agonies of German Defeat, 1943–1949* (Chicago: University of Chicago Press, 2005).
11. The literature on German victimhood has grown substantially since 2000 and has been dominated by a focus on the West Germany. See Bill Niven, ed., *Germans as Victims* (New York: Palgrave, 2006); Bill Niven, *Facing the Nazi Past: United Germany and the Legacy of the Third Reich* (New York: Routledge, 2002); Helmut Schmitz, ed., *A Nation of Victims? Representations of Wartime Suffering from 1945 to the Present* (New York: Rodopi, 2007). Richard Bessel has examined how Germans rapidly transformed themselves into the victims of the Nazis already in May 1945. See Richard Bessel, *Germany 1945: From War to Peace* (New York: Harper, 2009), 167–68.
12. German authorities during this period actively removed official monuments to Jewish victims erected shortly after the war. Perhaps the most infamous example is the research of Sonja Rosenberger in Passau, whose investigations prompted the Bavarian Interior Ministry to acknowledge that it had removed the names of Jews murdered during the Third Reich from a memorial tablet in the town. See the *60 Minutes* interview, "The Nasty Girl Still at Work," http://www.cbsnews.com/news/nasty-girl-still-at-work/.
13. For a discussion of the new monuments constructed in Berlin as part of this campaign, see Brian Ladd, *Ghosts of Berlin: Confronting German History in the Urban Landscape* (Chicago: University of Chicago Press, 1997), 217–236.
14. See, among others, Richard J. Evans, *In Hitler's Shadow: West German Historians and the Attempt to Escape from the Nazi Past* (New York: Pantheon, 1989).
15. On Germany as a "normal" nation, see Jochen Bittner, "What Germany Can Teach Japan," *New York Times*, April 16, 2014.

16. Takumi Sato, *8-gatsu 15-nichi no shinwa: shūsen kinenbi no media-gaku* (Tokyo: Chikuma Shinsho, 2005).
17. Toshihiro Tsuganezawa, ed., *Sengo Nihon no media ibento* (Tokyo: Sekaishisosha, 2002).
18. Kiichi Fujiwara, *Sensō wo kiokusuru* (Tokyo: Kodansha Gendai Shinsho, 2001).
19. Hadashi no Gen, 1973.
20. Yutaka Yoshida, *Nihonjin no sensōkan*, 1995.
21. Yoshiaki Fukuma, *Shōdo no kioku* (Tokyo: Shinyosha, 2011).
22. Osamu Yakabi, *Okinawa sen beigun senryōshi wo manabinaosu* (Tokyo: Seorishobo, 2009).
23. Hitoshi Koyama, *Kūshū to dōin* (Human Rights Research Institute, 2005).
24. Kim Puja, Toshio Nakano, ed., *Rekishi to sekinin* (Tokyo: Seikyusha, 2008).
25. Laura Hein and Mark Selden, *Censoring History: Citizenship and Memory in Japan, Germany, and the United States* (Armonk, NY: M. E. Sharpe, 2000).
26. Tony Judt, "The Past Is Another Country: Myth and Memory in Postwar Europe," *Daedalus* 121, no. 4 (Fall 1992), 99.
27. Henry Rousso, *The Vichy Syndrome* (Cambridge, MA: Harvard University Press, 1991).
28. Marcel Ophuls, *The Sorrow and the Pity* (1969).
29. Louis Malle, *Lacombe Lucien* (1974).
30. Richard Golsan notes that young writers were challenging the Gaullist myth while a new generation of filmmakers was gaining notoriety. In particular, he emphasizes the work of Patrick Modiano, who also co-authored the screenplay for *Lacombe Lucien*. See Richard J. Golsan, "The Legacy of World War II in France: Mapping the Discourses of Memory," in *The Politics of Memory in Postwar Europe*, ed. Richard Ned Lebow, Wulf Kansteiner, and Claudio Fogu (Durham, NC: Duke University Press, 2006), 73–101.
31. Robert Paxton, *Vichy France: Old Guard and New Order* (New York: Columbia University Press, 1972).
32. For an excellent synthesis on French memory of World War II, see Olivier Wieviorka, *Divided Memory: French Recollections of World War II from the Liberation to the Present*, trans. George Holoch (Stanford: Stanford University Press, 2012).
33. Golsan, "The Legacy of World War II in France," 76–77.
34. Robert Gildea, "Myth, Memory and Policy in France since 1945," in *Memory and Power in Postwar Europe*, ed. Jan-Werner Mueller (New York: Cambridge University Press, 2002), 59–75.
35. Henning Meyer, "Memory of World War II in France: National and Transnational Dynamics," in *Dynamics of Memory and Identity in Contemporary Europe*, ed. Eric Langenbacher, Bill Niven, and Ruth Wittlinger (New York: Berghahn, 2012), 136–148.
36. Toshiya Ika, *Sensō ha dō kioku sareru no ka?* (Tokyo: Kashiwa Shobo, 2014).
37. Research Society for Issues concerning War and Air Raids, *jūkeibakugeki to ha nani datta no ka?* Kobunken

Bibliography

Burma, Ian. *The Wages of Guilt: Memories of War in Germany and Japan*. New York: Farrar Straus Giroux, 1994.

Flath, James, and Norman Smith, eds. *Beyond Suffering: Recounting War in Modern China*. Vancouver: University of British Columbia Press, 2011.

Frei, Norbert. *Adenauer's Germany and the Nazi Past: The Politics of Amnesty and Reintegration.* New York: Columbia University Press, 1996.

Fujitani, T., Geoffrey M. White, and Lisa Yoneyama. *Perilous Memories: The Asia–Pacific War(s).* Durham, NC: Duke University Press, 2001.

Golsan, Richard J. *Vichy's Aftermath: History and Counter History in Postwar France.* Lincoln: University of Nebraska Press, 2018.

Gordon, Bertram M. *War Tourism: Second World War France from Defeat and Occupation to the Creation of Heritage.* Ithaca, NY: Cornell University Press, 2018.

Hein, Laura, and Mark Selden, eds. *Censoring History: Citizenship and Memory in Japan, Germany, and the United States.* Armonk, NY: M. E. Sharpe, 2000.

Herf, Jeffrey. *Divided Memory: The Nazi Past in the Two Germanies.* Cambridge, MA: Harvard University Press, 1997.

Langenbacher, Eric, Bill Niven, and Ruth Wittlinger, eds. *Dynamics of Memory and Identity in Contemporary Europe.* New York: Berghahn, 2012.

Lebow, Ned, Wulf Kansteiner, and Claudio Fogu, eds. *The Politics of Memory in Postwar Europe.* Durham, NC: Duke University Press, 2006.

Moeller, Robert. *War Stories: The Search for a Usable Past in the Federal Republic of Germany.* Berkeley: University of California Press, 2001.

Niven, Bill, ed. *Germans as Victims: Remembering the Past in Contemporary Germany.* New York: Palgrave Macmillan, 2006.

Nozaki, Yoshiko. *War Memory, Nationalism, and Education in Postwar Japan, 1945–2007.* New York: Routledge, 2008.

Olick, Jeffrey. *In the House of the Hangman: The Agonies of German Defeat, 1943–1949.* Chicago: University of Chicago Press, 2005.

Rousso, Henry. *The Vichy Syndrome: History and Memory in France since 1944.* Cambridge, MA: Harvard University Press, 1991.

Soh, C. Sarah. *The Comfort Women: Sexual Violence and Postcolonial Memory in Korea and Japan.* Chicago: University of Chicago Press, 2009.

Takenaka, Akiko. *Yasukuni Shrine: History, Memory, and Japan's Unending Postwar.* Honolulu: University of Hawai'i Press, 2015.

Wang, Zheng. *Never Forget National Humiliation: Historical Memory in Chinese Politics and Foreign Relations.* New York: Columbia University Press, 2012.

Wieviorka, Olivier. *Divided Memory: French Recollections of World War II from the Liberation to the Present.* Translated by George Holoch. Stanford, CA: Stanford University Press, 2012.

Index

For the benefit of digital users, indexed terms that span two pages (e.g., 52–53) may, on occasion, appear on only one of those pages.

A

Aachen, Germany
   American forces capture, 315
Abbot Laboratories
   features work of American artists, 553
Adam, Peter
   focuses on the political import of cultural production under the Nazis, 545–46
Addis Ababa
   captured by Italian forces, 58, 59
   railway line to, 56–57
Admiral Scheer (German warship
   sinks AMC *Jervis Bay*, 156–57
Adorno, Theodor
   critiques American cultural production, 552
Africa
   anti-colonial movements in, 41
   Germany explores transporting Jews to, 487
   increased harvesting of hardwoods from, 456
   missionary activity in, 415
   receives scant resources from UNRRA, 509
   send representatives to ecumenical meetings, 416
   soldiers from serve in Burma campaign, 328–29, 332, 336, 338
   southern region avoids sustained enemy attack, 375
   use of poison gas in, 58–59
African Americans
   as defense workers, 376
   experience significant discrimination, 377
   participate in war effort, 473–74
Air Corps Tactical School
   refines strategic bombing concept, 245–46, 247, 251

   texts consider the vulnerability of Japanese cities, 359
Akagi (Japanese flagship)
   sinking of, 347
Albania
   Greek counterattacks into, 103
   invasion of, 99–100, 195, 395–96
   war crimes committed in, 521
Alexander, Harold
   leadership of, 264
Alexander, Henry
   assesses impact of Allied air power, 252
Alexander, Martin
   interpretation of, 127
Algeria
   Jews held in concentration camps in, 426
   Setif rebellion erupts in, 265–66
   Vichy defense of, 258
al-Husseini, Amin
   meets with Adolf Hitler, 484
   supports Adolf Hitler, 417
Allen, Louis
   examines Japanese campaign in Burma, 328–29
Allied Military Government of Occupied Territories (AMGOT)
   minimizes civilian disruptions in battle zones, 264
Altmarck (German supply ship)
   capture of, 155
Amakasu Masahiko
   heads Manchurian Film Association, 550–51
   propagandist for Manchukuo, 542
American Friends Service Committee
   aids lawsuit of Gordon Hirabayashi, 504
   aids refugees, 423, 502–3
   waning role of, 509

Anglo-German Naval Agreement
  encourages Mussolini to invade Ethiopia, 60–61
Anglo-Japanese Alliance
  annulled, 24, 205
Anti-Comintern Pact
  Adolf Hitler betrays spirit of, 84
  formation of, 97, 98–99
  fosters shift in German Chinese policy, 78
  impact of Non-Aggression Pact on, 49
  influences course of Sino-Japanese war, 77–78
  Japan renounces, 100
  leads Josef Stalin to aid China, 85
anti-Semitism
  adopted as state policy in Germany, 483
  central to Nazi ideology, 48
  Christian basis for, 418
  denounced by Angela Merkel, 611–12
  as depicted in film, 609
  Federal Council of Churches condemns, 424
  fosters collaboration with Nazis, 45
  impact on American response to the Holocaust, 507–8
  increases in Romania, 276, 280
  limited purchase in Japan, 98–99
  strong sentiment in French North Africa, 265
  widespread acceptance of, 414–15, 420, 424–25, 502
Antonescu, Ion
  deposed, 106, 110, 296
  enacts anti-Semitic legislation, 280
  forms government, 279
  halt deportation of Jews, 282
  influences Adolf Hitler, 104–5
  institutes ethnic cleansing, 281
  meets with Adolf Hitler, 280
  opens negotiations with Western allies, 282–83
  sends forces to fight in Soviet Union, 280–81
  receives assistance from Adolf Hitler, 109–10
  seeks recovery of Transylvania, 282
  signs Tripartite Pact, 280

Antwerp, Belgium
  British forces seize, 313–14
  faces German rocket attacks, 436
  goal of German offensive, 316
  port opens, 311, 315
Arcadia Conference
  agrees on a Germany first strategy, 221
  clashes over British imperialism during, 222
  marks formal beginning of Grand Alliance, 221
  United Nations alliance proclaimed during, 221–22
Argentina
  British influence in, 230
  enters war, 231
  pursues neutrality, 2
  rise of fascist movements in, 45
Arita Hachiro
  announces expansion of Co-Prosperity Sphere, 213
  opposes rapprochement with Rome and Berlin, 100–1
Arkansas (American battleship)
  supports landing at Omaha beach, 308–9
Arnold, Henry "Hap"
  appoints Curtis LeMay to lead bombing campaign against Japan, 360–61
  appoints Haywood Hansell to lead bombing campaign against Japan, 360
  declares war has become vertical, 440
  demands maximum effort against Japan, 365
  ignores data on civilian casualties from fire raids, 365
  issues directives on bombing campaign against Japan, 360
  receives briefing from Curtis Lemay's staff, 364
  rushes deployment of B-29, 358–59
  seeks to prove worth of airpower and B-29, 360–61
  shielded from full knowledge of Curtis Lemay's plans, 361
  staff prepares target folders for Japanese targets, 359
  visits Curtis Lemay, 364
Ataturk, Mustafa Kermal
  pursues friendship agreements, 194–95

INDEX   619

Atienza, Juan Luis Beigbeder y
  favors neutrality, 399
Atlantic Charter
  and Allied decision to allow Vichy officials to remain in French North Africa, 259
  bolsters anti-colonial movements, 12–13
  clashes with opportunistic Allied policies in the Mediterranean, 261
  Franklin Roosevelt wants principles extended to European colonies, 564–65
  Joseph Biden and Boris Johnson issue new one, 573
  offers vision for new world order, 2, 220–21, 563–64
  outlines fundamental rights, 219–20
  reflects Allied unity, 108, 219, 221
  reflects liberal internationalism, 564
  suspended in deal with Pietro Badoglio, 259
  and the trusteeship system, 569
  wide diffusion of, 265
Atlantic Monthly (journal)
  war reporting in, 469
atomic bomb
  building of, 431, 437–38, 458
  Canada support development of, 224
  controversies surrounding, 9
  German research efforts, 437, 441
  and Japanese memory culture, 602, 605–6, 612
  leads to Japanese surrender, 553–54
  legacy of, 439, 468, 477–78
  lingering health impact of exposure to radiation, 475
  use against Japanese cites, 9, 353–54, 365–70, 384, 438–39, 453
Attlee, Clement
  serves as prime minister, 12–13
Auchinleck, Claude
  implements jungle training for troops in India, 332
Aung Sang Sun
  leads nationalist forces in Burma, 328
Auschwitz
  deportations to, 106, 491–92
  massive murder and slave labor complex, 491
  shapes perception of Nazi cultural productions, 545–46
  as a symbol, 482
  used to house ethnic German expellees, 592
  war crime trial of commandant of, 523
Australia
  cooperates with Allied war crime investigations, 529
  defense of, 344
  deploys troops to Great Britain, 141–42
  engages Japanese forces in New Guinea, 8–9, 349, 350
  forges closer ties with U.S., 225, 329
  gains experience in jungle warfare, 332
  holds war crimes trials, 527–28, 529
  Japanese seek to cut off from U.S., 345
  and logistical support of Marines at Guadalcanal, 349
  maintains camps for Italian prisoners of war, 504
  organizes commission to investigate war crimes, 525
  participates in ABDA, 210, 221, 343
  participates in Battle of Coral Sea, 345
  participates in Battle of Tobruk, 468–69
  participates in Tokyo war crime trials, 529–31
  passes Australian War Crimes Act, 526
  provides aviators to Far East Air Forces, 358
  regards many returning prisoners of war with suspicion, 503–4
  screening of potential military aviators, 472
  signs Declaration of United Nations alliance, 222
  submits proposal at San Francisco conference for greater role for UN General Assembly, 569
  troops deploy to North Africa, 148, 225
Austria
  Anschluss with Germany, 5, 99, 101–2, 502, 519
  Mussolini seeks to preserve independence of, 5, 60, 95–96
  rise of fascists movements in, 45
  sovereignty of, 5
  and Versailles settlement, 3
Austro-Hungarian Empire
  dismemberment of, 3, 19
  ethnic diversity of, 28
  as Germany ally, 16
  impact of Bulgarian armistice on, 17

Azores
   Allied access to, 400–2
   during Battle of the Atlantic, 166

B

Babi Yar
   mass killings at, 179
Backe, Herbert
   implements Hunger Plan, 505–6
Badoglio, Pietro
   announces armistice, 261
   communists join government of, 267
   heads new regime in Italy, 259–76
   lacks confidence in military commanders, 262–63
   opens negotiations with Allies, 105
Baldwin, Stanley
   adopts policy of non-intervention in Spanish Civil War, 66–67
Ball, Simon
   interpretation of, 260–61, 267–68
Barbie, Klaus
   trial of, 609
Battle for New Guinea
   American and Australians forces halt Japanese advance, 8–9
   Australian forces pursue Japanese across Owen Stanley Mountain, 349
   Australians gain experience in jungle warfare, 332
   Japanese forces threaten, 343
   Japanese pursue an overland campaign, 345–46
   Japanese transports destroyed by U.S. Fifth Air Force, 342–43
   JCS plans campaign to capture northern coast, 348
   MacArthur rapid advance speeds timetable for Philippines invasion, 352
   medical casualties during, 350–51
   Owen Stanley serves as natural defensive barrier for Allies, 344
   U.S. force battle up coast, 350
   U..S. Navy raids, 212
   U.S. Pacific fleet turns back invasion force, 212–13

Battle for Normandy
   Allied forces delay in closing Falaise Gap, 312–13
   Americans liberate Cherbourg, 311–12
   British efforts to seize Caen, 311, 312
   Germans face difficulty reinforcing Normandy positions, 311
   Omar Bradley attacks Brittany, 312
   turn back German counteroffensive toward Avranches, 312
   U.S. Forces use aerial bombardment to break German resistance, 312
Battle for Poland
   aftermath of, 127
   French Government promises offensive in West, 120
   Germans make effective use of combined arms warfare, 243
   lack of German planning for, 118
   Luftwaffe dominates skies over, 122, 242, 252
   Luftwaffe suffers significant losses, 239–40, 277
   myths surrounding, 116, 117, 118, 276
   perceived as ushering in a new way of war, 126–27, 131
   Polish cities bombed during, 131
   Polish defenses face eastward, 119
   Polish forces inflict significant losses on Wehrmacht, 276–77
   reasons for Polish defeat, 122
   role of Blitzkrieg in German victory, 472
   use of armored forces and air power in, 118–19
   use of tactical air power during, 237, 240
Battle of Adwa (1896)
   serves as turning point in Italo-Ethiopian relations, 56–57
Battle of the Atlantic
   Allied and Axis objectives during, 154–56
   Allied tonnage lost, 158
   and British diplomacy with Spain and Portugal, 400
   deciphering the Enigma Code crucial turning point for, 434
   fought in a zone of neutrality, 406
   Germans gain ports in Norway and France, 155–56

Germans use Spanish ports covertly, 69
Germans wolf packs clash with Allied navies.
    158–61
Germany deploys commerce raiders, 155,
    156–57
Italian participation in, 102–3
poses threat to British survival, 7
results in delays opening of second front,
    304–5
role of Latin American in, 229–30
Battle of Bataan
    American forces defeated in, 211–14,
        343–44
    Death March follows battle, 183, 351–52
    results in mass surrender of American
        forces, 316
Battle of Bismarck Sea
    achieves destruction of Japanese transports,
        350
Battle of Britain
    German failures during, 240
    Germans fail to prevail in, 434–35
    Luftwaffe bomb cities, 9, 146
    opening phase, 145–46
    role of signal intelligence during, 434
    Royal Air Force prevails, 7
    strategic significance of, 7, 155–56
Battle of the Bulge
    Adolf Hitler seeks to capture Antwerp, 316
    fosters inter-allied discord, 316–17
    U.S. forces defend Bastogne, 316
    Waffen SS murder American POWs, 316
Battle of Coral Sea
    American victory in, 202, 345
    impact on New Guinea campaign, 345
Battle of El Alamein
    German defeat in, 104, 190, 256
    strategic significance of, 9
Battle of Guadalcanal
    American forces initially unopposed, 9
    impact of malaria during, 11, 350
    Japanese lose naval battle of, 104
    Japanese seek to recover Henderson Field,
        349
    medical care during, 472–73
    U.S. invasion suffers major losses from
        Japanese attack, 348–49

U.S. Marines undertake amphibious
    landings, 348
Yamamoto withdraws, 349
Battle of Hurtgen Forrest
    Americans troops struggle in dense pine
        forest, 315
Battle of Iwo Jima
    fought in order to secure air bases, 352–53
    medical care during battle, 466
    Navajo code talkers aid victory, 434
Battle of Java Sea
    Allied forces suffer defeat in, 202, 210
Battle of Kohima and Imphal
    demonstrates strength of British and Indian
        forces, 335–36
    historiography neglects role of Indian army
        in, 333
    Japanese force advance at lay siege to
        Kohima, 333–34
    Japanese lay siege to Imphal, 334–35
    Japanese retreat, 335
    Japanese seek to strengthen defensive
        perimeter, 332–33
    siege of Kohima lifted, 334
Battle of Kursk
    Adolf Hitler orders attack, 105
    environmental impact of, 452
    German offensive halted, 290
    Josef Stalin overestimates ability to sustain
        offensives, 291–92
    Luftwaffe wins air superiority on first day,
        242–43
    shifts strategic balance, 7, 288, 291, 292–93,
        294
Battle of Kwajalein
    U.S. captures island with minimal losses,
        308–9
Battle of Leyte Gulf
    Japanese use of Kamikaze attacks, 352
    William Halsey pursues Japanese carriers,
        352
Battle of Midway
    characterized, 154
    intelligence plays crucial role, 9, 438–39
    strategic significance of, 9, 104
Battle of Narvik
    British naval success during, 125

Battle of Nomonhan
    Japanese army suffers defeat in, 84
    strategic impact of, 6, 85–86
Battle of Okinawa
    casualties during, 368
    Japanese commemoration of, 606
    Japanese launch kamikaze attack, 352–53
    media accounts of, 357
Battle of Santa Cruz
    Americans suffer loss of *Hornet*, 349
Battle of Shanghai
    Chinese army battle performance in, 5, 78
    Chinese face defeat in, 81–82
    photograph of abandoned baby shocks Westerners, 357–58
Battle of Smolensk
    strategic significance of, 175–76
Battle of Stalingrad
    Adolf Hitler's obsession with, 173–74
    after defeat Axis allies reconsider participation in war, 291
    aftermath prompts peace feelers by Hungary and Romania, 282
    civilian casualties during, 379
    German losses at, 267
    Hungarian and Romanian participation in, 281–82
    Hungarian, Italian, and Romanian troops routed, 104
    prompts proposal to create Polish auxiliaries, 277
    Soviet use stubborn defense of fixed positions to prevail, 288
    Soviet victory safeguards Allied scientific knowledge, 434
    strategic significance of, 7 , –9, 164, 173–74, 178–79, 191, 242–43, 268, 287–88
Battle of Tobruk
    bombing of medical facilities during, 468–69
    British garrison surrenders to Rommel, 191
Battle of Wuhan
    Chiang Kai-shek leads defense, 86
    Chinese forces attack Japanese aircraft, 85
    strategic significance of, 86
BBC
    suspends Swiss radio service, 402–3

Beck, Ludwig
    retirement of, 118
Becker, Karl
    leads German rocket development, 436
Belgium
    displaced persons from, 589
    embraces neutrality, 395
    establishes governments in exile, 266
    French army deployments in, 127
    French war plans regarding, 25–26, 121
    German invasion of, 7, 125, 144–45, 394, 434
    German massacre in, 316
    invades Ruhr region, 15–16
    Kaiser violates neutrality of, 394
    occupies Rhineland, 20
    participates in Inter-Allied Rhineland High Commission (IARHC), 20–21
    receives food relief, 497, 500–1
    signs Treaty of Locarno, 4
    tries war criminals, 519–20
Bechtolsheim, von, General
    orders murder of the Jews, 180
Bell, George (Bishop of Chichester)
    condemns bombing of German cities, 422
Benes, Edvard
    seeks expulsion of German minority, 591
    seeks expulsion of Hungarian minority, 593
Benjamin, Walter
    analyzes propaganda in authoritarian regime, 58–59
    describes anxieties presaging war, 539
    flees from German controlled areas, 545
Bergson, Peter
    publicizes plight of European Jewry, 505
Berlin, Germany
    battle for, 298–300, 318
    bombing of, 146, 248, 250
    hosts meeting of International World Baptist Congress, 419–20
    occupation of, 287
    rebuilding of, 453
    ruble in, 452–53
    revolutionary uprising in, 17–18
    serves as cultural center, 540, 549, 551–52
Berlin Olympics
    boycott of, 420
    filming of, 539

Bernard. Henri
　issues dissent during Tokyo war crime trials, 531
Bernays, Murray
　develops strategy for war crime trials, 517–18
Biddle, Francis
　weighs testimony of Chester Nimitz, 518–19
Biden, Joe
　issue new Atlantic Charter, 573
Bismarck (German battleship)
　destruction of, 157
Blitzkrieg
　countering of, 143–44
　failure of, 183, 184, 451
　myths regarding, 116, 117, 118, 122–23, 128–29, 131
　origins of terms, 118
　role of Luftwaffe in, 238–40
　success of, 7
Bloc, Marc
　examines reasons for French defeat, 116–17, 129, 130, 546–47
Blomberg, Werner von
　supports Sino-German military alliance, 78
Blue Division
　fights with Germans against Soviet Union, 70, 394, 399
Blum, Leon
　adopts policy of non-intervention in Spanish Civil War, 66–67
　initially favors aiding Spanish Republic, 66
　leads popular front, 25
　progressive policies of, 546–47
Bock, Fedor von
　favors Moscow as key objective, 175–76
Bohlen, Gustav Krupp von
　case against, 521
　indictment of, 518
　unavailable to stand trial, 518
bombing, aerial
　in advance of D-Day, 249
　against civilian targets, 439
　with bats, 370
　of British cities, 9, 147, 246, 378
　of British ports, 158–59
　of Chinese cities, 357–58
　of Chongqing, 380, 549–50, 611

　by Condor Legion in Spain, 67–68
　depictions in British war-time documentaries, 553
　devastates Japanese cities, 353, 605–6
　of Ethiopia, 58–59
　of German cities, 246, 250
　of German industrial targets, 248–49
　of German oil and refining capacity, 251
　of Germany heavy water plant in Norway, 437
　of Germany, Tokyo and Great Britain, 439
　of Hamburg, 452–53
　of Henderson Field, 349
　during Japanese siege of Imphal, 335
　of London, 146
　of Monte Cassino, 250
　of Polish cities, 131
　religious condemnation of, 422
　reluctance to authorize, 127–28
　of submarine pens, 246
　of Tokyo, 362–63
　of Tokyo by Doolittle raiders, 358
　unidentified planes bomb Kassa, 281
　of Wuhan, 85
Bonhoeffer, Dietrich
　resists Nazi regime, 422
Bonomi, Ivanoe
　forms government, 264–65
Bor-Komorowski, Tadeusz
　leads Home Army against German forces, 295
Bormann, Martin
　absent from Nuremberg war crime trial, 518
　indictment of, 518
　receives death sentence, 519
Borneo
　defense of, 206, 209–10
Bose, Subhas Chandra
　heads Indian National Army, 337
　travels to Germany, 105–6
Bradley, Omar
　fails to close Falaise gap, 312–13
　ignores advice on naval gunfire, 308–9
　launches Operation Cobra, 312
　losses control of First and Ninth Armies, 316–17
　orders attack on Hurtgen forest, 315
　seeks greater support for First and Third Armies, 314

Braun, Wernher von
  recruited to work in America, 440
Brazil
  Axis threat to, 229–30
  British influence in, 230
  pursues neutrality, 396, 398, 405–6
  rise of fascist organizations in, 45
  seeks to minimize German influence, 403
  site of cultural battleground, 402–3
  U.S. bases in, 401–2
Brest, France
  American forces besiege, 315
  Bismarck heads for, 155
  Hipper departs harbor, 156–57
Bretton Woods Agreement
  agreement blends laissez-fair economics and welfare-state intervention, 566
  key component of postwar order, 572, 573
  Soviet Union veers away from, 572–73
Bretton Woods Conference
  Americans and British differ on postwar economic order, 566
  serves as first multilateral North-South dialogue on global finance, 572–73
British Council
  undertakes programming in neutral nations, 402–3
Brooke, Alan
  anticipates German invasion, 147
  observes lack of readiness in ground troops, 145, 146
  replaces Edmund Ironside, 144–45
  war planning of, 147–48
Browning, Christopher
  interpretations of, 490
Browning, Frederick
  commands Allied First Airborne Army, 314
Buchanan, Andrew
  views of, 258, 260, 264–65, 269
Budapest, Hungary
  fall of, 296–97
  Jews deported from, 283
Bulgaria
  declares war on Germany, 106
  demands territory from Romania, 279
  German influence in, 395–96
  involvement in the Holocaust, 109
  joins Tripartite Pact, 103
  makes territorial demands on Romania, 279
  signs armistice, 17
  Soviets troops occupy, 296
  U.S. objects to pro-Soviet government installed in, 571
Bunuel, Luis
  denounces Salvador Dali, 547
  joins U.S. Government committee investigating propaganda, 547
Burma
  British deploy reinforcements to, 210–11
  British efforts to maintain control rule over, 228–29
  construction of rail line in, 524
  investigates war crimes, 525
  Japanese advances in, 8, 104, 202, 209, 211, 225–26, 342
  Japanese seek to exploit forest resources of, 456
  military campaign in, 328–38, 358
  nationalist support for Japanese, 213–14, 328
  participates in Tokyo war crime trials, 529–30
  provides crucial line of communication to China, 10
  Thailand seeks territory from, 396–98
Burma Road
  blockade of, 87
Bush, Vannevar
  heads Office of Scientific Research and Development, 433

C

Cadogan, Alec
  describes war-time atmosphere, 138
Cairo Conference
  considers plans for Korean independence, 228–29
  declares Allies will punish Japanese aggression, 525
  discuss strategy for Korean independence, 565
  reflects strength of Allied unity, 108
Cairo, Egypt
  Rommel threatens, 191

California
  Hiram Johnson represents in U.S. Senate, 22–23
  passes anti-Japanese legislation, 204
  site of World Student Christian Federation conference, 417
Calvert, Mike
  captures Mogaung, 336–37
Canada
  assists war crime investigations, 525, 527–28
  contributes to defense of Great Britain, 141–42, 224, 225
  economic mobilization of, 10
  enacts War Crimes Regulations, 526
  forges closer ties with U.S., 224, 231
  offers food relief for Bengal, 507
  participates in Tokyo war crimes trials, 529–31
  provides timber to Great Britain, 456
  role in Battle of the Atlantic, 7
  signs Union Nations alliance declaration, 222
  undertakes biological warfare research, 435–36
  wartime environmental damage to, 457
Carol, King (Romania)
  calls on Ion Antonescu to form government, 279
  expresses friendship with Germany, 279
Carson, Rachel
  expresses pessimism on relation between humans and nature, 458
Casablanca
  passage of Jewish refugees from, 502–3
  Vichy French defense of, 258
Casablanca Conference
  announces unconditional surrender policy, 422, 565
  formalizes Combined Bomber Offensive, 247
  gives priority to Battle of the Atlantic, 164–65
  orders planning for invasion of France, 305
  reflects strength of Allied unity, 108
Cassidy, David
  interpretations of, 441
casualties
  of Allied air crews in Europe, 249–50
  from Allied bombing campaign against Germany, 237–38, 250
  from atomic bomb attacks, 438–39
  from bombing of Durango, 67–68
  from British naval blockade in World War I, 366
  for China, 327–28, 380, 382
  civilians and combatants, 387
  for civilians at Leningrad and Stalingrad, 379
  data of civilian deaths from incendiary raids ignored by Hap Arnold, 365
  for D-Day landing, 310
  from disease on Guadalcanal, 473
  from executions in Italy, 519–20
  from famine, 505–7
  from firebombing of Hamburg, 452–53
  German losses in 1945, 299
  among German prisoners of war, 583–84
  for Germany, 385
  Hungarian war-time losses, 283
  during invasion Anglo-Soviet invasion of Iran, 405
  for Japanese force at Imphal, 336
  among Japanese prisoners of war, 585
  for the Mediterranean Theater, 268
  on Omaha Beach, 310
  projections for an Allied invasion of Japan, 368
  for Romanian forces on Eastern Front, 280–81
  on Saipan and Tinian, 351
  for Soviet forces in 1941, 181–82
  Soviet losses from Operation Barbarossa, 581–82
  among Soviet POWs, 180
  for Soviet Union, 173
  for the Soviet Union, 379
  from Tokyo fire raids, 362–63, 393
  in Vietnam from famine, 213–14
  at Wal Wal, 57–58
  for Warsaw, 278
censorship
  by Allied Control Commission in Italy, 264–65
  of the arts and culture, 540
  by German authorities of Hollywood motion pictures, 551–52

censorship (*cont.*)
  in Germany during World War I, 18
  imposed globally, 10–11
  by Iranian regime, 199
  in Italy, Soviet Union, Germany, and Japan, 541
  of Japanese front-line reporting, 551
  by neutral countries, 402–3
  of Pablo Picasso, 547
  in the Soviet Union, 543–44
  of *The Sorrow and the Pity*, 609
  by Turkish regime, 196–97
Chaban-Delmas, Jacques
  serves as military delegate to COMAC, 266
Chamberlain, Neville
  abandons policy of appeasement, 29
  assesses German war-time plans, 138–39
  negotiates Munich Pact, 28–29
  pursues policy of appeasement, 29, 119
Chanler, William
  deems Kellogg Briand Pact as legally binding, 517
Chapman, Herrick
  interpretations of, 130
Chastenet, Jacques
  interpretations of, 130
Chemical Warfare Service (U.S.)
  experiments with incendiary gel weapons, 458
  sprays DDT in Pacific Islands, 425–26
Chemical Weapons. *See* poison gas
Chennault, Claire
  clashes with Joseph Stilwell, 327
  commands Fourteenth Air Force, 358
  leads Flying Tigers, 357–58
  orders incendiary attack on Hankow, 359–60
  seeks support for Operation Matterhorn, 358–59
  urges bombing of Japanese industry, 359
Chevalier, Jacques
  names oak for Marshall Petain, 455–56
Chiang Kai-Shek
  adopts trading space for time policy in meeting Japanese invasion, 380
  appeals to League of Nations, 75, 79
  assessment of, 89
  clashes with Joseph Stillwell, 327, 328
  commands Chinese forces at Wuhan, 86
  declares war on Axis powers, 80–81
  defends Shanghai, 81
  and deployment of Chinese troops to Burma, 330
  distrusts Sun Li-Jen for actions in Burma campaign, 330
  envisions an alliance uniting the United States, Britain, and Soviet Union against Axis, 88
  historical assessments of, 328
  implements flood control measures, 506
  kidnapping of, 77
  meets with Roosevelt and Churchill, 565
  militarily unifies China, 549
  orders destruction Changsha, 381
  receive aid from the United States, 87–88
  receives British aid via Burma Road, 87
  resists Japanese aggression, 2, 5, 501
  seeks alliance with Germany, 5, 78, 82, 86–87
  seeks approval of Operation Matterhorn, 358–59
  seeks German mediation, 81–82, 83
  seeks immediate independence for Korea, 564–65
  seeks to avoid full scale war, 76–77
  seeks to end unequal treaties between China and imperial powers, 205
  seeks to expand relationship with United States, 88
  sees Tripartite Pact as drawing Soviets closer to China, 88
  signs Sino-Soviet Non-aggression Pact, 82
  takes part in uneasy truce with Chinese Communists, 381–82
  tries Japanese war criminals, 528
  wages war against Chinese communists, 549–50
  welcomes Soviet assistance, 85
children
  as subjects for oxygen deprivation experiments, 474–75
  efforts to aid refugee children in China, 381
  evacuated from British cities, 378
  Japanese expectations they serve the war effort, 383

lack of child care in U.S., 376
orphaned by air raid, 357–58
participate in Britain's Kindertransports, 502
protection of, 500
struggles to find adequate care for in Great Britain, 378–79
victims of Nazi euthanasia policies, 486–87
war-time death of, 501–2

Chile
British influence in, 230
Popular Front emerges in, 46

China
anti-Japanese protests in, 600–1
assists the UNWCC, 525
attracts Japanese artists and writers, 549
and Burma campaign, 10
champions rights of less developed countries at Bretton Woods conference, 567
Christian communities in, 418
civil war follows Japanese surrender, 382
comes under aerial bombardment, 357–58, 380
and command structure of China-Burma-India Theater, 327
commemorates Victory Day, 604–5
Communists triumph, 572
as counterweight to Japanese power, 229
course of war with Japan, 94
creates programs to aid refugee children, 381
Curtis LeMay seeks weather reports from, 361
deemed by Franklin Roosevelt as a great power, 220–21, 565
defends Wuhan, 86
deploys troops to Burma, 211
embarks on war with Japan, 79–81
emerges as new motor of global economy, 573
endures massive casualties during war, 380, 381, 382
endures massive war-time destruction, 381
engages in war with Japan, 5
experiences widespread famines, 506
faces humanitarian crisis, 501–2
favors iconographic painting and sculpture symbolizing political ideals, 544
fights Thai troops deployed to Burma, 397–98
flirts with fascism, 540–41
Franklin Roosevelts discussion with Josef Stalin regarding, 228–29
gains international support for resistance against Japan, 89
German agents in, 106
German colonies in, 97
gradual ascendancy of Communism in, 41
growing domestic pressure to challenge Japanese aggression, 77
holds war crime trials, 528, 611
impact of Great Depression on relations with Germany, 98
issues Pacific Charter, 564–65
Japan encourages foreign investors to return to, 100–1
Japanese conduct barbaric medical experiments in, 435–36
Japanese invasion of, 3, 5, 26, 28, 39, 47, 94, 98–99
Japanese occupation impact on the arts in, 550–51
Japanese POWs in, 585
lacks necessary structures for modern warfare, 89
loses German support, 26, 99
maintain close ties with Germany, 97, 98–99
and Manchurian Incident, 73–77, 98–99, 539
and memory of World War II, 1, 2
mobilizes literature and art to oppose Japanese aggression, 549–50
Nationalists and Communists maintain an uneasy truce, 381–82
as one of the Four Policeman in vision of Franklin Roosevelt, 233, 565
participates in Dumbarton Oaks Conference, 567–68
participates in Moscow Conference, 566
participates in San Francisco Conference, 569–70
participates in the Tokyo war trials, 529–30
and Prince Konoe's proclamation of New Order in Asia, 213

China (*cont.*)
    promotes independence for India, Korea, and Indochina, 564–65
    provides airfields for Operation Matterhorn, 358–60
    and the Rape of Nanjing, 82–83
    receives Americans supplies airlifted over the Hump, 329–30
    receives German support, 261–78
    receives Germany military aid, 5
    receives little support from Western democracies, 77
    receives support from Soviet Union, 84–85, 88
    receives U.S. support in war with Japan, 8, 87–88, 206, 207, 208
    receives veto on United Nations Security Council, 11
    relations with U.S. improve after Joseph Stilwell departs, 337–38
    scholarly assessment of war-time contributions of, 327–28
    seeks alliance with Nazi Germany, 86–75
    seeks apology from Japan, 601–2
    seeks German mediation, 81–82
    seeks to end unequal treaties, 205
    seeks united front against Japan, 88
    shifting memories of war, 610–11
    signs Declaration of United Nations alliance, 221–22, 564
    signs Potsdam Declaration, 525
    site of Japanese programs developing chemical and biological weapons, 370
    U.S. assesses Japanese forces in China, 209
    U.S. Fourteenth Air Force deployed to, 358
    U.S. seeks Japanese withdrawal from, 203
    U.S. seeks to improve Sino-Japanese relations, 205
    U.S. seeks to protect access to markets in, 203, 204–5
    WSCF invites religious representatives from China and Japan to discuss Sino-Japanese conflict, 417
Chongqing, China
    aerial bombing of, 357–58, 380, 611
    serves as headquarters for a branch of the UNWCC, 525
    serves as war-time capital, 86

Christianity and Crisis (journal)
    founding of, 425
Church of England
    leaders participate in Vatican exchanges, 422
    most leaders accept bombing of German cities, 422
Churchill, Winston
    accepts date for invasion of France, 305
    addresses crowds on V-E Day celebrations, 379
    addresses French people, 304
    addresses House of Commons, 143, 146–47
    agrees to food shipments to Greece, 507
    applauds American success at Battle of the Bulge, 316–17
    applauds victory over German forces at Tunisgrad, 105
    attends Casablanca conference, 565
    attends Teheran Conference, 198, 233, 565
    believes Singapore is Gibraltar of the East, 211
    bemoans lack of landing craft, 306
    bolsters British morale, 147
    brings Orde Wingate to Quebec Conference, 336
    characterizes nature of unconditional surrender, 582–83
    clashes with Franklin Roosevelt over colonialism, 8, 228–29
    clashes with Franklin Roosevelt over status of India and Dominions, 221–22
    condemns Munich Pact, 29
    coordinates statements on German war crimes with Franklin Roosevelt, 515–16
    criticizes neutrality, 394–95
    defends Allied naval blockade, 506–7
    deploys Australian and New Zealand troops to North Africa, 148
    electoral defeat of, 12–13
    embraces Great Power diplomacy in relationship with Josef Stalin, 227
    embraces *realpolitik* view of Soviet Union, 228
    expresses misgiving on Polish question, 228
    faces bleak military situation, 140
    favors Germany first strategy, 343
    forms multi-party government, 139–40

issues Atlantic Charter, 563–64
leadership of, 149
limits exportation of food to Nazi occupied Europe, 506–7
meets with Franklin Roosevelt, 160, 164
memoir largely ignore Kohima and Imphal, 333
as a navalist, 258
orders an invasion of Iran, 197
panders to Spanish and Portuguese sensitivities, 400
participates in Arcadia conference, 221
participates in Cairo Conference, 565
participates in Yalta Conference, 227–28, 568
places pressure on Turkey to declare war, 196–97
prioritizes Mediterranean Theater, 256, 258, 259–60, 267–69
provides aid to the Soviet Union, 7
raises possibility of summary execution of German war criminals, 516
receives report on British defenses, 144
refuses to grant immediate impendence to India, 225–26
rejects Canadian offer of food aid for India, 507
remains bullish during Battle of Britain, 146
seeks access to Iraqi petroleum, 194
seeks American built ships, 164
seeks to restore British glory, 220
signs United Nations declaration, 219
on success of Dunkirk evacuation, 140–41
uses rhetoric regarding moral underpinnings of western culture and society, 425
views Italian surrender as significant, 263
visits United States, 564
weak negotiating position at Yalta, 298
Ciano, Galeazzoe
condemns German actions, 100–1
confers with Adolf Hitler, 96–97
meets with Ribbentrop, 102
Citino, Robert M.
interpretations of, 122
Civil Affairs Corps
dispatched to Sicily, 263

civil defense
in Great Britain, 378
in Japan, 383
Clark, Kenneth
commissions war art, 553
Clark, Mark
assessment of, 264
Clausewitz, Carl von
views on causes of war, 29–30
Clemenceau, George
negotiates at Paris Peace conference, 18–19
seeks to maintain war-time alliance, 19
Clinchy, Everett
condemns extremism, 420–21
Coates, Peter
examines militarized landscapes, 450, 458–59
Cohen, Warren
interpretations of, 75
Cohn, Georg
offers conceptual model of neutrality, 396–97
Cold War
ability of United Nations Organization to enforce collective security wanes during, 11
builds on robust scientific and technological structures from World War II, 431
challenges United States for global dominance, 380
complicates decolonization, 12–13
encourages development of international religious networks, 427
and formation of National Liberation Army in Ethiopia, 59
fosters a discourse of peace in Japanese society, 605
fosters creation of regional security pacts, 569–70
fosters critical assessment of Franklin Roosevelt decisions at Yalta, 260
impact on Chinese memory of war, 610
impact on postwar planning, 563
impacts artists cultural production, 555
influences debate over use of atomic bomb, 368
influences memory of World War II, 1–2, 7

Cold War (cont.)
   leads to shift in treatment of war criminals in Japan, 529
   leads to surveillance of socialist and communist groups in Japan, 554
   loyalty of scientists suspected during, 440–41
   and role of Operation Paperclip in scientific-intelligence gathering, 440
   scholarly trends examining, 562–63, 572–73
   shapes historiography on evaluating Soviet combat effectives, 6, 173, 287
   shapes memory of war in Germany, 603
   and Soviet occupation of northern Iran, 199
   Soviet Union possesses powerful military during, 300
   storage of nuclear waste during, 452
   U.S. plays a major role in Middle East during, 200
   undermines Bretton Woods agreements on development, 567
   UNRRA bridges ideological chasm developing during, 509
   use of Axis POWs as bargaining chips, 585
   weapons systems created during World War II shape course of, 435
collaboration
   in China, 549–51
   among French artists in occupied Paris, 548
   Germans recruits Belarusian auxiliaries, 182–83
   among Italian artists and fascist regime, 543
   often rare in true form, 540
   in the Soviet Union, 523–24
   of Vichy regime, 528–29, 601, 607–10
Combined Bomber Offensive
   compared with British naval blockade of World War I, 366
   implementation of, 247
Combined Chiefs of Staff (COS)
   creates classification of disarmed enemy forces after V-Day, 583
   formation of, 8, 221
   grants Dwight Eisenhower control over bombers, 307
   orders planning for invasion of France, 305
   receives cable regarding conduct of Bernard Montgomery, 316–17
   supports long range penetration force in Burma, 336
Comintern
   considers reasons for Hitler's success in Germany, 46
   establishment of, 40
   inserts agent into Japan, 108
   paranoia in, 47
   stresses defense of Soviet state, 44–45
Conant, James B.
   raises concerns regarding biological warfare, 431
Condor Legion
   aids Francesco Franco, 67–68
   bombs civilians in Spanish Civil War, 67–68
Confessing Church
   contains members of German resistance movement, 422
   defends non-Aryan clergy and members, 419
   publishes memorandum critical of regime, 419
Congress, U.S.
   funds construction of Pearl Harbor naval base, 204
   issues report regarding Pearl Harbor attack, 211–12
   passes Johnson Debt Default Act of 1934, 22–23
   raises tariffs, 22
   refuses to admit children refugees, 502
Connelly, John
   interpretations of, 277
Conservative Party (Great Britain)
   supports social welfare initiatives, 24–25
Coolidge, Calvin
   remains committed to disarmament, 205
Copenhagen (play)
   explores career of Werner Heisenberg, 441
Corregidor, Philippines
   defense of, 212–13, 344
   fall of, 211–12, 213–14
Corse, Edward
   examines work of British Council in neutral countries, 402–3

Corsica
    bombers bases on, 268-69
    liberation of, 266
Crete
    German airborne units depleted after attack on, 108
    German use of air power against, 268
    mistreatment of POWs captured on, 519-20
Cripps, Stafford
    negotiates with Indian nationalists, 330-31
Croatia
    participates in final solution, 109
    receives eighty thousand deportees from Slovenia, 590-91
Cunningham, Owen
    serves as defense attorney at Tokyo war crime trials, 531
Curtin, John
    welcomes arrival of Douglas MacArthur, 344
Czechoslovakia
    Adolf Hitler plans to invade, 118, 519
    annexation of, 5, 483-84
    dismemberment of, 99, 275
    exchanges population with Soviet Union, 593
    expels Germans minority, 12, 591-92
    formation of, 19
    German minority in, 20, 28
    German occupation of, 29, 119-20
    joins alliance with France, 121
    Joins Little Entente, 25
    loses Sudetenland, 28-29

D

D-Day (June 6, 1944)
    Allies agree on date for, 305
    Allies use deception schemes to confuse Germans, 306
    American airborne forces scattered across Cotentin Peninsula, 308
    American meet with success on Utah Beach, 309-10
    British airborne units secure bridges, 308
    British forces fail to seize Caen, 309
    British forces reach Arromanches, 309
    Canadian forces push farthest inland, 309
    Combined Chiefs of Staff order planning to begin for, 305
    crucial need for landing crafts, 306
    destroyers attack enemy fortification on Omaha, 310
    Eisenhower uses air power to isolate Normandy, 307
    Germans fail to halt invasion, 310
    heavy bombers fail to hit target on Omaha Beach, 310
    impact of weather on landing, 308
    landing beaches selected, 306
    launches Allied forces into Northwest Europe, 304
    planners select Normandy as site for landing, 305
    pre-landing air and naval bombardment ineffective on Omaha Beach, 308-9
Daladier, Edouard
    negotiates Munich Pact, 28-29
    pursues policy of appeasement, 119
Dali, Salvador
    depicts Spanish Civil War, 547
Danzig
    becomes Polish city, 12
    serves as Polish corridor to sea, 19
Darlan, Jean-Francois
    equivocal behavior of, 261
    negotiates deal with Allies, 259-60, 263, 264, 266
    ponders possible Allied attack, 257-58
    seeks negotiations with Germany, 258
Dawes Plan
    provides German access to capital, 4
DDT (dichlorodiphenyltrichloroethane)
    sprayed to control malaria, 11, 350-51, 458
    testing of, 458
    value of, 438
De Bono, Emilio
    expands infrastructure in Eritrea and Somalia, 57
De Chirico, Georgio
    artistic career of, 542-43

De Gaulle, Charles
  absence from *Sorrow and the Pity*, 609
  American opposition to, 259–60
  assumes control over Algiers, 266
  improvises Free French government, 130–31
  liberates Paris, 548
  makes concession to Muslim population in Algeria, 265–66
  passed over, 259
  shapes memory of World War II. 1, 601, 608–9
Denmark
  casualties from German invasion, 405
  Germans acquire airfields in, 124–25
  holds crime trials in, 519–20
  indefensible, 121
  invasion of, 7, 101, 102, 124, 138, 394, 434
  postwar future of, 318
  remains part of the West, 318
Department of Defense (U.S.)
  emerges as largest patron of science, 440
Dieppe Raid
  Canadian forces participate in, 222
  failure of, 257
  indicates the problems facing D-Day planners, 304–6
Dietrich, Marlene
  acts in Hollywood motion pictures, 551–52
Dimitrov, Georgi
  embraces popular front, 46
  supports Non-Aggression pact, 50
displaced persons (DPs)
  demographic characteristics, 589
  efforts of UNRRA to assist, 509, 589–90
  many seek return to homelands, 590
  retribution against, 590
Dix, Otto
  produces antiwar art, 545
Douhet, Giulio
  predictions of, 237
Doherty, Thomas
  interpretations of, 551–52
Dominican Republic
  accepts refugees, 502
Donitz, Karl
  decisions regarding submarine deployments, 158–59, 162, 165
  defends conduct in waging submarine warfare, 518–19
  indictment of, 518
  receives prison sentence, 519
  seeks new submarines, 167
  seeks to break morale of British merchant seamen, 164
  uses Enigma machine for communication, 434
  withdraws forces, 165
Doolittle, James
  diligently identifies military target in Berlin, 250
  leads attack on Tokyo, 345, 358
  leads Eighth Air Force, 248
Doorman, Karel
  suffers defeat during Battle of Java Sea, 210
Douglass, R. M.
  interpretations of, 129
Dowding, Hugh
  leads Fighter Command, 146
Dower, John
  interpretations of, 209, 551–52
Dresden, Germany
  Chamber of Horrors based in, 544
  devastation of, 278, 452–53
  firebombing of, 250–51, 439
  prompts accusation of Army Air Force adopting terror attacks, 361
Duclos, Jacques
  plans for communist putsch, 266
Dulles, John Foster
  authors "Six Pillars of Peace" statement, 425
Dumbarton Oaks Conference
  considers plans for new international organization, 233, 567–68, 569
Dunkirk
  British evacuation of, 140–41, 142
  French troops defend, 130
  legacy of, 267
Dunant, Heri
  founds International Committee of the Red Cross, 499
Dupree, A. Hunter
  interpretations of, 433, 440–41
Durango, Spain
  bombing of, 67–68

Dutch East Indies
    civilian internees from, 329
    defense of, 209–10,
    defense of, 343
    fall of, 8–9, 202
    Franklin Roosevelt seeks self-government for, 222
    nationalists support for Japanese, 213–14
    petroleum resources in, 210

E

Eaker, Ira
    Carl Spaatz succeeds as commander, 248
    commands Eighth Air Force, 247
ecumenical movement
    denounces Holocaust, 423–24
    efforts to form ties between Christian and Muslim leader, 417
    emergence of, 415–17
    expands in postwar era, 427
    faces opposition from Roman Catholic and Orthodox Churches, 417
    interfaith organizations condemn Nazi anti-Jewish measures, 420, 502
    raise concerns regarding extremist movements, 420–21, 425–26
    seeks to influence postwar planning, 425
    seeks to prevent war, 422
Eden, Anthony
    adopts policy of non-intervention in Spanish Civil War, 66–67
    announces creation of Home Guard, 142
    reports on defense preparations, 144
    signs Four Power Declaration, 232
Edgerton, David
    interpretations of, 224, 441
Egypt
    British weaken power King Faruq, 191–92
    depends on Blue Nile, 56–57
    Italian army invades, 102, 191
    participates in Middle East Supply Center, 192
    receives deployment of Australian and New Zealand soldiers, 148
    serves as staging area for Allied forces, 225
    strategic location of, 190
    threatened by German-Italian forces, 104, 190, 191

Eichmann, Adolf
    implements Operation Reinhardt, 491
    oversees deportations in Hungary, 283
    promotes Jewish emigration, 483
    provides postwar testimony, 487, 490
    transports Jews from Germany, 485–86
    trial of, 12
Einstein, Albert
    plays role in Manhattan Project, 106, 367–68, 437–38
    receives sympathetic media coverage, 98–99
    visits Japan, 98
Eisener, Kurt
    urges Germans to admit war guilt, 18
Eisenhower, Dwight
    adopts broad front strategy, 315
    assumes command of ground operations, 314
    assumes control over all air forces between May and September 1944, 249
    avoids race to Berlin, 318
    critical of Mediterranean strategy, 259–60
    establishes courts to prosecute war criminals, 522
    modifies plans developed by COSSAC, 306
    and occupation of Italy, 264–65
    orders launching of D-Day, 308
    seek relief of Bernard Montgomery, 316–17
    seeks aerial death blow against Germany, 250
    seeks command of Allied air assets, 307
    seeks Operation Dragoon as necessary operation, 313
    serves as Supreme Allied Commander, 304
    views air superiority as a precondition of D-Day, 249
Enola Gay (bomber)
    drops atomic bomb on Hiroshima, 353, 367–68, 438–39
Esteva, Jean
    allows Axis forces to pour into Tunisia, 259
Estonia
    German troops isolated in, 296–97
    Soviet Union invades, 101–2

634 INDEX

Ethiopia
  artistic rendering of, 542–43
  bombing of, 67–68
  invasion of, 5, 25, 26, 43, 56–59, 70–71, 96–97
  impact on U.S. foreign policy, 231
  joins League of Nations, 60
  League of Nations fails to halt aggression against, 26, 60–63, 66
  liberation of, 59, 69
  response of Great Britain and France to invasion of, 5, 25
euthanasia
  Church protests against, 10, 421–22
  German implementation, 486–87
Evian Conference
  assessment of, 502

F
Falkenhorst, Nikolaus von
  war crime trial of, 519–20
Faruq, King (Egypt)
  makes concessions, 191–92
  position weakens, 191
Federal Council of Churches
  condemns destruction of European Jewry, 424
  founding of, 415–16
Fermi, Enrico
  plays role in Manhattan project, 106
  tests first nuclear reactor, 437–38
Finland
  Allies considering sending an expeditionary force to, 121, 142, 395
  avoids dictatorship, 109–10
  avoids participating in Holocaust, 109
  churches within align with Nazism, 425–26
  Italians attempt to aid, 100–1
  as non-belligerent, 394
  seeks return to old boundary with Soviet Union, 108–9
  seeks to leave war, 110, 291
  signs armistice with Soviet Union, 106, 293–94
  Soviet invasion of, 8, 26, 49–50, 393
  surrender of, 123–24
  takes part in Operation Barbarossa, 103–4, 178
  wildlife refuge on border, 452

fishing
  diminishes during war, 457
Fletcher, Frank
  deploys U.S. Marines on Guadalcanal, 348–49
  intercepts Japanese invasion force, 345
  launches planes, 347
Flick, Friedrich
  conviction of, 520–6
Florida
  weapons tested in, 458
  Winston Churchill visits, 221
  World War II transforms, 459
Flying Tigers (American Volunteer Group
  defeat of, 329–30
  recruitment of, 357–58
Foch, Ferdinand
  advocates independent state in Rhineland, 20
  critical of Treaty of Versailles, 25, 30, 50
  influence of, 130–31
food
  starvation widespread during World War II, 505
  Americans on Bataan lack, 212–13
  Bengal famine, 2, 330–31
  British dependence on imports of, 8–9
  British rationing of, 378
  British refuse to purchase Hungarian wheat surplus, 275
  British use Women's Land Army to increase production of, 378
  China experiences widespread shortages, 506
  Japan controls world's rice supply, 506
  costs rise in Iraq, 194
  efforts to avert famine in Europe, 500–1
  efforts to avert shortages in Middle East, 192
  famine in China, 506
  Germans implement Hunger Plan in East, 497, 505–6
  grown in Victory Gardens, 376
  impact of Allied blockade on access to, 506–7
  India experiences widespread shortages of, 507
  Japanese occupation policies in Vietnam, 213–14

obligations under international law to feed prisoners of war, 582–83
postwar shortages of, 475
Red Cross augments for prisoners of war, 504
relief effort to provide in World War I, 497, 499–500
rise of starvation in Japan's empire, 505
severe shortfall in Soviet Union, 379–80
shortages of agricultural workers to grow in United States, 376–77
Ukrainian famine, 43
United States increases production of, 377
widespread famines during war, 505
widespread hunger after V-E Day in Germany, 475
Four Freedoms
Winston Churchill's views regarding, 220
Allies fail to implement fully in French North Africa, 259
establishes a common set of values to strive for, 219–20
Franklin Roosevelt champions, 564
Norman Rockwell depicts, 552–53
stresses freedom of worship, 425
widespread diffusion of, 265
Four-Power Pact
framework for avoiding clashes in the Pacific, 24
Fourteen Points (Woodrow Wilson)
espouses ethnic self-determination, 3
fosters humanitarianism, 497
Germany seeks armistice based on, 17, 18
influences Atlantic Charter, 564
popularity of, 19
shapes Treaty of Versailles, 20
France
accepts German expellees as immigrants, 593
accepts U.S. trusteeship system under the United Nations, 569
acquires new postwar government, 380
Allied invasion of, 164, 166, 167, 244, 267, 304–14
allied invasion of French North Africa, 257–58, 259–60
and Allied Mediterranean strategy, 256–57

arts and culture in, 540
asks U.S. to moderate demand for full repayment of war debt, 21
and the Battle of the Atlantic, 394
builds concentration camps for Jews in North Africa, 426
builds Maginot line, 4
collapse of, 51
as a colonial power, 228–29, 564
commitment to Southeast Asia declines, 86
concession in Tianjin blockaded, 84
and conflict Italian-German conflict, 95–96
considered for membership of the UN Security Council, 567
criticized for seeking to punish Germany, 21
cultural production continues under German occupation, 548
declares war on Germany, 29
defines itself as non-belligerent, 394, 401–2
displaced persons from, 589
embarks on aviation building program, 239
embraces long strategy, 121
and end of Anglo-French alliance, 140
endures foreign occupation, 608
experiences war weariness, 539
faces challenges from fascism and communism, 50
faces defeat in Norway, 124
faces major German offensive, 16–17
faces security threat from Non-Aggression Pact, 28
faces tension in civil-military relations, 30
faces timber shortage, 455–56
fall of, 87, 130–32, 143, 155–56, 206, 224, 229–30, 231, 400, 487
financing Romanian rearmament fails, 275
German invasion of, 125–29, 139, 144–45, 174, 237, 240–24, 241, 243, 252, 398, 485–86
German military deployments to, 147, 268
Germans soldiers stationed in, 263
grapples with Vichy Syndrome, 548
has more to offer Hitler than Spain, 398–99
holds war crime trial for Klaus Barbie, 609
hosts anniversary commemoration of D-Day, 600
indicts popular front leaders, 129
invades Ruhr region, 15–16, 43–79

636 INDEX

France (cont.)
- Italy invades, 102
- lacks security guarantee from the United States, 26, 30
- legacy of Vichy regime, 1
- liberates Corsica, 266
- and Mein Kampf, 95
- as a member of the Five Policemen, 233
- military situation declines, 142
- mired in political turmoil, 24, 25
- naval losses of, 261
- offers refugee for Georgia De Chirico, 543
- offers refugee for Polish soldiers, 278–79
- opens hostilities against Germany, 94
- participates in Nuremberg war crime trials, 517, 529
- participates in Tokyo war crime trials, 529–30
- as a permanent member of the UN Security Council, 11
- permits German rearmament, 96
- polarized by Spanish Civil War, 25, 546–47
- popular front emerges in, 46
- postwar civil-military crisis in, 265
- postwar future of, 260
- prosecutes Japanese war criminals in Asia, 528–29
- provides security guarantees to Poland, 120
- provides security guarantees to Poland, Romania, Greece, and Turkey, 99–100
- pursues appeasement, 49
- RAF deployments to, 240
- rearms, 25
- rebuilding of army, 262
- reconciles with Germany, 600
- refuses to share military plans with Great Britain, 25–26
- refuses to supply aid to Republican Spain, 66
- relies on colonial economies, 540–41
- relies on merchant shipping, 154
- remembers World War II selectively, 607
- rift develops regarding Anglo-German Naval Agreement, 60–61
- rise of fascist movement in, 45
- role in starting World War I, 18
- seeks to build coherent military in French North Africa, 265–66
- seeks to demilitarize the Rhineland, 20
- seeks to maintain an alliance with Britain and the United States, 19
- seeks to prevent German-Italian alliance, 57, 60, 61
- seeks to retain world order unchanged, 38
- sends French workers to Germany, 520–21
- serves as bases for V-1 bombs, 436
- serves as port for German submarines, 102
- signs armistice, 138, 583
- signs Munich Pact, 28–29
- signs Non-Intervention Agreement regarding Spanish Civil War, 66–107
- signs of Treaty of Locarno, 26–27
- signs Tripartite Treaty regarding Ethiopia, 56–57
- signs Tripartite Treaty with Turkey, 195
- signs Washington Naval Treaty, 24, 500
- and Spanish neutrality, 70
- surrender of, 7
- takes part in Munich Pact, 275
- transitions to provisional government (GPRF), 266
- welcomes United Nations Organization as buttressing collective security, 570

France, Army of
- armored forces of, 125–17
- fails to fortify Ardennes sector, 126–27
- fails to mount defense of French North Africa, 257–75
- lacks capability to assist Poland, 120–21
- liberates Paris, 313–14
- makes ineffective use of airpower, 127–28
- Marc Bloc's indictment of, 116–17
- mobilizes reservists in French North Africa, 265
- participates in liberation of France, 256, 267
- participation of North African Muslins in, 262
- rebuilding of, 260
- suffers from lack of equipment, 262

Franck, James
- opposes use of atomic bomb, 437–38

Franco, Francisco
- emerges as leader of nationalist cause, 65
- German deploy to tanks to aid, 546–47
- maintains neutrality, 69–70, 398–401

receives support from Italy and Germany, 67, 96–97
receives support from Roman Catholic Church, 417–18
receives tacit support of Great Britain and France, 66, 67
Frank, Hans
 proposes Poles as possible German auxiliaries, 277
 receives death sentence, 519
 resists receiving Jewish deportees, 485–86
 trial of, 518
Frayn, Michael
 writes *Copenhagen*, 441
Freud, Sigmund
 influences scholarship on collective memory, 608
Frick, Wilhelm
 indictment of, 518
 receives death sentence, 519
Friedlander, Saul
 interpretations of, 488
Fritsche, Hans
 Indictment of, 518
 acquittal of, 519
Fuchikami Hakuyo
 influences Soviet photographic realism, 549
Fujita Tsuguharu
 makes documentary films of Japanese battles, 551
Fukuzawa Ichiro
 offers new interpretations of surrealism, 549
Fuller, J.F.C.
 proposes alternative to *Kesselschlacht*, 118–19
Fumimaro Konoe
 creates Imperial Rule Assistance Association, 45
 proclaims New Order in East Asia, 213
 seeks negotiated settlement with U.S., 207
Funk, Wal
 indictment of, 518
 receives life term, 519
Fussell, Paul
 applauds use of atomic bomb, 368

G

Galen, Clemens von (Bishop)
 protests euthanasia policies, 10, 421–22, 487
Gamelin, Maurice
 authorizes few bombing missions, 127–28
 fights German in Belgium, 127
 provides guarantees to Poland, 120
 replacement of, 130
 war planning of, 25–26, 121, 126–27
Garver, John
 Interpretations of, 82, 85, 88
Gellately, Robert
 interpretations of, 48
Geneva Convention (1864)
 International Committee works to publicize, 504
 signing of, 498
Geneva Convention (1929)
 German violations of, 522–23
 Germany and Western Allies adherence to, 503
 Japan fails to adhere to, 505
 protects medical personnel, 468–69
 Requires captors to feed prisoners of war adequately, 582, 583
 shortcomings in protecting prisoners of war, 503
 updates to protect prisoners of war, 500
 Western Allies abrogate provisions of, 583–85
Geneva Naval Conference (1927)
 discusses disarmament, 24
Gentile, Emilio
 interpretations of, 41
George, David Lloyd
 negotiates at Paris Peace Conference, 18–19
 seeks reparations from Germany, 19
George VI (British King)
 delivers stand down broadcast, 142
Georges, Alphonse
 identifies site of German offensive, 127
 restricts French air activity, 127–28
Gerasimov, Alexander
 paints official portraits of Joseph Stalin, 543–44
German Christians
 embrace anti-Semitism, 417–18
 seek to Nazify German Protestant Church, 419, 426

German Communist Party
  adheres to Comintern, 45
  expresses view they will gain power, 45
German Protestant Church
  bar non-Aryans from churches, 421–22
  divisions within, 419
  relations with Protestant denominations globally, 419–20
  supports for Hitler in, 419
Germany
  abandons Young Plan, 27
  achieves victories in Poland and the West, 101
  adopts Hunger Plan in East, 505–6
  aids disabled veterans, 476
  aligns with Japan, 83–84, 87, 99
  Allied occupation zone in, 20
  Allied strategy to defeat, 221
  and the Battle of the Atlantic, 154–68
  bombing campaign against, 268–69
  bombing of, 422, 439
  British assessment of, 138–39
  British dominions declare war against, 224
  carries out murder through T-4 program, 421–22, 486–87
  cedes territory to form Czechoslovakia, 19
  cedes territory to form Poland, 19
  as a center of science and technology, 432
  China declares war on, 80–81
  concedes Bessarabia to Soviet Union, 279
  conducts biological warfare research, 435–36
  conquers Greece and Yugoslavia, 103–4
  considers deporting Jews to Madagascar, 487–38
  contributes to Lytton Commission, 98–99
  creates Jewish ghettos, 485–86
  declares war on Great Britain and France, 86
  declares war on the United States, 88, 94
  defaults on reparations, 15–16, 20
  demands French timber, 455
  deploys forces to the Mediterranean, 256
  devastation of, 452–53
  develops jet propelled military aircraft, 434–35
  develops sophisticated system for wounded, 471
  dismemberment into zones occupations, 568
  disrupts food shipments to Great Britain, 378
  efforts to forge an alliance with Spain, 398–99
  embrace autarky, 23
  embraces Aryan science, 432–33
  embraces projects to create perfect citizenry, 39
  encourages human medical experiments, 474
  encourages physicians to participate in mass murder, 478
  encourages recycling, 456–57
  engages with East Asia, 74
  enlists women as military auxiliaries, 385
  evacuates ethnic Germans from Baltic countries, 101–2
  exercises significant influence in Eastern Europe, 395–96
  expects British to sue for peace, 138, 147–48
  exploits French prisoners of war, 583
  faces assertive Romanian and Hungarians governments in late 1942, 282
  faces loss of European allies, 106
  faces massive dislocation, 385
  faces military defeats, 104–5
  faces setbacks in Soviet Union, 401
  faces widespread epidemics after V-E Day, 475
  failed insurrection in, 44
  fails to defeat Soviet Union, 184
  fails to develop an effective alliance, 107–10
  favors iconographic painting and sculpture symbolizing political ideals, 544
  forms alliance with Italy, 62–63, 66, 96–97
  gains a new postwar government, 380
  gains collaborators among Belarusians and Ukrainians, 182–83
  gains support from neutral Spain, 69, 70
  genocidal policies of, 3
  given a new border at Teheran Conference, 565
  governmental structure in, 47
  growing power of, 57–58, 60, 61
  Holocaust has muted commemoration of victimhood in, 602

impact of Great Depression on, 22
impact of Treaty of Versailles on, 3, 15
implements Holocaust in Soviet Union, 179–80, 183–84
implements hunger plan in the East, 180, 505–6
imprisons Tunisian Jews, 426
informs Italy of invasion plans, 103
interactions with neutral nations, 392–93
invades Czechoslovakia, 29, 99–100
invades Denmark, 405
invades neutral nations, 394
invades Poland, 276–77
invades Soviet Union, 88, 173–78, 206
Iran declares war on, 198
Italy declares war on, 264–65
lacks resources for a war of attrition, 580
lacks sufficient resources to defeat Soviet Union, 287–88, 289
launches bombing offensive against Great Britain, 378
launches Kristallnacht against German Jewry, 420, 484–60
launches Operation Barbarossa, 206, 224, 274
leftist artists and intellectuals flee, 539, 547–48, 552
loots food and goods from Soviet Union, 380, 451
maintains economic ties with neutral nations, 404
maintains strong economic ties with Switzerland, 404
maintains strong ties with Iran, 197–98
mediates Sino-Japanese conflict, 81–82, 83
as member of the Triple Alliance, 95
mobilization of, 384–85
mounts forward defense in Italy, 262–63
murders European Jewry, 423–25, 482–83, 484, 487–92
murders Polish elites, 485
occupies Italy, 105
occupies northern Italy, 386
occupies the Netherlands, 202
paid reparations to the State of Israel, 601–2
participates in Munich Conference, 28–29
partners with China, 77–78, 97–98

place tight controls on arts and literature, 544–47
play pivotal role in formation of the Tripartite Alliance, 94–95
possibilities of Communist insurgency in, 266
postpones invasion of England, 400
prevails in Battle of France, 143–44
prisoners of war held in Germany repatriated, 581–82
pro-Chinese faction in, 86–87
produces Zyklon B insecticide, 457
pro-Japanese groups in, 98–94
provides aid to the Nationalists, 67–68
provides military aid to Francesco Franco, 25, 67–68
provides reparations to the Soviet Union, 451–52
radicalization of, 47
radicalizing impact of World War I, 41
rebuilding of, 453–54
receives assistance from allies on Eastern Front, 178
receives expressions of friendship from Romania, 279
receives raw materials form Japan, 105–6
receives support from neutral nations, 394
receives support from Spain, 399
receives transfer of Germans expelled from other countries, 591
receives troops from Romania for Eastern Front, 281
relations with Soviet Union, 3–4
religious life in, 418–20, 421, 426
removes military advisors from China, 84–85
reordering border of, 12
required to pay reparations, 568, 570–71, 572
requires few physicians to answer for war crimes, 474–75
resents Italianizing South Tyrol, 95
resettlement of displaced persons in, 509
resistance movement in, 422
resists occupation of the Ruhr, 20–21
response of Communist Party to rise of fascism in, 45, 46–39, 50
reunification of, 1

INDEX

Germany (cont.)
  seeks Allies in Eastern Europe, 274–76
  seeks annexation of Austria, 95–96
  seeks Lebensraum, 49
  seeks petroleum from Iran and Iraq, 190, 194
  seeks Spanish entrance into war, 70
  seeks to overturn Versailles Treaty, 21, 27, 29–30
  seeks to overturn world order, 38. , 5051–39
  seeks to resettle ethnic Germans in East, 485
  sends Polish priests to concentration camps, 423
  serves as a market for Hollywood films, 551–52
  shifts in memory culture in, 602–4, 612
  signs agreement with Sweden, 401–2
  signs Anti-Comintern Pact, 97
  signs economic agreement with Hungary, 280
  signs naval agreement with Great Britain, 60–61
  signs Non-Aggression Pact, 28, 49, 84, 100–1, 195, 379, 398
  signs Non-aggression Pact with Turkey, 195–96
  signs Non-intervention agreement, 66–67
  signs Non-Intervention Agreement regarding Spanish Civil War, 66–67
  signs Treaty of Locarno, 4, 26–27
  signs Tripartite Pact, 87–88, 102
  soldiers surrender after V-E Day not given POW status, 583–85
  Soviet efforts to export revolution to, 40
  strips German Jews of all rights, 483–84
  suffers defeat at Stalingrad, 178–79
  suffers defeat in World War I, 17–18
  support Pan Arab nationalists, 193
  supports atomic bomb research, 417–38, 441
  supports rocket development, 436
  supports scientific research, 432
  surrender of, 106
  territorial expansion of, 24–26, 28, 43
  threatens Egypt militarily, 191
  threatens Suez Canal militarily, 104
  totalizing dictatorship, 48
  trains Chinese forces, 81
  Turkey declares war on, 197
  uses enigma code to wage Battle of the Atlantic, 434
  uses slave labor to build wonder weapons, 435
  U.S. officials view of, 205, 206–7, 208
  and the war guilt question, 18, 21
  war-time production, 2–3
  weaponizes food aid, 507
  wrestles with crimes committed in war-time, 601
Gandhi, Mahatma
  launches Quit India movement, 225–26
Gentile, Emilio
  interpretations of, 41
Germany, East (GDR)
  commemorates World War II, 1
  memory of war seen through the lens of class warfare, 602
Gerow, Leonard
  supports proposal of Henry Dexter White, 208
Ghormley, Robert L.
  Bill Halsey replaces, 349
Gibraltar
  key deep water port for Britain, 400
  serves as barrier to German submarines, 159
  site of major British naval base, 61
Giffard, George
  views early defense of Kohima as crucial, 334
Gildea, Robert
  explores efficacy of political myths, 609–10
Glantz, David
  interpretation of, 173–74
Gneisenau (German battleship)
  attacks British shipping, 155, 156–57
  deploy to Norway, 157
  location of, 124–25
Goebbels, Josef
  issues public appeal for winter clothes, 394
  Praises *Battleship Potemkin*, 541
  supervises Nazification of the arts, 541, 543, 545, 546
Goring, Hermann
  cancels long-term research project after Polish campaign, 240

employs scientists, 440
favors alliance with China, 86–87
focuses on supporting ground forces in Operation Barbarossa, 241
plans for invasion of Great Britain, 147–48
receives death sentence, 519
seeks extermination of Jewry, 482–83, 489
sought a strategic bombing capability, 246
underestimates Allied production of aircraft, 239
underestimates Soviet adversary, 241
war crime indictment of, 518

Gort, Lord
orders retreat, 140

Goth, Amon
conviction of, 523

Govorov, Leonid
launches attack into Karelian Isthmus, 293–94

Graf Spee (German battleship)
destruction of, 155, 156

Great Britain
accepts children refugees from Germany, 502
accepts German reunification , 1
Adolf Hitler desires an alliance with, 95, 98–99
agrees on a site for D-Day, 305
agrees to Anglo-German Naval Agreement, 60–61
aids the Soviet Union, 7
as an ally of Japan, 97
asks U.S. to moderate demand for full repayment of war debt, 21
asserts vision of liberal imperialism, 50
begins rearming, 24–25
blockades Germany, 395, 403
commitment to Southeast Asia declines, 86
concession in Tianjin blockaded, 84
continues fight in June 1940, 7
contributes to Manhattan Project, 437–38
convenes military courts in Asia, 526
courts Mussolini as potential ally, 5
created Crown Film Unit, 553
creates public service posters, 552–53
debates morality of bombing, 10, 422
declares plans to hold war crime trials, 515–16
declares plans to punish Japanese aggression, 525
declares war on Germany, 86, 94
declares war on Japan, 80–81
declines to urge Poles to negotiate over Polish Corridor, 119
defends Versailles system , 4
delays repatriating Italian prisoners of war, 504
demobilizes after World War I, 586
demobilizes armed forces, 586–87
depends on imports, 8–9, 154, 156, 163
depends on petroleum from Iraq and Iran,, 194
develops radar, 439
develops sophisticated system for the wounded, 471
displays optimism regarding Norway, 124
does not support French strategy in Ruhr crisis, 20–21
draws on centuries of maritime experience, 156
efforts to forge anti-Axis alliance, 88
embraces long war strategy, 125
endures air attacks, 378
engages in area bombing of Germany, 9
envisioned by Franklin Roosevelt as one of the Four Policemen, 565
establishes Government Code and Cypher School, 434
establishes Middle East Supply Center, 192
evacuates British forces from France, 139–41
evacuates urban children to rural areas, 378
exploits timbers resources, 455, 456
expresses alarm at pro-Axis activities in Egypt, 191–92
faces challenges from fascism and communism, 50
faces possible German invasion, 102, 138
faces threat of war with Japan, 207
faces war weariness, 539, 551
fails to sustain Versailles system, 30
fosters economic penetration of Eastern Europe by Germany, 275
freezes Japanese assets, 206–7
funds scientific research with military application, 11, 432, 441

642   INDEX

Great Britain (*cont.*)
   as a future member of the Four Policemen, 233
   gains air superiority, 434–35
   and German war guilt question, 18, 21
   grants independence to Iraq, 193
   hostile to fascist ambitions, 49
   implements rationing, 378–79, 553–54
   influence in Latin America declines, 231–32
   intervenes in Middle East, 190
   invades Iran, 197–98
   invades Iraq, 193
   joins United Nations alliance, 8, 220
   joins United Nations Organization, 11
   launches First Chindit operation, 331–32
   maintains elaborate naval control of shipping, 159–60
   meets defeat in Burma, 329–31
   as member of the Grand Alliance, 226–29, 233–34
   miscalculate strategic balance, 132, 139
   mistrusts France, 25–26
   mobilizes for D-Day, 304
   mobilizes science for war effort, 432–33
   mobilizes women, 378, 383–84
   naval strength of, 124
   obtains Norwegian merchant marine, 123
   occupies Iceland, 394
   offers refugees for German artists and intellectuals, 545
   organizes Home Guard, 142–43
   outproduces Germany in aircraft, 239
   participates in Arcadia Conference, 221
   participates in Bretton Woods Conference, 566–67
   participates in Dumbarton Oaks conference, 567
   participates in Moscow Conference of Foreign Ministers, 232
   participates in Nuremberg war crime trials, 517
   participates in Paris Peace Conference, 18–19
   participates in Potsdam Conference, 570–72
   participates in the San Francisco Conference, 569–70
   participates in Tokyo war crime trials, 529–30
   participates in Yalta Conference, 568
   permits German rearmament, 96
   possibilities of settlement with Germany, 107
   prepares defenses against possible invasion, 143–45
   prevails at El Alamain, 191
   proposed alliance against, 78
   protest Hungarians permitting transit of German troops, 280
   provides assistance to veterans, 588
   provides food assistance to Iran, 198
   provides security guarantees to Poland, 120, 122
   provides security guarantees to Poland, Romania, Greece, and Turkey, 99–100
   purchases goods from Switzerland, 404
   pursues appeasement of Germany, 28–29
   receives assistance from British Commonwealth, 141–42, 148–49
   receives assistance from dominions and empire, 222–25, 328–29, 332, 333
   receives liberty ships from the U.S., 164
   receives substantial imports from U.S., 375–76
   refuses to aid Republican Spain, 25, 66–67, 68
   refuses to grant immediate independence to India, 225–26
   relies on colonial economies, 540–41
   religious leaders in, 422
   reneges on security guarantees to France, 26
   seek to avoid another bloodbath, 121
   seeks reparations from Germany, 19
   seeks Spanish neutrality, 398, 399, 400
   seeks to preserve world order unchanged, 38
   seeks to prevent German-Italian alliance, 57–58, 60, 61
   seeks to retain world order unchanged, 38
   signs Anglo-American Egyptian Treaty, 191
   signs Treaty of Locarno, 26–27
   signs Tripartite Treaty regarding Ethiopia, 56–57
   signs Tripartite Treaty with Turkey, 195
   signs Washington Naval Treaty, 23–24, 500
   and status of British dominions and India, 221–25

strong commitment to air power, 237, 238
subscribes to Atlantic Charter, 563–64
suffers major defeats in Asia, 329
supports the arts during war, 552–53
takes part in Munich Pact, 275
and treaty of alliance with Portugal, 400
undertakes biological warfare research, 435–36
urges Soviet Union to defer war crime trials, 523–24
wages land campaign in Burma, 8
welcomes home repatriated prisoners of war, 503–4
wins Battle of Britain, 7, 70, 145–48, 149, 155–56
wins Battle of El Alamein, 9
wins battle of production, 2
witnesses new postwar government, 380
Great Depression
impact of, 4, 22–23, 42, 98, 540–41
impact on Soviet experiment, 43
prompts support for the arts in U.S., 539–40
Greece
British influence in, 227–28
civilians hostages killed in, 521
German forces in, 256–57, 268, 269
German invades, 108
holds war crimes trials, 519–20
Italian occupation ends, 263
Italy invades, 103, 376
postwar future, 260, 266
receives British and French security guarantee, 99–100
receives food aid, 507, 509
Greenland
U.S. establishes bases in, 434–35
Greiser, Arthur
conviction of, 523
Groener, Wilhelm
replaces Erich Ludendorff, 17
Grosz, George
Adolf Hitler targets artwork of, 545
Groves, Leslie
manages production facilities for Manhattan project, 367–68
Groys, Boris
assesses Soviet Realism, 543–44

Guam
Carl Spaatz arrives in, 364–65
defense plans for, 343
fall of, 202, 209, 211–12, 342
serves as base for B-29, 353
Guderian, Heinz
considers Moscow key objective, 175–76
develops postwar myth of apolitical *Wehrmacht*, 179
executes a deep penetration attack, 128–29
seeks alternative to *Kesselschlacht*, 118
Guernica, Spain
bombing of, 67–68, 547
Gurkhas
aerve under Orde Wingate, 336–37
Gurlitt, Cornelius
maintains collection of "degenerate" art, 544

H

Haakon VII, King (Norway)
establishes government in exile, 123
responds to German invasion, 121
Haber, Fritz
receives favorable media coverage, 98–99
visits Japan, 98
Hague Convention (1899)
signing of, 498
Hague Convention (1907)
requires repatriation of former POWs, 583
signing of, 498
Hague Convention (1925)
bans use of chemical and biological weapons, 500
Hague Conventions
German violations of, 522–23
Halder, Franz
considers Moscow key campaign objective, 175–76
contemplates organizing a coup, 118
Halsey, William Jr.
invades New Georgia, 350
leads early offensive action against Japan, 345
pursues carrier force, 352
supports Douglas MacArthur's landing on Leyte, 352
takes aggressive action off Guadalcanal, 349

Hamburg, Germany
  fire bombing of, 452–53
  rebuilding of, 453–55
Hamilton, Maxwell
  supports proposal of Henry Dexter White, 208
Hanford, Washington
  production facilities in, 367–68, 437–38
  suffers from radiation pollution, 458
Hansell, Haywood
  embraces precision bombing, 365–66
  leads XXI Bomber command, 360–61
Harding, Warren G.
  diplomatic initiatives of, 205
  supports disarmament, 23–24
Harris, Arthur
  assumes command of Bomber Command, 246–47
  supports morale bombing, 250–51
Hart, B. H. Liddell
  expresses confidence in Maginot Line, 138–39
  seeks alternative to *Kesselschlacht*, 118–19
Hayashi Fumiko
  visits front-lines, 551
Hayashi Hisajiro
  receives report on railway system, 73
Heisenberg, Werner
  advocates use of heavy water for fission process, 437
  claims to slow advance of atomic bomb research, 441
Henderson Field
  Japanese forces attack, 349
  U.S. Marines capture, 348
Hess, Rudolf
  indictment of, 518
  receives life term, 519
Heydrich, Reinhard
  assassination of, 491
  discusses use of poison gas, 490
  orders ghettoization policy, 485
  organizes murder of Polish civilian leaders, 485
  prepares plan for Final Solution, 489–90
  receives appointment as head of Sicherheitsdienst, 483
  seeks extermination of Jewry, 482–83
  visits *Einsatzgruppen* and Waffen SS units, 489
High Commission on Refugees (League of Nations)
  creation of, 497, 510
  develops Nansen Passport, 500
High Commissioner for Refugees (United Nations)
  establishment of, 589–90
Himmler, Heinrich
  appoints Reinhard Heydrich as head of Sicherheitsdienst, 483
  employs scientists, 440
  implements Lebensraum policies, 485
  opposes creating Polish auxiliary, 277
  oversees murders of European Jewry, 488, 489, 490–91,
  oversees expulsion of German Jews, 485–86
  seeks extermination of Jewry, 482–83
  undertakes colonization scheme in Yugoslavia, 590–91
Hindenburg, Paul von
  asks Adolf Hitler to form a government, 27
  demands Germany seek an armistice, 17
Hinsley, Arthur
  promotes peace, 422
Hiranuma Kiichiro
  government falls, 77
Hirohito, Emperor
  announces surrender of Japan, 382, 384
  approves diplomatic initiatives of Prime Minister Konoe, 207
  condemns 1928 plot, 549
  favors surrender, 110, 353
  given immunity from prosecution, 530–31
Hirota Koki
  brings military officers into cabinet, 77
  seeks to establish Second Manchukuo, 77
Hiroshima
  attacked with atomic bomb, 106, 353, 366–, 67–, 369–70, 438–39, 453
  commemorates of atomic bomb attack, 606
  devastation of, 278
  and Japanese collective memory, 612
  radiation victims in, 475
  rebuilding of, 448–49

INDEX

Hitler Adolf
    abandons deportation as solution to Jewish Question, 486
    abandons idea of alliance with Japan, 84
    abandons Munich Agreement, 29
    abandons territory reluctantly, 296–97
    accommodates Italy regarding South Tyrol, 95–96
    adopts autarky, 23
    agrees to forward defense in Italy, 262–63
    alienates potential allies, 100–1
    Allies recommend pursuing a separate peace with Soviet Union, 104–5
    allies rethink commitment to war after defeat at Stalingrad, 291
    apathetic toward possible German invasion of Great Britain, 146
    appoints Albert Speer as official architect, 545–46
    approves Plan Z for Kriegsmarine, 124
    assassination attempt against, 106, 295
    assumes command of all Axis forces in Eastern Front, 103–4
    atrocities of, 366
    authors Mein Kampf, 48
    benefits from Allied strategic impotence, 120
    blames Allies for Stalingrad defeat, 178
    blocks tactical withdrawal after fall of Kiev, 292–93
    brings Hungary and Romania into Axis camp, 280
    builds Atlantic Wall, 310
    commits forces to Mediterranean, 256–57
    considers deporting Jews to Madagascar, 487
    consolidates power at home, 46–47
    continues euthanasia program in Germany, 487
    continues war, 299, 300
    controls deployment of armored reserves in France, 307–8, 310
    creates Dresden-based Chamber of Horrors, 544
    creating precedents, 591
    cultivates ties with Italy and Japan, 94–95
    decides not to focus German offensive on Moscow, 173–74
    declares war on the United States, 7, 88, 437
    delays attack on France, 127
    depictions in American propaganda films, 551–52
    did not seek Hungarian participation in war, 281
    diplomatic engagement with Romania and Hungary, 274
    distrusts Italians, 102–3
    efforts to appease diplomatically, 49
    embraces Non-Aggression Pact with Soviet Union, 6, 49–50, 94, 100, 101, 195–96, 398
    embraces plan to invade Denmark and Norway, 124
    embraces vision of creative destruction, 42
    emerges as leader, 4, 419
    employees scores of scientists in support of war effort, 440
    ends Operation Citadel, 290
    engages in war of attrition in Mediterranean, 267–68
    envisions strategic capability for Luftwaffe, 246
    expands aircraft and tank production, 432
    expansionist policies engender fear in Iran, 197
    exploits ethnic tensions in Czechoslovakia, 19, 28
    exploits French POW labor, 583
    expresses ambivalence on German invasion of Britain, 147–48
    faces setbacks in Eastern Front, 401
    as a failed artist, 545
    fails to develop atomic bomb, 437–38, 441
    fascist inspired revolution spreads globally, 45
    favors partnership with Japan, 83–84
    fears attack on Norway, 159
    forms government, 27
    Francisco Franco bans any comparison with Hitler's Germany, 70
    funds rocket research, 436
    genocidal mentality of, 131
    genocidal policies of, 563
    German commanders fault in postwar years, 179, 287, 289
    governing style of, 47

Hitler Adolf (*cont.*)
  grants Soviet Union eastern half of Poland, 591–92
  grants Transylvania to Hungary, 279
  Great Britain and France respond to Germany's rise, 57
  halts Kursk offensive, 291
  Herman Goring unwilling to admit mistakes to, 239
  implements Aktion T4 program, 486–87
  implements euthanasia, 10
  imposes control over cultural production, 541
  imposes humiliating armistice on France, 138
  installs Mussolini as head of Italian Social Republic, 105
  invades Soviet Union, 7, 45, 399, 543–44
  issues Directive No. 17, 145–46
  justifies Polish invasion, 129
  lacks sufficient industrial resources, 289
  launches Kristallnacht, 484
  launches offensive in the Ardennes, 288, 316
  launches Operation Barbarossa, 300
  leadership of, 542
  Leni Riefenstahl courts favor of, 546
  loses access to Romanian petroleum, 296
  marginalizes professional officers, 117–18
  mediates territorial dispute, 279
  meets with Axis leaders, 108
  meets with foreign minister Matsuoka Yosuke, 107
  meets with Francisco Franco, 70, 398–99
  meets with Ion Antonescu, 280
  meets with Marshall Petain, 398–99
  meets with Mussolini, 102
  meets with Oshima Hiroshi, 104
  Mein Kampf held up a literary model, 545
  minimizes impact of German capturing Moscow, 177
  miscalculates Soviet invasion plans, 297–98
  Neville Chamberlain miscalculates military plans of, 139
  orders attack toward Avranches, 312
  orders transport of German Jews to Poland, 485–86
  orders Wehrmacht not to prosecute soldiers for war crimes against civilians, 488
  overestimates number of collaborators in Norway, 129
  plans to wage aggressive war, 521, 522
  postpones invasion of Great Britain, 400
  pours resources in Mediterranean, 268–69
  precipitates war with Britain and France, 155
  pressures Poland to return territory to Germany, 19
  promises to bomb only military targets, 120, 131
  purges traditional conservatives, 99
  pursues German rearmament, 2–3, 66
  reaches settlement at Munich, 28–29
  receives blame for flawed strategy on East Front, 174, 177
  receives considerable support from German churches, 419
  receives memorandum from Confessing Church leaders, 419
  receives support from medical profession, 474
  receives support from Mufti of Jerusalem, 417
  redirects Luftwaffe to concentrate on British cities, 146
  regime embrace state of terror, 48
  repudiates Versailles Treaty, 96, 231
  resigned to defeat, 299
  reveals plans with regard to Austria and Czechoslovakia, 519
  role in German defeat at Stalingrad, 178–79
  Romanians share affinity with, 280
  rules until end of regime, 110
  seeks Caucasus oilfields, 177–78
  seeks de-Jewification of art, 545
  seeks destruction of Jewry, 109–10
  seeks extermination of Jewry, 482–83, 484–85
  seeks Hungarian support, 278–79, 281
  seeks Lebensraum, 49
  seeks popular support, 46
  seeks racist war of annihilation, 179, 183–84
  seeks to destroy ideologically demonized enemy, 48
  seeks to drag Italy into war, 100
  seeks to make Poland part of eastern frontier empire, 275

seeks to reorder populations of Europe, 580
seeks to resettle territories conquered in the East, 485
sees Germans lacking commitment to the Fatherland, 130
sees himself as genius, 288–89
sees Luftwaffe as working in close concert with ground commanders, 241
selects work for display in Great German Art Exhibition, 544–45
sends additional German troops to Italy after country's surrender, 263
sends reinforcements to Normandy, 312–13
sends scarce reserves to Hungary, 297
Soviet response to Hitler's success, 46, 50
SS members committed to following, 489
suffers significant losses in Southern France, 267
supplies aircraft to Francisco Franco, 67
supports Francisco Franco, 96–97
takes unilateral actions, 100
targets art work of Georg Grosz, 545
tasked Heydrich with preparing the Final Solution, 489
tests new weapons in Spanish Civil War, 539, 546–47
threatens Jews in public speech, 487–88
transfers German troops to Italy, 105
turns focus to Soviet Union, 148–49
turns forces to Ukraine, 175–76
turns south in response to Soviet strength, 176
vetoes proposals to create Polish auxiliaries, 277
view Normandy invasion as secondary operation, 306
views Futurists as degenerate, 542
views Moscow as secondary objective, 177
views regarding Western allies assisting Finland, 121
Western appeasement of, 119
Winston Churchill promises to meet the fight with, 143
withdraws Luftwaffe units from Eastern Front, 244, 252
world view of, 38–39, 42–44, 50
Hitler Youth
meet labor needs of home front, 385

Hlond, August (Cardinal)
urges Pius XII to speak out against atrocities, 423
Hoare, Samuel
seeks end of war in Ethiopia, 61
Hodges, Courtney
attacks German in Hurtgen Forest, 315
Hollande, Francois
give speech on French deportation of Jews, 609
organizes D-Day anniversary celebration, 600
Holocaust
absence from Yalta Conference agenda, 563
Allied response to, 12, 510
causes of, 482–83, 484–85, 487–88
Christian churches confront legacy of, 418, 427
establishment of Jewish ghettos and deportation, 485–86
French deportation of Jews remembered, 609
French support for, 426
German remembrance of, 602–4
Hungarian deportation of Jews, 283
ideological basis for, 38, 51
implementation by Axis Allies, 45, 109
key component of Eastern Front, 183–84
key war aim of Adolf Hitler, 109, 183–84
launching of Kristallnacht pogrom, 484
legacy of, 492
memory of, 1
as part of wider demographic conflict, 580
planning the Final Solution at Wannsee, 489–90
precedents established in eugenics policies, 486–87
proposed plan to resettle Jews in Madagascar, 487
religious response to, 423–25
religious responses to , 10, 418–22
requires scores of institutions and collaborators, 482
response of neutral powers to, 392
role of SS, 489
role of *Volkdeutsche* collaborators in, 485
role of Wehrmacht in, 488–89

Holocaust (*cont.*)
   Romanian participation in, 281
   scholarship on , 2
   systematic depriving Jews of human rights, 483–84
   totemic evil of, 524
   U.S. response to, 507–9
   use of death camps, 490–92
   use of Zyklon B in, 457
   Wehrmacht participation in , 179–80
   West German war crime trials related to, 601–2
Home Army (Polish)
   attacks Germans in Warsaw, 295–96
   size of, 277
Home Guard (Local Defense Volunteers)
   establishment of, 142
   man anti-aircraft batteries, 378
   role of, 143
homosexuality
   Himmler's obsession with, 489
   psychiatric discharges for, 467–68
Hong Kong
   cultural producers find refuge in, 549–50
   fall of, 202, 342
   war crime trials in, 527–28
Hooft, Willem Visse
   condemns Nazism and Communism, 426
   heads ecumenical office in Geneva, 425–26
Hoover, Herbert
   encourages disarmament, 205
   organizes humanitarian relief, 497, 499–501, 509
   raises tariffs, 23
   response to the Manchurian incident, 75
   seeks to break British blockade, 502–3
   suspends payment of Allied war debts, 23
Hoover, J. Edgar
   investigates loyalty of scientists, 432–33
Hopper, Edward
   paints Nighthawks, 553
Horkheimer, Max
   critiques American cultural production, 552
Hornbeck, Stanley
   discounts threat of war with Japan, 202
   rejects efforts for U.S. mediated Sino-Japanese peace talks, 206

Hornet (aircraft carrier)
   defends Midway, 346
   launches Doolittle raid, 212, 345, 358
   launches planes, 347
   loss of, 349
Horthy, Miklos
   halts Jewish deportations, 283
   sends troops to Eastern Front, 281
   views Jewish question as an internal matter, 282
Horton, Max
   orders withdrawal of escorts, 163
Hoss, Rudolph
   conviction of, 523
Hossbach, Friedrich
   takes notes regarding Hitler plans for acquiring living space, 519
Howard, John
   seizes bridge on Caen Canal, 308
Hughes, Charles Evans
   negotiates disarmament treaties, 23–24
Hull, Cordell
   attends Moscow Conference (1943), 566
   crafts new international organization, 232
   criticizes Franklin Roosevelt's decisions, 259–60
   issues statement on Iran's territorial integrity, 197
   negotiates with Japanese, 207, 208
   promotes Good Neighbor policy, 230–31
   rejects proposal for non-aggression pact with Japan, 206
   supports British blockade, 502–3
Hungary
   balks at surrendering Jews to Germany, 109
   demands territory from Romania, 279
   forces defeated at Stalingrad, 178
   German influence in, 395–96
   joins Tripartite Pact, 103
   and Paris Peace Conference, 3
   passes anti-Jewish legislation, 276
   seeks separate peace, 110
   seeks to expel German minority, 591–92
   sends troops to fight against Soviet Union, 281–82
   shelters Polish refugees, 278–79
   Soviet intervention in, 40

INDEX

Huntziger, Charles
   receives report French defense of Ardennes, 126–27
Huston, John
   directs *Let There Be Light*, 477
Hutton, Thomas
   leads Burmese Army, 330

I

Iceland
   aircraft based in , 160
   British establish bases in, 158
   merchant ships assemble in, 164
   neutrality of, 394, 405, 406
   no longer serves as escort relay point, 162
   U.S. establishes bases in, 160, 434–35
Ienaga Saburo
   sues Japanese Ministry of Education over textbook censorship, 607
I.G. Farben
   corporate officers tried for war crimes, 520–21
   develops chemical warfare agents, 457
Ikeda Hayato
   Policies usher economic miracle, 551
India
   assists war crime investigations, 525
   China supports immediate independence for, 564–65
   contributes to Allied war effort, 225
   examines history of World War II, 328
   and fall of Burma, 211
   famine in , 2, 12, 330–31, 507
   Franklin Roosevelt supports independence for, 226, 564
   independence movement in , 12–13, 105–6, 225–26, 330–31
   maintains prisoner of war camps, 504
   participates in Bretton Woods Conference, 567
   participates in Tokyo war crime trials, 12, 529–31
   provides airbases to US Army Air Force, 8,
   provides teak and hardwoods to, 456
   provides troops for invasion of Iraq, 193
   reopening of shipping lanes from the U.S., 257
   signs Declaration of the United Nations alliance, 221–22
   supports British war effort, 141
   views regarding Soviet system, 226–27
   Winston Churchill opposes independence of, 12–13
Indian Air Force (IAF)
   contributes to victory in Burma, 338
   participates in battles of Kohima and Imphal, 335–36
Indian Army
   capabilities of, 336, 338
   defends Burma, 329–30
   defends Malaya and Singapore, 329
   fight in battles of Kohima and Imphal, 332–36
   Orde Wingate's assessment of, 336
   participate in Chindit operation, 336–37
   participate in Operation Capital, 337
   participates in First Arakan campaign, 330–31
   participates in Operation Lioncloth, 331–32
   plays major role in Burma campaign, 10, 328–29
   training of, 332
Indian National Army
   fights as a formation, 337
Indochina
   anti-colonial movements in, 529
   China supports independence for, 564–65
   Franklin Roosevelts views regarding, 222
   invites Japan into Indochina, 528–29
   Japan occupies, 87, 88, 102, 103–4, 206–7
   Japanese aircraft based in, 210–11
   negotiations regarding, 207
   negotiations regarding, 565
   serves as major rice producing area, 506
   Thailand territorial claims regarding, 396–97
Inonu, Ismet
   becomes Turkish leader, 194
intelligence
   Allied code breaking success regarding, 434
   Allied miscalculations prior to Japanese attack on Pearl Harbor, 209
   Allied success in, 108
   American network in French North Africa, 257–58

intelligence (cont.)
    British limit sharing to France, 25–26
    British tracking of ship movements, 156
    confirms postponement of German invasion of Great Britain, 147–48
    crucial role in American success at Battle of Midway, 9
    Japanese obtain report on British defense in Asia, 102–3
    neutral government condone belligerent operations, 403
    predicts German attack through Ardennes, 127
    regarding German public opinion, 127
    Royal Navy lacks intelligence on Norwegian invasion, 124–25
    Soviet become masters of misdirection, 289
International Bank for Reconstruction and Development (World Bank)
    establishment of, 11, 233–34, 566
    Iran receives consideration from, 198
International Committee of the Red Cross
    arranges POW exchange, 503–4
    faces obstacles aiding prisoners held by Japan, 505
    facilities contact between families and POWs, 585
    founding of, 498–500
    humanitarian efforts, 497–98
    oversees POW camps holding Anglo-American prisoners, 503
    provides supplemental food to POWs, 504
    reports on detention facilities for German minorities, 592
    role under Geneva Convention, 582
    seeks end to Allied food blockade, 507
    sponsors relief efforts in Wuhan, 501–2
International Criminal Court
    establishment of, 594–95
International Labor Organization (ILO)
    as part of Franklin Roosevelt's vision for United Nations Organization, 233
International Monetary Fund (IMF)
    continued relevance, 573
    founding of, 11, 233, 566
International Refugee Organization (IRO)
    aids Displaced Persons, 589–90

International Tracing Service
    work of, 510
Iran
    Azerbaijan and Kurds seek to secede, 199–200
    British and Soviets invade, 197–98
    British and Soviets seeks concessions for petroleum concessions from, 199
    British depends on petroleum from, 194, 197
    casualties from Anglo-Soviet invasion, 405
    German seeks access to petroleum in, 190, 191
    impact of war on , 2
    participates in Middle East Supply Center, 192
    provides vital route for transporting supplies to Soviet Union, 198
    receives economic assistance, 198
    strictly censors press, 199–200
    war strengthens power of the state, 192
Iraq
    British depend on petroleum from, 194
    British invasion of, 193
    experiences shortages and rampant inflations, 194
    founding member of Arab League, 191–92
    German seeks access to petroleum in, 190, 191
    granted independence under mandate system, 193
    impact of war on , 2
    participate in Middle East Supply Center, 192
    war strengthens the power of the state, 192
Ireland
    munitions disposed in water off of, 457
    neutrality of , 2, 402–3
    security services comfortable dealing with belligerents, 403
    and support of British war effort, 403–4
Iriye, Akira
    interpretations of, 74
Iron Guard (Legion of the Archangel Michael)
    crushing of, 109–10
    embraces anti-Semitism, 417–18
Ironside, Edmund
    assesses German adversary, 147–48

given new role, 143–44
proposes Norwegian landing, 123–24
retirement of, 144–45, 147
Irvine, William D.
   interpretations of, 130
Irwin, Noel
   commands Eastern Army, 330–31
Ishikawa Tatsuzo
   writes of soldiers as human, but capable of atrocities, 551
Ishiwara Kanji
   plot Manchurian Incident, 74
   promotes new multiethnic culture in Manchukuo, 550–51
Israel, State of
   receives reparations from Germany, 601–2
   tries Adolf Eichmann, 12
Itagaki Seishiro
   plots Manchurian Incident, 74
Italian Air Force (*Regina Aeronautica*)
   Attacks Ethiopians with poison gas, 58–59
   lacks sufficient number of modern planes, 244
Italian Navy
   sends submarines to North Atlantic, 102–3
   ships sail to Malta, 261
Italy
   adheres to international norms, 95
   administers mandatory territory under League of Nations, 564
   adopts anti-Semitic legislation, 109
   aggression against Ethiopia goes unpunished, 26
   aligns with Germany, 25, 62–63, 66, 97
   and the Allied campaign in the Mediterranean, 256–57, 260, 268–69
   Allied invasion of, 13, 269, 304–5
   under Allied occupation, 264
   artistic styles favored by fascist regime, 544
   avoids communist-induced disorder, 267
   and career of Georgio De Chirico, 542–43
   China declares war on, 80–81, 88
   declares war on Germany, 264–65
   declares war on the United States, 103–4
   defines itself as non-belligerent, 394
   develops into a democratic republic, 260
   displaced persons from, 589
   embraces an alternative modernity, 51
   enters war in June 1940, 94, 102, 191
   faces imminent Allied invasion, 104–5
   faces political turmoil, 30
   faces setbacks in Greece and Libya, 102–3
   flirts with idea of creating a neutral bloc, 394
   forges bilateral relationship with Soviet Union, 45
   German commit atrocities in, 519–20
   German prisoners of war in, 583–84
   German war crimes committed in, 519–20
   Great Britain and France court Italy as potential ally, 5, 57, 60–61
   grows dependent on Germany, 96
   impact of Great Depression on, 540–41
   invades Albania, 195, 395–96
   invades Ethiopia, 58–60
   joins League of Nations, 4
   leaves Triple Alliance, 95
   and legacy of World War I, 41
   limited resources of, 3
   as member of Axis alliance, 94–95
   mobilizes women, 386
   permits multiple artistic styles to flourish, 10–11, 542–43
   postwar career of artists associated with fascist regime, 554
   practices aggressive foreign policy, 231
   prepares to invade Ethiopia, 57–58
   provides aid to Francesco Franco, 69, 96–97, 398
   provides substantial support for the arts, 542
   publicizes transcontinental flight to Asia, 104
   pursues policy of self-sufficiency in response to Great Depression, 23
   recognizes sovereignty of the Holy See, 416
   recognizes sovereignty of Vatican City, 386, 416
   relations deteriorate with Germany, 84
   relationship with Vatican, 417–18
   relations with Germany become strained, 100–2
   reluctance to grapple with fascist past, 387
   republic established in, 387

Italy (*cont.*)
  resistance movement in, 386
  rise of fascism in, 4
  seeks empire, 48
  seeks revisions in the world order, 38–39, 46–47
  seeks to preserve Austria's sovereignty, 95–96
  signs Munich Pact, 275
  signs Non-Intervention Agreement regarding Spanish Civil War, 66–67
  signs Treaty of Locarno, 26–27
  signs Tripartite Pact, 5, 87, 280
  signs Tripartite Treaty regarding Ethiopian, 56–57
  signs Washington Naval Treaty, 23–24, 500
  state intrudes on cultural life in, 541, 543
  and strategic bombing, 243
  strong influence Roman Catholic Church in, 386
  struggles against British Commonwealth forces, 108
  surrender of, 105–6, 110, 166–67, 259, 262–63, 572
  threatens Egypt and Sudan, 191
  U.S. seeks to deny access to strategic raw materials, 206

J

Japan
  admits Jewish refugees, 109
  adopts postwar constitution renouncing right to wage war, 602
  as ally of Germany, 107, 108
  as an ally of Thailand, 396 –97
  assists Germany navy, 102–3, 105–6
  attacked with atomic bomb, 9
  attacks Pearl Harbor, 88, 103–4, 202–3, 342–43, 434–35, 539–40
  augments economic, industrial, and technological resources, 432
  benefits from World War I, 28
  blockades British and French concessions in Tianjin, 84
  bombing of, 345, 353–54, 358–70, 384, 437–39, 453, 458
  bombs China, 357–58
  bombs Chongqing, 611
  captures Wuhan, 86
  Cold War concerns impact art in, 555
  commits atrocities at Nanjing, 82–83
  commits war crimes, 12
  continues to censor textbooks, 607
  continues to instill anxiety among neighbors, 604
  cosmopolitan art scene in, 549
  defeat of, 12
  defends Guadalcanal, 348–49
  difference in memory culture in Japan and Germany, 601–2
  disestablishes Shintoism as state religion, 426
  distributes public service posters, 552–53
  drives British out of Burma, 8, 104, 225, 329–30
  efforts to commemorate Battle of Okinawa, 606
  efforts to commemorate bombing of Japan, 605–6
  embraces imperialism, 41, 47–48, 213
  embraces kamikaze attacks, 352–43
  encourages Adolf Hitler to negotiate with Josef Stalin, 104–5
  engages in war with China, 5
  establishes date commemorating World War II, 604–5
  exploits timber resources, 455, 456
  face Anakim offensive in Burma, 330–31
  face First Chindit operation, 331–32
  faces criticism from Chinese government over history textbooks, 610
  faces defeat in New Guinea, 349–52
  faces defeats in China, 85
  faces formidable resistance in China, 89
  faces rebuke from League of Nations, 98–99
  faces resistance in Co-Prosperity Sphere, 213–14
  faces systematic air attacks against population, 250–51
  faces U.S. sanctions, 206–7
  faces war with the Soviet Union, 228, 298
  fails to adhere to Geneva Convention, 505
  fails to invade Midway, 346–48
  fails to protect the wounded, 469

fights Bolsheviks in Russia, 97–98
fights border war with Soviet Union, 28, 84, 85–86, 100
forces all churches to join Federation of Churches, 426
forges alliance with Germany, 83–84, 87–88, 94–95, 99, 101
fosters State Shintoism, 10
Franklin Roosevelt grants Kurile Islands and Southern Sakhalin to Soviet Union, 565, 568
gains control of ex-German colonies, 97
granted mandates under League of Nations, 564
grapples with war crimes, 606–7
ideological radicalization of, 46
impact of Great Depression on, 4, 98, 540–41
implements rationing, 383
influences of European art world, 540
interservice rivalries hinder science in, 436
invades China, 73–74, 79–82, 380, 418, 501–2, 506
invites businesses to invest in China, 100–1
joins Anti-Comintern Pact, 77–78, 98–99
joins Tripartite Pact, 5, 102
kills songbird and household pets for food, 456
lacks an ideological mass movement, 109–10
lacks peace-treaty with Russia, 13
lacks resources for a war of attrition, 580
lacks resources to sustain war of attrition, 2–3
launches attack on the United States, 7
launches Operation U-Go, 332–36
launches Pacific offensive, 209, 343–45
leadership shake-up in, 106
legacy of World War II, 2
loss of scientific and technological infrastructure, 431
maintains strong relationship with the United States, 612
minimizes responsibility for actions in World War II, 600–1
missionary impact in, 417
mobilization of, 382–83

mobilizes children, 383
mobilizes women, 383–84
nature of fascism in, 4
naval losses, 104–5, 107
negotiates with U.S., 207–8
occupies French Indochina, 88
Pacific Charter call for a complete defeat of, 565
permits human experimentation, 435–36, 467–68, 474–75
permits Lend Lease shipment to arrive in Vladivostok, 107
permits range of artistic expression, 10–11
persecutes leftists, 539, 541
political reconstruction of, 562
Potsdam Declaration calls for surrender of, 571–72
provides care for disabled veterans, 476
rebuilding of, 449, 453, 454
receives German and Italian submarines, 106
reconciles with the United States, 1
relations with Germany worsen, 84–85
religious life in, 420–21
religious policies in Korea, 416–17
resume cultural production during American occupation, 554
return of colonists and prisoners of war to Japan, 585
scientific reputation of, 432
seeks capture of Port Moresby, 345–46
seeks naval dominance in Pacific, 9
seeks new world order, 38–39, 50–51
seeks to foster pan-Asianist art scene, 550–51
seeks wonder weapon, 435
seizes Manchuria, 5, 74–77, 549–50
seldom provides restitution for war crimes, 611
sends artists and writers to front-lines, 551
signs non-aggression pact with Japan, 49–50
signs non-aggression pact with Soviet Union, 107
signs Washington Naval Treaty, 23–24, 500
suffers loss of Rangoon, 336–37
suffers three million deaths from war, 382

Japan (*cont.*)
  suppresses resistance movements brutally, 3
  surrender of, 110, 382, 439, 572
  territorial ambitions of, 24–25
  threatens British interests, 7
  Turkey declares war against, 196–97
  turns to militarism, 27–28, 44, 45
  U.S. containment of, 203–6, 229
  uses poison gas in Taiwan, 611
  welcomes visit of Albert Einstein, 98
  wins victories against American, British, and Dutch, 8–9
  witnesses new postwar government, 380
Japanese Americans
  internment of, 377, 504
Jeb, Eglantyne
  founds Save the Children, 500
Jervis Bay (AMC)
  sinking of, 156–57
Jews
  asylum for, 498
  confront Christian anti-Semitism, 418
  emancipation of, 414–15
  establish international organizations, 415
  flee Germany and Austria, 500
  Japanese attitudes toward, 98–99
  lose citizenship in Romania, 276
  lose citizenship under Vichy, 265
  lose civil rights in Hungary, 276
  ordered to wear Star of David, 421–22
  participate in tolerance movement in U.S., 415
  serve in French army, 262
Jodl, Alfred
  indictment of, 518
  receives death sentence, 519
Johnson, Boris
  issues new Atlantic Charter, 573
Johnson, Hiram
  condemns international bankers, 22–23
Johnson, Nelson
  views on Japanese intervention in China, 77
Joint Chiefs of Staff (U.S.)
  appoints commanders for invasion of Japan, 352–53
  approves Operation Matterhorn, 358–59
  briefs Harry Truman, 364
  creates Pacific Ocean Area command, 344–45
  decides to bypass Rabaul, 351
  frustrate Franklin efforts to provide merchant ships to Great Britain, 164
  order Dwight Eisenhower to investigate war crimes, 522
  outlines plan to reduce Rabaul, 348
  relationship with Douglas MacArthur, 344
  seek entry of Soviet Union in war with Japan, 368
  seeks maintenance of Allied unity, 228
  wrestles with options to defeat Japan, 368
Joint Distribution Committee
  aids refugees, 420
Jones, Edgar L
  condemns mistreatment of enemy, 469
Judaism
  emergence of Conservative and Reform traditions, 414–15
Juin, Alphonse
  briefly detained, 258
  discounts possibility of Allied landing, 257–58
  leads French Expeditionary Force, 256

K

Kaganovich, Lazar
  praises Stalin, 43
Kallay, Miklos
  rejects German demands on Jewish question, 282
Kaltenbrunner, Ernest
  indictment of, 518
  receives death sentence, 519
Kamikaze attacks
  against carrier *St. Lo*, 352
  American press coverage of, 357
  during Okinawa campaign, 352–53
  ineffectiveness of, 438–39
Kansteiner, Wulf
  examines postwar German memory, 602–3
Katyn Massacre
  perpetrated by Soviet Union, 504
Kautsky, Karl
  assembles documents regarding German war guilt, 18

Kawabata Yasunari
   sees Manchukuo as Pan-Asianist model, 550–51
Kaya Okinori
   becomes Japanese justice minister, 529
Keenan, Joseph B.
   serves at lead prosecutor at Tokyo war crime trials, 473–74
Keitel, Wilhelm
   anti-Semitic convictions of, 487–88
   defers to Hitler, 288–89
   indictment of, 518
   receives death sentence, 519
Kellogg-Briand Pact
   Mussolini signs, 95
   precedent for trying war criminals, 517
   regulates the conditions for war, 497
Kenney, George
   commands Far East Air Forces (FEAF), 358
   maintains controls over heavy bombers, 364–65
   maintains trust of Douglas MacArthur, 363–64
   orders attack on Japanese transports, 350
Kesselring, Albert
   defends against Allied invasion of Italy, 262–63
   war crime trial of, 519–20
Kevles, Daniel
   assessments of, 438–39
Keynes, John Maynard
   negotiates postwar economic arrangements, 566–67
Khrushchev
   delivers secret speech, 582
Kichisaburo Nomura
   negotiates with U.S., 207
Kikuchi Kan
   travels to front-lines, 551
King, Ernest J.
   advocates a Pacific offensive, 348
   distrusts Douglas MacArthur, 344–45
   initiates drive into Gilbert Islands, 351
   skeptical of intelligence regarding Midway attack, 346
King, William Lyon Mackenzie
   sends expeditionary forces to Britain, 142

Kirke, Walter
   replacement of, 143–44
Kishi Nobusuke
   becomes Japanese prime minister, 529
Kiszely, John
   interpretations of, 122–23
Kleist von, General
   Halts armored forces, 128
   makes limited use of air power, 128–29
Kluge, Gunther von
   ends *Citadel* offensive, 290
Knox, Geoffrey
   reports on Hungarian economy, 275
Kobe, Japan
   bombing of, 361, 605–6
Koch, Hal
   condemns extremist movements, 420–21
Koenig, Pierre
   military commander of resistance groups, 266
Kogoro Takahira
   negotiates with Elihu Root, 204
Kohl, Helmut
   absent from D-Day anniversary commemorations, 600
   seeks to craft a positive German identity, 603–4
Kogoro Takahira
   negotiates with Elihu Root, 204–5
Kollontai, Alexandra
   considers Soviet POWs deserters, 581–82
Konev, Ivan
   attacks across the Oder River, 299
   attacks west into Silesia, 297–98
   pauses offensive, 298
   reopens offensive, 298–99
   traps German forces at Korsun, 292–93
   turns South to Berlin, 299–300
Korea
   China supports immediate independence for, 564–65
   continued political division of, 13
   establishment of State Shinto in, 416–17
   Franklin Roosevelt's proposals for postwar future of, 228–29
   human experimentation in, 435–36
   Japanese artists visit, 549

656 INDEX

Korea (cont.)
    Japanese colonizers expelled from, 12
    Japanese occupation of, 416–17
    as part of Japanese empire, 44, 432
    political division of, 572
    U.S. recognizes Japanese hegemony over, 204
Korea, Republic of Korea
    seeks apology from Japan, 2, 601–2
Korean War
    causes of, 369
    energizes fears of Soviet Union in Japan, 554
    United States serves as imperial proxy during, 572
Korwin-Rhodes, Marta
    interpretations of, 129
Koshiro Oikawa
    approves of possible summit with Franklin Roosevelt, 207
Koval, George
    infiltrates Manhattan Project's Oak Ridge facility, 441
Kretschmer, Otto
    capture of, 158
Kriegsmarine (German navy)
    cooperates with Japanese navy, 105–6
    deploys U-Boats to attack Allied shipping, 157–68
    deploys surface raiders, 155, 156–57
    gains naval bases in Norway, 124–25
    limitations of, 123, 124
    losses during Norwegian campaign, 116, 124, 125
    operates in Indian and Pacific oceans, 102–3
    shortcomings of, 155
    withdraws from Norwegian waters, 123
Kristallnacht
    American religious leaders condemn, 420
    Nazi led pogrom against German Jewish community, 484
    prompts Evian Conference, 502
Krupp, Alfried
    faces war crime trial, 521
Krylova, Anna
    interpretations of, 183
Kube, Wilhelm
    protests killing of Jews, 180

Kwantung Army
    defeat of, 100
    fights Soviet forces, 84, 100
    miscalculates level of Chinese resistance, 76
    plot and execute the Manchurian Incident, 73, 74–75
    seizes Manchuria, 5, 205

L

Lampson, Miles (Lord Killearn)
    pressures King Faruq, 191–92
Lang, Cosmo (Archbishop of Canterbury)
    accepts World War II as just war, 422
Lange, Herbert
    uses gas vans to commit mass murder, 487
Lansing, Robert
    negotiates with Japan, 204–5
Latin America
    Allied forestry experts survey as source of timber, 456
    joins United Nations alliance, 8
    seeks development-friendly international order, 567
Latvia
    German troops isolated in, 296–97
    Soviet Union invades, 101–2
Laval, Pierre
    negotiates with Italy, 60
    responds to Operation Torch, 258
    seeks ends of war in Ethiopia, 61
League of Nations
    administers Danzig, 12
    and anti-colonial struggle, 41
    conducts inquiry on Manchurian incident, 74
    deems Japan an aggressor, 76
    founding of , 3–4, 15, 500
    French Socialists support of, 25
    German membership in, 26–27
    Haile Selassie's appeal to, 60, 61–63
    Italian role in, 95
    Japanese participation in, 97–98, 205
    Japanese withdrawal from, 98–99
    legacy of, 563
    loss of faith in, 130
    oversees mandatory territories, 564, 568
    refugee relief efforts, 502, 510

reports on Ethiopian-Italian border
    dispute, 58
response to aggression, 5, 26, 75, 79
role in interwar years, 42
sanctions Italy, 96
shortcomings of, 11, 16, 497, 501, 569,
    515–16
Ledo Road
    opening of, 8, 337–38
Lemay, Curtis
    assumes command of XXI Bomber
        Command, 193
    improves performance of XXI Bomber
        Command, 360–61
    estimates Japanese casualties from fire
        raids, 357
    executes Operation Matterhorn, 359–60
    implements changes in Eighth Air Force,
        247
    launches incendiary bombing raids against
        Japan, 250–51, 353, 361–64, 365–66
Lemkin, Raphael
    defines genocide, 523
Lend Lease
    aid flows through Vladivostok, 108
    angers Adolf Hitler, 487–88
    China receives, 87–88
    curtails British trade with Latin America,
        231–32
    fosters rise of Grand Alliance, 221
    helps Britain prevail in Battle of the
        Atlantic, 434
    provides Soviet forces with trucks, 289,
        294–95
    supports Soviet war effort, 240–41, 242
    use for rebuilding Soviet Union, 451–52
Lenin, Vladimir
    challenges liberal world order , 3–4
    death of, 543
    forms Comintern, 40
    imposes dictatorship of the proletariat,
        43–44
    seeks new world order, 39
    seeks to export revolution, 40
    unwavering in pursuit of power, 44
Leningrad
    civilian casualties in , 379

evacuation of Kirov Works from, 181
    German forces cut off, 183–84
    site of war crime trials, 524
    Soviet offensive end siege, 293–94
Lentaigne, Brigadier
    replaces Orde Wingate, 336–37
Leopold, Aldo
    expresses pessimism on relation between
        humans and nature, 38
Let There Be Light (documentary)
    banning of, 477
Lexington (aircraft carrier)
    intercepts Japanese invasion force, 345
    loss of, 345
Ley, Robert
    indictment of, 518
    unavailable for Nuremberg war crime trials,
        518
Libya
    Axis forces cleared from, 148
    Italian forces advance from, 102
    Italian forces face setbacks in, 103
    Italian threat from, 191
    use of poison gas in, 58–59
Lieber Code
    issuance of, 498
Life (magazine)
    features photograph of Japanese skull,
        351–52
    feature work of American artists, 553
Lifton, Robert Jay
    examines participation of Nazi physicians
        in mass murder, 478
Lincoln, Abraham
    promulgates Lieber Code, 498
Lisbon, Portugal
    passage of Jewish refugees
        from, 502–3
Lithuania
    churches align with Nazi Germany in,
        425–26
    Soviet invasion of, 101–2
Lloyd, Wilfrid
    leads 14th Indian Division, 327
logistics
    benefits British and Indian Army in Burma,
        336, 338

logistics (cont.)
  British import requirements, 156
  efforts to disrupt for German forces in Normandy, 307
  German army outruns supply lines in Eastern Front, 451
  Germans seek Soviet rolling stock and locomotives, 174
  hampers German army, 318
  hampers Western Allies advance in Europe, 313, 315
  hinders defense of Bataan, 212–13
  hinders Luftwaffe on Eastern Front, 242
  Lend Lease trucks in Soviet Union prove instrumental, 289, 294–95
  Luftwaffe supplies German forces in Norway, 123
  for Operation Torch, 163
  pillaging of Soviet population to support Wehrmacht, 179
  sites to support, 450
  stalls German offensives, 176
  strength of Soviet war effort, 181, 242
  support provided to Einsatzgruppe by Wehrmacht, 179
  supports XXI Bomber Command, 360
  use of airlift in CBI Theater, 8, 334, 337–38
  use of artificial harbors at Normandy, 309
  uses of airlift for Operation Matterhorn, 359
Lomax, Cyril
  given command, 330–31
London, England
  aerial bombing of, 9, 146, 147
  port closes, 158–59
  as hub of the Empire, 223
  target of German rocket attacks, 436
London Naval Conference (1927)
  leads to naval disarmament, 23–24
Long, Breckenridge
  blocks entrance of refugees, 508
Los Alamos, New Mexico
  site of atomic bomb development, 367–68, 437–38, 458
Los Angeles, California
  attracts German actors and filmmakers, 551–52
  expansion of, 377, 450

Ludendorff, Erich
  demands Germany seek armistice, 17
  launches offensive against France, 16–17
  resignation of, 17
Luftwaffe
  aircraft production falls short for, 242
  assessment of, 252
  attacks Dunkirk bridgehead, 140
  bombs London, 147
  close major British ports during Blitz, 158–59
  conducts deadly oxygen experiments, 474–75
  deploy forces into Tunisia, 259
  deploys Condor Legion to Spain, 67–68
  deploys forces in Mediterranean Theater, 244, 256–57, 268
  deploys troops to Oslo's Fornebu airfield, 123
  during Battle of Britain, 2, 7, 145–46
  expands air defense of Germany, 247, 248, 251
  faces logistical and weather challenges on Eastern Front, 242
  fails to win Battle of Britain, 147–48, 155–56
  gains air superiority in Polish campaign, 122
  lacks long range bomber, 239–40
  launches Blitz, 378
  loses air superiority, 249
  losses in Polish campaign, 277
  prevails in the Battle of France, 240
  provides limited air support to German armor in Poland, 118–19
  redeploys forces from Eastern Front to West, 252
  role in Battle of France, 128–29
  role in naval war, 155
  role narrows on Eastern Front, 242–43
  shifts targets during the Battle of Britain, 9, 146
  strafes Polish towns and cities, 131
  strikes civilian targets, 120
  suffers loses with deployment of P-51 Mustang, 248–49
  supplies German forces in Norway, 123
  supports ground troops, 238–39
  triumphs against Red Air Force, 240–41

U.S. offensive destroys as effective fighting force, 251
underestimates ability of Red Air Force to recover, 241–42
use women as ferrying pilots, 385
Lu Xun
protests against Japanese imperialism, 549–50
Lytton, Lord
chairs League of Nations commission, 76, 98

M

MacArthur, Douglas
bypasses enemy strongholds in New Guinea campaign, 351
expresses confidence in Philippine defenses, 202
gains control of land forces for invasion of Japan, 352–53
and the failed defense of the Philippines, 202, 212–13, 343–44
grants James Kenney autonomy, 358, 363–64
orders dismantling of State Shinto, 427
returns to the Philippines, 352
seeks to strike Rabaul, 348
serves as commander of Southwest Pacific Area, 344–45
shares divided command situation, 350
Macleod, Donald
retirement of, 330
Macmillan, Harold
witnesses parade in Tunisia, 262
McCarthy, Leighton
gains rank of ambassador, 224
McDonald, James
aids refugees, 502
views of, 508
McLeod, Roy
interpretations of, 441
McNair, Lesley J.
death of, 312
McNaughton, Andrew
assesses combat effectiveness of troops, 145
commands troops guarding Great Britain, 142
McNeill, John
examines unprecedented use of resources in World War II, 449–50

Madagascar
Adolf Hitler consider sending Jews to, 487
Maginot Line
confidence in, 120, 138–39
construction of, 4
French troop deployments behind, 127
lacks sufficient anti-aircraft guns, 126
serves intended purpose, 125–26
Mahan, Alfred Thayer
influence of, 342–43
malaria
campaign to eradicate, 468
endemic on Guadalcanal, 349, 472–73
impact on Burma campaign, 330–31
medical advance in treating, 336, 350–51
UNRRA establishes relief program in Greece, 509
use of atabrine to treat, 350–51, 471
use of DDT to control, 11, 458
Malle, Louis
releases *Lacombe Lucien*, 609
Malta
as base for British aircraft and submarines, 268
defense of, 243
major British naval base in, 61
reinforcement of, 257–58
Malaya
Allies view as war victim, 525
anti-colonial movements in, 529
British defense of, 210–11
British loss of, 202, 225
former Japanese prisoners of war rearmed in, 585
Japanese invasion of, 209, 329, 330, 342, 397–98, 401–2
Japanese prevails during invasion of, 358
receives reinforcements, 329–30
Thailand seeks recovery of lost territory from, 396–97
war crime trials in, 527–28
Maltzan, Ago von
seeks to improve relations with Soviet Union, 78
Manchurian Incident
as beginning of World War II, 548–49
escalates into full scale war between China and Japan, 76–77

Manchurian Incident (*cont.*)
　impacts Chinese cultural life, 549–51
　impacts global diplomacy, 74
　Japanese justification for, 213
　fosters persecution of leftists in Japan, 539
　plotted by Kwantung Army, 74–75, 86, 205, 539
　as reflective of ultra-nationalism on the part of Kwantung Army, 47
　represents first failure of collective security, 5, 62–63
　significance of, 73–74
　Western response to, 75–76, 77, 89, 98–99
Manhattan Project
　builds atomic bomb, 367–68, 437–38, 522
　delays in building bomb, 298
　infiltrated by Soviet agents, 431
　Roosevelt authorizes, 437–38
Manila, Philippines
　American forces withdraw from, 346
　becomes an open city, 212
　Japanese forces commit massacres in , 524
　site of Yamashita trial, 527
Mann, Thomas
　flees Germany, 542, 545
Manstein, Erich von
　develops postwar myth of apolitical *Wehrmacht*, 179
　ends Operation Citadel, 290
　fails to halt Soviet advance, 292
　orders murder of Jews, 179
　plans invasion of France, 127
　seeks to open Korsun pocket, 292–93
Manoilescu, Mihail
　dismayed by Second Vienna Award, 279
Mao Zedong
　allows American radio station at Yenan, 361
　gains power, 572
　historical assessments of, 89
　organizes war crime trials, 528
　signs truce with Chiang Kai-Shek, 5
Marco Polo Bridge Incident
　causes of, 79, 81
　triggers Sino-Japanese war, 5, 79, 80
Marinetti, Filippo Tommaso
　promotes futurism, 542

Marshall, George C.
　advice on amphibious assaults ignored, 308–9
　considers using poison gas against Japan, 370
　discounts threat of war with Japan, 202
　does not encourage Hull to purse a modus vivendi with Japan, 208
　expresses confidence regarding defense of Philippines, 212
　opposes Mediterranean campaign, 256–57, 259–60
　receives a briefing from Curtis LeMay, 364
　receives briefing from army intelligence, 207
　receives reports from Joseph Stillwell, 327
　supports strategic bombing, 245–46
Maruyama Tomoyoshi
　interacts with artists in Weimar-era Berlin, 549
Matsuoka Yosuke
　meets with Adolf Hitler, 107
Max of Baden, Prince
　appointed chancellor, 17
　reforms constitution, 17–18
medicine
　coping with malaria, 11
　human experimentation practiced, 3, 435–36, 467–68, 474–75
Mengele, Josef
　escapes to South America, 474–75
Merkel, Angela
　participates in D-Day anniversary commemoration, 600
　denounces anti-Semitism, 611–12
Merrill, Frank
　commands 5307th Provisional Unit in Burma, 336–37
Mexico
　farm workers from, 376–77
Meyer, Henning
　interpretation of, 609–10
Michael, King (Romania)
　becomes King, 279
　and response to the Holocaust, 282
Mikawa Gunichi
　attacks American fleet off Guadalcanal, 348–49

Milch, Erhard
  Recommends airborne troops assault Great Britain, 147–48
Miles, Sherman
  describes policymakers prewar views of Japan, 209
Mindlin, Mike
  produces *Hitler's Reign of Terror* documentary, 551–52
Ministry of Defense (MOD)
  claims sensitive to environment at military bases, 450
  conducts clean-up operations on Scotland's Gruinard Island, 458–59
missionaries
  foster colonialism, 415
  found ecumenical networks in Asia, 416
  maintain ties with African and Asian churches, 426
  opposition to, 416–17
Missouri (battleship)
  hosts surrender ceremonies, 353
Mitchell, William "Billy"
  advocates air powers, 245–46
Mitter, Rana
  interpretations of, 89, 327–28
Model, Field Marshal
  commits suicide, 317–18
Moeyes, Paul
  compares Dutch and Swiss neutrality, 405–6
Molotov, Vyacheslav
  delivers ultimatum to Romania, 279
  issues Four Powers declaration, 232
  negotiates Non-Aggression Pact with Germany, 28, 118
Moltke, Helmut von
  influence of, 118, 122, 128
Monroe Doctrine
  defines American sphere of influence, 230
Monte Cassino
  destruction of, 250
Montevideo, Uruguay
  Graf Spee takes refuge in, 155
Montgomery, Bernard
  captures Brussels, 313–14
  claims victory at Battle of Bulge, 316–17
  defeats Erwin Rommel, 191
  fails to close Falaise Gap, 312–13
  forces reach Baltic, 308
  launches Operation Plunder, 317–18
  opposes broad front strategy, 315
  pauses offensive, 317
  reviews plans for Operation Overlord, 306
  seeks to capture Caen, 311
  undertakes Operation Market-Garden, 314
  wages campaign to open Scheldt estuary, 315
Morgan, Frederick
  begins planning Operation Overlord, 305
Morgenthau, Henry Jr.
  curtails British trade with Latin America, 231–32
  favors execution of Nazi leaders, 516–17
Morocco
  concentration camps in, 426
  Vichy defense of, 258
Morocco, Spanish
  nationalist forces gain experience in, 65
  poison gas used in, 58–59
Moscow, Soviet Union
  civil disturbances in, 176
  German efforts to seize, 173–74
  German prisoners of war parade in, 295
  secondary objective for Hitler, 175–76, 177
motion pictures
  Crown Film Unit produces documentaries, 553
  explaining why American should fight, 107
  focusing on Vichy France, 608–9
  Marxist critiques of, 552
  Mussolini establishes Cinecitta film studio, 542
  national policy films produced in Manchukuo, 550–51
  portrayals of Japanese war effort, 551
  portrays Nazi regime, 551–52
  U.S. Army issues *The Negro Soldier,* 477
  U.S. bans *Let There Be Light,* 477
  work of Leni Riefenstahl exemplifies Nazi-sponsored film, 546
Mott, John
  founds World Student Christian Federation, 417
Moulin, Jean
  unifies French resistance groups, 266

Mountbatten, Louis
  expresses confidence in defense of Kohima, 334
  leads South East Asia Command, 332, 360–61
Mueller, Josef
  participates in German Catholic underground, 422
Mukden, China
  capture of, 73
Munich Pact
  criticism of, 29
  fosters German aggression, 5
  Hitler reneges on, 29
  negotiation of, 28–29
Murmansk, Russia
  convoys to, 8
Murphy, Robert
  establishes espionage network, 257–58
Muslims
  aid Jewish neighbors in North Africa, 426
  efforts to forge interfaith dialogue with, 417
  influence in Egypt grows, 191–92
  make up the majority of the population in French North Africa, 261
  provide assistance to Soviet war veterans, 588
  question French colonial rule, 265–66
  rescue Jewish neighbors during German occupation, 426
  serve in French Expeditionary Force (CEF), 262
Mussolini Benito
  accepts German annexation of Austria, 96
  Adolf Hitler flatters, 96–97
  Adolf Hitler seeks to avoid alienating, 70
  adopts autarky, 23
  arrest of, 105
  British and French governments seek to avoid provoking, 61
  brokers Munich Agreement, 28–29
  comparison with Adolf Hitler, 110
  courted as a potential ally, 5
  courted by Pierre Laval, 60
  demands apology from Ethiopia over Wal Wal incident, 60
  denounces German unilateralism and treaty violations, 96
  deploys bombers to Ethiopia, 67–68
  deploys poison gas against Ethiopians, 59
  dreams of Mediterranean empire, 38
  efforts to assert Italian power in Ethiopia backfires, 96
  entrenches state terror in Italian system, 48
  envisions fascism as foundation for new civilization, 42
  fall of, 110
  inclined to agree to peace settlement proposed by British and French, 61
  invades Greece, 103
  and invasion of Soviet Union, 43
  involves state in cultural production, 542
  and Italian memory of World War II, 387
  joins war as Germany's ally, 102
  leads march on Rome, 95
  meets with Adolf Hitler, 102–03, 104–5, 108
  moves closer to Germany, 66
  opposes German annexation of Austria, 96
  outraged at British for altering naval clauses of the Versailles Treaty, 60–61
  permits multiple styles in the arts, 542–43
  plans to invade Ethiopia, 57, 58
  popularity declines, 385–86
  rejects Adolf Hitler aesthetics, 542
  relationship with Franco obscured after, 69
  rise to power of, 4, 43
  rules Italian Social Republic, 105, 386
  seeks popular support, 46
  seeks support of Roman Catholic Church, 386
  seeks to aid Finland, 100–1
  seeks to avenge loss at Adwa, 56–57
  seeks to preserve Austria as client state, 95–96
  serves as mediator at Munich Conference, 99–100
  shocked by German invasion of Soviet Union, 103–4
  shocked by Non-Aggression Pact, 100
  urges Adolf Hitler to seek a negotiated settlement with Josef Stalin, 104–5
  vacillates over entering war, 100
  world view of, 39

Muto Tomio
  promotes utopian multiethnic culture in Manchukuo, 550–51
  propagandist in Manchukuo, 542

N

Nagai Kazu
  interpretations of, 79, 80
Nagasaki, Japan
  atomic bomb attack on, 353, 366, 367–68, 369–70, 384, –439, 441
  rebuilding of, 448–49, 453
Nagumo Chuichi
  commands First Carrier Striking Force at Midway, 346, 347
  fails to send a third wave to attack Pearl Harbor, 342–43
Nanjing, China
  anti-Japanese protests in, 76–77
  Chiang Kai-shek returns to, 75
  commemoration of, 610–11
  Japanese atrocities committed in, 82–83, 501, 610–11
  military academies in, 78
  U.S. ambassador in, 77
Nansen, Fridjof
  heads League of Nations High Commission for Refugees, 500
Napoleon
  artistic portraits of, 543–44, 554–55
Narvik, Norway
  Allied plans regarding, 116
  German military objective, 123
  naval battles at, 125
  surrender of, 129
National Council of Christian and Jews
  founding of, 415
  supports war effort, 425
National Defense Research Council
  replaced by Office of Scientific Research and Development, 433
National Southwest Associated University (Lianda)
  relocated, 380
Navajo
  derve as code-talkers in Pacific, 434

Netherlands
  as a colonial power, 222
  displaced persons from, 589
  freezes Japanese assets, 206–7
  holds war crime trials, 519–20, 527–28
  invasion of, 7, 87, 231
  issues Netherlands' Extraordinary Penal Law Decree, 526
  Japan pursues war against, 8–9
  neutrality compromised , 2
  participates Tokyo war crimes trial, 529–31
  rise of fascist movements in, 45
  seeks to maintain neutrality, 405–6
  site of V-1 bases, 436
Neuer Plan (New Economic Plan)
  Designed to prepare Germany for war, 274–75
Neurath, Constantin von
  indictment of, 518
  receives prison term, 519
Newfoundland
  contributes to defense of Great Britain, 141
  convoy battles off of, 156
Newsweek (magazine)
  escribe Pacific Theater as a war without quarter, 357
New York Times
  condemns postwar detention of prisoners of war, 586
  reports on fire raids against Japan, 357
  reports on forced population movements, 591–92
  reports on Four Power Declaration, 232
  reports on U.S. Army shielding war criminals, 474
New Zealand
  assists British war crime investigations, 527–28
  contributes to British war effort, 225
  declares war, 141–42
  forges closer ties with U.S., 225
  troops deploy to North Africa, 148
Nichols, J. Bruce
  interpretations of, 423
Niebuhr, Reinhold
  opposes isolationism, 425
Nimitz, Chester
  and control of bombers, 360–61
  champions carrier offensives, 346

Nimitz, Chester (*cont.*)
    commands U.S. naval forces in the Pacific, 344–45
    differs with Ernest King, 346
    expresses misgiving on landing at Kyushu, 369–70
    gives Bill Halsey command of Southwest Pacific area (SOPAC), 351–52
    participates in divided command structure, 348, 350
    provide interrogatory for Nuremberg War Crimes Tribunal, 518–19
    seeks islands closer to Japan, 352–53
    seeks to halt Japanese offensives, 345, 346
    uses carriers to support of amphibious assaults, 358
Nixon, Richard M.
    makes overtures to Beijing, 228–29
Nolde, Emile
    produces anti-war art, 545
Non-Aggression Pact (1939)
    allows Soviet Union to confront Japanese threat, 28
    concedes Bessarabia to Soviet Union, 279
    grants Soviet Union eastern Poland, 118
    Great Britain signs mutual assistance pact with Poland, 120
    Hitler abrogates, 7
    ideological basis of, 49–50
    leads to a deterioration in German-Japanese relations, 84, 100
    leads to invasion of Poland, 6, 86
    Mussolini's disillusionment with, 100
    strategic impact of, 94
    Western powers reaction to, 8
Norden bomb site
    development of, 245–46, 434–35
North Atlantic Treaty Organization (NATO)
    brings political stability to Europe, 594–95
    Helmut Kohl's strong commitment to, 600
    legal status under United Nations charter, 569–70
    seeks to draw lessons from Blitzkrieg warfare, 117
Norstad, Laura
    consults with Curtis Lemay on adopting new tactics, 361
    improves radar training, 361
    reports on air war on results of air war against Japan, 364–65
Norway
    fifth column activity in, 129
    German fears of British invasion of, 159, 306
    German invasion of, 7, 101, 122–24, 138, 139, 147–48, 394, 520
    German naval deployments in, 157, 161
    Germany acquires bases in, 124–25
    heavy water plant in, 437
    holds war crime trials, 519–20
    neutrality compromised. 2, 121, 394, 395
    proposed British actions in, 121, 142
    seeks to maintain neutrality, 395
    strategic value of, 155–56
Nuremberg Laws
    strips Jews of civil rights, 483
Nuremberg War Crimes Trial
    draws on Anglo-American and continental law traditions, 518–19
    embodies liberal internationalism, 572
    establishes important precedents, 12
    Indictments issued, 518
    initial proposals for, 515–17
    issues verdict on German aggression, 5
    issues verdicts, 519–20
    London Charter establishing, 517–18
    permits trials in Allied Zones of occupation, 519–20

O

Oak Ridge, Tennessee
    serves as production site, 367–68, 417–18
    suffers from radiation pollution, 458
Obama, Barack
    participates in D-Day anniversary commemoration, 600
Office of Scientific Research and Development (OSRD)
    establishment of, 433
Oldenziel, Ruth
    interpretations of, 457
Open Door
    U.S. seeks to protect, 75–76, 203–5
Operational Anvil
    French army part of, 267

Operation *Bagration*
   commemoration of, 543–44
   shatters German armies in East, 294–95
   success of, 291–92, 294–97
Operation Barbarossa
   Adolf Hitler unleashes, 103–4
   allies participating in, 178, 279
   combat effectives of Soviet forces debated, 173–74
   course of, 174–78
   delays launching of, 108
   essentially annihilates the Soviet army, 300
   failure of, 183–84
   German forces amassed for, 173
   Hungarian participation in, 281
   initiate mass shooing of Jews, 109
   Luftwaffe focuses on destruction Soviet Air Force, 241
   Romanian participation in, 280–81
   Soviet casualties as result of, 581–82
Operation Blau (Blue)
   depends on foreign troops to execute, 178
   Germans attack Kursk and Caucasus, 177–78
Operation Bolero
   U.S. forces land Great Britain in preparation of, 304–5
Operation Capital
   seeks to defeat Japanese forces on Shwebo plain, 337
Operation *Citadel*
   German offensive directed at Kursk salient, 290
Operation Cobra
   Allied forces seek breakthrough in Normandy, 312
   success of, 313
Operation Compass
   seeks to drive Axis forces out of Libya, 148
Operation Dragoon
   Allied amphibious landing in southern France succeeds, 256, 313
   execution coincides with Allied breakout from Normandy, 267
Operation Extended Capital
   leads to recapture of Rangoon, 337
Operation Gomorrah
   firebombs Hamburg, 452–53

Operation Grenade
   Ninth U.S. Army launches in support of Operation Veritable, 317
Operation Ichi-Go
   seeks to neutralize American airfields in China, 359
Operation *Kutuzov*
   initiates pattern of Soviet offensives, 291
   Soviet offensive breaks through Western and Bryansk fronts, 290
Operation Longcloth
   Orde Wingate launches irregular operation behind Japanese lines, 331–32
Operation Market-Garden
   failure of, 314
   makes massive use of airborne troops, 314
   seeks to penetrate the Ruhr, 314
Operation Mars
   seeks to destroy Army Group Center, 177
Operation Matador
   British planning for advance into southern Thailand, 210
Operation Matterhorn
   destroys Hankow as enemy base of operation, 359–60
   proves untenable, 360–61
Operation Meetinghouse
   plays role in Japanese surrender, 366–67
   targets Tokyo, 362–63
Operation MO
   seeks capture of Port Moresby, 345
Operation Paperclip
   brings Nazi scientists and physicians to United States, 440, 474–75
Operation Plunder
   leads to breakthrough across Rhine, 317–18
Operation Reinhard
   deports Jews from Warsaw ghetto to Treblinka, 491
Operation *Rumiantsev*
   Soviet meet fierce German resistance during, 291
Operation Sealion
   hastily produced plan, 147–48
Operation Storm (Burza)
   AK forces attack German forces, 278

Operation Thursday
    long range penetration operation led by
        Orde Wingate, 336–37
Operation Torch
    Allied troops diverted to, 304–5
    Allies land in Northwest Africa, 190
    Franklin Roosevelt commits to, 257
    impacts British shipping, 163
    makes Toulon the cemetery of French High
        Seas Fleet, 261
    results in collaboration with Vichy officials,
        259–60
    returns France to war, 265–66
    shapes postwar future of Greece and Italy,
        260
    Vichy response to, 258
Operation U-GO
    Japanese seeks to capture of Imphal, 332–33
Operation Veritable
    seeks to clear Rhineland, 317
Ophuls, Marcel
    releases *The Sorrow and the Pity*, 609
Oppenheimer, J. Robert
    leads Manhattan Project, 367–68, 437–38
    reflects on views of Henry Stimson, 366
Orlando, Vittorio
    negotiates at Paris Peace Conference, 19
Orthodox Church
    anti-Semitism in, 418
    Iron Guard aligns with, 417–18
    in Japan required to join Federation of
        Churches, 426
    provides assistance to Soviet veterans, 585
    response to ecumenism, 417
Oshima Hiroshi
    admires Adolf Hitler, 98–99
    encourages Hitler to consider making peace
        with the Soviet Union, 104–5
    messages to Tokyo intercepted, 108
    strategic visions of, 104
Ottoman Empire
    as ally of Germany, 17
    dissolution of, 194
Ottoman Red Cross
    adopts symbol of the Red Crescent, 499
Oxford Committee for Famine Relief (Oxfam)
    favors food shipments to Greece, 507

Ozawa Jisaburo
    seeks to lure William Halsey away from
        invasion force, 352

P

Pal, Radhabinod
    issues dissent at Tokyo war crime
        trials, 531
Palestine
    absence on Potsdam Conference agenda,
        563
    British mandate of, 417
    ecumenical efforts in, 417
    German forces threaten, 191, 197
    Orde Wingate serves in, 331–32
    Zionism as potent political force
        in, 267
Palmer, Matthew
    interpretations of, 276–77
Papen, Franz von
    acquittal of, 519
    indictment of, 518
Papon, Maurice
    trial of, 609
Paris, France
    as cultural center, 549
    entertainment world thrives under Nazi
        occupation, 548
    liberated by Free French forces, 313–14
Paton, William
    seeks to restore Christian values, 426
Patton, George S.
    army activated, 312
    assaults psychiatric patient, 470
    crosses Rhine River, 317
    halts Argentan, 312–13
    heads toward Metz, 313–14
    launches Ardennes counterattack, 267,
        316–17
    participates in deception operation, 306
Paxton, Robert
    examines Vichy France, 609
Pearl Harbor, Attack
    fails to cripple the Pacific fleet, 434–35
    featured in documentary by Fujita
        Tsuguharu, 551
    fuel tanks spared, 438–39

Japanese attack force departs for, 208
  results in loss of U.S. battleships, 9
Peiper, Joachim*
  murders American POWs at Malmedy, 316
penicillin
  heralds dawn of new era, 469-70
  increased production of, 431, 433, 438-39, 471
Percival, Arthur
  lacks experience of field command, 330
  surrenders, 211, 329
Petain, Phillipe
  commands anti-aircraft forces, 126
  enjoys loyalty of French professional soldiers, 265
  establishes People's Republic of China, 382
  meets with Adolf Hitler, 398-99
  oak tree named after, 455-56
  plans for defense of Ardennes, 126-27
  provides legitimacy to Vichy government, 130
  seeks support of peasantry, 506
  supports armistice, 130-31, 143
petroleum
  becomes scarcer for Germany, 438-39
  British depend on oil from Middle East, 194, 197
  as focus of air attacks, 245-46, 249, 251
  Japan seeks, 8-9
  Romania exports to Germany, 274-75
  shortages in Battle of France, 313
  shortfalls during Battle of the Atlantic, 164
  sources in the Middle East, 190
  U.S. bombing target German supplies and refining capacity, 251
Phibun Songkhram
  collaborates with Japanese, 397, 398
  embraces belligerency, 398-99
  seeks recovery of lost territories, 396-97
  seeks to capitalize on French difficulties, 397-98
Philippines
  Allied air attacks against, 344, 358
  American force land in Leyte, 352
  American reinforcement of, 202
  Douglas MacArthur plans to return to, 344-45

Fifth Air Force prevails over Japanese forces, 358
  holds war crime trials, 529
  interreligious activity in, 417
  Japanese aviators success in attacking, 358
  Japanese conquest of, 8-9, 202, 209, 212-13, 342
  Japanese express concern over threat posed by American bases in, 205
  Japanese forces stage landing at Luzon, 343-44
  Japanese prisoners of war in, 585
  participates IMT, 12, 529-30
  participates in Bretton Woods Conference, 567
  and plans to launch incendiary bombing attacks against Japan, 361
  provides airfields for B-29s, 353, 361
  receives promise of full independence, 222
  resistance organizations in, 213-14
  success in New Guinea speeds plans to retake Philippines campaign, 351
  Theodore Roosevelt seeks Japanese recognition of American control over, 204
  timber industry suffers war-time damage, 456
  transition from war to peace in, 369
  and trial of Yamashita Tomoyuki, 527
  United States purchases, 549
  War Plan ORANGE anticipates an attack on, 343
Picasso, Pablo
  paints *Guernica*, 547
Piccigallo, Phillip
  interpretations of, 531
Pius XII (Eugenio Pacelli)
  condemns suffering of innocent, 423
  connections with German underground, 422
  diplomatic career of, 416
  responds to the Holocaust, 424-25
Ploesti, Romania
  air raid against, 268-69
poison gas
  banning of, 500
  development of, 431, 440, 457

poison gas (cont.)
  George Marshall contemplates using, 370
  use in Ethiopian War, 58–59
  use by Japanese forces in Taiwan, 611
  use in Nazi death camps, 482, 486, 487, 490–91
Poland
  Adolf Hitler seeks to resettle ethnic Germans in, 101–2, 275, 485, 590–91
  AK Forces fight as part of Operation Storm, 277–78
  and Aktion Reinhard, 491
  alleged fifth column activity in, 129
  closing of death camps in, 491–92
  creation of Jewish ghettoes in, 485
  demands territory from Czech government, 275
  deportation of Jews to, 485–86, 487
  end of Cold War prompts reconsideration in, 283–84
  euthanasia program established in, 487
  exchanges population with Soviet Union, 593
  few collaborators in, 277
  German invasion of, 3, 5, 7, 15–16, 86, 88, 100–1, 116, 155, 257–58, 274, 277, 377, 398, 472, 484–85, 486, 539, 546
  granted Danzig Corridor, 19
  granted portions of eastern Germany, 591–92
  houses Nazi death camps, 282, 490–91
  Intelligentsia systematically killed by SS and Einsatzgruppen, 485
  Josef Stalin views as part of Soviet sphere of influence, 227
  Lenin seeks to export revolution to, 40
  military strength of, 125
  murder of Jews in, 482
  never surrenders to Germany, 277
  Polish forces transit through Hungary, 278–79
  Potsdam Conference consider postwar future, 570
  receives new borders in postwar era, 12
  receives security guarantees, 99–100, 120
  resistance forces in, 277
  resolving border disputes with Germany, 26–27
  Soviet forces fail to aid Warsaw uprising, 278, 295–96
  Soviet forces occupy, 298
  Soviet Union invades, 6, 50, 100, 393
  Soviets deport Polish citizens, 590–91
  Teheran Conference considers postwar future, 565
  treatment of Catholic clergy in, 423
  tries German war criminals, 523,
  Yalta Conference considers postwar future, 227–28, 568, 571
Pollack, Jackson
  U.S. Information Service funds European exhibition tours of work, 555
Port Moresby, New Guinea
  defense of, 344
  faces Japanese invasion force, 212–13, 345, 346, 349–50
Portugal
  cultural impact of war, 402–3
  neutrality of, 2, 398, 400–1
  signs Non-Intervention agreement regarding Spanish Civil War, 66–67
Potsdam Conference
  agree on new border for Poland and Soviet Union, 571
  avoids discussion of Holocaust, Jewish refugees, and Palestine, 563
  discusses reparations from Germany, 570–71
  discussions regarding development of atomic bomb, 437–38, 571
  issues declaration calling for Japanese unconditional surrender, 571
  Japan accept terms of declaration issued by, 568
  often viewed through lens of Cold War, 562–63
  reflects strength of Allied unity, 108
  seeks pause on expulsion of German minorities, 592
  Soviet Union does not sign declaration issued to Japan, 572
  underscores power of white Americans, Britons, and Russians, 570
Powers, Thomas
  interpretations of, 441

Preston, Paul
  interpretations of, 67
Prien, Gunther
  death of, 158
Prince of Wales (HMS)
  attacks Bismarck, 157
  sinking of, 202, 210–11
Princeton (American carrier)
  sinking of, 352
prisoners of war
  humanitarian efforts on behalf of, 2, 13, 497, 500, 503
  murder of, 517–18
Prisoners of war, Australian
  forced laborers on Burma-Thailand Railway, 329, 524–25
  greeted with suspicion when repatriated, 503–4
prisoners of war, British
  fear of retaliation against , 515–16
  forced laborers on Burma-Thailand Railway, 329, 524–25
  greeted with suspicion when repatriated, 503–4
  postwar care of, 379
  repatriation from Germany, 581
prisoners of War, Dutch
  forced laborers on Burma-Thailand Railway, 329, 524–25
prisoners of war, Filipino
  perish on Bataan Death March, 344
prisoners of war, French
  repatriation of, 581
prisoners of war, German
  French treatment of, 586
  mass capture of, 267
  parade through Moscow, 295
  provide useful intelligence, 146
  return from Japan, 98
  treatment by Soviet Union, 504, 586
  Western allies treatment of, 582–85
  wounded soldiers exchange, 399
prisoners of war, Indian
  serve in Indian National Army, 337
prisoners of war, Italian
  treatment of, 503–04, 586
prisoners of war, Japan
  treatment of, 585

prisoners of war, Polish
  capture, 277
  Soviet treatment of, 504
prisoners of war, Soviet
  considered deserters, 581–82
  at Bialystok-Minsk and Smolensk, 175
  liberation of, 290
  murder of, 179
  recruited to serve in German auxiliaries, 182–83
  starvation of, 180
  systematic murder of, 488
prisoners of war, U.S.
  attacks on , 522
  fear of retaliation against, 515–16
  Japanese atrocities against, 351–52
  massacred at Malmedy, 316
  mass surrender at Bataan, 344
  murder of, 522
  perish during Bataan death march, 212–13, 524
  repatriation from Germany, 581
production
  of aircraft, 434–35
  allies enjoy great capacity, 252–53
  of anti-aircraft guns in Germany, 252
  bolstered in Soviet Union by centralized planned economy, 180
  of British aircraft, 239, 240,
  Grand Alliance wins decisively, 2
  increases in Germany in 1945, 251
  of naval vessels, 159, 162
  of Soviet aircraft, 241, 242
  Soviets transfer production eastward, 181
  of steel in Japan, 28
  success at American conversion efforts, 375–76
prostitution
  Italian women turn to, 264
  use of comfort women by Japanese army, 2, 381, 524, 605, 607
psychiatry, military
  treatment of casualties, 470
public opinion
  regarding British morale, 147
  views regarding refugees, 502
Putin, Vladimir
  participates in D-Day anniversary commemoration, 600

Q

Quakers (Society of Friends)
  oppose slave trade, 498–99
  supports International Fellowship of Reconciliation, 415–16
  aid refugees, 423
Quebec Conference
  Orde Wingate attends, 336
Quezon, Manuel L.
  headquartered on Corregidor, 344
Quisling, Vidkun
  collaborates with Germany, 117

R

Rabaul
  Allies seek reduction of, 350
  Douglas MacArthur favors attack on, 348
  Japanese defense of, 350
  Japanese fleet seeks protection of, 348
  Japanese fortification of, 348
  JCS decides to bypass, 351
radar
  development of, 11, 431, 433, 435–36
  German advances shared with Japan, 105–6
  German use of, 269
  on escort vessels, 161, 163
  significance of, 438–39
  stations targeted in Battle of Britain, 145–46
  use during Battle of Britain, 240
  use during Battle of the Atlantic, 158, 163, 165, 166, 167
  use in bombing attacks, 360, 361, 362
  use in naval navigation, 348–49
Raeder, Erich
  assesses naval readiness, 155
  favors strategy of commerce raiding, 124
  indictment of, 518
  seeks naval bases in Norway, 124
  sentence of, 519
rape
  after Japanese capture of Nanjing, 82–83, 524
  against German expellees, 592
  by Soviet soldiers, 300, 385
rationing
  female British veterans given ration book to buy clothing, 588

  in Great Britain, 378–79
  in Japan, 383
  in Sicily under Allied Military Government, 264
  in Soviet Union, 379–569
  in the United States, 376
Red Air Force
  benefits from superior logistics, 242
  creates three all-female regiments, 242
  gains air superiority over Luftwaffe, 242–43
  gains numerical superiority over *Luftwaffe*, 241
  provides close air support, 241–42
  suffers losses during Operation Barbarossa, 240–41
  undergoes reorganization, 242
Red Army
  artists commemorate victory of, 554–55
  drives toward Warsaw, 40
  engage in sexual violence, 592
  historians assess capabilities of, 173–74
  losses during Operation Barbarossa, 173, 181
  mobilization of, 181
  postwar demobilization of, 586–87
  survives Nazi onslaught, 8
Reep, Ed
  serves as U.S. Army combat artist, 553
refugees
  aid diminishes after 1939, 423
  creation of Nansen Passport to aid, 500
  from Russian Revolution, 500
  Hungarian acceptance of, 278–79
Reichenau, Walther von
  supports Sino-German military alliance, 78
Renya Mutaguchi
  seeks to halt invasion of Burma, 332–33
religion
  atheistic character of fascism and communism, 40
  National Socialism fosters a secular one, 48
Remagen, Germany
  9th Armored Division seizes intact bridge in, 317
  POW enclosure in, 583–84
Repulse (HMS)
  sinking of, 202, 210–11

resistance movements
  assessing collaboration and resistance, 1, 10
  attracts German leftist intellectuals, 545
  in China, 3
  in Czechoslovakia, 491
  in France, 130–31, 266–23, 455–56, 601, 608–10
  in Germany, 422
  in Italy, 263
  in the Philippines, 213–14
  in Poland, 277–78
  in Soviet Union, 182
  in Yugoslavia, 267
Reynolds, Bruce
  interpretations of, 397
Rhineland
  fate of, 20
  demilitarization of, 20
  German militarization of, 5, 26, 96
  negotiations regarding, 27
Ribbentrop, Joachim
  forges alliance with Japan, 83–84, 98–99
  indictment of, 518
  meets with Ciano, 102
  negotiates non-aggression pact, 28, 118
  sentence of, 519
  urges Japanese attack on Dutch East Indies, 87
Richards, Hugh
  commands Kohima garrison, 333–34
Riefenstahl, Leni
  collaborates with Nazi regime, 546
  transits between Berlin and Los Angeles, 551–52
  "Triumph of the Will" 547
Riegner, Gerhart
  informs Western diplomats of Holocaust, 423, 424
  meets with church leaders, 423–24
Rochefort, Joseph
  decrypts Japanese naval transmissions, 346
Rochling, Hermann
  war-time trial of, 519–20
rocket
  British efforts to defend against, 378
  efforts to destroy launching sites, 314
  German development of, 436–38, 439, 440
  use by German fighters, 248
Rockwell, Norman
  depicts Rosie the Riveter, 552–53
Roer River
  flooding from, 315,
  American forces cross, 317
Röling, B. V. A.
  issues dissent during Tokyo war crime trials, 531
Roma
  victims of Holocaust, 10, 485, 486
Roma (Italian battleship)
  destruction of, 261
Roman Catholic Church
  aligns with Franco regime, 417–18
  faces persecution in Poland, 423
  rejects ecumenism, 417
  source of Spanish conservatism, 63–64, 399, 546–47
Romania
  accepts Reich Marks in trade with Germany, 275
  churches within align with Nazism,, 425–26
  fascist movements in, 45
  German forces secure oil fields in, 103
  German influence in, 395–96
  German minority population expelled from, 592–93
  losses during Battle of Stalingrad, 178, 295
  participates in final solution, 109
  receives security guarantees, 99–100
  returns Bessarabia to Soviet Union, 279
Rome, Italy
  roundup of Jews in, 424
Rommel, Erwin
  and Battle of El Alamein. 190
  defeat of, 104
  Hitler ignores advice from, 268–69
  oversees building of Atlantic Wall, 307–8
  threatens Egypt, 191–92
  victories of, 117
Roosevelt, Franklin D.
  accepts limits on Atlantic Charter regarding colonial holdings, 568
  accepts Soviet sphere of influence in Poland, 568

Roosevelt, Franklin D. (*cont.*)
    addresses Congress after Japanese attack at Pearl Harbor, 342
    announces unconditional surrender as Allied policy, 565
    gives assurance to French leaders regarding colonial status quo, 265
    calls on America to become Arsenal of Democracy, 450
    Chiang Kai-shek presses to speed pace of decolonization, 564–65
    Cold War critics condemn decisions made at Yalta, 260
    commits to Operation Torch, 257
    death of, 353
    decision enter Mediterranean bolsters Europe first strategy, 269
    declares Turkey vital to United States national security, 196
    declines to embargo exports to Japan in May 1941, 87–88
    discusses fate of German war criminals, at Teheran, 516
    discusses with Stalin creation of new United Nations Organization, 565
    gives Douglas MacArthur command of SWPA, 344
    engages in a debate with Winston Churchill on applicability of Atlantic Charter, 564
    envisions major role for Great Powers on Security Council for United Nations, 567
    establishes Office of Scientific Research and Development, 433
    expresses interest in Claire Chennault proposals, 359
    forges Grand Alliance, 8
    forges United Nations alliance, 219–20
    forges United Nations Organization, 233
    funds atomic bomb research, 437–38
    German efforts to influence, 487
    grants sphere of influence to Soviet Union in Far East, 568
    harbors realpolitik view of Soviet Union, 228
    ignores Japanese aggression in March 1933, 75–76
    imposes oil embargo on Japan, 88
    initiates Lend Lease, 434
    issues Atlantic Charter, 563–64
    issues statement regarding German reprisal shootings, 515–16
    JCS advice to seek an early entry of Soviet Union into war with Japan, 368
    limits resources deployed to Mediterranean, 268–69
    Marco Bridge incident fails to alter policy of his administration, 76
    meets with Churchill and Stalin in Tehran, 198
    meets with Winston Churchill, 160
    as a navalist, 258
    orders Douglas MacArthur to leave the Philippines, 344
    orders internment of Japanese Americans, 504
    outlines plan for United Nations Organization at Tehran, 233
    perceptions of Japan in administration of, 205–6
    and the Polish question, 227–28
    Prince Konoe seeks to arrange a summit with, 207
    promotes decolonization through United Nations declaration, 222, 226
    promotes Good Neighbor Policy, 230–31
    promotes religious engagement, 425
    proposes fact-gathering commission to investigate war crimes, 516
    pursues German first strategy, 343
    reaffirms Germany first policy, 221
    receives assurance American airpower can halt Japan, 212
    receives criticism for pursing Mediterranean strategy, 256
    receives letter from Albert Einstein, 367–68, 437–38
    recognizes importance of Mediterranean Theater, 258–59, 260–61
    recognizes Mediterranean as strategic overextension for Adolf Hitler, 267–68
    remembers France as pillar of Allied victory in World War I, 262
    responds to refugee crisis, 502, 507–8
    see Big Three plus China help maintaining world peace, 220–21

see Soviet-American cooperation as
    counterweight to Japanese power, 229
seek Soviet entry into war with Japan, 228
seeks aerial death blow against Germany,
    250
seeks democratization of Italy, 264–65
seeks independent relationship with Josef
    Stalin, 227
seeks Josef Stalin assistance to strengthen
    China, 228–29
seeks Josef Stalin support for termination of
    French colonial rule in Indochina, 565
seeks Soviet entry into war with Japan, 298
seeks to elevate status of China as a major
    power, 565
seeks to transform Europe into modern
    liberal democracies, 269
sets date for D-Day, 305
struggles with senior U.S. commanders, 164
support development of military aviation,
    245–46
supports decolonization to prevent future
    wars, 564
and United Nations Organization, 232
urges Queen Wilhelmina to grant self-
    government to Dutch East Indies, 222
view of Soviet Union as a continental
    power, 226–27
Roosevelt, Theodore
    contains Japanese expansion, 203–5, 206
Roosevelt, Theodore. Jr.
    lands at Utah Beach, 309–10
Root, Elihu
    negotiates agreement with Tokyo, 204
Rosenberg, Alfred
    indictment of, 518
    receives death sentence, 519
Rousso, Henry
    defines Vichy syndrome, 546–48, 608–10
Royal Air Force
    demobilization after V-J Day, 587
    acquires Supermarine Spitfire, 240
    airfields in Malaya, 210
    contributes to victory in Burma, 338
    deploys against German U-boats, 161
    engage in night bombing against Germany,
        237–38
    faces defeat in Battle for France, 240
    French hopes for, 130–31
    gains independence, 238
    losses during evacuation of Dunkirk, 140
    in the Mediterranean Theater, 243–44
    provide air support in defense of Kohima,
        334
    strength of, 141–42
    withdraws from Burma, 330
Royal Air Force Bomber Command
    attacks German cities, 246, 250
    contribution to Allied victory, 250–51
    creation of, 245
    joined in bombing campaign by Eighth Air
        Force, 247
    overhauls bomber force, 246–47
    relies on night-time raids, 246
    suffers high number of accidents and
        casualties, 249–50
    unable to mount pinpoint daylight raids,
        246
Royal Canadian Air Force
    deploys to Great Britain, 141–42
Royal Canadian Navy
    'assume operational control over convoys in
        a new command, 165
    closes gap in North Atlantic, 158–59
    engage in convoy battles in fall of 1941, 160
    equipment shortfall of, 160, 163
    establishes coastal convoys for North
        American waters, 161–62
    fights in the Battle of the Atlantic, 7
    keeps sea lanes to Murmansk open, 8
    leave convoys to chase U-Boats, 160–61
    participates in Mid Ocean Escort Force, 162
    send reinforcements to North Atlantic, 161
    strength of, 141–42
Royal Navy
    achieve significant victories at Narvik,
        124–25
    bear burden in North Atlantic, 162
    defends merchant shipping in Atlantic, 156
    develop formula for defeat wolf packs, 163
    fights in Battle of the Atlantic, 7
    issues convoy instructions, 160–61
    keeps sea lanes to Murmansk open, 8
    losses during evacuation of Dunkirk, 140–41

674 INDEX

Royal Navy (*cont.*)
    Newfoundland fishermen join, 141
    receives significant resources during
        interwar years, 432
    secures Monroe Doctrine, 230
    shifts escorts to convoys to Russia, 160
Rundstedt, Gerd von
    seeks to defend France with mobile armor
        reserve, 307–8
Russia
    as ally of France, 25
    exits World War I, 16, 30
    impact on death of Empress Elizabeth on
        Seven Years' War, 297
    invades Ukraine in 2022, 573
    military collapse of, 203
    military mobilization of, 18
    participates D-Day anniversary
        commemoration, 600
    suffers defeat against Japan, 41, 416–17
    suffers defeat in war with Japan, 203–4
    territory ceded from, 19
Russian Revolution
    attacks religious institutions, 417–18
    Bolshevik triumph triggers fear of
        revolutionary contamination, 39–40
    famine during, 497
    German and Japanese intervention in,
        97–98
    refugees from, 500
Russo-Japanese War
    Japanese victory in, 203–4, 416–17
    legacy of, 27–28, 41

S

Sachse, Carole
    Interpretations of, 441
Salazar, Antonio
    permits Allied access to Azores, 400–2
    strengthens ties with Spain, 400
Sato, General
    attacks Kohima, 334
Saturday Evening Post (magazine)
    features Rosie the Riveter on cover, 552–53
Sauckel, Fritz
    indictment of, 518
    receives death sentence, 519

Schacht, Hjalmar
    acquittal of, 519
    favors ties to China, 86–87
    indictment of, 518
Scharnhorst (German battleship)
    attacks British shipping. 155, 156–57
    finds safety in French port, 154
    deploy to Norway, 157
    location of, 124–25
Schepke, Joachim
    death of, 158
Schirach, Baldur von
    indictment of, 518
    receives prison sentence, 519
Schutzstaffel (SS)
    assist in executing Intelligentsia Operation,
        485
    characterized, 131
    deemed a criminal organization by
        International Military Tribunal, 518
    encourages violence through Honor Law, 489
    German women serve in, 385
    implement Final Solution in East, 482, 489
    introduce gas vans to murder medical
        patients, 487
    take part in *Kristallnacht*, 484
Scoones, Geoffrey
    defends Imphal and Palel, 332–33, 334, 335
    launches counterattack, 335
Selassie, Haile
    appeals to League of Nations, 60, 61–62
    describes use of poison gas, 58–59
    diplomatic miscalculations of, 57
    suffers defeat, 58
    returns to power, 331–32
Seven Years' War
    Adolf Hitler draws historical lessons from, 297
Sextant Conference
    Directs capture of Marianas Island, 358–59
Seyss-Inquart, Artur
    indictment of, 518
    receives death sentence, 519
Shanghai, China
    aerial bombing of, 357–58
    anti-Japanese demonstrations in, 76–77
    battle for, 5
    war crime trials in, 528

Shigemitsu Mamoru
  becomes Japanese foreign minister, 529
Shidehara Kijuro
  receives telegram on actions of Kwantung army, 73
Shi Liang
  founds Warfare Child Welfare Committee, 501–2
Shinto
  bolsters Japanese nationalism, 418
  imposed on Koreans, 416–17
  U.S. occupation policies regarding, 426
Shirer, William
  on location of Maginot Line, 125
Simon, John
  argues against war crime trials, 516
Singapore
  British bases in, 210
  fall of, 202, 209, 210–11, 212, 221, 222, 225–26, 329, 337, 343
  Japanese massacres in, 524
  Japanese plan to attack, 396–97
  mining waters off of, 104
  war crime trials in, 527–28
Slim, William
  commands Burma Corps, 330
  commands Fourteenth Army, 225
  cooperates with Joseph Stilwell, 327
  defends Impala and Patel, 332–34
  forms corps command, 330–31
  presses forces across Chindwin valley, 337
  receives air support, 358
Slovakia
  Becomes Nazi client state, 99–100
  Edward Benes seeks to expel Hungarian speakers from, 593
  halts deportation of Jews, 109
  joins Tripartite Pact, 103
Smolensk, Soviet Union
  Soviet forces retake, 291–92
  war crime trials in, 524
Smoot-Hawley tariff
  limits European imports, 23
Smyth, John
  orders demolition of Sittang Bridge, 330
  relief of, 330
Society of Friend. *See* Quakers

Song Meiling
  active in humanitarian relief organizations, 501–2
Sorge, Richard
  runs spy ring in Tokyo, 108
South Africa, Union of
  declares war, 141–42, 432–33
South Tyrol
  German residents want Germany to annex region, 101–2
  granted to Italy under Treaty of Saint-Germain, 95
  Hitler annexes, 105
  Hitler renounces claims over, 95–96
  impacts Italian and German relations, 5
Soviet Union
  accepts Germans reunification, 1
  art and the Cold War struggle, 555
  as member of Grand Alliance, 228
  border zone with Finland, 452
  challenges Western world order, 3–4
  convenes war crime trials, 519–20, 523–24
  defeats Japanese forces at Battle of Nomonhan, 84
  defeats Japanese forces, 6
  defense aided by geography and superior defensive firepower, 131
  early film makers influential in America and Germany, 541
  efforts of art to memorialize the war, 554
  embraces an ideology of coercion and consent, 48
  embraces projects for perfect citizenry, 39–40
  enlists war artists, 553
  enters Second Five Year Plan, 43
  excludes peasants from rationing system, 379–80
  favors Social Realist aesthetics, 543–44
  Franklin Roosevelt's assessment of, 226–27
  imposes censorship regime on the arts, 541
  invades Finland, 394
  invades Manchuria, 353
  invasion of, 7, 9–10, 43, 70, 104–5, 159, 173–84, 195–96, 208, 395–96, 401, 543–44
  Japan prepares for possible conflict with, 74
  Japanese fears of, 554

Soviet Union (*cont.*)
   make Comintern part of Soviet state, 40
   medical establishment unprepared for war, 471
   memorializes World War II, 554–55
   and memory of World War II, 1, 13
   military cooperation with Germany, 4
   makes demands on Turkey, 197–98
   occupies northern Iran, 197–98, 199–200
   participates in war against Japan, 228, 368
   plans to draft fifteen-year-olds, 357
   prosecutes Japanese war criminals, 529
   prospects of alliance with Britain and France, 121
   provide aids to China, 84–85
   receives aid by way of convoys, 159, 160, 163, 164
   refuses to renew friendship agreement with Turkey, 195
   religious developments in, 420–21
   relocates factories to interior regions, 380
   repatriates prisoners of war, 504
   resources for military medicine limited, 471
   Reza Shah views as threat to Iranian sovereignty, 197
   sanctions against, 26–27
   Scandinavian security concerns regarding, 395
   signs Non-Intervention Agreement regarding Spanish Civil War, 66–67
   signs Treaty of Brest-Litovsk, 16
   Soviet ambassador to Sweden, 581–82
   Spanish forces fight in, 399
   spurs industrialization, 4
   state killing of Cossack troops, 590
   suffers enormous death toll, 379
   supports creation of United Nations organization, 232–34
   supports scientific research, 432
   supports Spanish Republic, 68
   suppresses bourgeois science, 432–33
   threat of war with Japan, 28
   treatment afforded to prisoners of war by, 504
   views Great Power status in nationalistic terms, 220–21
   Winston Churchill's assessment of, 227, 228

Spaatz, Carl
   commands U.S. Army Strategic Forces (USASFAF), 248–49, 364–65
   focuses attacks on transportation and oil, 249, 251
   seeks military targets, 250
   willing to sacrifice accuracy, 249
   seeks to avoid urban-area bombing, 366
   views on bombing campaign against Japan, 365–66

Spain
   assists Italy and Germany during World War II, 69
   bans fascist salute, 70
   British Council organizes philatelic exhibits in, 402–3
   British seeks to keep neutral, 398–99
   considers itself a non-belligerent, 394
   neutrality of, 2
   neutrality of, 262
   as part of Italy's sphere of influence, 96–97
   popular front emerges in, 46
   remains aloof from Europe, 69
   remains divided society, 399
   sends Blue Division fight in Soviet Union, 70, 399
   shares common ground with Portugal, 400
   shifting allegiances of, 70
   uses poison gas in Spanish Morocco, 58–59
   value of belligerency declines, 400–2

Spanish American War (1898)
   legacy of, 63–64
   U.S. acquires imperial acquisitions, 548–49

Spanish Civil War
   attracts International Brigades to fight for Republic, 68
   Britain and France forge Non-Intervention Agreement, 66–67
   causes of, 63–64
   fosters left-wing mobilization, 43, 46
   German intervention in, 23, 26, 66, 96–97
   ideological divisions and the course of the war, 65–66
   impacts European thinking on war, 68–69
   Italian intervention in, 26, 67–68, 96–97, 99
   polarizes French society, 546–47
   religious impact of, 417–18

role of *Luftwaffe* in, 246–47
Soviet Union sells arms to Republic. 68
strategic significance of, 25
Western democracies views of, 5
worsens refugee crisis, 501–2
Speer, Albert
  conviction of, 519
  indictment of, 518
  offers postwar self-justifications for actions, 299
  promotes neo-classical architecture, 545–46
  supports development of atomic bomb, 437
  supports urban renewal, 454
Sperrle, Hugo
  reduces air support, 128–29
Spruance, Raymond A.
  avoids night engagement, 348
  launches planes to attack Japanese fleet, 347
Stagg, James
  provides weather report for D-Day landing, 308
Stahel, David
  interpretations of, 174, 175
Stalin, Josef
  able to develop bilateral relationship with fascist Italy, 45
  able to drive favorable bargain at Yalta, 298
  accepts date for opening of second front, 305
  adopts autarky, 23
  agrees to Non-Aggression Pact with Adolf Hitler, 15, 49–50, 100, 195, 398
  allows Orthodox and Moslem organizations to assist veterans, 588
  army's survive Nazi onslaught, 8
  artist support cult of personality surrounding, 543–44
  attends Teheran Conference, 198, 233, 584–85
  begins offensive to remove immediate threat to Leningrad, 293
  believes state had an obligation to support disabled troops, 476–77
  bolsters Soviet morale, 182
  characterizes impact of Bolshevik Revolution, 39–40
  compromises on veto question and United Nations Security Council, 569
  considers campaign to capture Berlin, 298
  constructs cities of science, 440
  controls Comintern, 45
  creates puppet government for Poland, 295
  death of, 554–55
  debates regarding decision to sign Non-Aggression Pact, 6
  decides to aid China, 85
  demands Second Front, 257
  deports kulaks from Ukraine, 43
  deports Polish citizens, 590–91
  defers war crime trials until end of war, 524
  discusses fate Nazi war criminals at Tehran, 516
  engages in private conversation with Franklin Roosevelt at Yalta, 228–29
  entrenches state terror into Soviet system, 48
  exerts complete control over the arts, 543
  expands support for China, 88
  expects attack on Moscow, 177–78
  faces peasant hostility over forced collectivization, 182–83
  fails to aid Home Army uprising in Warsaw, 295–96
  favors iconographic painting and sculpture symbolizing political ideals, 544
  finds a synthesis between government and ideology, 47
  Franklin Roosevelt seeks personal relationship, 227
  Franklin Roosevelt's view of, 226–27
  further consolidates power, 47
  Germany's appeasement of, 100–1
  grows to trust professional military competence, 289, 291–92
  implements First Five-Year Plan, 75
  initiates central planned economy, 180
  installs pro-Soviet governments in Eastern Europe, 590–91
  launches attacks on Posen and Breslau, 298–99
  launches major winter offensive, 297–98
  limits application of Atlantic Charter, 220
  and Mediterranean campaign, 256, 260
  Mussolini encourages Adolf Hitler to negotiate with, 104–5

Stalin, Josef (*cont.*)
  orders German prisoners of war paraded through Moscow, 295
  orders Palmiro Toglietti to join Badoglio government, 267
  permits Konev to race for Berlin, 299–300
  pledges to enter the war against Japan, 568
  possesses formidable military in 1945, 300
  presses for offensives too quickly, 177, 291–92
  prioritizes establishing a Soviet-friendly government in Poland, 568
  privately discusses creating United Nations Organization with Franklin Roosevelt, 565
  receives news of atomic bomb, 381, 437–38
  refuses to return eastern half of Poland, 591–92
  regains mastery of Soviet system, 177
  regime survives Nazi onslaught, 287
  relationship with Winston Churchill, 227
  relieves Georgi Zhukov from command, 177
  relocates factories to Urals and Siberia, 181
  remains in power in postwar era, 380
  responds to rise of Nazi Germany, 3–4
  seeks narrow role for Soviet air force, 241–42
  seeks new world order, 39
  seeks to avoid direct conflict with Japan, 85
  seeks to end influence of AK and London based Polish Government, 277–78
  seeks to train more physicians, 471
  sees Warsaw uprising as primarily about postwar status of Poland, 295–96
  selects Georgi Dimitrov to head the Comintern, 46
  signs Non-Aggression Pact with Chiang Kai-shek, 82
  speeds timetable for attacking Berlin, 299
  and the state involvement in the arts, 542
  success in establishing a revolutionary regime rivaling bourgeois modernity, 48
  tries member of Polish underground for war crimes, 524
  views Soviet POWs as deserters, 581–82
  Winston Churchill characterizes, 227–28
Stark Harold
  supports proposal of Henry Dexter White, 208
  welcomes more time to prepare for war, 208

Stevens, Anthony
  analyzes Nazism, 48
Stilwell, Joseph W.
  abilities of, 328
  advances into Myitkyina, 336–37
  clashes with Chiang Kai-Shek, 89, 327, 337–38
  commands Chinese forces, 330–31
  criticizes Chindits and Merri Merrill's Marauders, 336–37
  serves as deputy to Louis Mountbatten, 332
Stimson, Henry
  argues for war crime trials, 516–17
  army intelligence recommendations regarding negotiations, 205
  backs military commanders, 259–60
  discounts threat of war with Japan, 202
  expresses concerns regarding Japanese actions, 75
  expresses confidence regarding defense of Philippines, 212
  expresses misgiving on air war, 357, 366
  strategic vision of, 260
Stolfi, R. H. S.
  interpretations of, 174
Streicher, Julius
  conviction of, 519
  indictment of, 518
Stresemann, Gustav
  death of, 27
  leads pro-western faction, 78
  negotiates Treaty of Locarno, 26–27
Strughold, Hubertus
  commits atrocities, 474–75
Student, Kurt
  murders POWs in Crete, 519–20
sulfa drugs
  shortages of, 473
  widespread use of, 467–68, 469–70
Suner, Ramon Serrano
  favors alignment with Axis, 399
Sun Yat-sen
  seeks alliance with Soviet Union, 78
  seeks partnership with Germany, 77–78
Sweden
  Allies consider expedition to seize iron mines in, 121

best place to alleviate Europe's suffering, 392
British Council sponsors lectures by
  English poet in, 402–3
environmental damage to, 457
German leverage on, 124
impact of war on postwar political
  trajectories, 402–3
neutrality of, 2, 406
permits transit of German troops, 401–2
sells iron ore to Germany, 121, 124
views regarding Germany, 395
Switzerland
  exiles in, 547
  neutrality of, 2, 392, 394, 402–3
  source of iron ore for Germany, 121
  war-time trade, 404, 432–33
Szilard, Leo
  assists in developing atomic bomb, 106
  drafts letter to Franklin Roosevelt, 437–38
  opposes use of atomic bomb, 437–38

T

Taft, William Howard
  accepts Japanese hegemony over Korea and
    Manchuria, 204
  mismanages relations with Japan, 204–5
  signs executive agreement with Japan, 204
Taittinger, Pierre
  reports on vulnerabilities at the Ardennes,
    126–27
Taiwan
  Allies consider a victim community, 525
  atrocities in, 607
  as part of Japanese Empire, 213, 549
  social welfare programs in, 501–2
  uses of poison gas in, 611
  war crime trials in, 528
Tajima Nobuo
  interpretations of, 78
Tamura Hiroshi
  war crime trial of, 517
tariffs
  impact on Great Depression, 23
Tashiro Kanichiro
  submits occupation plan, 79
Taylor, A. J. P.
  interpretations of, 117–18, 120

Taylor, Jay
  interpretations of, 77, 81, 89
Tedder, Arthur
  enlists assistance of Solly Zuckerman, 307
Tehran Conference
  affirms territorial integrity of Iran, 198
  clears way for United Nations Organization,
    233
  considers fate of Nazi war criminals, 516
  considers Franklin Roosevelt's plan for the
    United Nations organization, 233
  considers plan for Franklin Roosevelt's Plan
    for a United Nations Organization, 233
  decides Germany will be partitioned into
    zones of occupation, 565
  discusses fate of French Indochina, 565
  reaffirms territorial sovereignty of Iran, 198
  recognizes Iranian support of Allied war
    effort, 198
  sets date for opening of second front, 305
Teleki, Pal
  Sees need for Hungary to align with
    Germany, 278–79
Temple, William (Archbishop of Canterbury)
  accepts World War II as just war, 422
  seeks immediate aid for European Jewry,
    424
Tennessee Valley Authority
  federal funding of, 432
Terauchi Hisaichi
  receives occupation plan report, 79
Terkel, Studs
  examines why Americans view World War
    II as good war, 387
Thach, James
  Observes attack on Japanese aircraft
    carriers, 347
Thailand
  British consider preemptive advance into,
    210
  declares war against Great Britain and the
    United States, 397–98
  embraces belligerency, 398–99
  Japanese forces invade, 342
  permits Japanese use of territory to invade
    Malaya, 401–2, 405
  seeks to maintain neutrality, 396–97, 405–6

Thirty Years' War
  legacy of, 498
Thomas, Georg
  favors ties with China, 86–87
Thorez, Maurice
  returns to France, 263
Thorne, Andrew
  commands XII Corps, 144
The Times (newspaper)
  reports on arrival of troops from the Empire, 141
Timoshenko, S. K.
  issues Directive No. 3, 177
  prepares large-scale offensive, 177
Tito, Josef
  defeats Germans, 267
  executes pro-German Yugoslavia, 590
  forces Italians to flee Yugoslavia, 593
Toglietti, Palmiro
  Joins Badoglio government, 267
Tojo Hideki
  approves diplomatic initiatives of Prime Minister Konoe, 207
  continues negotiations with U.S., 207, 208
  ousted from power, 106
  testifies in Toyko Tokyo War Crime trials, 531
  seeks war, 214
Tokyo, Japan
  bombing of, 362
  devastated by fire-raids, 353, 362–63, 367–68, 439, 453, 605–6
  Doolittle raid against, 345, 358
  as potential target for bombing, 359
  rebuilding of, 453–54
Tokyo War Crimes trial
  assessment of, 524–25
  embodies liberal internationalism, 572
  initial criminal investigations, 525, 529
  initial proposals for, 525
  international character of, 12
  international character of court, 529–30
  Tokyo Charter establishes, 526
  verdicts rendered, 529, 530–31
Touvier, Paul
  Tried for war crimes, 609
Toyoda Soemu
  war crime trial of, 531

Trautmann, Oskar P.
  mediates between Chinese and Japanese governments, 82 , –83
Treaty of Lateran
  affirms sovereignty of Vatican City, 416
Treaty of Locarno
  settles boundaries of Western Europe, 4, 26–27
Treaty of Rapollo
  establishes diplomatic ties between German and Soviet Union, 4
Treaty of Saint-Germain
  awards Italy South Tyrol and Istria, 95
Treaty of Versailles
  benefits Italy, 95
  as cause of second world war, 116, 118
  demilitarizes Rhineland, 20–21
  diminishes German territory, 20
  efforts to modify, 27
  establishes League of Nations, 500,
  establishes new European states, 39–40
  failure of, 15–16, 21–22, 25–26, 30, 50.
  Hitler's violates terms of, 96, 231
  impacts Japanese-American relations, 205
  imposes war guilt on Germany, 21
  Japan helps negotiate, 97–98
  legacy of , 3–4
  limits Germany sovereignty, 15
  preserves imperial inequities, 500, 563
  prohibits aviation development in Germany, 432
  provides a modicum of stability, 4
  radicalizes Japan, 41
  shapes German naval development positively, 124
  support for modifying terms of, 119
  uniliteral modifications of, 60–61
  unites Germany in opposition to, 27
Tripartite Pact
  additional countries join, 103, 280
  limitations of, 108–10
  minor cooperation continues after Germany's surrender, 106
  provides level of mutual military coordination, 102–3
  strategic impact of, 5, 87–88, 94–95, 102, 103–4, 203

Truman, Harry S.
  approves use of atomic bomb, 353–54, 368–58
  believes U.S. can defeat Japan without Soviet Union, 572
  delivers radio address, 353
  discusses fire raids with Henry Stimson, 366
  endorses proposal of Murray Bernays, 517
  informs Josef Stalin of existence of atomic bomb, 437–38
  JCS seeks entry of Soviet Union into war with Japan, 368
  orders a resumption of bombing against Japan, 365
  recognizes need for cooperation with Soviets at Potsdam Conference, 571
  seeks plan from JCS for defeat of Japan, 364
  seeks to avert joint occupation of Japan with Soviet Union, 571, 572
Tuchman, Barbara
  interpretations of, 89
Tucker, Richard P.
  examines impact of World War II on forests, 449–50, 505
Tunisia
  Allied campaign to invade, 256
  Anglo-American armies prevail against Wehrmacht in, 265, 267–68
  Axis troops pour in to defend, 259
  French participation in campaign to retake for Allies, 262
  Jews held in concentration camps in, 426
  offers piecemeal resistance to Allied attack, 258
  provides French navy with shipyard, 261
Turing, Alan
  cracks the Enigma Code, 434
Turkey
  deals cautious with Axis and Allied Powers, 197–98
  declares war on Germany, 196–97, 198
  ecumenical leaders seek with Muslim leaders and Christian leaders, 417
  freezes Japanese assets, 206–7
  Great Britain applies pressure on, 197
  impact of war on, 2
  maintains sovereignty during war, 200
  maintains strict press censorship, 199
  mobilizes large army, 196
  receives aid from the United States, 196
  receives guarantees from British and Soviets regarding territorial integrity, 197
  receives security guarantee, 99–100
  secret service entertains relations with belligerents, 403
  seeks to avoid entering war, 194–96
  seeks to stabilize a weak economy, 196
  strategic position of, 190
Turner, Richmond Kelly
  serves as amphibious force commander for Guadalcanal landing, 348–49

U

Ukraine
  churches within align with Nazism, 425
  famine in, 43, 505–6
  German occupation of, 16, 182–83, 451
  Josef Stalin deports kulaks from, 43
  Russian invasion of, 573
  war crime trials in, 524
ULTRA
  alerts Americans of German plans counterattack toward Avranches, 312
  allows rerouting of convoys, 159
  confirms Germans will require air superiority before invading Great Britain, 146
  directs USN Hunter-Killer groups, 166
  fails when Germans introduce a new rotor to Enigma machine, 164
  indicates presence of panzer formations near Arnhem, 314
  informs Allies of diminishing strength in Normandy, 312
  intelligence restored, 164, 165
  value declines when Germans halt routine signaling, 167
United Nations (alliance)
  and the Grand Alliance, 226–29
  formation of, 8, 219–23, 563–65
  Franklin Roosevelt seeks a new multilateral world through, 226
  participation of Latin Americans in, 231
UNESCO (United Nations Educational, Scientific, and Cultural Organization
  founding of, 440

United Nation Organization
  admits Turkey to membership, 196–97
  aids in the establishment of religious networks, 427
  conducts investigations Spanish neutrality, 69
  discuss structure of organization at Teheran Conference, 233, 565
  Dumbarton Oaks begins drafting charter for, 233, 567–68
  embodies liberal internationalism, 572–73
  expectations for, 589–90
  fosters global interactions, 555
  fosters multilateralism. 233–34, 562–63
  founding of, 11, 562
  Moscow Conference of Foreign Ministers announces plan for, 232
  negotiations at San Francisco complete charter, 588–70
  precedents established by League of Nations, 510, 563
  proposals regarding Security Council considered at Yalta, 568
  role of State Department in formation of, 232
  Russian veto prevents Security Council acting on Ukraine, 573
  sanction military operations, 602
  serves as key component of postwar order, 572
United Nations Relief and Rehabilitation Administration (UNRRA)
  aids Displaced Persons, 589–90, 594
  provides food relief to Soviet citizens, 509
  provides humanitarian relief, 508–9, 589–90
United Nations War Crimes Commission (UNWCC)
  establishment of, 516
  regional office in Asia, 525
United States
  acquires Philippines, 549
  as adversary of Japan, 44, 73–74, 79–80, 86, 87
  as adversary of the Axis Powers, 107–9
  as an ally of China, 88
  assesses political loyalty of scientists, 221
  bolsters defense of Western Hemisphere, 229–30, 231
  captures supply of uranium oxide, 106
  charts strategy at Arcadia Conference, 203–21
  and Chinese declaration of war on Japan, 80–81
  clashes with Japanese negotiators at Versailles, 205
  commits opening a second front, 304–5
  conducts war crime trials in the Philippines and Japan, 527
  confronts Japan, 202
  continues to maintain segregation, 376
  creates militarized landscapes, 458
  creates Women's Land Army, 377
  denies strategic materials to Japan, Germany, and Italy, 206
  deploys American forces to China-Burma-India Theater, 327–28
  deploys forces to Pacific, 343
  devotes resources to signals intelligence, 434
  displace British influence in Latin America, 230
  dominates war in the Pacific, 9
  efforts to aid German Jews, 502–3
  embraces internationalism, 11
  embraces isolationism, 121
  embraces neutrality, 94
  emerges as superpower, 51
  emerges as world power, 379, 380
  enacts high tariffs, 22–23
  encourages women to enter defense factories, 376
  engages in biological warfare research, 435–36
  enters World War II, 7–9
  establishes GI Bill of Rights, 477
  establishes laws of war, 498
  establishes Office of Scientific Research and Development, 433
  excels in experimental physics, 432
  experiences few civilian deaths from enemy attack, 375
  experiences incendiary attacks in Pacific Northwest, 370
  experiences second industrial revolution, 432
  experience ssignificant demographic shifts, 396

extends Lend Lease to Britain, 231–32
faces defeat in Pacific, 202
faces major defeat in Pacific, 342
faces stiff resistance from Germans in Italian campaign, 262–63
fails to deter Japan, 202–3
fails to join the League of Nations, 26
fears rocket attack, 167
forges closer relations with Australia and New Zealand, 225
forges closer relations with Canada, 224
forges United Nations alliance, 219–20, 221–22
forges United Nations Organization, 232–34
freezes Japanese assets, 206–7
and French intervention in the Ruhr, 20–21
and German reparations, 22, 23
as the good war, 387
historically champions neutral rights, 393
holds war crime trials in American zone of occupation in Germany, 520–23
implements Project Paperclip, 440
implements rationing, 376
imposes sanctions on Japan, 88, 103–4
increases harvesting woods, 456
initiates Works Progress Administration, 541
interns Japanese Americans, 377, 504
judges neutrality as reprehensible, 404
and League of Nations sanctions against Italy, 61
limits international responsibilities, 21–22, 30, 50, 75
maintains economic interests in Shanghai, 81
maintains global network of military bases after the war, 449–50
maintains segregated military, 473–74
as a major center of scientific research, 432
as major petroleum exporter, 190, 194
makes widespread use of DDT, 458
Marxist critiques of cultural life in, 552
as member of the Grand Alliance, 226–29
mobilizes arts for war effort, 551–53
mobilizes economy, 375–76, 450
mobilizes society, 10–11
negotiates with Italian regime, 263
negotiates with Japan, 207–8

occupies Japan, 554
offers refugee for cultural producers, 539, 551
opens front in Mediterranean, 256–61
participates in ABDACOM, 343
participates in Nuremberg war crimes trials, 518–20
participates in Tokyo War crimes trials, 529–31
patronizes sciences in postwar era, 440
planners offer visions of urban renewal, 453–54
plays important role in organizing Tokyo war crimes trial, 525–26
plays major role in Middle East, 200
plays pivotal role in organizing Nuremberg war crimes trials, 515–18
proclaims neutral zone in western Atlantic, 159–60
promotes abstract expressionism globally, 555
promotes disarmament, 23–24, 205
promotes Good Neighbor Policy, 230, 231
provides assistance to China, 87–88
provides food aid to Iran, 198
provides home to evacuated British children, 378
provides public supports the arts, 539–40
ramps up production of penicillin, 471
rearms France, 262
recognizes Iranian sovereignty, 198
reconciles with Japan and Germany, 1
religious life in, 415–16, 417, 418, 420, 422–521
remains non-committal toward European neutrality, 393
responds to Manchurian Incident, 5, 75–76, 77, 89
responds to Marco Polo Bridge incident, 79
revitalizes Germany economy, 4
seeks a return to normalcy, 553–54
seeks full repayment of Allied war loans, 21, 22–23
seeks to deter Japanese expansion, 205–6
seeks to promote principles of the Atlantic Charter, 563–65
seeks wonder weapon, 435

United States (cont.)
  seek to promote Open Door in China, 203–5
  support for incendiary bombing raids, 357
  supports a neutral Turkey, 196
  supports Anglo-Soviet invasion of Iran, 198
  supports French efforts to retain Indochina, 12–13
  surpasses Germany in aircraft production, 434–35
  terminates 1911 Japanese-U.S. Treaty, 84
  Thailand declares war against, 397–98
  underestimates Japanese strength, 209
  undertakes atomic bomb research, 437–38
  viewed as good war, 13
  wins battle of production, 2
United States Army Air Force
  airlift of supplies from India to China, 327
  attacks Japanese transports at Bismarck Sea, 350
  attacks targets prior to D-Day landing, 307–206
  builds air bases in China, 359
  deploys B-17s to Philippines, 212
  deploys in Pacific under George Kenney, 358
  drops atomic bombs on Japan, 353, 367–70, 437–38
  effectiveness of ETO air campaign, 251–53
  efforts to execute precision bombing of Japan, 360–61
  embraces strategic bombing, 245, 247, 249, 571
  experiences of air crews serving in, 249–50
  faces combat losses, 247, 248
  gains long range escort, 248
  greater autonomy, 238–39
  launches Doolittle raid, 358
  launches incendiary raid against Hankow, 359–60
  launches incendiary raids against Japanese cities, 353, 361–8, 439, 453
  morality of air campaign waged by, 250–51
  organizes Tactical Air Commands, 244
  participates in Combined Bomber Offensive, 247
  planning for bombing of Japan, 358–59
  recognizes importance of gaining air superiority, 243–44
  spray jungle with DDT, 350–51
  suffers heavy losses in the defense of the Philippines, 343–44
  supports D-Day invasion, 249
  targets German transportation infrastructure, 249
  undertakes airlift to China, 8
  wins air superiority against *Luftwaffe*, 248–49
United States Navy
  advance through Solomons, 350
  commands South Pacific area, 348
  decides against convoys for coastal trade, 161–62
  deploy Hunter Killer groups against German U-Boats, 166
  destroys naval base on Truk, 351
  develops war plan against Great Britain, 30
  engages in Battle of Atlantic in 1941, 159–60, 262
  enlists combat artists, 553
  faces rifts with U.S. Army, 344–45
  fights for naval dominance off Guadalcanal, 348–49
  forestall invasion of Port Moresby, 345–46
  funds research to use Mexican freetailed bats as bombers, 370
  gains dominance in the Mediterranean, 261
  isolates Japanese island garrisons, 506
  launches Dolittle raid, 212, 345
  losses from Japanese attack on Pearl Harbor, 211–12, 342–43
  participates in Battle of Java Sea, 210
  prevails at Battle of Leyete Gulf, 352
  prevails at Battle of Midway, 346–48
  skilled at deep-ocean U Boat hunting, 167
United States Supreme Court
  affirms legality of interning Japanese Americans, 504
  upholds conviction of Yamashita Tomoyuki, 527
University of Chicago
  site of first nuclear reactor, 437–38
U.S. Army
  faces logistical difficulties in France, 313

fail to close the Falaise gap, 312–13
paratroopers attack on D-Day, 308
captures Avranches, 312
combat effectiveness of, 318
contributes to Burma campaign, 336
creates fictional army to deceives Germans, 306
defends against German forces in Battle of the Bulge, 316–17
defends Bataan and Corregidor, 344
defends Philippines, 212–13
develops effective system for caring for the wounded, 466–67
enlists combat artists, 553
face obstacles on Omaha Beach, 310
faces rifts with U.S. Navy in the Pacific, 344–45
gains experience in jungle warfare, 327
launches invasion of Salerno, 268
launches offensive against Germany, 317–18
launches offensive in Hurtgen Forrest, 315
launches Operation Dragoon, 267, 313
liberate Cherbourg, 311–12
meet with success on Utah Beach, 309–10
occupies liberated Italy, 263–65
outbreaks of malaria hinder combat effectiveness, 350–51
Participates in Operation Market-Garden, 314
provides intelligence on Japanese intentions, 209
pursue Japanese forces in New Guinea, 349
seizes St. Lo, 312
triumphs against *Wehrmach*t in North Africa, 265, 267–68
U.S. Marines
defend Wake Island, 212
enlists combat artists, 553
invade Iwo Jima, 352–53
invades Guadalcanal, 348–49
suffer high casualties on invasion of Tarawa, 351

V

Vanderbilt, Cornelius (IV)
sponsors sensational Hitler's *Reign of Terror* documentary, 551–52

Vandegrift, A. A.
commands U.S. Marines at Guadalcanal, 348
Vargas, Getulio
declares war on Germany, 401–2
Vatican
aligns with Franco, 219, 417–18
condemns suffering of innocents, 423
fosters exchanges for negotiated peace, 422
neutrality of, 2
relations with Germany and Italy, 10–11
signs concordat with Germany, 386, 419
sovereignty recognized, 416
veterans, British
receive modest benefits, 588
veterans, German
disabled seek government support, 476
veterans, Japanese
receive few benefits, 476
veterans, Soviet
receive meager benefits, 588
veterans, U.S.
former prisoners experiencing post-traumatic stress disorder, 588
receive GI Bill or Rights, 587–88
Victor Emmanuel (King)
abdication of, 264–65
actions of, 262–63
proclaimed emperor of Ethiopia, 58
remains on throne, 259
Vietnam
Japanese occupation of, 213–14
Vietnam War
anti-war protests draw links to American bombing of Japan, 605–6
British military authorities re-impose colonial order in, 585
scholarly focus on, 328
use of Agent Orange in, 449
U.S. serves as imperial proxy, 572
Vlasov, Andreevich
execution of, 581–82

W

Wainwright, Jonathan
surrender of, 212–13

Wake Island
  defense plans for, 343
  fall of, 202, 209, 211–12, 342
Walker, Mark
  interpretations of, 441–43
Wang Jingwei
  collaborates with Japanese, 528, 550–51
Wannsee Conference
  adopts plans for murder of Jewry, 490
  impact of German campaign in the Soviet Union, 183
war crime trials, Chinese
  Communists deem Nationalists as war criminals, 516–17, 528
  continue despite civil war, 528
war crime trials, France
  issues harshest sentence, 528–29
  tries Vichy officials, 609
war crime trials, German
  tries perpetrators of the Holocaust, 601–2
war crime trials, Great Britain
  convene twelve military courts in Asia, 527–28
  issues Royal Warrant outlining war crime procedures, 526
war crime trials, Poland
  prosecutes perpetrators of Holocaust, 523
war crime trials, Soviet Union
  pursues cases against Unit 731, 529
  tries collaborators, 524
War Crime Trials, U.S.
  establishes legal concept of command responsibility, 527
  tries over 546 cases of suspected Japanese war criminals, 527
war crime trials, U.S. Occupation Zone in Germany
  for atrocities at concentration camps in Germany, 522–23
  for crimes against American POWS, 522
  holds several trials concurrently, 520
  for murdering hospital patients, 522
  prosecutes SS and military physicians, 520
  tries high ranking business officials, 520–21
  tries military leaders for murder of civilians, 521–22
  tries military leaders for waging aggressive war, 522
Warfare Child Welfare Committee
  serves as model of social welfare programs in China, 502
Warner Brothers
  produce anti-Nazi motion pictures, 551–52
War Plan Orange
  MacArthur unable to implement, 212–13
  predicts Japanese military threat, 343
War Production Board (U.S.)
  establishes priorities, 375–76
War Refugee Board (U.S.)
  establishment of, 508
War Relief Control Board (U.S.)
  oversees U.S. relief groups, 508
Warsaw, Poland
  bombing of, 131
  falls to Soviet forces, 297–98
  Jewish ghetto in, 485, 491
  rebuilding of, 453
  Red Army drive toward, 297
  uprising in, 278, 295–96
Wartime Child Welfare Protection Association (WCWPA)
  aids refugee children, 381
Washington Naval Treaty (1922)
  Japan adheres to, 97–98
  reduces naval fleets, 23–24, 500
Wavell, Archibald
  appoints Orde Wingate commander of 77th Indian Infantry Brigade, 331–32
  appoints Thomas Hutton commander of Burma Army, 330
  convenes infantry committee meeting, 332
  leads America, British, Dutch and Australian Command, 221, 343
weather
  hinders *Wehrmacht* and *Luftwaffe*, 242
  impact on war against Soviet Union, 173
  impacts Allied bombing offensive, 249–50
  meteorological advances, 433
Webb, William F.
  investigates Japanese war crimes, 525
  presides over Tokyo war crimes trials, 531
Weber, Heike
  Interpretations of, 457

Wedemeyer, Albert
  criticizes Franklin Roosevelt in postwar memoirs, 259-60
  orders incendiary attack on Hankow, 359-60
  replaces Joseph Stilwell as commander, 337-38
Wehrmacht
  effectives of Polish resistance against, 277-78
  faces inadequate logistics in Eastern Front, 242, 294-95
  historical assessments of, 318
  lacks sufficient. Industrial base to support, 289
  losses during Polish campaign, 276-77
  Luftwaffe subservient to, 238-39
  military effectiveness of, 131
  military preparedness of, 117-18
  operational doctrine of, 118-19
  participates in the Holocaust, 179-80, 482, 488-89
  reduced to infantry army during Italian campaign, 268
  relationship with Adolf Hitler, 176, 287-89, 307-8
  victories of, 116-17
Weinberg, Gerhard L.
  views on medical advances, 469
  Views on use of atomic bomb, 369-70
Weise, Hubert
  reorganizes German air defenses, 247-48
Weizsacker, Ernest von
  favors alliance with China, 86-87
Welles, Sumner
  assists in crafting United Nations Organization, 232
  undertakes diplomatic mission to Europe, 393
Wells, H.G.
  predictions of, 237
Westing, Arthur H.
  examines impact of war on environment, 449
Weygand, Maxime
  announces end of Battle of France, 143
  assumes command of French forces, 130
  seeks armistice, 130-31

Wheeler, Keith
  reports on medical care, 466
White, Harry Dexter
  negotiates postwar economic arrangements. 566-67
  proposes peace plan for Japan, 208
Wilhelm II
  abdication of, 3, 17-18
  accepts resignation of Erich Ludendorff, 17
Wilhelmina (Queen)
  Franklin Roosevelt expresses views regarding fate of Dutch East Indies to, 222
Williams, E.T.
  compares Japanese to defeated Germans, 205
Wilson, Woodrow
  contains Japanese expansion, 204-5, 206
  dictates terms of German surrender in 1918, 17, 18, 565
  Fourteen Points and Treaty of Versailles, 20
  liberal internationalism of, 564
  participates in Paris Peace conference, 18-19
  promotes self-determination, 3, 97
  refuses to cancel Allied war debt, 22
  seeks League of Nations, 11, 497
  seeks U.S. membership in League of Nations, 26
  views of economic causes of war, 564
Wingate, Orde
  undertakes irregular operations, 331-32, 336-37
  views Indian troops as inferior, 336
Wise, Stephen (Rabbi)
  early opponent of Nazism, 423
women
  artistic portrayals of American war workers, 553
  British Government conscripts women for national service, 378
  British women join Women's Voluntary Service (WVS), 377
  British women participate in work force, 378-79
  conditions in Germany deteriorate over course of war, 384-85
  endure widespread rape, 385
  engage in passive resistance in China, 550-51

women (cont.)
  forced sterilization of, 486
  humanitarian work of, 501–2
  provide humanitarian relief, 502
  resistance to women serving armed forces, 262
  serve as combat aviators, 242
  serve in Germany military, 385
  serve in Red Army, 380
  serve in Soviet military, 183
  serve in Women's Land Army (U.S.), 377
  sexual exploitation of, 2
  under Allied occupation in Italy, 264
  work in U.S. defense factories, 376, 434–35
Woodward, Rachel
  examines environmental sensitivity claims of British military, 450, 458–59
Work Progress Administration (WPA)
  commissions artwork depicting ordinary Americans, 552–53
World Bank
  see International Bank for Reconstruction and Development
World Council of Churches
  founding of, 415–16
World Health Organization (WHO)
  founding of, 497–98, 509
World Jewish Congress
  calls for immediate rescue of Jewish communities, 424
  founding of, 414
  informs Western diplomats of Holocaust, 423
World Missionary Conference (Edinburgh)
  forges international connections, 415
World Parliament of Religions (Chicago)
  meeting of, 415, 416
World Student Christian Federation
  founding of, 417
  maintains ties to African and Asian Churches, 426
World War I
  Allies fail to document German war crimes, 515–16
  attritional nature of, 175–76
  became the chemists' war, 431
  benefits Japan, 27–28, 97–98
  British artists support propaganda effort, 553
  British Woman's Land Army in, 378
  characterized, 264, 562–63
  demobilization in Great Britain, 586
  devastates forests, 449–50, 455
  discredits imperialism, 213
  ends in German defeat, 16–18
  fosters appeasement policies, 119
  fosters rise of fascism and communism, 40, 41
  fosters war weariness in Great Britain, 551
  France serves as pillar of Allied victory in, 262
  French memories of Verdun recalled, 126–27
  fundamental differences with World War II, 563
  German civilians deaths from British naval blockade in, 366
  heightens class divisions in Italy, 542
  humanitarian response to, 497, 509, 510
  leads to dissolution of Ottoman Empire, 194
  legacy of, 15, 29–30, 41
  new nations in Middle East emerge after, 194
  origins of, 18, 21
  reasons for Germany's loss, 131
  results in Germany losing dependencies in Asia, 78
  results in Italy and Japan administering mandatory territories, 564
  U.S. limits export of steel plate to Japan during, 204–5, 206
  witnessed German invasion of neutral Belgium, 394
Wuhan, China
  battle of, 86
  bombing of, 85
  Japanese aircraft destroyed in, 85
  refugees in, 501–02

Y

Yakovlev, Vasili Nikolaevich
  paints portrait of Georgi Zhukov, 540, 543–44
Yalta Conference
  agree to make use of German and Hungarian POWs to labor for victors, 584

Cold Warriors criticize Franklin Roosevelt's participation, 260
considers fate of Poland, 227–28, 571
convenes at conference in San Francisco conference, 568
determines zones of occupation, 318
discusses fate of German war criminals, 516
establishes new borders for Poland, 568
fails to resolve trusteeship question, 568
Franklin Roosevelt and Josef Stalin in conversations with regard to Far East, 229
military situation favors Josef Stalin, 298
resolves structure of Security Council for United Nations, 233, 567
scholarly assessments of, 562–63
shapes postwar world order, 568
Winston Churchill confident Josef Stalin will fulfill promises made at, 227–28

Yamamoto Isoroku
conceded Guadalcanal to the Americans, 349
death of, 350
expresses disappointed regarding Pearl Harbor attack, 342–43
plans Midway operation, 345–46
sought to pursue Americans, 348

Yamashita Tomoyuki
war crime trial of, 527, 531–32

Yang Hucheng
kidnaps Chiang Kai-shek, 77

Yank Magazine
Features work of American artists, 553

Yellow River
flooding along, 381, 501, 506

Yergin, Daniel
interpretations of, 438–39

Yorktown (aircraft carrier)
intercepts Japanese invasion force, 345
launches fighter planes, 347
loss of, 348
rapidly repaired, 346
receives heavy damage, 345–46

Yoshiya Nobuko
visits front-lines, 551

Young, Louise
Interpretations of, 550–51

Young Plan
German government abandons, 27

Yugoslavia
communists success in, 260, 267
displaced persons from, 589
executes pro-German Yugoslavs, 590
expels German minority from, 592–93, 594–95
German deportations in, 591
German influence in, 395–96
German invasion of, 103, 108
German replace Italian troops in, 263
joins Little Entente, 25, 121
Soviet liberation of, 296
unleashes state terror against Italian population, 593
violent break-up of, 593–94
war crime trials in, 519–20

Z

Zeitzler, Kurt
Week position of, 288–89

Zhang Xueliang
kidnaps Chiang Kai-shek, 261

Zhang Zuolin
assassination of, 549

Zhukov, Georgi
attacks Berlin, 299–300
launches Operation Mars, 177
participates in Operation Bagration, 294–95
pauses offensive, 298
portrait of, 543–44, 554–55
skill of, 289
Stalin relieves, 177
takes command of 1st Belorussian Front, 297–98

Zionism
oppenents of, 417
support for, 264, 414–15

Zionist Organization of America
Membership increases, 420

Zuckerman, Solly
recommends targeting for bombing, 307